Talcott Parsons
1902–1979
Dean of American sociology in the mid-1900s promoted a conception of society as a social system with subsystems of human action in which individuals fulfill the systems needs of the societies of which they are members.

Herbert Blumer
1900–1987
American student of ... who coined the term 'symbolic interactionism'.

Everett C. Hughes
1897–1983
... an sociologist studied economic ...ization, work occupations, ethnic relations, ...g a key study ...thnic division ...r' in Quebec.

Samuel Delbert Clark
1910–2003
Canadian historical sociologist and educator founded the University of Toronto's Department of Sociology (1963).

Theodor Adorno
1903–1969
German Frankfurt School philosopher argued that philosophical authoritarianism is inevitably oppressive.

Oswald Hall
1908–2007
Canadian educator researched the sociology of work and medicine and served on the Royal Commission on Health Services and the Royal Commission on Bilingualism and Biculturalism.

Robert K. Merton
1910–2003
American sociologist and educator developed middle-range theory, which sought to bridge the gap between high-level theories and low-level observations.

Erving Goffman
1922–1982
Canadian-born sociologist advanced microsociology and studied social roles, deviance, stigma, and 'total institutions'.

John Porter
1921–1979
Canadian sociologist examined connections between ethnicity and barriers of opportunity in Canadian society, which he characterized as a 'vertical mosaic'.

C. Wright Mills
1916–1962
American critical sociologist studied power structure in the US and coined the term 'sociological imagination'.

Guy Rocher
b. 1924
Canadian educator and pioneer in the sociology of education, law, and medical ethics has sat on several commissions and boards of inquiry at the provincial and federal levels and wrote a lucid and highly regarded introduction to the discipline, Introduction à la sociologie (1968).

Michel Foucault
1926–1984
French thinker, famous for historical studies of madness and civilization, imprisonment and sexuality, portrayed science as an arbitrary instrument for control and power, and constructed a theory of power as actions and relations.

Dorothy Smith
b. 1926
English-born Canadian sociologist developed standpoint theory, which sought to frame and understand everyday life from a feminist standpoint.

Jean Baudrillard
1929-2007
French cultural theorist influenced postmodernism and showed how capitalist consumer society erases distinctions between reality and reference, leading to a loss of meaning.

Margrit Eichler
b. 1942
Canadian sociologist has studied family sociology, feminist research methods, and gender inequality.

1900 — 1950 — 2000

1960
Negroes in Toronto: A Sociological Study of a Minority Group, by US-Canadian activist and Ontario Human Rights Commissioner Daniel Hill (1923–2003)

1962
The Developing Canadian Community, a study of US influence on Canada's cultural development, by S.D. Clark

1964
'Institutional Completeness of Ethnic Communities and Personal Relations of Immigrants', an examination of why and how some ethnocultural communities survive while others do not, by Canadian sociologist Raymond Breton

1965
Lament for a Nation: The Defeat of Canadian Nationalism, an examination of the dangers of Canadian cultural absorption by the US, by Canadian social philosopher George Grant (1918–1988)

The Vertical Mosaic: An Analysis of Social Class and Power in Canada, a ground-breaking and influential study of Canada's class structure, depicting a complex system of groups organized in hierarchy across lines of ethnicity and class, by John Porter

1968
Introduction to the Mathematics of Population, a landmark contribution to the field of population studies, by Canadian demographer Nathan Keyfitz (b. 1913)

1969
Doctors and Doctrines: The Ideology of Medical Care in Canada, an examination of Canada's healthcare system in terms of role strains, conflict in values, and relations to the public, by Bernard Blishen

1975
The Rise of a Third Party: A Study in Crisis Politics (1975), a sociological analysis of the growth of nationalist politics in Quebec, by Maurice Pinard

The Canadian Corporate Elite: An Analysis of Economic Power, a response to *The Vertical Mosaic* examining corporate elites and their impact on class and social stratification, by Wallace Clement

1978
The Double Ghetto: Canadian Women and their Segregated Work, a study of gender inequality in the labour force and the home, by Pat Armstrong and Hugh Armstrong

1983
Green Gold: The Forest Industry in British Columbia (1983), an early study in the social, political, and economic aspects of a particular staples industry, the BC forest industry, by Patricia Marchak

1986
'The "Wets" and the "Drys": Binary Images of Women and Alcohol in Popular Culture', a study of gender inequalities and mass media, by Thelma McCormack

1987
The Everyday World as Problematic: A Feminist Sociology, an argument that sociology has developed without proper insight into women's experiences, by Dorothy Smith

1988
Quebec Society: Tradition, Modernity, and Nationhood, a study of Quebec's rising middle class and the separatist movement, by Hubert Guindon

Families in Canada Today: Recent Changes and Their Policy Implications, a study of how the way we think and talk about gender roles pre-empts useful changes in family policy, by Margrit Eichler

1989
The Social Significance of Sport, a study of how individuals take control of and participate in society through voluntary association, by James Curtis (1943–2005)

1996
The Barbershop Singer: Inside the Social World of a Musical Hobby, a study of leisure and hobbies in society, by Robert Stebbins

2002
The Impact of Feminism on Canadian Sociology (2002), a study of the rise of sociology as a feminist discipline, by Margrit Eichler

2004
Perspectives de Recherche en Santé des Populations au Moyen de Données Complexes (2004), an analysis of the Quebec healthcare system, by Paul Bernard

Milestones in Canadian Sociology

Sociology

Second Edition

A Canadian Perspective

Tepperman ▸ Curtis ▸ Albanese

OXFORD
UNIVERSITY PRESS

OXFORD
UNIVERSITY PRESS

70 Wynford Drive, Don Mills, Ontario M3C 1J9
www.oup.com/ca

Oxford University Press is a department of the University of Oxford.
It furthers the University's objective of excellence in research, scholarship,
and education by publishing worldwide in

Oxford New York
Auckland Cape Town Dar es Salaam Hong Kong Karachi
Kuala Lumpur Madrid Melbourne Mexico City Nairobi
New Delhi Shanghai Taipei Toronto

With offices in
Argentina Austria Brazil Chile Czech Republic France Greece
Guatemala Hungary Italy Japan Poland Portugal Singapore
South Korea Switzerland Thailand Turkey Ukraine Vietnam

Oxford is a trade mark of Oxford University Press
in the UK and in certain other countries

Published in Canada
by Oxford University Press

First published 2008

Library and Archives Canada Cataloguing in Publication

Sociology : a Canadian perspective / edited by Lorne Tepperman, James
Curtis and Patrizia Albanese. — 2nd ed.

Includes bibliographical references and index.
ISBN 978-0-19-542559-8

1. Sociology—Textbooks. 2. Canada—Social conditions—1991– —Textbooks.
I. Tepperman, Lorne, 1943– II. Curtis, James E., 1943–2005 III. Albanese, Patrizia

HM586.S62 2008 301 C2007-907247-X

Cover Image: Fancy Photography/Veer

1 2 3 4 – 11 10 09 08
This book is printed on permanent (acid-free) paper ∞.
Printed in the United States of America

Contents

Tables, Figures, and Boxes xii

Preface xvi

Introduction:
Why Not Become a Sociologist? 2
Lorne Tepperman and Patrizia Albanese

Part I Theory and Methodology

1 **Three Empirical Traditions of Sociological Theory** 12
Neil McLaughlin and Antony Puddephatt

2 **Research Methods** 38
Bruce Arai

Part II Major Social Processes

3 **Culture and Culture Change** 66
Shyon Baumann

4 **Socialization** 98
Sue Wilson

5 **Statuses, Roles, and Identities** 128
Cheryl Albas and Dan Albas

6 **Groups and Organizations** 155
Lorne Tepperman

7 **Deviance** 190
Vincent F. Sacco

Part III Social Institutions

8 **Families and Intimate Relationships** 218
Maureen Baker

9 **Education** 244
Terry Wotherspoon

10 **Work and the Economy** 276
Pamela Sugiman

11 **Health Issues** 312
Juanne Clarke

12 **Religion** 340
Lorne L. Dawson

13 **Politics and Political Movements** 370
Peter R. Sinclair

14 **Social Movements** 402
John Veugelers and Randle Hart

Part IV Social Inequality

15 **Class and Status Inequality** 432
Julie Ann McMullin

16 **Gender Relations** 458
Pat Armstrong

17 **Sexuality** 484
Patrizia Albanese

18 **Ethnic and Race Relations** 514
Nikolaos I. Liodakis

Part V Canadian Society and the Global Context

19 **Global Society** 552
Michael R. Smith

20 **Population and Society** 578
Frank Trovato

21 **Cities and Urbanization** 610
William Michelson

22 **Mass Media and Communication** 640
David Young

23 **The Environment** 674
G. Keith Warriner

Glossary 709

References 729

Contributors 763

Index 765

Detailed Contents

Tables, Figures, and Boxes xii

Preface xvi

Introduction: Why Not Become a Sociologist? 2
Lorne Tepperman and Patrizia Albanese
Introduction 4
A Definition of Sociology 5
How Sociology Differs from Other Academic Fields 7
Conclusion 8

Part I Theory and Methodology

1 Three Empirical Traditions of Sociological Theory 12
Neil McLaughlin and Antony Puddephatt
Learning Objectives 12
Introduction 14
What Is Sociological Theory? 16
Multivariate Theory 17
Interpretive Theory 19
The Historical-Comparative Tradition 23
Three Contemporary Examples of Sociological Theory 25
The Case for Theoretical Diversity 30
Conclusion 35
Questions for Critical Thought 36
Recommended Readings 36
Recommended Websites 37

2 Research Methods 38
Bruce Arai
Learning Objectives 38
Introduction 40
Sociology as a Science 41
Theory and Research 42
Research Techniques 47
The Context of Sociological Research 58
Conclusion 61
Questions for Critical Thought 62
Recommended Readings 62
Recommended Websites 63

Part II Major Social Processes

3 **Culture and Culture Change** 66
Shyon Baumann
Learning Objectives 66
Why Study Culture? 68
What Is Culture? 68
The Role of Culture in Social Theory 76
Cultural Realms 82
Cultural Dynamics 87
Canadian Culture 91
Conclusion 95
Questions for Critical Thought 96
Recommended Readings 96
Recommended Websites 97

4 **Socialization** 98
Sue Wilson
Learning Objectives 99
Introduction 100
Forms of Socialization 101
Theories of Socialization 103
Agents of Socialization 105
Socialization Outcomes 116
Future Directions 124
Conclusion 125
Questions for Critical Thought 126
Recommended Readings 126
Recommended Websites 127

5 **Statuses, Roles, and Identities** 128
Cheryl Albas and Dan Albas
Learning Objectives 128
Introduction 130
The Social Nature of Status, Role, and Identity 130
Status, Role, and Identity 131
Identity 140
Where Role and Identity Come Together 148
Macro-Societal Implications: Authority
and Its Basis in Statuses, Roles, and Identities 150
Conclusion 152
Questions for Critical Thought 153
Recommended Readings 153
Recommended Websites 154

6 **Groups and Organizations** 155
Lorne Tepperman
Learning Objectives 156
Introduction 157
Sets of People 158
Cliques 164
Bureaucracies 167
Evolving Organizational Theory and Research 173
How Bureaucracies Actually Work 180
Conclusion 187
Questions for Critical Thought 188
Recommended Readings 188
Recommended Websites 189

7 **Deviance** 190
Vincent F. Sacco
Learning Objectives 190
Introduction 192
What Is Deviance? 192
Deviance as a Sociological Concept 193
Researching Deviance 195
The Sociology of Deviant Behaviour 197
Making Sense of the 'Facts' of Deviant Behaviour 204
The Sociology of Deviant Categories 206
Conclusion 214
Questions for Critical Thought 215
Recommended Readings 215
Recommended Websites 216

Part III Social Institutions

8 **Families and Intimate Relationships** 218
Maureen Baker
Learning Objectives 218
Introduction 220
Family Variations 220
Explaining Family Patterns and Practices 224
Recent Issues in Canadian Families 228
Reforming Canadian Family Policies 238
Future Families 239
Conclusion 241
Questions for Critical Thought 242
Recommended Readings 242
Recommended Websites 243

9 Education 244
Terry Wotherspoon
Learning Objectives 244
Introduction 246
The Changing Face of Education 246
Alternative Accounts of Educational Growth and Development 255
Educational Participants 262
Educational Policy, Politics, and Ideologies 263
Education, Work, and Families 266
Education and New Technologies 266
Educational Opportunities and Inequalities 267
Conclusion 272
Questions for Critical Thought 273
Recommended Readings 273
Recommended Websites 274

10 Work and the Economy 276
Pamela Sugiman
Learning Objectives 276
Introduction 278
World Economic Systems 279
The Global Economy 284
The Capitalist Economy: Where People Work 286
Managerial Strategies of Control 290
The Social Organization of Work Today 292
The Changing Face of Labour: Diversity among Workers 297
Workers' Coping and Resistance: The Struggle for Dignity and Rights 304
Conclusion: Work in the Future, Our Future as Workers 308
Questions for Critical Thought 310
Recommended Readings 310
Recommended Websites 311

11 Health Issues 312
Juanne Clarke
Learning Objectives 312
Introduction 314
Theoretical Perspectives 315
The Sociology of Health, Illness, Disease, and Sickness 319
Sociology of Medicine 330
Conclusion 336
Questions for Critical Thought 337
Recommended Readings 337
Recommended Websites 338

12 Religion 340
Lorne L. Dawson
Learning Objectives 341
Introduction: Why Study Religion? 342
The Nature of Religion: Definition and Dimensions 345
Classical Sociological Theory and the Functions of Religion 351
Religion vs Modernity: The Ambiguous Legacy of Secularization Theory 354
The Religious Life of Contemporary Canadians 361
The Future of Religion 365
Questions for Critical Thought 368
Recommended Readings 368
Recommended Websites 369

13 Politics and Political Movements 370
Peter R. Sinclair
Learning Objectives 371
Introduction 372
Core Concepts 372
Modern State Institutions 376
Perspectives on the Democratic State 380
Democracy and Politics in Canada 386
Challenging Issues and Political Movements 392
Conclusion: Future Developments 397
Questions for Critical Thought 399
Recommended Readings 400
Recommended Websites 401

14 Social Movements 402
John Veugelers and Randle Hart
Learning Objectives 402
Introduction 404
What Is a Social Movement? 404
Theoretical Approaches 407
The Analysis of Social Movements 416
Conclusion 425
Questions for Critical Thought 427
Recommended Readings 428
Recommended Websites 428

Part IV Social Inequality

15 Class and Status Inequality 432
Julie Ann McMullin
Learning Objectives 433
Introduction 434
What Is Social Class? 435

Defining and Measuring Social Class 444
Social Class and Inequality 446
Conclusion: Does Class Matter? 455
Questions for Critical Thought 456
Recommended Readings 456
Recommended Websites 457

16 Gender Relations 458
Pat Armstrong
Learning Objectives 459
Introduction 460
Theories of the Sexes 460
Growing Up Feminine or Masculine 464
The Division of Labour by Sex 467
Community and Social Life 475
Explanations for Inequality: Making Connections 477
Strategies for Change 478
Looking Ahead 479
Conclusion 480
Questions for Critical Thought 481
Recommended Readings 481
Recommended Websites 482

17 Sexuality 484
Patrizia Albanese
Learning Objectives 485
Introduction 486
Sexuality over the Centuries 489
The Scientific Study of Sex 491
Sociology of Sex: Theoretical and Methodological Approaches 494
Sexual Citizenship and Sexuality in Canada 501
Sex and the Workplace 507
Cybersex, Pornography, and the Internet 508
Sexual Offences 509
Conclusion 510
Questions for Critical Thought 511
Recommended Readings 511
Recommended Websites 512

18 Ethnic and Race Relations 514
Nikolaos I. Liodakis
Learning Objectives 515
Introduction 516
A Brief History of Ethnicity and Race 517
Building One Nation or Two: Canada's Development through Immigration 520
The New Mosaic: Recent Canadian Immigration Trends 523

Multiculturalism and Its Discontents 526
Prejudice and Racism 532
Culturalism and Political Economy:
Explanations of Socio-economic Inequalities 536
The Vertical Mosaic Then and
the Colour-coded Mosaic Today 538
Earnings Differentials within Ethnic Groups:
The Role of Class and Gender 540
Conclusion: The Future of Race and Ethnicity 544
Questions for Critical Thought 547
Recommended Readings 547
Recommended Websites 548

Part V Canadian Society and the Global Context

19 Global Society 552
Michael R. Smith
Learning Objectives 552
Introduction 554
What Is Globalization? 555
The Effect of Globalizing Mechanisms 560
Conclusion 574
Questions for Critical Thought 575
Recommended Readings 575
Recommended Websites 576

20 Population and Society 578
Frank Trovato
Learning Objectives 578
Introduction 580
Demographic Change and Social Change 580
World Population 581
Age Compositions of Developed
and Developing Countries 586
Theories of Population Change 586
Canada's Population: An Overview 595
Conclusion 606
Questions for Critical Thought 608
Recommended Readings 608
Recommended Websites 609

21 Cities and Urbanization 610
William Michelson
Learning Objectives 611
Introduction 612
Urbanization 612

Urbanism 617
Ecology 622
Structural Analysis 631
Conclusion 637
Questions for Critical Thought 638
Recommended Readings 638
Recommended Websites 639

22 Mass Media and Communication 640
David Young
Learning Objectives 641
Introduction 642
Sociological Theories of the Media 642
Political Economy and the Media 645
Cultural Studies of the Media 656
The Internet: Extending Political Economy and Cultural Studies 666
Conclusion 669
Questions for Critical Thought 671
Recommended Readings 671
Recommended Websites 672

23 The Environment 674
G. Keith Warriner
Learning Objectives 675
Introduction 676
The Basics of Environmental Sociology 677
The Environment and Ecological Scarcity 679
The Environment and Social Theory 685
The Environment and Social Movements 693
Conclusion 702
Questions for Critical Thought 705
Recommended Readings 705
Recommended Websites 707

Glossary 709

References 719

Contributors 763

Index 765

Tables, Figures, and Boxes

Tables

2.1 Guidelines for Designing Good Survey Questions 50
2.2 Population by Marital Status and Sex, Canada, 1998–2002 57
2.3 Percentage of 25- to 64-Year-Olds Graduating from Upper Secondary (High School) Programs, by Country, 1998 58
3.1 Radio Listening Time by Format and Age Group, Fall 2006 71
3.2 Top 20 Names for Baby Girls Born in Illinois by Race, 1989, 1940, and 1920 90
3.3 Population by Language Spoken Most Often at Home, Canada, 1991, 1996, and 2001 92
4.1 Poor Parenting Practices 107
4.2 Teens' Concern About Violence by Religion, Community Size, and Birthplace 113
4.3 Prevalence of Bullying and Victimization in Canada 114
4.4 Parental Expectations About Education and Career 116
7.1 Robert Merton's Paradigm of Deviant Behaviour 199
7.2 Rates of Persons Charged, by Gender, Montreal and Vancouver, 2003 205
7.3 Types of Deviant Behaviour 211
8.1 Percentage of Families in Canada by Type, 1981 and 2001 221
8.2 Canadian Labour Force Participation Rates for Mothers and Fathers with Children Under 15 Years of Age, 2001 228
8.3 Poverty Rates of Households with Children in Various Countries, by Working Status of Parents 234
8.4 The Establishment of Social Benefits in Canada 239
9.1 Educational Attainment in Canada, by Percentage of Population Aged 15 and over, Selected Years, 1951–2005 248
9.2 Full-Time Enrolment in Canada, by Level of Study, Selected Years, 1870–2003 250
9.3 Summary of Digital Divide: Inequalities in Internet Access in Eight Countries 268
9.4 University Degrees Awarded by Field of Study and Gender, Canada, 2004 270
10.1 The Largest 25 Employers in Canada, 2007 283
10.2 Employment by Industry and Sex, 2006 287
10.3 Full-time and Part-time Employment by Sex and Age Group, 2002–6 295
10.4 The Union Advantage, 2003 308
11.1 Health Indicators: Canada, 2003 321
11.2 Leading Causes of Death, Canada, Twentieth Century 322
11.3 Health Expenditures, 2000–4 332
12.1 Weekly Service Attendance in Canada, 1957–2000 357
12.2 Religious Identification of Canadians, 1871–2001 362
12.3 Belief in God in Canada, 1985–2000 364
12.4 Claims of Experiencing God, 1975–2000 365
13.1 Political Development, States and Colonies, 1900–2000 380
13.2 Key Features of Perspectives on Liberal-Democratic States 381
13.3 Women as Percentage of Legislatures, Most Recent Election, Regions and Selected Countries, Ranked by Lower House Representation 387
14.1 Approaches to the Study of Social Movements 407
14.2 Frequency of Types of Protest among Native Bands in Canada, 1981–2000 415
14.3 Support for Socialist Parties in Western Europe Prior to 1914 422
15.1 Samuel Clark's Status Variables 440
15.2 Clement and Myles's Conceptualization of Social Class 446
16.1 Rates of Labour Force Participation by Educational Attainment and Sex, 2005 469
16.2 Average and Median Hourly Wages by Union Coverage, Industry, and Sex 470
17.1 Disapproval and Non-Acceptance of Children's Sexual Behaviour by Age, Gender, and Religious Service Attendance 503
17.2 Discussing Sexuality by Age and Region 504
17.3 Acceptance of Sexual Relations and Approval of Legal Abortion by Age Cohorts, 1975 and 2000 505
18.1 Percentages of Immigrants to Canada by Major Source Area, 1950–5 and 200–4 523
18.2 Top 10 Source Countries of Immigrants to Canada, 2005 524
18.3 Immigration to Canada by Province or Territory of Permanent Settlement, 2006 527
18.4 The Class Composition of Ethnic Groups, 2001 543
18.5 Earnings Differentials among Ethnic Groups, 2001 544
18.6 Earnings Differentials within Ethnic Groups, 2001 545
19.1 Shares of Cultural Imports into Canada, 1996–2000 572

20.1 Estimated and Projected Population of the World, Major Development Groups and Major Areas, 1950, 2000, and 2050, According to Different Projection Variants 585
20.2 Canada's Population and Growth Components, 1851–2001 597
20.3 Interprovincial Migratory Balance in Canada over Five Decades, 1950 to 2000 606
21.1 Urbanization by Continents, 2005 614
21.2 The 20 Largest Cities in the World in 2005 616
21.3 The Size and Suburban Proportion of Canada's Largest Census Metropolitan Areas, 2006 624
22.1 The Leading Media Organizations in Canada, 2005 647
22.2 Stages in Conflict between Cultural Institutions and Ethno-racial Minorities over Representation in the Arts 664
23.1 Population by Level of Development and World Regions, 1950, 2005, and 2050 681
23.2 A Comparison of the Human Exemptionalism Paradigm and the New Ecologic Paradigm 688

Figures

2.1 The Traditional View of Sociology as a Science 40
2.2 Another View of Sociology as a Science 42
2.3 Randomization 53
3.1 Regular Internet Use in Canada, by Gender, Age, Education, and Household Income 84
3.2 Allophone Groups That Increased or Decreased the Most from 1996 to 2001, Canada 92
3.3 Relative Costs and Revenues of Canadian Content and US Simulcasts in Television 95
4.1 Average Weekly Hours of Television Viewing, Canada, 1995–2004 110
6.1 Social Networks for Social Support 160
6.2 Ontario Municipal Board Organizational Hierarchy 171
7.1 The Normal Curve 193
7.2 Provincial Variations in Rates of Homicide, 2005 203
7.3 Suicide Rates by Sex and Age, 2003 206
8.1 Dependent Children by Party to Whom Custody Was Granted, 1995 and 2002 235
9.1 Level of Education in Selected OECD Countries, 2004 253
9.2 Total Educational Spending in Canada, by Direct Source of Funds 265
10.1 Measures of Time Scarcity 301
10.2 Distribution of Annual Earnings, Visible Minorities and Non-Visible Minorities, 2001 302
11.1 Components of Health 320
11.2 Adults and Children Estimated to Be Living with HIV/AIDS as of the End of 2001 323
11.3 Increase in Medical Use by Seniors in Good and Bad Health, Manitoba, 1971–83 335
13.1 Occupations of Members of Parliament, Canada, 1867, 1945, and 2000 383
13.2 Popular Vote by Party, Canadian Federal Elections, 1953–2006 388
13.3 Percentage of Distribution of Votes and Seats by Party, Federal Election, 2006 390
13.4 Armed Conflicts in 2002 395
14.1 The Impact of Environmental Movements 405
14.2 Number of First Nations Protest Collective Events by Year, 1981–2000, Canada 414
14.3 'Old' and 'New' Repertoires in Western Europe and North America 425
15.1 Edward Grabb's Theoretical Framework on Social Inequality 441
15.2 Eric Olin Wright's Class Divisions 446
15.3 Highest Education Attainment of Parents or Guardians of Dropouts and Graduates 453
16.1 Rates of Labour Force Participation by Sex and Five-year Age Categories, 2005 468
16.2 Percentage of Spouses, with Children, Who Do 30 or More Hours of Unpaid Housework per Week, by Labour Force Status, 1996 472
17.1 Kinsey's Heterosexual–Homosexual Rating Scale . . . Applied 493
17.2 Percentage of Canadian Grade 9 and 11 Students Who Have Had Intercourse, 1988, 2002 506
17.3 Number of Sexual Partners among Grade 11 Students Who Have Had Intercourse, 1988, 2002 506
18.1 Immigration in Historical Perspective, 1860–2004 521
18.2 Categories of Immigrants Admitted to Canada, 2005 526
19.1 OECD Imports 563
19.2 Net Public and Private Social Expenditures as a Percentage of GDP 566
19.3 Trade Policy and the Third World 568
20.1 The World Population Explosion 583
20.2 Comparison of Age Structures: Population by Age, Sex, and Development 587
20.3 The Classical Demographic Transition Model and Corresponding Conceptual Types of Society 591
20.4 Schematic Representation of Demographic Transition: Western, Delayed, and Transitional Models 592
20.5 Age-Sex Pyramids of Canada, 1881, 1921, 1951, 1991, 2011, and 2036 604
21.1 Timeline of Significant Events in the Development of Urbanization 614
21.2 Urbanization by Development Level, in Five-Year Intervals 615
21.3 Urbanization of Canada, by Province and Territory, 2001 618
21.4 Payment by Average Residential Property Owner in Toronto (2006) for Types of Service 632
22.1 Home Computer Access, Ages 16–65, by Household Income Quartiles, 2003 667
23.1 The World Model from The Limits to Growth 684

Boxes

Chapter 1
In the First Person Neil McLuaghlin, Antony Puddephatt 15
Sociology in Action Émile Durkheim (1858–1917) 18
Sociology in Action Max Weber (1864–1920) 20
Sociology in Action Georg Simmel (1858–1918) 21
Sociology in Action Karl Marx (1818–1883) 24
Sociology in Action Dorothy E. Smith (b. 1926) 31
Sociology in Action W.E.B. Du Bois (1816–1963) 34

Chapter 2
In the First Person Bruce Arai 41
Human Diversity Are Leaders Born or Bred? 43
Open for Discussion Max Weber And Verstehen 47
Sociology in Action Asking the Right Questions about Survey Data 52
Global Issues Research Ethics in Global Perspective 61

Chapter 3
In the First Person Shyon Baumann 69
Global Issues Fashion and Religion Don't Mix in Toronto 72
Open for Discussion Uniting Iraq's Disparate Cultures a Challenge, Experts Say 81
Sociology in Action Patients with AIDS 87
Human Diversity China's Youth Look to Seoul for Inspiration 93

Chapter 4
In the First Person Sue Wilson 102
Sociology in Action The National Longitudinal Survey of Children And Youth 108
Global Issues Children's Preference for Violent Media 111
Human Diversity Early Childhood Socialization and 'the Troubles' in Northern Ireland 118
Open for Discussion Do the Media Contribute to Disordered Eating Among Young Adolescent and Pre-Adolescent Girls? 119

Chapter 5
Open for Discussion Philip Zimbardo's Stanford Prison Experiment 138
Sociology in Action Seymour Lieberman's Workplace Study 140
Human Diversity Karen March: 'Who Do I Look Like?' 142
Global Issues Milgram's Experiment on Obedience to Authority 151

Chapter 6
In the First Person Lorne Tepperman 159
Open for Discussion *Gemeinschaft* and *Gesellschaft* in a World of Cultural Variety: Cairo 162
Sociology in Action Organizations and Individualism 164
Global Issues Global Virtual Groups Provide New Varieties of Organization 182
Human Diversity Society and Bureaucracy in Ghana 184

Chapter 7
Global Issues Deviance and Diffusion 194
In the First Person Vince Sacco 195
Open for Discussion Is the Sociology of Deviance Dead? 196
Human Diversity What's in a Name? 211
Sociology in Action Disclaimer Mannerisms in University Examinations 212

Chapter 8
In the First Person Maureen Baker 222
Human Diversity A Maori Lone-Mother Family on Social Assistance, New Zealand 223
Open for Discussion Medically Assisted Conception 231
Sociology in Action The Emotional Scars of Family Violence 237

Chapter 9
In the First Person Terry Wotherspoon 249
Open for Discussion Debating Alternatives to Public Schools 252
Global Issues Towards Global Progress on Education 254
Sociology in Action Dimensions of Educational Participation 259
Human Diversity Education for Canada's Aboriginal People 271

Chapter 10
In the First Person Pam Sugiman 279
Global Issues Global Sweatshops: Nike in China 285
Open for Discussion Hard Work Never Killed Anyone 291
Human Diversity Offshore Migrant Farm Workers: A New Form of Slavery? 298
Sociology in Action McDonald's and Unions 306

Chapter 11
In the First Person Juanne Clarke 315
Global Issues Warfare and Human Health 319
Human Diversity Health and Aboriginal Canadians 326
Open for Discussion The Power of Medicalization 333
Sociology in Action Population Aging 335

Chapter 12
In the First Person Lorne Dawson 343
Sociology in Action 'The Battle Hymn of the Republic' 344
Open for Discussion New Religious Life and the Internet 356
Human Diversity The New Religious Diversity 366

Chapter 13
Sociology in Action The Impact of Research on Political Practice: The Aalborg Project 374
In the First Person Peter R. Sinclair 375
Human Diversity Equalization Payments and Oil Revenues 382
Open for Discussion Controversy Over Health Care Reform 392
Global Issues Colombia: 'Everybody Is Full of Terror' 396

Chapter 14
Sociology in Action Craig Kielburger and Free The Children 406
In the First Person Randle Hart 409
Open for Discussion The Free-Rider Program 411
Human Diversity Activism After September 11 417
Global Issues The Clayoquot Standoff 423

Chapter 15
In the First Person Julie Mcmullin 435
Open for Discussion The Lessons of Kimberly Rogers's Death 436
Human Diversity Images of Child Poverty in Canada 449
Global Issues UN Finds Global Inequality Rising 455

Chapter 16
Global Issues Changing Views of Men 463
Sociology in Action More Work for Mother 473
Open for Discussion The High Cost of an Interrupted Career 478

Chapter 17
Open for Discussion Heteronormativity in Nursing 487
In the First Person Patrizia Albanese 488
Human Diversity Incest and Taboo 495
Sociology in Action Sexual Scripts and Sexual Double Standards in Popular Magazines 498
Global Issues HIV/AIDS: A Global Crisis 507

Chapter 18
In the First Person Nik Liodakis 518
Global Issues The Points System For Skilled Workers: Would You Make It? 525
Open for Discussion Reasonable Accommodation, Xenophobia, and Islamophobia 534

Chapter 19
Open for Discussion The International Monetary Fund and the World Bank 556
In the First Person Michael Smith 559
Global Issues Stiglitz on Globalization and the Third World 562
Human Diversity Foreign Competition: The Case of the Canadian Clothing Industry 565

Chapter 20
In the First Person Frank Trovato 581
Open for Discussion Sex Ratio Imbalances in the Marriage Market 588
Human Diversity Youth in the International Labour Market 590
Global Issues The HIV/AIDS Epidemic: A Snapshot 599

Chapter 21
In the First Person William Michelson 613
Global Issues The Gap Between the Real World and Statistical Measures 617
Open for Discussion Individual Identity in a World of Strangers 620
Human Diversity Gender and the Everyday Use of Urban Contexts 622
Sociology in Action Improving Women's Safety 630

Chapter 22
In the First Person David Young 643
Global Issues The Global Music Industry 651
Open for Discussion Do We Need Cancon Regulations for Radio? 655
Sociology in Action Watching Homeless Men Watch *Die Hard* 662

Chapter 23
Global Issues Energetics 686
Sociology in Action Cancer City 698
Human Diversity Environmental Justice 702

Preface

From the Publisher

While preparing this second edition of *Sociology: A Canadian Perspective,* the general editors, contributing authors, and publisher kept in mind one paramount goal: to produce the most authoritative, comprehensive, yet accessible and interesting introduction to sociology available for Canadian students.

The revision builds on the strengths of the well-received first edition and incorporates many new features designed to enhance the book's usefulness for students and instructors alike.

Chapter 17 Sexuality 501

The sex trade and poverty are worldwide phenomena that seem to go hand in hand. Here, sex workers buy fresh goat milk while waiting for clients outside their rented rooms on '*La Linea*' ('The Strip') in Guatemala City. (CP/AP Photo/Alexandre Meneghini)

Sexual Citizenship and Sexuality in Canada

Former Prime Minister Pierre Trudeau, when he was Justice Minister in 1967, played a key role in helping to legally redefine sexuality for Canadians. For the first 100 years after Confederation, homosexuality was illegal in Canada and considered to be a mental illness. In December of 1967, Trudeau introduced a controversial new omnibus bill in the House of Commons (Bill C-150) that challenged this and some other restrictions placed on sexuality. Trudeau's legislation brought issues like abortion, homosexuality, and the divorce law to the forefront, changing the sexual landscape of Canada. At the time, Trudeau famously stated that 'there's no place for the state in the bedrooms of the nation.' Despite considerable opposition, by 1969 homosexual acts had been decriminalized and women had more control over sexual reproduction and their bodies. It was not until the year 2000, however, with the passing of Bill C-23, that same-sex couples were granted the same rights and obligations as common-law couples, and 2005, when the Liberal government passed 'equal marriage' legislation. On 20 July 2005, Bill C-38, The Civil Marriage Act, recognized the right of same-sex couples to have access to civil marriage, without discrimination.

Over the past 40 years there have also been changes to the laws governing the legal age of consent to have sex in Canada, with major changes in 1988. That year, the introduction of Bill C-15 created the offence of 'sexual interference' and prohibited adults from engaging in virtually any kind of sexual contact with either boys or girls under the age of 14, regardless of consent. The notion of

Time to Reflect

Despite legal changes, in the spring of 2002 the Durham Catholic School Board unanimously voted to deny a gay Oshawa high school student, Marc Hall, the right to attend his high school prom with his same-sex partner. In light of the legal changes, do you support the school board decision? Why? Why not?

New chapter on sexuality

A brand-new chapter dealing with the sociological implications of sexuality and gender has been added to this edition. Written by Patrizia Albanese, the new chapter reflects both cutting-edge research and age-old questions in what has become a central area of sociological inquiry. Discussion of current topics such as same-sex marriage helps to anchor discussion of key concepts in the real world and provides an opportunity for discussion and reflection.

New treatment of theory and research methods

In response to feedback from reviewers, the chapters on sociological theory and research methods now are found at the beginning of the book, to better emphasize and explore the tools and concepts used in social research and to lay the groundwork for the chapters that follow.

1 Chapter

Three Empirical Traditions of Sociological Theory

Neil McLaughlin and Antony Puddephatt

Learning Objectives

New contributing authors

For the second edition, we welcome aboard several new contributing authors: Nikolaos Liodakis (race and ethncity), Patrizia Albanese (sexuality), David Young (mass media and technology), and Neil McLaughlin and Antony Puddephatt (sociological theory)

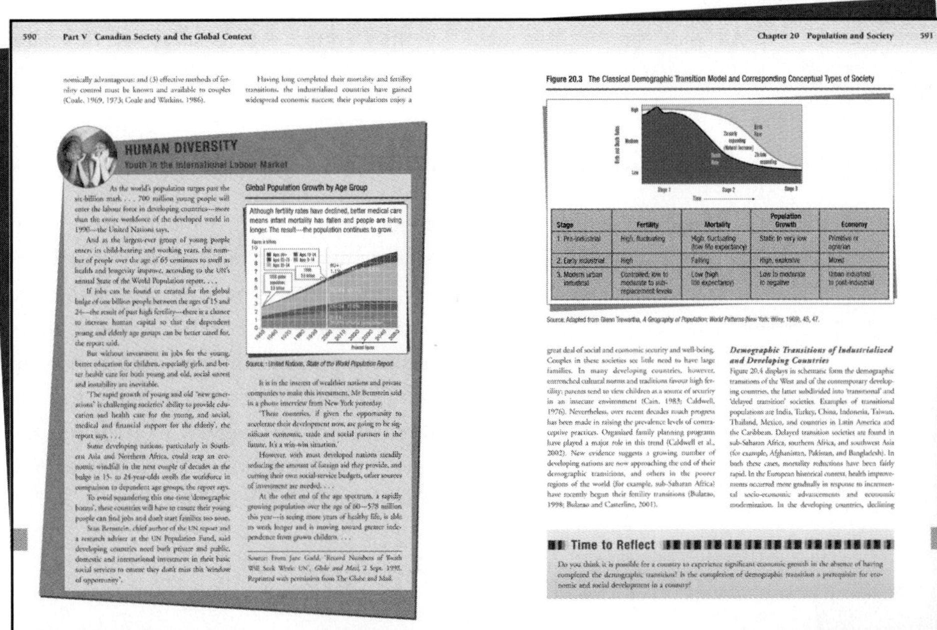

New design

The book has been completely redesigned in a contemporary four-colour palette intended to enhance readability while reflecting the vibrancy of Canadian sociology as an academic discipline.

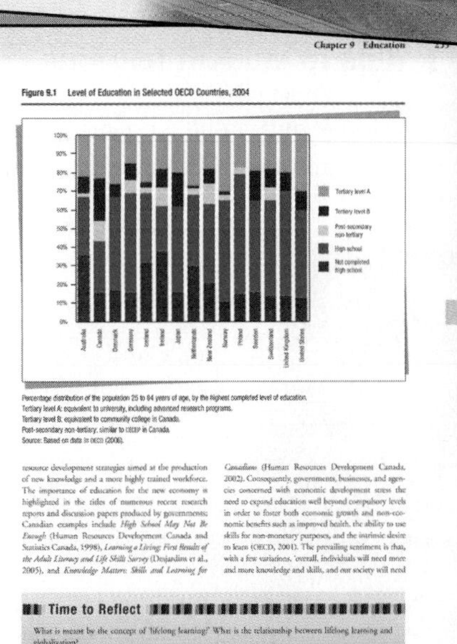

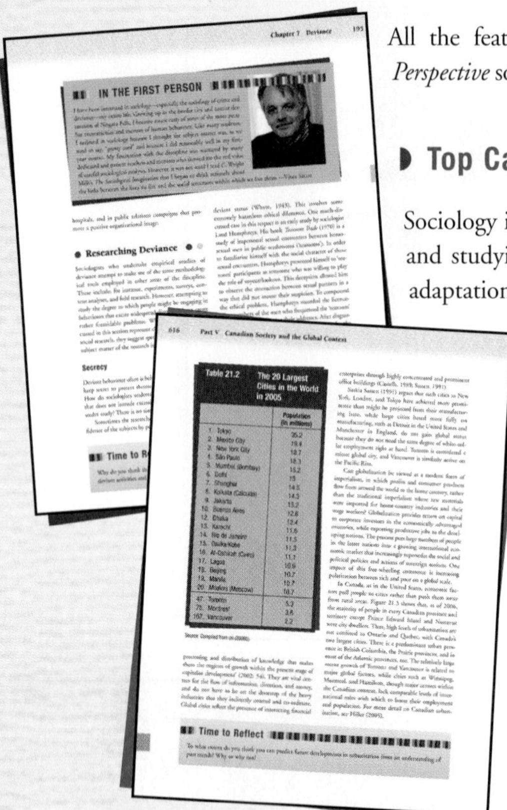

Chapter 7 Deviance 195

IN THE FIRST PERSON

Researching Deviance

Secrecy

Time to Reflect

616 Part V Canadian Society and the Global Context

Table 21.2 The 20 Largest Cities in the World in 2005

	Population (in millions)
1. Tokyo	35.2
2. Mexico City	19.4
3. New York City	18.7
4. São Paulo	18.3
5. Mumbai (Bombay)	18.2
6. Delhi	15
7. Shanghai	14.5
8. Kolkata (Calcutta)	14.3
9. Jakarta	13.2
10. Buenos Aires	12.6
12. Dhaka	12.4
13. Karachi	11.6
14. Rio de Janeiro	11.5
15. Osaka-Kobe	11.3
16. Al-Qahirah (Cairo)	11.1
17. Lagos	10.9
18. Beijing	10.7
19. Manila	10.7
20. Moskva (Moscow)	10.7
47. Toronto	5.3
75. Montreal	3.6
107. Vancouver	2.2

Time to Reflect

All the features that made the first edition of *Sociology: A Canadian Perspective* so popular have been retained in this revision:

Top Canadian contributors

Sociology is a global discipline, but one to which sociologists working in and studying Canada have made unique contributions. Not merely an adaptation of a book originally written for American undergraduates, this text was conceived and written from the ground up as a Canadian perspective on this fascinating field. Experts in their particular sub-disciplines not only examine the key concepts and terminology of sociology as an academic discipline, but also use those concepts to shed light on the nature of Canadian society and Canada's place in the world.

Global perspective

Although this is a book written by and for Canadians, the editors and authors never forget that Canada is but one small part of a vast, diverse, and endlessly fascinating social world. Along with Canadian data, examples, and illustrations, a wealth of information about how humans live and interact around the world is presented in every chapter.

Theoretical balance

The very mention of the term 'theory' seems to make first-year undergraduates uneasy, but the overriding goal in *Sociology: A Canadian Perspective* has been not just to make the theories that underpin the discipline comprehensible, but to show how they inform an understanding of the data that sociologists gather—and how the choice of which theoretical perspective to employ can yield new and surprising insights. Throughout the text, emerging paradigms are also discussed where they shed new light on longstanding questions.

Aids to student learning

A textbook must fulfill a double duty: while meeting instructors' expectations for accuracy, currency, and comprehensiveness, it must also speak to today's students, providing them with an accessible introduction to a body of knowledge. To that end, numerous features to promote student learning are incorporated throughout the book. These include:

Chapter 15

Class and Status Inequality

Julie Ann McMullin

Learning Objectives

- ***Learning Objectives*** at the start of each chapter, providing a concise overview of the key concepts that will be covered.

- ***Theme Boxes*** illustrating important points and providing examples of how sociological research sheds light on the 'real world'.

- ***Graphs and Tables.*** Though qualitative research methods have grown in importance in recent years, one of the characteristics that still distinguishes sociology from some of the other liberal arts and social sciences is its emphasis on using quantitative data and analysis as a crucial tool for understanding society. Colourful graphs and charts make such data clear in a way that sometimes text cannot.

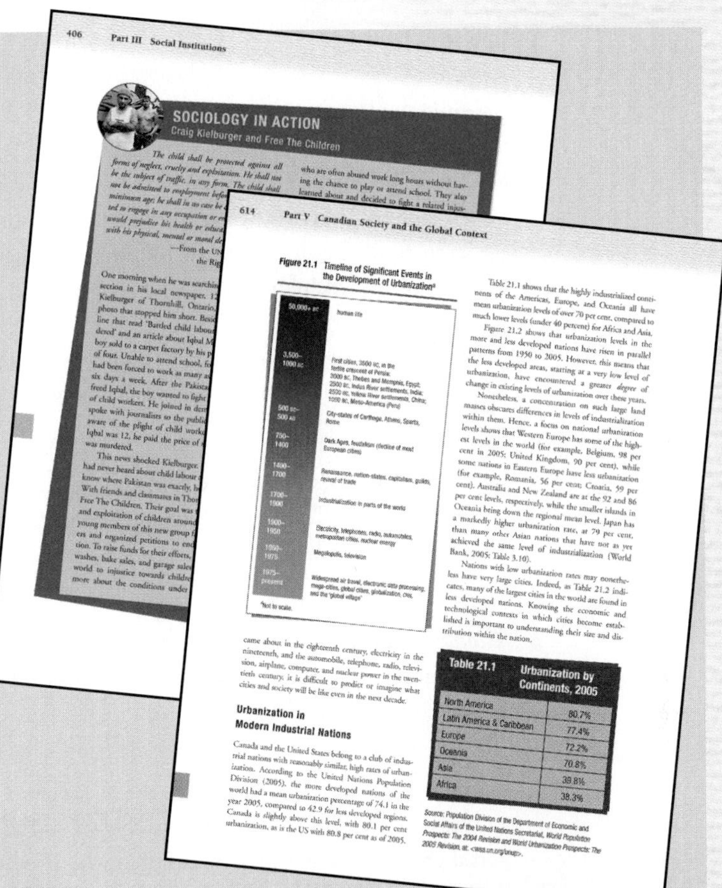

406 Part III Social Institutions

SOCIOLOGY IN ACTION
Craig Kielburger and Free The Children

614 Part V Canadian Society and the Global Context

Figure 21.1 Timeline of Significant Events in the Development of Urbanization

Urbanization in Modern Industrial Nations

Table 21.1	Urbanization by Continents, 2005
North America	80.7%
Latin America & Caribbean	77.4%
Europe	72.2%
Oceania	70.8%
Asia	39.8%
Africa	38.3%

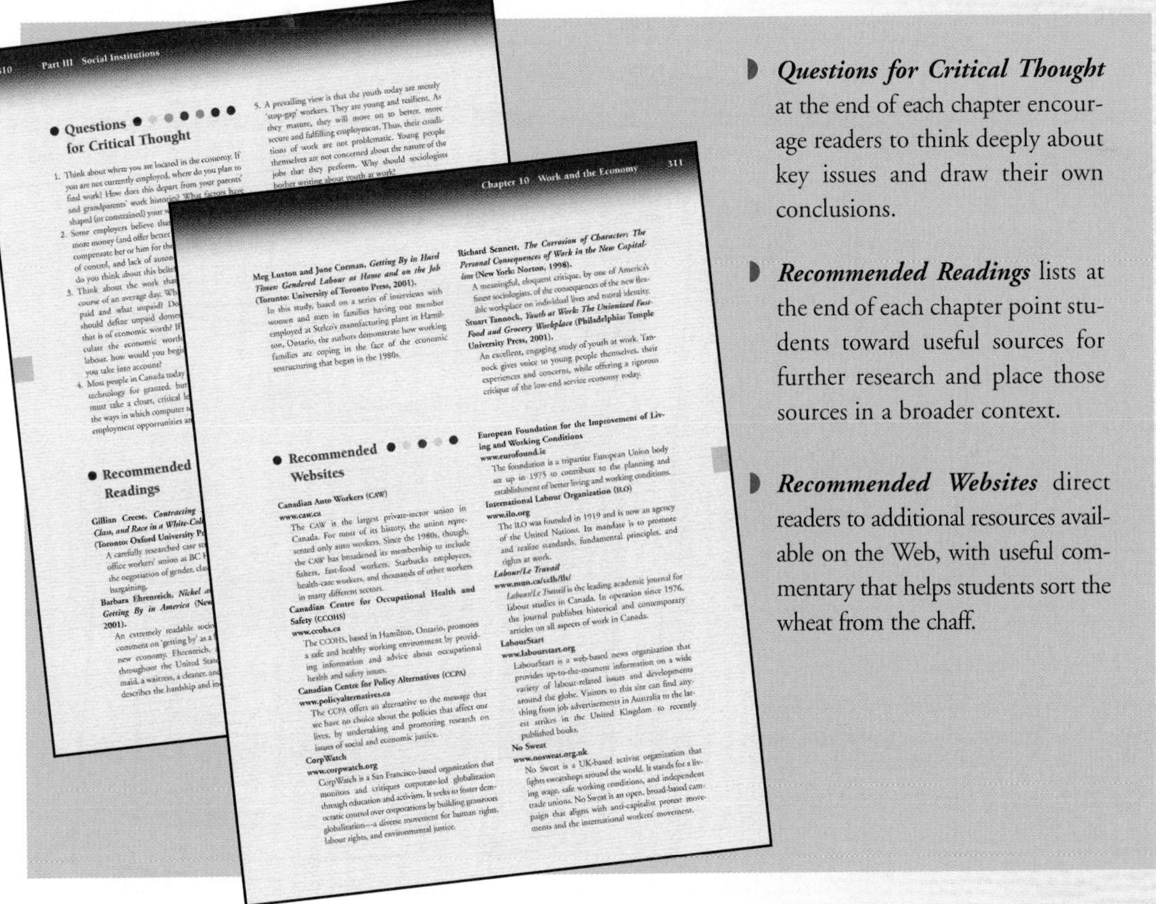

310 Part III Social Institutions

Questions for Critical Thought

Recommended Readings

Chapter 10 Work and the Economy 311

Recommended Websites

- ***Questions for Critical Thought*** at the end of each chapter encourage readers to think deeply about key issues and draw their own conclusions.

- ***Recommended Readings*** lists at the end of each chapter point students toward useful sources for further research and place those sources in a broader context.

- ***Recommended Websites*** direct readers to additional resources available on the Web, with useful commentary that helps students sort the wheat from the chaff.

Theme boxes

'Why study sociology?' is a question frequently asked by students enrolled in their first sociology course. There are all kinds of reasons, of course, but among them are that sociology provides a unique insight into the nature of the human world; that it shows us things about society and ourselves that we might not otherwise know; and that the lessons of sociology can be intriguing, touching, tragic, even fun. The dozens of theme boxes scattered throughout the text illustrate all these dimensions of the discipline.

- ***Sociology in Action*** boxes show how sociological research can help us better understand the everyday world, from issues surrounding women's safety to sexual double standards in popular magazines.

- ***Open for Discussion*** boxes use contemporary social issues and debates to focus understanding of core sociological concepts. Examples range from medically assisted conception to new religious life on the Internet.

- ***Global Issues*** boxes draw upon examples from around the world to illustrate the effects of globalization and show what sociologists have to say about, for instance, energetics or the effects of warfare on human health.

- ***Human Diversity*** boxes recognize the overwhelming and unavoidable fact of human diversity, and seek to introduce students to the ways of life and world views of different cultures and social groups, whether they be children who lived through 'the Troubles' in Northern Ireland or Aboriginal Canadians fighting diseases of development and impoverishment.

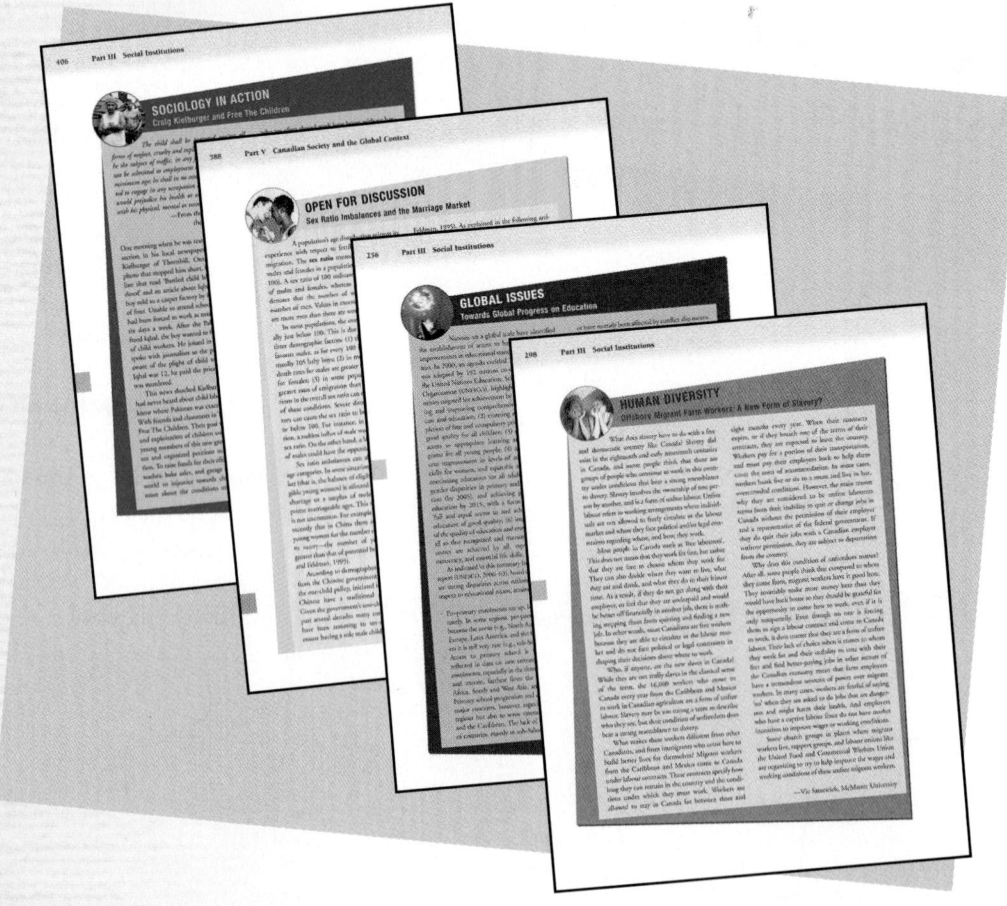

Sociology as a human pursuit

Sociology: A Canadian Perspective celebrates the fact that while sociology is an academic discipline with a distinguished pedigree, it is also a very human pursuit—a fact that becomes clear in the brief *In the First Person* narratives now included in every chapter, in which the authors discuss why they chose careers in sociology. The text's contributors first encountered the discipline at the same age as many of the students now using this text in 'intro soc'. Sociology is, above all, the study of human beings interacting within society in all their wonderful complexity, and *In the First Person* provides an intriguing glimpse into why this particular group of individuals chose to make that study their lifework.

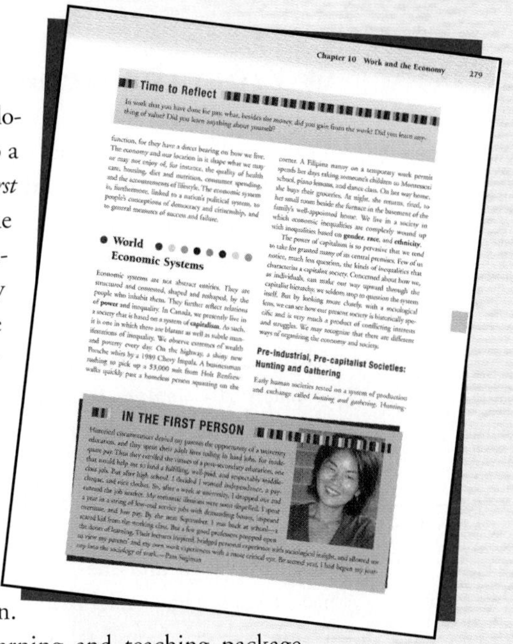
Chapter 10 Work and the Economy 279

Time to Reflect

World Economic Systems

Pre-Industrial, Pre-capitalist Societies: Hunting and Gathering

IN THE FIRST PERSON

Supplements

Today's texts no longer are volumes that stand on their own. Rather, they are but the central element in a complete learning and teaching package. *Sociology: A Canadian Perspective* is no exception. The book is supported by an outstanding array of ancillary materials for both students and instructors.

For Instructors

- **Online Instructor's Manual**
  This fully revised online resource includes comprehensive outlines of the text's various parts and chapters, additional questions for encouraging class discussion, suggestions on how to use videos to enhance classes, and extra resource material for use in lectures.

- **Online Test Generator**
  A comprehensive electronic test item file—now employing cutting-edge test generator technology that allows instructors a wide array of options for sorting, editing, importing, and distributing questions—provides over 2,400 questions (more than 100 per chapter), in multiple-choice, short-answer, and true/false formats.

- **PowerPoint® Slides**
  Hundreds of slides for classroom presentation—newly updated and enhanced for this edition—incorporate graphics and tables from the text, summarize key points from each chapter, and can be edited to suit individual instructors' needs.

- **CBC News DVD**
  This extremely popular collection of video clips has been completely revamped to accompany the second edition of the text. News stories from across Canada and around the world make key issues in sociology come alive for today's students.

For Students

- **Companion Website**
  A comprehensive online study guide site provides automatically graded study questions, annotated links to other useful Web resources, additional review questions, applied exercises, and other material designed to enhance student learning.

From the General Editors

The two editors of this book—formerly teacher and student, now colleagues—are happy to bring enthusiastic readers a new edition of a text that tries to explain sociology, and Canadian society, to a new generation of Canadian students. We think that, in this second edition, *Sociology: A Canadian Perspective* continues to provide an up-to-date picture of Canadian society and Canadian sociology at the beginning of the twenty-first century. As always, we remain committed to providing the best, most reader-friendly presentation of social facts and theories. Our publisher, Oxford University Press Canada, has helped us do so, and we are grateful for this help. *Sociology: A Canadian Perspective* has received strong support from the topmost levels of Oxford University Press Canada, including David Stover, president of the Canadian branch. Thank you, David. Oxford knows that it wants a Canadian sociology list and knows how to produce it.

Working with us on this edition of *Sociology: A Canadian Perspective* was copy editor Richard Tallman, a veteran of our earlier *Social Problems* textbook. Richard is a true professional, thorough and provocative, and one of the best we have met in decades of writing books. Richard's help has been encouraging, enlightening, and inspiring. We also thank Richard for his endless patience. Thank you, developmental editor Dina Theleritis, managing editor Phyllis Wilson, and, especially, Eric Sinkins at Oxford for taking care of the backstage practical matters. You made sure that all the pieces came together when and where they were supposed to. And thanks to Eric, too, for his role in selecting photographs, and to all those talented people who took the photos that appear in this great-looking book.

We are also grateful for help received from Lorne's University of Toronto work-study undergraduates, who last year included Jason Jensen, Matt Kopas, Achire Mbanwi, Jenny Wong, Alina Smirnova, and Joanna Guerriere. Your help was invaluable and inspiring.

Our main thanks go to the contributing authors, without whom this book simply would not exist. They put up with our (seemingly endless) demands, and somehow we got from A to B without any catastrophes or other unseemly emotional displays. It has been a great privilege working with this distinguished group of top Canadian scholars from all over the country. Thank you, authors.

Finally, in closing, we dedicate this book to our friend and colleague Jim Curtis, who passed away just before work on this new edition was to begin. Jim had co-edited the first edition of this book, and he was a singular collaborator, not to mention a singular human being. Replacing Jim in full was impossible, but Patrizia was kind enough (and honoured) to take up the challenge. We two editors have enjoyed working on this book together. What's more, Jim would have been proud of the result. Jim, we miss you. Your hope that our textbooks might contribute to Canadian sociology and the education of young Canadian scholars remains alive and in good hands. We think the readers of this book will agree.

Lorne Tepperman, University of Toronto
Patrizia Albanese, Ryerson University

This book is dedicated to a friend and leading Canadian sociologist, James (Jim) Curtis, who passed away on 27 May 2005. Jim was convinced that good sociology could improve our society. His desire to teach another generation of sociologists lives on in this book.

Introduction: Why Not Become a Sociologist?

Lorne Tepperman and Patrizia Albanese

Photo: Mike Manzano/iStockphoto

Introduction

Why do people become sociologists? There are many answers to this question, and it is likely that everyone at one point or other has been on the brink of becoming a sociologist. We say this because all people experience odd facts of social life that affect their opportunities, and they try to understand them. This is where sociology begins for most people. When people continue from here, there is even more motivation to do sociology. What can be more fascinating, more empowering, and more personal than to begin to understand the society that shapes our lives? For these reasons, sociology is an inherently attractive area of study, and many people do study it.

Maybe as a child you noticed that:

- Parents sometimes treat their sons differently from their daughters.
- Teachers often treat pretty little girls better than plain-looking ones.
- Adults treat well-dressed children better than poorly dressed children.
- Movies typically portray people with 'accents' as strange or ridiculous.

If you noticed these things, you may have wondered why they happen. They may even have affected you, as a daughter or son, a plain-looking or attractive person, a poorly dressed or well-dressed person, or a person with or without an 'accent'. You may have felt ashamed, angry, or pleased, depending on whether you identified with the favourably treated or the unfavourably treated category of people.

Perhaps you grew up in a small town and have moved to a big city, or grew up in a big city and now live in a small town. You noticed that:

- People are not like the media portrayed them.
- The ethnic and racial composition of the people around you is not what you are used to.
- The gap between rich and poor is more pronounced.
- People interact with each other differently than back home.
- They have strange reactions to strangers.
- They talk differently, dress differently, eat different kinds of foods.

If you noticed these things, you may have wanted to understand them better. These are the kinds of circumstances in which sociological curiosity begins. All sociologists somehow, sometime or another, got hooked on trying to better understand their own lives and the lives of people around them. They came to understand that common sense gave them only incomplete explanations about what happened to people, about people's behaviour and the society in which they live. They were not satisfied with the incomplete explanation and wanted to know more.

For many people, and for much of what we do, common-sense understanding is just fine. Still, for anyone who wants to understand how society works, it is not good enough. You may already realize there are many questions common sense cannot answer adequately. For example:

- Why are some people so different from you, and why are some so similar?
- Why do apparently similar people lead such different lives?
- How is it possible for different people to get along?
- Why do we treat some people as if they are more 'different' than others?
- Why do we often treat 'different' people much worse than others?
- What do people do to escape from being treated badly?
- Why do some aspects of society change quickly and others hardly at all?
- What can citizens do to make Canadian society a more equitable place?
- What can young people do to make their elders think differently?
- Can we bring about social change by changing the laws of the country?

Sociologists try to answer these questions by studying societies methodically. In fact, their task is to study people's lives—their own and others'—more carefully than anyone else. Sociologists want to understand how societies change and how people's lives change with them. Social changes, inequalities, and conflicts captivate sociologists because such issues—war and peace, wealth and poverty, environmental destruction and technological innovation, for example—are important for people's lives. Sociologists know that 'personal problems' are similar across many individuals. They also know that many of our personal problems are the private side of public issues. American sociologist C. Wright Mills called this knowledge or ability 'the sociological imagination'. With this ability or approach, we know we need to deal with personal problems collectively and, often, politically—with full awareness that we share these problems and their solution with others.

In the 1950s, American sociologist C. Wright Mills was a famous rebel *with* a cause. He pushed the sociological community towards a more historically informed, politically committed engagement with the world. (Photo © Yaroslava Mills)

However, solving problems entails clear thinking and careful research. So, social theorists and social science researchers have developed concepts, theories, and research methods that help them study the social world more effectively. Our goal as sociologists is to be able to explain social life, critique social inequities, and work towards effecting social change. In this book, you will learn how sociologists go about these tasks, and some of what sociologists have found out about the social world.

Our starting point here is a formal definition of *sociology*, comparisons of sociology with other related fields of study, and a discussion of sociology's most basic subject matter.

A Definition of Sociology

Scholars have defined **sociology** in many ways, but most practising sociologists think of their discipline as the systematic study of social behaviour in human societies. Humans are intensely social beings and spend most of their time interacting with other humans. That is why sociologists study the social units people create when they join with others. As we will see in the following chapters, these units range from small groups—comprising as few as two people—to large corporations and even whole societies (see, for example, Chapter 6, on groups, cliques, and bureaucracies). Sociologists are interested in learning about how group membership affects individual behaviour and, reciprocally, how individuals change the groups of which they are members. In most social life, at least in Canadian society, there is a visible tug-of-war between these two forces: the group and the individual.

However, it is impossible for any sociologist to study all social issues or to become an expert in all the subareas of sociology. As a result, most sociologists specialize in either macrosociology or microsociology—two related but distinct approaches to studying the social world—and choose problems for study from within these realms.

Teams, like other social groups (e.g., bands, gangs, classrooms) all need communication, co-ordination, leadership, shared identity, and ritual. Many teams have uniforms and other insignia to increase their solidarity. (moodboard/Corbis)

Macrosociology is the study of large social organizations (for example, the Roman Catholic Church, universities, corporations, or government bureaucracies) and large social categories (for example, ethnic minorities, the elderly, or college students). Sociologists who specialize in the macrosociological approach to the social world focus on the complex social patterns that people form over long periods (see many examples in Parts III and V of this volume, on social institutions and global society, respectively).

On the other hand, **microsociology** focuses on the typical processes and patterns of face-to-face interaction in small groups. A microsociologist might study a marriage, a clique, a business meeting, an argument between friends, or a first date. In short, he or she would study the common, everyday interactions and negotiations that together produce lasting, secure patterns (see many examples in Chapters 4 and 5, on socialization and on roles and identities, respectively).

The difference in names—**macro** versus **micro**—refers to the difference in size in the social units of interest. Macrosociologists study large social units—organizations, societies, or even empires—over long periods of time: years, centuries, or millennia. Microsociologists study small social units over short periods of time—for example, what happens during a conversation, a party, a classroom lecture, or a love affair. As in nature, large things move (and change) slowly and small things move more quickly. As a result, macrosociologists are likely to stress how slowly things change and how persistent a social pattern is as it plays itself out in one generation after another. An example is the way society tends to be controlled by its elite groups, decade after decade. The connection between business elites and political elites is persistent. By contrast, microsociologists are likely to stress how quickly things change and how elusive is that thing we call 'social life'. In their eyes, any social unit is constantly being created and reconceived by the members of society. An example is the way one's friendship group changes yearly, if not more often, as one moves through the school system or the world of work. Some people remain our close friends over years, but many are close friends for only a short while.

Combining macro and micro approaches improves our understanding of the social world. Consider a common social phenomenon: the domestic division of labour—who does what chores around the home. From the micro perspective, who does what is constantly open to negotiation, a result of personal characteristics, the history of the couple, and other unique factors. From a macro perspective, different households tend to have similar divisions of labour, despite differences in personal history. This suggests the answer lies in a society's history, culture, and economy. It is far from accidental that, across millions of households, men enjoy the advantage of a better salary and more social power both in a great many workplaces and at home.

While these approaches are different, they are also connected. They have to be: after all, both macro- and microsociologists are studying the same people in the same society. All of us are leading unique lives within a common social context, faced by common problems. The question is, how can sociologists bring these elements together? As noted above, C. Wright Mills (1959) gave the answer when he introduced the notion of the **sociological imagination** as something that enables us to relate personal biographies—the lives of millions of ordinary people like ourselves—to the broad sweep of human history. The sociological imagination is what we need to use to understand how societies control and change their members and, at the same time, are constantly changed by the actions of their members.

All of this is the subject matter of sociology. We may choose to focus on problems of microsociology or macrosociology because of our preference to understand one or the other, but a proper or full understanding of most problems will need us to consider elements of both, because the two types of processes are closely connected.

How Sociology Differs from Other Academic Fields

Sociology is just one of several fields of study designed to help describe and explain human behaviour; others include journalism, history, philosophy, and psychology. How does sociology differ from these other endeavours? Canadian sociologist Kenneth Westhues (1982) has compared sociology's approach with those of the other fields. He stresses that journalism and history describe real events, as does sociology. However, journalism and history only sometimes base their descriptions on a **theory** or interpretation, and then it is often an implicit or hidden theory. Sociology is different. It strives to make its theories clear to test them. Telling a story is important for sociologists, but less so than the explanation on which the story is based. Besides, stories often make the news because they are unusual; sociologists instead are drawn to issues because they are common events or are recurring patterns. Sociology may be good preparation for doing history or journalism, but it differs from these disciplines.

Sociology also differs from philosophy. Both are *analytical*—that is, concerned with testing and refining theory. However, sociology is firmly *empirical*, or concerned with gathering evidence and doing studies, while philosophy is not. Philosophy has greater concern with the internal logic of its arguments. Sociological theories must stand up logically, but they must also stand up to evidence in a way philosophical theories need not. Sociologists, no matter how logical the theory may be, will not accept a sociological theory whose predictions are not supported by evidence gathered in a sound way.

Finally, sociology differs from psychology, which is also analytical, empirical, and interpretive. The difference here lies in the subject matter. Psychologists study the behaviour of individual humans (or, sometimes, animals), and generally under experimental conditions. Sociology's subject matter is social relationships or groups viewed in society. The family, the educational system, the media, the way work is organized, and the total society are the matters of inquiry. Sociology and psychology come close together in a field called *social psychology*, but this field is defined differently by sociologists and by psychologists. Studies conducted by sociologists in this field are more likely to focus on the effects of group living on the views or behaviours of individuals, while psychologists are more likely to be concerned with particular individuals and how they respond under certain experimental conditions.

Another way of characterizing sociology and what makes it unique has been put forward by Earl Babbie (1988). He states that sociologists hold some basic or fundamental ideas that set them apart from those in other fields:

1. Society has an existence of its own.
2. Society can be studied scientifically.
3. Society creates itself.
4. Cultures vary over time and place.
5. Individual identity is a product of society.
6. Social structure must satisfy survival requirements.
7. Institutions are inherently conservative.
8. Societies constrain and transform.
9. Multiple paradigms or fundamental models of reality are needed.

Sociology is just one of the fields of study designed to help describe and explain human behaviour. It differs from others, such as psychology, in its focus on social relationships or groups observed in society. (Volker Kreinacke/iStockphoto)

As we will see in the chapters that follow, these are many of the most basic ideas or assumptions of sociology. However, some sociologists would disagree about which of these are most important, or whether there are other ideas that are just as important or more important. Part I of this collection (Chapters 1 and 2) introduces the theoretical underpinnings and methodologies of sociology. In Part II the work of several sociologists and sociological approaches focus on understanding major social processes like culture (Chapter 3), socialization (Chapter 4), roles and identities (Chapter 5), groups and organizations (Chapter 6), and deviance (Chapter 7). In Part III you will learn about different social institutions that shape and constrain our lives, including the family (Chapter 8), education (Chapter 9), work and the economy (Chapter 10), health (Chapter 11), religion (Chapter 12), politics (Chapter 13), and social movements (Chapter 14). Part IV presents different forms of inequality experienced by some in society, through chapters on class and status (Chapter 15), gender relations (Chapter 16), sexuality (Chapter 17), and ethnic and race relations (Chapter 18). Increasingly, understanding society involves understanding global issues—the focus of Part V of this book. In this section you will read about global society (Chapter 19), population (Chapter 20), cities and urbanization (Chapter 21), the mass media (Chapter 22), and the environment (Chapter 23).

Conclusion

Sociology is a good idea. It pays off by enlightening us, and it has worthy goals. It is the systematic study of how society and patterns of social behaviour within society are structured and change.

It is a broad field of study. This is obvious in the broad theoretical perspectives used to guide much sociological research. The breadth of the field of study is further evident in the idea that sociology highlights both micro- and macro-level analyses and the complex relationships between the two as highlighted in Mills's concept of the sociological imagination. Sociology also covers a broad subject matter—consider the subject matter of the following chapters, ranging across deviance, family, education, religion, politics, the economy, health, and beyond.

Sociology allows people to move beyond a purely common-sense approach to better understanding social life. It allows them to use more powerful methods of investigation that reveal the multi-faceted and elaborate ways that aspects of social life are interconnected. In the process, much **common-sense knowledge** is shown to be faulty. Sociology will help you see that things are not always what they seem.

Sociology stresses the relationships among individuals, social structure, and culture. Social structure and culture are shown to constrain the behaviour of individuals, yet they are essential for the persistence of human life and society. In addition, social structure and culture are creations of humans through social interaction and, therefore, are subject to future change by individuals acting in group settings. Strong constraints are placed on certain forms of social and cultural change, however, by the actions of powerful interest groups.

Sociology has obvious personal relevance, since it addresses everyday life issues. And, finally, sociology has an important goal overall: to contribute positively to the future of humanity. Our sincere hope is that this text will set you on your way to developing your own sociological imagination.

Part I

Theory and Methodology

1

Chapter

Three Empirical Traditions of Sociological Theory

Neil McLaughlin and Antony Puddephatt

Learning Objectives

In this chapter, you will:

- Learn about three major approaches to sociological theory: multivariate, interpretive, and historical-comparative.
- Understand how sociological theories are linked to quantitative, qualitative, or historical-comparative research methods and evidence.
- Identity some of the advantages and disadvantages of each type of theoretical approach and data-gathering method.
- Gain insight into suicides in Quebec, relationship breakups, and Canadian–American cultural differences.
- Understand the ways in which contemporary sociologists combine the three major approaches to theory to explain aspects of society.

Figure/ground by Warren Collins, Tasmania, Australia, collage

camera til

Introduction

Have you ever known someone who seemed reasonably happy and content one day, only to find the person later killed himself (or herself), leaving a suicide note to loved ones? Why would someone do this? Have you ever known the perfect and happy romantic couple, who would surprise their friends and family suddenly with a bitter and angry divorce proceeding? What are the sociological stages that accompany divorce and separation? Do you ever wonder what makes Canada different from other nations? If you have not spent much time outside of Canada, you probably rely on the media—movies, television, books, the Internet—to give you a sense of how other countries differ. How did Canada come to be the kind of country it is, and how are Canadians different from Americans? Sociological theorists address these types of questions by looking for the patterns that underlie social life through empirical research. They make sense of these patterns using the conceptual tools provided by sociological theory.

Sociological theory provides the analytic tools to understand the relationship between people's individual lives and their surrounding social world. American sociologist C. Wright Mills (1959) called this attempt to link seemingly personal experiences with larger historical and social trends the **sociological imagination.** This involves fitting individual events into larger patterns of association, conducting research to better understand group structures and processes. This sociological imagination allows for the creation of general sociological theories to make sense of the complexities of the social world. Too often, sociological theory is considered separately from the empirical research traditions that created it. As a result, we often forget that good sociological theory is based on carefully gathered evidence, and that the most interesting and useful evidence often comes from theoretically informed research. There are three major empirical traditions that contributed to sociological theory along different levels of analysis. **Level of analysis** refers to the size and scale of social life under examination. Macro-level theories analyze relations between large numbers of people who may never interact personally, yet who are connected by social factors operating at regional, national, or global levels. In contrast, micro-level theories deal with the social processes and dynamics of small groups, networks, and individuals. Meso-level theories deal with the scale of society in between the macro and the micro levels, for example, organizations and institutions such as businesses, schools, and governments. Sociological theory is designed to examine all three levels of analysis. But what are the major types of sociological theory?

Most textbooks categorize theory into four major camps: (1) **functionalism**, (2) **conflict theory**, (3) **symbolic interactionism**, and (4) **feminism**. Functionalism refers to theories that try to explain the social world in terms of how it fits together and how each part helps the whole to run smoothly. Conflict theory tends to see social life in terms of power and inequality, focusing on the gap between the 'haves' and 'have-nots' in the social world. Symbolic interactionism emphasizes the social meanings actors give to and take from their own and others' social behaviour and how we need to understand these personal meanings if we are to understand their everyday actions. Finally, feminist theories emphasize how male dominance over women is embedded in institutions and culture, treating gender as a central analytical lens to understand society. These theoretical distinctions are important, yet also serve to divide theory, rather than unite it around empirical research questions or substantive issues. Thus, conflict theorists analyze private schools, for example, in terms of how they reinforce class inequality. Functionalists, in contrast, tend to treat private schools as an unquestioned good, stressing how well they function to educate our youth and instill values and norms. Neither camp listens to the other side, since their assumptions about society lead them to view the world in only one way (either in terms of co-operation or conflict). If theorists saw their commonality in a similar topic and level of analysis, they might correct each other's blind spots, thus gaining a more balanced and empirically informed picture of the case at hand. Therefore, it is important to use different kinds of sociological theory together, considering co-operation, conflict, and negotiation as they manifest themselves differentially in particular social contexts.

For these reasons, we will organize this chapter in terms of three distinct empirical traditions of sociological

Time to Reflect

Is society characterized more by shared values, consensus, and co-operation (the functionalist view) or by struggles for authority and power (the conflict view)? Why do you think this is?

theory: (1) **multivariate theory**, (2) **interpretive theory**, and (3) **historical-comparative theory**. Of course, many theories combine these research methodologies and are applicable at more than one level of analysis. These categories are not always clear-cut, often overlapping in practical research designs (Alford, 1998). Still, different methodological approaches allow for different questions to be asked and give rise to different theoretical claims. We hope that an emphasis on empirical research will help to bridge opposing camps in sociological theory, uniting them in a close dialogue with evidence. Theory is not to be simply admired or adhered to, but applied, tested, and refined in light of ongoing research.

Because of this emphasis on evidence, the best sociologists from the classical era still have valuable things to teach us about contemporary society. Often seen as the 'founders' of modern sociology in nineteenth- and early twentieth-century Europe, Karl Marx, Émile Durkheim, Max Weber, and Georg Simmel each laid out a provocative and original vision for sociological theory in dialogue with empirical research traditions. Although these classical theorists cannot be easily categorized into only one theoretical logic, Durkheim's writings on suicide demonstrate the multivariate logic, Weber and Simmel provide early examples of the interpretive approach, and Marx's writings on capitalism illuminate historical-comparative theory. The objective of this chapter is to show how the best classical sociological theory has stood the test of time and can be usefully applied to contemporary problems.

After introducing these three logics of the classical theorists, we will introduce recent examples of sociological theory that draw on the classical tradition to help explain contemporary issues. These are: (1) the relationship between suicide in Quebec and the Stanley Cup

IN THE FIRST PERSON

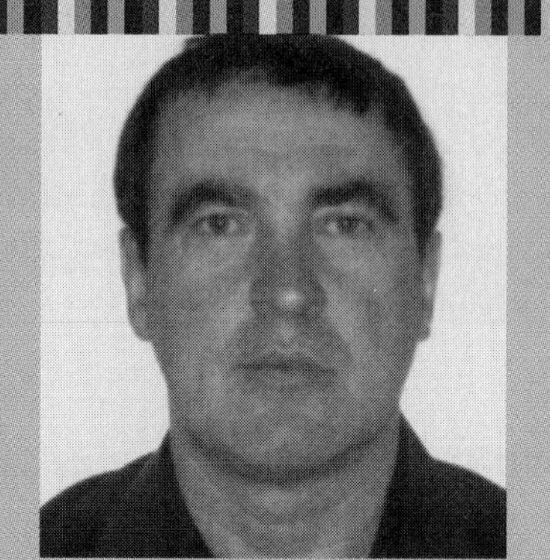

Born in Scotland and raised in Two Mountains (Deux-Montagnes), Quebec, north of Montreal, I became interested in sociology after enrolling at Cleveland State University on a soccer scholarship after trying to play professionally in Scotland. Learning about the civil rights movement in undergraduate classes and travelling around the United States playing soccer created a new-found desire for knowledge that sociology helped to satisfy. I was exposed to Marx, Weber, and Durkheim by reading the German psychoanalyst Erich Fromm's best-selling classic, *Escape from Freedom* (1941), a work passed on to me by a high school friend who had been taught by an American draft resister at Vanier College in Montreal. I then learned Marx from Michael Harrington, a famous American socialist scholar, at the City University of New York (CUNY), and was trained in the scholarly tradition of the sociological imagination by CUNY professor Robert Alford, himself a former student of Seymour Martin Lipset. It is for these reasons that I feel personally connected to a long history of sociological theorists and remain committed to global intellectual exchange beyond my home in Canada.—Neil McLaughlin

I am currently teaching in the Department of Sociology at Lakehead University. I got interested in sociology after taking an early course in ethnographic methods at the University of Waterloo. For my research project, I studied the active decision-making processes of nursing home residents in managing their everyday lives. This research opened my eyes to the utility of ethnographic methods and the power of the sociological imagination. Since then, I have studied the culture of amateur chess players, the dynamics of interdisciplinary collaborations, and George Herbert Mead's social theory of science. It is the breadth of our discipline that I find so appealing, in that so many topics are fair game for sociological analysis.—Antony Puddephatt playoffs; (2) the painful dynamics associated with divorces and relationship breakups; and (3) the social and political differences that exist between Canada and the United States. While these different sociological arguments represent 'pure' examples of each type, the final section of the chapter will discuss how some theorists have attempted to combine the strengths of different approaches (multivariate, interpretive, and historical) to gain a more comprehensive analysis of society. This final section of the chapter will draw from the feminist writings of Canadian theorist Dorothy Smith, the attempt of American sociologist Randall Collins to combine 'macro' and 'micro' theory, and the emphasis on race and racism pioneered by the great African-American scholar W.E.B. Du Bois. Since ultimately it will be up to you to decide what theories you find most useful, we end this chapter by talking about some ways that you, as students, might think critically about the various sociological theories you encounter. What factors help explain why some theories and not others are important and influential among sociologists? How should you go about deciding which theory or combination of theories to use when trying to answer a question of interest to you? After learning about these three theoretical traditions, you will be ready to assess and choose among competing theories, developing your own sociological imagination from a perspective grounded in the Canadian experience.

What Is Sociological Theory?

Theories in sociology are abstract and general ideas that help organize and make sense of the social world. Theories highlight the place of the individual within larger cultural contexts and social structures. By 'abstract' we do not mean ideas that are out of touch with reality or unconnected to research findings. Theories in sociology must go beyond mere common-sense descriptions of particular people, places, and events. Sociologists instead look for generic concepts and theoretical relationships that are relevant across a wide variety of empirical cases. It is this general nature of sociological theories that makes them so powerful. This is why we still find inspiration in Marx, Durkheim, and Weber today. Indeed, we will demonstrate how the best sociological theories have stood the test of time, and how they can help us to understand and explain the social world around us.

Sociological theories involve systematic efforts to link concepts with empirical evidence, which can then be tested and evaluated by others. Sociological theorists do not always gather evidence themselves. There is value in 'meta-theoretical' work that builds on existing theory and evidence gathered by other researchers to generate original arguments. From our perspective, however, the best sociological theory engages with empirical evidence and systematic data-gathering, which can be categorized into three major types: (1) statistical data, based on measuring large numbers of observable social phenomena; (2) observational data, based on qualitative interviews or notes taken through observing people in their everyday activities; and (3) historical-comparative data, based on written, photographic, and/or oral records of lives, institutions, and events in different places and times. These three types of empirical data are used in multivariate, interpretive, and historical-comparative theory, respectively.

These different theoretical traditions should *not* be seen as entirely distinct ways of understanding the world, never to be combined in research practice. Sociology, more than any other modern discipline, attempts to combine these different theoretical traditions to give informed explanations of social phenomena at a number of levels. By doing this, sociologists gain a more comprehensive view of the social world. This is accomplished by combining theoretical strategies to study the interrelationship of social-psychological processes with larger social structures and broad historical traditions. This makes the discipline of sociology relatively unique. In sociology, more than is the case in any other major discipline, these methodological divisions are increasingly breaking down, as scholars are learning the value of using multiple methods, to 'triangulate' findings from each theoretical approach in practical research designs.

Each type of theory operates with a different set of assumptions about reality and the social world. Each type of theory also contains its own type of **epistemology**, or 'way of knowing', positing different criteria for how we are able to gain knowledge about the world. In addition, different theorists and schools of thought make use of distinct metaphors or ways of describing reality through the use of language. Multivariate theory sees society as being made up of objectively identifiable patterns that we can understand by using the language of hypothesis testing and empirical measurement. Interpretive theorists emphasize the unique nature of human behaviour in contrast to the natural world, and argue that studying the conscious and self-aware character of group life requires a method that is sensitive to these features. Reality itself, for most interpretive theorists, is a social product relative to the particular social group in question, and is a product of their own unique perspective. Historical-comparative sociologists are less focused on cultural or group definitions of 'meaning' and instead place emphasis on the importance of historical processes and events of particular times and places. From this perspective, societies will be very different from each other today as a result of their evolution from separate and distinct pasts. Now let us turn to each major type of theoretical logic, beginning with multivariate theory.

Multivariate Theory

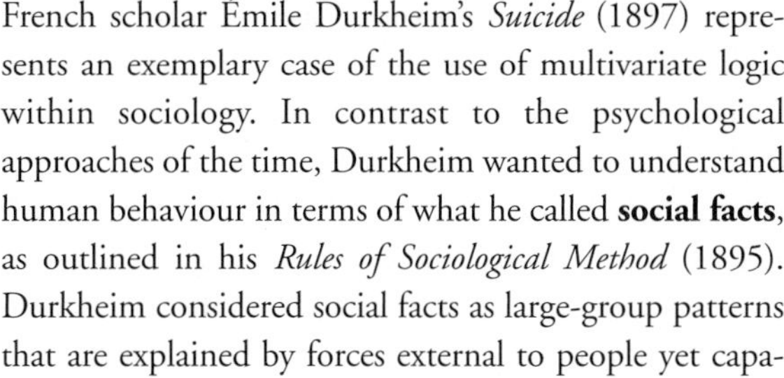

French scholar Émile Durkheim's *Suicide* (1897) represents an exemplary case of the use of multivariate logic within sociology. In contrast to the psychological approaches of the time, Durkheim wanted to understand human behaviour in terms of what he called **social facts**, as outlined in his *Rules of Sociological Method* (1895). Durkheim considered social facts as large-group patterns that are explained by forces external to people yet capable of acting on them and directing their behaviour. Thus, Durkheim suggested that social behaviour could be explained based on an adequate understanding of the social facts deemed relevant to the case at hand. From this perspective, theories can be seen as clusters of factors that underlie large-scale patterns of behaviour. Durkheim used this multivariate approach to write a pioneering and still influential analysis of suicide throughout Europe in the nineteenth century. He provided a *social* explanation of suicide rates, in contrast to individual accounts that were often put forth by psychologists and philosophers. More importantly, this early example of multivariate sociology would set the precedent for later scholars who would make use of large-scale surveys and increasingly sophisticated statistical analyses.

In political terms, Durkheim's writings on suicide were part of a general trend in social thought in the late nineteenth century. European countries were modernizing rapidly, and were thus trying to come to terms with the social consequences of the changes brought about by the Industrial Revolution. Durkheim used suicide as an

A Vietnamese monk sets himself aflame to protest the war. (CP/Everett Collection)

indicator of deeper 'pathological' problems of society in ways that other approaches did not. Economists, for example, stressed economic self-interest, arguing that suicides are most common during economic crises. Psychologists stressed individual psychological pathology and mental illness as the major cause of suicide. Durkheim offered a creative *social* explanation of the phenomenon by focusing not on individual cases of suicide, but rather on *rates* of suicide among different sectors of the population. If such large-scale rates were different and varied by the social facts characterizing the groups, then suicide is not merely an individual problem but a product of larger social forces. For example, Durkheim observed an increase of suicide rates in Western European cities over what was common in earlier feudal and agricultural societies. He also observed that those with more income in large urban centres were more likely to commit suicide and that suicide rates increased during economic booms as well as crises. Thus, a purely economic explanation of group suicide rates was inadequate. Durkheim argued that increased rates of suicide accompanying large-scale economic crises had less to do with poverty than with rapid social change and an accompanying lack of social stability. From Durkheim's perspective, increasing suicide rates were a sign of the pathological aspects of the modernization of society and the erosion of community. Thus, suicide serves as an important indicator of social cohesion in periods of rapid industrial change.

Durkheim examined a great deal of data on suicide rates throughout Europe in the nineteenth century. He compared men and women, married and single men and women, Protestant and Catholic religious affiliations, and even different seasons and times of the day in which suicides were committed. The most important finding was that Protestants had higher rates of suicide than Catholics, while single people were more likely to kill themselves than people who were married with children. Since the Catholic religion emphasizes community cohesion, while Protestantism emphasizes individualism, Catholics have a higher level of social solidarity. Similarly, married people with children also have a stronger basis for belonging and social solidarity. Thus, Durkheim concluded that the level of social solidarity was the most important factor in determining rates of suicide among different groups.

In addition to drawing our attention to an analysis of a society's health, Durkheim's pioneering work on suicide helped create the multivariate perspective that dominates mainstream sociology today. As a result, contemporary training in the field of sociology requires researchers to be skilled in quantitative data-gathering and statistical variable analysis. More importantly, Durkheim contributed a marvellous study that shows the sociological basis for patterns of individual action. Scholars of the human condition could no longer turn a blind eye to multivariate theoretical analysis, which highlights how larger social structures influence individual behaviour.

Some Recent Examples

The most important and influential multivariate sociological theorist of the twentieth century may have been Robert K. Merton, an American who was based at Columbia University. Merton, along with his teacher Talcott Parsons (1937), developed a theoretical approach known as 'functionalism' that dominated the discipline from the 1940s through to the early 1970s. This functionalist approach represents a more modern version of multivariate scholarship. Functionalists, influ-

SOCIOLOGY IN ACTION

Émile Durkheim (1858–1917)

Born to a deeply religious Jewish family, Durkheim was an excellent student as a young man and went on to become one of the most influential scholars at the most elite French universities. Initially a professor of education, Durkheim was a widely trusted scholar who helped reform the French national education system. More so than the other major classical theorists we have discussed, Durkheim made the development of a separate discipline of sociology a major life goal. When he died the same year his son was killed fighting for France in World War I, he left a rich legacy of sociology professorships and journals that shaped twentieth-century sociology and anthropology throughout the Western world.

enced by Durkheim, tend to be most interested in understanding the social origins of social stability and order. They emphasize how the various elements of society work together to promote the common good of a society organized around shared values. Sociologists starting in the 1960s, in particular, would later come to see functionalism as a conservative theory that downplays conflict in society and uncritically supports the status quo. After the emergence of the civil rights movement in United States in the late 1950s and 1960s and the feminist movement in the 1970s, race, gender, and class became increasingly central to analysis across various emerging 'conflict'-oriented theories. These conflict theories would emphasize the divisions and social injustice in society, over and above its cohesion. Nonetheless, the basic theoretical approach represented by Merton's vision has had an enormous influence on modern sociology.

Merton rejected his teacher Parsons's (1937) emphasis on 'grand theory' that attempts to generate universal theories for all aspects of social life. In contrast, Merton (1949) thought sociological theory should operate at the 'middle range'. **Middle-range theory**, from this perspective, would address concrete questions in specific subfields in sociology separately, as opposed to a 'grand theory' of the whole society. Just as Durkheim tried to predict suicide rates according to various 'variables' such as religion, age, and marital status, Mertonian scholars tried to identify sociological factors that offer an explanation of specific topics. In this way, Merton provided middle-range explanations for deviance, voting behaviour, reward systems in science, and the adoption of innovations in professional life. Despite Merton's association with the functionalist sociology of the 1950s, the basic theoretical approach of measuring concepts using quantitative data to test and refine larger theoretical models has become the dominant approach in sociology today.

While Merton's theory remains influential, not all versions of multivariate analysis are functionalist. For example, feminist multivariate theory is an important approach that rejects functionalist assumptions. Feminist sociological theory gave rise to an increasing awareness of gender inequality, whereby women were given less pay, prestige, and power in many aspects of social life. Feminist multivariate theorists are inspired by a general commitment to equality for women, but they translate their political commitments into testable hypotheses that can be measured. Barbara Reskin (2003) is an example of a feminist sociologist who has argued for an increased emphasis on operationalizing and testing hypotheses derived from theories of gender, race, and class inequality using variable analysis. How does marital status or number of children influence the rewards given to women as compared to men? With all else being equal, how does the pay for women compare to the pay for men? Do perceptions of attractiveness affect how people are judged at work, and does this have more impact on women? These are the kinds of issues that feminist multivariate theorists and researchers would address in an effort to learn how gender helps to explain important patterns of inequality in society.

Interpretive Theory   

Multivariate theorizing is not the only way that sociologists approach their research. Interpretive theory in sociology is based on data in the form of observations and interviews. This tradition has its roots in two late nineteenth- and early twentieth-century German theorists, Max Weber and Georg Simmel. The interpretive tradition was solidified in America at the University of Chicago, thanks to Robert Park and Everett Hughes, as well as the symbolic interactionist school inspired by George Herbert Mead and formally developed by Herbert Blumer. We will consider the various contributions of these theorists in this section.

Max Weber can be seen as an early exemplar of the interpretive perspective, emphasizing ***verstehen***, which refers to understanding the meanings carried by actors that lead them to make decisions. For example, in Weber's *The Protestant Ethic and the Spirit of Capitalism* (1904), he focused on the religious beliefs of Calvinism, which came from John Calvin, the sixteenth-century Swiss Protestant leader in the Reformation, whose influence was broad throughout much of European Protestantism. Calvinists believed in the doctrine of predestination, which is the idea that one's fate in the afterlife is predestined from birth. As such, there is no way to earn your way to heaven, so Calvinists were desperate to find signs of their potential salvation. Their belief that hard work was a sign that they were among the chosen to get to heaven led them to work hard and resist the temptations of luxury. By living a self-disciplined ascetic lifestyle, they would engage in a sort of 'wishful thinking' that this behaviour was not a result of their own will, but rather a sign of their eternal salvation in heaven. This unique religious culture, Weber believed, fostered the rise of a related 'spirit of capitalism' associated with economic success. Weber believed this cultural spirit, begun by deep religious beliefs, not merely by technological development, formed the basis of rapid industrialization and the

SOCIOLOGY IN ACTION

Max Weber (1864–1920)

The son of a powerful and authoritarian German politician and a shy and religious Protestant mother, Max Weber dealt with issues of politics and religion in a lifetime of extremely influential scholarly works. Trained in law, history, and economics, Weber became one of the central founders of sociology in Germany. Weber's wife Marianne was an important early feminist in Germany, and Weber helped to educate and support some of the most creative German intellectuals of the time, including his friend Georg Simmel. Weber inherited a large amount of money from his father, and thus focused his energies on writing rather than teaching. As a consequence of this and his own natural talent, Weber left an enormous legacy of historical and intepretive sociology that is still being used today. Ever a practical as well as a theoretical intellectual, Weber died in 1920, not long after serving as a hospital administrator in the German war effort in World War I.

expansion of capitalist societies in Europe and America. This was especially the case because many of the notable early capitalists and industrialists lived in relatively plain personal circumstances, turning their vast profits back into their businesses to make even more profit, rather than enjoying all the trappings their wealth could buy. Not all historians and sociologists agree with the specific argument Weber made about the importance of the 'Protestant ethic' for the development of capitalism (see Hamilton, 1996). Nonetheless, Weber's theoretical argument for the importance of meaning would leave a lasting impact on the interpretive approach.

Another important influence on interpretive theory is Georg Simmel (1950b). Simmel was a controversial German sociologist who had an enormous influence on American sociologists in the early twentieth century. In addition to writing philosophical essays, Simmel wrote sociological pieces on everyday life, including fashion, rumours, the culture of interaction in cities, male and female differences, and even yodelling. Unfortunately, Simmel has become a relatively neglected thinker over the past 40 years. One reason for this is that, as a Jew, Simmel suffered from the anti-Semitism common in Europe until well into the twentieth century. Further, his writing and lectures tended to be oriented to popular audiences, and consequently other academics accused him of 'playing to the crowd' rather than engaging in real scholarship. Nonetheless, his influence on later theories in symbolic interactionist research is clearly evident and his contributions to sociology have been more widely recognized in recent years. He is now often considered the 'father' of microsociology, especially as it regards the dynamics of small groups and networks.

One of Simmel's foundational theoretical contributions was an emphasis on the *forms of association* in social life (see Simmel, 1950b). That is, he emphasized the patterns and regularities of social interaction over and above their specific content. Thus, the same group dynamics would hold for dyads as opposed to triads no matter the content of the communication. Simmel often referred to the law of 'small numbers', emphasizing that the size of an interactive group carries unique patterns of association despite the type of group or activity they engage in. For example, Simmel highlighted the value of external conflicts to unite a group internally against a common threat. Simmel's ideas help us see the similarities in social dynamics across a range of situations. Consider the feelings that are set in motion when an outsider criticizes a member of your family, or how an authoritarian professor creates a cohesive sense of identity among undergraduates who feel unfairly treated. Simmel's theory also sheds light on why Americans became united as a nation, at least for a time, after the terrorist violence of 9/11.

This German tradition of interpretive social theory would have a major influence on the school of symbolic interactionism. The philosopher and social psychologist George Herbert Mead (1934) spent time studying in Germany, where he would encounter much of the social psychology that forms the basis of the contemporary interactionist tradition. Mead's student, Herbert Blumer (1969), would go on to formally define the research tradition of symbolic interactionism and give it its name.

Moneychanger and Wife, by Marinus Van Reymerswaele. Oil on wood, 1539. (The Granger Collection)

SOCIOLOGY IN ACTION

Georg Simmel (1858–1918)

As much an artist as a scientist, Simmel lived his life on the margins of the German university system. Initially trained as a philosopher, Simmel made the case for a micro approach in sociology in a series of essays and entertaining public lectures. He died from cancer right before the end of World War I. Because he was both Jewish and an unconventional thinker, Simmel was excluded from good jobs in the German university system until just a few years before his death. Simmel was active in German intellectual life, often associating more with artists, journalists, and writers than with other sociologists. An example of how ideas from the margins can often have enormous influence on scholarship, Simmel is widely regarded as one of the key founders of sociological interpretive theory and the school of symbolic interactionism.

Rituals and symbolic objects all around let us communicate to one another the values we hold above all others. Often, they identify the heroes and villains who (we believe) shape our world. (CP/Erik C. Pendzich/Rex Features)

Distrusting the reduction of social life to 'objective' social forces in the way of Durkheim, Blumer would argue for the centrality of meaning in the formation of action and decisions. Unlike Weber, however, Blumer would incorporate the influence of the ethnographic methods used by Robert Park to emphasize the importance of up-close observation to gain an 'intimate familiarity' with the social group under study. For Blumer, only by participating and spending time with the group, and forming concepts based on the meanings the members carry, can one achieve an accurate understanding of group life. This general calling laid the basis for the development of modern ethnographic research and qualitative analysis.

Some Recent Examples

One of the most interesting contemporary representatives of interpretive theory and ethnographic research is Erving Goffman, who was born and raised in western Canada and trained at the University of Toronto and the University of Chicago. Goffman's (1959) *The Presentation of Self in Everyday Life* is a classic account of how individuals manage impressions in daily interactions. The book was based on examples taken from novels, newspaper and magazine clippings, personal observations, and fieldwork off the north coast of Scotland in the Shetland Islands. Goffman argued that social life can be seen as a stage, where people are actors who play roles in

Time to Reflect

What is the best way to explain social behaviour? Is it the meanings individuals carry as a result of their interaction in group life or the 'social facts' external to individuals that influence their behaviour? How do you justify your choice between these alternatives?

order to portray themselves in the best possible light. Thus, people eagerly display their 'front-stage' selves to others, while keeping the 'back-stage' self from view. The 'back stage' is where secrets, mistakes, backroom deals, shameful behaviour, and the personal, private self are carefully concealed. People do not only construct presentations alone, but often work in teams to convey the best possible images to clients. Consider the teamwork necessary to maintain the front-stage impression at a high-class restaurant or a wedding procession. Goffman also wrote about the dynamics of human interaction in elevators, on park benches, in mental health institutions, and in the public spaces of streets and stores. He developed his dramaturgical theory of personal interaction by drawing on the insights of interpretive theory, his unique talent for observation, and an amusing and entertaining writing style. Representing a modern continuation of the tradition pioneered by Simmel, Goffman was awarded the presidency of the American Sociological Association shortly before he died in 1982. Goffman's theoretical work is used today among numerous Canadian sociologists working in a range of specialized subfields.

Interpretive theory sometimes offers us a direct challenge to the assumptions of multivariate sociology, as in the case of Donna Gaines's provocative book, *Teenage Wasteland: Suburbia's Dead-End Kids* (1991). Multivariate theorizing often carries with it the assumption that one can explain the social causes of suicide by examining quantitative data alone. Gaines, in contrast, uses ethnographic research to explore the highly publicized 'pack' suicide of four teenage 'burn-outs' in 1987 in Bergenfield, New Jersey. Gaines provides an alternate account of this event from what was documented by the national and local media. For the most part, the media blamed the suicides on heavy metal music. Focusing instead on the economic conditions facing these young people in the late 1980s and Gaines's own ethnographically informed analysis of heavy metal culture, her book paints a different picture of the social origins of suicide. Gaines spent months in Bergenfield getting to know the culture of the teenagers who lived there, many of whom knew the teenagers who had committed suicide. Her explanation of the suicides stresses the lack of opportunities and respect that many 'burn-outs' faced in that town, as well as the pervasive adult control over their lives. Her book suggests that blaming teen suicides on heavy metal music shows a lack of the sociological imagination. One may find her explanation of this tragic event incomplete, since not all, in fact, hardly any, teenagers who lack economic opportunities and social respect commit suicide. However, her attention to the meanings held by these teenagers in the context of their lives challenges Durkheim's reliance on quantitative data alone to explain suicide.

The Historical-Comparative Tradition

Researchers also make use of the historical-comparative approach in contemporary sociology. The historical-comparative tradition explores specific processes that explain a sequence of contingent events that occurred across time (Alford, 1998: 45). Historical theorizing usually relies on empirical evidence in the form of texts, documents, artifacts, and oral histories, often sought in historical archives, library collections, and museums. This evidence is then organized using theoretical inferences to judge their significance and their relation to the events of the time. This process of moving back and forth between theory and evidence allows for the creation of empirically based sociological theory in relation to specific or broadly sweeping historical events.

The origins of historical-comparative sociology can be traced to the nineteenth century and the works of the French thinker Alexis de Tocqueville and the German émigré intellectual and political radical Karl Marx. Tocqueville authored the famous two-volume *Democracy in America* (1835, 1840). He also pioneered the comparison of different national histories in order to explain differences in culture, political structures, and individual behaviour. Tocqueville was a member of the French aristocracy, a group of people who owned massive amounts

Time to Reflect

When considering the issue of suicide, do you think it is best to focus on social facts (in the tradition of Durkheim) or shared meanings (in the case of Gaines) to understand this most fully? How might these two approaches complement each other?

of land and ruled France along with King and the Catholic Church before the Revolution of 1789. Tocqueville had originally visited the United States because he wanted to observe the prison system, since it was widely regarded as more humane and well run than the prisons of France. In the course of his travels in America, he made the case for the value of this New World democracy against the elitist politics of France. Many elites at that time felt that the elimination of the rule by King, Church, and aristocracy brought about by the French Revolution had led to cultural chaos, political anarchy, and the creation of the 'tyranny of the majority'. As a member of the elite himself, Tocqueville shared some of these concerns about the levelling of cultural standards in democracy. But he made a compelling case that the decentralization of the American Republic, the tendency of Americans to join voluntary associations and organizations, and the checks and balances of the new system would lead to an attractive new democratic culture. He predicted this system would soon spread to the 'Old World' of Europe. Tocqueville's analysis still has much to offer the contemporary study of the political system of the United States and the culture of democracy in general.

Writing in the second half of the nineteenth century, Marx became one of the most influential theorists in sociology, developing a 'historical materialist' analysis of contemporary capitalism in Europe (Marx, 1887). Specifically, Marx linked the rise of the textile industry in Great Britain to the 'enclosure movement' that forcibly removed the peasantry from their means of subsistence on feudal lands. Since these peasants were removed from their land to make room for the expanding wool industry, they were forced into cities, where they were exploited for cheap labour in factories. Thus, the material relations of production surrounding the textile industry in England gave rise to separate classes of bourgeois owners and proletariat workers. Marx provided a historical account of how the modern-day class structure arose, which was associated with the shift from feudal to capitalist society in England under the changing market pressures on lords and landowners and the restriction of the means of production for peasants, who were transformed from self-subsistent workers to a new proletariat class. Marx's theorizing has been central to the development of the conflict paradigm in sociology, which focuses our attention on social class and power relations, and seeks to bring about egalitarian social change.

Some Recent Examples

Historical sociology went out of favour in the middle of the twentieth century as sociologists were turning to statistical analysis and ethnographic research. More recently, since the 1960s, historical-comparative sociology has seen a revival, partly inspired by the influence of the Harvard sociologist Barrington Moore (1966). Moore's *The Social Origins of Dictatorship and Democracy* analyzes the historical processes leading to democracy in France, England, and the United States and fascism and communism in Germany, Japan, China, and Russia. He explains the role played by the landed upper class of elites in the development of both democratic and totalitarian antidemocratic movements in these various nation-states.

SOCIOLOGY IN ACTION

Karl Marx (1818–1883)

Born in Trier, Germany, to a Jewish couple with a long tradition of rabbis on both sides of the family, Marx inherited a moral approach to politics and scholarship. Forced to drop out of academic philosophy and then made to leave his native Germany as a consequence of persecution for his political views and his defence of freedom of the press, Marx settled in Belgium, France, and eventually England, where he died within two years of his wife and the same year as his oldest daughter (both named Jenny). More of an activist than a scholar, Marx was not himself a sociologist per se but his focus on class conflict played a central role in the development of both historical-comparative and conflict theories in our discipline. Marx was relatively poor most of his life and was supported by his long-time friend and collaborator, Friedrich Engels, the wealthy German-born son of an English factory owner.

From Moore's perspective, when peasants remained working on the land under the control of the aristocratic elite, dictatorships were most likely to arise, as in the case of Soviet Communism. When the class of landowners is defeated politically or militarily, as in the American South during the Civil War, a society populated by workers and capitalists arises instead.

The American sociologist Theda Skocpol's *States and Social Revolutions* (1979) offers us a further example of the value of historical-comparative theory. Skocpol, who studied under Moore at Harvard, examines the extensive historical record of the French Revolution of 1789, the Russian Revolution of 1917, and the Communist revolution led by Mao Zedong in China that finally succeeded in overpowering the nationalist Kuomintang in 1949. From comparing these popular revolutions, she argues against dominant theories that stress the importance of conflicts between classes or the actions of influential 'great men'. In contrast, Skocpol analyzes the state bureaucracy and the role of military conflict in each of these three cases to understand how the stability of these governments was undermined. This undermining of government, Skocpol argues, is what leads to revolutionary change.

Some of the most important historical-comparative work today involves an analysis of countries outside of Europe. Mounira Charrad's (2001) *States and Women's Rights: The Making of Post-Colonial Tunisia, Algeria and Morocco* explains the different levels of women's legal equality in each of these countries after they gained independence from European powers. Like Moore and Skocpol, she uses historical-comparative theory. Tunisia today has a relatively high level of women's rights because the Tunisian government was forced to break the historical relationship between extended kin groups and the state. In contrast, clan-based forms of government and family alliances retained greater strength in Algeria and especially in Morocco. From this perspective, one cannot understand the state of women's rights in each of these three countries by doing a survey or making observations. Only a historical analysis of the roots of women's relative freedom in Tunisia and relative oppression in Morocco allows us to see how history shapes social life today. For Canadians who have followed the debate about *shariah*-based Islamic law in Ontario, Charrad's historical-comparative perspective suggests that to understand social issues we cannot simply measure variables or observe interactions. We have to consider how history shapes behaviour, institutions, and the law today, the great strength of the historical-comparative perspective.

Three Contemporary Examples of Sociological Theory

Sociological theory is often generated by interesting questions that matter to people. What role does hockey play in Canadian culture today? Why do people continue to commit suicide in societies that are relatively wealthy, modern, and educated? How do two people manage to separate from the deep emotional connections and practical economic arrangements in long-term intimate relationships? What social processes are involved in the 'we' of a romantic couple becoming two separate individuals no longer linked by sexual, emotional, and legal connections? How is Canadian society different from American society? Is Canadian national identity created simply by *not* being an American, as the famous 'Joe Canadian' from the Molson beer commercial seems to suggest? Or are Canadian culture and society characterized by a different set of values and ways of organizing social life than is in the case in the United States? We cannot answer these questions conclusively in one short textbook chapter, yet the discussion of how these questions are addressed will help to demonstrate the use of theory in an understanding of contemporary society.

First, we will discuss Frank Trovato's article on suicide in Quebec as an example of innovative multivariate theory related to Durkheim's landmark study of suicide. Second, we will consider Diane Vaughan's *Uncoupling* (1986), on the social processes associated with how intimate couples separate, which provides a compelling example of interpretive theory. Vaughan's book revisits Simmel's earlier emphasis on the forms of association and the importance of secrets in social relations. Finally, we will assess the lively debate about the controversial American sociologist Seymour Martin Lipset's (1950) theory of the differences between the United States and Canada (Curtis and Grabb, 2005; Adams, 1997). This will help illustrate a style of historical theorizing in sociology and demonstrate the lasting influence of Alexis de Tocqueville's views of North American culture. These examples will help us explore sociological theory as they are connected to three empirical traditions of research.

Do Quebecers Kill Themselves When the Habs Lose?

Drawing on Durkheim's approach to studying suicide, Canadian scholar Frank Trovato (1998) wrote a fascinating study titled 'The Stanley Cup of Hockey and Suicide in Quebec, 1951-1992'. This article illustrates how classical sociological theory and the multivariate/quantitative research tradition can help answer important questions about Canadian society. Building on theoretical suggestions left to us by Durkheim, modern **ceremonial theories** suggest that major holidays and sporting events may be responsible for lowering suicide rates. The logic of this hypothesis is that the ceremonial occasions that draw people together for social interaction will likely provide much-needed social support to lonely individuals who are more at risk of committing suicide. Trovato builds on this research tradition by asking whether the Stanley Cup playoffs in Quebec may, in fact, be such a ceremonial occasion that reduces the rate of suicide in the province. In addition, Trovato asks whether the performance of the Montreal Canadians has any effect on suicide. Following Durkheim's approach, Trovato tests these hypotheses with a range of statistical tests performed on annual data about suicide rates in Quebec over a period of 42 years. The results provide a clear example of the benefits of multivariate designs and quantitative sociological theory.

The first step taken in many good quantitative studies is to choose a concrete case for testing a particular theory. Trovato's choice of Quebec and the Stanley Cup playoffs represents an excellent place to build on Durkheim's work on suicide. Historically, people in Quebec have been fanatical about hockey. The Montreal Canadians are among the most successful professional hockey teams, having won the Stanley Cup an unprecedented 23 times. Important players in the history of Les Canadians, including Maurice 'the Rocket' Richard, Jean Beliveau, Ken Dryden, and Guy Lafleur were heroes throughout Canada, but especially in Quebec, the 'hockey mad' home province of the Canadians. If a sporting event was going to have an effect on suicide rates, the case of the Montreal Canadians and the Stanley Cup playoffs makes an excellent test case.

Trovato presents data on all the suicides that occurred in Quebec for each year from 1951 to 1992. He then attempts to sort out the influence of the Stanley Cup playoffs by the use of statistical methods. Building on Durkheim, Trovato knew that marriage negatively affects suicide rates. Married people are less likely to commit suicide than single or divorced individuals. Gender and age were two other important factors that Travoto had to take into account. Men are more likely to be successful in killing themselves than women, although women attempt suicide more often. The most likely suicide in the population is by a single or divorced man over the age of 35. Using hypotheses based on these Durkheimian 'social facts', Trovato was able to refine his approach so that he was not looking for those most likely to watch and be affected by the Stanley Cup playoffs, which are single men (not elderly grandmothers!).

The results are illuminating and show the importance of administering empirical tests. Trovato found no evidence to support the claim that the playoffs lowered the rate of suicide in Quebec by creating a ceremonial event. Considering the population as a whole, the period during the Stanley Cup playoffs did *not* show a statistically significant decline in suicide rates. In fact, when the analysis is focused on single men between the ages of 15 and 34, we see an *increase* in suicides when the Habs are eliminated early from the playoffs. This cannot be explained simply by the agony of defeat. The data suggest that there is no variation in the suicide rates according to whether the Habs win or lose the Stanley Cup in the final series. The key variable, as multivariate theorists would call it, is the early elimination of the Canadians from the playoffs. Single male Quebecers aged 15–34 do not commit suicide because the Habs lose, but a statistically higher number from this group do kill themselves when Montreal is eliminated early.

How should we make sense of these findings? Building again on Durkheim, the key element in Trovato's interpretation involves the centrality of social solidarity. For Durkheim as well as for Trovato, human beings are happiest when well integrated in society. People get into trouble when they are socially isolated. Trovato argues that the small core of lonely and unstable men in the province between 15 and 34 years of age who are at risk of suicide are given opportunities for needed social integration and interaction during the playoffs. Since members of Quebec society often watch the games while drinking alcohol, this can serve to put more vulnerable people at risk. For some of these men, particularly when they have drinking problems to begin with, the premature ending of this intensive period of ritualistic social activity leads to a jarring effect and feelings of loneliness, leading to higher rates of suicide.

In addition to explaining the function that hockey plays in Quebec popular culture, this adaptation of Durkheim's theory of suicide and his multivariate approach opens up a range of other issues that researchers could examine. What role does American football or baseball play in the culture of our southern neighbours, and what could we learn about how society is held together by studying the relationship between international soccer and suicide rates around the world? As society changes, and women become more solidly incorporated into the previously male-dominated world of work and competitive sports, will female suicide rates begin to look more like the rates of their male counterparts? These questions are just the kinds of things that sociologists who are influenced by Durkheim study using multivariate theories.

Secrets and Lies: Breaking Up Is Hard to Do

While the multivariate approach centres on the *why* of social phenomena, interpretive theorists are far more interested in *how* social life operates. One of the best examples of interpretive theory is Diane Vaughan's study, *Uncoupling* (1986). Vaughan examines the processes by which couples end long-term romantic relationships. *Uncoupling* is one of the top-selling sociology books of all time, showing that sociological theory can often go beyond the classroom to engage the general reader. Vaughan combines the interpretive theories of Simmel with extensive interviews with those who have undergone the dissolution of an intimate relationship. Using these interviews, Vaughan attempts to capture the sociological patterns that characterize this painful social process.

Vaughan's basic thesis is informed by two key elements from the classical interpretive theorist Georg Simmel. First, Vaughan focuses on the 'forms of association' that underlie social life. Vaughan argues that despite the fact that every single divorce and separation that occurs has its own particular reasons and particular set of issues, there are always generic **forms of association** common among the individual stories. When one looks at the narratives of people's experiences that Vaughan recorded in the course of over 100 interviews, one sees a general pattern despite the very different circumstances of individuals involved in each particular case. Vaughan builds on Simmel's insights to make the case that interpretive theoretical work can help identify the sociological patterns that shape human experience.

Second, Vaughan's account of divorce and separation draws on another of Simmel's ideas: the sociological function of the secret. When one looks at the history of relationships that end, one generally sees that the beginning of the breakup starts in the form of a secret. One participant keeps his or her unhappiness in the relationship from the other, often for many years. At the beginning, the knowledge of this unhappiness may be unconscious, that is, it's a secret to the very person experiencing it. The process of the break-up tends to evolve further when this secret comes out in the open. This begins as the unhappy member of the relationship tries to get the partner to change some aspect of his or her behaviour. Later, the couple enters into a stage Vaughan calls 'trying' as they work on a relationship that both partners now acknowledge is in trouble. If the relationship is not repaired, and the break-up moves to the next stage, the 'secret' is no longer kept within the couple but is shared to friends, families, and other social networks. Once this has been made public, the relationship is much more difficult to repair, since the problematic issues have been socially defined and made to feel more real and concrete. If this progresses further, the 'initiator' in the process usually makes the final and public break, which usually culminates in the creation of two separate individuals out of the ruin of the failed relationship.

It is remarkable how often Vaughan heard the same story, as she listened to people who either had been left by a partner or had left a relationship. The 'initiator' would often claim that she or he had tried to communicate unhappiness in the relationship to the former partner in an honest and clear way. Over and above the cases where one partner really was dishonest and involved in the relationship for insincere reasons, initiators never seem to manage to communicate their unhappiness in a clear way. This is because in the early stages of the breakup, the initiators have not yet decided to leave and are thus hesitant to be too open about their unhappiness, even to themselves. The secret is thus expressed in indirect ways through hints and signs that the former partner can only understand *after* the relationship is over. The person who is left often misses the signs of trouble and unhappiness because they are veiled rather than clear and direct. This is partly because the initiator is giving mixed signals but also because the person who is being left was not emotionally ready to see the truth and not yet in a social position to build a new life and networks of social support.

The process evolves in stages. While the initiator starts to withdraw emotionally from the relationship in the same 'stages' that the partner will later experience, the initiator gains the benefit of starting the process earlier since he or she is the first one to know the secret. The partner who is left almost always goes through more pain and social trauma because that person is taken more by surprise and has not had the opportunity to carve out a new life beyond the failed relationship. Further, this person has not had time to come to terms emotionally with the history of the soon-to-be failed relationship. Both partners will go through the same stages of exit, albeit at different times, and they both eventually come to some new understanding, moving on to create a new life and identity outside the once all-encompassing relationship.

Vaughan's powerful qualitative analysis is limited, of course, by the small sample of uncoupled people that she talked to, most of whom had come to emotional peace with their former relationship or who were in the process of doing so. Some people kill or are violent towards their partners and others carry the hurt, shame, abandonment with them down through the rest of the years of their lives without ever finding healing or creating a truly viable new life and identity. In addition, the dynamics of divorce and separation are profoundly shaped by the historical context of the particular family form and culture we are concerned with; things play out very differently when divorce is not legal or when traditional family norms and religion influence intimate personal relationships in ways not common in modern Western societies. Vaughan's qualitative research on a particular subset of divorced and separated individuals, however, illuminates certain types of experiences and suggests numerous possibilities for further qualitative, quantitative, historical-comparative research that can give us a more complete picture of the dynamics of uncoupling.

Vaughan's book is popular among readers precisely because it helps to make sense of a painful personal experience that seems unique but is actually shared by millions of people. The book may also help couples whose relationships are in trouble, since understanding the process of breaking up can sometimes ease the emotional pain involved and perhaps give couples a better chance to stay together. People have options in their lives, and people do, of course, manage to save troubled relationships. *Uncoupling*, despite the limitations outlined above, remains an important contribution to the development of interpretive theory and qualitative research in the classic sociological tradition of Georg Simmel.

I Am Not American: The Culture of Canadians

The multivariate and interpretive traditions of sociological theory, despite their many differences, share one characteristic. Both approaches tend to conduct their analysis as if suicide rates or the experience of divorce, for example, could be analyzed apart from its specific genesis through major historical events. The third type of sociological theory and research tradition that we will discuss, the historical-comparative paradigm, is important precisely because it stresses the value of looking at how the specific history of different societies leads to important national differences in the contemporary period. We will illustrate the use of this historical-comparative theoretical tradition by discussing the controversial and provocative work of Seymour Martin Lipset (1950). Lipset, an American sociologist, has written extensively about the similarities and differences between the United States and Canada (Lipset, 1990). We will also consider a number of contemporary Canadian critics of Lipset, who argue for a different take on the similarities and differences between the two countries (Curtis and Grabb, 2005; Adams, 1997).

Lipset's (1990) work is rooted in the nineteenth-century tradition of historical-comparative sociology represented by Tocqueville, Marx, and Weber. Lipset used Tocqueville's central methodological approach, reading as much about the history of Canada and the United States as he could and travelling widely in both countries. Lipset then captured elements of the culture of both nations that could be identified by comparing them to each other. For Lipset, one cannot fully understand one's own country without a thorough comparison to others. Lipset also drew from the 'historical materialism' of Karl Marx, who argued that the economic history of a nation was central to understanding its present culture and politics. Drawing on these influences, Lipset was interested in the significance of slavery to producing cotton in the US South and the economic dependency on Great Britain that shaped early Canadian history. Lipset's *Agrarian Socialism* (1950) stresses how the economy of Saskatchewan in the early twentieth century shaped the emergence of the Co-operative

Are Canadians and Americans really that different? (© Vance Rodewalt, *Calgary Herald*)

Commonwealth Federation (CCF) in the early 1930s, which three decades later morphed into the New Democratic Party (NDP), thus explaining the rise of the three-party political system in Canada in contrast to the two-party system of the United States.

Lipset also relies on Weber's pioneering focus on values and culture, as well as the role played by unique historical events in understanding contemporary society. From Lipset's perspective, the United States and Canada, while very similar, differ in significant ways because of a unique event in American history. This event is the American War of Independence (1775–83). The United States was formed initially when 13 colonies broke away from the British Empire and the King, establishing their own distinct national identity. The area of North America that would later become Canada, in contrast, remained loyal to the British monarchy and rejected the values and culture enshrined in the American Constitution. Americans, the story goes, became a nation committed to 'life, liberty, and the pursuit of happiness' while Canada became a nation oriented to 'peace, order, and good government'. These are significant differences: one is oriented towards liberal individualism, the other towards conservative collectivism.

Lipset's (1990) analysis of the differences between the United States and Canada exemplifies the historical-comparative commitment to using unique events from the past to explain the behaviour, culture, and institutions of the present. Due to the influence of the American Revolution, Lipset argues that Americans are more individualistic, more skeptical of the role of government, and more prone to violence than their neighbours to the north. Canadians, according to Lipset, are more group-oriented, rely more on government, and are less violent and aggressive than Americans. Lipset's analysis relies on public opinion polls, historical accounts of both countries, and quantitative data on divorce, rates of unionization, crime, and protests. Lipset argues that Canadians are more likely to join unions and support state-run social programs such as national health care, but are less likely to support civilian gun ownership and protest government actions. This supports his claims that Americans are more individualistic and anti-authoritarian, while Canadians are more collectively oriented and culturally deferential. At the core of his argument is the idea that historical events and traditions are important in understanding a nation's culture, values, and institutions today.

Lipset's analysis gave rise to enormous controversy among Canadian sociologists. From the perspective of James Curtis and Edward Grabb (2005), Lipset's theory exaggerates the evidence for the 'revolutionary' elements of American culture and neglects regional differences within each of the countries. Curtis and Grabb argue that Lipset's quantitative data suggest only small differences between Americans and Canadians. In addition, not all the historical and contemporary evidence suggests the kinds of differences Lipset's theory would predict. For example, the fact that Canadians have legalized gay and lesbian marriage, while Americans have not, suggests a problem with the notion that Canadians are conservative supporters of traditional authority. Most importantly, Curtis and Grabb argue that North America is best understood in terms of four distinct regions: the American South, the northern United States, English Canada, and Quebec. When framed this way, the southern United States with its history of slavery and primarily French-speaking Quebec with its links to French culture are indeed distinct regions shaped by different religious traditions, political cultures, and values. However, Curtis and Grabb argue that English Canada is remarkably similar in culture, behaviour, and political attitudes to the American North. For example, crime rates in English Canada are basically the same as crime rates in the northern US, with the only difference being that Americans are more likely to commit murder. The fact that Canadians commit as many burglaries as Americans raises a question about Lipset's thesis regarding the peaceful and deferential culture in Canada that allegedly flowed from an acceptance of British authority. Nonetheless, Lipset could certainly argue that the number of murders in the US has something to do with the availability of guns, a cultural tradition that flows from a rejection of state authority rooted in the original rebellion of the American Revolution.

This debate between Lipset and his critics continues today (Carroll, 2006). Sociologist and opinion pollster Michael Adams, for example, wrote an entertaining empirical analysis of Canadian and American differences titled *Sex in the Snow* (1997). Arguing against the Lipset thesis, Adams uses opinion poll data to suggest that 'despite their mythological adherence to the ideal of personal freedom, Americans, in fact, harbour a far greater confidence in many institutions than do Canadians. In general, Americans have a greater faith in the family, the state . . . religion and the market' (Adams, 1997: 164). Yet, contrary to the importance that Curtis and Grabb place on four regions, Adams argues that 'French and English Canadians have far more in common with each other in terms of values than either group has with the Americans' (ibid., 195). In fact, Adams concludes that 'in spite of our growing intimacy with American commerce and culture, Canada remains a distinct society' (ibid.). Whatever the answer to these issues about Canadian identity, the historical-comparative research tradition clearly provides the best avenue for understanding.

The strength of the historical-comparative perspective is that it calls on us to examine the specific histories of various nations (or groups or regions) before attempting to generalize based on theories that are often generated from research within only one nation or time period or group of people. Our examination of the questions raised about Canadian and American value differences shows that a multivariate focus on statistical data in dialogue with historical arguments is indispensable for contemporary sociologists. In addition, while Lipset's macro analysis of the history of Canada and the United States leads him to suggest that Canadians accept traditional authority more than Americans, his historical-comparative approach clearly requires 'testing' with the kind of qualitative micro research on how people actually behave in public and everyday life.

We have presented the multivariate, interpretive, and historical-comparative theoretical traditions as separate and sometimes competing perspectives, but the reality is they each are most effective when combined together for a more comprehensive understanding. The following section explores the importance of combining theoretical logics.

The Case for Theoretical Diversity

Sociology has a unique contribution to offer social science in that it is able to effectively combine these three types of social analysis in productive ways. Even the best works of social science within one of the three major theoretical paradigms tend to be blind to the challenge posed by competing modes of theorizing. Combining multivariate, historical, and interpretive logics of analysis offers a very powerful approach. For example, Durkheim's classic work *Suicide* tells us much about the systematic patterning of suicide rates that can be predicted by such sociological variables as religion, marital status, and gender. However, his commitment to multivariate analysis blinds him to the symbolic meanings central to suicidal behaviour at the micro level (Alford, 1998). Suicide is a profoundly social-psychological act as well as being a part of larger social trends.

Donna Gaines's (1991) ethnographic analysis of teen suicides in New Jersey, for example, suggests the value of theorizing based on close qualitative observations rather than the more remote quantitative analysis of variables. Identifying structural correlations alone does not, as Gaines's study suggests, provide more precise explanations of the specific social processes that operate within these larger relationships. The interpretive approach helps to connect structural patterns to the real, lived experiences and interpretations that actually cause suicide. Durkheim's use of aggregate statistical data, moreover, leads him to implicitly suggest that suicidal acts can be understood without an account of the historically specific contexts that influence human action. The historical-comparative perspective might suggest that the same level of social solidarity may have different effects on suicide across different national contexts and historical periods.

The same criticism could be raised against approaches that put too much emphasis on interpretive sociology and historical-comparative approaches. The kind of arguments made in Weber's and Simmel's works, for example, are often criticized for a lack of rigour in sampling procedures and quantitative testing. Qualitative interviews with small numbers of people or extended participant observation with subgroups of the population are no substitute for systematic sampling of large populations. For example, Diane Vaughan's theory of uncoupling may operate differently in regard to gender, social class, race, ethnicity, or sexual orientation. A multivariate model could be used to answer these questions and measure how the process of breaking up differs among various segments of the population.

It would be a major mistake to dismiss too easily the contributions of statistical approaches to the study of social life, something that can also be seen when looking at Lipset's work on Canadian–American differences. There is enormous value in taking a historical perspective on Canadian society, revolutions in France, China, or Russia, and gender relations in the Middle East. At

Time to Reflect

What makes sociological theory different from our common-sense understandings of the world? Try to think of at least two major differences.

the same time, grand generalizations that attempt to explain Canadian character, the success of different revolutionary movements, or the human rights situations of women should also be tested by the kind of careful empirical statistical analysis at the core of the multivariate approach. Social science is best served by trying to combine the three types of theorizing we have outlined above. This helps overcome the specific shortcomings of each of the approaches when used alone. We will now illustrate this point about the value of methodological diversity with three examples from important theorists who combine these three logics of inquiry.

Dorothy Smith's Feminist Ethnography

Few feminist scholars have had as much influence as the Canadian theorist Dorothy Smith, trained by Erving Goffman at the University of California at Berkeley. She was also influenced by Harold Garfinkel, the founder of an important approach to sociology known as **ethnomethodology**. Ethnomethodologists stress the value of studying the methods and routines of everyday life that people must use to make sense of and establish order in their everyday lives (Garfinkel, 1967). Smith's involvement in the feminist movement in the 1960s and 1970s suggested to her the importance of looking at this everyday world from the perspective of women. The world looks different, Smith (1987) argues, according to where you are placed within the hierarchies established by traditional forms of male dominance. Smith's advocacy of 'standpoint theory' challenged the dominance of the male perspective in sociology. Scholars influenced by Smith's theory do research using an approach known as 'institutional ethnography'. This method examines how social life and traditional 'relations of ruling' by men are created and reinforced in the context of activities both in public workplace organizations and the private space of the family. Further, by focusing on the specific standpoints of those who struggle under relations of power, Smith has argued that an understanding of these structures comes into clearer focus. This has created an exciting new tradition of scholarship that studies power relations in society that is informed by the strategy of qualitative research methods. This theoretical approach is designed to understand the power relations linked to institutions and organizations by exploring the first-hand perspectives of those negatively affected by these traditional arrangements.

The innovative nature of Smith's (1987) contributions flows from the way in which she combines ethnographic research with the insights of the Marxist version of historical-comparative theory. Marxist theories tend to emphasize how class inequality is reinforced through the history of economic and social relations. Some versions of Marxism, following in the tradition of his collaborator Friedrich Engels, attempt to explain the origins of the subordination of women in the history of the family. As such, Smith is part of this long tradition of Marxist feminists. Her work combines a concern with how everyday gender relations are embedded in a broader history of what feminists call patriarchy: the legal, political, economic, and cultural dominance of men over women. Like Marx, Smith is concerned with changing society and not simply understanding it, and is one of the most influential sociological theorists today. She has attained her success partly because of the way

SOCIOLOGY IN ACTION

Dorothy E. Smith (b. 1926)

Born in England and educated in sociology at the London School of Economics and University of California at Berkeley in the 1950s and 1960s, Dorothy Smith has spent the most productive and innovative years of her career in Canada as our major feminist sociological theorist. Influenced by Marxism, the women's movement, and various micro-interpretive theories, Smith pioneered an approach to sociology that puts women's experience at the centre of the discipline. She taught one of the first Women's Studies classes in Canada at the University of British Columbia and taught for many years at the Ontario Institute for Studies in Education (OISE) at the University of Toronto. Retired now and teaching at the University of Victoria, Dorothy Smith works with various former students on the development of what she calls 'institutional ethnography'.

she combines both the interpretive and historical-comparative traditions. In doing so, she argues against ethnographies and interpretive theories that do not link their observations to structures of inequality. Some sociologists feel that Smith's analysis is excessively subjective and does not make enough use of quantitative and traditional historical-comparative approaches. One could also argue that she does not give adequate weight to the changes in gender norms that the feminist movement created over the past 30 years. Despite these criticisms, Smith forged a sociology that would help to understand and thus change the experiences of women and disadvantaged people everywhere by understanding their place within powerful institutions.

Randall Collins's Micro Theory of Stratification

Not all combinations of interpretive and historical-comparative perspectives must be rooted in the Marxist

Social stratification has been a central concern of sociology since its founding. Even non-sociologists have long understood their lives are shaped by the class structure. (University of Washington Libraries, Special Collections, UW1535)

tradition. Randall Collins's (1975, 2004) influential micro theory of **stratification** successfully combines Max Weber's theories of class, status, and power with the micro-sociology pioneered by Goffman. Traditional Marxist conflict theorists often stress how social classes (capitalists versus workers) are engaged in conflict over the control and use of economic resources and profit. From the Marxist perspective, those who control the means of production in society are accorded the most status, political power, and prestige, not to mention better meals and more fun at the cottage. Thus, for Marxists, economic well-being is the most important factor in determining status, power, and prestige. Following Weber, Collins stresses how status and power differences are played out in society over a broader range of conflicts than simply economic class alone. For Collins, society is pervasively dominated by battles over social prestige, racial, ethnic, religious, and gender differences, and local cultural distinctions. In addition, contemporary Weberian scholars such as Collins (1975) stress the importance of institutions—armies, the police, the state—that serve to control people through the use of force and violence.

Unlike Marxists, Collins believes that scholars should understand social inequality but not be primarily concerned with challenging it. For Collins, attempting to change society (the role of the activist) is a very different thing from trying to understand the world in an objective way (the role of the scholar). Thus, Collins combines the commitment to objective science with research into social inequality. Collins has studied topics as wide apart as the sociology of the family and sexual relations, the creation of 'credential inflation' in schools, and the fall of communism in the former Soviet Union. The common link across this work is a close attention to how conflicts of power, prestige, and economic resources play themselves out in society.

Collins's (2004) theory of inequality derives from Weber's emphasis on the importance of status and prestige as well as Goffman's micro-interpretive work. Most of the multivariate and historical-comparative theorists we have talked about tend to understand the world through a focus on large-scale structures of society. This tends to leave everyday interactions far less explored. Goffman's work in *The Presentation of Self in Everyday Life*, you will remember, challenged this bias in traditional sociological theory. Collins follows this emphasis to extend the study of inequality to micro-sociological processes as well as macro-sociological structures. Traditional surveys, for example, tend to place people in one socio-economic category, which they are supposed to carry around with them at all times. In reality, Collins argues, one's status is always connected to local interactions, something missed when one studies inequality with quantitative surveys. Thus, a professor may enjoy status and respect at the university but becomes a virtual unknown at a baseball game. This same professor would take on an even lower status while strolling through an inner-city ghetto, where he or she is forced to show deference to gangs on the street. To fully understand how social status plays out in real life, it is important to study work, leisure, and other ritual settings across a number of contexts that intersect in people's everyday lives.

Collins's (2004) focus on everyday interactions has provided interesting insights into the changing nature of status in society that the quantitative tradition is less likely to pick up. Have you ever noticed how informal servers in restaurants have become, often engaging in friendly and even personal interactions with diners? This is very different from the almost stiff formality one sees in old movies. In addition, movie stars and popular musicians today often appear in public unshaven and in torn jeans. This is something that would have been incomprehensible to someone from the generation of Marilyn Monroe or Frank Sinatra. Perhaps more dramatically, a politician today caught speeding in his/her private car would be far less likely now than in the past to get off without a ticket. In the past, taking advantage of one's government authority to avoid paying the ticket might work, yet today, it would be seen as corrupt. Collins's theory of micro-stratification helps explain these examples of changing norms in everyday interaction as a function of larger transformations in societal attitudes towards elites, traditional authority, and the importance of formal hierarchies. The amount of status and power one has in a particular situation, Collins argues, is no longer so closely linked to the formal institutions and power relations of the larger society. Thus, from Collins's perspective, we need to do sociological work that looks closely at status and inequality in micro-interactions, as Goffman once argued. This means supplementing quantitative data on income or status with up-close observations of smaller contexts of interactions to see how social inequality plays itself out.

The Neglected Theory of W.E.B. Du Bois: The Problem of the Colour Line

Not all theorists are given as much recognition as they deserve. One of the most important sociological theorists is W.E.B. Du Bois. Du Bois was an African-American scholar who wrote at the same time as Durkheim and Weber. Du Bois never became as famous in sociology for a variety of reasons. For one thing, as a black scholar working in the United States, Du Bois suffered from racial discrimination. In addition, Du Bois was a committed political intellectual, so he spent a lot of his energy working on behalf of the movement for black rights in America. As a consequence, he did not formulate his theories as systematically as did scholars such as Durkheim or Weber. Moreover, as a researcher as well as theorist, Du Bois's contributions have had more influence in particular subareas of sociology (race relations, community studies, and historical sociology) than in sociological theory. Nonetheless, his legacy is impressive, and he exemplifies the need to combine the different logics of historical-comparative, multivariate, and interpretive theories.

Du Bois's *Black Reconstruction in America* (1935) is a historical analysis of the ways in which slaves were freed in the American South after the Civil War. Du Bois illustrates how blacks were first liberated from slavery, but then subordinated again through the creation of a system of legal segregation. Not satisfied with a purely historical approach, Du Bois's *The Philadelphia Negro* (1899) was one of the most important early urban studies to make use of up-close observations and interviews. It is also an excellent example of multivariate sociology in that he gathered statistics regarding the black poor, as well as presenting a detailed ethnographic account of urban African-American Philadelphia. The study convincingly illustrates the lack of opportunities afforded to blacks at that time, and shows how their opportunities for employment were closely linked to their everyday deference to whites. Finally, *Souls of Black Folk* (1903) draws on the interpretive theories of the self learned from German scholars such as Weber and Simmel. Like many American sociologists in the early twentieth century, Du Bois visited Germany to become educated in social psychology. Du Bois uses Weber's insights to develop his own theory about the complicated psychology experienced by people who are discriminated against because of the colour of their skin. African Americans, Du Bois argues, were created by American history and became rooted in the United States after their ancestors were shipped to the New World from Africa as slaves. American blacks were part American then, since most of them, at the time Du Bois was writing, had been born and raised in the United States. The psychology of African Americans, however, has also been shaped by the experience of being looked down upon and discriminated against by the white majority. This is a condition that creates, Du Bois argues, a complicated dual consciousness. In Canada, 'visible minorities' and Aboriginal Canadians experience a different psychology from the white majority because of similar dynamics of discrimination.

The irony here is that the major insight that Du Bois brings to contemporary sociological theory is the reason why he was ignored as a theorist for so long. Du Bois argued that the major theoretical, political, and moral problem of the twentieth century was 'the problem of the colour line'. Earlier theorists such as Weber, Marx, Simmel, Tocqueville, and Durkheim were white European theorists who tended to ignore the importance of race and racism. To be fair, both Marx and Tocqueville wrote critically about the domination of non-whites by the

SOCIOLOGY IN ACTION

W.E.B. Du Bois (1868–1963)

Fortunate to get a quality education in the United States at a time when most blacks were denied such opportunities, W.E.B. Du Bois earned a Ph.D. at Harvard and went on to become one of the most influential American thinkers of the twentieth century. Du Bois began his academic career teaching Greek and Latin at Wilberforce, a black college in Ohio. He also taught at the University of Pennsylvania and Atlanta University. Active in the National Association for the Advancement of Coloured People (NAACP) and, more controversially, the American Communist Party, Du Bois was an activist scholar in the tradition of Karl Marx. Du Bois's uncritical attitude later in life regarding communism in the Soviet Union is the one flaw in what was otherwise an extraordinary life of sociological scholarship, political involvement, and commitment to racial justice. He died as an honoured leader of the black civil rights movement shortly after having moved to and become a citizen of Ghana in 1963, ironically, the day before Martin Luther King Jr's famous 'I Have a Dream' speech at the March on Washington.

Time to Reflect

Pretend you are a sociologist interested in developing a sociological theory about poverty in any major Canadian city. How would you draw on each of the three theoretical logics (historical, multivariate, and interpretive) sketched in this chapter to understand and study poverty in this city more carefully?

European great powers and in the United States. Nonetheless, only Du Bois made race central to his sociological theorizing. In contemporary sociology, questions about racism directed at non-white immigrants to Canada, the continuing tragedy of massive AIDS-related deaths throughout Africa, and the negative view about America that many non-white citizens of the world hold can be illuminated by Du Bois's sociological imagination.

Conclusion

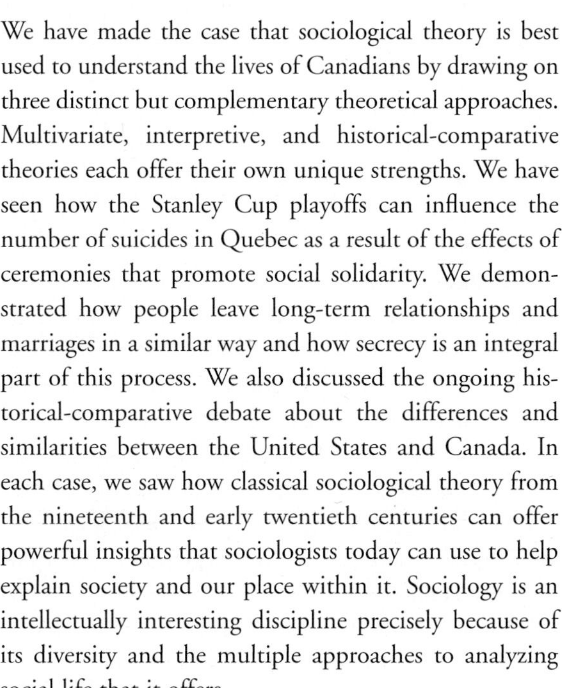

We have made the case that sociological theory is best used to understand the lives of Canadians by drawing on three distinct but complementary theoretical approaches. Multivariate, interpretive, and historical-comparative theories each offer their own unique strengths. We have seen how the Stanley Cup playoffs can influence the number of suicides in Quebec as a result of the effects of ceremonies that promote social solidarity. We demonstrated how people leave long-term relationships and marriages in a similar way and how secrecy is an integral part of this process. We also discussed the ongoing historical-comparative debate about the differences and similarities between the United States and Canada. In each case, we saw how classical sociological theory from the nineteenth and early twentieth centuries can offer powerful insights that sociologists today can use to help explain society and our place within it. Sociology is an intellectually interesting discipline precisely because of its diversity and the multiple approaches to analyzing social life that it offers.

We also stressed that these different theories should *not* be seen as wholly separate. In contrast, the most exciting and interesting types of sociological research are those that *combine* different theoretical orientations and types of evidence. The research possibilities are endless and will be best conducted by complementing one theoretical sensibility with others. Choosing the theory most relevant to your research project will involve decisions based on the type of questions you want to answer. Questions that involve differences between various large groups require multivariate theories. That is, if you want to know the differences in crime, birth, or death rates between Canadians in different regions of the country, you will likely find multivariate approaches most useful. Questions that involve the dynamics of social processes tend to be best handled with the use of interpretive theories, examining, for example, how people interact in public, bury their dead, or celebrate at weddings. Making use of a historical-comparative perspective will help you see how the issue you are interested in is a product of long-term historical processes, which may differ across distinct countries or parts of the world. The specifics of how to actually *do* research according to these three approaches are discussed in Chapter 2. For now, we have provided a broad sense of the types of sociological theories available, as they are rooted in these three diverse methodological approaches.

It is important to remember that the best theory is linked closely to empirical research. Sociological theory is not here to be worshipped as the wisdom of 'great thinkers' from the past. The ideas of Durkheim, Simmel, Weber, and Marx are used today because they have been useful in framing issues and explaining patterns important within contemporary society. Sociology can best contribute to people's understanding of their lives when research is guided by a diverse set of theoretical questions. We can be interested in explaining *why* certain things happen, explore *how* people go about certain aspects of their lives, and look at society with an eye to what *historical comparisons* can help to understand contemporary behaviour. We hope you will keep your minds open to these diverse ways of thinking as you encounter the various sociological theories on Canada and the world presented in the remainder of this book.

Questions for Critical Thought

1. Durkheim emphasized the importance of ceremonies that encourage social solidarity in society, reducing the isolation of individuals. The presence of lonely and isolated individuals is often a serious problem on university campuses in North America. What can universities—administrations, faculties, students—do to try and increase ceremonial activities in ways that might bolster social cohesion?
2. From your perspective, and thinking about Dianne Vaughn's study of uncoupling, how do you think separations in long-term intimate relationships might vary according to gender, social class, ethnicity, and sexual orientation?
3. How do you think differences that exist between Canada and the United States might shape how residents and citizens of these two nations interact in public? How could we study these kinds of issues?
4. How might W.E.B. Du Bois's analysis of race and racism be applied to the experiences of First Nation and visible minority people in contemporary Canada?
5. What are some of the strengths of each of the three major theoretical approaches we have discussed: multivariate, interpretive, and historical-comparative? What are some of the weaknesses of each approach?

Recommended Readings

Robert Alford, *The Craft of Inquiry* (Oxford: Oxford University Press, 1998).

The argument that sociological theory can be divided into the three major approaches (multivariate, interpretive, and historical-comparative) is developed in this clearly written guide to the research process. Perhaps a difficult read on the first attempt, this book is extremely helpful when you are engaging in your own research. It outlines the process by which you can frame a research question using sociological theory and explains what methods to use to answer a question you are interested in.

Lewis Coser, *Masters of Sociological Thought: Ideas in Social and Historical Context*, 2nd edn (New York: Harcourt, 1977).

This is an entertaining and engaging account of the lives of the major sociological theorists, including Marx, Weber, Durkheim, and Simmel. Clearly written by a major sociological theorist in his own right, Coser's text stresses the relationship between biography and historical context in the emergence of sociological theory.

Fred Pampel, *The Sociological Lives and Ideas* (New York: Worth, 2006).

This is a well-written short introduction to the basic ideas of Marx, Weber, Durkheim, Simmel, Mead, and Du Bois. Following in the tradition of Coser, Pampel's text does a particularly nice job of linking the lives and historical context of each of these classical sociological theorists with their sociological concepts. If we were to recommend one short introduction to classical theorists, this would be it.

Theda Skocpol, ed., *Vision and Method in Historical Sociology* (Cambridge: Cambridge University Press, 1984).

A particularly useful introduction to the historical-comparative approach edited by one of most famous and productive scholars in historical sociology, a professor at Harvard University.

Irving Zeitlin, *Ideology and the Development of Sociological Theory*, 7th edn (Englewood Cliffs, NJ: Prentice-Hall, 2001).

Zeitlin, who taught at the University of Toronto for many years, is particularly valuable for highlighting the historical context for the emergence of sociological theory in the conservative reactions to the French Revolution. The ideas of Marx are given particular attention in this classic text.

Recommended Websites

American Sociological Association Theory Section
www.cas.sc.edu/socy/faculty/deflem/theory/default.html

An excellent place for contemporary discussions, debates, and news surrounding sociological theory in the American Sociological Association.

Émile Durkheim Archive
durkheim.itgo.com

Designed for undergraduate students, this site provides links to selections from Durkheim's major writings.

Marxists.org Internet Archive
www.Marxists.org

If Marxist-oriented sociology is for you, this site will give you links to the major writings of Marx and Engels as well as a range of resources on contemporary Marxism.

Sociosite: Sociological Theories and Perspectives
www2.fmg.uva.nl/sociosite/topics/theory.html

A valuable source on the most famous sociological theorists and their major ideas.

Verstehen: Max Weber's HomePage
www.faculty.rsu.edu/~felwell/Theorists/Weber/Whome.htm

A nice place to get a basic introduction to Weber's approach to both interpretive and historical-comparative sociological theory.

WWW Virtual Library: Sociology—Sociological Theory and Theorists
www.mcmaster.ca/socscidocs/w3virtsoclib/theories.htm

A comprehensive website that provides links to the key texts of major sociological and social theorists.

Kellogg's
ALL-BRAN PLUS
now with calcium
Kellogg's
FROOT LOOPS
ONLY £1.69
Kellogg's
Just Right
HALF THE FAT OF MUESLI
Kellogg's
All-Bran
Kellogg's
CORN FLAKES
Kellogg's
RICE BUBBLES
Kellogg's
FROSTIES
Kellogg's
CHOCO CORN FLAKES
Kellogg's
ALL-BRAN BITE-SIZE
light, crispy, tasty
NUTRI-GRAIN
Kellogg's
COCO POPS
ONE FREE
Kellogg's
RICE KRISPIES
Kellogg's
CRUNCHY NUT
Kellogg's
CORN FLAKES
FROOT LOOPS
Today's Tally
Today's Tally
VOTE
Today's Tally
FROOT LOOPS
VOTE
VOTE
Today's Tally
COCOA KRISPIES
VOTE
VOTE
Today's Tally
VOTE
VOTE

Chapter 2

Research Methods

Bruce Arai

Learning Objectives

In this chapter, you will:

- Become familiar with the traditional model of science and with the more sophisticated model that has superseded it.
- Differentiate between quantitative and qualitative approaches to sociology.
- Differentiate between validity and reliability.
- Appreciate the importance of ethics in sociological research.
- Learn the different approaches to validity in qualitative and quantitative methods.
- Explore the influence of feminist theory on sociological methods.
- Gain a better grasp of social survey design.
- Learn about field research, interviewing, and ethnographic research.
- Study the different types of existing data and how they are analyzed.

Photo: Jeff Greenberg/PhotoEdit Inc.

Introduction

In the previous chapter, you read about the major theories that sociologists use to understand social life. In this chapter, we focus on the methods that sociologists use to collect the data that have informed these theories and produced the many findings you will read about throughout this text. Among other things, you will learn about the debate over the scientific status of the discipline of sociology, the major techniques of data collection, and the influence of research ethics and the rise of feminism on sociological research methods.

Sociology departments in Canada belong to many different faculties. At your university or college, is the sociology department located in the faculty of arts, the faculty of social sciences, or somewhere else? This may seem like an unimportant issue, but it gives you some indication of the different ways in which sociology is perceived. Many sociologists think of sociology as a science or as a social science, others view it as an arts or humanities discipline, and still others choose not to categorize it at all.

How we view sociology is important for this chapter because the methods that we use to produce sociological knowledge are intimately related to whether it is seen as a science, an art, or something else. Viewed as a science, sociological research is often designed to measure and quantify social life; this is called quantitative sociology. Viewed as an art or humanity, sociological research is often designed to get at the rich meanings that people attribute to their lives; this is called qualitative sociology. This distinction between quantitative and qualitative sociology is not absolute, and many sociologists prefer not to use it. It is used occasionally in this chapter to organize the discussion, and also to show how the distinction itself has become irrelevant to some scholars. The chapter begins by exploring a scientific view of sociology, because the founders of the discipline certainly thought of it this way and because it remains one of the most dominant views of the discipline today. The scientific view of sociology is also used as a backdrop for understanding other perspectives on the discipline.

Sociology as a Science

We often imagine that a science has several distinguishing characteristics (see Figure 2.1), including these:

- Knowledge is based only on facts.
- Facts are part of the real world and can be observed.
- When making scientific observations, we do not let our personal emotions or biases interfere with our observations; this is called 'objectivity'.
- We usually use the scientific method, including experiments, to collect and analyze data and to draw conclusions.
- Science gives us the best understanding of the way the world works. In other words, if we follow the proper procedures of science, we will discover the truth about the world, and this truth will be better than other truths.

Figure 2.1 The Traditional View of Sociology as a Science

(© Brenda Brown. Reprinted with permission.)

We usually base these ideas on what we think of as 'real science'—something like physics, astronomy, chemistry, or perhaps biology. Compared to these fields of study, sociology seems to be a lesser science, perhaps not even a science at all. It is debatable whether any social science can ever live up to the rigorous standards of scientific inquiry set by these other disciplines. So, it is not just sociology that fails to meet the standards; but also the other social sciences, including psychology, economics, and political science.

However, the perception that the social sciences are lesser sciences than their more hard-nosed cousins is based largely on an outdated, unrealistic understanding of what actually happens in disciplines like physics, astronomy, chemistry, and biology. As Sandra Harding (1986) has argued, what physicists actually do when they do physics is only one very particular way of doing science, and it is not clear that most sciences follow this model. Instead, there are a great many ways of doing science, and what physicists do is only one of them. Stanley Lieberson (Lieberson and Lynn, 2002), a past president of the American Sociological Association, recently has argued that sociologists should not model themselves on what happens in physics because the subject matters differ too much. What we should be doing is to pay more attention to what biologists are doing and use biology as a more appropriate model of how we might study society scientifically.

If we look at what scientists actually do and the methods they use to produce their scientific claims, whether in chemistry, biology, sociology, or economics, we see many different ways of doing science. Not all of them involve experiments, or even the collection of data. Some science can be done with only a paper and pencil. Sociologists, anthropologists, and others who have studied the actual behaviour of scientists have shown convincingly that the production of scientific knowledge depends heavily on things like informal negotiations between scientists, drama, and rituals (Latour and Woolgar, 1987; Lynch, 1985). In other words, it is not just the scientific method and **objective** observations that lead to scientific conclusions. Personal opinions, biases, and cultural understandings are at the very heart of most scientific endeavours.

In addition, completely objective observations of the world are impossible. Nobody can separate himself or herself completely from his or her prior knowledge of the world when making observations. Indeed, it is impossible even to make observations of the world, much less record them and communicate them to others, without knowing a language. And since languages are not unbiased, accurate reflections of the world, the fact that we have to make and express our observations of the world through language makes total objectivity impossible (see Chalmers, 1999).

This would seem to be a serious threat to the possibility of science in general. Scientific findings should not be influenced by the emotions, thoughts, prejudices, or language of any individual scientist. Instead, they are supposed to be true, accurate recordings of the real world. Does this make science impossible?

One answer is 'yes', and some people argue that if objectivity is impossible, then science is impossible. The reason for this opinion is that without the claim to objective knowledge, science ceases to be useful. We should abandon science, or at least alter it radically. This point of view is often associated with **relativism**—the belief that there is no ultimate truth.

But another answer is 'no', that it is possible for sociology and other disciplines to be scientific. The reason is that the criticisms of objectivity, convincing as they are, do not undermine science because objectivity is not necessary for

IN THE FIRST PERSON

The person who really solidified my interest in becoming a sociologist was the late Jim Richardson, my master's supervisor at the University of New Brunswick. Most of us like to think that we make most decisions independently, from the kind of music we listen to, to the kinds of restaurants we prefer, even to our choice of girlfriends, boyfriends, and partners. But the reality is that strong social forces shape and constrain the choices we make. Sociology shows us how our seemingly individual decisions are shaped by these larger social pressures. Jim had a keen eye for this, and one of his extraordinary gifts was to be able to make those processes crystal clear for me and for his many other students.

But the two people who started me thinking sociologically were Tullio Caputo (now at Carleton University) and Lesley Miller at the University of Calgary. Dr Caputo's classes were filled with his energy, humour, and incisiveness, which made sociology both relevant and fun. And the best class I've ever taken at university was my third-year sociological theory course with Dr Miller. As we read works by Marx, Durkheim, Weber, Parsons, Berger and Luckman, and Goffman, she led us to think abstractly and comparatively about these ideas. She was able to show us the power of sociology as a way to understand the world we live in. I feel lucky to have met these three people, and to share a passion for sociology; I hope you will have similar experiences.—Bruce Arai something to be called 'scientific'. All that we require is that science be defined as 'guidelines or rules of thumb or conventions that produce claims that are defensible when called upon, though not perfect' (Goldenberg, 1992: 19). The 'eight items or less' rule in grocery stores, seen in Figure 2.2, is simply a rule we use to make our lives easier. The rules we use in science are more important than 'eight items or less', but they are not ultimate or final statements.

Figure 2.2 Another View of Sociology as a Science

(© Brenda Brown. Reprinted with permission.)

What this means in practical terms is that sociologists can and do develop rules for what constitutes 'good sociology' and for how it can be differentiated from 'bad sociology'. Physicists, chemists, and psychologists do the same thing, developing rules for 'good' and 'bad' physics, chemistry, and psychology. Many of these rules concern the proper methods used to collect, record, and analyze data. We will cover some of these basic rules or conventions in the next two sections of this chapter on the connections between theory and research and on the major techniques of sociological research.

Theory and Research 

For most sociologists, it is important that their research be closely connected with a **theory** or set of theories. Briefly, *theories* are abstract ideas about the world. Most sociological research is designed to evaluate a theory, either by testing it or by exploring the applicability of a theory to different situations. As can be seen throughout the many chapters in this text, sociologists investigate substantive problems and try to use their theories to help them understand these problems better. For instance, sociologists may be interested in understanding crime, the family, the environment, or education, and they will almost always use their theories to provide a deeper appreciation of these issues.

Sociologists use theories as models or conceptual maps of how the world works, and they use research methods to gather data that are relevant to these theories. Thus, theories and methods are always intertwined in the research process. There are hundreds of different theories in sociology, but most of them can be grouped into the four main theoretical perspectives that can be found throughout this text: structural functionalism, conflict theory, symbolic interactionism, and feminism. Theories cannot be tested directly, because they are only abstract ideas. Theories must be translated into observable ideas before they can be tested. This process of translation is called **operationalization**.

Time to Reflect

To engage in science, or anything else for that matter, we must use language. Imagine if you were asked to determine the temperature at which different liquids reach a boiling point. Presumably, this would tell you something about the properties of these liquids. But to do this experiment, you would need to understand a language to make your observations. So doing science of any kind is dependent on language. Yet languages are always imperfect and biased, not just reflections of the world around us. This makes 'objective science' impossible. How could you record a boiling point if you didn't know what it means for a liquid to boil, or you didn't know what a temperature scale or thermometer was? Does this make you skeptical about science being 'objective'?

HUMAN DIVERSITY

Are Leaders Born or Bred?

Every organization needs leaders. Companies need CEOs to increase profits or to turn around a run of bad years. Churches require strong leaders and universities need visionary presidents to ensure that they remain dynamic and relevant. The Liberal Party of Canada spent months searching its ranks for a new leader, and at the end of its leadership convention in late 2006 the party chose Stéphane Dion over Bob Rae, Michael Ignatieff, and Gerard Kennedy, who had been the other main candidates.

But, are leaders born or bred? Sociologically, this is an important question because if they are born (that is, most of the essential features of a good leader are determined at birth or a young age) then the hundreds of leadership programs available across North American are largely ineffective. If leaders are bred, then a very different story emerges.

This discussion shows how important theory is to the definition of a problem. If leaders are born, we can do little but sit back and hope that the right people end up in the right positions. But if leaders are bred, 'leadership training' as a concept starts to make sense.

The prevailing view at present is that leaders are bred. Perhaps this is because so many organizations are offering leadership training programs, and they all have an interest in this position! But if leaders are bred, then it becomes possible to evaluate the quality or effectiveness of different training programs. A great number of studies attempt to do just that. Sometimes the evidence seems to suggest that these programs work (Mighty and Ashton, 2003; Nichols, 2002) and at other times they don't (Allio, 2005; Fossey and Shoho, 2006).

Methodologically, the interesting point about all of these discussions is that it has proven almost impossible to develop a widespread and consistent theory of leadership. Generally speaking, we have moved past the idea that leaders possess special qualities such as superior intelligence, morality, or motivation to the idea that leadership arises from the relationships among people. Leaders emerge from a group in times of crisis to legitimately move an organization forward. But why has it proven so difficult to identify leaders except after the fact? And consequently, why is it so hard to evaluate these training programs?

At one level, the answer is simple. People are far too diverse in what determines who they will follow and why for anyone to be able to develop a reliable standard measure of either leadership or program success. Some people will follow the head of an organization simply because that person is the head. Others will follow a clerk in the mail room as long as the clerk possesses qualities that inspire them. Others will follow a person of compassion and strong moral character because they find those qualities admirable.

Despite the fact that leadership is critical to the success of virtually all modern organizations, human diversity makes it almost impossible to predict who will follow when. And this in turn makes it extremely difficult to evaluate whether or not these programs are successful.

Operationalization

Operationalization is the process of translating theories and concepts into hypotheses and variables. Theories are abstract ideas, composed of concepts. **Concepts** are single ideas. Usually, theories explain how two or more concepts are related to each other. For instance, as discussed in Chapter 14 on class and status inequality, Karl Marx used concepts such as 'alienation', 'exploitation', and 'class' to construct an abstract explanation (theory) of capitalism.

Once we have a theory, we need some way to test it. The problem is, we are not able to test theories directly. We need an observable equivalent of a theory, or at least a set of observable statements that are consistent with our theory. These are called hypotheses. In the same way that theories express relationships between concepts, **hypotheses** express relationships between variables.

Unlike the typical definition of a hypothesis as simply an 'educated guess', it is important to point out that hypotheses must be observable or testable. This means they must be composed of or express relationships between variables.

Variables are the empirical or observable equivalent of concepts. The two key points about a variable are that it must be observable and that it must have a range of different values it can take on. For instance, ethnicity, age, years of schooling, and annual income are variables. We can collect information on all of these items (that is, they are observable), and people can have different ages, ethnicities, and so on. 'French', '45 years old', '12 years of schooling', and '$50,000 per year' are not variables because although these are observable, they do not vary. They are *values* of variables, not variables in themselves, and it is important not to confuse the two.

In most cases, our hypotheses contain a minimum of two types of variables: independent variables and dependent variables. Independent variables are roughly equivalent to causes, and dependent variables are roughly equivalent to effects. Another way to keep these straight is to remember that the value of a dependent variable depends on the value of an independent variable. For instance, if you wanted to investigate differences between the average earnings of men and women, then sex or gender would be the independent variable and earnings would be the dependent variable. This is because peoples' earnings may depend on their gender. Indeed, it is easy to keep the independent and dependent variables straight in this example because it makes no sense to say that a person's gender can depend on his or her earnings.

Validity and Reliability

In the process of operationalizing our theories and concepts into variables and hypotheses, it is important that this process of translation be as clean as possible. That is, we want to ensure that our variables and hypotheses accurately reflect our theories and concepts. In particular, we want to ensure that when we go out and collect our data, we are using measures that are both valid and

Albert Einstein famously said, 'God does not play dice with the universe', meaning that we can successfully study the world through systemic research. Popular games of chance carry no such guarantee of success. (Simon de Trey-White/Photofusion Picture Library/Alamy Images)

reliable. The most important step in this process is the construction of *operational definitions* of our concepts. These are definitions that specify what we are going to observe, how we are going to make our observations, and how we are going to differentiate observations from non-observations (or how we will know which possible elements to exclude from our study).

Validity

The **validity** of an empirical indicator is always related to the concept it is supposed to capture. A valid measure is one that adequately represents the concept, and an invalid measure is one that does not. There are no valid or invalid measures as such, and the validity of an indicator is always a matter of degree. A measure can be perfectly valid in relation to one concept but invalid for another. For instance, sociologists often use a person's years of schooling as an indicator of educational attainment, and most sociologists consider it a valid (if imperfect) indicator of this concept. However, a person's years of schooling is not a valid indicator of ethnic origin.

It is probably fairly obvious to you that a person's years of schooling is a better indicator of her or his educational attainment than of her or his ethnicity. But this is really only one of several validity criteria, one called *face validity*. An indicator has high face validity when it seems to fit nicely with our mental image of the concept it is supposed to measure. There are several other types of validity that are often used in social sciences research, but we will cover only two more of them here.

Construct validity assesses how well an indicator of one concept performs against indicators that measure other, related concepts. A measure with high construct validity will behave as expected in relation to indicators of these other concepts. For example, you may be interested in the concept of political involvement, and you may choose to use the number of political rallies or events that a person attended in the past year as a measure of this involvement. You might also think that a person's political involvement should be positively related to his or her level of political awareness, and you could develop an awareness score for your respondents based on their answers to a series of questions about politics and current events. If you find that people's scores on your political awareness measure correlate well with the number of rallies and events they have attended, then your measure of political involvement probably has good construct validity.

The *content validity* of a measure refers to the degree to which that measure captures the various meanings of a concept. A measure with high content validity will cover all or most of the meanings of a concept without overlapping onto other concepts. For example, one commonly used measure of educational attainment in high school is a student's score in math, or sometimes the difference between a student's math scores in Grade 10 and in Grade 12 (Morgan and Sorensen, 1999). These variables have reasonably high content validity for the concept of math ability but fairly low content validity for concepts like intelligence and school success. School success is often measured by a student's overall average, and IQ is sometimes used to measure intelligence.

In addition to discussing the content and construct validity of specific measures or variables, sociologists also talk about two types of overall validity of a piece of research: the external and internal validity of a study also need to be established. The *external validity* of a piece of research refers to the extent to which the results from that research can be generalized to a larger population (that is, the generalizability of the findings beyond, or external to, the specific **sample** used in the study). The two main areas of concern in establishing external validity are the proper selection of the sample of people or elements to be studied and the specific techniques used in the research.

Ensuring that a sample is chosen using a properly random procedure usually satisfies concerns about sample selection. It is important, however, to distinguish randomness from haphazardness, because choosing a truly random sample is a much more intentional process than the name suggests. For instance, if you are working for a bottled water company and are asked to find out which of the company's two brands people prefer, you could do this in a number of ways. If you choose to stand in front of a mall and ask people which brand of water they prefer, the external validity of your research would be very low because there is no obvious connection between the sample of people you talked to and a larger population. You could say that the population is the total number of people who went to that mall on that day, but clearly that population is not of significant scholarly interest. Alternatively, if you had a list of current customers of this company, you could deliberately choose every tenth name on the list, mail them a questionnaire, and analyze the results. In this case the external validity of your research would be pretty high because there is a direct and unbiased connection between your sample and the population of current customers.

The threat from the procedures themselves is most commonly that there may be a reason to suspect that the results are a product of something in the study itself and not completely reflective of real-life situations. In other words, if there is a reason to think that people acted or answered differently during the research than they would in real life, then there is a threat to the external validity of the study. For instance, people may answer questions differently if they know they are being tape-recorded, and people may act differently simply because a researcher is present.

The *internal validity* of a study concerns the degree to which the conclusions from the study are actually supported by the data and methods that were used. Internal validity is threatened when the effects that are attributed to specific variables or processes in the study (for example, the effect of more education on the amount of money a person earns in his or her first job) are actually produced by other factors. For instance, if people perform better on a math test after taking a math class than they did on a test before taking the class, it might be tempting to conclude that the class was a good one because peoples' grades went up. However, there are many other reasons why math grades might have gone up, including the fact that the students will have a better idea of the types of questions that will be asked on the second test than they did on the first one. If these and other factors are not accounted for in the research, then the internal validity of the study is lower than it could be (Campbell and Stanley, 1970).

Reliability

The **reliability** of a measurement process refers to its level of consistency. A reliable measurement process is one that produces the same measurements of the same phenomenon again and again. For instance, you can get a sense of the reliability of a supermarket scale by weighing an apple on it several times in succession. If you get very similar weights each time, the scale is reliable. However, if you get very different weights each time, it is not. In sociology, assessing the reliability of our measurement processes is rarely this straightforward. The details of these assessment procedures are beyond the scope of this chapter, but you can learn more about them in sociology research methods courses.

Another Approach to Validity and Reliability

Another way of assessing the validity and reliability of our measurement processes is an approach most often associated with qualitative research and is based on the depth of understanding that a researcher has of her or his topic. In this approach, researchers usually refer to the validity and reliability of their findings rather than to their measurement processes, in part because many qualitative researchers do not see themselves as 'measuring' social phenomena so much as 'recording' or 'understanding' them. Indeed, sociologists often demonstrate a hesitancy to speak of *validity* and *reliability* because these terms are closely associated with the idea of precise, often quantitative, measurement.

One of the main goals of a great deal of qualitative research is to gain a better understanding of the topic or group being studied. But in order to acquire this better understanding, it is important that the results of the research be both valid and reliable. The reason is simply that we cannot have a better understanding of the topic if our results are unreliable and invalid. Wendy Griswold (1987), for instance, has developed one of the only sophisticated models for assessing the validity of qualitative cultural data.

To achieve a level of validity and reliability in qualitative research, we do not usually engage in an extensive process of testing the different dimensions of validity and reliability as we do in quantitative research. Instead, we establish it by making a convincing argument that we have properly understood our topic or group. In other words, we demonstrate to our readers that we have gained enough understanding of our topic to ensure that our results are valid. We do this in several ways, including spending enough time with the people we are studying to fully understand their point of view, interviewing group members until we begin to see the same ideas come up again and again, or conducting extensive analyses of written records and documents on our topic of interest. (For a readable and irreverent discussion of these issues in qualitative research, see Stoddart, 1986.)

Bias and Error

Even with solid conceptualization and operationalization, a study can be threatened by the existence of both *biases* and *errors*. Although the words, bias and error are often used interchangeably in everyday conversations, they have two distinctly different meanings in social science research.

Error refers to the unintentional, accidental mistakes that inevitably creep into a piece of research. These errors are often referred to as 'random errors', reflecting the understanding that these mistakes are unintentional and unpredictable. Random errors have many sources, including having the wrong people participate in research, respondents making mistakes when they fill out a survey or answer questions, errors in coding (the process of preparing data for analysis), and errors in analysis. There are ways of checking for some types of random errors, but there are no foolproof checks that will catch all of them. Obviously, our goal is to minimize the number of random errors in our research.

OPEN FOR DISCUSSION

Max Weber and *Verstehen*

In many of the chapters in this text, you will come across the ideas of Max Weber. One of his most enduring contributions to research methods in sociology is his elaboration of a concept he called '*verstehen*' (German for 'to understand'). His idea is that in order to properly study the cultures of other peoples, a researcher needs to develop more than knowledge, but an 'empathetic understanding' of their lives in order to see the world as that group sees it.

Verstehen became a cornerstone of qualitative sociology, as researchers tried to understand the lives of others 'from the inside'. In Weber's view, developing *verstehen* was a bit of an art, but in theory anyone who was good at it could understand the world view of any other group. In other words, the views of any group could be understood regardless of the personal characteristics of the researcher.

But this view has been criticized as too simplistic. That is, some researchers have argued that there are limits to *verstehen* because the personal characteristics of the researcher will affect how the group reacts to her or him. And this will limit the depth of *verstehen* or understanding that a researcher can achieve. For instance, Margaret Mead's classic anthropological study in Somoa has been criticized because the Somoans later claimed that they were not completely honest with her. Similarly, men will be able to reach only a certain limited level of understanding with women. And because of this, it may not even be appropriate for men to study women, or vice versa. If we relate this to Killingsworth's (2000) study of mom and tot groups discussed in this chapter, it may be the case that as a male, he may not have had the same access to the ongoing discussions around motherhood and child care. On the other hand, are there factors that would also limit the level of *verstehen* that a researcher can achieve? And if so, what are those factors and how do we identify them? At its extreme, this would mean that a researcher would have to match up with her/his participants on everything from gender, to education level, to hair colour, to fashion sense. So neither extreme position is particularly convincing, but exactly where we draw this line remains 'open for discussion'.

Bias is different from error—it refers to systematic inaccuracies in our data or analysis. Biases are usually unintentional, but they can be more serious than errors because they distort our findings in systematic ways. They also have multiple sources, but most researchers are concerned primarily about *respondent biases.* Two of the most common forms of respondent bias are *acquiescence bias,* where respondents simply check off answers to questions without thinking about them, and *social desirability bias,* where they try to answer questions the way they think the researcher wants them to instead of answering the way they want to themselves.

Even though *bias* and *error* mean two different things in social science research, something that starts out as a random error can turn into a systematic bias. For instance, when entering data from a survey into a computer, numbers are usually used to refer to different possible answers to each question. So instead of entering 'French' or 'Korean' for a person's ethnic background, a researcher will arbitrarily assign numbers to these categories (1 for French and 2 for Korean, for instance) and then enter the numbers into the computer. If, during the course of entering the data, a researcher mistakenly starts to enter the number 2 for people who are French, the data will be systematically biased.

• Research Techniques 

Having covered many of the more general issues in social scientific research, we now turn our attention to some of the specific techniques that sociologists and other social scientists use to conduct research. Again, this chapter will not cover these in great detail but rather try to give you a sense of what these techniques are, and when and how they are used. Before doing so, let us return for a moment to the traditional vision of what methods a scientist might use.

A popular image is that the primary method scientists use to conduct research is the experiment. However, even in the natural sciences, experiments often are the exception rather than the rule. A great deal of biology, astronomy, and other sciences is not done—and, in many cases, cannot be done—experimentally. Nevertheless, the image persists, and has traditionally been the standard against which science of all types, natural or social, has been measured.

The main advantages of experiments is that (1) they provide a controlled environment in which it is possible to (2) manipulate specific factors in an attempt to determine their effect on an outcome. Experiments can show the effects of one variable on another variable quite convincingly because of these two features.

However, sociologists do not use experiments very often for two reasons. First, we cannot manipulate many of the variables we are interested in, for either practical or ethical reasons. Sociologists are often interested in the effects of variables like gender, ethnicity, and social class on other variables like educational outcomes, earnings, or health status. But it is neither ethical nor practical to alter peoples' ethnicity or gender just so we can observe what happens to their educational outcomes. Nor can we simply move a person from an upper-class home into a lower-class home (or vice versa) just so we can find out what effect this might have on his or her eventual choice of career.

Second, one of the enduring criticisms of experiments is that it is not always clear that what happens under the controlled conditions of an experiment will also happen when we try to apply our findings to the 'real world' (that is, external validity). For instance, many of the experiments in medical research are done first on rats and other animals, and it is always a question whether or not what happens to rats will also happen to humans. Similarly, in social scientific research, it is never clear that what we observe in a controlled social experiment will also happen to people in their daily lives. Yet, it is what happens in the real world that is often of most interest to sociologists. So, the findings from a social experiment may not be interesting for us until it can be shown that the results are relevant in the real world as well.

Despite the fact that sociologists do not use experiments very often, the logic of the experiment still dominates at least one of the major techniques of sociological research. Surveys almost always collect a great deal of extra information from respondents in an attempt to recreate the controlled environment of the experiment after the fact. Surveys are often referred to as *quasi-experimental* designs because they are only able to construct a controlled environment after the data have been collected. In other words, in true experiments the controlled conditions are set in place and then the experiment is allowed to run, while in quasi-experiments observations of 'naturally occurring' phenomena are made and an attempt is made to remove the effects of confounding variables during the analysis stage.

Surveys

Surveys are the most widely used technique in social scientific research. Sociologists, economists, political scien-

The systematic study of public opinion is well developed in sociology and plays an important role in political life and public decision-making. (Ivy Images)

tists, psychologists, and others use them regularly (Gray and Guppy, 2003). They are an excellent way to gather data on large populations that cannot be studied effectively in a face-to-face manner. The goals of almost all social scientific surveys are to produce detailed data that will allow researchers to describe the characteristics of the group under study, to test theories about that group, and to generalize results beyond those people who responded to the survey.

You have probably participated in a survey or opinion poll before, although perhaps not in one used for social scientific research. Many polls done by political parties or polling organizations to find out about the political preferences of the electorate are very well done. The need to be able to generalize results from a sample of people to the preferences of voters in general is extremely important, and consequently most of these organizations put a great deal of effort into constructing and administering their polls properly. The one disadvantage of many of these polls is that they are very focused on time-sensitive issues or candidates, so they are only useful for a limited range of social scientific research topics. However, studies of voting behaviour and other political processes have profited immensely from public opinion polls.

Many 'surveys' are done for purposes other than social scientific research, and most of these will not produce data that are amenable to social science research. Designing and administering a good survey is much more difficult than it seems, but respondents rarely see all of the work that goes into producing a good survey. This may partly explain why surveys seem easy to create, and it may also contribute to the proliferation of pseudo-surveys in many different forms.

Pseudo-Surveys

A great deal of marketing and customer satisfaction research does not meet the standards of a social-scientific survey, despite the fact that generalizable results remain an important goal. That is, companies do this research only to find out what their customers and potential customers want and do not want to see in their products and services. But if their results apply only to the specific people who answered the survey and not to their customers and potential customers more generally, then they have very limited value. The usual problem in these surveys is that not enough attention is paid to the selection of the people to whom the survey will be sent or administered or to ensuring that enough of the surveys actually are returned. Both of these factors jeopardize the generalizability of the results.

Typically, a customer satisfaction survey will be sent to a selection of customers, perhaps all customers during the past year, in the hope that some of these customers will send it back. But the keys to being able to generalize the results of a survey are that the sample be chosen using a randomized selection procedure and that enough people return the completed survey to ensure that there are no important differences between people who did and did not return it. Unless the company chooses its sample randomly, the results will apply only to those who actually answered the survey.

Moreover, it is not unusual for a company to send a survey to all of its customers yet receive only 20 per cent of them back. Why did so many people not return it, and are these people different from those who did return it? Probably, some people moved and did not get it, but likely others did not return it because they were unhappy with the service or product they received. To improve a product or service, you need this 'negative' information as much as or more than the positive information from the people who did respond.

You may have seen TV shows that ask you to register your opinion about something by phone or website. Perhaps you have seen people in shopping malls asking passersby for their opinions, or have come across a survey on an Internet site, or have read a mail-in questionnaire in a magazine. Sometimes the results of these questionnaires are released with outrageous claims, like '46 per cent of Canadians think X.' The problem with many of these questionnaires is that respondents are chosen according to convenience and luck rather than randomly. The respondents to these questionnaires have to watch the TV show, read the magazine, or be in the mall in order to find out about the survey in the first place and for those reasons alone these groups of people might not be representative of the larger population. Indeed, one of the main purposes of TV and radio shows, magazines and newspapers, and shopping malls is to appeal to specific, and often quite special, parts of the population. Clearly, the results of any of these polls are not generalizable to larger populations.

A relatively new class of pseudo-surveys comprises push polls, sales pitches disguised as surveys, questionnaires designed to create mailing lists, and other gimmicks. *Push polls* usually are phone interviews designed to influence rather than record public opinion by 'pushing' people into believing certain things. Political parties (or lobby groups) run them to spread damaging facts or rumours about opposing candidates in the hope that the bad publicity will push people into supporting their favoured candidates.

Some companies also use surveys as a cover for their sales pitches. These take many forms: people are called and asked to participate in a survey about their buying habits, or perhaps about their concerns about their health or the environment. Then, a week or two later, they get calls from companies selling products that fit their buying habits.

To alleviate some of the confusion around surveys and pseudo-surveys, and also to remove the derogatory connotation of the latter category, it is useful to distinguish between surveys and questionnaires. The pseudo-surveys mentioned above can be classified as questionnaires, but not as surveys. A *questionnaire* is any set of questions administered to a group of people. A *survey*, on the other hand, is a properly designed set of questions systematically administered to a randomly chosen sample from a population. In other words, all surveys are questionnaires, but not all questionnaires meet the standards of a survey. What sets a survey apart are the design of the questions, the goal of collecting data rather than manipulating people, the method of administration, and how the sample is chosen.

Constructing Survey Questions

Having summarized what social scientific surveys are not, it is also important to describe some of the key characteristics of a good survey. Surveys consist mainly of questions, and there are many issues to consider in designing good survey questions (see Table 2.1 for a summary of key points to consider when constructing survey questions).

At first glance, it might seem that designing good questions for a survey would be easy. The reality is that it is quite difficult—sociologists can spend months trying to figure out what questions they will ask, how they will word them, and the order in which they will ask them. One of the reasons that it is so difficult is because each question must be unambiguous for both the respondent and the researcher. A question with several different interpretations is not useful because respondents may answer it from a different perspective than is intended by the researcher. Similarly, questions that are too complicated for respondents to answer, or that presume a level of knowledge that respondents do not have, will not produce useful data. There are many, many

Table 2.1	Guidelines for Designing Good Survey Questions
Focus	Each question should have one specific topic. Questions with more than one topic are difficult to answer, and the answers are often ambiguous.
Brevity	Generally, shorter questions are preferable to longer questions. They are easier to understand for respondents. An important exception to this guideline is when asking about threatening topics, where longer questions are often preferable.
Clarity	Use clear, understandable words and avoid jargon. This is especially important for general audiences, but if you are surveying a distinctive group or population (such as lawyers), then specialized language is often preferable.
Bias	Avoid biased words, phrases, statements, and questions. If one answer to a question is more likely or is more socially acceptable than others, then the question is probably biased and should be reworded. For instance, if you are asking people about their religious preferences, do not use words like 'ungodly', 'heathen', or 'fanatic' in your questions, or else you will bias your answers.
Relevance	Ensure that the questions you ask of your respondents are relevant to them and to your research. Also, in most surveys, some questions will not be relevant to all respondents; filter questions allow people to skip questions that are not pertinent to them. For instance, if you want to know why some people did not complete high school, you should first filter out high school graduates and ask them not to answer the questions about not completing high school.

Source: Adapted from George Gray and Neil Guppy, *Successful Surveys: Research Methods and Practice*, 3rd edn (Toronto: Nelson Thomson, 2003).

issues to consider in designing good questions and the order they appear on the questionnaire, but we will talk about just four of them in this chapter.

First, sociologists must avoid the use of double-barrelled questions in surveys. *Double-barrelled questions* are those that have two or more referents or subjects, and that can therefore be answered honestly in more than one way. For instance, 'Do you think that the government should increase taxes so that it can spend more on environmental protection?' is a double-barrelled question. The problem is that a yes or no answer to this question is impossible to interpret. 'Yes' may mean that a person agrees with the whole statement, or only with the environmental protection component or only with the increasing taxes component. 'No' may mean that the person disagrees with increased taxes but may nonetheless want more environmental protection, or that he or she disagrees with the entire statement. A researcher will not know which of these interpretations is correct for any individual respondent. The way to avoid this confusion is to formulate two separate questions, one about tax increases and one for environmental spending.

A second problem occurs when researchers do not pay sufficient attention to respondents' abilities to answer questions accurately. It may seem straightforward to ask a person how much he or she earned last year, but very few people know to the actual dollar how much they earned over the last 12 months. And even fewer people will be willing to look it up on their latest tax return. So, while you can ask people for their specific annual income, most of the answers you get will be wrong. Some people round off their income to the nearest $1,000, others round it off to the nearest $5,000, and others simply guess at the actual dollar amount. You then have no way of correcting for these different reporting procedures. The solution is to offer people categories, because people often know to the nearest $5,000 or $10,000 how much they earn in a year.

Third, in some surveys, it is deemed necessary to ask people about uncomfortable topics, topics that they may perceive as threatening. Surveys of criminal activity, sexual practices, and criminal victimization imply socially threatening questions. However, it is impossible to predict how individuals will react to any question, and even the most innocuous question may be perceived as threatening. Asking people about their incomes generally is perceived as somewhat threatening, and care must be exercised in how you ask about this.

Strategies for reducing the threat of questions include making the behaviour or attitude you are asking about less threatening by positioning the respondent at some distance—by asking about it in hypothetical terms or asking about it as one of a series of questions. For instance, instead of asking people directly if they have been victims of crime, you could ask people about how they feel about their own safety, how much media coverage of criminal activity they receive, and whether or not they have been victimized. No single strategy will work for every question, topic, or sample.

Finally, the order in which you ask questions can have a significant effect on respondents' answers, and even on whether or not they will complete the survey. As a general rule, it is better to ask threatening questions near the end rather than at the beginning of a survey. By asking easier questions up front, researchers have an opportunity to establish a rapport with the respondent, in phone and interview surveys through conversation, and in paper surveys by leading the respondent to identify with the topics and issues on the survey. Second, if threatening questions turn off respondents so much that they refuse to participate further in the research, then at least they have completed part of the survey already. If this happens at the beginning of the survey, no usable data are collected at all.

Random Sampling, Sample Size, and Response Rates

The idea of choosing samples using a random procedure was emphasized in the discussion of pseudo-surveys. Random sampling is so important because it is the only way that we can be confident that our sample is representative of (that is, that it looks like) the population we are interested in. If our sample is representative, then we can be fairly confident that the patterns we find among our sample also will be present in the larger population. If it is not representative, then we have no idea if what we found in our sample also is present in our population. Using a proper randomization procedure ensures that we do not deliberately bias our sample and guards against any unintentional biases that may creep into our selection process. And although randomization does not guarantee that our sample will be representative, by minimizing both intentional and unintentional biases we maximize our chances that the sample will be representative. Additionally, randomization does not solve all problems in sociological research, and is not always appropriate or necessary in field research.

There are many procedures for choosing a truly random sample, but all are based on the principle that each person (or element) in a population has an equal (and non-zero) chance of being selected into the sample. The simplest random-sampling procedure is known as *simple*

SOCIOLOGY IN ACTION

Asking the Right Questions about Survey Data

Rudner (1999) investigated the relative performance of high school students who graduated from a traditional high school as compared to those who had been home-schooled, on two standardized tests. Interestingly, his results showed that home-schoolers did as well or better than their counterparts who went to traditional school. His results were based on an analysis of over 20,000 home-schooled students whose test scores were compiled by Bob Jones University Press, the publishing division of a small, religious college in South Carolina.

Rudner found that on average, those who were home-schooled scored between the 70th and 80th percentile on the Iowa Test of Basic Skills and the Test of Achievement and Proficiency, two widely accepted tests of scholastic ability in the US. By definition, students from traditional schools on average score at the 50th percentile. He claimed that these results show that home-schoolers outperform their counterparts who went to regular school.

This may well be true on average, but unfortunately the data in his study cannot be used to support this conclusion. This is because this sample is not representative of the larger population of US home-schoolers. This sample has low external validity for at least three reasons. First, most home-schoolers do not ever write standardized tests. So those who do are clearly different from the norm. Second, when the test is voluntary for home-schoolers but mandatory for children in school, as in this case, there is a good reason to believe that what is being compared here is the top end of the spectrum of the home-schooling category against all schooled children. After all, if you are a home-schooler and you know you are a weak student, what incentive do you have to take a voluntary test? Institutionally educated children were not given this choice, so they were being compared to the top end of the home-schoolers and found wanting.

Finally, the claim that over 20,000 home-schooled students were used in the study, thus making the claims generalizable to a larger population, is patently false. Always be wary of studies that emphasize how large the sample is as the basis of their validity. Somebody either doesn't know what he or she is doing in the area of sample selection, or is hiding something. Luckily for you, a good grounding in research methods will prevent you from making the same mistakes!

random sampling: each person in a population is put on a list and then a proportion of them are chosen from this list completely at random. The usual way of ensuring that people are chosen at random is to use a table of random numbers either to select all of the people or to select the starting point in the list from which the sample will be chosen.

Actually, the adjective 'simple' in 'simple random sampling' does not refer to the degree of difficulty—simple random samples are quite difficult to construct. Generating truly random samples is not as easy as is suggested in Figure 2.3. The problem lies not in choosing the actual people or elements but in constructing a complete list of every person or element in the population. For this reason, other sampling techniques such as stratified sampling and cluster sampling frequently are used to choose samples, even by large government agencies like Statistics Canada.

It is also important to consider the issue of sample size in designing a proper survey. How big a sample do you need in order to be able to generalize your results? Actually, this is the wrong question to ask—it is not the size of the sample but rather how it is chosen that determines how confident you can be that your results are applicable to the population. That is, even a very large sample, if it is not chosen randomly, offers no guarantee about the generalizability of the results. On the other hand, a small sample, properly chosen, can produce very good results. So never assume that because a sample is large it must be representative. Always make sure you find out about how the sample was chosen before making any judgements about its generalizability.

Another crucial factor in determining the generalizability of survey results is how many people from the original sample actually complete the survey. This percentage is called the *response rate*, and is an important,

Figure 2.3 Randomization

(© Brenda Brown. Reprinted with permission.)

although not the only, issue to consider in determining the generalizability of the results of a survey. The reason it is important is that unless a large proportion of the people in the original sample actually complete the survey, it is quite possible that the people who do not respond to it are different from those who do respond.

Field Research

In surveys, the primary aim is to collect quantitative or numerical data that can be generalized to a larger population. In contrast, field researchers are concerned about collecting qualitative or non-numerical data that may or may not be generalized to a larger population. In field research, the aim is to collect rich, nuanced data by going into the 'field' to observe and talk to people directly. Researchers spend time getting to know their subjects in order to be able to capture their world view. Some of the classic sociological field studies, such as William Whyte's *Street Corner Society* (1943) and Elliot Liebow's *Tell Them Who I Am* (1993), are vivid portrayals of what life is like for certain groups of people—in the former case, the members of a lower-class urban community, and in the latter case, of homeless women.

Several separate techniques fall under the rubric of field research. These include participant observation or ethnography, in-depth interviewing, and documentary analysis. In many studies, more than one of these techniques is used.

Ethnographic or Participant Observation Research

In *ethnographic* or *participant observation* research, the researcher participates in the daily activities of his or her research subjects, usually for an extended period of time. This may include accompanying them on their daily activities (such as following police officers on patrol), interviews and discussions about their lives, and occasionally even living with them. During these activities, researchers take field notes (or make recordings) either during or after an episode in the field.

A good example of participant observation research is Killingsworth's study (2006) of how mothers interact with each other in a 'moms and tots' playgroup to construct ideas about what a good mother is, and how they can reconcile that with the consumption of alcohol. Killingsworth participated in a playgroup of mothers and toddlers in Australia over a period of several months. As is typical of participant observation research, he did not have a rigid research design that he followed strictly over the time he was in the field. Rather, his main interest was in the women's conversations about alcohol and their own personal consumption of it, and how they used these conversations to define, alter, and reconstruct ideas about 'good mothers'. He did not direct the women's conversations or ask them to focus their talk on particular issues. Instead, he simply participated in the playgroup and allowed the conversations to occur naturally. He found that the women were able to reconcile their understandings of good motherhood with the consumption of alcohol by recapturing the importance of alcohol to their previous identities as childless women and using that to build ideals of themselves as women first and good mothers second.

Time to Reflect

Now that you understand some of the major points about surveys, perhaps you will be more critical of some of the questionnaires you read about in the newspaper or see on TV. And if you're asked to participate in a survey in a mall or over the phone, would you be willing to ask the interviewer about the sampling procedures and questionnaire design? After all, you are the one giving up your time to answer the questions, so don't you want the results to be meaningful?

Sociologists, like anthropologists, often study subcultures from the inside, using well-established techniques of ethnographic research. At times, however, they run risks in studying deviant subcultures. (Ivy Images)

Killingworth's research is interesting for several reasons, but one is particularly relevant to his use of participant observation. By focusing on naturally occurring conversations, he was able to show how cultural ideals about things like motherhood and womanhood are embedded in and recreated by seemingly mundane discussions among mothers. In other words, ideals about good mothers do not just appear out of nowhere and exert pressure on people through 'norms' or 'society'. Instead, ideals about good mothers are defined, interpreted, and reconstructed by actual people in actual interactions.

In-Depth Interviews

In-depth interviews are another popular field research technique and may be used in conjunction with participant observation. *In-depth interviews* are extensive interviews that are often tape-recorded and later transcribed into text. In some cases, these interviews are highly structured and neither the researchers nor the respondents are permitted to deviate from a specific set of questions. At the other extreme, unstructured interviews may seem like ordinary conversations in which researchers and respondents simply explore topics as they arise. In many cases, researchers use semi-structured in-depth interviews that ask all respondents a basic set of questions but that also allow participants to explore other topics and issues. Striking the right balance between structured and unstructured questions can pose problems for sociologists, as can asking the right questions.

Elizabeth Murphy investigated the connections between health-care conversations (2000) and images of childhood (2007) and ideals about good mothers. Obviously, field research techniques can be used to investigate many more issues than motherhood, but Murphy's and Killingsworth's studies provide a nice illustration of how different field methods can be used to study similar topics. In her earlier article, Murphy used theories about how people understand and respond to risks as the basis of her research on breast-feeding and motherhood. In her later article, her focus was on how feeding, and breast-feeding in particular, allowed women to negotiate different conceptions of childhood. She interviewed 36 British mothers six times each, from one month before the birth of their babies to two years after birth. Each interview was semi-structured. In Murphy's sample, 31 women breast-fed their babies initially, but only six were still breast-feeding four months after birth. This is interesting in light of current medical advice about the importance of exclusively breast-feeding infants for at least four months, and many health practitioners recommend continuing up to two years of age. Did the women in this study who stopped breast-feeding before four months think of themselves as bad mothers? Or were they able to set aside this medical advice and still think of themselves as good mothers? Murphy found that almost all of the women who had stopped breast-feeding recognized formula feeding as inferior but that none of them perceived this as a threat to their status as good mothers. Rather, they were able to justify their decisions because other people were at least partly—and, in many cases, primarily—responsible for the switch to formula feeding. Also, breast-feeding and the demands of the children were critical in shaping how mothers viewed their children, in relation to 'Appolonian themes of natural goodness and innocence' (Murphy, 2007: 122).The interviews revealed that some women encountered health-care workers who were unsupportive of breast-feeding or who did not diagnose medical or mechanical problems that prevented breast-feeding. Other women had babies who were either unco-operative or could not do it because of 'incompetence' (Murphy, 2000: 317).

One of the strengths of Murphy's research is the flexibility of her semi-structured interview technique. By directing the women to discuss their breast-feeding decisions and then following their leads, Murphy was able to gain a much deeper understanding of these choices. Had she not imposed some structure on the interviews, it is possible that the women might not have talked about their breast-feeding choices at all. Instead, her research presents us with a better understanding of how women can reconcile individual decisions to stop breast-feeding with seemingly contradictory ideals about 'good motherhood'.

Documentation

In some field studies, researchers will have access not only to people, but also to documents. This is more common when studying formal organizations like police forces or law firms, but can also be true when studying churches, political groups, and even families. These documents (case records, files, posters, diaries, even photos) can be analyzed to provide a more complete picture of the group under study.

The elaborate procedures needed to choose a sample for a survey are not necessary for selecting the research site and the sample in field research. Strictly following a randomization protocol is necessary only if statistical analysis and generalization are the goal of the research. Field research is done to gain greater understanding through the collection of detailed data, not through generalization. Nevertheless, it is important to choose both the research site and the subjects or informants carefully.

Conducting Field Research

The first criterion in choosing a site for field research is the topic of study. A field study of lawyers or police officers likely will take place at the offices and squad rooms of the respective groups. Choosing which offices and squad rooms to study depends on many factors, including which ones will be most useful for the purposes of the research. But a practical element impinges on much field research—the actual choice of research site can come down to which law offices or squad rooms will grant access. This is not a criticism of field research, but a recognition of the realities facing scholars doing this kind of research.

Once the site has been chosen, the issues of whom to talk to, what types of data to record, and how long to stay in the field become important. Some things can be planned in advance, but many things may be decided during the course of the field research. The selection of key informants—those people who will be most valuable in the course of the study—cannot always be made beforehand. Similarly, figuring out what to write down in field notes, who to quote, and which observations to record cannot always be determined until after the research has begun.

Deciding when to leave the field is almost always determined during the course of the research. Most researchers stay in the field until they get a sense that they are not gaining much new information. In many cases, researchers decide to leave the field when they find that the data coming from new informants merely repeat what they have learned from previous informants. This is often taken as a sign that the researcher has reached a deep enough level of understanding to be

Time to Reflect

The research by Murphy and Killingsworth reveals that mothers do not simply accept social norms about things like alcohol consumption and childhood. For instance, mothers who drink alcohol are able to talk about how they can drink and still be good mothers, despite all of the messages they receive about the harmful effects of alcohol on babies. This is a clear example of why it is wrong to say that 'society tells us . . .'. Society tells us nothing. Rather, people talk about things they hear and believe, and in turn they refine their thoughts. What are some of the messages that you hear that you have modified in your talk with your friends?

confident that he or she will not learn much from further time in the field.

This flexibility during the course of the study is one of the great advantages of field research over survey research. Mistakes in research design and the pursuit of new and unexpected opportunities are possible in field research but are not usually possible in quantitative survey research. Once a survey has been designed, pre-tested, and administered to a sample, it is impractical to recall the survey to make changes. This is one of the reasons why pre-testing is so important in surveys.

Existing Data

Both in surveys and in field research, sociologists are involved in collecting new, original data. However, a great deal of sociological research is done with data already collected. Of the several different types of existing data most are amenable to different modes of analysis. Some of the major types of existing data are official statistics and surveys done by other researchers; books, magazines, newspapers, and other media; case files and records; and historical documents.

Secondary Data Analysis

The analysis of official statistics and existing surveys—also known as *secondary data analysis*—has grown immensely with the development of computers and statistical software packages. It has become one of the most common forms of research reported in the major sociological journals, such as the *American Journal of Sociology* and the *American Sociological Review.* Statistical analyses of existing surveys also can be found in almost every issue of the *Canadian Journal of Sociology* and the *Canadian Review of Sociology and Anthropology* for at least the past 10 years.

Quantitative data can be presented in tables like Table 2.2. However, tables can be designed in many different ways, and the type of information being presented will determine the types of comparisons that can be made. In Table 2.2, on marital status in Canada, comparisons can be made within or across the values of marital status (for example, how many people are married versus single), by sex, and across five different years.

As an example, we can see that the number of divorced males increased by over 93,000 between 1997 and 2001 (641,734 – 547,914 = 93,820) and the number of divorced females has risen by over 125,000 (868,037 – 742,671 = 125,366), while the numbers of married men and women have increased by 87,500 and 106,136 respectively. However, the table does not tell us anything about why these numbers may have changed, nor can we make any comparisons with the number of married and divorced people in other countries.

In Table 2.3, though, comparisons between countries are possible. Some of these results may seem surprising, depending on your impressions of high school graduation rates here in Canada versus other countries. Many media portrayals of the US school system suggest that it is inferior to the Canadian system, yet it has a higher graduation rate than Canada.

This table also reveals some of the problems tables may present, especially with data from different countries. First, the school systems vary widely between countries, and despite careful efforts by the Organization for Economic Co-operation and Development (OECD) to standardize the data, all of these numbers should be viewed with caution. Many could change significantly depending on the way graduates are counted, and especially in reference to how each country reports its data to the OECD. Second, data may simply not be available, as in the case of Slovakia in Table 2.3.

Personal computers, statistical software packages, and the ready availability of many national and international data sets have made secondary data analysis possible for almost every social scientist. The advantages of secondary analyses are that the coverage of the data is broad and that the hard work involved in constructing and administering a survey has already been done, usually by an agency with far more expertise and resources than most individual researchers. The disadvantages are that the data collected are often not precise enough to test the specific ideas that interest researchers and that mastering the techniques to analyze the data properly can be challenging.

Historical Research and Content Analysis

The analysis of historical documents, print and other media, and records and case materials can be done by several methods. The two most common forms of analysis are historical research and content analysis. Historical sociology relies on *historical research* into all kinds of historical documents, from organizational records, old newspapers, and magazines to speeches and sermons, letters and diaries, and even interviews with people who participated in the events of interest. In *content analysis*, documents such as newspapers, magazines, TV shows, and case records are subjected to careful sampling and analysis procedures to reveal patterns.

One of the major issues facing historical sociologists is that someone or some organization has created the records used in their analyses, but the potential biases and reasons for recording the information in the documents are not always clear. Further, some documents are

Table 2.2 Population by Marital Status and Sex, Canada, 1998–2002

	1998	1999	2000	2001	2002
Total					
Both sexes	30,248,412	30,499,323	30,770,834	31,110,565	31,413,990
Male	14,978,787	15,107,404	15,236,964	15,405,773	15,552,644
Female	15,269,625	15,401,919	15,543,870	15,704,792	15,861,346
Single					
Both sexes	12,797,263	12,911,946	13,031,272	13,175,106	13,304,129
Male	6,849,478	6,912,620	6,979,618	7,059,481	7,131,973
Female	5,947,785	5,999,326	6,051,654	6,115,625	6,172,156
Married[a]					
Both sexes	12,979,263	12,911,946	13,031,272	13,175,106	13,304,129
Male	7,299,132	7,337,226	7,381,266	7,431,522	7,476,537
Female	7,331,041	7,374,567	7,425,428	7,482,244	7,541,593
Widowed					
Both sexes	1,489,388	1,503,843	1,518,633	1,534,232	1,550,367
Male	263,490	269,220	274,910	280,748	286,940
Female	1,225,898	1,234,623	1,243,723	1,253,484	1,263,427
Divorced					
Both sexes	1,331,588	1,381,741	1,434,235	1,487,461	1,541,364
Male	566,687	588,338	611,170	634,022	657,194
Female	764,901	793,403	823,065	853,439	884,170

[a] Includes persons legally married, legally married and separated, and living in common-law unions.
Source: Statistics Canada, CANSIM database, at: <cansim2.statcan.ca>, Table 051–0010.

lost or destroyed with the passing of time, so the historical sociologist must be aware that the extant documents may not give a complete picture of the events or time period under study. Why have certain documents survived while others have not? Is there any significance to the ordering or cataloguing of the documents? These and other issues must be dealt with continually in historical research.

Content analysis can be done in a number of ways, but it usually involves taking a sample of relevant documents and then subjecting these documents to a rigorous procedure of identifying and classifying particular features, words, or images in these documents. For instance, in studying political posters, content analysis could be used to determine whether the posters from particular parties put more emphasis on the positive aspects of their own party or the negative aspects of other parties. These results could then be used to better understand styles of political campaigning in a particular country or time period. In *manifest content analysis*, words, phrases, or images are counted to provide a sense of the importance of different ideas in the documents. In *latent content analysis*, researchers focus less on specific word or phrase counts and more on the themes implicit in the documents.

Selecting a Research Method

To summarize, all of the methods described here are used by sociologists to collect data on particular research problems, and they use theories to help them understand or solve these problems. Any of these methods can be used to investigate problems from any of the theoret-

Table 2.3 Percentage of 25- to 64-Year-Olds Graduating from Upper Secondary (High School) Programs, by Country, 1998

	Percentage Graduating from Upper Secondary
Canada	79.7
Mexico	21.2
United States	86.5
Japan	79.9
Korea	65.4
Australia	56.0
New Zealand	72.7
Belgium	56.7
Czech Republic	85.3
Denmark	78.4
Finland	68.3
France	60.7
Germany	83.8
Hungary	63.3
Italy	41.0
The Netherlands	64.3
Norway	83.0
Poland	54.3
Portugal	20.1
Spain	32.9
Slovakia	–
Sweden	76.1
Turkey	17.7
United Kingdom	60.2
OECD Mean	61.2

Source: Organization for Economic Co-operation and Development (OECD), at: <www.oecd.org/pdf/M00019000/M00019568.pdf>. Reprinted by permission.

ical perspectives encountered in this text, although some methods are almost never used in some perspectives. For instance, symbolic interactionists rarely if ever use quantitative surveys, while most conflict theorists prefer surveys to participant observation.

How do you know which method to use with which theory or theoretical perspective? A complete answer to this question is beyond the scope of this chapter, but the rule of thumb in sociology has been that you let the problem determine the method. For example, if you want to find out something about the national divorce rate and how divorced people differ from those who remain married, then you need a method that will give you data from people all over the country, such as a survey. But if you want to find out how nurses manage the many pressures of their jobs, then participant observation is a more appropriate method.

As with any generalization, there are exceptions. Sheldon Goldenberg (1992) and others have argued that letting the problem determine the method is not as straightforward as it seems. A sociologist can become much more comfortable using a particular technique. This leads to a tendency to frame research questions in ways that allow those familiar techniques to be used. In other words, the comfortable methods can come to determine the questions considered for investigation.

The Context of Sociological Research

We have discussed the scientific status of sociology, the connection between theory and research, and some of the major research techniques used by sociologists, but we have said little about the context in which this research takes place. In this final section, we consider three of the many possible issues that affect the way in which sociologists do their research: the different purposes of sociological research, the rise of feminism and feminist methods, and research ethics.

Purposes of Research

Sociological research has several different purposes. Some research is *exploratory* or descriptive, where the goal is to find out more about a particular group or topic. For instance, research on home-schoolers (people who educate their children at home) likely will be exploratory because not much is known yet about this particular group (Arai, 2000). Other studies are designed to be *explanatory*. Usually, these studies test different theories against each other to determine which theory provides the best explanation for the phenomenon. Explanatory studies may test whether a theory developed from one group or time period applies to

Time to Reflect

If you were to read a piece of research, would you be more inclined to believe the results if they were based on quantitative analysis or on field research? Why?

another group or time period. A good example of an explanatory study is Stephen Morgan and Aage Sorensen's test of James Coleman's 'social capital' theory applied to why students in Catholic high schools tend to outperform students from public high schools (Morgan and Sorensen, 1999).

Other research aims to be able to predict future patterns of behaviour. Many early studies of criminal recidivism (convicted criminals' committing of further offences after being released from prison) were designed to enable people to make better predictions about which criminals would be more likely to reoffend once they were released from jail. Note that although they sometimes are related, prediction and explanation are not the same thing. It is fairly easy to predict that night will follow day, but this does not mean that night causes or explains day—the two phenomena have a common cause.

Still other research aims to empower the group being studied. In the past, anthropologists would often become very involved with the concerns of the people they studied and would become advocates for that group. This was generally frowned upon, and anthropologists were accused of 'going native'—becoming one of the people they were studying—instead of objectively studying them. Nowadays, many researchers specifically want to empower the people they study. For instance, *participatory action research*, in which researchers are guided at least as much by the goals and wishes of their respondents as they are by their own theoretical concerns, has become more popular in sociology as well as in such other disciplines as psychology and social work. In Canada, there are government grants available specifically for social scientific research that is guided primarily by the needs and concerns of community groups rather than by the purist academic concerns of the researchers.

Feminism and Research Methods

The goal of empowering the people being studied is an important component in feminist research. **Feminism** has had an enormous impact on many disciplines, including sociology. This influence has affected the topics that sociologists study, the perspectives they use to study them, and even the methods they use. The topics and perspectives influenced by feminism are covered in other chapters in this book, but it is important here to mention the influence of feminism on research methods in sociology.

Over the last 30 or so years, feminists have increasingly criticized the visions of science that inform the methods used by social scientists to study the world (Harding, 1986). In particular, the values of objectivity and detachment from the subjects that underlie a scientific view of the world have been heavily criticized on two grounds. First, these values are associated most often with men, while attributes like emotionality and intuition that are supposedly non-scientific are associated with women. The implication is that a scientific view of the world, based as it is on the 'male' characteristics of reason and objectivity, is a better way to understand the world than a typically female view, which is coloured by emotion and intuitive reasoning. The result of this has been a systematic exclusion of women from science and the subordination of women's perspectives on the world to those of men.

Second, feminists and others have shown convincingly that a detached, unbiased science of society is not possible. Much of this demonstration is based on some of the criticisms of objectivity outlined in the first section of this chapter. Social scientists all have biases, and to claim a position of objectivity is simply to hide one's biases. It is far more preferable, for feminists and for others, to acknowledge biases up front than to hide them behind a curtain of supposed objectivity (Loughlin, 1993).

One of the hallmarks of feminism is the recognition and even the celebration of diversity. Feminists have responded to the challenge of science in several different ways. Some feminists have deliberately abandoned science of any sort, preferring the contradictions of relativism to the straitjacket of science. Others have done the opposite, trying to apply the rules of science as precisely as possible to show that science can be a useful tool in eradicating the suppression of women.

Still others have worked to articulate a feminist 'standpoint' theory that takes the lived experiences of women as the critical starting point for a less distorted understanding of the world than that produced through science (Smith, 1990). Briefly, the standpoint of women is crucial for better understanding because of the unique positions of women as research subjects and of women as scientists. Women as subjects, largely excluded from mainstream sociological research, can provide researchers a fresh view of the world relative to the historical preponderance of male research, because they are in some senses on the outside looking in. Women as researchers also have a privileged standpoint for understanding the experience of exclusion and working with the women they study to empower them to make positive changes in their lives.

This diversity means that there is no single method that can be properly called a 'feminist method'. Indeed, most feminists would reject any attempt to define a singular feminist method as an example of male-centred, or *androcentric*, thinking. Feminists use a variety of methods. But what often sets their research apart from that of other researchers are a commitment to the empowerment of their research participants and the modification or rejection of social scientific methods to meaningfully incorporate women into the philosophy and practice of social science research.

Research Ethics

Our final topic in this chapter is the ethics of social research. While too broad and complicated to cover in any detail here, we can summarize some of the main issues confronting researchers. It is a topic with increasing relevance in the social sciences, but also one with a long history.

A turning point in the history of research ethics in the social and natural sciences was the Nuremberg trials of Nazi doctors and concentration camp officials after World War II. Research performed on prisoners in these camps had produced valuable insights into human physiology, but only as a result of the prisoners' having been subjected to horrific experiments (Guillebaud, 2002). The moral imperatives on the protection of research subjects during the acquisition of knowledge has guided the development of ethical principles for social and natural scientific research ever since.

In North America, one of the most important principles of research ethics to arise from these trials is the principle of *voluntary participation*. This means that people can be asked to participate in any piece of research, regardless of its potential damage, as long as they voluntarily agree to be a part of that research. People must not be coerced or tricked into participating, and they must be able to withdraw from the study at any time, without penalty.

The principle of voluntary participation cannot be fully realized unless its complementary principle of *informed consent* also prevails. Potential participants must give their consent to participate in the research with a full knowledge of the potential costs and benefits to themselves and to the researchers. Indeed, participation cannot be considered to be voluntary unless a person is fully informed about the research before giving his or her consent.

One of the implications of informed consent is that research should be designed without deceiving the subjects unnecessarily. If deception is used at all, it must outweigh the harms associated with the deception and be absolutely necessary to the project and the benefits of the research. In most cases in sociology, this problem does not arise, but there are topics that require the use of deception. For instance, studying people's discriminatory attitudes is often not possible without deception. One way of doing this that has been particularly successful is to have people evaluate fictitious resumés of job applicants on which all of the details of the resumé are the same except for the gender of the applicant. The idea is to determine whether or not people evaluate the abilities of men and women differently based not on their reported abilities but simply on their gender. Telling people that the gender of the applicants will be switched around beforehand would defeat the purpose of the study (Foschi et al., 1994). Another classic example of potential harm in sociological research is the series of 'breaching experiments' conducted by Harold Garfinkel (1967). In one of these, he asked his students to pretend to be boarders in their own homes—to speak only when spoken to, to address people formally, and to steer clear of personal topics and conversations. The reactions from family members were often strongly emotional. And in a few cases, the anxiety and harm caused by these experiments lasted a long time.

The identity of research participants must be protected in North America, either through an assurance of *confidentiality* or through *anonymity*. Sometimes these terms are used interchangeably, but they are quite different. To assure participants of anonymity, a researcher must not collect any identifying information about his or her respondents. This is possible only in mail-in surveys. In most interviews, field research, and telephone surveys, researchers either have met their participants or possess identifying information about them.

It is more common to assure respondents of confidentiality, whereby identifying information is collected but deliberately withheld in the publication of any results. This is possible in all types of research, but note that the protection of a subject's identity is weaker with

GLOBAL ISSUES

Research Ethics in Global Perspective

In the discussion of research ethics you may have noticed the phrase 'in North America' a couple of times. This may seem unnecessary, for after all, aren't ethical principles by their very nature applicable at all times and in all places? Ironically, in the case of research ethics, this definitely is not true.

Research participants in many parts of the world do not enjoy the protections that have been explained in this chapter. In many countries, particularly those with more repressive political regimes, coercion of participants and violations of confidentiality and of other research protections are commonplace. Additionally, even when rights are respected some strong cultural factors influence issues of how these rights are established. For instance, establishing that someone has provided informed consent to participate in a study usually is affirmed via signed waivers. But in many cultures, agreements are concluded with a handshake or some other informal mechanism. A signed agreement makes people suspicious and in many cases people won't sign an agreement even though they're perfectly happy to participate in the study. Research ethics truly is a global matter because of many such differences. One might think that ethical research principles would be universal, but their application, at least, turns out to be very context-oriented and country-specific. As the amount of international research continues to grow, this issue will become increasingly relevant.

confidentiality than it is with anonymity. For instance, researchers asked by a court to reveal the identities of their subjects may have to decide between breaking a promise to their subjects or disobeying a court order. If they have not collected identifying information about participants, they will have nothing to reveal.

Many researchers today are getting around the potential conflict of confidential information by promising to keep subjects' identities secret unless they are ordered to reveal them by court order. While this arrangement has weakened the confidentiality protections in many studies, it allows potential subjects to make a more informed decision about participating in the research in the first place.

A final principle, often attributed to the Nuremberg trials, is that research should not involve any unnecessary harm to the participants. The Nazi doctors were completely unconcerned about the well-being of their subjects and did not take any precautions to protect them from harm. Most researchers find this abhorrent, and their research usually only involves some inconvenience to participants. In most sociological research, the greatest inconvenience to participants is the time they have to spend talking to researchers, filling out surveys or diaries, or, to some extent, allowing the researchers into their lives. However, there are instances in which real psychological damage can occur, and researchers have an obligation to be aware of this and guard against it.

Conclusion

This chapter has introduced you to some of the major methods that sociologists use in their research and to some of the issues they face when conducting that research. A simplistic understanding of science is not helpful—for sociology or any other science. But a more sophisticated view of science does underpin how many sociologists view their discipline, although some sociologists reject the idea that sociology is a science at all. Nevertheless, establishing the validity and reliability of their results remains important to almost all sociologists.

The three main techniques—surveys, field research, and the analysis of existing data—were then reviewed, and the chapter ended with a discussion of research ethics and the influence of feminism on sociological methods. And while it has not been possible to cover all topics in detail in this chapter, you should have a better appreciation for the difficulties and the joys of finding out about the world sociologically.

Questions for Critical Thought

1. What was your understanding of science before reading this chapter? How has it changed?
2. When you read about a social scientific finding in the newspaper, what kinds of evidence convince you of its veracity? In other words, do you need quantitative, statistical results, are you convinced by detailed accounts of individuals, or are both equally convincing?
3. If you were going to investigate across Canada the effects of a person's ethnicity on his or her educational attainment, what method would be most appropriate? Why?
4. If you wanted to find out more about the motivations of parents who send their children to a particular private religious school, what methods would be most appropriate? Justify your answer.
5. Outline the two different approaches to establishing validity.
6. Summarize the criticisms of science outlined in this chapter. Which one is most convincing, and why?
7. It was argued in this chapter that there is no single feminist method. Do you agree with this? Why or why not?
8. It is often difficult to distinguish between a survey and a pseudo-survey, especially if you are a respondent rather than a researcher. Summarize the key points necessary for a proper social scientific survey and how these are violated in each of the types of pseudo-surveys discussed in this chapter.

Recommended Readings

Earl Babbie, *The Basics of Social Research*, 2nd edn (Toronto: Wadsworth Thomson Learning, 2002).

Babbie's books are used in more research methods courses across North America than those of any other author. This one is a comprehensive treatment of research methods.

Bruce Berg, *Qualitative Research Methods for the Social Sciences*, 4th edn (Boston: Allyn and Bacon, 2001).

Berg's book is the current standard for qualitative research methods courses.

Sheldon Goldenberg, *Thinking Methodologically* (New York: HarperCollins, 1992).

This sophisticated research methods text is more difficult to read than the other texts listed here, but is well worth the effort.

George Gray and Neil Guppy, *Successful Surveys: Research Methods in Practice*, 3rd edn (Toronto: Nelson, 2003).

Gray and Guppy have written an accessible and comprehensive introduction to survey research methods. The book can be used as a step-by-step guide for conducting a basic survey.

Sandra Harding, *The Science Question in Feminism* (Ithaca, NY: Cornell University Press, 1986).

This is arguably Harding's most influential book, although most of her writings have had a significant impact. It begins with the issue of the underrepresentation of women in science and moves to the issue of the sexist nature of science more generally.

Don G. McTavish and Herman Loether, *Social Research: An Evolving Process*, 2nd edn (Boston: Allyn and Bacon, 2002).

Another popular methods book, this one is more focused on quantitative methods than qualitative methods. Loether and McTavish have also written statistics texts that have been used in many social statistics courses across North America.

Charles Ragin, *Constructing Social Research: The Unity and Diversity of Method* (Thousand Oaks, Calif.: Sage, 1994).

Ragin's book covers the main topics of social research but is shorter and less comprehensive than Babbie, Goldenberg, or McTavish and Loether. Nevertheless, it is an excellent introduction to social research methods.

Shulamit Reinharz with Lynn Davidman, *Feminist Methods in Social Research* (New York: Oxford University Press, 1992).

Reinharz's book is the starting point for informed discussions of feminist methods. By reading this book first, you'll have a better appreciation of the more recent writings on feminist methods, many of which cite this book as a key source.

Recommended Websites

Inter-university Consortium for Political and Social Research
www.icpsr.umich.edu

This is one of the first—and one of the best—social science data archives in the world. As a college or university student, you can use many of the datasets from the ICPSR for class and research purposes, at no charge.

Organization for Economic Co-operation and Development (OECD)
www.oecd.org

The OECD collects data on economic, political, social, environmental, and industrial conditions in member countries (including Canada) and non-member countries (particularly developing countries). Data, publications (on-line and paper), and special reports are available at this site.

PAR-L: A Canadian Electronic Feminist Network
www.unb.ca/PAR-L/

PAR-L (Policy, Action, Research List) is a network of feminist groups and individuals engaged in research and policy discussions on women. This site is a great collection of links to feminist and advocacy organizations, as well as to publications and resources on feminist issues in Canada.

Qualpage
www.qualitativeresearch.uga.edu/QualPage/

This site is dedicated to qualitative methods. It lists new books, conferences, and many other resources for people interested in qualitative research.

Research Methods Resources on the WWW
www.slais.ubc.ca/resources/research_methods/content.htm

This useful site lists both qualitative and quantitative methods resources, originally developed at the University of British Columbia library. Resources include on-line books, data, journals, and more.

Society for the Study of Symbolic Interaction (SSSI)
http://sun.soci.niu.edu/~sssi/

This society is open to anyone interested in qualitative social science research, in particular, symbolic interactionist research. The society publishes a journal and holds annual meetings at which members and others present their work. The journal *Symbolic Interaction* publishes high-quality qualitative research.

Statistics Canada
www.statcan.ca

This is one of the most useful sites on the Internet for Canadian sociologists. Many of the surveys listed at this site can be used for class projects and research papers through your university or college, at no charge to you. Ask at your computing centre or library for details on the Data Liberation Initiative. If you go to only one of the sites listed here, make it this one.

US Census Bureau
www.census.gov

Like Statistics Canada, the US Census Bureau provides a wealth of resources and data, some of it free to use. You can also order publications, view them on-line, and download some US data from this site.

Part II

Major Social Processes

Chapter 3

Culture and Culture Change

Shyon Baumann

Learning Objectives

In this chapter, you will:

- See that culture has many meanings and dimensions.
- Observe that culture is ubiquitous, thoroughly a part of our lives, and necessary for social life.
- Learn that culture is powerful: it integrates members of society but can also cause great conflict.
- Learn that culture quintessentially carries meaning and facilitates communication.
- See that change in culture is inevitable: it is within the nature of culture to evolve.
- Find that sometimes culture change is caused by socio-structural factors and other times culture change is spurred by other cultural factors.

Photo: Ivy Images

TORONTO
Parks, Forestry & Recreation
Canadian Heritage
Patrimoine canadien
CANADA
DUNDAS

Why Study Culture?

Why do sociologists care about culture? Briefly, we want to know because **culture** is an amazingly powerful social force that influences events as diverse as whom we marry and whether we go to war. Marriage and war are interesting examples—while they seem unrelated, they are similar insofar as they both involve the bonds between people, in one case bringing people closer together and in the other pushing them further apart.

Let us consider how culture is implicated in each of these events. How we choose whom to marry is incredibly complicated, but what is clear is that in general people like to marry other people with whom they share interests and experiences. Such shared ideas and preferences create a feeling of comfort and familiarity, which are things we enjoy about being with other people. If we like the same music and the same kind of movies, if we share a belief in the importance of family and the role of religion in our lives, if we share a notion of the different roles and responsibilities of men and women, if we support the same political ideals, then we feel more connected to each other. In all these ways, culture is influencing how we relate to others. Culture includes all these preferences and ideas and notions, and these are the things that allow us in our daily lives to feel connections to other people. Cultural similarities influence our decisions not only about getting married, but about all kinds of connections—with whom we become and stay friends, even with whom we work.

Just as we often are brought closer to other people, so too we often experience social divisions, some relatively minor and others quite significant. Like marriage, war is an enormously complicated phenomenon; it can result from a wide array of social, economic, and geopolitical factors. But it is also clear that culture can play a role in creating or worsening the divisions between groups or societies that can lead to war. While a conflict of material interests usually sets the stage for war, culture can play a large role in determining whether war is engaged. If we differ in fundamental **beliefs** about such things as democracy and human rights, if we speak different languages and cannot easily communicate, if we cannot understand others' religious concepts and practices or strongly oppose them, if we do not share preferences for what we consider to be the normal and good ways to live our lives, then we feel less connected to each other. In all these ways, culture plays a role in dividing us from others, and it is only in the presence of such divisions, when we feel essentially different and disconnected from others, that we are able to pursue as drastic a course of action as war. In addition, culture plays a role in many more minor social divisions that are not as significant as war, the various social cleavages between many **social groups** within the same society.

Culture, then, is important because it is the key to understanding how we relate to each other; specifically, it is behind both what unites us and what divides us. Our cultural differences and similarities are continually coming into play, in our daily face-to-face interactions and on a global scale. To truly understand the dynamics of war and peace, love and hate, and more, we need to look at the ways culture facilitates or inhibits the bonds and the rifts between us.

The goals of this chapter are to review the many nuances to the meaning of culture and to explain how culture is implicated in many important social processes. First, we will further specify what culture is through a clear conceptualizing of culture's many dimensions. Second, we will summarize how culture is used in sociological theorizing about society and examine how culture fits into causal explanations of the way society works. In this chapter, we are also interested in a description of those realms of social life that are primarily cultural—the loci of culture. The nature of culture change is a third focus of this chapter, and we will examine the reciprocal relationship between culture change and social change. Finally, we will discuss the insights of this chapter as they pertain to Canadian culture.

What Is Culture?

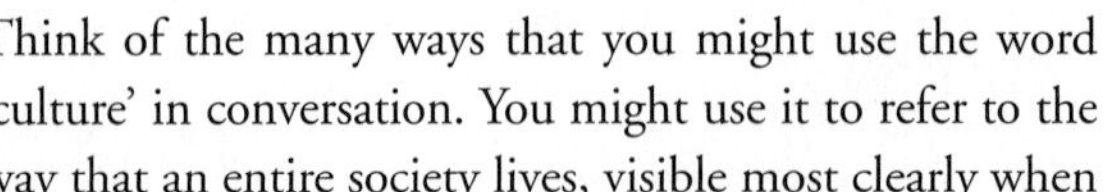

Think of the many ways that you might use the word 'culture' in conversation. You might use it to refer to the way that an entire society lives, visible most clearly when

Time to Reflect

Aside from marriage and war, what other social phenomena are influenced by culture's ability to bring people together and to keep them socially distant?

it is foreign to you, as perhaps in 'Thai culture'. You might use 'culture' to refer to the refined aesthetic productions that 'cultured' people enjoy, such as art shows, symphony concerts, or theatrical performances. Culture takes on a still different meaning in a phrase such as 'consumer culture', which focuses on a major pattern of people's behaviour and a set of economic institutions in contemporary society. Or, you might use 'culture' to refer to the practices and preferences of a subgroup of people, for example, 'jock' or 'geek' or 'skater' culture, who are nonetheless part of the larger society, in whose culture they also participate. Perhaps no term in the sociological vocabulary has as many meanings as 'culture'. Although some of these meanings are closely related to each other, others are remarkably divergent. For a concept that has traditionally been viewed as central to much sociological analysis, this is a strange state of affairs and one that complicates any attempt to provide a succinct and definitive summary of the sociology of culture. In lieu of a concise definition that would miss too many crucial nuances, this chapter will explain what culture is through a discussion of its most important dimensions.

Distinctively Cultural Elements of Social Life

Concepts like culture are most useful when it is clear what they do and do not refer to. At its most expansive, culture can be conceived of as the sum total of human creation; everything that is a product of a human mind, no matter how small or large, how concrete or abstract, how individual or widely shared, constitutes an element of culture. The first clear distinction, then, is that between culture and the natural world as it exists apart from human interaction. For the purposes of sociological analysis, when we speak of culture we do not refer to the physical reality of our natural environment, the complex ecological system billions of years in the making. This first distinction, however, still leaves quite a lot under the rubric of culture, namely all of social reality, and this begs for further clarification.

Defining culture as the sum total of the human-influenced and human-created environment, anything and everything that is the product of a human mind, leaves us with a rather bloated notion of the term's meaning. This expansive definition rests on the notion that all of our thought processes are conditioned and shaped by the **social environment** into which we are socialized. Without this social environment, without this culture, we would have nothing to form our thoughts except for our natural instincts and desires. All human societies, however, develop distinctive ways of life that can significantly shape the minds of individuals and allow them to develop into socialized members of that society. Insofar as this **socialization process** influences all that we do—if not directly then at least indirectly—we can plausibly call all of social life cultural.

Although culture can mean all of this, the concept is really only useful for making sociological arguments and drawing sociological insights if we can limit it further. In practice, we are usually interested in determining the relative influence or functioning of cultural factors in society compared to other, non-cultural, but still social, factors. We therefore often employ various, more restricted senses of the term and strive to set apart certain elements of social life as 'cultural' from those

IN THE FIRST PERSON

At the most general level, I chose to study sociology because it helps us to figure out how the world works. More specifically, though, I am interested in understanding the role of culture in shaping social inequality. The reasons why some people have more wealth and status in society are varied and complex. Cultural factors are a part of this story—that is, people can draw on and manipulate cultural resources as a conscious or unconscious strategy for helping them to succeed socially and economically. What is fascinating about the role of culture in social inequality, however, is that culture is not *just* a tool for conflict. People sincerely appreciate and identify with cultural objects and productions—their cultural tastes are genuine. So it is interesting to determine how and when culture performs these different functions.—Shyon Baumann elements that are not. To add to the complicated nature of defining 'culture', among sociologists persists a certain amount of disagreement over which elements of social life are properly 'cultural'.

For the sake of giving initial form to the idea of culture as it is discussed here, we can create a list of specific things that are always or usually classified as 'culture' in sociology. Languages, symbols, discourses, texts, knowledge, values, attitudes, beliefs, norms, world views, folkways, art, music, ideas, and ideologies all are 'culture'. In sociological analysis, these social phenomena are differentiated on the basis of inherent cultural qualities. To better understand why these things are 'culture', we need to think about their characteristics.

Culture is different between places and at different times. We also need to examine the ways that sociologists distinguish between the cultural and the non-cultural. Two major distinctions employed in the sociological literature to specify the elements of culture are the difference between culture and structure, and the difference between the symbolic and the non-symbolic.

Culture in Place and Time

Culture quite often refers to the entire social reality of particular social groups in comparison to other social groups. Perhaps the largest cultural groupings frequently in use differentiate between large regions of the globe—Western culture, for example. While encompassing tremendous variation these groupings convey a notion that coheres in contradistinction to the history and present reality of, for example, Eastern and Near Eastern cultures. Such a broad distinction obscures the many similarities and historical continuities between these cultures and instead emphasizes how they differ. Nonetheless, it is a first step in limiting the concept of culture to a more useful definition, namely the entire social environment of people from within a circumscribed physical space.

It should be immediately clear that we often think of culture in more specific geographic terms than just Western or Eastern. We frequently think in national terms, with fairly strong ideas of what we mean by, for example, Japanese culture, Italian culture, or Mexican culture. These ideas exist in our minds as stereotypes or generalizations about the kind of lives inhabitants of these countries lead. Among many other things, we might think of Japanese rituals of politeness and a preference for sushi, the sights and sounds of Italian opera and the speed of Vespa scooters, and small Mexican towns where elaborate, solemn Catholic ceremonies can give way to lively and colourful festivals. Likewise, you might have noticed when talking to people from other countries that they sometimes impose expectations on you based on stereotypes of Canada and Canadians: 'Do you play hockey?' 'Ski?' 'Have a snowmobile?'

Whatever the accuracy or generalizability (frequently low) of such stereotypes as images of the typical culture of these countries, their pervasiveness points to the reality that culture can vary systematically between nations, even in ways we commonly are unaware of. Nation-states have often (although not always) coalesced around a common cultural foundation, or if one was not clearly defined from early on, they have tended to promote such a cultural foundation for the sake of national unity and cohesion.

Despite the definitional clarity that a notion of national culture offers, on closer inspection we can see that, like the larger generalizations of 'Western culture' or 'Eastern culture', national cultures also entail a great deal of regional and local variation. For example, in a large country such as the United States, the culture of the politically liberal, highly urbanized, and economically successful Northeast can be contrasted with the culture of certain of the politically conservative and less affluent states in the South. Such a contrast points to the differences between the whole way of life of northeasterners and southerners; however, we need to be mindful that both share a culture that is more generally 'American' and that they therefore share countless cultural features as well.

We can continue to spatially limit our concept of culture by pointing to the general social differences between various cities and even between parts of cities. The culture of downtown Toronto, for example, brings up notions of a lifestyle and a built environment that are business-oriented, cosmopolitan, and culturally rich. Toronto's **urbanism** is often cited for its impersonality and inward-looking character, and contrasts with the habits, manners, and interaction styles of, for example, St John's, Newfoundland. Remember that, as with the differences in regions, such local cultural variations exist in a broader cultural environment of greater similarities than differences.

However, just as with the differences between regions, we must be careful not to overstate the precision with which we can delineate a concept of culture based on physical space. Cultural similarities are bound to exist between various physical spaces—no matter how narrowly we draw our boundaries—on account of social spaces being shared. Just as we can identify culture as the human environment of specific geographic locations, so we can identify culture as the human environment of groups who are similar socially despite being geographically disparate. Therefore, we can think of the culture of, for example, adolescent males as distinct from adolescent females and from adult males, whether their geographic location is Vancouver or Halifax. (See also Table 3.1 on radio listening times across genders and age groups, broken down by musical genre.) Acknowledging culture's social, not just physical, boundedness provides us with a second dimension for understanding and limiting the meaning of culture.

Age and **gender**, the social groupings in the above example, are just two of many social boundaries that can differentiate between cultures. Other social lines along which cultural features may fall include **race** and **ethnicity**, sexual orientation, religion, and many other ways that people see fit to distinguish themselves. Another social space with important cultural implications is that of social **class**. Stereotypes of distinct working- and upper-class cultures are at least as pervasive as national stereotypes. We have firm ideas about the typical speech, mannerisms, dress, culinary preferences, occupations, and leisure activities of the working class and the upper class.

At this point it is necessary to point out again that, just as the cultures of urban Ontario and rural Alberta share more similarities than differences, the culture of different social groups within a society likewise share more similarities than differences. By enumerating the ways in which, for example, social classes in Canada differ, we neglect myriad ways in which they are similar: difference in accent is trivial to the overall nature of a language; a similar reliance on automobiles overshadows any consideration of whether those automobiles are foreign or domestic; and a propensity to vote for different political parties cannot diminish the tremendous importance of a shared faith in parliamentary democracy.

In addition, it is necessary to point out that the dimensions of physical and social space are relatively

Table 3.1 Radio Listening Time by Format and Age Group, Fall 2006

	All Ages	Teens 12–17	Men (18 and over)	Women (18 and over)
Adult contemporary	22.3	23.0	17.3	27.2
Album-oriented rock	6.0	9.3	8.0	3.8
CBC	11.6	2.7	10.7	13.1
Contemporary	8.8	24.8	8.5	7.8
Country	10.0	8.5	9.4	10.8
Dance	0.5	2.7	0.4	0.4
Easy listening	3.6	0.9	3.2	4.2
Golden oldies/rock	13.9	14.2	17.0	10.9
Middle-of-the-road	2.8	0.5	2.5	3.3
Sports	1.0	0.5	1.9	0.2
Talk	10.2	2.0	11.0	10.0
US stations	3.0	6.2	3.1	2.6
Other	6.3	4.6	7.0	5.8
Total listening time	100.0	100.0	100.0	100.0

Note: Figures may not add up due to rounding.
Source: Statistics Canada, at: <www40.statcan.ca/l01/cst01/arts17.htm?sdi=radio>.

but not entirely independent of each other. In some instances there is considerable overlap, when a social grouping exclusively or almost exclusively inhabits a physical space. For example, if we were to study the culture of retirement communities, we would see that these are physical spaces populated mostly by a specific social group defined by age. The social boundedness of culture by age (the culture of an older generation) overlays a physical boundedness of culture by residential location (the culture of a retirement community). Likewise, there is a great deal of overlap between, for example, the physical space of Anglican churches and the social space of Anglicans.

Notice that cases in which the physical and social spatial dimensions of culture intersect to the exclusion of other social groups are fairly narrowly circumscribed. For the most part, our social lives are messier, and different **subcultures** interact with each other all the time. Sometimes the young visit their grandparents in their retirement homes; quite frequently individuals of various social classes occupy the same classrooms, malls, arenas, and workspaces (although with different functions within those workspaces); segregation on the basis of race sometimes occurs residentially, though for the most part the common venues in which daily life is played out are racially integrated.

Adding to the fuzziness of cultural boundaries, borrowing across cultures happens all the time. Often such borrowing occurs without anyone noticing, but sometimes it can happen in ways that are thought to be illegitimate, leading to charges of cultural appropriation. In those cases, the borrowing of culture across social boundaries can offend a group's sense of identity and cultural heritage (see Global Issues box).

GLOBAL ISSUES

Fashion and Religion Don't Mix in Toronto

In their zeal to cash in on the trendiness of all things Bollywood, organizers of Toronto's biggest fashion event have stepped into a cultural minefield, outraging thousands of South Asians worldwide.

Hyped as a synergy of East and West—'Bollywood bling meets rhinestone cowboy'—the theme of this year's gala Fashion Cares has sparked an international protest among Hindus, who say the event appropriated their culture and was disrespectful to their religion.

About 5,000 people attended the annual fashion extravaganza organized by the AIDS Committee of Toronto (ACT) to raise money for AIDS prevention and treatment, held at the Metro Toronto Convention Centre on Saturday.

'The reaction is massive. It's not just locally people who are upset, it's internationally', said Tushar Unadkat, owner of a Toronto advertising agency. He said he has received thousands of e-mails from Canada, the United States, the United Kingdom and India since he posted a letter about the show on his website earlier this week.

The head of the Vishnu Hindu temple in Richmond Hill is organizing a protest to be staged in front of ACT offices. 'It's totally despicable to present a nude exhibition of a goddess. Hindus are docile and laid-back people, and they (ACT) obviously took advantage of that, but we won't stand for this', said Dr Budhendra Doobay, adding he wants a full public apology from ACT in the mainstream press.

ACT, which expects to raise more than $1 million from the event, has issued an apology on its website. 'ACT regrets any offence that was caused. Our intention was to have a great event to raise money for a worthwhile cause', said Karim Karsan, an ACT spokesperson and board member. . . .

Protestors say that despite the Bollywood theme, South Asians were largely absent from the show, aside from a performance by a hip hop bhangra group, a South Asian DJ spinning tunes and a song by a *Bombay Dreams* cast member. Clothes by South Asian fashion designers were not featured, and there were few South Asian models.

Some groups, like the National Anti-Racism Council of Canada, also found the pairing of cowboys and Indians, with its 'connotation of colonial conquest', problematic.

The cover of the Fashion Cares program, handed out at the show, depicts a model in a stylized pose of the multi-armed Lakshmi, goddess of wealth. She is sitting cross-legged in the lotus position and nude except for strategically placed sparkles.

'India has a very exotic image attached to it, especially now, and I'm totally for the mainstream embracing our culture, but they took it too far. These deities are sacred to us. How dare they do this', said Mitra Sen, a former director of the *Degrassi Junior High* television series, now a teacher in Toronto.

Unadkat said he was horrified to see drag queens dressed as the goddesses Durga, Saraswati and Lakshmi, smoking and drinking at the event, and white models dressed as Krishna and Radha, handing out postcards of Hindu gods and goddesses—images that had drinks spilled on them and were trampled underfoot when dropped. . . .

'I'm all for cultural fusion and all that fun stuff, but you can't mess with religion that way', said [Abhishek] Mathur, festival director of Masala! Mehendi! Masti!

About two dozen activist groups, including the Alliance for South Asian AIDS Prevention, brought the issues to ACT's attention a month before the show.

The storm began to brew after the Fashion Cares April 13 launch party, which featured white models dressed as goddesses, and go-go dancers with their skin painted in Krishna blue serving alcohol. Karsan now admits ACT should have consulted more broadly within the South Asian community before going ahead with the show. ACT made some changes to its marketing materials after it got negative responses, but it was too late to pull the program cover depicting a nude Lakshmi, he added.

The hullabaloo serves as a wake-up call to the sometimes complacent South Asian community, said Krishan Mehta, chair of the South Asian group. 'It's all about politics of inclusion. The mainstream still sees our culture as song-and-dance dinnertime entertainment, but if we want to be real players with a voice at the table, we need to push them to get beyond that.'

The incident shows how 'clued out' most so-called mainstream organizations, both corporate and non-profit, are when dealing with ethnic groups, said Andil Gosine, a professor of race and cultural studies at York University. 'They're not as engaged with the multicultural reality of Toronto as they ought to be, and they don't realize how much they're losing out because of that. The lesson here is to be really willing to deal with the people you claim to serve and not just have a distant relationship with them', Gosine said. 'My feeling is this kind of show results because there are not enough people of colour engaged in these institutions. They are so lost in how so much of Toronto's population thinks and reacts because of this.'

However, not everyone found the show offensive. Toronto filmmaker Deepa Mehta, who attended, said she doesn't know what all the fuss is about. 'This appropriation of culture makes me slightly uncomfortable, but surely we should be a bit more secure in our culture. Bollywood is good fun, glitzy, not to be taken seriously. It's just a fashion show, as opposed to an affront to our goddesses, and I'm a good Hindu', said Mehta.

In India, people are typically much more relaxed about such things, said Mehta, recounting a costume party she attended in New Delhi last year where everyone came dressed as a deity.

'We leave a culture behind in India and we become very protective about it, and we let that define who we are. I think it's very sad. When someone apologizes, we should accept it and move on.' . . .

Source: Abridged from Prithi Yelaja, 'For Hindus, it's fashion careless', *Toronto Star*, 9 June 2005, A1. Reprinted with permission—Torstar Syndication Services.

Finally, we can recognize that culture varies over time. The temporal dimension is an important qualifier because of the magnitude of differences that accumulate to produce cultures that are vastly different from what came before. In other words, culture evolves.

Leaving aside the precise mechanisms of cultural evolution for now, we can recognize that for the most part culture is never static. It is always developing new features and characteristics. Therefore, Western culture of today is remarkably different from 500 years ago and is in many ways quite different from even 10 years ago. The temporal dimension of culture is independent of its physical and social locations—culture changes over time in all countries and regions and for all social groupings.

Norwegian culture today is different from what it was in 1900; French-Canadian culture, irrespective of actual geographic roots, has evolved over the century as well; and the culture of Canadians in their sixties has changed dramatically over time—the leisure and work options and the values and ideals of older Canadians bear little resemblance to what they were in earlier time periods. Many observers of culture argue that cultural changes are occurring more frequently in recent time periods—the rate of cultural change is increasing. When we turn to the specifics of cultural dynamics, we will learn more about the reasons behind this increase in the rate of change.

Culture and Structure

While a description of culture's dependence on time and location shows us the changing nature of culture, we also need a clear idea of what 'counts' as culture and what does not. To help us to draw this boundary, we can consider the distinction between *culture* and **structure**, two terms that have specific meanings within formal sociology. This distinction, as described by Philip Smith, sees culture primarily as the realm of the 'ideal, the spiritual, and the non-material' and opposed to the 'material, technological, and the social-structural' (2001: 3–4).

The meanings of these terms merit further elucidation. One might characterize the *ideal*, the *spiritual*, and the *non-material* as things that exist primarily in people's heads, limited to an essentially mental existence. That is to say, this version of culture privileges the distinction between thoughts, emotions, beliefs, and the more abstract elements of organized social life on the one hand and the 'concrete' elements of society that literally are embodied and enacted by actual things and people on the other hand. Drawing the boundaries of culture in this fashion allows us to classify, for example, attitudes about gender roles and about the kinds of work that are appropriate for men and for women as 'cultural'. Such attitudes are shared modes of thinking, and to the extent that they are only mental constructs, they properly are cultural.

At the same time, the fact that there exists a high degree of occupational segregation by gender, with some jobs (for example, elementary school teachers) primarily done by women and others (for example, elementary school principals) primarily done by men, is not cultural. Rather, this segregation is 'structural'. It is an enduring pattern of social behaviour, existing primarily not at a mental level but at a level of lived experience. The idea that it is normal or proper for men to be principals and women to be elementary school teachers is a cultural value. The fact that this pattern exists in our society (although changing) is a structural property of our society.

We can find another example in the realm of **politics**. In Canada the widely held preference for representative democracy and a belief that it is a legitimate and necessary form of self-government represent a deep-rooted aspect of Canadian culture. This political orientation is related in a significant way to many other beliefs about authority, individual rationality, and justice, and so it is an element of culture that is enmeshed in a web of other important cultural elements. In contrast, representative democracy is not merely an idea, it is a practice that involves a tremendous amount of material resources and engenders longstanding patterns of social behaviour. Known in the sociological literature as **the state**, our democratic government is a structural dimension of social life. It is related in significant ways to many aspects of citizens' daily existence; it influences, among other things, our work lives, our consumption patterns, our health outcomes, and our educational outcomes, and so it is a material element of social life that is clearly enmeshed in a web of other important structural elements.

Culture as Symbolic

A second way in which culture frequently is defined in sociology is according to the role that it plays in creating meaning. In this view, culture is those elements of social life that act as symbols and are subject to interpretation. These elements are produced in order to be received and understood by individuals who derive meaning—a personal understanding—through the reception process. Any element of society that has meaning for its creator and its audience, even if there is a discrepancy between the intended and the perceived meanings, is part of the symbolic order. Culture, then, is both a product of **social interaction** and the social force that enables social interaction because it allows people to communicate meanings to each other.

In contrast to the symbolic, many things in life play an instrumental role for purposes other than communication or expression. For example, houses provide shelter from the elements, and planes exist to transport people and cargo. In these roles, houses and planes are not cultural. Admittedly, this is a fine distinction because meaning can often be found wherever we look hard enough, especially by those with a postmodern sensibility that encourages a view of all social objects as 'texts' that can be 'read' for the meanings that society has imbued them with. However, it is of practical importance to limit culture to those things that are intended to be interpreted and to hold meaning, even if people's interpretations of those meanings might vary.

Going back to the political example demonstrating the difference between culture and structure, we can see the state as an instrumental **social institution** designed to achieve governance. It does not qualify as culture because it is not in itself a symbol; it does not exist to be received and understood as having a meaning. However, there is no shortage of politically oriented culture or of political symbols existing in a wide array of forms. Political ideologies of the left, centre, and right, expressed in political discourses, in conversations, newspaper articles, and books, both fiction and non-fiction, are squarely in the realm of culture. The national anthem and the Canadian flag are both explicit political symbols. The neo-Gothic Parliament buildings in Ottawa, while serving as the venue for federal politics, also serve as a political symbol, not only through the 'messages' associated with their stately, traditional, European style of architecture (they are not pagodas or pyramids), but also because they are sufficiently well known to conjure an association with the federal government and so can represent the country as a whole. Their very image has gained interpretive currency and so can be effectively used as a tool for communication.

The symbolic view of culture bears much similarity to the view that opposes culture to structure. In both views, the roles of ideas and mental states are important elements of culture. The two views do differ, however. Where the opposition between culture and structure emphasizes the distinction between the material and the non-material, the symbolic view of culture, with its focus on the expressive function of culture, recognizes that meaning is conveyed through symbols that take material form.

By combining the insights of each perspective, we can recognize that culture is ideas, beliefs, emotions, and thoughts and their direct physical embodiments, such as paintings and newspapers. First, the two views together provide a more comprehensive description of what constitutes culture than either does alone, but without being unduly or impractically broad. Second, those manifestations that are clearly 'culture' from both perspectives are generally closer to the core of the concerns of the sociology of culture. For example, language—non-material words spoken or otherwise transmitted to convey meaning—is a phenomenon that is a cultural subject par excellence. Third, the two perspectives show us that there are multiple ways of viewing social phenomena. It is possible that certain things can be analyzed as culture while they are simultaneously understood as being outside the realm of culture.

To take a technological example, the automobile can be analyzed on different levels. On the one hand, automobiles are material objects that are instrumental in facilitating social needs. They are part of the structural side of social life, namely, our transportation system. On the other hand, automobiles are designed with an aesthetic dimension to them, and as such they are the embodiment of ideas about taste and style, which are cultural elements. They play a role in self-expression for many people. On a deeper level, attitudes towards automobile use and the kind of lifestyle that their use engenders are known as 'car culture', and in this sense automobiles are implicated in the realm of social culture in a second way.

A Detailed Picture

To this point, our view of culture is, on the one hand, that we can separate the cultural from the non-cultural and, on the other hand, that we can recognize the contingency of the cultural on physical and social location and on time. We can be very specific now about what we mean by culture and how it is represented in sociological study.

The sociology of culture has tackled topics such as the reading experiences of middle-class women in the American Midwest in the 1980s (Radway, 1984); the influence of religion on civic engagement and individualism in the United States (Bellah, 1996); the attitudes, values, and morality of French and American upper-middle-class males (Lamont, 1992); the tension between morality and economic imperatives in the late-twentieth-century West (Bell, 1979); and the organizational and economic foundations for the ideology that developed after 1800 in Vienna to distinguish the 'serious' music of genius from ordinary classical music (DeNora, 1991).

As in any subfield of sociology, studies within the sociology of culture often gain analytical leverage through comparisons. We can increase our understanding of current values, for instance, by comparing them to values of a different time, to values of a different social group, or to values of a different place. Comparative work exists in many forms and covers many topics within the sociology of culture. Cross-national comparisons, which sample across physical space, help to outline the contours of national cultural features, such as political values. Sociologist Seymour Martin Lipset (1990) has helped us to understand Canadian values through work that contrasts Canada with the United States. Comparisons of men and women, across social space, can highlight the gendered nature of language use (Weatherall, 2002). Historical studies, by comparing

Time to Reflect

Provide examples of things that can serve both cultural and structural roles simultaneously and explain how these roles can coexist.

present-day and historical elements of culture, can provide tremendous insight into the time-contingent nature of such things as our ideas about human rights or appropriate and inappropriate public behaviour (Elias, 1994).

Culture is always changing. What cultural evolutions have you personally observed?

The Role of Culture in Social Theory

Now that we have a clear idea of what culture is, we can gain an understanding of how it has figured in the works of some of the major sociological theorists. In this section, we will outline how these thinkers have employed culture in their writings about the fundamental driving forces of society.

Above all else, theories explain things. That is to say, the defining feature of a theory is that it tells why or how something is the way it is. Social theories, then, are explanations of social things—they tell us why certain aspects of society are the way they are. A great deal of social theory, it turns out, is strongly concerned with culture. This concern, however, appears in different forms: social theories are concerned with culture for a variety of reasons. Below, we consider the place of culture in five major social theoretical perspectives.

Orthodox Marxist and Neo-Marxist Theories

One of the most influential theoretical perspectives in sociology is **Marxism**. In developing his theory of society, Karl Marx was responding directly to previous philosophical arguments about the central role of ideas (squarely cultural) in determining the path of history and the nature of social reality. In such arguments, the general cultural environment worked at the level of ideas to shape people's thoughts and actions, and so was in principle the root cause behind events and social change. This 'spontaneous unfolding' of the spirit or culture of a given time could explain the course of history (Smith, 2001: 13).

By contrast, in Marxism, social reality is seen as determined primarily by the prevailing **mode of production**, evolving through history from agrarian societies to slave ownership to feudalism and then to industrial **capitalism**. This perspective posits that the best way to explain social facts—and all of history—is by recognizing that they are outcomes, direct or indirect, of the economic organization of society.

Societies shift from one mode of production to the next in a historical progression, the current state being industrial capitalism. The economic organization of society forms the base on which the rest of society, the superstructure, is founded. In a strict reading of Marxism, the superstructure responds to, but does not cause, changes in the base. Culture, in all its forms—ideas, beliefs, values, art, religion, and so on—is part of the superstructure and must be understood as essentially a product of the base.

In today's society, then, all aspects of our culture are shaped by the needs and dictates of industrial capitalism. One of the most important cultural productions of capitalism is the **dominant ideology**. This ideology is a system of thoughts, knowledge, and beliefs that serves to legitimate and to perpetuate capitalism. Our mental lives and our entire thought modes are shaped to minimize criticism of capitalism and to maximize participation in and support of capitalism.

Neo-Marxist perspectives do not adhere so strictly to the view that culture is entirely dependent on society's mode of production. While they borrow extensively from Marx's insights, they also modify these insights, and in so doing they provide a significantly different view of culture. These perspectives share with Marxism a focus on the role of culture in maintaining and supporting capitalism, but they differ from Marxism insofar as they seek to explain culture as more than simply the reflection of the underlying economic base.

Neo-Marxists recognize that culture can be shaped by specific groups and individuals who seek to achieve certain social outcomes. For example, Antonio Gramsci (1992) argued in the 1920s and 1930s that intellectuals within spheres such as politics, religion, the mass media, and education provide knowledge, values, advice, and direction to the general population that serve to perpetuate the status quo and to suppress revolutionary tendencies. To take another example, members of the Frankfurt School, who began writing in the 1920s, identified pro-capitalist functions in much of popular culture, which promotes capitalist ideals and stifles critical, independent thinking. The groups responsible for the creation and promotion of popular culture within the entertainment industry are themselves significant members of the **bourgeoisie**. In the view of the Frankfurt School, the entertainment industry is of great use to the capitalist order through the cultural products it creates.

It is important to note that neo-Marxists make a fundamental advance in their view of culture insofar as they see it as more than simply an artifact of the economic base. Culture, they argue, can also help to determine other facets of social reality—not merely reflective of other things in society, it also helps to shape society. A significant continuity between Marxist and neo-Marxist views of culture is that culture is implicated in the essentially conflictual nature of society. Culture, in a sense, supports dominant groups in their efforts to maintain their dominance.

Cultural Functionalism

A contrasting approach to understanding culture can be found in work that is based on the theoretical insights of Émile Durkheim. In contrast to the conflictual emphasis of the Marxists and neo-Marxists, the views on culture that are based on Durkheimian sociological insights focus on the integrative ability of culture. Rather than pointing to the ways in which culture can create social fissures, Durkheim (1995 [1912]) identified the ways in which culture can create social stability and solidarity, focusing on how culture unites us rather than on how culture divides us.

Culture, in terms of norms, values, attitudes, and beliefs, is not reflective of the economic mode of production. Instead, these cultural elements are generated according to the needs of society by its form as a more or less complex system. Culture rises out of a particular society's **social structure** to produce a general consensus about the goals and nature of society. As such, our values about, for example, the importance of education evolve in response to the changing needs of a modernizing society in which higher general levels of education allow for a more smoothly functioning society. In this sense, culture serves a necessary function: through common values and beliefs, society is able to remain coherent and all the different parts of society can effectively carry out their specific purpose.

Durkheim paid special attention to the role of religion as a motivating force in society, one that made possible the affirmation of collective sentiments and ideas, and one therefore that could play an important role in strengthening social bonds that then strengthened and reinforced the fabric of society.

Symbolic Interactionist and Dramaturgical Perspectives

A third important perspective treats culture as a product of individuals' interactions. In **symbolic interactionist** thought, culture plays the role of a vehicle for meaning (hence 'symbolic') and is generated by individuals in face-to-face encounters (hence 'interactionist'). Culture is the enacted signals and attitudes that people use to communicate effectively in order to go about their daily lives. Body language and the signals we send through it, however subconsciously, are a clear element of culture in this perspective. The decisions we make and carry out to reveal or to suppress certain pieces of information about ourselves are also culture.

Social interaction can be analyzed to reveal layers of meaning behind routine actions. It becomes evident that there is a communicative element in a great deal of our interactions although we are not always conscious of its presence or of the nature of the messages we send. The result of our interactions is (usually) the successful management of our relationships with others.

In terms of its view on culture, the symbolic interactionist approach contrasts with Marxist and functionalist approaches insofar as it attributes more responsibility to individuals as the active creators and implementers of culture. Rather than originating from an economic order or indirectly from the general social structure, culture is a product of creative individual agents who use it to manage their everyday tasks and routines.

One of the most influential theorists to write about the interactions of individuals was Erving Goffman. Goffman developed an analytical framework that analogizes social interaction to what goes on in a theatre. For that reason, it is known as a dramaturgical perspective. In a theatre, there are actors with roles to play for an audience. Likewise, when we interact with people, we assume a role for the situation we find ourselves in and perform that role according to a well-known script that defines the boundaries of what is expected and acceptable for the role. We learn these rules of social behaviour through the ordinary process of socialization. We use these rules to create meaningful and effective interaction with others. When we are interacting with others and are in our roles, we are managing impressions and performing in a front-stage area. When we let down our guard and behave informally and in ways that would embarrass us in front of others, we are in the back-stage area.

Culture plays a part in the dramaturgical perspective that is in one sense quite central: social order is constituted by the creation and use of meanings embodied in interaction. The sending and receiving of signals and messages is the key to understanding why society functions at all when there is so much potential for chaos. When you think about it, we are remarkably efficient at maintaining social order most of the time, and this achievement is made possible through the shared meanings in face-to-face interactions.

This view of culture, however, is one that is perhaps less rich than that offered by the cultural functionalist perspective. Rather than culture playing a fundamental role in shaping individuals' very consciousness, as the functionalist perspective would argue, the dramaturgical perspective sees culture as a tool for creative individuals to manipulate strategically. Rather than persons being fully subject to the influence of culture, culture is subject more to the influence of individuals.

The Cultural Studies Tradition

Cultural studies is a field with roots in British literary scholarship and in sociology. The 'Birmingham School' theorists at the Centre for Contemporary Cultural Studies at the University of Birmingham showed in the 1970s how subcultural groups on the margins of society, such as skinheads and punks, both appropriate elements of the dominant culture by imbuing them with alternative meanings and shape their own alternative subcultures in an attempt to create a separate space for themselves in the larger society. Much of the work accomplished in this tradition builds on the work of Marxism and neo-Marxists. The specific insight that cultural studies borrows from neo-Marxists is that culture can be shaped and manipulated by dominant groups and employed to maintain hegemony. Cultural studies practitioners agree that culture can function to maintain social divisions, keeping some groups dominant over others. Where they break from Marxists and early neo-Marxists is in the recognition that class conflict is only one of many sites of ideological dominance. As Smith writes of cultural studies, 'a move has gradually taken place away from Marxism toward an understanding of society as textured with multiple sources of inequality and fragmented local struggles' (2001: 152). Dominant groups can be defined not only by class position, but also by race, gender, geography, and sexual orientation.

In addition to a focus on the multiple forms of domination, cultural studies has provided a more sophisticated understanding of the ways in which meaning functions in society. One of the main figures in this tradition from the Birmingham School is Stuart Hall, who has produced some of the seminal concepts of cultural studies. As Hall (1980) explains, communication of meaning requires both **encoding** and **decoding**. By this he means that such things as an advertisement or a television show are created in such a way as to convey a particular perspective. The predominant beliefs of the creators are encoded into these cultural productions (or texts) in subtle and sometimes subconscious ways. A fresh, critically informed reading of such texts is required to see how they encode assumptions and messages about such things as gender and social class relations. Another significant insight of Hall's is that meaning does not simply exist as part of cultural creations, but instead is constructed by individuals through the process of receiving and interpreting culture. Meaning is created by people while they make sense of the culture they consume or take in.

As evidence, note how the very same cultural products may carry very different meanings for different individuals or for different groups. For example, a study of the meaning of Hollywood Westerns showed that the movies were interpreted quite differently by 'Anglos' and by Native Americans: the films' messages about the frontier, Native–European relations, and the value of authority and independence were construed quite differently by the Anglo and the Native viewers (Shively, 1992). While those who create cultural products may intend them to convey a certain meaning, there is, nonetheless, opportunity for individuals to read or understand messages, texts, and symbols in oppositional or idiosyncratic ways, deriving meanings through a process that is influenced by the individuals' backgrounds and interpretive abilities.

The 'Production of Culture' Perspective

The 'production of culture' perspective takes as an object of study those aspects of culture that are created through explicit, intentional, and co-ordinated processes. This approach focuses on material culture, and studies taking this perspective focus on mass media, technology, art, and other material symbol-producing realms such as science and law. The guiding insight of this perspective is that culture is a product of social action in much the same way as non-cultural products are. The implication of this view is that culture is studied best according to the same methods and analysis that are standard in other fields of sociology.

A key figure in the development of the production of culture perspective, Richard A. Peterson (1994), notes that the perspective developed to account for perceived shortcomings in the prevailing 'mirror' or 'reflection' view that posited that culture was somehow a manifestation of underlying social-structural needs or realities. This view, held by orthodox Marxists and by functionalists, is quite vague about the specific mechanisms through which culture is created. The metaphor of a mirror is descriptive of the content of culture—it represents the true nature or character of society—but is mute about culture's production.

Such a view would find, for instance, that the contours of Canadian national identity are visible through studying the literary output of Canadian authors. As a body of work, Canadian literature takes on the characteristics of and reflects the essence of Canadian society. Likewise, Baroque art forms are seen as expressions of society in the Baroque period, and modernist art is explained as an expression of societal sentiments and values in the early decades of the twentieth century.

By contrast, the production of culture perspective is insistent on specifying all the factors involved not only in cultural production per se, but also in how culture is 'distributed, evaluated, taught, and preserved' (Peterson, 1994: 165). Through a thorough analysis of all these processes, we can better account for the specific

Sometimes art is employed to achieve ideological ends. This painting by Franklin Carmichael, a member of the Group of Seven, depicts the landscape of the Canadian North. The Group sought to express their nationalistic sentiments through paintings of scenes that were uniquely Canadian. (Franklin Carmichael [1890–1945] *Northern Tundra*, 1931. Oil on canvas. 77.4 x 92.5 cm. Gift of Col. R.S. McLaughlin. McMichael Canadian Collection. 1968.7.14)

Time to Reflect

Which of the above theoretical traditions do you find most useful for understanding culture's role in social inequality?

content of culture. We need to examine the resources and constraints that specific actors were working with and that influenced the kind of art or other symbols that they created. In this way, the production of culture perspective provides us with the means of explaining the shape of culture.

Conflict, Integration, Origin, and Autonomy

It is useful to compare these various perspectives according to their views on several key features of culture. Marxists and neo-Marxists are clear in their argument that culture is a tool of conflict in society, a view that contrasts with functionalists, who emphasize the integrative function of culture. Functionalists are interested in explaining social order, and they see culture as a key factor in creating social stability.

For symbolic interactionists, culture is primarily the means by which individuals create order out of potentially chaotic and unpredictable social situations, and so they support an integrative view of culture. The cultural studies tradition, building on the work of neo-Marxists, has an explicit focus on the many ways in which culture is implicated in various forms of domination and conflict in society.

The production of culture perspective has little to say about characterizing culture as integrative or as implicated in conflict. But while it has the least to say about that dimension of culture, it says the most about another dimension, the origin of culture, because it developed out of dissatisfaction with the views of Marxism and functionalism on the origin of culture. While these older perspectives relied on a 'reflection' metaphor to explain where culture comes from, the production perspective locates cultural origin in 'purposive productive activity' (Peterson, 1994: 164). Cultural studies does not provide quite so articulate an account of cultural origin, but neither does it merely rely on vague notions of reflection. Instead, it sees culture as originating in the work of hegemonic leaders who create the texts, symbols, and discourses that embody particular ideologies. Symbolic interactionists also provide an explanation for the origin of culture: it is produced in the meanings that people create through social interaction at the micro level.

Finally, the various perspectives place different emphases on what we can call the 'autonomy of culture'. *Autonomy of culture* refers to the place for culture within causal explanations. Is culture primarily a dependent **variable**, something that deserves to be explained but does not warrant recognition as a fundamental cause of social outcomes? Or is culture autonomous—does culture merit a place at the core of sociological explanation, wherein it is the key to understanding the contours of social reality?

Orthodox Marxism clearly denies the autonomy of culture by making it a reflection of the economic base of society. Functionalism views culture as far more autonomous: culture is, in and of itself, the predominant stabilizing force in society and can account for social order. Symbolic interactionists are less sympathetic to the autonomy of culture, preferring instead to privilege the role of spontaneous human creativity in understanding how social order is maintained. Culture is more appropriately viewed as the product of action than as the motivator of action. The cultural studies tradition gives us a view of culture as enjoying a significant degree of autonomy; the crucial role of ideology in various forms of dominance portrays culture as primarily shaping the conflictual nature of social life. The production of culture perspective, to conclude this summary, is largely concerned with the ways in which myriad social processes create cultural products, and so finds little room for the autonomy of culture.

Time to Reflect

Which of the traditions are most similar, and which are most different? Why?

OPEN FOR DISCUSSION

Uniting Iraq's Disparate Cultures a Challenge, Experts Say

24 April 2003

Constructing a representative government from the ashes of Saddam Hussein's totalitarian regime is a daunting challenge for Iraq. 'If you look at an ethnic map, you'd say that Iraq's political geography is at odds with its cultural geography', says geographer Harm De Blij, distinguished professor at Michigan State University.

'As with most of the nations in that region, the boundaries [of Iraq] are the result of political decisions, mostly arbitrary, by the colonial powers early last century', said James P. Reams, retired Army Artillery Field officer and former West Point geography instructor. 'That the boundaries have lasted into the 21st century is more a tribute to the series of local despots that have run these "countries" since the colonial powers left.'

Now that Iraq's regime has been toppled, the old cultural divisions are again surfacing. How and if different ethnic and religious groups can be united under one peaceful, stable system of government remains to be seen.

Modern Iraq was created after the defeat of the German-allied Ottoman Empire in World War I, when the victorious British and French carved up the territory of their defeated rival. One of their decisions was the establishment of the new nation of Iraq under the rule of King Faisal I. The monarch had led the Great War's Arab revolt—popularized by *Lawrence of Arabia*—and had captured Damascus from the Ottomans in 1918.

Within the country's borders, three major groups—each with an identity and an agenda—occupy fairly distinct geographic regions: Sunni Muslims, Shiite Muslims, and Kurds. Each calls Iraq home, but each is unsure of what its role will be in the new Iraq. If the country's territorial integrity is to be respected, they must somehow work together.

In northern Iraq, the Kurds have recently begun to shake off decades of oppression. These traditionally pastoral people dwell in a region split by four different nations (Iraq, Iran, Turkey, and Syria). Though most Kurds are Muslim, they represent a unique group that has long held its own national aspirations. 'They are a distinct people with a distinct language (related to Persian or Farsi), much as Basques are different from Spaniards', explained David Miller, senior editor for National Geographic Maps.

The Kurdish minority was persecuted under the regime of Saddam Hussein. The Kurds took refuge in the mountainous north of Iraq where they enjoyed some degree of autonomy from Baghdad during the period between the Gulf War and the 2003 war that ousted the Hussein regime. . . .

'Numerically, they represent optimistically only a fifth of the population and that's not a lot', said Harm De Blij. 'Everyone talks about how much influence they'll have, but with their location and lack of presence elsewhere in the country I don't know how much they will be able to expect', De Blij said, while noting that the Kurds are themselves divided into two rival regional authorities. . . .

'They will demand no less autonomy than that which they had under Saddam', Reams said of the Kurds. 'However, I think they will realize that they cannot demand so much autonomy that they will incur Turkish wrath and even Turkish military incursions.' Turkey is ever wary of Kurdish aspirations because of the sizable and often restive Kurdish minority within Turkey. 'Since 1991, they've periodically staged raids into northern Iraq to get Turkish Kurd rebels who've fled to [Kurdish] Iraq to escape the armed forces', Miller added. 'Hussein's government had protested these incursions, but couldn't do much about them.' . . .

The rift between Iraq's Shiite and Sunni Muslims is primarily one of divergent religious viewpoints, which has its beginnings with the line of succession after the death of the Prophet Muhammad. Regional and cultural differences also exist, but Harm De Blij noted that the two lived rather harmoniously in Iraq until the rise of Baath Party power.

'What exacerbated this [difference] was a secular political movement—the Sunni Baath party. If there is one thing Shiites are not, they're not secular. As shown by the example of the Iranian revolution, religion is very central in their lives, and that's not the way Sunnis looked at it', De Blij said.

Saddam Hussein's sometimes brutal treatment of Shiites during his long reign has left a potentially deep rift between the groups—with many Shiites persecuted though they were numerically in the majority. 'It's one of the tragedies of Iraq', De Blij said, 'that because of that animosity a division was created that hadn't really been there before. . . .'

Salving these long-standing wounds won't be easy, as mistrust and animosity have grown over the years. Western officials at work in Iraq must recognize and account for such distinctions at all levels.

'Local ayatollahs toting sidearms with posses of loyal followers carrying AKs and knives will make these tribal and cultural differences an inescapable consideration in the attempts to transition to some form of democracy and representative government', said Reams.

A priority of any new Iraq government is balancing recognition and representation of the nation's distinct cultural entities with a central, national government that can rule for the good of all. How much regional autonomy is too much? How to get all groups fairly represented under the same tent? They are tough questions, but they should be at the forefront of rebuilding a nation that was from the beginning an amalgamation of disparate groups.

'The talking heads we see on TV have maps but they only seem to show tanks, planes, roads, and forts', said De Blij. 'I don't see many of them talking about the cultural, social geography of Iraq—and I hope somebody somewhere is looking at it that way.'

Source: Abridged from Brian Handwerk, for National Geographic News, at: <news.nationalgeographic.com/news/2003/04/0423_030423_iraqcultures.html>.

Cultural Realms

The stage is now set to discuss some of the attributes of those realms of social life most commonly located at the core of the sociology of culture. Although we could discuss the cultural dimension of almost any area of society, we will limit our discussion to language and discourse, the mass media, religion, and art. Within each realm, we will highlight the insights that the sociology of culture can bring to bear.

Language and Discourse

As mentioned above, language is a cultural subject par excellence. But before describing more fully the interest of sociology in language, it will be useful to distinguish it from the related concept of communication. *Language*, a system of words both written and spoken, is but one means of communication. **Communication** is the sharing of meaning, by which the thoughts of one person are made understandable to another. Communication can occur through a variety of signs and symbols, but we reserve a special place for the study of language because it is the primary means by which our communication takes place.

Languages are complicated systems of many symbols deployed according to a set of rules, and their use gives rise to a number of interesting social phenomena. It is argued, for instance, that the presence of language structures our very thoughts and consciousness, that without a vocabulary with which to label events (as is the case for infants) we cannot remember them. The character of social reality is tied to language insofar as we make sense of all our experiences in terms of the linguistic devices of and the logic made available through the language we speak.

As evidence of the consciousness-determining nature of language, we can point to examples of concepts and thoughts that exist in one language and are not entirely translatable to other languages, such as the German concepts of *Kultur* and *Geist*, or the French concepts of *ennui* and *joie de vivre*. Speakers of a language are said to share a certain mentalité that differentiates their mindset and world view. Likewise, it has been argued that the advancement of science in the West was in part related to the structure of European languages that encourages linear, causal thought patterns.

Discourse is a linguistic phenomenon that refers to a set of ideas, concepts, and vocabulary that recur in texts. A text can be broadly defined as any material or non-material communication act. Discourse is a habitual way of speaking about and understanding a topic or issue. Discourses abound in society. We encounter them constantly, but rarely do we explicitly recognize their features even when we are ourselves employing them. That is because it is natural for us to adopt a singular way of understanding an issue, and so a singular way of discussing or talking about an issue.

Take, for example, the issue of crime. In talking about crime, we might employ an *individualist discourse* that understands crime as the actions of a self-interested individual who is presented with options and makes certain choices. Crime in this discourse is conceived as something that one person does to one or more others, and it occurs in discrete instances. This discourse of crime encourages an understanding of the psychological factors involved in criminal behaviour and leads to solutions that work at the level of the individual. An individualist solution might suggest that if we alter the attractiveness of the option of committing crime by making penalties harsher for those who are caught, the individual will, we hope, no longer choose to commit crime.

In contrast, a *collectivist discourse* of crime also exists. This discourse views crime as a social problem. Crime is conceived as a feature of society that can be more or less prevalent. The focus is on crime rates and on the social conditions that influence the likelihood that crime will be committed in society. This discourse encourages a view more sociological than psychological of the factors contributing to crime, focusing on the social level rather than on the individual level. Just as the problem is conceived at the group level, so the ideas and terminology of a collectivist discourse promote a conception of solutions at the group level. For example, an effort to reduce crime might be based on information gained from a comparison of low- and high-crime societies to determine how certain social differences influence crime rates.

As the example of discourses about crime shows, discourses have the potential for great influence. The promotion of certain discourses throughout society, by those with the power to do so, can have the effect of setting the public agenda for certain issues. A discourse of abortion as an issue of privacy, for example, portrays the central concern as autonomy. It privileges the discussion of government impingement on the right of women to control their own bodies. But an opposing discourse surrounding abortion privileges a discussion of the social need to uphold all human life, no matter how inchoate that life appears to be. In this discourse, the primary concern is the idea that human life is so important to the society that it should not be compromised.

Such discourses play a role in the **social construction** of the categories and definitions we use to understand and to analyze social life. In our daily lives, we constantly refer to these categories and definitions in order to make judgements about good and bad, right and wrong, desirable and undesirable, how to distinguish between 'us' and the 'other', as well as to understand the very nature of things—Is abortion murder? Is killing in warfare murder? Are movies an art form, an educational medium, a propoganda tool, or entertainment? Is eating animals a question of morality? Is 'race' about biological differences? Is crime an individual failing? Is crime a collective failing of the society? For all these questions, our answers will be influenced by the way predominant discourses shape and frame our notions of the issues central to them.

Mass Media

The mass media are powerful social forces. They constitute a key realm of cultural production and distribution and can be seen to play a variety of social roles. The **mass media** are those technologically based methods and institutions that allow a single source to transmit messages to a mass audience. The mass media in Canada include print (newspapers, magazines, books, and journals), film, radio, television (broadcast, cable, and satellite), and the Internet. The Internet is a special case because, although it can function as a mass medium, it is also much more—a network medium by virtue of its ability to allow multiple message sources. Potentially every person on the Internet can be a source of mass media content. (See Figure 3.1 on the ways in which Canadians are using the Internet.)

The mass media are a central cultural concern because of the nature of the content that they bring to the vast majority of people. That content can be categorized both as *information* and as *entertainment*.

Let us first consider the mass media as the primary source of news information in society. They are the means by which we find out about important political, economic, and social happenings. We rely on them for the information we need to understand our local, regional, national, and global contexts. In addition to information that is delivered as news per se on news programs and in newspapers, the mass media provide us with a wealth of other information about the world that we might never have access to through first-hand experience. Through the mass media, we can read about the modernization of industries in China, we can see what the skyline of Buenos Aires looks like, we can hear about the best way to invest money in a sluggish economy, we can find information about our diagnosed disease and likely find a supportive group willing to share their experiences with the ailment. In short, the mass media bring a world of information to us, and their capacity to do so has greatly increased with the advent of the Internet, which allows us to access only information we desire, when we desire it, if we can locate it.

Figure 3.1 Regular Internet Use in Canada, by Gender, Age, Education, and Household Income (%)

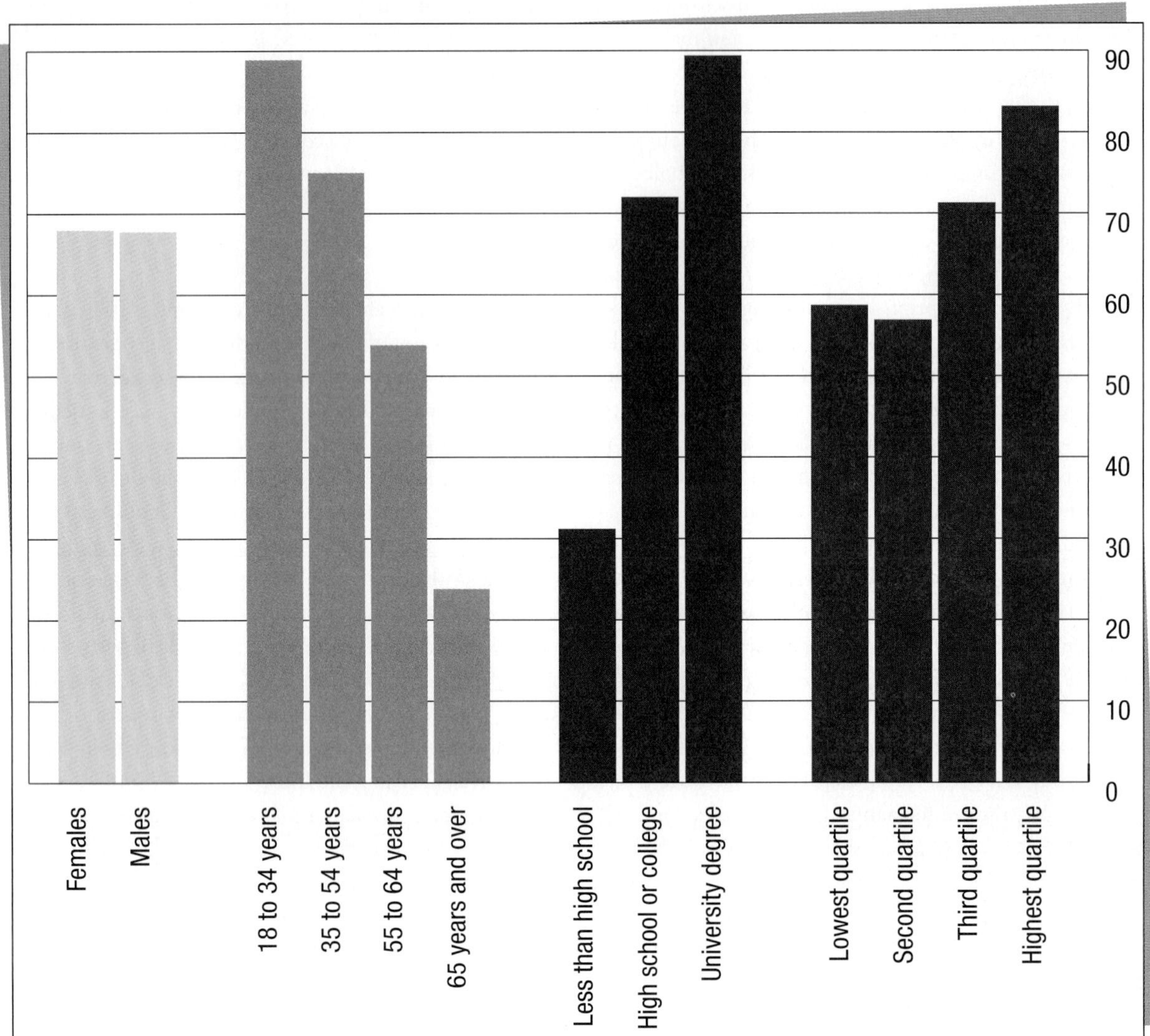

As the providers of so much information, the mass media have an enormous amount of influence on people's attitudes and behaviours, which are dependent on the state of our knowledge. For example, some people will alter their eating habits based on information they learn from magazine articles about the dangers and benefits of certain foods, some people will form an opinion about strengthening environmental protection regulations based on stories they watch on television news programs, and some people will relocate and change their lifestyles based on information about the effects of global warming. Because the mass media select a limited amount of information to present to audiences from a virtually infinite supply, they serve as informational gatekeepers (White, 1950). This gatekeeping function can account for much of their influence. However, just as important as what they present is the question of how they present media content. There is a connection here to the preceding discussion of discourses, because it is through the mass media that most discourses are disseminated to the general public.

The mass media are also the primary source for popular culture. While high culture (discussed below) is only rarely made available through the mass media, popular culture is everywhere. The popular culture productions brought to us by the mass media are argued to be linked to deep-seated social problems. This link is specified as the ability of the mass media to warp or corrupt our culture: television shows, movies, music, and so on are argued to have a profoundly negative impact on our entire way of life.

An important criticism of mass media content finds fault with the materialistic values the mass media explicitly and implicitly advocate. By constantly connecting depictions of happiness and success to material wealth, the mass media have been a principal cause of the development of a consumer culture that focuses our attention and energies on gaining and spending money and away from spiritual, moral, ethical, and social issues. The mass media also are blamed for a culture of violence: it is argued that they contribute to high levels of violence in society insofar as portrayals of violence incite violent acts and desensitize people to the presence of violence. At the same time, it is argued that the mass media contribute to an unhelpful, unrealistic, and shallow understanding of and response to this violence. The list of social problems linked to the ways in which the mass media may distort and negatively influence our culture is long, including such serious issues as body consciousness and eating disorders, racism, and sexism, exacerbated through stereotypical and misleading depictions.

Religion

Religion is a sociological subfield of its own, but it merits its inclusion in a discussion of culture because it has had such a large impact on the development of values and cultural traditions in most countries, Canada included. The case for the importance of religion as a cultural force was strongly made by Durkheim (1995 [1912]), who saw religion as providing the basis for social solidarity, as noted earlier in this chapter. More generally, we often characterize Western countries as belonging to a Judeo-Christian tradition, a tradition that denotes a specific history and related social institutions and dominant values. It is important to realize that it does not require a specifically religious mindset to be influenced by Judeo-Christian values in general. These values permeate our culture and are seen in such things as predominant views on the role of authority; the moral code undergirding much of the legal system; beliefs in the value of punishment and the possibility of rehabilitation; social action on behalf of the underprivileged, sick, disabled, and terminally ill; and attitudes towards work and leisure.

Culture carries aesthetic meanings through various signs—clothing, hairstyle, and so on—that go in and out of fashion. Do you recognize this pop cultural icon? (Michael Ochs Archives/Corbis)

Perhaps the best-known thesis in sociology regarding the influence of religion on culture is Max Weber's argument in *The Protestant Ethic and the Spirit of Capitalism* (1958 [1904]). Weber argues that several aspects of Protestant (specifically Calvinist) doctrine specifically encouraged the values and behaviour of economic rationalism, thereby promoting the rapid advancement of capitalism in Protestant societies. The accuracy of this argument and its strength as a single explanation of economic development has been questioned, but its importance for an understanding of the cultural role of religion remains.

Art and Aesthetics

In common usage, 'culture' often is synonymous with 'art', though for the reasons described in this chapter there is good reason for distinguishing between the two. Art is best seen as one element, albeit a unique element, of our larger culture, but most people use their artistic capacities in everyday life, just as they use their abilities to speak, write, and communicate in gestures and with facial expressions and other dramatic forms of movement. Children develop their artistic forms of expression in school; they go on to make choices about clothing, furniture, and personal and home accessories, and create environments in house, garden, and office based on their personal aesthetics. They draw, paint, take photographs, make home movies, and make things of aesthetic appeal for themselves and others. Some use the skills they have developed therapeutically. Some turn these abilities towards commercial ventures in applications from letterhead and business cards to store window decoration, restaurant decoration, or other means of communicating with the buying public. However, one of the concerns of those who want to spend most of their time creating 'art' has always been, 'Will it sell?'

The realm of art is, above all, an expressive area of social life. Whereas much of our behaviour is oriented towards the practical achievement of a useful goal, art stands out as an activity that is done to communicate through **aesthetic** means and the goal may be no more (or less) practical than to induce feelings. The *New Shorter Oxford English Dictionary* (1993) defines *aesthetics* as 'a system of principles for the appreciation of the beautiful', which begs the definition by failing to define beauty! Today, many artists would eschew the word 'beauty' for 'important' (and some might narrow that idea to 'what is important to me'). Art, then, employs a set of rules or principles embodied in many different forms and pertaining to the artist's notions of what is beautiful or important. This makes art—whether visual, musical, or literary—a special form of communication: it is an expression of thoughts and emotions not communicated through the ordinary means of language. Instead, it relies on the much more implicit and intuitive rules that people in general use to assess beauty or truth or, for that matter, societal strengths, values, and shortcomings.

Art is an inherently imprecise form of communication, in which particular works carry implicit messages that may require an educated sense of appreciation for the aesthetic principles at play to be received. That is why we can read a novel and generate many different ideas about what the novel 'is really about' or what the author 'is really saying', just as we can for paintings, sculpture, plays, and other forms of art. Moreover, we tend to think of truly good art as the expression of artistic genius. 'Masterpieces', we tend to believe, are the works of geniuses, people of special technical and intellectual ability whose ideas and forms of self-expression represent ideals for human creativity and thought. The very best of art represents the very best of humanity, and so art occupies an honoured place in society.

As discussed above, we often distinguish between 'popular culture' and 'high culture'. This distinction points to the existence of a *cultural hierarchy*, in which certain forms of culture are granted greater legitimacy and prestige. Oil painting is higher on the hierarchy than filmmaking, which in turn is higher than television. Works by certain artists command higher prices than those of others. It is important to recognize that such status distinctions are themselves cultural productions. That is to say, our categories of 'high' and 'popular' or 'low' are socially constructed. These categorizations represent more than tangible differences in the characteristics of cultural productions. They also reflect differences in the social contexts in which the artifacts of culture are produced, distributed, and received.

Take, for example, Italian opera. North Americans have a clear notion of opera as high art. The dominant discourse of art portrays art as the product of artistic minds and as inherently special—there is something about art that allows us to recognize it when we see it. So long as we are informed about the value of art, we will never confuse Italian opera with popular culture. This discourse neglects the reality that our definitions involving status reflect an entire social process involved in bringing art to audiences. Our ideas about Italian opera as high art are based partially on an array of cues, such as its high cost, the status of its audiences, the costly training of its performers, the physically distinct and opulent venues in which it is performed, the extravagance of its production values, its non-profit status (we pretend to oppose art to commerce), and intellectual analyses of Italian opera to explain why it is great art. If one goes to Italy, however, one finds that opera is much more an art of the people. The audiences are much more broadly based in terms of class, the vanishing of the language barrier removes an arcane quality to the production and demystifies both attendance and understanding of the production. People do not have to pay as much, relatively, to attend productions, and are much more likely to leave singing snatches of the arias without an appearance of flaunting class distinctions.

This approach to art highlights several of art's sociologically significant features. First, as explained by the production of culture perspective, art does not just spring out of a **collective consciousness**, or even out of an individual's consciousness. Instead, art is a collective activity that requires collaboration between many actors in an art world (Becker, 1982). It is this collective activity that helps to determine how artistic genres may be legitimated or become prestigious and how they may be viewed in the wider society.

Second, the socially constructed nature of distinctions between high and low in art also points to the significance of art in helping to determine the contours of social stratification. This link is rooted in the notion of **cultural capital**: the knowledge, preferences, and tastes that people have concerning art and aesthetics. Having abundant cultural capital usually means sharing the knowledge, preferences, and tastes that are common among those of high status in society. The link between cultural capital and stratification is based on the power of high cultural capital to provide access to informal interpersonal connections that can influence our occupational and economic prospects. Sharing similar artistic tastes and consumption patterns with those in economically privileged positions provides us with access to networks and opportunities not open to those who do not have the necessary aesthetic preferences and expertise. In sociological terms, our cultural capital can increase our economic capital. (This is an interesting inversion of the Marxist logic whereby the cultural realm is determining, or influencing, the economic realm.)

Third, and perhaps even more significant, is the role that artistic consumption plays in creating social groupings in society. The enjoyment of products of aesthetic quality is deeply related to our conceptions of our own identities, of who we really are, and of the kind of people with whom we wish to be associated. In this way, our tastes are profoundly implicated in how our lives are structured. We've already seen how artistic tastes can interact with our class position, but tastes can also be a way of expressing racial, gender, regional, and age-based identities.

Take the example of youth culture. Although this term refers to many aspects of how young people live their lives, one important way in which adolescents and young adults set themselves apart is through the music they listen to, the publications they read, the television shows and channels they watch, the films they see, and, increasingly, the websites they visit and create. Knowledge of and participation in this particular set of aesthetic preferences allow young people to experience group belonging. Through aesthetics, they can distinguish themselves from prior generations.

Cultural Dynamics

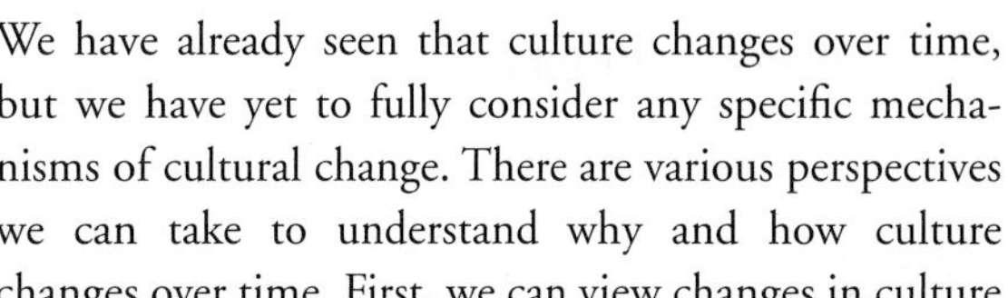

We have already seen that culture changes over time, but we have yet to fully consider any specific mechanisms of cultural change. There are various perspectives we can take to understand why and how culture changes over time. First, we can view changes in culture

SOCIOLOGY IN ACTION
Patients with AIDS

AIDS presented a serious challenge to established identities—and patterns of trust and control—in the treatment domain. A knowledge and treatment vacuum emerged as a result of a very public display of scientific uncertainty and institutional impotence in the face of this new crisis. Suddenly, old understanding about who was knowledgeable, who could and could not be trusted, and who should and should not be granted control, were open to contestation. For example, early on in the epidemic, the expertise of the 'doctor' was in doubt. Not only did physicians *not* have the expertise to deal with this new challenge, some were patently unwilling to acquire it or even to act in the interests of their patients. Many early AIDS patients were abandoned, as discrimination, bigotry, and fear led to some doctors 'dumping' their patients.

PWAs ['persons with AIDS'] began to reject the identity of 'patient' and the victimhood it implied. 'Patients' (from the French '*patienter*', which means to wait, as in a physician's waiting room, and originally from the Latin, where it means 'to suffer') would be 'patient' and suffer in silence no longer. '*Silence = Death*', an expression made popular by the activist group ACT-UP, became the call to action for HIV/AIDS patients seeking to redefine themselves and their role within the domain. Community members stressed that they were neither 'patients' nor 'victims', but 'people living with AIDS'. . . .

The identity of PWAs, collectively, is thus very different from that of traditional patient groups. The notion of patients as passive, ignorant, requiring the medical expertise of an elite was successfully deconstructed and replaced with a notion of a patient group as empowered, informed, and organized decision-makers.

Source: Steve Maguire, Nelson Phillips, and Cynthia Hardy, 'When "Silence = Death", Keep Talking: Trust, Control and the Discursive Construction of Identity in the Canadian HIV/AIDS Treatment Domain', *Organization Studies* 22, 2 (2001): 296. Reprinted by permission of Sage Publications Ltd.

Time to Reflect

What characteristics of each of the above four social phenomena—language, mass media, religion, and art—make them particularly cultural rather than structural?

as responses to particular social-structural changes; we will focus on the cultural ramifications of economic changes and of technological changes. Second, we can also view changes in culture as responses to other cultural developments, a view that emphasizes the weblike, interconnected nature of culture.

Economic, Technological, and Cultural Change

At the most basic level, all of culture can be seen as human adaptation and ingenuity to better control and survive in the physical environment. Beyond that most basic level, but in keeping with the premise that culture allows us to deal with our surroundings, it also gives us the means to function effectively in our social environment, in our dealings with other people. Changes in that social environment, then, encourage and enable corresponding cultural changes.

The discussion of Marxism earlier in this chapter reviewed the case for the economic foundation of culture. In Marxism, culture is a reflection of the underlying economic basis of society. But it is not necessary to adopt Marxists' assumptions of culture merely as a reflection of economics to see that important economic changes are capable of provoking specific changes in culture. An example of such a change is the liberalization of attitudes towards women and work. In the mid- to late nineteenth century and in the first half of the twentieth century, there was a strong belief in Western societies that it was most appropriate for women, especially married women, not to work outside the home but rather to find fulfillment in their roles as mothers and housewives. While the reasons for the change that has occurred in this attitude are many, it can be argued that an important cause of the change was economic. Maintenance of a middle-class standard of living increasingly required a second income. Changing attitudes about women and work, in this view, were an adaptive response to a changing economic reality.

Over the same period of time, rising levels of affluence made it possible for teenagers to possess a certain amount of disposable income. The development of youth culture, while deriving from various causes, was facilitated by the economic changes that created consumers out of young people and thereby encouraged cultural producers to target and cater to youth. The continued growth in spending power of teenagers has also allowed them to become the primary demographic target of Hollywood film studios. Because young people see films in theatres more often than do older groups, a great deal of film production is tailored to their tastes and expectations. This dynamic is representative of the more general dependence of the content of cultural industries on economic conditions.

Technological change can also be viewed as the source of a great deal of the change in our culture. Perhaps the clearest and most significant technological influence on culture has been the development of the mass media. The printing press, invented by Johannes Gutenberg in 1452, has been credited with transforming European culture in diverse ways. For example, the printing press—by making reproduction fast—reduced the value of a book and eventually brought the cost down to allow many people to personally own Bibles and read them and interpret them apart from what they were instructed by priests to believe and think: a precondition for the Protestant Reformation. The invention of the telegraph, which vastly hastened the speed with which information could travel over great distances, has been cited as changing our attitudes concerning the pace of life and punctuality, and even our very definitions of the proportions of space and time.

Television is arguably one of the most powerful technologies ever invented. It has wrought profound cultural changes. First, a specific form of cultural content has developed for the purposes of the medium, shaping our tastes for and expectations of dramatic entertainment, but also, and more fundamentally, influencing our perceptions of social reality and of the nature of the world outside our daily lives. Second, this technology has brought a major leisure activity into our homes, promoting the growth of television culture, in which we spend at least some of our free time in a one-way relationship with a screen rather than interacting with others or engaging in community-based activities.

It would be impossible to enumerate all the ways in which technology has created cultural change. To take an example of a broad cultural pattern, the very idea of 'nightlife' and all its attendant activities is predicated on the existence of electricity and the light bulb. Much more narrowly, the technological innovation of the electrification of musical instruments has influenced tastes in musical styles. Suffice it to say that technological change frequently has the potential to create cultural reverberations, sometimes of limited significance and other times life-transforming.

Recognition of the influence of technological, economic, and other (for example, demographic) changes on the shape of culture is in no way a denial of the transformative power of culture. The relationship, to be sure, is reciprocal. Cultural changes can at times influence these very same structural features of society.

Change for the Sake of Change

Despite the strength of the relationship between culture and social structure, culture also has internal dynamics that can account for cultural change. In this view, cultural change is inevitable because culture, as representative of individual and collective self-expression, is inherently progressive, evolutionary, volatile, and unstable: it is the nature of culture to evolve.

The validity of this view is perhaps best exemplified by the phenomenon of fashion. *Fashion* is change for the sake of change in the realm of aesthetics. Ongoing change is built into the very idea of fashion. Moreover, fashion is not just the styles of clothes that are popular, although that is one of its most visible manifestations. Rather, elements of fashion can be found in a many areas of social life.

Consider, for instance, how vocabulary choices acknowledge that some words are 'in' while others are 'out'. To express approval, one might have heard adjectives in the past such as 'swell', 'groovy', or 'mod', words that sound dated now despite the fact that the need to express approval has not gone away. New, more fashionable words do the job today. Consider also how changes in furniture and interior design occur gradually but consistently enough to evoke associations with particular decades. Few of these changes are linked to changes in function or technological innovations. Finally, consider how fashion operates to change the popularity of first names (Lieberson, 2000). The Ethels, Mildreds, and Eunices of yesterday are the Emilys, Hannahs, and Madisons of today (see Table 3.2). The function of naming remains constant, while the aesthetic element of naming

Fashions in dress come and go. What social changes can you infer by comparing the dress and look of the '1830 woman' with the '1930 woman'? What might the '2030 woman' look like? (Left: Lebrecht Music and Arts Photo Library/Alamy Images; Right: Gonzalo Fuentes/Reuters/Corbis)

reveals continuous modification. The kinds of aesthetic modifications that are made today are dependent on the nature of the aesthetic modifications of the past.

Although aesthetic changes do not serve any practical or functional purposes, they may still be related to a social purpose: they satisfy needs for self-expression. In this sense, the aesthetic dimension of life is symbolic—we communicate to others and articulate (however obliquely) for ourselves certain thoughts, values, identities, and senses of group affiliation. Change in aesthetics results from shifts in the meanings or understandings commonly attributed to certain aesthetic elements, such that they no longer connote what they used to.

To see how this is so, consider Georg Simmel's theory of fashion (1957). This argument has become known as the trickle-down model. In this model, fashion is triggered by the status concerns of high-status groups who seek to distinguish themselves by adopting a new fashion, which they have the means to afford. Those elements of fashion that they adopt then come to connote high status by their association with a high-status group—that is the symbolism of the fashion. Lower-status groups then adopt this fashion for themselves to share in the high status, but in doing so they change the meaning of the fashion: it no longer expresses exclusiveness. High-status groups thus no longer find the fashion appealing or useful, and so they adopt a new fashion. Although this model cannot in fact explain much of the fashion world today, which often appropriates the symbols of lower-status groups, it is nonetheless a clear illustration of how

Table 3.2 Top 20 Names for Baby Girls Born in Illinois by Race, 1989, 1940, and 1920

1989		1940		1920	
Shared by Blacks and Whites		**Shared by Blacks and Whites**		**Shared by Blacks and Whites**	
Ashley	Jessica	Barbara	Joyce	Alice	Helen
Brittany	Michelle	Beverly	Margaret	Anna	Margaret
Christina	Nicole	Carol	Mary	Catherine	Marie
		Dorothy	Patricia	Dorothy	Mary
		Joan	Sandra	Elizabeth	Mildred
			Shirley	Evelyn	Ruth
				Frances	Virginia
White Only	**Black Only**	**White Only**	**Black Only**	**White Only**	**Black Only**
Amanda	Alicia	Carolyn	Betty	Betty	Ethel
Caitlin	Amber	Donna	Brenda	Eleanor	Gladys
Catherine	Ariel	Janet	Dolores	Florence	Lillian
Elizabeth	Bianca	Judith	Gloria	Lorraine	Louise
Emily	Candace	Karen	Gwendolyn	Marion	Lucille
Jennifer	Crystal	Linda	Helen	Marjorie	Thelma
Kelly	Danielle	Marilyn	Jacqueline		
Lauren	Dominique	Nancy	Loretta		
Megan	Ebony	Sharon	Yvonne		
Rachel	Erica				
Rebecca	Jasmine				
Samantha	Kiara				
Sarah	Latoya				
Stephanie	Tiffany				

Source: Stanley Lieberson, *A Matter of Taste: How Names, Fashions, and Culture Change* (New Haven: Yale University Press, 2000), 204. Reprinted by permission of Yale University Press.

Time to Reflect

Based on the information above, why might the rate of cultural change be increasing?

culture can evolve according to an internal set of principles that do not reflect social-structural change.

Canadian Culture

The concepts and arguments reviewed in this chapter can help us to understand the current state of Canadian culture, along with some of the more contentious issues facing Canadian society. Because of its unique history, Canadian culture is unlike any other national culture, with a unique set of challenges and a unique set of opportunities.

Distinct Societies

One of the defining features of Canadian culture is its basis in 'two founding peoples', French and English. The term *peoples* refers, of course, not only to the actual members of the French and English colonies, but also to their respective ways of life—their cultures. How different or similar are the cultures of French and English Canada? On a global scale, they are quite similar to one another in comparison with, for example, Pakistani or Indonesian culture. However, they differ in important ways still. Most obvious is the linguistic basis for the distinction (see Table 3.3). As discussed earlier, language is a core component of culture, with significant implications for social life. The ability to communicate with verbal and written language is a key element to social bonding—without this form of communication, opportunities for social interaction are limited. Differences in other cultural traditions exist as well, ranging from cuisine and leisure activities to political values and views on marriage and family.

The challenge for Canada has been and continues to be the forging of a unified Canadian culture that respects the unique characteristics of both traditions. To this end, we employ a policy of **official bilingualism** and we foster cultural events and new traditions that embrace both French and English cultural elements. The great concern over the success of this endeavour has been with us for decades and remains. The movement for sovereignty within Quebec is to a large extent based on the belief that the health of French-Canadian culture, and especially the vigour of the French language in Quebec, can only be adequately maintained and nurtured separate from a wider Canadian culture. The challenge for our country is to capitalize on the potential for Canadian culture to unite us rather than to divide us.

Multiculturalism

The conception of two founding peoples can be seen as primarily a legal construct rather than as an accurate historical depiction. In reality, there have always been more than two cultural traditions in Canada. The Aboriginal cultures of **First Nations** and Inuit peoples were, of course, present before the idea of a Canadian society or culture was ever proposed.

The Mounties' iconic red coats were selected when the force was established in 1873, because Native peoples retained respect for the British Army—the 'redcoats'. (Alamy Images)

Table 3.3 Population by Language Spoken Most Often at Home, Canada, 1991, 1996, and 2001

	1991	1996	2001
English	18,440,535 (68.3%)	19,294,835 (67.6%)	20,011,535 (67.5%)
French	6,288,425 (23.3%)	6,448,615 (22.6%)	6,531,375 (22.0%)
Non-official language	2,265,075 (8.4%)	2,784,645 (9.8%)	3,096,110 (10.5%)

Source: Adapted from Statistics Canada, *Profile of Languages in Canada: English, French and Many Others* (Ottawa: Statistics Canada, 2002); at <www12.statcan.ca/english/census01/products/analytic/companion/lang/contents.cfm#nine>.

More recently, increased immigration from a large number of countries and the formation of an equally large number of ethnic communities in Canada have added to the number of cultural traditions we have to work with (see Figure 3.2 on Canada's increasing linguistic diversity). As a society, we have adopted a stance of official **multiculturalism**, although the merits of this position engender a good deal of debate. We should distinguish between multiculturalism as a fact of contemporary Canadian society—there are ethnic subcultures that are thriving—and multiculturalism as a policy—the tolerance and encouragement of the maintenance of the national cultures that immigrants bring with them from their countries of origin.

Proponents of multiculturalism point to its helpfulness in easing the transition of new immigrants into

Figure 3.2 Allophone Groups[a] That Increased or Decreased the Most from 1996 to 2001, Canada (Population in Thousands)

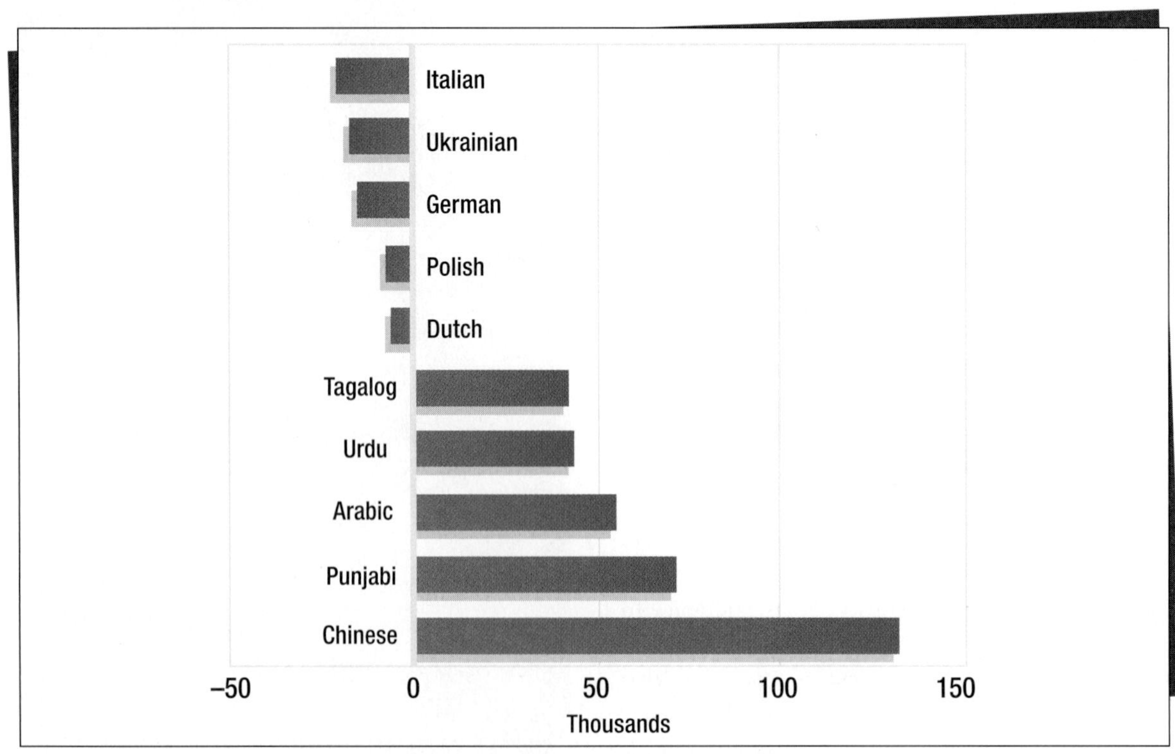

[a] Groups of people who possess the same non-official language as their mother tongue.

Source: Adapted from Statistics Canada, *Profile of Languages in Canada: English, French and Many Others* (Ottawa: Statistics Canada, 2002); at <www12.statcan.ca/english/census01/products/analytic/companion/lang/contents.cfm#nine>.

Canadian society. This happens through the fostering of ethnic communities that can provide social support. In addition, proponents argue that multiculturalism is a policy that is properly respectful to all Canadians and that enriches the wider Canadian culture. Detractors, on the other hand, argue that multiculturalism only makes it more difficult to create a unifying Canadian culture. Moreover, they question the wisdom of a policy that encourages, to however small a degree, self-segregation rather than facilitating the full cultural integration of immigrants into Canadian life. Again, just as with the question of two founding peoples, the challenge here is to balance culture's potential for unifying us with our desire to maintain certain cultural partitions.

Globalization and American Cultural Imperialism

Globalization typically refers to the fact that goods, services, information, and labour, now more than ever, can easily flow between distant countries. Of particular concern for us is the cultural influence that globalization brings. There are various implications of globalization for Canadian culture. Technological advancements in mass media have made possible easy and abundant access to the sights and sounds of geographically distant locales. Through media representations we can be made aware of cultural elements from across the globe, and the potential exists to incorporate these elements into Canadian culture. In a sense, one effect of globalization is the internationalization of national cultures as they increasingly are exposed to one another. The mass media, then, are the key channels of the cultural diffusion occurring through the mutual influence of many national cultures.

Globalization, however, can bring with it many difficult cultural challenges. Chief among these challenges is the need to manage the global export of American popular culture. Popular culture, in the form of films, television shows, music, and websites, is one of the largest American exports, reaching every corner of the

HUMAN DIVERSITY

China's Youth Look to Seoul for Inspiration

At Korea City, on the top floor of the Xidan Shopping Center, a warren of tiny shops sell hip-hop clothes, movies, music, cosmetics and other offerings in the South Korean style.

To young Chinese shoppers, it seemed not to matter that some of the products, like New York Yankees caps or Japan's Astro Boy dolls, clearly have little to do with South Korea. Or that most items originated, in fact, in Chinese factories.

'We know that the products at Korea City are made in China', said Wang Ying, 28, who works for the local branch of an American company. 'But to many young people, "Korea" stands for fashionable or stylish. So they copy the Korean style.'

From clothes to hairstyle, music to television dramas, South Korea has been defining the tastes of many Chinese and other Asians for the past half decade. As part of what the Chinese call the Korean Wave of pop culture, a television drama about a royal cook, *The Jewel in the Palace*, is garnering record ratings throughout Asia, and Rain, a 23-year-old singer from Seoul, drew more than 40,000 fans to a sold-out concert at a sports stadium here in October.

But South Korea's 'soft power' also extends to the material and spiritual spheres. Samsung's cellphones and televisions are symbols of a coveted consumerism for many Chinese. Christianity, in the evangelical form championed by Korean missionaries deployed throughout China, is finding Chinese converts despite Beijing's efforts to rein in the spread of the religion. South Korea acts as a filter for Western values, experts say, making them more palatable to Chinese and other Asians.

For a country that has been influenced by other cultures, especially China but also Japan and America, South Korea finds itself at a turning point in its new role as exporter.

The transformation began with South Korea's democratization in the late 1980s, which unleashed sweeping domestic changes. As its democracy and economy have matured, its influence on the rest of Asia, negligible until a decade ago, has grown accordingly. Its cultural exports have even caused complaints about cultural invasion in China and Vietnam.

Historically, Christianity made little headway in East Asia, except in South Korea, whose population is now about 30 per cent Christian and whose overseas missionary movement is the world's second largest after the United States.

Today, in China, South Korean missionaries are bringing Christianity with an Asian face. South Korean movies and dramas about urban professionals in Seoul, though not overtly political, present images of modern lives centering on individual happiness and sophisticated consumerism.

They also show enduring Confucian-rooted values in their emphasis on family relations, offering to Chinese both a reminder of what was lost during the Cultural Revolution and an example of an Asian country that has modernized and retained its traditions.

Three Guys and Three Girls and *Three Friends* are South Korea's homegrown version of the American TV show *Friends.* As for *Sex and the City*, its South Korean twin, *The Marrying Type*, a sitcom about three single professional women in their thirties looking for love in Seoul, was so popular in China that episodes were illegally downloaded or sold on pirated DVDs.

'We feel that we can see a modern lifestyle in those shows', said Qu Yuan, 23, a student at Tsinghua University here. 'American dramas also show the same kind of lifestyle. We know that South Korea and America have similar political systems and economies. But it's easier to accept that lifestyle from South Koreans because they are culturally closer to us. We feel we can live like them in a few years.'

'They seem to have similar lifestyles', Ms. Qu said. 'They have friends and go to bars. They have good mobile phones and good cars and lead comfortable lives.'

Her classmate, Huo Kan, 23, said, 'American dramas are too modern.'

Ms. Qu said, 'They're postmodern.'

Ms. Huo added, 'Something like *Sex and the City* is too alien to us.'

Jin Yaxi, 25, a graduate student at Beijing University, said, 'We like American culture, but we can't accept it directly.'

'And there is no obstacle to our accepting South Korean culture, unlike Japanese culture', said Ms. Jin, who has studied both Korean and Japanese. 'Because of the history between China and Japan, if a young person here likes Japanese culture, the parents will get angry.'

Politics also seems to underlie the Chinese preference for South Korean-filtered American hip-hop culture. Messages about rebelliousness, teenage angst and freedom appear more palatable to Chinese in their Koreanized versions.

Kwon Ki Joon, 22, a South Korean who attends Beijing University and graduated from a Chinese high school here, said his male Chinese friends were fans of South Korean hip-hop bands, like H.O.T., and its song 'We Are the Future'. A sample of the song's lyrics translate roughly as: 'We are still under the shadows of adults/Still not Free/To go through the day with all sorts of interferences is tiring.'

To Mr. Kwon, there is no mystery about the band's appeal. 'It's about wanting a more open world, about rebelliousness', he said. 'Korean hip-hop is basically trying to adapt American hip-hop.'

Like many South Koreans, Oh Dong Suk, 40, an investor in online games here, said he believed that South Korea's pop culture was a fruit of the country's democratization. 'If you watch South Korean movies from the 1970s or 1980s, you could feel that it was a controlled society', Mr. Oh said. . . .

Source: Abridged from Norimitsu Onishi, 'China's Youth Look to Seoul for Inspiration'. From *The New York Times*, 2 Jan. 2006.

globe. The sheer volume of American cultural export has led to the term cultural imperialism, describing the scope of the global dominance of American culture.

The reaction to this state of affairs in Canada has been one of alarm and a concerted effort has been mounted to maintain the integrity of Canadian culture. The importing of American cultural products is seen as dangerous to Canadian culture because the many pre-existing similarities with American culture threaten to overwhelm the differences by which we recognize our culture as distinct and, for us, preferable. In order to promote Canadian cultural production, the federal government has for several decades enacted policies that require Canadian broadcasters to make a sizable proportion of their content of Canadian origin. In addition, a variety of programs exist to subsidize Canadian film, television, music, and book production (see Figure 3.3 on the relative costs of production).

This policy of Canadian cultural protectionism has clearly achieved some measured successes. Scores of Canadian artists have achieved a level of success that would have been unlikely if left to compete on the unequal playing field with American artists who are promoted by vast media conglomerates. Yet despite these successes, and despite the strict requirements of Canadian content regulations, Canadians consume tremendous amounts of American popular culture. There is no question that the continuing distinctiveness of Canadian culture and identity is threatened by the extensive consumption of American cultural products. There is an unfortunate contradiction between Canadians' preference for their own national norms, values, attitudes, and beliefs on the one hand and their preference for American popular culture on the other.

Figure 3.3 Relative Costs and Revenues of Canadian Content and US Simulcasts in Television

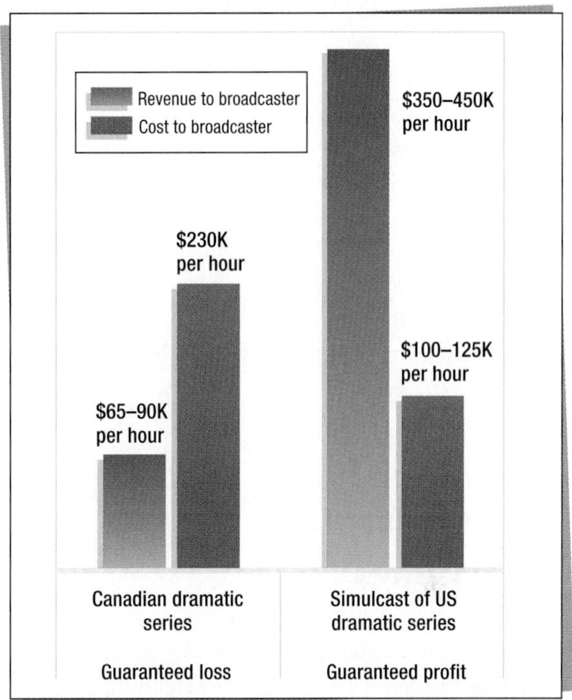

Source: CBC, *The Economics of Canadian Television* (cbc Fact Sheet) (2002); at <http://cbc.radio-canada.ca/htmen/pdf_rtf/CBCfacts-economics-finale.pdf>. Reprinted by permission of the publisher.

Conclusion

Culture is undoubtedly one of the most difficult sociological terms to pin down—it has many meanings—but through careful analysis sociology can bring those multiple meanings into focus and can explain why we have them. Many different social phenomena can be called 'cultural'. We need to understand what those various phenomena have in common to cause them all to be considered 'culture'. Culture is always evolving and is intimately tied to other social changes and to other cultural changes. Finally, we need to be aware of the role of culture in social life because it is the key to understanding some of the most important events in our society and in the world today. Culture is implicated in the social dynamics both of conflict and of people coming together, and for that reason as well as others it is an essential subject for sociological analysis.

Time to Reflect

What are the arguments for and against multiculturalism in Canada? Which do you find more persuasive?

Questions for Critical Thought

1. What is Canadian culture, and what are its most important or distinctive facets?
2. What subcultures are you a member of? What are the characteristics of those subcultures? How did you enter them?
3. How much do you know about other cultures and how did you learn about them? How do you know if your impressions are accurate?
4. Where does culture come from? How could you begin to research such a question? What dimensions of culture are particularly amenable to such a research question?
5. What role do art and music play in your life? Do your friends like the same art and music that you like? Do these art forms bring you together?
6. Who gets to decide what is good literature, painting, films, television, or music, and on what bases? Should you listen to experts on these matters, or can you decide for yourself?
7. How would you go about measuring cultural change? Moreover, how would you try to explain such change?
8. Is cultural change beneficial to society? Is it conceivable to have no changes in our culture?

Recommended Readings

Victoria D. Alexander, *Sociology of the Arts: Exploring Fine and Popular Forms* (Oxford: Blackwell, 2003).

This book is a clear, engaging, thorough, and sophisticated overview of this area of study.

Peter Berger and Thomas Luckmann, *The Social Construction of Reality: A Treatise in the Sociology of Knowledge* (Garden City, NY: Doubleday-Anchor, 1966).

This is a seminal work in the sociology of culture, laying the groundwork for social constructionist thought.

Laura Desfor Edles, *Cultural Sociology in Practice* (Malden, Mass.: Blackwell, 2002).

Edles's book is a good survey of many issues and studies, both old and new, in cultural sociology.

Wendy Griswold, *Bearing Witness: Readers, Writers, and the Novel in Nigeria* (Princeton, NJ: Princeton University Press, 2000).

This is an excellent demonstration of the complexity of cultural analysis, examining cultural production, subculture, and the influence of national values and beliefs.

Eric Klinenberg, *Cultural Production in a Digital Age: The Annals of the American Academy of Political and Social Science* (Thousand Oaks, Calif.: Sage, 2005).

Taking a broad view of what counts as culture, this edited volume investigates how the technological advances of the digital age have influenced the methods and outcomes of cultural production.

Michele Lamont, *The Dignity of Working Men: Morality and the Boundaries of Race, Class, and Immigration* (Cambridge, Mass.: Harvard University Press; New York: Russell Sage Foundation, 2000).

This is a thoughtful analysis of the complex ways in which the many dimensions of culture act to shape the lives of working-class men and their understandings of status distinctions.

Nelson Phillips and Cynthia Hardy, *Discourse Analysis: Investigating Processes of Social Construction* (Thousand Oaks, Calif.: Sage, 2002).

This short book provides a concise and insightful review of the theory and research in sociology and related fields on the role of discourse in social life.

Lyn Spillman, ed., *Cultural Sociology* (Malden, Mass.: Blackwell, 2002).

Spillman provides an entertaining overview of many excellent empirical studies in the sociology of culture as well as many intriguing theoretical works.

Recommended Websites

Canadian Broadcasting Corporation (CBC)
www.cbc.ca
In addition to finding the news, you will also find links to the corporate history of the CBC, the broadcasting entity charged with strengthening Canadian culture and identity.

Canadian Heritage
www.canadianheritage.gc.ca
There are many agencies within this federal government department actively involved in promoting the health of Canadian culture.

Canadian Radio-television and Telecommunications Commission (CRTC)
www.crtc.gc.ca
Here you'll find the public policy behind our broadcasting regimes. The CRTC is the quasi-independent agency responsible for regulating the entire broadcast industry.

Culture & Tradition
www.ucs.mun.ca/~culture/
The bilingual journal *Culture & Tradition* focuses on Canadian folklore and folk culture, both French and English.

Culture/Online
www.ibiblio.org/culture
This is the site of the American Sociological Association's section on the Sociology of Culture. Here you can find links and news about new work done in the field.

National Film Board of Canada (NFB)
www.nfb.ca
There are countless interesting links at the website of the NFB, which is especially renowned for its documentary and animated productions.

Poetics
www.elsevier.nl/inca/publications/store/5/0/5/5/9/2/
The electronic version of the journal *Poetics: Journal of Empirical Research on Culture, Media and the Arts* is here.

UNESCO
www.unesco.org
The United Nations Educational, Scientific and Cultural Organization deals with, among others, issues of cultural diversity and preservation.

Chapter 4

Socialization

Sue Wilson

Learning Objectives

In this chapter, you will:

- Gain an understanding of the process of socialization.
- Understand and develop the capacity to apply basic concepts in the study of socialization.
- Reflect on personal experiences growing up in terms of socialization.
- Think about ways the hidden curriculum in educational institutions reproduces inequalities of gender, class, and race.
- Think critically about the ways in which the media both shape and reinforce social values.
- Learn about the National Longitudinal Survey of Children and Youth as a resource for studying Canadian children.

Photo: World of Stock

Introduction

Peter Berger (Berger and Berger, 1975) defined **socialization** as the process by which people learn to become members of society. For every individual, this process starts at birth and continues throughout life.

The most intense period of socialization is infancy and early childhood. Almost from the moment of birth, children begin to learn the basics of **social interaction**; they learn to recognize and respond socially to parents and other important people in their lives. In the process of interacting with parents, siblings, and other caregivers, children typically acquire the necessary cognitive and emotional skills to get along in their society. Moreover, as they adjust to daily routines, they learn to conform to adult expectations about a wide range of behaviour: where and when to sleep and eat, what to wear and play with, what is funny and what is serious, and so on. At the same time, children develop an individual **identity**, a self-concept.

Language is an important aspect of socialization. As children learn to understand words and later to use them, they simultaneously learn to categorize their experience. Children also begin at an early age to evaluate their own behaviour and that of others. Indeed, one of the first words many children say is NO!

In time, children learn to identify social **roles**—first the roles of family members, and later, as their experience broadens, those of others with whom they interact. They begin to identify consistent patterns in relatives, teachers, doctors, religious leaders, and to know how they should act around these others. They also develop an understanding of status differences and the ways in which roles interact with **race**, **class**, and **gender** to create a complex social structure. When children respond appropriately, conforming to social expectations, they are said to have internalized behavioural **norms**.

Socialization patterns vary with class, ethnicity, family structure, gender, and birth order. The way people are socialized is therefore affected by whether they grow up in Vancouver or Moncton; whether they speak English or Cantonese at home; whether they worship at a church, a synagogue, a mosque, or not at all; whether they grow up in a single-parent or a two-parent household; and whether their parents are strict or lenient in their discipline, among many other factors. Despite such

Early childhood socialization, based on a close attachment between child and regular caregiver, sets the stage for all later personality development and social adjustment. (iStockphoto)

differences, the research cited throughout this chapter shows that there are certain interesting patterns in socialization practices and outcomes. According to Eleanor Maccoby, for example, as a result of socialization, most people acquire a package of attitudes, skills, and behaviours that enable them to '(a) avoid deviant behaviour; (b) contribute, through work, to the economic support of self and family; (c) form and sustain close relationships with others; and (d) be able to rear children in turn' (1992: 1006).

Parents (or parent substitutes) control much of the early learning environment of their children. But children are not simply passive receptors in the processes of socialization. Because of individual differences, some children thrive on routine; others resent it. Some grow up wanting to be like their parents; others react against parental models. Even within the same family, children will experience socialization differently.

Socialization, then, occurs in the process of social interaction. The two major accomplishments of socialization are the development of a self-concept and the internalization of social expectations. This chapter will examine some of the processes by which the complex learning that is socialization occurs and will discuss a number of theories of socialization. As you will see, families, schools, peer groups, and the media all play a part in socializing children. Moreover, adolescent socialization is a process that prepares young people for adult family and employment responsibilities. The chapter closes with a brief look at future directions in socialization.

Forms of Socialization

Socialization is complex and multi-dimensional. In many ways, socialization is an umbrella concept: it takes in all social contacts and continues from birth to death. This section will consider the various forms of socialization experienced throughout life.

Primary Socialization

The most intense learning, **primary socialization**, occurs from birth through adolescence. The family is the most important agent of primary socialization. This socialization is both intentional and unintentional, imposed and reciprocal. Parents socialize their children intentionally in countless ways as they teach them how and what to eat, what to wear, what to play with, what is funny, what is sad, how to address and treat others, which behaviours are rewarded and which punished, and so on. At the same time, unintentional socialization takes place as children learn about power and authority; gender, age, class, and ethnic differences; love, affection, and intimacy. Furthermore, the family's status in the community will affect the responses of others to the child, as well as where and with whom the child will play or go to school.

Although it is not entirely a 'top-down' process, primary socialization is largely imposed, because children have less power and are less competent than adults. Yet, although the relationship is far from equal, there will be some elements of reciprocity in parent–child interactions. On the other hand, the relative power of parents will not guarantee socialization outcomes: children do not simply absorb life lessons from their parents.

Secondary Socialization

Secondary socialization is an ongoing process of 'recalibrating' throughout the life cycle as people anticipate and adjust to new experiences and new situations. In changing jobs, marrying, having children, coping with life crises, and so on, people are continually being socialized.

In many ways, socialization is a reciprocal process: children learn from their parents, but parents also learn from their children. Thus, as children learn social interaction from their parents, parents learn how to parent. Reciprocal socialization is not confined to parents and children. Students learn from teachers, teachers from students. Family members, friends, and co-workers also socialize one another. In learning related to digital media, children are typically far more sophisticated than their parents and teachers. Much of this high-tech learning will involve children teaching adults.

Settersten (2003: 16) suggests that the life course provides a lens that shifts attention from a primary focus on childhood socialization to 'what adults learn in the central settings of their lives, why they learn it and how they learn it'. As Settersten points out, 'the socialization experience in childhood and adolescence is clearly not enough to meet the demands of the adult years' (ibid.). In many cases, what is learned in childhood is outdated by adulthood.

In early adulthood we acquire new work and family statuses. Status losses (e.g., divorce or widowhood, the death of friends or retirement) are more likely to occur later in life (ibid., 21). Not all status losses carry regret. Some people will look forward to retirement or an empty nest. Some will move on with anticipation following divorce.

Adult socialization differs from childhood socialization because it is based on accumulated learning and

IN THE FIRST PERSON

I could reconstruct my career as a series of logical steps, although of course that is not what happened. Two or three threads have guided my choices over the years. The first is that I have always been passionate about applied sociology—the *so whats?* and *what ifs?* of the body of knowledge that is sociology. So while it might seem odd from the outside for a sociologist to find an academic home in a School of Nutrition, doing community-based research, the opportunity was indeed like coming home for me. I am privileged to work in an institution that is vibrant, and full of possibilities, on projects that are wide-ranging and—most importantly—personally relevant. Along the way I worked with hundreds of wonderful students, and students who became colleagues. I recently had the chance to work on a project about feminist mothers and daughters with my daughter! It's been fun and it's been interesting—I couldn't ask more of working life.—Sue Wilson

previous experience. Frances Waksler likens the difference between primary and secondary socialization to the difference between being born into a religion and converting from one religion to another: 'In the latter process, one has both more choice (e.g., the very choice of converting or abandoning the endeavour) and more limits (e.g., the difficulty or even impossibility of coming to believe something that one had previously thought unbelievable)' (1991: 14).

Anticipatory Socialization

In most situations, previous experience provides the capacity to imagine new experiences, so people become adept at **anticipatory socialization**. People mentally prepare themselves for future roles and responsibilities by means of anticipatory socialization, which Robert K. Merton defined as 'the acquisition of values and orientations found in statuses and groups in which one is not yet engaged but which one is likely to enter' (1968: 438–9). Many college and university students, for instance, are engaged in anticipatory socialization as they acquire necessary academic skills and credentials for their future occupations.

The effectiveness of anticipatory socialization will depend on the degree of ambiguity of a new situation, as well as on its similarity to previous experience. According to Diane Bush and Roberta Simmons, 'if the individual is prepared ahead of time for a new role, in the sense of understanding the norms associated with the role, having the necessary skills to carry it out, and becoming aware of expectations and rewards attached to the role . . . he or she will move into the new role easily and effectively' (1981: 147). This sums up very well the assumption underlying the concept of anticipatory socialization.

Many vehicles exist to ease the process of anticipatory socialization. Familiar examples include high school and university initiation, new employee orientation programs, parenting courses, and pre-retirement courses.

Resocialization

Most people would not be able to anticipate successfully what it would be like to join the armed forces or a religious cult, to experience the sudden death of a loved one, or to be fired. When people encounter such situations, they must learn new rules. When new situations are so unique that people cannot rely on their previous experience to anticipate how to act, they may encounter a period of **resocialization**.

Some institutions, such as prisons and psychiatric hospitals, are specifically designed to resocialize 'deviants'. Timothy Seiber and Andrew Gordon (1981) introduced the idea of socializing organizations as a way of understanding socialization. Socializing organizations include total institutions such as prisons, as well as schools, job-training programs, counselling centres, and voluntary associations. These organizations are formally mandated to bring about some change in their members, but often the explicitly stated aims are less important than the latent messages they impart. In the words of Seiber and Gordon, 'as recruits participate in the organization they learn its social and speech etiquettes, modes of self-presentation, rituals, routines, symbolic codes of deference, and other patterns of social relations' (1981: 7).

Prisons and other 'total institutions' try to resocialize people who have been unable or unwilling to obey society's rules. In practice, these efforts are often unsuccessful and carry undesired, unexpected side effects. (John Zich/Corbis)

Therapy or self-help groups are significant sources of change for adults as they initiate self-resocialization to replace old beliefs with new ones. 'For many, adulthood is a period of recovery from negative childhood experiences; it is a period in which problematic early socialization must be unlearned and relearned' (Settersten, 2003: 33).

Theories of Socialization

The questions sociologists ask, and often the methods they use, depend on which theoretical perspective they adopt. Some sociologists take **social structure** as their point of departure; others begin with individual interaction. Alan Dawe calls these two approaches, respectively, the *sociology of social system* and the *sociology of social action*: 'One views action as the derivative of system whilst the other views system as the derivative of action' (1970: 214).

These two contrasting views of socialization are the focus of this section. The sociology of social system—'action as the derivative of system'—is best represented by the functionalism of Talcott Parsons (1955), who was interested in how individuals internalize social norms and become conforming members of society. **Symbolic interactionism**, by contrast with functionalism, explains how individual self-concepts develop in the process of social interaction.

Time to Reflect

Explain the difference between primary and secondary socialization. Think of an occasion when you have gone through an experience of resocialization. Perhaps it was moving away from home to attend university or college. What aspects of your early socialization had to be 'unlearned and relearned'?

The Functionalist Perspective

Sociologists who take the functionalist perspective, such as Talcott Parsons, describe socialization as a process of internalizing socially approved norms and behavioural expectations. People who grow up in a particular culture internalize a similar set of norms and values. The more widespread their acceptance, the more smoothly the group will function. Sociologists refer to a smooth outcome as *social integration.*

According to functionalist thinking, conformity is the consequence of internalizing behavioural expectations. This sounds very deterministic—as if norms necessarily make individuals conform. Indeed, the functionalist emphasis on individual conformity to group norms amounts to, as Dennis Wrong (1961) put it, 'an oversocialized view' of humankind. To say that people are socialized does not imply that they have been completely moulded by the norms and values of their culture.

The Feminist Critique

Sexist socialization practices were one of the first targets of **feminist** critiques of sociology in the 1970s. Feminists were highly critical of Parsonian analysis because of the implication that differences between men and women could be understood as differences in socialization. In the first place, to describe inequities as the result of socialization avoided the issue of the structural barriers faced by women. Second, the socialization approach begged the question of change: how could parents socialized in traditional ways adopt non-sexist child-rearing practices? Therefore, feminists typically do not use socialization to explain gender differences, viewing them instead as consequences of systemic inequalities.

Gender socialization will be discussed in more detail later in the chapter. An extensive literature documents differential socialization practices, both implicit and explicit, and the ways these contribute to establishing gender differences in adolescents and adults.

The Symbolic Interactionist Perspective

The symbolic interactionist approach, in contrast to the functionalist perspective, assumes that individuals actively participate in their own socialization. George H. Mead and Charles H. Cooley, two American sociologists who were active around the beginning of the twentieth century, were leading figures in developing the symbolic interactionist perspective. Perhaps more than any other theorists, these two men influenced how most sociologists understand socialization.

Both Cooley and Mead were interested in the way individuals develop a sense of **self** and in the importance of family interaction in this process. Cooley believed that children were born with an instinctive capacity for self-development, which matured through interactions in *primary groups*, which he defined as 'characterized by intimate face-to-face association and cooperation' (1962 [1909]: 23).

Adults communicate their attitudes and values to their children primarily through language, and children develop a self-concept on this basis. In other words, people begin to see themselves as they imagine others see them. This sense or awareness—'I feel about me the way I think you think of me'—Cooley called the **looking-glass self**. The looking-glass self has three elements, according to Cooley: 'the imagination of our appearance to the other person; the imagination of his judgment of that appearance; and some sort of self-feeling, such as pride or mortification' (1902: 184). The reaction of others, then, is important in determining how people feel about themselves.

Mead (1934) was also interested in the development of self-concept, which he considered to have two components: the Me, the socially defined self that has internalized society's norms and values, and the I, the spontaneous, creative self. The I is what makes every person different from others. The Me induces people to conform to behavioural expectations.

Mead emphasized the importance of children's imaginative play in early socialization, believing that through play children become sensitive to the responses of others. He believed that people learn symbolically, by taking roles, to present themselves in different social situations. This process consists of four stages. At first, children's behaviour is a combination of instinctive behaviour and imitation. This Mead called the *pre-play stage*. Later, when children pretend to be a parent, teacher, doctor, and the like, they are in effect role-playing. Mead called

Time to Reflect

Why do feminists not consider socialization to be an adequate explanation of gender inequality?

this the *play stage*, in which children learn to assume the roles of others and to objectify that experience by seeing themselves from the point of view of others. In the next stage, the game stage, children learn to handle several roles at once, to anticipate the behaviour of others and the expectations others have of them. Finally, children learn to internalize general social expectations by imagining how any number of others will act and react. At this **generalized other** stage, a child has a sense of self and can react in a socially approved way.

Marlene Mackie (1987) regards the pre-play stage as lasting until the age of about two, the play stage as extending from two until the entry to school, and the game stage as continuing until puberty. Judy Dunn, however, argues that children have an early and sophisticated sense of the emotional states of family members, and respond appropriately. On the basis of her study of British families, Dunn asserts that by two years of age, children have developed 'powers to anticipate the feelings and intentions of other family members' and 'powers to recognize and transgress social rules and to understand that jokes about such transgressions can be shared with other people' (Dunn, 1986: 112). Nonetheless, because social meanings are based on assumptions concerning the understanding and intentions of others, they are always more or less ambiguous and subject to ongoing interpretation and reinterpretation.

Psychological Theories of Socialization

Sociologists owe a considerable debt to psychological theories of development, including the psychoanalytic theories of Sigmund Freud (1856–1939). According to Freud (1973 [1938]), the emotional development of children can be measured as a progression through five stages: oral, anal, phallic, latent, and genital.

The *oral stage* occurs in the first year when children are fed and experience positive sensations through suckling. At this stage, too, children begin to explore the world by putting objects in their mouths. The *anal stage* focuses on toilet training and is the child's first experience with self-control (Collier et al., 1991). Gender differences in development begin at the phallic stage, when children become aware of sex differences. This is followed by a latent period during which a child's sex drive is dormant before being awakened in adolescence.

Phase theories of development that focus on particular life tasks accomplished at specific stages in the life cycle inevitably build on Freud's work. Erik Erikson (1982), for instance, identified eight stages, or 'turning points', from infancy to old age. Each stage involves a conflict whose resolution creates a specific human capacity. For example, in the first phase, infants resolve the conflict between trust and mistrust, developing hope in the process. In the final stage, old age, the conflict is between integrity and despair, and people develop wisdom from the resolution of this conflict.

Another way Freud influenced the thinking of social psychologists was through his theory of personality development (Freud, 1974 [1923]). Indeed, awareness of the three components of personality (the id, the ego, and the superego) has seeped into popular culture and become part of everyday parlance. For Freud, the ego mediates between the id—our basic instincts—and the superego—internalized values. The insight for sociologists is that both the ego and the superego develop socially—in other words, in the process of socialization: 'One of Freud's central theses is that society forces people to suppress basic human impulses such as sex and aggression, so that they must find expression in indirect and often distorted ways' (Collier et al., 1991: 105).

Behavioural theories, by contrast, describe socialization as a process of learning through identification or reinforcement. Reinforcement, typically by parents, encourages some behaviours and discourages others. Albert Bandura (1973), whose work on children's imitation of violence has been very influential, developed his social learning theory based on observations of children imitating parents and other models. While we have all seen children imitating parents, and may have family stories that centre on such imitative behaviour, it is hard to explain all learning in terms of this model.

There are, then, two views of socialization: action as derivative of system, and system as derivative of action. Those who focus on ways individuals *internalize* social norms and values fall into the first group. This perspective was the focus of early feminist critique of socialization theories. Mead and Cooley, in contrast, focus on ways individuals are active participants in socialization—that infants are born with the capacity for self-development. Students interested in understanding more about this topic are encouraged to read original versions of the work of Freud, Mead, Cooley, and Erikson.

● Agents of Socialization ●

Agents of socialization are those social institutions in children's environments that have the greatest effect on their socialization. The principal agents of socialization are the family, friendship or peer groups, the education system, the media, religious institutions, and the neighbourhood or community. The socializing effect of these agents varies over time and is different for different children.

For most children, the family is the most important agent of socialization. Although it is reasonable to assume that children today spend fewer of their preschool years in the exclusive care of a family member, it is still the case that children learn basic life skills and develop their values and beliefs in the course of family interaction. The other important agents of socialization to be discussed here are schools (including daycare centres and preschool), friendship or peer groups, and the media. Parents and schools have legally defined responsibility for socializing children; peer groups do not.

The Family

Most children today have early and extensive experience of the world around them. Nevertheless, the family is still the most impressive agent of socialization. In families, children learn how to relate to other people, express intimacy, and resolve conflict. Parents play a major part in the lifelong social adjustment of their children. To cite Maccoby, 'successful socialization of children involves not only bringing about their outward conformity to parental directives, but also enabling them to become self-regulating, and motivating them so that they become willing to cooperate with parental socialization efforts' (1992: 171).

How do parents encourage their children to internalize social norms and values and to behave in socially appropriate ways? On the surface, it might seem that parental control of scarce resources would be sufficient inducement. However, asserting parental power is only effective in the short term. Longer-term effects are achieved when children have a say in setting the standards with which they are expected to comply (ibid.). The parenting style that seems to be most effective in developing high self-esteem and encouraging self-regulating skills is a combination of warmth and discipline. Diana Baumrind (1971) called this style *authoritative parenting.* Authoritative parents are affectionate but clear in their expectations for pro-social, responsible behaviour. An authoritative parenting style is balanced between the two extremes of authoritarian and permissive parenting.

The family is the child's window to the world. A child's experience of the world will be framed by his or her family's social class, religion, ethnicity, and so on. 'Contemporary families are tall and narrow in form, with many generations alive at once, few members in each generation, and each generation significantly different from each other in age' (Settersten, 2003: 29–30). More of us are part of multi-generational households so that children are socialized by parents, grandparents, siblings, and so on—and they in turn socialize or resocialize their parents, grandparents, and even great-grandparents. Baker (1991) suggests that the influence of dead partners or relatives can be as great or greater than living family members. At best they can be influential role models. At worst they can prevent people from moving on.

Families today are also far more varied structurally than families in the past. More children are born to single women, live in single-parent households, or enter reconstituted families. What effect do these outcomes have on socialization? Do socialization practices differ by type of family? Many researchers have considered these questions. Sociologists Elizabeth Thomson, Sara McLanahan, and Roberta Curtin, for instance, argue that 'the most consistent findings from studies of family structure and socialization are that single parents exert weaker controls and make fewer demands on children than married parents' (Thomson et al., 1992: 368). The researchers wondered why this was so. Was it because one parent can exert only half as much control as two, or because single mothers have not been socialized to display traditional paternal control behaviours? They concluded that socialization differences are determined primarily by the structural conditions of being a single parent, not by gender. In other words, the primary reason for the greater leniency of single parents is their lack of time.

Does parenting style matter? According to the National Longitudinal Survey of Children and Youth, it does indeed. Sarah Landy and Kwok Kwan Tam (1996) looked at the effect of parenting style on children who were also at risk because of family characteristics. Four styles were identified: ineffective, aversive, consistent, and positive. *Ineffective parents* are often annoyed with their children and prone to telling the child he or she is bad, or not as good as others. *Aversive parents* raise their voices when children misbehave and use physical punishment. *Consistent parents* discipline the same way for the same behaviour. *Positive parents* praise their children and play and laugh together. Risk factors that might negatively affect physical or mental development include living in a single-parent household, a teenage mother, family dysfunction, low social support, and low income (Landy and Tam, 1996: 103). Fewer than 4 per cent of the children in the survey were significantly at risk, and these children had four or more risk factors. The authors found that parenting practices had a greater

Time to Reflect

Since families are so influential in early socialization, what chance is there for successful adulthood adjustment for children raised by uncaring and distant parents?

impact on outcomes than risk factors. Indeed, positive parenting practices significantly contribute to child outcomes and protect children who are at risk: 'Children in at-risk situations who enjoyed positive parenting practices achieved [outcome] scores within the average range for children in Canada' (1996: 109). The parenting style that most strongly predicts delinquent behaviour in children aged 8–11 is the ineffective style, followed by the aversive and inconsistent styles (Stevenson, 1999; see also Table 4.1).

Do children learn to be violent from observing their parents? Moss (2004) used the National Longitudinal Survey of Children and Youth (see 'Sociology in Action' box) to investigate the effect of witnessing family violence on children's behaviour. The survey asked the person most knowledgeable—usually the child's mother—how often the child witnessed violence in the home. Although we might expect a certain degree of under-reporting, the results show that 8 per cent of children aged 4–7 witnessed violence at home. Witnessing violence was related to poorer families and lone-parent families. Low education also made a difference. 'Higher rates of witnessing violence were reported for children whose parents gave little positive feedback, or were quite hostile or punitive in their interactions with the child' (Moss, 2004: 14).

Because data in the National Longitudinal Survey of Children and Youth is collected over time it was possible to see the effect of observing violence on subsequent violent behaviour. As we might predict, children who observed violence at home were more likely to show signs of bullying, fighting, and other aggressive behaviours. These children were also more likely to have higher levels of anxiety (ibid.).

Children gradually move beyond their experience of the family. As they become involved in groups in the neighbourhood—other families, playgroups, school classes, church groups, and the like—they gain social experience, deal with conflicting demands, and become increasingly sophisticated social actors. Nevertheless, at the base of this experience of the world is their initial experience of family, which acts as a benchmark throughout life.

Table 4.1 Poor Parenting Practices

	Children with Conduct Disorder	
Parenting Style Used	**Frequency**	**%**
Ineffective	Rarely	4
	Sometimes	24
	Very often	63
Aversive	Rarely	7
	Sometimes	22
	Very often	40
Consistent	Rarely	38
	Sometimes	24
	very often	16
Positive	Rarely	27
	Sometimes	19
	Very Often	14

Source: Adapted from Kathryn Stevenson, 'Family Characteristics of Problem Kids', *Canadian Social Trends* (Winter 1999), Catalogue 11-008, 4.

SOCIOLOGY IN ACTION

The National Longitudinal Survey of Children and Youth

The National Longitudinal Survey of Children and Youth (NLSCY) was initiated in 1994. Its purpose is to follow Canadian children by interviewing them every other year until 2018. The initial national sample comprised 22,500 individuals aged newborn to adult.

Information is gathered about the children and their families from the person most knowledgeable—usually the child's mother. Teachers and school principals also contribute information about school performance. Children aged 10 and 11 are asked about their experiences with friends, family, and school.

The study was designed to support the analysis of child and youth characteristics over time and to allow for the investigation of the impact of social and physical environments on outcome measures such as sociability and success in school.

Longitudinal studies such as this one allow researchers to identify factors in a child's environment that affect later life abilities, capacities, health, and well-being. The NLSCY includes key development indicators such as family composition, employment, economic well-being, parenting styles, and community resources. Some of the research cited in this chapter is taken from this survey. To find out more about the survey, go to the study website: <www.hrdc-drhc.gc.ca/sp-ps/arb-dgra/nlscy-elnej/home.shtml>.

Media

The **mass media**, including newspapers, magazines, television, radio, films, and the Internet, are more than sources of entertainment or information. They are influential agents of socialization. The media are instrumental in transmitting and reinforcing certain values, social behaviours, and definitions of social reality. By focusing on some groups and not others or by stereotyping social characteristics, the media provide important lessons about power and influence. In this way, the media contribute to racial and sexual stereotypes. Stereotyped portrayals of men and women, racial or ethnic minorities, homosexual men or women, older people, or those with varying abilities shape viewer understandings and socialize. The impact is circular. Media representations are indicative of 'who counts' in our society and in turn provide lessons in who counts.

One of the first targets of feminist critique was the media, for contributing to the stereotyping of men and women. One would expect that there would be less stereotyping now than in the past because of this criticism and because women have made economic and political gains in the last four decades. It is therefore surprising to find that television commercials continue to reflect a gender imbalance. Robert Bartsch and colleagues (2000) replicated two earlier studies of stereotyping in television commercials and found that most voice-overs continue to be male, and men are still more likely to appear in all commercials except those advertising domestic products. The authors did find some movement, however. The proportion of male voice-overs dropped from approximately 90 per cent to approximately 70 per cent, and the proportion of women advertising non-domestic products increased (Bartsch et al., 2000: 739–40).

What about advertisements in non-Western media? In India, magazines, not electronic media, are the primary vehicle for advertising. Mallika Das (2000) studied changes in portrayals of men and women in Indian magazine advertisements in 1987, 1990, and 1994. Interestingly, the results showed that the 1990 ads portrayed women in less traditional situations than the earlier or later ads. At the same time, men were portrayed in more traditional ways in 1990 than before or after. In North American media, men and women are most typically shown in athletic roles in advertisements. This is far less evident in India. On the other hand, Indian women are less likely to be portrayed as sex objects than women in British media. Das writes, 'In India the trend seems to be to portray women less often as housewives or concerned with looks, but not more often in non-traditional, career-oriented, or authority figure roles' (2000: 713). Das suggests that this may reflect the patriarchal values of Indian society.

Concern about media violence has been long-standing. Today, concern focuses on violence and pornography in digital media; 20 years ago it was television, particularly music videos; but movies, comics, and magazines have all been considered potentially dangerous sources of influence, especially for young people. In the 1950s, Frederic Wertham published his book *Seduction of the Innocent* (1954) to protest violence in comic books, as there was a concern regarding the popularity of comic books and the rise of violence in the United States. Those concerned about media violence feel that the negative effects of the media are self-evident, that the sheer amount of violence speaks for itself. They are concerned that children will imitate what they see on television or on the Internet. A second, more subtle, more pervasive problem is the media's role in creating definitions of social reality. For example, we may tolerate high levels of violence because we have come to think that 'that's the way life is.'

Media effects have been studied by psychologists in laboratory experiments. Under laboratory conditions, subjects display more aggressive behaviour than control groups when exposed to television portrayals of violence (see Bandura, 1973). It is not clear, however, whether the kinds of imitative behaviour that occur in the laboratory also occur in normal social interaction. Experiments may confidently conclude that the response (aggressive behaviour) was triggered by the stimulus (violent media portrayals) but not that it will also occur outside the lab (Singer and Singer, 2000). In natural set-

Debate continues about the extent to which television socializes young people, and whether the types of resulting socialization (e.g., attitudes to sex and violence) are benign or malignant. (Ivy Images)

tings, the difficulty lies in controlling extraneous variables. In other words, how can we be sure that the behaviour we observed was, in fact, triggered by the media and not by something else?

Two social scientists at the Université de Montréal in Quebec studied the effect of listening to rap music on French-Canadian adolescents (Miranda and Claes, 2004). Adolescents listen to a great deal of rap music—some of which is explicitly anti-social in its messages. Does this encourage anti-social behaviour in young people, or are deviant adolescents drawn to particular kinds of music? The study found that rap music is related to deviant behaviours including violence, street gang involvement, and 'mild' drug use, such as tobacco, alcohol, and cannabis. Rap music that originates from France is more strongly associated with deviant behaviour while hip-hop/soul is significantly linked to less deviant behaviours. Miranda and Claes (2004: 120) suggest that adolescents who already present anti-social values select anti-social music because it reinforces their values. In this regard, it might be noted that rap had its origins in the 'toasts'—belligerent, boastful, misogynist, racist folk poetry—that developed out of the urban US black pimp/drug dealer subculture of a half-century and more ago (see, e.g., Abrahams, 2006 [1964]; Wepman et al., 1976).

Surveys indicate that television takes up the third largest amount of time in our lives, after work or school and sleep. Interestingly, the number of hours Canadians spend watching conventional television has decreased over the past two decades. Canadians watched television for an average of 21.4 hours a week in the fall of 2004—down slightly from 2000 (see Figure 4.1). The average ranged between 23 and 24 hours a week during the 1980s. Young men (aged 18–24) spent the least amount of time watching television—only 12.3 hours a week. Women watched an average of five more hours of television than men, although for both sexes viewing time increased with age (Statistics Canada, 2006a).

Television is the primary medium accessible to young children and is a potent agent of socialization. While we might worry about the amount of television children watch and about the way television contributes to a sedentary lifestyle, the amount of time children spend watching television has, like adult viewing, decreased. According to Statistics Canada figures, adolescents watch an average of 12.9 hours a week and children watch 14.1 hours. Both averages have dropped since 2000. One reason for the drop in viewing time was the cancellation of the 2004–5 NHL hockey season. Another obvious reason is the increased use of the Inter-

Figure 4.1 Average Weekly Hours of Television Viewing, Canada, 1995–2004

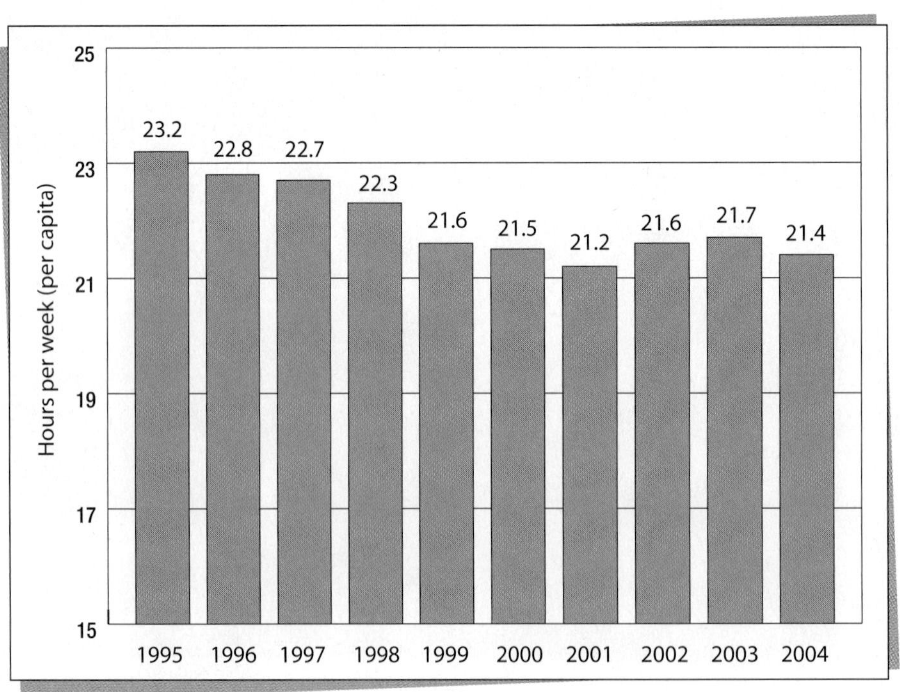

Source: Statistics Canada, 'The Daily', *Television Viewing*, 31 Mar. 2006, at <http://www.statcan.ca/Daily/English/060331/d060331b.htm>.

net. Unfortunately, the survey did not ask about time spent playing video games, so we can only guess that this preoccupation accounts for another part of the decline.

In 1997, Statistics Canada began to collect data about Internet use. The 2004 Canadian Internet Use Survey, which included 30,000 respondents, provides an interesting picture of Internet use in Canada. In 2005, 61 per cent of Canadian households were connected to the Internet. Internet use is related to income, education, age, and having children living at home (Statistics Canada, 2006b).

In his book *Growing Up Digital*, Don Tapscott (1998) refers to what demographers have called the *baby-boom echo generation* (born between 1977 and 1997) as the *Net generation*. The media sometimes call this group *screenagers*. While their parents, the baby-boom generation, were shaped by television, which influenced their values, their political beliefs, and how they spent their leisure time, the Net generation are immersed in digital media, with perhaps more far-reaching effects, for digital media are an educational tool in a way that television was never able to be. The Net generation also use the Internet to communicate with friends and to establish and maintain community. Young people have, according to Tapscott, become bored with the unidirectional medium of television, preferring the engagement required by digital technology. Indeed, they watch far less television than their parents did when they were young. The Net gener-

GLOBAL ISSUES

Children's Preference for Violent Media

The media are important contributors to children's socialization experiences. Because characters in children's television reflect gender stereotypes, including aggressive male behaviour, they perpetuate the stereotypes and contribute to a cultural climate of aggressive and stereotypical behaviour. This is a universal observation, not one limited to North American media. A number of studies conclude that early viewing of television violence is associated with aggressive behaviour in adolescence (Knobloch et al., 2005: 124). It is not clear to what extent media self-selection on the part of children influences the socializing effect of the content. In modern societies, children are technologically sophisticated and have some control over the media they watch. It is quite possible that children's selective exposure to particular media content cultivates behaviour reflecting that content.

Knobloch and colleagues recently published a cross-cultural study of children's media choices. The three societies studied were China, Germany, and the United States. The study was conducted in daycare centres and schools. The researchers showed children pairs of videotape covers and asked them which of the two tapes they would like to watch. For six of the choices, one of the tapes was apparently aggressive and one was not. For these choices the protagonist was the same—three were male, three were female.

While it is clear that the kind of media children are drawn to is an important variable in these kinds of studies, very few researchers have asked children about their preferences. More typically, the parents are asked to describe the child's media tastes. Parents' views will inevitably reflect their biases and their need to respond in a socially approved way. An advantage of the study described here is that it asked children about their preferences, not those of their parents.

The researchers hypothesized that boys would prefer violent, competitive content and girls would be drawn to content with more nurturing, co-operative themes. They expected these patterns to be stronger for Chinese children than for Western children.

The findings supported the gender difference in preference for violent or nurturing content. However, there was no difference between China and Western countries in preference for violent content. 'Boys, compared to girls, uniformly across cultures and to the same degree prefer violence' (Knobloch et al., 2005: 130). In other words, boys' preference for violent content begins at an early age and appears to be universal. What is not clear is whether this tendency is due to nurture or nature. Are boys socialized to prefer violence at ages younger than four so that by the time they are in the age group studied—4–6 years old—they have already developed a preference?

ation are also sophisticated users of the new technology, far surpassing their parents or their teachers.

Two aspects of shifting media use are worth noting. The first is that media use is increasingly a solitary activity. Today there are more televisions and fewer people per household. In other words, more people are watching television alone. We also watch more videos and go to fewer movies. Again, going to the movies is usually a social activity; video viewing may not be. Typically, entertainment and communication on the Internet are solitary. The second point concerns what Tapscott (1998) calls the *digital divide*: the class and educational difference in digital media use. This has created a system of information haves and have-nots. The digital divide occurs within societies like Canada and the United States, and it occurs between societies where dramatic differences in access distinguish the developing and the developed world.

The Statistics Canada General Social Survey of 2000 asked Canadians about their Internet use. There were 3,300 young people (aged 15–24) among the respondents, 56 per cent of whom were connected to the Internet at home. Almost half of these young people used the Internet every day. Frequent users also access the Internet at school and at work. Nevertheless, those with home access indicated far more hours of use than those without home access. Men use the Internet for more hours per week than women. E-mail is the most popular Internet activity for young Canadians (Rotermann, 1999: 5–6). Internet use for 15- to 24-year-olds is lower in Quebec than in the rest of Canada. This is presumably because much of the content of the Internet is in English only, a factor that affects usage worldwide.

The Peer Group

Patricia Ramsey writes, 'For both children and adults, friends enhance our pleasure, mitigate our anxieties and broaden our realm of experience' (1991: 3). As you have seen, the family is the first reference group for most people, that is, the group with which children compare their behaviour, ideas, and values. But starting at an early age, the peer group also becomes very important. Because so many parents are now in the labour force, more children are spending more time with children of the same age, and at a younger age. Peer groups have therefore gained increasing recognition as important socializing agents for even very young children. The success of children's peer relationships is linked to their later psychological development and to school success. It has also been suggested that children with poor peer relationships may experience job-related and marital problems in later life (Ramsey, 1991).

Playgroups provide important opportunities for children to learn to relate to others and increase their social skills. By interacting with their peers in playgroups, children develop a frame of reference not based on adult authority. Gerald Handel (1988: 17) asserts that 'it is in these peer groups that a child learns to function more independently, to acquire and test skills and beliefs that earn him a place among people of the same generation, to develop new outlooks that reflect youthful interests rather than adult ones.'

The peer group assumes great influence in adolescence. In developmental terms, the task of adolescents is to begin to establish emotional, social, and economic independence. By the age of 13 or 14, adolescents typically spend most of their leisure time with peers. In an international survey, Klaus Hurrelmann found, for example, that Western adolescents report spending more time talking to peers than on any other single activity—and are happiest doing just this (1989: 16).

Adolescence is commonly depicted as a period of testing limits. It is not a surprise that more adolescents are killed in accidents than die from health-related problems. If we were to rely on the mass media, we might be persuaded that youth violence is increasing in this 'age of Columbine'. Certainly there have been a few spectacular incidents of adolescent violence in Canada and in the United States. On the other hand, official statistics suggest that the incidence of violent crime is declining and that only a small proportion of young people are involved in physical violence. When Canadian sociologist Reginald Bibby surveyed Canadian young people, he found that many were fearful of encountering violence: 22 per cent of young people did not feel safe in school—a smaller proportion than found in comparable US studies (2001: 84, 88; see also Table 4.2).

Time to Reflect

Where does the responsibility lie for ensuring that children are protected from violent television or video content? From sexual predators on the Internet?

Table 4.2 Teens' Concern About Violence by Region, Community Size, and Birthplace (Percentages)

	School Violence a Very Serious Problem	Close Friend Attacked at School	Not Safe at School	Not Safe at Home	Close Friend Physically Abused at Home
Nationally	50	32	22	7	31
British Columbia	51	30	19	7	30
Prairies	49	32	17	5	30
Ontario	53	32	22	7	32
Quebec	43	33	27	7	33
Atlantic	54	30	21	8	27
North	53	34	19	2	31
Cities, towns					
<30,000	53	29	21	8	33
30,000–99,999	56	36	28	7	31
100,000–399,999	51	32	21	7	34
>400,000	44	35	21	5	32
Rural					
Non-farm	52	32	18	7	27
Farm	50	24	19	6	25
Born in Canada	50	31	21	7	32
Born outside Canada	47	35	26	6	28

Source: Reginald W. Bibby, *Canada's Teens* (Toronto: Stoddart, 2001), 84.

Why is it that some adolescents resort to physical violence and others do not? The National Longitudinal Survey of Children and Youth (NLSCY) provides some interesting information about aggressive behaviour among Canadian pre-adolescents. Indeed, children become less, not more, violent as they become older. The age at which children are most likely to hit, bite, or kick was 27 to 29 months (Tremblay et al., 1996: 129), suggesting that most Canadian children 'benefit from the socializing impact of their families and other socialization agencies' (ibid., 130). Children who are physically aggressive are also often hyperactive and suffer inattention problems. They also have lower self-esteem, tend to exhibit high levels of indirect aggression and high emotional disorder, and tend not to help other children (ibid., 132).

Families have an important impact on the aggressive behaviour of pre-adolescents. Boys and girls who have siblings with behavioural problems are more likely to be aggressive themselves. They are also more likely to live in families with high levels of parent–child conflict and sibling conflict. Aggressive children have poor peer relationships and are more likely to be victimized by other aggressors (see Table 4.3). Will these young people outgrow their adolescent behaviour? Richard Tremblay and colleagues (1996) suggest that because the aggression stems from family interaction problems, this appears unlikely. Without support, these children are more likely to continue aggressive behaviour into adulthood. It is, however, important to keep in mind that these children represent a small proportion of all Canadian children. Most children are not inappropriately aggressive. In

Table 4.3 Prevalence of Bullying and Victimization in Canada (Percentages)

	Parent's Report		Children's Self-Report[a]	
	Boys	Girls	Boys	Girls
Ages 4–6				
Bullying	14.4	9.4	–	–
Victimization	4.9	4.4	–	–
Ages 7–9				
Bullying	14.8	7.9	–	–
Victimization	4.0	7.4	–	–
Ages 10–11				
Bullying	13.0	9.2	17.2	8.7
Victimization	8.6	9.1	13.6	8.1

[a] Self-report data were not collected in the 4–6 and 7–9 age groups.
Source: Wendy Craig, Ray Peters, and Roman Konarski, 'Bully and Victim: Child's Play or Unhealthy Schoolyard Behaviour?', from Human Resources and Social Development Canada, *Applied Research Bulletin* (Fall 1999): 17. Reproduced with the permission of Her Majesty the Queen in Right of Canada 2008.

addition, they are, as Bibby (2001) points out, highly resilient. In the face of family problems and economic and educational disadvantage, Canadian adolescents are optimistic about the future.

Judith Harris in *The Nurture Assumption* (1998) argues that children are socialized primarily by other children—not by their families. Others argue that Harris overstates the case. 'Socialization in families is a complex phenomenon encompassing multiple and interacting processes and mechanisms that are manifested in a number of domains with different effects' (Putney and Bengtson, 2003: 179). Although much is made of the idea of adolescent rebellion, there will generally be considerable correspondence between parental and adolescent values. Because parents want their children to be well liked and want good relationships with them, they are generally supportive of their children's activities. Peer-group influence is tempered by parental influence because parents control scarce and valued resources, including their approval. Certainly some adolescents rebel, but for most young people learning to be independent adults, adolescence is not a particularly turbulent time.

School

Schools do more than instruct students in the three R's; they also provide an important environment for the transmission of social values. Next to the family, the school is probably the most important locus of childhood and adolescent socialization because it is central to a young person's social life and acts as a filter for future occupational choice. Children's readiness to learn is an important factor in success at school. A recent study used the National Longitudinal Survey of Children and Youth to look at school readiness among five-year-olds. Not surprisingly there were significant gender differences. In factors that measure school readiness girls showed greater development regarding communication skills and greater attention to self-control and impulsive

Time to Reflect

When does the influence of parents on children's socialization shift to the peer group? Is this transition universal?

behaviour. Boys were more developed in terms of curiosity. Children from affluent homes did better on many dimensions of readiness to learn. However, regardless of income—children who have been read to daily, who have positive interactions with their parents, or who are involved in sports or the arts show greater readiness to learn (Thomas, 2006: 49).

A key component here seems to be the effect of positive reactions by parents and teachers on a child's self-concept. Doris Entwisle and Leslie Hayduck (1988) report that parental and teacher reactions measured in Grade 3 had a significant effect on achievement almost a decade later. As they explain, children in the early grades are building their 'academic self-images'. During transitions, such as starting school, moving, or adjusting to family changes like a new sibling or a parental separation, children depend on significant others—family members, teachers—for support: 'getting off to a good start gives them a competitive advantage from then on' (Entwisle and Hayduck, 1988: 158).

Self-concepts are particularly fragile when adolescents are in middle school (senior public or junior high). David Kinney (1993) reports that older adolescents remember this as a difficult time. Students universally recall a rigid social structure dominated by a popular (and powerful) group. Unpopular adolescents remember being ridiculed, shunned, and ignored by their popular classmates. Fortunately, the impact of popularity is short-lived. In high school, student culture is more open and more diverse. There are far more reference groups with which to identify, and the social structure is less hierarchical (Kinney, 1993).

As children mature, they increase their experiences and contacts. However, these events and associations will not be random but, rather, are largely compatible with earlier experience. It is therefore unlikely that the school environment will promote different values from those already learned by a child. For example, middle-class children will attend school with other middle-class children, who for the most part will value school achievement.

Yet much of what is learned in school is implicit, sometimes referred to as the **hidden curriculum**. The hidden curriculum comprises unspoken rules and practices such as the acclaim given by students and teachers alike to academic versus athletic endeavours and the behaviours that are punished versus those that are excused; the age, sex, race, and ethnic structure of the administration, the teaching staff, and the student body; and the similarity or difference between a student's friends' and his or her family's expectations for the student's success. The greater the disjunction between the behaviours reinforced at school and those reinforced by the family or the peer group, the smaller the likelihood that the student will see success in school as relevant.

Parental involvement, including helping children with homework, encouraging them to study, having contact with the school and teachers, and attending events at the school, has a positive effect on children's academic performance. This relationship holds for younger as well as older students.

Many immigrant parents in particular have high expectations for their children regarding education. As shown in Table 4.4, the majority are actively involved in their children's education and want their children to go to university. Canadian-born children of Canadian-born parents are much less likely to want to choose their children's career or to expect their children to go to university. They are, however, among the most likely parents to help their children with school. L.P. Salazar and colleagues (2001) studied the family socialization processes used by Filipino-Canadian parents living in Winnipeg to motivate their children in school. The children, who were in Grades 7 through 12, completed a self-report questionnaire about parenting styles, parent involvement, the importance of family reputation, attribution of success, and student involvement. The results suggest that student involvement in school was promoted by parental involvement (as perceived by their adolescents) and authoritative (not authoritarian) parenting. Authoritative parents encourage psychological autonomy and exert firm behavioural guidelines. Authoritarian parents, in contrast, are strict, demand obedience, and are emotionally distant. Adolescents indicated that they felt obliged to do well in school to maintain their family reputation. Those students who were concerned about family reputation were inclined to believe that effort and interest, not academic ability, were the basis of student success. That these findings corresponded closely to findings of a study done of Filipino immigrants in San Francisco suggests that, indeed, the emphasis on family reputation as a mediating factor in school success may be characteristic of Filipino adolescent immigrants.

In schools throughout the world, adolescents are 'sorted' during secondary schooling. High school grades and course selection will determine whether a student attends a post-secondary institution, whether he or she graduates, and whether or not the student makes a successful transition to paid employment. One of the most important variables influencing which of these paths is taken is gender.

Table 4.4 Parental Expectations About Education and Career (% of Teens Agreeing)

	Caribbean[a]	Chinese[a]	East European[a]	Latin American[a]	South Asian[a]	Canadian[b]	All
My parent(s) want to choose a career for me	15	26	17	19	26	8	19
My parent(s) expect me to go to university	69	89	70	68	77	45	70
My parent(s) think high marks in school are important	92	87	91	81	90	75	84
I feel a lot of pressure from my parent(s) to do well in school	50	55	49	52	60	45	52
If I have problems at school, my parent(s) are ready to help me	76	64	71	81	78	80	73

[a] Children not born in Canada or whose parents were not born in Canada.

[b] Children born in Canada to Canadian-born parents.

Source: Barbara Helm and Wendy Warren, 'Cultural Heritage and Family Life', *Transition Magazine* (Ottawa: The Vanier Institute of the Family, Sept. 1998): 7. Reprinted by permission of the publisher.

Socialization Outcomes

This section will look at the effects of gender, race, and class on socialization practices. It will also examine how children learn to make gender, race, and class distinctions and how to understand their implications. For children, adolescents, and adults alike, gender identity and perceptions of socio-economic status are fundamental aspects of the development of self-concept. Gender and class infuse social interaction as children develop physically, cognitively, and emotionally and as they anticipate adult family and economic roles.

The Social Reproduction of Gender

Individuals develop an understanding of gender through a complex interweaving of individual and environmental factors, predispositions, and expectations. In the course of gender socialization, children are exposed to many models of behaviour and gain a sense of masculinity or femininity from a variety of sources. Furthermore, individuals receive inconsistent messages even from the same sources.

How much of what we are is determined by socialization, and how much is inborn? This question is often

Time to Reflect

Given the importance of early learning, what if anything can be done in the community to ensure that all children are ready to learn when they enter kindergarten?

referred to as the *'nature versus nurture' debate*. The assumption that nature dominates is called **biological determinism**. The opposite of biological determinism is what is described as 'an oversocialized view' of human nature (Wrong, 1961) that implies that people are largely moulded by their socialization experiences.

In the past, people believed that behavioural differences were largely genetically determined, that children were born with certain aptitudes and dispositions—including a predisposition to good or evil. This assumption of inherent characteristics was taken to apply to differences between races as well as between men and women. This line of reasoning is now regarded as fallacious. It is one thing to suppose that nature helps explain individual differences, quite another to say the same thing about group differences. Nevertheless, the question of nature versus nurture remains a focus of continuing research, with much attention given to differences between females and males. Are sex distinctions in adults better explained in terms of biological differences or in terms of differential socialization?

Gender differences have been the subject of thousands of studies. Much of the research has focused on the behaviour of infants and young children. Reviews of this body of work, including an early review by Eleanor Maccoby and Carole Jacklin (1974) of 1,400 studies, find few behaviours that consistently differentiate males and females. In many cases, studies investigating similar behaviours have had contradictory results. For instance, consistent gender differences have been reported in aggression and in a preference for certain toys. In fact, most studies have found that the actual distinctions between boys and girls are minor. Most children are not aggressive, and they spend most of their time playing with toys that are not gender-related. Furthermore, since boys are handled more roughly from birth onward, it is predictable that there will be some sex-related differences in behaviours such as level of activity or aggressiveness; however, these differences may have more to do with socialization practices than with biology. Most adult behaviours do not have clear antecedents in early childhood. The important differences between adults—**status** distinctions, for example—are unrelated to the differences typically found in children.

Some researchers argue that gender differences develop because of parental reaction to innate differences (see Ruble and Martin, 1998). That is, girls become more verbally skilled because they are more receptive to verbal interactions, while boys become more physically aggressive because they respond more positively to aggressive play. Others argue that parents reinforce behaviour in a way that is consistent with their own expectations and stereotypes. Parents have different expectations of their infant boys and girls in language and in cognitive and social development (see Ruble and Martin, 1998). This may or may not also extend to motor development. E.R. Mondschein, K.E. Adolph, and C.S. Tamis-LeMonda (2000) measured mothers' expectations regarding crawling and compared this to crawling ability. Mothers of boys had higher expectations of their sons than did mothers of daughters regarding the crawling tasks. Although the infant boys and girls in the study did not differ in motor abilities, mothers expected them to differ. This difference in expectation has significant implications for later motor development and risk-taking.

Very young children show sex-stereotyped toy preferences and sex-stereotyped activities. Research evidence seems to favour a socialization explanation. Television ads, catalogue layouts, toy packaging, and the organization of toy departments all seem to collude to steer the toy purchaser in the direction of stereotyped choices. It is no surprise that toys and other aspects of the physical environment of very young children are differentiated according to gender. Andrée Pomerleau and colleagues (1990) found that boys under the age of two tended to be given sports equipment, tools, and large and small vehicles, while girls were presented with dolls, fictional characters, child's furniture, and other toys for manipulation. They also observed the traditional pink–blue differences in the room decoration of the children in their sample.

Socialization is, to a large extent, based on nuance and subtlety. By the age of two, children are perceptive readers of their **social environment**. They observe patterns of interaction in the home, including the genderrelatedness of household tasks. Even in homes where both parents are gainfully employed, women take greater responsibility for housework and child care than men. Socialization to such divisions of labour presumably affects the family and occupational choices of young people. Children grow up with gendered names, toys, clothes, games, and room decorations. By the time they get to school, **gender stereotypes** are well established. The structure and practices of education, then, reinforce rather than challenge these earlier perceptions.

As argued earlier in the chapter, the media are a significant source of gender stereotyping. Studies of media content continue to find that women are under-represented, stereotyped, and trivialized. Susan Losh-Hesselbart (1987) made the interesting discovery that heavy television viewers show more rigidity in gender stereotyping than occa-

HUMAN DIVERSITY

Early Childhood Socialization and 'the Troubles' in Northern Ireland

Protestants and Catholics in Northern Ireland have been engaged in a long period of conflict. From the late 1960s until the mid-1990s the country was engaged in armed conflict, euphemistically called 'the Troubles'. Over 3,600 people died and thousands were injured during this 30-year period (Connolly et al., 2006: 265). A 1994 ceasefire signalled the beginning of a relatively peaceful period.

Little research has been done to find out the impact on young children of living in a divided society like Northern Ireland. One study (Connelly et al., 2002) found that it is not until age five or six that children develop a sense of 'us and them' in such a setting. While three-year-olds in Northern Ireland do not have a strong sense of the divisions, they implicitly have preferences for their respective communities (ibid.). When three-year-olds were shown the British Union flag and the Irish tricolour flag, most of the Protestant children (60 per cent) chose the British flag and the majority of Catholic children (64 per cent) chose the Irish one.

Recently there has been an effort to devise a way to encourage children in Northern Ireland to learn to respect diversity of race, ability, and religion. To this end, three one-minute cartoons were created for television accompanied by curricular materials developed for use in preschool. The program is called the Media Initiative for Children—Northern Ireland. The decision to focus more broadly was taken to gain support for the program. It was anticipated that a program that focused only on religious difference would not gain acceptance among parents and would be stressful for children.

The short cartoons were developed using computer animation. The scripts were crafted by a storyteller respected by both Protestants and Catholics. The cartoons can be viewed on-line (www.pii-mifc.org). The four cartoon characters are Jenny, Jim, Kim, and Tom. Tom wears an eye patch. Kim is Chinese—the largest racial minority group in Northern Ireland. The other two characters wear soccer shirts that represent Protestant and Catholic teams.

(CP/Peter Morrison/AP)

A pilot project conducted in 2004 consisted of running the cartoons on television for six weeks and at the same time introducing the companion curricular materials in selected playgrounds. The evaluation of the pilot program showed that children who took part were better able to recognize instances of exclusion presented to them and better able to say how being excluded makes someone feel. They were also slightly more willing to include a person who was being excluded. Children in the pilot study showed that they were more likely to play with children who were 'different':

> The programme therefore appeared to have achieved some measurable success in terms of encouraging young children to be more inclusive of others in relation to disability and 'race', [but] it did not seem to have had any effect in relation to the third difference—Catholic and Protestant children's attitudes towards one another. (Connolly, 2006: 273)

Children in the pilot group were too young to have formed opinions about 'the other' in religious terms, although they already held such opinions about a child with a disability and a child of a different race. The initiative continues to be used throughout Northern Ireland, with an additional cartoon about bullying planned for the near future.

sional viewers. It is hardly surprising, then, that one of the women's movement's first targets among traditional socialization practices was the gender stereotyping in children's books and television programming. These criticisms have met with some success. A study of children's picture books by Carole Kortenhaus and Jack Demarest found that newer books show a greater representation of female characters: 'Prior to 1970, children's literature contained almost four times as many boys as girls in titles, more than twice as many boys in central roles, almost twice as many boys in pictures, and nearly four times as many male animals as female animals' (1993: 225). After 1970, there were more female characters in all categories—but still not an equal number. Kortenhaus and Demarest also noted that activities depicted in books were strongly stereotyped by sex, with males dominating in instrumental behaviours and females in passive, dependent roles. Again, however, they found some improvement over time.

Childhood experiences have lifelong implications. Patricia Coats and Steven Overman (1992) compared childhood play and other early socialization experiences of women in traditional and non-traditional professions. They found that women in non-traditional fields had received different forms of parental encouragement as children than women in traditional professions. Women in non-traditional (business) professions participated in more competitive activities as children and continued to seek competitive recreational activities as adults. The members of this group also had more male companions when they were children. Interestingly, the fathers of all the professional women encouraged their daughters' competitiveness. Mothers of women who entered non-traditional professions echoed that encouragement, whereas mothers of women who entered traditional professions encouraged more traditional values.

Data from a US intergenerational panel study of parents and children provide an opportunity to see the effect of childhood socialization practices regarding household division of labour on the next generation (Cunningham, 2001). Women in this sample were interviewed first in 1962 and again in 1977, and their 18-year-old daughters were interviewed in 1980. Indeed, the mothers' attitudes during their children's early years had a strong influence on the children's ideal division of household labour at 18. The family division of labour also had an important impact: adolescent women whose fathers had shared housework were more apt to support men's participation in stereotypically female household tasks.

A number of studies support the conclusion that black husbands and fathers do more housework than men of other races. This involvement seems to reflect early 'socialization for competencies' (Penha-Lopes, 2006). Penha-Lopes conducted in-depth interviews with 45 black fathers of young children to find out more about their engagement in housework and how they made sense of their choices. The majority (90 per cent) of the men in the study either shared (did at least 50 per

OPEN FOR DISCUSSION

Do the Media Contribute to Disordered Eating Among Young Adolescent and Pre-adolescent Girls?

Most women in fashion magazines, movies, and television are pencil-thin. Indeed, the media create an impression that thinness is highly valued in Western society. Viewers of all ages use these images as points of comparison when evaluating their own body image. No wonder body dissatisfaction is universal. Kevin Thompson and Leslie Heinberg (1999) connect exposure to unrealistically thin images in magazines and television with body dissatisfaction and disordered eating among girls and women. Their solution is to counter these extreme images: 'The media itself is one potential vehicle for communicating productive, accurate, and deglamorized messages about eating and shape-related disorders' (ibid., 339).

What do you think about this issue? Are girls susceptible to images of ultra-thin models? Are girls more susceptible than young boys? In what other ways besides the mass media is thinness reinforced? How do we reconcile media images with reports of increased numbers of obese children and youth? Does the solution lie, as these authors suggest, in changing the images in the media, or is it a larger and more complex problem?

cent of the housework) or helped (did at least one-third of housework) as adults. They had done housework from the time they were six and by age 10 or 11 were actively involved in cooking and cleaning. Their parents did not have different expectations for sons or daughters, so the men in this study grew up with the expectation that they had a responsibility to help at home. Housework was not sex-typed in the homes they grew up in, 'regardless of their living arrangements, mothers' employment status, and the presence of sisters'. The men in this study 'formed ideas about housework as a matter of competence, self-sufficiency, and masculinity, rather than [as] the exclusive domain of femininity' (ibid., 272).

Gender stereotypes continue to frame our understanding of the social behaviour of males and females from infancy to old age. Minor behavioural and attitudinal differences in childhood are reinforced through adolescence and become pronounced in adults. However subtly, people react to boys and girls, men and women, differently, and in the process encourage different behavioural responses. The differential reactions may be quite unintentional. Parents tend to say they have similar expectations for their children with regard to dependency, aggression, school achievement, and so forth, although fathers are typically more concerned than mothers about gender-typed behaviour in their children.

The gender stereotyping of occupational choices has important implications for a young person's future. Occupational stereotypes frame educational, occupational, and interpersonal choices, especially for women, and are the basis of discriminatory practices in education and the workplace. Nonetheless, significant changes have occurred in the family and in the occupational responsibilities of both women and men during the past three decades. These changes indicate that behaviour can be modified, even for those whose primary socialization was highly traditional.

The Social Reproduction of Race and Class

Racial socialization refers to all of the ways parents shape children's learning about race and race relations (Hughes and Johnson, 2001). Racial socialization is an important component of child-rearing among ethnic and racial-minority families. It appears that efforts to instill racial pride are successful. Generally, children whose parents have emphasized racial pride have higher self-esteem and greater knowledge of their ethnic or racial group (see Marshall, 1995).

Racial socialization, like gender and class socialization, is an iterative process. Children are not simply sponges. Their reactions and needs interact with their parents' own experiences of being socialized and with their parents' experiences in the world to determine parental racial socialization strategies.

D. Hughes and D. Johnson (2001) used reports of 94 dyads of African-American parents and Grade 3, 4, and 5 children to determine if socialization practices were influenced by whether or not children had experienced racial **discrimination**. Most parents reported that they talked to their children about their own and other ethnic groups, and most talked to their children about the possibility that the child might experience discrimination. Only about one-fifth of parents reported that they had cautioned or warned their children about other racial or ethnic groups. Hughes and Johnson refer to this strategy of talking about the possibility of discrimination as 'promotion of mistrust'. Not surprisingly, promotion of mistrust was related to parents' reports that their children had received unfair treatment from adults as well as to children's reports of unfair treatment from peers. Interestingly, parental promotion of mistrust was not related to their own experiences of discrimination.

How does racial socialization work when parents and children are of different races? Tracy Robinson (2001) studied this issue by analyzing interviews of white mothers of mixed race (white–Maori) children in New Zealand. These mothers described the importance of exposing their children to both white (*Pakeha*) and Maori culture and their frustration in the face of the discrimination their children experienced. One woman discussed tearfully the difficulty her child encountered in finding an apartment. Her daughter had phenotypical characteristics (brown skin, dark hair, and brown eyes). One day the

Time to Reflect

Why does gender inequality persist? What are the most significant barriers to be overcome in achieving gender equity?

daughter said, 'Mum, you come along with me so that I can get the apartment' (Robinson, 2001: 180).

Another important context of socialization is socio-economic class. The kinds of work adults perform and the coping strategies they employ to make sense of their work have fundamental implications for the socialization of their children. As in gender socialization, children begin at a very young age to absorb the implications of class in society. They learn early 'who counts' and where they fit into the social hierarchy.

Alwin (1990) argues that there was a general shift in North American parental values over the five decades leading up to his study. Whereas parents used to want their children to be obedient and conforming, they were now more inclined to want to instill a sense of independence or autonomy. He looked at five studies measuring parental socialization values from the 1920s through the 1980s. Public opinion surveys done in Detroit in 1958, 1971, and 1983 revealed some interesting differences (Alwin, 1984). Parents were asked the following question:

If you had to choose, which thing would you pick as the most important for a child to learn to prepare him for life?
(a) to obey
(b) to be well-liked or popular
(c) to think for himself
(d) to work hard
(e) to help others when they need help. (Ibid., 365)

Respondents were asked to rank their top four choices. Alwin found that 'to think for himself' was the most preferred quality and that the number of parents citing it as most important increased over time. 'To be well-liked or popular' was the least preferred and became even less important over time. Obedience also decreased in importance, while hard work increased. The number of parents who valued the quality of helpfulness remained stable. In other Western countries, too, there seems to be a similar parental concern for developing independence in children (Alwin, 1990).

The transition from school to work is a rite of passage into adulthood. It is also a period of anxiety as students try to figure out how to turn their academic credentials into wages. (Tim Mantoani/Masterfile)

What accounts for this shift in focus? Alwin feels it results partly from increased education, partly from increased secularization. Predictably, increased education is associated with the valuation of autonomy and with a decrease in the value of conformity. Parental preference for obedience is linked to levels of church attendance, which have declined over recent decades. Finally, it is interesting that some evidence exists that the youngest cohorts are slightly more inclined towards conformity and obedience than older cohorts. Nevertheless, parental values are only one part of the equation. Myriad factors combine to influence children's behaviour. The fact that parents claim to value self-reliant behaviour does not necessarily imply that children will respond accordingly.

Social Reproduction of Adult Family and Work Roles

Childhood, adolescence, and adulthood are social constructs that broadly define periods of social, psychological, and biological development. They are generally, but not absolutely, determined by age. Because life-cycle stages do not follow a predictable or orderly track, there is no specific point at which an adolescent is declared to be an adult, for example. Some young people will have assumed adult roles of marriage, parenthood, or economic independence before their eighteenth birthday. Others remain in school and financially dependent on parents well into their twenties. Still others return to the parental home after divorce or job loss. Some of these adult children will have children themselves, thus creating a temporary three-generation household. During the past quarter-century, the transition from adolescence to adulthood has been altered by such trends as increased schooling and a rise in the age at first marriage. Now, young adults enjoy a period of independent living before marriage. Two or three decades ago, this period of independence was shorter, as both men and women typically married in their early twenties. Ceremonies such as graduation or marriage may therefore be more appropriate than age as signals of the transition to adulthood.

José Machado Pais (2000) has argued that the transition to adulthood takes longer now than in the past. One of the reasons for this is uncertainty about future education, work, and family roles. The transitional process from youth to adulthood is affected by past socialization experiences and by expectations about the future. To the extent that the future appears uncertain, the transition to adulthood is stalled. Leaving school, starting a job, or making a commitment to a relationship does not necessarily signal permanent departure or the assumption of adult responsibilities.

A second characteristic of the transition to adulthood today is that it is reversible. Education, employment, relationships, and living arrangements all are more transitory than they were in the past; young people may return to school, or again live with parents at the end of a romantic or employment relationship. Pais calls this reversibility the 'yo-yo-ization' of the transition to adulthood. Parents of youth in transition are also affected by this pattern because of the societal dominance of youth culture. Parents adopt aspects of youth culture in an effort to forestall aging.

One of the greatest challenges of adolescence is preparation for adult family and work responsibilities. Dating is one of the vehicles for this learning. Even though dating is much less formal than it was in the past, it still helps develop social and communication skills and contributes to the development of self-esteem. In our culture, dating provides opportunities for anticipatory socialization for future cohabitation or marriage.

Adolescents are also required to make decisions about educational options that will affect their future opportunities in the labour force. While not irreversible, decisions such as quitting school or selecting math and science rather than languages and history will open some doors and close others.

Not all of the socialization children receive for adult roles is positive. For instance, violent or abusive adults have internalized this inappropriate response to stress or frustration through socialization. In the area of family violence, researchers have just begun to clarify the links between experiences in childhood and adult behaviour. Judith Seltzer and Debra Kalmuss predicted that people who have experienced violence in their homes as children 'may incorporate abuse into the behavioural repertoires they bring to intimate relationships that they establish in adulthood' (1988: 475). Their findings support this prediction: 'Early childhood exposure to family violence has a substantially greater effect on spouse abuse than does . . . exposure to recent stressful experiences or chronic economic strain' (ibid., 487). Furthermore, observing parents' marital aggression has more of an effect on children than being hit by a parent.

However, the relationship is not absolute. Some adults have violent marriages even though they did not grow up in violent homes. Moreover, not all children growing up in such homes become abusive adults. Extra-familial socialization agents, including peer groups, dating partners, and the media, explain the discrepancies (ibid.).

Socialization for Parenthood

Do adolescent boys and girls anticipate parenthood differently? A New Zealand study by Barbara Calvert and Warren Stanton found considerable evidence to support the conclusion that adolescent males and females were equally committed to becoming parents. Among the respondents, 89 per cent answered 'Yes' to the question, 'Would you like to have children of your own?' When asked whether they would want to adopt if they were unable to have children, 83 per cent of the girls and 72 per cent of the boys answered in the affirmative (Calvert and Stanton, 1992: 317). Both boys and girls wanted to have their first child when they were in their mid-twenties, and both genders listed 'fond of children' as an important quality in a spouse. All the young people in the study expected to combine family and employment responsibilities, although the majority thought that, ideally, one parent should stay home with young children. Interestingly, 82 per cent of the boys and 85 per cent of the girls said it did not matter whether the mother or the father was the caregiving parent (ibid., 319). Other responses indicated that both girls and boys expected both parents to nurture and perform child-care tasks.

The major gender difference between these teenagers was not in attitudes, but in experience; the boys had considerably less exposure to young children and less experience in caregiving. As Calvert and Stanton suggest, this difference could result in a definition of the women as more expert and promote a gendered division of labour when the adolescents form families of their own. The study also found strong evidence to suggest that children will be strongly influenced by the child-rearing practices to which they were exposed when growing up: 'Most respondents expected to do pretty much as their parents had done' (ibid., 325).

Studies of new parents find that many are ill-prepared for the time and energy demands of caring for a newborn. Not surprisingly, Renee Steffensmeier (1982) found that anticipatory socialization had a significant effect on the transition to parenthood. The more previous experience new parents had, or the better they were prepared by training for the experience of parenting, the more satisfying they found it. Jay Belsky (1985) found that women were more likely than men to experience a disjunction between their expectations and their experiences regarding childbirth and, consequently, to report less satisfaction. Since women hold the greatest responsibility for infant care, this is hardly surprising. While the household division of labour tends to become more traditional following birth, the mothers in Belsky's sample were more involved in infant care relative to the fathers than either the mothers or the fathers had anticipated, and this was a major source of dissatisfaction.

While most men marry, and while attitude surveys indicate that men give high priority to family life, early socialization does little to prepare them to be fathers. To some extent, low involvement by fathers is a self-fulfilling prophecy. Men have very little preparation for the care of infants or young children, and they are likely to feel awkward; they therefore experience failure in their attempts to help. Alice Rossi's investigations of interactions between fathers and infants suggest that men 'tend to avoid high involvement in infant care because infants do not respond to their repertoire of skills and men have difficulty acquiring the skills needed to comfort the infant' (Rossi, 1984: 8). She sees a solution in teaching fathers about parenting and so encouraging their participation. Rossi assumes that men are not more active parents because they have not been socialized to anticipate this role.

In recent years, it has become more the rule than the exception for fathers to attend prenatal classes, to assist during labour, and to be present during the birth of their child. Other trends, such as high divorce rates, have brought about an increase in the number of 'weekend fathers'—divorced men who have periodic responsibility for their children. Such parenting experiences seem to pave the way for increased male involvement in child care.

However, no amount of compensatory socialization will alter the structural barriers to equal involvement in child care and other domestic tasks. Primary caregiving fathers in a study in Australia had made a decision to be involved in child-rearing and household tasks, although only half the sample defined housework and child care as

Time to Reflect

How could we better prepare young men for fatherhood and the sharing of domestic tasks? Why are black men more involved in housework than men in other races? Will this change in future?

their primary tasks (Grbich, 1992). In Australia, the role of caregiver is not considered appropriate for men. The fathers all recognized that parenting and housework have low status, and one-third of them were uncomfortable with their role for this reason. Some of the fathers mentioned that they received verbal put-downs from neighbours, shopkeepers, and others. They reported a number of subtle tactics used to marginalize them, including sexual labelling, avoidance, ostracism, active confrontation, lowered expectations of their performance or capabilities, and non-payment of child allowances (ibid.). Clearly, it will take much more than changes in individual behaviour to change the structures of sexual inequality.

Socialization for Employment

Professional schools are important socializing agents for adults. Medical schools in particular have been studied in this regard. What students learn during their years in medical school goes well beyond the acquisition of technical skills: they are learning to behave like doctors. Some researchers, however, feel that the similarities in attitudes and values among medical school graduates have more to do with selective recruitment of middle- and upper-class students than with any training they receive. In their panel study of Canadian medical students, Neena Chappell and Nina Colwill (1981) found that students recruited to medical schools shared certain attitudes at the outset. Interestingly, these viewpoints seemed unrelated to either social class or gender. Although the researchers do not discuss their findings in terms of anticipatory socialization, it seems that a medical student's orientation to the profession begins long before he or she enters medical school.

Frederic Jablin (1984) describes three stages of socialization to employment. The first is the period of *anticipatory socialization.* Prospective employees form expectations about the job on the basis of their education, training, and previous employment. The second stage is the *encounter phase,* during which the employees 'learn the ropes'—what the organization and its members consider to be normal patterns of behaviour. If anticipatory socialization experiences have created an accurate sense of the work environment, the encounter phase will be a relatively smooth transition. From the organization's point of view, effective socialization of new employees is a key to organizational stability. Most organizations therefore formalize the encounter phase through new employee orientation. The final *metamorphosis stage* continues throughout each employee's career in the particular organization.

Much adult socialization is self-initiated. Some is formal, such as the training provided in professional schools or work-related courses; some is informal. Increasingly, formal training is available in areas previously left to the family, the schools, or other agents of socialization, or in areas for which socialization was once taken for granted. Thus, prospective parents can take prenatal and, later, parenting courses, while people anticipating retirement can sign up for courses in retirement planning. When adults join such organizations as Weight Watchers or Parents Without Partners, they do so because they seek the social support these groups provide. It is during transition periods, as one moves from an established role to a new, possibly unexpected role, that this support is most needed.

Future Directions

It is not new to suggest that family life has undergone major changes over the past few decades. Marriage rates have declined, while divorce rates have increased. More couples live together instead of marrying, and more children are born to single mothers. More children live independently, many of them on the street. At the same time, work demands and economic insecurities create stressful situations for many families. In the past decade, increased concern has been expressed for the plight of children worldwide, much of it arising from a concern about family instability and change. Thus, in the future, we might expect more research to focus on understanding the dynamics of early childhood development and socialization in order to provide the kind of support to families that will optimize their positive development.

Sociology has been criticized for not paying sufficient heed to children, but this inattention is likely to change in the future. In an aging society such as that of Canada (and Western nations generally), with birth rates well below replacement levels, children will become an increasingly valued resource. An important goal for the future, then, is to create a central place in the discipline of sociology for children. This place should be based on a deeper understanding of the role of children, not just as recipients of adult socialization practices, but as active agents in the lifelong socialization of the people with whom they interact.

Conclusion

Sociologists view socialization as a lifelong process influenced by all of an individual's social interactions. The two main accomplishments of socialization are the development of a self-concept and the internalization of social expectations.

Sociologists who take the functionalist perspective have tended to describe socialization as being imposed on individuals. By contrast, symbolic interactionists such as Cooley and Mead have helped to shed light on the active engagement of individuals in their own socialization.

All socialization takes place in a social context. For most people, the enduring and intimate nature of family relations makes socialization in the family the most pervasive and consequential experience of childhood. Parent–child interactions are differentiated by class, race, and ethnicity and are framed by the relationships between the family and the community. They are further affected by family size, birth order, family structure, and household composition. Patterns of influence are extremely complex, and become more so as children increase their contacts to include friends, neighbours, and schoolmates. The messages people receive from others are inconsistent and sometimes contradictory, and all draw their own conclusions from these competing influences.

Individual life chances are also strongly influenced by structural variables, the most important of which are gender and social class. Gender and social class have considerable influence on socialization and on the development of self-concept throughout life. The socialization of children and adolescents anticipates their adult work and family responsibilities. The competencies people develop in the course of primary socialization enable them to anticipate, prepare for, and deal with the ups and downs of adulthood.

Questions for Critical Thought

1. Far too many children grow up in the face of societal conflict. When so many children are socialized in this way, is there a realistic hope for peace?
2. What are the implications of the research finding that few characteristics consistently differentiate very young females and males?
3. Why do gender stereotypes persist in the media despite the women's movement, the rise in female labour force participation, and other signs of structural change?
4. Talk to your parents and other family members about what they considered to be important values in your early development. What differences do you anticipate in raising your own children?
5. Ask students who have come to your university or college from another country to describe the resocialization they experienced in making the transition.
6. Can you link early socialization experiences to your decision to attend a post-secondary institution? to the courses you have chosen to focus on? to your anticipated career?
7. As you look back can you identify aspects of the hidden curriculum in your public school, your high school, or your university?
8. What, if anything, can be done to protect children from exposure to inappropriate content on the Internet?

Recommended Readings

Reginald Bibby, *Canada's Teens: Today, Yesterday and Tomorrow* (Toronto: Stoddart, 2001).

Canadian sociologist Reginald Bibby has written a number of books based on his analysis of national surveys. This book documents attitudes and experiences of Canadian teenagers regarding violence, sex, and drugs and compares current patterns to past trends.

Gerald Handel, ed., *Childhood Socialization* (New Brunswick, NJ: Aldine Transaction, 2006).

This is a much-awaited second edition of what has been a classic reference in the study of socialization. The second edition adds 11 new readings to the anthology, retaining nine of the originals.

Margaret Norrie McCain and J. Fraser Mustard, *Reversing the Real Brain Drain: Early Years Study: Final Report* (Toronto: Canadian Institute for Advanced Research, 1999).

This report, commissioned by the government of Ontario, argues that without positive nurturing and stimulation before the age of six, children suffer emotionally, socially, and economically in later life. This is not simply a class problem. The authors argue that many of the approximately 15 per cent of Ontario children who are at risk are middle-class children. The study is available on the Canadian Institute for Advanced Research website or from the Children's Secretariat of the Ontario government.

Mary Pipher, *Reviving Ophelia: Saving the Selves of Adolescent Girls* (New York: Ballantine, 1994).

This book, written by a clinical psychologist, examines the roots of young adolescent women's angst. Pipher addresses the question of young girls' feelings of low self-esteem and the high incidence of depression, suicide, and eating disorders among adolescent girls.

William Pollack, *Real Boys: Rescuing Our Sons from the Myths of Boyhood* (New York: Henry Holt, 1998).

This book is in many ways a companion to *Reviving Ophelia*; it, too, is written by a clinical psychologist. Pollack documents the 'silent crisis' affecting young boys in the United States. Stereotypical expectations of manliness are as damaging to young boys as are stereotypically feminine expectations to young girls.

Don Tapscott, *Growing Up Digital: The Rise of the Net Generation* (New York: McGraw-Hill, 1998).

This book is an examination of the 88 million children of the baby boomers in the United States and Canada to have grown up with the Internet. This generation, Tapscott argues, is destined to be a force for social transformation.

Eleanor Thomas. *Readiness to Learn at School among Five-year-old Children in Canada.* Catalogue no. 89-599-MIE no. 004. (Ottawa: Statistics Canada, 2006).

This Statistics Canada study takes an in-depth look at what factors contribute to school readiness among Canadian five-year-olds and how these vary by social class, gender, and so on.

Douglas Willms, ed., *Vulnerable Children: Findings from the National Longitudinal Survey of Children and Youth* (Edmonton: University of Alberta Press; Hull, Que.: Human Resources Development Canada, Applied Research Branch, 2002).

This is a collection of papers based on the NLSCY, investigating the effect of community, family life, and school on the well-being of Canadian children.

Recommended Websites

Canadian Research Policy Networks
www.cprn.org/cprn.html

The family network at this site is dedicated to advancing public debate on policy issues that have an impact on Canadian families and on the circumstances in which they live. Its research ranges from public values about children and families to broader concerns of social cohesion within communities and society as a whole.

Childcare Resource and Research Unit (CRRU), University of Toronto
www.childcarecanada.org

Here you will find links to information about published and ongoing research, policy developments, and print materials related to child-care policy. The Resources section contains print and web resources, including bibliographies, complete texts of CRRU publications, and links to useful child-care, social policy, and research websites.

Growing Up Digital
www.growingupdigital.com

This website is a companion to Don Tapsott's book of the same title (see above), about those children and youth who have grown up surrounded by digital media. This, according to Tapscott, makes them a force for change. The website includes summaries of the main themes of the book and links to discussion groups related to this topic.

Health Canada
www.healthcanada.ca

Health Canada's website provides links to a wide range of information, including research reports about the health and well-being of Canadians of all ages.

The National Longitudinal Survey of Children and Youth (NLSCY)
www.statcan.ca

The National Longitudinal Survey of Children and Youth (NLSCY) is a comprehensive longitudinal survey designed to measure and track the development and well-being of Canada's children and youth over time.

Statistics Canada
www.statcan.ca

The Statistics Canada website is a fundamental tool for all students of sociology. It provides links to volumes of current information about all aspects of Canadian economic and cultural life. Here is where you will find current data on demographic trends, labour force patterns, consumption, media use, and more.

Today's Parent
www.todaysparent.com

This is the website for the Canadian magazine *Today's Parent.* Despite the advertising, the site contains practical and useful information for parents presented in an accessible way.

Vanier Institute of the Family
www.vifamily.ca

The vision of the Vanier Institute of the Family is to make families as important to the life of Canadian society as they are to the lives of individual Canadians. The Institute advocates on behalf of Canada's 8.4 million families because it believes that families are the key building block of society. This website is designed to help build public understanding of important issues and trends critical to the well-being and healthy functioning of Canadian families.

Chapter 5

Statuses, Roles, and Identities

Cheryl Albas and Dan Albas

Learning Objectives

In this chapter, you will:

- Learn what statuses, roles, and identities are and how they relate to each other.
- Understand how it is possible to interpret statuses, roles, and identities from different theoretical perspectives.
- See how theoretical perspectives concerning statuses, roles, and identities can be used to understand face-to-face interaction in everyday life.
- See how statuses, roles, and identities constrain us and shape us.

Photo: World of Stock

Introduction

To understand sociology we must realize that **social structure** and **social interaction** constitute social life and that theoretical understandings of the nature of how social life is formed and changed are the substance of sociological inquiry. In regard to both of these concepts, the main subsidiary concepts used by theorists are: **statuses**, **roles**, **identities**, **prestige**, and **authority**. Different sociologists use these concepts in a variety of ways to explain human behaviour in society. For example, are statuses, roles, and identities imposed on people from 'above' as Durkheim suggests, or are they invented and negotiated in face-to-face interaction as Mead indicates?

The Social Nature of Status, Role, and Identity

The subjects of this chapter—statuses, identities, and roles—are social attachments we acquire over the course of our lives as we interact with others. **Identities** are the names we give ourselves (female, male; child, adolescent, adult; friend, academic, worker, athlete; attractive, unsociable, ordinary, unusual) or who we announce ourselves to be in word, manner, and appearance that enable others to respond to or place us in particular ways (Stone, 1981).

Our first placement by others is when we are introduced to an expectant audience shortly after birth. As children learn the meaning of this placement by others, they usually identify with it and begin to present (or 'announce') themselves accordingly. By the time they are grown-ups they cannot interact comfortably with others without mutual identification in terms of their gender. Throughout a lifetime of establishing identities, we act parts in the game of life by playing out scripts organized in the form of normative expectations called roles, which are attached to social positions, or statuses. These roles include gender roles, age roles, occupation roles, and a multiplicity of others.

On the one hand, roles provide scripts that permit and oblige us to behave in certain ways. For example, at a party everyone can say, 'It's getting late; I've got to go to sleep'—except the host. On the other hand, roles can be thought of in a more dynamic fashion, as expectations that emerge in the give and take of social interaction. For example, a student reports that during an exam he was passed a note by his friend sitting in the next seat requesting 'help' for a particular question. Terrified that the instructor might notice the interaction, the student attempted to resolve the dilemma by eating the note, mercifully 'very short and written on a small piece of paper' (Albas and Albas, 2005: 25).

Thus, *role enactment*, or *role-playing*, can be viewed either structurally, in terms of fixed expectations, or interactionally, as dynamic and developmental. In other words, we can view social behaviour as the learned performance of scripts that follow agreed-on rules or as negotiated arrangements that people work out with one another to solve unique problems of spontaneous interactions.

What is the use of studying the concepts of roles and identity? The answer is that, as agreed-to expectations for behaviour, roles generally facilitate interaction in society. We don't realize just how dependent we are on **role expectations** to co-ordinate our acts with others until those expectations are violated. Similarly, in order to play roles, we need to know the identities of others as well as our own. Roles may also polarize and distance people from one another. The expectations that persons may hold of others can work as barriers to communication and socialization, also. We need to understand roles in order not to be unwitting slaves to them.

As we will see, roles and identities are complementary and intertwined. The roles we play give us a sense of what and where we are relative to others with whom we interact. This sense of identity allows us to act in ways that are coherent and purposeful. Every role we play has an identity awaiting us, and taking on that identity makes the role come to life. When role expectations are breached, people tend to feel as if trust has been betrayed and may feel bewildered and insecure. Unmet expectations lead us to question who we—and others in the situation—really are.

Consider an example of how roles and identities work. The American sociologist Harold Garfinkel (1997) believed that we could best understand the constraints of social structure by breaking the hidden rules. To do this, he instructed his university students to return to their homes and behave in ways that breached the normal expectations of their family lives, by acting as if they were boarders and their parents were the landlords. Students were to be extremely polite, addressing their parents formally as 'Mr' and 'Mrs' and speaking only when spoken to. Approximately 80 per cent of students who actually went through with the experiment reported that their parents were stupefied, shocked, and embarrassed. Many worried that their children had 'lost their minds'—that the pressures of school, work, and everyday life had 'gotten to them'. Others thought their children were being mean, inconsiderate, and impolite. In short, they couldn't make sense of this rule-breaking behaviour.

In one instance, a father even followed his son to the bedroom and said in a very concerned tone of voice, 'Your mother is right. You don't look well and you're not making sense. You had better get another job that doesn't require such late hours.' The son replied that he appreciated their concern but that he felt fine and only wanted a little privacy. The father went into a rage: 'I don't want any more of that out of you', he shouted. 'And if you can't treat your mother decently, you'd better move out' (Garfinkel, 1997: 401–2).

How can we understand these common, disturbed reactions to **deviance** from the expectations people in society place on us? As was noted in Chapter 1, sociology as a discipline offers a variety of perspectives. Also called *theoretical frames of reference* or **paradigms**, these perspectives vary from theorist to theorist and change from time to time. A number of different problems can be analyzed within the same paradigm, and any one problem can be analyzed from the standpoint of more than one paradigm. All discussions of problems involve concepts—their definitions, the ways they relate to each other, and the logical sense these relationships make for their solutions, in effect, constructing theory.

In this chapter, the focal issues of our theorizing are status, role, and identity and the major theoretical paradigms to be used are **structural functionalism**, **symbolic interactionism**, and **conflict theory**.

Status, Role, and Identity

The Structural-Functional Paradigm

The structural-functional paradigm generally stresses the part played by factors that exist independent of individuals and that constrain them to act, think, or feel in particular ways. From this perspective, the roles of persons in 'real life' are described as 'expected behaviour corresponding to their positions in the "real world"', positions termed 'statuses'. The term *status* is used also to describe society's ranking of roles relative to each other, which, in turn, can determine a corresponding amount of prestige for the individual involved. Prestige adheres to the person who occupies high status and derives from it a degree of authority and the expectation of deference from others.

Émile Durkheim's initial orientation to the concepts of role and status was considerably elaborated, systematized, and reinforced by the anthropologist Ralph Linton (1936) as follows: status is a position to which are attached specific rights and duties, which, in turn, confer reciprocal rights and duties on others who occupy interacting statuses. From this perspective, then, in the case of students and teachers, teachers have the right to expect that students come to classes, are attentive during class, join class discussions, and study conscientiously: these are student duties.

An example of this mutual interplay of status and roles between teacher and students was observed in a large introductory-level university class. Two students started conversing with each other in tones loud enough to interrupt the order of the classroom and to distract the professor; that is, their behaviour constituted a breach of courtesy to the professor, a lack of consideration for other students, and a violation of their duty as students to be attentive. The professor's response to the miscreants was a polite inquiry as to whether they had a question—intended also as a reminder that they were not fulfilling their duties. When the professor returned to lecturing, the students returned to their chatter. After class, the professor stopped them and reminded them of the requirement of considerate behaviour in class and of their duties to the other students in the class, to themselves as students, and to himself (the professor). The professor's suggestion that they no longer sit together in the class was met with the aggressive complaint that 'we weren't doing anything'—a clear breach of the students' duties of basic courtesy to the authority based on his status and a clear indication that they were failing in their own responsibilities to themselves as university students by engaging in disruptive behaviour. Their role enactment as students certainly was not 'ideal' role enactment, and as such, it would be termed 'dysfunctional'.

Students have reciprocal rights and expectations regarding their teachers. They can, for example, expect teachers to demonstrate expertise, mastery, and patience, to show up for class well-prepared, and to treat their students with respect and civility. These rights and obligations are well-known and accepted by everyone. When people do not fully know or embrace these agreed-on rights and duties, interaction breaks down and the situation becomes chaotic and confusing.

However, such breakdowns, at least according to the functional perspective, are remarkably rare. Sociologist Talcott Parsons (1949), perhaps the best-known structural-functionalist theorist, explains this by emphasizing that society is organized around many common values that are the source of stability and social order; this is Durkheim's concept of *exteriority* (1964 [1893]). It is only when socialization is imperfect or inadequate that people break the rules. Then others reinforce conformity by public sanctions, such as shame—Durkheim's concept of *constraint*.

One of Parsons's students, sociologist Robert K. Merton, makes more explicit this structural aspect of society in general, and of roles in particular. In fact, the problem facing us is that we all play so many different roles and, therefore, take on many different rights and responsibilities. Merton terms the specific collections of statuses we occupy status sets and the collections of roles in a specific single status (which Linton did not identify) a *role set*: 'By role-set I mean that complement of role-relationships in which persons are involved by virtue of occupying a particular social status' (Merton, 1957: 110). The multiplicity of statuses and, consequently, of roles individuals occupy and play, respectively, in their lifetimes follow recognizable patterns that Merton terms *status sequences*.

These concepts of role sets, status sets, and status sequences underlie the recognition of order and structure in society as structural functionalists view it. More specifically, for example, a physician's status set may include the collection of statuses of a spouse, a parent, an administrator, and a soccer coach as well as a medical specialist. For each status in this status set, the physician has a number of roles to play, every one of which requires considerable expertise, tact, and discretion for its performance. This collection of roles is termed a role set.

For example, a physician's role in a hospital or medical office involves interaction with a variety of other roles—nurses, paramedics, janitorial staff, clerks, medical colleagues, and patients—each interaction demanding different role behaviour. Consequently, physicians interact differently with each other than they do with other members of the medical team or with patients. Whereas physicians must routinely request that patients remove clothes so that their bodies can be examined, the same request to a ward clerk or nurse would be completely inappropriate to those role sets.

The norms governing the role of physician also demand professional decorum, no matter how dramatic

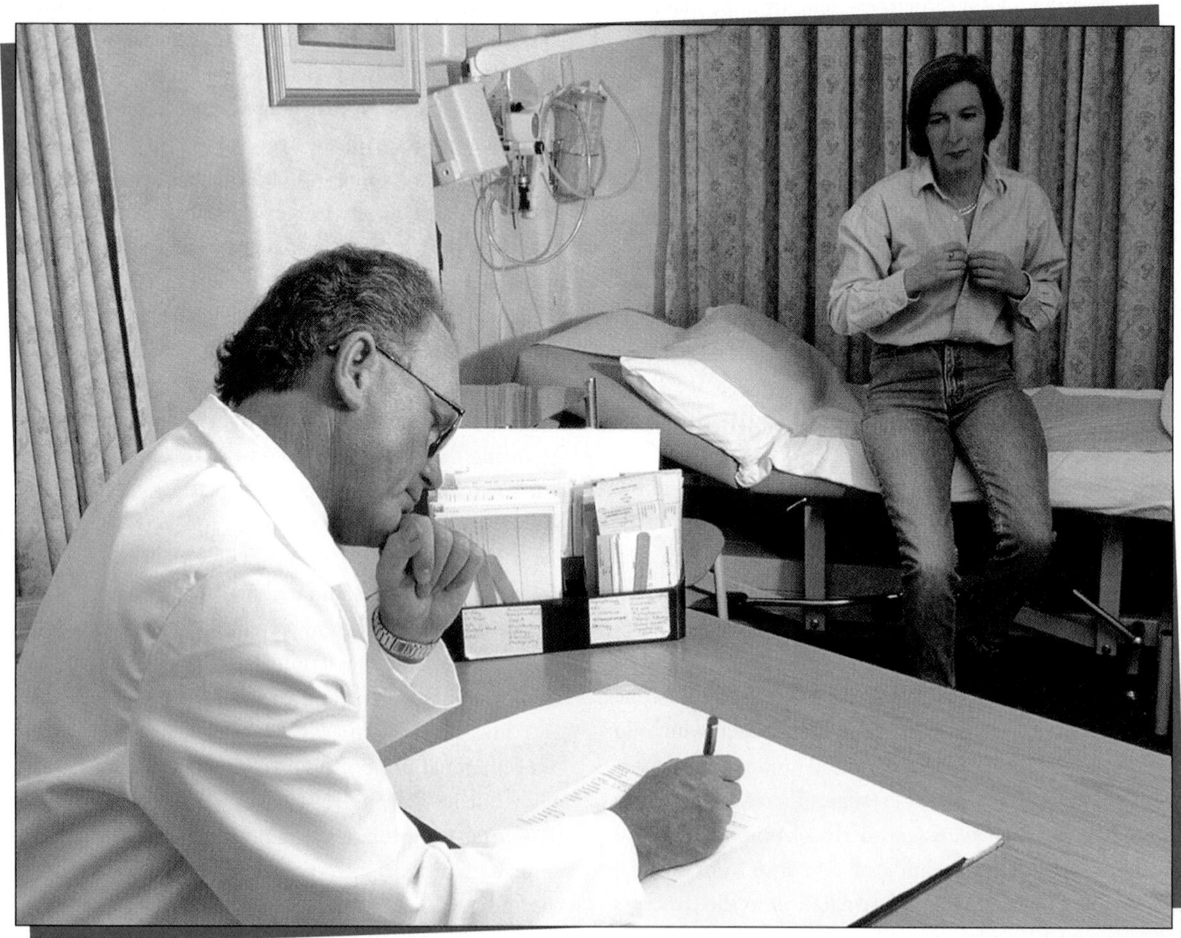

It is precisely because of the clear definition—and regulation—of the physician's role that patients feel confident about undressing and otherwise revealing private, intimate information about themselves. (Image State/Alamy Images)

the circumstances. For example, years ago a plane carrying a soccer team crashed high in the Andes Mountains of South America. The flight was intended to be a short one, so the chartered plane carried no supply of food. The passengers not killed in the crash survived only because they ate the flesh of the others who died during and subsequent to the crash. When rescued and asked by the attending physician what he had been eating during the ordeal, one survivor responded 'human flesh'. The physician indicated that his 'stomach turned' and he felt extreme 'revulsion'—a completely normal reaction to the situation. However, the physician also noted that professional protocol required that he not allow the 'normal' reaction of revulsion to show, so he simply continued with the examination of the survivor as if it were a routine event.

A good synonym for Merton's concept of status sequence is *career*. An individual progresses from high school student to university student to medical intern to medical resident to qualified physician. Each phase of the sequence carries with it specific rights, duties, associated prestige, and authority—generally, medical students do not have the right to carve up patients' bodies without supervision until they become fully fledged surgeons, at which time the carving process will be termed 'surgery' and the knife will be designated a 'scalpel'.

When individuals occupy a number of different statuses and accordingly play a number of different roles, they consequently acquire varying amounts of prestige attached to each. Nonetheless, there is normally a single status and accompanying prestige that most distinctly characterizes each person. Everett C. Hughes (1945) terms the overarching, distinguishing status a **master status** and the other statuses in the status set auxiliary statuses. This distinction was originally used to distinguish occupational statuses from other ones. As Hughes indicates, if we know nothing about a person, the status that tells most about her or him as a whole is occupation, which, in turn, probably provides a very good idea of level of education, income, and lifestyle. The term *master status* is now used not only to cover occupational 'achieved' statuses, which are arrived at by our own efforts, but also 'ascribed' statuses, over which we have no control and that are attributed to us on the basis of characteristics such as sex, appearance, and age.

Role Strain

Despite the tendency towards order just described, a tendency towards disorder in every society and in every life may be observed. When roles compete or even conflict with each other, they produce *role strain* for the person. Strain above a critical level results in distress that we may describe simply as 'stress'. William Goode, Merton's student and a structuralist in the Mertonian tradition, states, 'Role strain—difficulty in meeting given role demands . . . is normal. In general, the individual's total role obligations are over-demanding' (1960: 485). Role strain may undermine the tendency to order and interfere with people's ability to play their roles as expected.

The major sources of strain that constantly challenge the established order include *inadequate socialization*, that is, people simply not knowing the rules of appropriate behaviour. Consider this example: Almost three decades ago, a northern trapper came to the 'big city', and his son took him to a relatively posh restaurant for dinner. On the way home, the father admonished his son, saying, 'You're pretty careless with your money. You left some on the table, but I took care of it.' His isolated northern way of life at that time had taught him nothing about the convention of tipping; as a result, he violated the city restaurant rules. Both parties in this interaction experienced a degree of strain—the father because of his unfamiliarity with the restaurant setting, the son because he then felt responsible for **resocializing** his father.

Another illustration of role strain comes from first-year university students who are inadequately socialized to the 'looseness' of their new role. High schools have fairly tight institutional structures in that the rules students must follow are laid out explicitly and clearly. Students are constantly observed and supervised by teachers and administrators who restrict their behaviour with a variety of rules and sanctions, ranging from mild to severe reprimands and to the ultimate possibilities of reporting them to their parents or expelling them. This tight role is reinforced by daily attendance-taking, specific directions as to pages and paragraphs to be read, and frequent testing.

In contrast, universities, for students, are more loosely structured institutions. Students frequently find themselves unrecognized by instructors who rely heavily on course outlines that specify broad topics to be covered and due dates for exams and assignments. Given the impersonality of the university situation, many students feel as if their instructors don't care how they are doing until the time comes to assign a final grade based on highly weighted, infrequent exams and a major term paper. In the context of this loose structure, many students fail to keep up and fall by the wayside.

Sometimes, role strain is due to a bad fit between personality and the requirements of a role. In this instance, people's natures and personalities clash with the expectations of the new role they are called on to perform. For example, tender-hearted employees may experience personality–role conflict when ordered by their bosses to call customers with outstanding debts and put 'the squeeze' on them even though both are aware that the customer is in dire economic straits. Likewise, highly extroverted students may experience more personality–role conflict than introverted students when it comes to studying because serious study is usually a solitary activity. W. Furneaux notes in a 1957 report that university students who score high on extroversion on personality inventories do not perform as well on examinations as do those who score high on introversion. These differences in performance are not evident in high school. He suggests that stricter supervision (that is, 'tight' role) in high school checks the socializing tendencies of extroverts (see Entwhistle and Entwhistle, 1970).

Role conflict occurs when individuals are called on to play two or more roles that make incompatible demands such that conformity to one role necessarily means violation of the other. For example, an athlete who becomes the coach of the team and is required to select members for the next year will experience role conflict when choices must be made regarding whether to select outstanding new players or buddies and friends from the previous year. A student working for her father during the summer formed friendships with other employees. When those new friends disparaged her father, she found it particularly difficult to cope with roles both of loyal daughter and of friendly co-worker.

Role competition, which can also cause strain, exists for almost everyone because our many and varied roles compete continually for our energy and our time. For example, students might plan to spend a night with their books when friends call and ask them to go out. As long as there is enough time before the exam to study and catch up with work, they think they can do both. However, closer to the exam, they face role overload and must evaluate their roles as students and as friends and decide which roles to prioritize.

The same principle applies to workers—especially women, who are trying to balance multiple roles, such as paid worker, parent, spouse, elder caregiver, and household worker. They, too, are faced with choices between competing tasks and competing loyalties. They experience role overload in terms of their time or energy and must choose the demands of one role at the expense of others. Some women in a study by Hochschild and Machung (1989: 9) spoke longingly of sleep 'the way a hungry person talks about food'.

Merton (1957) identifies some social mechanisms that help people to articulate role sets and status sets more clearly, thus reducing strain. For example, people can appeal to hierarchies already established in society that distinguish between roles and order them in terms of institutional priority. In our society, the student role is valued and given high priority, so families and workplaces often give special concessions to students that allow them more study time.

Another way to reduce role strain is to abide by recognized **power** differences between roles. For example, school principals, who must mediate altercations between teachers and students, are almost always expected to support and defend teachers unless teachers' behaviour actually breaches the legal code for that role as, for example, by sexual misconduct. Few principals who fail to publicly support their teachers survive in their roles for very long. At the same time as this power relationship is being affirmed in the public schools, an aspect of the authority structure of society is publicly confirmed and reinforced.

Sometimes role strain is reduced when roles can be compartmentalized. Thus, families may separate and isolate the affectionate parent role from the affectionate spouse role and compartmentalize them into separate spaces in the home by installing locks on 'master', parental bedrooms.

Finally, role strain can be reduced by providing opportunities for relinquishing a role. When parental roles become overwhelming, some employers allow employees to take time off. Likewise, when life circumstances become generally overwhelming, employees may be granted some form of stress leave or offered compensation if they completely relinquish the role.

As adults performing multiple roles, we function better and make more fully informed choices when we understand what defines those roles, what they involve for ourselves and others, the strains inherent in the roles, the sources of those strains, and, sometimes, the societal mechanisms that can reduce some of those strains. Few of us in modern life have learned to play all our roles as smoothly and effortlessly as we should.

The Interactional Paradigm

The concept of role in sociology was borrowed from the world of the theatre to describe the behaviour of actors playing parts in the drama of life. As Shakespeare wrote in *As You Like It*:

> All the world's a stage,
> And all the men and women merely players.
> They have their exits and their entrances;
> And one man in his time plays many parts.

This analogy suggests two possible avenues of interpretation for the concept of role. In the theatre, an actor speaks or behaves in a particular way that produces a response from other actors on the stage. These speeches and responses were scripts, originally written on rolls (which later came to be called 'roles'), which were spoken and acted out in such a way as to appear dynamic, changing, and spontaneous.

However, the difference between roles in the theatre and the roles people play in everyday life, from the interactional perspective, is that in society actors' roles are not completely scripted. They have opportunities for mutual and reciprocal action and reaction to what other actors say and do. Thus, the social role is really a dynamic one in a constantly changing drama. George Herbert Mead (1934), the first social scientist explicitly to use the concept of role, refers to this ongoing drama as **role-taking**.

Mead and Turner

George Herbert Mead's outstanding contributions to role theory (1934) incorporate the concepts of significant **symbols** (language), role-taking, mind, self, and society. The concepts are linked theoretically as follows. First, intelligent human interaction rests on mutual understanding of the current symbols of meaning in society. Second, during interaction our response to others' behaviour towards us is based on our interpretation of it. Third, a further aspect of role-taking is the impression of **self** provided by the other's reaction to us. Fourth, when we have a distinct sense of self, we can name and recognize objects in the environment and make decisions about the appropriate reaction to them. We make these decisions in the process of an internal conversation with self—what Mead terms a **mind**.

Mead postulates that, as humans, we are universally vulnerable and our only hope for survival rests on our co-operation with others. In new situations, we use ingenuity to develop new ways of co-operating. During a major mine disaster a few years ago in Pennsylvania, nine miners were trapped together underground in one part of the mine. Soon they became hungry, started to suffer from hypothermia, and were in real danger of being swept away by a strong current in the underground river that had broken through the mine wall.

The miners' story of survival made headlines all over the world. We can translate their story into Mead's concepts to understand how their co-operation made survival possible. After 18 hours, when their hopes for rescue seemed bleak, one miner took out a pen, wrote a letter to his wife on the side of a cardboard box he found, and passed the pen around to the other eight miners so they could do likewise. The process of role-taking enabled him to know that they needed and wanted to do the same thing. As experienced underground workers, they were able to relate meaningfully and successfully to all the objects (that is, symbols) surrounding them in the mine shaft. The man's generous gesture generated a strong feeling of camaraderie in the group and created in each man an image of himself as a significant contributor to the enterprise of survival—something that might not have happened without that initial contribution.

As the hypothermia became more pronounced, it was obvious that the men had to find a way to warm themselves or they would perish. Among the multiplicity of work paraphernalia in the mine shaft was a long piece of rope. Despite the fact that in our society males frequently are uncomfortable being in too close bodily contact with each other, the exigencies of their plight overcame any reluctance the miners might have felt and they tied themselves closely together to generate as much body heat as possible to lessen the hypothermia. Thus, according to Mead's terminology, 'mind' was brought to bear on the problem and the most rational alternative employed to solve it. The miners overcame traditional role expectations and created new ones through meaningful interaction. They all survived.

Meadian theory has been considerably refined and extended by Ralph Turner (1962), who regards the more structuralist approach put forth by Linton and Merton as being far too rigid and static. According to Turner, 'The actor is not the occupant of a [fixed] status for which there [are] a neat set of rules—a culture or set of norms—but a person who must act in the perspective supplied in part by his relationship to others whose reactions reflect roles that he must identify' (1962: 23). In effect, Turner shifts the focus from role-playing to the reciprocal joint processes of role-taking and **role-making**. He expands the concept of status from a static one to a dynamic one.

In role-making, we 'devise' performances on the basis of an imputed other role. Role-taking is the gestalt that we impute to be the role the other appears to be devising. As we might expect, there is the possibility of considerable inaccuracy and attempts to reinterpret the imputations involved. Turner refers to this process as 'shifting axis', which involves our continually testing the validity of our presumptions. Actors involved in role-making attempt to create a gestalt for each other so that they can more effectively role-take. To this end, they use the symbolism involved in things such as clothing, gestures, eye contact, and tone of voice to communicate clearly with each other.

A student illustrated the role-making/role-taking process involving a relationship between herself and a male friend, a relationship that, to this point (as she inferred from role-taking), had been on a casual level. They frequently attended movies together, visited in each other's homes, and engaged in games like pool. She assumed it was a non-romantic relationship and that he was a friend because this was the gestalt implied by his actions towards her to that point. Then, one evening as they walked towards a movie theatre, the axis shifted and the friend appeared to transform his role of friend into a role of lover. Instead of just walking side by side, he placed his hand on her upper hip. This unaccustomed and unexpected action on his part shocked her and presented her with a problem of how to validly interpret his role: he was clearly role-making, and she was attempting to role-take accurately, but was uncertain.

Was it an accidental slip of the hand, or was he attempting to demonstrate to approaching friends that they had become a couple? Had the relationship changed from friendship to romance? She looked for cues to help her define an accurate, valid interpretation of the situation: she glanced at him, he looked embarrassed and glanced away quickly, and when he finally did speak it was in a hoarse croak; she then noted with surprise that he was better dressed than usual; and when they reached the theatre, contrary to their custom of 'going dutch', he paid for her ticket to the movie. Further confirmation of the transformation of the relationship into a romantic one occurred when the movie began and he reached for her hand to hold.

Thus, Turner's approach to the concept of role is interactive and symbolic; it involves mutual testing of the images projected by symbols. Because of the tentativeness of meanings, interaction is always highly fluid. Although Turner's role theory deals mainly with interpersonal interaction at the individual level, it can also have a macro aspect in that the 'other' may be the '**generalized other**' constituted by society at large. Even self or 'ego' can be thought of as a group (for example, industrial workers) carrying on role-taking. Relationships between groups, like relationships between individuals, shift constantly and effect changes in the social order (shifting axes).

For example, there is debate in Canada about the amount of painkillers physicians should be allowed to administer to dying patients and whether large doses constitute merciful relief as implied by some physicians and members of the public (role-making) or murderous euthanasia (role-taking) as implied by some other physicians and other members of the public. In at least one instance a physician was prosecuted in the courts for this difference in perception of the therapy. However, a more recent shift in the axes of this perception has resulted in a decrease in the distance between the two points of view. This concordance has been partly achieved by the creation of slightly more clear-cut regulations drawn up by the medical profession for medical personnel to follow—a process that represents a definite change in the public order.

Both theoretical approaches to role—structural and interactional—have weaknesses. The **structural approach** faces difficulties explaining change, and the interactional has difficulty explaining stability. As a result, it is useful to employ them both when analyzing sociological problems.

The Conflict Paradigm

The conflict paradigm emanates from the thinking of Karl Marx (1967 [1867]). Marx considers that the control of the distribution of material goods and the ownership and control of the instruments of production, along with family heritage, produce divisions between the two major classes that, under **capitalism**, could be termed the **bourgeoisie** and the **proletariat**. Bourgeoisie own and control the **means of production** and employ the workers of the proletariat, who are compelled, sometimes by force, to contribute to the maintenance and enhancement of the capital accumulations of their employers. This situation of forceful exploitation of one class by the other, maintained by power and exemplified

Time to Reflect

Mead explains social behaviour on the basis of five concepts: symbols, role-taking, self, mind, society. How would you define each concept? How would Mead synthesize the workings of these concepts in problem-solving? How does Turner employ the concepts of role-taking, role-making, and shifting axes to understand social interaction?

by contrasting lifestyles (comfort and leisure versus impoverishment and toil), leads to hostility on both sides. The bourgeoisie fear the loss or reduction of their profits because of the resentment, lack of co-operation, and even rebellion by the workers who are the source of their profits; the workers come to resent their exploitation, travail, and relative impoverishment.

W. Peter Archibald (1976, 1978) deals with the micro aspects of role from a conflict perspective and focuses on Marx's concept of **alienation** from others (Marx, 1964). According to Archibald, alienation from others is characterized by four features: (1) we feel indifference or separation; (2) when we approach others, it is for narrow, egoistic purposes; (3) when we interact with others, we are more controlled than in control; and (4) when we relate to others, it is with feelings of dissatisfaction and even hostility. Archibald develops these four features in generalizations that can also be considered aspects of the symbolic interactionist paradigm as it is elaborated by Erving Goffman in his chapter 'Nature of Deference and Demeanor' in *Interaction Ritual* (1967).

In the case of indifference or separation—really a detachment generalization—Archibald (1976) notes that people of different classes, statuses, and power groups tend to avoid each other. In factory settings, for example, management tends to have separate maintenance facilities, such as entrances, elevators, washrooms, and cafeterias. Similar principles apply in a **macrosociology** realm. For example, in her historical study of urban transformation, Lyn Lofland indicates that zoning ordinances emerged in the nineteenth century as a 'result of a desire on the part of the upper and middle classes to separate themselves from the "dangerous classes"' (1973: 74). Developers took these sentiments to heart and did their best, creating district after district of similarly valued homes and 'protecting' those values through covenants and 'gentlemen's agreements'.

Archibald (1976) argues that the two classes avoid each other because each feels threatened by the other. The position of the privileged depends on continued deference from the underprivileged. But such compliance is not always assured, and when it is not forthcoming it signals a loss of face and undermines one's superiority. In addition, revealing slips in the presence of subordinates give evidence that one may not be a superior person. People in lower positions feel even more threatened by those in higher positions. Studies (see, e.g., Cohen and Davis, 1973) demonstrate that performing in front of high-status audiences is more anxiety-producing (as measured by the Palmar Sweat Index) than performing before an audience of peers. Interacting with, or at least within hearing distance of, bosses may result in giving out information that can be used against one. Consequently, avoidance is a useful strategy in dealing with enemies and rivals. As Goffman states, 'The surest way for a person to prevent threats to his face is to avoid contacts in which these threats are likely to occur' (1967: 15). Archibald concludes that 'avoidance as a self-protective strategy is . . . a very plausible explanation for the "detachment generalization"' (1976: 822).

Archibald's second principle is the means–ends generalization. That is, when the two classes do interact there is a tendency (especially on the part of subordinates) for it to be on a role-specific basis rather than on a personal basis. As one former student said of his summer job, 'I am a very conscientious worker. When my boss asks me questions pertaining to work I'm happy to answer them . . . they make me look responsible . . . but I don't like him asking questions about my life outside of work. It's none of his business . . . it makes me look

All social situations, especially workplaces, have a backstage area where people can rest, eat, smoke, gossip, and view others. (Profimedia International s.r.o./Alamy Images)

OPEN FOR DISCUSSION

Philip Zimbardo's Stanford Prison Experiment

Commonly held stereotypes portray prisons as pathological places because of the personalities of the prisoners (low impulse control, problematic character structure, sociopathologies) and guards (surly, sadistic, megalomaniac). However, psychologist Philip Zimbardo and colleagues (1972) thought otherwise and suspected that social roles were the major factors in determining prisoner–guard interactions.

To test their hypothesis, they set up a mock prison and advertised in a local newspaper for subjects to participate in a two-week experiment on prison life in return for modest remuneration. All of the more than 75 male applications were subjected to a rigorous screening process to ensure that they were mature, emotionally stable, and 'normal.' From this original group, 21 college students from middle-class homes were selected to participate in the experiment. Approximately half of the subjects (11) were randomly assigned to the status of prison guard, the remainder (10) to the status of prisoner. Guards were issued khaki uniforms, billy clubs, whistles, and handcuffs. Prisoners were dressed in smocks resembling hospital gowns and in nylon stocking caps.

Initially, subjects approached their role-playing in a light-hearted fashion, but it did not take long before they began to fall into stereotypical behaviour characteristic of their roles. The guards became increasingly callous and began to demonstrate inventiveness in the application of arbitrary power (Zimbardo, 1972). They refused prisoners permission to go to the toilet and forced them to do tedious and useless work (such as moving cartons back and forth, and picking thorns out of blankets that had been dragged through thorn bushes). Guards issued commands to prisoners to do push-ups and occasionally stepped on their backs in the process. They also forced prisoners to do humiliating tasks such as scrubbing toilets with bare hands.

As early as the second day, the prisoners began to rebel, and the guards responded with increased force and threats of violence. In turn (given the reciprocal nature of roles), prisoners became increasingly passive and began to 'adopt and accept the guards' negative attitude towards them. . . . The typical prisoner syndrome was one of passivity, dependence, depression, helplessness, and self-depreciation' (Haney, Banks, and Zimbardo, 1973: 79).

The result was that prisoners began to develop serious pathologies. One prisoner developed a psychosomatic skin rash over his whole body, and others developed symptoms of severe depression and acute anxiety. The experiment had to be aborted after six days. As Zimbardo states,

> At the end of only six days we had to close down our mock prison because what we saw was frightening. It was no longer apparent to most of the subjects (or to us) where reality ended and their roles began. The majority had indeed become prisoners or guards. . . . There were dramatic changes in virtually every aspect of their behavior, thinking, and feeling. . . . We saw some (guards) treat others as if they were despicable animals, taking pleasure in cruelty. While other boys (prisoners) became servile, dehumanized robots who thought only of escape, of their own individual survival, and of their mounting hatred for guards. (Zimbardo, 1972: 5)

less responsible and reliable because I'm a teenager who loves to party and drink on weekends.'

This emphasis on role specificity is hypothesized to be the result of a desire, especially on the part of workers, for predictability. When subjects in the research study of J.L. Cohen and J.H. Davis (1973) were told what high-status audiences were looking for (that is, when they experienced role specificity), their anxiety levels were lower than when they were told nothing (that is, when they experienced role diffuseness). Archibald states, 'restricting the number of roles and the scope of activities associated with each role permits one to get some of what one wants from the person in a different class or power position while at the same time minimizing threat' (1976: 820–1).

Once again drawing on Goffman, Archibald (1976) explains that high-status individuals' reliance on the formalities of role relationships helps maintain the status quo. As for the low-status role point of view, Goffman states that 'adherence to the formalities one owes others can be a relatively protective matter, guaranteeing that one's conduct will be accepted by others' (1961b: 128). For example, one student reported that her boss at her summer job always asked her how her weekend was, and she always said something general like 'fine' or 'too short'. This way she was sociable enough to show respect and guarded enough to maintain her privacy. Thus, she not only protected her privacy and smoothed her relationship with her boss (the micro aspect of the interaction) but also maintained the macro system by demonstrating her acceptance and approval of the expected convention. This personal interaction that may seem insignificant can and does have an impact on the wider social system.

Archibald's third principle is the control-purposiveness generalization. Archibald maintains that higher-class, higher-status, and higher-power individuals are more likely than lower-class, lower-status, and lower-power ones to initiate activity and influence others. Goffman notes that 'in American business organizations, the boss may thoughtfully ask the elevator man how his children are, but this entrance into another's life may be blocked to the elevator man, who can appreciate the concern but not return it' (1967: 64). This point about the control-purposiveness generalization is further illustrated by experiments showing that drivers of expensive, high-status cars are more likely to honk at low-status cars in front of them (Diekman et al., 1996). Anthony Doob and Alan Gross (1968) report that when low-status cars stall and block traffic behind them, they are more likely to be honked at than are high-status cars and, in a couple of cases in their study, stalled low-status cars were actually bumped by impatient drivers behind them. The fact that drivers of low-status cars are less likely to initiate such action illustrates conformity to the principle of the control-purposiveness generalization.

On the other hand, William Whyte's 1949 study of the social structure of the restaurant presents an apparent contradiction of Archibald's generalization. In one busy restaurant, the workforce consisted of cooks, other kitchen workers, service pantry workers, bartenders, supervisors, and waitresses. The waitress group was submitted to the greatest level of stress because they came in contact with anywhere from 50 to 100 customers a day, who were frequently in a hurry, impatient, and sometimes verbally abusive; the waitresses also had to deal with the other categories of workers, who were predominantly male. In order to satisfy the urgent customer demands, waitresses (females, who in this instance were assumed to be subordinates, and not expected to be aggressive) were often forced to shout orders urgently—something the predominantly male cooks (assumed to be superordinate in the institutional hierarchy of the restaurant) and other workers took as an affront from the subordinate females. In response, cooks often turned a deaf ear to the orders, frustrating the waitresses even more and causing angry customers to exert even greater pressure when food orders were not forthcoming.

At this point it might be noted that, whereas in the study by Diekman and colleagues (1996) the generalization of the initiation of activity (that is, honking) by drivers of high-status cars is taken for granted, in Whyte's restaurant study the converse appears to be true: when lower-status waitresses shouted orders to cooks, they were objected to and ignored. This anomaly illustrates what happens when interaction is organized in a manner contrary to the generally accepted principles of everyday life.

Whyte relates that one restaurant solved the problem by installing a spindle wheel on which orders were placed, thus eliminating the necessity for personal contact and potential animosity between waitresses and cooks. One cook stated that never in all his life had he worked in such a 'wonderful place'. He described earlier experiences in other restaurants where there was no such insulating mechanism: 'The girls could call their orders in—an ordeal to which no man should be subjected' (Whyte, 1949: 308).

Archibald's fourth principle is the *feelings generalization*: an element of hostility underlies much and perhaps most interaction between non-equals; occasionally there is outright rebellion. An example would be low-power workers who rejoice at a manager's misfortune. In one instance, a lawyer had his parking privileges at work revoked because he used his wife's parking pass and attempted to gain the use of two spaces for the price of one. His misfortune gave so much satisfaction to his clerk in the law firm that she said she felt like a cat who just caught a mouse. Expressions of such feelings of hostility become particularly virulent during strikes.

The conflict paradigm provides a perspective to view status and role in their perhaps less acceptable, institutional aspects and to examine their underside of dissatisfaction, turbulence, and coercion—even their tendency to violence and revolution. So, while the structural-functional paradigm asserts that order in society is achieved by wide cultural consensus and achieves considerable stability and longevity, the conflict paradigm suggests that stability and any degree of permanence is

SOCIOLOGY IN ACTION

Seymour Lieberman's Workplace Study

Seymour Lieberman (1956) studied the attitudes (that is, orientations towards a person, group, or social process) of 2,354 rank-and-file workers in an appliance factory towards unions and management. He demonstrated, as did Peter Archibald (1976) later, the Marxian hypothesis concerning the effect of status on attitudes and the resulting attitude of mutual hostility between upper and lower classes in society.

After the initial survey was completed, the usual workplace processes continued; 23 men were promoted to the rank of foreman and 35 people were elected by their work groups as shop stewards. After 15 months, promoted foremen and shop stewards whose attitudes had originally been recorded in the first survey were retested and the results compared with their answers on the first survey. The results of the second test showed an increase in pro-management attitudes on the part of the promoted foremen and an increase in the pro-union attitudes on the part of the shop stewards. However, the increase in the pro-management attitudes of foremen was greater than the increase in pro-union attitudes of the shop stewards. Lieberman says that these differences should have been predicted because the move from rank-and-file labourer to foreman is greater than that of worker to shop steward.

After two more years, business conditions for the company changed and fewer foremen were needed in the plant, so eight of them were demoted to their former positions. Lieberman then conducted a third survey to compare the attitudes of foremen who were demoted with those who retained their positions. The results indicated that individuals who were demoted now had much stronger pro-union than pro-management attitudes—a clear reversal compared to the situation when they were at the level of foreman. In effect, all of the test results in Lieberman's study support Archibald's (Marxian) theories of inter-class, particularly industrial world, attitudes.

achieved by the dominance of one group over the other and by the force used to maintain this dominance.

Identity

The Symbolic-Interactionist Approach to Identity

We turn now to the third element in our discussion of social structure and the way it constrains us. Identity is the way in which people define themselves and are defined by others. It is a result of the things people do (their roles) and the ways in which their acts are evaluated (accorded prestige) and reacted to. As John Hewitt says, 'A role in itself is lifeless—an unplayed part that has no substance until the individual claims it for his or her own and breathes life into it through identification with it' (2000: 97).

Hewitt (2000) classifies several aspects of identity. **Situated identity** focuses on identity as it emerges through and affects face-to-face interaction with others. *Social identity* is based on identification with groups (e.g., family, ethnic, and occupational groups) and significant social categories (e.g., age and gender), which define us in terms of our similarities with some groups and our differences from other groups. *Personal identity*

Time to Reflect

How do structural functionalists and conflict theorists differ in their explanations of order and stability in society? In the work world, what are the differences between workers and management? What may be the consequences of these differences in status, authority, and prestige?

consists of factors that make us different from others (including physical characteristics such as height, weight, and skin colour) as well as aspects of our past we have incorporated into our sense of self based on how other people have reacted to us and typed us. Personal identity and social identity are parts of our *biographical identity* and, as such, provide continuity as we step into and out of various situated identities. Identities are established by our announcement of ourselves and by others' placement of us. Howard (1995) says that members of dominant groups are more likely to emphasize distinguishing achievement (i.e., personal identities) while members of oppressed groups are more likely to emphasize their similarities to others like themselves (i.e., social identities).

Classical Theorists on Identity: Cooley and Mead

Charles Horton Cooley (1902) is best known for formulating the concept of the **looking-glass self** to describe how identity is formed. Cooley states, 'Each to each a looking glass / Reflects the other that doth pass' (1902: 52). In effect, then, our identity is what we think others think of us. This reflected (hence 'looking-glass') self emerges as we imagine how we appear to others, then imagine how others judge that appearance, and finally come to some self-feeling such as pride or mortification.

A male student sat at the back of a crowded classroom with three vacant seats between him and the next person. Three female students came to class late and entered through the back door, then struggled past the knees of the back row of students already seated. The first girl stopped at the empty seat farthest from him; the next girl passed the first to take the seat beside her, and the third latecomer passed those two to sit beside the male student. It seemed to him that they would have been far more sensible to reverse their seating order and save themselves from having to crawl over each other's knees; so, he began to reflect on their actions as a comment on their perception of him. He felt embarrassed and mortified, and he hoped that other students would not notice this 'real putdown'.

Of course, the female students may have had other reasons for their seating procedure and may have been completely unaware of its 'reflective' effect on him. The first girl may have wanted not to seem to be taking the favoured position nearest to the male; or she may have been embarrassed by the spectacle she was making of herself and have taken the quickest way out of her predicament. Similarly, some professors feel they are being slighted when students walk out of the room while they are lecturing. Not surprisingly, according to Cooley (1962 [1909]), self-image is reflected most strongly in primary, intimate face-to-face groups such as playgroups, family, or even work groups.

Cooley anticipates later work by Goffman on the dramaturgical model of identity not only by asserting that 'the imaginations people have of each other are the solid facts of society' (1902: 107), but also by noting that children quickly learn how to control their appearance so as to be seen and treated as they wish: 'The young performer soon learns to be different things to different people. . . . If the mother or nurse is more tender than just, she will almost certainly be "worked" by systematic weeping' (ibid., 197).

Mead extended Cooley's ideas by emphasizing the cognitive skills acquired through role play and through learning the rules of games. Mead's best-known distinctions in the area of self-development are the definitions of the *play stage* and the *game stage* (1934). In the play stage, children 'play at' being, for example, a mother or father and speak to themselves as the mother or father might. Consequently, they assume for themselves the identity of the label applied by parents. For example, a little girl fiddling with the television dial—an explicitly forbidden act—was observed to tap her own extended hand with the other and say 'bad girl'—an assumed identity, however temporary.

In the game stage, according to Mead (1934), there is a clear-cut, and in some circumstances intricate, organization of roles to be played. This complexity involves reciprocity on the part of the players. Overall, a set of rules structures the game, but players must nevertheless respond appropriately to the specific acts of other members of their own team as well as to members of the opposing team. As the game progresses, these conditions, acts, and reciprocal acts change constantly and must be adjusted to and coped with by effective role-taking. For example, in the game of baseball, when the pitcher throws the ball to the batter, the first reaction is by the batter, and the batter's reaction determines the reaction of the fielders according to the rules and objectives of the game.

Games involve a number of players having to enact expected roles quickly and efficiently, anticipating others' actions and reacting to their own acts and to the anticipated outcomes of those acts. This complexity of organization, interaction, and outcome functions not only in games but within society generally and develops within us a concept of society at large that Mead refers to as the *generalized other*.

HUMAN DIVERSITY

Karen March: 'Who Do I Look Like?'

Karen March's study 'Who Do I Look Like? Gaining a Sense of Self-Authenticity Through Physical Reflections of Others' (2003) focuses on the components of identity and identity trouble that emerge when there is a disjunction between announcement and placement. She describes the situation of adoptees who lived during the period when it was illegal to reveal who their biological parents were. The adoptees describe feelings of a 'deep gap' in their personality and an 'incompleteness' of self-image (that is, personal and social identities).

To understand the phenomena, March contrasts the table-talk experiences of individuals from biologically intact families with those of adoptees. In biologically intact families, it is not unusual for people to hear casual comments about how so-and-so has the nose, eyes, ears, body, or build of their parent, aunt, uncle, or grandparent. This seemingly trivial talk builds family bonds and constructs identity in family terms. In the case of adoptees, however, there is rarely such talk, and if it does occur, it is often problematic. A 35-year-old female adoptee put it very well: 'You come into a room, or you're sitting there, and they talk about how so and so looks like Uncle Jim. They ignore you. Or they notice you and stop talking. Or they change the subject. It makes you [feel that] a piece is missing. . . . You feel a bit on the outside. I feel phoney' (March, 2003: 319). These experiences of incomplete placement marginalize adoptees and contribute to their feelings of inauthenticity. As the adoptee notes, 'It makes you want something that is biologically yours.'

When secrecy laws were eventually relaxed and face-to-face contacts achieved, adoptees reported feelings of completeness, authenticity, and relief, especially if there was biological matching. They said things such as 'I immediately knew I belonged there', 'I felt real for the first time', and 'It made me feel connected.' In essence, contact provided adoptees with a more complete framework for further development of their social and personal identities. As March states, 'It validates the source of self as a physical being. Furthermore, biological matching substantiates one's unrivaled position within an intergenerational group of physical beings possessing unique characteristics' (2003: 321).

March's article on the identity troubles of adopted children is echoed by a 40-year-old test-tube baby, who bemoans the fact that not only does she not know her father as a person, but she knows only that he 'is a glass jar [with] a blob of sperm in it': 'If my mum had had an affair at least there would have been sex and lust, something human rather than something so cold, scientific and clinical. My parents never even met.' The effects on her identity are dramatic: 'I feel like a freak, a fake, I don't feel I know who I am any more' (Woodward, 2003: 24).

The development of identity, particularly biographical identity, is the result of a series of impulses to act and the resultant actual responses to those impulses. For the most part, the impulses are spontaneous and even unconscious, whereas reactions are more deliberate. Mead terms the spontaneous motivations of the individual the 'I' aspect of the self and the deliberately chosen behaviour the 'Me' aspect of the self. Over time, the chosen behaviour characteristics of an individual come to characterize that individual's self. Thus, identity corresponds to the Me—to that part of self most sensitive to the expectations of others; the I is based more on impulse and provides energy and propulsion to the act. There is a continuing dialogue (and frequently an outright struggle) between the I and the Me, and **social control** is usually a matter of self-control in each and all of the society's individuals. In the song 'Will You Love Me Tomorrow?' by Gerry Goffin and Carole King, the singer states the internal 'urge to merge': 'Tonight the light of love is in your eyes'; this is the I speaking. The singer then asks, 'But will you love me tomorrow?' One way to interpret this is that the Me agonizes over whether yielding to the impulse of the I will result in a loss of self-esteem and to lack of respect from the other person.

Contemporary Theorists on Identity: Blumer, Stone, Goffman

The structural view of interaction, as we have seen, emphasizes the relative stability and permanence of the social world. Symbolic interactionism, on the other hand, views social life as a series of processes involving continual interactions. Out of these interactions emerge new situations and new interactions within them, producing, in turn, different identities and coping strategies. Following the lead of Cooley and Mead, Herbert Blumer (1969) named this view of social interaction, that is, interaction as an exchange of meanings through symbols (i.e., words), *symbolic interactionism*, and he is considered the pre-eminent exponent of this school of social analysis. These situated coping strategies and identities rest on and are recognized additionally by material symbols, for example, the uniform identifying a police officer or the vestments identifying a priest.

In this ongoing social process, Gregory Stone (1981) recognizes two kinds of identity: *identification of*, when placement coincides with announcement, and *identification with*, when the person who does the announcing enjoys a comfortable compatibility with the one who does the placement; an identification of the other is necessary before role-taking can occur, which, in turn, makes possible an identification with the other.

One example of identification of and identification with is the process sometimes called 'gaydar' where gays and lesbians in public places signal their identities to one another (Nielsen, 2007). Nielsen notes that lesbians wear short hair, baggy jeans, masculine (i.e., comfortable) shoes, and adopt an 'open' body stance. This identity announcement is so effective, one lesbian said, she can 'spot queers a mile away' [identification of], which usually leads to feelings of **solidarity**. Another noted: 'I feel affirmed, energized, empowered and proud of myself and the lesbians I encounter. It makes

'All the world is a stage', and people spend much time off stage or backstage, learning their lines, preparing their costumes, and readying themselves to play their 'big scene'. (CuboImages srl/Alamy Images)

me feel I'm not alone in the world and that I'm ok' [identification with].

Erving Goffman is perhaps the most lucid and imaginative exponent of identity analysis (though he does not label it as such); significantly for this discussion, his analysis also involves the concepts of role and status. Goffman places the concept of role squarely back on the stage, thus suggesting its structural aspect while also explicitly indicating an interactionist orientation. In the case of the structuralist aspect of self-presentation, Goffman (1959) uses theatrical analogies to distinguish the two zones of open and explicit role-making 'in the front stage' from the hidden role-making 'in the back stage'. Between the front stage and the back stage are 'barriers to perception' that buffer one area from the other.

Presentation of self in the front-stage area is analyzed in terms of three factors: (1) setting—the spatial aspects of things that function as sets and props; (2) appearance—the actor's age, sex, clothing, appearance; and (3) manner—behaviour indicating how one intends to perform the role, for example, haughty or friendly, formal or informal. These three factors combine to create *front*—a set of abstract, stereotyped expectations that prepare audiences for the ensuing performance and help them come to an appropriate definition of the situation (ibid.). Front adds 'dramatic realization' to performances because it helps performers convey everything they wish to convey on any given occasion.

Goffman also indicates that whether performances of social roles are honest or dishonest, they still have the same general characteristics: 'Whether an honest performer wishes to convey the truth or whether a dishonest performer wishes to convey a falsehood, both must take care to enliven their performances with appropriate expressions, exclude from their performances expressions that might discredit the impression fostered and take care lest the audience imputes unintended meanings' (ibid., 66). In addition, 'impressions given' are intended and designed to convey a desired identity, whereas 'impressions given off' are accidentally conveyed (for example, by a slip of the tongue or an uncontrolled gesture) and represent actors in an undesirable light from their own point of view (ibid., 7). These aspects of front must be consistent to produce a convincing identification of the actor.

An example of interaction gone awry because of such inconsistencies involves the case of Ahmed Ressam, the so-called Millennium Bomber, who, in 1999, was stopped at the Canada–US border by a US customs officer. The culprit attempted to identify himself to the officer as a routine commuter. The first inconsistency that emerged was that the car carried British Columbia licence plates but the driver was from Montreal. Furthermore, it could be logically presumed that, as a 'regular commuter', he would be fully familiar with British Columbia and matters pertaining to that province. When questioned, though, he seemed completely ignorant of both. In addition to these inconsistencies, his manner was diffident and faltering. He soon began to sweat, a strong cue that something was untoward. The setting was an international border crossing where the drug trade was a serious problem. The customs officer became very suspicious and, in Turner's terms (1962), 'imputed the role' of drug dealer to him. She asked him to open the trunk of the car, where, instead of the drugs she had suspected, she discovered a stock of explosives. In effect, then, the three aspects of front (setting, manner, and appearance) were present, leading to impressions that contradicted an identity Ressam had tried to project and which the customs officer did not accept.

The back stage is a region characterized by privacy that hides accidents, disagreements, and conflicts between actors on the team (that is, those who co-operate to present a performance). For example, a waiter in a restaurant accidentally dropped a plate of food, destined for a customer, on the kitchen floor. Disgusted and frustrated with himself, he uttered a stream of profanities, then scooped up the food, neatly rearranged it on a clean plate, and presented it with a big smile to the customer. Another waitress reported the incident to the owner, who told her to mind her own business. The customer, left unaware by these 'barriers to perception', expressed verbal satisfaction with the service and left a generous tip. In this example, the different types of interaction in the respective areas of kitchen and dining room dramatize the distinctions between back-stage and front-stage behaviour.

Goffman's treatment of presentation of self and the establishment of identity involves the concepts of role, status, and prestige presented by an actor and recognized by an audience. Goffman states emphatically that the recognition and granting of high status and the accompanying prestige it deserves are an actor's 'moral right': 'Society is organized on the principle that any individual who possesses certain characteristics has a moral right to expect that others will value and treat him in an appropriate way' (Goffman, 1959: 13). In the process of self-presentation to others, Goffman says that we overplay the two basic strategies of self-revelation and concealment. Self-revelation allows us to project ourselves in the best possible light when our worthy qualities might not be fully apparent to others, while concealment allows us to hide aspects of ourselves that could be discreditable.

Another aspect of identity projection is **altercasting** (Weinberg and Deutschberger, 1963). Altercasting is the strategy of projecting a characteristic of some kind—favourable or unfavourable, obligatory or privileged—onto another person with the object of achieving some advantage for oneself. It is the counterpart of Goffman's concept of **impression management**, whereby, in effect, actors engage in self-casting.

In altercasting, this process of fixing an identity on another in order to elicit a specific role could be considered role-making in reverse. In essence, the other person is put on the spot, forced to interact in a way he or she may not wish to but that forces the drama into the pattern intended. For example, Premier W.A.C. Bennett, who had dominated British Columbia's legislative assembly for years, attempted to put down Dave Barrett, the new, admittedly upstart, leader of the opposition, by responding to the young member's first attempt at government criticism with the accusation, 'You are a Marxist.' The response, which came with great alacrity, was 'Which one, Harpo, Groucho, or Chico?' Members roared with laughter and the Premier was cast into the role of a comic foil. The Premier—not yet aware that he had met his match—then went doggedly on and accused the opposition leader of being a 'Waffle' (a member of the well-known radical wing of the New Democratic Party in the early 1970s), but he was duped again by the quick response, 'That makes you, Mr Premier, a pancake.' The identity negotiation continued with the Premier mainly on the losing end, which probably ultimately contributed to his political downfall in the next election.

Another illustration of the concept of altercasting is the case discussed above in reference to Turner's concept of 'shifting axis' and we noted how the male moved the axis from friendship to romance. The first phase of the altercasting act was putting his hand on her upper hip, the second was paying for the movie, and the final phase was taking her hand. Another familiar example of altercasting is when some acquaintance becomes uncommonly friendly as the presage to a request for a special favour.

Identity Troubles: Embarrassment

Embarrassment occurs when an announced identity is not supported or is even distorted, resulting in unsatisfactory placement (Gross and Stone, 2005). Typical instances of embarrassment resulting from dissonance between announcement and placement are a result of bodily accidents, which cause embarrassment because they project a less than fully mature persona, or possibly a careless one.

A dramatic illustration occurred when a female university student went to Banff with a youth group. She was particularly attracted to one of the young men in the group and was delighted when he invited her to climb part way up one of the mountains. They reached their destination and were sitting close together enjoying the splendour and romance of the setting sun, when he leaned over to kiss her. As their lips met, the strong emotional arousal, combined with the excitement and tension, was just too much for her to cope with, and she lost control of her sphincter. Mortified and humiliated, she raced down the mountain with her friend in hot pursuit. When he finally caught up to her, he assured her that it really didn't matter and leaned over to give her another kiss; once more she lost control. This was clearly a case of distorted announcement and unsatisfactory placement.

A second cause of embarrassment is insufficient support for identity announcement. Consider a self-confident student who consistently receives A's emerging from the exam room proclaiming 'I aced it' only to find out when grades are posted that the performance was worthy of a mere B. Or consider what happens when you go to a cashier's counter and announce yourself as paying with cash only to discover that you've left your wallet at home. Yet another example was recounted by a university student: when she was about 10, she got her hair cut very short and was pleased with the result, until she struck up a conversation with some peers, one of whom mistakenly took her for a boy. She was so embarrassed that she became a virtual recluse for the time it took for her hair to grow back.

A third source of embarrassment is *mistaken identity placement*, in which a person may adequately document an identity but fail to have others place it because of distraction or inadequate attention. For example, a young woman who worked as a waitress went to serve two customers seated at a table. She placed napkins on the table and, without observing the customers very closely, greeted them with 'Hi there, ladies.' Only then did she glance up and realize that one of them was a man, who pointedly said, 'Excuse me!' Both she and the customers were deeply embarrassed. She apologized quickly and tried to smooth things over with humour, but neither technique seemed to work. The customers did not leave a tip. Mistaken identity placement also occurs when we use the wrong name for a person when introducing her or him to someone else, or when we say something disparaging about someone to a third party only to discover later that the two of them have a close relationship.

Mismanagement of superfluous identities is a fourth cause of embarrassment. In most encounters there are more activities (roles) and identities than are necessary for ensuing transactions. For example, at parties people eat and drink (subordinate role) while they converse (dominant role). The subordinate roles and identities must be managed so that they remain in the background and don't interfere with what people have come together to do—their dominant roles. A misalignment of these subordinate and dominant roles and identities can result in embarrassment. This occurs when subordinate roles and identities impose themselves on dominant ones. A subordinate activity that properly belongs to a situation may suddenly become the dominant focus of the occasion. For example, at one dinner party the guests were engaged in serious discussion. As they munched on their salads, which contained small cherry tomatoes, one guest, who related this story to the authors, bit into an especially ripe specimen and accidentally squirted the host, who was sitting across the table. The shocked guests and host all noted what happened, which superseded the main objective of the occasion and caused great embarrassment for all.

Embarrassment also occurs when reserve identities inappropriately surface on the dominant identity (Gross and Stone, 1981). For example, one of Gross and Stone's respondents, a judge, said that he stumbled on the way up to the bench, exposing his golfing clothes (reserve identity) beneath his robes. Similarly, if a student's cellphone rings during a lecture, a reserve identity (friend) imposes itself on the dominant identity (student).

We also experience embarrassment when a relict identity—an element of our biographical identity we no longer wish to announce—resurfaces (ibid.). For example, a young man whose new girlfriend admired his sweater and asked where he got it blurted out spontaneously that his ex-girlfriend had knitted it for him. The new relationship was short-lived. A more extreme case was that of a student who took his new girlfriend home to meet his parents for the first time. At one point his mother produced a small formaldehyde-filled vial and proudly announced that it contained the remains of her son's foreskin from when he was circumcised as an infant.

Identity Management: Defensive Practices

Goffman (1971) says that embarrassment causes us to 'lose **face**', and that when we do, we attempt to compensate for the loss by engaging in *remedial work*, that is, *face-work*, or face-saving. Remedial work manifests itself in a variety of forms, including avoidance, accounts (justifications or excuses), and disclaimers, all of which are designed to prevent or remedy damage to our identities (Goffman, 1971; Scott and Lyman, 1968; Stokes and Hewitt, 1976).

Avoidance

Goffman's term for face-saving work to prevent identity damage in the first place is *avoidance*. For example, university students who suspect they have failed an exam frequently do not attend classes on the day the tests are to be returned, and students who do attend class and find that they have received very low or failing grades generally attempt to avoid the students who received high grades. In other words, we attempt to avoid situations wherein we are likely to be embarrassed. Those students who bomb on tests and exams ('Test Bombers') not infrequently make remarks like 'You want to avoid them [Aces] because you emerge looking like the "dumb one"', or 'It makes you feel like you're lazy or unreliable.' Understandably, Bombers become particularly sensitive to the signs of success Aces display—things like 'sitting tall' at their desks, 'broad grins', 'sparkling eyes', and 'jaunty walks'. Bombers often use these signs as cues to identify whom to avoid (Albas and Albas, 2003).

Disclaimers and Accounts

Two related defence strategies to save face are disclaimers and accounts. *Disclaimers* are excuses that come before the act for which face-saving is expected to become necessary. *Accounts* are excuses and justifications that follow embarrassing acts. According to Stone (1981), both disclaimers and accounts can be verbal, in what he terms the *universe of discourse*, or they can be non-verbal mannerisms, in the *universe of appearance*. In the past, almost all research in this area of identity has focused on verbal disclaimers and accounts in the universe of discourse. More recently, however, there has been increased interest in the non-verbal mannerisms we employ in public places where talk is difficult or impossible.

Verbal disclaimers—excuses that come before a potentially problematic act that may damage our identity—come in a multitude of forms. For example, when a professor asks a university class an 'open question', students who do take the risk and respond when they are not entirely certain they have the 'right' answer may attempt to set up the situation to defend their identity beforehand, hedging by using verbal disclaimers such as: 'I may be wrong on this, but . . .' Likewise, students state that they do not study for tests long in advance because 'if I study early I'll only forget it' or 'I study best under pressure.' Verbal disclaimers, especially hedging, are rampant just before exams, when students offer many excuses why others should not expect too much from them. In fact, it's not unusual for a sort of contest to emerge as to why each will do worse than the other—'I'm going to outfail you!'

Another verbal disclaimer comes in the form of *sin licence*, when, if we know we are going to break a rule, we argue that we have good reason to do so. Thus, the professor feeling himself badly underpaid announces to his partner that he will not declare on his income tax return his royalties on the American edition of his novel.

Verbal accounts are offered following a faux pas, and are 'statements made to explain unanticipated or untoward behavior' (Scott and Lyman, 1968: 46). Accounts, in turn, can be subdivided into excuses and justifications. *Excuses* are 'accounts in which one admits that the act in question is bad, wrong, or inappropriate but denies full responsibility' (ibid., 47)—for example, 'I did not know'; 'I was coerced.' *Justifications* are statements wherein we accept responsibility for an act but deny the negative implications associated with it. For example, drivers may admit that they park in prohibited zones using a disabled notice, but argue that it 'was okay because I'm driving my mother's car and she really is disabled and might have been the person using the parking space.' People may mistreat others but argue that 'it's okay because they're not important enough to worry about anyway' or that 'they deserve what they get.' In all cases, accounts serve to 'repair the broken and restore the estranged' (ibid., 46).

Actors can also use accounts to negotiate a more positive identity for themselves after a disruptive interaction. Two students persisted in talking to each other during lectures. After the first request by the professor (not one of the authors), the talking ceased, and there was compliance for the next couple of classes. In subsequent classes, though, the talking resurfaced, and when confronted once again by the professor, the students offered the account that they were only doing what 'everyone else' was. One of the students accused the professor of 'picking on him'. In this case, the students attempted to switch their identity from that of troublemaker to that of innocent victim by condemning the condemner. In a more successful negotiation to reposition oneself with a more positive identity, a young woman, whose rent payment was late, was curt and unpleasant when the apartment owner asked her for the overdue amount. The next day she apologized for her rudeness, accounting for her actions by reminding the owner that she was a single mother and explaining that she had just lost her job. The apartment owner's reaction was tolerant and she offered the young woman two weeks' period of grace to find another job and make up the arrears.

Non-verbal forms of disclaimers and accounts are termed *motive mannerisms*; these occur within a universe of appearance when talk is difficult or impossible (Albas and Albas, 2003; Stone, 1981). As noted earlier, this is an area of identity management that increasingly is being recognized.

An illustration of 'face-saving' occurred to a former student who, at a high school social, emerged from the bathroom unaware that she had caught the end of the toilet paper in her skirt and that she was trailing it behind her. The startled looks of others soon alerted her that something was amiss. When she realized what was happening, she gathered up the toilet paper behind her and wrapped it around herself while dancing in perfect step with the music. She received a loud round of applause and managed to salvage heroism from embarrassment.

Disclaimer mannerisms (that is, excuses) prior to the problematic act can be seen regularly in traffic when a driver cuts in front of another vehicle and the offender then waves to the other driver, implying that the latter has generously allowed the privilege. It is possible that in this process ruffled feathers are smoothed and chances of road rage are decreased. Similarly, shoppers often take self-conscious precautions to avoid looking suspicious by making exaggerated shows of innocence, for example, by tying a knot at the top of every bag they are carrying to give a clear message that nothing else could have been added.

Identity Management: Protective Practices

Protective practices are to some extent altruistic and show consideration of the other. They function to protect the user as well as the communal assembly in which these practices are used because gaffes by a single person disrupt the interactional tone and thereby embarrass the entire group. Protective practices provide the user with some degree of self-protection because everyone is always vulnerable and considerate people are more likely to have consideration directed to them than are people who are thoughtless and unsympathetic. As Goffman (1959) notes, actors form a moral pact to support each other's fostered impressions of themselves.

Protective practices include studious inattention to small lapses in appropriate behaviour of others. For example, we might pretend not to notice a quiet burp emitted by the person next to us. Goffman (1959) refers to this face-saving device as *studied non-observance*. Studied non-observance can also be active; women who need to breast-feed their infants in a public place usually appreciate a courteous lack of attention.

The previous illustrations are of small lapses in appropriate behaviour. However, the process applies just as well when the lapses are much more significant. An illustration of pretended non-observance to a large lapse in appropriate behaviour comes from the Hans Christian Andersen tale of 'The Emperor's New Clothes', in which an unsophisticated child alone from among the crowds surrounding the emperor dares to state the truth, namely, that the emperor is wearing no clothes. As Goffman states emphatically in regard to nakedness, 'When bodies are naked, glances are clothed' (1971: 46). It is also taboo in nudist colonies to stare at the intimate parts of other people's nude bodies (Weinberg, 1997).

Protective practices also come in the form of being considerate and refraining from possibly embarrassing the other. A student once approached one of the authors of this chapter after a lecture and asked how to spell a word (*Kamikaze*) she had used. When asked why the request had not been made at the time the word was used, the student, a former teacher, said, 'I didn't want to embarrass you in case you didn't know.' It is also common for students to inform professors before class that they have to leave early; in so doing, the students remove the implication that they are leaving because the lecture is boring.

Refraining from gloating over our own successes and providing feasible excuses to the unsuccessful for their failure to do as well is also a protective practice. It happens when, after an exam is returned in class, high-scoring 'aces' merely gloss over their grade ('I did okay') when talking to low-scoring 'bombers'. Aces also often offer bombers face-saving excuses such as the difficulty or unfairness of the test, or remind them of disclaimers: 'As you said, you hardly had any time at all before the test to study.' Similarly, when 'Oscars' are handed out at the Academy Awards, many of the winning recipients offer to 'share' their awards with competitors who are lauded by the winners as equally deserving.

Self-mockery (Ungar, 1992) is another protective practice we use frequently to save our own image, but also to save the image of the other. For example, on a visit to Canada, US President Ronald Reagan was heckled by a particularly vocal crowd. To prevent then Prime Minister Pierre Elliott Trudeau from being embarrassed by the rude treatment his guest was receiving, the President quipped, 'They must have been imported to make me feel at home' (*U.S. News and World Report*, 1981, cited in Ungar, 1992: 50).

Where Role and Identity Come Together

Three concepts that demonstrate strikingly how role and identity overlap are role distance, role embracement, and role exit. *Role distance* (Goffman, 1961b) designates the behaviour of actors who play roles in such a way as to announce identities that will have others place them at a distance from the identities they seemingly are announcing. *Role embracement* occurs when actors attempt to convey by their role-making actions the specific and correct self-images by which they wish others to identity them.

Goffman's examples of these concepts are based on his observations of boys on a merry-go-round. First, role embracement begins at about age four or five, when they have to expend every effort just to hang on to the reins, and often also to the horse's neck or ears, and so, literally as well as metaphorically, embrace the role of rider. As Goffman states, 'to embrace a role is to disappear completely into the virtual self available in the situation, to be seen fully in terms of the image, and to confirm expressively one's acceptance of it' (ibid., 106).

Role embracement represents the polar opposite of role distance; it can be observed when boys reach the age of 11 or 12 years. By this point, maleness 'has become a real responsibility. . . . It is necessary to stay away or exert creative acts of distance' from childhood (ibid., 108). Boys accomplish role distance by treating the wooden horse as if it were a racehorse, or by pretending they are stunt riders or comedians, jumping from horse to horse, all the while making faces at friends and passersby. The purpose of these acts, of course, is to display distance from the role of a merry-go-round rider.

A contemporary example of role distance is practised by teenagers who no longer wish to be viewed as children and instead want to establish an identity of independence and maturity, and do so in part by insisting that parents drop them off around the corner from their destination. David Snow and Leon Anderson found that role-distancing also is common among the homeless, especially the recently homeless; they quote one man as saying, 'I'm not like other guys who hang down at the Sally [Salvation Army]. If you want to know about the street people, I can tell you about them; but you can't really learn about studying street people from studying me, because I'm different' (1993: 349).

Role exit is the disengagement from a role that is central to one's self-identity (Ebaugh, 1988). This relinquishment usually brings with it a continuing identity 'hangover' from the past, which influences the playing of a new role. Helen Ebaugh, a former nun, used her own case as an example in her study and interviewed 69 other former nuns as well as another 116 'exes', including transsexuals, police officers, convicts, doctors, divorced people, and air traffic controllers. Drawing on Robert Prus (1987), she formulates a generic social process involved in becoming an 'ex'.

First, there are feelings of frustration, unhappiness, uncertainty, and burnout, which Ebaugh terms *first doubts*. This uncertainty on the part of people about to exit a role leads to what she terms *unconscious cueing*, whereby they begin to change the image they project to others. For example, nuns in this early phase of becoming an 'ex' begin to let their hair grow. Consequently, their announcement leads to a tacit placement, which accordingly encourages or discourages the contemplated move.

Second, depending on whether there has been encouragement or discouragement in the first phase, role alternatives are considered and weighed, and a new role identity is tentatively decided on. In this process, the person inevitably chooses and begins to identify with a new reference group, which will help to consolidate and confirm the new identity. For example, transsexuals, to identify with the opposite sex, cross-dress and take on new mannerisms and occasionally undergo sex-change surgery (ibid.). Role exit occurs after this anticipatory socialization in and by the contemplated new reference group, and finally the new reference group and the new membership group become one.

A fourth and final stage involves accommodating the new identity to the old one. This process is always problematic because the old identity constantly intrudes itself on the new one. Ebaugh cites examples of former police officers who find it difficult to interact affably with people they knew in their previous roles to be involved in shady activities.

Role exit is a predominant characteristic of modern society. In the past, people generally lived their entire lives in one community, gender, occupation, marriage, and religion. In today's society, these statuses and their

Body language tells a story. What caption would you make up for this picture, considering the signs of disappointment, degradation, and status inequality? (CP/Edmonton Sun/Dan Riedlhuber)

accompanying roles and identities are taken on and shed with increasing frequency.

Macro-Societal Implications: Authority and Its Basis in Statuses, Roles, and Identities

Authority is the 'right' of individuals in a given status to expect compliance of others in related subordinate statuses; reciprocally, it is the 'duty' of those in subordinate statuses to comply. In turn, these rights and duties result in specific roles and identities depending on whether subordinates choose to comply (i.e., conformity), or not (i.e., rebellion). The weighty impact of authority can lead to a subdued conscience and compromised morality of those in a subordinate status. For example, the Holocaust against the Jews and other minorities in Nazi Germany raised the issue of what social limits there are, if any, to subordinates' willingness to comply with the dictates of authority. Milgram (1974) attempted to investigate experimentally these types of conditions (see 'Global Issues' box).

The experiments are relevant and important because they shed light on a highly significant historical event. Also, the social dynamics involved continue to occur with considerable regularity in other circumstances (e.g., the My Lai massacre in Vietnam; the 'killing fields' of Cambodia; episodes of 'ethnic cleansing' in Rwanda, Bosnia, and Kosovo; various military and political acts in the course of warfare and the questioning of prisoners).

These experiments also provide a basis to review, display, and illustrate how structural functionalists and symbolic interactionists use concepts introduced in this chapter to interpret and explain a particular set of experimental findings. In one set of Milgram's experiments 64 per cent of subjects complied with orders to inflict pain and suffering on an innocent stranger. Their callousness in ignoring the protests and pleas for mercy from victims (i.e., 'learners') affirms the influence that structural functionalists attribute to the status–role identity–authority complex as something that supersedes an expected 'normal' humane response to suffering.

Symbolic interactionists offer an equally plausible explanation of why authority can override the expected 'humane' tendencies to sympathy in situations such as those described in Milgram's experiments. Symbolic interactionists stress that in every successful interaction actors must come to an agreement as to who each is relative to the other (i.e., negotiation of identities). In Milgram's experiments, the experimenter makes identity claims or announcements to competence and authority. In essence, subjects come to the experimenter's laboratory located in a university *setting*, find the experimenter *dressed* in a laboratory coat (i.e., representing the institution of science), and acting in a 'take-charge' authoritative *manner*. To the extent that subjects go along with the 'front' the experimenter presents, then the identity announcement effectively is recognized. This public agreement, which Goffman (1959) calls a 'working consensus', carries the weight of a social contract.

As was noted earlier, society is organized on the principle that an individual recognized to have a measure of status and prestige has 'a moral right to expect that others will value and treat him in an appropriate way' (ibid., 185). To refuse to go along with the experimenter's prods (i.e., 'the experiment requires that you continue') is to reject that individual's identity claims to competence and authority and directly challenges his ethics! As Milgram (1974: 150) notes, there is no way for 'the subject to stop shocking the learner without violating the experimenter's self-definition and eventually leading to feelings of social awkwardness and embarrassment. Goffman's argument that most people try at all cost to avoid feeling awkward and embarrassed helps to explain why so many subjects obeyed the experimenter's orders, even against their wishes.

Finally, the 'teacher' subjects used accounts (Scott and Lyman, 1968) both as excuses and justifications to salve their consciences and thereby facilitate compliance with malevolent authority. They admitted that their actions were 'bad, wrong, or inappropriate' but denied full responsibility by asserting that they were only following orders. This logic was also the defence used by German officers at the Nuremberg war trials after World War II. More recently, American military personnel involved in the My Lai massacre during the Vietnam War and in the torture and dehumanizing treatment of prisoners at Abu Ghraib prison in Iraq claimed to have been doing simply what had been ordered and expected of them.

Some soldiers involved justified their actions by blaming the victims. This technique was also employed by some of Milgram's subjects, who asserted that the 'learners' (i.e., victims) were 'so stupid and stubborn' that they 'deserved to get shocked' (1974: 10). Similarly, German Jews were described by Nazis as 'egotistical, cunning, and arrogant' (Bain, 1992: 184) and, therefore, presumably 'deserving [of] their fate'.

GLOBAL ISSUES

Milgram's Experiment on Obedience to Authority

More than 1,000 subjects in the United States were recruited through newspaper advertisements to participate in a series of experiments. They were adults (20–50 years) representing every income level and roughly reflective of the population characteristics that perpetrated the Holocaust during World War II. In the experiment of interest in this instance subjects arrived individually at the experimental site at Yale University and were greeted by a stern-looking, thirtyish, male wearing an 'authoritative' looking laboratory coat over his regular clothing. Also present was someone who appeared to be another subject—a male, fiftyish, slightly overweight, and obviously a little nervous—in reality, he was the experimenter's assistant (i.e., confederate). The experimenter explained to the subject and the confederate that they would be involved in a pioneering study of the effects of punishment on learning. To reinforce the message, on a table in the room and in clear sight of the subjects was a huge tome titled *The Teaching–Learning Process*. The participants then drew slips of paper marked as either 'teacher' or 'learner' to assign them to their respective roles. In reality, the process was 'rigged' so that the confederate always became the 'learner' and the subject became the 'teacher'.

All three moved to an 'adjacent room and the learner was strapped into an 'electric chair' apparatus. The experimenter explained that the straps were to prevent excessive movement while the learner was being shocked. The effect was to make it appear impossible for him to escape from the situation. An electrode was attached to the learner's wrist, and electrode paste was applied 'to avoid blisters and burns'. Subjects were told that the electrode was attached to the shock generator in the adjoining room.

To add credibility the experimenter declared, in response to a question by the learner, 'Although the shocks can be extremely painful, they cause no permanent tissue damage' (Milgram 1974: 19). The experimenter and subject 'teacher' then went into yet another room containing a realistic-looking shock generator with multiple switches, each of which controlled a level of power ranging from 15 volts at one end to 450 volts at the other end. Under the switches were designations of 'slight shock' through 'Danger Severe Shock' to an ominous 'XXX!'

During the experiment the 'teacher' punished the 'learner' for each incorrect answer to a multiple-choice question by administering electrical shocks of increasing intensity. As the experiment progressed, and according to plan, the 'learner' made many errors. Before long the 'teacher' was placed in a position of having to administer the highest shock levels recorded on the machine while listening to the increasingly excruciating cries of pain and protest from the 'learner'. When the 'teacher' protested and balked at administering any more shocks, 'the experimenter responded with a sequence of "prods" [ranging from 'Please continue' to 'the experiment requires that you continue' to 'it is absolutely essential that you continue' and finally 'you have no other choice, you *must* go on] using as many as necessary to bring the subject into line' (ibid., 21). The result was that 64 per cent of subjects, even against their wishes, succumbed to the experimenter's orders and administered the highest shock voltage to the learner.

If, as we have seen, authority structures—even artificial ones—impose obedience, then malevolent authority reinforced by resources of the state makes what happened in Nazi Germany more understandable, although by no means whatsoever justifiable. Indeed, as Sabini and Silver (2005: 199) state, the answer to the question of how these atrocities can occur lies in the 'bureaucratization of evil'. This observation will become clearer in Chapter 6, which deals with the characteristics of organizations, especially bureaucracy.

Time to Reflect

The degree of compliance with authority is apt to vary with the presence or co-presence of: (1) the authority figure and subordinate agent, and (2) the agent and the object of his/her aggression when it violates the agent's conscience. How would structural functionalists and symbolic interactionists explain these two propositions?

Conclusion

The concepts of status, role, and identity can be viewed and analyzed from a variety of theoretical perspectives: structural functionalism, interactionist theory, and conflict theory. Status, role, and identity are complex, far-reaching, yet related entities.

Role is related to identity in that role involves a script of action, and that identity is a result of actions and how they are categorized, judged, and evaluated by others. Every role has an accompanying identity, and enacting the role shapes both action and actor. We usually become that which we play at. Identity troubles, as manifested in episodes of embarrassment, make continued role performance difficult, if not impossible, raising the question of embarrassment management, which in turn involves strategies such as avoidance.

The study of statuses, roles, and identities stands at the intersection of society, culture, and personality. As such, it is inevitably connected with socialization—the process by which infants become socially competent—and with the formation and maintenance of communities. The process is social because it is through interaction with others and in response to social pressures that people acquire the culture—the language, perspective, and skills, the likes and dislikes, the cluster of **norms**, **values**, and **beliefs**—that characterizes the group to which they belong.

Society determines many of the ways we think and act, much of what we say, and the values and norms we live by. At the same time, we—all of us together—constitute society. We are both the actors and the acted on. Freedom and determinism, transformation and constraint, are central features of social life. Socialization, accordingly, is often defined as the social learning process a person goes through to become a capable member of society. As people go through the socialization process, they actively participate in learning. They generalize, apply rules, and use language in a creative way. They continue to invent roles and invent identities, and they struggle with the conflict between their various roles and identities.

Having a concept of the generalized other is possible because there is a rough consensus among members of the **society** or **subculture** to which we belong. The I is spontaneous, impulsive, and self-interested. All of us also have a Me, a part of the self that is the result of socialization and is therefore conscious of social norms, values, and expectations. A significant stage of a child's development is the period around two years of age at which the child begins to develop a coherent sense of self and to differentiate itself from others.

In the first few years of life, we also learn such basic facts about ourselves as whether we are male or female and what that means about who or what we are expected to be. In this sense, gender socialization stands as an example of all **primary socialization**. Gender roles and gender identities are among our most central, and therefore most complex, defining roles and identities. Throughout this book, in studying socialization and gender, work and family, we return again and again to the concepts of status, role, and identity.

As we have also seen, the creation and transmission of roles and identities is shaped by technology—currently, by new information technology. The result is a new set of problems and opportunities, and the need for a continual improvement in our theories about how social structure works and about the place of statuses, roles, and identities in this process.

Questions for Critical Thought

1. What do you think are proper professor–student expectations and obligations?
2. How is it possible to interact confidently with a complete stranger?
3. In the work world, what are the differences between workers and management? How are these differences expressed in roles?
4. What is the difference between the interactionist view of role and the structuralist view of role?
5. Where does one's sense of identity come from?
6. How is identity related to role?
7. What is the difference between 'identification of' and 'identification with'? Can you illustrate this from your own life?
8. How does embarrassment relate to role and identity?

Recommended Reading

Kathleen Charmaz, 'The Body, Identity, and Self: Adapting to Impairment', in Kathleen Charmaz and Debora Paterniti, eds, *Health, Illness and Healing: Society, Social Context and Self* (Los Angeles: Roxbury, 1999), 95–112.

This study reveals that the stable nature of self-concepts makes them resistant to change. Experience (in this case, illness) changes more rapidly than self-concept, and so self-concept frequently lags, especially when the experience is overwhelming.

Helen Ebaugh, *Becoming an Ex: The Process of Role Exit* (Chicago: University of Chicago Press, 1988).

Ebaugh details how people disengage from social roles that previously were central to their self-identity.

Victor Gegas and Peter Burke, 'Self and Identity', in Karen S. Cook, Gary Alan Fine, and James S. House, eds, *Sociological Perspectives on Social Psychology* (Boston: Allyn and Bacon, 1995).

This article is a review of the literature concerning self and identity.

Erving Goffman, 'Role Distance', in *Encounters: Two Studies in the Sociology of Interaction* (Indianapolis: Bobbs-Merrill, 1961), 85–152.

Goffman describes how people use distancing techniques (here, role distance) when they do not wish others to identify them with a 'self' implied in a particular role, especially if the role in question is considered beneath them.

David A. Snow and Leon Anderson, *Down on Their Luck: A Study of Homeless Street People* (Berkeley: University of California Press, 1993).

The authors describe how people with low self-concept cope with themselves and with everyday life.

Vered Vinitzky-Seroussi, *After Pomp and Circumstance: High School Reunion as an Autobiographical Occasion* (Chicago: University of Chicago Press, 1998).

The author provides a touching account of how people's experience of high school reunions leads them to reflect on themselves.

Kath Woodward, *Understanding Identity* (London: Arnold, 2003).

This work explores personal and collective identities by drawing on experiences that highlight the importance of ethnicity and race, gender, and place in the production of meanings about who we are.

Recommended Websites

ALS Survival Guide
www.lougehrigsdisease.net/index.html
This website discusses how illness/disability is a master status that supersedes gender, race, and religion. It details the social, medical, emotional, and psychological aspects of Lou Gehrig's disease (amyotrophic lateral sclerosis).

Erving Goffman: *The Presentation of Self in Everyday Life*
www.cfmc.com/adamb/writings/goffman.htm
Adam Barnhart's article elaborates upon Goffman's influential book.

ETHNO/CA NEWS
www.pscw.uva.nl/emca/index.html
This site has a great deal of very basic information about all aspects of contemporary work in the field of ethnomethodology and conversation analysis.

The Presentation of Self in Electronic Life: Goffman on the Internet
ess.ntu.ac.uk/miller/cyberpsych/goffman.htm
Hugh Miller's article relates Goffman's description of face-to-face interaction to interpersonal communication in cyberspace.

Chapter 6

Groups and Organizations

Lorne Tepperman

Learning Objectives

In this chapter, you will:

- Learn about the different sociological 'sets' of people.
- Distinguish between spontaneous and formal organizations.
- Learn the history of the bureaucratic form of organization.
- Understand the characteristics of a bureaucracy.
- Identify the differences between the model or ideal bureaucracy and the real-world bureaucracy.
- Read about the significance of the Hawthorne studies.
- Distinguish between the main points of organizational theories.
- Identify recent changes in the structure of organizations.

Photo: Productions Oracle

The general fact is that the most effective way of utilizing human energy is through an organized rivalry, which by specialization and social control is, at the same time, organized co-operation.

Charles Horton Cooley

Introduction

Wherever you turn these days, you come face-to-face with groups and **organizations**. People work, study, and teach in them, and often play and pray in them, too. We spend more and more of our lives dealing with large organizations—with colleges, governments, hospitals, department stores, and so on. Yet few of our experiences with these organizations, whether as workers or as 'customers', are pleasant. In fact, often they make us feel fake and inhuman. This effect is because large organizations have their own impersonal cultures, which will be discussed in this chapter. And because they bring together large numbers of strangers, large organizations use special ways of preserving social control. To do this, they invent large bodies of rules and regulations. Often, large organizations are so complex that no one knows all the rules. The result—a huge, powerful collection of strangers following rules that almost nobody knows—can be frightening.

This chapter is about basic elements of social structure—namely, groups and organizations. In fact, you could say that, along with the previous chapter on roles and identities, this chapter maps the most fundamental elements of social structure, the subject matter of sociology itself. This chapter is about 'social organization' in its broadest sense, and touches on two main questions. (1) How do people typically act in social groupings of different size and arrangement? (2) How could we organize social groupings to increase the chances that people would act in specific ways? These general questions can be addressed to a wide variety of social groupings ranging upwards in size from (two-person) dyads, to cliques, small groups, large groups, social networks, communities, and formal organizations—among others.

We begin the chapter by discussing different ways of organizing people; they include networks, groups, and cliques. We will start small and build up to bureaucracies, because large and small organizations are more similar than you might think.

First, as we shall see, all bureaucracies contain networks, groups, and cliques. These small, informal organizations perform much of the work of large, formal bureaucracies. Sometimes, they also subvert the plans and efforts of these bureaucracies. Second, many of the same organizational principles that shape small groups, cliques, and communities also shape large, formal organizations. As we shall see, processes of leadership, commitment, control, and exchange, among others, shape all organizations, whatever their size. That means that what you already know about families, classrooms, and clubs can be applied—with a little ingenuity—to things you know less about, like bureaucracies, societies, and empires (for example).

Large organizations of the kind we see today (and discuss in this chapter) are still fairly new to human history, and in some ways they are a major human accomplishment. Yet, somehow, this great ambition has gone wrong. This chapter discusses the problem of large organizations: namely, that they are so effective and yet potentially so dangerous. Large organizations are as likely to frustrate and disappoint as they are to satisfy our wishes. Often, they control us more effectively than we humans can control them. Next, we trace the development of organizational theory from its crude beginnings at the turn of the twentieth century. In general, this development reflects the growth of sociological knowledge about human groups. The chapter ends with an examination of the ways that large organizations actually work, compared with the ways they are supposed to work.

Sets of People 

Imagine five sets of 20 people. Call them *categories, networks, communities, groups,* and *organizations.* Sociologists will study these five sets differently, because they are organized differently and have different effects on their members. This section will briefly discuss these sets and explain why they would interest sociologists in different ways.

Categories

Imagine, first, that these 20 people are a mere collection of people unconnected with one another—say, a random sample of Canadian 19-year-olds—but fall into the same category: in this case, they are the same age. These teenagers do not know one another and are not in contact with one another, but they have age in common.

This sample of teenagers is of interest to sociologists if they represent the attitudes and behaviours of 19-year-olds across the country. Knowing these attitudes and behaviours may help us predict the future behaviour or explain the current behaviour of 19-year-olds. It will be

IN THE FIRST PERSON

People come to sociology by strange routes, but they usually reproduce family influences. I remember my teacher George Homans telling me that he had wanted to become a poet and his parents had suggested instead that he become a minister of religion. He said he compromised and went into sociology—a field that encourages us to write a lot (like a poet, if you were George Homans) and to promote social improvement (like some ministers of religion).

I had wanted to become a musician—particularly, a composer. When that proved impractical, my father—a physician—proposed a career in medicine. However, studying biology, physics, and chemistry didn't catch my imagination so I began to think about a career in law. Meanwhile, I needed an undergraduate degree and my best friend was majoring in sociology. Why not sociology, I thought? I could always go into law later. That might have happened but for Aunt Toby and Uncle Oscar, who were both literary and radical. They encouraged me to see in sociology a way to help change the world. In the end, I stayed with sociology but retained a skeptical 'hard science' turn of mind, like my father.

Today, 40 years later, I have learned a lot more about the reasons to become a sociologist. The discipline offers ever-new opportunities to view and explore a changing reality, using evolving tools, methods, and concepts. And it allows us to re-explore the founding documents—the classical thinkers—who brought sociology to our attention in the beginning. Sociology remains a way of exercising our minds to see social reality in what Weber called a state of 'disenchantment'—a kind of informed skepticism—but also wonder at the patterns and complexity of human life.—Lorne Tepperman

of particular interest to market researchers who want to sell products to 19-year-olds and to political pollsters who want to shape their voting preferences. However, for the most part, sociologists will not be interested in such samples of people. Since they are unconnected, people in categories have no social structure of interest, and it is **social structure**—the invisible feature of social life that controls and transforms our behaviour—that is mainly of interest to sociologists.

However, categories become sociologically interesting when societies dramatize (or socially construct) meanings for the boundaries between one category and another. No such meaningful boundaries exist for 19-year-olds, compared with 18- and 20-year-olds. However, important cultural boundaries exist between the categories named 'male' and 'female', 'young' and 'old', and, in some societies, 'white' and 'black'. As a result, these categories assume social importance. Yet, they assume importance only when the categorical differences are dramatized, the boundaries are enforced, and categorical differences result in social and cultural differentiation—for example, in the form of communities or of **social movements**.

Networks

Generally, sociologists are more interested in what they call networks, or **social networks**. Imagine the same 20 people all connected to one another, whether directly or indirectly. By *direct connections*, we mean links of kinship, friendship, and acquaintance among all 20 people, each connected to the other. In this set of 20 people, there can be $[20(19)]/2 = 190$ such pairwise connections—obviously, many interesting relationships and combinations of relationships to study.

Indirect connections also are of interest to sociologists. In fact, some sociologists such as Mark Granovetter (1974) argue that *weakly tied networks*, based largely on indirect links, may be even more useful than *strongly tied or completely connected networks*. Information, social support, and other valuable resources flow through incompletely connected, or weakly tied, networks (see Figure 6.1). Also, rumours, diseases, innovations, and job information all spread geographically through (indirectly linked) networks of weak ties, because weakly tied networks have a vast outreach. They connect large numbers of weakly tied people (for example, acquaintances) at a few removes, unlike tightly connected networks, which tend to circulate the same information or resources repeatedly through the same set of people (for example, close friends).

The pairwise connections (which sociologists call *dyadic relationships*) that make up social networks are based on regular patterns of social exchange. In stable dyadic relationships, people give each other things they want and need. So long as these relationships satisfy their needs, people stay in these relationships. People usually act in their own best interests—when they are aware of these interests. They are rational and sensible, and they preserve **social relationships** that are useful to them. So, people enter, leave, and stay in the social networks in which their valued dyadic relations are embedded. Over time, as people enter and leave relationships, networks change in their size and composition. This, in turn, affects the resources flowing to other members of the network.

Figure 6.1 Social Networks for Social Support

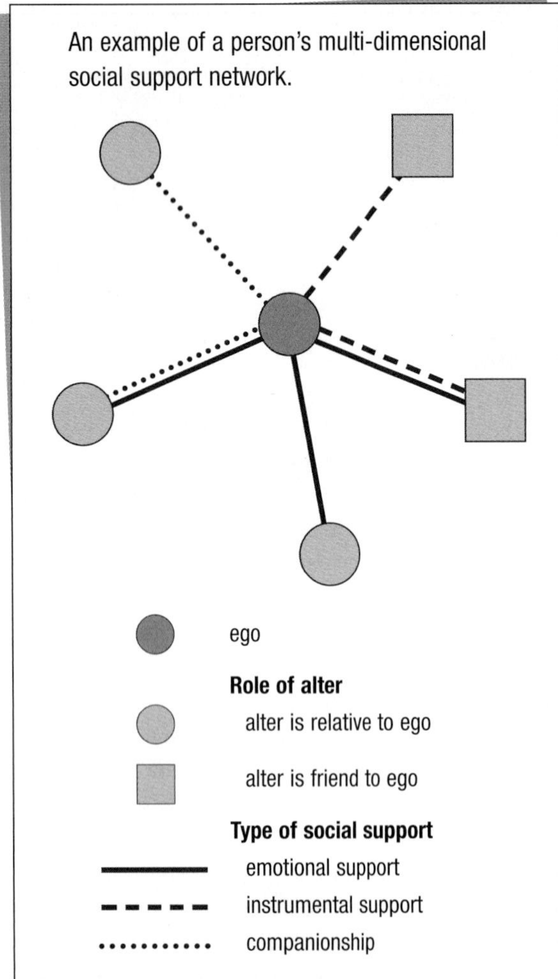

Source: Filip Agneessens, Hans Waege, and John Lievens, 'Diversity in Social Support by Role Relations: A Typology', *Social Networks* 28, 4 (Oct. 2006): 427–41. Copyright 2006, reprinted with permission of Elsevier.

In recent years, Internet-based social networking services such as LinkedIn, Friendster, and Facebook have rapidly increased in popularity. These services collect information from an individual's profile and their list of social contacts to create a display of their personal social network. This display publicizes how the contacts within the network are interconnected. These on-line services are often provided free to users, although individuals must disclose personal information to register and use these on-line networking sites. These sites are built on the premise that individuals may merely be a few 'links' removed from a desirable business or social partner and not even know it. Such networking services claim that by allowing members to 'get to know one's friends of friends [they can] expand their own social circle' (Adamic and Adar, 2005: 188). Increasingly, people are setting up virtual networks of relationship in cyberspace, as well as real ones.

As you can see from this glimpse, social networks are important and interesting. There is a huge and growing sociological literature on social networks. However, much of social life is not well understood in terms of networks. That is because networks lack several key characteristics. First, people in networks lack a sense of collective identity, such as a community would have. Second, people in networks lack an awareness of their membership and its characteristics, such as a group would have. Third, people in networks lack a collective goal, such as an organization would have.

Communities

Sets of people with a common sense of identity are typically called **communities**, and there is a long history of community studies in sociology. Imagine, for the sake of consistency, that we are thinking of a community of only 20 people—say, a community of like-minded people living together on the land (perhaps a hippie commune in 1960s British Columbia or a utopian farming community in nineteenth-century upstate New York) or in the city (perhaps a community of anarchist or bohemian youth living in a broken-down squat in twenty-first-century Amsterdam).

These are likely to be people drawn together by common sentiments; or they may be people who have grown up together and share strong values uncommon to the rest of society. The nineteenth-century German sociologist Ferdinand Tönnies (1957 [1887]) took great pains to distinguish the foundations of community life, or what he called *Gemeinschaft*, from the foundations of non-community life, which he called *Gesellschaft*. Tönnies also associated community life with rural areas and non-community life with urban areas. At least since medieval times, the city has been represented as a place distinct from both rural communities and from the natural environment.

Gemeinschaft refers to the usual characteristics of rural and small-town life, which include a stable, homogeneous group of residents with a strong attachment to one particular place. Residents of the community interact around similar qualities and lead similar lives. Not only are their lives similar, they are also linked by intimate, enduring relationships of kinship, friendship, neighbouring, and (often) working together. Because rural people share so much, it is not surprising they also share similar moral values, and moral guardians such as the church, school, and local upper classes protect these values. In social structure, the *Gemeinschaft* is marked by dense or highly connected networks, centralized and controlling elites, and multiple social ties.

By contrast, the ties among people in a city take the form of a *Gesellschaft*. This includes a fluid, heterogeneous group of residents with a weak sense of place. According to Tönnies, the residents have different personal histories and impersonal, brief relationships. They interact around similar interests, not similar characteristics or histories. They share few moral values and few moral guardians to enforce a common moral code. In social structure, city networks are less connected, less centralized, less cliquish, and less redundant. In short, the *Gesellschaft* demonstrates less cohesion and has less social control.

The question that several generations of sociologists have debated since Tönnies is whether *Gesellschaft*—or city life—represents a loss of community or a new kind of community. Most sociologists in the first half of the twentieth century believed the former: they saw city life as disorganized and lacking in the cultural and social benefits of community. However, in the second half of that century, sociologists came around to another view. They showed that people are not as isolated and atomized in large cities as previous sociologists thought. Rather, the majority form small communities based on residential closeness

Cliques organize the flow of information to ensure that some people are included and others are excluded—even mocked, ridiculed, and mistreated. (Heide Besner/zefa/Corbis)

and social likeness, or on friendship and support networks among geographically scattered people. (For more about this, see the 'Open for Discussion' box on *Gemeinschaft* relations in the city streets of Cairo.)

Communities, whether urban or rural, real or virtual, are important because people are aware of their membership in them. They want the community to survive and may make large personal sacrifices to see that it does.

Groups

Sometimes, groups can be like small communities: engrossing and demanding of loyalty. In other cases, groups are much less so. What all groups have in common is an awareness of membership. Also, members are all connected with one another (directly or indirectly), and to varying degrees they communicate, interact, and conduct exchanges with one another. To continue our example, a 20-student classroom is one kind of group. It is more highly connected than a 20-person category, more self-aware than a 20-person network, but shows less solidarity (based on common values) than a 20-person community.

Since Charles Horton Cooley (1962 [1909]) wrote in the early twentieth century, sociologists have distinguished between primary groups and secondary groups. *Primary groups* are small and marked by regular face-to-face interaction; an example is a family household. Cliques, which we will discuss shortly, and work groups also fall into this category of primary groups. *Secondary groups* are larger, and many members may not interact with one another on a regular basis. However, even in secondary groups there is a clear membership, at least some members interact, and there is an identifiable nor-

OPEN FOR DISCUSSION

Gemeinschaft and *Gesellschaft* in a World of Cultural Variety: Cairo

In Shéra Dokki there is a strong sense of *Gemeinschaft* for those living and working in this street. The street belongs to this core community. For those who merely pass through the street on their way somewhere else, however, the street will appear in a different light. Although for those who live in this street, life goes on very much as it would in a country village, people never forget that a busy urban street runs through their community. For women, in particular, the street is always the scene of possible censure and criticism. People laugh and talk with friends on the street. Public scrutiny very much influences what women in particular wear in public. The body is on show in the street. The clothes worn indoors are very different from the clothes worn on the street. Poorer women wear a black gallabaya over more colourful clothes; black is seen as a respectable colour for older women to wear in the street.

There are many reasons why people go into the street. Perhaps they are simply going through this street to somewhere else. Here, the intimate act of eating takes place in the public street. No one censures these men for eating in the street, although young children are told not to eat in the street as they walk along. For them the street is home, they do everything but sleep here. Other people who spend all their time in the street are the street sweepers; dressed in orange clothing and pushing their bins in front of them, they speak only to other sweepers. Street children also live in the street, begging by day and scrounging a living any way they can, they sleep under the flyover in Medan Dokki. It is hard to calculate the number of people supported by this one street.

Many, however, just pass through the street on their way somewhere else. The lower the social class the more at ease people are in the street, the more the public and private blend. The street is a place of work, buying and selling, eating and drinking, repairs, ironing, learning, killing animals, resting on chairs, drinking public water from earthenware jugs, sleeping, praying, parading new clothes. Danger and the need for policing are associated with streets both in East and West. One of the big differences between the streets in Cairo and the streets in Europe is that the Cairo streets are full of stationary people either selling their wares or just sitting talking, or perhaps praying. It appears that Cairo streets were never designed to be walked on in a hurry.

Source: Abridged from Isobel Ryan, 'City and Place. The Urban Village: "Gemeinschaft" and "Gesellschaft" Revisited', in *Lianes*, 27 Feb. 2006.

Time to Reflect

Explain the differences between *Gemeinschaft* and *Gesellschaft*. Evaluate the strength and quality of social ties and the general character of social life in each.

mative order and a shared sense of collective existence (as in a community).

Typically, groups are less engrossing than communities. However, they have organizational structures and do what social structures are expected to do: namely, control and transform their members. All groups, even small groups, have clearly defined familiar roles: for example, husband–wife, parent–child, or brother–sister in families, leader–follower in cliques, or teacher–student–teacher's pet in classrooms. These roles, as we saw in the chapter on roles and identities, carry interactional expectations, and people are identified (and identify themselves) with the roles they play. Even in small groups, behaviours become scripted. Robert Bales, in the 1950s, found that in the discussion groups he studied, three roles—task leader, emotional leader, and joker—regularly emerged. Bales (1950) inferred that groups 'need' these roles to survive.

As we will see later in this chapter, informal work groups emerge within large formal organizations. Within these work groups, informal leadership roles and group norms emerge. These control and transform the behaviour of group members, sometimes to the dismay of the people who manage the formal organization. This discovery is one of sociology's most important contributions to the study of organizations.

Secondary groups, though less strongly integrated than primary groups, are no less important. We spend most of our waking hours as members of secondary groups, interacting, communicating, and exchanging resources with other people. Secondary groups are also the staging area for much social learning. They bind people in fairly stable patterns of **social interaction**. Formal organizations, which will be discussed at length later, are subtypes of secondary groups, and bureaucracies are subtypes of formal organizations. So, in the end, almost everything in this chapter—except the discussion of cliques—is about secondary groups.

Organizations

As just noted, organizations are secondary groups that have a collective goal or purpose. An organization can be a giant **multinational corporation**, such as General Motors, or a small corner variety store; a political party or a government; a church, a school, a sports club, or a search party. Given the endless variety of organizational forms and the millions of specific examples, what do all organizations have in common?

Every organization is a group of people working together and co-ordinated by communication and leadership to achieve a common goal or goals. Within this general definition, however, organizations vary considerably. The group of people in question—that is, the **social group**—may come together spontaneously or deliberately. The division of labour within that organization may be crude or complex. The communication and leadership may be *informal* or *formal* (these terms will be defined shortly). The organization may have one specific goal or various loosely related goals.

One important distinction to make about organizations is between spontaneous and formal organizations. Both types fit the general definition of an organization, yet the two are different in important ways. A **spontaneous organization** is one that arises quickly to meet a single goal and then disbands when the goal is achieved or thought to be beyond reach or when the organization is absorbed by a formal organization. A clique, though informal, is not a spontaneous organization. Perhaps the most commonly cited examples of spontaneous organizations are bucket brigades and search parties. Each has a single goal—keeping a barn from burning down or finding a lost child. Each arises spontaneously and its leaders emerge informally, without planning. Each has a crude division of labour—for example, filling buckets, passing them along, emptying them on the fire. Nevertheless, each is much more likely than an unco-ordinated mob to achieve its goals. Compare the chance that a mob, running off in one direction, has of finding a lost child with that of a group conducting a co-ordinated search pattern. Spontaneous organizations disband as quickly as they form. The bucket brigade will scatter when it achieves its goal of putting out the fire or the barn has burned down or the fire department arrives on the scene.

Organizations that have loosely related goals and are fairly unstructured, with little differentiation between their members, are considered **informal organizations**. One familiar example of informal organization is the

SOCIOLOGY IN ACTION

Organizations and Individualism

You may have noticed, living in North America, that there seems to be an organization for every social ill, common interest, and shared goal. Is this a new phenomenon of the information age? Not at all. Alexis de Tocqueville, in his classic work, *Democracy in America* (1945 [1835, 1840]) noticed this trend while studying American society in the 1800s. He believed that individualism was a unique characteristic of democratic societies, such as the United States of America. He also believed that it could be very destructive, leading people to abandon societal concerns and turn inward to their own interests. Looking at the United States, he asked: 'how do the Americans combat the effects of individualism?' His answer was organizations, or, as he called them, 'free institutions'.

Tocqueville realized that urban life was much different from traditional rural living. People had fewer strong ties and often dealt with strangers in their daily work. This produced a new sense of individualism, where it became difficult for people to see that they were not independent of their fellow citizens. Organizations, Tocqueville said, helped people see that they were not as independent as they thought. These associations were often political, but he also saw how people organized in thousands of different ways—religious, moral, commercial, and otherwise.

Why were these groups so important in democratic societies? Coming from an aristocratic family himself, Tocqueville thought that voluntary associations performed the same function that the aristocrats did in traditional society: they served as an intermediary between the king and the people. In the case of the modern society, voluntary organizations were between the state and the people. Still, Tocqueville was a conservative at heart, and didn't think that these associations could replace what he saw as being lost in the move away from aristocratic society: community.

—Written by Matt Kopas

clique. Cliques seem very different from the formal organizations to be discussed in most of this chapter, yet, paradoxically, they share common features. Also, as we will discover later, cliques and other informal organizations can usually be found nested within formal organizations, doing much of the work.

Cliques

Defining the Clique

Dictionaries variously define *clique* as 'a small exclusive set', a 'faction', a 'gang', or a 'noisy set'. This meaning comes from the French *cliquer*, meaning 'to click', or 'to make a noise'. People in cliques—especially the most popular ones—make a lot of noise, pumping themselves up and ridiculing others.

To come closer to our current sociological meaning, we would define 'clique' as a group of tightly interconnected people—a friendship circle whose members are all connected to one another, and to the outside world, in similar ways. Usually, clique members feel strong positive sentiments or liking for one another and contempt for outsiders. They spend more time with one another than with non-clique members, share their knowledge with one another, and think and behave similarly. They try to ignore or exclude outsiders—people not like themselves, and not friends of their friends.

In short, cliques are groups characterized by friendship, likeness, interaction, exclusion, and the flow of valuable resources: information, support, and opinions (among others). In these respects, cliques are mini-communities, like mini-states. Like states, they amass **power** and resources. They receive, censor, and direct information flow. Like states, cliques remain distinct; resources (such as information) flow readily within the clique and less readily outside its borders. Cliques gather and redirect information. They also produce information, distort it, and send information out as gossip and rumour. Cliques, like other organizations, create and concentrate information flow. Because they produce and control the

American popular artists Currier and Ives captured nineteenth-century North American conceptions of 'community', in this case, the pleasure of sharing one another's company in a simple holiday pastime—skating on the frozen river. (Courtesy of the Currier & Ives Foundation)

flow of information effectively, cliques are stable structures (on this, see Carley, 1989, 1991). They survive largely through what psychologist Irving Janis (1982) called 'groupthink'.

Sometimes it helps to view the familiar through unfamiliar lenses. The first thing we learn when we study cliques in this way is that they satisfy human needs for interaction and support. Lloyd Siegel and Arthur Zitrin (1978), for example, in a classic study of New York male-to-female transsexuals on public welfare, found that all the people they were studying lived with one or more transsexual friends. Besides, a transsexual community had seemingly come into existence, creating its own subculture. A citywide informal network provided transsexuals with information concerning particular needs, and reportedly worked to create a feminine environment and appearance for clique members. The community, made up of multiple cliques, was stable, cohesive, and supportive. Transsexual friends often accompanied clients to welfare centre interviews and provided other practical help. The authors infer that this subcultural community helped transsexual men to foster their illusion of being female, often without their having to undergo surgery.

The second thing we learn when we study cliques and communities is that they produce new roles, rules, and cultural values. An example is the supposedly anarchic world of 'bohemians'. Bohemians are people who, for artistic or other reasons, have rejected the middle-class lifestyle. Paradoxically, once freed from middle-class conventions, they create their own conventions. In a classic study of bohemians, Patricia Nathe (1978) writes that although 'Bohemia' is a classless society, there are distinct circles of membership: at the core are the true career artists and intellectuals; then their disciples, known as pseudo- or professional bohemians; then the weekend or part-time bohemians; then the entrepreneurs who profit from the bohemian scene; and in the 'outer circle', the voyeurs, relatives, reporters, detectives, and groupies. These various 'types' interact in cliques regularly, filling recognizable roles and playing out scripts based on the romance of art, poverty, self-expression, and identification with other socially vulnerable groups.

Though seemingly without goals, cliques have an unstated 'mission' or purpose: to raise the status of clique members at the expense of non-members. Though lacking an organizational chart or stated division of labour, school cliques have a clear hierarchy of influence and popularity, with the leader on top surrounded by his or her favourites. In this sense, then, a clique is a group of people working together and co-ordinated by communication and leadership to achieve a common goal or goals.

Cliques in School Settings

Cliques form in every area of life, even within bureaucracies and other formal organizations. However, cliques are most familiar to us from our childhood school experience. In school settings, cliques typically have a well-defined membership. Clique members are typically similar to one another in background and behaviour (Ennett and Bauman, 1996). Cliques typically have rituals that exclude outsiders and integrate insiders. Cliques also have a leader, who is the most popular member of the clique and who dominates the other members. Usually, the leader defines the group boundaries, invents group rituals, and chooses the membership.

Cliques are not only organizations: they are communities and miniature societies. In cliques, children first learn the rules and expectations of society outside their family home. Through games and play with clique members, children internalize the beliefs, values, and attitudes of their group. By these means, children also form judgements of themselves. For example, they learn what it means to be 'good-looking', 'sexy', and 'popular', to be chosen or passed over. Children's activities, their friendships, and their feelings about themselves are tied up with their involvement in the cliques that organize their social landscape (Crockett et al., 1984).

Cliques, though often supportive, can also offer excellent examples of structured cruelty, and they can be found everywhere. It was perhaps unavoidable that the reach of cliques would extend into cyberspace. On-line bullying carried out by clique members is a new phenomenon and potentially just as damaging as the bullying that occurs face-to-face. With on-line or e-bullying, youth can constantly harass their victims over the Internet, through instant text messaging on cellphones and postings on bulletin boards and on their blogs. Thanks to technology, which makes more pervasive and unrelenting forms of bullying possible, victims are always within reach.

Cliques form when people meet others like themselves. The social structuring of activity itself—for example, grading of activities such as education, entertainment, or work by age—increases the likelihood that people will meet others like themselves (Feld, 1982). Also, since class or ethnicity often separates neighbourhoods, and since children usually attend neighbourhood schools, they are likely to meet other children of the same class and ethnic background. The more homogeneous the people they meet, the more children will form relationships with others who are similar. It is, first, this structuring of acquaintances that leads to creating cliques.

However, an element of choice is involved. Cliques carefully screen people for membership. Once formed, cliques preserve themselves by continuing to ensure that members remain similar. Cliques change as individuals enter and leave the group. Those at the clique's centre—the leaders—are most influential in the recruitment process. They use their power, based on their popularity, to decide which potential members are acceptable and which are not.

Cliques control their members by defining the behaviours that are proper and acceptable. Leaders are skilled in exercising control. They often do so by building up the clique members and then cutting them down (Adler and Adler, 1995). One technique is to draw new members into an elite inner circle, allowing them to enjoy brief popularity, then humbling them by turning the group against them. Leaders also take advantage of quarrels to divide and conquer the membership. They degrade and make fun of those who are lower in the hierarchy or outside the group. All of these tactics allow leaders to build up their own power and authority. Such rites of degradation also foster clique solidarity by clarifying the norms for acceptance and rejection.

The cohesion of a clique is based mainly on loyalty to the leader and loyalty to the group. This loyalty, in turn, is based as much on exclusion as it is on inclusion. First, group members hive themselves off from non-members. Lack of contact with outsiders allows members to believe that outsiders are different and less socially desirable than themselves. Also, clique members use gossip to reinforce their ignorance of outsiders and keep social distance from them. They also use gossip to ridicule and spread nasty rumours about outsiders. Finally, they may pick on or harass outsiders. Doing so instills fear, forcing outsiders to accept their inferior status and discouraging them from rallying together to challenge the power hierarchy.

Cliques and the rituals of inclusion and exclusion on which they rely are more than mere children's games. They are small-scale models of how organizations state, teach, and enforce rules; as such, they provide a lesson in social control. Cliques remind us that every inclusive action is, at the same time, an exclusive action. Organizations like cliques can have shared goals that are unstated but real, norms that are unwritten but compelling, hierarchies that are undocumented but powerful, divisions of labour that are effective but unplanned.

Life in the Animal House

Many university students, especially those on the outside looking in, consider fraternities and sororities to be formally organized cliques. Recent research in the United States would seem to confirm certain differences between those who live off-campus or in residence halls as opposed to those in Greek houses.

A survey at a public American university (Page and O'Hegarty, 2006) compared male students living in fraternities with males living in apartment complexes and residence halls. It found that the fraternity men drank more alcohol, engaged more often in heavy episodic drinking, and drank more when 'partying'. A similar pattern was true for females living in sororities compared with female students living in apartment complexes and residence halls. Wherever they lived, most students drank less than what they believed to be the socially accepted drinking norm. However, students living in fraternities and sororities estimated the highest average levels of socially acceptable drinking. Thus, it appears that higher-than-average estimates of acceptable drinking may contribute to extremely frequent and heavy alcohol use, chiefly among members of fraternities and sororities. These results also confirm that students' choice of residence is a main influence when it comes to drinking behaviour.

In another research study, a male experimenter took digital pictures of all the images of women displayed in the rooms of 30 fraternity men and 30 non-fraternity men at a small liberal arts college. The men also filled out a rape myth acceptance scale. Ninety-one images were found in the form of posters, 'pin-ups', advertisements, or computer screen savers. Researchers found that fraternity men had significantly more images of women displayed in their rooms and the images were rated significantly more degrading than those in the rooms of non-fraternity men. Fraternity men were found to have significantly higher scores on a rape supportive attitude scale (RSA). RSA scores, in turn, were positively related to the amount of degradation in the images found in men's rooms (Bleecker and Murnen, 2005).

Bureaucracies

Formal Organizations

Organizations are *formal* if they are deliberately planned and organized. This planning may occur when people found a new university, for instance. Or it may occur gradually, as happens when the people who form a bucket brigade find that enough fires are starting that they would do better to organize themselves into a volunteer fire department.

Within formal organizations, communication and leadership are provided through consciously developed and formalized statuses and roles. Often formal organizations have multiple goals, and they usually have a long lifespan. The Roman Catholic Church is a formal organization that has lasted nearly 2,000 years. Besides this, formal organizations normally have access to far greater resources and more complex technologies than spontaneous organizations. We can define a **formal organization** as a deliberately planned social group in which people, resources, and technologies are consciously co-ordinated through formalized roles, statuses, and relationships to achieve a division of labour intended to gain a specific set of objectives. This is similar to the general definition of organizations. A formal organization will have an overarching set of goals framed by its leaders and more or less accepted by its members. But we cannot assume that these are the only goals of the membership. Workers, professionals, and managers will have their own occupational goals as well.

There is a huge literature, containing many lively debates, that addresses the question of why some organizations are more successful and powerful than others. The most common explanations cite the degree to which an organization fills a social need (either real or successfully promoted by the organization itself), controls or has access to needed resources and technologies, tailors its goals to match the goals of its members, and adapts to or

Time to Reflect

Do cliques provide useful socialization for children? What are the advantages and disadvantages of childhood exposure to cliques?

causes changes in its environment. The main form of the large, powerful, and long-lived formal organization in the twentieth century is the **bureaucracy**.

'Bureaucracy' has negative connotations for most people. In everyday use, the word carries little of its original meaning and is often used as a disparaging term. We hear about how bureaucracies impede business, how people battle against them, and, most of all, about how frustrating they are. The word calls to mind images of red tape, an overemphasis on rules and regulations, inefficiency, and unwieldy government organizations moving at a tortoise-like pace. To sociologists, however, a bureaucracy is merely a particular type of formal organization that thrives in both the public and the private sectors, in capitalist and socialist societies alike. The fact that bureaucracy is the main organizational form taken by competitive corporations shows that it can be very efficient.

The Emergence of the Bureaucratic Form of Organization

In a bureaucracy, the *superordinate*, or boss, of the organization personally owns none of its resources. All resources belong to the organization. Further, all resources are meant to flow from superior to inferior persons based on authority or office-holding position alone—not based on personal attachment. In turn, office-holding is (ideally) based on expertise and effectiveness alone.

In bureaucracies, people move through positions, or *offices*, in the organization based on their merit. The resources remain attached to offices; they do not follow the individual movers. Besides, there are elaborate written rules to govern many (if not all) of the relationships in the organization. *Organization charts* are made to show the (ideal) chains of responsibility, authority, and communication between superiors, subordinates, and equals.

It was obvious to Max Weber (1978 [1908])—the first sociologist to study bureaucracies—that this form of organization held enormous advantages over earlier organizational forms, such as patrimonialism or *clientelism*, in which clients are tied to their boss or patron by personal loyalty. First, bureaucratic organization holds the potential for rational planning. In bureaucracies, goals are stated clearly, strategies are planned and communicated, the most capable people are hired and trained, resources are mobilized, effectiveness is evaluated, and organizational improvements are carried out. How different this makes IBM or the University of British Columbia—both bureaucracies—from the Italian Mafia or the court of Louis XIV, which are patron–client organizations!

Bureaucracy in its modern form arose under three important historical conditions: European nation-building, capitalism, and industrialization. The modern state is a bureaucratic apparatus of rule that rests on a particular structure of legitimation, leadership, and policy, complete with symbolic instruments—signatures, offices, seals, and registers—to establish impersonal, interchangeable power (Bourdieu, 1997b). Nation-building—and by extension imperial conquest and colonization—created the need for effective tax collection and military capability. Kings cannot run countries, or wars, without taxes. They cannot raise taxes without the help of honest and hard-working tax collectors who are loyal to the king. An honest and effective military is needed to beat down the local aristocrats, and to fight the armies of other countries.

With nation-building and international warfare—especially in the eighteenth and nineteenth centuries—rulers quickly discovered that their armies were not properly organized, provisioned, and led. The weakness of command, usually, was because the positions for officers were filled through patronage or the purchase of commissions, a system that provided no assurance that military officers were competent to lead, or that authority was linked in any way to competence. The results were ineffective leaders and, often, disastrous outcomes, as demonstrated by Britain's lengthy failure to control Napoleon's armies. Eventually one nation after another—Prussia, Great Britain, France, and others—realized there was a need to reorganize the military and the civil service along bureaucratic lines, or the nation could never achieve its ruler's goals (see Bensman, 1987; Gorski, 1995; Kiser and Schneider, 1995; Spittler, 1980; Tyrell, 1981).

Capitalism imposed similar demands. Under capitalism—a system devoted to the pursuit of maximum profits—people quickly discover that some forms of social and economic organization yield higher rates of

Time to Reflect

If bureaucracies are so very efficient, why do so many people complain about bureaucratic 'red tape'?

profit on investment than others. The rationality of bureaucratic organization is well-suited to the rationality associated with a pursuit of profits. The bureaucratic structure is capable of growing as large as necessary, through a growth of roles, yet remains highly controlled from the top. This is less possible, if possible at all, in clientelist systems based on personal loyalty. The legal idea of 'limited liability' allows a bureaucracy to manage investment and profits impersonally, in a way that protects both the owners and the workers. This impersonality also makes bureaucracy different from clientelist systems.

Finally, industrialization also favoured the rise of bureaucracies. Bureaucracies are good at controlling large workforces—even highly educated and differentiated workforces. As the size of an organization grows, its degree of differentiation typically increases. Related problems of co-ordination and control—formalization, decentralization, and supervision—must be solved (Marsden et al., 1996). Reorganization may be called for, especially if the number of personnel is growing rapidly (Raadschelders, 1997). As industrial enterprises grew larger with the mechanization of work, control structures (that is, for management and administration) had to grow similarly larger. This has been equally true in post-industrial enterprises that process information and turn out services (or other information) rather than manufactured goods. The twentieth-century development of professional management and administration reflects the enormous importance of bureaucratic organization in modern work life. Modern organizations—embedded in diverse networks of ties to external sources, growing rapidly, and responding to continuous changes in the environment—became continuous adopters of new technology and administrative technique (Kelley and Helper, 1997).

On a broader scale, Weber (1978 [1908]) traced the rise of bureaucracy, capitalism, and the modern state to the **rationalization** of human activity. Indeed, rationalization is central to Weber's general conception of history. For Weber, rationalization refers to the movement away from mystical and religious interpretations of the world to the development of human thought and belief based on a methodical collection of evidence. Also associated with rationalization is the rise of impersonal authority based on the universal application of a codified set of rules and laws.

The value system associated with rationalization prizes efficient, effective administration in government and in the production of goods and services. In Weber's view, these values spurred the growth of bureaucracy, because bureaucracies organize human activity in a logical, impersonal, and efficient manner. Or so he thought.

The Characteristics of Bureaucracy

Weber first analyzed the particular features of the bureaucratic form of organization. In his study of the major organizations of his day, Weber (1958 [1922]) identified seven essential characteristics of bureaucracy:

- a division of labour,
- a hierarchy of positions;
- a formal system of rules;
- a reliance on written documents;
- a separation of the person from the office;
- hiring and promotion based on technical merit;
- the protection of careers.

Division of Labour

In earlier eras, workers handcrafted specific articles from start to finish to produce society's goods. Gradually, this production process gave way to specialization and the division of labour. Adam Smith noted the overwhelming productive superiority of specialization as long ago as 1776 (Smith, 1976 [1776]). A specialized division of labour became the foundation of modern industry and bureaucratization. An automotive assembly line is perhaps the typical modern example of such a division of labour.

As on an assembly line, every member of a bureaucracy performs named and distinguished duties. The bureaucracy itself provides the facilities and resources for carrying out these duties. Workers work with equipment they do not own; in other words, they are separated from the **means of production**. Also, administrators manage what they do not own. The goals of this combination—task specialization based on technical competence plus

Time to Reflect

Brainstorm several types of business where clientelism is still employed. List reasons bureaucracy has not been able to entirely replace the old system of company–customer relationships.

All organizations depend on a division of labour that is usually hierarchical and brings together expertise and technology to complete a specific task. (CP/AP/Eugene Hoslip)

the centralized provision of resources—are increased efficiency and productivity.

Hierarchy of Positions

We can imagine the structure of an organization as a pyramid, with authority centralized at the top (see, for example, the organizational chart in Figure 6.2). Authority filters down towards the base through a well-defined hierarchy of command. Thus, the structure plainly identifies both the range and the limits of authority for people in each position. Within this hierarchy, each person is responsible *to* a specific person one level up the pyramid and *for* a specific group of people one level down.

The organizational chart of any large corporation is shaped roughly like a Christmas tree, in that the number of workers increases (and the division of labour specializes) as you move down towards the base of the hierarchy. With the other characteristics of bureaucracy, this feature serves to increase efficiency: all communications flow upward to 'control central' from large numbers of workers 'at ground level'. However, formal communication within a bureaucracy can be awkward. What if a Halifax, Nova Scotia, sales representative wishes to discuss a special order with a craft worker in the Moncton, New Brunswick, plant? Does the sales rep have to communicate through intermediaries, all the way up and down the structure, until he reaches the craft worker in Moncton? No. In real life, people work to avoid such unwieldy communication channels, often forming informal communication networks, which will be examined later in the chapter.

Rules

Bureaucracies work according to written rules. The rules allow a bureaucracy to formalize and classify the countless circumstances it routinely confronts. For each situation, decision-makers can find or develop a rule that provides for an objective and impersonal response. The rules, therefore, guarantee impersonal, predictable responses to specific situations. Impersonality and objectivity help the organization to achieve its objectives.

Separation of the Person from the Office

In a bureaucracy, each person is an office-holder in a hierarchy. The duties, roles, and authority of this office all are clearly defined. That is, the rights and responsibilities of a Level 3 supervisor are spelled out in relation to a Level 4 supervisor (her superior) or Level 2 supervisor (her subordinate). The relationships between positions in a bureaucracy are, thus, impersonal relationships between roles, not personal relationships between people. This separation of person and office means that people are replaceable functionaries in the organization: people come and go, but the organization remains intact. It also means that personal feelings towards other office-holders must be subordinated to the impersonal demands of the office. Equally, relationships are confined to the official duties of office-holders and—ideally—do not invade their private lives.

To illustrate: Charlie Brown, as sales manager, has the right to issue specific orders to his sales force. The sales representatives follow these orders because they come from the sales manager, not because they come from Charlie personally. And they follow the orders only because these relate to each salesperson's official duties. Next week, if Charlie is transferred to a different job, he can no longer issue the same orders to the same people, because he will hold a different office.

Figure 6.2 Ontario Municipal Board Organizational Hierarchy

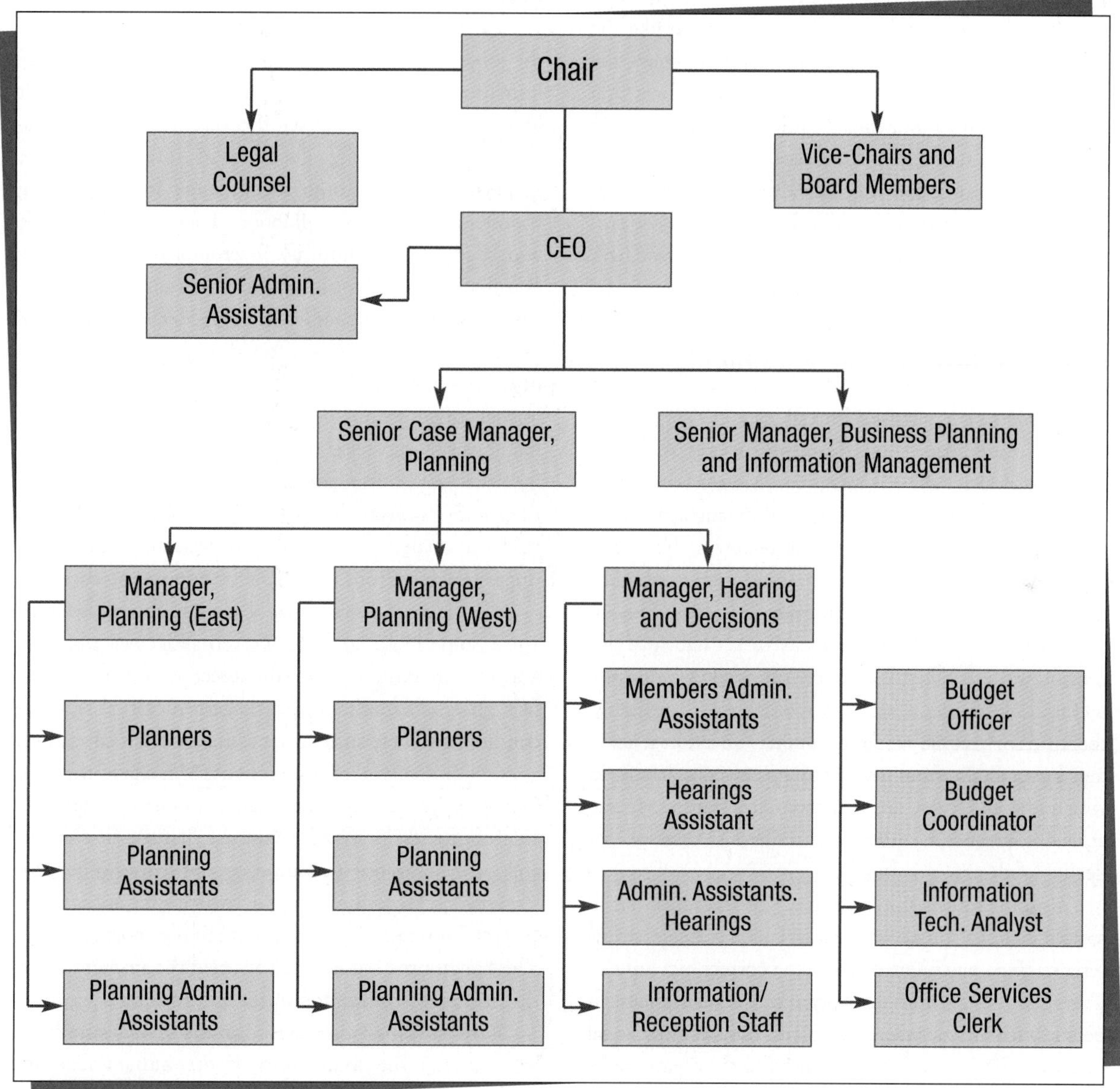

Source: Ontario Municipal Board, at: <www.omb.gov.on.ca/About/Annual%20Report/images/orgchart20012002.gif>.

Hiring and Promotion Based on Technical Merit

A properly functioning bureaucracy hires on the basis of impersonal criteria such as technical competence, not by ascribed, inborn characteristics such as gender, race, or ethnicity. Promotion is based on technical competence, or sometimes on seniority. People are neither discriminated against nor favoured because of such personal criteria as their personalities or their kinship connection to a person at the top of the hierarchy.

Protection of Careers

The final characteristic of bureaucracies is that people's careers are protected within them. People can look forward to long careers in a bureaucracy because they are not subject to arbitrary dismissal for personal reasons. So long as they follow the rules attached to their office or position, they are secure in their jobs. Generally speaking, their income will continue to arrive at the end of each month.

Compare these characteristics with the cliques, communities, or spontaneous work teams considered earlier.

In a bureaucracy, we find a much more detailed division of labour and a much longer hierarchy of positions than one finds in the typical clique, for example. The system of rules in a bureaucracy is formal, or written, unlike the informal rules in a clique. A bureaucracy separates the person from the office, whereas there are no offices in a clique, only distinct individuals. Hiring and promotion in a bureaucracy are based on technical merit; in a clique, they are based on popularity, friendship with the leader, toughness, or attractiveness. Finally, a bureaucracy provides people with secure, often lifelong careers; as we have seen, clique memberships may be brief and insecure.

Merton's Bureaucratic Personality

Robert Merton's analysis of bureaucracy (1957) focused on the pressure placed on bureaucrats to act in ways that serve to weaken the organization. Merton compared bureaucrats to overtrained athletes. Bureaucracies place great pressure on their members to conform. This pressure, combined with intensive training, overemphasizes members' knowledge of the bureaucracy's rules. This, in turn, makes it easy for bureaucrats to act habitually in routine ways. In Merton's words, they follow rules in a methodical, prudent, and disciplined way. Inevitably, the routines become similar to blinkers on a horse, keeping bureaucrats from recognizing new situations in which the old rules are inappropriate. Thus, Merton argued, bureaucrats develop a 'trained incapacity' for dealing with new situations.

Also, the routine application of rules requires that all situations must somehow be classifiable by objective criteria so they may be made to fit the correct pigeonhole. The result is that bureaucrats cannot see their clients as people with unique wants and needs, only as impersonal categories. This viewpoint is harmful to the organization since it causes bureaucrats to fail to meet the unique needs of individual clients. The result may be efficient but not effective, seemingly productive but unsatisfying and inhumane.

Informal Organizations in Bureaucracies: The Hawthorne Studies

Although bureaucracy is intended to be an impersonal form of organization, actual people fill the bureaucratic roles. As human beings, workers resist becoming faceless cogs in the bureaucratic machine (replaceable cogs, at that). So, they develop complex personal and informal networks that work within the formal organization. Collectively, these networks make up the informal organization—bureaucracy's human face. Within formal organizations, we find informal organizations, even cliques of the kind discussed earlier in this chapter.

Informal networks among people who interact on-the-job serve many purposes. First and foremost, they humanize the organization. They also provide support and protection to workers at the lower levels of the hierarchy, serve as active channels of information (the grapevine), and become mechanisms for exchanging favours and exerting influence. They provide people with a sense of community, a sense of inclusion. They also direct the flow of information, enforce moral standards, and exclude people they consider inferior. All of these informal processes affect the operation of formal organizations. Paradoxically, informal networks within formal organizations—though similar to cliques in many ways—can serve to free people from the limits of formal organization and, occasionally, allow them to protest and subvert their working conditions. They also confer human meaning on otherwise impersonal settings, as we see from the classic Hawthorne studies.

The Hawthorne studies were conducted between 1927 and 1932 at the Western Electric plant at Hawthorne, Illinois, under the direction of Elton Mayo. In a series of experiments, management varied working conditions to determine what effect different conditions would have on worker productivity. Mayo held the view that workers were non-rational, emotional beings. His studies provided a massive database that social scientists still are using to test a wide variety of theories. They also spawned a huge literature, of which the account by George Homans (1951) is probably the most readable. The Hawthorne studies first revealed the importance of the informal organization in formal organizations.

Early conclusions drawn from the Hawthorne studies provided the foundation of the human relations school. One of the first conclusions became known as the **Hawthorne effect**. This proposition holds that when people know they are subjects of an important experiment and receive much special attention, they tend to behave the way they think the researchers expect them to. The Hawthorne effect has influenced the design of social-psychological experiments ever since, as researchers try to control for this distortion.

Other conclusions drawn from the studies dealt with the social aspects of work: the relationships among the members of the informal group, the norms developed by the informal group, and types of supervision. The relationships among the women in Phase II of the research were happy and supportive—and associated with higher productivity—while those among the men in Phase IV were not. This finding led human relations theorists to infer that happy group relationships may even increase productivity. The Hawthorne studies also found that group relationships can limit productivity, particularly in the absence of rigid, formal supervision.

A prime example of the usefulness of this approach is demonstrated by the work of sociologist William Foote Whyte (best known as author of the sociology classic *Street Corner Society*), who invented a tool for reducing costly conflict between chefs and servers in restaurants. Whyte (1948) discovered that status differences between restaurant wait staff (typically female) and the (male) chef led to conflicts, because chefs disliked taking orders from women. The revolving order spindle to which waitresses could attach an order and spin it in the direction of the kitchen, which resulted from Whyte's study, allowed customer orders to be conveyed impersonally, reducing workplace conflict and improving communication. Other research-based products include decision supports such as checklists to guide a performance review or action plans to conduct meetings in ways that build consensus (e.g., Mohrman and Mohrman, 1997), effectively translating the evidence into guides for action.

Decades later, further analyses of the Hawthorne studies by Perrow (1972) and others changed the original conclusions, however. In fact, they produced a different idea of informal groups. Starting from the premise that people will respond rationally to the constraints placed on them by organizations, Perrow and other researchers studied the objective conditions surrounding the original Hawthorne studies. They found the Hawthorne plant, like most others, had a long history of raising the productivity standard once workers had consistently reached a certain level. As a result, workers had needed to achieve an increasingly fast pace to keep their incomes. It is logical, then, that workers would try to keep a balance between productivity and earnings, protecting their jobs by not producing too much. This analysis forces organizational theorists to reject the early human relations idea of non-rational workers and group norms.

Other reanalyses of the Hawthorne data by Brannigan and Zwerman (2001) have also raised doubts about the truth and significance of the Hawthorne findings. These authors point out that in the first set of experiments, the productivity of the Western Electric employees increased over time with every variation introduced in their working conditions. Because the workers knew they were being watched, they did their best to show themselves in a positive light. However, in a second set of experiments, the gains in productivity were modest and inconsistent.

This later research has led to the conclusion that informal organization can either help the formal organization to arrive at its goals, or hinder it. Which end it does achieve will depend largely on the quality of the relationship between the workers and their managers. Often-cited examples of hindrance are the British coal industry and Canada Post, both of which have a long history of bitter labour–management conflict. In short, workers are not as non-rational or irrational as managers might have wanted to believe, nor are they entirely focused on the paycheque.

Evolving Organizational Theory and Research

Scientific Management

Why was the assumption that workers might rationally seek to improve their well-being so radical? Perhaps the answer lies with the primitive state of organizational thinking in the early twentieth century. Shortly after the turn of the century, Frederick W. Taylor's view of workers as mere machine cogs became extremely influential.

One of the earliest statements of organizational theory was Taylor's 1911 *Principles of Scientific Management*, which attracted great attention in North America and Western Europe during a period of industrial strife. Taylor's aim was to end labour–management conflict over 'shares of the pie' by providing a bigger pie. Taylor saw the worker as *homo economicus*: an economically rational being who works solely for economic rewards, that is, for money. Therefore, reasoned Taylor, if the worker is shown how to produce more and is paid more as profits increase, everyone will be happy—workers, managers, and corporate shareholders alike.

To arrive at this end, Taylor and his followers rigorously trained time-and-motion study experts to break down every task into its essential motions. In the process, they hoped to strip away all non-essential motions. The experts then trained each worker to perform specific tasks in the precise way their studies showed was the most efficient. Then they timed them with a stopwatch to develop a 'standard time', which became the basis of their piecework rates. The result was often a spectacular, but short-lived, increase in productivity.

Taylor's **scientific management** approach developed the specialized division of labour to the fullest extent. It produced an extreme vertical division of labour within which workers repeated their narrowly defined tasks over and over. It also introduced a new horizontal division of labour. No longer could workers use their experience to improve the efficiency of their task performance. Instead, the workplace was now divided into thinkers (managers and experts) and doers (workers). This style of management even infiltrated such seemingly distant areas of activity as modern ballet, which has moved away from a focus on ballerinas and onto the 'creative' choreographer and composer (Van Delinder, 2005).

The mindless, repetitive work proposed by Taylorism and the alienation it produced are one reason scientific management gradually became more subtle. Many present-day uses of information technology to watch and control workers build on the original assumptions of Taylorism (Harris, 2006), for example. And, in an age of global planning, new strategies of governance based essentially on principles of Taylorist scientific management continue to shape work activities as different as the global production and consumption of food (Phillips and Ilcan, 2003) and the global provision of management advice (Djelic, 2004). Taylorist principles connected to so-called Fordist notions of regulation still are relevant in the modern world of work. And, in many areas of production, the assembly line—that most distinctive invention associated with Henry Ford and Fordism—is still to be seen.

Recall that in an assembly-line form of manufacture workers merely repeat an identical physical task throughout the workday. Such assembly-line methods are common in manufacturing in the low-wage developing countries—for example, in the foreign-owned assembly plants known as maquiladoras in Mexico (Livingston, 2004). Introducing these assembly methods transforms—some say, worsens—gender, family, and other social and economic relations, even while bringing money into the local community (see, for example, Jose Castillo and Lopez Calle, 2002–3). Some critics have even connected this change to a growth in gendered violence against women (Garwood, 2002).

In North America, many traditionally professional, semi-professional, or at least semi-independent occupations have been 'proletarianized' for closer control, faster work, and higher profits. The legal profession offers one prime example of this change; so does the profession of journalism. Gans (2003), for example, notes that increased profit-seeking in the news media coupled with a change to assembly-line style news production contributes to a decrease in investigative journalism and critical news analysis. In short, we are far from seeing the end of Taylorist notions of management that treat workers as *homo economicus*.

The Human Relations and Behavioural Schools: The Happiness Era

In the early 1930s, organizational theory shifted away from seeing organization as merely structure (in the tradition of Taylor) to viewing it more in terms of people. This new focus dominated the field through the 1960s.

Growing out of the famous Hawthorne studies, discussed earlier, the early human relations school focused on relationships within informal groups. It assumed that happy group relationships increased job satisfaction, which, in turn, increased productivity. The school studied the effects of supervision on this equation. Since workers were seen as emotional and non-rational, management's task was to instill both happiness and rationality in work groups. The basic objective, though, was productivity. Happiness and rationality were viewed as means to this end. The central idea was that socially connected workers were happy workers, and happy workers were productive workers.

Like the other approaches we discuss in this chapter, the human relations approach continues to change and inspire new research. For example, a recent study (Castilla, 2005) examined the role of referral contacts on workers' performance, on the assumption that referred workers will be more connected, therefore happier and more productive workers. The author examined the performance of new workers in a call centre and found that people referred to the job are initially more productive than people who are not referred, largely because they have more initial connections within the firm. However, post-hire social processes also affect the connectedness, happiness, and productivity of new workers. For example, referred workers also have lower than average turnover rates. This study shows that the effect of referral ties continues beyond hiring, having long-term effects on employee attachment to the firm and on performance.

The **behavioural school** developed out of a fusion of human relations theory and a psychological conception of human needs. In the 1940s and 1950s, the psychologist Abraham Maslow (1954) developed his idea of the hierarchy of needs, which changed the view of workers forever. No longer were organizations seen as being composed of just two groups, workers and managers. They were now viewed as associations of complex human beings who responded to inner drives that Maslow ranked in the following hierarchy, from lowest to highest: physiological needs, security, social needs, esteem, and self-fulfillment.

Douglas McGregor developed and popularized Maslow's path-breaking work. His 1960 publication *The Human Side of Enterprise* had a huge influence on managers. McGregor and other members of the behavioural school felt the chief leadership style of their era had been autocratic and task-centred. They proposed that managers should adopt a participative employee-centred leadership style instead. The collective result of the ideas of these two schools was a rapid increase of management-training programs aimed at improving the relationship between superiors and subordinates and increasing the happiness of workers.

The debate between Taylor's 'scientific management' approach and the 'humanistic' approach taken by Mayo, Maslow, and McGregor can be viewed as, finally, a dispute about the relative importance of 'extrinsic' (especially, material) work rewards and 'intrinsic' (non-material, especially social) work rewards. This debate about extrinsic versus intrinsic rewards continues today. However, researchers have come to understand that these rewards cannot be either/or; both types are important. So, for example, Kashefi (2005) uses data from the General Social Survey to show that extrinsic rewards must meet workers' basic needs before the value of intrinsic rewards starts growing. Only after employee incomes rise significantly are employees likely to take income for granted and turn their attention to intrinsic rewards (such as job complexity, autonomy, and opportunities for sociability).

Findings like these, repeated scores if not hundreds of times, show that work must satisfy the most basic human needs for food, shelter, and income security Maslow described. Only then can work begin to satisfy the 'higher needs' for belonging and self-actualization that Maslow described also. Even inmates working in prison industries satisfy their intrinsic needs through their work, in much the same way as free workers, as Wignall (2004) has shown.

Systems Theory: The Organization as Organism

The sociological influence on organizational theory emerged again with **systems theory**, an approach in which organizations are viewed as open systems. An organization receives inputs from its environment, processes them, and produces outputs for consumption. These outputs must be acceptable to the environment if the organization is to survive. Survival is a basic theme of systems theory, which sees organizations and their goals as shaped by the interests of their participants and their environments.

Philip Selznick's famous 1949 study of the Tennessee Valley Authority (TVA), *TVA and the Grass Roots*, showed how this particular organization co-opted important elements of its environment to gain support for its operations. However, support came at a price, as these co-opted elements became participants in the TVA's decision-making. Selznick shows that even public agencies and their management must make concessions to secure support in their environment. It may even involve sacrificing the primary policy agenda to survival, particularly if that agenda involves social change.

Organizational leaders and policies struggling to secure themselves in a difficult environment may, in turn, be 'co-opted' by existing interests. So, for example, leadership of the TVA gave up their agricultural policy goals to powerful local interests in return for political support they needed to push TVA's electrical power generation agenda. This shows how the support of powerful interests comes at a price. The more that public programs intend to change the existing order, the more they threaten those who benefit most from the status quo. As a result, those who are best-positioned to shape the details of the program are best-positioned to capture the benefits of the program during its execution.

Research on the institutionalization, leadership, and co-optation of progressive movements has continued to blossom in the field of organization studies. For example, the institutionalization of family planning programs aimed at reducing fertility levels and slowing population growth in the developing world has led some researchers to wonder about their future relevance. The danger of co-optation is always present. Interviews and focus-group discussions with insiders in population studies revealed four possible courses of action for the movement: (1) forming strategic alliances with other movements, specifically HIV/AIDS prevention; (2) redefining the family-planning message to mobilize and strengthen support; (3) improving service delivery to broaden public acceptance and contraceptive method use; and (4) nurturing new leadership. It is too soon to know whether the future course of the movement will hold up against co-optation by overlapping movements or will demonstrate revitalization (Blanc and Tsui, 2005).

Systems theory stresses the effects of the environment on organizations. However, as critic Charles Perrow (1972) notes, it ignores the effects of large and powerful organizations on their environments. He asks us to consider how the 'normal accidents' at Chernobyl, Bhopal, and Three-Mile Island affected the surrounding communities. As a result, researchers like Perrow following the system approach examine the reasons 'normal accidents' occur, and conclude that systems that are too complex and too tightly coupled are most likely to suffer error that is unanticipated and outside the control of human operators.

In recent years, such ideas have gained even wider currency. John Urry (2005) notes the cultural and social sciences have experienced a 'complexity turn' in the past decade. The main characteristics of the 'complexity turn' are a concern with the human behaviour of large populations; examination of systems that are flexible over time; engagement with a post-Newtonian, relativistic idea of time; the expression of chaos theory and its chief conclusion that small causes can produce large effects; an understanding that undisturbed populations may not always reach a balanced state within nature; the appearance of diseases and viruses that are highly adaptable; and recognition that organizations, like other organisms, often reproduce and change themselves.

Systems theory regards organizations as similar to organisms—that is, as intricately interdependent systems of functional parts. Consider this analogy: just as blood poisoning from an infected cut on the hand affects the whole body, so an ineffective sales department or a hostile workforce can endanger the success of an entire organization. This approach produces an almost certain emphasis on the uniqueness of organizations. It also often focuses on the *ripple effect*, that is, how changes in one part produce (often unforeseen) changes in other parts of an organization.

Labour Process Theory: Worker Exploitation

Arising in the 1970s, **labour process theory** is a neo-Marxist approach to organizations and the conduct of work. It focuses on the *alienation* of the worker and on power relationships between capitalists and workers.

Alienation is an important idea in Marx's analysis of capitalism. It comprises four elements, which have been summarized by James Rinehart (2001) as follows:

- *Alienation of workers from the products of their labour.* As soon as workers sell their ability to work to their employers, they receive wages in return rather than any interest in the products they produce. The products belong solely to the employer.
- *Alienation of workers from the labour process.* Wage workers must surrender to their employer the control of how and when a product will be produced.
- *Alienation of workers from themselves.* Because of the first two elements of alienation, work is no longer a central life activity or a means of self-expression. It becomes, instead, merely a means to the end of obtaining income for life satisfaction off the job.
- *Alienation of workers from others.* Under capitalism, workers are separated from their employers because the two sides hold opposing interests in the control of and benefits from the labour process. Workers are also alienated from each other as they compete for jobs.

From these assumptions, it logically follows that rational workers will resist efforts by capitalists and management to convert the labour time they buy into increased effort. This perspective sees the 'human engineering' of the behavioural school as a misguided and superficial effort that does nothing to change the power relations of the wider society or those at the point of production (Braverman, 1974). Harry Braverman's classic work, *Labor and Monopoly Capital: The Degradation of Work in the 20th Century*, continues to explain many recent changes in the workplace. Understanding what has happened to workers in the past 20 years requires knowledge of how craftsmanship has been destroyed by capitalism and workers have been degraded (Staples and Staples, 2000).

An important strand in the labour process perspective is the intensification of management control over the workplace that has occurred since the turn of the century. Taylor's scientific management, the introduction of assembly lines, and the use of technology to convert workers into tenders of machines all typify this trend. Labour process theorists regard all these as parts of a strategy to replace the skilled craftsperson of a bygone era with a modern unskilled, easily replaceable counterpart (Braverman, 1974). Many historical studies have supported the idea of the decline of the artisan. However, as Wallace Clement (1988) points out, the deskilling process is complex, with new skills replacing old ones often.

The labour process approach is usefully applied to any situation where managerial strategies are transparently applied to manipulating worker productivity through fear or loyalty. So, for example, Videla (2006) examined the labour process at a high-end garment factory in central Mexico. Her ethnographic research consisted of nine months of work at the factory and in-depth interviews with 25 managers and 26 workers. Achievement of 'lean production' in this factory was an organizational and social feat. Besides a focus on quality, just-in-time production, and flattened hierarchies, lean production was based on a management-sponsored 'community of fate' ideology. In this case study, the 'community of fate' ideology devised by managers—with its discourse of loyalty and sacrifice—convinced workers to extend their physical, intellectual, and emotional labour to the firm. What managers failed to

Modern offices not only divide the labour, they divide the labourers by barriers that represent their isolation and simplify their subordination. (Jagadeesh/Reuters/Corbis)

understand was that in workers' eyes, the 'community of fate' belief also tied the firm to the workers. When management reneged on this social pact, workers not only resisted management's efforts to regain control over the shop floor, but also actively used the team system to thwart the firm's economic viability. In the end, instead of controlling workers, lean production simplified worker radicalization and mobilization.

Another central element of labour process theory has been an analysis of the evolution of different forms of control exercised by capitalists over the workplace. Richard Edwards's influential study (1979) argued that the first of these was the simple person-to-person domination of the owner or supervisor over the worker. As firms grew, such control became impractical. Edwards suggests that capitalists then consciously developed technology that improved their ability to govern the pace and execution of work. Thus, technological control replaced face-to-face domination. The automotive assembly line, first set up by Henry Ford in 1913, would be a clear example of this form of control.

Technological control of this kind made power relations more impersonal but did nothing to motivate the workers. The increasing worker resistance that resulted led to the arrival of today's bureaucratic control, which represents the institutionalization of control. Rules and procedures now govern the conduct of each specific task, the penalties for poor performance, and the rewards for good performance. In this form of control, power relations became impersonalized and embedded in the structure of the organization. Still, to quote Edwards, 'top-echelon managers retain their control over the enterprise through their ability to determine the rules, set the criteria, establish the structure, and enforce compliance' (1979: 173).

In some respects, this control represents a subtle form of indoctrination or brainwashing at the highest levels of the organization. At lower levels it can be viewed as simply the inculcation of a 'proper attitude', as can be seen in studies of sales staff, for example. Consider Schweingruber's (2006) study on the use of a motivational philosophy called 'positive mental attitude' (PMA) by door-to-door salespersons. While PMA works as a form of worker control, the flexibility of PMA also makes it useful to salespersons that draw on it to deal with everyday work problems. Like method actors, dealers and sales staff draw on their personal goals, values, and experiences to form motivational foci—the content of the positive thinking they wish to preserve—and try to keep these thoughts in mind through motivational practices learned during their training.

According to regulation theory, changes in managerial strategy have occurred in various guises and to various degrees throughout the industrial world, in the transition to what some have called post-Fordism. 'Fordism' attempted (in the first half of the twentieth century) to control workers through the use of high wages, tall bureaucratic management structures, union-management co-operation, and technical control (i.e., fast-moving assembly lines). By contrast, post-Fordism—since 1965–75—has attempted to control workers with low wages, flat administrative structures, avoidance of unions, threat of global competition and unemployment, and meritocratic ideologies.

These changes, involving a decline of state control over markets, have affected work life in the public sector as well as the private sector. So, for example, recent reforms to UK education have led to significant organizational changes in primary school and higher education. Regulation theory also examines two main theoretical explanations for these, namely post-Fordism and New Managerialism. Up to the mid-1980s, publicly funded educational organizations did display bureaucratic features, including rules, staff hierarchies, and complex procedures. However, professionals employed in these organizations kept discretion and autonomy in their work. Since then, the introduction of an audit culture and a greater emphasis on management and control of the work of teachers and academics has decreased discretion and autonomy (Brehony and Deem, 2005).

Labour process theory proposes that this transformation of forms of workplace control has been driven by the capitalists' need to extract the most possible effort from the wageworker. Critics of labour process theory argue, in contrast, that alienation, deskilling, and the coming of bureaucratic control occur in socialist and capitalist societies alike. While deplorable and even degrading, they are specific aspects of Weber's more general idea of bureaucracy. This criticism may contain truth. Nevertheless, we can learn much from labour process theory about the reality of work and the problems faced by workers in repetitive, mind-numbing jobs.

The Structural Approach: The Organization Makes the Person

Another prominent perspective that offers great promise is the **structural approach**. In the Weberian tradition, it focuses on the structural characteristics of organizations and their effect on the people within them. One objective of present-day **structural analysis** is to devise changes in organizational structures that will make bureaucracies more effective by making them more humane. Perrow (1972), for example, argues that analyses of the famous Hawthorne studies show that bureaucratic effectiveness depends on the degree to which a bureaucracy can complete changes that will increase the congruence between the goals of the formal and the informal organizations.

Nobel laureate Herbert Simon (1986, 1997) was an important pioneer of the structural approach. Noted mainly for his work on decision theory, Simon also pointed out the importance of structural constraints on organizational decision-making. In doing so, he provided 'the muscle and flesh for the Weberian skeleton' (Perrow, 1972: 146). Simon's studies led him to infer that Weber's six elements of bureaucracy define the situation for decision-makers and shape the assumptions on which they base organizational decisions. In other words, bureaucratic structures impel their members to make decisions consistent with those made at the top of the hierarchy.

Thus, organizations differ in the degree to which their various parts are connected or 'coupled'. Top-down control implies a high degree of organizational coupling, but Perrow shows that this can carry high risks: highly complex, tightly coupled organizations are the most likely to suffer disastrous effects from failures in any part of the organization and what Perrow calls 'normal accidents'. Equally, the coupling between formal and informal sources of control can itself lead to 'bureaucratization'—an intensified version of rule-making and bureaucratic control. This is explained in a study by Hallett and Ventresca (2006), who return to Alvin Gouldner's classic study, *Patterns of Industrial Bureaucracy* (1954), to re-examine the 'coupling' idea in present-day institutionalism in a way that engages the following question: How do new institutional forms emerge?

Time to Reflect

Contrast labour process theory to scientific management. What criticism did labour process theory make against Taylor's scientific management?

Gouldner's study had concluded that new bureaucratic rules are a result of conflict between labour and management; in short, rules are attempts by management to control, not to improve productivity. Building on Gouldner's detailed observations of work in a gypsum mine, Hallett and Ventresca argue that coupling processes help us to understand how the institution of bureaucracy emerges through an interaction with previous social orders of authority and control. Gouldner's account of coupling at the mine is a story of formal and informal power struggles and active conflict over meaning and legitimate control.

An influential structural analysis of modern bureaucracy is Rosabeth Moss Kanter's *Men and Women of the Corporation* (1977). Kanter explains the behaviour of people in organizations in light of three key variables: the structures of power, of opportunities for advancement, and of proportional representation. Her evidence suggests that those who have power make good leaders—not because of their relationship with subordinates, but because they can gain for their whole group a favourable share of the organization's resources. On the other hand, 'accountable but powerless' people react rationally to their unfortunate situation in ways harmful both to the organization and to their leadership. Those who are upwardly mobile support the organization and its goals. Those whose mobility is blocked salvage their dignity by withdrawing their support from the organization and by trying to gain recognition elsewhere (for example, from subordinates or from sources outside the organization).

Finally, Kanter suggests that those who make up a small part of a group—for instance, women and ethnic minorities among managers—are treated as tokens. The results, which include stereotyping, exclusion from leaders' networks, and intense scrutiny, produce a self-fulfilling prophecy. Tokens perform moderately well at best because of structural constraints, not individual flaws. Thus, their numbers fail to become large enough to break the bonds of tokenism. To change this, Kanter recommends changing the structures of power and mobility, and proportions recruited from different groups.

Feminist Perspectives: Gender Matters

Until three decades ago, most organizational theorists seemed to have ignored the fact that organizations comprise women as well as men. A notable exception is Rosabeth Moss Kanter (1977). However, Kanter took a structural approach in accounting for the disadvantaged positions of women. Women are, indeed, disadvantaged because they are heavily over-represented in lower-level clerical and service occupations and under-represented in management (Armstrong and Armstrong, 1984).

A new wave of feminist theories has developed to address this organizational issue, using gender as an important explanatory concept. Earlier theorists either ignored gender or assumed that organizations were gender-neutral. However, feminist theorists, including Joan Acker (1991), have pointed out that, historically, men have dominated organizations, with the result the organizational image of the manager and the worker is a male image. This bias has several important results.

First, the hierarchical structure of bureaucratic organizations and the accompanying sets of rigid rules and procedures are incompatible with female gender characteristics. Kathy Ferguson (1984) has suggested that women press for more open and democratic organizational systems not only for their own sakes, but also because they believe such changes would make their organizations more effective. However, women are rarely in positions of enough power and authority to change the organization. Thus, organizations remain bastions of male power.

Second, as Acker (1991) asserts, the dominant male image excludes and marginalizes women. Almost by definition, women cannot achieve the qualities of a 'real' worker because to do so is to become like a man. Also, women's bodies and sexuality are stigmatized in organizations often and used as grounds for control and exclusion.

Third, the male image of the organizational worker causes women's gender roles to be regarded as deviant. Women are seen as being incompatible with organizational life because of their (assumed) ties to marriage and responsibility for children (Cuneo, 1990). As Cynthia Cockburn charges, even attempts to make organizational adjustments to ease women's role conflicts are unproductive: 'The more women are permitted various kinds of flexibility in relation to work to enable them to cope with motherhood and other domestic responsibilities the more they can be dismissed as "different", less serious than male employees' (1990: 92). Cockburn goes on to point out that all women become dismissed as deviant because of the potential role conflicts of some.

Today, studies continue to probe the effects of gender on hiring, promotion, and career trajectory, as mediated by factors like marriage, child-rearing, and family caregiving responsibilities. So, for example, Maume (2006), using data from the National Study of the Changing Workforce, finds that in the presence of family and work-related controls, women are less likely than men to have unused vacation time. Men's work schedules, supervisory duties, and concerns about job security significantly reduce the duration of their vacations. Even though family factors have no direct impact on women's vacation use, women's concerns about the success of their family lives increase with the number of unused vacation days. These findings suggest the persistence of traditional work–family priorities.

Drago et al. (2006) analyze bias avoidance behaviours, whereby employees respond to biases against caregiving in the workplace by strategically lessening or hiding family commitments. They divide bias avoidance behaviours into productive types that improve work performance and unproductive types that are inefficient. Original survey data from faculty in 507 US colleges and universities suggest both types of bias avoidance are fairly common and women more often report both types of behaviour. Regression analyses find supportive supervisors associated with reported cuts in bias avoidance, and suggest that low levels of bias avoidance for women are linked to institutional gender equity.

Finally, Morgan and Martin (2006) note that many women professionals pass through settings beyond the office in their work, but research on women professionals rarely follows them out of the office. Using a large data set of focus groups with sales professionals, the authors ask how work in out-of-the-office settings affects women's careers. They find that, in 'heterosocial' settings, interaction rules are traditionally and normatively gendered. Women and men in these settings are understood by others as heterosexually linked pairs, women (and men) become targets of gossip, and some women report sexual advances and sexual harassment. In 'homosocial' settings such as golf courses and strip clubs, women's disadvantage takes the form of exclusion.

In short, gender differences have not ceased to be a source of significant differentiation in careers, professions, groups, and organizations.

How Bureaucracies Actually Work

Weber's concept of bureaucracy, as we have seen, is a very useful model for the study of this complex form of organization. It calls our attention to central features of bureaucracy. But it is a simplification, an idealization, like the notion of a perfect vacuum in physics or of a feather falling through space without meeting any wind resistance. Such images are good for starting to think theoretically, but they are not the real world. In the real world, bureaucracies have flaws, and sociologists since Weber have spent a great deal of time discussing these flaws. This section presents the more obvious and troubling discrepancies between ideal bureaucracies and actual bureaucracies.

Ideally, every member of a bureaucratic organization is knowingly enmeshed in a network of reporting relationships. In graphic form, a bureaucracy is a Christmas-tree-shaped structure that repeatedly branches out as you go down the hierarchy. Thus, at the bottom of the hierarchy there are a great many people whose job it is to (1) carry out orders from above and (2) report work-related information up the tree to their superiors. At the top of the hierarchy, there are a few people whose job it is to (1) issue orders to their subordinates, (2) process information received from below, and (3) maintain linkages between the organization and its (political, economic, and social) environment. Also at the top, information is shared between the heads of planning, manufacturing, shipping, public relations, and other sectors of the organization.

In practice, organizations do not work this way, as sociologists since Weber have pointed out. They could not afford to work this way, and human beings aren't constructed to work this way. Thus, alongside the ideal or formal structure—which prescribes how a bureaucracy ought to work—there is an actual or informal structure, which is how it *really* works.

Actual Flows of Information

In theory, a failure to report information up the hierarchy would never occur. In practice, it occurs all the time, because workplaces are politically 'contested terrains' (Edwards, 1979), and controlling the flow of information from below is a means of changing the balance of power between superiors and subordinates. And, as the French sociologist Michel Crozier (1959) showed, bureaucracies work differently in different societies. This is because people raised in different cultures have different ideas about inequality, deference, openness, and secrecy. For example, people raised in France or Russia will be much more alert to the inequality of bureaucratic relations and the power of information control to equalize relations than workers raised in the United States. French and Russian workers behave differently, and as a result bureaucracies work differently in these countries.

Bureaucracies also appear to work differently for men and women, as has already been noted. When playing a managerial role, women adopt a collaborative, relational approach derived from qualities used in familial relations, whereas men emphasize purely economic considerations. Women's managerial styles emphasize the establishment of good employer–employee relations and the sharing of information and power (Occhionero, 1996).

In practice, workers everywhere make friends and acquaintances. As a result, they casually share work information. Much of the information that flows within an organization is shared orally, not in writing, to introduce civility and negotiation between work teams (Grosjean and Lacoste, 1998). In many cases, workers use information purposely to help one another. In a few cases, they may even leak information for personal gain or to subvert their boss or the organization as a whole.

Thus, within organizations based ideally on strangers relating to other strangers on the basis of written rules, we find workers forming what amount to secret organizations or subcommunities that obey their own rules. Political actors below the top level cannot employ routine channels or resources to negotiate in the idealized manner. 'Politics from below' includes all the actions that defy, oppose, or sidestep the rules or roles of the organization (Brower and Abolafia, 1997).

The basis of this informal organization is trust, which relies on friendship, acquaintanceship, and gossip about third parties that strengthens existing ties (Burt and Knez, 1996). In the end, the same materials that build cliques build the informal, often hidden, infrastructure of bureaucracies.

As in cliques, trust in bureaucracies is built gradually, maintained continuously, and easily destroyed (Lewicki and Bunker, 1996). When trust is violated, the result is often revenge or another disruptive response—confrontation, withdrawal, or feuding, for example (Bies and Tripp, 1996). Trust is easier to generate within organizations than across organizations, since it is within organizations that managers, serving as third parties, can monitor and enforce reciprocity. The result is that organizational boundaries work effectively to restrict intellectual diffusion (Zucker et al., 1996). Within organizations, the flow of information is harder to contain.

Often team structures are created by management to cut across the bureaucratic hierarchy, enabling workers to co-operate in the solution of a cross-branch problem. This solution is undertaken with the recognition that requiring all information to flow to the top and then across is a slow and ponderous way of solving problems. Thus, increasingly, organizations have adopted horizontal, as well as vertical, reporting relationships. In many instances, this has improved organizational learning and given the organization a competitive advantage (West and Meyer, 1997).

Such temporary, cross-cutting groups rely on what is called *swift trust.* In these temporary systems, a premium is placed on making do with whatever information is available and in which swift judgements of trust are mandatory. Generally, trust develops most rapidly when (1) there is a smaller labour pool and more vulnerability among workers; (2) interaction is based on roles, not personalities; (3) behaviour is consistent and **role expectations** are clear; (4) available information allows a faster reduction in uncertainty; and (5) the level of interdependence is moderate, not high or low (Meyerson et al., 1996).

New information technology also makes it easier for horizontal groupings to form, since distant employees can easily exchange information through a large organizational computer network (Constant et al., 1996). New cultures emerge when computers, linked together to form intra-organizational networks, create a virtual organization parallel to but independent of the traditional bureaucratic hierarchical organization (Allcorn, 1997). As well, telecommuting, or teleworking, now occupies an important place in the world of information work, posing new problems (Di Martino, 1996). It may reduce costs by externalizing or delocalizing work, but we are far from knowing how it will affect work organization and productivity (Carre and Craipeau, 1996). For example, the increased use of computer-mediated communication appears to increase user satisfaction in task-oriented organizational cultures and to decrease user satisfaction in person-oriented organizational cultures (Kanungo, 1998).

Nowhere is the role of new communication technology in organization more apparent than in the development of huge, seemingly shapeless 'virtual teams' of workers. Their size, ingenuity, and passion often produce unexpected discoveries, as information in the 'Global Issues' box on the next page indicates.

Organizational Cultures and Flexibility

In temporary or other horizontal groupings, a worker reports to more than one superior, which may create conflicts or inconsistent demands. Sometimes, it becomes

Time to Reflect

Do you think new technologies will improve the communicating process from top to bottom in bureaucracies?

GLOBAL ISSUES

Global Virtual Groups Provide New Varieties of Organization

One of the differences between human teams and some biological teams is sheer scale in terms of number of members. Human teams rarely exceed 50 and a typical large single human organization might contain 10,000 members. Human organizations much bigger than this exist, but they tend to organize themselves into smaller independently managed subunits. However, biological teams, such as ant or bee societies, can contain up to a million members in a single mature colony or hive—all of whom can act as a unit. This has meant that some dimensions of biological teamwork and group behaviour were not possible in human teams and organizations due to this lack of scale. The Internet might change all this. *Businessweek* (www.businessweek.com/magazine/content/05_25/b3938601.htm) reports that 'mass collaboration on the Internet is shaking up business'.

'Scale' enables some particularly useful characteristics in teams, such as:

- *Reduced vulnerability to individual member failure.* Individual member actions are unlikely to alter the overall group outcome due to the sheer numbers involved.
- *Swarm intelligence.* Simple individual behaviours can produce amazingly sophisticated collective results. Examples of this include bird flocking, schools of fish, and, of course, ants' amazing scheduling and routing capabilities.
- *Emergent behaviour.* Swarming and school formation create emergent behaviour. An emergent behaviour can appear when a number of simple entities (agents) operate in an environment, forming more complex behaviours as a collective. The property itself is often unpredictable and unprecedented, and represents a new level of the system's evolution. The complex behaviour or properties are not a property of any single such entity, nor can they easily be predicted or deduced from behaviour in the lower-level entities.
- *Give and take.* The Voice over IP (VoIP) start-up has attracted 41 million users and is changing the face of the global telecommunications industry. 'When users fire up Skype, they automatically allow their spare computing power and connections to be borrowed by the Skype network, which uses that collective resource to route others' calls. This creates a self-sustaining phone system requiring no capital investment based on users' spare capacity' (www.skype.com). However, Skype is just one example of the power of **distributed or grid computing,** which has already been exploited by a number of other non-commercial initiatives.
- *Participation through passion.* The innovative power of individuals can be remarkable once they are provided with the opportunity to be creative in an area that stimulates them.

We won't be able to fully predict what happens next. One of the most interesting aspects of these phenomena is the fact that they all demonstrate *emergent behaviour*, which means we cannot predict exactly how they will evolve. For example, Internet mass collaborations may evolve into even more valuable forms of mass collaboration by starting to operate as networks (with connections between individual members). Today they operate more as star formations (with connections mostly between individual members and the centre). Alternatively, it may turn out that some of the most advanced forms of collaboration are available only to small teams and not accessible to teams of the size we are starting to see in Internet mass collaborations.

Source: Adapted and abridged from Ken Thompson, 'Virtual Teams, Virtual Groups, and Virtual Crowds', 23 June 2005, at:<www.bioteams.com/collaboration_research_science.html>. Ken Thompson, Belfast, Northern Ireland c/o www.bioteams.com

unclear where a worker's main duties lie and, therefore, how that person's work should be evaluated and rewarded. Greater flexibility and co-operation must be sought from the workers as well as built into the organizational structure itself.

Organizations require increasingly more flexibility from workers, which is possible only if those workers receive continuing education and training and participate in planning (de la Torre, 1997). Yet worker motivation, recruitment, and training all pose problems for bureaucracies. The motivational problem is greatest in organizations where professional expertise and judgement are most required, as in universities, law firms, and technology-development firms. There we find the greatest attention given to matters of organizational culture and career development. It is only by giving these workers considerable autonomy and rewards for strong identification with the firm that the most able workers can be induced to join, stay, and carry out their duties in conformity with organizational goals. Along with this structure comes a need for thorough organizational **socialization**, which begins at the stage of recruitment and interviewing and is never completed (Edwards, 1979).

Some organizational cultures are more effective than others in creating a high level of worker commitment and high rates of employee retention, and societies vary in their use of one or another kind of organizational culture. For example, in Japan, Korea, and China, people are more receptive to a collective (or group) culture than we find in North America.

Some organizations manipulate organizational culture to tackle the perceived shortcomings of bureaucracy and to empower the workers. They espouse open management, teamwork, continuous improvement, and partnership between customers and suppliers without replacing bureaucratic principles of standardization, differentiation, and control through a single chain of command. In the end, senior management has merely used these techniques to restructure management roles, justifying increased corporate control and intensifying work.

However, people usually form stronger attachments to other people than they do to 'the organization' as an abstract entity. Thus, patterns of clientelism develop even within bureaucracies. In the end, bureaucracies are organizations in which two principles—rule-based rationality and person-based clientelism—contend for dominance, with neither being able to win decisively at the expense of the other.

The Problem of Rationality

Bureaucracies are thought to be rational in the ways they make and execute plans. They are indeed more rational—in a limited sense—than patron–client relations. This is because, over the long term, by making impersonal decisions and rewarding excellence, they are more able to pursue long-term organizational goals with huge amounts of wealth and power.

However, the sheer size of large bureaucracies and their long-term outlook introduce certain types of irrationality that, in the end, may undermine the organization. A concern with the mere survival of the organization may undermine shorter-term concerns with the quality of decisions, products, and services the organization is providing to its customers. The much-hated 'red tape'—or administrative delay—by bureaucracies persists not because of inadequate technology or personnel, but because it serves positive (as well as negative) functions for the organization (Pandey and Bretschneider, 1997). The bureaucratic demand to eliminate subjectivity and individuality actually undermines the productivity of institutions. By creating boundaries between the institution and outside influences, the institution loses touch with the individuals who are both the subjects and the objects of their efforts (Imershein and Estes, 1996).

Managerial tools such as corporate statements, corporate culture, performance appraisal, and reward systems are means for the **social construction** of homogeneity. Obedience is valued because it is interpreted as the willingness to adopt and internalize dominant ideas, values, rationality, and, more generally, normative systems (Filion, 1998).

In bureaucratic organizations, the presumption of knowledge, heavy reliance on official records and procedures, and the predominance of routine all cushion 'pape-reality'—a world of **symbols**—from other forms of representation. This inhibits both forgetting and learning (Dery, 1998). Another result is the creation of a *bureaucratic personality*, which substitutes proceduralism at the expense of any moral impulse or ethical concern with outcomes (Ten Bos, 1997). Anonymity and distance from decision-making make moral indifference likely, if not inevitable. Rule-making and record-keeping proliferate, particularly in private organizations. There is evidence that managers who are more alienated and more pessimistic make more rules (Bozeman and Rainey, 1998).

The bureaucratic characteristic of relying on the rules as written can create another problem. As a bureaucracy grows and more rules are added, the system

HUMAN DIVERSITY

Society and Bureaucracy in Ghana

Bureaucracy is a new and increasingly dominant form of human organization, but it is not the only one. Many communities and organizations function using a clientelist model, which emphasizes personal relationships, as opposed to the impersonal rules of bureaucracy. Traditional societies usually operated in such a manner, and there are even remnants of this model in our bureaucratic culture. It's easy to see how the rules that govern a bureaucracy can fail when met with the human element. Even as bureaucracy has become so prevalent in many societies, it causes problems when people ignore the rules in favour of other values. This raises the question: what would be the result of introducing bureaucracy into a society that is based on traditional familial obligations? Robert Price wrote about this issue in *Society and Bureaucracy in Modern Ghana* (1975), where he looks at the effects of implementing a bureaucratic civil service in Ghana.

In his study, Price discovered a conflict between the ideals and rules required to run a bureaucracy and the traditional values of Ghanaian society. There was also a conflict between the roles Ghanaian civil servants were expected to play—that of the bureaucrat and that of a family member. Price conducted the study in southern Ghana, where he said 'descent groups . . . are corporate in nature and are the foundation of social organization.' Thus, he found it hardly surprising that research pointed to family matters as the primary focus of traditional morality.

To study this conflict, he presented an imaginary situation where a civil servant experienced role conflict between bureaucratic and family roles. By presenting this situation together with various questions to civil servants, Price hoped to discover which role they thought should determine behaviour in a conflicting scenario. He also asked how respondents thought the typcial Ghanaian civil servant would act and how a family member would expect to be treated in the same situation. His findings showed that 75.3 per cent of the civil servants polled believed that universalistic behaviour was the legitimate one in the situation ('universalistic' meaning following the rules of bureaucracy that apply to all). Yet only 19.4 per cent thought that the typical Ghanaian civil servant would act in such a way.

The reason for this discrepancy is found in the last question asked. A full 92.6 per cent of respondents thought that the family member in the situation would expect the civil servant to act in a particularistic way (treating them as better than non-relatives). Thus, Price concluded that 'when presented with imaginary organizational situations involving conflict between bureaucratic and familial role obligations, there is a consensus among the civil servant respondents that the family role-set will consider its obligations binding, expect them to be fulfilled, and mobilize its considerable sanctional resources in instances of their violation.'

Source: Adapted from Price (1975: 56–82).

becomes increasingly complex. This can lead to a situation where no one person knows all of the rules and different offices act independent of each other, creating rules that conflict with one another.

Rule by offices undermines personal responsibility for decisions the organization may take. No member of the bureaucracy is asked, or obliged, to take responsibility for collective decisions. As a result, so-called collective decisions—typically taken by the top executives—are liable to be foolish, harmful, or even criminal. Corporate and government entities are unique in that their deviant behaviour may be caused by systemic patterns in their organizations rather than only by individual malfeasance. However, once deviant behaviour has occurred, they are well positioned to evade responsibility. Managers may often refuse responsibility by hiding behind organizational structures or by adopting the view that they were merely following orders. The deviant behaviour of big business and big government occurs because of limited information, the establishment of norms and rewards that encourage deviant outcomes, or the implementation of actions by organizational elites.

Such deviance is usually initiated by managerial elites and subsequently institutionalized into organizational culture. It will normally continue unchecked until it is challenged from inside or outside the organizations. Organizations themselves are rarely penalized for deviant behaviour (Ermann and Lundman, 1996). Such deviance is rarely prosecuted and punished. A recent prominent example was the prosecution of top leaders of Enron for falsifying records and manipulating information for their own personal benefit, at the expense of thousands of investors and millions of American citizens. Enron's collapse in 2001 wiped out more than 5,000 jobs, more than $60 billion in market value, and more than $2 billion in pensions.

Twenty-four people besides the Enron president, Kenneth Lay, were convicted or pleaded guilty in Enron cases. Four of the 24 had convictions reversed on appeal, and more appeals are pending. Investors are suing to recover more than $30 billion in stock market losses. Lay, 64, died of heart disease while vacationing in Aspen, Colorado, in July of 2006. The government filed a civil forfeiture case in October 2006 against Lay's estate, seeking $12.5 million for victims of Enron's collapse. It sought a jury trial to re-establish Lay's responsibility for the fraud, though in May 2006 he had been convicted of 10 counts of fraud, conspiracy, and lying to banks in two separate cases. District Judge Simeon T. Lake III subsequently declared that Lay's death vacated his conviction on fraud and conspiracy charges because Lay couldn't challenge the conviction.

Even more recently, the US federal government has been equally assertive in its efforts to convict former Canadian businessman Conrad Black of white-collar crime. He was facing 13 charges over claims he stole $60 million from investors in Black's newspaper firm, Hollinger International. Thanks to evidence from his former second-in-command, David Radler, the former media baron was found guilty of obstructing justice and of three counts of mail fraud. This followed a 15-week trial in Chicago and more than two weeks of jury deliberation. Black, 62, who was cleared of racketeering and tax evasion, could face 35 years in jail when sentenced on 10 December 2007. Black may now regret giving up his Canadian citizenship to accept a knighthood from the British government; US prosecutors and prisons are allegedly harsher than Canadian ones.

Despite a few headline-making 'successes' by the courts, historically, charges and convictions of white-collar criminals have been hard to secure. As a legal person, the corporation is able to employ many more resources than individuals who are seeking redress for their injuries by the corporation. The result may be fraudulent practices, dangerous commercial products, or even, as in Nazi Germany, death camps.

The administrative bureaucracies that carried out the extermination of the Jews progressed through several steps, ending in incarceration in concentration camps, starvation, and eventual annihilation. Once the machinery had been put into place, it was not confined to Jews but spread to treatment of other groups, including Gypsies, asocial individuals, and Polish prisoners of war. It is true that the managers responsible for this program experienced psychological repulsion. However, most managers rationalized their behaviour in terms of their duty in the bureaucratic system and the supposedly evil nature of the Jewish race (Hilberg, 1996).

Relations with the Outside World

Ideally, the bureaucratic organization relates to the outside world as though it is looking through one-way glass. The outside world, composed of competitors, customers, and other bystanders, cannot see into the organization. However, the organization can see out as well as it needs to. In principle, the main contact between the organization and the outside world is by means of its top executive. It is the top executive, in full possession of organizational intelligence, who can act publicly in the organization's interests.

The separation of decision-making authority from front-line experience is also likely to create an 'us versus them' point of view within the organization. As customers criticize the organization for unresponsiveness to their concerns, the organization takes a stance of embattled resistance to change. Union-based protest and organized citizen or customer protest movements put

Time to Reflect

What problems are inherent in the organizational style of bureaucracy? How can the different features of bureaucracy degenerate?

pressure on the bureaucracy. The result may be 'groupthink', a resistance within the organization to taking criticism seriously, considering a wide variety of options, or conceding the need for change. Nowhere is this organizational strategy more starkly depicted than in what Erving Goffman has called *total institutions.*

Total Institutions

As Goffman (1961a) pointed out, mental hospitals, convents, prisons, and military installations have a lot in common as organizations. True, they have different institutional goals and provide different services to society; they also employ different kinds of experts and oversee different kinds of 'customers'. However, what they have in common organizationally far outweighs these differences.

First, they have total control over their 'customers'—whether mental patients, nuns, convicts, or soldiers-in-training. Twenty-four hours a day, seven days a week, they are able to watch and, if desired, control behaviour within the institution. Though they can see their customer pool perfectly, none of them—whether as psychiatrists or nurses, priests or mothers superior, guards or officers—can be watched unknowingly or unwillingly. Thus, their relationships in the flow of information are highly unequal.

Total institutions offer an extreme example of the bureaucratic organization and the bureaucratized society. They are founded on principles of efficiency and procedural rigidity that are potentially in conflict with the values to which public organizations are expected to assign priority: particularly, democratic participation by employees and by those affected by organization practice (Davis, 1996).

What Goffman (1961a) tells us about mental institutions and prisons reminds us of what we have heard about life in **totalitarian** societies like Nazi Germany and Soviet Russia. Under both Nazism and Communism, governance is further complicated by the competition between two bureaucratic hierarchies: the government (based on expertise) and the party (based on loyalty). (For details on East Germany, see Bafoil, 1996, 1998; on China, see Zang, 1998.) Moreover, in practice, both are dominated by a patrimonial ruler, making neither a true bureaucracy (Maslovski, 1996).

In fact, totalitarian societies are not only like total institutions, they also make liberal use of total institutions to punish, brainwash, and **resocialize** unco-operative citizens. Thus, as Weber warned, modern bureaucratic society is an 'iron cage' in which we are all trapped by aspirations to career, efficiency, and progress (1958 [1904]: 181). Bureaucracy has an enormous potential for enslavement, exploitation, and cruelty. It also has an enormous potential for promoting human progress through economic development and scientific discovery, high-quality mass education, and the delivery of humane social services to the needy. It is to gain the second that we have risked the first. The jury remains out as to whether, in the twentieth century, the gain justified the cost.

Indeed, Blau (1963), drawing on the work of Michels (1962), points out a paradox in the relationship between two essentially different forms of social organization: bureaucracy and democracy. *Bureaucracy* is an organization formed to achieve set objectives. Its organizing principle is efficiency, and its organizing structure is the hierarchical relationship of dominance and subordination. *Democracy*, on the other hand, is an organization established to find out the objectives of a human group. Its organizing principle is the freedom of dissent necessary to permit majority opinions to form, and its organizing structure is essentially egalitarian.

Democratic forms of social organization are well suited to making choices between alternative policies, but they are not well suited to implementing them. This is the role bureaucracy fills so efficiently. Hence, the two forms of organization complement each other: democracy depends on bureaucracy to implement its policies. But paradoxically, as Blau recognized, by concentrating power in the hands of a very few, bureaucracy is a constant threat to the very survival of democratic institutions.

In the end, Weber was ambivalent about bureaucracy. Its superiority over other organizational forms—for example, organizations based on friendship or kinship, charismatic leadership or tradition—greatly impressed him. He concluded that a bureaucracy is an extremely powerful tool for whoever controls it. For that very reason, Weber (1978 [1908]) expressed disquiet over the immense power a bureaucracy can wield in society, citing the domination by Otto von Bismarck's bureaucracy of the weak German parliament of the day. The fate of 'grey-faced bureaucrats' was also of concern to Weber in his writings about bureaucracy (1978 [1908], 1958 [1922]). Bureaucracies posed problems because they shared many of the shortcomings of cliques, yet they were infinitely more dangerous since more likely to achieve their goals.

Time to Reflect

Do you agree with Blau and Michels that bureaucracy and democracy are at odds? If so, can democracy ever be sustainable in a country whose government and economy are organized into bureaucracies?

Conclusion

As we have noted, wherever you turn these days, you see organizations. Large organizations are daunting: they have their own impersonal cultures, they bring together large numbers of strangers, and they devise special ways of maintaining social control. However, it is unclear whether small tightly connected organizations, such as cliques, are any better than large tightly connected organizations, such as bureaucracies.

This chapter has reviewed a variety of different 'sets' of people. These included categories, networks, communities, groups, cliques, and organizations. Sets of people with a common sense of identity are typically called communities, and there is a long history of community studies in sociology. Communities, whether urban or rural, real or virtual, are important because people are conscious of their membership and make personal investments in remaining members. Formal organizations combine many of the features of networks, groups, cliques, and communities.

The main form of the large, powerful, and long-lived formal organization of the twentieth century is the bureaucracy. The goals of bureaucracy—task specialization based on technical competence plus the centralized provision of resources—are increased efficiency and productivity. Owing to its social importance, the chapter has discussed bureaucratic organization at length.

Theories about formal organization, in turn, mirror changes in society and changes in organizations over the twentieth century. This chapter has reviewed a variety of theories about organization, starting with Taylorism. Taylor's intention was to end labour–management conflict over 'shares of the pie'. However, the mindless, repetitive work advocated by Taylorism and the alienation it produced is one reason scientific management gradually faded from prominence. The human relations approach was more humane. Since workers were seen as emotional and non-rational, management's task was to instill both happiness and rationality in work groups. This approach, however, ignored real inequalities of power in the workplace. Labour process theory paid attention to problems of exploitation in the conduct of work. Under capitalism, workers are separated from their employers, because the two sides hold opposing interests in the control of and benefits from the labour process. More recent feminist theories pay attention to the importance of gender differences and inequality in formal organizations.

Finally, this chapter considered total institutions. As Goffman pointed out, mental hospitals, convents, prisons, and military installations have a lot in common as organizations. All of these are organizations that have total control over their 'customers'—whether mental patients, nuns, convicts, or soldiers-in-training. Myths and **ideologies** are propagated to justify the differences between rulers and ruled. Total institutions offer an extreme example of the bureaucratic organization and the bureaucratized society.

Questions for Critical Thought

1. You have learned that there is a discrepancy between the theoretical model of the bureaucracy and the real-world bureaucracy. Why does this discrepancy exist? Is there a way to better align the two?
2. Is it possible to control total institutions in a more egalitarian or democratic manner? How could this be accomplished? Are communities a way of exercising social control?
3. What types of organizations would you expect to see in the absence of social order and control—for example, immediately after natural disasters? What is the 'natural' organization of human beings?
4. What is/are the main goal(s) of cliques? How do they control their members and interact with the outside world? What are the characteristics of leaders of cliques? How about members?
5. In the groups and organizations discussed in the chapter, is size totally irrelevant when discussing the characteristics of each? For example, could a family be a community, or is it too 'small' to be a community?
6. How can the informal organization help the formal organization meet its goals? How can it also hinder these goals?
7. When discussing the downfalls of today's bureaucracies, one is likely to mention the problem of the 'red tape'. What is the 'red tape' and in which ways does it benefit the bureaucratic organization? Overall, suggest ways in which bureaucracies could become more humane and customer-centred.
8. The question that several generations of sociologists have debated since Tönnies is whether *Gesellschaft*—or city life—represents a loss of community or a new kind of community. What side of the debate do you agree with? Why?

Recommended Readings

Bengt Ambrahamsson, *Why Organizations? How and Why People Organize* (London: Sage, 1993).
An in-depth look into organizational theory, this book offers cross-continental analysis of organizations and explores the universal functions of organizations and the social forces that regulate their operations.

Michel Crozier, *The Bureaucratic Phenomenon* (Chicago: University of Chicago Press, 1964).
The French sociologist Michel Crozier found that Weber's idealized bureaucracy in practice varies from one culture to another. Each bureaucracy is a political subculture nested within a larger culture; as a result, bureaucracies may operate differently in different societies, despite the same set of formal principles.

Erving Goffman, *Asylums: Essays on the Social Situation of Mental Patients and Other Inmates* (New York: Anchor Doubleday, 1961).
This classic work notes the remarkable yet often ignored similarities between institutions that, whatever their stated goal, act to warehouse and closely control large numbers of people. These institutions transform people's identities as inmates learn to lead new moral careers entirely defined by the organization itself.

George Homans, *The Human Group* (New York: Harcourt Brace and Company, 1950).
The author uses famous sociological and anthropological field studies to argue that groups should be treated as social systems and studied organizationally, in terms of reinforcement, exchange, control, authority, ritual, and equilibrium,.

Charles Perrow, *Normal Accidents: Living with High-Risk Technologies* (New York: Basic Books, 1984).
According to this book, man-made disasters are almost inevitable when high-risk technologies are used. The two characteristic features of a normal accident are unexpected interactions between faults that, individually, are tolerable; and *tight coupling* that sets off a chain reaction of failures once a fault occurs.

Andrew Ross, *No Collar: The Humane Workplace and Its Hidden Costs* (New York: Basic Books, 2003).
This text focuses on the changes in the American workplace over recent years. The changing structure of workplace organizations is one product of downsizing and workers' increased mobility. Ross examines the implications of these changes by looking at employees' quality of life and satisfaction with their work environment.

Daniel A. Silverman, *Queen Victoria's Baggage: The Legacy of Building Dysfunctional Organizations* (Lanham, Md: University Press of America, 1999).
This book offers a cross-cultural analysis of what the author calls 'dysfunctional' organizations. Silverman examines the classroom and community as sites in which different cultural concepts of discipline exist.

Robert Westwood and Stephen Linstead, eds, *The Language of Organization* (London: Sage, 2001).
Taking a more micro approach, the articles in this collection focus on language as a form of social control. The volume looks specifically at the kinds of words we use to describe organizations generally, the day-to-day interactions within organizations, and the components of organizations.

Recommended Websites

Bureaucracy and formal organizations
www2.pfeiffer.edu/~lridener/DSS/formorg.htm
This website provides many links to relevant sites about bureaucracies and other formal organizations.

Correctional Service Canada
www.csc-scc.gc.ca
The website of Correctional Service Canada, like all Canadian government sites, offers a wealth of literature on a variety of topics, including prisons as total institutions.

Encyclopedia of Organizational Theory
faculty.babson.edu/krollag/org_site/encyclop/encyclo.html
This site provides almost everything you need to know about organizations. Every concept and theory is summarized nicely.

Inside Canada's Prisons
www.cbc.ca/prison/index.html
The CBC offers an interactive tour of a Canadian prison, giving clues to how it would feel to be a prisoner. As well, this link offers articles and analysis concerning prisons and further links for those interested.

Major organizational theories
faculty.babson.edu/krollag/org_site/org_theory/theory_index/theory_toc.html
This website provides links to a wide variety of journal articles that talk about the major organizational theories.

Managementlearning.com
managementlearning.com/index.html
This commercial site aims to educate users about behaviour within an organization. The main goal of the literature the site supplies is efficiency. Try following any of these sublinks: 'Research', 'Library', 'Articles', 'Topics'.

PROFITguide.com
www.profitguide.com
This site has a clear objective: profits. Focusing on this goal, the site has articles and step-by-step guides to help managers increase their profits by organizing their workplace according to certain principles. Try the 'How To' link.

Sociology of organizations
www.sociosite.net/topics/organization.php
This website contains links to many journals and articles on the sociology of organizations.

Chapter 7

Deviance

Vincent F. Sacco

Learning Objectives

In this chapter, you will:

- Learn to define deviance and social control as sociological concepts.
- Think critically about the images of deviance that we regularly encounter in the popular media.
- Learn to describe the major problems confronting researchers who study deviance.
- Identify the major questions that sociological theories of deviance and control are intended to answer.
- Compare and contrast various sociological explanations of deviant behaviour.
- Examine some of the social and demographic factors that are related to particular forms of deviant conduct.
- Learn how behaviours and people come to be categorized as deviant.

Photo: World of Stock

Introduction

In a suburban house on a quiet, tree-lined street, two teenagers sit in the kitchen and discuss how they will spend Friday night. They decide that one of them will try to get a fake ID in order to buy some beer for a party they are planning to attend. An older brother of one of the teenagers approaches the house. He picks the daily newspaper off the front step and glances at the front page, where the headline announces the mayor's resignation—it was discovered that the mayor had been giving untendered contracts to a construction firm owned by someone who made large, regular contributions to her recent political campaign. The teenagers stop discussing their plans when the older brother, who is a student at the local university, enters. He instructs them to stay off the computer because he is waiting for a 'very important' e-mail. What he doesn't tell them is that the e-mail is from a friend at another university who has promised to send a copy of an A+ essay, which the recipient plans to submit as his own work in a course he is failing.

Across town, in a gleaming corporate office, several managerial staff members of a clothing company meet to consider the bad press they have been getting since it was revealed that their clothing lines are made by children in sweatshops in developing countries. Rather than considering how they might improve employees' working conditions, they decide to launch a publicity blitz that denies the charges and calls into question the honesty and motivations of their accusers. One of the executives finds it difficult to concentrate on business because she is distracted by the situation at home. Her husband's occasional violent outbursts have become more frequent, and she worries that she and her children may be in some real danger. Before the meeting, she sneaked outside for a quick cigarette. She felt guilty doing it because she knows that the people with whom she works view smoking as a disgusting habit of weak-willed people. She hopes that the mint she has popped into her mouth will hide evidence of what she thinks of as 'my addiction'.

What do all of these situations have in common? On the surface, it might seem that the answer is 'very little'. However, some important common themes run through these examples and relate to the central concerns of this chapter: the sociological nature of deviance and control. All of these situations raise questions about the nature of disvalued social action, why some people engage in it, and why others react to it in particular ways.

This chapter will attempt to accomplish several objectives. First, it will explain what the terms **deviance** and **social control** mean when they are used in sociological discourse. Next, it will consider some of the major problems faced by researchers who are interested in the empirical investigation of deviance and social control. Finally, it will focus on the three major theoretical questions that occupy the time and attention of sociologists who study deviance.

What Is Deviance? 

Any discussion of the sociology of deviance and social control must begin with some consideration of what these terms mean. This is not a straightforward task. These terms have been defined in many different ways, both within and beyond the discipline of sociology. Formal sociological conceptualizations of deviance can be contrasted with more popular views that define *deviance* by illustration, statistically, and in terms of a notion of harm.

By Illustration

When students are asked to define *deviance*, a first response typically is to list types of people or types of behaviours they think deserve the label. Most of us would have no trouble coming up with a long list of deviants, which could include (but would not be restricted to) criminals, child molesters, drug addicts, alcoholics, the mentally ill, members of religious cults, chronic liars, and more. Of course, who goes on the list and who does not is very much a function of who is doing the listing and when and where the listing is being done.

The major problem with these stand-alone lists is that they are incomplete. On their own, they tell us nothing about why some types of people and behaviour are (and why other types are not) included. In short, we are left in the dark regarding the definitional criteria being employed.

In Statistical Terms

Statistical rarity suggests a more explicit way of thinking about the meaning of *deviance*. In this sense, deviant behaviour and deviant people are identifiable by their rarity. On the face of it, this makes a certain amount of sense. Many of the kinds of people we think of as deviant are, in a statistical sense, relatively unusual.

A major problem with statistical definitions of deviance is illustrated by Figure 7.1. The area between points X_1 and X_2 represents typical performance levels across some characteristic. The shaded area on the far left represents the minority of statistically rare cases that

Figure 7.1 The Normal Curve

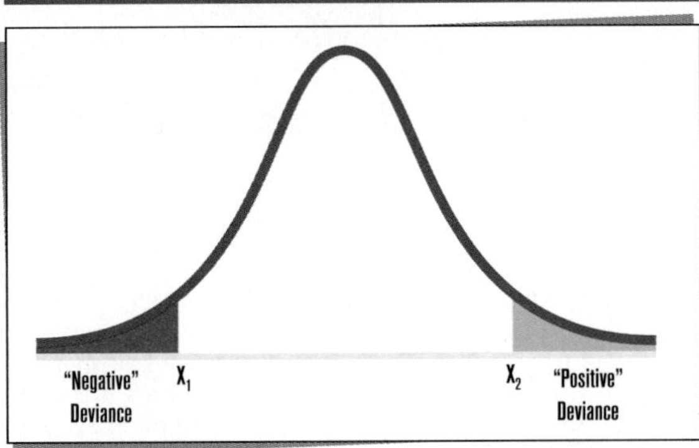

Statistical definitions of deviance make it difficult to distinguish 'negative' deviance from 'positive' deviance.

fall well below the average. On an examination of basic knowledge of their hometowns among Canadians, for instance, the people who fail very badly would be represented there. We might tend to think of such people as 'deviants' in the conventional sense of 'inferior'.

However, the shaded portion on the far right-hand side also suggests a statistically rare performance—but in the positive direction (Fielding et al., 2006; Spreitzer and Sonenshein, 2004). On an examination, these people would show superior knowledge about their town or city. Statistical definitions obscure distinctions between people who exceed and people who fall short of certain expectations.

As Harmful

Another familiar way of defining *deviance* is in terms of harm. In this sense, we equate deviant action with action that produces destructive outcomes. Once again, many of those who would appear on most shortlists of deviants would also seem to be encompassed by this definitional criterion. Murderers, thieves, liars, sexual abusers, and wife-assaulters all can be said to be authors of real and tangible harm.

But any attempt to equate deviance with harm also is fraught with difficulties. While many of the people treated as deviant in this society are the authors of harm, it also is true that many so treated are not. The developmentally delayed, the genius, the mentally ill, the exceptionally altruistic, gays and lesbians, the verbally unproficient, and many others outside of the mainstream are treated as deviant although it is difficult to ascribe harm to their differentness or to document the harm that they cause. In contrast, greedy corporate executives and unethical politicians may be able to manage how others see them so as to appear socially benign, even though their actions may result in considerable damage to life and property. We tend to reserve the label of 'deviant' in our society for other categories of people (Pearce and Snider, 1995; Woodiwiss, 2005).

'Harm' may be as much a matter of judgement and opinion as is 'deviance'. Considerable disagreement persists in our society about what is and what is not harmful to the individual and to the society and whom we do and do not need to fear (Glassner, 1999; Siegel, 2005). Indeed, historical and anthropological evidence shows that judgements about harm may change over time and from one culture to another.

Deviance as a Sociological Concept

As sociologists, we are interested in deviance as a product of **social interaction** and group structure. In other words, we understand the study of deviance to be the study of people, behaviours, and conditions that are subject to social control. Conversely, we can define social control as the various and myriad ways in which members of **social groups** express their disapproval of people and behaviour. These include name-calling, ridicule, ostracism, incarceration, and even killing. The study of deviance is about ways of acting and ways of being that, within particular social contexts and in particular historical periods, elicit moral condemnation.

When sociologists talk about deviance in this way, they sometimes create confusion for those who are used to thinking about the subject in a more conventional manner. When the sociologist says, for instance, that homosexuality is an appropriate subject for the scholarly study of deviance, the implication is not that the sociologist thinks of homosexuality as deviant; rather, that homosexuals are the targets of various forms of social control in our society. As sociologists, we are interested in why those with the power to exert social control regard gays and lesbians in this way and what the consequences of such actions are (Alden and Parker, 2005; Nylund, 2004).

In the study of deviance, it is important to distinguish between the *objective* and the *subjective* character of deviance (Loseke, 2003). The former refers to particular ways of thinking, acting, and being, the latter to the moral status accorded such thoughts, actions, and characteristics. It is important to keep this distinction in mind at all times. From the perspective of sociology, the 'deviant' character of certain behaviours or world views or physical features is not implicit in those behaviours,

GLOBAL ISSUES

Deviance and Diffusion

Because we can think about deviance as resulting from a claims-making process, it is possible to conceptualize claims about the disreputability of behaviour as separate from the behaviour itself. This means that it is possible to ask questions about the 'performance' of these claims. Such questions have been posed by Joel Best (2001, 2008) and other writers who have attempted to determine how claims about deviance and social problems diffuse from one social setting to another. In other words, when a way of acting is seen as troublesome in one place, how do these definitions of the behaviour travel within and across national boundaries?

It is a reasonable question. After all, clothing styles, musical fashions, and other cultural trends certainly do travel in this way. There is every reason to expect that problem claims do also. The task of the sociologist interested in these issues is to understand the conditions under which such diffusion takes place and why some kinds of claims travel with greater ease or difficulty than others.

An interesting case study for the diffusion process concerns the relationship between Canada and the United States (Sacco and Ismaili, 2001). In this respect, it can be argued that many of the new forms of deviance that are constructed by the American cultural industries work their way northward in rather short order. For example, Canadians found themselves worrying about such problems as school violence, ritual abuse, stalkers, home invaders, rap music, and Internet predators quite soon after these issues had begun to attract widespread attention south of the border.

There are several reasons why this diffusion occurs as it does. Similarities in the linguistic and political cultures of the two countries facilitate similar styles of discussion and debate of such topics. In addition, the American mass media exert a remarkable influence on Canadian images of what is worrisome in the contemporary world.

However, differences in cultural settings can seriously impede the diffusion of claims about deviance. The moral panic about satanic crime that originated in the United States in the 1980s travelled easily to Canada, Great Britain, and Australia. Despite a remarkable lack of evidence, many residents of these countries, like the Americans who preceded them, came to believe that Satanists were kidnapping and molesting children, desecrating bodies, influencing the content of youth music and other forms of leisure, and conducting ritual human sacrifices. In France and elsewhere, however, these claims were met with ridicule and the satanic panic was never able to take root.

world views, or physical features, but is conferred on them by the society. To be deemed 'deviant' by a sociologist, a particular behaviour must not only hold the potential for being called deviant (e.g., be unusual or rare behaviour or be considered deviant in another society), but also must be labelled as 'deviant' by powerful others who are willing to use the labels.

Of course, as sociologists, we recognize the need to focus our attention on both sides of the deviance issue. We need to be alert to the fact that not everything that could be labelled 'deviant', say, statistically, is necessarily labelled 'deviant' by the society. In an East Asian neighbourhood, the blue-eyed and light-skinned person may be anomolous, but the neighbours probably do not consider that individual deviant. Or, the fact that women wore long skirts in the Victorian period and would have considered a woman with a knee-length skirt to be deviant does not mean that a contemporary woman in a short skirt will be considered deviant.

The ability of some in society to use available resources in order to resist the efforts of others to consider them deviant also is of sociological interest. For example, even though corporations engage in activities that undermine health or safety or that weaken the economic well-being of many in society, they are able to define themselves as moral and respectable corporate citizens. They do this, most commonly, through their support of sporting events, donations to universities and

IN THE FIRST PERSON

I have been interested in sociology—especially the sociology of crime and deviance—my entire life. Growing up in the border city and tourist destination of Niagara Falls, I became aware early of some of the more peculiar eccentricities and excesses of human behaviour. Like many students, I majored in sociology because I thought the subject matter was, as we used to say, 'pretty cool' and because I did reasonably well in my first-year course. My fascination with the discipline was nurtured by many dedicated and patient teachers and mentors who showed me the real value of careful sociological analysis. However, it was not until I read C. Wright Mills's *The Sociological Imagination* that I began to think seriously about the links between the lives we live and the social structures within which we live them.—Vince Sacco

hospitals, and in public relations campaigns that promote a positive organizational image.

Researching Deviance

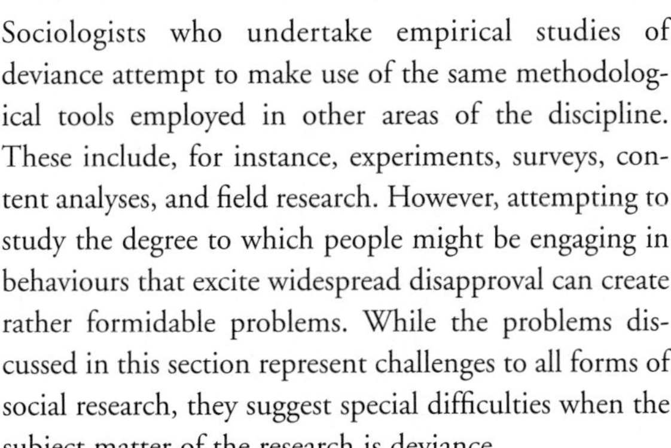

Sociologists who undertake empirical studies of deviance attempt to make use of the same methodological tools employed in other areas of the discipline. These include, for instance, experiments, surveys, content analyses, and field research. However, attempting to study the degree to which people might be engaging in behaviours that excite widespread disapproval can create rather formidable problems. While the problems discussed in this section represent challenges to all forms of social research, they suggest special difficulties when the subject matter of the research is deviance.

Secrecy

Deviant behaviour often is behaviour that people wish to keep secret to protect themselves from social reactions. How do sociologists undertake valid research in a way that does not intrude excessively into the lives of those under study? There is no simple answer to this question.

Sometimes the researcher attempts to gain the confidence of the subjects by posing as one who shares their deviant status (Whyte, 1943). This involves some extremely hazardous ethical dilemmas. One much-discussed case in this respect is an early study by sociologist Laud Humphreys. His book *Tearoom Trade* (1970) is a study of impersonal sexual encounters between homosexual men in public washrooms ('tearooms'). In order to familiarize himself with the social character of these sexual encounters, Humphreys presented himself to 'tearoom' participants as someone who was willing to play the role of voyeur/lookout. This deception allowed him to observe the interaction between sexual partners in a way that did not arouse their suspicion. To compound the ethical problem, Humphreys recorded the licence-plate numbers of the men who frequented the 'tearoom' and was able to determine their addresses. After disguising his appearance, he went to their homes, under the pretense of conducting a public health survey, in order to learn more about them. Needless to say, when his research techniques were discovered they provoked a firestorm of controversy. Generally, sociologists do not believe that such deception is ever excusable.

Discovery of Reportable Behaviour

If research subjects confide in the researcher and reveal information about illegal or harmful circumstances, does the researcher have an obligation to report that wrongdo-

Time to Reflect

Why do you think that movies, television, and most other forms of popular culture seem to be so focused on deviant activities and deviant people?

OPEN FOR DISCUSSION

Is the Sociology of Deviance Dead?

For years some sociologists have been arguing that the field known as the sociology of deviance is dead. This position was first articulated by American sociologist Alexander Liazos (1972) and British sociologist Colin Sumner. In 1994, Sumner published a book entitled *The Sociology of Deviance: An Obituary*, which has come to be seen by many as a manifesto that describes everything wrong with this area of study. The essence of the argument is that the field of deviance has outlived whatever usefulness it might have had. It no longer has any theoretical vitality and it lacks any real relevance to either the broader field of sociology or to the wider society.

Critics argue that, despite the sloganeering value of the 'deviance is dead' position, those who make this argument either don't really understand what the sociology of deviance is all about, or are just seeking to advance their own ideological agendas.

Sociologists like Erich Goode (2003, 2004) and Patricia and Peter Adler (2006), who maintain that rumours of the death of deviance are greatly exaggerated, say that critics of the field need to consider the following:

- Enrolments in courses in the sociology of deviance at universities and colleges that offer such courses remain consistently high.
- The study of rule-breaking and of the condemnation of those who are thought to break rules is inseparable from the key developments in the history of the discipline of sociology. One need only recall Émile Durkheim's classic study of suicide to appreciate this fact.
- Critics worry too much about what they think are the politically incorrect implications of the sociology of deviance. In other words, they are uncomfortable with the suggestion that gay, lesbian, or transgendered lifestyles or the physically disabled or those with eating disorders are 'deviant'. But defenders of the field say that anyone who raises this objection really doesn't appreciate what the sociologist of deviance really does. To call something deviant is not to express the moral position of the sociologist, but to recognize that within a given society a particular way of acting or being was or is the object of moral denunciation. Indeed, the factors behind the denunciation are understood as an important part of the puzzle.
- Defenders of the field ask, 'How in the world could anyone come to the conclusion that the sociological study of deviance is not immediately relevant to the study of contemporary society?' The processes on which these sociologists focus are central to all the aspects of social life that concern us most. Whenever we talk about election campaigns, terrorism, social movements for equality, the effects of the Internet and other new technologies, or the relationships between the genders or between age or ethnic groups, we will end up talking about how some in society violate the expectations of others and how these violations provoke denunciation. Such processes can't be ignored without ignoring most of what is important and interesting about society. Even if we choose not to call it 'the sociology of deviance' we would end up calling it something else and studying it anyway.

ing to authorities? The problem is brought about by the cross-pressures that the researcher experiences (Bostock, 2002). On the one hand, the researcher has a professional obligation to respect the confidentiality of information that research subjects divulge. On the other hand, one has a social and moral obligation to protect the safety of the public, including the research subject.

Some of the complexities relating to reportability are illustrated by the case of Russel Ogden, who in 1994 was an MA student in the School of Criminology at Simon Fraser University in British Columbia. Ogden's study involved an investigation of the process of assisted suicide among terminally ill HIV/AIDS patients. Shortly after he defended his thesis, he was summoned by a coroner's inquest, which asked him to reveal the sources of his information. Ogden refused, citing the pledge of confidentiality he had provided to his research subjects. He was subsequently charged with contempt of court. Despite his having little formal support from his university, he won the case. The court later ruled that social science researchers have a qualified privilege to maintain confidentiality because such research contributes substantially to Canadian society (Palys and Lowman, 2000).

Safety

Closely related to the problems of reportable behaviour are those related to the safety of respondents. In short, researchers should take no action that could result in harm to those who participate in the research. While we tend to think only of physical harm in this respect, the injunction is much broader and includes emotional, mental, and economic harm.

There are many ways in which research could produce harmful outcomes. In the case of one major survey of female victims of male violence, for instance, there was a real concern on the part of researchers that calling women and asking questions about violence in their lives could put them in danger if, for instance, a woman's abuser might be sitting next to her when she received the phone call and started answering questions (Johnson, 1996). As a result, it was necessary to take several special precautions, for instance, training interviewers to be sensitive to cues that the respondent might be under some immediate stress.

Research can put study subjects at risk in a more general sense as well. It is important to remember that, by definition, research into the disvalued nature of people and behaviour involves looking into the lives of the most vulnerable members of society. These could include the poor, the homeless, and others with whom society associates designations of deviance. The sociologist needs to remain aware that research findings can often be used *against* these vulnerable groups, especially when sufficient care is not taken to qualify conclusions or to suggest appropriate interpretations of research evidence.

The Sociology of Deviant Behaviour

We have defined *deviance* as ways of thinking, acting, and being that are subject to social control—in other words, as kinds of conditions and kinds of people who are viewed by most of the members of a society as wrong, immoral, disreputable, bizarre, or unusual. In so doing, we recognize that deviance has two distinct yet related dimensions: objective and subjective. *Objective* refers to the behaviour or condition itself, *subjective* refers to the placement of that condition by the members of society in their system of moral stratification.

To choose a simple example, sociologists do not confuse the physical act of someone smoking marijuana with the designation of marijuana-smoking as a deviant act. While each suggests a distinct realm of experience, each is an appropriate object of sociological attention. It is one thing to ask why people smoke marijuana, and it is quite another to ask why some (the social institution of the law, for example, and those who support it, for another) consider this deviant conduct. However, both types of questions are significant in sociology.

We can identify several problem areas that have been the focus of theoretical attention in the sociology of deviance. These include questions about (1) the causes and forms of deviant behaviour, (2) the content and character of moral definitions, and (3) the issues that arise over labels of deviance.

While sociologists are interested in a broad array of issues, questions about why deviants do what they do have attracted the lion's share of attention. However, the 'Why do they do it?' question contains a number of important (if unstated) assumptions. (1) It implies that most of us share a conformist view of the world in which the important thing to understand is why some deviant minority refuses to act the way 'we' act. (2) The moral status of deviant behaviour is never called into question. In a sense, the 'Why do they do it?' question proceeds from the assumption that—by and large—society is a pretty stable and orderly place, that there is generally widespread agreement about what is right and what is wrong, and that we therefore need to

Time to Reflect

Based on your own reading, do you think that sufficient ethical safeguards are in place to protect the subjects of deviance research?

understand what pushes or pulls some off the path the rest of us travel.

Most (but not all) of the theoretical thought in this respect reflects the influence of functionalist perspectives. Three dominant ways of thinking about 'why they do it' can be identified—strain theory, cultural support theory, and control theory (Cullen et al., 2006).

Strain Theory

Strain theory derives from the writings of the famous American sociologist Robert Merton, who in 1938 published a very influential paper entitled 'Social Structure and Anomie'. Merton sought to understand why, according to official statistics, so many types of nonconformity are much more pervasive among members of the lower social classes. Crime, delinquency, drug addiction, alcoholism, and other forms of deviance, Merton recognized, seem to emerge as more significant problems the further one moves down the socio-economic structure. As a sociologist, Merton was interested in trying to understand this issue in a way that made the structure of society—rather than the personalities of individuals—the central explanatory mechanism.

Merton argued that the answer could be found in the malintegration of the cultural and social structures of societies. In other words, it is the lack of fit between the *cultural goals* people are encouraged to seek and the *means* available to pursue these goals that creates a kind of social strain to which deviant behaviour is an adjustment. Merton's logic is elegant and compelling. In a society like the United States, there is little recognition of the role that **class** barriers play in social life. As a result, everyone is encouraged to pursue the goal of material success—and everyone is judged a success or a failure in life based on his or her ability to become materially successful.

Merton knew, though, that there are many people near the bottom of the class hierarchy who, because of their ethnic or regional or class origins, may not be able to achieve that overpowering social goal of material success. This, Merton said, is a type of socially induced strain to which people must adjust their behaviour, and often these adjustments take deviant forms. When people steal money or material goods, for instance, it can be said that they are attempting to use 'illegitimate means' to achieve the trappings of success. When they take drugs (or become 'societal dropouts'), they can be seen to have pulled out of the competition for stratification outcomes. For Merton, these problems are most acute in the lower social classes because it is there that people are most likely to experience the disjuncture between the things they aspire to and things that are actually available to them (see Table 7.1).

Later critics have pointed out certain problems with Merton's arguments (Downes and Rock, 2003; Vold et al., 2002). Merton proceeds from the assumption that the distribution of crime and deviance that we find in official statistics is accurate, which it may not be. Merton does not extend his argument to explain how it happens that acts of crime and deviance also occur within middle- and upper-class populations.

Despite these limitations, Merton's argument has had a great deal of influence on the way sociologists think about the causes of deviant behaviour (Laufer and Adler, 1994). For example, sociologists Richard Cloward and Lloyd Ohlin (1960) expanded on Merton's ideas in an effort to explain lower-class gang delinquency. They agree with Merton that juvenile crime is prompted by the inability of lower-class youth to achieve the things that their culture encourages them to seek. However, they suggest that there is a need to explain why different kinds of delinquent behaviour patterns emerge in different types of neighbourhoods.

For these researchers, delinquency patterns are like rare plants that require specialized conditions to flourish. Cloward and Ohlin identify three kinds of delinquent adaptations. The first, which they refer to as the *criminal pattern*, is characterized by instrumental delinquency activities, particularly delinquency for gain, in which those involved seek to generate illegal profits. We might think of drug-dealing or the theft and fencing of stolen goods as examples of this kind of crime. The second, the *conflict pattern*, is characterized by the presence of 'fighting gangs' who battle over turf and neighbourhood boundaries. The third, the *retreatist pattern*, is organized around the acquisition and use of hard drugs.

A more recent version of strain theory has been proposed by Robert Agnew (1985, 2006; Agnew and Broidy, 1997). Agnew theorizes that the inability to achieve the things we want in life is only one type of socially induced strain and that there are at least two others. A second source of strain involves an inability to avoid or escape some negative condition. For example, the youth who cannot avoid an abusive parent or bullying at school might turn to drugs, run away from home, or become aggressive with others as ways of coping with the strain his living situation creates. A third kind of strain results from conditions in which individuals lose something that they value. For example, a child who is forced to move and thus to leave important friendships, the person whose parent has died, and a boyfriend or

Table 7.1 Robert Merton's Paradigm of Deviant Behaviour

Robert Merton argued that there are essentially five ways of adjusting to a social structure that encourages large numbers of people to seek objectives that are not actually available to them. Four of these adaptations represent types of deviance. Each type can be understood in reference to the goals and means of the culture.

	Attitude to Goals	Attitude to Means	Explanation/Example
Conformity	accept	accept	Most people accept as legitimate the culturally approved ways of achieving those goals. In Merton's example, most strive for material success by working hard, trying to get a good education, etc.
Innovation	accept	reject	The bank robber, drug dealer, or white-collar thief seeks success, too, but rejects the conventional means for achieving that success.
Ritualism	reject	accept	Some people seem to simply be going through the motions of achieving desired social goals. In large organizations, we use the term 'bureaucrat' to describe people who are fixated on procedures at the expense of outcomes.
Retreatism	reject	reject	Some people adjust to strain by 'dropping out' of the system. Such dropping out could include losing oneself in a world of alcohol or illegal drugs or adopting some unconventional lifestyle.
Rebellion	reject/accept	reject/accept	Rebellion includes acts intended to replace the current cultural goals (and means) with new ones. In this category we might include the radical political activist or even the domestic terrorist.

girlfriend experiencing the breakup of the relationship all experience loss strain.

Despite differences, these arguments hold certain features in common. First, they take as their point of reference the need to explain why some individuals but not others behave in ways that invite social sanction. Second, they share an explanatory logic that focuses on how the organization of our social relations creates problems that require solutions. In this paradigm, the causes of deviant behaviour are located in patterns of social life that are external to but impact individuals.

Cultural Support Theory

A second explanation of deviant behaviour, **cultural support theory**, focuses on the way patterns of cultural beliefs create and sustain such conduct (Cohen, 1966). According to arguments of this sort, people behave in ways that reflect the cultural values to which they have been exposed and that they have internalized. In this way, it can be said that you are attending university or college because you value education and learning and come from a home or cultural setting that similarly values education and learning. If conventional values support conventional behaviour, it should also follow that deviant values support deviant behaviour. The important task of such theories is to understand how the cultural meanings people associate with deviant conduct make that conduct more likely.

One of the earliest explicit statements of this position was provided by a sociologist associated with the University of Chicago, Edwin Sutherland (Sutherland,

'Deviant' behaviours such as excessive drinking are not always deviant, from a statistical standpoint. Among young men, many risky behaviours (such as binge drinking) are celebrated as signs of masculinity and group conformity. (Chuck Savage/Corbis)

1947). Writing in the 1930s, Sutherland proposed that people become deviant because they have been exposed to learning experiences that make deviance more likely. In short, people end up deviant in the same way that they end up as Catholics, as stamp collectors, as saxophone players, or as French film fans—that is, as a result of exposure to influential learning experiences. People become deviant because they have learned in the context of interpersonal relationships how to become deviant.

But what does learning to be deviant actually involve? Most important, according to Sutherland, is the learning of what he called the 'specific direction of drives, motives, attitudes and rationalizations' (1947: 7). In other words, we must learn to think about deviant conduct as acceptable to ourselves. Why do we not kill people who make us angry? It cannot be because we don't know how (most of us do) or even, in many cases, because we fear getting caught. Most commonly, we refrain from murderous violence because we have come to define such action as morally repugnant, that is, as unacceptable to ourselves. For Sutherland, it was this learning to accept or to value criminal or deviant action that in a very real sense made such action possible.

Sutherland's cultural insights help us to understand how people come to value actions the rest of the society might despise. But other writers in this tradition have shown that the culture of deviant action is even more complicated. The complication concerns the fact that we live in a society that seems simultaneously to condemn and to support deviant behaviour. Is it possible to simultaneously believe in and to break important social rules? Most of us think, for example, that stealing is wrong, and we have learned to be wary of thieves. However, most of us also have stolen something of value (perhaps at work, perhaps from a corner store or a family member). This is possible because we have learned to define these deviant situations as ones to which the rules really do not apply. When we steal at work, for instance, we might not see this as theft. We tell ourselves (and others) that we are underpaid and deserve whatever fringe benefits we can get, or that our employers actually expect people to steal and build the cost of such losses into their budgets. From this perspective, the broader culture both condemns deviance and makes available for learning the techniques to neutralize the laws that prohibit deviant action (Fritsche, 2005; Matza and Sykes, 1957).

Like strain arguments, cultural arguments have been very influential in the sociological study of deviant behaviour (Akers and Jensen, 2006). Some critics have charged, however, that arguments that use culture to explain deviance ultimately are tautological (Maxim and Whitehead, 1998), that is, employ a kind of circular reasoning. Cultural theories tell us that deviant beliefs and values are the source of deviant conduct. Yet, how do we ever really know what people's beliefs and values are? Usually, we observe how people behave and then, on the basis of their behaviour, infer that they hold certain values. Is it appropriate, then, to use the value we have inferred from observations of behaviour to explain that behaviour? If we observe people stealing and then infer that they have come to acquire values that are supportive of stealing and that these values explain the stealing, we have reasoned in a circle and have explained nothing at all.

On the other hand, arguments of this type have proven more useful than strain arguments in making sense of corporate crimes. Whereas strain theories typically proceed from assumptions of disadvantage as a cause of crime, cultural theories do not. One may argue that corporate crime, at least to some extent, is rooted in a 'culture of competition' that legitimates organizational wrongdoing (Calavita and Pontell, 1991).

Control Theory

The logic of the strain and cultural support theories contrasts quite sharply with the logic of a third point of view known as **control theory**. Advocates of control theory argue that most types of deviant behaviour do not require a sophisticated form of explanation. People lie, cheat, steal, take drugs, or engage in sexual excess when and if they are free to do so. Lying and cheating can be the most expeditious and efficient ways of getting what we want in life. Experimenting with drugs and sexual promiscuity can be more fun than working or studying. The important question we need to ask, according to control theorists, is not 'Why do some people break rules the rest of us abide by?' Instead we need to ask, 'Why don't more of us engage in "forbidden" behaviour?' For control theorists, deviant behaviour occurs whenever it is allowed to occur. Thus, we expect to find deviance when the social controls that are supposed to prevent or check it are weak or broken. Seen in this way, deviance is not a special kind of behaviour that requires a special kind of motivation. Rather, it is behaviour that results from the absence of pressures that would check or constrain it.

This idea is a very venerable one in sociology—it can be traced to the writing of Émile Durkheim (1966 [1897]). In his classic study of suicide, Durkheim sought to explain why some groups in society experience higher suicide rates than others and why suicide rates vary over time. Catholics, he found, have lower suicide rates than Protestants, and married people have lower rates than single people. As well, suicide rates increase in times both of economic boom and of economic depression. What is varying in all of these cases? Durkheim suggested that the crucial variable might be social regulation (or what we call *social control*). Social regulation forces people to take others into account and discourages behaviours that are excessively individualistic. Catholicism—with its mandatory church attendance and practices such as confession—might suggest more social regulation than various strands of Protestantism. Married life implies more external regulation (in terms of obligations, duties, and so on) than single life. Periods of both boom and depression throw large numbers of people out of the customary social grooves in which they have been living their lives and disconnect them from social regulations. In short, suicide is more likely when people are left to their own resources.

In more recent times, sociologist Travis Hirschi (1969) has been the most influential social control theorist. Like many other sociologists interested in the study of deviant behaviour, Hirschi focused on the study of juvenile crime. In a very influential book published in 1969, Hirschi attempted to use social control logic to explain the conduct of youthful offenders. For Hirschi, the problem of juvenile crime could be understood in reference to the concept of the bond to conventional society. Each of us, to a greater or lesser degree, has a bond or connection to the world of conventional others. In the case of youth, the world of conventional others is the world represented by their parents, teachers, and members of the legitimate adult community. Hirschi reasoned that if youthful bonds to conventional others are strong, youths need to take these others into account when they act; if the bonds are weak, however, they are free to act in ways that reflect much narrower self-interest. Much of what we call crime and deviance, he reasoned, is evidence of this self-interested behaviour.

More recently, in collaboration with Michael Gottfredson (Gottfredson and Hirschi, 1990), Hirschi has proposed a general theory of crime and deviance that has been the object of a great deal of attention (Gottfredson,

2006). Gottfredson and Hirschi argue that crimes of all types tend to be committed by people who are impulsive, short-sighted, non-verbal risk-takers. The underlying social-psychological characteristic of such people, they maintain, is low self-control. Further, individuals who have low self-control not only are more likely to commit crime, they are also more likely to engage in a wide range of deviant practices, including drinking, smoking, and activities that result in getting into accidents (Baron, 2003; Junger et al., 2001; Nakhaie et al., 2000). For Gottfredson and Hirschi, the problem of low self-control originates in inadequate child-rearing that fails to discourage delinquent outcomes.

Social control theories remain very influential, but they have been criticized for their assumption that motivation is essentially irrelevant to the study of crime and deviance (Bohm, 1997). As well, some writers argue that while these ideas make a certain amount of sense when we are talking about crime and deviance among the more marginalized segments of society, they do an inadequate job of explaining why those members of society whose bonds to the conventional world seem strongest also engage in prohibited acts (Deutschmann, 2007).

The Transactional Character of Deviance

Despite their sociological character, strain, cultural support, and social control arguments tend to focus attention on the individual: people, according to these theories, commit deviant acts because they respond to strain, because they are exposed to learning environments that support deviance, or because they are free from social constraints. Other writers, however, encourage us to understand deviant behaviour as an interactional product. From this perspective, we understand deviant behaviour as a joint or collective, rather than individual, outcome.

When most of us seek to explain murder, we tend to focus on the murderous acts of the individual (see Figure 7.2 for homicide rates in Canada). As sociologists, we might try to understand how people who commit acts of lethal violence do so in response to social strain (Pratt and Godsey, 2003) or as a result of an affiliation with a culture of violence (Chilton, 2004; Wolfgang and Ferracuti, 1967). Alternatively, we might try to understand how murder results from particular kinds of interactions.

David Luckenbill (1977), for example, has attempted to show how murder can in many cases be understood as a **situated transaction**. This means that some murder, at least, may be seen not as an individual act, but rather as an interaction sequence in which the participants (the eventual murderer, the eventual victim, and, perhaps, an audience) interact in a common physical territory. Based on a study of 70 homicides in the state of California, Luckenbill concludes that many murders move through six common stages:

- *Stage 1.* The transaction starts when the person who will end up the victim does something that the person who ends up the offender could define as an insult or as an offence to 'face'. This could be quite trivial. The victim might call the offender a liar, refuse to share a cigarette, or make a sexually suggestive comment about the partner of the eventual offender.
- *Stage 2.* The offender defines what the victim has said or done as threatening or offensive.
- *Stage 3.* The offender makes a countermove intended to respond and save face. This could involve a verbal response or a physical gesture.
- *Stage 4.* The victim responds in an aggressive manner. At this point, a working definition of the situation as one that will require a violent resolution seems to be emerging. The problems may be aggravated by the presence of onlookers who jeer the participants, offer to hold their jackets, or to block a convenient exit.
- *Stage 5.* At this stage, a brief violent exchange occurs. It may involve a fatal blow, a thrust with a knife, or the pulling of a trigger. Typically, it is over quickly.
- *Stage 6.* The battle, such as it was, is over and the offender either flees or remains at the scene.

Luckenbill's work shows us how murder can be understood as a social product. This does not imply an absence of guilt on the part of people who murder, and

Time to Reflect

Do you think that some explanations of deviant behaviour, such as strain theory, can be faulted for excusing such behaviour?

Figure 7.2 Provincial Variations in Rates of Homicide (Number of Homicides per 100,000 Population), 2005

For reasons that are not entirely clear, the rate at which the situated transaction we refer to as homicide varies from province to province.

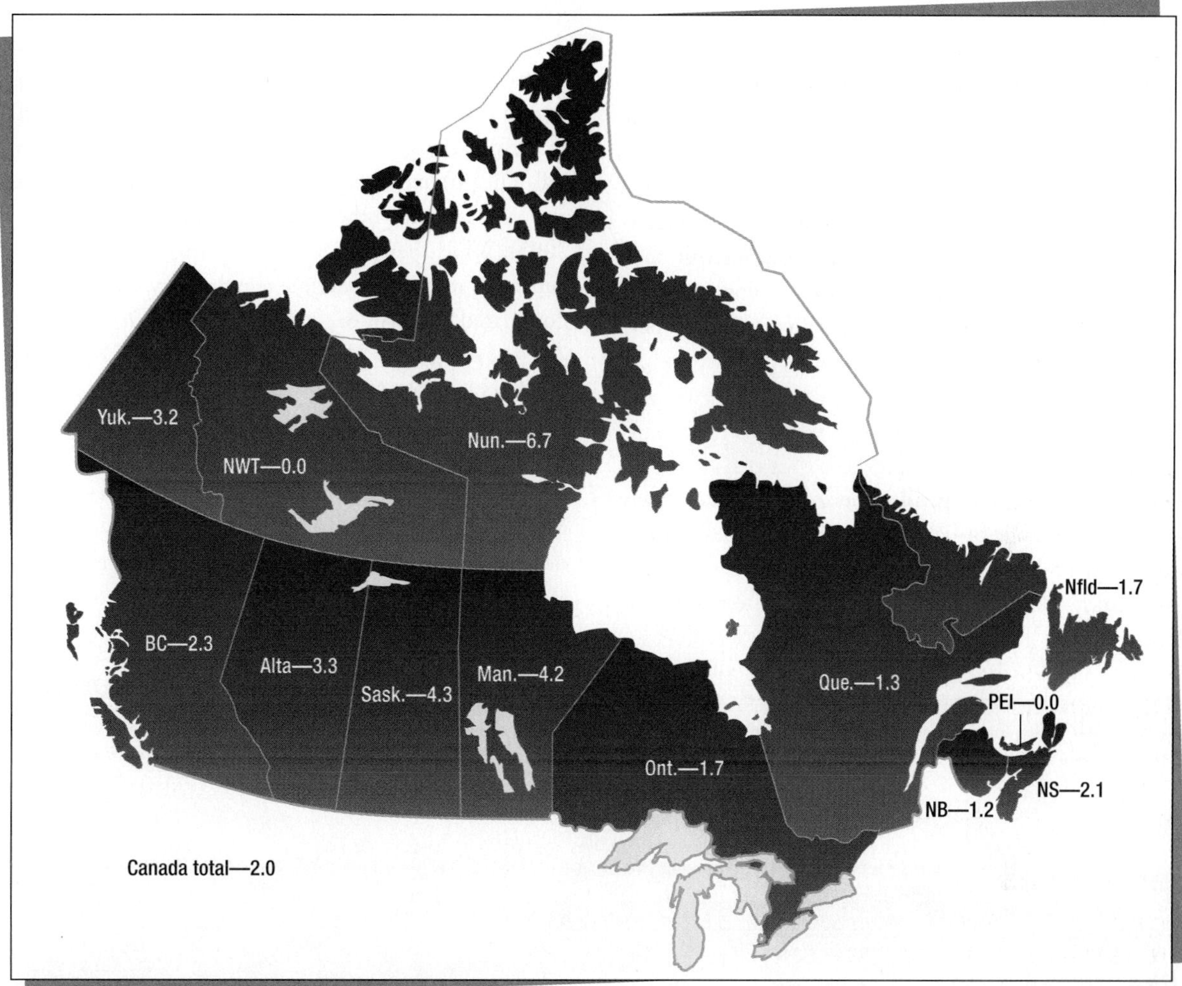

Source: Statistics Canada, 'Crime Statistics in Canada, 2005', *Juristat*, Cat. 82-003, vol. 26 no. 04, released 20 Jul. 2006, available at <http://www.statcan.ca/english/freepub/85-002-XIE/85-002-XIE2006004.pdf>.

it is not offered as an excuse for killing. It does show that acts of deviance can be quite complex and can involve significant interactional dimensions. For this reason, some students of deviant and criminal behaviour argue that it is more useful to think of murder, or theft or similar other forms of deviance as 'social events' rather than the acts of individuals in isolation (Sacco and Kennedy, 2007). To say they are social events is to imply that they involve much more than an individual behaving badly. The outcome of a homicide event does not just depend on what the 'killer' does. It also depends on what bystanders do, whether the parties to the conflict are alone or with friends, how quickly the police or paramedics arrive, etc.

Time to Reflect

Do theories that focus on situated transactions blame victims for their own victimization?

Making Sense of the 'Facts' of Deviant Behaviour

Sociologists interested in the study of deviant behaviour have repeatedly demonstrated that deviant acts—especially the kinds of acts that seem to concern the average member of the society most—are not randomly distributed in the population. Instead, people with some kinds of social and demographic characteristics seem much more likely to be involved in such behaviour than others. The task for sociological explanations that focus on the deviant act is to explain these levels of differential involvement.

Gender

It is well-known that **gender** tends to correlate closely with a wide range of behaviours. This is no less true in the study of deviance than in the study of other areas in sociology. Males and females differ in terms of the amounts and the kinds of disapproved behaviours in which they engage.

Males are more likely to be involved in those behaviours of which most members of Canadian society would say they disapprove. Males are much more likely than females to be involved in criminal behaviour (crimes related to prostitution are an important exception in this regard). In 2003, males made up 81 per cent of persons charged by the police and this pattern is typical. The differential is greatest in cases of violence but is also very large for other kinds of crime (Gannon et al., 2005). While there has been some narrowing of the gender gap in recent years, crime remains very much a male-dominated activity (Sacco and Kennedy, 2007). Table 7.2 shows gender differences in crime for two of Canada's largest cities.

Males are more likely to consume both legal and illegal drugs, including tobacco, alcohol, marijuana, and cocaine (Canadian Centre on Substance Abuse, 2005). Males are more likely to commit suicide, and when they do so, they are more likely to use guns or explosives (Langlois and Morrison, 2002). Overall rates of mental

Bullying is a common form of 'deviance' in schools and playgrounds. Usually the work of cliques (discussed in the last chapter), bullying uses exclusion, ridicule, and sometimes even violence to turn ordinary kids into outcasts and victims. (Michael Newman/PhotoEdit Inc.)

Table 7.2 Rates of Persons Charged, by Gender, Montreal and Vancouver, 2003

	Violent Crime		Property Crime	
	Male	Female	Male	Female
Montreal	1,362	204	924	200
Vancouver	1,001	112	1,535	301

Source: Statistics Canada, 'Exploring Crime Patterns in Canada', *Crime and Justice Research Paper Series*, Cat. 85-561, no. 5, p. 14, released 29 Jun. 2005, at <http://www.statcan.ca/english/research/85-561-MIE/85-561-MIE2005005.pdf>.

illness do not differ markedly between men and women, although there are significant variations by type. Women are more likely to be diagnosed as suffering from depression and anxiety, while men are more likely to experience problems relating to various forms of addiction and psychosis (Health Canada, 2002).

Several feminist writers have argued that there has been a marked tendency in the sociological literature to systematically ignore the deviant behaviour of women (Miller and Mullins, 2007). To be sure, most of what is written about crime and deviance concerns the behaviour of men, both as deviants and as police and other agents of social control. Moreover, many sociologists have assumed that female deviant behaviour could be explained using the same theoretical ideas and models that have been used to make sense of male behaviour—a position with which many feminists do not agree.

The failure to be sufficiently attentive to the gendered nature of criminal and deviant behaviour has been an empirical problem, also. Most research has dealt with the actions of men, either explicitly or implicitly. Sociologists tended, historically, not to be terribly interested in acts of crime or deviance that did not have a significant male dimension (Boritch, 1997). Only through the work of feminist social critics did researchers come to focus on problems that affect women more directly. These include, for instance, various forms of deviance that tend to uniquely victimize women, such as intimate violence and sexual harassment (Chasteen, 2001; Comack et al., 2000).

Age

Age, like gender, is strongly associated with many kinds of deviant behaviour (Tanner, 2001). Crime rates are greatest during the late teens and early adulthood and decline very sharply after that (Sacco and Kennedy, 2007). This pattern characterizes even violence in the home: young husbands (those under 30) are much more likely than older husbands to treat their wives violently (Mihorean, 2005). However, this pattern does not hold for all kinds of crime. White-collar crimes (professional fraud, cheating on taxes, and so on) tend to occur somewhat later in the life cycle (Gottfredson and Hirschi, 1990).

Alcohol use and illicit drug use are more heavily concentrated among young people (Canadian Centre on Substance Abuse, 2005). But while suicide rates among young people are a cause of considerable concern, such rates actually tend to be lower among younger Canadians (Langlois and Morrison, 2002; see Figure 7.3). While older people are traditonally assumed to be those most likely to experience a variety of forms of mental illness, the onset of most mental illness occurs during adolescence and young adulthood (Health Canada, 2002).

Class and Ethnicity

As with gender and age, relationships between indicators of socio-economic disadvantage and various forms of deviant behaviour are of considerable interest to sociologists. Many of the studies on this subject say that poorer people and people from minority groups are more likely to be involved in many forms of crime and delinquency, to use drugs and alcohol, and to develop various kinds of mental illness. Indeed, a great deal of sociological theorizing about the 'causes' of deviant behaviour has taken as its central issue the need to explain why social and economic precariousness is related to deviant outcomes. This is very clear, for instance, in most versions of strain theory.

However, a consensus in the research literature does not exist regarding how concepts such as poverty, economic inequality, ethnicity, or minority group status should be measured for research purposes (Braithewaite, 1979; Hagan and Peterson, 1995; Wortley, 1999), and there is less consistency in research findings. While some studies seem to say that working-class youth are more

Figure 7.3 Suicide Rates by Sex and Age (Rates per 100,000), 2003

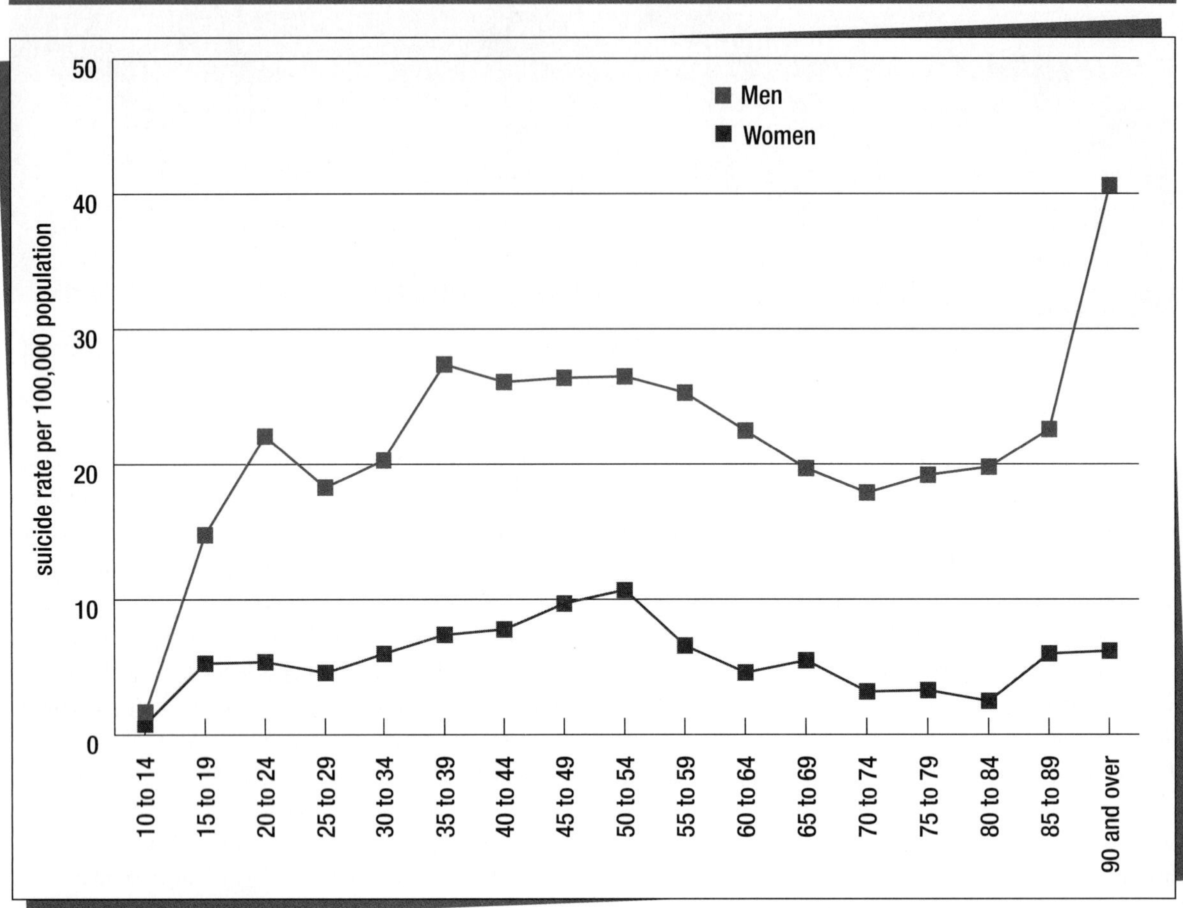

Source: Statistics Canada data.

likely to be delinquent, other studies tell us the opposite (Tittle et al., 1978). As well, while minority group status seems to be related to higher rates of crime in some cases, for example, with **First Nations** people, it seems to be related to lower rates of crime in others, for example, with Asian immigrants in British Columbia (Gordon and Nelson, 2000; Brzozowski et al., 2006).

Other interpretations of the significance of the relationship between social disadvantage and deviant behaviour point in the direction of a more general fault line that runs through the sociology of deviance. These other interpretations encourage us to ask different types of questions. Are poorer or minority people more likely to be deviant, or are they just more likely to get caught and labelled as 'deviant'? Even more profoundly, do our definitions of what constitute crime and deviance themselves reflect class biases? Poor people, for instance, are less likely to commit many kinds of crimes, such as fraud and embezzlement. They are even less likely to manufacture faulty products, to engage in false advertising, to profit from political corruption, or to engage in various kinds of stock market swindles.

These observations suggest that while questions about who commits deviant acts and who does not are interesting and important, there is a need to move beyond them and to ask questions about the subjective character of deviance. Why are some ways of thinking, acting, and being more likely than others to excite indignation and disapproval, and why are some people more likely than others to become the objects of social control? It is to these questions that we now turn our attention.

The Sociology of Deviant Categories

As stated at the beginning of this chapter, the sociology of deviance is also the study of moral stratification. To call something or someone 'deviant' is to articulate a

Time to Reflect

Are the locations and activities that host large numbers of young people (especially young males) more likely to be characterized by high levels of deviance?

judgment that the thing or person is disreputable. An important set of issues in the sociology of deviance relates to the creation of categories—some deviant and some not—by which people and actions are sorted (Loseke, 2003).

In the course of living our lives day to day, we tend to treat these distinctions as common sense. The deviant qualities of people and acts, we convince ourselves, reside within the people and acts themselves. However, judged from another standpoint, known as **social constructionism** (Miller and Holstein, 1993; Spector and Kitsuse, 1977), this logic is flawed. Acts and people are not inherently deviant but are defined as such by those in society with the power to do so.

Proceeding from this assumption, we are led to another set of questions. For example, how do we make the moral distinctions that we make? This perspective maintains that there is nothing self-evident or commonsensical about the deviant quality of people and their behaviour. Instead, the deviant quality assigned to people and behaviour is itself problematic and requires investigation.

Further, we need to recognize that the character of social condemnation is fluid and dynamic over time (Curra, 2000). It is easy to think of behaviours that were once widely viewed as deviant but that have come to be considered much less deviant in recent years. 'Living together', having a child outside of marriage, or being gay might only a few years ago have been widely seen as grounds for social exclusion. While there is some resistance to these behaviours in the society at large (and a great deal of resistance in particular sectors of society), societal attitudes have moderated considerably.

At the same time, it is equally easy to think of many ways of acting or ways of being that were once widely tolerated but that now seem to draw considerable

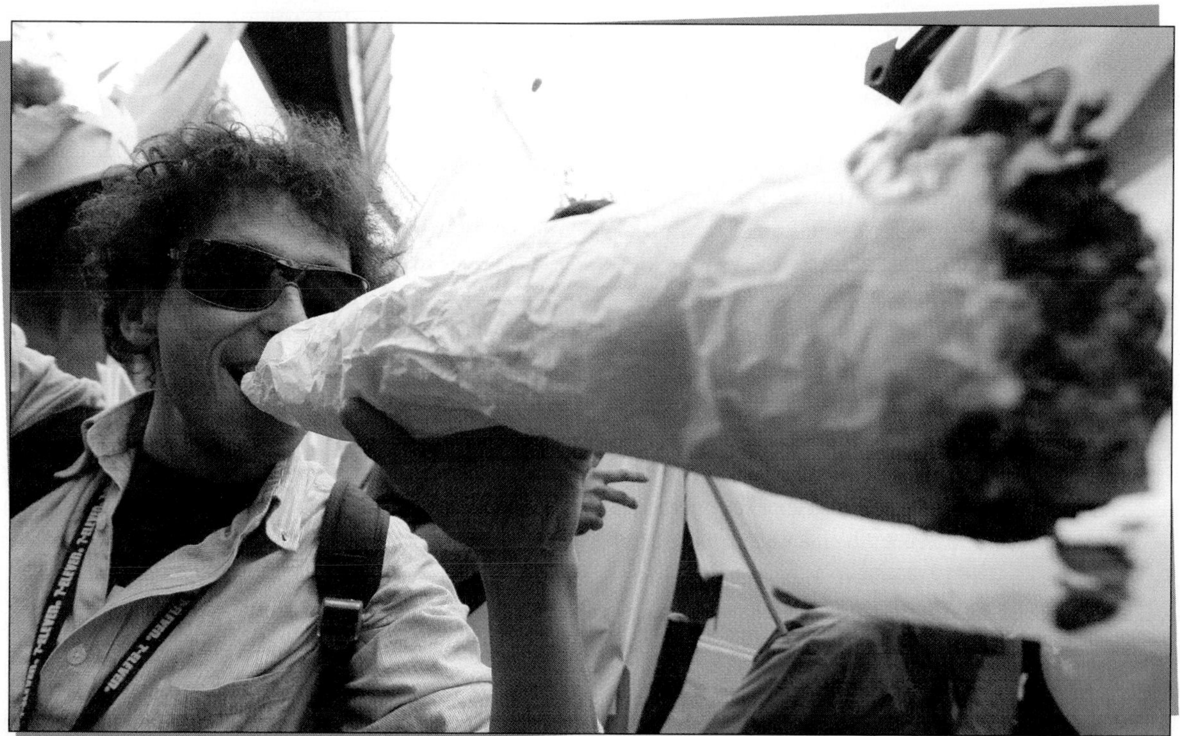

Illegal behaviours such as marijuana smoking are common among young people. Some believe that marijuana use should be decriminalized since non-enforcement of the law brings all lawmaking into disrepute. (Reuters/Daniel Aguilar)

disapproval. One clear example is cigarette-smoking (Tilleczek and Hine, 2006; Troyer and Markle, 1983; Tuggle and Holmes, 1999). Only a few decades ago, cigarette-smoking was widely approved of, even imitated as glamorous. People smoked on elevators, in restaurants, and around children—even while attending sociology classes. That view of smoking contrasts sharply with the present-day view. Today, smokers are pariahs in many circles, and their habit is the object of scorn (Balkne and Silva, 2004). Increasingly, they are the objects of a variety of forms of legal and extra-legal control (Wagner, 1997). Other examples of behaviour for which social tolerance has decreased in recent years include drinking and driving (Asbridge et al., 2004; Gusfield, 1981), wife assault (Johnson, 1996), and sexual harassment (Stewart, 2002).

Deviance as a Claims-Making Process

What are the sources of the distinctions that the members of a society make between what is and what is not deviant? Social constructionist writers understand this to be a **claims-making** process (Best, 2001; Spector and Kitsuse, 1977). This refers to the process by which groups assert grievances about the troublesome character of 'other' people or their behaviour. Claims-making thus involves the promotion of a particular moral vision of social life. In a practical sense, we recognize claims-making in many different sorts of activities that could include voting for 'reform' candidates in a local election, debating some exotic sexual practice on a daytime talk show, marching in protest to have the police do something about local crime, and providing expert testimony before a parliamentary committee. In short, claims-making is anything anybody does to propagate a view of who or what is deviant and what needs to be done about it (Loseke, 2003).

As a social process, claims-making is directed towards the achievement of three broad types of objectives:

1. *Publicizing the problematic character of the people with the behaviour in question.* Before they come to see people as troublesome, the members of a society generally need to be convinced that there is some tangible reason to regard those in question as troublesome. Claims-makers may endeavour to convince us that deviants are dangerous or irresponsible or that their behaviour is contagious (Best, 1999; Macek, 2006). In many cases, there is no objective basis to the claim, but the claim may be understood by many as a valid statement about the world.
2. *Shaping a particular view of the problem.* Deviants can be defined in many different ways, and it matters greatly whether we see people as troubled or as troublesome (Gusfield, 1989). Generally, claims-makers want not only to convince us that certain people are a problem, but that they are problems of a particular type. 'Problem drinking', for instance, can be constructed in many different ways (Holmes and Antell, 2001). We might see it as a sin, which implies that it is a religious problem. We might see it as a crime, which implies that it is a legal problem. Or we might see it as a sickness, which implies that it is a medical problem. In all cases the behaviour in question remains the same, and in all cases it is seen as deviant. What changes is the kind of deviant the problem drinker is understood to be. These differing constructions have very different implications for what it is we think we need to do about the deviant person.
3. *Building consensus around the new moral category.* Claims-makers endeavour to build widespread agreement about the correctness of a particular moral vision (Heimer, 2002; Macek, 2006). This is accomplished by winning the support of the media, officialdom, and the general public (Hilgartner and Bosk, 1988). As consensus is built, dissenting views are relegated to the margins of legitimate discourse. It is precisely the establishment of consensus and the marginalization of dissenting views that give the deviant categories in our society their common-sense character.

Who Are Claims-Makers?

The movement to 'deviantize' people and behaviour originates in the perceptions (however narrowly shared at the outset) that something is troubling and needs correction. Howard Becker (1963) coined the term *moral entrepreneur* to describe those who 'discover' and attempt to publicize deviant conditions. Becker says that moral entrepreneurs are crusading reformers who are disturbed by some evil that they see in the world and who will not rest until something is done to correct it.

In the early stages, definitions of deviance often are promoted by those who have some direct connection to the problem. In the case of drinking and driving, for instance, claims-making to heavily criminalize this conduct originated with victim groups such as MADD (Mothers Against Drunk Driving), whose members had a powerful emotional stake in the issue (Reinarman, 1996). In contrast, many of those involved in the construction of deviance have no vested interest in or emotional connection to the problem or the outcome. Lawmakers, journalists, daytime talk show hosts, and the producers of television drama frequently play a very significant role in the promotion of particular designations of deviance (Hilgartner and Bosk, 1988; Sacco, 2005). However, their social distance from the issue is often greater than that of victims' groups, and for many of them, the construction of deviance is just another day at the office.

What Are Claims?

When social constructionists speak of *claims*, they are talking about the actual message content that conveys a moral vision of deviance and non-deviance. What do claims-makers say, for example, in interviews on television talk shows, in pamphlets, in newspaper editorials, and on picket signs to convey the message that something or someone deserves the appellation of 'deviant'? The study of claims is the study of rhetorical communication, since such communications—by design or in effect—persuade audiences.

Successful claims-making rhetoric can demonstrate the gravity of a problem in several ways, including these:

- *Using compelling statistics.* Statistics are used to impress on consumers of the media the size of a problem and that the problem is getting worse (Best, 2001; Gilbert, 1997). Statistical estimates of a problem's dimensions that suggest that a large problem is getting worse legitimate concern and provide compelling evidence of the urgency of a problem.
- *Linking an emergent concern to problems already on the public agenda.* In this way, familiar moral language can be used to provide ready reference points for the emergent problem. For instance, because addiction is widely recognized as a problem in North America, new problems may be described as 'addictions'. We use the term 'addiction' in a very liberal way and speak of, for instance, 'pornography addicts', 'gambling addicts', and 'Internet addiction' (Butters and Erickson, 2000).
- *Using emotionally compelling examples to typify the seriousness and character of the threat posed by the behaviour* (see Bromley and Shupe, 1981). For example, the killings at Columbine High School in Colorado are applied in a rhetoric to exemplify the problem of school violence, even though such incidents are extremely rare and most school crime in no way resembles this incident (Fox and Levin, 2001).

Deviance Ownership

Claims-making is not just a matter of seeing particular types of people or behaviour as problems, it is also seeing them as particular *kinds* of problems (Gusfield, 1989). What is at stake is the 'ownership' of the problem: how a problem is framed determines who will be responsible for responding to or dealing with the problem (Sasson, 1995). If problem drinking is understood as a legal problem, we might expect the courts and police to do something about it. If it is understood as a religious problem, then we look to the clergy and theologians for solutions. If it is understood as a medical problem, we turn to doctors and psychiatrists.

One dominant trend in the way we think about deviance solutions concerns *medicalization* (Adler and Adler, 2006; Conrad and Schneider, 1980). Increasingly, we have come to think that many behaviours are forms of medical disorder that require treatment rather than punishment (Dworkin, 2001). More and more, it seems we have come to use the language of sickness, health, and disease when talking about conditions as diverse as violence, gambling, obesity, drug use, underachievement, and rampant consumerism. It can be argued that this shift suggests a more benign approach to deviants, since it implies that individuals are not entirely to blame for their behaviour; the stigma associated with deviant conduct is therefore reduced (Appleton, 1995). At the same time, it can be argued that medicalization encourages us to ignore structural contexts when we think about various kinds of deviance. In other words, medical models imply that these problems occur because individuals 'get sick' and not because social structural conditions make some kinds of behaviour more likely, which would shift some of the responsibility for the condition of the individual onto society in general.

Deviance and Social Conflict

Moral differentiation suggests processes of social conflict. Disagreement exists in society regarding who or what should be seen as disreputable (Hier, 2002). These conflicts are evident in the battle over abortion, the movement to legalize marijuana, and efforts to control cigarette-smoking. In other cases, the conflict is less evident only because effective claims-making has resulted in consensus.

While sociology makes available to us a large number of versions of **conflict theory**, two broad types can be distinguished: conservative and radical (Williams and McShane, 2003). These theories suggest different ways of understanding the wider social dynamic of the claims-making process.

From the perspective of conservative conflict theory, social conflicts regarding the moral meaning of conduct emerge from diverse sources (Turk, 1976; Vold et al.,

2001). As members of various ethnic, religious, professional, lifestyle, or cultural groups seek to pursue their social interests, they may come into conflict with other groups over scarce resources. In the context of such models, **power** is seen as relatively diffuse and thus not concentrated in any one sector of the society (Gusfield, 1963). Instead, various **status groups** come into conflict, often over specific issues. From this perspective, the study of moral differentiation is the study of how some groups in society are able to influence systems of social control so as to allow them to compete more effectively in their struggle to achieve their goals.

The creation of new categories of deviance may facilitate the pursuit of social goals in many different ways. Social control bureaucracies may find that the resources made available to them become more plentiful when they can identify new forms of danger that require control (Becker, 1963; Jenkins, 1994). Alternatively, new or struggling medical specialities can find their social status enhanced if the members of a society become convinced that they are indispensable to the solution of some pressing social problem (Pfohl, 1977).

Often the struggle to define deviance reflects a much more evident cultural difference regarding what is or what is not moral. Contemporary debates over abortion, for instance, can be seen as debates about who will, in the end, get to call whom 'deviant'. Similarly, those whose cultural or religious beliefs lead them to oppose a movement for gay rights may think of gay people as deviants. At the same time, gays and lesbians (and others in society) may think of those who actively (or even violently) oppose the movement for gay rights as suffering from a psychological malady known as *homophobia.* Both examples suggest status struggles over whose moral vision shall prevail and, conversely, over who shall be thought of as deviant.

In contrast, radical conflict theory draws on the Marxian understanding of society (Spitzer, 1975). Thus, it views the economic organization of society as the key to understanding moral stratification. From this point of view, the **social construction** of deviance must be understood as reflecting the economic realities of capitalism and the class exploitation capitalism engenders.

From a Marxian position, the internal logic of capitalism gives deviance both its objective and its subjective character. Capitalism requires a large pool of labour that can be exploited by keeping wages low. But this means that there will always be more workers than jobs and some people inevitably will be marginalized. These marginalized populations will have little stake in the system and will be at greater risk of criminal involvement and of being labelled as criminal.

The Sociology of Deviant Stigma

A third key area of study in the sociology of deviance concerns the ways in which deviant stigmas are applied to people and how stigma is managed (see, for example, Table 7.3). This body of research and theory focuses attention on the social interaction between those who exercise social control and those who are thought of in society as disreputable. In this respect, questions about the application and consequences of deviant stigma tend to be more micro- than macrosociological.

The Process of Labelling

People come to be seen as deviant because of what others believe they have done or what others believe them to be. The labels of 'deviant' that are assigned to people are not benign. Rather, they are charged with a great deal of emotion. Such labels sort through the thousands of acts in which a person has engaged and indicate that the person's identity is best understood in terms of the act according to which the label is affixed (Erikson, 1966).

The assignment of stigma suggests what sociologists refer to as a **master status**. This means that the label of deviant overrides all other status considerations (Becker, 1963). To be known as a murderer, for example, is to possess a status characteristic that trumps any other status characteristics the person might have. Whatever else one might be (bright, interesting, poor, blond, left-handed), one is a murderer first.

Sociologists use the term **status degradation ceremony** to refer to the rituals during which the status of 'deviant' is conferred (Garfinkel, 1956). These ceremonies, like other public ceremonies such as marriage or

Time to Reflect

Do you think that the contemporary concern over 'Internet predators' is another example of exaggerated deviance construction?

Table 7.3 Types of Deviant Behaviour

Howard Becker (1963) suggested that once we recognize that deviant stigma is separable from the deviant act, it is possible to recognize at least four types of deviants. These types are created by the contrast between what people actually do (breaking rules or keeping them) and what they are perceived as (deviant or not deviant).

		Behaviour	
		Obedient	Rule-Breaking
Perception	Perceived as deviant	Falsely accused	Pure deviant
	Not perceived as deviant	Conforming	Secret deviant

graduation, publicly and officially acknowledge a shift in social **roles** and the emergence of a new identity. Status degradation ceremonies, including incompetency hearings, psychiatric examinations, and courtroom trials, mark the movement from one social position to another as the individual at the centre of the ritual is officially declared deviant. While we have designed ceremonies to move people into the status of 'deviant', we don't have comparable ceremonies to move them out of these statuses and back to 'normality'.

Resistance to Labelling

Of course, many people do not submit willingly to the imposition of labels of deviance. The ability of some in society to confer the status of 'deviant' on others reflects differentials in social power. When people have access to power resources, they are able to more effectively negotiate the status of 'deviant' (Pfuhl and Henry, 1993). A high-priced legal team can effectively counter-challenge efforts by the state to impose the status of 'deviant'. Plea-bargain negotiations, as the name implies, suggest straightforward attempts to negotiate moral status.

People might use a range of other strategies to avoid or negotiate a label of deviance. One obvious method involves efforts to undermine social control efforts through *evasion*. Such statuses are negotiated most effectively, perhaps, by avoiding their assignment in the first place. 'Successful' deviants learn to engage in prohibited conduct in ways that decrease the likelihood of getting caught (Becker, 1963).

HUMAN DIVERSITY

What's in a Name?

Does it matter how we label behaviour? Consider each of the pairs of labels below. In your view, do the labels in each pair refer to the same kinds of behaviour and people or to different kinds of behaviour and people? If they are different, then how are they different?

Terrorist	Freedom Fighter
Prostitute	Sex Worker
Sex Assault Victim	Sex Assault Survivor
Cult Leader	Religious Leader
Disabled	Differently-Abled
Pro-Life	Anti-Choice
Pro-Choice	Pro-Abortion
Addiction	Bad Habit

Individuals also try to avoid or negotiate stigma through what Goffman calls *performance* (Goffman, 1959). Many of us are quite explicitly aware of the dramatic roles we might perform if we are stopped by the police officer who suspects we have been speeding; the performance is intended to neutralize the efforts of the police to impose a deviant designation (Piliavin and Briar, 1964). Under some conditions, people use what are called *disclaimer mannerisms.* These are actions intended to signal to agents of social control that they are not the appropriate targets of deviant attribution.

Deviant Careers and Deviant Identities

One potential consequence of the labelling process is what is known as *deviancy amplification*: the ironic situation in which the very attempt to control deviance makes deviance more likely (Lemert, 1951; Tannenbaum, 1938). Efforts to describe how labelling processes result in more rather than less deviance usually distinguish between primary and secondary deviance (Bernberg et al., 2006; Lemert, 1951). *Primary deviance* is the deviance in which we all engage from time to time and that has no real consequence for how we see ourselves or

SOCIOLOGY IN ACTION

Disclaimer Mannerisms in University Examinations

Sociologists Daniel Albas and Cheryl Albas (1993) undertook a study of how students attempt to distance themselves from charges of academic dishonesty while writing examinations. Data of several sorts were collected, including interviews with students and observations of students writing exams. The authors note that people writing examinations are at high risk of stigmatization. Invigilators patrol the rooms on the lookout for suspicious behaviour. Too often, neither the professor (who may or may not be at the exam) nor graduate assistants have any direct knowledge of the individuals writing the exam. For these reasons, students take many steps to ensure that they will not be falsely accused of cheating.

The authors were able to define two major types of strategies: actions that students take and actions that they attempt to avoid taking.

Actions taken include the following:

- *Picayune overconformity with regulations.* This involves the demonstration of conformity with even the most minor examination rules. Students are careful, for instance, to hand in their papers before gathering up their possessions to leave. In this way, there can be no suspicion that anything untoward is occurring. A student who needs to blow his or her nose will be sure to wave the tissue around first so it is clear that it is nothing other than a tissue.
- *The expression of repression of creature releases.* Creature releases are those aspects of the self that steal through the facade of social control, including sneezes and yawns. A student who needs to use the bathroom during the exam might make very exaggerated gestures to impress upon invigilators the urgency of the situation.
- *Shows of innocence.* Students know, for instance, that a lack of activity might be read as indicative of a lack of preparation. So when they are not writing, they might be underlining or circling words or phrases on the exam sheet.

Actions avoided include these:

- *Control of eyes.* Students know that they are not supposed to have roving eyes, so they are careful where they look. One preferred strategy is to stare at the ceiling or the head of the person behind whom the student is sitting.
- *Control of notes.* Students might frisk themselves before they enter the exam room to ensure that they are not carrying anything with them that could get them into trouble.
- *Morality of place.* Students worry that where they sit can send a message about their trustworthiness. A student might be careful, therefore, not to sit next to a very good student or someone whom they believe is perceived as a potential cheater.

for how other people see us. For instance, all of us from time to time might lie, might cheat, might drink too much, or might engage in some other prohibited behaviour. *Secondary deviance*, in contrast, is marked by a life organized around deviance. Secondary deviance suggests emergence in a deviant role rather than ephemeral acts of deviance. It is one thing to steal on occasion; it is quite another to be a thief. While any of us might tell an occasional lie, most of us do not think of ourselves or are thought of by others as liars.

Some researchers have asked what sometimes turns primary deviance into secondary deviance. The answer is societal reaction. It is argued that the ways in which agents of social control respond to initial acts of deviance—through stereotyping, rejection, and the degradation of status—can actually make future deviance more rather than less likely (Markin, 2005; Tannenbaum, 1938).

One of the key intervening mechanisms in this process, it is argued, is the transformation of the **self**. Consistent with social psychological theories (such as the one advanced by Charles Horton Cooley, 1902) of how the self emerges and is maintained, labelling theorists have argued that individuals who are consistently stigmatized may come to accept others' definition of their deviant identity. To the extent that individuals increasingly come to see themselves as others see them, they may become much more likely to behave in ways that are consistent with the label of 'deviant'. In a sense, individuals become committed to a life of deviance largely because others have expected them to. Deviance becomes a self-fulfilling prophecy (Tannenbaum, 1938).

Managing Stigma

How do those who have been labelled 'deviant' manage these labels? People may employ various strategies that allow them to control information about their deviant identity or to alter the meaning of their stigma so as to reduce the significance of the deviance in their lives (Hathaway, 2004; Park, 2002).

In any discussion of stigma management, it is important to distinguish between the *discreditable* and the *discredited* (Mankoff, 1971). In the former case, we are talking about people who might become discredited if knowledge about their stigma were to become public. In the latter case, the stigma is either evident or it can be assumed to be known.

Because the discreditable and the discredited face different sorts of problems, they have differing options available to them for the management of stigma. For the discreditable, the pressing need is to control information others have about them. If people have a kind of stigma others may not know about, they face the constant worry that others they care about may reject them if information about this stigma becomes public (James and Craft, 2002). Victims of a sexual crime, those suffering from stigmatized diseases, and those who hold unpopular religious beliefs need, in many cases, to keep aspects of their lives secret because they fear the rejection of others.

In other cases, the discreditable may attempt to 'pass'—to fraudulently assume an identity other than the one for which they might be stigmatized. A gay man, for instance, might 'stay in the closet' to allow others to assume that he is 'straight'. An individual whose unpopular political opinions are kept secret may laugh publicly at the jokes directed at people who think the same way that she does.

The discredited face a different problem. Their stigma tends to be apparent, so there is no need to keep it secret. Rather, they need to restrict its relevance to the ways others treat them. One obvious way this might be accomplished is through some form of purification, in which the stigmatized individual attempts to convince others that he or she has left a deviant identity behind (Pfuhl and Henry, 1993). Some sort of redefinition of the self is intended to restrict the interactional relevance of the stigma by locating it in the past. This occurs when stigmatized individuals tell others that they have become religious or that they have 'finally grown up'. One of our contemporary definitions of a hero is someone who has left a deviant stigma behind. Helen Keller and Christopher Reeve, for instance, are thought of as heroic largely because they rose above the stigmatizing character of particular physical conditions.

The discredited may also invoke some collective form of stigma management. This means that individuals who are the bearers of stigma may join together to form some sort of association intent on changing public perceptions of their disvalued character. Organizations intended to 'undeviantize' behaviour have been formed in recent years, including the National Organization for the Reform of Marijuana Laws (NORML) and COYOTE (Call Off Your Old Tired Ethics), which promotes the rights of sex workers. Collective stigma management may involve attempts to influence media coverage of the group in question or the use of terms used to describe members of the group (Bullock and Culbert, 2002). For instance, groups organized around collective stigma management have advocated that the terms 'disabled', 'retarded', and 'AIDS victim' be replaced in popular and official discourse with 'differently abled', 'developmentally delayed', and 'AIDS survivor', respectively (Titchkosky, 2001).

Time to Reflect

If deviance is a source of stigma, why are so many kinds of deviants in our society (e.g., gangsta rappers, misbehaving actors and athletes) treated like celebrities?

Conclusion

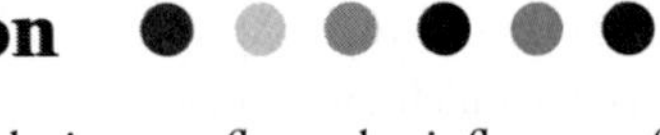

Our experience with deviance reflects the influence of the cultural context and the historical period in which we live. As times change, so do the categories of people and behaviour society finds troublesome. While gay and lesbian lifestyles were once viewed as highly deviant, today they are seen as less so. While drunk driving, wife assault, and cigarette-smoking were once regarded as normal, they are now viewed as highly deviant. Deviance is thus a dynamic process, and the future will present further permutations and innovations. By way of example, we need think only about the large number of newly constructed forms of deviance that we already associate with computer use, such as cyberporn, cyberstalking, and Internet addiction.

In the most general terms, the sociology of deviance is concerned with the study of the relationships between people who think, act, or appear in disvalued ways and those who seek to control them (Sacco, 1992). It seeks to understand the origins, the character, the consequences, and the broader social contexts of these relationships.

Deviance can be thought of as having two dimensions: the objective and the subjective. The objective aspect is the behaviour, condition, or cognitive style itself. The subjective aspect is the collective understanding of the behaviour, condition, or cognitive style as disreputable. A comprehensive sociology of deviance needs to consider both dimensions. Thus, we want to know why some people rather than others act in ways the society forbids, but we also want to know why some ways of acting rather than others are forbidden.

Correspondingly, it is possible to identify three major types of questions around which theory and research in the sociology of deviance are organized. First, how do we understand the social and cultural factors that make prohibited behaviour possible? Strain theory argues that people engage in deviant behaviour because it is a form of problem-solving; cultural support theories focus on the ways in which people acquire definitions of deviant conduct that are supportive of such behaviour; and control theories maintain that deviance results when the factors that would check or constrain it are absent.

Second, what is and what is not viewed as disreputable is not obvious and there is a need to explain the prevailing system of moral stratification. Definitions of deviance emerge from a process of claims-making. The establishment of consensus around such definitions gives categories of deviance a taken-for-granted quality.

Finally, we need to ask questions about the application and management of deviant stigma. Being labelled 'deviant' is a complex process that creates a large number of problems for the person who is the object of social control attention. It is important, therefore, to understand who gets labelled and how people cope with social control. In particular, we need to be alert to the manner in which the imposition of labels can worsen the very problems that the application of social control is meant to correct.

Questions for Critical Thought

1. What images of crime and deviance dominate coverage in the local media of the community in which you live? What sorts of images do they create of troubled and troublesome people?
2. Why do people cheat on university examinations? How might this question be answered alternatively by proponents of strain, cultural support, and control theories?
3. In your view, why are young males so much more likely than other groups in society to engage in a range of behaviours that many in society find troublesome?
4. What evidence do you see in your own social environment of the disvalued character of cigarette-smoking and smokers?
5. Aside from the examples given in the text, can you suggest behaviours or conditions that have undergone a shift in moral status in the last few years? How would you account for these changes?
6. How might Marxian and more conservative conflict theorists differ in their interpretations of the legal and moral battle in our society regarding the use of 'soft' illegal drugs, such as marijuana?
7. How might you explain to an interested layperson the difference between the ways in which sociologists think about deviance and the ways in which journalists do?
8. In your opinion, does it make sense to speak of something called 'positive deviance'? Why or why not?

Recommended Readings

Deborah Brock, *Making Work, Making Trouble: Prostitution as a Social Problem* (Toronto: University of Toronto Press, 1998).

This study provides a comprehensive treatment of the social problem of prostitution in Canada. The author's analysis illustrates the value of a constructionist approach to the study of specific forms of social deviance.

Francis T. Cullen, John Paul Wright, and Kristie R. Blevins, eds, *Taking Stock: The Status of Criminological Theory* (Edison, NJ: Transaction, 2007).

This collection of essays provides a detailed and comprehensive examination of the major varieties of sociological theories of nonconformity. Each of the theories is explained and assessed with respect to available empirical evidence.

John Curra, *The Relativity of Deviance* (Thousand Oaks, Calif.: Sage, 2000).

The aim of this book is to show that deviance cannot be considered an absolute and that what is subject to social control varies by time and place. The analysis of necessity calls into question many common assumptions about the nature of problematic people.

Frederick J. Desroches, *The Crime that Pays: Drug Trafficking and Organized Crime in Canada* (Toronto: Canadian Scholars' Press, 2005).

This book offers a systematic and highly readable treatment of the problem of organized drug-trafficking. The author's insightful analysis highlights the social organizational character of this kind of deviant activity.

Erving Goffman, *Stigma: Notes on the Management of Spoiled Identity* (Englewood Cliffs, NJ: Prentice-Hall, 1963).

This is the classic discussion of how people who are defined as 'deviants' by the society in which they live manage stigma. The book was formative in the development of the sociology of labels of deviance.

Donileen Loseke, *Thinking about Social Problems.* 2nd edn (New York: Aldine de Gruyter, 2003).

Loseke provides an introduction to the social constructionist perspective as it applies to the study of troublesome people and behaviour.

Vincent F. Sacco, *When Crime Waves* (Thousand Oaks, Calif.: Sage, 2005).

This book exlores the phenomenon known as the crime wave. In so doing, it addresses both the objective and subjective character of deviance.

Lorne Tepperman, *Deviance, Crime, and Control: Beyond the Straight and Narrow* (Toronto: Oxford University Press, 2006).

A detailed discussion of the contemporary field of the sociology of deviance. The book focuses both on the theories that structure the field and on their substantive application.

Recommended Websites

Canadian Sociology and Anthropology Association
www.csaa.ca/structure/Code.htm
This website contains the rules, regulations, and principles relating to the ethics of professional sociological research.

Crimetheory.com
crimetheory.com
This site provides a very comprehensive discussion of deviance and crime theory for educational and research purposes.

Florida State University School of Criminology and Criminal Justice
www.criminology.fsu.edu/cjlinks/default.htm
This collection of links relating to the sociologies of crime, deviance, and social control is extremely comprehensive.

Sex Professionals of Canada
spoc.ca/
This page contains resources for professional sex workers and provides some interesting insights into how those involved in professional pursuits that others regard as deviant think about their own lives.

Society for the Study of Social Problems
itc.utk.edu/sssp/
This is the main page for the Society for the Study of Social Problems (SSSP). The journal of this society, *Social Problems*, has been very influential in the development of the sociology of deviance.

Statistics Canada
www.statcan.ca
This is the main page for Canada's national statistical agency, Statistics Canada. Many different sorts of reports, tables, and graphs relating to a variety of forms of deviance can be located at this site.

The Surveillance Project
www.queensu.ca/sociology/Surveillance/
This page contains a wealth of information relating to the Queen's University Surveillance Project. The project is concerned with the study of the increasingly large number of technologies and social practices employed for the purpose of social control.

Part III

Social Institutions

Chapter 8

Families and Intimate Relationships

Maureen Baker

Learning Objectives

In this chapter, you will:

- Learn to differentiate popular myths about family life from actual research results.
- Gain a clearer understanding of variations in family life.
- Understand how sociologists have conceptualized and explained family patterns.
- Gain some insight into several contentious issues in Canadian families.
- Identify current demographic trends in Canadian families.
- Understand how predictions are made about family life in the future.

Photo © Sophia Fortier

than on feelings of attraction, love, and obligation or the services intimates provide for each other. These definitions always include heterosexual couples and single parents sharing a home with their children, but until recently, few definitions encompassed same-sex couples. Most definitions include dependent children, while some also take into account childless couples or those whose children have left home. Still others extend the definition of family to grandparents, aunts, uncles, and cousins who are sharing a dwelling.

Sociologists and anthropologists used to talk about 'the family' as a monolithic **social institution** with one acceptable structure and common behavioural patterns (Eichler, 2005). Academic researchers used to assume that family members were related by blood, marriage, or adoption and that they shared a dwelling, earnings, and other resources; that couples maintained sexually exclusive relationships, reproduced, and raised children together; and that family members cherished and protected each other. Nevertheless, academics have always differentiated between **nuclear families**, which consist of parents and their children sharing a dwelling, and **extended families**, which consist of several generations or adult siblings with their spouses and children who share a dwelling and resources. Both kinds of families continue to be a part of Canadian life although the nuclear family is more prevalent.

The most common definition used in policy research is Statistics Canada's **census family**, which includes married couples and cohabiting couples who have lived together for longer than one year, with or without never-married children, as well as single parents living with never-married children. As of 2006, couples can be same-sex or heterosexual but this definition says nothing about the larger kin group of aunts, uncles, and grandparents, or about love, emotion, caring, or providing household services. Yet a common definition must be agreed upon when taking a **census** or initiating policy research.

The Canadian government also uses the concept of **household** in gathering statistics relating to family and personal life. Household refers to people sharing a dwelling, whether or not they are related by blood, adoption, or marriage. For example, a boarder might be part of the household but not necessarily part of the family. Table 8.1 shows the percentage of Canadians living in various family types in 2001 compared to 1981.

In a culturally diverse society such as Canada, it is inaccurate to talk about 'the family' as though a single type of family exists or ever did exist. In fact, cultural groups tend to organize their families differently, depending on their traditions, religious beliefs, socio-economic situation, immigrant or indigenous status, and historical experiences, though most Canadians live in nuclear families comprising parents and their children (VIF, 2004).

Nevertheless, the extended family, in which several generations (or siblings and their spouses and children) share a residence and co-operate economically, remains important as a living arrangement as well as a support group, especially among recent immigrants from parts of the Middle East or South Asia. Even when family

Table 8.1 Percentage of Families in Canada by Type, 1981 and 2001

Type of Family	1981	2001
Legally married couples with children	55.0	41.4
Legally married couples without children	28.2	29.0
Lone-parent families	11.3	15.7
Common-law families without children	3.7	7.5
Common-law families with children	1.9	6.3
Same-sex couples as % of all couples	—	0.5
% of male same-sex couples with children in household	—	3.3
% of female same-sex couples with children in household	—	15.2
Stepfamilies as % of all families	—	12

Source: Vanier Institute of the Family (2004: 40, 42, 58). Reprinted by permission of the publisher.

members do not share a residence, relatives may live next door or in the same neighbourhood, visit regularly, telephone daily, assist with child care, provide economic and emotional support, and help find employment and accommodation for one another (Paletta, 1992). When relatives do not share a household but live close by and rely heavily on one another, they are said to be a **modified extended family**.

In the 1950s, American sociologists lamented the isolation of the modern nuclear family, suggesting that extended families used to be more prevalent prior to industrialization (Parsons and Bales, 1955). Since then, historians have found that nuclear families were always the most prevalent living arrangement in Europe and North America (Goldthorpe, 1987; Nett, 1981), but extended families were and still are widespread among certain cultural groups, such as some **First Nations** peoples, Southern Europeans, and some Asians. They are also more prevalent among those with lower incomes and at certain stages of the family life cycle, for example, in order to provide low-cost accommodation and practical support for young cash-strapped couples, lone mothers after separation, or frail elderly parents after widowhood.

Many immigrants come to Canada from countries where people live in extended families, yet the percentage of 'multi-family households' (a term used by Statistics Canada that approximates an extended family) declined from 6.7 per cent in 1951 to 1.1 per cent in 1986, when immigration rates were high (Ram, 1990: 44). The explanation for this decline is that more Canadians began to live alone during that period and that immigrants tend to change their family practices to fit in with the host country. In a study of immigrants who came to Canada in 1985, 43 per cent initially lived with established relatives in 1986, but this declined to 26 per cent by 1996 (Thomas, 2001: 18). In contrast, only 11 per cent of Canadian-born people lived with relatives in 1986 compared to 13 per cent in 1996. Living with relatives was more prevalent among female immigrants and among those with lower educational qualifications and lower incomes (ibid., 21).

In this chapter, the term 'families' will be used in the plural to indicate the continued existence of different family structures. Qualifying phrases, such as 'male-breadwinner families', 'lesbian families', and 'stepfamilies', will be used for clarification. Although sociological definitions formerly focused on who constitutes a family, more researchers and theorists now emphasize what makes a family. This approach downplays the sexual preference of the couple and the legality of the relationship, focusing instead on patterns of caring and intimacy (Eichler, 2005).

Monogamy and Polygamy

In Canada it is against the law to marry more than one spouse at a time but **polygyny**, or having several wives at a time, is practised in some countries in Africa and Western Asia, especially those using Islamic law. In sub-Saharan Africa, about half of married women aged 15–49 were in polygynous unions throughout the 1990s in Benin, Burkina Faso, and Guinea, and over 40 per cent in Mali, Senegal, and Togo (UN, 2000: 28). Wealthy men are more likely than those with fewer resources to take on more than one legal wife (Barker, 2003).

Polygynous unions, which lead to a proliferation of stepchildren and step-relatives, tend to be associated with patriarchal authority and wider age gaps between husbands and wives. They are more common among rural and less-educated women, as well as those who do not formally work for pay outside the household (ibid.). Multiple wives, who are sometimes sisters, may resent

IN THE FIRST PERSON

I first became interested in sociology after I worked for a sociologist as a research assistant at the University of Toronto in 1968. I was just completing my second year of university. That work experience and more undergraduate sociology courses led to several similar jobs working for sociology professors, who encouraged me to continue with graduate studies. Since completing my doctorate in sociology at the University of Alberta in 1974, I have worked in three different countries (Australia, Canada, and New Zealand) as a university teacher, freelance consultant, parliamentary researcher, and social policy adviser.—Maureen Baker

Time to Reflect

How would you characterize the family structure in which you grew up? Was this ideal for you, or did you ever long to be part of a different kind of family?

their husband taking a new partner but they may also welcome her assistance with household work, child care, and horticulture, and may value her companionship in a society where marriage partners are seldom close friends. Furthermore, the husband's second marriage elevates the rank of the first wife, who then becomes the supervisor of the younger wife's household work.

Polygamy refers to the practice of having more than one spouse at a time but polygyny is much more prevalent than **polyandry** or marriage between one woman and several husbands. When polyandry does occur, the husbands are often brothers and the practice may relate to the need to keep land in one parcel (Ihinger-Tallman and Levinson, 2003). However, most societies prefer polygyny because more children can be born into marriages with multiple wives and this could be important if children are the main source of labour for the family or community. Also, the identification of the father is particularly important in **patrilineal** societies because children take their father's surname, belong to his kin group, and inherit from him, and married men are responsible for supporting their children. Knowing who the father is would be difficult with multiple husbands, so this is not usually an acceptable form of marriage in patrilineal systems. As most societies have been patriarchal, men have ensured that marriage systems suit their own interests.

Arranged versus Free-Choice Marriage

Marriages continue to be arranged in many parts of the world in order to enhance family resources, reputation, and alliances and because parents feel more qualified to choose their children's partners. The family of either bride or groom may make initial arrangements, but marriage brokers or intermediaries with extensive contacts are occasionally used to help families find suitable mates for their offspring.

Middle Eastern and South Asian immigrants living in Canada sometimes have their marriages arranged, which may involve returning to the home country to marry a partner selected by family members still living there, or being introduced to a suitable partner from the same cultural group living in Canada. Young people expect to have veto power if they strongly object to their family's choice, but in the home country considerable pressure exists to abide by the judgement of elders (Nanda and Warms, 2004).

HUMAN DIVERSITY

A Maori Lone-Mother Family on Social Assistance, New Zealand

'. . . from Friday to Sunday it's pretty much mayhem here. I can have anything up to 13 kids. Nieces, nephews, the *mokos* (grandchildren), the neighbours. Last weekend I had their baby, a 15-month-old baby from next door. Because they were having a big party and they were out of babysitters and I said, well just chuck him over the fence and we'll be right and she can sleep here the night so you can . . . pick her up in the morning. So they did that. My niece had to go to a funeral and she's got a three-week-old baby and she popped her over to me with a little bottle of breast milk as well. So I had those two babies and . . . my son had his friend over for the night because his mother was next door partying and so while everybody does their thing, I have the kids and I had another little girl 'cause her mother was there too and I don't really know them.'

Source: Excerpt from an interview with a Maori lone mother on social assistance in New Zealand, Maureen Baker, 2002.

Family solidarity, financial security, and potential heirs are more important in arranged marriages than sexual attraction or love between the young people. New partners are urged to respect each other, and it is hoped that love will develop after marriage. Often, arranged marriages are more stable than free-choice unions because both families have a stake in marriage stability. Furthermore, divorce may be legally restricted, especially for women, and may involve mothers relinquishing custody of their children and struggling to support themselves outside marriage.

In cultures with arranged marriage systems, dowries have sometimes been used to attract a partner for daughters, to cement alliances between families, and to help establish new households. Dowries involve payments of money or gifts of property that accompany brides into marriage and become part of marriage agreements. Although the types of payment vary considerably, they might include household furnishings, jewels, money, servants, or land. If a woman has a large **dowry**, she can find a 'better' husband, which usually means one who is wealthier, healthier, better educated, and from a more respected family. In some cultures, the dowry money becomes the property of the groom's family and in others it is used to establish the bride and groom's new household. Dowries have also been used to provide brides with some measure of financial security or insurance in case of partner abuse, divorce, or widowhood, but this depends on how much control women have over the money or property (Barker, 2003).

In other societies that practise arranged marriage (such as eastern Indonesia), the groom's family is expected to pay the bride's parents a **bride price** for permission to marry their daughter. If the bride is beautiful or comes from a wealthy or well-respected family, the price rises. If the groom and his family are short of assets, the bride price could sometimes be paid through the groom's labour.

Although dowries and bride prices are associated with arranged marriages, free-choice marriages have retained symbolic remnants of these practices. For example, trousseaus, wedding receptions, and the honeymoon are remnants of dowries, while the engagement ring and wedding band given to the bride by the groom are remnants of a bride price.

Patterns of Authority and Descent

Most family systems designate a 'head', who makes major decisions and represents the group to the outside world. In both Western and Eastern societies, the oldest male is typically the family head, in a system referred to as **patriarchy**. An authority system in which women are granted more power than men is a **matriarchy**, but matriarchal systems are rare. Some black families in the Caribbean and the United States have been referred to as matriarchal, or at least **matrifocal** (Smith, 1996), as have been the Tchambuli people of New Guinea (Mead, 1935). In both examples, wives and mothers make a considerable contribution to family income and resources as well as to decision-making. Although Canadian families used to be patriarchal, men and women now have equal legal rights and men are no longer automatically viewed as family heads. However, in some cultural communities, men are still regarded as family heads.

When Canadian young people marry, they usually consider their primary relationship to be with each other rather than with either set of parents or siblings. In most cases, however, the newly married pair is expected to maintain contact with both sides of the family and to participate in family gatherings, and could inherit from either side of the family. This situation is termed a **bilateral descent pattern**. In some other societies, the bride and groom are considered to be members of only one kin group, in a system called patrilineal descent if they belong to the groom's family, matrilineal descent if they belong to the bride's. Patterns of descent may determine where the couple live, how they address members of each other's family, what surname their children will receive, and from whom they inherit.

In Canadian families, bilateral descent is common for kinship and inheritance, but **patrilineal descent** has been retained for surnames in some provinces. The surname taken by a wife and by the couple's children has traditionally been the husband's name—a symbol of his former status as head of the new household. This tradition has been changed in Quebec, where brides are required to retain their family name. In Ontario, brides have a choice between keeping their family name or taking their husband's name. Where there is some legal choice, couples may also abide by their cultural traditions.

Explaining Family Patterns and Practices

All social studies are based on underlying philosophical assumptions about what factors are responsible for the structure of human society, what influences social change, and what should be the focus of social research. These assumptions, often called theoretical frameworks, cannot be proven or disproven but guide our research and help to explain our observations (Klein and White, 1996). In this section, several theoretical frameworks used to study families will be examined, including their basic premises, strengths, and weaknesses.

The Political Economy Approach

The basic thesis of the political economy approach is that people's relation to wealth, production, and power influences the way they view the world and live their lives. Family formation, interpersonal relations, lifestyle, and well-being are all affected by events in the broader society, such as economic cycles, working conditions, laws, and government programs. This perspective originates in the nineteenth-century work of German political philosophers Karl Marx (1818–83) and Friedrich Engels (1820–95). In *The Origin of the Family, Private Property and the State* (originally published in 1882 but reprinted in 1942), Engels discussed how family life in Europe was transformed as economies changed from hunting-and-gathering societies, to horticultural, to pre-industrial, and finally to industrial societies.

The political economy approach has been debated and modified over the years. Political economists argue that social life always involves conflict, especially between the people who have wealth and power and make social policies and those who do not. Conflicting interests remain the major force behind societal change. In the nineteenth century, men's workplaces were removed from the home, which gradually eroded patriarchal authority and encouraged families to adapt to the employer's needs. Furthermore, many of the goods and services that people formerly had produced at home for their own consumption were eventually manufactured more cheaply in factories. This meant that families eventually became units of shared income and consumption rather than units of production. Once the production of most goods and services took place outside the home, people began to see the family as private and separate from the public world of business and politics. Nevertheless, the two are actually related, as unpaid labour within the family helps keep profits high and wages low in the labour market (Bradbury, 2005; Luxton and Corman, 2001).

The impact of industrialization and workplace activities on family life become the focal point of the political economy approach, as well as the belief that economic changes transform ways of viewing the world. Political economists would argue, for example, that the surge of married women into the labour force after the 1960s occurred mainly for economic rather than ideological or feminist reasons. The service sector of the economy expanded with changes in domestic and foreign markets, requiring new workers. While married women had always worked as a reserve labour force, the creation of new job opportunities, as well as inflation and the rising cost of living, encouraged more wives and mothers to accept paid work. These labour market changes led to new **ideologies** about family and parenting. Political economists focus on the impact of the economy on family life, on relations between **the state** and the family, and on the social conflict arising from these political and economic changes. In doing so, they downplay voluntary behaviour and interpersonal relations.

Structural Functionalism

The basic assumption of structural functionalism is that behaviour is governed more by social expectations and unspoken rules than by economic changes or personal choice. Individuals cannot behave any way they want but must abide by societal or cultural guidelines learned early in life. Deviant behaviour that violates rules is always carefully controlled.

Within this approach, 'the family' is viewed as a major social institution that provides individuals with emotional support, love and companionship, sexual expression, and children. Parents help to maintain social order through socializing and disciplining their children. Families co-operate economically and help each other through hard times by sharing resources. They often protect their members from outsiders. Finally, people acquire money and property through inheritance from family members, which suggests that social **status** is largely established and perpetuated through families.

Talcott Parsons and Robert F. Bales (1955) theorized that with the development of industrialization and the shift to production outside the home, the small and relatively isolated nuclear family began to specialize in the **socialization** of children and in meeting the personal needs of family members. These authors assumed that the family has two basic structures: a hierarchy of generations, and a differentiation of adults into instrumental and expressive **roles**. Parsons and Bales argued that the wife necessarily takes the expressive role, maintaining social relations and caring for others. The husband, on the other hand, assumes the instrumental role, earning the money for the family and dealing with the outside world (Thorne, 1982).

Structural functionalists have been criticized for their conservative position, as they often write about the family as though there is one acceptable family form rather than many variations. They believe that behaviour is largely determined by social expectations and family upbringing, and, therefore, is difficult to alter. Structural functionalists have also implied that a gendered division of labour was maintained throughout history because it was functional for society, when it may actually have benefited heterosexual men more than others (ibid.). In addition, change is seen as disruptive rather than as normal or progressive, and individual opposition to social pressure has been viewed as deviance. Consequently, the structural functionalists have not dealt with conflict and change as well as have those taking a political economy approach. Nor have they focused on the dynamic nature of interpersonal relations. For these reasons, many researchers who want to examine inequality, conflict, and change find this theoretical perspective less useful than others to explain the social world.

Systems theory accepts many of the basic assumptions of structural functionalism but focuses on the interdependence of family behaviour and the way that families often close ranks against outsiders, especially when they are in trouble. This approach has been particularly useful in family therapy.

Social Constructionist Approach

The **social constructionist** approach refutes the idea that people behave according to unwritten rules or social expectations. Instead, it assumes that we construct our own social reality (Berger and Luckmann, 1966). Life does not just happen to us—we make things happen by exerting our will. This approach, also called **symbolic interactionism**, originated with the work of Americans Charles H. Cooley (1864–1929) and George Herbert Mead (1863–1931), who studied how families assist children to develop a sense of **self**. Within this perspective, the way people define and interpret reality shapes behaviour, and this process of interpretation is aided by non-verbal as well as verbal cues. Social constructionists also theorized that part of socialization is developing the ability to look at the world through the eyes of others and anticipating a particular role before taking it (called **anticipatory socialization**).

Studies using this approach often occur in a small-groups laboratory, using simulations of family interaction and decision-making. Researchers observe the interaction in this kind of setting between parents and children, among children in a playgroup, and between husbands and wives. Sometimes behaviour will be videotaped and the subjects will be asked to comment on their own behaviour, which is then compared to the researchers' observations. Research is often centred on communication processes during everyday experiences, but it is not enough to observe what people do. In addition, it is essential to understand how they feel and why they feel this way. People's perceptions and their definitions of the situation, rather than events or constraints in the external world, are thought to influence their actions or behaviour. This perspective could be seen as the precursor of postmodernist theory, to be discussed later in this chapter.

Feminist Theories

Feminist theorists have focused on women's experiences, on written and visual representations of women, and on socio-economic differences between men and women. These perspectives developed and proliferated as more researchers concluded that women's experiences and contributions to society have been overlooked, downplayed, or misrepresented in previous social research.

Some feminist researchers have used a **structural approach** to analyze the ways in which inequality is perpetuated through social policies, laws, and labour market practices (Baker, 1995; O'Connor et al., 1999). Others have concentrated on interpersonal relations between men and women, examining non-verbal communication, heterosexual practices, and public discourse (Baines et al., 1998; Krane, 2003). Still other feminist theorists are attempting to create a more interpretive feminist analysis that takes women's experiences and ways of thinking and knowing into consideration (Butler, 1992; D. Smith, 1999).

Feminists typically argue that **gender** differences are social and cultural, are developed through socialization, and are maintained through institutional structures and practices. Most argue that differences in interests, priorities, and achievements between girls and boys grow out of their unique psychological and sexual experiences, which are shaped by different treatment by parents, teachers, relatives, community leaders, and employers (Brook, 1999). Nancy Chodorow (1989) combines psychoanalysis and feminist theory, showing how unconscious awareness of self and gender, established in earliest infancy, shapes the experiences of males and females as well as the patterns of inequality that permeate our culture. Carol Gilligan argues in *In a Different Voice* (1982) that women's moral development is quite different from men's: while men tend to focus on human rights, justice, and freedom, women's sense of morality is typically based on the principles of human responsibility, caring, and commitment. Feminist scholars have also argued that whatever is considered 'feminine' in our culture is granted lower status than 'masculine' achievements or characteristics.

Feminists note that housework and child care are unpaid when performed by a wife or mother but paid when done by a non-family member but that, in both cases, the work retains low occupational status and prestige. Although most adult women now work for pay, they continue to accept responsibility for domestic work in their own homes (Bittman and Pixley, 1997; Fox, 2001a; Hochschild, 2001). The unequal division of labour within families, as well as women's 'double shift' of paid and unpaid work, is considered to interfere with women's attempts to gain employment equity.

Post-feminists question the very nature of feminist analysis by arguing that vast differences remain between individual women depending on their unique experiences, social position, and cultural background (Fraser and Nicholson, 1990). Others criticize the feminist perspective because it glosses over men's experiences or does not always compare men with women, but feminists argue that men's experiences and views are already well represented by traditional social science. Much of social science is now permeated by feminist ideas and the work of female scholars. The incorporation of this perspective into mainstream academic theory has been promoted by greater acceptance of the postmodernist idea that there is no absolute truth and that perception and knowledge depend on one's social position.

Postmodernist Approaches

The postmodernist analysis of families argues that truth is relative and depends on one's social position, gender, race, and culture. Furthermore, vast differences exist in family life, and the traditional nuclear family is more a myth than a historical reality. In contemporary countries of the OECD (Organization for Economic Co-operation and Development), sexuality is increasingly separated from marriage, and marriage is being reconstructed as a contract that can be ended. Child-bearing and child-rearing are no longer necessarily linked with legal marriage, and the division of labour based on gender is continually renegotiated (Beck-Gernsheim, 2002). These demographic and social trends have led to a theoretical reworking of what defines family in the twenty-first century.

Another focus is on how families are constructed in everyday language and policy discourse (Muncie and Wetherell, 1995). By deconstructing—or analyzing the origins and intended meanings of beliefs about the family, researchers are able to see how images of this institution have been socially constructed and are historically situated. Nancy Fraser (1997) argues that historical conceptions of the nuclear family, upon which many Western countries built their welfare systems, were premised on the ideal of the male-breadwinner/female-caregiver family. Labour market changes (including the casualization and feminization of the workforce) and new lifestyle possibilities have encouraged both men and women to question this gender order. Fraser suggests that we need to rethink the social construction of gender and the organization of work in order to facilitate a new order based on equity and recognition of the interdependence of work and family.

The legal assumption of the heterosexuality of couples has also been criticized, and Martha Fineman (1995) proposes a reconceptualization of family away from the current focus on sexual or horizontal intimacy (between spouses or partners). She argues for abolishing marriage as a legal category and placing greater emphasis on a vertical or intergenerational organization of intimacy (between parents and children). This would redirect attention away from sexual affiliation and encourage policy discussions about support for caring. Elizabeth Silva and Carol Smart (1999) suggest that 'normative heterosexuality' is being challenged by lesbians and gays who dispute the old saying, 'You can choose your friends, but you can't choose your relatives.' These families embrace friends, lovers, co-parents, adopted children, children from previous heterosexual relationships, and offspring conceived through alternative insemination (Weeks et al., 1998). Critics of the postmodernist approach often argue that too much emphasis is placed on personal choices and minority family situations rather than focusing on the ways that most people live or the practical constraints on their life choices (Nicholson and Seidman, 1995; Baker, 2007).

Time to Reflect

Which theoretical approach to the study of families do you find of most relevance to your own experience as a family member? Why?

Recent Issues in Canadian Families

In the past few decades, many aspects of family life have come to be seen as conflictual or even as social problems. In this section, we consider a number of these, with specific reference to Canadian families. First, we examine issues relating to the gendered division of labour.

Sharing Domestic Work

Over the past 20 years, patterns of paid work between husbands and wives have changed dramatically. While 50 per cent of families depended only on the husband's income in 1975, by 2002 only 15 per cent had a single male earner because so many wives have entered the job market (Statistics Canada, 1998a: 22; VIF, 2004: 83). The second earner in a dual-earner family with children increased the household income by 35 per cent (VIF, 2004: 87). Table 8.2 shows that fathers are still more likely than mothers to be working for pay, regardless of the age of their children. In addition, fathers are more likely than mothers to work full-time and overtime and to earn higher wages.

Canadian adolescent women expect to have paid jobs in the future. They tend to perceive household tasks as 'women's work', but not as a viable option for themselves, except among working-class girls (Looker and Thiessen, 1999). Furthermore, both adolescent males and adolescent females see jobs normally done by women as less desirable than those usually performed by men.

Research typically concludes that most heterosexual couples divide their household labour in such a way that husbands work full-time and perform occasional chores around the house, usually in the yard or related to the family car. Most wives are employed for fewer hours per week than their husbands, but they usually take responsibility for routine indoor chores and child care, even when employed full-time. Wives are also expected to be 'kin keepers' (Rosenthal, 1985), which includes maintaining contact with relatives, organizing family gatherings, and buying gifts. In addition, wives and mothers usually retain responsibility for emotional work, such as soothing frayed nerves, assisting children to build their confidence, and listening to family members' troubles (Ranson, 2005).

Despite this prevalent division of labour, wives who are employed full-time tend to perform less housework than those who work part-time or who are not in the labour force, and employed women did less housework in 2005 than in 1986 (Statistics Canada, 2006c). Wives employed full-time may lower their housework standards, encourage other family members to share the work, or hire someone to clean their houses or care for their children. Yet most women continue to retain all or most of the responsibility for indoor housework and child-rearing tasks, including the hiring and supervision of cleaners and care providers (Bittman and Pixley, 1997; Luxton, 2001; Ranson, 2005). Many employed mothers report feeling exhausted and drained by their attempts to earn money when they also accept most of the responsibility for child care and homemaking.

Younger, well-educated couples with few or no children tend to share domestic work more equitably. However, some wives in dual-earner families are employed full-time but still retain sole responsibility for housework, especially older women and those who did not complete high school. Wives' bargaining power may increase slightly when they earn an income comparable

Table 8.2 Canadian Labour Force Participation Rates (%) for Mothers and Fathers with Children Under 15 Years of Age, 2001

Family Type	Mother	Father
Lone parent with children under 6	60	76
Married parent with children under 6	71	94
Lone parent with youngest child 6–14	76	83
Married parent with youngest child 6–14	81	94

Source: Vanier Institute of the Family (2004: 74), derived from Statistics Canada, 2001 census. Reprinted by permission of the publisher.

to their husbands', as these wives are better able to persuade their husbands to do more housework (Statistics Canada, 2006c) and they tend to be less willing to relocate with their husbands' jobs. An unsatisfactory division of housework with their partner was given as a valid reason for divorce by 17 per cent of respondents in a 1995 Canadian study, but men were more likely to hold this attitude than women (Frederick and Hamel, 1998).

Why do wives accept the responsibility for housework even when they work for pay and prefer more sharing? Lorraine Davies and Patricia Jane Carrier (1999) examined the division of labour in dual-earner Canadian and US households using 1982 data, which allows them to say little about the current division of labour. Nevertheless, they concluded that the hours of work and the income earned by marital partners are less important than marital power relations in determining the allocation of household tasks. These power relations are influenced by gender expectations, opportunities, and experiences in the larger society, and gender intersects with race, ethnicity, and social class to influence these relations.

Based on 66 interviews with Australian women in and around Melbourne, Ken Dempsey (1999) concluded that few wives want to retain control over the domestic realm but that most are unable to persuade their husbands to take more responsibility for indoor household tasks. Husbands use a variety of tactics to avoid doing housework, such as waiting to be asked each time by their wives, saying they do not know how to do the task, arguing that it does not really need doing yet, and delaying completion of the task.

Only 1 per cent of Canadian families have adopted a role reversal, with the husband performing domestic work and child care at home while the wife works full-time (Marshall, 1998). In these families, most of the men are unemployed and have not necessarily chosen this lifestyle. Other North American research suggests that unemployed husbands feel that they would lose power in their marriages if their wife earned most of the household income, and that this view is shared by the wider community (Potuchek, 1997). Considerable research suggests that even when men have time available, they do not choose to spend it on domestic work (Shelton and John, 1996). Husbands will lend a hand if their wives are pressed for time, but housework and child care remain the responsibility of wives (and female relatives) throughout much of the world. Furthermore, women who have attempted to resist the gendered consequences of marriage by living in common-law arrangements find that they often slip back into conventional arrangements (Elizabeth, 2000). Cohabiting couples seem to have a less gendered division of labour than legally married couples (Wu, 2000), but relative power differences in heterosexual relationships continue to influence patterns of housework.

An uneven division of labour has many implications. More mothers than fathers develop close ties with their children, through years of physical and emotional caring work. In addition, some wives supported by their husbands are able to pursue hobbies and friendships during the day. At the same time, accepting most of the responsibility for housework and child care reduces the likelihood of obtaining employment qualifications, of working full-time or overtime, or of being promoted to higher-paying or more responsible positions. Furthermore, the consequent lack of income may reduce women's confidence in their ability to earn a living outside marriage. This may translate into reduced decision-making power in marriage and less income in the event of widowhood or divorce (Baines et al., 1998). And when women accept responsibility for domestic work, they also reinforce traditional role models for their children (Duffy and Pupo, 1992). Many women feel they have little control over the household division of labour but would like their husbands to accept a larger share of household and caring work (Dempsey, 2002).

Low Fertility and Assisted Conception

Common-law marriage, same-sex partnerships, divorce, and remarriage have complicated marriage and family relationships in the twenty-first century, but reproductive and genetic technologies may be in the process of fundamentally reshaping families (Eichler, 1997). This reshaping includes separating biological and social parenthood, changing generational lines, and creating the possibility of sex selection. A wide range of procedures have now become routine, such as egg retrieval, in vitro

Time to Reflect

What is your personal attitude towards the division of housework between partners? Do you think your gender affects your response?

fertilization, and reimplantation into a woman's womb. Frozen sperm and embryos make conception possible after their donors' death, post-menopausal women can bear children, and potential parents can contract surrogates to bear children for them (Baker, 2005).

Eichler (1996) argues that reproductive technologies tend to commercialize human reproduction: we can now buy eggs, sperm, embryos, and reproductive services—all of which are produced and sold for profit. These technologies tend to raise the potential for eugenic thinking and enable us to evaluate embryos on their genetic makeup. Prenatal diagnoses allow us to determine whether or not a fetus is worthy of being born (ibid.). However, we have very little research on the impact of these technologies on family life, such as how parents involved in artificial insemination reveal their children's background to them and how children deal with this knowledge.

Most men and women intend to reproduce. Fertility is important for social acceptance and gender identity, and conception problems contribute to feelings of guilt, anger, frustration, and depression and to marital disputes (Doyal, 1995). Low fertility may be caused by many factors, including exposure to sexually transmitted diseases, long-term use of certain contraceptives, workplace hazards, environmental pollutants, hormonal imbalances, and lifestyle factors such as tobacco smoking, excessive exercise, a large consumption of caffeine or other drugs, and prolonged stress (Bryant, 1990). The probability of conception also declines with women's age. Some couples spend years trying to become pregnant, while others place their names on adoption waiting lists. The number of infants available for adoption, however, has dramatically decreased in the past two decades with more effective birth control, greater access to abortion, and social benefits enabling single mothers to raise their own children. Consequently, more couples with fertility problems are turning to medically assisted conception.

Infertility is usually defined as the inability to conceive a viable pregnancy after one year of unprotected sexual intercourse, although many fertile people take longer than that to conceive. This short-term definition encourages some fertile couples to seek medical attention prematurely. Access to reproductive technologies is often limited to those considered most acceptable as parents: young heterosexual couples in a stable relationship with no previous children. Private clinics charging fees, however, may be less selective, and many women around 40 years of age approach fertility clinics for assistance. Most treatments last for several months and involve the use of drugs that can produce side effects such as depression, mood swings, weight gain, and multiple births. Some treatments continue for years (Baker, 2005).

Fertility treatments are also expensive, although those who end up with a healthy baby may find these costs acceptable. Many individuals pay privately for medically assisted conception but any complications will probably be treated within the public health system. The chances of complications following in vitro fertilization (IVF) are higher than with natural conception; about 25 per cent of IVF pregnancies end in miscarriage (Baird, 1997). Furthermore, the success rate is not always as high as couples anticipate. British research indicates that in vitro fertilization ends in success for less than one-third of those who embark on it (Doyal, 1995: 149) and for only about 15 per cent per treatment cycle. In Australia, the viable pregnancy rates were 14.9 per cent after one cycle of IVF, 15.9 per cent for insemination with sperm, and 18.1 per cent for egg transfer. If these products are frozen or thawed, the pregnancy rates fall (Ford et al., 2003: 100). Australian research also shows that adverse infant outcomes, such as pre-term delivery, low birth weight, stillbirth, and neonatal death, are higher among assisted conception births compared to all births (ibid.). Medically assisted births and their complications tend to use greater public health resources and also place financial and time constraints on new parents.

Those unable to reproduce even with the assistance of medical technology have sometimes turned to surrogacy arrangements. Surrogate mothers are usually low-income women who view pregnancy and childbirth as a relatively easy way to earn money, while the childless couple is often financially comfortable (McDaniel, 1988). Patricia Baird (1997) suggests that commercial surrogacy arrangements are unethical because they are premised on the idea that a child is a product that can be bought on the market and because they allow women to be exploited. In the United States, the substantial cost of surrogacy arrangements means that the commissioning couple is likely to be of a much higher economic and educational status than the woman gestating, and the brokers work on behalf of the paying couple (Baker, 2001).

Eichler (1997) argues that reproductive and genetic technologies represent a quantum leap in complexity by blurring the role designations of mother, father, and child. For the child in a surrogacy relationship, who is the mother—the woman who gave birth or the woman who was part of the commissioning couple? What does it now mean to be a father? Does a man become a father if he impregnates a woman but has no social contact with the child? Does he become a father when he contracts another woman to use his sperm to make a baby, which he then adopts with his legal wife? Although sociologists have always been interested in the impact of absent fathers on family life, they are now talking about the 'new absent fathers': sperm donors (Jamieson, 1998: 50). Social researchers are also interested in the increasing number of lesbian couples who are using self-insemination to create families without men (Albury, 1999; Nelson, 1999).

Sociologists and feminists have been ambivalent about medically assisted conception. On the one hand, it offers hope and opportunities for parenthood for those who might otherwise be excluded. However, some of the technologies are experimental and intrusive. These technologies also medicalize the natural act of child-bearing, reinforce the pressure for all women to reproduce, and provide costly services unavailable to the poor. Feminist scholars have also been concerned that patriarchal societies will use sex selection to reinforce the cultural preference for sons rather than daughters and that working-class women will be exploited, both financially and emotionally, through surrogacy arrangements. These scholars seem to be most supportive of new reproductive technologies when they discuss self-insemination within lesbian relationships (Nelson, 1999), perhaps because of the assumption that unequal power relationships and coercion are minimized.

Sociologists are also concerned that the widespread availability of medically assisted fertility treatments could place additional pressure on childless women, who are already perceived to be either unfortunate or 'morally flawed' (Morell, 1994). Research suggests that adoptive mothers are not always seen as real mothers, even by other women. These persistent attitudes help explain why some women and couples go to extreme lengths to reproduce or acquire a baby.

OPEN FOR DISCUSSION

Medically Assisted Conception

'We tried IVF [in vitro fertilization] and we got pregnant the first time. So it was very successful and obviously we are very pleased. I would say the IVF process was very cruel, even though we succeeded. I take my hat off to people who have it two or three times because it was extremely tough. It is very impersonal. You can't fault the treatment or the staff, but all the injection, different phases—it's like a roller coaster. You think you're ahead. Then you have a setback, bad news. One of the most stressful times for me was when I was in the room and they were harvesting the eggs from [my wife's] ovaries the first time—one egg. It felt terrible because we were hoping to get 12. We got five off the second so that was great but you still feel pretty disappointed. Then they fertilize and you only get two embryos and we were pretty depressed. Then a day later, we were up to four, so we were elated. Their goal was to try for five or six to choose. We had four but one was a bit dodgy so we had three good embryos—you get that news a day later and you're down a little bit. Then during the IVF we had always envisaged that they would insert two embryos, which is extremely common—most people have two put in. We only had one because [my wife's] uterus is a bit dodgy and they didn't want twins with a uterus shaped like that. They didn't want a prem baby [premature] so all of a sudden you think that your chances are halved, which wasn't quite true. Then we had three great embryos and they chose the best one and it took, which is very pleasing. The other two are cryogenically frozen just like Austin Powers, waiting for their day in the sun.'

Interviewer: 'Amazing isn't it when you think of the technology?'

'Yes it is and we wouldn't have got pregnant otherwise. . . . One of the senior doctors said that this was just the start and there were plenty more ups and downs. We are in the process now where there is lots of worry. [My wife] is worried about what she should and shouldn't eat. She worries that the baby will be born with some fault because she didn't take enough care. I'm very much in the reassuring mode—I'm sure it will be fine. I'm sure that once it is born then more worries start. It is an intriguing game, becoming a parent, I'd say.'

Source: Interviews with couples experiencing fertility treatments in Auckland, New Zealand, Maureen Baker, 2002.

Affordable and Regulated Child Care

The dramatic increase in the proportion of employed mothers within the past 40 years has led to a higher demand for non-family child care and to public concerns about the need to regulate the quality of care. Yet the demand still outstrips the supply, the assurance of quality continues to be a problem, and child-care costs are unaffordable for many parents. Since the 1960s, Canadian governments have subsidized child-care spaces for low-income and one-parent families, generally in not-for-profit centres or licensed homes. However, there are insufficient spaces for eligible families and two-parent families with higher incomes must pay the full cost (Clevedon and Krashinsky, 2001).

Canadian governments offer two forms of support for child care: a federal income tax deduction of up to $7,000 per child for employed parents using non-family care (with no family maximum), which is most useful for middle-income families paying higher taxes. In addition, the provincial governments (assisted by federal transfers) subsidize child-care spaces for low-income families and for sole parents (Baker, 2006). Unlike other Canadian provinces, Quebec offers heavily subsidized child care for all parents who need it, regardless of their household income or work status, at a cost to parents of only $7 per day (Albanese, 2006). Not surprisingly, the employment rates of mothers with children under six are much higher in Quebec than in the rest of Canada (Statistics Canada, 2006d).

Idealized or romanticized images of family life—so common in the mass media—give many people the sense they or their family is failing in some important respect; otherwise, wouldn't they be happier? (Popperfoto/Alamy Images)

Across Canada, many not-for-profit child-care centres have long waiting lists. Furthermore, they do not usually accept children under the age of two unless they are toilet-trained. Even if space is available, parents want to ensure that the centre employs an adequate number of staff to keep the infants clean, fed, and stimulated. In addition, some parents are concerned about the spread of infectious diseases in centre care. Finding a qualified babysitter to come to the child's home or who will welcome an extra child in her home is also difficult, although licensed family homes are available in most jurisdictions (Doherty et al., 1998).

Sitter care is unregulated by any level of government, yet it remains the most prevalent type of child care for employed parents. Grandparents (usually grandmothers) are sometimes able and willing to provide child care while the parents are at work, and care by grandmothers can save money, provide culturally sensitive care, and create a more solid bond between generations. Yet it could also lead to disagreements about child-rearing techniques between the parents and the grandparent, who is likely to have retained more traditional cultural values. Child-care concerns have encouraged some mothers to remain at home to care for their own children, although most can no longer afford this option.

Most centre-based care operates during regular office hours, but some parents need child care in the evening and weekends. In two-parent families, employed parents may be able to share child-rearing if they work on different shifts, but it is difficult to maintain their own relationship or to engage in family activities. Parents whose children have special needs also experience problems. Before institutions and hospitals were built in the 1960s, mothers were the main caregivers of these children. This source of unpaid labour is once again being examined as a way to reduce health and chronic-care costs with policies of deinstitutionalization since the 1980s. Yet many mothers are now in the labour force, and without some remuneration and community assistance, they will be unable to supervise their disabled children (or frail relatives) because of their own work responsibilities.

Many parents and activists are concerned about the quality of care both in licensed centres and by babysitters in private homes. In some jurisdictions (such as Alberta), neither the employees of child-care centres nor babysitters are required to have special training. These jobs pay the minimum wage or less and have difficulty attracting and retaining trained workers. A number of advocacy groups have formed around child-care concerns. These groups have asked governments to tighten regulations; to improve training, fringe benefits, and pay for child-care workers; and to allocate more public money to child care for employed parents. However, the extent of government involvement in the funding and regulation of child care remains contentious in many jurisdictions.

In the early 1980s, two Canadian commissions studied child-care issues, and after considerable lobbying by child-care advocacy groups the Conservative government under Prime Minister Brian Mulroney introduced a National Strategy on Child Care in 1987. However, only the tax reforms were implemented from this Strategy and the proposed national child-care program was delayed. As child care falls under provincial jurisdiction, the federal government was unable to persuade the provinces to create a program with national standards. This meant that federal child-care subsidies to the provinces continued to be channelled through the Canada Assistance Plan, which was a program for funding welfare.

Since this program ended in 1996, the federal government has been giving block grants to the provinces to use for a variety of health, social, and educational services. Friendly (2001) argues that after many years of lobbying, Canadian child-care programs have not developed beyond a rudimentary level and even deteriorated in the 1990s. She attributed some of the problems to disputes over federal–provincial jurisdiction. In the 2004 Canadian election, however, child-care shortages became a major election issue for the Liberal Party, which won a minority government.

Some conservative politicians still argue that child care is a family matter that should be of no concern to governments or employers. Yet conservative women's lobby groups, such as REAL Women of Canada, have argued for more income-tax relief for single-earner families and for higher social benefits to allow women to make a choice about working for pay or caring for their children at home (Baker and Tippin, 1999). For governments to provide mothers with a real choice, however, the social benefits would need to approximate women's potential earnings. This suggests that taxes would have to rise considerably.

Divorce and Repartnering: The Impact on Children

When divorce rates increased in the 1970s and 1980s, researchers began to devote their attention to the social consequences, especially for children. In 2001, researchers estimated that about 38 per cent of marriages would be expected to end in divorce before their thirtieth anniversary, but only half of all Canadian divorces involve children (VIF, 2004: 33). Many studies have concluded that children from one-parent families experience more negative outcomes than do children from two-parent families, including lower educational attainment, behavioural problems, delinquency, leaving home earlier, premarital pregnancy for girls, and higher divorce rates when they marry. The main research question typically focuses on whether negative outcomes result from the parental conflict during marriage, the trauma of separation, the absence of a father, or some other factor. As Figure 8.1 shows, mothers typically retain custody of the children.

Despite negative media attention given to single-parent families, most children from these families do not experience problems, although they have a higher risk of problems than do children from two-parent families. Furthermore, when studies control for changes in household income after marital separation, the incidence of problems declines, although it does not disappear (Elliott and Richards, 1991; Kiernan, 1997). The Canadian National Longitudinal Survey on Children and Youth (NLSCY) found that about 19 per cent of children from low-income families headed by a lone mother experience a conduct disorder, compared to 9 per cent of children from two-parent families. For those from higher-income families, this percentage drops to 13 per cent for lone-mother families and 8 per cent for two-parent families (Lipman et al., 1996: 88). Socio-economic conditions, however, are not always held constant in research projects.

Many lone-parent families experience economic disadvantage before divorce as well as after, as people from lower socio-economic groups tend to have higher rates of bereavement, separation, and divorce (Pryor and Rodgers, 2001). When children are raised in low-income families, they are more likely to suffer disadvantages that continue into adulthood. Using British National Child Development Study data, Kathleen Kiernan (1997) found that children from separated families were more likely than those from intact families to experience low earnings, low family income, unemployment, and social housing as adults. As Table 8.3 indicates, most children in one-parent families live in poverty in Canada and the English-speaking countries, especially if their mother is not working for pay.

Distinguishing between the impact on children of low socio-economic status and of parental separation is difficult for researchers. Lower status after separation seems to be a mediating factor for some outcomes but not for others. It accounts for a decline in educational attainment but not for rates of delinquency, psychosomatic illnesses, cigarette smoking, or heavy drinking in adulthood (Hope et al., 1998). Even in intact families, being raised in lower socio-economic households is associated with negative behavioural outcomes. These include delayed school readiness, lower educational attainment, a greater number of serious childhood illnesses, higher childhood accident rates, premature

Table 8.3 Poverty Rates of Households with Children in Various Countries, by Working Status of Parents

Country	1 parent, no worker	1 parent, 1 worker	2 parents, no worker	2 parents, 1 worker	2 parents, 2 workers	Poverty rate for all children
United States	93.8	40.3	77.9	30.5	8.3	21.7
Canada	89.7	27.7	75.3	22.9	3.5	13.6
United Kingdom	62.5	20.6	37.4	17.6	3.6	16.2
Australia	58.7	11.7	43.3	5.4	3.3	11.6
Netherlands	42.8	17.7	50.7	7.8	1.7	9.0
Finland	25.0	7.2	25.8	5.4	1.3	3.4
Sweden	34.2	5.6	13.7	8.2	1.1	3.6

Source: Based on EQ3.2, 'Poverty rates are much higher for families with jobless parents' (p. 57), from *Society at a Glance: OECD Social Indicators 2005*, © OECD 2005.

death, high rates of depression, high rates of smoking and alcohol abuse as young adults, and more trouble with school authorities and the law, to name only a few (NLSCY, 1996). For this reason, social researchers and theorists must consider socio-economic status as an important variable in all discussions of the outcomes of children after divorce.

Many studies indicate that children who live with their mothers after divorce are likely to experience diminished contact with their fathers and to suffer distress from this loss (Cockett and Tripp, 1994; Smyth, 2004). As children grow older, the time they spend with the non-resident parent decreases, and about a third lose contact completely (Amato, 2004). However, father/child contact is not the deciding factor in children's adjustment after their parents separate, as frequent contact with their father may negatively impact on children's well-being if there is a high amount of conflict between father and child or between parents over the children. If conflict is absent or contained, children both want and benefit from frequent contact with both parents (ibid.). In general, a close relationship with both parents is associated with a positive adjustment in children after divorce (Pryor and Rodgers, 2001). Furthermore, whether or not the father continues to pay child support may influence both the children's adjustment and the socio-economic status of the lone-parent family.

Adult children of divorced parents are more likely than those from intact marriages to end their own marriages with divorce (Beaujot, 2000). This may result from poor role models in childhood, from the simple observation that there is life after marriage, or from the fact that divorce becomes more personally acceptable as a solution to an unhappy marriage if it has already happened in one's own family.

There is no simple or direct relationship between parental separation and children's adjustment, although many studies do find differences between children from intact and separated families. Parental separation clearly adds stress to children's lives through changes in relationships, living situations, and parental resources. Although most studies find that psychological and behavioural stress are prevalent for children from separated parents, few studies conclude that psychological disturbance is severe or prolonged (Emery, 1994). Instead, most research finds that the first two years after separation require adjustments by both parents and children.

Never-married mothers who become pregnant before their education is completed are particularly vulnerable to low income as well as to disciplinary problems with their children. These mothers often repartner within a few years of the child's birth, but the socio-economic disadvantages of bearing a child at a young age may linger (Dooley, 1995; Edin and Kefalas, 2005). Their children are most likely to spend their childhood in one or more stepfamilies, which are often conflictual (Marcil-Gratton, 1998). These factors may partially account for higher rates of behavioural problems in the children of never-married mothers.

Research suggests that stepfamilies are difficult to establish and that considerable negotiation is required to maintain them. Children living in stepfamilies are at the

Figure 8.1 Dependent Children by Party to Whom Custody Was Granted, 1995 and 2002

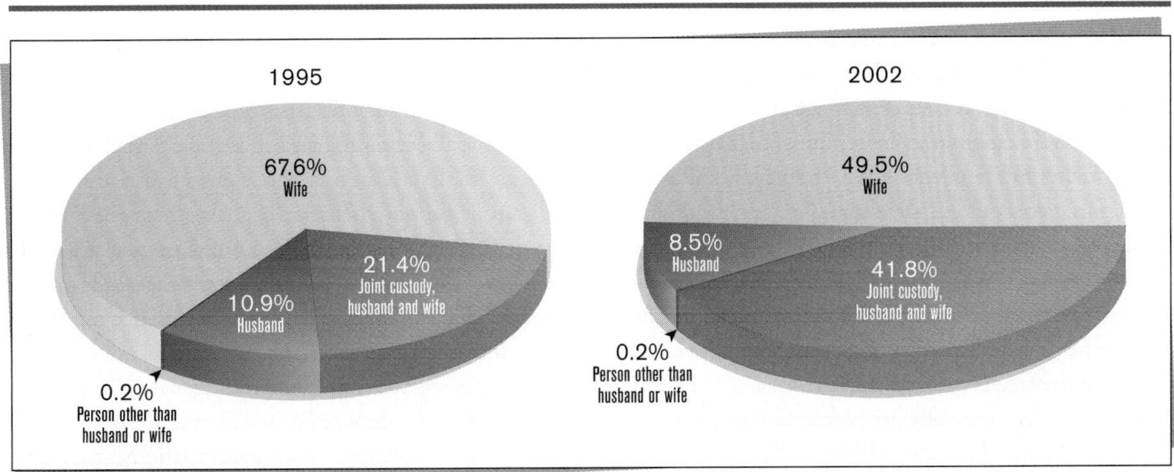

Source: Adapted from Vanier Institute of the Family, *Profiling Canada's Families III* (Ottawa: Vanier Institute of the Family, 2004), 38. Reprinted by permission of the publisher.

same risk of behavioural problems and distress as children growing up in lone-parent families. Neither a higher household income nor having two adults in the home ensures good outcomes for these children (Pryor and Rodgers, 2001). One explanation is that parental conflict and separation have a lasting effect on children. Another is that step-parents do not relate to their stepchildren with the same warmth and concern as they do with their biological children because they do not see them as their own children and have not spent their formative years together.

Although researchers usually study separation and divorce as negative life events, parents often experience relief and contentment after the initial adjustment of leaving an unhappy marriage. This is reflected in their general outlook and in their interactions with their children. Consequently, most researchers agree that children living in stable lone-parent families are better off than children living in conflict-ridden two-parent families (Booth and Edwards, 1990). Furthermore, children of employed lone mothers tend to accept more egalitarian gender roles, as they see their mothers supporting the family and managing tasks that were previously defined as men's jobs (Baker, 2001). This suggests that separation and divorce could have positive as well as negative outcomes for both parents and children.

Wife Abuse

Beginning in the 1980s, when domestic violence appeared to be on the increase, sociologists became more interested in studying this phenomenon. Feminist sociologists argued that the very term 'family violence' implies that this behaviour is randomly distributed within families, when men actually are the perpetrators in the vast majority of cases that come to the attention of police and social workers (Dobash et al., 1992).

The Canadian Urban Victimization Study found that in cases of 'spousal violence', physical abuse is not an isolated event. Some abused women are assaulted on numerous occasions by their male partners and have sought help many times from friends, neighbours, social workers, and the police. Furthermore, separated women are more likely to be assaulted than divorced or married women (DeKeseredy, 2005). Women are also more vulnerable if they see their partner as the head of the household, if they are financially dependent on him, or if they live in a housing development with other single mothers. Violence may also become normalized when it is continually viewed as a form of entertainment in films and sports events.

Murray Strauss and Richard Gelles (1990) found that marital violence actually decreased in the United States throughout the 1980s even though the reporting of this behaviour increased. They argued that reporting was influenced by the women's movement, by police campaigns to prosecute perpetrators, and by the availability of more options for women wishing to leave violent marriages. Yet they also made the controversial claim that women are as likely as men to abuse their partners, although they acknowledged that this behaviour is less likely to be reported to the authorities, is less consequential in terms of physical harm, and often is a form of self-defence. Walter DeKeseredy (2005) criticized the conflict tactics scale used by Strauss and Gelles, which counts incidences of violence but fails to examine their social context. He agreed that women's 'violence' against men often is in self-defence.

Wife abuse may represent men's rising concern that they are losing authority in their families, especially those men who are experiencing unemployment or other personal problems. This kind of violence is also aggravated by alcohol and substance abuse but represents much more than an interpersonal problem. The fact that most victims of reported violence are women and that separated women are often the targets indicates important social patterns in this behaviour relating to gender and power.

In the past, the police failed to respond in a serious way to calls about violent wife abuse because they thought women did not want charges laid or would later withdraw them (ibid.). Policies have now been implemented in most jurisdictions for police to charge men who batter. Yet many wives remain with abusive partners because of shortages of low-income and temporary housing, an inability to support themselves and their children, and a lack of knowledge about where to turn for assistance. Abuse is also permitted to continue because some women feel that they deserve it, especially those abused as children and those who suffer from low self-esteem. In addition, many women fear reprisal from spouses or former spouses who have threatened to kill them if they go to the police or tell anyone about an incident. The enormous publicity recently given to women killed by their partners indicates that, in many cases, fear of reprisal is entirely justified.

Women's groups, social service agencies, police, and researchers have developed new ways of dealing with violence against women in intimate relationships. Many of the programs are crisis-oriented and focus on women, helping them develop a protection plan that could involve laying charges against a spouse or ex-spouse,

SOCIOLOGY IN ACTION

The Emotional Scars of Family Violence

'I was raped by my uncle when I was 12 and my husband has beat me for years. For my whole life, when I have gone to the doctor, to my priest, or to a friend to have my wounds patched up, or for a shoulder to cry one, they dwell on my bruises . . . that's for sure. . . . I don't look like anything like I did 15 years ago, but it's not my body that I really wish could get fixed. The abuse in my life has taken away my trust in people and in life. It's taken away the laughter in my life. I still laugh, but not without bitterness behind my laughter. It's taken away my faith in God, my faith in goodness winning out in the end, and maybe worse of all, it's taken away my trust in myself. I don't trust myself to be able to take care of the kids, to take care of myself, to do anything to make a difference in my own life or anyone else's. That's the hurt I would like to fix. I can live with my physical scars. It's these emotional scars that drive me near suicide sometimes.'

Source: Dekeseredy and Macleod (1997: 5).

finding transitional housing, engaging a lawyer, and, if necessary, acquiring social assistance to cover living costs. Through either individual counselling or group therapy, battered wives are also helped to restructure their thinking about violence and to view it as unacceptable regardless of their own behaviour.

The male abuser is now more often charged with an offence. He is also given opportunities for counselling, including accepting responsibility for his acts of violence rather than blaming his partner, learning to control his emotions, developing better communication skills, and learning non-violent behaviour from positive male role models. Action against family violence has also included sensitization workshops for professionals, such as teachers and judges, to increase their knowledge of program options and of the implication of this form of violence for women, their families, men who batter, and the wider society (ibid.). In addition, more support services have been provided for families in high-risk circumstances.

Although governments at all levels have voiced their concern about violence against women and children, money is a major impediment to establishing new programs and transitional housing. Transition houses are usually funded by private donations, staffed by volunteers, and operated with uncertain resources. Follow-up therapy and counselling may also be necessary for the entire family, but these services also cost money to establish and maintain. Despite the serious nature of marital violence, new program funding for the rising number of reported victims and their abusers is difficult to find (Se'ver, 2002).

A correlation has been noted between 'courtship' violence and marital violence. K. O'Leary and colleagues (1989) found that the probability of spouse abuse in the United States was over three times greater if violence had also occurred during courtship. They also found that adults who abuse their spouses or children have often come from families where their parents engaged in similar behaviour.

Three broad explanations of marital violence arise from these studies. The intergenerational theory suggests that solving conflicts through physical or verbal violence is learned from early family experiences. The solution within this perspective focuses on improving conflict resolution and parenting skills in order to reduce marital violence. A second theory sees marital violence as a misguided way of resolving conflicts that is used by husbands who feel that their authority within the family is being

Time to Reflect

What sources of support and help are available for someone in an abusive relationship? Which of these might people turn to first and which might be seen as a last resort? Why?

threatened. The solution to the problem within this systems framework is to offer therapy sessions to men or couples to improve their communication skills, learn to control emotions, and become more assertive about their feelings and needs without resorting to violence.

In contrast, feminist theories argue that marital violence is actually violence by men against their female partners. This behaviour is symptomatic of women's lack of interpersonal power in families, the way in which the patriarchal state has permitted husbands to control their wives, and the social acceptability of violence towards those considered most vulnerable (Se'ver, 2002). Changing public attitudes towards physical and sexual abuse means that more people now report such activity and that social services are needed to assist them. Consequently, this kind of behaviour, which always existed, now appears more prevalent.

These theories are not entirely incompatible: not everyone becomes abusive who has witnessed abuse or who feels threatened by lack of power in their workplace or at home. Furthermore, everyone lives in a society that condones certain kinds of violence and a lower status for women. None of the theories can explain by itself the perpetuation of violence in intimate relationships. Yet it is clear that violence against women and children cuts across national, cultural, and class boundaries and that it is not confined to marriage or cohabitation. In fact, separated women are more vulnerable than married women.

Reforming Canadian Family Policies

When Canada was established as a nation in 1867, jurisdiction over policy was divided between the federal and provincial governments. Over the years, new social policies and programs were established to meet the needs of the changing society. In the nineteenth century, the federal government developed ways to count the citizens and to require them to register marriages, births, adoptions, divorces, and deaths. The provincial governments also enabled married women to control their property, equalized the guardianship rights of mothers and fathers over their children, and established basic social services in the 1920s. As Table 7.4 indicates, income security programs for families were developed by both levels of government, mainly from the 1940s to the 1970s, but these have been modified considerably since then. Provincial governments have also tightened abuse and neglect laws as well as the enforcement of child support and eligibility for 'welfare' during the 1980s and 1990s (Baker, 2006; Ursel, 1992).

In recent years, the extent of government intervention in family life has been questioned but there will always be a need to regulate certain aspects of family life, especially to protect vulnerable family members, and to assist those in serious financial difficulty. Families also require health and social services to ensure healthy and safe pregnancy, childbirth, and childhood, and these services need government regulation and financial support. Regulation of life events by the state is designed to prevent incestuous and bigamous marriages, adoptions by inappropriate parents, and hasty divorces, and to ensure that spouses and parents understand and fulfill their basic support obligations. Governments also need to gather basic statistics about populations in order to plan future social services and facilities. They must be able to predict the size and structure of the future labour force and the numbers of future voters, taxpayers, and consumers. Some of these statistics also prove useful for the business sector in their marketing and growth plans.

Since the 1980s, labour markets have been restructured, full-time jobs have become harder to find, and more households now need two or more earners to pay the bills, but high rates of marriage instability mean that more households contain only one parent. These socioeconomic trends have raised the cost of social programs for governments, encouraging more taxpayers and politicians to express concern about the high levels of taxes needed to maintain the welfare state at existing levels and to question the effectiveness of anti-poverty strategies. In addition, many politicians and researchers continue to worry about the state's ability to sustain social programs with an aging population, growing structural unemployment, and high rates of marriage dissolution. While several provincial governments have cut back on 'welfare' benefits since the 1990s, the federal government has tightened eligibility for unemployment benefits but enhanced child benefits. However, Canadian parents are increasingly expected to rely on their own resources for family well-being rather than depending on state assistance.

Throughout Canadian history, the desirability of government involvement in family life has been debated, although these debates have usually focused on the cost of state income support. Recently, federal and provincial governments have trimmed the costs of social services and focused more on personal and family responsibility rather than on state support. At the same time, they have

Table 8.4 The Establishment of Social Benefits in Canada

Family Allowance	This universal allowance was created in 1945 and paid to mothers for each child.
Old Age Pension	Originally established in 1926 as a pension for those with low incomes, in 1951 it was converted to a universal pension.
Mothers'/Widows' Pensions	These pensions were developed around 1920 but the date varies by province.
Unemployment Insurance	UI was established as a federal social insurance program in 1941; in 1971 maternity benefits were added.
Hospital/Medical Insurance	Hospital insurance was established in 1958; universal medical insurance (medicare) was established in 1966.
Canada Pension Plan	This broad social security program, effectively a retirement program, began in 1966, financed by contributions from employees and employers and from government; CPP also pays survivor benefits and disability benefits to contributors.
Spouses Allowance	Set up in 1975, this is an income-tested pension for spouses (mainly women) aged 60–4 of old-age pensioners.
Child Tax Benefit	The former Family Allowance and tax deductions/credits for children were rolled into this targeted tax benefit for lower- and middle-income families in 1993.
Parliamentary Resolution to end 'Child Poverty'	An all-party agreement was passed in 1989 to end child poverty by the year 2000.
Canada Child Tax Benefit	The Child Tax Benefit and Working Income Supplement were rolled together to form this benefit in 1998.

Sources: Ursel (1992); McGilly (1998); Baker and Tippin (1999).

tightened laws on spousal and child abuse, but these laws have been difficult to enforce because this behaviour often occurs within the privacy of people's homes and without witnesses. The careful monitoring of at-risk families suggests that the state regulates family life as a form of social control as well as merely for assistance, information-gathering, and future planning.

Future Families

Sociologists often use current family trends as an indicator of future patterns, but predicting the future is always complex. Nonetheless, from what we know about patterns in family formation, we might assume that cohabitation will become more prevalent in the future (Wu,

Time to Reflect

You are a senior policy adviser to the social services minister in your province and she has asked you to develop a new and comprehensive family policy to be included in the party platform for the upcoming election. What issues will you emphasize, and which ones will you steer away from? Why?

2000). As the distinction between common-law and legal marriage becomes socially and legally blurred, the average age of legal marriage will increase slightly and legal marriage rates will continue to fall. Living together will become more socially acceptable as a preliminary step to the public commitment of legal marriage. Particularly young people from divorced families and older divorced adults will be reluctant to enter legal marriage without some previous experience of living with their partner. Furthermore, those who are ideologically opposed to traditional gender roles will continue to see cohabitation as a preferable alternative to legal marriage, even though research suggests that the differences in gender roles between cohabiting and married couples become minimal over time (Baxter, 2000).

As more households rely on two incomes, men's opportunities to move to jobs in new locations may be limited by their partners' employment. These husbands could find it harder to encourage their wives to give up their jobs because their families could not survive on one income. More couples may be forced to live apart for short periods in order to further their education or obtain work. Commuter marriages could become more prevalent as professional and managerial positions become harder to find, as the labour market becomes more globalized, and as women become more career-oriented.

Delayed marriage and delayed child-bearing are definitely on the increase in Canada. This suggests that more individuals and couples will live for longer periods in non-family households, in a lifestyle that focuses on work, career development, leisure pursuits, and travel. Some will become accustomed to this lifestyle and will choose a marriage without children. If substantial numbers of Canadians make this choice, however, policymakers will become concerned about the future of the nation's population. An increase in child-free marriages could also lead to higher divorce rates, as it is easier to divorce without children. Higher rates of cohabitation also suggest greater marriage instability in the future because couples who lived together before legal marriage

In the transition from large to small families, many of us have lost the opportunity to experience relationships with cousins, aunts, and uncles. (David Young-Wolff/PhotoEdit Inc.)

have a higher probability of divorce than those who have not lived together. In addition, children from divorced parents have a higher probability of divorce, suggesting the greater impermanence in marriage in the future.

Most demographers predict that declining birth rates will continue because children are increasingly costly in modern urban environments and because combining work and family life is difficult when both parents are employed. Many working parents experience problems finding affordable and high-quality child-care services. Although government reports have said that children are our greatest future resource, little has been done in many Canadian provinces to help parents combine paid work and child-rearing.

Young people tend to remain at home with their parents for longer periods now than in the 1970s. The greater need for higher education, the longer time required to find a secure job, and the higher cost of housing prolong the period of active parenting. At the same time, more women are in the full-time labour force in mid-life, which means that they have neither the time nor the energy to supervise their young adults adequately.

As **life expectancy** increases and fertility declines, more people will live beyond the age of 75 and more frail elderly people will continue to require care. More parents, especially women, could be trying to provide attention, emotional care, and domestic services for both children and aging parents. Furthermore, middle-aged people will have fewer siblings to help them care for frail parents. In the future, they will also need to remain in the labour force longer to counteract job insecurity throughout their lives and lower work-related pensions. To deal with rising public pension costs as well as employees' need for more income in later life, an increasing number of governments are proposing to end or change mandatory retirement regulations.

As more people remarry in later life, attitudes towards aging, marriage, and leisure may gradually change. Family relationships will become more complicated, with stepchildren and ex-partners and with older men repartnering and reproducing with younger women. A global economy and high rates of migration could also mean that more elders remain in their home communities while their children migrate to find work, taking the grandchildren far away. This may lower the frequency of family activities, but it could also strengthen friendship ties for both generations. Yet keeping in touch will become even easier with e-mail, long-distance telephone, and text messaging, as well as new, as-yet-unforeseen communications technologies.

Conclusion

Intimate relationships remain central to most people, yet family life has changed substantially over the past few decades. Cohabitation and divorce are now more prevalent than a generation ago, while legal marriage and fertility rates are declining. Cultural variations are becoming more noticeable with new immigration sources. In addition, more people are creating or modifying their own intimate arrangements in response to changes in the larger society, but governments continue to clarify the rights and responsibilities of family members within these new arrangements.

Social scientists have used different theoretical frameworks to study changes in family patterns and practices, each emphasizing different aspects and issues. The five theoretical frameworks presented in this chapter suggest that family theorists differ in their focus. This chapter also discussed five of the many conflictual issues in family life. The first is the sharing of domestic work; despite dramatic increases in women's paid work, wives still do the major portion of housework and child care. The second issue relates to the apparent rise in infertility and to feminist and sociological concerns about medically assisted conception. The third issue relates to the high cost and quality of care of the children of employed parents, making it difficult, especially for mothers, to combine paid work and child-rearing. The fourth discusses the contradictory evidence of the impact of separation, divorce, and repartnering on children, suggesting that separation is not always a negative solution, but neither is remarriage always the best solution for children. And the fifth issue relates to wife abuse and why it continues despite public efforts to reduce it.

This chapter has shown that more people now cohabit, separate, repartner, and live with more than one partner over their lifetime. Nevertheless, not all of our family cicumstances represent personal choices. Most Canadians still hope to develop loving and stable intimate relationships and to watch their children grow into adults. However, few people anticipate the ways that work requirements, money problems, social policy changes, new ideas, and the actions of other people shape their family experiences.

Questions for Critical Thought

1. In your opinion, does the way in which family is defined make a difference? Why or why not?
2. Would you expect societies that practise arranged marriages to have more stable and happier marriages than societies that allow free-choice marriage? Why or why not?
3. How would you explain the rise in maternal employment, with reference to (a) feminist perspectives, (b) structural functionalism, and (c) political economy theory?
4. Why are more young people living together? Does this behaviour indicate a rejection of marriage?
5. Should parents stay together for the sake of the children or is parental conflict more detrimental to children?
6. Should cohabiting couples (both same-sex and heterosexual couples) be permitted to use the services of fertility clinics at the public's expense? Give reasons for your viewpoint.
7. Should governments contribute more or less than now to child-care services for employed parents?
8. Is there any reason to believe that Canadian birth rates will rise again in the near future?

Recommended Readings

Maureen Baker, *Choices and Constraints in Family Life* (Toronto: Oxford University Press, 2007).

This book argues that our personal choices about partners and living arrangements are shaped by economic circumstances, cultural expectations, popular culture, and events in the larger society, including labour market changes and political discourse.

Walter DeKeseredy, 'Patterns of Family Violence', in Maureen Baker, ed., *Families: Changing Trends in Canada*, 5th edn, (Toronto: McGraw-Hill Ryerson, 2005), 229–57.

This chapter discusses recent research and theorizing about various forms of family violence, including wife abuse, child abuse, sibling violence, and elder abuse.

Margrit Eichler, *Family Shifts: Families, Policies, and Gender Equality* (Toronto: Oxford University Press, 1997).

Eichler examines major new shifts affecting families today, including gender equality as a legal and moral principle and the potential impact of biotechnology.

Lynn Jamieson, *Intimacy: Personal Relationships in Modern Societies* (Cambridge: Polity Press, 1998).

The author discusses whether a new type of intimacy is being sought in Western societies or if relationships are still fundamentally shaped by power and economic considerations.

Susan A. McDaniel and Lorne Tepperman, *Close Relations: An Introduction to the Sociology of Families*, 2nd edn. (Scarborough, Ont.: Prentice-Hall Allyn and Bacon, 2004).

This Canadian text provides an overview of research on and theories of family life.

Jan Pryor and Bryan Rodgers, *Children in Changing Families: Life after Parental Separation* (Oxford: Blackwell, 2001).

This book, which covers international research on the impact on children of parental separation and stepfamily formation, offers insights into why some survive family change better than others.

Vanier Institute of the Family, *Profiling Canada's Families III* (Ottawa: Vanier Institute of the Family, 2004).

This book contains numerous tables and charts about family trends and patterns, accompanied by a discussion of their relevance.

Recommended Websites

Australian Institute for Family Studies
www.aifs.gov.au
This website contains details about new research and recent publications from this Australian government research centre on family issues.

Campaign 2000
www.campaign2000.ca
Campaign 2000, created in 1989 to monitor 'child poverty' in Canada, publishes an annual report card.

Centre for Families, Work and Well-Being
www.worklifecanada.ca
The website of the Centre for Families, Work and Well-Being at the University of Guelph contains information about research projects.

Child and Family Canada
www.cfc-efc.ca
This website offers public education from numerous non-profit organizations.

Childcare Resource and Research Unit
www.childcarecanada.org
The website of the Childcare Resource and Research Unit at the University of Toronto includes Canadian and cross-national research and other material on child-care issues.

National Association for the Education of Young Children (NAEYC)
www.naeyc.org
This US-based association publishes the journal *Young Children*, which includes reviews of research and practical information.

Statistics Canada
www.statcan.ca
Statistics Canada provides a wide range of census documents and statistics relating to families and households.

Vanier Institute of the Family
www.vifamily.ca
The Vanier Institute of the Family in Ottawa provides educational material, news items, and research on Canadian families.

Chapter

Education

Terry Wotherspoon

Learning Objectives

In this chapter, you will:

- Understand how and why formal education has become a central social institution in Canada and other nations.
- Identify the main dimensions and challenges associated with the growth of formal education systems.
- Gain a critical understanding of various forms of lifelong learning beyond formal education.
- Understand the major theoretical perspectives and theories that sociologists employ to explain educational institutions, practices, and outcomes.
- Understand the relationships between education and social inequality.
- Explore how education and educational outcomes are shaped by relationships between educational institutions and participants and how the social contexts within those institutions operate.
- Critically evaluate contemporary debates and controversies over major educational issues.

Photo: Al Harvey/The Slide Farm

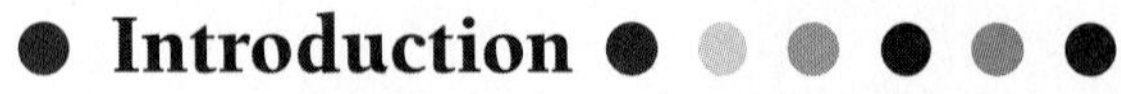

Introduction

The chief economist for the World Bank recently highlighted the importance of education as 'critical to participation and productivity in economic life'. 'A healthy, literate labor force', he said, 'will both increase the amount of growth realized from establishing a sound investment climate and strongly re-inforce the poverty reduction benefit from that growth' (Stern, 2002: 21). Probably few people would take issue with these comments. What do they mean, though, to people in different situations? Consider the following cases of students in a Canadian high school:

- a recent immigrant who speaks little English or French
- a teen who has difficulties with reading comprehension but has stayed in school until now because it is required in order to play on a competitive sports team
- new arrivals who find the school much larger and more regimented than elementary schools in nearby **First Nations** and rural communities
- a student pressured by parents who feel the school's poor academic and disciplinary standards are impeding the student's ability to gain entry into a prestigious university
- a high school student tempted to leave school to take a high-paying job in the energy sector
- a youth whose repeated conflicts with students and teachers in a previous school, combined with substance abuse and domestic problems, have made regular school attendance difficult

These situations reveal much about education's significance in the context of what is often called the *knowledge* or *learning society*. Education has been thrust into a central role as individuals, organizations, and nations struggle to keep pace with demands for new knowledge and credentials regarded as essential for jobs, career advancement, and economic and social development. We expect educational institutions to educate and prepare learners with a wide range of technical, social, and personal competencies for changing, often uncertain, futures. We also look to schools to respond to the needs of diverse students and communities.

Sociologists are interested in several issues associated with educational processes and outcomes and in the environments within which education operates. This chapter examines several key questions that sociology addresses in its concern to understand education:

- Why is formal education so important in contemporary societies, and how did it get to be that way?
- What are the main dimensions of education and education systems in Canada and other nations?
- How do sociologists explain the growth of education systems and the outcomes associated with education for different groups?
- What are the main educational experiences and outcomes for different social groups?
- What are the main challenges facing education systems in Canada and other nations?

The Changing Face of Education

Education is generally understood as the formal learning that takes place in institutions such as schools, colleges, universities, and other sites that provide specific courses, learning activities, or credentials in an organized way. Informal learning also occurs as people undertake specific activities to learn about distinct phenomena or processes. Both formal and informal education are part of the broader process that sociologists typically call **socialization**, which refers to all direct and indirect learning related to humans' ability to understand and negotiate the rules and expectations of the social world.

Nearly all Canadians engage in formal education for extended periods of time, a situation that was not always the case. In the late nineteenth century, educational participation tended to be secondary to other pressing concerns. Ian Davey observes that factors such as 'cyclical depressions and crop failures affected school attendance because in good times more parents sent more of their children to school and sent them more regularly. Yet, lower attendance during bad times resulted largely from a magnification of those factors which caused irregular attendance throughout the nineteenth century—transience and poverty' (1978: 230). At the beginning of the twentieth century, only three out of five pupils enrolled in public school attended on a regular basis, and many of those were not in school for extended periods during the school year. Many communities lacked schools or qualified teachers. Children often did not begin their **schooling** until they were seven or eight years old, and typically left school by their early teen years (Guppy and Davies, 1998).

A comparison of today's educational settings and classrooms with those of a century ago yields both striking similarities and profound differences. Massive, architecturally designed complexes have replaced self-contained one- or two-room wooden buildings; sophisticated equipment often takes the place of chalk and slate boards; and most students are exposed to a diverse range of teachers, subject

A century ago, schools were often segregated by class and age. Here, young ladies are learning to sketch a live model—a skill that will give them cultural capital when they pass into adult social life. (Courtesy of the Bishop Strachan School Museum & Archives)

choices, and work projects unthinkable in 1900. Today's students and teachers are likely to exhibit a far greater array of personal, stylistic, and cultural variation than was apparent a century ago, and they have access to many more learning and community resources.

Despite these changes, the casual visitor to classrooms in either time period is not likely to mistake schools for other settings. Groupings of children and youth, under the instruction and regular scrutiny of adult teachers, are guided both through regimented activities—at least for part of the time in rows or other arrangements of desks—and through periods allocated for recreation or personal expression. Education is a unique social institution at the same time as it reveals characteristics that are integral to the society in which it operates.

Dimensions of Educational Growth

Educational expansion accelerated rapidly after World War II. In 1951, over half (51.9 per cent) of all Canadians aged 15 and over had less than a Grade 9 education, while just under 2 per cent had a university degree and only about one in 20 aged 18 to 24 was enrolled in university (Clark, 2000: 4–6; Guppy and Davies, 1998: 19). At the beginning of the twenty-first century, by contrast, Canadians have unprecedented levels of education, distinguishing Canada with one of the most highly educated populations in the world.

Table 9.1 provides an overview of the increasing educational attainment of Canadians in the last half of the twentieth century. The proportion of the population

Time to Reflect

What is the difference between education and socialization? How has the introduction of formal schooling influenced the relationship between these two phenomena?

who had less than a Grade 9 education diminished rapidly, especially in the 1960s and 1970s. By contrast, very few had taken or completed post-secondary studies at the start of the period, whereas nearly half of the population now hold post-secondary credentials. The average number of years of formal education held by Canadians has risen from just under 12.5 at the beginning of the 1990s to over 13 a decade later, ranking Canada in 2004 sixth among highly developed nations, just below Norway at 13.9, Denmark and Germany at 13.4, and the United States and Luxembourg at 13.3, but above the average for the developed countries of the Organization for Economic Co-operation and Development of 11.9 (OECD, 2006: 41). Growing emphasis on the importance of formal education and credentials has been matched by three interrelated factors: the overall expansion of educational opportunities and requirements, increasing levels of educational attainment among people born in Canada, and recent emphasis on the selection of highly educated immigrants.

The fact that many people did not have substantial amounts of formal education in the late nineteenth and early twentieth centuries was not as significant as it may seem in retrospect because only a few occupations required educational credentials. Most people relied on schools to provide some basic skills and knowledge, discipline, and social training, and as a service to provide something for children to do when their parents were too busy to attend to them. Formal learning was often subordinate to other concerns. School superintendents and other educational authorities devoted their efforts to enforcing school attendance and improving the quality of instruction in schools. Annual reports and other documents maintained by provincial education departments are filled with references to concerns such as the need to maintain proper order and discipline in the classroom; attention to habits and duties; routine procedures and daily records of pupil attendance, school visitors, and recitations drawn from various subjects; and the desire for teachers who were not so much good instructors as proper role models with good manners and high moral standing (for examples, see Lawr and Gidney, 1973).

Early advocates of public schooling undertook a mission to convince the public, and especially members of influential groups, of the merits of the educational system. They promoted schooling as an efficient enterprise that would serve the public or general interest. Other institutions or sites, such as families, churches, and businesses, were by contrast more narrow and selective in scope.

Table 9.1 Educational Attainment in Canada, by Percentage of Population Aged 15 and over, Selected Years, 1951–2005

	Less than Grade 9	Grades 9–13	Some Post-secondary	Post-secondary Certificate or Diploma	University Degree	Median Years of Schooling
1951	51.9	46.1	–	–	1.9	–
1961	44.1	53.0	–	–	2.9	–
1971	32.3	45.9	11.2	5.8	4.8	10.6
1981	20.1	44.3	16.1	11.5	8.0	11.8
1986	17.7	42.5	19.3	12.3	9.6	12.2
1991	14.4	43.8	8.8	21.9	11.4	12.5
1996	12.3	39.4	8.9	25.9	13.3	12.7
2001	9.7	36.9	9.2	28.3	16.0	13.0
2005	8.4	35.0	8.6	29.8	18.2	–

Note: Figures are rounded.
Source: Compiled from Statistics Canada, census data (1951–86) and labour force survey, annual averages (1991–2005).

IN THE FIRST PERSON

I became interested in sociology almost by default. Like many students, I had little concept of the discipline until a friend suggested a sociology course as an interesting elective at university. Sociology proved to offer several useful skills, understandings, and connections to significant issues, but after completing my BA I did not return to it until my role as a schoolteacher led me to question many aspects of educational processes and the relationship between schooling and various dimensions of students' lives and life chances. When I returned to university to complete graduate work, I began to take sociology more seriously as I came to apply the discipline to my experiences and emerging interests. Sociology is continually changing, even when focused around a core set of disciplinary focuses and attributes, and I find that I can continually make new linkages as I attempt to connect academic life with communities and policies related to education and other aspects of social life.—Terry Wotherspoon

Education systems adopted a degree of flexibility that made it possible to integrate new tasks and curricula. School authorities had to make concessions when funds to build and run schools or hire the preferred quality of teachers were scarce. Some people resented having to pay or be taxed for schooling. Schools could also be victims of their own success, as demands for education or population growth in communities outpaced the ability to provide school facilities, textbooks, teaching materials, and qualified teachers. In many parts of Canada, especially in smaller communities and rural areas, school operations remained highly uncertain or irregular until well into the twentieth century because of sporadic pupil attendance, resignation of teachers or the community's inability to attract teachers, lack of funds, or disputes between school board and community members. A single teacher provided the schooling that was offered for all grades in rural one-room schools, whereas cities and larger districts tended to have better-equipped schools with a full range of programs and a complement of trained, more specialized teachers.

Across Canada centralized schools and districts gradually replaced smaller units. School district consolidation began in 1900, though amalgamation into larger schools and school districts did not fully take hold until the period between the mid-1940s and the late 1960s. Amalgamation has continued since then, accelerating in the 1990s as the number of school boards has declined in each province, in many cases by as much as half to two-thirds and in one, New Brunswick, by abolishing all school boards between 1996 and 2001 (Pierce, 2003). Consolidation was hastened by financial and administrative difficulties in many districts and by the development of transportation networks and support linkages that made it easier to concentrate schools in selected centres. By 1970/1, there were just over 16,000 public schools in Canada (a figure that has since declined by a further five hundred), nearly 10,000 below the number that had operated a decade earlier (Statistics Canada, 1973: 104; Statistics Canada, 2005a).

Pressure to build and maintain larger schools intensified as more people began to stay in school longer, extending into and beyond the high school years. The **baby boom** that occurred after World War II resulted in unprecedented sizes of cohorts of children who were entering and moving through the school system. The figures in Table 9.2 demonstrate that, while total enrolment in Canadian public elementary and secondary schools in 1950 was just over double what it had been in 1900, enrolment doubled again over the next decade and a half. The average number of pupils per school increased in Canada from 66 in 1925–6 to 156 in 1960–1 and nearly doubled over the next decade to reach 350 in 1970–1, a level that has remained relatively stable since then (Manzer, 1994: 131).

The data in Table 9.2 demonstrate how formal education has expanded throughout the life course. Children have begun their schooling at progressively younger ages over the past five decades. Kindergarten is now compulsory in most Canadian jurisdictions, and many children also attend various preschool and early childhood education programs.

Meanwhile, people have been extending their formal education well past high school into post-secondary

Table 9.2 Full-Time Enrolment in Canada, by Level of Study, Selected Years, 1870–2003 (000s)

	Pre-elementary	Elementary and Secondary	Non-university Post-secondary	University Undergraduate	University Graduate
1870	–	768	–	2	–
1880	–	852	–	3	–
1890	–	943	–	5	<1
1900	–	1,055	–	7	<1
1910	–	1,318	–	13	<1
1920	–	1,834	–	23	<1
1930	–	2,099	–	32	1
1940	–	2,075	–	35	2
1950	–	2,391	–	64	5
1955	103	3,118	33	69	3
1960	146	3,997	49	107	7
1965	268	4,918	69	187	17
1970	402	5,661	166	276	33
1975	399	5,376	221	331	40
1980	398	4,709	261	338	45
1985	422	4,506	322	412	55
1990	468	4,669	325	468	64
1995	542	4,895	392	498	75
2000	522	4,867	408	522	81
2003*		5,289	461	616	101

*Pre-elementary figure for 2003 is included in elementary and secondary total.

Sources: Compiled from various editions of Dominion Bureau of Statistics/Statistics Canada, census data, 'Education at a Glance', *Education Quarterly Review*; Patric Blouin, Marie-Josée Courchesne, and Isabelle Thony, *Summary Public School Indicators for the Provinces and Territories, 1997–1998 to 2003–2004* (Ottawa: Minister of Industry); and Canadian Association of University Teachers, *CAUT Almanac of Post-Secondary Education in Canada 2006* (Ottawa: CAUT, 2006).

studies. The larger cohorts of students moving through schools and completing high school, combined with increasing emphasis on higher education in particular fields and more general reliance on educational credentials as a means for firms to select employees, contributed to massive growth in post-secondary studies. The data in Table 9.2 demonstrate that, whereas in 1950–1, only about 69,000 people were enrolled in full-time university studies, university enrolment exploded to over 200,000 by the mid-1960s, and has now surpassed 700,000 (with over 100,000 in graduate studies alone).

A similar pattern followed in other post-secondary institutions, which until the 1960s had encompassed mostly specific occupational and vocational certification

Time to Reflect

To what extent has educational enrolment increased in Canada over the past century? Which factors account for this growth?

programs in areas such as nursing and teacher education as well as pre-university studies in Quebec and other provinces. However, the introduction and expansion of the community college system in the 1960s and 1970s provided numerous options for post-secondary study both for students seeking certification in specialized trades or vocations and for students taking courses that could be employed for university credit. Sociologists have been concerned with issues related to the bureaucratic organization of education and educational inequality as school size and complexity increased.

Education in the Learning Society

The organization and nature of schooling across Canada remain varied. Initiatives to implement greater conformity and consistency across jurisdictions run parallel with increased numbers of alternative schools and educational services. Educational diversity is a product, in part, of the fact that elementary and secondary education is a formal jurisdiction of the provinces under constitutional legislation, while other forms of education, including adult and post-secondary education and vocational training, are controlled, operated, or funded by a variety of governments (federal, provincial, and First Nations) and by private sources. Increased emphasis on education and training has been accompanied by considerable expansion of educational opportunities and programs offered at all levels. Many people are turning to additional sources, such as distance education and Internet-based course offerings that originate both within and outside Canada.

Formal schooling is compulsory for Canadians aged 6 to 16 in most provinces (with an overall range between 5 and 18 years). However, most people engage in education well beyond these limits. The growing popularity of terms such as *information society*, *learning society*, and **lifelong learning** signifies the central place that education holds within the context of what is commonly designated as the **new economy** or *knowledge-based economy*. The new economy has gained prominence through increasing reliance on rapidly changing information technologies and scientific advancements that have affected not only business and the workplace, but virtually every major sphere of social life. Learning is central to all dimensions of the new economy, including the need to train qualified personnel; to conduct research for continuing innovation; to develop, test, and market new products and services within firms; to process the vast amounts of new information being created; and to ensure that people have the capacities to employ new technologies at work and at home (Wolfe and Gertler, 2001). In this climate, what counts is not so much the knowledge that we acquire, as the capacity to learn and apply that knowledge to emergent situations. People are expected not simply to learn more, but to develop different ways of learning and transferring knowledge.

These expectations have contributed to extensive levels of and variations in educational qualifications and experiences. With respect to formal learning, nearly 6.5 million Canadians (about one-fifth of the entire population) identified in Table 9.2 are engaged in full-time schooling, and well over 300,000 more are involved in part-time studies. About half of the Canadian population aged 16 to 65 (ranging between less than one-quarter of those with the lowest literacy levels and over two-thirds of those with the highest levels of literatcy) indicate, as well, that they are involved in some adult education, whether in the form of in-person, correspondence, or private courses, workshops, apprenticeships, or arts, crafts, or recreation programs (Desjardins et al., 2005: 98).

The phenomenon of informal learning has also attracted growing attention. *Informal learning* involves distinct efforts arranged and undertaken by individuals or groups to acquire new knowledge that can be applied to work, personal, or community circumstances. Such activities include initiatives to learn a new language on one's own or with other people, to learn computer skills or software programs, or to gain competencies that can be used for volunteer work or family situations. Surveys in Canada and the United States estimate that over three-quarters of the adult population undertake well over 300 hours of informal learning projects per person every year. Nearly all people, regardless of education, are heavily involved in informal learning activities although, as with adult education, there is a general pattern of correspondence between levels of active participation in informal learning and formal educational attainment (Livingstone, 2004: 36–7; Desjardins et al., 2005: 89).

OPEN FOR DISCUSSION

Debating Alternatives to Public Schools

Although strong public support exists for public schooling in Canada, many individuals and groups have advocated the need for alternative forms of schooling within public school systems or through various types of privately operated schools. These demands, often based on dissatisfaction or rising expectations regarding existing school systems, are emerging at a time when the importance of education is growing both for basic social participation and for advanced economic competitiveness.

Some critics are calling for greater school choice, viewing education as a marketplace in which parents can 'shop' for the kinds of education best suited to their children's needs. Private schools, voucher programs, home schooling, and other measures are viewed as mechanisms that may ensure that schools become more responsive and accountable to the varied interests of educational consumers (Stein, 2002).

Other initiatives are emerging through calls for reform within public education systems. Saskatchewan, for example, has adopted a model of schools as community-based centres of learning and services called School^PLUS, while other provinces have complemented existing schools with more specialized school programs or institutional arrangements. Schools under First Nations control have introduced many innovations or modifications to public models of education, while other groups are seeking more specialized schools in response to particular concerns or interests.

Sociologist George Sefa Dei is among those who propose the need for black-focused schools to address high dropout and failure rates and related social problems such as violence, unemployment, and drug abuse among inner-city black youth. Arguing that present educational practices contribute to youth alienation through disconnection from students' real concerns, Dei (2006: 28) argues that African-centred or black-focused schools would be guided by 'a new vision' that stresses:

> the development of a culture of youth affirmation that fosters a sense of pride by helping to build strong personal, social and cultural identities. For example, such a culture can be achieved when teachers introduce alternative forms of school discipline to replace suspensions, expulsions or the summoning of law enforcement.

Still other researchers indicate that increasing diversity in Canada's public school populations can be most beneficial for all students, creating opportunities for critical reflection and broadened understanding of what it means to live and function in a truly global society.

Canada ranks high on international comparisons of education, although Canadians are not unique in their growing pursuit of education and training. Among the OECD nations represented in Figure 9.1, Canada has the highest proportion of the population with formal educational credentials beyond high school, but it ranks behind the United States, Denmark, the Netherlands, and Iceland with respect to the percentage of the population with a university degree, and it is also lagging behind many nations in the advancement of literacy levels across the population.

Emphasis on formal training and lifelong learning is a phenomenon associated with **globalization** and competitiveness across national settings. Throughout the twentieth century, the degree to which a population was educated came to be recognized as a significant indicator of modernization and development status. The more education one has, the higher the chances of having a job, better income, good health status, and many other factors positively associated with a high standard of living. Conversely, rates of poverty, unemployment, crime, serious illness and injury, and other less desirable indicators rise when formal education is limited.

Many nations are accelerating the pace of educational advancement as they undertake economic and human

Figure 9.1 Level of Education in Selected OECD Countries, 2004

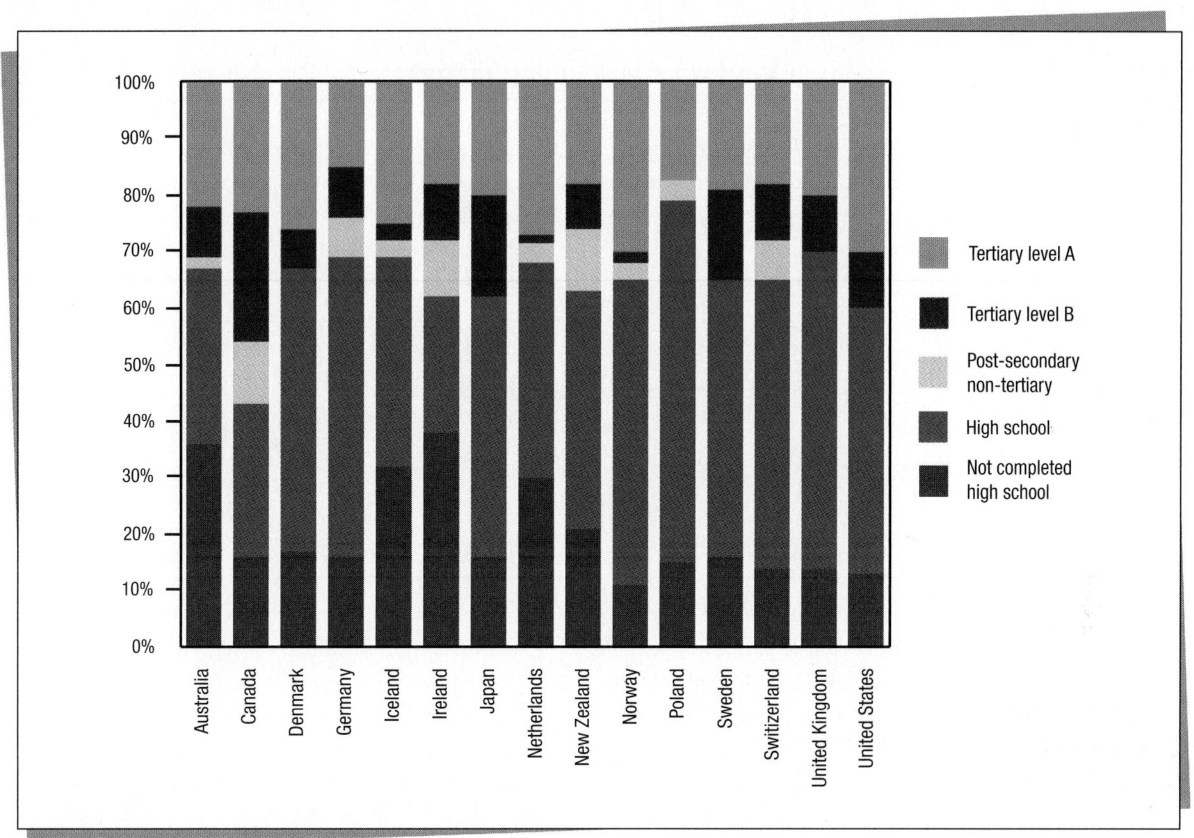

Percentage distribution of the population 25 to 64 years of age, by the highest completed level of education.
Tertiary level A: equivalent to university, including advanced research programs.
Tertiary level B: equivalent to community college in Canada.
Post-secondary non-tertiary: similar to CECEP in Canada.
Source: Based on data in OECD (2006).

resource development strategies aimed at the production of new knowledge and a more highly trained workforce. The importance of education for the new economy is highlighted in the titles of numerous recent research reports and discussion papers produced by governments; Canadian examples include *High School May Not Be Enough* (Human Resources Development Canada and Statistics Canada, 1998), *Learning a Living: First Results of the Adult Literacy and Life Skills Survey* (Desjardins et al., 2005), and *Knowledge Matters: Skills and Learning for Canadians* (Human Resources Development Canada, 2002). Consequently, governments, businesses, and agencies concerned with economic development stress the need to expand education well beyond compulsory levels in order to foster both economic growth and non-economic benefits such as improved health, the ability to use skills for non-monetary purposes, and the intrinsic desire to learn (OECD, 2001). The prevailing sentiment is that, with a few variations, 'overall, individuals will need more and more knowledge and skills, and our society will need

Time to Reflect

What is meant by the concept of 'lifelong learning?' What is the relationship between lifelong learning and globalization?

GLOBAL ISSUES

Towards Global Progress on Education

Nations on a global scale have identified the establishment of access to basic education and improvements in educational standards as core priorities. In 2000, an agenda entitled 'Education for All' was adopted by 192 nations co-ordinated through the United Nations Education, Science and Cultural Organization (UNESCO), highlighting six main priorities targeted for achievement by 2015: (1) expanding and improving comprehensive early childhood care and education; (2) ensuring access to and completion of free and compulsory primary education of good quality for all children; (3) ensuring equitable access to appropriate learning and life-skills programs for all young people; (4) achieving a 50 per cent improvement in levels of adult literacy, especially for women, and equitable access to basic and continuing education for all adults; (5) eliminating gender disparities in primary and secondary education (by 2005), and achieving gender equality in education by 2015, with a focus on ensuring girls' full and equal access to and achievement in basic education of good quality; (6) improving all aspects of the quality of education and ensuring excellence of all so that recognized and measurable learning outcomes are achieved by all, especially in literacy, numeracy, and essential life skills.

As indicated in this summary from the monitoring report (UNESCO, 2006: 63), based on 2004 data, there are strong disparities across nations and regions with respect to educational access, attainment, and quality:

- Pre-primary enrolments are up, but not very significantly. In some regions, pre-primary education has become the norm (e.g., North America and Western Europe, Latin America, and the Caribbean); in others it is still very rare (e.g., sub-Saharan Africa).
- Access to primary school is improving, a fact reflected in data on new entrants and on primary enrolments, especially in the three regions that were, and remain, farthest from the goal: sub-Saharan Africa, South and West Asia, and the Arab States. Primary school progression and completion remain major concerns, however, especially in these same regions but also to some extent in Latin America and the Caribbean. The lack of data for a number of countries, mainly in sub-Saharan Africa, that are or have recently been affected by conflict also means the global picture is not as positive as that painted by examining only countries for which data exist.
- The number of children not in school has declined but remains much too high. Moreover, there is some evidence that countries which are getting within closing distance of UPE are finding it very difficult to succeed in the final stages of attracting the most marginalized children and retaining them through the full primary cycle.
- Considerable progress is being made towards gender parity, in particular in countries where gender differences in education are still high, but disparities remain predominant, particularly in secondary education. About two-thirds of countries with data available for 2004 have achieved gender parity in primary education; in the remainder, the disparities mainly favour boys. However, in only one-third of the countries with data available for secondary education has gender parity been reached at that level, and disparities in secondary are much more pronounced than in primary education; they can favour either girls or boys.
- No major new information is available on learning outcomes, but new analyses of past assessments, together with a new evaluation report from the World Bank, confirm that quality remains a major issue, particularly for children from poorer backgrounds. Key teacher indicators suggest the same: while pupil/teacher ratios have generally improved slightly, they remain much too high, as do the proportion of teachers who are not qualified and trained, and the rate of teacher absenteeism. The issue of quality is not confined to the three regions with the greatest enrolment challenges. It is also a concern in East Asia and the Pacific, and in Latin America and the Caribbean.
- The scope of the global literacy challenge remains much as depicted in the 2006 Report, which had literacy as its special theme: about one in five adults is still not literate (one in four adult women) and those who are not literate live mainly in South and West Asia, sub-Saharan Africa, and the Caribbean.
- Monitoring instruments remain to be developed for the learning needs of youth and adults, and for the literate environment.

a class of highly educated and trained people to prosper' (LeBlanc, 1994: 15).

Regardless of the widespread acceptance of and participation in education as an essential feature of contemporary life, not everyone encounters and benefits from education in the same way. Educational experiences, outcomes, and achievements differ considerably among individuals and groups and are interpreted in different ways.

Alternative Accounts of Educational Growth and Development

There are various ways of understanding education, just as there are diverse orientations to what education should be. These orientations are concerned with the politics of education or represent different ideological positions. Specific visions may be related to particular issues, such as what kinds of education a society should have, who should control and pay for education, and what should be taught in schools. Sociological theories of education, by contrast, are more concerned with describing and explaining education systems, educational processes, and educational change, although they sometimes draw from or influence educational **ideologies**.

Several major theoretical perspectives that have been applied to an understanding of the education system are outlined here: the structural-functionalist approach, symbolic interactionist and interpretive theories, conflict theory, feminist theories, and more recent integrative orientations to the analysis of education.

Structural Functionalism

Structural functionalism is concerned primarily with understanding how different parts of the entire social system are interconnected in order to keep the system going. It addresses questions of how societies perpetuate themselves, how individuals come to be integrated within social frameworks, and how social change can occur without upsetting the social order. Structural functionalism examines education, like any other aspect of society, in terms of its contributions to social order and stability. Education gains importance in modern societies as an institution that provides participants with the core understandings, capabilities, and selection criteria necessary to enable them to fit into prescribed social and economic roles. As society becomes more complex and specialized, schools and other educational institutions take on many of the functions previously managed by families, communities, and religious organizations to ensure that children and youth—and eventually adult learners, also—are equipped for work and adult life.

The structural-functionalist perspective presents an image of the properly functioning society as one in which the **transition** from early childhood and family life into schooling and eventually the labour force is relatively seamless, relying on the co-ordination and integration of all of the significant contributors. Disruptions and changes are posed as problems of adjustment, either within the social system or within individuals who do not 'fit'. Social pathologies must be monitored, like periodic automobile maintenance or health check-ups, and repaired through proper diagnosis and treatment in order to maintain the system in a state of healthy balance.

In the early twentieth century, Émile Durkheim (1956 [1922]: 123), who wrote extensively about education in his efforts to establish sociology as a distinct scientific discipline, described education as 'the means by which society perpetually re-creates the conditions of its very existence'. Education cultivates within each person knowledge as well as moral obligation and commitment to other members within a social framework governed by definite rules, regulations, and expectations.

Talcott Parsons (1959) later extended this analysis to a North American context, highlighting the two central functions that schooling fulfills within contemporary societies. First, schooling allocates individuals into selected occupational pathways and social positions in order to match social requirements with the available pool of skills, talents, and interests. Second, it socializes people by providing them with the general aptitudes and knowledge that they need to operate successfully in their society and by preparing them more specifically for the adult roles that they will occupy. Schooling is organized in such a way that people move in the primary grades from home environments where highly personal, emotional ties prevail, through the senior grades marked by progressively greater degrees of competition, merit, and instrumentality intended to prepare the individual for integration into work and other institutional settings crucial to adult life.

Robert Dreeben (1968) shows further the importance of school practices, in and out of the classroom, in cultivating characteristics essential for contemporary work and public life. Four essential **norms** are independence (students' acting according to expectations without supervision), achievement (students' actions to meet accepted standards of excellence), universalism (students' impartial treatment of others based on general categories), and specificity (students' developing selected individual characteristics as opposed to the person as a whole). Teachers are expected not only to convey knowledge and the opportunity to practise these norms for their students, but to model these behaviours for them as well.

Structural functionalism offers a possible explanation of educational expansion both by connecting schooling with the growth of complexity in the occupational structure and by highlighting its increasing importance to citizenship in industrialized societies. A related form of analysis, sometimes referred to as *technical functionalism*, links educational growth with the increasing technical sophistication of jobs and knowledge production (Bell, 1973). Functionalist analysis typically assumes a broad social consensus about what should be taught in schools and how educational institutions should be organized. Moreover, it tends not to question either the legitimacy of educational credentials to determine entry into specified labour market positions or the fairness of the way the education system operates.

Functionalist analysis tends to portray deviation from these ideals as abnormalities or temporary problems that warrant minor reforms rather than as challenges to the education system as a whole. It tends to descriptions of what schools should be like, within liberal democratic ideologies, than to explanations of how schooling came about. Functionalism presents education as a meritocratic ideal, a means of enabling people to gain opportunities for social or economic success regardless of their social backgrounds. Societies require a careful fit among capability, talent, effort, training, and jobs as social tasks become more complex and specialized. These claims have led to subsequent research into the definition and measurement of educational inequality, calling into question the degree to which educational realities match the needs of industrial democratic societies.

Human capital theory, an approach with some affinity to structural functionalism, emphasizes education's role as a critical tool for developing human capacities to create and apply new knowledge. The human being is regarded as an input, along with material and economic resources, that contributes to economic productivity and development. **Human capital** can be enhanced when adequate investment is made in the form of proper training, education, and social support; this approach has been used to justify massive investment by governments that contributed to the significant enrolment growth in post-secondary education observed in Table 9.2. Modified versions of human capital theory have gained renewed currency as attention turns to the importance of advanced training and educational credentials in 'knowledge-based' societies.

Despite evidence that levels of employment, income, and other benefits improve with educational attainment, structural functionalism and related theories, such as human capital theory, are unable to account for the presence of persistent inequalities in educational opportunities, outcomes, and benefits. The theoretical emphasis on consensus limits consideration of differences in educational values, content, and practices; of how some things get incorporated into schooling while others do not; and of how these differences affect people from different social backgrounds. Alternative theoretical approaches to education attempt to address some of these issues.

Symbolic Interactionism and Microsociology

In contrast to structural functionalism's focus on education systems and institutional arrangements, *microsociology* or *interpretive theories* are concerned more with interpersonal dynamics and how people make sense of their **social interactions**. **Symbolic interactionism**, the term applied to one of the most influential branches of microsociology, focuses on how meanings and **symbols** are integral to social activity. Symbolic interactionism moves the analysis directly into the lives and understandings of social participants.

Interpretive analysis examines diverse questions central to the sociological study of education, such as how schooling contributes to the development of personality and **identity**, how some forms of knowledge and not others enter into the curriculum, and how students and teachers shape the learning process in and out of the classroom. This work stresses the importance of examining the meanings and possibilities that social actors bring to social settings. Willard Waller depicts schools as

Time to Reflect

What are the main functions of education identified by structural functionalist approaches to the understanding of schooling?

'the meeting-point of a large number of intertangled social relationships. These social relationships are the paths pursued by social interaction, the channels in which social influences run. The crisscrossing and interactions of these groups make the school what it is' (1965 [1932]: 12). Peter Woods (1979) explores schooling as a series of **negotiations** among teachers, students, and parents, expressed in such phenomena as how pupils select the subjects they take, the role of humour and laughter in the classroom and staff room, and teacher reports on student progress. Howard Becker (1952) shows how teachers' backgrounds influence their construction of images of the ideal pupil, which in turn affect how they treat and assess students.

These examples illustrate symbolic interactionists' depictions of societies and institutions as fluid rather than as fixed entities. Institutional patterns are the result of recurrent daily activity and of people's capacities to shape, interpret, reproduce, and modify social arrangements through their social relations. *Ethnomethodology*, a variant of interpretive sociology, examines in detail the methods or approaches that people draw on to construct a sense of reality and continuity in everyday life. Understood this way, the likelihood that classrooms in one place resemble those in another is less a product of a given model of schooling than an outcome of actions based on images about what is expected of us and how we are supposed to act.

Symbolic interactionism and ethnomethodology offer interesting insights, but they tend to fail to account for broader concerns and limiting factors by focusing too much on the details of ongoing social activity. Classroom dynamics or how one interprets the curriculum cannot be understood fully without reference to educational policy, power structures, social change, and persistent social inequalities that strongly influence educational processes and outcomes.

Some researchers have combined interpretive sociology, with its insights into practical social activity, with other approaches that pay greater attention to the social contexts in which social action takes place. Several British sociologists, under the banner of the 'new sociology of education', extend this analysis by attempting to break down barriers between **micro-** and **macrosociology**, and by shifting attention away from educational problems defined by educational administrators and policy-makers. Their concern is how society constructs educational knowledge and practices and makes them part of the taken-for-granted assumptions that guide the actions and understandings of teachers and other educational participants. This work has focused 'on the curriculum, on the "educational knowledge" imparted by the school, and on the school's conception of "what it is to be educated"' (Blackledge and Hunt, 1985: 290). Furthering this analysis, Basil Bernstein (1977) highlights the various ways that **power** and control enter into the authority structure of schools and classrooms as well as through the expectations and assumptions around which the curriculum and educational policies are framed. Bernstein's contributions to a systematic understanding of micro and macro levels of analysis have influenced writers working within diverse theoretical traditions (Sadovnik, 1995).

Conflict Theory

Conflict theory, arising in Marxism, encompasses approaches to social analysis that emphasize competition between and power relations among social actors, groups, or forces. Much greater concern prevails in conflict theory than in other approaches regarding how institutional structures and social inequalities are maintained or changed through conflict and struggle.

Samuel Bowles and Herbert Gintis, like structural functionalists, emphasize schools' role as mechanisms that select and prepare people for different positions in labour markets and institutional life. Their Marxist orientation reveals schools' inability to fulfill the democratic ideology they purport to enact, namely, that all students have fair chances to succeed. Their view is that the labour market is conditioned more by capitalist interests than by general consensus about social values and needs. Bowles and Gintis (1976: 49) posit education, historically, as 'a device for allocating individuals to economic positions, where inequality among the positions themselves is inherent in the hierarchical division of labor, differences in the degree of monopoly power of various sectors of the economy, and the power

Time to Reflect

How do symbolic interactionist theories differ from functionalist and conflict approaches to the study of education?

of different occupational groups to limit the supply or increase the monetary returns to their services'.

Conflict theorists emphasize that education-related inequalities are not simple imbalances that can be eradicated with minor modifications or reforms. Deeply rooted relations of domination and subordination create persistent barriers to opportunity and advancement. This critical sociological orientation denies the functionalist and human capital theory accounts of educational expansion as being a result of rising technical requirements of jobs. Different **social groups** are understood to employ education and educational ideologies as tools to pursue their own interests. Employers rely on formal educational credentials—regardless of the skills demanded by the job—to screen applicants and assess a person's general attributes. Professions control access to education and certification as a way to preserve the status and benefits attached to their occupations. New knowledge and technological advancements in areas such as medicine, nursing, teaching, engineering, and information-processing may appear to produce a demand for increasingly more advanced, specialized training. But more often, credential inflation occurs as occupations preserve special privileges by simultaneously claiming the need for superior qualifications and restricting entry into these kinds of jobs (Collins, 1979).

Technological developments are not necessarily accompanied by increasing skill requirements for many jobs. Machines and information technology often substitute their routine technical operations for human input or influence the content of 'new jobs' in which people are required to do little but read gauges, respond to signals, or key in information. Under these conditions, schools may function more as warehouses to delay people's entrance into the labour force and to dissipate their dissatisfaction with the economy's failure to provide sufficient numbers of satisfying jobs than as places where effective learning and occupational training take place. Harry Braverman suggests that 'there is no longer any place for the young in this society other than school. Serving to fill a vacuum, schools have themselves become that vacuum, increasingly emptied of content and reduced to little more than their own form' (1974: 440). **Capitalism**, in this view, has contributed less to skills upgrading through technological advancement than to an ongoing process that erodes working skills, degrades workers, and marginalizes youth.

Other conflict theorists highlight the biases and inequalities that are produced directly or indirectly through the curriculum and classroom practices. Students and parents have different understandings, resources, and time that affect the extent to which they can participate in and benefit from educational opportunities. Government cutbacks and changes to school-funding formulas exacerbate many of these inequalities. In Ontario, for instance, many schools report difficulty raising funds even for basic school materials and supplies: 'funding levels are so low, parents are having to make up for programs that aren't paid for—so then it depends on where you live and who you are. . . . There is a growing concern about equity. There is a growing gap between the "have" and "have-not" schools' (L. Brown, 2002: A1, A26).

In post-secondary education, decreased government funding has led to rising tuition fees, which, accompanied by higher costs for textbooks and technology support, living expenses, and other factors, make it increasingly difficult for students without sufficient resources or unable or unwilling to take on mounting student loans to attend colleges and universities. Conflict analysis also points to concern about the growing reliance by educational institutions on corporate donations and sponsorships to make up for shortfalls in government funding.

Conflict theories of education, in short, stress that expectations for schooling to fulfill its promise to offer equal opportunity and social benefits to all are unrealistic or unattainable within current forms of social organization. Barriers that exist at several levels—access to schooling, what is taught and how it is taught, ability to influence educational policy and decision-making, and differential capacity to convert education into labour market and social advantage—deny many individuals or groups the chances to benefit from meaningful forms and levels of education. Conflict theories offer varying assessments of what must be done to ensure that education can be more democratic and equitable. Some analysts stress that educational institutions and organizations themselves must be transformed, while others suggest that any kinds of school reform will be limited without more fundamental social and economic changes to ensure that people will be able to use, and be recognized for using, their education and training more effectively.

Feminist Theories

Feminist analyses of schooling share similar observations with other conflict theories, though with an explicit emphasis on the existence of and strategies to address social inequalities based on **gender**. Feminist theory stresses that social equity and justice are not possible as long as males and females have unequal power and status through **patriarchy** or gendered systems of domination.

In the eighteenth century, Mary Wollstonecraft (1986 [1792]) saw access to education as a fundamental right for women; by being denied such a right historically, women were degraded as 'frivolous', or a 'backward sex'. Later waves of feminism have continued to look to education as a central institution through which to promote women's rights, opportunities, and interests.

There are multiple feminisms in the analysis of education, rather than a single feminist orientation; each poses different questions for educational research and proposes different explanations and strategies for change (Gaskell, 1993; Weiner, 1994). In general, though, feminist analysis shows that influential mainstream studies of schooling have most often concentrated on the lives of boys and men, with little recognition that girls and women have different experiences and little chance to voice their concerns. Much research in the 1970s and 1980s focused on how such things as classroom activities, language use, images and examples in textbooks and curriculum material (including the absence of women and girls in many instances), treatment of students by teachers, and patterns of subject choice reflected gender-based stereotypes and perpetuated traditional divisions among males and females (Kenway and Modra, 1992).

SOCIOLOGY IN ACTION

Dimensions of Educational Participation

In Canada and most other nations, educational participation rates and attainment levels are increasing, regardless of social background. Sociologists have debated the extent to which these trends do or do not reflect the ability of education to fulfill its promise to provide social and economic opportunity, especially in relation to demands associated with labour markets that require more skilled and highly qualified workers.

Exploration of these issues offers a useful opportunity to apply a *sociological imagination*, described by C. Wright Mills (1959) as the ability to link one's personal biography or background and circumstances with historical sensitivity to wider social structures and processes.

Begin by examining your own educational and career pathways. What level of formal education have you attained so far? What level would you like to attain? What other kinds of education (such as informal learning through self-directed or group study, special interest courses, adult education, or on-the-job training) have you engaged in? Have there been any gaps or interruptions in your studies? What experiences (positive or negative) have affected your interest and ability to gain the level of education you desire or have completed? What jobs (if any) have you been engaged in? What is the relationship between your educational background, including any specific skills, knowledge, or credentials you have, and the job itself? (Examine both the starting qualifications for the job and the actual tasks involved in the job.) What future employment do you desire, and how is this related to your educational plans and qualifications?

Second, consider your own educational experiences in relation to your social background and context. How typical or different are your own educational and work experiences in comparison with your family and members of other social groups you have associated with (such as your grandparents, parents, childhood peers, and community members) or those you consider yourself part of now? Relate your educational experiences and aspirations with other important characteristics or aspects of your social background (including your gender, race, ethnicity, family income, regional and national origin, place of residence such as urban or rural, age, and other factors you consider important).

Third, engage in broader comparisons between your own education and working experiences and those of others. Examine data from various studies cited in this chapter and from extensive records maintained on the Statistics Canada website. What is the relationship between your experiences, those of other persons from your family and home community, and wider trends evident from these data?

Finally, explain the major patterns and conclusions derived through your inquiries. What do these findings reveal about the nature of education and its social and economic importance?

Feminist analysis seeks to do more than simply demonstrate how these social processes contribute to inequalities, in order to change the conditions that bring these practices about. This focus has shifted as some aspects of the agenda on women's rights and issues have advanced successfully while specific barriers continue to restrict progress on other fronts. For instance, school boards have policies, enforced through human rights legislation, to restrict sexist curricula and to prohibit gender-based **discrimination** in educational programs and institutions. Educational participation rates of and attainment by females have come to exceed those for males. Yet, gender parity has not been achieved in several important respects, as reflected in concerns that relatively few females take courses or programs in areas such as computer programming, engineering, and some natural sciences, that some gender-based barriers exist in other areas of schooling, and that educational achievements do not always contribute equitably to successful social and economic outcomes.

Feminist analysis of education also explores the gender structure of the teaching force. The feminization of teaching, as female teachers came to outnumber male teachers by the end of the nineteenth century, carried significant implications for the occupation and its members. Teachers often lack the professional recognition that might otherwise accompany the demands and training their work involves. Teachers—and women teachers in particular—have been heavily regulated by governments and by school boards. During the early part of the twentieth century, guidelines often specified such things as what teachers could wear, with whom they could associate, and how they should act in public (Wotherspoon, 1995). Until the 1950s, legislation in many provinces required women to resign their teaching positions upon marriage. Although today's teachers have much greater personal and professional autonomy than those of the past, teachers' lives and work remain subject to various forms of scrutiny, guidelines, and informal practices that carry gender-based assumptions or signifi-

Much of what is learned in schools occurs in groups, as we learn with and from other people, including our classmates. Eventually, group work gives way to individualistic competition. (O. Bierwagen/Ivy Images)

cance. Female teachers predominate in the primary grades, while men tend to be overrepresented in the upper grades and in post-secondary teaching positions, especially in the most senior teaching and educational administrative positions.

Feminist analysis also addresses interrelationships among gender and other social factors and personal characteristics. Gender-based identities, experiences, and opportunities are affected by race, region, social class, and competing expectations and demands that people face at home, in the workplace, and in other social spheres (Acker, 1999). Students and teachers from different backgrounds encounter diverse experiences, concerns, and options, even within similar educational settings, which in turn affect subsequent educational and personal options.

Emerging Analysis and Research in the Sociology of Education

Educational researchers make distinct choices about which theoretical positions are most useful or relevant to their analysis. Since theory is a tool to help understand and explain phenomena and guide social action, sociologists commonly employ insights from several models or orientations.

Critical pedagogy is an approach that draws from different theoretical positions, including conflict theory, feminist theory, and postmodernist challenges, both to explore how domination and power enter into schooling and personal life and to seek to change those aspects that undermine our freedom and humanity (Giroux, 1997; McLaren, 1998; Darder et al., 2003). Anti-racism education shares similar orientations, stressing further the ways in which domination builds on notions of racial difference to create fundamental inequalities among groups that are defined on the basis of biological differences or cultural variations (Dei, 1996).

Pierre Bourdieu (1997a; Bourdieu and Passeron, 1979) has explored how **social structures** (the primary focus of structural functionalism and conflict theory) become interrelated with the meanings and actions relevant to social actors (the main concern of symbolic interactionism or interpretative sociology). Bourdieu, as a critical theorist, emphasizes that education contributes to the transmission of power and privilege from one generation to another as it employs assumptions and procedures that advantage some groups and disadvantage others. Educational access, processes, and outcomes are shaped through struggles by different groups to retain or gain advantages relative to one another. However, the mere fact that people hold varying degrees of economic, social, and cultural resources does not guarantee that these will be converted automatically into educational advantage. Competition for educational access and credentials increases as different groups look to education to provide a gateway into important occupational and decision-making positions.

Canadian research, influenced by Bourdieu's analysis and other integrative approaches such as life course theory, demonstrates the complex interactions among personal and social structural characteristics that affect the pathways taken by children and youth through education and from schooling into work and other life transitions (Andres Bellamy, 1993; Anisef et al., 2000). In order to understand schooling fully, it is necessary to take into account several interrelated dimensions:

- how educational systems are organized and what happens inside schools;
- how school experiences are made sense of and acted on by various educational participants;
- the relationships between internal educational processes and external factors, including governments and agencies that set and administer educational policy, employers that demand particular kinds of education and training and that recognize particular types of credentials, political frameworks composed of competing values and ideologies about what education should be and about how resources should be allocated for education in relation to other priorities, and broader structures of social and economic opportunity and inequality;
- the relations among transformations occurring on a global scale with more specific economic, political, and cultural structures that alternatively provide opportunities for, and systematically exclude, democratic participation by specific social groups (Apple, 1997; Torres, 1998).

Time to Reflect

What are the main bases of inequality emphasized in conflict theories and feminist theories of education, respectively?

Time to Reflect

What advantages do integrative approaches to the analysis of education offer in comparison with other theories presented earlier in this chapter?

Educational Participants

Educational institutions reveal considerable complexity in their organization and composition. Comprehensive schools may have 2,000 to 3,000 students and dozens of teachers and support staff, while colleges and universities can exceed the size of small cities. Consequently, sociologists are interested in questions related to the changing nature of who attends and works in these institutions (with respect to gender, racial, ethnic, religious, socio-economic, and other factors), what positions they occupy, and what barriers and opportunities they encounter.

Increasing diversity in education is a consequence of several factors. The educational participation of girls and women has increased significantly since World War II, especially at the post-secondary level. Immigration has also contributed to changing educational profiles, particularly in the largest cities. The immigrant population, in turn, contains increasing numbers and proportions of students classified as visible minorities and of those who speak languages other than English or French when they arrive in Canada. Combined processes of rural-to-urban migration, policy changes, and population growth have increased the concentrations of Aboriginal students in elementary and secondary schools, especially in western

Modern universities are like factories in their efforts to mass-produce a product—educated graduates. Some believe that, in this environment, people mainly learn how to submit to regimentation. (Carlos Osorio/Torstar Syndication Services)

and northern Canada. Economic changes have exacerbated many inequalities, including the perpetuation or magnification of gaps between high- and low-income families. Poverty and economic marginalization affect up to one-quarter of Canada's children. Classrooms today integrate students who historically have been excluded, such as teen parents or those with physical or learning disabilities. Numerous additional factors such as religious orientations, the health of regional economies, and distance to essential educational and support services affect educational participation and outcomes.

Significant questions arise concerning how educational institutions attend to the diverse circumstances and needs of their student bodies. Sociologists are interested in much more than simply how the curriculum and formally structured activities affect students' learning and chances for success. Educational organization, rules, expectations, and practices also contain a **hidden curriculum**, the unwritten purposes or goals of school life. School life has a daily rhythm, through repeated variations between structured learning situations and informal interactions, channelling students into selected directions and contributing to taken-for-granted understandings about order, discipline, power relations, and other aspects of social life (Lynch, 1989). These educational processes are likely to reflect selected interests or issues while they ignore others. Benjamin Levin and J. Anthony Riffel observe that 'low socio-economic status is more strongly associated with poor educational outcomes than any other variable. Yet educators are quite ambivalent about the meaning of poverty for their work and the conduct of schooling' (1997: 117). Schooling often has limited connection with—and produces negative consequences for—the students and communities it is intended to serve (Dei et al., 2000; Royal Commission on Aboriginal Peoples, 1996).

Two mechanisms—referred to as *silencing* and the *banking model*—illustrate how common educational practices can have indirect and unequal consequences for students, their identities, and their educational experiences and outcomes. *Silencing* refers to practices that prevent educational participants from raising concerns that are important to them (such as when teachers do not give students the opportunity to talk about current events or matters of student interest), as well as to indirect processes that make students question their own cultural background or that discourage parents from talking to teachers because of their discomfort with the authority represented by the school. The *banking model* of **pedagogy** (Freire, 1970) refers to educational practice in which material is pre-packaged and transmitted in a one-way direction, from the educator to the student. This practice limits the forms of knowledge that are presented as valid, leaving students from alternative backgrounds with a sense that their experiences, questions, and capacities are invalid or irrelevant.

Many educators have modified their approaches as they have gained sensitivity to the impact of their actions on students and have responded to new skill priorities in areas such as critical thinking. However, educators are under considerable pressure to balance public demands for improvement in the quality of education with attention to the multi-faceted problems and interests they must deal with in their work. As resources and energies are directed to special needs students or to programs to accommodate students from diverse cultural backgrounds, there tends to be less time and funding for core areas that must also be covered.

The high profile given to concerns such as bullying and violence in the classroom and schoolyard is in part symptomatic of tensions encountered both by staff and by students. Teachers are becoming increasingly frustrated with many aspects of their jobs as they find they are given little time and recognition for all that they are called on to do (Council of Ministers of Education Canada, 1996). While teachers are considered to be professionals, with the expectation that they are responsible for planning and carrying out educational functions, their professional status is constrained by extensive regulations and scrutiny.

Educational Policy, Politics, and Ideologies

Educational policy is established and administered in quite different ways in other countries. Many nations, such as Sweden and Japan, have highly centralized systems of education. Canada and the United States, by

Time to Reflect

What does an understanding of the hidden curriculum tell us about the nature and purposes of schooling?

contrast, do not have uniform or centralized education systems because education is constitutionally defined as an area of provincial and state authority. Canada exhibits what Paul Axelrod describes as an 'educational patchwork, particularly in comparison with the more uniform approaches of other countries' (1997: 126). In nearly all nations, however, competing demands for more co-ordinated educational planning, national standards, and consistency across jurisdictions coexist with competing reforms seeking greater responsiveness and **accountability** to local concerns (Manzer, 1994).

Provincial and territorial governments in Canada have the authority to create legislation and guidelines that outline virtually all aspects of the education system, including how it is organized, the length of the school year, curriculum and graduation requirements, teacher qualifications and certification, and educational funding. The specific details related to setting and carrying out educational policies and operating schools are normally delegated to elected local school boards or similar regional bodies.

In recent years, almost all provinces and territories have begun to propose and initiate significant changes in the ways education is organized and administered, particularly at the school board or district level. Along with a shift to larger school units, noted earlier, new bodies, including parents' advisory councils and community school programs have been established to seek greater local representation (Council of Ministers of Education Canada, 2001).

Public education at elementary, secondary, and post-secondary levels has experienced significant financial changes since the early 1990s. Total education spending, estimated to be over $80 billion in 2006, has risen by nearly $30 billion since 1991. However, the rate of increase has slowed considerably (with education expenditures falling for a brief period in the mid-1990s), with education spending as a proportion of the nation's gross domestic product (GDP, or total expenditures) declining from 8 to 6 per cent since 1992 (Statistics Canada, 2004: 54). Education spending now represents about 6 per cent of GDP although total educational spending has recovered and increased in the new century, often through more selective or targeted forms of funding. Selected educational priority areas, such as materials, innovation, and training related to new technologies, have expanded, whereas other areas have languished. Figure 9.2 shows that the predominant source of education funding in Canada is provincial and territorial governments, but a reliance on private and individual sources is growing.

These fiscal trends have placed higher burdens on students and others who have come to be defined as 'educational consumers'. Educational inequalities increase when students from less privileged backgrounds cannot afford to enrol and remain in advanced educational programs. Post-secondary tuition fees doubled during the 1990s and have continued to grow dramatically. Increases in the numbers of students incurring student debt and in the extent of student debt loads have accompanied rising costs of education and living expenses (Allan and Vaillancourt, 2004).

Elementary and secondary schools are facing difficult choices as they weigh the costs and benefits of seeking higher taxes to finance schools, increasing school fees, fundraising, relying on corporate sponsors to cover educational expenses, or cutting school programs and services. Following changes to its provincial school funding formula, Ontario has concerns about what some observers have identified as an increasing inequity between 'have' and 'have-not' schools (L. Brown, 2002: A26). Similarly, results from a national survey by the Canadian Teachers' Federation (2006: 12–13) demonstrate fundraising initiatives, once employed primarily for school trips or extracurricular activities, are being relied on increasingly to cover core areas:

- 49 per cent of all schools reported fundraising for library books (including 60 per cent of elementary schools);
- 24 per cent of all schools reported fundraising for school programs and 18 per cent for school supplies;
- 92 per cent of full-time educators contribute some of their own money (an average of $344 each in the 2004–5 school year) for classroom materials and class-related activities for their students.

Educational funding decisions are accompanied by growing concern over the extent to which education systems are able to prepare learners for contemporary economic and social conditions. There are competing viewpoints (often expressed through concerns about educational quality and excellence) about what role governments should play within this changing environment.

Neo-liberal critics promote the need for governments and the services they deliver, including education, to operate more like businesses guided by market principles. High-quality education is defined in terms of the excellence of educational 'products', measured by such things as standardized test scores, parental choice, and public accountability. Parents and learners are commonly viewed, in this way, as 'consumers' who should have the opportunity to approach education like decision-making about other purchases, with the added importance that it is their children and not some material object that is of

Figure 9.2 Total Educational Spending in Canada, by Direct Source of Funds

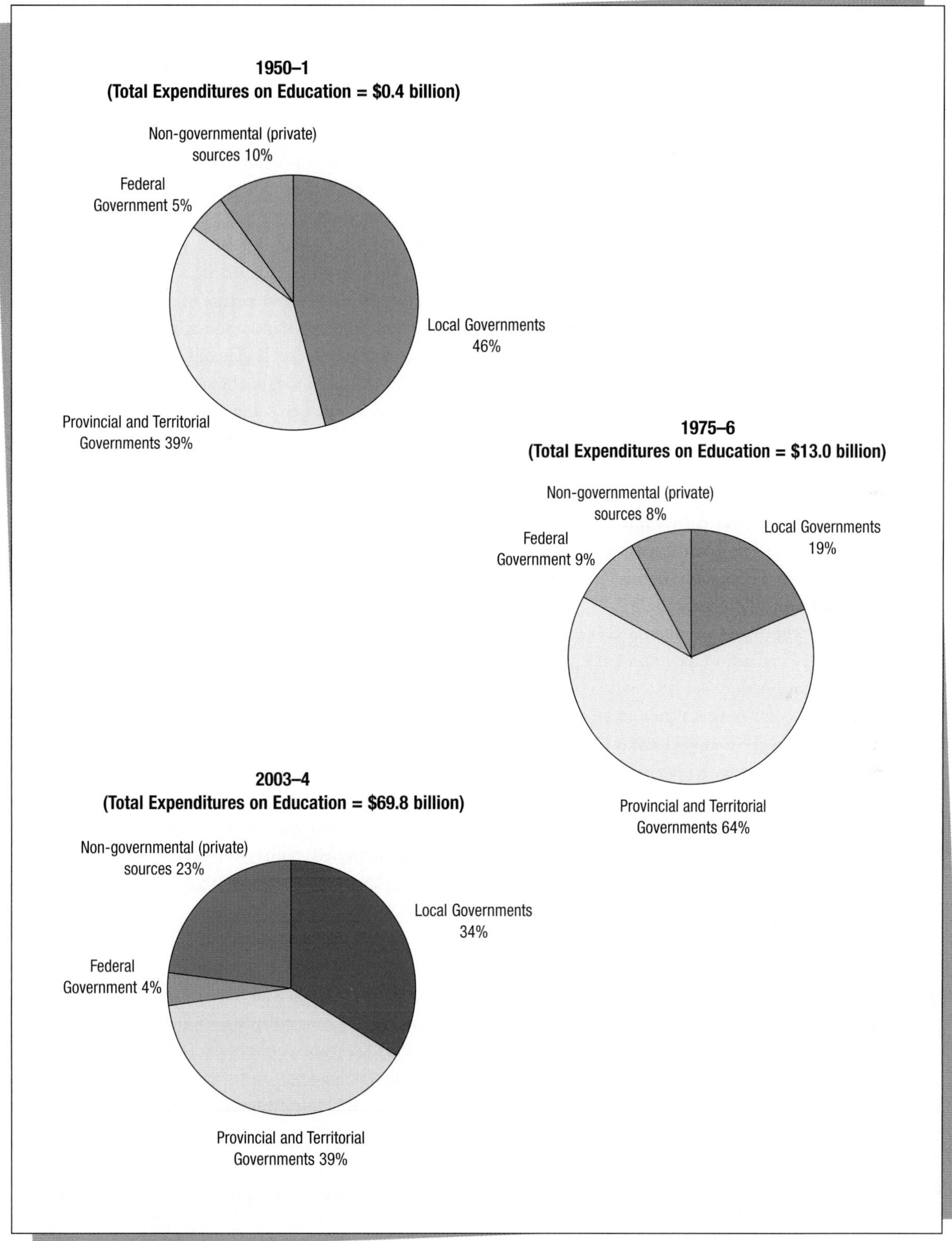

Sources: Based on data from Statistics Canada, *Historical Compendium of Education Statistics: From Confederation to 1975* (Ottawa: Statistics Canada, 1978); Statistics Canada, *Advance Statistics of Education* (Ottawa: Statistics Canada, annual); and estimates calculated from OECD (2006) and Statistics Canada CANSIM data tables 385–0002 and 385–0003.

concern, with the tools to make personal choices about the kinds of schooling they desire.

These criticisms have had some impact on education systems, particularly as governments look for ways to restrict expenditures and reorganize public services. Some observers view the recent directions in educational reform as a dangerous shift in public priorities to serve the needs of vocal interest groups who are more concerned with their own economic interests or catering to narrowly defined family and group demands rather than a commitment to community participation and high-quality education (Osborne, 1999). Matters of educational quality, accountability, and choice often are framed by a limited number of factors that can be measured in quantifiable terms, such as standardized test results. These kinds of indicators, and the manner in which they are interpreted, can be misleading when they do not account for the full range of activities and competencies encompassed by schooling. Ironically, many reformers who claim to increase educational 'choice', public accountability, and decentralization of educational decision-making in fact concentrate control over such matters as finance, curriculum, and provincial testing at the provincial or territorial level or in central bodies outside of formal education systems (Gidney, 1999; Kachur and Harrison, 1999; Sears, 2003).

Education is the focus of intense debate in part because of its social and economic importance. It is both a central institution in the lives of children and youth and a strategic focus for policy related to emerging economic realities. Given these concerns, it is important not to forget that there has been fairly consistent consensus over time about the general nature and purposes of education: schooling is to be responsive, as much as possible, to the needs and interests of the communities it serves while it must also prepare people for effective participation in broader social, cultural, and economic contexts.

Education, Work, and Families

Changes in the nature and composition of learners' families and the varied demands from workplaces for particular kinds of qualified labour-force participants have made it even more crucial to understand how education systems interact with other institutions.

The nature of childhood and adolescence is changing profoundly as students and their families experience various life challenges. Few people experience 'traditional' linear pathways from home to school to work. Periods of work and study often overlap. Children and their parents undergo substantial stress as they experience family breakdown, economic crises induced by job layoffs or persistent poverty, or difficulties in securing adequate child-care arrangements. Family, work, and community responsibilities create multiple demands on both children's and parents' time, often making it difficult to provide strong support for learning and extracurricular activities that rely on extensive student–parent interaction. Tensions often spill over from one site of social life to another, expressed in public concern over phenomena such as bullying, violence, gang warfare, and 'risk' among children and youth. Unfortunately, these issues may be regarded in a highly sensationalist way that distorts the true nature of childhood and youth activity and that ignores the strong motivations and positive contributions to leadership and mutual support prevalent among much of the student population.

Students, teachers, and educational environments face additional stresses through the growing general emphasis on education as an entry point to subsequent occupational and economic success. Taking their cue from the market model of education, many parents view their children's education as an investment, making significant demands both on their children (in order to guarantee high performance) and on teachers and educational administrators (in order to deliver a high-quality product that will yield the best results in the marketplace). Parental education, along with emphasis on early reading and literacy skills, factors heavily as an influence on children's subsequent educational attainment and success (Statistics Canada, 2006e). Parents and community members from diverse backgrounds frequently have divergent expectations about the way education should be organized and delivered. Some immigrants, for instance, may feel the Canadian education system is too unstructured and undemanding in comparison with the systems they were familiar with prior to arriving in Canada, while others take the opposite view (Campey, 2002). Aboriginal people look to schools to reconcile the need to prepare youth for a meaningful place in global society with the need to make strong connections with Indigenous people, their cultural heritage, and their contemporary circumstances (Royal Commission on Aboriginal People, 1996).

Education and New Technologies

Education, like other institutions, has been significantly affected by the introduction of computers and other new technologies. Information technology, in a few cases, has revolutionized education. Some institutions have replaced traditional instructional settings with fully wired teaching/learning centres in which participants can not only communicate with each other, but also draw upon material and interact with individuals on a global basis (Gergen, 2001). Schools in remote regions have gained access to varied learning resources and connections through the Internet and through initiatives such as SchoolNet, which aims to provide web-based learning resources to all Canadian schools. Adults can subscribe to an unprecedented range of continuing and post-secondary study options. Schools and universities are just beginning to explore fully the opportunities that new technologies are making available to them (even though the origins of the World Wide Web lie, in part, in the development of a tool that could be used to produce and share new knowledge among university-based researchers).

New technologies and their use in and impact on education give rise to several important questions. Levin and Riffel, reviewing different perspectives on the role that new technologies play in school settings, conclude that 'it may be that technology is not living up to its promise because it has been seen as an answer to rather than a reason to ask questions about the purposes of schools and the nature of teaching and learning' (1997: 114). Two issues are especially critical in this respect.

First, a significant 'digital divide' separates those who have access to computers and electronic connections—and the skills and know-how to use and take advantage of new technologies—and those who do not. This divide is most commonly posed in global terms, distinguishing richer, more technologically developed nations, such as those in North America, Europe, parts of Southeast Asia, and Australia and New Zealand, from developing nations in Asia, Africa, and Latin and South America. Canada, in this regard, is in a highly favourable situation in comparison to all or nearly all other nations, with one of the highest proportions of its population who use and own computers and employ Internet connections at home and at work. However, even within regions and nations, regular access to computers and the ability to employ them regularly at higher levels depend on such factors as a steady job, income and education levels, gender, social class, and racial characteristics (see Table 9.3).

A second issue related to the impact of new technologies on education arises from an examination of how and why new technologies are being adopted as tools and expectations in education. Clearly, information technology offers many advantages to users, contributes to important educational innovation, and may provide greater employment and economic opportunities outside of school. The rapid expansion of new technologies and applications, from text messaging, blogging, and communities involved in the dissemination of public information resources such as Wikipedia, to gaming and electronic surveillance devices, is transforming everyday life for students and their families. However, students and teachers are not always equipped and supported to use such technologies to their advantage, or to understand fully their implications and limitations.

Issues related to the adoption of computer technologies in education reflect more enduring concerns about the relationship of what happens in the classroom with structures and processes outside of schooling. Educational practices are strongly influenced by social, technological, and economic developments and innovations, though they also reveal their own peculiarities and rhythms. Demands for education to prepare people for the changing workplace sit side by side with parallel demands for producing better citizens and persons with multiple competencies to function in a global society.

Educational Opportunities and Inequalities

Questions about the relationship of education to social inequality and opportunity structures have long been central to the sociological study of education. This is due, in large part, to public expectations about education's contributions to social and economic advancement in post-industrial or knowledge-based societies. Despite compelling evidence that much of this promise has been fulfilled, significant inequalities persist in educational experiences and outcomes.

Differences between groups are apparent within the significant increases in levels and rates of educational participation and attainment across the population as a whole. One of the most striking trends within the general pattern of educational growth has been the strong

Time to Reflect

What are the main ways in which the introduction of new technologies has influenced formal education?

Table 9.3 Summary of Digital Divide: Inequalities in Internet Access in Eight Countries

Country	Socio-economic Status	Gender	Life Stage	Region
US	Declining yet persistent	No appreciable divide	Declining yet persistent	Declining yet persistent
UK	Increasing	Declining yet persistent	Declining yet persistent	Declining yet persistent
Germany	Increasing	Increasing	Declining yet persistent	Declining
Italy	Large divide based on education	Increasing	Younger use the Internet more	Northern Italy leads the south
Japan	Declining yet persistent	Declining yet persistent (reversed digital divide in mobile Internet	Younger use the Internet more	Major cities have higher Internet diffusion than smaller cities
Korea (Rep.)	Increasing	Persistent	Increasing	Declining: Seoul still the most wired city in country
China	Huge yet slightly declining	Declining yet persistent	Slightly declining	Huge, yet slightly declining
Mexico	Huge	42 per cent of Internet users are women	Younger make up the majority of Internet users	Very uneven: users still concentrated in centre, Guadalajara, and Monterrey

Source: Chen and Wellman (2004: 43). Reprinted by permission of the publisher and the authors.

advancement of educational opportunities for women, particularly in post-secondary education. With respect to the increase in overall education levels during the period between 1951 and 1991, Neil Guppy and Scott Davies point to two key trends related to gender: 'First, at the low end of the educational distribution, men remained less likely than women to complete at least Grade 9 and this difference did not narrow over the 40-year interval. Second, at higher education levels, women have surpassed the lead that men clearly held in 1951' (1998: 87). Among persons most likely to have completed their education recently, the proportion of the population in the 20–9-year-old age cohort with a post-secondary degree or diploma increased from 37 per cent for both men and women in 1981 to 54 per cent for women and only 45 per cent for men in 2001 (Statistics Canada, 1998b: 1; Statistics Canada, 2006e). In 2003, 60 per cent of all persons who received university degrees were women, although the reverse was true at the highest end, where 58 per cent of Ph.D.s were awarded to men (Statistics Canada, 2005f; see also Table 9.4).

The shift in the gender balance of educational attainment has drawn attention to other aspects of education. Findings from numerous surveys that girls have begun to outperform boys on a number of indicators have generated controversy over suggestions that gender inequality has reversed to the point that the education system is now 'failing' boys. For example, the comprehensive Programme for International Student Assessment (PISA), conducted in 2000 and 2003 to compare

New learning technology rapidly passes into the school curriculum, and children often know more about the technology than their teachers or their parents. (Bonnie Jacobs/iStockphoto)

student performance in core areas, has posed a concern for policy-makers that girls in Canada and at least 30 other participating nations consistently demonstrate stronger test outcomes in reading (Bussière et al., 2001; Bussière et al., 2004: 38). However, the findings from PISA and similar studies also demonstrate the complex nature of gender inequalities in education. For instance, in most provinces, and in many dimensions of mathematics and science performance, relatively few pronounced gender differences appear while in some instances boys outperform girls. Moreover, the survey highlights how similarities and differences based on gender cannot be understood without reference to a broad array of other family, school, and individual characteristics, notably family socio-economic background (Bussière et al., 2001).

Many gender-related differences are obscured through simple comparisons between boys' and girls' test results (Epstein et al., 1997). Women outnumber men in post-secondary enrolment and graduation, but there are strong gender differences in fields of study and types of training programs (see Table 9.3). Programs in areas such as business, management, and commerce, some arts and social sciences, protection and correction services, and languages are relatively popular among both men and women. Women are much more heavily concentrated in a few fields such as education, nursing, and social work or social services. Men tend to be more widely dispersed over more fields but outnumber women considerably in areas such as engineering and electrical technologies, computer science, and primary industries.

Differences in fields of study reflect a combination of personal choices and circumstances, institutional characteristics (such as cues or levels of comfort and discomfort that direct students into some areas and away from others or the compatibility between particular programs and responsibilities to care for dependent children), and broader socio-economic factors (Statistics Canada, 1998b; Wotherspoon, 2000). Employment options and life pathways are generally associated with the kinds of education and credentials that people attain. Nonetheless, rising levels of education do not always translate fully into gains in labour market positions, incomes, and other equitable outcomes for women (Kenway et al., 1998).

Parallel with gender comparisons, educational differences between racial and ethnic groups appear to have disappeared or diminished significantly in recent decades (Guppy and Davies, 1998). Immigration policies have simultaneously emphasized the recruitment of immigrants with high educational credentials and made Canada less dependent on immigrants from Western Europe and the United States. These policies have contributed to a growing proportion of highly educated or professionally qualified visible-minority immigrants who place a high value on their children's educational advancement. Racial diversity has been accompanied by increasing sensitivity to the impact of racial discrimination and other mechanisms that historically have excluded or discouraged racial minority students from advancing through the Canadian education system.

Nonetheless, as in the case of gender inequalities, much of the analysis of racial and ethnic inequality in education points to a complex series of factors and interactions that do not lead to any straightforward conclusions. The short answer to the question of whether some groups are advantaged or disadvantaged in relation to racial and ethnic criteria is, 'It depends.' Guppy and Davies (1998), in common with many other commentators who have reviewed census data and education indicators over time, observe that Canadians in most categories (based on gender, race, region, age, class, and other factors) have benefited from the expansion of education systems. However, specific groups, including

Table 9.4 University Degrees Awarded by Field of Study and Gender, Canada, 2004

Field of Study	Number of Graduates	Rank Order for Female Graduates	Female Graduates in Field as % of All Female Graduates	Females as % of All Graduates in Field	Rank Order for Male Graduates	Male Graduates in Field as % of All Male Graduates	Males as % of All Graduates in Field
Business, management and public administration	43,200	2	19.0	54.9	1	23.2	45.1
Social and behavioural sciences, and law	41,800	1	22.4	66.7	2	16.4	33.0
Education	25,400	3	15.5	76.0	7	7.2	24.0
Humanities	22,400	5	11.6	64.7	4	9.3	34.8
Health, parks, recreation and fitness	20,100	4	12.2	75.6	8	5.8	24.4
Architecture, engineering, and related technologies	17,500	8	3.5	25.1	3	15.6	74.9
Physical and life sciences, and technologies	15,200	6	7.0	57.2	6	7.6	42.1
Mathematics, computer and information sciences	11,100	9	2.6	29.7	5	9.1	69.4
Visual and performing arts, and communications technologies	7,300	7	3.9	67.1	9	3.0	34.2
Agriculture, natural resources and conservation	3,600	10	1.5	52.7	10	2.0	47.2
Other	1,700	11	0.8	58.8	11	0.7	35.3
All Fields	209,100		100.0	59.7		99.9	40.3

Source: Compiled with data from Statistics Canada, 'The Daily', *University Enrolment*, Cat. 11-001, 7 Nov. 2006, at <http://www.statcan.ca/Daily/English/061107/d061107a.htm>.

CULTURAL DIVERSITY

Education for Canada's Aboriginal People

The educational experiences of Aboriginal people in Canada are instructive for an understanding of how education can both advance and restrict social and economic opportunities. Historical practices and inequities have contributed to a legacy of widespread failure, marginalization, and mistrust, but considerable optimism also accompanies many new initiatives.

Many Aboriginal people in the late nineteenth century looked to schooling as a way to ensure integration into contemporary societies. Tragically, while some education-related treaty promises were fulfilled, the residential school system and continuing problems with other forms of educational delivery had devastating consequences that many Aboriginal communities and their members are still struggling to cope with. The report of the Royal Commission on Aboriginal Peoples (1996) endorsed the long-standing principle of First Nations control over education along with other measures to ensure that all educational institutions would provide more receptive schooling for Aboriginal people.

Mixed results have been accomplished so far, as one of the co-chairs of the Royal Commission has observed:

> Considering the primary importance of children in aboriginal cultures, it is not surprising that education was one of the first sectors where aboriginal nations and communities are now administered locally, and where possible they incorporate aboriginal languages and cultural content in the curriculum. . . . More young people are staying in school to complete a high-school diploma, though a gap still exists between graduation rates of aboriginal and non-aboriginal people. . . . Aboriginal youth are especially vulnerable. They are less likely than mature adults to have attained academic and vocational credentials and they are hardest hit by unemployment. (Erasmus, 2002: F6–7)

The accomplishment of educational improvement is a difficult one in the context of considerable diversity among Aboriginal populations and their educational options, aspirations, and circumstances. Some successful schools or programs, for instance, have developed strong foundations in Aboriginal cultures and indigenous knowledge systems, while others have been more concerned to provide services oriented to students' immediate needs and future plans. Marlene Brant Castellano, Lynne Davis, and Louise Lahache, reviewing recent trends, conclude that:

> the promise of education is that it will enable Aboriginal people to sustain well-being while meeting their responsibilities in the circle of life. Those responsibilities are seen to reach further today than in any previous generation. Fulfilling the promise will require preparing successive generations to participate fully in their own communities and to assume their place as Aboriginal citizens and peoples in global society. (2000: 255)

However, the legacy of failed promises continues, according to a 'report card' issued by the Assembly of First Nations (2006: 16–17) on the tenth anniversary of the Royal Commission report, which assigned failing grades to all but three of 11 specific recommendations in the section on education.

Aboriginal people, those from working-class backgrounds, francophones within Quebec, Portuguese Canadians, and the disabled, continue to face strong disadvantages relative to most other groups. Social class has a strong impact on post-secondary attendance and educational attainment. These general trends are compounded by considerable variation in educational success and attainment within groups.

Research on education for Aboriginal people is instructive in this regard. Many significant initiatives have been undertaken as researchers, policy-makers, and educators have come to acknowledge the combined impact of significant barriers to educational advancement faced by Aboriginal people. Education has long been regarded by Aboriginal people, as for any other group, as an important vehicle for gaining meaningful employment and social participation. Many First Nations, for instance, expressed their desire in the treaty-making process in the nineteenth century to have access to formal education in order to keep pace with contemporary social and economic demands.

However, subsequent developments, including the often damaging legacy of residential schooling, lack of acceptance or discriminatory treatment in provincial schools, and other social, cultural, and economic factors, have left Aboriginal people's overall education levels (especially for registered Indians who live on reserve) well below national levels (Schissel and Wotherspoon, 2003). Data from the 2001 census reveal that, despite continuing increases in the levels of educational attainment by Aboriginal people, Aboriginal people aged 25 to 40 years remained two-thirds as likely as non-Aboriginal people to have a post-secondary degree or diploma, one-quarter as likely to have graduated from university and over twice as likely not to have completed high school (based on data in Hull, 2005: 6).

Sociologists and other researchers have identified numerous factors, such as cultural differences, lack of individual motivation and family or community support, and social and educational discrimination, to explain these educational inequalities. These typically occur through a complex chain of interrelated cause-and-effect mechanisms. Increasing attention has been paid to the importance of early childhood development and to the family and social environments in which children are raised for the development of literacy and language skills, thinking processes, and other capacities that are central to educational success. These conditions, in turn, depend on the socio-economic circumstances of parents, the availability of support networks in the home and community, labour market opportunities for parents and students coming out of the education system, the extent to which people in particular communities or regions have access to high-quality educational programs and services, and numerous other factors. There are strong associations between social class or socio-economic background and educational attainment. Parents' education levels and household income are strong predictors, both independently and in combination with one another, of the likelihood that a person will continue into post-secondary education (Knighton and Mirza, 2002).

Educational institutions are implicated in these broader processes in several ways. Schooling makes a difference in many ways, such as how well institutions are equipped to deal with students from diverse cultural and social backgrounds; the kinds of relationships that prevail between and among teachers, parents, and students; curricular objectives and materials; standards for assessing and evaluating students; and the general social climate within educational institutions. Social class and cultural differences are evident, for instance, in the grouping and **streaming** of students into specific educational programs that contribute, in turn, to diverse educational pathways.

There is general agreement, in the context of global economic developments that place a premium on knowledge and learning, that education is important for all people. The same consensus does not exist, however, with regard to how education should be arranged to fulfill its promise on an equitable basis.

Conclusion

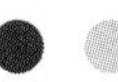
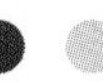

This chapter has examined several dimensions of education and its relevance for sociological inquiry. It has highlighted the phenomenal growth of formal systems of education since the nineteenth century and the accompanying increases in general levels of education throughout the population. It has linked that growth to a strong degree of public faith in the ability of education to contribute simultaneously to individual development and to address social needs for knowledge, innovation, and credentials. Educational growth, processes, and outcomes have been understood from four major theoretical perspectives: structural functionalism, which analyzes education in terms of its contributions to dominant social and economic requirements; symbolic interactionism and microsociology, which highlight the roles and interactions of various participants within educational processes; conflict theories, which emphasize education's contributions to social inequality and power relations; and feminist theories, which stress gender-based educational differences. The chapter has also addressed the changing significance of formal schooling to the experiences and social and economic opportunities of different social groups, particularly with respect to gender, race and ethnicity, and social class. All groups have benefited from educational expansion, though in varying degrees. Adequate sociological analysis of education requires an ability to integrate an understanding of what happens in and as a result of formal education with the social context in which education is situated.

Questions for Critical Thought

1. Why is education in most nations organized formally through schools and related institutional structures rather than through some other arrangement, such as families or community-based agencies? To what extent should education be a private as opposed to a public responsibility?
2. Explain how and why employers and other agencies have come to rely on formal educational credentials or qualifications as legitimate mechanisms to determine applicants' eligibility for positions in their organizations.
3. Compare and contrast schooling (formal education) with other major social institutions, including businesses, families, prisons, and religious organizations. Describe and explain the major similarities and differences.
4. What is the impact of emerging emphases on lifelong learning and the new economy on education systems? What kinds of alternatives to formal schooling are being developed in response to increasing demands for lifelong learning? Explain and critically discuss the changes (or lack of change) you have identified.
5. What factors account for the rising levels of education in Canada and other, similar nations? Discuss and explain the extent to which increasing levels of education are required to perform essential tasks associated with new technologies and information systems in a global economic framework.
6. Discuss the extent to which education is, and should be, organized in the interests of the communities in which educational institutions are located as opposed to interests shaped by national and global concerns. Illustrate this with reference to your own educational experiences.
7. To what extent has education in Canada fulfilled its promise to provide greater opportunities for social and economic advancement to all social groups? Explain your response with reference to at least three different theoretical frameworks.
8. Discuss the relative impact that particular social groups or forces (including students, teachers, administrators, parents, policy-makers, and selected interest groups) have had on educational decision-making and processes. To what extent are the arrangements you describe satisfactory, and to what extent should they be changed? Justify and explain your answer.

Recommended Readings

Paul Anisef, Paul Axelrod, Etta Baichman-Anisef, Carl James, and Anton Turrittin, *Opportunity and Uncertainty: Life Course Experiences of the Class of '73* (Toronto: University of Toronto Press, 2000).

A comprehensive account of the life transitions that people undergo after high school, this book traces for a period of over two decades the educational, work, and family dynamics experienced by Ontario students who were in Grade 12 in 1973.

Madeleine Arnot, Miriam David, and Gaby Weiner, *Closing the Gender Gap: Postwar Education and Social Change* (Cambridge: Polity Press, 1999).

This book highlights, from a primarily British perspective, the closing and apparent reversal of the gender gap in education, detailing the processes by which girls' and boys' educational experiences and outcomes have changed in recent decades.

Sandro Contenta, *Rituals of Failure: What Schools Really Teach* (Toronto: Between the Lines, 1993).

Contenta discusses how schools' hidden curricula both restrict future prospects for many students and limit the extent to which true education is accomplished through schooling. The author concludes with a proposal to reorient schools to foster critical thinking and social change.

George J. Sefa Dei, Irma Marcia James, Leeno Luke Karumanchery, Sonia James-Wilson, and Jasmin Zine, *Removing the Margins: The Challenges and Possibilities of Inclusive Schooling* (Toronto: Canadian Scholars' Press, 2000).

Diverse research and experiential backgrounds highlight the authors' call for a more inclusive form of education. The work outlines a series of strategies that can enable schools to benefit all students by drawing from the varied resources and capacities available in diverse community settings.

Neil Guppy and Scott Davies, *The Schooled Society: An Introduction to the Sociology of Education* (Toronto: Oxford University Press, 2006).

The authors integrate their discussion of core concepts and theories in the sociological analysis of education with material drawn from sociological research and case studies. Both historical and contemporary issues and developments are covered.

Hugh Lauder, Phillip Brown, Jo-Anne Dillabough, and A.H. Halsey, eds, *Education, Globalization, and Social Change* (Oxford: Oxford University Press, 2006).

This is one of the most comprehensive collections of analyses of education from various perspectives in sociology and other disciplines, containing influential chapters from different national settings that examine the impact of political and economic changes on education, cultural diversity, new conceptions of knowledge and curricula, the reshaping of teaching, and the dynamics of inequality and exclusion in relation to formal education.

D.W. Livingstone, *The Education–Jobs Gap: Underemployment or Economic Democracy* (Toronto: Garamond, 2004).

Livingstone systematically analyzes the relationships between education and work in the current economic context. Both education and the extent to which it is related to actual employment situations are explored through several dimensions, integrating statistical data with people's accounts of their own education and work experiences.

Terry Wotherspoon, *The Sociology of Education in Canada: Critical Perspectives*, 2nd edn (Toronto: Oxford University Press, 2004).

Various dimensions of Canadian education are explored from a critical orientation that emphasizes inequalities based on class, race, gender, region, and other factors. The book addresses contemporary aspects of Canadian education in the context of various theoretical perspectives and historical factors.

Recommended Websites

Canadian Education and Educators Resources
www.oise.utoronto.ca/canedweb/

Maintained through the Ontario Institute for Studies in Education (OISE), University of Toronto, this website provides a comprehensive range of links and directories that pertain to education in or relevant to Canada.

Canadian Teachers' Federation
www.ctf-fce.ca/

This website provides an educators' perspective on important educational matters, ranging from factual information on education systems and significant educational developments to position papers and analyses of pressing educational issues.

Council of Ministers of Education, Canada
www.cmec.ca

The Council of Ministers of Education provides access to major reports and studies conducted through that organization, as well as links to each of the provincial and territorial ministries of education and other important Canadian and international education bodies.

Educational Resources Information Center (ERIC)
www.eric.ed.gov/ERICWebPortal/Home.portal

The ERIC database is a comprehensive collection of information (mostly abstracts of journal articles and reports) on various aspects of and fields related to education, including the sociology of education.

Organization for Economic Co-operation and Development (OECD)
www.oecd.org

The OECD website provides useful and up-to-date information for major international comparisons and developments. It includes report summaries, statistics, and links to major documents on education and related thematic areas that highlight significant trends and issues for 30 member countries and several dozen other nations.

SchoolNet
www.schoolnet.ca

SchoolNet was established by the Canadian government in the late 1990s. In 1999, Canada became the first nation in the world to link all public schools and libraries to the Internet in order to provide ready access for educators, students, and numerous educational partners to common sites and to an extensive resource base to support teaching/learning and educational activities.

Section on Sociology of Education, American Sociology Association
www2.asanet.org/soe/

This site, though directed primarily to professionals and researchers, contains a summary description of the sociology of education and emerging issues and many useful links to other databases and relevant sites.

Social Science Information Gateway
www.sosig.ac.uk/roads/subject-listing/World-cat/soceduc.html

The Social Science Information Gateway, based in the United Kingdom, offers a substantial and useful set of links to significant reports, databases, journals, publishers, government bodies, and other organizations pertinent to the sociology of education in numerous national settings.

Statistics Canada
www.statcan.ca

Statistics Canada provides a comprehensive body of data and information on education on its website and through its links with other sites.

Chapter 10

Work and the Economy

Pamela Sugiman

Learning Objectives

In this chapter, you will:

- Come to understand the different types of paid and unpaid work that people carry out in this society.
- Examine the different ways in which work has been socially organized by employers.
- Be introduced to some of the main concepts that are used in the sociological analysis of work.
- Learn some of the recent trends in employment.
- Highlight the ways in which workers experience work and sometimes resist.
- Recognize the impact of the new flexibility strategies on workers who are located differently in a society stratified by race, gender, and class.

Photo: World of Stock

Introduction

In the last decade, we have witnessed a waning interest, if not a discernible disinterest, in the study of work in Canada. Many students have abandoned courses on work, labour, and occupations in favour of the more popular topics of deviance, popular culture, sport, and sexuality. The first step in confronting this challenge has been to pose the question, Why does the sociology of work no longer seem inspiring to young people today? Perhaps the answer is that we have moved too far away from the original sources of inspiration: the workers and workplaces. Perhaps scholars have placed too much emphasis on abstract and seemingly impersonal forces, numbers, and aggregate trends. In doing so, they may have taken people and agency out of the picture. How, then, to bring people back into the analysis and thereby re-engage students in a discussion of work?

Let us begin by making three straightforward assertions. These assertions are the premises on which this chapter is based. First, most of us will spend the better part of our lives working, because work is central to our economic well-being. Second, work is a social product and, as such, it is subject to **negotiation** and change by human actors. Third, people seek meaning in the work that they perform: there is a close relationship between work, life, and **identity**. Let us look more closely at each of these points.

1. *Work remains central to our existence.* In recent years, some social commentators have predicted the demise of work. In this view, people will invest more time in leisure activities and will be shaped primarily by their relationship to the consumer economy. But try to imagine a life without work. What would it be like if you never held a job? Unless you were incredibly wealthy, unable to work as a result of disability or poor health, or willing (or forced) to live on social assistance or handouts on the street, it is unlikely that you could live without work. If you are like most people, you have no choice but to work in order to secure for yourself the basic necessities (food, clothing, a hospitable living environment). Most of us will spend most of our days working; the majority will work for someone else, on another's terms. This holds true whether you bus tables, drive a truck, trade on Bay Street, or teach in a school. The very wealthy rely heavily on investment income for their economic well-being, and the extremely poor depend on social welfare (transfer payments). But the majority of people in the middle- and highest-income groups in Canada (from $50,000 to over $100,000 household income per year) count on wages and salaries for their existence (Jackson and Robinson, 2000: 11). A recognition of the strong link between work and life calls for a critical examination of the world of work. It is imperative that students today confront the topic for it has strong implications for how you will live your lives.

2. *Work is a social product.* The second point emerges from the observation that most Canadians view the work they do as a given. Work is something that we either have or do not have (Gorz, 1999), that we must prepare ourselves for, that we may escape at the end of a day or the end of a career. Discussions of work, therefore, tend to revolve around a specific, narrowly circumscribed set of concerns, namely, job growth, unemployment, and job-related training (Lowe, 2000). But just as we need to face up to the fact that work is what we will do for the good part of our lives, it is also important to understand that there is nothing inevitable about how work presently is organized. Work is a social product. The way work is structured, the nature of jobs, the rewards of work—these are the products of **social relationships** between different groups of people. Hence, over time and across cultures, work has taken varied forms. Students need to examine critically its current forms and organization with the knowledge that these can be questioned and perhaps even transformed.

3. *People seek meaning in their work.* Although most of us work in order to survive and to live comfortably, we also work for more than mere economic survival or comfort of living. Sociologist Graham Lowe (2000) highlights the importance, therefore, of moving discussions about the quantity of work (unemployment statistics, job counts, and work hours) to its quality. After all, the quality of work matters to workers, young and old. According to Workplace 2000, this country's first national work-ethic study, when Canadian workers were asked what they would do if they won a million dollars, only 17 per cent said that they would quit their jobs and never work again; 41 per cent of respondents claimed that they would remain in their current job, 17 per cent would embark on a different career, and 24 per cent would start their own business (Lowe, 2000: 52). Canadians have a strong attachment to their work.

In order to understand work fully, it is necessary to think about the wider economy in which it is situated. We may define the *economy* as a social institution in which people carry out the production, distribution, and consumption of goods and services. Discussions of the economy sometimes are presented in inaccessible language that easily mystifies those untrained in the discipline. Talk of gross domestic product, gross national product, inflation, and recession can be confusing. Yet, it is critical that we understand how economic systems

Time to Reflect

In work that you have done for pay, what, besides the money, did you gain from the work? Did you learn anything of value? Did you learn anything about yourself?

function, for they have a direct bearing on how we live. The economy and our location in it shape what we may or may not enjoy of, for instance, the quality of health care, housing, diet and nutrition, consumer spending, and the accoutrements of lifestyle. The economic system is, furthermore, linked to a nation's political system, to people's conceptions of democracy and citizenship, and to general measures of success and failure.

World Economic Systems

Economic systems are not abstract entities. They are structured and contested, shaped and reshaped, by the people who inhabit them. They further reflect relations of **power** and inequality. In Canada, we presently live in a society that is based on a system of **capitalism**. As such, it is one in which there are blatant as well as subtle manifestations of inequality. We observe extremes of wealth and poverty every day. On the highway, a shiny new Porsche whirs by a 1989 Chevy Impala. A businessman rushing to pick up a $3,000 suit from Holt Renfrew walks quickly past a homeless person squatting on the corner. A Filipina nanny on a temporary work permit spends her days taking someone's children to Montessori school, piano lessons, and dance class. On her way home, she buys their groceries. At night, she returns, tired, to her small room beside the furnace in the basement of the family's well-appointed home. We live in a society in which economic inequalities are complexly wound up with inequalities based on **gender**, **race**, and **ethnicity**.

The power of capitalism is so pervasive that we tend to take for granted many of its central premises. Few of us notice, much less question, the kinds of inequalities that characterize a capitalist society. Concerned about how we, as individuals, can make our way upward through the capitalist hierarchy, we seldom stop to question the system itself. But by looking more closely, with a sociological lens, we can see how our present society is historically specific and is very much a product of conflicting interests and struggles. We may recognize that there are different ways of organizing the economy and society.

Pre-industrial, Pre-capitalist Societies: Hunting and Gathering

Early human societies rested on a system of production and exchange called *hunting and gathering*. Hunting-

IN THE FIRST PERSON

Historical circumstances denied my parents the opportunity of a university education, and they spent their adult lives toiling in hard jobs, for inadequate pay. Thus they extolled the virtues of a post-secondary education, one that would help me to land a fulfilling, well-paid, and respectably middle-class job. But after high school, I decided I wanted independence, a paycheque, and nice clothes. So, after a week at university, I dropped out and entered the job market. My romantic illusions were soon dispelled. I spent a year in a string of low-end service jobs with demanding bosses, imposed overtime, and low pay. By the next September, I was back at school—a scared kid from the working class. But a few good professors propped open the doors of learning. Their lectures inspired, bridged personal experience with sociological insight, and allowed me to view my parents' and my own work experiences with a more critical eye. By second year, I had begun my journey into the sociology of work.—Pam Sugiman and-gathering (also called *foraging*) societies were characterized by a simple *subsistence economy*—relatively small groups of people lived off the land (gathering nuts, berries, and other forms of wild vegetation), hunting game, and, in some cases, fishing. Such societies were characterized by considerable physical mobility as groups would move from one geographic location to another in accordance with the food and water supply. Production among hunter-gatherers was largely for *consumption*, or immediate use. In other words, food gathered would be divided among people and eaten with little excess, or surplus. Without the accumulation of surplus, a system of exchange was minimal, and there was no private accumulation of wealth. Hunting and gathering societies are thus considered to be among the most egalitarian in human history.

Furthermore, the division of labour among hunter-gatherers was simple, based on sex and age. Women tended to perform gathering activities, often with children in tow, while men hunted. Some anthropologists have argued that this sex-based division of labour did not translate, however, into inequalities between the sexes. While men and women performed different functions, the divisions were not as rigid as they are currently. The work that women performed was not devalued. Indeed, insofar as hunting-and-gathering societies looked largely to vegetation (and not scarce meat) for their dietary needs, women made a greater productive contribution to the maintenance of the group than did men.

Agricultural Societies

The development of *agriculture* (the breeding of animals, the cultivation of plants, and human settlement) brought about many changes in the social and economic organization of societies. These changes were connected to an increase in productive power, a more dependable and stable food supply, and the accumulation of surplus leading to the establishment of market exchange.

Prior to the nineteenth century, Canada was largely an agricultural society based on a family economy: most economic activities were located in or nearby family households. The **household** thus served both as a place of work and of residence. This type of economy, further-

Family production was the key to all production in the earliest societies, and though work was differentiated by age and sex, it was shared by all in a familiar home setting. (Anthony Bannister/Gallo Images/Corbis)

more, featured a more elaborate division of labour (than in the past) based on age and sex (Nelson and Robinson, 2002). Family survival during this period, though, depended on the interdependent and collective labours of household members. Work was organized according to the market, but also according to nature, seasonal cycles, and personal need.

Capitalism

Unlike earlier economic systems, capitalism is based on private ownership of the **means of production**, an exchange relationship between owners and workers, an economy driven by the pursuit of profit, and competitive market relations.

In order to understand capitalism, let us turn to the ideas of the social theorist Karl Marx. Marx ([1867] 1967) wrote about the profound changes he observed in nineteenth-century England. He witnessed in England a gradual but dramatic transition from a feudal agricultural society to an industrialized, capitalist economy. Under capitalism, the capitalist class (or **bourgeoisie**) owns the means of production, while the majority of people, the working class (or **proletariat**), does not. Means of production is a concept that refers to wealth-generating property, such as land, factories, machines, and the capital needed to produce and distribute goods and services for exchange in a market. While many of us own a car, a computer, or perhaps a house, these items do not constitute the means of production insofar as they are for our personal use only (a place to live, a tool for writing your research papers) and not for the production of wealth.

In a capitalist society, furthermore, capitalists and workers are engaged in a relationship of unequal exchange. As workers do not own the means of production, they have no choice but to sell their labour to a capitalist employer in exchange for a wage. Working people are forced into this relationship because in this type of economy, it is almost impossible to survive without money. One can try to feed a family with the produce of a home vegetable garden, wear home-made clothes, and live without electricity, but at some point it is necessary to purchase market goods and services. For example, you will need to buy fabric, sewing needles, seeds, and a plot of land.

The capitalist class organizes production (work) with the specific goal of maximizing profits for personal wealth. For this reason, it structures work in the most efficient way imaginable, pays workers the lowest possible wages, and extracts the greatest amount of labour from the worker within a working day. And, lastly, capitalism is based on a freely competitive market system and therefore a laissez-faire ('hands-off') government. Under capitalism, the market forces of supply and demand are supposed to determine the production and distribution of goods and services, with no government interference.

Capitalism and Industrialization

People sometimes use the terms capitalism and industrial society interchangeably. However, conceptually, they are distinct. While capitalism is a broad economic system, industrialization refers to a more specific process that has consequences for the nature and organization of work as well as for the division of labour.

In Canada, as in England, industrialization resulted in a transformation of capitalist production. The rise of industrial capitalism in the late nineteenth and early twentieth centuries constituted one of the most fundamental changes in our society. Industrialization involved the introduction of new forms of energy (steam, electricity) and of transportation (railroads), **urbanization**, and the implementation of new machine technology, all of which contributed to the rise of the factory system of production and the manufacture and mass production of goods. These changes greatly facilitated and heightened capitalist production. As well, and in profound ways, they have shaped the ways in which people worked and organized their lives.

The proliferation of factories led to the movement of work from homes and small artisanal workshops to larger, more impersonal sites, to the concentration of larger groups of workers under one roof, and to the introduction of *time discipline* (by the clock), in addition to a more specialized division of labour.

This movement of work, furthermore, resulted in the departure of men from the home and family. While

Time to Reflect

Would you characterize your family of origin as 'bourgeoisie' or 'proletariat'? In what ways, if any, do you believe that your family background affects your attitudes towards work and workplace rights?

single women were employed in some textile factories, married women were prohibited from most factory jobs. Many women thus continued to work in the home or were employed as domestics in private households, took in boarders, or did other people's laundry in exchange for a small cash sum (Bradbury, 1993). These changes in the economy had far-reaching consequences for the construction of femininity and masculinity, marriage, and family life.

During the period of industrial capitalism economic inequalities became increasingly visible and conflict between classes grew. While successful capitalists made huge amounts of money, working-class men toiled in factories or mines for a pittance, women combined long hours of domestic drudgery with sporadic income-generating activities, and children were sent off to factories or domestic work. Many people lived in poverty and misery.

Family Capitalism

In the mid- to late nineteenth centuries, industrial capitalism was in its early stages. Throughout this period, a small number of individuals and families owned and controlled most of the country's wealth—major companies and financial institutions. Because wealth accrued from business enterprises was passed on within families, from generation to generation (for example, the Fords and Rockefellers in the United States and the Eatons and Seagrams in Canada), this era is aptly termed that of *family capitalism*.

Corporate Capitalism

The subsequent phase of economic development, occurring in the late nineteenth to mid-twentieth centuries, is called *corporate* (or *monopoly*) capitalism. This phase witnessed the movement of ownership from individuals and families to modern corporations (and their shareholders). A *corporation* is defined as a legal entity distinct from the people who own and control it. As an entity, the corporation itself may enter into contracts and own property. This separation of enterprise from individuals has served to protect owners and chief executives from personal liability and from any debts incurred by the corporation.

Insofar as the Canadian economy has traditionally been resource-intensive, many of the corporations that have dominated our industrial development have been American-owned. Consequently, Canadians have witnessed the establishment of numerous branch plants of companies whose head offices are located in the United States (for example, IBM Canada and GM Canada). This fact has raised important concerns about our political sovereignty, our culture, and our distinctiveness as a people and a nation.

Under corporate capitalism, furthermore, there has been a growing concentration of economic power (that is, power in the hands of a few large corporations). One way in which capitalists have increased their economic power is through mergers. By merging, large corporations have been able to create situations of monopoly and oligopoly. We have a monopoly when one corporation has exclusive control over the market. Obviously, this situation is undesirable for consumers, as it restricts their market 'choices'. The Canadian government has, as a result, implemented various controls to curb the monopolization of an industry.

An *oligopoly* exists when several companies control an industry. The insurance, newspaper, and entertainment industries all are characterized by oligopolistic control. Increased revenues by way of mergers and acquisitions obviously is desirable to corporate owners but may occur at the expense of industrial development and employment. In 2005, profits of the top 500 firms internationally reached a halting $610 billion. In fact, these economically powerful firms, known as the Fortune 500, have doubled their economic power over the last half-century. In 2005, Fortune 500 revenues were up by 10.2 per cent. Yet, during this same period, employees or what economists term 'head count', increased by a mere 2 per cent. Although the 10 largest employers provided jobs for 5 million workers, these employers included such companies as Wal-Mart, McDonald's, Sears, Home Depot, and Target, all of which are retailers known for offering low wages and few opportunities for training and advancement. Workers have not benefited from this growing wealth (www.laborresearch.org/story2.php/417; see also Table 10.1).

Welfare Capitalism

In the real world, of course, examples of pure capitalism and pure socialism cannot be found. In Canada, as well as in parts of Western Europe, the economy is market-based; at the same time, the government intervenes with regulations and controls. Economists call this type of system *welfare capitalism*. Under this system, state-sponsored programs such as universal health care and public education address the needs of different groups of people within the country. Many government controls, such as tax credits for corporations, act in the interests of business.

Table 10.1 The 25 Largest Employers in Canada, 2007

Rank	Company (Year End)	Number of Employees	Location of Head Office	Revenue per Employee ($)	Profit per Employee ($)
1	Onex Corp. (De06)	167,000	Toronto, Ont.	$120,341	$6,000
2	George Weston (De06)	155,400	Toronto, Ont.	$207,857	$779
3	Magna International (De06)[a]	83,000	Aurora, Ont.	$292,253	$6,361
4	Royal Bank of Canada (Oc06)	70,000	Toronto, Ont.	$514,929	$67,543
5	Metro Inc. (Se06)	65,000	Montreal, Que.	$168,398	$3,892
6	Alcan Inc. (De06)[a]	64,700	Montreal, Que.	$365,394	$27,604
7	Canadian Tire (De06)	56,559	Toronto, Ont.	$146,203	$6,270
8	Bombardier Inc. (Ja07)[a]	56,000	Montreal, Que.	$267,375	$4,786
9	BCE Inc. (De06)	54,434	Montreal, Que.	$326,469	$36,870
10	Bank of Nova Scotia (Oc06)	53,251	Toronto, Ont.	$422,189	$67,210
11	Toronto-Dominion Bank (Oc06)	51,147	Toronto, Ont.	$436,037	$89,996
12	Garda World Security (Ja07)	50,000	Montreal, Que.	$13,660	$421
13	Jean Coutu Group (My06)[a]	47,115	Longueuil, Que.	$236,714	$2,203
14	Shoppers Drug Mart (De06)	44,040	Toronto, Ont.	$176,804	$9,593
15	Sears Canada (De06)	41,107	Toronto, Ont.	$144,752	$3,712
16	CIBC (Oc06)	40,559	Toronto, Ont.	$497,202	$65,238
17	Alimentation Couche-Tard (Ap06)[a]	39,500	Laval, Que.	$257,438	$4,967
18	Empire Company (My06)	37,000	Stellarton, N.S.	$356,565	$8,022
19	Quebecor Inc. (De06)	36,588	Montreal, Que.	$268,911	$–2,566
20	Bank of Montreal (Oc06)	34,942	Toronto, Ont.	$519,518	$76,212
21	Nortel Networks (De06)[a]	33,760	Brampton, Ont.	$343,661	$829
22	Extendicare REIT (De06)	33,700	Markham, Ont.	$51,794	$–1,060
23	Thomson Corp. (De06)[a]	32,375	Toronto, Ont.	$205,869	$34,595
24	ACE Aviation Holdings (De06)[b]	32,256	Saint-Laurent, Que.	$331,318	$12,649
25	Telus Corp. (De06)	30,000	Vancouver, B.C.	$289,777	$37,417

[a]Company reports in U.S. dollars.

[b]Figures have been annualized in previous 3 through 5 years.

Figures for fiscal periods other than 12 months are annualized for rankings and calculating returns. Foreign currencies are converted into Canadian dollars at the end of the relevant period for balance sheet items and at the average exchange rate for the relevant period for earnings items.

Source: Excerpted and adapted from 'The Top 1000', *Globe and Mail Report on Business Magazine* (2007); available at <http://www.reportonbusiness.com/v5/content/tp1000-2007/index.php?view=top_50_employers>. Reprinted with permission from The Globe and Mail.

As well, in our society, the means of production are owned by both private citizens and governments. In spite of moves towards their **privatization**, we still have a number of *Crown corporations* (businesses owned by the federal or provincial governments) such as Canada Post, the Canadian Broadcasting Corporation (CBC), and the Canada Mortgage and Housing Corporation (CMHC).

Socialism

Marx (Marx and Engels, 1986 [1848]) believed that in a capitalist society, workers would eventually revolt against their **exploitation**, develop a consciousness of themselves as a class, and overthrow the system of capitalist production, replacing it with a socialist economy. It was not clear how this revolution was to proceed (except that it would be led by a communist party). In the first stages after victory, workers would establish a 'dictatorship of the proletariat' and the economy would be socialized. This would involve the elimination of private property and public ownership of the means of production (in other words, workers' control). Once this had been accomplished, the state would gradually wither away and socialism would give way to *communism*. Under communism, work would be organized on the basis of a radically different division of labour. In particular, the production and distribution of goods and services would be in accordance with ability and need within the population, rather than shaped by market forces and the pursuit of profit for individual gain.

Like capitalism, socialism and communism never have existed in a pure form. Many revolutions, successful and not, have been attempted in its name (for example, the Bolshevik revolution in Russia in 1917, China's in 1949, and Cuba's in 1959), but these societies have never reached the vision laid out by Marx. During the 1980s, the Soviet Union experienced a series of economic and political crises that ultimately led to the disintegration of its economic base and political structures. This economic crisis was based on the inability of this form of 'command economy' to adapt rapidly to the changing global economy. The last two decades have witnessed the breakup of the Soviet empire and attempts by Russia and the various 'new' countries, such as Hungary, Czechoslovakia, Poland, Ukraine, Latvia, Estonia, and Lithuania, to make the transition from command to capitalist economies, or some variation between the two (Storey, 2002).

According to Robert Storey, 'for the present, capitalism seems triumphant. If so, however, given the historical and contemporary inequalities, not to mention capitalism's intimate association with war and environmental degradation, it is a triumph that has many human and natural costs' (ibid.).

The Global Economy

Today, economic activity knows no national borders. Most large companies operate in a global context, setting up businesses in Canada, the United States, and various parts of Asia, Africa, and India. These companies may be called *transnational* or *multinational*. The head offices of transnational corporations are located in one country (often the United States), while production facilities are based in others. We see the products of the global economy everywhere we turn. Look at the clothes you wear, the car you drive, the food you eat. Where are they from? Products of the new global economy typically move through many nations.

Clearly, the goal of transnational corporations is profit. Capitalists are rapidly moving beyond national boundaries in an effort to secure the cheapest available labour, lowest-cost infrastructure (power, water supply, roads, telephone lines), and production unencumbered by health and safety regulations, minimum-wage, and hours-of-work laws, maternity provisions, and the like. Unprotected by legislation and typically without union representation, labour in **developing countries** is both cheaper and easier to control than workforces in Canada.

Critics have pointed to the negative cultural, social, and economic consequences of **globalization**. Some argue, for example, that globalization has resulted in a homogenization of **culture**. Media giants Time Warner and Disney, for instance, distribute many of the same cultural products (television shows, films, videos, books) to audiences across the globe. Among many other holdings, Time Warner owns well over 1,000 movie screens outside of the United States and the second-largest book publishing business in the world. The company furthermore boasts that CNN, its popular news network, aggregates approximately two billion audience impressions worldwide every day (www.timewarner.com/corp/businesses/detail/turn_broadcasting/index.html). Admittedly, corporate capitalists of the early twentieth century wielded great power, but the power of transnational firms in the current era is immense. According to Anthony Giddens, 'half of the hundred largest economic units in the world today are nations; the other half are transnational corporations' (2000: 315).

Furthermore, global capitalism has had an uneven impact on different groups of people both within Canada and around the world. Media exposés of children sewing Nike soccer balls in Pakistani sweatshops for the equivalent of six cents an hour have brought worldwide attention to sweatshop abuses in the garment and sportswear industries. More hidden, says the Maquiladora Solidarity Network, are the teenage girls, often single mothers, who sew clothes in the maquiladora factories of Central America and Mexico for major North American retailers such as Wal-Mart, The Gap, and Northern Reflections (Maquiladora Solidarity Network, 2000). Some of these are 12- and 13-year-olds working illegally, while others, 15- and 16-year-olds, are legal employees. Both groups of young people, however, work 12- to 18-hour days, often without overtime, under unsafe conditions and in the face of physical, verbal, and sometimes sexual abuse.

It is no coincidence that many sweatshop employees are women, and of colour—people who have no choice

GLOBAL ISSUES

Global Sweatshops: Nike in China

Nike's presence in China is estimated at 50 contracted factories, manufacturing sneakers and clothing and employing approximately 110,000 workers. Forty per cent of Nike's footwear is produced in China. The Sewon factory is a South Korean investment that has produced exclusively for Nike since 1989. Average wages for a worker in a shoe factory in South Korea are US $2.49/hour, or more than twelve times the cost at Sewon. Is it any wonder that Nike produces such a considerable amount of shoes and garments in China?

The New York-based National Labor Committee (NLC) researchers uncovered that working time is excessively long and three factories show evidence of gender and age discrimination. These factories prefer to hire young, single women, specifically stating in job recruitment advertisement that proof of marital status is necessary for the application. One company fires employees at the age of 25 when they become 'used up' (exhausted).

Nike's Code of Conduct guarantees that '. . . partners share the best practices and continuous improvement in . . . management practices that recognize the dignity of the individual' and that 'there shall be no discrimination based on race, creed, gender, marital or maternity status, religious or political beliefs, age, or sexual orientation.' Obviously, on these points, Nike has failed in China.

Source: Canadian Labour Congress, 'Nike in China', *Sweatshop Alert* (Nov. 2000): 9; at: <www.clc-ctc.ca>.

Nike in China: Five Factories

Factory	Location	No. of Workers	Wages ($US)	Working Hours	Time Off	Remarks
Sewon	Jiaozhou City, Shandong Prov., Liuhizai Ind. Area	1,500, mostly women aged 18–25	Base wage: 20¢/hr	11- to12-hr shifts, 6 days/wk	1 day/wk	Sewon would not hire 27 yrs of age
Hung Wah & Hung Yip Keng Tau	Huijou City, Guangdong Prov.	2,000–2,500, mostly women aged 16–32	Average: 22¢/hr	Peak season: 15-hr shifts, 7 days/wk	1 day/mo.	Workers never heard of Nike's Code of Conduct; 12/room
Keng Tau	Keng Tau Industrial Zone	1,000–1,200	11–36¢/hr	Peak season: 14 hrs/day, 7 days/wk	1 day/mo.	No overtime premium; 16/room
Tong Ji	Chongzhan Prov.	500 migrant workers	Average: 27¢/hr	57.5 hrs/wk	1 day/wk	Nov. 1999: 72.5 hrs/wk
Wei Li	Guangdong Prov.	6,100, mostly women aged 16–25	Average: 56¢/hr	Normal: 8 hrs/day, 5 days/wk; Peak: 12-hr shift	Normal: 2 days/wk; Peak: 1 day/ 2 wks	Employs only single women; require certificate of marital status

Source: China Labour Bulletin and National Labour Committee.

but to endure these conditions in order to survive. Garment manufacturers in Central America's free-trade zones, Mexico's maquiladora factories, and Asia's export-processing zones say that they prefer to hire young girls and women because 'they have nimble fingers. Workers suspect that children and young people are hired because they are less likely to complain about illegal and unjust conditions. And more importantly, they are less likely to organize unions' (ibid.). We are seeing the intensification of divisions of labour, globally, along the lines of class, sex, and race.

These developments, furthermore, have direct consequences for the organization of work, and for the collective power of working people in Canada. Many Canadians now work under the constant threat of company relocation to lower-cost areas. And this has resulted in a weakening of the political power of workers and their unions. In light of this threat, many people in Canada have agreed to concessions (that is, giving up past gains) such as pay cuts, loss of vacation pay, and unpaid overtime. In a study of clerical workers employed at a major telecommunications firm, Bonnie Fox and Pamela Sugiman (1999) found that top management relied on television monitors in the employee cafeteria to broadcast warnings that jobs would be lost if the workers did not make special efforts (including concessions) in the interest of the firm's survival. One employee explained, 'the axe is falling. People are afraid. . . . They'll do what they need to do to keep their jobs' (Fox and Sugiman, 1999: 79). In the long term, the lingering threat of job loss affects the standard of living in the country as a whole.

Around the world, modern industrial technology remains central to producing wealth—despite the increased importance of knowledge and information. (Keith Dannemiller/Corbis)

The Capitalist Economy: Where People Work

Most of us contribute to the economy in one way or another. Just as the economy undergoes change throughout history, so does our relationship to work. With the expansion of some economic sectors and the contraction of others, our opportunities for certain kinds of jobs also change. Social scientists identify four major economic sectors in which people in this country find employment: primary and resource industries, manufacturing, the service sector, and social reproduction (see Table 10.2).

Primary Resource Industry

Years ago, most Canadians worked in primary (or resource) industry. It is likely that your grandparents or great-grandparents performed primary-sector work. Though not always for pay, **First Nations** people have had an important history in the resource industry (Knight, 1996). Work in the primary sector involves the extraction of natural resources from our environment. Primary-industry jobs may be found, for instance, in agricultural production (farming, skilled and unskilled agricultural labour), ranching, mining, forestry, hunting, and fishing.

Throughout the eighteenth and nineteenth centuries, the primary sector represented the largest growth area in Canada. However, in the twentieth century, it began to experience a dramatic decline. Many forces have contributed to its contraction, notably the demise of small family farms and small independent fishing businesses, along with a corresponding rise in corporate farming (or 'agribusiness') and large fishing enterprises. These devel-

Table 10.2 Employment by Industry and Sex, 2006

	Number Employed (000s)		
	Both Sexes	**Men**	**Women**
All industries	**16,484.3**	**8,727.1**	**7,757.2**
Goods-producing sector	*3,985.9*	*3,065.7*	*920.2*
Agriculture	346.4	239.5	107.0
Forestry, fishing, mining, oil and gas	330.1	269.1	60.9
Utilities	122.0	92.5	29.5
Construction	1,069.7	946.8	122.9
Manufacturing	2,117.7	1,517.8	599.9
Services-producing sector	*12,498.4*	*5,661.4*	*6,837.0*
Trade	2,633.5	1,340.4	1,293.2
Transportation and warehousing	802.2	616.2	186.0
Finance, insurance, real estate, and leasing	1,040.5	442.7	597.8
Professional, scientific, and technical services	1,089.9	620.1	469.9
Business, building, and other support services[1]	690.0	366.1	323.9
Educational services	1,158.4	410.4	748.0
Health care and social assistance	1,785.5	312.8	1,472.7
Information, culture, and recreation	745.0	394.2	350.8
Accommodation and food services	1,015.0	402.2	612.8
Other services	701.0	327.9	373.1
Public administration	837.4	428.4	409.0

1. Formerly Management of companies, administrative and other support services.
Source: Statistics Canada, at: <www40.statcan.ca/l01/cst01/labor10a.htm>.

opments have resulted in dwindling opportunities for many people. Moreover, because of the geographic concentration of primary-sector jobs, this decline has devastated some towns (for example, Elliot Lake, Ontario) and entire regions (for example, Atlantic Canada).

Manufacturing

Into the twentieth century, growing numbers of Canadians began to work in the *manufacturing* (or *secondary*) *sector*. Manufacturing work involves the processing of raw materials into usable goods and services. If you make your living by assembling vans, knitting socks, packing tuna, or piecing together the parts of Barbie dolls, you are employed in manufacturing. Though the popular image of a manufacturing employee is a blue-collar male, the industry's workforce now reveals much more diversity along the lines of sex, as well as race and ethnicity.

On the whole, the manufacturing sector in Canada has experienced a slower decline than primary industry. The decline in manufacturing began in the early 1950s. In 1951, manufacturing represented 26.5 per cent of employment in Canada, but by 1995, the employment share of manufacturing had been cut nearly in half, to 15.2 per cent (Jackson and Robinson, 2000: 11). The industry nonetheless continues to be an important employer of Canadians. Job losses in manufacturing are largely attributable to technological change and the relocation of work to various low-wage sectors in Mexico, parts of Asia, and the southern United States.

The Service Sector

In *The End of Work* (1995), Jeremy Rifkin wrote about the relationship between job loss and technological change. Rifkin predicted that technological innovation would result in the loss of a great many jobs (except for an elite group of knowledge workers such as computer technicians and scientists) and would thus constitute an end to work. For various reasons, Rifkin's predictions have not come true. First, many employers prefer to hire dirt-cheap human labour rather than purchase expensive machines. Second, unions have exerted some power in resisting the wholesale implementation of technological change. And third, a massive number of new jobs have been created in the rapidly expanding service (or tertiary) sector. Study after study demonstrates that employees who lost jobs in manufacturing have been absorbed by the service industry. Indeed, many of you are no doubt currently employed in part-time or temporary service jobs. If so, you are not unlike many Canadians.

In recent years, the service sector has expanded dramatically. Among the world's largest industrialized economies—Canada, France, the United States, and the United Kingdom—the percentage of employment in the service sectors now surpasses 70 per cent in. In addition, in Germany, Italy, and Japan, service-sector work constitutes close to 65 per cent ot total employment (www.ilo.org/public/english/bureau/inf/magazine/41kilm.htm). The rise of the service industry has been linked to the development of a post-industrial, information-based economy and to the rise of a strong consumer culture. All of this has resulted in a growing need for people to work in information-processing and management, marketing, advertising, and servicing. In the course of a day, you will encounter dozens of service-sector employees. Airline reservation agents, taxi drivers, teachers and professors, daycare staff, bank employees, computer technicians, crossing guards, librarians, garbage collectors, and Starbucks barristas—all these are service workers.

As you can see from these examples, the service sector embraces a wide range of jobs. So dissimilar are these jobs that some people speak of a polarization of work. In other words, there are some 'good', highly skilled, well-paid jobs at one end of the spectrum and many 'bad', poorly paid, dead-end jobs at the other. Jobs in retail trade and food services are at the low end of the hierarchy, while those in finance and business, health, education, and public administration tend to be at the high end.

The experience of service work is also qualitatively different from that of manufacturing. Much service employment involves not only the physical performance of a job, but also an emotional component. In the face of an intensely competitive market, how does a company vie for customers? Service. And service rests on a big smile and (artificially) personalized interactions. In *The Managed Heart* (1983), Arlie Hochschild explored the emotional work of flight attendants. According to Hochschild, emotional labour, typically performed by women, is potentially damaging to workers because it involves regulating one's emotional state, sometimes suppressing feelings and often inventing them.

Also problematic is the frequently tense relationship between workers and their bosses. Low-end service work is characterized by low-trust relationships. With the expectation that their workforces will have only weak loyalties to the company and its goals, managers attempt to control employees largely through close direction and surveillance (Tannock, 2001). It is now common practice for employers to use electronic equipment to monitor telephone conversations between employees and clients and to install video security cameras to keep an eye on retail clerks. Another form of surveillance, more common in the United States than Canada, is drug testing (through urinalysis) of prospective employees. Such testing is standard, for example, at Wal-Mart stores (Ehrenreich, 2002; Featherstone, 2004). But at the same time that such work is subject to routinization and close surveillance, it necessitates high levels of self-motivation and investment on the part of the workers. In consequence, the most common complaint among workers in low-end service jobs is a high level of stress (Tannock, 2001).

Social Reproduction

All the work we have discussed so far is conducted in what social scientists call the *sphere of production*. Production typically occurs in the public world of factory, office, school, and store. Moreover, it involves monetary exchange. The study of work in this country has largely been biased towards production. When we think of work and workers, who comes to mind? Steelworkers, garment workers, plumbers, secretaries, farmers, and lawyers. What is common to all of these occupations? They are all done in exchange for money—a wage, salary, or income.

However, in Canada as well as in other parts of the world, many people spend hours and hours each day doing work that is not officially recorded as part of the economy. This type of labour may be called **social reproduction**. Social reproduction involves a range of activities for which there is no direct economic exchange. Often, though not always, this work is performed within family households. Typically, it is done by women. We do not view as economic activity the hours women (and, less often, men) spend buying groceries; planning and cooking meals; washing dishes; washing and folding laundry; chauffeuring children; buying clothes; vacuuming, washing floors and sinks, and cleaning the toilet bowl; managing the household budget; caring for aging relatives; and supervising homework. The instrumental value of such activities has long been hidden. Rather than being viewed as work, they are deemed a labour of love (Luxton, 1980).

But what would happen if women and other family members no longer performed this labour? How would it get done? Equally important, who would pay for it? If capitalist employers or the state had to ensure that workforces got fed, clothed, nurtured, and counselled, what would be the cost? These kinds of questions perplex economists and social statisticians. Says economist Marilyn Waring, breast-feeding, for example, is 'a major reproductive activity carried out only by women, and this thoroughly confuses statisticians' and economists' production models. The reproduction of human life also seems conceptually beyond their rules of imputation. But bodies most certainly have market prices' (1996: 86). In the United States, the cost of reproducing another life through artifiical insemination ranges from $1,800 for artificial insemination to $10,000 to over $30,000 for a surrogate mother to carry the child (en.wilkipedia.org/wilki/Surrogatemother). According to a Canadian estimate, if unpaid work were replaced for pay, it would be worth $275 billion to the Canadian economy (GPI Atlantic, n.d.).

The system of capitalism benefits tremendously from the performance of unpaid labour. Yet the unpaid services of housewives and other family members are not only excluded from traditional economic measures, for many years sociologists did not even consider them to be 'work'. This is perplexing insofar as such work is essential to basic human survival and to the quality of our lives.

The Informal Economy

Also hidden from official growth figures—as well as from public conscience—is a wide range of economic activities that are not officially reported to the government. These activities make up the **informal** (or *underground*) **economy**. Some are legal; others are not. They include, for example, babysitting, cleaning homes, sewing clothes, peddling watches, playing music on the streets, gambling, and dealing drugs. As you make your way through the downtown areas of most major cities in Canada and the United States and almost anywhere in the developing world, you will see people of all ages trying to eke out a living in the informal sector.

Of course, we do not know the precise size of the underground economy. We have only estimates of its share of officially recognized economies and see much variation across the globe. According to the International Labour Organization, (ILO), in developing countries as a whole, the informal economy has been estimated to involve one half to three quarters of the non-agricultural labour force. In North Africa, it represents 48 per cent of employment; 51 per cent in Latin America, 65 per cent in Asia, and 72 per cent in sub-Saharan Africa. Furthermore, in the developing world, informal employment is generally a larger source of employment for women than for men. For example, in sub-Saharan Africa, 84 per cent of women non-agricultural workers are active in the informal economy compared to 63 per cent of male agricultural workers; in Latin America, these informal workers' statistics are 58 per cent for women and 48 per cent for men; and in Asia, the proportion of women and men in the non-agricultural informal economy is roughly equivalent (www.ilo.org/public/english/employment/gems/download/women.pdf).

Informal economies have flourished for a long time in most nations, but this sector has been growing in importance, largely because of economic hardship related to restructuring, globalization, and their effects of dislocation and forced migration. Increasingly, people are turning to 'hidden work' in order to survive in the midst of contracting opportunities in the formal economy. It has become a safety net of sorts for the poorest groups in society. Without doubt, workers in this sector have had to be enterprising. Some are highly motivated and possess valuable skills; others lack formally recognized credentials. Unfortunately, most people who rely on the informal economy for a living face precarious, unstable 'careers' in unregulated environments.

Time to Reflect

Have you or anyone you know ever worked in the informal or 'hidden' economy? Was this out of choice or necessity?

Managerial Strategies of Control

Scientific Management

To assess the new world of work, it is important first to understand the old one. So, let us go back in time. Since the days when Marx observed the rise of the factory system, capitalist goals of efficiency and profit-making have shaped the organization of work. Writing in the nineteenth century, Marx declared that work should be a central source of meaning and satisfaction in a person's life. In his words, 'the exercise of **labour power**, labour, is the worker's own life-activity, the manifestation of his own life' (cited in Rinehart, 2001: 13). But he noted that for most labouring people, work had lost meaning and creativity. Under capitalism, the worker 'works in order to live. . . . Life begins for him where this activity ceases' (cited ibid., 3).

By the early twentieth century, with the spread of mass production, much work (most notably in manufacturing) was being further divided into ever more unconnected and meaningless parts. The twentieth century witnessed the large-scale implementation of so-called **scientific management**, one of the most influential and long-lasting managerial strategies. Scientific management was a method of organizing work and controlling workers that was introduced by American engineer Frederick Winslow Taylor, so scientific management is also referred to as *Taylorism.*

Taylor applied the principles of 'science', or efficiency, to the human performance of labour. On the basis of his close observations of workers performing their jobs, he broke work processes down into simple tasks, each of which could be timed and organized into formal rules and standardized procedures. Taylor believed that once the work was subdivided, workers did not need to understand the entire process of production. Scientific management, in this sense, resulted in the separation of mental and manual labour, the conception of work from its execution. In short, it contributed to the deskilling of the worker.

Also in the twentieth century, Henry Ford, founder of the Ford Motor Car Company, applied the principles of scientific management (in tandem with the bureaucratic organization of work) to mass production of the automobile. Even if you have never stepped foot in an auto-manufacturing plant or other mass production facility, you are probably familiar with the assembly line. Richard Edwards (1979) called the moving assembly line an example of *technical control.* Technical control refers to the control of a workforce not directly by supervision (for example, by a foreperson), but indirectly by a machine.

While early researchers highlighted the application of Taylorism to manufacturing, this principle is now applied to many different types of work. In one form or other, scientific management has been implemented in offices (Lowe, 1987), schools, hospitals, and restaurants. Esther Reiter (1991) describes how the fast-food industry has carefully broken down the process of serving a burger from laying down the buns to evenly spreading the ketchup to distributing precisely half an ounce of onions. The total preparation time for a Burger King Whopper is 23 seconds—no more, no less.

Though efficient and 'rational', critics have argued that work broken down into simple parts results in degradation and dehumanization (Braverman, 1974). The most minute opportunities for individual decision-making and judgement are subverted. Marx introduced the concept of 'alienation' to describe the consequences for working people. **Alienation** is a structural condition of powerlessness that is rooted in a worker's relationship to the means of production. Insofar as workers have little or no control over their labour, work is no longer a source of fulfillment. According to Marx, under these conditions, workers become estranged from the products of their labour, from the work process itself, from each other, and from themselves (Rinehart, 1996).

Faced with the problem of alienated workforces, some employers have attempted to motivate workers with financial incentives. In the 1930s, Henry Ford introduced the 'Five Dollar Day'. In that era, five dollars constituted a relatively high rate of pay that would supposedly cover the living costs of not only the male autoworker but also his (dependent) wife and children. Decades later, J.H. Goldthorpe and colleagues' study of workers' orientations to work (1969) further supported the view that some people have an instrumental relationship to work. In this view, people can be compensated for meaningless work. Work can be a means to an end rather than an end in itself.

Two central problems contend against the assumption that money makes up for the meaninglessness of work. First, only a minority of employers do in fact compensate their employees for performing degraded and dehumanized work. In the popular media, we hear stories about $30 hourly wage rates for auto and steelworkers. But we must keep in mind that Ford, GM, and Stelco workers represent the privileged of the working class. The fact is that most employers are not willing to pay high wages—though they can be forced to do so, under the

OPEN FOR DISCUSSION

Hard Work Never Killed Anyone

Hard work never killed anyone! This is an old and familiar phrase. Teenagers are likely to hear it from their parents when they balk at having to cut the grass or shovel snow. Steelworkers, miners, and loggers hear it bellowed at them by their supervisors when they do not want to clean out filthy and toxic steel-making furnaces, work overtime to dig out more coal, or climb steep hills to cut down that next stand of trees.

But hard work does injure and kill. In 2004, 340,000 Canadian workers were injured on the job severely enough to lose time from work. In the same year, workers' compensation boards across the country accepted 928 fatality claims. Many would regard these as highly conservative estimates. That is, tens of thousands of workers who have accidents while at work do not report them, while official statistics of workplace fatalities fail to take into account the daily wear and tear of jobs that can take years off one's life—not to mention the problem of occupational disease.

Canadian workers are injured and killed on the job in at least three ways. First, some jobs such as mining, logging, fishing, and farming are very dangerous, and accident and fatality rates are unacceptably high. Second, accident rates are related to how fast and how long a person works at a job. The more hours a person works in a day, the greater the likelihood of an accident. Why? Fatigue. If you get tired shovelling snow, you can stop. If you are paid according to the number of laptops, shirtsleeves, or telephone calls you make, you are likely to push yourself beyond safe limits. And, if you are manipulating a fast-paced machine with sharp cutting tools, even a brief lapse in attention can result in serious injury. Third, years of working hard can lead to various occupational diseases that are both debilitating and fatal.

The change from an industrial to a 'post-industrial' or 'information' society has altered the patterns of workplace accidents somewhat. Over 30 years ago, the dominant form of injury compensated by provincial compensation boards involved crushed or severed limbs. Now, one-half of all accident/injury claims are related to strains and sprains, especially of the lower back and upper limbs. Why? Musculoskeletal injuries are on the rise because we are being asked to work harder and faster in jobs that are poorly designed and highly repetitive. Under such conditions, our bodies break down. We lose time from work. We may even lose our jobs. What we do not lose, however, is the chronic neck, shoulder, arm, and back pain.

But this is just the tip of the iceberg. The workers' compensation figures cited above apply overwhelmingly to injuries caused by identifiable workplace accidents. But what about occupational disease? Numerous studies link long-term exposure to toxic substances and chemicals such as asbestos, lead, benzene, and arsenic to cancer and other deadly diseases. So, too, waiters in bars and casino workers must deal with second-hand smoke, unruly customers, sexual harassment—all of which can lead to high levels of stress and subsequent health problems such as heart disease. Yet, these serious workplace health and safety problems rarely find their way into official accident and compensation statistics.

Again, we ask, why? One reason lies in strong business resistance: employers do not want such illnesses recognized as work-related as they would then have to pay some of the enormous costs associated with compensating occupational diseases. Another reason has to do with establishing proof. Given that most cancers and other serious illnesses have an incubation period ranging from 10 to 20 years from the moment of first exposure, what evidence is scientifically sufficient to prove that an exposure to a toxic chemical at some point in time caused her/his cancer? And what if the person also smoked cigarettes? And what if the person had changed jobs a few times? Every year, thousands of Canadians get ill and die from a work-related disease. They don't know this and the statistics do not show it.

Workers and unions in Canada have long protested these alarming scenarios. In the 1970s, such protests resulted in the passage of occupational health and safety laws that gave workers the right to know about the substances they were working with, the right to participate with management in identifying unsafe and unhealthy working conditions, and the right to refuse work they believed to be unsafe. While these rights apply to the majority of workers, unionized workers are the most knowledgeable about their health and safety rights and are most likely to exercise them on a regular basis.

In 1994, Sean Kells, a 19-year-old from Mississauga, Ontario, was killed when flammable liquid he was pouring into a vat was ignited by electricity. It was his third day on the job. The plant in which he was working was not unionized. He had received no safety training or safety information from his employer. He was not aware of his health and safety rights, including his right to refuse unsafe work. He might still be alive if his employer had obeyed the law.

—Robert Storey, Labour Studies and Sociology, McMaster University

pressure of strong unions such as the Canadian Auto Workers and the United Steelworkers of America. Consequently, the majority of people do not receive high monetary compensation. Most Canadians perform boring jobs and are not paid handsomely for doing so.

Second, this view overlooks the importance of workers' needs for *intrinsic satisfaction*—the need of human beings to find meaning in the work that they perform. As stated, whether they are Supreme Court judges, car assemblers, letter carriers, caretakers, or retail clerks, people need to find meaning in the work that they perform day in and day out. We have a basic human need for respect and dignity at work (Hodson, 2001). This holds true whether you are a man or woman, Canadian-born or a recent immigrant or a migrant labourer, in middle age or youth, in a part-time job or a career.

The Early Human Relations School

In the 1930s, social psychologists and managerial consultants began to recognize this basic human need. In a series of experiments at the Western Electric Company's Hawthorne plant in Chicago, an industrial psychologist named Elton Mayo discovered that attention to workers resulted in a significant improvement in their productivity. The Hawthorne studies played an important role in spawning a new school of management thought known as the **human relations** approach. The basic idea on which the human relations approach rests is that if managers want productive, motivated workers, they should recognize workers' social needs.

In contemporary workplaces, many early human relations principles are embedded in an array of organizational initiatives such as 'human resource management', 'total quality management', and 'quality of work life' programs. Employee-of-the-week schemes, employee suggestion boxes, quality circles, and job enrichment all reflect such managerial methods. All of these schemes highlight employee motivation by promoting a discourse of co-operation (rather than of conflict) between managers and workers, with the belief that happy workers are better workers.

A fundamental problem with the human relations approach to managing, however, is that such programs do not constitute real workplace democracy. Under such schemes, employers often create the illusion that workers are important and respected, their ideas valued and rewarded, but there is no real redistribution of power and control. Over time, employees begin to recognize the limits of their involvement. Moreover, some research has demonstrated that workers' suggestions for organizing work may backfire against them, resulting in layoffs for some and in the further rationalization of the work process for those who remain (Robertson et al., 1993).

The Social Organization of Work Today

Revolutionary New Technology

Today, popular writers and scholars alike are talking about the emergence of a new world of work, one that is rooted in a 'knowledge society'—a world that offers opportunity, an increase in leisure time, an experience of work that is far more positive than in the past. Are these assertions founded? Do people now have better jobs than their parents and grandparents? Have we rid the economy of many of the low-paying, dead-end, and routine jobs that characterized the past? In short, has work been transformed?

According to Daniel Bell (1973), the answer to these questions is 'Yes'. In *Post-Industrial Society*, Bell argues that we are now living in a post-industrial era, a new information economy, one based on the use of sophisticated microelectronic technology. With the decline of Taylorized manufacturing jobs and the rise of knowledge work, argues Bell, people are becoming highly skilled and jobs are becoming intrinsically rewarding.

Admittedly, most people agree that the new technology may eliminate routine, repetitive tasks, thereby freeing people to perform more challenging work. Think, for example, about preparing a research paper without a computer, printer, and access to the Internet. Moreover, the technology has had a positive impact on job creation. In fact, in Canada, information technology has created more jobs than it has eliminated. In a comparison of firms that relied extensively on sophisticated information technology with other, low-tech firms, the Conference Board of Canada found that the former produced more jobs than the latter (Lowe, 2000).

Notwithstanding these findings, some sociologists argue that, at the same time, the technology has created new forms of inequality and exacerbated old ones. While it has resulted in new, more challenging jobs for some people, many others have lost their jobs (or skills) as a result of technological change in the workplace. In the **service economy**, for instance, employers have relied extensively on computers and the new microelectronics to streamline work processes. In banking, many of the decisions (such as approving a bank loan) that used to be made at the discretion of people are now computer governed. And the introduction of automated bank machines has made redundant the work of thousands of tellers. As well, in various industries, computers have taken over the supervisory function of employee surveillance. With state-of-the-art computer equipment, and without the direct intervention of a supervisor, firms can now effectively enforce productivity quotas and monitor workers, especially those who perform highly routine tasks (Fox and Sugiman, 1999).

Another problem is that the technology is rapidly changing. Competence with the technology thus necessitates continually learning new skills and making ongoing investments in training. Often workers themselves assume the costs of such training. In the past, says Graham Lowe, employment was based on an implicit understanding of loyalty in exchange for job security; today, this idea has been replaced with a system based on 'individual initiative and merit'. Workers who go above and beyond, who contribute what managers sometimes call 'value added', who hone their skills—these are the workers who will be recognized and rewarded (Lowe, 2000: 61).

Moreover, opportunities for extra job-related training are unequal. Not surprisingly, they are closely linked to an employee's income and level of education. Lowe notes that only 3 in 10 Canadian workers annually receive training related to their present or future employment (ibid., 65). University graduates are twice as likely as high school graduates to be involved in such training. One in five workers who earns less than $15,000 participates in training, compared to half of those earning in excess of $75,000.

Flexible Work

Alongside information technology, some writers are extolling the benefits of related innovations in management methods. In business circles today, one hears buzzwords such as 'workplace restructuring', 'downsizing', and 'lean production'. All of these concepts are part of a relatively new managerial approach called flexibility. Flexibility (most often in tandem with technological innovation) has, as they say, 'held out the hand of promise'. It has been promoted as an improvement over the old human relations approach and an alternative to the Taylorist and Fordist methods that have long stripped workers of control and dignity (Sennett, 1998). Critics, on the other hand, say differently. Smart, young managers trained in the postmodern language of flexibility may introduce seemingly new forms of managing and organizing work and adapt them to an increasingly competitive and precarious global context, but on close inspection, they claim, such strategies are firmly grounded in earlier approaches.

Most contemporary flexibility strategies are based on one or a combination of two approaches: *numerical flexibility* and *flexible specialization* (also called *functional flexibility*).

Numerical Flexibility

Numerical flexibility involves shrinking or eliminating the core workforce (in continuous jobs, and full-time positions) and replacing them with workers in *non-standard* (or *contingent*) *employment.* **Non-standard work** is a term used to describe various employment arrangements such as part-time work, temporary (seasonal and other part-year) work, contracting out or outsourcing (work that was previously done in-house), and self-employment. Non-standard work is, in short, based on an employment relationship that is far more tenuous than those of the past (Jackson and Robinson, 2000; Vosko, 2000, 2003).

When you hear about non-standard work, what comes to mind? If you are like most Canadians, you think of jobs in the fast-food or retail industries—

'McJobs'. But in the current economy, non-standard work arrangements now characterize most spheres of employment. We need look no further than the university or college, for example, to see the employment of people in non-standard jobs. In these institutions of higher learning, you may discover that many of your courses are taught by part-time or sessional instructors, some of whom hold Ph.D.s, others of whom are graduate students. These individuals are paid by the university to teach on a course-by-course or session-by-session basis. Sessional or part-time instructors typically do not work on a full-time basis, and they seldom receive assurances of stable employment.

According to the Economic Council of Canada, non-standard labour represents the fastest growing type of employment in this country (Duffy et al., 1997: 53). While 6 per cent of all employed persons worked part-time (fewer than 30 hours per week) in 1975, that proportion had risen to over 18 per cent by 1997 (Nelson and Robinson, 2002: 239). Today, non-standard work represents over one-third of all jobs. Though this form of employment may be found in all industries, non-standard workers are most likely to be found in the primary and utilities industries, accommodation and food services, and construction or trades (www.statcan.ca/Daily/English/041215/d041215c.htm).

Many writers have cogently argued that the growth of non-standard work is closely linked to the corporate goals of flexibility and global restructuring (Harvey, 1989). Not unlike the 'reserve army of labour' described by Karl Marx, non-standard employees provide owners and managers with a ready supply of labour to 'hire and fire' as the market demands. Employers invest minimally in these workers and offer them only a limited commitment. In order to remain competitive in the global market, it is argued, corporations must reduce labour costs through downsizing, that is, laying off permanent, full-time workers and replacing them with part-time, temporary, and contract labour (Vosko, 2000).

Yet, unyielding market forces notwithstanding, there is also evidence that 'precarious jobs have become the norm much faster in some countries than in others' (Jackson and Robinson, 2000: 50). For example, in the United States, non-standard work grew quickly in the 1980s, but in comparison to Canada, in the 1990s, its growth has been limited by low unemployment. Moreover, in much of Europe, unions and employment laws have (until recently) limited the growth of contract work and substandard part-time work. In the Netherlands, a country known for having one of the most flexible labour markets in continental Europe, part-timers receive equal wages and benefits with full-time employees, and contract workers must be given a permanent job within a specified time period (ibid.).

Another offshoot of the increasingly precarious relationship between employers and workers is the growth in self-employment. In the 1990s, one driving force behind self-employment was the move of large firms and governments to contract out work that formerly had been performed in-house by a core workforce (ibid.). In fact, throughout the 1990s, growth in self-employment was a leading labour market trend. In 1998, self-employed individuals accounted for 18 per cent of all employment in Canada, and between 1989 and 1997, self-employment constituted about 80 per cent of all job growth (Lowe, 2000). In fiscal 2004–5, self-employment in Canada increased by 61,400, thereby outgrowing paid employment, though the share of all jobs to self-employment has declined since 1997–8 (www.hrsdc.gc.ca/en/ei/reports/eimar2005.shtml).

Contrary to romantic images of the self-employed as benefiting from flexible work schedules, autonomy, and economic success, research indicates that they are not always better off than their waged or salaried counterparts. Most self-employed people work alone, often in small enterprises. Only a minority run companies that employ others (Lowe, 2000). Furthermore, they tend to work excessively long hours and, on average, accrue about the same earnings as regular employees. In addition, gender-based pay differentials are more pronounced among the self-employed, and work is highly polarized. In other words, recent growth in self-employment has been especially strong at the top of the job hierarchy (for example, among engineers and accountants) and at the bottom (for instance, among domestic cleaners and salespeople).

Part-time and temporary workers tend to be women and young people, though not exclusively (see Table 10.3). Because of these demographics, people assume that the casual employment relationship is not problematic; indeed, some believe it to be desirable. Admittedly, there are individuals who choose non-standard work in the hope that it will offer heightened flexibility to facilitate the competing demands of job and family or job and school. Yet, many other people accept these employment terms on an involuntary basis, largely because they have no alternatives. Moreover, studies suggest that many non-standard work arrangements do not in fact provide employees with greater flexibility (Vosko, 2000) or that they offer flexibility only to favoured employees (Sennett, 1998).

Furthermore, non-standard workers as a whole receive relatively low wages and few benefits. Consequently, many people who rely on this type of work must resort to holding multiple jobs in an effort to make ends

Table 10.3 Full-time and Part-time Employment by Sex and Age Group, 2002–6 (000s)

	2002	2003	2004	2005	2006
Both sexes					
Total	15,310.4	15,672.3	15,947.0	16,169.7	16,484.3
15–24 years	2,399.1	2,449.4	2,461.0	2,472.5	2,535.8
25–44 years	7,575.6	7,571.5	7,594.0	7,597.5	7,610.7
45 years and over	5,335.7	5,651.4	5,892.0	6,099.7	6,337.8
Full-time	12,439.3	12,705.3	12,998.1	13,206.2	13,509.7
15–24 years	1,323.1	1,344.3	1,361.4	1,370.2	1,419.8
25–44 years	6,627.0	6,624.7	6,671.2	6,684.7	6,730.9
45 years and over	4,489.1	4,736.3	4,965.5	5,151.3	5,359.0
Part-time	2,871.1	2,967.0	2,948.9	2,963.5	2,974.7
15–24 years	1,076.0	1,105.1	1,099.6	1,102.3	1,116.0
25–44 years	948.5	946.8	922.8	912.8	879.9
45 years and over	846.6	915.0	926.5	948.4	978.8
Men					
Full-time	7,287.9	7,423.0	7,559.3	7,664.0	7,781.0
15–24 years	763.9	774.9	781.2	782.5	809.2
25–44 years	3,831.1	3,832.2	3,834.1	3,832.6	3,845.6
45 years and over	2,692.9	2,815.9	2,944.1	3,048.9	3,126.2
Part-time	896.5	925.0	921.3	930.7	946.1
15–24 years	460.4	468.3	467.1	456.5	467.7
25–44 years	197.4	196.9	189.8	199.5	189.7
45 years and over	238.8	259.8	264.4	274.7	288.7
Women					
Full-time	5,151.4	5,282.3	5,438.8	5,542.3	5,728.7
15–24 years	559.2	569.4	580.2	587.8	610.5
25–44 years	2,796.0	2,792.5	2,837.2	2,852.1	2,885.3
45 years and over	1,796.2	1,920.4	2,021.4	2,102.4	2,232.8
Part-time	1,974.6	2,041.9	2,027.6	2,032.8	2,028.5
15–24 years	615.6	636.8	632.4	645.8	648.4
25–44 years	751.2	749.9	733.0	713.3	690.1
45 years and over	607.8	655.2	662.1	673.7	690.0

Source: Statistics Canada, at: <www40.statcan.ca/l01/cst01/labor12.htm>.

meet. People carve out a living by stringing together a host of low-paying, part-time, and temporary jobs. Often this involves moonlighting or doing shift work, situations that no doubt put added strain on families.

Interestingly, along with the expansion of the non-standard workforce, there has been an increase in overtime work for full-time employees. And while there has been a significant rise in overtime hours for both sexes, men are especially likely to work beyond the standard 40-hour week. As well, the lengthening of the work day has been more pronounced among managers than among employees. And on the whole, more of this overtime is unpaid. Paid overtime tends to be concentrated in unionized workplaces and in blue-collar manufacturing and construction jobs (Jackson and Robinson, 2000). Unpaid overtime, in comparison, is more marked in the female-dominated public sector such as in teaching and social work (suggesting that women are more likely to put in overtime without pay), as well as among managers and professionals.

There are many reasons for the recent increase in overtime work. First, as a result of downsizing and restructuring, people simply must put in longer hours to get the job done. Say Andrew Jackson and David Robinson, 'the survivors have to pick up the work of those who have left as a result of layoffs or early retirement' (ibid., 86). Fear of future job loss is also a potent factor behind putting in extra hours. In a 'survival-of-the-fittest' corporate culture, long hours are viewed as evidence of effort and commitment. Undoubtedly, many workers also internalize the ethic of doing more with less, particularly those who are serving the public and helping to make up for cuts through unpaid work. In short, in the face of general labour market uncertainty, many core employees feel pressured to work overtime, whether or not they so desire. As a result, we now have, 'side by side, underemployment and overemployment, with high levels of insecurity and stress on all sides' (Duffy et al., 1997: 57).

In light of these trends, for most Canadians, the concept of a career is a remnant of the past. The gold watch for 50 years of continuous service to the same company is not attainable in the new workplace scenario. Says Richard Sennett, 'flexibility today brings back this arcane sense of the job, as people do lumps of labor, pieces of work, over the course of a lifetime' (1998: 9). Living in this era of economic uncertainty, with the attendant worry about layoffs and job loss, is, not surprisingly, a major source of stress for people in Canada (Jackson and Robinson, 2000).

Flexible Specialization

Another component of the new flexibility is **flexible specialization** (or *functional flexibility*, often called *flex spec*). Flexible specialization involves multi-skilling, job rotation, the organization of workers into teams, and the concentration of power—without the centralization of power. Flexible specialization has been called the antithesis of the system of production embodied in Fordism (Sennett, 1998). Under the new system, the old auto assembly line has been replaced by 'islands of specialized production'. These new work units, or *islands*, allow businesses to respond quickly to fluctuations in market demand, especially in industries such as fashion and textiles where there is a short product life.

Typically, flex spec is also accompanied by a goal of co-operation and flexible arrangements between labour and management rather than adversarial relations based on strict contractual agreements. Where Taylorist management strategies have rationalized production by eliminating the need for workers to make decisions, a flex-spec organization attempts to eliminate 'waste' by employing workers' knowledge of their jobs in the rationalization process. Working in teams, employees are given responsibility for scheduling, planning the work, rotating workers among jobs, and meeting quotas (Fox and Sugiman, 1999). By increasing workers' responsibility, team organization diminishes the need for supervision—although it provides employees with no added authority.

Finally, information technology has been an integral component of flexibility strategies. Flexible specialization is suited to high technology: 'Thanks to the computer, industrial machines are easy to reprogram and configure. The speed of modern communications also has favoured flexible specialization, by making global market data instantly available to a company' (Sennett, 1998: 52). Unlike the earlier mechanization, the new telecommunications technology enables employers to relocate work easily from one site to another, thereby scattering workforces to various parts of the country, continent, or world. As a result of teleworking, you can make a hotel reservation or check your credit level from Picton, Ontario, and be speaking to a reservation agent or debt collector in Tennessee. Likewise, with the availability of portable computers, fax machines, cell phones, Blackberries, and other Internet connections, some people may simply do their work from home rather than in an office or factory. Work can now follow people home.

Flexibility for Whom?

We may now point to a polarization of jobs. At one end of the spectrum are the good jobs, at the other the bad. There is no bulging middle. There has, in other words, been a widening of inequalities. Good jobs offer decent pay and intrinsic rewards (fulfillment, autonomy, the opportunity to exercise knowledge and acquire skill).

Time to Reflect

Have you ever worked or do you now work at what could be termed a 'McJob'? Did it or does it fulfill your needs? In what ways? In what ways, if any, did or does it fall short? Would you like to work at a 'McJob' for the rest of your working life? Why or why not?

When you next order a pizza, complain about the non-arrival of a package, or report a lost credit card, you may find yourself talking to someone in India—thanks to the globalization of work and the export of Canadian jobs. (Amit Bhargava/Corbis)

But while the new information society has created some good jobs, these are not held by all, or even most, people in this country. And whether they work in the primary, manufacturing, or service economy, as manual labourers or as professionals, people are facing increasing uncertainty in the labour market.

Downsizing, the resulting increase in non-standard employment, and the **globalization of work** have all contributed to this uncertainty. Says Sennett, 'What's peculiar about uncertainty today is that it exists without any looming historical disaster; instead it is woven into the everyday practices of a vigorous capitalism. Instability is meant to be normal' (1998: 31).

The Changing Face of Labour: Diversity among Workers

Just as places of work have changed dramatically over time, so too has the workforce itself. Workplaces today, whether they be offices, factories, hospitals, or classrooms, are becoming increasingly diverse. Only a minority of families relies on a single paycheque. First Nations people make up a growing proportion of the paid labour force in certain geographic areas. People of colour, some of whom are immigrants to this country, many Canadian-born, currently have a stronger-than-ever presence, particularly in big cities such as Vancouver, Toronto, and Montreal. As well, the workforce has become more highly educated and younger. As a result of these changes, students of work must turn their attention to some pressing new problems.

Gendered Work

The participation of women in the paid labour force has increased steadily over the past four decades. In Canada today, women constitute approximately 47 per cent of the labour force (www.statcan.ca/english/freepub/89F0133XIE2003000.pdf). Most striking has been a rise in the employment rates of married women and mothers of children under the age of six. Recent census

HUMAN DIVERSITY

Offshore Migrant Farm Workers: A New Form of Slavery?

What does slavery have to do with a free and democratic country like Canada? Slavery did exist in the eighteenth and early nineteenth centuries in Canada, and some people think that there are groups of people who continue to work in this country under conditions that bear a strong resemblance to slavery. Slavery involves the ownership of one person by another, and is a form of unfree labour. Unfree labour refers to working arrangements where individuals are not allowed to freely circulate in the labour market and where they face political and/or legal constraints regarding where, and how, they work.

Most people in Canada work as 'free labourers'. This does not mean that they work for free, but rather that they are free to choose whom they work for. They can also decide where they want to live, what they eat and drink, and what they do in their leisure time. As a result, if they do not get along with their employer, or feel that they are underpaid and would be better off financially in another job, there is nothing stopping them from quitting and finding a new job. In other words, most Canadians are free workers because they are able to circulate in the labour market and do not face political or legal constraints in shaping their decisions about where to work.

Who, if anyone, are the new slaves in Canada? While they are not really slaves in the classical sense of the term, the 16,000 workers who come to Canada every year from the Caribbean and Mexico to work in Canadian agriculture are a form of unfree labour. Slavery may be too strong a term to describe who they are, but their condition of unfreedom does bear a strong resemblance to slavery.

What makes these workers different from other Canadians, and from immigrants who come here to build better lives for themselves? Migrant workers from the Caribbean and Mexico come to Canada under labour contracts. These contracts specify how long they can remain in the country and the conditions under which they must work. Workers are allowed to stay in Canada for between three and eight months every year. When their contracts expire, or if they breach one of the terms of their contracts, they are expected to leave the country. Workers pay for a portion of their transportation, and must pay their employers back to help them cover the costs of accommodation. In some cases, workers bunk five or six to a room and live in hot, overcrowded conditions. However, the main reason why they are considered to be unfree labourers stems from their inability to quit or change jobs in Canada without the permission of their employer and a representative of the federal government. If they do quit their jobs with a Canadian employer without permission, they are subject to deportation from the country.

Why does this condition of unfreedom matter? After all, some people think that compared to where they come from, migrant workers have it good here. They invariably make more money here than they would have back home so they should be grateful for the opportunity to come here to work, even if it is only temporarily. Even though no one is forcing them to sign a labour contract and come to Canada to work, it does matter that they are a form of unfree labour. Their lack of choice when it comes to whom they work for and their inability to vote with their feet and find better-paying jobs in other sectors of the Canadian economy mean that farm employers have a tremendous amount of power over migrant workers. In many cases, workers are fearful of saying 'no' when they are asked to do jobs that are dangerous and might harm their health. And employers who have a captive labour force do not have market incentives to improve wages or working conditions.

Some church groups in places where migrant workers live, support groups, and labour unions like the United Food and Commercial Workers Union are organizing to try to help improve the wages and working conditions of these unfree migrant workers.

—Vic Satzewich, McMaster University

data indicate that the two-breadwinner (also called *dual-earner*) family is now the norm.

Decades—indeed, over a century—of struggle and activism by feminists have resulted in important gains. Paid work is one arena in which these gains have been most prominent. In Canada, we now have employment equity legislation (albeit limited) in the federal government and laws enforcing equal pay for work of equal value. It is important to remember, though, that many of these breakthroughs are relatively recent. Into the 1950s, companies and governments still restricted the employment of married women, overtly defined work as 'female' and 'male', and upheld gender-based seniority systems (Sugiman, 1994).

Today, many young women and men entering the labour force are unaware of the blatant sexual inequalities of the past. Whether or not they self-identify as feminists, women today are building their careers on a feminist foundation. If not for the challenges posed by women's rights activists, university lecture halls would be filled exclusively by men, women would not be permitted entry into the professions or management, and paid employment would simply not be an option after marriage.

But just as women's historical breakthroughs are instructive, so too are the persisting inequalities. In spite of a dramatic increase in female labour-force participation, women and men are by no means equal in the labour market. The **social institution** of work is still very much a gendered one. It is important that women have made inroads in non-traditional fields of manual labour, the professions, and management and administration, but the majority of women remain concentrated in female-dominated occupations such as retail salesperson, secretary, cashier, registered nurse, elementary school teacher, babysitter, and receptionist, while men are more commonly truck drivers, janitors, farmers, motor vehicle mechanics, and construction trade helpers, for example. Particularly troubling is the finding that Canadian women who have completed university or community college are three times more likely than their male counterparts (24 per cent and 8 per cent, respectively) to move into a clerical or service job (Nelson and Robinson, 2002: 226). To the extent that occupational segregation by sex has lessened somewhat over time, it is more because of the entry of men into female-dominated occupations than the reverse.

As well, women (as well as youth of both sexes) are more likely than men to be employed on a part-time and temporary basis. For years now, women have made up approximately 70 per cent of the part-time workforce in Canada. And while the majority of the self-employed are men, the 1990s witnessed a rapid growth in women's self-employment. In comparing the sexes, we also see that self-employed men are more likely than self-employed women to hire others—male employers outnumbered females three to one—and that businesses operated by men are more likely to be in the goods sector whereas female-run businesses are likely to be in the less lucrative service sector (ibid., 242).

These trends—labour market segregation by sex and the overrepresentation of women in precarious employment—have contributed to gender-based differences in earnings. While the pay gap between women and men employed full-time and full-year has narrowed over time, on average, women still earn less than men even when we take into account, occupation, age, and education. Furthermore, the narrowing of this wage gap was largely the result of an increase in time worked for women and of falling or stagnant wages for men, with only a modest increase in women's earnings. In addition to this, gender-based earnings differentials may, to a large degree, be attributed to women's concentration in part-time and temporary work. When we compare women employed on a full-time basis with their male counterparts, the gap narrows—though, as noted above, it does not disappear. Currently, a woman employed full-time earns 72.5 cents for every dollar earned by a man (www.betterchoice.ca/en/payequity.htm).

All women are not, of course, in the same position. Immigrant women, women of colour, and Aboriginal women bear the brunt of income and occupational polarization by sex. In consequence, their average annual earnings are disproportionately low. In her research on various categories of women, Monica Boyd (1999) concludes that earnings differentials increase between Canadian-born women and foreign-born women, especially when the latter group are of colour and when they are not fluent in English or French. In addition, foreign-born women who are currently residents of Canada are more likely than Canadian-born women to be employed in particular segments of the service sector—namely, those that are typically labour-intensive, poorly paid, and dominated by small firms (Vosko, 2000). While men of colour are concentrated in either professional occupations or service jobs, women of colour are more likely than Canadian women as a whole to perform manual labour. Aboriginal women likewise are concentrated in service or clerical work (Aboriginal men are more likely to perform manual labour than other kinds of work).

Faced with multiple forms of **discrimination**, working-class women of colour and some female immigrants have come to occupy job ghettos. Indeed, many of the jobs that typically are performed by working-class people of colour have a 'hidden' quality: the work they do is not noticed; the workers are rendered invisible. All too often, we regard private domestic workers and nannies, hotel and office cleaners, taxi drivers, health-care aides, and dishwashers—all of whom perform indispensable labour—as simply part of the backdrop (Arat-Koc, 1990; Das Gupta, 1996). Not only are they physically out of sight (in basements, in kitchens, working at night when everyone else has gone), they are out of mind.

In documenting sex-based inequalities in employment, social scientists have produced reams of statistics. But there are many other ways in which we may speak of the gendering of work, some not easily quantifiable. Joan Acker (1990) writes about the process by which jobs and organizations come to be gendered, regardless of the sex of job-holders. The bureaucratic rules and procedures, hierarchies, and informal organizational culture may rest on a set of gender-biased assumptions, for example. In *Secretaries Talk* (1988), Rosemary Pringle highlights the ways in which gendered family relationships are reproduced in workplace relations between bosses (fathers) and secretaries (wives, mistresses, daughters). Pringle describes how male bosses determine the boundaries between home and work, public and private, whereas 'secretaries do not have this luxury. Male bosses go into their secretaries' offices unannounced, assume the right to pronounce on their clothes and appearance, have them doing housework and personal chores, expect overtime at short notice and assume the right to ring them at home' (Pringle, 1988: 51).

There are many formal and informal mechanisms that prevent women from entering male-dominated occupations. Cynthia Cockburn (1983) explores the ways in which a culture of manhood became very much a part of the printing trade. For years, the link between masculine identities, masculine culture, and the printing trade was so strong that it made the occupation completely impenetrable to women. Sugiman (1994) describes how women attempted to carve out for themselves 'pockets of femininity' in the male-dominated auto plants of southern Ontario during World War II. By the war's end, however, women's presence was no longer welcome. Most were hastily dismissed from the industry.

Women work in the assembly department of the British Munitions Supply Company in Verdun, Quebec, *c.* 1916–18. (NAC, PA-024435)

Today, many young women plan to both have a professional career and raise a family, but they are not quite sure how they will combine the two. Feminist researchers have demonstrated how the very concept of 'career' is gendered, built on a masculine model. Career success depends on the assumption of a wife at home—a helper who will pick up the children from school, arrange dinner parties, and generally free the 'breadwinner' to work late at nights or on weekends and for out-of-town business travel.

Furthermore, feminist analysis has called attention to the complex link between paid and unpaid labour, employment and family. With two breadwinners, both of whom are spending increasing hours in their paid jobs, families are under enormous pressure (see Figure 10.1). While the demands of paid work have risen over time, so too have pressures on family life. Government restructuring and cutbacks in resources have affected public daycare, after-school programs, special needs programs, and care of the elderly and the disabled. Who picks up the slack? The family. One consequence has been an intensification of (unpaid) family work and growing tensions within families as people try to cope.

In a study of working-class families in Flin Flon, Manitoba, Meg Luxton (1980) introduced the concept of a *double day* of labour—the combination of paid and unpaid labour that must be performed in the course of a day. Usually, notes Luxton, this double burden is carried by women. Every day, millions of people put in a 'second shift' of unpaid labour after they get home from their paying jobs. According to Hochschild and Machung, (1989), this second shift amounts to one extra month of 24-hour days of work per year. Hochschild (1997) also speaks to the experiences of millions of North American families in her study of the 'time bind'. The time bind has resulted in overworked, stressed people and in the downsizing and outsourcing of family responsibilities. Children are cranky, parents are rushed, and the concept of 'leisure' is laughable. Hochschild suggests that rather than leave families with the 'leftovers' of paid work, people should start challenging employers to more seriously consider the conflicting needs of family and employment.

Race and Racialized Work

The trends we have so far discussed (precarious work, heightened job insecurities, and underemployment) have had a disproportionate impact on groups who have long faced discrimination in the labour market and in society as a whole: women, people of colour, and indigenous people. But though we now have an abundance of

Figure 10.1 Measures of Time Scarcity

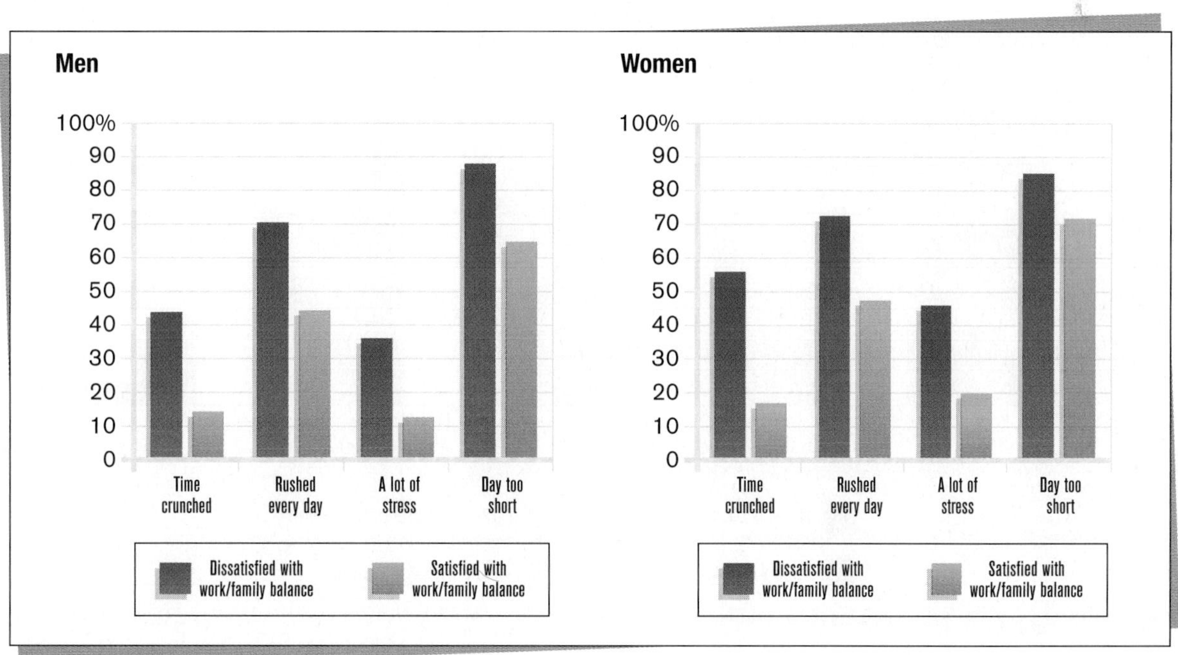

Source: Adapted from Statistics Canada, *General Social Survey*, 1998.

research on the gendering of work, sociologists in Canada have paid far less attention to the relationship between race, citizenship, and employment.

Barriers faced by people of colour, by Aboriginal Canadians, and by some immigrant groups are most often demonstrated in unemployment and earnings disparities. Aboriginal peoples comprise only a tiny percentage of the working-age population, yet this group is growing rapidly and already constitutes a sizable share of the labour force in some cities (Jackson and Robinson, 2000: 70). **Unemployment rates** for Aboriginals are disturbingly high, more than double that for the Canadian population as a whole (24 per cent for Aboriginal men and 22 per cent for Aboriginal women. In addition, over half of Aboriginals are in part-time employment—jobs that offer little security—and they are concentrated in marginalized sectors of the economy where they face low pay, seasonal jobs, and high levels of discrimination in hiring (canadianlabour.ca/index.php/Aboriginal Workers/464). Furthermore, the economic prospects for those who live on reserves are even more bleak. Close to half of the off-reserve Aboriginal population live in poverty (Jackson and Robinson, 2000: 71).

The category 'people of colour' is quite diverse, containing significant differences according to class, education, and citizenship status. In Canada, about one in 10 workers is defined as being of colour (the official census term is 'visible minority' and excludes Aboriginal Canadians), and over 80 per cent of this group are relatively recent immigrants (ibid., 69). Today, immigrants of colour (compared to earlier generations of immigrants) are finding it extremely difficult to close the employment gap with native-born Canadians, as it is, more generally, for visible minorities in Canada (see Figure 10.2). In 2000, the average annual earnings of Canadian-born workers of colour was $21,983, compared to $25,205 for immigrant workers of colour and $30,141 for other persons born in Canada (labourfutures.ca/Section%206.pdf). And these gaps persist even when we control for age and education. Typically, recent immigrants are younger than the labour force as a whole, but they also have more schooling. One problem is that foreign credentials are not always respected in Canada, thus contributing to a high concentration of immigrants of colour in low-wage jobs (Jackson and Robinson, 2000: 69–70).

Figure 10.2 Distribution of Annual Earnings, Visible Minorities and Non-Visible Minorities, 2001

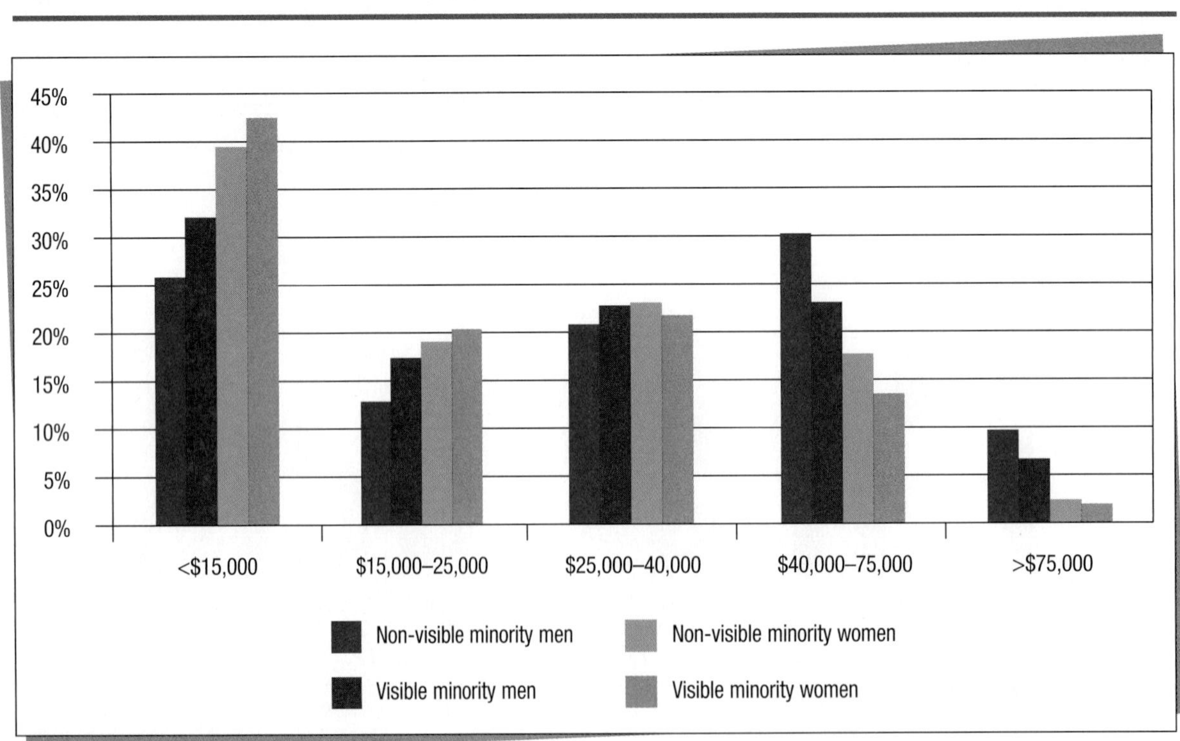

Source: Adapted from Statistics Canada, *Statistical Area Classification: Highlight Tables, 2001 Counts, For Canada, Provinces and Territories,* 2001 Census, Catalogue no. 97f0024, 27 Feb. 2004.

Likewise, recent immigrants are far more likey to experience unemployment in their first five years in Canada as compared to migrants who have been in this country for longer. For example, in 2001, the unemployment rate among men aged 25–44 who arrived between 1996 and 2001 was 11 per cent. Among women it was even higher at 15.8 per cent. These statistics merit concern about whether certain immigrant groups are being constrained from converting relatively high human capital (such as a university education) and a desire to work, into strong economic performance and socio-economic mobility. Equally alarming is the finding that immigrants who arrived in this country in the latter part of the 1980s and through the 1990s, have faced an even greater earnings gap relative to native-born Canadians. Moreover, this gap has not rapidly closed as immigrants spend more time in this country (www.migrationinformation.org/Profiles/display.cfm?ID=348).

It is not surprising, then, that many immigrants who reside in large cities such as Toronto, Montreal, and Vancouver experience high levels of poverty. While low-income rates among the Canadian-born generally dropped across the country, throughout the last decade, low-income rates for people living in our major cities actually rose, as did the low-income rate for immigrants who have resided in Canada for fewer than 20 years (www.migrationinformation.org/Profiles/display.cfm?ID=348).

Strong economic need also is experienced disproportionately by some groups of native-born Canadians. Roughly 45 per cent of black households in Canada , for example, live in poverty. Furthermore, there is evidence of race-based inequities in earnings. On the whole, people of colour earn about 15 per cent less than the total Canadian workforce (Jackson and Robinson, 2000: 70). And among this group, the pay gap is much greater for men than women (though we must consider that women generally have much lower earnings than men). These lower earnings are in part a result of this group's concentration in low-paying, relatively low-skilled jobs, their underrepresentation in skilled jobs, and their higher rates of unemployment.

Though telling, these statistics reveal only one dimension of the research on disadvantaged groups. It is equally important to recognize that because of racial and cultural differences, people experience the work world in distinct ways. In their study *Who Gets the Work*, Frances Henry and Effie Ginzberg (1985) found a striking incidence of discrimination directed at job seekers. For example, when whites and blacks with similar qualifications applied for entry-level positions that had been advertised in a newspaper, jobs were offered three times more often to whites than to black applicants. Similarly, of the job seekers who made inquiries by telephone, those who had accents (especially South Asian and Caribbean) were often quickly screened out by employers.

Furthermore, the role of the Canadian state historically in promoting or facilitating racialized work has been documented extensively (Schecter, 1998). Agnes Calliste (1993) notes that between 1950 and 1962, Canadian immigration authorities admitted limited numbers of Caribbean nurses, but under rules different from those for white immigrant nurses. Black nurses were expected to have nursing qualifications superior to those demanded of whites. Several scholars (Arat-Koc, 1990, 1992; Bakan and Stasiulis, 1994, 1995; Daenzer, 1993) have also discussed the role of the Canadian state in addressing the need for cheap child-care workers by importing women from the developing world (the Caribbean and the Philippines, in particular) to perform domestic labour, without granting them full citizenship rights.

Often, jobs and occupations come to be racialized (that is, to adopt a racial label) as a result of formal and informal barriers that prevent their holders from exiting (Calliste, 1993; Das Gupta, 1996). In a study of black workers in automotive foundries, Sugiman found that after years of intense discrimination, workers themselves may come to circumscribe their 'choices'. Over the course of many decades, most black men remained where they had started—in the foundry. In the words of one foundry worker, 'Their idea was, "well, the white man don't want you up there no how, so why . . . put yourself in a position where you know you're not wanted"' (Sugiman, 2001: 102).

Youth

In Canada today, youth (persons 15–24 years old) constitute a much smaller share of the population than in past years (Lowe, 2000: 110). Nevertheless, the youth labour market is expanding at a significant rate. Curiously, young people still receive relatively little attention in studies of work. But young people today are facing harsh economic conditions, with the youth unemployment rate roughly 50 per cent higher than that of the population as a whole. Throughout the 1990s, in Canada, the overall high unemployment rate, government deficit-cutting, public- and private-sector downsizing, and various other wage-reduction strategies resulted in a contracting job market. In consequence, large numbers of youth withdrew from the labour market, returning to school or staying in school for longer periods (ibid., 109).

The research presents us with a woeful picture. Study after study suggests that young people are in important ways no different from the majority of Canadian workers. They want high-quality work—work that is interesting and challenging and that provides a sense of accomplishment (ibid.). And youth have been increasing their human capital to acquire such jobs. Notably, young people are acquiring more education. (While a university degree does not guarantee a job, young people are still better off if they have the formal credentials.) But while Canadian youth are better-schooled on the whole, they are also working less, and in jobs for which they feel that they are overqualified. Young people are most likely to be employed in low-paying service-sector jobs such as fast food restaurants, clothing stores, and grocery stores. For most students, contingent work is all that is available.

Some writers argue that the youth labour market makes a perfect accompaniment to the new goals of managerial flexibility. Employers invest in the belief that young people will have a limited commitment to the goals of the firm and that they expect to stay in jobs temporarily, as a stop-gap measure discontinuous with their adult careers and identities (Tannock, 2001). Stuart Tannock explains that youth themselves partially accept the popular **ideology** that positions them 'as a separate class of workers who deserve less than adult workers do. Good jobs are predominantly the privilege of adulthood. Young workers must be content at first to spend their time in a tier of lower-quality service and retail employment. Dreams of meaningful work must be deferred' (ibid., 109). Many young people compare themselves not to other workers across the spectrum, but exclusively to other youth workers (Sennett, 1998). Consequently, youth are more pliable and passive. Also, because their jobs are viewed as transient, youth are not as likely to become unionized. All of these features render them an extremely exploitable source of labour.

But as Tannock points out, youth are not stop-gap workers simply because they are young: they are also stop-gap workers because of the poor conditions under which they have to labour—conditions that have been created by employers in the service sector. But despite the popular view that young people are not especially concerned about their conditions of work, there is now much evidence that points to the contrary: 'Teenagers and young adults working in these industries, who expect to have long lives ahead of them, worry that their jobs, which are supposed to be meaningless, stop-gap places of employment, will have lasting and detrimental effects on their bodies and future life activities' (Tannock, 2001: 54).

Workers' Coping and Resistance: The Struggle for Dignity and Rights

Finding Meaning in Work

Regardless of the many differences among Canadian workers today, one point remains clear: most Canadians want work that is personally fulfilling (Lowe, 2000). People have a powerful desire to maintain dignity at work (Hodson, 2001). Some of us are fortunate to hold jobs that offer challenge, jobs in which we can exercise autonomy and from which we can reap fruitful economic rewards. But even the 'good jobs' are not always meaningful. And there are many jobs that are rarely rewarding. How do people cope with their work?

Sociologists have found that no matter how meaningless the job, people seek meaning in their work. Sometimes this is done through the culture of the workplace. People who have boring, routine jobs, for example, may make a game out of their work, varying repetitions, altering pace and intensity, imagining the lives of customers. As well, the social component of work (peer relations) is frequently a source of pleasure. In some workplaces, employees regularly exchange gossip, flirt, engage in sexualized play, share personal problems, debate politics, ridicule management. Relationships with co-workers often make the job itself more bearable, if not meaningful. In cases where the organization of work permits such exchanges, the lines between employment and leisure can become blurred.

Job satisfaction studies suggest that work is not all that bad. Most people report that they are generally satisfied with their jobs (Lowe, 2000). On close examination, though, discontent broods near the surface. At the same time that they report satisfaction, a majority of workers say that their jobs are somewhat or highly stressful, that they are not sufficiently involved, recognized, and rewarded, and that their talents are underutilized (ibid.). In addition, there are high rates of absenteeism, oppositional attitudes, slacking off, pilfering, and even destruction of company property. Some workers simply quit their jobs. But in the face of a competitive job market, family responsibilities, consumer debt, and, for some, few marketable skills, this is not a viable option. Furthermore, it is telling that even though they themselves claim to like their jobs, many people add that they do not want their own children to end up doing the same kind of work (Sennett, 1988).

Faced with unfair, unsafe, and sometimes unchallenging work, workers will be discontent. They will find ways to make changes, to resist. The question is, how? Individual acts of coping and resistance may give workers the feeling of agency and control, but insofar as they are individual acts, they rarely result in a fundamental or widespread change in conditions of work. In order to effect large-scale change, people must resort to collective measures.

Professions and Negotiating Professional Control

Securing professional control is an option for middle-class people who possess formally recognized credentials and can claim expertise in an area. When we think of a *professional*, who comes to mind? Physicians, educators, psychiatrists, dentists, lawyers, engineers, accountants. Some sociologists (proponents of trait theory) have attempted to define professionals with reference to a checklist of characteristics (Freidson, 1970). This checklist includes, for example, possession of a body of esoteric or abstract knowledge, reliance on a specialized technical language or vocabulary, and membership in associations that control entry and membership in the occupation through licensing, accreditation, and regulation.

Critics, however, argue that trait theory does not fully explain how and why some occupations come to be defined as professional while others do not. Rather than list a series of traits that define a profession, Terence Johnson (1972) highlights the resources available to different occupational groups. These resources have enabled physicians, psychologists, and lawyers to define themselves as distinct from other groups such as managers, clerical workers, and massage therapists. In focusing on the process of professionalization, critical theorists have noted that at the heart of the struggle to professionalize are relations of power and control. Feminist scholars have recently offered a more nuanced analysis of the ways in which **patriarchy** (a system of male dominance), too, structures the process of securing professional authority and control (Witz, 1991).

Labour Unions and Labour's Agenda

But the struggle to professionalize is not one in which many Canadians will be engaged—it is largely an exclusive one. Greater numbers of people in Canada, and globally, turn to another form of collective action to secure their rights and dignity in the workplace: they look to unionization. Just as campaigns to secure professional control have had a middle-class base, the struggle to unionize in this country has traditionally been one of white men in blue-collar jobs. In the latter part of the twentieth century and into the present time, however, increasing numbers of women, people of colour, white-collar workers, and middle-class employees have joined the ranks of the labour movement.

When most of us think of unions, strikes come to mind. Some of us may view trade unionists as just a bunch of greedy, overpaid workers demanding higher wages and, in the process, disrupting our lives, transportation, communication—even our garbage collection. We may owe this perception to dominant media representations of unions, their members, and their leaders.

The labour movement in this country goes far beyond this narrow and unfair characterization. The basic premise of the organized labour movement is to take collective action through the process of bargaining a contract. This *collective agreement* is the outcome of days, weeks, or even months of negotiations between two parties: worker representatives and company representatives. The contract is a legally binding document, an agreement that has been signed by both the employer and the union. Only if the two parties cannot reach an agreement is there potential for strike action. The actual incidence of strikes in Canada is, in fact, low. In 2001, the estimated work time lost through strikes and lockouts was 0.07 per cent, one-sixth the level of 20 years earlier (Statistics Canada, 2002e: 3). The strike is usually a measure of last resort. The vast majority of contracts that come up for renewal are settled without resorting to strike action. Indeed, some would argue that the leadership of unions acts to contain militancy on the part of its rank-and-file membership.

Workers in the nineteenth century first struggled to secure union representation in an effort to protect themselves against excessively long work days, extremely hazardous work environments, low pay, and blatant favouritism on the job. Critical to the survival of the labour movement in Canada was the passage of the Rand formula at the end of World War II. The Rand formula, named for Supreme Court Justice Ivor Rand, ensured the automatic deduction of union dues by the employer in a unionized workplace.

Today, labour–management conflict arises over a host of issues. Not only are wages an item of dispute, but companies and union representatives also negotiate benefits packages, job security, the implementation of technological change, outsourcing, concessions, and anti-harassment policies. Because of the struggles of union members, Canadian workers in offices, stores, and factories now

SOCIOLOGY IN ACTION

McDonald's and Unions

A Quebec trade union has signed a labour contract with a McDonald's fast-food franchisee, the first in North America and only the second in the world.

'We had so many problems, so much repression,' said Jean Lortie, a division president with the Quebec Confederation of National Trade Unions in Montreal. 'But we didn't give up.'

It took more than a year of often bitter negotiations to get a contract with the fast-food outlet in the tiny resort town of Rawdon, in the Laurentians north of Montreal. The process, Mr Lortie said, was so unpleasant and lengthy that by the time the union won only two of the 25 original signatories were still on staff.

The CNTU nearly became the first union in the world to get a labour contract with McDonald's, but a French union signed up a McDonald's restaurant only six weeks ago, said Len Ruel, area director of the Canadian Auto Workers in British Columbia.

The French union had to strike for six months to get a contract. By contrast, the Quebec contract was negotiated through the normal arbitration channels without a work stoppage. 'All parties negotiated in good faith,' said Maureen Kitts, a spokeswoman for McDonald's Restaurants of Canada Ltd in Toronto. She said McDonald's pays fair and equitable wages. Employees often start at the minimum legal wage with merit increases that are based on performance.

Rawdon is the first Canadian McDonald's outlet to sign a labour contract. Several other Canadian outlets have been certified by provincial labour authorities, but were unable to reach a first contract.

Ms Kitts said an outlet in Squamish, BC, was the first to be certified in North America. But Mr Ruel said the company decertified that union before he was able to negotiate a first contract.

Unions have organized other outlets in recent years, notably in Orangeville, Ont., in Montreal, and in St-Hubert, Que.

But Mr Lortie said those outlets were closed or decertified shortly after. Another outlet, in the United States, was bulldozed by the franchisee shortly after it was certified, Mr Ruel said. 'The company does everything it can to stop the union,' he said.

With the first contract, the McDonald's workers in Rawdon will get a base pay of $7 an hour and a raise of 10 cents every six months on the job. 'It's not a very good deal, but it's a start,' Mr Lortie said. 'This is the first time that everybody will get the same wage. There will be no favouritism.'

More important, he said the workers will get seniority rights and layoff protection, a key factor in a resort town where the work is highly seasonal. The company has also agreed to stiffer safety regulations, a contentious issue in a restaurant that fries potatoes in boiling oil.

The labour contract in Rawdon will not apply to other McDonald's outlets because it is owned by an independent franchisee.

The two union leaders said McDonald's fought hard to stop the union coming in. They say the company and the franchisee harassed the union leaders by moving them to midnight shifts, giving them dirty jobs or by neglecting to call them into work.

'They had so many problems, they quit,' Mr Lortie said. 'They were only getting $7 a hour, so it wasn't worth it for them.'

'We had to rebuild the union from scratch after they pushed out the union officers,' he added. 'It was a tough job to implement the new agreement.'

Source: Oliver Bertin, 'Quebec Union's Labour Contract with McDonald's Is Landmark', *Globe and Mail*, 18 Apr. 2002. Reprinted with permission from The Globe and Mail.

have the right to refuse unsafe work, the right to participate in company-sponsored pension plans, and, in some cases, access to on-site daycare centres.

The gains of unionized workers, moreover, spill over into the wider society. Both unionized and non-unionized workers now have employment standards, (un)employment insurance, a standard work day of eight hours, a five-day work week, overtime premiums, vacation pay, health benefits, and sick-leave provisions. Unions have been pivotal in lobbying governments to introduce worker-friendly provincial and federal legislation.

Union Membership

In the first half of 2004, union membership in Canada was 4.1 million (of 13.4 million paid employees). This represented an increase from 4 million in the first half of 2003). Women accounted for nearly all of this increase. In 2004, the rate of union membership among women was 30.6 per cent, for the first time surpassing that of men, which dropped slightly to 30.3 per cent (www.childcareadvocacy.ca/resources/pdf/union_update2004.pdf). In part, growth in female membership reflects the high rate of unionization in the (female-dominated) public service (for example, in Crown corporations, public schools, and hospitals). It is also, in part, a result of recent union organizing in private services (Jackson and Robinson, 2000). In comparison, the unionization rate for men has dropped since the 1960s. This is largely attributable to a shrinking proportion of jobs in traditionally male-dominated and heavily unionized sectors, such as primary/resource, manufacturing, and construction (ibid.).

Union membership also varies with terms of employment. Almost one in three full-time employees belongs to a union, compared to one in four part-time workers. Similarly, close to one in three permanent employees is a union member compared to about one in four non-permanent employees (Statistics Canada, 2002e: 2). We can, furthermore, see variations by age. Employees aged 45–54 (41.6 per cent) are more likely to be unionized than those aged 15–24 (13.3 per cent). Education is also a factor. A higher-than-average unionization rate can be found among men with post-secondary credentials (34.7 per cent) and those with less than a Grade 9 education (34 per cent). For women, the highest rate is for those with a university degree (40 per cent), reflecting unionization in health care and teaching (ibid., 3).

Global comparisons reveal that the rate of union membership in Canada is higher than those in the United States and Japan and lower than those in most Western European nations. The dramatic decline in union membership in the United States has been a particular source of concern. The US unionization rate fell from 30 per cent at the end of the 1960s to less than 15 per cent in the current period (Jackson and Robinson, 2000: 25). This drop can be explained by a variety of forces, not the least of which are the electoral success of anti-union governments and the growth of anti-union employers such as Wal-Mart and Radio Shack. The assault on trade unions has been blatant in the United States.

The Union Advantage

There is absolutely no doubt that unionization benefits workers (see Table 10.4). Collective bargaining has secured for employees advantages in wages, benefits, job security, and extended health plans. This has been called the *union advantage*. The union wage premium in particular is greatest for (traditionally disadvantaged) workers who would otherwise be low-paid. Unionization tends to compress wage and benefit differentials and thereby promote an equalization of wages and working conditions among unionized workforces (ibid.). In 2003, for example, average hourly earnings of unionized workers in Canada were $21.01, while for non-unionized workers the average hourly rate was $16.65. Thus, the union advantage as a percentage of the non-union hourly wage was over 26 per cent. The difference in wage between unionized and non-unionized women was even greater, at 37 per cent. As would be expected, the advantage for union workers was least in the public sector, where most employees are union members. Part-time unionized workers also are in a better position than non-union part-timers; in 2001, the hourly wage figures were $17.31 and $10.60, respectively. In addition, unionized part-timers also tended to work more hours per week than their non-unionized counterparts. Consequently, their average weekly earnings were nearly double—$343.94 compared to $181.65 (Statistics Canada, 2002e: 3).

The advantages of unionization to women are perhaps the most obvious. In 2001, unionized women working full-time received on average 90 per cent of the hourly earnings of their male counterparts, and female part-time workers earned 9 per cent more than men who were in part-time work (Statistics Canada, 2002e: 3). Women in unionized jobs are more than twice as likely to be included in pension plans than are women in non-unionized jobs (Jackson and Robinson, 2000).

According to the 1995 *World Employment Report* of the International Labour Organization (ILO), it is

Table 10.4 The Union Advantage, 2003

	Union	Non-Union	Union Advantage	Union Advantage as % of Non-Union
Median hourly wage				
All	$20.00	$14.00	$6.00	42.9%
Men	$21.00	$15.98	$5.02	31.4%
Women	$18.75	$12.02	$6.73	56.0%
Average hourly wage				
All	$21.01	$16.65	$4.36	26.2%
Men	$22.00	$18.69	$3.31	17.7%
Women	$19.94	$14.55	$5.39	37.0%
Age 15–24	$12.66	$9.88	$2.78	28.1%
Public sector	$23.10	$22.09	$1.01	4.6%
Private sector	$18.70	$16.17	$2.53	15.6%
Sales and service occupations	$13.16	$11.28	$1.88	16.7%
Processing and manufacturing occupations	$18.11	$14.76	$3.35	22.7%

Source: Statistics Canada, *Guide to the Labour Force Survey, 2004*, Catalogue no. 71-543, 17 Feb. 2004.

erroneous to believe that unions or good labour standards are the 'fundamental cause of unemployment, and it is important to recognize the positive impacts for society in terms of greater equality and less poverty'; collective bargaining efforts should be regarded as an 'important source of social well-being' (ibid., 96).

Conclusion: Work in the Future, Our Future as Workers

Workers and unions, of course, have limited powers. While newspaper headlines promote the 'big' collective bargaining gains of the most strongly organized unions, most unionized workers across the country are still struggling to attain basic rights that others managed to secure years, if not decades, ago. Every day, in small workplaces, employees (unionized and non-unionized) negotiate their rights. More often now than in the past, these are women, people of colour, the disabled—not members of the dominant groups in this country.

These struggles have been difficult, and continue to be so, particularly in the context of the current assault on unions. Powerful corporations such as Wal-Mart and McDonald's effectively curb workers' rights to organize by simply closing down stores, mounting strong union decertification campaigns, or stalling when it comes time to bargain a first contract. In Ontario, furthermore, the Harris-led Conservative government curbed the power of the Ontario Labour Relations Board by intro-

Time to Reflect

Imagine that you are employed in a non-unionized workplace and a union organizer seeks to enlist union members and certify your workplace. Would you support this action? Would you if it meant you might be fired from your job?

ducing legislation that removes the board's right to give union certification to workers who have faced (illegal) intimidation by anti-union employers. The power of workers and their movements is being even more severely circumscribed by the aggressiveness of global capitalists, many of whom are openly supported by networks of governments in both developing and developed nations. Whether you work part-time at The Gap, labour a 60-hour week in a steel factory, freelance as a consultant, or find sporadic office employment through a temporary help agency, you are faced with a challenge.

Regardless of theoretical perspective or political agenda, scholars today are debating the nature of the challenge of the transformation of work. Young people entering the labour market for the first time and middle-aged people confronting reconfigured jobs and refashioned workplaces both are part of this transformation. Workers, young and old, must work in order to survive, to nurture families, to participate in life. Given this reality, it is crucial to know the debate, engage in it, and perhaps transform the world of work according to your own vision.

Questions for Critical Thought

1. Think about where you are located in the economy. If you are not currently employed, where do you plan to find work? How does this depart from your parents' and grandparents' work histories? What factors have shaped (or constrained) your work-related aspirations?
2. Some employers believe that if you pay a worker more money (and offer better benefits), then you can compensate her or him for the boredom of work, loss of control, and lack of autonomy on the job. What do you think about this belief?
3. Think about the work that you perform in the course of an average day. What proportion of this is paid and what unpaid? Do you believe that we should define unpaid domestic activities as 'work' that is of economic worth? If you were asked to calculate the economic worth of unpaid domestic labour, how would you begin? What factors would you take into account?
4. Most people in Canada today take the new computer technology for granted, but as a sociologist, you must take a closer, critical look. Consider some of the ways in which computer technology has reshaped employment opportunities and the nature of work.
5. A prevailing view is that the youth today are merely 'stop-gap' workers. They are young and resilient. As they mature, they will move on to better, more secure and fulfilling employment. Thus, their conditions of work are not problematic. Young people themselves are not concerned about the nature of the jobs that they perform. Why should sociologists bother writing about youth at work?
6. Do you believe that who you are (that is, female or male, Aboriginal, of Asian or European or African descent, young or middle-aged, working-class, educated) is an important indicator of the type of work you will perform? If so, in what ways? If not, explain.
7. Even though women's workforce participation rate is now almost the same as men's, there are many persisting gender-based inequalities in employment. Identify some of these inequities. What are some of the formal and informal barriers to equality between women and men in the labour market today? How would you confront them?
8. Labour unions have long faced challenges in capitalist societies. Some people would argue that today union leaders and members face new challenges, perhaps more formidable than those of the past. Identify and discuss some of the new challenges that confront the labour movement in this country.

Recommended Readings

Gillian Creese, *Contracting Masculinity: Gender, Class, and Race in a White-Collar Union, 1944–1994* (Toronto: Oxford University Press, 1999).

A carefully researched case study of the white-collar office workers' union at BC Hydro. Creese uncovers the negotiation of gender, class, and race in collective bargaining.

Barbara Ehrenreich, *Nickel and Dimed: On (Not) Getting By in America* (New York: Henry Holt, 2001).

An extremely readable sociological (and personal) comment on 'getting by' as a low-wage worker in the new economy. Ehrenreich, a sociologist, travelled throughout the United States, working as a hotel maid, a waitress, a cleaner, and a Wal-Mart clerk. She describes the hardship and indignity of it all.

Ann Eyerman, *Women in the Office: Transitions in a Global Economy* (Toronto: Sumach, 2000).

In presenting the stories of 12 female office workers in Canada, the author makes a highly accessible critique of new managerial approaches in the context of global competition, corporate restructuring, computer technology, and the rise of contingent work arrangements.

Randy Hodson, *Dignity at Work* (Cambridge: Cambridge University Press, 2001).

Based on an examination of 109 organizational ethnographies, Hodson sensitively highlights the ways in which workers search for dignity and self-worth on the job.

Graham S. Lowe, *The Quality of Work: A People-Centred Agenda* (Toronto: Oxford University Press, 2000).

A refreshing and informative empirical analysis, by one of Canada's experts on the sociology of work, of the quality of work performed by Canadians today.

Meg Luxton and June Corman, *Getting By in Hard Times: Gendered Labour at Home and on the Job* (Toronto: University of Toronto Press, 2001).

In this study, based on a series of interviews with women and men in families having one member employed at Stelco's manufacturing plant in Hamilton, Ontario, the authors demonstrate how working families are coping in the face of the economic restructuring that began in the 1980s.

Richard Sennett, *The Corrosion of Character: The Personal Consequences of Work in the New Capitalism* (New York: Norton, 1998).

A meaningful, eloquent critique, by one of America's finest sociologists, of the consequences of the new flexible workplace on individual lives and moral identity.

Stuart Tannock, *Youth at Work: The Unionized Fast-Food and Grocery Workplace* (Philadelphia: Temple University Press, 2001).

An excellent, engaging study of youth at work. Tannock gives voice to young people themselves, their experiences and concerns, while offering a rigorous critique of the low-end service economy today.

Recommended Websites

Canadian Auto Workers (CAW)
www.caw.ca

The CAW is the largest private-sector union in Canada. For most of its history, the union represented only auto workers. Since the 1980s, though, the CAW has broadened its membership to include fishers, fast-food workers, Starbucks employees, health-care workers, and thousands of other workers in many different sectors.

Canadian Centre for Occupational Health and Safety (CCOHS)
www.ccohs.ca

The CCOHS, based in Hamilton, Ontario, promotes a safe and healthy working environment by providing information and advice about occupational health and safety issues.

Canadian Centre for Policy Alternatives (CCPA)
www.policyalternatives.ca

The CCPA offers an alternative to the message that we have no choice about the policies that affect our lives, by undertaking and promoting research on issues of social and economic justice.

CorpWatch
www.corpwatch.org

CorpWatch is a San Francisco-based organization that monitors and critiques corporate-led globalization through education and activism. It seeks to foster democratic control over corporations by building grassroots globalization—a diverse movement for human rights, labour rights, and environmental justice.

European Foundation for the Improvement of Living and Working Conditions
www.eurofound.ie

The foundation is a tripartite European Union body set up in 1975 to contribute to the planning and establishment of better living and working conditions.

International Labour Organization (ILO)
www.ilo.org

The ILO was founded in 1919 and is now an agency of the United Nations. Its mandate is to promote and realize standards, fundamental principles, and rights at work.

Labour/Le Travail
www.mun.ca/cclh/llt/

Labour/Le Travail is the leading academic journal for labour studies in Canada. In operation since 1976, the journal publishes historical and contemporary articles on all aspects of work in Canada.

LabourStart
www.labourstart.org

LabourStart is a web-based news organization that provides up-to-the-moment information on a wide variety of labour-related issues and developments around the globe. Visitors to this site can find anything from job advertisements in Australia to the latest strikes in the United Kingdom to recently published books.

No Sweat
www.nosweat.org.uk

No Sweat is a UK-based activist organization that fights sweatshops around the world. It stands for a living wage, safe working conditions, and independent trade unions. No Sweat is an open, broad-based campaign that aligns with anti-capitalist protest movements and the international workers' movement.

11

Chapter

Health Issues

Juanne Clarke

Learning Objectives

In this chapter, you will:

- See how health, illness, and disease are distinct in the sociology of health, illness, and medicine.
- Learn that health, illness, disease, and death are integrally related to social inequality throughout world through a number of intermeshing levels.
- Examine medicare as a system that embodies five principles: portability, universality, comprehensive coverage, public administration, and accessibility.
- See how privatization is increasing in the Canadian medical system.
- Learn that medicalization is a powerful cultural force.
- Discover that there are significant problems in the medical profession.

Photo: CP/Richard Lam

WELCOME TO
insite
OPEN DAILY
10:00AM - 4:00AM
Front door closes at 3:15 am daily
Ph: 604.OUR.SITE

Introduction

This chapter is an investigation of health and medical issues from the perspective of sociology. What do you think are some significant health issues facing you today as a student, as a young man or woman, as a Canadian? Do you think immediately of HIV/AIDS, alcoholism, cancer, or heart disease? Do you think of eating disorders, depression, unwanted pregnancies, or sexually transmitted diseases (STDs)? Or do you think of the medical-care system and topics in the news such as long waiting lists for emergency service, the lack of available physicians, or home-care services? This chapter will introduce you to a sociological perspective on topics such as these that are related to the sociology of health, illness, and medicine.

Health is linked inextricably to the social order. Its very definition, its multitudinous causes, and its consequences all are social. What is considered healthy in one culture or society may not necessarily be considered to be healthy in another. What was thought of as good health at one time is not the same as what is considered to be good health at another. Rates, as well as understandings, of sickness and death vary across time and place. Social classes differ in their definitions of good health. What a woman considers health may be different from a man's definition of health. Moreover, **class** and **gender** differences lead to varying levels of health and sickness and different rates of death.

One example of historically based cultural differences in the experience of health and illness comes from a tale told by the early Canadian writer Catharine Parr Traill in *The Backwoods of Canada* (1966 [1836]). This account is based on Traill's letters home to England from 1832 to 1835, while she and her husband were homesteading near what is now Peterborough, Ontario. She wrote,

> My dear husband, my servant, the poor babe, and myself, were all at one time confined to our beds with ague. You know how severe my sufferings always were at home with intermittents, and need not marvel if they were no less great in a country where lake-fevers and all kinds of intermittent fevers abound. Few persons escape the second year without being afflicted with this weakening complaint; the mode of treatment is repeated doses of calomel, with castor-oil salts, and is followed up by quinine. Those persons who do not choose to employ medical advice on the subject dose themselves with ginger-tea, strong infusion of hyson, or any other powerful green tea; pepper, and whiskey; with many other remedies that have the sanction of custom or quackery. (Traill, 1966 [1836]: 107)

I doubt that you have heard of or suffered from lake-fever or intermittents. I also doubt that you have used quinine, pepper, or whiskey as a treatment when you were ill, although many of you may have your own family healing traditions, such as chicken soup, mustard plaster, or brandy for a cold. Yet, the diseases and the treatments described by Traill were believed in as fervently as we believe in treating cancer with chemotherapy, radiation, and surgery today.

Similar stories of the experiences of new immigrants from various parts of the world to all of the provinces in Canada would provide interesting insights into some of the culturally distinct threads of the Canadian 'mosaic' of health's meanings. The interpretation of health varies not only historically and culturally, but also between men and women, people of different educational and social class backgrounds and religious traditions, and so on. Think a little about how your male and female friends, your brothers and sisters, and your parents differ with respect to how they think and talk about and act with regard to what they consider sickness. Think, too, about how illness and medicine are portrayed on popular television programs such as *Grey's Anatomy*. The first part of this chapter will examine several health issues: the changing health of Canadians over the nineteenth and twentieth centuries, HIV/AIDS, environmental health problems in different parts of Canada including the Walkerton water crisis, social inequality, **social capital** and health, the sense of coherence, obesity and eating disorders, and health among Aboriginal Canadians.

The sociology of health issues is not only about **health**, illness, and **disease**, but also about medical or health systems of diagnosis, prognostication, and treatment. Conventional medicine—sometimes called **allopathic medicine** because it treats by means of opposites, such as cutting out or killing germs, bacteria, or other disease processes through medications, surgery, or radiation—is taken for granted in much of the Western world. In fact, much of the history of the sociology of health and medicine is based on assuming the primacy of the work of the allopathic system and its practitioners. However, naturopathic (treatment through 'natural' remedies and procedures, such as herbs or massage), chiropractic (treatment through spinal adjustment), and homeopathic medicine (treatment with similars) all are examples of CAM, or *complementary and alternative medicines* and are of increasing importance in the Western world. The second part of this chapter will investigate some of the most important trends and social policy issues in the area of medical sociology, including **medicalization**, the future of the health-care system, and **privatization**.

IN THE FIRST PERSON

My initial intention at university was to major in psychology, but I was more intrigued by my first-year course in sociology. Having grown up in one of the monolithic suburbs of Toronto, I was naive about the diversity of values and the impact of social structures on people's lives. In particular, I was fascinated and 'empowered' by the sociological perspective on gender differences, and was influenced by early papers on pain and culture by Irving Zola and by Ivan Illich's *Limits to Medicine* (1976). Hence, I decided to specialize in health and medical studies within sociology, and now teach courses in this area and in research methods at Wilfrid Laurier University. Because a number of people in my family suffered with cancer I have focused much of my research and writing on the social aspects of this disease, including a personal account of childhood cancer (*Finding Strength*, 1999) written with and about my daughter Lauren. At the present time my research is largely related to the media portrayal of illness, disease, and the medical system.—Juanne Clarke

Theoretical Perspectives

Four theoretical **paradigms** of sociological thought are considered to be the most significant approaches to understanding health and medicine sociologically: structural functionalism, conflict theory, symbolic interactionism, and feminism.

Structural Functionalism

From the **structural functionalist** perspective, health is necessary for the smooth running of the social system. In a stable society, all institutional forces work together to create and maintain good health for the population. Your university or college assumes your good health as it organizes its courses and exams—you probably have to get a letter from a doctor for exemption from writing a test or an exam. The smooth functioning of societies depends on the good health of their members. Societies are organized to support a population up to an average **life expectancy** and at a given level of health and ability. This normative standard of health and normative age at death are reinforced by political, economic, cultural, and educational policy.

It has been suggested, for example, that the reason that governments continue to allow cigarette smoking is because to do so reaps economic benefits for **the state** through the high levels of taxation. Not only does the availability of cigarettes with their high taxation rate contribute to the income of the state, but the relatively fast death from lung cancer as compared to other cancers, for instance, saves the government in health-care costs. Although some may find this too cynical an analysis, it does make clear that there are interesting and thought-provoking social structural ways of thinking about the potential relationships between the health and life expectancy of a population and institutional and political forces.

Assertions about the interrelationships among institutions all fit within the structural functionalist theoretical perspective. A classic statement of this perspective is found in the work of Talcott Parsons (1951), in particular in his concept of the sick role. The sick role is to be thought of as a special position in society. It exists to prevent **sickness** from disrupting the 'ongoingness' of social life. The sick role also provides a way of institutionalizing what might other-wise become a form of deviant behaviour. It does this by articulating certain rights for those who claim sickness in a society so long as they fulfill certain duties.

Specifically, in Parsons's thinking, there are two rights and two duties for those who want to claim sickness and engage in the sick role. The rights include the right to be exempted from normal social **roles** and the right to be free of blame or responsibility for the sickness. The duties are to want to get well and to seek and co-operate with technically competent help. However, that these theoretically derived ideas do not always have empirical support is evident in a number of ways. For example, it is well known that the right to be exempt from the performance of social roles depends in part on the nature of the sickness. A hangover, for instance, may not be considered a good enough reason to claim the sick role as an excuse for an exam exemption. There is also a great deal of evidence that people with AIDS were seen as culpable, especially in the early days of the disease in North America—in fact, it was called the 'gay plague' by some (Altman, 1986). And, with respect to duties, not everyone is expected to want to get well. Indeed, those with a chronic disease such as multiple sclerosis are expected to accept their condition and to learn to live with it. Parsons assumed the dominance of allopathic medicine in his statement that a sick person was to get technically competent help. Today, however, many people believe that the best help may not always come from allopathic medicine even though it is the state-supported type of medical care. Indeed, a substantial minority—approximately 40 per cent—of North Americans now rely on complementary and alternative medicines, or CAMs (Statistics Canada, 2001a: 17; Eisenberg et al., 1998) and between one-fifth and one-quarter of Canadians use alternative health-care providers (Statistics Canada, 2006g: 161).

Conflict Theory

From the perspective of **conflict theory**, health and ill health result from inequitable and oppressive economic conditions. The primary focus of analysis is the distribution of health and illness across the **social structure**. Questions driving this perspective include: Are the poor more likely to get sick? Is the **mortality rate** (the frequency of death per a specified number of people over a particular period of time) among the poor higher than among the rich? Are women more likely than men to get sick? Do men die at younger ages? Does racism affect the **morbidity** (sickness) **rate** (the frequency of sickness per a specified number of people over a particular period of time)? In this perspective, health is seen as a good that is inequitably located in society.

A classic statement of this position is found in the work of Friedrich Engels, who often wrote with Karl Marx. In his book *The Condition of the Working Class in England* (1994 [1845]), Engels demonstrates the negative health consequences of early **capitalism**. He

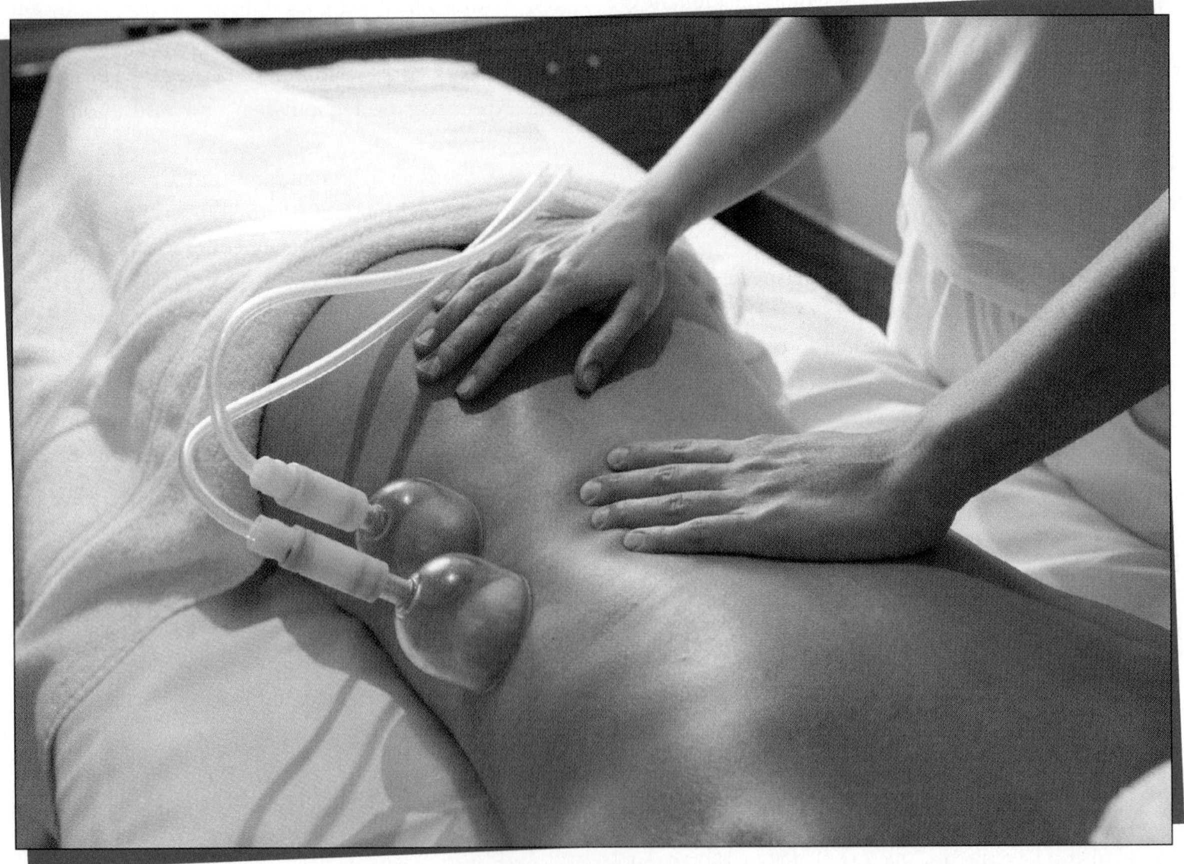

Moxibustion is an alternative treatment for allergies and skin irritations in which moxa—an extract from the leaves of an Asian plant—is burned on or near the skin. (Atlantide Phototravel/Corbis)

Time to Reflect

Why do you think a growing number of people choose to go to alternative health-care providers? Use sociological reasoning.

describes how the development of capitalism advanced mechanism in agriculture and forced farm workers off the land and into the cities to survive. Capitalists in the cities sought profit regardless of the costs to the well-being of the workers. Owners maintained low costs for labour through poor wages and long hours of back-breaking work in filthy and noisy working conditions. Even children worked in these unhealthy circumstances.

As a consequence, poor labourers and their families lived exceedingly rough lives in shelters that offered little or no privacy, cleanliness, or quiet. They had very little money for food, and the quality of the foodstuffs available in the cities was poor. The slum-like living conditions were perfect breeding grounds for all sorts of diseases, and because of the high density of living quarters, the lack of facilities for toileting and washing, and the frequent lack of clean drinking water, the morbidity and mortality rates in the slums were very high. Infectious diseases such as tuberculosis (TB), typhoid, scrofula, and influenza spread quickly and with dire results through these close quarters and malnourished populations.

Epidemics were almost common in nineteenth-century industrial cities, where overcrowding, overflowing cesspits, garbage piled all around, and unsafe water were the norm. It was only when there were new discoveries in bacteriology and it became clear that many of the worst diseases were spread by bacteria and viruses in the water, air, and food that governments enacted public health measures. These new prevention policies included sewage disposal, garbage removal, clean filtered drinking water, and hygienic handling of food. The death rates began to abate (Crompton, 2000). Even in the 1920s in Canada, infectious diseases such as influenza, bronchitis, and pneumonia, TB, various stomach and digestive ailments such as gastritis, and communicable diseases were important causes of death.

Conflict theory has been given a feminist emphasis, also, as in the work of Hilary Graham. In *Women, Health and the Family* (1984), Graham documents how inequality affects the various types of home health-care work done by women in order to protect the good health of their families. In particular, she articulates four different components of women's home health-care work: (1) maintaining a clean, comfortable home with an adequate, safe, and balanced diet as well as supportive social and emotional intra-familial relations; (2) nursing family members when they feel ill or are debilitated; (3) teaching family members about health and hygiene, including such things as sleeping, bathing, cleaning, and toileting; and (4) liaising with outsiders regarding the health-care needs of family members, such as taking children or a partner to the doctor, clinic, hospital, or dentist.

As Graham notes, the ability of women to fulfill these four roles varies significantly depending on the socio-economic, health, spiritual, and emotional resources that women have or to which they are able to gain access. Moreover, these resources are inequitably distributed over the socio-economic hierarchy.

Symbolic Interactionism

Interpretation and meaning are the hallmarks of sociology within the **symbolic interactionist** perspective. What is the meaning, for example, of anorexia and bulimia? Are they medical conditions? Are they the result of a moral choice? Or could they be considered 'socio-somatic' conditions, that is, caused by society (Currie, 1988)? Various authors have attributed them to

Time to Reflect

There are new infectious diseases occurring around the world today. The avian flu is an example. Investigate the extent to which the reasons for the decline in infectious diseases in previous centuries may be relevant for preventing diseases such as 'bird flu' today.

women's 'hunger strike' against their contradictory positions, against culturally prescribed images, and against lack of opportunities in contemporary society. They have been conceptualized as a means 'through which women, both unconsciously and consciously, protest the social conditions of womanhood' (ibid., 208). Dias (2003) has documented the way many people with various eating disorders support their 'lifestyle choice' through involvement in pro-ana (anorexia) websites.

Stigma often is attached to the person with HIV/AIDS, cancer, depression, inflammatory bowel disease, diabetes, or asthma. By some, these diseases are thought to have connotations of morality or immorality. Good health is even associated with being a good person. The following research addresses some of the paradoxes of stigma in respect to Asperger's syndrome, often considered to be a mild form of autism. This study, in the symbolic interaction tradition, is an analysis of the blogs of people who self-identify as having Asperger's (AS) and parents or caregivers of those thought to have the disorder (Clarke and Van Amerom, forthcoming). It used a qualitative content analytic technique to describe and compare the similarities and differences between people self-identifying as having AS and their parents or caregivers. The findings indicate that these two groups held not only different but even oppositional views regarding AS. People who self-identified as having Asperger's rejected the stigma of AS. They called themselves Aspies. They called others NTs or neurotypicals. They said they were proud of who they were and of the way they thought. They said that they felt the major problems they faced were not due to the 'disorder' or the 'limitatations' they suffered because of AS but resulted from the stigma of AS and the way that others perceived and acted towards them. Parents and caregivers, on the other hand, expressed worry about their children's problems in schooling and in their social lives. They accepted the dominant and pathologizing view of AS, while the bloggers who self-identified as having AS expressed pride and mutual solidarity. The paper demonstrates the value of an 'up close and personal' investigation of the world views of people, particularly those who are vulnerable to stigmatization or marginalization.

Feminism

Feminist health sociology recognizes the centrality of gender to social life as well as to inequity in the worlds of and in relations between men and women. Feminist health sociology investigates whether, how, and why men and women have different health and illness profiles, as well as different causes and average ages of death. Feminist health sociology also includes consideration of such things as **ethnicity**, sexual preference, and ability/disability as fundamental characteristics of social actors and social life. These axes of inequality, therefore, are central issues to be included in designing research, uncovering social injustice, and planning and making social change.

Women's health has been a central issue and in many ways a major impetus for the recent women's movement. The health-related book *Our Bodies, Our Selves*, when first published in 1971, became a major rallying document for women. Translated into many languages, and more recently revised and updated, this book from the Boston Women's Health Collective offers a radical critique of medical practice and medicalization and provides women's views of their own health, sickness, and bodies.

Another example of work within the feminist paradigm is Anne Kasper and Susan Ferguson's *Breast Cancer: Society Shapes an Epidemic* (2000), which suggests that among the reasons for the growing incidence (number of new cases in a year) and prevalence (number of cases within a given population) of the disease is that it is largely a women's disease and is therefore not given the serious and systematic research attention that it would have received had it been primarily a male disease. Contributions to this book by scholars and practitioners from a wide variety of fields, including sociology, zoology, social and health policy, anthropology, law, and biology, examine the social and political contexts of breast cancer as a social problem, arguing that gender, politics, social class, race, and ethnicity have affected the type of research that is done, the types of treatments that have become dominant, the rates of growth in the morbidity and mortality of breast cancer, and even the ways in which the disease is experienced by women. Indeed, they suggest that one of the reasons for the continuance of the epidemic is that it is not only primarily a women's disease but that it is located in their breasts.

Kasper and Ferguson's collection provides a thought-provoking look at one of the major causes of worry, sickness, and death among women in Canada and the United States. Despite the fact that both heart disease and lung cancer are more frequent causes of death for Canadian women, women in Canada fear breast cancer more and even think of their breasts as essentially flawed and vulnerable to disease (Robertson, 2001). This is undoubtedly related to the enormous mass media attention the disease has received in the last 15 years or so. During this time, first in the United States and then in Canada, powerful lobby groups of women activists founded highly successful breast cancer advocacy coalitions, lobbied governments and corporations, and received substantial increases in the funding levels for research into the disease and its

GLOBAL ISSUES

Warfare and Human Health

Human health depends on the complex interaction of manifold social determinants that operate across a number of levels as portrayed in Figure 11.1. An important part of this picture is international and intra-national conflict. The twentieth century was the most violent century in history. Almost three times the number of people who had died in conflict in the previous four centuries died in the twentieth century. This is partly due to the huge numbers massacred in World Wars I and II and partly due to the overall frequency of conflict. The Rwandan genocide in 1994, for instance, resulted in the deaths of approximately 1 million people. The civil war in the Democratic Republic of the Congo decimated 7 per cent of the population of that country and the several-decades-old conflict in Sudan has resulted in 2 million deaths and the displacement of 6 million people. Over time, conflict has increasingly occurred in the poorest countries of the world. By the 1990–2003 time period low-income countries accounted for more than half of the world's conflicts. In fact, approximately 40 per cent of the world's conflicts are in Africa.

The consequences of conflict for health are many. Wars inevitably result in death, disability, and rape. They also result in the destruction of the infrastructure necessary for everyday living for the masses of people affected. This decimation occurs in food production, storage, and distribution systems. It occurs in limiting or obviating access to potable water, sewage systems, and electricity, not only for homes but for hospitals. Fundamentals such as roads, homes, schools, and health-care facilities are also affected and frequently destroyed or damaged. Other negative consequences include chronic and acute psychological trauma and distress. The majority of the countries that have experienced war have child death rates that have either stagnated or worsened after the conflicts.

The World Bank has suggested that a civil war reduces the growth of a nation's economy by about 2.2 per cent per year and costs an average of $54 billion for a low-income country. The longer a conflict lasts the greater the toll on all fronts, from the human to the economic. Violence also sets in motion uncertainty about the future that inevitably has long-term health consequences for people within the countries engaged in the conflict as well as interacting countries around the world.

treatment. There is, of course, a painful irony in the fact that the increased attention and financial investment have been coupled with a proliferation of stories in the mass media that have served to increase anxiety and fear of risk of disease among Canadian women. King, in *Pink Ribbons, Inc.*, also demonstrates how the focus on consumer activism in the breast cancer movement, 'shaped as it is by an ideology of individualism and an imperative for uncomplicated, snappy marketing slogans, has allowed for the emergence of a preoccupation with early detection to the virtual exclusion of other approaches to fighting the epidemic (e.g., prevention) and a failure to address the barriers, financial or otherwise, to treatment' (King, 2006: 117–18). She argues that the corporations involved in breast cancer awareness and fundraising have benefited from their involvement. It is possible that this corporate advantage has been to the detriment of accessibility to treatment for all American women equally.

The Sociology of Health, Illness, Disease, and Sickness

At the broadest level, sociologists compare within and between societies around the world and over time with respect to the rates of, causes of, and treatments for health and sickness and to rates and causes of death. Here, factors such as wars, famine, drought, epidemics, natural disasters, air and water quality, quantity and quality of foodstuffs, transportation safety, level and type of economic development, technology, available birth control, immunization, antibiotics, medicalization, culture, and political economy all are considered relevant.

At the next level, sociologists examine morbidity and mortality within societies and cultures and compare people of different social class, educational levels, genders, religiosity, rural/urban locations, occupations, ethnicities, family statuses, and so on. A further level of investigation concerns the way socio-psychological factors, such as level of stress and sense of coherence, are implicated in illness, disease, and sickness.

The next level is an examination of the relationships between various 'lifestyle' behaviours, such as smoking, seat-belt use, alcohol consumption, diet, risk-taking behaviours, sexual activity and protection, drug use, and health. Finally, the existential considerations, including the meaning and the experience of morbidity and mortality to individuals, are studied. Figure 11.1 shows these links, beginning from the person.

In this chapter, we will look at specific and limited topics within each of these levels of analysis, beginning with the changing health of Canadians over the nineteenth and twentieth centuries, HIV/AIDS in Canada and around the world, and the water crisis in Walkerton, Ontario, as examples of first-level concerns. At the second level, we will look at social inequity and social capital, along with Aboriginal health issues. At the third level, the focus will be on sense of coherence. Fourth, we will investigate eating-disordered behaviour and attitudes, including obesity. The fifth and final level will be illustrated by a discussion of popular conceptions of illness as well as an illustration through poetry of the experiences of one mother when her child had cancer.

You will not be surprised to learn that this separation into levels is artificial and done only for reasons of analytical clarity. In fact, each of the levels influences all the other levels.

Comparative Analyses

The Changing Health of Canadians

People generally are living longer and healthier lives today than they did in the past. The increase in health and the decrease in mortality rates over the past 150 years has been substantial. In the nineteenth century, infectious and communicable diseases such as cholera, typhoid, diphtheria, and scarlet fever were responsible for enormous suffering and death for early Canadians. Wound infections and septicemia were frequent results of dangerous and unhygienic working, living, and medical conditions. Puerperal fever killed many women during and after childbirth. The health experiences of early Canadians have been described well in some general non-fiction (see, e.g., Bliss, 1991, 1992) and in personal memoirs, such as Susannah Moodie's *Roughing It in the Bush* (1995 [1852]), on settler life in the 1800s. Even fiction can help us understand how people have experienced health. Margaret Atwood's *The Edible Woman* (1994 [1968]), for example, foreshadows the contemporary issue of eating-disordered attitudes and behaviours.

In 1831, the average life expectancy for Canadian men and women was 39.0 years—38.3 for women, and 39.8 for men (Clarke, 2000: 50). Today, life expectancies are about double this for Canadian men and women. Today's women can expect to live to 82, men to 77 (*Canada Year Book*, 2006: 161). What has happened to cause this dramatic shift? You might think first of medical interventions and vaccinations. However, the most important causes of the increase in life expectancy are related to public health measures that were able to forestall the spread of disease. These included improved nutrition, better hygiene through sanitation and water purification practices, and advances in birth control. Interventions such as these brought the average life expectancy to 59 in the 1920s and, largely because of dramatic declines in infant mortality, to 78 in 1990–2 (Crompton, 2000: 12).

Figure 11.1 Components of Health

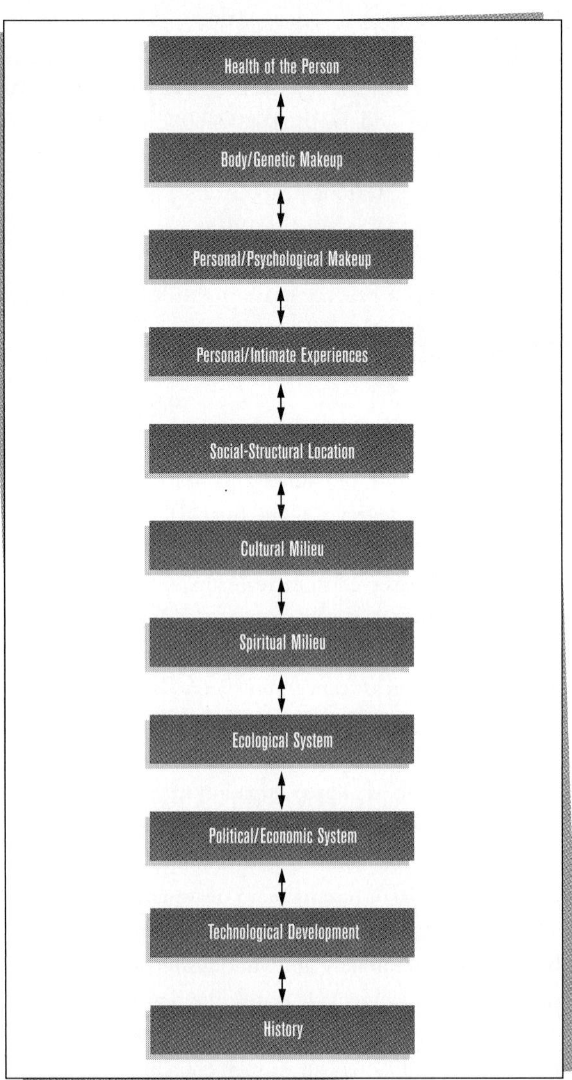

Table 11.1 Health Indicators: Canada, 2003

	Males	Females
Life expectancy at birth (years)	77.4	82.4
Health-adjusted life expectancy at birth[1] (years)	68.3	70.8
Infant mortality rate (deaths per 1,000 live births)	5.7	4.8
Babies with low birth weight (%)	5.4	6.3
Total fertility rate (number of live births per woman)	—	1.5
Daily smokers (%)	19.4	16.2

[1]Data for 2001.

Source: Statistics Canada, 'Canada Year Book', 2006, Cat. 11-402, p. 160, released 28 June 2006.

In the 1920s, the most common causes of death became heart and kidney disease, followed by influenza, bronchitis, and pneumonia, and the diseases of early infancy. Widespread use of newly discovered vaccines and antibiotics (vaccines against diphtheria, tetanus, typhoid, and cholera were developed in the late nineteenth and early twentieth centuries, and antibiotics were introduced in the 1940s and 1950s) made a significant difference in the twentieth century (ibid.). While heart disease remains the most common cause of death, it has declined dramatically over time, probably as a result of lifestyle changes such as declines in smoking and dietary fat, improvements in exercise, and better medical treatments. Lower infant death rates today have resulted primarily from better nutrition and improved hygiene in pregnancy, secondarily from medical and technological advances. For example, prematurity, a frequent cause of infant death in the past, is now more often prevented through educational programs and prenatal care and effective management in hospitals.

The incidence of diseases such as measles, scarlet fever, and whooping cough was cut virtually to zero until some people abandoned the vaccines in the 1990s. For a short time, the incidence of these diseases increased, but by the late 1990s they had declined again when public health authorities became alerted to the issue and became more diligent about universal vaccinations in Canada.

One other important feature of the declines in mortality or gains in life expectancy is the gap between men and women and how this gap has changed over time. From 1920 to 1922, women lived an average of two years longer than men; from 1990 to 1992, they lived an average of six years longer than men. Part of the explanation for women's greater benefit from the changes of the twentieth century relates to the decline in maternal mortality over this period. Another part of the explanation is the greater tendency for men to engage in risk-taking behaviours such as cigarette smoking and drunk driving.

Today, among the most important causes of death are, for men, cardiovascular disease, followed by diseases of the heart and then cancer, and for women, cardiovascular disease, followed by cancer and then diseases of the heart. The rates per 100,000 for men are 316.9, 238.7, and 234.7, and for women, 193.8, 150.3, and 134.8, respectively (Statistics Canada, 2001a).

But these rates do not take age into account. Potential years of life lost, or **PYLL**, is a statistical representation of death that does take age into account: the younger the average age of death for a given disease, the greater the number of years of life lost. PYLL allows us to see the years of life lost by disease type, taking 70 years as the cut-off point for age. Here, the importance of suicide and accidents, occuring as they often do among younger people,

Time to Reflect

What might be some of the other sociological explanations for the growing gap in life expectancy in men as compared to women?

Table 11.2 Leading Causes of Death, Canada, Twentieth Century

	Cause of Death[a]	Rate per 100,000
1921–5	All causes	1,030.0
	Cardiovascular and renal disease	221.9
	Influenza, bronchitis, and pneumonia	141.1
	Diseases of early infancy	111.0
	Tuberculosis	85.1
	Cancer	75.9
	Gastritis, duodenitis, enteritis, and colitis	72.2
	Accidents	51.5
	Communicable diseases	47.1
1996–7[b]	All causes	654.4
	Cardiovascular diseases (heart disease and stroke)	240.2
	Cancer	184.8
	Chronic obstructive pulmonary diseases	28.4
	Unintentional injuries	27.7
	Pneumonia and influenza	22.1
	Diabetes mellitus	16.7
	Hereditary and degenerative diseases of the central nervous system	14.7
	Diseases of the arteries, arterioles, and capillaries	14.3

[a]Disease categories are not identical over time.
[b]Rates are age-standardized.
Source: Adapted from the Statistics Canada publication, *Canadian Social Trends*, Catalogue 11-008, Winter 2000, p.13.

increases (www.statcan.ca/english/freepub/82-221-XIEI/2004002/hlthstatus/deaths4.htm).

These two sorts of information have different implications for such things as government health promotion planning. For example, the PYLL figures tell us that younger people are more likely to die of accidents and suicide and that the numbers of deaths in these categories are large. One can then consider what sorts of things might be done to prevent different sorts of accidents and suicides as compared to the chief causes of death—those sometimes called 'diseases of civilization'—cancer and cardiovascular and heart diseases.

HIV/AIDS

All of us have heard of HIV/AIDS. It is a disease of pandemic proportions around the world today (see Figure 11.2). Many people in North America have come to associate the disease with certain categories of other people. In particular, North Americans tend to think of HIV/AIDS as the 'gay disease' (Crossley, 2002). In an international context, however, HIV/AIDS is almost as common among heterosexual women as among men: in 1997, 59 per cent of those diagnosed internationally were male and 41 per cent were female; by 2005, 52 per cent were male and 48 per cent female (UNAIDS, 2001b: 1). In sub-Saharan Africa, however, more women than men are HIV-positive (this means that they carry the precursor virus but have not yet developed AIDS). In some of the sub-Saharan African countries where the disease has taken its highest toll, teenage girls are five to six times as likely to be infected as boys. Whether because they themselves are diagnosed with the disease or because they are much more likely to act as caregivers to others who are sick, women are substantially more affected by the AIDS epidemic than men in Africa. Already, too, in Africa, more than 1 million children are living with HIV and 12.1 million children have been orphaned by the disease. The number of orphans is expected to double by 2010. Children who are orphaned because of AIDS bear additional burdens of stigma and decreased access to health and education. In turn, they are more susceptible to becoming infected by

HIV/AIDS (UNAIDS, 2001a: 2). At present there are estimated to be about 38.6 million people living with HIV and there were approximately 4.1 million new cases of HIV diagnosed in 2005 (www.unaid.org).

What is this disease that has caused so much havoc in the last 20 years? AIDS (acquired immune deficiency syndrome) is a disease of the immune system that most scientists believe comes from HIV (human immunodeficiency virus). It is spread from person to person through bodily fluids such as semen, blood, vaginal fluid, and breast milk. Sexual intercourse, needle sharing, and mother-to-fetus transmission are currently the most common means of transmission. In the end, though, it is not HIV/AIDS per se that causes death, but rather such diseases as cancer, pneumonia, and tuberculosis that the vulnerable immune system is too weak to resist.

Even though the incidence and prevalence of HIV/AIDS are much lower here, Canada is not exempt from this epidemic. By 2005, there had been a cumulative total of 20,353 AIDS cases in this country. Females comprised 7 per cent of AIDS cases reported from 1979–94. By 2005, women comprised 23 per cent of the cases identified in Canada. One of the most worrying trends is the increase in rates of AIDS among young women aged 15–29. In 2005 this age group comprised 35 per cent of all those diagnosed with AIDS (www.avert.org/canstar.htm).

The most common means of transmission in Canada has been among men who have sex with men (MSM)—75.6 per cent of cases have been attributed to MSM (this category also includes other high-risk behaviour) and an additional 9.9 per cent to men who inject drugs. Among women, 59.6 per cent of cases are attributed to heterosexual contact, 21.9 per cent to injection drug use, and 9.6 per cent to receipt of blood and blood products (UNAIDS, 2002: 6).

HIV/AIDS is especially prevalent among Aboriginal people. Between 1996 and 1999, the number of Aboriginal people infected with HIV grew from 1,430 to 2,740—almost doubling. In 2000, a study by the Canadian Aboriginal AIDS Network concluded that Native people were five times more likely than non-Native people to become HIV-positive (*Ottawa Citizen*, 2000: A7). In 2001, Aboriginal and African-Canadian people accounted for 3.3 per cent and 2.2 per cent of the population of Canada, respectively. In the same year these groups were diagnosed with 6.6 per cent and 15.1 per cent of the AIDS cases with known ethnicities.

Figure 11.2 Adults and Children Estimated to Be Living with HIV/AIDS as of the End of 2001

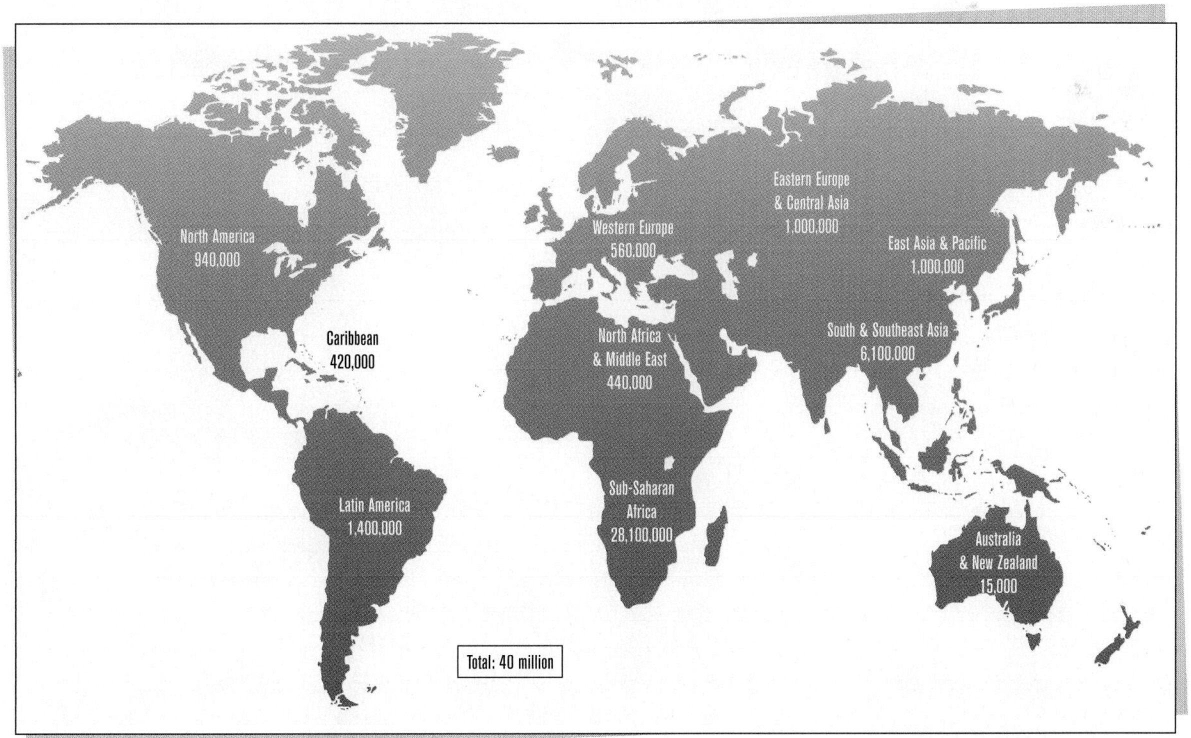

Source: From <http://www.unaids.org/worldaidsday/2001/EPIgraphics2001/EPIcore_en.ppt>. Reprinted with permission from UNAIDS.

Environmental Issues across the Country

At the broadest level, our health is dependent on the natural environment and the ways in which we as societies maintain the health of the natural environment. Water, air, and soil are among the basic and determining factors. Do you know how safe your drinking water is? Do you know how it is purified or how much is available and for how long? I must admit that I don't. Is there enough water for your generation, for your children and their children, and so on? Good and healthy land and soil are prerequisites to health because they are the basis for the production of foodstuffs. However, there are threats to the environment all across Canada.

Alberta Oil Sands

In Alberta the extraction of oil from the oil sands is an ongoing challenge to the health of the people and the environment. While the amount of oil is immense (there are said to be 175 billion barrels of proven oil, second only to the 260 billion barrels in Saudia Arabia), the processes needed to access this oil essentially require the strip mining and consequent removal of the sand to extract the infused oil. This affects soil organisms and water flow in the Athabasca River and water levels in the river and, downstream, in Lake Athabasca (huge amounts of water are required to extract the oil, but the water cannot be returned to the river because of its toxicity). In addition, mining of the oil sands displaces animals, increases erosion, and decreases carbon sequestration. Moreover, the energy required to access the oil is already causing public health problems, air pollution, and global warming. Some argue that the damage will be repaired naturally within a decade. Others say that 30 years after mining the oil sands there is still no reforestration.

The Walkerton Water Crisis

Water is fundamental to our good health. Walkerton, a small town nestled among rolling hills beside the

A heroin addict in Vancouver's Downtown Eastside, a neighbourhood notorious for its drug addicts and dealers. The area is also home to North America's first safe injection site, set up to counter the spread of HIV and AIDS among the neighbourhood's drug users. (Christopher Morris/Corbis)

Saugeen River in southwestern Ontario, was, at least from the outside, a perfect picture-postcard town—until May 2000. That was when the drinking water became polluted with a virulent strain of E. coli bacteria that was ingested repeatedly by the townspeople, leading to seven deaths and to illness in 2,300 others. The 2002 report of the Walkerton Inquiry, written by Justice Dennis R. O'Connor, details the causes of these tragic deaths and sicknesses and suggests that individual behaviours, cultural values, and social structural arrangements all were causes of the suffering of the people of Walkerton.

Let us examine these causes. First, what were the causes at the level of individuals? Two brothers, Stan and Frank Koebel, were particularly implicated in the tragedy. According to the O'Connor report, Stan Koebel neglected several essential aspects of his job with the Public Utilities Commission (PUC) as the general manager responsible for water chlorination and safety. In addition, he repeatedly lied to officers in the health unit and, even after many people had taken sick, reported that the water was 'okay'. Some of his actions were the result of his lack of understanding of the health consequences of his work. Some were due to the fact that the norms in the PUC culture had been lax for at least 20 years, before Koebel was hired. As the report states, 'It had been the practice of PUC employees not to measure the chlorine residuals on most days and to make fictitious entries for residuals in the daily operating sheets' (O'Connor, 2002: 7).

As well, there were structural causes for this tragedy. These included the fact that Stan and Frank Koebel were certified on the basis of their experience ('grandfathered') and were not required to take any courses or pass any examinations for continued certification. Another structural deficiency related to the fact that the Ministry of the Environment failed in its responsibility to regulate or to enforce regulations pertaining to the construction and operation of municipal water systems. Budget reductions at the provincial level were also implicated because they led to the privatization of lab testing and to failure to regulate the reporting responsibilities (to the Ministry of the Environment and the local Medical Officer of Health) of private labs whenever unsafe water was detected, and to ensure that proactive water quality interventions were made.

Sydney Tar Ponds

On the other side of the country, the 'tar ponds' at Sydney, Nova Scotia, contain dangerously contaminated soil and sediment as a result of decades of steel and coke production. The process of heating coal to produce coke for the manufacture of steel produces toxic chemicals such as benzene, kerosene, and napthalene. These have accumulated in the harbour in Sydney. 'More than 80 years of this type of coke-oven operation left the ground water and surface water in the area seriously contaminated with arsenic, lead and other toxins.' There were about 700,000 tonnes of chemical waste and raw sewage here (www.cbc.tarponds). In 2005, after years of public lobbying, a $400 million cleanup was announced.

Clearly, in the cases both of the oil sands and the tar ponds, economic gains have been privileged over the possibilities of long-term health deficits. This could be seen as an example of hope (i.e., that the damage done will be insignificant or that scientists and others will find a solution to the resulting problems before they cause too much damage) or greed (i.e., a focus on profit and economic well-being regardless of threats to people or environments along the way).

Intra-societal Analyses

Social Inequality and Health

The degree of economic inequality has been increasing in Canada, especially recently, in the last decade of the twentieth century and into the twenty-first century. Consider the following statistics. In 1996, the top 20 per cent of the Canadian population earned 43.2 per cent of the total income, while the bottom 20 per cent earned 2.3 per cent (Ross and Roberts, 1999: 26). Many people are aware of the widening gap between the rich and the poor, the 'haves' and the 'have-not's in Canada. What you might be less familiar with is that there is a direct link between income inequality and health. A classic illustration of this relationship can be found in the Whitehall studies, which followed the health of more than 10,000 British civil servants for nearly 20 years and found that both the experience of well-being and a decline in mortality rates were associated with increases in the ranks in the occupational hierarchy of the British civil service (Marmot et al., 1978, 1991). Positive health benefits were found *in each increase in rank*. Remember, too, that this is a study of the civil service. Thus, all of the jobs under scrutiny were white-collar, office jobs with 'adequate' incomes. It is interesting that this finding held true even among people who engaged in health-threatening behaviours such as smoking. Thus, for instance, 'researchers found that top people who smoked were much less likely to die of smoking-related causes' than those nearer the bottom who did not smoke (National Council of Welfare, 2001–2: 5).

Poverty exacerbates health problems from birth onward. In 2004, the poverty rate in Canada was 15.5 per cent, the child poverty rate 14.1 for males under 18 years and 17.6 for females under 18 (www40.

statcan.ca/101/cs+01/famil41a.htm). The rate of poverty for children from one-parent families is 60 per cent as compared to 13 per cent for those from two-parent families;. Forty-three per cent of children of visible-minority parents and 52 per cent of Aboriginal children live in poverty (www.cich.ca). Poor women are more likely to bear low-birth-weight babies. Low birth weight is associated with myriad negative health, disability, learning, and behavioural effects. Children born in the poorest neighbourhoods in Canada (the lowest 20 per cent) live shorter lives, by 2 to 5.5 years. They also tend to spend more of these shorter lives with some degree of disability. Children at the lower end of the social hierarchy have a greater variety of health and developmental deficits than those higher up on the socio-economic status ladder. It is also important to notice that these results, like the Whitehall study results, are situated in the context of a nationally funded medical care system. Moreover, the number of children living in poverty grew by 700,000 between 1981 and 1996. It is also interesting to note that in a global context the rate of childhood poverty is high (www.cich.ca). It is also important to point out that the rate of childhoood poverty in Canada is *higher* than in other developed nations such as Sweden, where the incidence of childhood poverty is 3 per cent; the Netherlands, where it is 6 per cent; France and Germany, 7 per cent; and the United Kingdom, 10 per cent (ibid.).

HUMAN DIVERSITY

Health and Aboriginal Canadians

One of the most troubling health issues faced by Canadians today is the relatively poor health and shorter lives of Aboriginal Canadians. For instance, in the Northwest Territories, where more than half of the population is Aboriginal, the life expectancy is more than five years less for men and women, at 75 and 70 respectively (Helwig, 2000: 681). The infant mortality rate, one of the most sensitive indicators of the overall health of a people, is 1.5 times higher among First Nations people at 8 deaths per thousand as compared to 5.5 for all Canadians (Adelson, 2005). While this rate reflects a great improvement over the past 30 years, there is still reason for concern. Moreover, the major causes of death among First Nations people include diseases of development and impoverishment such as injury, poisoning, and respiratory disease along with the causes more common among other Canadians such as heart disease and cancer. Suicide and self-inflicted injury are the chief causes of death among those aged 10–44. This is followed by motor vehicle accidents, drowning, and homicide. Violence, including physical abuse, sexual abuse, and rape, is also significant problem. Aboriginal people are three to five times more likely to suffer from diabetes (non-insulin-dependent diabetes mellitus). Tuberculosis is eight to ten times more frequent. HIV/AIDS is also increasing dramatically among this population. The rate of infection grew from 1.0 per cent in 1990 to 7.2 per cent in 2001.

First Nations people also do very poorly in respect to the social determinants of health, including employment rates and household income (where household incomes average $25,040 as compared with $46,606 for other Canadians). This results from the fact that most Aboriginal Canadians live in the rural north of Canada, where there are fewer employment opportunities, as well as from 'the complex interplay of job market discrimination, lack of education, cultural genocide, and loss of land and sovereignty that affects employment status, and, ultimately, the degree of poverty faced by those who are caught in a circle of disadvantage' (ibid.). Aboriginal Canadians also are more likely to live in inadequate and crowded housing. For instance:

1. Homes are twice as likely to need repair.
2. Houses are 90 times as likely (9.4 per cent as compared with 0.1 per cent) to lack piped water.
3. Homes are five times more likely to lack bathroom facilities (3.2 per cent as compared with 0.6 per cent)
4. Households, on average, include four rather than three people, which is the Canadian average today.

The continuation of these inequities in the lives of Aboriginal Canadian reflects their historical position in Canadian governmental and social policy.

Even though there are substantial links between income inequality and both ill health and death, Canadian health policy continues to involve substantial investments in the health-care system rather than in community-level interventions such as a guaranteed annual wage, job creation, a national daycare program, or proactive prenatal care for low-income mothers. This is despite the fact that repeated studies have documented that interventions at these levels would have more widespread effects on the health of the population than do medical initiatives directed towards individuals.

The ways in which economic inequality affects health outcomes are complex and contested. Certainly, material needs are part of the explanation. For example, differential ability to pay for ample healthy foodstuffs and for clean, quiet, and temperature-appropriate living quarters are a part of the explanation. What the Whitehall studies suggest, however, is that there is likely something beyond material differences contributing to the explanation. One finding of the Whitehall studies was that while all levels of the civil service had elevated stress levels while at work, blood pressure levels of the senior administrators dropped when they went home; in contrast, the stress levels remained high for those lower in the hierarchy (National Council of Welfare, 2001–2). Socio-psychological issues related to perceptions of well-being and of relative advantage and disadvantage also appear to be implicated in inequities in health outcomes. In other words, people also feel stress and appear to have consequent health difficulties as a result of comparing their socio-economic positions (negatively) to those of others (Marmot et al., 1978, 1991).

Despite the fact that links beteween poverty, inequality, and health have been documented over a long period of time both within Canada and around the world, Canada's social and health policy-makers have continued largely to ignore the link (Franzini et al. in Aday, 2005). Coburn (2005: 340) argues that this is because of the dominance of neo-liberal doctrine, which holds that the market and market forces are the 'most efficient allocators of resources'. Intervention through redistributive social policies,(such as a guaranteed annual wage or full employment)—from the neo-liberal perspective—would impede the 'normal' functioning of markets. (344).

Social Capital

It is clear from all types of research done today and in the past, and in this and in other societies, that social status and health are related. Much of this analysis compares individuals who differ in health and **social status**. However, when the level of analysis moves from the individual to the society as a whole, the link between status and health remains. Societies with greater degrees of inequality have poorer overall health outcomes regardless of their overall wealth. Thus, for rates of health and illness, the overall wealth of a society appears to be less important than the degree of inequity among societal members with respect to rates of health and illness.

This interesting paradox needs clarification. Explanations for the individual-level correlation have suggested that people with higher incomes, higher occupational prestige scores, and higher educational levels are more able to prevent ill health through eating and drinking wisely, avoiding serious threats to health such as cigarette smoking and excessive alcohol consumption, and engaging in prescribed early detection such as mammograms and PSA (a test for prostate cancer). When those in these higher levels are sick, they are able to get immediately to the doctor and take advantage of the most sophisticated and effective new treatments. They are also, as the Whitehall studies intimated, able to maintain a sense of well-being through various socio-psychological processes.

Why would the degree of inequality in a society be more important than the average living standard and income of persons in a society in predicting health and illness outcomes? A recently developed theoretical explanation is that it is the degree of social cohesion, social capital, or trust that is the link between inequity and health (Mustard, 1999). A society characterized by inequity is one in which 'there is a pronounced status order' (Veenstra, 2001: 74). As people compare themselves to one another, it is possible—indeed, likely—that those lower in the status hierarchy 'will feel this shortcoming quite strongly, given the width of the gap, and consequently will suffer poorer health' (ibid., 75). This may result from 'damaging emotions such as anxiety and arousal, feelings of inferiority and low self-esteem, shame and embarrassment, and recognition of the need to compete to acquire resources that cannot be gained by any other means' (ibid.).

A number of researchers have suggested that societies with high degrees of inequality are also low in *social cohesion* (or *social capital*), and it is social cohesion that mediates between social status and illness. Social cohesion is thought to be evident in societies to the extent that people are involved in public life and volunteer to work together for the good of the whole. A society with little social cohesion might, for instance, be dominated by market values and characterized by transactions in the interest of profit. Current social policies in Canada that favour market dominance over state intervention exacerbate the degree of inequity in society.

Many researchers are now looking at the processes whereby societies in which there is a high degree of citizen involvement, communication, and community feeling (social cohesion or social capital) maintain relatively high levels of good health.

Socio-Psychological Factors: The Sense of Coherence

The *sense of coherence* is a socio-psychological concept articulated first by Aaron Antonovsky (1979). Rather than asking what makes people sick, Antonovsky wondered what kept people healthy. Having thought about this and reviewed available research, he defined *sense of coherence* as an orientation to the world and to one's place in it that leads a person to a long-lasting and dynamic feeling of confidence that 'things will work out' because (1) life is basically comprehensible, understandable, and predictable; (2) there are sufficient resources for the individual to be able to cope with whatever circumstances arise; and (3) life makes sense or has meaning. These three components of the sense of coherence enable individuals to manage life experience in a positive manner and to establish a basis for resisting disease and handling suffering. Recent research on the sense of coherence has found that there is a continuing link between the sense of coherence and health outcomes. (Kivimaki et al., 2000; Suominen et al., 2001).

Lifestyle Behaviours: Obesity and Eating Disorders

A number of recent articles in the *Canadian Medical Association Journal*, and indeed in the mass media, have reported on seemingly opposite health concerns: obesity, on the one hand, and eating disorders such as anorexia and bulimia, on the other. It seems that both are increasing among children and adults and that both herald other serious medical problems. Why are so many young people facing such problematic and contradictory issues related to food, body image, and control of eating?

Obesity is now pandemic (Katzmarzyk, 2002), affecting millions of people around the world, especially in rich countries, where between 10 and 20 per cent of the population are obese. In poor countries there are few obese people. *Obesity* is defined as an excess of fatty or adipose tissue; it 'results from un-balanced energy budgets. An overweight person consumes food energy in excess of expenditure and stores the surplus in body fat' (Obesity Canada, 2001). Recent research also suggests the use of certain plastics used as food and beverage containers may be creating larger and more permanent fat cells that are not affected by food intake reduction or exercise (toxsci.oxfordjournals.org/cgi/content/full/76/2/247). Other research, from the University of Wisconsin (www.eurekalert.org/pub_releases/2006-01/aps-coi012506.php), suggests particular viruses (Adenovirus-37) to which animals and humans are exposed create metabolic changes that store fat rather than allowing the body to burn it. Excess body fat is associated with higher rates of premature morbidity and death from diseases such as coronary heart disease, stroke, type 2 diabetes mellitus, gallbladder disease, and some cancers. Adult obesity is associated with 2.4 per cent of total direct medical costs (Katzmarzyk, 2002). Children are vulnerable, too, and the incidence of obesity among children is growing because of both an increase in calories and a decrease in exercise (Tremblay and Willms, 2000). The rate of growth from 1981 to 1996 is estimated at 92 per cent in boys and 57 per cent in girls (ibid.). Our sedentary lifestyle, typified by television viewing and computer games, has played a role in this growing health concern. Children who watch four or more hours of television a day have higher body mass indices and thicker skin folds than those who watch fewer than two hours per day. In addition, caloric intake is positively associated with television viewing (ibid.). By 2004, 26 per cent of children and adolescents ages 2–17 were overweight or obese, compared with 15 per cent in 1978–9.(*Canada Year Book*, 2006: 165).

While some children are gaining too much weight, others are losing or trying to lose too much. For example, in a survey of 1,739 adolescent females, 23 per cent were dieting to lose weight (Jones et al., 2001: 549). Binge eating was reported by 15 per cent, self-induced vomiting by 8.2 per cent, and the use of diet pills by 2.4 per cent. Disordered attitudes towards eating were found in over 27 per cent of the young women surveyed. Consistent with other studies, disordered eating behaviours and attitudes seemed to increase gradually during adolescence and were more common among girls with higher body mass indices (BMI), an international standard for measuring over-

Time to Reflect

What processes in the university or college encourage or discourage your involvement in extracurricular activities (which might enhance your social cohesion while at university)?

Thanks to those sweet and salty foods we love to eat, our society has produced the largest-ever crop of overweight and obese people. (Karen Kasmauski/Corbis)

weight and obese (Jones et al., 2001: 549–50). This link between obesity and disordered eating attitudes and behaviours is confirmed by studies showing that dieting on and off (yo-yo dieting) frequently leads not to weight loss but to obesity, partly because people use diet pills and laxatives to achieve weight loss.

The Existential Level

How do you experience illness? What sorts of illnesses have you had? Have you always gone to the doctor when you have felt ill? Have you gone to a naturopath, chiropractor, or acupuncturist? Have you always been able to get a diagnosis when you have sought to find out what is wrong with you? People around the globe and even within the variety of cultures and classes within Canada experience illness in different ways. There are competing and overlapping popular conceptions of illness, too. One compilation of popular notions of illness includes illness as choice, illness as despair, illness as secondary gain, illness as a message of the body, illness as communication, illness as metaphor, illness as statistical infrequency, and illness as sexual politics (Clarke, 2000).

Illness as choice refers to the notion that we choose when to become sick, what type of illness we will have, and so on. In other words, illness episodes are viewed as a reflection of the deep tie between the mind and the body. That illness is a sort of despair is a related notion. Primarily, however, the idea is that illness results from emotional misery. It reflects unresolved grief and unhappiness.

The notion of secondary gain emphasizes the idea that people sometimes benefit from illness—for instance, an ill

Time to Reflect

What other social factors are related to disordered eating behaviours and attitudes among adolescents?

student might not be able to write an exam for which he or she also happens to be unprepared. Closely related to this notion is the philosophy of illness that suggests that physical symptoms are a means through which the body communicates a message to the consciousness. And related to this, in turn, is the idea that the symptoms are meant to reflect a particular message, a particular set of unmet needs. For example, a cold, with its running nose and eyes, may be said to represent a frustrated desire to cry.

Susan Sontag (1978) has described some of the metaphors attached to diseases such as tuberculosis, AIDS, and cancer. One illustration of disease metaphor is the idea of a disease as an enemy and the subsequent necessity for a war against the disease. Illness as statistical infrequency, in contrast, is simply a numerical definition that names as 'illness' a bodily functioning or symptom that is infrequent in the population.

Finally, the idea that illness reflects gender politics is related to the **patriarchy** of the medical profession and its consequent tendency to see women's bodies as basically flawed and women's behaviours as more likely to be pathological (for example, meriting psychiatric diagnosis) than those of men. These medical views reflect gender and gender roles in society (see Clarke, 2000).

All of these different popular conceptions of illness have been taken up at one time or another by Canadians.

The existential level of analysis also now includes a new way of sharing research findings through art and poetry. The following prose poem was written to express the feelings of a mother whose child had cancer and whose symptoms (which immediately after this writing almost killed him) from the side effects of treatment were not taken seriously. The prose poem is in the words of the mother and taken from a transcript of an interview in a recent study on the home health-care work of mothers whose children have cancer (Clarke and Fletcher, 2004). The poem, in this context, is a means of expressing a key theme in a qualitative sociological study. (Note: the significance of chicken pox is that it is the one disease that parents are told that they must avoid or get immediate treatment for during the time that their child is sick with cancer and undergoing chemotherapy.)

A Mother's Lament

When we were sent home on a weekend
Benjamin was having abdominal pains
Severely
We called and it was the other oncologist
And it wasn't ours.
She said,
He is just constipated
And
to keep him at home
I ended up with a counter full of medications
and . . .
Finally
Rich rushed him into emergency in the
middle of the night.
The child
was
like a woman
in labour
Without an epidural.
His eyes were dilated and you could see the
contractions coming on . . .

We brought him in
And we found chicken pox on his abdomen
Rich brought him in
At 4 o'clock
in the morning . . . and
Emergency sent him home with a
prescription . . .

We were sent home.

The experience of illness has been portrayed in theatre (in plays such as M. Edson's *Wit*, 1999), movies (such as *Lorenzo's Oil*, 1992), poetry, and other art forms, such as the quilts made to honour those with breast cancer or HIV/AIDS. Perhaps these may also be effective means for the transmission of social science findings.

Sociology of Medicine

The sociology of medicine examines the location, definition, diagnosis, and treatments of disease. It includes an examination of the various health-care institutions such as hospitals, clinics, co-operatives, and home care, along with medically related industries and the training, work, and statuses of medical and nursing professions and other health-care providers today and in historical context.

Because the history of the twentieth century has been characterized by the increasing dominance of allopathic medicine and its spreading relevance to more and more of life (Zola, 1972), the term **medicalization** (the tendency for more and more of life to be defined as relevant to medicine) has provided an important conceptual framework for critical analysis. In this part of the chapter we will discuss the medical care system in Canada today.

The Canadian Medical Care System

Our present medical care system was first implemented in 1972 after a Royal Commission on Health Care (Hall, 1964–5), under Justice Emmett Hall, recommended that the federal government work with the provincial governments to establish a program of universal health care. While hospitalization and some medical testing had been covered before that, the new program was designed to cover physicians' fees and other services not already covered under the Hospital Insurance and Diagnostic Services Act (1958).

Four basic principles guided the program. The first was universality. This meant that the plan was to be available to all residents of Canada on equal terms, regardless of prior health record, age, income, non-membership in a group (such as a union or workplace), or other considerations. The second was portability. This meant that individual benefits would travel with the individual across the country, from province to province. The third was comprehensive coverage: the plan was to cover all necessary medical services, including dentistry, that required hospitalization. The fourth was administration. This referred to the fact that the plan was to run on a non-profit basis.

The Canada Health Act of 1984 added a fifth principle, accessibility. The costs of the plan were to be shared by the federal and provincial governments in such a way that the richer provinces paid relatively more than the poorer provinces; thus, the plan would also serve to redistribute wealth across Canada. Doctors, with few exceptions (found mostly in community health clinics), were not salaried by the government. Instead, they were and continue to be private practitioners paid by the government on a fee-for-service basis.

Privatization

Despite the presence of the universally available and federally supported national medical care system, there is considerable evidence of privatization within the system. Moreover, the degree of privatization varies across the provinces. By the late 1990s approximately 75 per cent of the Canadian system was public, 25 per cent private (Fuller, 1998). These figures, however, exclude physicians, who are in a somewhat anomalous position because, though most receive money from the state, they do so as private entrepreneurs compensated on the basis of the number of patients they see and the type of diagnosis and treatment they offer.

The private aspects of the Canadian system are dominated by multinational corporations involved in providing a variety of health-related goods and services, including additional medical insurance, information technology services, food and laundry for hospitals, long-term and other institutional care, drugs, medical devices, and home care (ibid.). The most important impetus for growth in the medical system is in the private sector, particularly in drugs and new (and very expensive) technologies such as MRI, CAT scan, and mammography machines and other increasingly popular diagnostic technologies, such as the PSA test for prostate cancer (ibid.).

Table 11.3 portrays the increase in personal expenditures on medical care from 2000 to 2004. Notice especially the relative rate of growth in expenditures for other health-care professionals (which could include, for example, providers of complementary and alternative health care) and for pharmaceuticals as well as other (unspecified) expenses.

There is considerable debate today about whether or not Canada can continue to afford a publicly funded and universally available medical care system. The mass media are full of stories of overcrowded emergency rooms and impossibly long waiting lists. These sorts of concerns often seem to lead to the argument that the problem is the publicly funded system. Consistent with the move to the political right both in Canada and throughout the Western world is an emphasis on the value of the free market, arguing that a private health-care system would be both more efficient and more cost-effective. However, evidence from a wide variety of sources does not support this point of view (Canadian Health Services Research Foundation, 2002). For example, Calgary recently moved to some degree of privatization: cataract surgery services are now bought from private companies. This has resulted not only in more costly cataract surgery, but also in longer waiting times than in the nearby cities of Lethbridge and Edmonton.

US studies on the effect of governments' buying of medical services from private companies also demonstrate problems with privatization. For instance, dialysis and kidney transplants are funded through the federally run Medicare program, which buys services from both for-profit and not-for-profit dialysis centres. Johns Hopkins University researchers compared over 3,000 patient records and found that the for-profit centres had higher death rates, were less likely to refer patients for transplants, and were less likely to treat children with the dialysis method most likely to be of benefit to them (ibid.).

Most US-based research suggests that for-profit (private) care costs more, pays lower salaries to staff, and incurs higher administrative costs but does not provide higher-quality care or greater access. Between 1990 and

Table 11.3 Health Expenditures, 2000–4 ($ millions)

	2000	2001	2002	2003	2004
Hospitals	30,554.5	32,199.0	34,375.1	36,808.7	36,896.8
Other institutions	9,331.3	10,104.7	10,776.5	11,547.6	12,456.1
Physicians	12,977.0	13,978.0	15,050.7	16,012.6	16,785.2
Other professionals	11,586.6	12,576.7	13,116.8	13,891.0	14,635.6
Drugs (prescribed and non-prescribed)	15,085.8	16,660.8	18,408.7	20,002.9	21,758.4
Other expenditures	18,368.3	20,791.8	22,313.9	24,741.0	25,743.7
Total health expenditures*	97,903.4	106,302.0	114,041.6	123,003.7	130,275.2
Health expenditures as % of GDP	9.1	9.6	9.9	10.1	10.1

*Totals may not be precise due to rounding.
Source: Adapted from *Canada Year Book* (2006: 166).

1994, for-profit hospitals billed approximately $8,115 (US) for every discharged patient, whereas not-for-profit hospitals charged $7,490 per person even though quality of care, according to some indices, was better in not-for-profit institutions. For instance, not-for-profits tend to provide higher rates of immunization, mammography, and other preventive services (ibid.). On average, people lose two years of life when they are treated in for-profit hospitals (Devereaux et al., 2002: 1402).

Some claim that private systems offer more choice. The inference is that public systems are restrictive because of bureaucratic government interference. In fact, however, the interference by insurance companies in medical decision-making in private, for-profit systems appears to be more problematic than state interference. The other aspect of the argument for choice is that a combined system would allow individuals the possibility of choosing between private and public services for different services. This argument, by and large, flies in the face of the repeatedly confirmed value orientations of Canadians, who continue to identify medicare as one of Canada's most important social programs.

Medicalization

Medicalization is the tendency of more and more of life to be defined as relevant to medicine. Irving Zola (1972) is one of the social theorists who has been critical of this process. He defined medicalization as including the following four components:

1. an expansion of what in life and in a person is relevant to medicine;
2. the maintenance of absolute control over certain technical procedures by the allopathic medical profession;
3. the maintenance of almost absolute access to certain areas by the medical profession;
4. the spread of medicine's relevance to an increasingly large portion of living.

The first area of medicalization is the expansion of medicine from a narrow focus on the biomechanics of the human body to a broader concern by medicine with the 'whole' person. The second area refers to the fact that there are things that only doctors are allowed to do to the human body, such as surgery. The third refers to the fact that doctors, through medicine, have been able to transform into medical problems areas of life such as pregnancy and aging that were formerly viewed as normal, neither as pathological nor as medically relevant processes. The fourth pertains to the way in which medicine increasingly has jurisdiction in areas formerly considered to be of relevance to the criminal justice or religious systems, such as criminality and alcohol addiction.

Medicalization has been shown to be evident in the tendency for more and more of life to be defined by the medical profession. Ivan Illich (1976) attributes the growth of medicalization to bureaucratization. Vincente Navarro (1975) claims that medicalization, or medical dominance, is more related to class and class

OPEN FOR DISCUSSION

The Power of Medicalization

The power of medicalization can be illustrated by the case of Tyrell Dueck. He was 13 when, in early October 1999, he was diagnosed with osteogenic sarcoma or bone cancer. Treatment upon diagnosis usually begins immediately with chemotherapy to shrink the tumour and stop the spread of the disease. Surgery is used next to remove the tumour or sometimes the whole limb if the disease is found to have spread. Chemotherapy may then continue. With immediate treatment and localized disease the prognosis can be excellent for full recovery.

At the point of diagnosis Tyrell's father, Tim Dueck, said that the family did not want Tyrell to undergo chemotherapy and surgery but wanted him to try alternative treatments. By 11 December, now a couple of months after the diagnosis, the hospital went to court in Saskatchewan and received a court order giving the Saskatchewan Minister of Social Services guardianship over Tyrell. This gave the minister the right to consent to treatment on Tyrell's behalf. After two rounds of chemotherapy doctors decided Tyrell's leg would have to be amputated and that this surgery would give him a 65 per cent chance for survival. The doctors were also clear that they believed that he would die without the amputation of his leg.

Nevertheless Tyrell decided that he did not want to have his leg removed. Nor did he want more chemotherapy. This created a new dilemma. The court order of guardianship had taken the power of consent for treatment from Tyrell's parents. It had not taken it from Tyrell himself. Another hearing began on 13 March. A psychologist and a psychiatrist gave contradictory evidence regarding whether Tyrell was legally mature and thus capable of making the decision against treatment on his own. The media were highly involved by this time and debate raged about the issue. It became clear that the Duecks believed that a combination of prayer and complementary health care in Mexico would heal Tyrell.

By 18 March the court decided that Tyrell was a 'mature minor' and therefore was to be required to have the prescribed medical treatment. But by this time further medical investigations revealed that the time lapse had decreased Tyrell's chances for survival to 10 to 15 per cent. At this point the Minister of Social Services withdrew the order of treatment and the Duecks were free to pursue alternative treatment in Mexico. They did so. Tyrell received the treatment. Nonetheless, Tyrell died a few months later (Rogan, 1999: 43–52).

Who do you think should have the power to decide in a situation like this, the state, the doctors, the parents, or the young person?

conflict, in particular the upper-class background and position of physicians. He also relates medicalization to the work of physicians who operate as entrepreneurs in the definition of health and illness categories and their relevant treatments.

Disease Mongering

Furthering this argument about the role of capitalism in the growth of medical dominance is the instrumental role that the pharmaceutical corporations play in 'disease mongering'. Through a series of suggestive anecdotes, Ray Moynihan, Iona Heath, and David Henry (2002) argue for critically examining the ways in which the pharmaceutical industry plays a significant role in defining as diseases conditions for which they have developed an effective drug. The researchers illustrate this practice through descriptive case histories of a process whereby a drug is manufactured and then a disease is newly highlighted as problematic. Three cases are highlighted: a baldness tonic for men, a drug for 'social phobia', and osteoporosis medication for aging women.

Ostensibly involved in public education about new diseases and treatments, and often working alongside doctors and consumer groups, the pharmaceutical industry has promoted as problematic conditions that may well be better seen as part of life. For example, the medicalization of baldness by Merck occurred after the development of their anti-baldness drug, Propecia, in Australia. Around the time of the patenting of the drug,

Time to Reflect

Some people argue that Canadian society is increasingly medicalized. Others argue that it is increasingly demedicalized. What social forces do you see that would support each of these points of view?

a major Australian newspaper reported on a new study that indicated that about one-third of men experienced hair loss (Hickman, 1998). Further, the article emphasized, hair loss sometimes led to panic and other emotional difficulties and had a negative impact on job prospects and well-being. At the same time, the paper featured news of the establishment of an International Hair Study Institute. What the newspaper failed to report was that both the study and the institute were funded by Merck and that the 'expert' quotations were from the public relations firm hired by Merck.

GlaxoSmithKline, another pharmaceutical company, along with the medical communications firm In Vivo, developed a three-year 'medical education program' to create a new understanding of irritable bowel syndrome (IBS) as a specific and treatable disease. According to documents from In Vivo, one of several companies specializing in corporate-backed medical 'education', the key aim of the education program was to ensure the following: 'IBS (irritable bowel syndrome) must be established in the minds of doctors as a significant and discrete disease state' (Moynihan et al., 2002: 886). The steps for this education program were all laid out, beginning with the establishment of an advisory board comprised of key opinion leaders from each state in Australia, who would provide information about what was currently believed about IBS and how this could be changed. Another strategy was to produce and distribute a newsletter that would reinforce the seriousness of the syndrome.

These two steps are just illustrations of some strategies used by pharmaceutical industries who have been advised in Britain's *Pharmaceutical Marketing* magazine to 'establish a need and create a desire' (Cook, 2001, cited ibid.). The report cited is based on several anecdotes. More and systematic research on the extent of these practices is needed, but even these few examples raise questions about what may be invisible and unregulated attempts to 'change public perceptions about health and illness to widen markets for new drugs' (ibid., 891).

Morale and Bullying among Doctors

Recent research in the United Kingdom has identified workplace bullying as a major source of stress at work for health-care professionals (Quine, 2002). One study among doctors who worked for the National Health Service found that one in three reported that they had been bullied in the year previous to the study (Quine, 1999). Another study found that bullying, racial harassment, and discrimination were everyday occurrences in the work lives of Asian and black doctors in the United Kingdom (Coker, 2002). In the United States, too, a few studies have identified mistreatment and bullying experienced by medical students, interns, and residents (Kassebaum and Cutler, 1998).

Lyn Quine developed a 'bullying' scale that includes 21 bullying behaviours, then sent a questionnaire containing this scale, a definition of bullying, and socioeconomic information questions to 1,000 doctors randomly selected from the British Medical Society list of doctors and representing various levels of responsibility and status. Thirty-seven per cent of the doctors surveyed reported that they had been bullied in the previous year, and 84 per cent had experienced at least one of the behaviours included on the 'bullying scale'; 69 per cent reported that they had observed others

(Mike Adams, www.NewsTarget.com. Copyright © Truth Publishing. Reprinted by permission of the publisher.)

being bullied (Quine, 2002: 878–9). Asian, black, and female doctors were significantly more likely to report having been bullied than white male doctors. The experiences of being bullied occurred all of the way up and down the job hierarchy.

Thus, even though doctors tend to be recruited from higher social class and educational backgrounds, they are not immune to discrimination on the job. While these studies of bullying have not been done in Canada, there is reason to think that the patterns might be generalizable to this country. However, the research needs to be done. It is particularly important as increasing numbers of Canadian-educated doctors are both female and from visible-minority backgrounds.

Bullying is not the only cause of increasingly poor morale among doctors around the world (Edwards et al., 2002). Poor morale is partly the result of doctors' increasing workload accompanied by a relative decrease in remuneration. However, according to extensive research, the declining morale of doctors is also, and perhaps more importantly, related to the changing social compact between doctors and the societies in which they practise. Doctors who were previously sole practitioners and operated as independent entrepreneurs within a private—even, many suggest, 'sacred'—doctor–patient relationship are now under intense surveillance by governments and corporations (such as insurance companies). They are presently faced with strict and pervasive accountability to organizations that not only monitor their work, but may even decide whether or not certain prescribed treatments are justified.

Evidence-based medicine may also contribute to decreasing morale. This new approach to medical practice removes the clinical judgement from the doctor and

SOCIOLOGY IN ACTION

Population Aging

You have probably heard the concern voiced that the health-care system will be stressed as the population ages in the next several decades in Canada as a result of the increase in age among the baby-boom generation. In fact, people over 65 are no more likely to be ill than adults at other ages. They are, however, more likely to use the health-care system when they are ill. Recent research from the Canadian Health Services Research Foundation demonstrates that the increasing utilization by seniors is not the result of their increasing numbers in the population but rather their relatively higher utilization rates. There is evidence that it is not the sick seniors who are responsible for the increase in costs but rather healthy seniors. The rate of doctor visits among the well, for example, in Manitoba between the 1970s and 1983 increased 57.5 per cent among specialists and 32 per cent for general practitioners. Unhealthy seniors' rates increased only 10 per cent or less. It appears that the elderly routinely receive more care than they formerly did. The cost of health-care increases, due to the simple aging of the population, is estimated to be only 1 per cent of the total health-care costs. The significant impact of population aging, then, appears to be the result of some degree of over-treatment of the elderly. Although such interventions as flu shots, hip replacement, and cataract surgery may be necessary, others may not (www.chsrf.ca/mythbusters).

Examine the following figure. What is the obvious explanation for what is portrayed? Having read the above paragraph, what do you think are the more complex and interesting explanations?

Figure 11.3 Increase in Medical Use by Seniors in Good and Bad Health, Manitoba, 1971–83

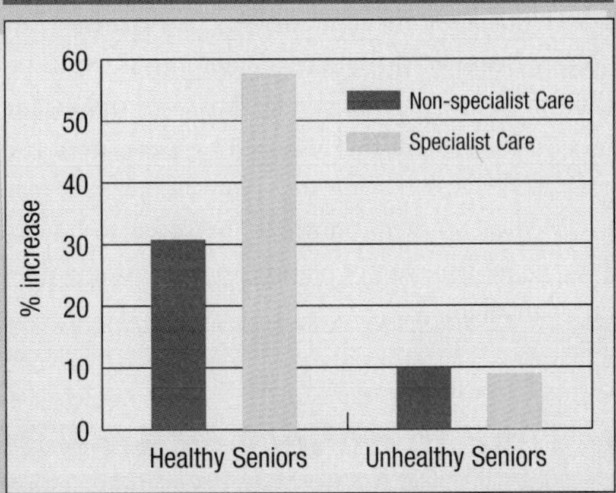

Source: Canadian Health Services Research Foundation, *Mythbusters*.

puts it into the hands of epidemiologists and other scientists who determine best-practice principles that doctors are expected to follow. In these conditions, medical decisions are not the sole purview of individual doctors working their craft and exercising their clinical experience in the midst of a 'sacred' professional relationship, but rather according to the results of research findings. Moreover, best-practice findings are no longer published only in arcane medical journals, but often are easily accessible to insurance company personnel and to individual patients through numerous, disease-specific Internet sites.

The Socio-economic Background of Medical Students in Canada

There are substantial differences between the backgrounds of medical students and those of the rest of the Canadian population. Doctors are not drawn, in a representative way, from across the socio-economic and socio-demographic variation of the whole population of citizens.

Specifically, medical students have been more likely to have had fathers who were doctors. This continues to be true today. In 1965, 11.8 per cent of medical students had fathers who were doctors. Today, 15.6 per cent have (Dhalla et al., 2002: 1032). Rural students, in contrast, were underrepresented in the mid-1960s and continue to be underrepresented today. Whereas 30.4 per cent of Canadian high school students lived in rural areas in 1965–6, only 8.4 per cent of the medical students did. Rural students are slightly better represented today (ibid.). In 1965–6, the fathers of 7.5 per cent of the population had attended university, while 38.0 per cent of the fathers of medical students had done so. Today, 39.0 per cent of the fathers of medical students earned graduate or doctoral degrees, compared with only 6.6 per cent of the whole population of the same age (ibid.). With respect to gender, however, significant changes have occurred. In 1965–6, 11.4 per cent of the medical students were female. Now about half are (ibid.). Medical students continue, however, to be less likely than the general population to be Aboriginal or African Canadian.

These findings are important in practical terms as well. For example, medical students who are from rural areas are more likely to practise in (underserviced) rural areas. And poorer people have poorer health outcomes, yet students from the poorest neighbourhoods are seven times less likely to attend medical school than those from the richest neighbourhoods (ibid.).

The trend towards privatization in Canadian universities can only exacerbate these discrepancies in adequate representation of medical students. Rising tuition fees in Ontario since 1997 have already affected the equitable representation of doctors such that there has been an increase in the self-reported family incomes of students in medical schools while they are graduating with more debt, are more likely to consider finances when choosing a place to practise, and are more likely to report financial stress while in school (Kwong et al., 2002).

Conclusion

In many ways, health issues are fundamentally social issues. The rates, definitions, and meanings of illness, sickness, disease, and death have varied and continue to vary around the world and over time. Within Canadian society, these differences, particularly in rates, reflect culture and social structure and mirror inequality and marginalization. They are affected by large external physical forces such as characteristics of the physical environment and by smaller lifestyle, existential, and psychosocial factors.

Medical care is dominated by allopathic medicine today. However, a sizable minority of Canadians are now choosing complementary and alternative care. Still, there is continuing evidence of the dominance of medical definitions of reality (medicalization) in many parts of life. As well, evidence increases of the manipulation of medicalization by the pharmaceutical industry and its entrepreneurial disease-defining work. While there is substantially more privatization in the Canadian medical care system today, it has tended not to reduce costs or to provide better medical service but the reverse. Finally, it appears that doctors in the system are experiencing low levels of job satisfaction and morale today.

Time to Reflect

Do you think it is important for the backgrounds of physicians to reflect the cultural, ethnic, and other diverse features of Canada? Explain.

Questions for Critical Thought

1. What are the implications of developing health policy on the basis of the mortality rate from the chief causes of death in Canada as compared to PYLL?
2. Discuss the evidence for an increasingly medicalized society.
3. What are the costs and benefits of medicalization?
4. Assess the opportunities for social cohesion in your college or university. Are there things to do available to you in class or extracurricularly that give you chances to get to know and trust people from different programs and years at your university?
5. What challenges to your health are evident in your school? In your answer include challenges related to the physical plant, the organization of learning and testing, and the social life available to students.
6. Discuss the water or air quality of the town where you are going to school. Discuss the strategies that you have used to get information about the air or water quality. Assess the quality of the information to which you have gained access.
7. Examine three magazines that you commonly read for their health-related messages. Include both articles and advertisements in your analysis. Consider the portrayal of issues such as gender, ethnicity, and social class in your discussion.
8. Compare the sense of coherence and social cohesion. To what extent are these concepts related to one another?

Recommended Readings

Pat Armstrong and Hugh Armstrong, *Wasting Away: The Undermining of Canadian Health Care* (Toronto: Oxford University Press, 1996).

This book is based on interviews, observation, and documentary evidence regarding the effects of the 'cuts' to and privatization of health care in Canada. The focus here is especially on the effects of the changes on workers and patients.

Pat Armstrong, Hugh Armstrong, and David Coburn, eds, *Unhealthy Times: Political Economy Perspectives on Health and Care in Canada* (Toronto: Oxford University Press, 2001).

This is a fascinating book on the ways that economics and politics influence health in Canada and globally. Topics covered include globalization and its impact on health and the health-care system, the pharmaceutical industry, health-related ideologies such as neo-liberalism, the impact of capitalism on the curriculum of pharmaceutical sciences, women's health issues related to health-care reform, the relationship between work and health globally, environmental contamination and political ecology, and poverty, social disintegration, and health among Canadians.

Sharon Batt, *Patient No More: The Politics of Breast Cancer* (Charlottetown, PEI: Gynergy, 1994).

This award-winning story of the politics of breast cancer in Canada and the Western world begins with the experience of the author's own diagnosis and moves from this through the larger world of breast cancer science, medicine, and charities.

David Coburn, Carl D'Arcy, and George Torrance, eds, *Health and Canadian Society: Sociological Perspectives*, 3rd edn (Toronto: University of Toronto Press, 1998).

This excellent reader provides an overview of the socio-historical development of the medical system, health-care costs, and the health status of Canadians. It also provides a number of empirically based commentaries on various social factors known to be related to health and illness.

Daniel Drache and Terry Sullivan, eds, *Market Limits in Health Reform: Public Success, Private Failure* (London: Routledge, 1999).

The essays in this collection are written largely from a political economy perspective. The book focuses on the tensions between a nationally funded medical care system and a growing move towards a market-driven economy, comparing the UK, the US, and Canada with respect to the effects of privatization and rationalization on health and on health costs.

Colleen Fuller, *Caring for Profit: How Corporations Are Taking Over Canada's Health Care System* (Vancouver: New Star, 1998).

Fuller is a health-care activist and researcher who wrote this book while she was a research associate at the Canadian Centre for Policy Alternatives. After discussing the beginnings of the medicare system in Canada, Fuller charts medicare's history up to the current period of privatization. She documents examples of privatization across the country to demonstrate that medicare is no longer a universal system.

Anne Kasper and Susan J. Ferguson, eds, *Breast Cancer: Society Shapes an Epidemic* (New York: St Martin's Press, 2000).

This reader is written with a multi-disciplinary perspective, including sociology, women's health activism, environmentalism, medicine, health policy, and health management. It makes the case that the breast cancer epidemic is socially constructed from the very diagnosis to ideas about treatment and early detection.

Samantha King, *Pink Ribbons, Inc.: Breast Cancer and the Politics of Philanthropy* (Minneapolis: University of Minnesota Press, 2006).

This book examines the corporate face of fundraising for breast cancer with a series of interrelated papers on various aspects of funding medical research.

Michael Rachlis and Carol Kushner, *Strong Medicine: How to Save Canada's Health Care System* (Toronto: HarperCollins, 1994).

Written by a physician and a journalist, this is an accessible account of various problems in the Canadian system. The authors advocate fundamental structural reform in the interests of quality and efficiency while maintaining universal medical care.

Recommended Websites

Health Canada
www.hc-sc.gc.ca

Health Canada, a government department, provides health-related information on topics such as healthy living, health care, diseases and conditions, health protection, and media stories. You can also find here the latest statistics regarding health, illness, death, PYLL, medical care system characteristics, and current issues.

Globe and Mail
www.theglobeandmail.com/health/

This is the website of Canada's national daily newspaper. It provides journalistic accounts of the latest in imporant health-related news stories in Canada.

The Hunger Site
www.thehungersite.com

This is a site for those who are concerned about world hunger, who want to keep informed on the situation and to take action.

National Institutes of Health
www.nih.gov

The National Institutes of Health in the US provides access to research, health news, and various health-related resources.

National Network on Environments and Women's Health
www.yorku.ca/nnewh/english/nnewhind.html

This is one of the five federally funded Centres of Excellence for Women's Health. It focuses on women's health and workplaces, including paid and unpaid work, unemployment and labour force restructuring and adjustments, health systems (both conventional and unconventional forms of health care), formal and informal practices, women's understandings of health and health risks, and policy.

National Women's Health Information Center
www.4woman.gov

The Office on Women's Health and the Department of Health and Human Services of the US federal government provides an excellent site for the latest findings regarding health research, particularly as it pertains to women (there is also an internal link to men's health issues included on the home page). Topics include screening and immunization information, advice on how to quit smoking, action strategies regarding breast-feeding, information about violence against women, body image, women with disabilities, and health information for 'minorities'. This site would also be of use as a document for content analysis regarding current definitions of significant health issues and their treatments.

Public Health Agency of Canada
www.phac.asac.gc.ca/

The Public Health Agency of Canada offers access to research and working papers on the social determinants of health, health promotion, and population health perspectives.

Statistics Canada
www.statcan.ca

Statistics Canada publishes myriad studies on Canadian society, including statistics relevant to morbidity, mortality, disease incidence, birth rates, and so on.

United Nations Statistics Division
http://unstats.un.org/unsd/

This site provides global statistics on the populations, families, health, education, communication, work, human rights, and political decision-making of people in nations around the world.

World Health Organization
www.who.int/

The World Health Organization provides information, fact sheets, various reports, and news about health issues around the world. It also covers essential information regarding worldwide epidemics and news about outbreaks of various illnesses in a worldwide context, including epidemic and pandemic alerts and responses.

Chapter 12

Religion

Lorne L. Dawson

Learning Objectives

In this chapter, you will:

- Learn about the prominent place religion has held in all human societies in the past.
- Think about the basic dimensions of religion.
- Learn about the crucial functions that the great sociological theorists thought religion served in all societies.
- Discover that the supposed demise of religion in modern societies may be misleading.
- Learn that the forms in which religion is expressed in modern Western societies may be changing, but that the basic demand for religious answers persists.
- Study how the religious life of Canadians has changed since the middle of the twentieth century.
- Find out how the Internet and non-European immigration are changing contemporary religious life in North America.

Photo: AFP/Getty Images

Introduction: Why Study Religion?

To the best of our knowledge, humankind has always been religious. Until very recently, every aspect of human social life was imbued with meaning and regulated by religious systems of beliefs and practices. People's very sense of time and space were organized by religious principles and marked by ritual activities. The cycle of the year followed the calendar of holy days and festivities, while the temple or cathedral lay at the physical heart of every town or city. *Sacred* (which means 'set apart') *places,* where the gods or other supernatural forces were thought to reside, were secure refuges from the cruelties of nature and enemies. In these special places people could call on the strength of their gods to protect them and to assure them that there was life after death for the faithful. The time and space dedicated to making contact with and preserving the integrity of the sacred gave structure to the profane time and space around people. Birth, death, and every major life transition in between were understood in terms of religious **rites of passage** (for example, baptisms, marriages, and funerals) that made these events meaningful and legitimate. The great events of the world, from wars to the coronation of kings and the launching of ships, were marked by ceremonies designed to gain the favour of supernatural powers, while the events of daily living, from planting crops to cursing an unco-operative neighbour, were suffused with words and gestures that acknowledged and invoked a spiritual presence. Religious beliefs and behaviours were so common that until a few centuries ago most societies did not even have a word like 'religion'. Religion was so much a part of everyday life that there was little need to distinguish it.

With the rise of science and the material comforts and security that came with industrialization, much of this has changed for the prosperous nations of Europe, North America, parts of Asia (such as Japan), and elsewhere. We live in societies that are much less manifestly religious. Yet, as the great sociologist Max Weber reasoned, the root causes of religious belief have not been significantly displaced by our recent progress in achieving either prosperity or knowledge. We may no longer sense as strong a need to curry the favour of the gods in our daily lives, but Weber (1963 [1920–1]) suggested there is an inner compulsion on the part of humanity to understand the world as a meaningful cosmos, and a consequent desire to take a consistent and unified stance towards this cosmos. Throughout most of our history humans have been unwilling to live in uncertainty about the ultimate meaning of life. This impulse, which can be very intense, has taken on a life of its own in human history driven by the need of humans, as a species and as individuals, to cope with the reality of various forms of suffering in their lives.

In this sense, Weber finds at the heart of all religious systems what Christian theology calls **theodices**. A theodicy is an attempt to explain and justify why God or other supernatural forces would allow the suffering we all experience, from nature and human causes. In particular, many people need some way to account for the suffering of the innocent and of the righteous. While today a mother can know that a specific disease was responsible for how her child died, her need to reconcile her child's death with the world she still inhabits is as great as that of any mother in the past. Her need is not to explain this suffering as justifiable, but to place it in a framework of meaning that renders it bearable and that strengthens her resolve to face whatever life brings of joy or sorrow. Without this resolve, in Weber's view, societies themselves would wither and die.

Over the course of human history, religious beliefs have changed, prompting sweeping changes in the social conditions of life. The world is a different place because of the past actions of military and political leaders, figures like Napoleon, Lincoln, and Stalin. But few individuals have transformed the world so completely and lastingly as Abraham, Moses, Confucius, Lao-tzu, the Buddha, Jesus, and Muhammad. In reshaping the thoughts and feelings of even the lowliest citizen of any society, religious reformers have exerted more influence on human affairs than anyone else. People respond to the prophet's call, Weber argues, when their desire for greater meaning, order, and justice is frustrated. This frustration is the result of the discrepancies between the expectations and explanations we learn from our societies and our actual experiences. In the face of the seeming irrationality of so much that happens to us, the suffering caused by natural events and experienced at the hands of our fellow human beings, a plethora of religious views have arisen, some gaining acceptance and spreading, others disappearing, almost without a trace.

The collapse of certain forms of religious expression in some societies of the advanced industrial West is indicative of a growing discontent with the existing religious institutions. The church-centred Christianity that satisfied the needs of so many Canadians from the founding of our nation through to about the 1960s appears to be losing its relevance. But the data collected by sociologists continue to reveal a strong and ongoing desire for

IN THE FIRST PERSON

I was on my way to becoming a lawyer when I took some courses in religious studies, especially a fourth-year seminar in the sociology of religion. Within a year I was doing graduate work in the latter. Perhaps my interest stems from the fact that religion is one of the most difficult subjects to study sociologically; yet almost all societies are shaped profoundly by their religious heritage. What does it mean to be human? What is the ultimate purpose of the societies we build? The answers to these basic questions are codified in our diverse religious visions. I wanted to understand the nature, wisdom, or folly of these visions, and their consequences for everyday life. I was intrigued by the sheer intellectual challenge of determining how such a subjective phenomenon could be studied scientifically. The mysteries of religious life continue to make its study a stimulating challenge. The things people do in the name of religion—good and bad—leave us no end of important issues to investigate.—Lorne Dawson

meaningful responses to the ultimate issues of life. We undoubtedly live healthier and more materially comfortable lives than our predecessors, so our religious orientations have changed. We no longer turn to God so readily to help us survive a long journey or to make our crops grow. But the kinds of suffering that Weber saw as fundamental to the religious impulse remain an unavoidable presence in our lives. Illness, accidents, heartbreak, loneliness, and death still punctuate and disrupt, and sometimes define, our lives, and with the advent of mass media every Canadian is now embroiled, if only emotionally, in the catastrophic or senseless suffering of thousands or millions of others around the world.

The force of the interrelatedness of societies was demonstrated by the public response in Canada to the tragic events of 11 September 2001 in the United States. A hundred thousand Canadians gathered on Parliament Hill in Ottawa three days after members of the terrorist group al-Qaeda crashed the planes they hijacked into the twin towers of the World Trade Center and into the Pentagon. Canadians gathered to share their grief and show their solidarity with their American friends and allies. Similar memorial services, redolent with religious symbols, prayers, and other invocations of God, were held across Canada.

In the United States, which is a much more religious society to begin with, the shocking attack, seemingly unprovoked by Americans, spurred public officials from the President to the mayor of New York City to set aside the constitutional separation of church and state and call on their citizens to pray for the salvation of the thousands who had lost their lives and for the future safety of their country. Levels of church attendance rose markedly for weeks after, and throughout Manhattan memorials with candles, flowers, and pictures honouring the dead were created in parks, on church steps, and around the lampposts where pictures of missing loved ones had been posted.

It would be difficult to imagine how Canadians or Americans could have responded to this disaster without religion, and in honouring the anniversary of this tragedy people turn to their faith in a higher being, no matter how implicit or vague, to seek the appropriate words of solace and significance to commemorate the shocking events and tragic loss of lives. The first anniversary began with a moment of silence in the United States and ended with a plea from President George W. Bush to pray that God 'will see us through and keep us worthy'. The citizens of the most powerful, modern nation in human history struggled to cope with what had happened while listening to the stirring sentiments of traditional hymns such as 'Amazing Grace' and 'The Battle Hymn of the Republic'. These songs, known by almost everyone, related those who grieved to one another, to the struggles of their nation's past, and to the promise of a better future—in line with God's providence. Americans believe this faith, variously defined, makes them stronger, and perhaps in the end it does. That is a difficult judgement for a sociologist to make, as it is unclear what kind of evidence could be used to prove the case. But Émile Durkheim, another great sociologist of religion, suspected strongly that societies needed something like the unifying force of a common religion to succeed. Yet, he could see that a shared religious world view was

SOCIOLOGY IN ACTION

'The Battle Hymn of the Republic'

The stirring words of this classic American hymn were sung by the soldiers of the Union Army as they marched into battle in the US Civil War. It was set to the tune of the anthem of the American anti-slavery movement, 'John Brown's Body'. The verses refer to the second coming of Christ to defeat evil and judge humanity, as foretold in the last book of the Bible, the Book of Revelation. It is easy to see why contemporary Americans could still find comfort in these words in the face of threats to their nation.

Mine eyes have seen the glory of the coming of the Lord;
He is trampling out the vintage where the grapes of wrath are stored;
He hath loosed the fateful lightning of his terrible swift sword;
His truth is marching on.
Glory, glory, hallelujah! His truth is marching on! *[repeat after each verse]*

He hath sounded forth the trumpet that shall never call retreat;
He is sifting out the hearts of men before his judgment seat.
O be swift, my soul, to answer him; be jubilant, my feet!
Our God is marching on!

In the beauty of the lilies Christ was born across the sea,
With a glory in his bosom that transfigures you and me;
As he died to make men holy, let us live to make men free,
While God is marching on!

He is coming like the glory of the morning on the wave;
He is wisdom to the mighty, he is succour to the brave;
So the world shall be his footstool, and the soul of time his slave:
Our God is marching on!

—Julia Ward Howe (1819–1910)

increasingly unlikely in the complex societies of the future, and he feared what the consequences of living without religion might be.

As a Canadian, especially if you are a young Canadian, you probably would find it hard to imagine how prevalent religion once was, since we live in one of the few truly secularized societies in the world. The role of religion in our social life seems to be in decline, a process that sociologists call **secularization**. From colonial times until the 1960s, much of community life was centred on the church and its activities; today, however, people dedicate most of their time, money, and energy to other pursuits and institutions. The religious symbols and leaders who formerly shaped the consciences and habits of most Canadians have been displaced by other leaders and influences of a decidedly more secular nature, whether political, economic, or social. Now, it appears that popular music fads, rather than religion, are more prominent in the lives of most Canadian teenagers, and the public presence of religion has dissipated dramatically for all Canadians. Until recently, the churches played a prominent role in educating Canadians and meeting their medical and welfare needs through the hospitals and charities they sponsored. You could not shop on Sundays, get an abortion, or have an alcoholic drink at a table outside of a hotel, because these behaviours offended the religious sensibilities of most citizens. In the last 50 years this has changed, and with the spread of modernization most sociologists thought the same would be true in the rest of the world. But things have not turned out as expected.

We are inclined to think that what has happened here will soon happen everywhere, and hence that we need not pause to consider how our experience may be different and could bias our understanding. But the

Houses of worship, with their familiar architecture, are finding new uses as community and cultural centres—even retail outlets—to supplement their dwindling role as places of prayer. (Ivy Images)

experience of Canadians, we now know, is not typical. In fact, it is atypical in some important regards. We are inclined to overlook this fact because the changes in the practice of religion in Canada seem to be in line with the expectations of some of the influential commentators on religion, from Karl Marx (Marx, 1957 [1844]) and Sigmund Freud (1961 [1927]) through to Peter Berger (1967). Other nations, such as Sweden, Holland, Britain, and Australia, share our experience of secularization. But this is not the case in much of the Muslim world, South America, Africa, and, perhaps most curiously, the United States. In the last few decades many millions of Americans have experienced a religious revival, and one need only turn on the radio or TV in most US cities to become aware of this differernce. The citizens of the world by and large still are religious, though often in new ways; and the onset of modernity does not mean religion will cease to be important.

If the Canadian experience is analyzed and compared with what is happening elsewhere, we can see that the reality that has evolved here is much more complex and sociologically significant than sociologists first expected. Most sociologists of religion speak now of the changing face of religion in societies living with the conditions of late modernity, not of its simple demise. Though at present just what this means in terms of social structures is unclear, the widespread demand for a religious or spiritual aspect in their lives persists among contemporary Canadians and sociologists are more likely to observe that complete secularization of the society is unlikely.

It is not my intention to suggest that religion simply is about coping with pain, fear, and the unknown. Most religious activity happens at a more mundane and daily level, and religions serve many other important functions in society, in intended and unintended ways. But for contemporary Canadian society, in which secularization has made deep inroads, where people's experience of conventional church-oriented religion seems increasingly tangential to their lives, it is important to stress the ways a primal need and desire for religion persist. Moreover, there is reason to believe that even in Canada we may be on the cusp of a great shift in the form and functioning of religion as an integral part of social life. Most sociologists of religion are convinced that the outward appearance of secularization in many modern Western nations belies a deeper continuity in the ways people will be religious, one that assures a significant, though somewhat different, expression of religion in humanity's future.

To understand the debate over the future place of religion in modern societies like Canada, we must begin to discuss what religion is: its dimensions and functions. This leads us to the influential insights of the classical theorists of sociology, Karl Marx, Émile Durkheim, and Max Weber. Then we can turn our attention to some new ways of thinking about the process of secularization and discuss how religious practice seems to be changing in Canada, the United States, and elsewhere around the world. Religion is likely to continue to be a significant force for good or evil in human affairs in the twenty-first century, compelling sociologists to learn more about its nature and functioning.

The Nature of Religion: Definition and Dimensions

To determine how significant a presence religion has become in the modern world, and whether its nature has changed, we first need to have a clear idea of what we mean by the term. The task is more difficult than initially it might seem. Most of us have an understanding of what religion is, but our view likely is based on limited experience. We derive our ideas largely from what traditionally was considered religious in our society. Most Canadians realize, however, that going to church to pray, to listen to a sermon, and to sing hymns is only one of many ways of being religious. The diversity of ways people around the world express religious belief and feeling, some of them bringing their practices to Canada as well, raises issues with our traditional definitions of 'religion'. Can we identify some features that all religions share? How have sociologists tried to define religion?

Defining Religion

When we refer to some behaviour or set of behaviours as a 'religion' what precisely do we mean? There is no consensus in sociology. The diversity of things people have held sacred through the centuries and the practices they have adopted relative to these sacred things are so vast as to defy inclusion under any one definition. When pressed, most sociologists revert to a pragmatic definition suited to their immediate empirical task or theoretical interest. These definitions tend to reflect a range of possibilities configured along a continuum anchored by substantive definitions at one end and functional definitions at the other.

Substantive definitions try to delineate some crucial feature assumed of all religious activity. They focus on what religion *is*. A classic and simple example is provided by the eminent British anthropologist Edward Tylor (1903), who defined religion as 'belief in Spiritual Beings'. Functional definitions focus, alternatively, on what religion 'does', and a simple and classic example is provided by the American sociologist of religion Milton Yinger: 'Religion [is] a system of beliefs and practices by means of which a group struggles with [the] ultimate problems of human life' (1970: 7). Each approach has its well-known limitations, and many sociologists have devised definitions that attempt to blend the two perspectives while minimizing their liabilities.

Substantive definitions tend to be too exclusive. Tylor's definition, for example, has been criticized on three counts. First, the definition suggests that religions primarily are sets of **beliefs**. However, this frequently is not the case in any strict sense for the religious practices of most preliterate peoples—and even for the followers of some more contemporary forms of religious expression, such as neo-pagans and Wiccans (adherents of various forms of witchcraft). Their beliefs are quite fluid and not encoded in any definitive set of texts accepted by all as authoritative. Moreover, in some religious traditions holding certain beliefs is secondary to participating in specific rituals and other shared activities (for example, in Hinduism and Taoism). Orthopraxis ('right practice') may take precedence over orthodoxy ('right belief'). The stress on 'belief' in our sociological definitions may manifest an **ethnocentric bias** since orthodoxy is characteristic of the major religions of the West: Judaism, Christianity, and Islam. These are called 'religions of the book' (that is, the Torah, the Bible, and the Qur'an) for their emphasis on their sacred writings, and Tylor's definition reflects this bias.

Second, the specification of 'spiritual beings' would also exclude some forms of religion. Contemporary neo-pagans and some Buddhists, for example, either see such a belief as optional or formally deny it. There is no absolute God or, strictly speaking, any gods at all for the Theravada Buddhists living throughout Southeast Asia. In other regards, however, most observers would identify these groups as religious, and little is gained empirically by excluding them from the category. The Buddha is worshipped, rituals are performed, holy days are celebrated, and moral standards are derived from a set of sacred scriptures.

Third, Tylor's substantive definition of religion raises a problem very common to most definitions of religion: it relies on terms that are themselves in need of definition. In this case, for instance, we might ask what constitutes a 'spiritual being'.

Functional definitions suffer from the opposite tendency: that of being too inclusive. Their terms of reference tend to be so broad that it is difficult to distinguish true religions from what sociologists call 'functional equivalents' (an intense involvement in sport, commerce, or theatre, for example). Furthermore, they too frequently invite an infinite regress of definitional questions. Yinger's definition focuses on struggles with the

Time to Reflect

Whether you are religious or not, can you avoid it having an impact on your life?

ultimate problems of human life, but what constitutes an 'ultimate problem'? Additional specification is needed, and disagreements are likely with any list of problems or criteria of 'ultimacy'. Is it appropriate to suggest that the world view of radical environmentalists is their religion? What if they display an abiding concern with being good environmentalists, perhaps even at the cost of laying down their lives to protect some endangered species or ecological niche? Does the inclusion of such activities within the bounds of religion help, or does such talk simply blur the boundaries between phenomena in a way that is analytically unhelpful? Too many things become 'religious', critics charge, when the functionalist perspective is adopted.

In framing their definitions of religion, sociologists must seek to balance the relative strengths and limitations of these options in the service of their immediate research objectives. Some of the most famous definitions of religion have incorporated elements both of the substantive and of the functional approaches. Durkheim, for instance, defined religion as 'a unified system of beliefs and practices relative to sacred things . . . which unite into one single moral community . . . all those who adhere to them' (1965 [1912]: 62). The substantive element here is concern with the sacred, which is used to differentiate religion from other activities. The functional element is reflected in the identification of religion with the creation of moral communities. Does this approach dissolve the definitional dilemma or merely compound it? It is difficult to say in the principle, and much will depend on how it is used.

Recently many researchers have chosen to stress the contextual nature of all our conceptions of religion. These sociologists contend that ideas and practices called 'religious' are **social constructions** born of specific times and places and that it is futile to search for any universal or essential features or functions. But if we simply say that whatever people call religion is religion, then we lose the ability to make systematic comparisons and generalizations about this phenomenon, let alone to be analytical. In thinking about religion we inevitably are working with some implicit definition, no matter how leery we are of making generalizations. So, making our definitions explicit and known, though provisional, avoids our falling prey to unintended biases and untested assumptions. Most sociologists seek to strike a balance between the exclusive and inclusive tendencies of substantive and functional definitions, and are content to follow the lead of the philosopher Ludwig Wittgenstein, who suggests that almost all of our concepts operate through a principle of 'family resemblance'. There is no definitve list of criteria for assessing whether or not something is a religion, any more than there is for such other social phenomena as sports, music, or medicine. In the practice of science, just as in life, we make sense of things by bringing a cluster of related atrributes to bear on a situation and then making a judgement about whether something belongs to that category. Some things display more of some of the features we have in mind, others display more of other features. But as long as we find sufficient overlap we are inclined to identify them as being the same kind of thing. Still, it is useful to think about the attributes we associate with any phenomenon. Educating oneself about the range of possibilities for categories ensures clearer judgements about what should and should not be included, though the possibility for debate remains.

Dimensions of Religion

However one decides to divide religions from non-religions, all religions seem to share certain dimensions or elements, though some non-religions have them as well. These dimensions have been conceived in different ways (e.g., Glock and Stark, 1965; Smart 2000), but every religion of which I am aware recognizes a set of beliefs, practices some rituals, makes claims about certain special experiences, and is a shared or communal activity. By briefly considering each of these dimensions of religious life we can identify some of the things sociologists must bear in mind when studying religion, and may gain a sense of the complex nature of religion as a subject of study.

Belief

Most obviously, religions are systems of beliefs. To be religious is to 'believe' something about the nature of the world that you have been taught by others who hold similar beliefs, based on the authority of some respected teacher—a guru, prophet, or saviour. Religious life has a cognitive aspect; it is about knowing certain things and thinking in certain ways. Religions provide people with highly generalized understandings of life that can be called world views. These world views explain why things are the way they are, and they tell us what can be done, accordingly, to make our lives better or more complete. More often than not these teachings are grounded in some kind of primary belief in the existence of another level or type of reality, another world—of supernatural beings, heaven, nirvana, or the complete, blissful unity of all things—that is considered more important in some ways than this world. The other world can or often does exert a significant influence on how things happen in this world. From the sociological perspective it is not important that this presumed other world, of supernatural beings or whatever, be real in the same way as sensorily perceived reality. Whether they exist is not relevant, as long as people believe them to be true, because sociologists are interested in studying the consequences of holding these beliefs. If a person believes in the existence and effect of evil spirits in this world, then they are 'real' in the consequences for how that person leads his or her life. The social effects are real, whether or not the beliefs are 'true'.

The word 'religion' normally calls to mind the formal creeds and sets of doctrines that people hold. One might say that Buddhists differ from Christians because they believe different things, as laid out in their respective teachings. The Buddha taught that there is no God, and that we must seek our salvation from a world of perpetual rebirth by discovering the right way to live through the practice of meditation. Jesus taught that we can find salvation from our sins by placing our faith in a creator God, who loves us like a father, can be communicated with, and expects us to love one another during our one brief life on this earth. Yet, for most believers the daily practice of their religion is less a matter of formal teachings than of the lessons learned about leading the good life that are found in the myths, stories, images, and music of its tradition. This other less formal kind of knowledge shapes people's values and guides their behaviour. The great religious leaders of the world set an example for us, and we practise a religion by honouring and emulating how they lived as much as by what we are told they said. The feelings evoked by the sights, sounds, and experiences of our childhood, of our first exposure to religion, are more important than anything else in determining if and how we are religious.

Ritual

As children we participate in the performance of rites often before we have a grasp of what they mean. Being religious entails doing things, especially actions meant to arouse affective states, to engage our emotions. Religious meanings are given concrete form; they are enacted, through the repeated use of bodily gestures and actions, whether crossing oneself before the altar as a Catholic or prostrating oneself towards the east and Mecca during prayers at the mosque as a Muslim. Rituals can be simple, barely attracting notice (e.g., saying 'bless you' after someone sneezes), or elaborate and conspicuous (e.g., the coronation of a king or queen). The range of rituals humans have devised is enormous and varied, and the study of rituals—what they are, how they operate, why they matter—is a complex field. It is hard to imagine a religion without some regular, repeated, and prescribed actions that are intended either symbolically (to remind us of the teachings of our religion) or literally (to elicit the response of the otherworldly powers) to bring us to the heart of religious belief. Such rituals include, for example, the Catholic mass, formulaic prayers, animal sacrifices, chanting or singing, processions, communal meals, the burning of incense and candles, the donning of special clothing, the pouring of water or wine or milk or other libations, the bestowing of flowers and food on images, and so on.

One of the categories of rituals most commonly performed in Canadian society is the rite of passage. These rituals, which entail the symbolic stripping of an old identity and the assumption of a new one, are used to

An 18-metre granite figure of the Jain saint Bahubali is anointed with scented waters, milk, rice flour, and flowers during a mahapuja performed in the year of its thousandth anniversary. Jainism is one of the world's oldest religions. This figure is located at Shravanabelagola in Karnataka, southern India. (Courtesy of Darrol Bryant)

mark, commemorate, and sometimes legally accomplish transitions in life, from birth (baptism, circumcision, naming ceremonies), through coming of age (first communion, bar mitzvah and bat mitzvah, confirmation, confession, vision quests, purification or atonement ceremonies), to vocational commitments (graduations, ordinations, the taking of vows) and coupling (marriage), to death (wake, funeral, burial and reburial rites). Such rites provide a structured context for encouraging or expressing strong emotions, whether of pride, joy, loyalty, shame, love, obligation, or grief, that society associates with common, significant changes in life. Rites guide and control the thoughts and motivations of those experiencing the transitions (in most cases), but also those of witnesses to these events, who will be affected by the transition—family, friends, and whole communities. While only a minority of Canadians now regularly attend religious services, the majority of Canadians continue to celebrate these life transitions with religious rites. Comparing national survey data from 1987 and 2000, Reginald Bibby (2002: 53, 89) found that little had changed for adults and teenagers. In 1987, for example, 87 per cent of teenagers said they anticipated being married by 'a minister, priest, rabbi, or some other religious figure'. In 2000, the number was 89 per cent. Surprisingly, even 34 per cent of adult Canadians declaring they had 'no religion' said they were anticipating a religious funeral. Many people still feel the need, it seems, to legitimate these changes with traditional forms of blessing or through association with enduring social institutions. But as Joel Thiessen and Lorne Dawson (2008) argue, no one has undertaken the qualitative research required to understand why Canadians turn to these services and what they think they derive from them. In Britain, John Walliss (2002) discovered that there were several non-religious reasons why people chose to get married in a church.

Experience

To be religious is not just to think or believe certain things, it is about having feelings directed in certain ways as well. If religions were just sets of beliefs and rites, with little emotional effect on us, it is unlikely religions would exist or persist. In fact, many Canadians no longer find the rituals performed in their churches, synagogues, and temples meaningful because they experience them as empty and boring. They seem dead, in part, because we can no longer relate the messages conveyed to the contexts of our lives. We are unmoved by our experiences during religious services. However, this was not the case in the past, and still is not the case for many Canadians who attend services, and does not appear to be true for many other people around the world.

Durkheim was impressed with the reality of religion, sociologically, because he was convinced that rituals had power. 'The believer who has commmunicated with his god is not merely a man who sees new truths of which the unbeliever is ignorant', he said, 'he is a man who is stronger. He feels within him more force, either to endure the trials of existence, or to conquer them' (1965 [1912]: 464). However we may choose to characterize such feelings, all religions rest on claims of access to a special kind of experience of great force and significance. The experience, we are told by religious leaders, is analogous to the excitement we associate with sex, love, or being in the presence of great beauty, but it exceeds any of these comparisons and involves some hard-to-explain element that is *sui generis*, unique to religion. We can know it, and even induce it in others, but we can never really capture it in words. Yet it is what bonds people together in loyalty to certain traditions.

In fact some prominent scholars of religion have gone so far as to insist that the study of religion requires researchers to have some prior personal knowledge of this mysterious experience (e.g., Eliade, 1969; Otto, 1923; Smith, 1959). Thus, as sociologists confine their attention to what is empirically available, all sociological accounts of religion are inevitably incomplete, and more often than not, dangerously reductive, since they tend to reduce religion to those things that can be observed, measured, and compared in some way. In turn, most sociologists are willing to admit that their personal experience may be limited, that their claims need to be circumscribed, and that an element of mystery remains about the possible role of uniquely religious forces in human affairs. But, they ask, how can we base the scientific study of religion on such claims? How are we to test the credibility of the statements made by those who would appeal to such privileged and idiosyncratic sources of knowledge (e.g., Flood, 1999; Idiniopulos and Yonan, 1994; McCutcheon, 1999)?

In speaking of religious experience it is common to think first of the extraordinary visions recorded by the prophets and mystics of the great religious traditions, or perhaps of the altered states of consciousness induced by shamans to communicate with the spirit world. But the full range of subjective states identified with religious involvement is much broader. Religious experiences may be momentary or prolonged, curious or profound. They may entail a sense of abiding peace, joy, and well-being or they may be marked by terror and instill anxiety. Some religious groups encourage personal religious experiences, some do not, while others seek to suppress them for fear they may become too disruptive. Some groups differentiate between types of experiences, developing procedures for cultivating only certain kinds (e.g., Zen Buddhism, Santiera), while others exercise much less care and expect some spontaneity in the ecstatic experiences and behaviour of participants (e.g., in many expressions of Pentecostal Christianity, such as the Toronto Airport Christian fellowship in the 1990s, many voodoo rites, Hindu ceremonies in Bali such as the annual Barong ritual, and the Muslim dervishes). Some groups think spiritual experiences should be open to all, while others confine the practices associated with the experiences to religious 'virtuosi'. But whatever the practice, it is hard to find a religion that is not grounded in some promise of extraordinary experience, or of an ecstatic or transformative state. In most cases, however, the daily experience of the devotee is much simpler, yet considered essential. When asked if they have experienced God's presence, for example, 40–50 per cent of Canadians consistently say either 'definitely' or that they 'think so' (Bibby, 2002: 147). This response has held constant for decades, even though the conventional indicators of religious involvement (e.g., church attendance, saying grace before meals) have plummeted. But what actually do they mean?

Community

Religion seems to be an inherently social phenomenon. It is a community-forming activity, whether people intend it to be or not. Religious beliefs and practices gain their plausibility from being shared, and for the most part they are ideas intended to be shared. In principle one could have a private religion, but it is extremely unlikely that an individual's private religion would be of much significance from a sociological point of view. Even if the sociologist encounters a highly idiosyncratic religious practice by an individual, surely, to be recognized as a 'religious' practice the person's views and actions would be reliant on the content and authority of recognized traditions to be identified as 'religious'—and in that way it, too, would be a social phenomenon. When people agree about particular ways of making sense of this world, especially in what they believe to be an ultimate sense, it is natural for them to bond together; and if they believe they have found a truth that is beneficial, a compulsion to persuade others generally follows.

Second, most religions are concerned with ethics. They are systems of beliefs and practices focused on the regulation of people's behaviour and relations with each other. Religions tell people how to lead a good or acceptable life; a life that protects and promotes what is thought to appease the gods or to be in everyone's best interests. In particular, religions tend to be preoccupied with guiding, and when necessary sanctioning, how we behave, even in our most initimate family relationships, immediate and extended, and in our local communities. For it is here—around issues of love, sexuality, loyalty, work, and authority—that we are most prone to abuse others, or most vulnerable to be abused. These are the relationships that religions traditionally have tried to control through the imposition of taboos and moral rules designed to encourage and compel us to do what is supposedly in the best interests of our community. Religions usually offer an 'ultimate' reason for controlling our actions: God, or the gods, or other supernatural forces can know what we are thinking, so we must sincerely strive to do what is expected of us, for example, to be honest, compassionate, and wise in thoughts as well as in our words and deeds. Of course, the gods can also set an example to us in how to be wily, proud, and violent, justifying all manner of cruelties from infanticide and slavery to genocide.

Before the onset of mass communication, mass media, and mass transportation, in a time when most people lived their whole lives in a single and relatively small community, the church, synagogue, or temple was the hub of social life. It was the place where people gathered with regularity, shared meals, met potential mates, learned the news of the neighbourhood, and sought advice or help in times of trouble. A primary source of entertainment, as well, it exposed people to music, sermons, stories and plays, and art that were otherwise not readily available. Today all of these sorts of cultural resources are available elsewhere, but religious institutions continue to serve many of these functions, and many people find the kind of social support they need in order to be happy in the communities created by the participants in religious rites. New immigrants, for example, often are more religious in their adopted homeland than they were in their native lands, because their religion helps them to preserve some of their old ways, and hence their identity, while adapting to a strange, new place.

Different religions, even different traditions within a religion, give more emphasis to some dimensions over others. Catholics commonly tend to see participation in certain rites as more important, while most Protestant groups stress matters of doctrine and belief. Theravadin Buddhists place more emphasis on meditative experience, while Mahayanist Buddhists favour ritual and worship. Pentecostal Protestants highlight the role of particular religious experiences (glossolalia, manifestations of the 'gifts of the Spirit', exuberant worship services), while Anglicans organize worship around traditional ritual forms and ceremonies. Each particular dimension, however, can be traced in each of these religious traditions, and in studying religious life sociologists must be attentive to its cognitive and affective aspects, as well as to its individual and collective expressions. As the anthropologist Clifford Geertz (1973: 90) notes of religious systems in general, they equip people with a conception of how the world really works, what really matters, and they reinforce this world view with intensely cultivated sentiments. Neither the ideas nor the sentiments may stand up to sharp scrutiny, but each is sustained by the 'borrowed authority of the other'. This makes religion a powerful motivator and justification for all kinds of important social actions, especially those involving self-sacrifice, from serving the needs of the poor in dangerous parts of the world to being a suicide bomber.

With a better sense of the nature of religion in mind, let us look at some of its social functions. Sociologists of religion still take their primary cue from the insights of the founding figures of sociology, who discussed some of the macro functions of religion for society.

Classical Sociological Theory and the Functions of Religion

The principal founding figures of sociology, Karl Marx (1818–83), Émile Durkheim (1858–1917), and Max Weber (1864–1920), were not personally religious. In fact, Weber declared himself to be 'religiously unmusical', while Marx was a scornful critic of the Christian heritage of Europe. Yet, each saw the analysis of religious life as essential to his work. Durkheim and Weber, indeed, dedicated much of their lives to its study. The great common concern of these theorists was the investigation of the sweeping changes in social conditions gripping their societies as they were transformed into modern industrial states.

The traditional social order of every society prior to the modern era had been suffused with religious institutions, symbols, and sentiments. Religions legitimated the dominant institutions of the day and provided a 'cosmic' approval for the **norms** that guided almost every aspect of daily life. One of the marks of modernity, as first experienced in Europe, was the declining presence and influence of religious symbols and institutions. Nationalism and a pragmatic stake in economic interests seemed to be displacing religion as the unifying forces of society. Religion became an increasingly private matter, a personal concern, of diminishing significance in the lives of an ever-growing number of people. Secularization appeared to be a hallmark of modernization.

Comprehending the social functions of religion, Marx, Durkheim, and Weber realized, might improve their grasp of the causes of the social discord and **alienation** that had become characteristic of modern life. To know the contours of the emerging new social order and to ease the sufferings it imposed, they sought to understand the foundations of order on which societies had always relied—which most certainly included religion. Could societies be strong without the presence of a common religion?

The studies of Marx, Durkheim, and Weber enhanced our appreciation of religion's intended and unintended contributions to three fundamental aspects of social life: Marx examined the ways in which religion can act as an agent of **social control**; Durkheim examined the role of religion in promoting social solidarity; and Weber showed how religious beliefs and practices may prompt sweeping social changes.

Marx and Social Control

Marx (1957 [1844]) insisted, contrary to the Biblical view of the world, that God did not make humanity, humanity made God. This atheistic proposition was not new when Marx penned it, but few others had expressed it more forcefully or stipulated so well the social sources of the human need for 'an illusion like God'. Religions exist, Marx argued, to legitimate the right to rule of wealthy and powerful elites and to make that rule possible by distracting the poor and oppressed masses from

Time to Reflect

Have you had a religious experience, while participating in a religious activity or otherwise? What made it 'religious' for you?

grasping the real causes of their suffering. The **ideology** and rites of religion provide people with a harmless way of venting the fears, hopes, and grief they feel in the face of the hardships imposed on them. In the pithy and famous phrase of Marx, religion is 'the opium of the people' (Marx, 1957 [1844]: 38). The promises of rewards for good behaviour in the next life and the admonitions to cultivate humility and forgiveness in the face of hardship act like a powerful sedative, subduing and diverting the people's attention from the social and economic sources of their lowly lot in life. Religion gives voice to the distress of the oppressed, and its communal bonds provide some much-needed comfort. But the struggles with temptation and sin and the worship of God or gods do little to end the political and economic **exploitation** that is the true reason for their suffering.

Yet, Marx argues, those who rule, the classes that 'owned the **means of production**', are equally deluded. They tend to support fervently the religious institutions of their day, believing in a cosmology that conveniently justifies their authority and comfort as either their God-given right or just as part of the natural order of things. Church and state (the instruments of the ruling class of any society) collude to the mutual benefit of the ruling classes.

The first step, Marx asserts, to the communist revolution that will usher in the classless society that will finally liberate humanity is the critique of religion. For the revolution even to begin, enough people must realize that their religious beliefs and practices essentially are fantasies and that they constitute a harmful system of social control. But only with the overthrow of the political tyranny founded on the wage slavery of the modern capitalist state will the suffering of humanity be relieved sufficiently to end the condition of need that fosters the illusory compensations of religion. When equality is achieved, the church will wither away.

Durkheim and Social Solidarity

Durkheim, like Marx, was essentially an atheist. But he was more keenly aware of the role played by religion in holding societies together in the face of adversity and, even more, of controlling the destructive, anti-social impulses of their own members. Religious beliefs and practices, he argued (Durkheim, 1965 [1912]), have been instrumental in protecting the moral integrity of social relations and hence assuring the very survival of societies. Divine sanctions serve to suppress the natural selfishness of individuals and to encourage the unselfish behaviour that all groups need to prosper. The members of any society must be willing to make personal sacrifices, perhaps even to lay down their lives, for the benefit of others or of future generations if that society is to survive in the struggle for resources with others. Religion provides the ultimate reasons and justifications for such sacrifices.

These reasons, with their supernatural cast, may well be illusory, Durkheim thought, but believed he had discovered why people continue to believe in the special powers of the sacred—to protect humanity. At the heart of religion lies a real experience of power, he argues, that people find exhilarating and comforting. They may attribute this feeling incorrectly to the various sacred objects they worship. But the experience is real, as are its benefits. In fact, Durkheim proposes, it is the experience of society itself, in its most fundamental form, that inspires the religious convictions that serve society's needs so well.

Durkheim's theory of religion rests on a set of interrelated observations and assumptions. He begins by stipulating that the unique mark of the religious world view is the division of reality into two kinds of phenomena, the sacred and the profane. The sacred is that which is thought to possess tremendous power, and it is set apart and treated with special awe and respect. Throughout the course of human history, a great many things have been deemed sacred, from natural phenomena, such as trees, rocks, streams, and stars, to objects crafted by human hands. The sacred is not marked by any intrinsic features. What marks the sacred is our attitude towards it, and the consequences of our attitude. The sacred acts as the fixed and eternal, yet volatile, focal point of reality, around which the chaos of the profane world happens. Religious rites and the institutions that provide them offer people a stable and safe way to contact this power and to harness it to stave off the threatening uncertainties of profane existence. But how, Durkheim asks, could this extraordinary division of reality into the sacred and the profane have arisen 'though nothing in sensible experience seems able to suggest the idea of so radical a duality?' (ibid., 57). The answer lies, he proposes, with two other observations derived from his study of (what he took to be) the most primitive religion in the world: that of the Australian Aborigines. In studying these seemingly simple beliefs and practices, he thought he had gained an insight into the core nature of all religious experience.

When the Aborigines perform their sacred rites, Durkheim notes, they are moved by feelings of heightened strength. In his words, 'The believer who has communicated with his gods is not merely a man who sees new truths. . . . He is a man who is stronger. He feels within him more force, either to endure the trials of existence, or to conquer them' (ibid., 464). This feeling of empowerment, Durkheim argues, is marked by three features: the strength is felt to come from a source greater than themselves, from outside of themselves, and independent of their will. It has a kind of sovereignty over them. These features provide a crucial clue, Durkheim reasons, to the true source of their experience. Durkheim argues that if, as scientists, we discard the possibility of a supernatural source, then we must find the cause in the religious activity itself. By participating collectively in the performance of religious rites of worship and sacrifice, people are brought into dramatic contact with two powerful aspects of social life: **collective conscience** and **collective effervescence**.

Religion, unlike magic or mere superstition, Durkheim insists, is always a social undertaking. It is a shared activity. In fact, for most of human history, the enactment of religious rituals marked one of the few regular occasions when relatively large numbers of people would purposefully gather together. In the performance of solemn and elaborate rituals, often entailing specific attempts to induce ecstatic states through rhythmic drumming, chanting, and the use of incense and colourful imagery, people would be lifted out of their ordinary existence and worries. Through symbols and myths they would be exposed to a larger horizon of understanding and the cumulative wisdom of their society—to the 'collective conscience'. They would be imbued with a profound sense of their participation in a cultural whole that transcends them and that seeks to instruct and protect them. The reassurance this provides is reinforced by a contagious emotional enthusiasm set in motion by the sheer presence of so many people united in an activity of celebration. They are gripped by a 'collective effervescence' that inspires a sense of power and possibility far outstripping their solitary experience. Like soldiers marching to battle or participants in political rallies or large sporting events, they feel transported for a time to a place where their personal woes are of little consequence and their collective strength is unimpeachable.

People mistakenly believe that the mythic entities they are worshipping are the source of these feelings, of their strength. So, at the heart of religion, for Durkheim, lies a great error. But the illusion serves a worthy and most important social function: it boosts and maintains the social solidarity of a people. It is the unifying result that counts. In circular manner, the practice of religion bonds people together; these bonds fortify the strength of every individual, and this feeling of empowerment helps to perpetuate the belief in the sacred that in turn bonds people together. By Durkheim's reasoning, society is the 'soul of religion', but then religion is the soul of society. This makes it difficult to imagine a stable society in the absence of religion.

Weber and Social Change

Weber devised a comprehensive sociological theory of religion encompassing an encyclopedic range of historical information. He wrote books and essays on the religious history of the Western, Chinese, and Indian civilizations, as well as on ancient Judaism and Islam. In the introduction to this chapter, the basic principles of his understanding of religion were discussed, but in its scope and critical insight, Weber's analysis of religion defies easy summary. At the core of his thought, however, is a famous and reasonably simple argument that has become part of the canon of sociological knowledge, what is known as the **Protestant ethic** thesis. We will confine our attention to this important argument.

Weber's chief concern was the origin and nature of modernity. Like Marx before him, he identified modernity with the emergence of **capitalism**. He recognized that many factors contributed to the creation of the capitalist economic, social, and political order of Western Europe—the driving force of modernity around the world. The capitalist system was dependent on the discovery of everything from double-entry bookkeeping to the steam engine. There could have been no capitalism without the growth of a large pool of labourers free to leave the land and take jobs in the new factories of the eighteenth and nineteenth centuries, or without the new resources and markets opened up by colonialism. But capitalism, and modernity in its diverse forms (such as bureaucratic administration and autonomous legal systems), was also marked by an attitude, a motivational pattern, that was equally unique and essential. Weber

Time to Reflect

As there is no overarching religious consensus in Canada, how do we get people to incur the sacrifices required for our society to succeed? Why would someone die for Canada?

identified this 'spirit of capitalism' as the 'ascetic ethic of vocation' (Weber, 1958 [1904]).

In *The Protestant Ethic and the Spirit of Capitalism*, Weber argues that the early capitalists were distinguished from their more traditional predecessors by a proclivity to resist spending the profits of their labour on the luxuries of life. Instead, they favoured reinvesting their profits in their businesses. In other words, they peculiarly chose in the present to deprive themselves—to be ascetic—in order to establish ever-growing businesses, and hence more profits to invest as capital. With constant reinvestment, their enterprises prospered, and the substantial capital required to lay the foundation for the modern industrial economy accumulated.

But what could have led people to adopt this new approach to their work, to turn to an ascetic ethic of vocation? Prompted by studies indicating that Protestants, when compared with Catholics, were disproportionately employed in business and other related professions, Weber turned to the legacy of the Protestant Reformation for an answer. He traced the spirit of capitalism to the unique influence of two religious doctrines advanced by the Protestant reformers in their rebellion against the Catholic Church. The first was Martin Luther's concept of 'the calling'. The second was John Calvin's doctrine of predestination.

Seeking to return people to the purity of the early Christian church, free of what he saw as the institutional corruption of Catholicism, Luther proposed that all people are called, in their ordinary walks of life, to the service of God. He affirmed 'the priesthood of all believers', whereby each person, in completing the calling of God to the best of his or her ability, as farmer, lawyer, carpenter, wife, or whatever, was doing the bidding of God. The religious virtuosi—the monks praying in their cells or the bishops ruling the church—no longer had a special status in the eyes of God. Everyone was elevated in importance, in principle, while the church's role through its priesthood in intervening with God was demoted.

But this change had two unforeseen and related consequences. First, it made Protestants more acutely aware of the significance of all their daily deeds, most particularly their work. They became more methodical in their labours and more careful and honest in all their dealings. If one should fall into sin, there was no escape from the consequences, because the Reformation had cast off the rites of confession and priestly absolution in rejecting the Catholic Church. Second, this inducement to dedication to one's calling understandably helped businesses to thrive. But other factors limited the impact of these developments until later in the Reformation, when the social consequences of Luther's innovations were reinforced by Calvin's doctrine of predestination.

If God is all-knowing, everywhere present, and all-powerful, then all things must have been determined by him from the beginning of time, Calvin reasoned. God knows who is saved or damned, and all efforts to influence our fate are not only futile, they are an affront to God, calling into question his majesty. Our fate lies in his hands alone; it is predestined. Our duty, as prescribed by his teachings, is to have faith in God and to believe in our salvation. Doubt of our salvation reveals that we are susceptible to temptation and may be evidence that we are not saved. Faced with this spiritual conundrum, Weber surmises, the very devout and sincere Protestants of the early modern era were driven to find some psychological relief in the discovery of covert signs of salvation. Agonizing over their fate, Protestants were advised by their pastors to allay all doubts by redoubling their labours at their callings. Idle hands, as the saying goes, are the devil's helpmates. With time, success in one's calling became an unofficial sign of salvation, while the humility required of true believers helped to further assure that the wealth accrued from this success was ascetically reinvested and not squandered on ostentatious displays of self-importance or on the corrupting pleasures of the flesh.

Thus, the conditions required for the accumulation of capital sufficient to lay the foundations of the modern industrial order grew out of the religiously motivated desire to secure peace of mind and social prestige in the community of believers. By this means, Weber concludes, religion unintentionally played an instrumental role in the birth of capitalism, and thus in the eventual spread of modernity around the world. It had become a world-transforming agent of social change, but in ways quite contrary to the original intentions of any of the leaders of Christianity. In this instance, religion was the agent of a series of unintended and sweeping changes that, ironically, would push religion itself to the periphery of social life. Or so most sociologists have believed until recently.

Religion vs Modernity: The Ambiguous Legacy of Secularization Theory

Over the course of the twentieth century, a vast research literature has accumulated exploring aspects of religion's role as an agent of social control in society, a force for social solidarity and order, and a source of social change.

In our society, the traditional and the sacred are repeatedly jostled by the modern and the mercantile. (Gunter Marx Photography/Corbis)

In these studies, religion has been both the independent variable—the cause of other social events and developments—and the dependent variable—a phenomenon significantly affected by other events and developments in society. In characteristic manner, religion has been shown to be both a force for the maintenance of systems of social stratification and inequality, or racial **prejudice** and sexism, and, simultaneously, a key influence in efforts to reform society and correct its ills (see, e.g., Christiano et al., 2002; Roberts, 1995). Everything depends on the style of religion being examined, the social and historical circumstance of its practice, and numerous other factors, such as the leadership exercised by individuals in the groups studied.

In the southern United States, for example, the same evangelical Christianity that fostered the civil rights movement in the 1960s also served to undergird the white segregationists fervently opposed to the extension of civil rights to blacks. Extremist groups such as the Ku Klux Klan operated as quasi-religious organizations, invoking a Christian heritage to legitimate their discriminatory beliefs. But the great leaders of the civil rights movement, such as Reverend Martin Luther King Jr and Reverend Jesse Jackson, employed a Christian rhetoric to rally opposition to the Klan and all that it stands for. Both sides claimed the approval of God for their cause and reverted to the Bible to support their views.

In Canada, the Christian churches played a leading role in helping the government to suppress and assimilate the Native population, running the residential schools that ultimately did so much physical and mental harm to generations of young Native people. Yet, many of the same churches were in the forefront of efforts to raise the consciousness of Canadians about the rights of Aboriginal peoples, the value of their culture, and the need for the government and the churches to redress their grievances (Lewis, 1993; Miller, 1996) and make reparations. Religious persons interact in diverse and complex ways with their surrounding societies.

Beneath all the research, however, the assumption of the classical theorists persisted that the significance of religion would diminish in the modern world. By the

1970s, although there were significant variances in the patterns emerging in Western Europe, Canada, and the United States, it seemed clear that the citizens of the most advanced nations on earth were turning their backs on organized religion in ever-increasing numbers. In Europe, for example, the numbers of churchgoers had been declining for decades, and though various official state churches continue to be supported with tax dollars (for example, the Lutheran Church in Germany and, until recently, in Sweden as well), these societies have become more or less completely secular. In Canada and the United States, there was a great surge of religious activity following World War II, as the soldiers returned home, got married, had children, and moved to the suburbs. Thousands of new churches were built, and people flocked to Sunday services as never before. But by the time their children, the baby-boom generation, began to come of age, many denominations had begun to experience serious declines. In Canada, the slide has been constant, with levels of church attendance dropping from 50 per cent in the 1950s to about 20 per cent in 2000 (see Table 12.1).

In the United States, the so-called mainstream and liberal denominations (for example, Congregationalists,

OPEN FOR DISCUSSION

New Religious Life and the Internet

Religion is abundantly present on the Internet. Every major world religion is represented, major and minor Christian denominations, almost all new religious movements, thousands of specific churches. Countless web pages are operated by individual believers, self-declared gurus, prophets, shamans, apostates, and other moral entrepreneurs. In addition, the Internet has spawned its own religious creations, from megasites of cyberspirituality to virtual 'churches' and strictly on-line religions. To this mix, we can add numerous commercial sites wishing to turn a profit on our spiritual appetites, providing us with religious news, selling us religious paraphernalia, and acting as network nodes for links to hundreds of other sites. There are also sites launched to educate the public or to pursue a diverse array of religious causes (for example, sites based on university courses or anti-cult crusades).

On the Internet, people can read about religion, talk with others about religion, download religious texts and documents, buy religious books and artifacts, take virtual tours of galleries of religious art or the interiors of religious buildings, search scriptures using electronic indexes, locate churches and religious centres, vote on organizational propositions, see images of their religious leaders, watch video clips, and listen to religious music, sermons, prayers, testimonials, and discourses. They can also participate in rituals or meditation sessions, share intercessory prayers, or undertake virtual pilgrimages. Soon they may even be able to feel the texture of objects appearing on their screen or smell the aroma of the virtual incense burning on the computer-generated altar to their gods. The technology exists to simulate both.

The Pew Internet and American Life Project reports that approximately 3 million Americans turn to the Internet each day to meet their spiritual and religious need (Larsen, 2001), and 28 million Americans say they have used the Internet for religious purposes at some time.

Every religion can benefit from being on-line, but the Internet has proved to be especially beneficial for the thousands of new religious movements operating around the world. In this and other ways, the Internet may be a new and significant force for religious change, magnifying the religious pluralism that is developing in our societies. Never has it been so easy for new religious ideas to gain a public voice. Anyone with a small investment in some computer hardware, software, and training can soon mount a web page and operate it at little expense. With the right placement, the page may become rapidly available to a potential audience of millions.

The Internet is expanding at an astronomically rapid rate, and most users are drawn from the very segments of society that new religions wish to contact in their quest to mobilize resources (that is, to acquire members with money, skills, and influence). There is a pronounced overlap between those who have joined new religions in the last few decades—relatively well-educated, if somewhat disaffected, middle-class young adults—and the primary users of the Internet. Through the Internet, new religions can circumvent the political and commercial control of the conventional broadcast media by social elites intent on maintaining the status quo.

The Internet provides an unparalleled means for people to stay in touch with each other. New religious communities can be formed and operate over vast geographical distances, as 24-hour contact can be maintained in a relatively inexpensive manner. The monthly newsletter can be supplemented or even replaced by daily messages of inspiration and instruction, with the added possibility of immediate interaction between the leadership and distant followers, and between followers themselves. The Internet also opens up the possibility of much more direct and frequent contact between representatives of new religious organizations and other potentially helpful members of society, such as scholars of religion, advocates of civil rights, and journalists. This networking can greatly enhance the ability of such groups to rally allies in the face of legal challenges, negative media reports, government persecution, and the other crises that arise from time to time.

The relative anonymity of communicating on-line allows new religious movements to circumvent the social constraints and biases born of systems of social stratification and of ethnic and cultural differences. The anonymity can be used to great advantage by groups intent on fashioning a new global community of individuals united above all else by their shared beliefs and interests.

Source: Adapted for this volume from Lorne L. Dawson, 'Doing Religion in Cyberspace: The Promise and the Perils', *Council of Societies for the Study of Religion Bulletin*, 30, 1 (2001): 3–9, and Lorne L. Dawson, 'Religion and the Internet: Presence, Problems, and Prospects', in Peter Antes, Armin Geertz, and Randi Warne, eds, *New Approaches to the Study of Religion* (Berlin: Verlag de Gruyter, 2003).

Episcopalians, and Methodists) showed the greatest change, with overall levels of membership and attendance declining quickly for a time. During the 1960s, things were beginning to look bleak for the institutional church, and the United States, a very religious nation by most standards, seemed destined to replicate the secular trajectory set in Europe. In the late 1970s and the early 1980s, however, the US numbers began to reverse them-

Table 12.1 Weekly Service Attendance in Canada, 1957–2000 (as Percentage of Whole Population)

	1957	1975	1990	2000
Total	53	31	24	21
Protestant	38	27	22	25
Conservative	51	41	49	58
Mainline	35	23	14	15
Roman Catholic	83	45	33	26
Outside Quebec	75	48	37	32
Quebec	88	42	28	20

Sources: Reginald Bibby, *Restless Gods: The Renaissance of Religion in Canada* (Toronto: Stoddart, 2002), 73; Gallup poll, March 1957; for 1975, 1990, and 2000: Bibby, Project Canada surveys.

selves. Taken as a whole, over the last 50 years, the United States has maintained a remarkably constant level of reported church involvement of about 40 per cent (Greeley, 1989).

Sociologists also began to notice a phenomenon Grace Davie (1994) aptly called 'believing without belonging'. Even in the countries where the traditional indicators of religious involvement were in sharp decline, surveys revealed a continued interest in the basic questions at the heart of religion, such as the meaning of life and of life after death. Most people still claimed to believe in God and felt a need for some spiritual guidance and development in their lives. Reginald Bibby reports survey data showing that 75 per cent of Canadians acknowledge they have 'spiritual needs' (Bibby, 2006: 184). So, perhaps it is not surprising that many billions of dollars are spent each year on a wide array of religious periodicals, books, and other inspirational materials and activities (videos, audio tapes, lectures, yoga and meditation classes, religious retreats and tours). Clearly, religious institutions are nowhere near as prominent or influential as they were just a few decades ago, yet a fairly strong demand for religious beliefs and practices persists. Sociologists are uncertain what to make of this curious new state of affairs.

Changing Views of Secularization

In 1967, the American sociologist Peter L. Berger published a highly influential book, *The Sacred Canopy*, which helped to shape the academic and popular consensus that the process of modernization was inextricably linked to the secularization of society. By the 1990s, however, Berger had reversed himself, declaring his earlier pessimism about the future of religion to have been a mistake (Berger, 1999). This change of viewpoint is characteristic of a broader shift in sensibilities among sociologists of religion. By looking briefly at Berger's ideas we can come to understand how many sociologists now think that religions may coexist with modernity, perhaps in some instances even thrive.

The plight of religion in the modern world, Berger originally argued, is a 'plausibility crisis' brought on by two changes: increasing social and cultural pluralism, and the privatization of religion. Following Weber, Berger thinks that the roots of these two closely related yet distinct processes can be traced to historical features of the Biblical religions of the West that reached their natural culmination in the Protestant Reformation. In casting off the religious monopoly of the Catholic Church, the Protestant reformers placed a premium on the faith, knowledge, and practice of the individual believer. With time, this emphasis transmuted religion from something into which one was born, to a private matter. In principle, at least, religious commitments have become a matter of evangelism and individual choice. Such beliefs cannot be legitimately imposed on populations from above, and people should not take the beliefs to which they have been socialized by their family and society for granted. Religious beliefs can and probably should be subjected to critical scrutiny. These new norms, in combination with the exposure to other cultures that accompanied the universal spread of Western capitalism, made it possible for a plurality of religious systems to either develop in or be imported into the cultures of North America and Europe. So, we live in societies where there are a large number of quite different and seemingly equally valid religions. But the relative plausibility of all religious systems today impairs the ability of any one religion to offer the kind of absolute claims to truth that are the hallmark of all traditional religious systems. And privatized conceptions of religion will not support a common universe of meaning for the members of a society, a lack of support that severely impairs the traditional functioning of religion as an agent of social control and social cohesion, and perhaps of sweeping social change as well. The societal impact of religion has been undermined, Berger laments, by religious individualism.

Religions in the modern world, Berger stipulated, are compelled to choose between two options: (1) they can accommodate themselves to the dominant social order and seek to find their place in the growing leisure and service economy, serving the needs of spiritual consumers in piecemeal fashion, or (2) they can 'entrench themselves and continue to profess the old objectivities as much as possible as if nothing had happened' (Berger, 1967: 153). In other words, they can adapt to modernity or reject it. Neither option sounds promising for the future of religion as a significant feature of social life. Many mainstream Christian denominations appear to have pursued the first course of action and watched their memberships shrink because these institutions have lost their distinctiveness and cannot compete with other sources of knowledge, fellowship, entertainment, and comfort in the modern world. The latter option appears to characterize various separatist and fundamentalist religious groups that have taken a stance in stark opposition to the dominant **values** and behaviour of modern societies (for example, Hasidic Jews, Jehovah's Witnesses, most Baptists, and various forms of Pentecostalism). These groups have grown in numbers and strength, surprising the proponents of secularization. Yet, in the last analysis, some sociologists argue, they will be more or less permanently confined to the margins of society (Bruce, 1996; Wilson, 1982).

Many were convinced by Berger's arguments about the implausibility of religion in the modern world, but eventually even Berger expressed strong doubts. He continued to state that modernization had some very real secularizing effects. But the effects varied greatly from place to place, and he stressed that modernization 'has also provoked powerful movements of counter-secularization' (Berger, 1999: 3). Three developments led him to suspect that his reading of the options available to modern forms of religion had been too limited and pessimistic: (1) the revival of religion in the United States, particularly what is called the 'New Christian Right', (2) the resurgence of conservative forms of religion around the world, and (3) the apparent survival of religion, even in secularized societies, at the level of individual consciousness.

In the 1980s, evangelical forms of Protestantism began systematically to assert themselves on the US scene, setting off what came to be known as the 'cultural wars' (Hunter, 1991). Aligning themselves with conservative elements in US politics, a rising tide of born-again Christians reasserted the role of Christian values in American public life. They sought to reverse court decisions and laws such as those banning prayers in the schools or banning the posting of the Ten Commandments in courts and other public buildings. They sought to end the support for such things as more liberal abortion laws and gay rights. The relevant laws have not changed, but a broadly Christian and conservative social agenda has achieved prominence in much of American political life. Since the 1970s few American Presidents have felt they could afford to ignore or offend the religious right, and Ronald Reagan and George W. Bush actively sought their support as conservative denominations continue to dominate an ever-greater share of the US religious market.

Elsewhere in the world, much the same sort of social change has happened, with the sharp rise in fundamentalist movements in Islam and the creation of Islamic states following the successful Iranian revolution of 1978, the revival of the Orthodox Church in Russia following the collapse of the Soviet Union, the spread of conservative forms of Catholicism in Africa and elsewhere in the developing world, the resurgence of evangelical Protestantism in Latin America, and the rise of Hindu nationalism in India. Throughout the world, the role of religion as a focal point for group and national identity is increasing rather than diminishing. Likewise, religion has re-emerged as a significant factor in many social conflicts around the world, from the violent clashes between Muslims and Hindus in India and between Christians and Muslims in Bosnia-Herzegovina, Nigeria, and the Philippines to the persecution of Christians and thousands of members of the Falun Gong spiritual movement in Communist China.

Most important, as indicated, it also appears that the public decline in the membership and influence of the traditional Christian institutions of the modern West has not been matched by a decline in the religious concerns, inclinations, and even practices of the majority of people in modern secular societies (see, e.g., Bibby, 1993, 2002; Davie, 1994, 2000; Roof, 1999). People continue to believe in God, to worry about life after death, and to pray with regularity, even if they have stopped going to church. We must distinguish, it seems, between secularization at the institutional and individual levels.

A New Theoretical Perspective

In the 1980s the American sociologist Rodney Stark, in conjunction with several colleagues (Finke and Stark, 1992; Stark and Bainbridge, 1985, 1996; Stark and Finke, 2000), proposed a theory of religion that accounts for—that even anticipated—these exceptions to the conventional consensus on secularization. Stark's views have exerted a strong influence on the field in recent years, though many researchers disagree with some of his premises and conclusions.

Like Weber, Stark based his theory of religion on the assumption that the need for religion probably is a constant of the human condition and that, consequently, the current secularization of parts of the world is more a historical aberration than a permanent feature of all future societies. The theory is based on four simple assumptions, borrowed in part from exchange theory and rational choice theory in economics and sociology.

The first premise is that religions are about the operation of the supernatural in people's lives. Many social involvements may become quite all-consuming for individuals and hence play a religious-like role in their lives, but it is the reference to the supernatural that truly distinguishes a religious phenomenon. The second premise is the simple utilitarian principle that most of human behaviour, including religious behaviour, is governed by the pursuit of what we perceive to be rewards and by the avoidance of what we perceive to be costs. The third premise is that the rewards most highly prized by people are usually scarce and that the rewards at the heart of the religious quest seem to be things least readily available, like true peace of mind or life after death.

The fourth premise is that in the absence of these most valued real rewards, people are inclined to create, exchange, and accept what Stark and William Bainbridge (1985, 1996) call **compensators**. In daily life, we often appease people for incurring some sacrifice today by promising some appropriate reward in the future—every household and work environment in the world operates on this basis. In many cases these promised rewards are quite specific—in the case of children, an ice cream cone for good behaviour at the mall; in the workplace, a good pension for loyal employees. But religions deal in the most general of compensators: ultimate relief from suffering, immortality for the virtuous, and knowledge of the meaning of life. These compensations require belief in the operation of a supernatural agency or force in this world.

Religions, then, are organizations that provide general compensators based on belief in the supernatural, and Stark thinks that if we keep this simple truth in mind, there can be little doubt that religions will persist—under the conditions of modernity or otherwise—because, in the end, the scientific world view cannot compete with religions in meeting certain needs. 'Systems of thought that reject the supernatural lack all means to promise credibly such rewards as eternal life in any fashion. Similarly naturalistic philosophies can argue that statements such as "What is the meaning of life?" or "What is the purpose of the universe?" are meaningless utterances. But they cannot provide answers to these questions in the terms in which they are asked' (Stark and Bainbridge, 1985: 7–8).

With this perspective in mind, Stark argues that the process of secularization should be conceived of as a recurring and cyclical phenomenon. Secularization is not a uniquely modern development that entails the eventual demise of religion. Rather, it should be understood in terms of the periodic collapse of support for certain dominant forms of religion as they become complacent and overly accommodated to non-religious features of the societies in which they developed. Secularization should not be confused with the loss of all need for supernatural compensators, but should be associated with the failure of established religions to provide sufficiently vivid and consistent supernatural compensators. As such, secularization is an intrinsic and limiting feature of all religious economies, guaranteeing the periodic renewal of religious institutions.

This renewal may come in the form of revival, which Stark associates with the formation of religious sects, or of innovation, which he associates with the creation of **cults** or new religious movements. Sects are offshoots of mainstream religions that are seeking to recapture the purity of some tradition and to reform the world on this basis. Cults are groups that introduce more unconventional and often totally new religious ideas into a society, often with the intent of initiating an even more revolutionary change in the character of the society. All of the great religious traditions of the contemporary world began as either sects or cults, and with time they will likely be replaced by others (see Stark, 1996).

In addition to postulating the importance of a relatively steady 'demand' for religion at the individual level, undercutting the assumption that the decline of certain institutions is indicative of the complete secularization of society, Stark and his colleagues (Finke and Stark, 1992; Stark and Finke, 2002; Stark and Innacconne, 1994) have argued that many of the differences in rates of secularization detected between countries can be accounted for by examining how religion is 'supplied'. This so-called **supply-side theory** argues, contrary to Berger, that pluralism acts as a stimulus to religious growth by encouraging competition between religious groups, like companies struggling for a share of a market. Competition makes the leadership of the religions more responsive to the needs of the people, resulting in higher levels of religiosity overall. This is why the United States, one of the most modern nations in the world, is still a very religious society. The guarantee of religious freedom provided by the First Amendment of the US Constitution has fostered a diverse and competitive religious market.

In many European countries, however, various Christian denominations acquired a more or less full monopoly (for example, the Catholic Church in Italy, the Lutheran Church in Germany, the Anglican Church in England). These established churches became complacent because they were able to suppress any effective competition, often with the official help of the governments of these nations. They were stripped of any incentive to remain responsive to the changing needs of their constituencies, and in modern times these societies have become largely secular. The veracity of this supposition has been put to the test through various empirical studies, generating considerable controversy (e.g., Finke, 1997; Finke et al., 1996; Froese, 2001; Olsen, 1999). While many sociologists are now persuaded of the value of Stark's arguments, the jury is still out and a final verdict has yet to be rendered.

Time to Reflect

Can you be religious without a belief in the supernatural? If so, in what sense is this possible?

The Inevitability of Secularization?

Some sociologists, such as Steve Bruce (2001, 2002), think Berger was too quick to recant his views and doubt that the data will support Stark's theories in the long run. Briefly stated, he argues that the so-called revival of religion in the United States is likely to be short-lived and shallow. Secularization, he stresses, is the by-product of certain larger social processes associated with modernization, such as **urbanization** and the advancement of a scientific world view. The United States simply lags behind its European counterparts, Bruce asserts, arguing that there 'is certainly considerable evidence that church membership and attendance is now declining in the United States' as well (Hadaway et al., 1993, cited in Bruce, 2001). Moreover, as several other prominent scholars have argued before (e.g., Luckmann, 1967; Wilson, 1966), the religion of Americans has been secularized from within. It is a diluted and comfortable religion of conformism that offers broad support to the most basic cultural values of the United States without really demanding much from its practitioners. In other words, it is a pale ghost of its former self, and even the recent turn to the religious right has rapidly dissipated as the new evangelicals become increasingly like everyone else in their behaviour, if not in their stated ideology.

Likewise, in the developing world, the resurgence of religion is tied to social conditions of either rebellion or repression (e.g., in Iran, Lebanon, or India). In the face of the political, economic, and cultural threats posed by **globalization**, religion has become once again a potent force for the protection of **ethnicity** and national sovereignty. Its use is facilitated, moreover, by the absence of any liberal democratic order in most of these societies. They need not support any significant religious pluralism—one of Berger's original forces of secularization—in the name of democracy. But historically, Bruce is confident, this is a transitory state of affairs that will change as these societies are compelled to find their place in a new global order marked at its heart by the attributes of the Western societies. In truly modern and secularized societies, such as Germany, Britain, the Netherlands, and Denmark, there are no signs of a return to religion, despite the formal creation of conditions of religious pluralism and the introduction of many new minority religions. The data are not congruent with Stark's expectations, Bruce argues, but they continue to offer support for Berger's original theory of secularization.

In the end, scholars are awaiting the data that will demonstrate whether the continued religiosity of Americans is an exceptional state of affairs, defying the slow but steady secularization of the world, or whether the continued secularity of Western European nations is the exceptional case, defying a world that always has been and will continue to be religious.

But what about the Canadian situation? How does the evidence about our attitudes and behaviour factor into the equation? We share much of our cultural experience and religious history with the United States, and until recently our religious profiles were very similar. Since the 1960s, however, the religious habits of Canadians have come to resemble those of Western Europeans. We seem to fall somewhere between the American and the European cases. What does our religiosity tell us about whether it is the Americans or the Europeans that are exceptional?

The Religious Life of Contemporary Canadians

The prognosis for organized and conventional religion in Canada has seemed quite bleak for several decades. Beginning in the 1960s, all of the major indices of religious membership and activity began to decline steadily. Yet, in his latest detailed analyses of religion in Canada, Bibby (2002, 2006) finds some evidence of rejuvenation. Moreover, as Berger stresses and as Bibby has consistently documented in the Canadian context (1987, 1993), the religiosity of individuals has not significantly diminished with time. Most Canadians, like their British and European counterparts (Davie, 2002; Lambert, 2004), still display an apparent interest in religious concerns even though they have stopped going to church.

Beginning in the 1960s, Canadian and American churches experienced what Wade Clark Roof and William McKinney (1987) aptly call 'the collapse of the middle'. In both nations, the large mainline and liberal Protestant denominations that had dominated religious life started to lose members and to experience declining attendance at services. These groups had held the middle ground on a religious spectrum for almost two centuries, with more radical and largely new or alternative religions on the left, and more conservative, even fundamentalist, religious orientations on the right. In the United States, the Congregational, Episcopalian, Presbyterian, and Methodist churches suffered the blow, along with the more doctrinally liberal segments of the Lutheran and Baptist churches. In Canada, the Anglican, Presbyterian, Lutheran, and United churches felt similar losses. The collapse in support was more precipitous in Canada, however, and its consequences more severe since the vast majority of Canadians belonged to these few Protestant churches or to the Catholic Church, which has experienced serious declines as well (see Table 12.2).

In the United States, the decline of the mainline Protestant denominations was balanced by a remarkable and unexpected increase in religious activity on the right, and even some modest growth on the left (for example, the rise of such diverse new religious movements as neo-paganism/witchcraft and various imported Eastern religions). In Canada, however, no such compensation occurred. Weekly churchgoing for the mainline Protestant denominations in Canada dropped from 35 per cent in the 1950s to 23 per cent in the 1970s, and to a mere 14 per cent in 1990s (Bibby, 2002: 20). Attendance at conservative services in Canada dipped slightly during this period as well, but by 1990 had returned to the levels of the 1950s (49 per cent). Unlike the trend in the United States, no sweeping turn to the right in religious matters occurred in Canada in the 1980s. There was, however, a modest yet significant increase in the actual percentage of Canadians involved in more conservative churches (for example, various Baptist and Pentecostal groups), which grew by about 8 per cent in the 1990s. But very few Canadians turned to any of the alternative religions identified with the left end of the religious spectrum (Bibby, 2002: 62–4).

Roman Catholic levels of attendance fell equally precipitously in Canada, from a high of 83 per cent in 1957 to 33 per cent in 1990. Measures of Catholicism in Canada, though, are complicated by the cultural differences between Quebec and the rest of the country. Figures that were consistently higher inside Quebec than outside the province now show a trend consistently the reverse, with non-Québécois Catholics displaying higher levels of church attendance.

Overall church attendance figures in Canada have dropped from a high of 53 per cent in 1957 to a low of 19 per cent in 2000 (Bibby, 2002: 75). This figure is still significantly higher than the single-digit figures common in most Western European nations and Britain (Davie, 2000), but it presents a startling contrast with the figure of approximately 40 per cent regular service attendance that Americans have maintained with some consistency for the last 50 years (Greeley, 1989).

Can we account for these differences using Stark's theories? Canada is not simply a more modern nation than the United States. Could the answer lie with Stark's supply-side notions and the varying degrees of religious pluralism fostered historically in each nation? Americans have long spread their religious allegiances over a much greater array of religious choices. Perhaps by taking their political ideal of freedom through revolution into their church disagreements, schisms have created dozens of minor or sub-denominations in older, established churches. Hundreds of denominations have flourished throughout their history, and they have given birth to several successful new religions, such as the Church of Jesus Christ of Latter-day Saints (Mormons), the Seventh Day Adventists, the Jehovah's Witnesses, and Pentecostalism. The religious history of Canada, however, has been marked by what the British sociologist David Martin (2000) calls 'shadow establishments'. No single church has been formally established in Canada as the state religion since the mid-nineteenth century, but the extended colonial ties with Britain in English Canada did secure the pre-eminence of the Anglican and Presbyterian churches among the nation's economic, political, and social elites. These few churches, along with the United Church (which was formed out of elements of

Table 12.2 Religious Identification of Canadians, 1871–2001 (Percentage of Total Population)

	1871	1901	1931	1961	1991	2001
Protestant	56	56	54	49	36	29
Roman Catholic	42	42	41	47	46	43
Eastern Orthodox	<1	<1	1	1	1	2
Jewish	<1	<1	1	1	1	1
Other faiths	2	2	2	1	3	5
No religion	<1	<1	<1	<1	12	16

Sources: Reginald Bibby, *Restless Gods: The Renaissance of Religion in Canada* (Toronto: Stoddart, 2002), 85; Statistics Canada, 2001 census data.

As Canada assimilates people from around the world, many still retain their religious traditions. Here, sisters Shreeya and Sejal Thakrar of Mississauga light diyas—small clay lamps—as part of Diwali, a major Hindu festival honouring Lakhmi, the goddess of prosperity. (CP/Hans Deryk/*Toronto Star*)

the Methodist, Presbyterian, and Congregational churches in 1923), have monopolized Protestant religious life in Canada. In Quebec, the Catholic Church exerted an overwhelming control over almost all aspects of life until the Quiet Revolution of the 1960s. Catholicism was synonymous with the French-Canadian identity, protecting the culture of the province from the incursion of the larger English-speaking society of North America. How might these historical differences have contributed to the reduced religious institutional involvement of contemporary Canadians?

In Quebec, for example, everything changed dramatically in the 1960s, when a secular form of Quebec nationalism began systematically to replace the Church's traditional control over education, health care, and other aspects of social welfare. Within 30 years, Quebec was transformed from one of the most religious societies in the world to one of the least religious. Today, Quebec most resembles Europe in its secularity, a result in line with Stark's assumptions about the negative consequences of religious monopolies.

The same explanation may hold true for the increased secularization of English Canada as compared to the United States. In English Canada, however, a lesser degree of religious monopoly existed, one offset by a measure of denominationalism. Seeing themselves as denominations and not as universal churches with a right to impose their beliefs on others, most religious groups in English Canada were content to recognize that they represented but one of many ways of embodying Christian truths. This hybrid situation may account for the in-between status of Canada in considering the arguments for either the European case or the American exception to secularization. At present it is still too early to tell what will transpire in Canada, and there are many other complex factors to consider (see, e.g., Beyer, 1997, 2000; Reimer, 1995). Clearly, though, as the Canadian sociologist Peter Beyer (1997, 2000) asserts, there is no single 'master trend' for religion in modernity. Regionally specific and unique developmental patterns have to be taken into consideration.

At the institutional level, Canada appears to be secularized, though Bibby has raised some doubts (2002, 2006). He notes, for example, that by 2000, church attendance figures in Canada had stopped declining, and in fact the liberal Protestant denominations had begun to post some modest increases in membership and attendance. Moreover, Canadian churches in general were maintaining or even increasing the levels of participation of teens and other young people in their activities. But the single most significant factor currently giving sociologists pause is the persistent strength of measures of individual or private religiosity in Canada and the rest of the Western world. People may be 'unchurched', but it is clear that they have not become irreligious.

In his repeated surveys of the religious views of Canadians (begun in 1974), Bibby has documented certain constants other than the decline in church attendance. First, most Canadians continue to identify themselves with some specific religious group—usually that of their parents and grandparents—even if they no longer participate in most of its formal or institutional activities. They show little inclination, moreover, to switch from this traditional religious identity. Second, most Canadians state that they will continue to use the religion with which they identify to perform various important rites of passage in their lives, like baptisms, marriages, and funerals. Third, most Canadians say they believe in God (see Table 12.3) and that they think God cares about them.

Fourth, most Canadians continue to ask themselves such fundamentally religious questions as what happens after death, why is there suffering in the world, and what is the purpose of life. What is more, almost half of all Canadians say they have actually experienced God's presence in their lives (see Table 12.4, and Bibby, 2006: 190, where he provides a new figure for 2005 of 49 per cent), and 74 per cent acknowledge that they pray privately, with 3 in 10 saying they do so daily. In light of these and other kinds of longitudinal results, Bibby (2002: 164) concludes:

> The empirical data are decisive: God has not disappeared from the lives of the vast majority of Canadians. The average people we pass on sidewalks and roadways and see in supermarkets and malls may not often say it out loud, but most of them believe in God, converse with God, and in nearly one in two cases think they have experienced the presence of God. That's a lot of people. These are not anomalous beliefs, practices, and experiences.

But what are we to make of these findings? Similar data have been produced for Britain and Europe (Davie, 2002; Lambert, 2004) and for the 'unchurched' in the United States (Roof, 1999). Are these results definitive disproof of the secularization thesis? Or, as Bruce would argue, are they merely evidence of a process of cultural lag, of resistance to social change that will eventually succumb to a more secular world view? After all, the percentage of Canadians claiming to have 'no religion' has been steadily increasing, moving from 12 per cent in 1991 to 16 per cent in 2001 (Statistics Canada, 2001 census data). Even in the United States this figure has doubled in the last decade, reaching an all-time high of 14 per cent. For the first time in US history, the overall increase in religious affiliation (8.8 per cent) did not keep pace with the rate of population growth (13.2 per cent) (Smith, 2002).

But the increase in the 'no religion' category, Bibby and others (e.g., Hout and Fischer, 2002) argue, may be deceptive. The 'no religion' category is like a revolving door, with more members flowing constantly in and out than staying. Data suggest that the increasing numbers reflect an increase in the proportion of the population in a process of transition in their lives and in a temporary condition of religious disaffiliation more than to a sheer

Table 12.3 Belief in God in Canada, 1985–2000 (Percentage of Total Population)

'Do you believe that God exists?'	1985	1990	1995	2000
Yes	84	82	80	81
Yes, I definitely do.	61	56	57	49
Yes, I think so.	23	26	23	32
No, I don't think so.	10	10	11	13
No, I definitely do not think so.	6	8	9	6

Sources: Reginald Bibby, *Restless Gods: The Renaissance of Religion in Canada* (Toronto: Stoddart, 2002), 140; Bibby, Project Canada Survey Series.

Table 12.4 Claims of Experiencing God, 1975–2000 (Percentage of Total Population)

'Do you believe that you have experienced God's presence?'	1975[a]	1980[a]	1985	1990	1995	2000
Yes	48	43	44	43	41	47
Yes, I definitely do.	22	21	25	20	20	20
Yes, I think so.	26	22	19	23	21	27
No	52	57	56	57	59	53
No, I don't think so.	–	–	32	31	33	31
No, I definitely do not.	–	–	24	26	26	22

[a]In 1975 and 1980, the question read, 'Have you ever had a feeling that you somehow were in the presence of God?' with the response options, 'Yes, I'm sure I have,' 'Yes, I think I have,' and 'No.'

Source: Reginald Bibby, *Restless Gods: The Renaissance of Religion in Canada* (Toronto: Stoddart, 2002), 147; Project Canada Survey Series.

increase in confirmed religious dropouts. Those claiming no religious affiliation are more likely to be young and, in many cases, in the process of switching religious affiliation rather than of leaving religion behind altogether. With age and the onset of family responsibilities, or the completion of other major disruptions such as geographic migrations, many of them will push their way through the revolving door again back to a religious affiliation. In fact, Bibby says that if we track Canadians who claim to have no religion over time, within five years 1 in 3 will have re-identified with a religion, and within 10 years the figure increases to 2 in 3 (2006: 201).

Of course, all analyses of religion in the Western world must now contend with a new religious pluralism. While most Canadians, Europeans, and Americans remain overwhelmingly Christian—at least nominally—there are growing communities of Hindus, Buddhists, Muslims, and those of other faiths. How will their presence alter the overall pattern of religious life in Western societies? Under the influence of these new religious communities, new ways of being religious are emerging in Canada and elsewhere. Perhaps these recent additions to the competitive market of religious options will work to reduce or reverse the effects of secularization, as Stark's theory suggests. But with the passage of time, will the followers of these imported traditions, like most of their Christian counterparts, simply become less religious or even non-religious?

The Future of Religion

For thousands of years, humankind has been deeply religious and almost every aspect of social life has borne a religious significance. Little has changed fundamentally in the fate of individuals and nations. We still live with uncertainty, fear, disease, and death. We still yearn to be blessed and somehow spared from the harsher realities of human existence. We find it difficult to live with the knowledge of our demise and seek some eternal happiness or peace. Religious beliefs still play a key role in assuring the civility of our societies. Religion has not disappeared from our world—not even from the most scientific and prosperous parts.

Viewing matters from one perspective, there is little reason to doubt that the inhabitants of the late twenty-

Time to Reflect

Does religious pluralism strengthen the role of religion in society or undermine it?

HUMAN DIVERSITY

The New Religious Diversity

The religious landscape of North America is changing as Muslim mosques, Hindu and Buddhist temples, and Sikh gurdwaras begin to appear in Canadian and American cities. More people immigrated to the United States between the 1960s and the 1990s than during the so-called heyday of immigration at the height of the Industrial Revolution from 1890 to 1920. But now the immigrants are coming from India, Pakistan, China, Indonesia, Korea, and other countries throughout Asia and the Middle East, not from Europe. As these millions of people settle into their new lives in their adopted, yet still strange, homelands, they have brought their religious traditions with them.

As sociologists have long recognized, religious organizations commonly play a crucial role in helping immigrants to maintain their cultural traditions while providing the physical and social support required to make the transition. In fact, in the face of a foreign society in which immigrants' language is not spoken or their customs known and respected, religious beliefs and practices often surge to the fore as a bulwark of cultural identity. For a generation or two, the devotion of immigrants is likely to be greater than that of people in their native lands. But with time, assimilation frequently sets in and many members of later generations enter more completely into the dominant culture, often through marriage to people of other faiths and cultures.

For the Canadian communities into which these new immigrants have moved, though, things have changed forever. On any street in Montreal, Toronto, Winnipeg, Edmonton, or Vancouver, a Catholic church is as likely to have a Gujarati Hindu temple as its neighbour as it is a Lutheran church. This new visible presence of other traditions from around the world is inevitably changing the cultural and religious consciousness of Canadians. It is part of the process of globalization happening all around us. The national policies and rhetoric of multiculturalism are taking concrete form in unusual yet inspiring ways, in the elaborate facades of the Hindu temples and the large and shining domes of the Muslim mosques being built in our cities. Canadians are learning to accept and understand a much wider array of religious traditions, and some are even choosing to practise them. As the Christian legacy of Canada fades in the face of secularization, our strong and persistent curiosity about religious and spiritual issues is finding new avenues of expression. There is no going back to the narrow Judeo-Christian heritage that shaped the first centuries of our nation. As Canadian life is increasingly infused with the practices of cultures from around the world, and as people are exposed on a daily basis to distant lands through mass communications, air travel, and business contacts, a new and unparalleled religious diversity is slated for our future.

The consequences of this diversity are as yet unknown. But in recent years, scholars have begun to turn their attention to the study of these groups (for example, the Pluralism Project led by Diana Eck at Harvard University; see <www.pluralism.org>). Many important studies have been completed, though much more research is required (see, for example, Ebaugh and Chafetz, 2000; McLellan, 1999; Warner and Wittner, 1998).

All the same, we must be careful not to exaggerate the changes underway. In 2001, only about 5 per cent of the Canadian population were Hindus, Buddhists, Muslims, Sikhs, or members of other non-Christian religions. The Canadian census reveals that this was true of 2 per cent of Canadians in 1871 (Bibby, 2002: 85). The rate of growth is steadily increasing, but the real numbers are still quite small. The recent growth of these groups in the United States has been more rapid, but they still constitute only a small fraction of Americans. They constituted 0.8 per cent of the population in the late 1970s and about 2.6 per cent of the population in 2000 (see Smith, 2002: 578). To gain some perspective, it might be noted that the membership of the twelfth largest Christian denomination in the United States, the United Church of Christ, is about the same as the entire American Muslim population (1.7 million and 1.5–1.9 million people, respectively). With 62 million Catholics alone, for example, it will be some time before these new religions have a statistically significant impact on the United States (Glenmary Research Center, 2002).

Nevertheless, the change that is underway is already forcing our dominant institutions to adapt (for example, legal, medical, and educational institutions), especially in cities like Toronto, where, for example, over 254,000 Muslims now live. These institutions are being drawn increasingly into the dialogue of religious differences and similarities as they attempt to serve the needs of a new range of Canadians.

first century will be as religious, in some sense, as their forebears. But from another perspective, we must consider just how much some aspects of society have changed in a historically short period of time. In just a few centuries, religion has fallen from its place of pre-eminence among social institutions to become only one of many segmented aspects of our lives. It persists in the hearts and minds of most people, but it no longer appears to exert as much influence over our education, business choices, social activities, or commitments. Canadians, unlike many Americans, do not choose their political leaders because of their religious convictions, nor are the religious orientations of our neighbours as much of a concern to us as they once were. Recently, for example, the Catholic Church was criticized sharply for suggesting that any Canadian politician who is a Catholic and who voted in favour of the legalization of same-sex marriages should be denied access to the sacraments, while the evangelical convictions of the leader of the Reform Party, Stockwell Day, were ridiculed in the Canadian press because journalists feared his beliefs might unduly influence his approach to public policy. In the small Ontario town where I grew up during the 1960s, Catholic and Protestant kids did not associate, even though they were neighbours. We were strangers to each other and fights between groups of Catholic and Protestant boys often occurred. Yet no one, it seemed, gave this situation much thought. Is that still the case in this neighbourhood today? I suspect not. The face of religion has changed in the modern Western world, and probably permanently (short of a complete socio-economic collapse). But it would be premature to try to predict what the real consequences will be of the changes religion is undergoing, especially with regard to its very existence. Care must be taken to realize that elsewhere the face of religion has changed little.

As cautioned in the introduction to this chapter, the view of religion we have from our experience in Canadian society is far from universal. More traditional, conservative, 'supernatural', and collectively oriented religious movements are spreading rapidly and gaining strength throughout the world. Religion may have become a very individual and private affair in much of the Western world, but fundamentalist versions of Islam and evangelical and Pentecostal versions of Christianity are ascendant in many parts of Africa, Latin America, and Asia. Where the populations of the world are growing fastest, so are the most traditional and fervent forms of religious life. Religion is bound to play an increasingly important role in the clash of interests and sensibilities between the developed and developing worlds over the course of the next century (see Jenkins, 2002).

Questions for Critical Thought

1. How would you define religion?
2. Are there aspects of religion that cannot be measured or analyzed by the social sciences?
3. Can you describe a recent situation in which religion acted primarily as an agent of social control?
4. Have you ever experienced the social effervescence that Durkheim says is crucial to religion? Under what circumstances, and what was it like?
5. If you attend religious services with some regularity, why? If you do not, why not?
6. Do you think Stark's supply-side theory of secularization explains why church attendance has dropped off so sharply in Canada?
7. Bibby reports that half of all Canadians claim to have experienced God's presence in their lives. How would we go about investigating what this means?
8. Judging by events happening in the world today, do you think that religion is going to play a significant role in social developments in the twenty-first century?

Recommended Readings

Peter L. Berger, *The Sacred Canopy: Elements of a Sociological Theory* (New York: Doubleday, 1967).

This modern classic has exerted a tremendous influence on the study of religion. Berger delineates one of the most fundamental theories of the basic nature and social function of religion and provides a classic statement of the theory of secularization, developing the ironic Weberian theme that Christianity sowed the seeds of its own destruction.

Reginald W. Bibby, *Restless Gods: The Renaissance of Religion in Canada* (Toronto: Stoddart, 2002).

This is one of a series of books written by this Canadian sociologist providing a detailed overview of the religious beliefs and practices of contemporary Canadians based on comprehensive and longitudinal survey data. Bibby provides an effective summary of his earlier findings. The latest data indicate that the declining fortunes of mainstream religions in Canada may be changing.

Lorne L. Dawson, *Comprehending Cults: The Sociology of New Religious Movements*, 2nd edn (Toronto: Oxford University Press, 2006).

This book provides a concise overview of the results and insights of the social scientific study of new religious movements since the onset of the contemporary controversy over cults in the 1960s, including questions of brainwashing, violence, and cultural significance.

Paul Heelas and Linda Woodhead, *Spiritual Revolution: Why Religion Is Giving Way to Spirituality* (Oxford: Blackwell, 2005).

Heelas and Woodhead present the results of a comprehensive study of the religious life of the population of Kendal, a small city in northern England. The book provides an unprecedented snapshot of the process of religious change, documenting the slow but steady rise of a new and more individualistic, yet coherent, style of religiosity based on a number of largely non-Christian forms of holistic spirituality.

H. Richard Niebuhr, *Christ and Culture* (New York: Harper, 1951).

Niebuhr, one of America's earliest and most gifted sociologists of religion, who was also a theologian, neatly captures the paradoxical and perplexing nature of the relationship between religions and their surrounding cultures. Niebuhr describes five different scenarios, relating them to elements of Christian scripture and doctrine, different historical traditions, and prominent spokespersons: Christ against culture, the Christ of culture, Christ above culture, Christ and culture in paradox, and Christ the transformer of culture.

Wade Clark Roof, *Spiritual Marketplace: Baby Boomers and the Remaking of American Religion* (Princeton, NJ: Princeton University Press, 1999).

This book provides one of the best overviews of religious life in the contemporary United States, using extensive survey research data and detailed interviews. Roof argues that the religious culture of America has fragmented into five distinct subcultures: dogmatists, born-again Christians, mainstream believers, metaphysical believers and seekers, and secularists.

Rodney Stark and Roger Finke, *Acts of Faith: Explaining the Human Side of Religion* (Berkeley: University of California Press, 2000).

Stark and Finke provide an excellent and very readable overview of the 'religious economies' approach to the study of the most basic elements of religious life and the heated debate over secularization. Religious preferences and behaviour are framed in terms of our understanding of broader human decision-making processes.

Max Weber, *The Protestant Ethic and the Spirit of Capitalism*, trans. Talcott Parsons (New York: Scribner, 1958 [1904–5]).

Weber argues that the Protestant Reformation had a profound and unanticipated impact on the modern world. The Protestant quest for personal salvation set in place a world view that stimulated the development of the economic ethos undergirding the rise of the capitalist system that dominates all aspects of life throughout the contemporary world.

Recommended Websites

Academic Info
www.academicinfo.net

This non-profit academic reference service provides access to many pages listing websites that deal with most religious groups present in North America and a wide variety of related religious topics (under the headings Humanities and Social Science).

Beliefnet
www.beliefnet.com

This is the largest and best-known commercial 'zine site dedicated exclusively to religion, with many features designed to educate and entertain the public and to sell religious goods of all kinds. This sophisticated site has regular columnists and special essays by experts; covers religion in the news; profiles groups, festivals, and places; reviews books; discusses TV shows, movies, and other websites; and has numerous chat lines.

The Cauldron
www.ecauldron.com

This large and sophisticated US-based neo-pagan website is meant to meet every possible need of the committed and the curious, with feature articles and forums on all aspects of belief and practice and on the integration of paganism into American religious and popular culture.

GodWeb
www.godweb.org

This is one of the first and most successful efforts to create a virtual Christian community, or at least a church presence that is exclusively on-line. It offers visitors a wide array of traditional church services, sermons, prayer groups, Bible studies, Biblical texts and indices, movie reviews, book reviews, chat rooms, and information on Christian developments from around the world.

Ontario Consultants on Religious Tolerance
www.religioustolerance.org

This private effort has received international acclaim for its efforts to promote religious understanding by providing profiles of many different religious groups, including new religious movements, and careful information and discussion of many controversial religious topics (for example, assisted suicide, evolution, and creation science).

Religion in the News
www.trincoll.edu/depts/csrpl/RIN.htm

The website for *Religion in the News*, a serial academic publication of the Leonard E. Greenberg Center for the Study of Religion in Public Life at Trinity College, Hartford, Connecticut, provides links to numerous articles and books published on a wide array of religious topics by academics and journalists.

The Religious Movements Homepage
http://religiousmovements.lib.virginia.edu

The Religious Movements Homepage at the University of Virginia is an excellent source of information on a wide array of new religious movements (NRMs) and for essays on aspects of the study of such controversial groups. The page was created by a prominent sociologist of religion, the late Jeffrey Hadden, and contains many contributions from his students and other scholars.

Wiccan Church of Canada
www.wcc.on.ca

The Wiccan Church of Canada is one of thousands of neo-pagan groups operating in North America. The website is designed to provide basic information on this group and to provide links to the wider neo-pagan community.

ELECTIONS CANADA

Chapter 13

Politics and Political Movements

Peter R. Sinclair

Learning Objectives

In this chapter, you will:

- Be introduced to concepts that help illuminate political life.
- Become aware of different forms of the contemporary state.
- Come to appreciate the value of comparing different societies.
- Review and evaluate competing perspectives on democratic societies.
- Consider the global dimensions and implications of many political issues.
- Grasp why women, the poor, and minority ethnic groups have been poorly represented in political life.
- Appreciate the forces that generate internal and international terrorism.
- Understand why many problems require answers at a regional or even global level and why solutions are difficult to put into practice.

Photo: Getty Images

Introduction

11 September 2001. On this day, international terrorism shocked North America with new ferocity and massive loss of life. Four planes were hijacked after taking off from US airports. Their pilots were replaced at the controls by men bent on a suicide mission to destroy core symbols of American power and to kill as many civilians as possible. Two hijacked jets ripped into first the north and then the south towers of New York City's World Trade Center. About one hour after the first strike, a third plane smashed into the Pentagon, the Washington, DC, home base of the US military, with the subsequent loss of almost 200 lives, including those on the plane. Meanwhile, raging fires weakened key parts of the superstructures of the twin towers, which collapsed in clouds of debris within half an hour of each other. Although many by this time had escaped to the streets, nearly 2,800 employees, passengers, and rescue workers perished in this devastating spectacle. Minutes after the collapse of the south tower, the fourth plane crashed into a Pennsylvania field, probably after a struggle on board, with a further loss of 45 lives, as hijackers tried to fly it to Washington.

As the events unfolded, it became evident that Islamic extremists conducted the attacks to strike back at the United States and international capitalism for supporting regimes they perceived as corrupt and immoral. When the United States became convinced that Osama bin Laden's al-Qaeda network had orchestrated the assaults from its sanctuary in Afghanistan, American and allied forces first bombed that country and then joined Afghans on the ground to attack both the Taliban (the fundamentalist Islamic rulers of Afghanistan) and al-Qaeda. President George W. Bush demanded that all countries support his 'War on Terror', and received backing from most Islamic states, including Pakistan. By early December, the Taliban regime had collapsed and al-Qaeda forces had dispersed into the mountains, possibly to Pakistan and other countries where they might find refuge.

After the United States sustained such a violent and successful attack on its own territory, there could be little doubt that the scale of response would be enormous and that the inevitable anti-terrorist measures would disrupt movements of people and products, especially across borders. Long delays occurred on the busy crossing points between the United States and Canada. Stock markets plunged. Many people cancelled all but essential travel. Airlines, the travel industry, and all those linked to it suffered from declining business. In these ways, the terrorists were successful. US policy and the views of the general population hardened after the attacks. There was no sign of rethinking the directions of international capitalism or US foreign policy in ways more sympathetic to poor countries and particularly to Palestinians, as al-Qaeda supporters desired.

In the following years, the US and its allies tried to support a sympathetic, secular government in Afghanistan while also attempting to hunt down Osama bin Laden and his followers. Canada contributed several hundred troops and aid personnel beginning in 2002. In 2006, when NATO (the North Atlantic Treaty Organization) took command of military operations, Canada increased its commitment to 2,200 troops posted to the southern region of Kandahar, which long was a centre of Taliban support. Indeed, it soon was apparent that Taliban forces had reorganized and NATO troops found themselves fighting a series of military battles and searches for Taliban rather than engaging in peacekeeping and development activities. By the fall of 2007, the number killed and injured in fighting and from suicide bombers was mounting with no end in sight.

The events of 11 September and their aftermath were dramatic and extraordinary, but politics enters into everyone's life every day in much more routine ways; there is almost nothing we do that the state does not in some way limit or regulate. Through its laws, regulations, and system of enforcement, the state influences people's lives from the cradle to the grave. At the same time, the state's power is under threat from **globalization** trends, terrorist opposition, popular disenchantment, and environmental disasters, to name only some of the most pressing problems. Despite the obvious importance of politics, people are unequally involved and their interests unevenly satisfied. This chapter provides sociological concepts and perspectives that should help explain the state and politics in Canada and elsewhere.

Core Concepts

Politics and Power

Politics is the process by which individuals and groups act to promote their interests, often in conflict with others. It is intimately connected to social and economic **power**. In all spheres of action, power reflects the extent to which available resources both constrain and enable people's actions (Giddens, 1979). Resources provide the means for action, but they also provide a limit on what action is possible. Following Max Weber (1978 [1908]), one of sociology's outstanding social theorists of the early twentieth century, power is often defined as the

US foreign policy has come under attack in recent years. In the aftermath of 11 September 2001, the United States hunted down potential terrorists in Afghanistan, forced a regime change in that country, and invaded Iraq. Many peace movements around the world protested the war with Iraq. In this photograph, a man protests by diving onto riot police at the entrance to the Al-Azhar mosque in Cairo. The demonstration came after a leading cleric in the Muslim world expressed sympathy for the Iraqi people. (Marwan Naamani/Agence France-Presse/GettyImages)

ability of a person or group to achieve their objectives, even when opposed. Power typically becomes concentrated in society because some people consistently have greater discretion in controlling what others do (Barnes, 1988). However, in some situations power is more or less equal, as in most friendships.

Thus, power is about capacity to act in a desired way, and politics is the process of mobilizing these capacities. Politics is most visible when it involves struggle between opposing forces, but it is also evident in what people do to avoid conflict and maintain their domination. Examples include controlling agendas and the timing of decisions, even how other people define their interests (Lukes, 1974). John Gaventa (1980) demonstrated the way power was maintained for generations in his investigation of why Appalachian miners remained politically inactive, despite much poverty, from the late nineteenth century until 1975. Apart from brief periods when recessions weakened the position of landowners and mine operators, this local elite wielded effective power. In particular, the poor miners and their families accepted existing conditions because their opponents controlled not only vital resources—jobs, houses, land, stores, access to medical facilities, even the local electoral process—but also the opinion-forming institutions of the area: schools, churches, and the media.

An excellent example of the difficulty of challenging power-holders is Bent Flyvbjerg's study (1998) of the politics of urban planning in Aalborg, Denmark. Flyvbjerg provides careful documentation of the ill-fated attempt to reduce the use of private cars in the centre of Aalborg and to make conditions more favourable for other forms of transportation. This study investigates the process of winning and losing, how reason is argued and manipulated in the exercise of power. Local business people believed that restrictions on automobiles would reduce their sales. Through the Chamber of Industry,

SOCIOLOGY IN ACTION

The Impact of Research on Political Practice: The Aalborg Project

Social research can have an effect on what is studied by helping to change the way people conduct their affairs. Bent Flyvbjerg's investigation of Aalborg's transportation system (1998) uncovered how effectively the local business elite was able to bypass formal democratic processes and achieve its objectives over a period of 15 years. However, Flyvbjerg (2001) was also committed to research that would be critical and reflexive. This required placing the results of his research back into the political arena in the hope that improvements might take place—here, in the functioning of democracy. Flyvbjerg therefore presented his results in the mass media and in public meetings. For example, he demonstrated that, contrary to expectations, traffic accidents in the centre of Aalborg increased over the life of the plan without officials apparently noticing, and that 'the increase in accidents was caused by city officials allowing the rationality of the Chamber of Industry and Commerce to slowly, surely, and one-sidedly, influence and undermine the rationality of the Aalborg project' (Flyvbjerg, 2001: 157).

Initially, those whose positions were threatened by his evidence challenged Flyvbjerg by claiming his information was inaccurate, but a determined defence of that evidence was eventually accepted by the alderman responsible for city planning. After that, dialogue developed. Dialogue is understood as a respectful exchange of ideas, a requirement of the democratic process, in contrast with mere rhetoric and polemic, which impede informed judgement.

As the public debate proceeded, the alderman and his officials realized that reports about the research were influencing the public and that the Aalborg plan had to change. They could no longer defend what was demonstrably not working, especially as the project was by this time receiving much international attention. A new plan emerged based on an open democratic process. The city government invited a variety of interest groups to join the planning and implementation processes. The European Union, inspired by Flyvbjerg's research and determination that it should be noticed outside the academy, recognized this new practice by commending Aalborg for its innovative, democratic planning process.

they prevented measures to control cars while supporting aids to buses, bicyclists, and pedestrians. Much of this activity was covert, unnoticed by the general public. In the end, the environment and virtually every citizen lost out when all forms of traffic increased. Yet this study paradoxically shows the practical value of sociology.

Power is often hidden in relationships. For power to be observed, those subject to it must actively resist. However, opposition will be rare if people believe they have no chance of successfully resisting the demands being placed on them; and it will not appear when power-holders enjoy authority, which may be defined as power considered legitimate by those subject to it.

Types of Authority

To hold authority over others is a critical resource in the conduct of politics. Where authority is widely accepted, politics will likely follow peaceful, established patterns, but when it does not exist, intense conflicts are probable sooner or later. In order to understand how authority becomes established, the work of Max Weber, almost a century ago, remains important. Weber (1978 [1908]) identified three types of authority according to the grounds on which it was accepted by those subject to it. These types seldom appear in pure form because actual relationships usually involve combinations.

Traditional authority is evident when people obey because that is the way things have always been done. The power-holder enjoys 'the sanctity of immemorial traditions' (ibid., 1: 215) and may expect obedience as long as these established rules are followed. Examples include chiefs and elders who ruled tribal societies by customary practice and acceptance of their rights. Authority of this type is more secure when it is grounded in the belief that it derives from a revered spiritual source. Thus, to oppose one's leader would also be to oppose one's god.

Charismatic authority rests on belief in the exceptional qualities of an individual person, someone of exemplary or heroic character who reveals how life will unfold, perhaps involving new social **values** and patterns of conduct. The person with charisma is thought to be able to resolve problems beyond the capacity of ordinary people and may build a devoted following, sometimes rooted in religious faith, as with the Hebrew prophets, or in secular **ideologies**, as with Mao Zedong and Adolf Hitler. Charismatic leaders are innovative, even revolutionary, but their authority is fragile, being dependent on their personal qualities and the appearance of results. One of the best Canadian examples is William Aberhart, a fundamentalist preacher who spread his message through radio broadcasts from his Calgary Prophetic Bible Institute (Irving, 1959; Bell, 1993). Aberhart turned his rhetorical skills to politics and became Premier of Alberta from 1935 until his death in 1943. Initially, he persuaded people that the rather mysterious economic theory of social credit would solve the problems of farmers and other small business people during the Great Depression. The theory required that the government distribute social credits to producers to compensate for their low incomes, which were related to high costs of production. It required control over banks and money supply, and could not be implemented against federal opposition. Aberhart and the Social Credit League continued in power aided by the focus on the war effort from 1939 and, after Aberhart's death and the end of the war, by the discovery of oil at Leduc in 1947.

Rational-legal authority is based on formally established rules, procedures, and expertise in which an individual's acknowledged right to command is limited to his or her official position. Personal characteristics of the office holder and those subject to command are irrelevant to the conduct of business. It is expected that each person will be treated as any other, which gives rise to formal procedures both for appointment to positions and for the treatment of citizens. This form of authority is characteristic of bureaucratic structures, both public and private, where those in higher-ranked positions may command those in lower positions within the limits of their jurisdiction. Thus, the manager who attempts to obtain sexual services from a secretary engages in behaviour that is considered illegitimate in that context. Specialized knowledge or expertise is another modern basis of authority, as when a physician persuades a patient to endure unpleasant and undignified procedures that the patient does not fully understand.

Modern states develop bureaucratic structures based on claims to rational-legal authority, though backed by the capacity to draw on the means of force should there be opposition. Of course, bureaucratic officials, in practice, are at times corrupt (which means that some people are treated with special favour in return for unofficial personal payments) or obstructionist. These departures from the rules weaken the legitimacy of the **bureaucracy** and may increase the likelihood of radical opposition to the regime in control of the state.

Although power and politics are dimensions of all **social relationships**, 'politics' in common use refers, in the first instance, to processes of government and regulation within and between modern states. It is this more

IN THE FIRST PERSON

I went to the University of Aberdeen in 1964 thinking I wanted to study how people behaved. A year later I discovered the new subject of sociology, which captured me immediately with its focus on social relationships and issues of social justice. More important, I was forced to challenge many beliefs I assumed to be true, to recognize that other ways of behaving were plausible and sometimes preferable. Since then, over many years, I have been rewarded by countless opportunities to research and teach about things that excite me—such as how people can act collectively to challenge what disturbs them in society; how inequality affects the way people conduct their lives; why people have destroyed so many of the natural resources on which they depend. One of the many rewarding aspects of doing sociology is the opportunity to help young people achieve their potential and challenge what is taken for granted.—Peter R. Sinclair specific understanding of politics that will be developed in this chapter.

Political institutions are established rules and procedures for the conduct of political affairs, including the government of society. They constitute a network of power relationships. Specialized political institutions were evident in some form in most earlier societies but became more complex in the industrial countries of the modern world, on which we focus here. There is no uniform course of development, but several important trends can be identified: increasing scale of government, growing political intervention in social affairs, the rise of the nation-state, and various forms of bureaucratic administration (Bottomore, 1979) including attempts at organization more inclusive than the state, particularly the United Nations and its component frameworks and sub-groups. We can analyze these networks of power in light of their internal structures and their links to the rest of society. Special interest groups, **social movements**, and political parties connect various segments of the public to the state, which is the core political frame of contemporary complex societies.

In modern societies, state institutions are both objectives of political struggle and resources in these struggles. In Weber's famous definition, **the state** is 'a human community that (successfully) claims the monopoly of the legitimate use of physical force within a given territory' (1946 [1922]: 78). Residents consider the use of force to be acceptable only when state leaders call on it, and probably only when it is applied according to widely held rules. However, it is common for physical coercion to be deployed within a particular territory without that force being viewed as legitimate by most residents. Tyrants, dictators, and zealots can rule effectively for long periods. Unless we insist that states exist only when rule is legitimate, another definition is called for. Thus, the state may be considered to be that set of procedures and organizations concerned with creating, administering, and enforcing rules or decisions for conduct within a given territory. Here, legitimacy is not assumed.

Pre-industrial states were usually rudimentary in form, for example, extensions of the household of a ruler. They were also small, as reflected in the Greek city-states. **Monarchy** is rule by a single individual who claims legitimacy based on royal lineage. Today's monarchs, as in Canada, Britain, and the Netherlands, have survived the transition to democratic constitutions, but their powers are only formal, their practice essentially ceremonial.

Modern nation-states certainly vary in scale, but they typically are much more complex, with their legislatures, governments, public bureaucracies, police, judiciary, and military components. Remembering the complexity and scale of these states, it is misleading to assume that 'the state' is coherently unified; in practice, the parts are loosely integrated and often work at cross-purposes. Canada's federal Department of Finance, for example, may wish to reduce taxes at the same time as the Department of Health and Welfare is pushing for a better-funded health-care system. The federal structure also creates layers of government with overlapping jurisdictions and potential conflicts.

Modern State Institutions

The structure of states varies in the degree to which power is centralized, civil rights are equally distributed, opposition is permitted, and military forces are subject to civilian control—key dimensions for the analysis of state

Emperor Maximilian of Mexico. In the centuries when dynasties, aristocracies, and monarchies prevailed, rulers personified the pomp and power of the states they ruled. In the truest sense, the personal was political. (Schalkwijk/Art Resource, NY)

political institutions. The forms of the state are usefully summarized as authoritarian, totalitarian, and liberal-democratic. Since the nineteenth century, the importance of the idea of nationhood to many cultures means that a society within the territorial boundaries of a state is often referred to as a nation-state, even though state and national boundaries rarely coincide perfectly. We shall see that attempts to establish truly national states often have generated severe conflict in the last 50 years.

Authoritarian States

In authoritarian states, public opposition is forbidden and the population as a whole is under great pressure to accept and comply with the expectations of political leaders. At a minimum, authoritarian leaders insist on compliance in all public life and depend on control of military force to maintain their positions if challenged.

Absolutist monarchies, which combine tradition and force to control the population, were common in pre-industrial societies in which the labour of ordinary people supported an elite. Although this type of state became rare in the late twentieth century, one example was the regime of the Shah of Iran prior to that country's Islamic revolution of 1979. Some contemporary states come close to this model. Thus, the Saudi royal family rules Saudi Arabia with an appointed advisory council and imposes a strict *shariah* code of conduct on all residents. There is no parliament and no formal opposition is permitted, but covert opposition and resistance challenge the notion that power really is absolute (e.g., see Ménoret, 2005). In 2005, the introduction of municipal elections (for men only) was the first sign of concession to some form of popular representation.

Military dictatorships have frequently taken power in Asian, African, and Latin American countries following their independence from colonial rule. Usually these seizures are claimed to be temporary measures until corruption or ethnic conflicts can be solved. Nigeria, Haiti, Myanmar, Chile, and Argentina are among many countries that have experienced military rule at least once. Military regimes lack popular legitimacy and may be short-lived. At times, experimental democratic regimes and military dictatorships replace each other in a cyclical pattern. The Chilean case (Martínez and Díaz, 1996; Meller, 2000) shows the difficulty of achieving radical change by democratic means when it is opposed by local elites and the US. In 1973, Salvador Allende, Chile's elected socialist President, who had nationalized several foreign corporations, was replaced in a military coup supported by the Chilean elite and tacitly approved, if not directly promoted, by the US. Many leftist supporters, probably more than 3,000, were killed or 'disappeared' as the new state crushed opposition and opened the economy to market forces with minimum regulation. General Augusto Pinochet ruled supreme for 17 years, but lacked enough popular support, despite improvements in the economy, to win a referendum in 1988 that would have continued his presidency for eight more years. Pinochet did accept the election of a new president in 1990, but remained commander of the army until 1998 (Meller, 2000).

Totalitarian States

Totalitarianism is more extreme than authoritarianism because it involves intervening in and controlling all aspects of both public and private life. It demands cultural homogeneity in every important respect. Totalitarianism is best considered as a strategy for achieving total domination through a centralized repressive state apparatus. Although no case perfectly fits the concept, Nazi Germany is often considered an example of totalitarianism because the Nazi Party (the National Socialist German Workers' Party) mobilized cultural institutions (mass media, schools, religion) to promote its ideology and tried to eliminate any opposition. Such states usually function in alliance with established classes and corporations, although the rhetoric of their leaders may be populist; for example, they may appeal to the anger of ordinary people, who may be suffering economic pain or political humiliation, by selecting visible minorities as targets for extremist action. Drawing on widely held racist assumptions, Hitler brought the Nazi Party to power by appealing to nationalists who felt devastated by the country's defeat in World War I and to middle-class Germans who felt threatened by the economic problems that followed the war and culminated in the Depression of the 1930s. The Nazis targeted socialists, Communists, Jews, and the post-war democratic state as dangerous sources of weakness inside Germany. They demanded order and demonstrated that they could use violence to achieve it (Bessel, 2004; Childers, 1983).

Once in power (elected by a minority of voters in 1933 shortly after Hitler had been handed the chancellorship), the Nazis soon established a compromise with big business and the assault on liberty accelerated. Parliament was closed and all other parties banned. Unions were eliminated and their leaders imprisoned in concentration camps. In later years, the Nazis rounded up millions of Jews and other minorities from Germany and other European countries and transported them to these infamous camps where they provided forced labour and were put to death in gas chambers. Secret police crushed any known opposition. Nazi beliefs in German cultural and political supremacy were promoted by any means possible until finally the Allied forces defeated Hitler's Germany in 1945 (Fox, 2004; Kershaw, 2001; Leitz and James, 1999).

Socialist states that follow the organizational structure of the former Soviet Union are also totalitarian, but ideologically quite different from Nazi Germany in that they are committed to a revolutionary transformation of **capitalism** (hence the rationalization for controlling all political, cultural, and economic institutions without permitting open dissent) to break the old order and bring a new socialist society to life. In the Soviet Union, most productive property was collectively owned, but control was centralized in the bureaucracy of the Communist Party rather than dispersed among collectives or workers.

In practice, totalitarian homogeneity never existed in the Soviet Union. Although the Soviet state was highly centralized, it was not a monolithic entity that excluded all debate and dispute. Even in the years before Mikhail Gorbachev's leadership (1985–91), interest groups and factions struggled for control within the Communist Party. There was, for example, long-standing competition between advocates of a more decentralized economic system and those who believed that modern information-processing technologies could permit centralized planning to a high degree, even in a complex industrial economy. Until the 1980s, the latter position dominated, but the rise of Gorbachev and his commitment to a more decentralized structure in economic and political affairs—to the reform of state socialism from within—changed the balance, with serious

As the institution exercising the state's monopoly over the legitimate use of force, the military has always played an important political role. In some states, questions rightly arise over whose interests the military is protecting. (Rueters)

consequences for the whole system and its final collapse in 1991 (e.g., Brown, 1996; McCauley, 1993).

Although few commentators foresaw the end of the USSR until it was practically upon us, with hindsight it is possible to suggest plausible factors leading to its collapse. Perhaps the most significant of these are the internal contradiction of state socialism and the lack of legitimacy. The contradiction lay between the need to raise productivity and living standards, which increasingly required more individual initiative and 'company' autonomy in some kind of market system, and the need to maintain central control of the social structure (Sinclair, 1982). A system created on the basis of bureaucratic control and centralized planning could not easily be reconciled with the decentralization required by effective local initiatives. Openness and criticism (*glasnost*), once genuinely released, could not be contained. The second factor, lack of legitimacy, had to do with popular frustration resulting from inadequate material living conditions in comparison with the advanced capitalist societies, resentment against authoritarian rule, and the suppression of ethnic and religious cultural identities. In the case of the nations of Eastern Europe, hostility towards the USSR as a colonizing power was an additional factor.

By 1989, it was clear that Gorbachev would not maintain Soviet influence in Eastern Europe by force, and populist democratic pressures in all the satellite nations swept the old Communist parties from power. In the Soviet Union itself, reformers, who felt that recent changes were too limited, and old socialists, who feared loss of power and, perhaps genuinely, the harshness of the free market system, challenged Gorbachev's position. In 1991, Boris Yeltsin, although himself an opponent of Gorbachev, spearheaded popular resistance in Russia to the old-style Communist Party elite, who attempted a coup to unseat both Gorbachev and Yeltsin. The Yeltsin-led radicals were successful in defeating the coup, but then deprived Gorbachev of any effective power and within months were able to ban the Communist Party in Russia. The old USSR was dead. In its place are Russia, Ukraine, and other republics in which somewhat fragile democratic institutions have been established and a capitalist economic structure is emerging (e.g., McFaul, 2001).

Liberal-Democratic States

Literally, *democracy* means 'rule by the people', but who is to count as 'the people' and how ruling takes place can vary enormously. *Direct democracy*, in which all citizens discuss and vote on all issues of importance to them, can function effectively only in small settings such as utopian communities or the classical Greek city-states. That said, liberal-democratic states are characterized by institutions that allow representation of the views of ordinary citizens through political parties that compete for the power to govern. These states may be *constitutional monarchies*, like Norway and Canada, in which the head of state is a hereditary position, or *republics*, like France and the United States, in which the head of state is elected.

At the heart of democracies are their election practices. These electoral institutions are quite varied. Some create legislatures by electing members from small areas (*constituencies*) within the state. In a sense, such societies (such as the United Kingdom and Canada) conduct a set of mini-elections all at the same time. Other democracies count votes for the whole society and candidates are elected from a party list in proportion to the party's share of the total votes cast. These *proportional representation* systems are found in many countries, including Israel and Italy.

The rapid spread of democracy has been one of the world's great dramas over the last 50 years. As Table 13.1 indicates, democratization proceeded rapidly in the twentieth century. These data are open to challenge because they depend on the Freedom House definitions and procedures for allocating cases, but they do clearly indicate general trends. In 1900, no society qualified as fully democratic because the first democracies of Europe, North America, Australia, and New Zealand restricted voting rights to men. After 1945, many societies emerged from colonial rule, sometimes to continuous democratic politics (like India), sometimes to unstable democracies

Time to Reflect

Political leaders in the West, particularly in the United States, speak of introducing democracy to formerly authoritarian and totalitarian states. Do you think this is a reasonable or laudable objective? What possible reasons would the liberal-democratic countries have for 'exporting' democracy to other states?

Table 13.1 Political Development, States and Colonies, 1900–2000

	2000	1950	1900
Democracy[a]	120 (62.5%)	22 (14.3%)	0
Restricted democratic practice[a]	16 (8.3%)	21 (13.6%)	25 (19.2%)
Constitutional monarchy	0	9 (5.8%)	19 (14.6%)
Traditional monarchy	10 (5.2%)	4 (2.6%)	6 (4.6%)
Absolute monarchy	0	2 (1.3%)	5 (3.8%)
Authoritarian regime	39 (20.3%)	10 (6.5%)	0
Totalitarian regime	5 (2.6%)	12 (7.8%)	0
Colonial dependency	0	43 (27.9%)	55 (42.3%)
Protectorate	2 (1.0%)	31 (20.1%)	20 (15.4%)
Total	**192**	**154**	**130**

[a]Freedom House defines democracies as competitive party systems in which 'opposition parties have a legitimate chance of attaining power or participating in power', whereas restricted democratic practices are systems that preclude 'meaningful challenge' to ruling parties.
Source: Freedom House, Democracy's Century report, 1999, at: <www.freedomhouse.org>. Reprinted by permission of Freedom House.

with periods of military rule (like Nigeria). In addition, many Latin American states formally established in the nineteenth century did not transform effectively to democratic institutions until the latter part of the twentieth century. Although China continues to try to maintain authoritarian central control in political life while opening the economy to market rules, it has proven exceptionally difficult to restrict individual freedom to the marketplace in socialist societies. After 1989, the spread of democracy accelerated for several years with the dramatic appearance of fledgling democratic political institutions when the Soviet Union and its East European allies collapsed, as indicated above.

Perspectives on the Democratic State

Sociologists have attempted to explain the politics of the modern state by analyzing the connection between political institutions and the social groups of which society is composed. Sociological theories of the state revolve around the question of whose interests are represented in institutions and actual policies. (See Table 13.2 for summary statements.) Do all these approaches provide part of the answer, or does the evidence fit some better than others?

Old Foes

The Ruling Elite

Until the 1970s, the chief contending perspectives stressed either elite domination or pluralism. The 'ruling elite' approach pointed to a small clique that effectively dominated political decisions on all matters that were central interests of its members. C. Wright Mills argued for the existence of a power elite at the national level in the United States—'those political, economic and military circles which as an intricate set of overlapping cliques share decisions having at least national consequences' (1956: 18). This power elite was not a fixed group whose members, in conspiratorial fashion, made all decisions; rather, it was composed of people who knew each other, shared an upper-class background, and consulted each other on issues of fundamental importance to society. Other researchers identified elites that effectively controlled decision-making at the local level (Hunter, 1953). Thus, the vision of elite domination encompassed all levels of the state.

Mills believed that the corporate elite was the most powerful segment of the power elite. Closer to Marx's

Table 13.2 Key Features of Perspectives on Liberal-Democratic States

	Social Bias of the State	Basis of Political Power	Possibility of Major Change
Power/Ruling elite	Captive of the elite: leading members of state, military, and especially economic elite	Common socialization process and control of key political resources	Highly unlikely because the mass public lacks effective organization
Pluralism/Elite competition	Neutral arena for debate: wide range of interest groups and public as a whole benefit	Success in persuading electorates in open competition plus interest group mobilization	Normal rotation of parties and effective interest groups; no structural change
Neo-Marxism	Serves the capitalist class and, to a lesser extent, the service class	Control of wealth and, indirectly, of the political elite	Unlikely but occasionally possible through revolutionary class action
Autonomous state	State elite and more powerful interest groups	Control of means of force, taxation, and votes	Possible if balance of resources shifts among key social groups
Feminism	Reflects male values and organizations; state helps maintain patriarchy	Male control of institutional patterns; limited participation by women	Unlikely without radical transformation of gender attitudes

concept of the ruling class is William Domhoff (1990), who believes that the corporate wealthy (about 1 per cent of the US population) are able to limit government to actions that serve the interests of the capitalist class. Similarly, Wallace Clement (1975) describes at length a ruling class in Canada intimately interconnected at the highest levels of corporate power and between private boardrooms and the national government.

The image of the state implicit in 'ruling elite' theory is one that puts little emphasis on administration. Instead, it focuses on policy, which is linked to the interests of those who hold key institutional positions. In all cases, this theory agrees that the interests of ordinary people are ignored whenever they might clash with those of the elite. Without explicitly writing about the state, these theorists create a vision of the state as necessarily anti-democratic. The state becomes nothing more than a means of domination, even when policy is couched in formally democratic procedures.

Pluralism and Elite Competition

Mills and his followers wrote partly in criticism of pluralism, whose advocates presented a benign view of American democracy as a forum in which any person or group had a fair chance of being represented. In turn, they themselves were attacked by those identifying a pluralist structure in US politics. Robert Dahl (1961), for example, cautioned that Mills had merely pointed out a group with high potential for control but had failed to demonstrate that this group actually dominated decision-making. Furthermore, Dahl insisted that only issues on which a clear difference of position could be observed in public debate ought to be considered. He also adopted the restrictive view that power is not exercised in situations where people are persuaded by others to adopt their attitudes. Dahl's own research, particularly in the city of New Haven, Connecticut, led him to conclude that democracy was alive and well in the America of the 1950s.

The pluralist approach recognizes that modern states all have intermediate organizations between government and the people—namely, parties and interest or lobby groups, which represent those with particular issues to promote in the state. Interest groups attempt to influence parties but rarely offer their own candidates for election because their objectives are limited to particular issues. Pluralists claim that no one interest is able to dominate the state and that democracy is protected by the competition between interests. Political leaders will be swayed by mass opinions because of their desire to win elections.

HUMAN DIVERSITY

Equalization Payments and Oil Revenues

The distribution of wealth is an important indicator of human diversity and is frequently the subject of political dispute. In Canada, this problem is complicated by the country's federal structure. Recognizing that the provinces vary in their capacity to ensure that their residents have comparable programs for health care, education, and welfare, the federal government introduced a system of 'equalization' payments in 1957. Since then, the formula for calculating these payments has changed. In 2006, the federal government compared the per capita income of the provincial governments to the mean of Quebec, Ontario, Manitoba, Saskatchewan, and BC. Any province below this mean receives a payment from the federal treasury to bring it up to the mean. All but Ontario, Alberta, and Saskatchewan benefit from this formula. The recipients are free to spend this money as they please.

Although equalization payments recognize and try to counteract the social impacts of economic diversity across Canada, they are challenged by the governments of wealthier provinces and even by some recipients who wish to change the method of calculation. Especially contentious is the current practice of counting oil and gas revenues in assessing the provinces' fiscal capacity—but not in Alberta. Alberta, Newfoundland and Labrador, and Saskatchewan have been especially opposed on the grounds that non-renewable resources provide only temporary benefits to the provinces that own them. Most others claim that transfers are artificially low because Alberta's revenues are excluded from the current base formula, and consequently the equalization payments are less than they should be. Ontario, which would not gain from the change, adopted a neutral position and opposed increasing the volume of payments that would be necessary if oil revenues were included (Canadian Press, 2006a; CBC News, 2006d; Holden, 2006).

The new Conservative government came to power in 2006 committed to removing oil and gas revenues from the calculation. Indeed, both Nova Scotia and Newfoundland and Labrador had already negotiated exclusion of their resource revenues for eight years early in 2005. However, in August 2006, a new government report recommended an intermediate position. Fifty per cent of revenue from non-renewable resources should be included in the calculation and a cap should be instituted to guarantee that no province in receipt of equalization revenue could achieve greater fiscal capacity than one that did not (CBC News, 2006d). Adopting the recommended 10-province standard would thus include Alberta's oil revenues. How this issue, which highlights provincial against pan-Canadian interests in a fragmented state, works out remains to be seen.

Evaluation

If pluralism is correct, the more disadvantaged groups in society (workers, women, minorities, and the poor) will not consistently lose to other groups. The pluralist position is justified to the extent that these groups sometimes achieve their objectives. Rights to organize and strike, extension of the franchise to women, equal-pay legislation, medicare, language legislation, land claims agreements with Aboriginal peoples, unemployment insurance, and welfare state payments are among the most important state actions that point to an element of pluralism in the Canadian system. This system might be viewed as one of elite competition for popular support. However, these policies could also be interpreted as elite concessions, implemented because they were socially and politically expedient. Clearly, an extreme ruling-elite perspective is unwarranted, but so is the uncritical image of a political system functioning without bias.

A fundamental problem for the pluralist perspective is that men and elites dominate political parties, the key groups in the political system. Of course, there is no assured link between social background and political views. As A. Paul Williams (1989) showed in his study of Canada's political elite, a person's social background is no guarantee that he or she will understand or support the interests typical of that group. Nevertheless, it is a disadvantage for any group to have to rely on the sympathetic perceptions of others. In research in the 1980s, Neil Guppy, Sabrina Freeman, and Shari Buchan (1987) found that the New Democratic Party (NDP) elected more people from lower-status groups than the other parties, but that the middle class still predominated.

As Figure 13.1 reveals, representation in Parliament shows a strong class bias that has persisted throughout Canada's history. White-collar workers in routine jobs (clerical and sales) and blue-collar workers, the majority of the population in the twentieth century, have always been severely under-represented, whereas business and middle-class professionals have dominated all parliaments. The increasing proportion of people from business and administration reflects the growing significance of corporate managers. Comparing 2000 with the two earlier years, we see that the number of lawyers declined sharply, while that of other professional groups, mainly educators and social scientists, increased. Information on the Parliament elected in 2006 is not reported in categories comparable to those in Figure 13.1, but only 11.7 per cent of members reported occupational backgrounds other than business, administration, or professional (Canada, 2006) compared with 16.4 per cent in 2000.

The extent to which Canada's tiny capitalist class occupies the pinnacles of state power has also been the subject of considerable research by such sociologists as John Porter (1965), Wallace Clement (1975), Denis Olsen (1980), and John Fox and Michael Ornstein (1986), although much of this work is now dated (Ogmundson, 2005). During the nineteenth century, the wealthy were often directly represented in the state apparatus; in the late twentieth century, this became less common, but connections were still close.

For 1946–77, Fox and Ornstein investigated the convergence between those in leading state positions and those sitting on the boards of Canada's largest corporations. At the federal level, they examined the cabinet, deputy ministers, major Crown corporations, the Senate, senior courts, and the Governor General; at the provincial level, cabinets, deputy ministers, major Crown corporations, and lieutenant-governors. In addition, they looked at the 20 largest universities and the 15 largest hospitals. They found that, 'overall, more than

Figure 13.1 Occupations of Members of Parliament, Canada, 1867, 1945, and 2000 (Percentage of Total Membership)

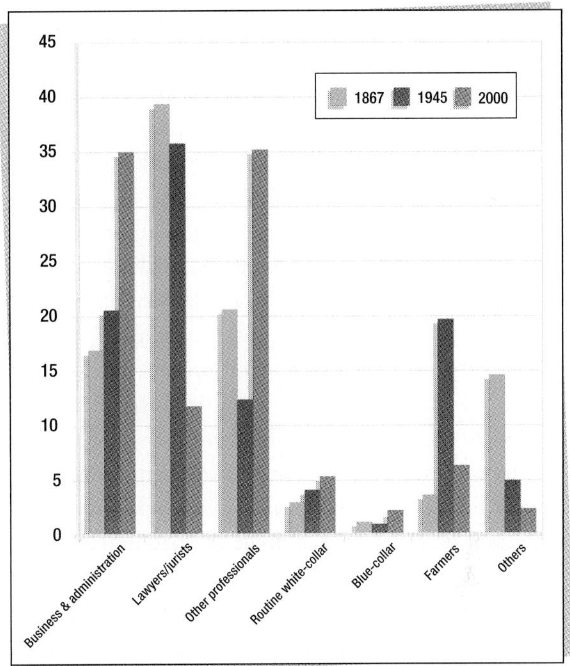

3,300 ties connect the 148 state organizations and 302 private organizations' (Fox and Ornstein, 1986: 489–90). Manufacturing and finance firms were especially well-connected to the federal cabinet, the Senate, and the state bureaucracy. Provincial governments were much less likely than the federal government to be linked to corporations. Moreover, the degree of convergence increased substantially over the three decades. The weight of this evidence is behind a 'ruling elite' position. However, it is not decisive because the association between the social ties of decision-makers and their actions should be demonstrated, and it is possible that the social ties themselves are now less pronounced.

Political Economy Perspectives

Neo-Marxism

Since the late 1960s, political economy perspectives have focused discussions on the state, which is seen as

Time to Reflect

Who are the elite and how did they get there? Do you believe you are a member or potential member of the elite? Why or why not?

the core of the political system. For the most part, these modern thinkers abandoned the old Marxist view, associated with Vladimir Ilyich Lenin, that the state was merely the instrument of capital designed to solve periodic problems of accumulation. Although they have disputed the degree to which the state should be seen in this simplistic way, neo-Marxists usually consider the state to be structured or even programmed so that it acts in the long-term interests of capitalists as a class. Consequently, these authors de-emphasize the evidence that workers appear not to be against capitalism, and see reformist labour or social democratic parties as fulfilling a need for capitalism to make concessions in order to maintain legitimacy and continuity. Similar to ruling-elite theory, the liberal-democratic processes are thought to function at a secondary level in the power structure.

Nicos Poulantzas (1978) developed the neo-Marxist perspective most fully, arguing that the state must be relatively autonomous from class conflict in the production process if it is to serve the needs of the dominant class. Here, *autonomy* does not mean independence from class control, but rather that the state is not directly representing dominant class interests. The key role of the state is to attain cohesion by 'individualizing' the workers—that is, by contributing to their sense of **identity** as individuals and as part of a nation rather than as members of a class. Legal and ideological structures resting on claims of equality among citizens conceal from workers the fact that they are engaged in class relations. To achieve this outcome, the state may act to protect certain economic interests of the dominated classes, but it never challenges the political power of the dominant class. The state may have to resist certain short-term demands of capitalists (for example, reduced taxes and reduced public spending) to meet the long-term needs of capitalism as a whole (for example, maintaining an appropriately educated labour force). From this perspective, the expansion of public welfare against capitalist opposition is interpreted as a move to shore up the future of capitalism by smoothing over some of the discontent engendered by unemployment, poor health care, and unequal access to education.

The Partially Autonomous State

Theda Skocpol (1979) and Fred Block (1980), among others, put forward another theory of the state. These theorists claim a genuinely independent source of power for state officials based on the resources of the state that these officials control. This position challenges Marxist theory by claiming, first, that the continuation of capitalism is not necessary; second, that other forms of state or institutional action might meet the 'needs' of capitalism; and, third, that much state action is opposed by those very persons for whom it is thought to be essential.

Block's answer to the key question of why state managers should act in the interests of capitalism is that they need capitalists to continue investing, or the state will lose income and political legitimacy. Nevertheless, state intervention often takes a form opposed by capital, because the state is forced to respond to working-class political pressure and because state managers have an interest in expanding their sphere of influence. Depending on the relative flow of power among these groups, state policies can be expected to oscillate. In this model, the state becomes a third effective force, although it is tied to the perpetuation of capitalist interests.

In a more radical version of this thesis, Skocpol argues persuasively that the state should be recognized as a 'structure with a logic and interests of its own not necessarily equivalent to, or fused with the interests of the dominant class in society or the full set of member groups in the polity' (1979: 27). Here, we are directed to the interests of state actors themselves, as well as to the process of policy formation, to explain the policy that is actually produced. Skocpol does acknowledge that the state often protects dominant class interests, but not in all circumstances—in particular, not when such protection would threaten political stability. Hence, according to Skocpol, 'the state's own fundamental interest in maintaining sheer physical order and political peace may lead it—especially in periods of crisis—to enforce concessions to subordinate class demands' (ibid., 30). Skocpol charges neo-Marxists with a failure to accord sufficient independence to state and party and with an unjustified insistence that the state must work towards the reproduction of capitalism. Without accepting the idea that politics is a free-for-all competition among equals, this position goes some way towards the pluralist interpretation by recognizing that the capitalist class is not consistently dominant.

Evaluation

As indicated earlier, Canadian data show that the links between capital and the state are substantial—certainly substantial enough to permit direct input of capitalist interests into the state arena. Fox and Ornstein conclude, however, that 'the data demonstrate nothing like a fusion of state and capital' (1986: 502). Thus, a simplistic view of the state as the instrument of capital will not hold true. Power can, of course, be exercised indirectly when interest groups lobby government and appeal to popular opinion. For example, David Langille (1987) claims that the most powerful corporate group, the Business Council on National Interests, was the effective architect of Canada's free trade policy, while Jack Richardson (1992) demonstrates how this policy fitted squarely with the interests of finance capital.

What are the implications for state policy and practice? On the basis of their exhaustive study of Canadian industrial policy, Michael Atkinson and William Coleman (1989) claim that Canada, unlike societies such as France, has not developed a tradition of strong state intervention. They suggest that Canadian business and political elites share critical values on such matters as minimizing state intervention, that industrial policy is largely consistent with business interests, and that the organization of political representation tends to render agrarian and labour interests ineffective. This is not to deny considerable variation, particularly by the industrial sector. Peter Sinclair's research on fisheries policy (1987) shows, for example, that the interests of small inshore fishers in Atlantic Canada were partly protected by a state that both limited the access of corporate fishing companies to critical stocks and provided subsidies or income support to small operators.

The state elite is not a mere tool of capital. One reason for the independence of the state elite is that capitalists seldom present a united front on specific policies; another is that the state controls such key resources for independent action as legal authority, lawful force, and information. The elite accommodates deprived groups to some degree in order to guarantee the legitimacy and stability of the political structure in which their own careers are located. That said, it is also true that the ideological compatibility between the state elite and Canadian capitalists, together with the complementarity of their interest in maintaining the social structure from which they benefit, works to inhibit radical institutional change. Over 30 years ago, Robert Presthus argued that the unequal distribution of political resources permits those with a vested interest in the status quo to enjoy more meaningful and successful political participation. His crisp conclusion remains valid: 'The perhaps inevitable inequalities of political resources among interest groups mean that government, to some extent, is pushed into the anomalous position of defending the strong against the weak' (1973: 349).

Feminist Perspectives

Most theories of the state focus on class issues to the exclusion of **gender** and **ethnicity**. By contrast, feminist theory makes gender a central component in the analysis of politics and the state, as it does for social life generally. Specifically, the **feminist perspective** has brought attention to the state as a contributor to the subordination of women and as an institution permeated by gender inequality. However, there is no single feminist position. Judith Allen (1990), for example, even asserted that feminists have no need for a theory of the state because the concept of the state is too vague and unitary to be applicable to women's political strategies, which must focus on specific local conditions or 'sites'.

Nonetheless, other feminists have considered state theory important. In her influential paper, Mary McIntosh (1978) argues that the state supports a system in which men control women in the household, where they work without pay to maintain capitalism's labour force, and from which they can be drawn as needed to supply cheap labour. Referring mainly to the United Kingdom, McIntosh reviews the ways in which the state indirectly subordinates women by staying out of certain areas such as family life, which are left to the control of men, and through legislation, such as husbands' tax allowance, which privileges employed, married men. In a sense, McIntosh contends, women are hidden in the family or household to serve the needs of men and capitalism.

Jill Quadagno claims, with justification, that the explanation of the development of the welfare state has emphasized class analysis, while ignoring the welfare state's 'organization around gender' (1990: 14). Feminist theorists often claim that welfare programs maintain male dominance insofar as their rules of eligibility favour male breadwinners. Women are more often subject to means tests for social assistance programs, whereas men are more likely to qualify for universal entitlement programs. However, Quadagno notes that some social programs could advance women's interests by reducing their dependence on men. But the development of 'gender-equal policies' requires women to become mobilized as effective political actors. The latter point is effectively supported by Quadagno's analysis of the defeat of the US Family Assistance Plan in 1972. Had it been implemented, this program would have improved the economic position of both women and blacks in the southern states.

Quadagno's view is consistent with the earlier work of Varda Burstyn (1983), a Canadian feminist, who also identifies the state as acting to maintain domination both by capitalism and by men, and with subsequent studies of how state policies often discriminate against women's interests or simply fail to address them (Brodie, 1996). Burstyn explains the gender-biased actions of the state largely by the massive extent to which men occupy higher-level state positions. The most extreme bias in the state's structure is the inadequate representation of women. Most Canadian women achieved federal voting rights only in 1918—in Quebec, not until 1940. The 65 women elected between 1921 and 1984 amount to 0.8 per cent of all elected members of the House of Commons (Brodie, 1985: 2–4). Since then, the situation has improved, with women constituting 20.8 per cent of MPs in 2006 (Cool, 2006), about the same as their share based on elections held since 1997. Still, Sylvia Bashevkin's generalization that the more powerful the position, the fewer the women (1985) remains apt for both party and state. Only one woman has been Prime Minister—Kim Campbell, for several months in 1993, until her Conservative government was defeated.

Does representation matter? While there is no reason to expect women to hold views different from those of men on many issues, it is more likely that the interests of women would be effectively represented if they were present in decision-making positions. Manon Tremblay's analysis of women in Parliament in the mid-1990s (Tremblay, 1998) gives some support to this position (see also Ogmundson, 2005). Although women's issues (women's rights and traditional areas of women's involvement, such as elder care) were marginal in House activities, when discussion did take place women were more involved than men. MPs who were women gave greater importance than did men to women's issues; they were more likely to report interest in these matters and to feel that they should be given priority. Yet differences were moderate. Regardless of whether or not women would be better protected by greater political participation, their absence from positions of power is unacceptable, since it seems to rest purely on the ascriptive criterion of gender.

The position of Canadian women in politics is barely intermediate when compared with other societies, as Table 13.3 demonstrates. In the Scandinavian countries and the Netherlands, women fare much better, holding over 35 per cent of electoral seats in 2003, while the United States, with 15.2 per cent, did not rank in the top 50. Rwanda (1), Costa Rica (3), Cuba (8), and Argentina (10) are developing societies that now rank in the top 10 for representation of women in their legislatures. Women also have made substantial advances since the 1980s in holding executive positions. As of December 1990, women headed just six of the United Nation's 159 member states, while in 93 countries women held no ministerial positions (United Nations, 1990: 31). Since then, it has been much more common to find a woman holding the highest office. Thus, between 1990 and 2000, 36 women were elected as heads of state (Lewis, 2002). In European Union countries, women held an average of 24.6 per cent of cabinet positions in 2001, with parity actually achieved in Sweden (FCZB, 2001).

Women are dismantling the bastions of male political dominance, but the process is slow and depends on reorienting attitudes towards gender roles. The **socialization** process must change before this form of discrimination will disappear. Although some men are sensitive to women's issues, male-controlled legislatures in Canada and elsewhere have been slow to act on many matters of importance to women. Can it be purely coincidental that women are primarily responsible for child-care prior to school but that the state provides inadequate assistance for mothers who wish to be employed? As of 2006, there was still no national day-care policy; rather, a patchwork of provincial programs and federal payments of $1,200 per child (under six years old) to parents to spend as they wish. Yet, daycare facilities do not meet the demand (CBC News, 2006a). Furthermore, child-care workers are unable to earn the professional salaries that would justify the necessary training and commitment. In the labour market generally, part-time workers are disproportionately women and receive inferior job protection. Legislation that would end pay discrimination in the private sector based on gender has been slow to arrive and is difficult to enforce. These are only a few examples of the gender-related problems that remain to be solved in Canada and most other societies.

Democracy and Politics in Canada

Party Politics

A **political party** is an organization dedicated to winning political power by controlling government. In liberal democracies, this means winning a general election. Canada is a federation with a complex structure in

Time to Reflect

What steps might be taken to ensure that more women and minorities are elected to public office? Do you believe greater representation of women and minorities is desirable or even matters? Why or why not?

Table 13.3 Women as Percentage of Legislatures, Most Recent Election, Regions and Selected Countries, Ranked by Lower House Representation

	Lower or Combined House	Upper House
Countries		
1 Sweden	45.3	—
2 Denmark	38.0	—
3 Finland	37.5	—
4 Netherlands	36.7	26.7
5 Norway	36.4	—
6 Cuba	36.0	—
7 Belgium	35.3	—
8 Costa Rica	35.1	—
9 Austria	33.9	21.0
10 Germany	32.2	33.3
36 Canada	20.6	32.4
59 United States	14.3	13.0
Regions		
1 Nordic countries	39.7	—
2 Americas	17.7	17.2
3 Europe: OSCE[a] members including Nordic countries	17.7	14.5
4 Europe: OSCE members excluding Nordic countries	15.6	14.5
5 Asia	15.4	13.8
6 Sub-Saharan Africa	14.1	15.6
7 Pacific	12.1	25.9
8 Arab states	5.9	3.6

[a]Organization for Security and Co-operation in Europe.
Source: Inter-parliamentary Union, *Women in National Parliaments*; data available at <www.ipu.org/wmn.e/classif.htm>.

which the powers of legislation are divided between federal and provincial governments. The organization of parties mirrors this institutional arrangement, and securing as much electoral support as possible within this structure is the key to their success.

At the federal level, only the Liberal and Conservative parties had ever governed until 2006, and the Liberal Party had been dominant. This is evident in Figure 13.2, which shows party support since the 1953 election. Until the 1990s, these two parties competed with each other for control of the state by following a brokerage strategy in which the parties would attempt to appeal to diverse social groups in order to establish a winning combination. Usually, this meant avoiding controversial ideological issues and adopting broadly similar positions on major issues. An exception was the 1988 election campaign in which the Progressive Conservatives championed free trade and claimed victory after a bitter struggle.

The Co-operative Commonwealth Federation (CCF) and its successor, the NDP, have taken positions similar to European labour and social democratic parties but have never succeeded at the federal level in gaining Ontario-based support outside several industrial or peripheral areas. In Quebec, the CCF/NDP has failed to establish itself. With this weak performance in the most

Figure 13.2 Popular Vote (%) by Party, Canadian Federal Elections, 1953–2006

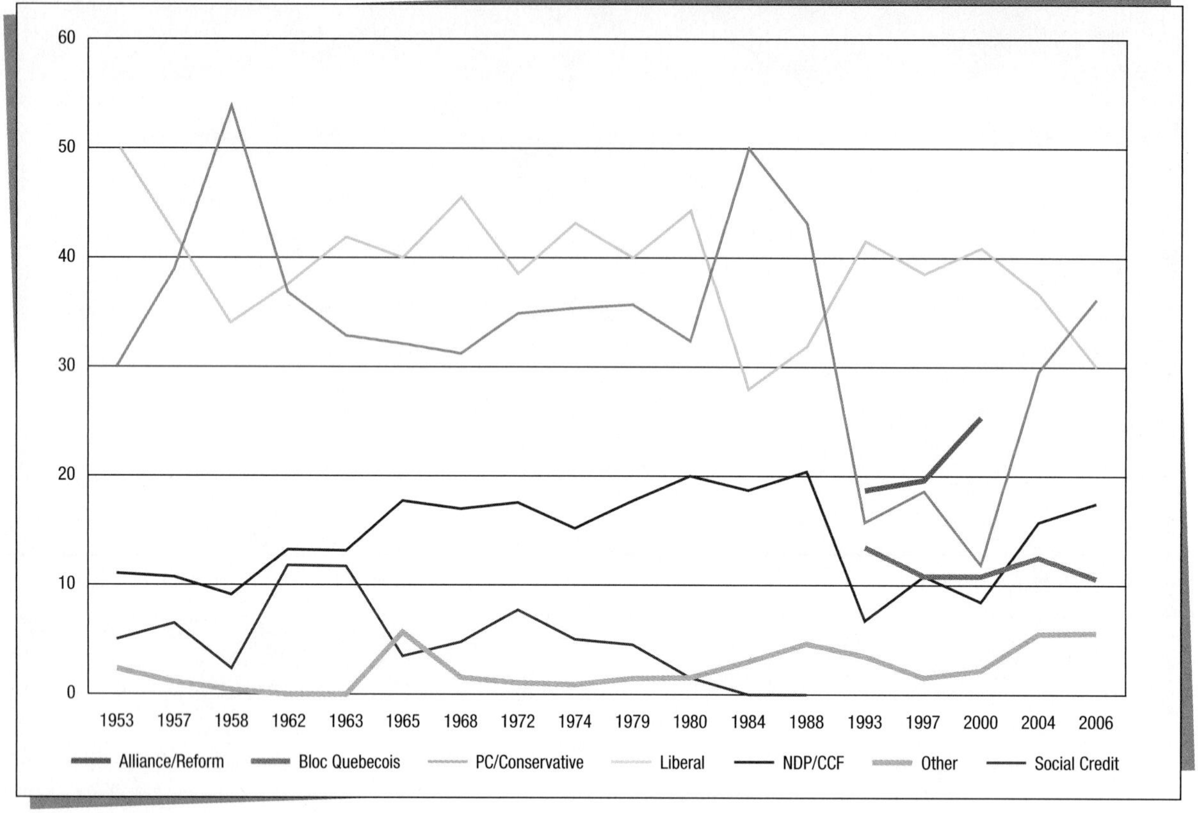

Source: Calculated from Elections Canada data.

populated provinces, the CCF/NDP has been unable to exceed 20 per cent of the vote after more than 70 years of campaigning. From 1988 to 2000, the party appeared to be in serious trouble with its vote hovering around 10 per cent as the rise of neo-conservatism pushed some NDP voters to prop up the Liberal centre. NDP prospects revived in the last two federal elections with considerable support among young voters in 2004 (Gidengil et al., 2006).The NDP has consistently failed to translate its support in provincial elections into equivalent federal votes, with the exceptions of Saskatchewan, Manitoba, and BC. This may be due to a perception that the provincial NDP governments, especially in Ontario, could not enact sufficient legislation to favour the interests to which the party has appeared committed (workers, the poor, minorities, and women). Also, the party's more popular policies, such as medicare and subsequent support for public health systems, were adopted by the mainstream parties when it was expedient to do so.

In the 1990s, important new parties emerged in federal politics. The Bloc Québécois, paradoxically, has represented separatist voters in the national Parliament since 1993, but this party, like the provincial Parti Québécois, is social democratic as well as nationalist. That made it quite different from the other newcomer to federal politics, the Canadian Alliance, which began its existence as the Reform Party. The Alliance was a socially conservative, populist party that emerged from Alberta and spread eastward with decreasing success beyond Manitoba except for pockets of support in Ontario and the Maritimes. The populist dimension was reflected in the party's formal commitment to direct democracy and members' control of the organization, although this was seldom evident in practice, despite sharp attacks on the elitism of established parties. The Alliance found core support among Canadians who wanted lower taxes, reduced public spending, a smaller state presence in their lives, a more punitive approach to crime control, curtailment of abortion rights, and more restrictive immigration policies. This Canadian version of the New Right agenda climbed to 25 per cent of popular support in the election of 2000, but the party lost favour as a result of a bitter internal struggle to remove Stockwell Day from the leadership that ultimately was successful in 2002. The chief casualty of the emergence of Reform/Alliance was the Progressive Conservative Party, whose support plummeted after 1988 to a level not much greater than that of the NDP. This decline was soon followed by a merger with the Alliance in 2003 into what has become a socially conservative party, the Conservative Party of Canada ('Progressive' was dropped from the name of the old PC Party), which achieved minority government status in the 2006 federal election following corruption scandals in the Quebec wing of the federal Liberals.

The Electoral System

Canada's electoral system has several advantages. Citizens may be able to approach their local area's member of Parliament (MP), although it would be impossible for everyone actually to do so. More important, this system usually produces a majority, and thus a stable government. But it clearly makes some people's votes more influential than others, depending on where they live, and often produces a Parliament that does not reflect the wishes of the population as a whole.

Most people vote for the party rather than for the individual candidate. The electoral system, however, provides no assurance that the party receiving the most votes over the whole country will win the election. If two parties have roughly equal total support but one party has voters equally distributed and the other much more concentrated, the party with equal distribution will certainly win. In fact, it can win even if its total votes are fewer, as has happened several times in Canadian history. Thus, the majority does not necessarily elect the governing party. Indeed, in only three of the 18 elections between 1953 and 2006 did the governing party receive more than 50 per cent of all votes. Moreover, since it is rare for more than 75 per cent of those eligible to vote actually to cast a ballot, there has never been a Canadian government voted to office by a majority of citizens.

None of this makes Canada unusual. Rule by minorities occurs because more than two parties contest the elections, and the system of competition in constituencies spread across the country means that popular vote does not translate directly into representation in Parliament. Indeed, in three elections (1957, 1962, and 1979), the Progressive Conservatives formed the government after having received fewer votes than the Liberals. Getting more than 40 per cent is usually enough to assure success. For example, in the election of 2000, the Liberal Party translated 40.8 per cent of the votes cast into 57.1 per cent of the seats. The elections of 2004 and 2006 led to minority government with no party able to reach 40 per cent of the popular vote. Figure 13.3 shows that the Conservatives formed the government by turning 36.3 per cent of the votes into 40.3 per cent of the seats. Except for the Bloc Québécois, the smaller parties received a higher percentage of the vote than seats. The Bloc's vote was obviously concentrated in Quebec ridings, many of which it won. The other parties (the NDP and the Green Party) had moderate support widely scattered across constituencies with the consequence that they could win few seats.

The constituency system often leaves supporters of minority parties with little or no representation. It is especially difficult for new parties to be successful in this system because they have difficulty translating their support into seats and political visibility. Thus, a party that obtains 10 per cent of the votes may not win a single seat unless those votes are concentrated in a few ridings. This discourages participation and makes it difficult for new parties to become established and considered as viable options by the electorate as a whole. Proportional representation is designed to avoid these problems. Had such a system functioned in Canada with the same voting distributions, the country would have had a minority or coalition government in 2000 and in 12 other elections from 1949 until then. Political compromises would have been necessary, but many societies achieve stable governments with election by proportional representation. Usually, a party must obtain a minimum of 5 per cent of electoral support in order to obtain any seats; this prevents excessive fragmentation of the legislature. Because the party that governs and benefits from the present system would have to support a change, it is extremely unlikely that Canadians will adopt a more representative system in the foreseeable future.

Time to Reflect

Canada's 'first-past-the-post' electoral system favours some parties and disadvantages others. Would you like to see some kind of proportional system in place, and how would such a system change the political landscape of the country?

Figure 13.3 Percentage Distribution of Votes and Seats by Party, Federal Election, 2006

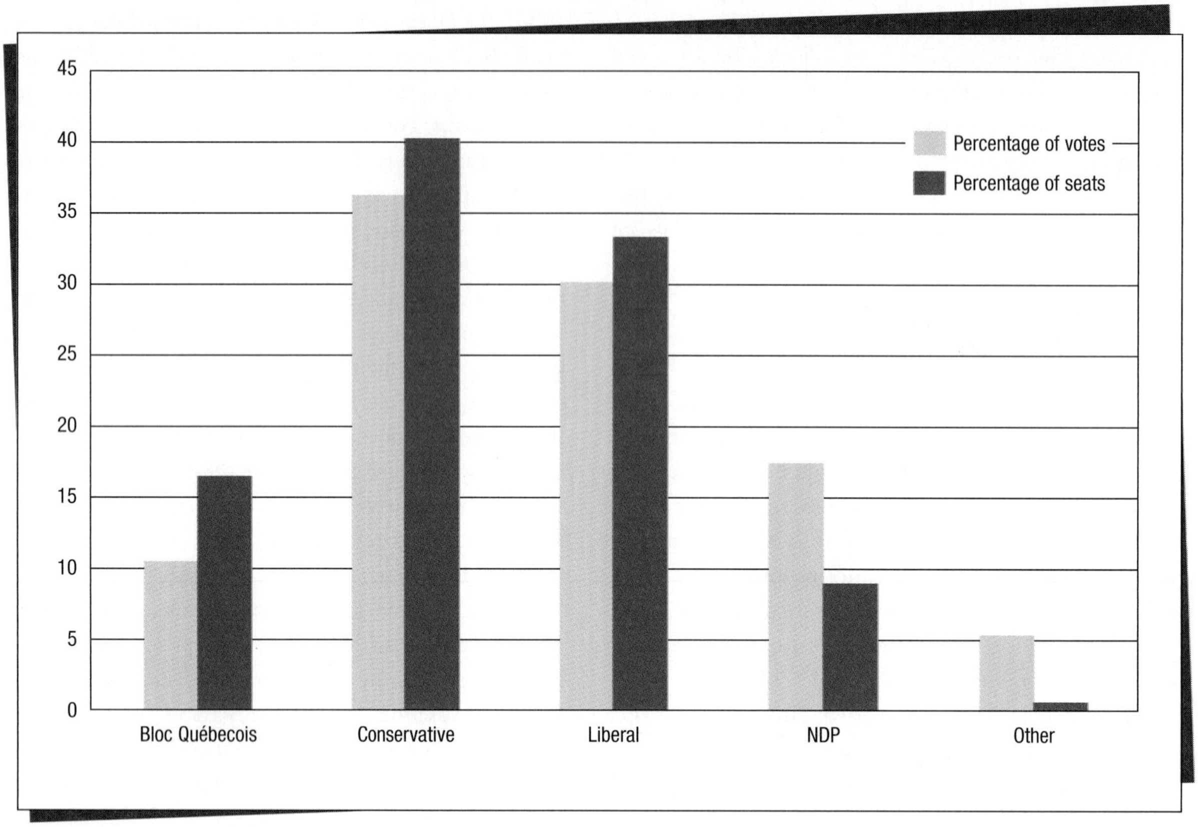

Source: Calculated from Elections Canada data.

Political Participation

Participation in the political process varies from informal discussion, listening to media reports, and voting to more demanding activities such as attending meetings, assisting with campaigns, contacting politicians in order to influence them, and even running for office. For most Canadians, political participation is limited to discussion and voting for candidates to the various levels of government. However, it appears that the public is becoming increasingly cynical about politicians; turnout at elections is falling, with federal elections now attracting about 60 per cent of eligible voters.

Sociologists are interested in the social characteristics that may influence participation. However, a great deal of research has demonstrated that there is no necessary link between a person's social background and the party he or she supports. Harold Clarke's team (1991) examined the variables of class, gender, ethnicity, religion, region, community size, and age, and found that they all have some effect on Canadians' voting preferences, but much less than political variables such as prior voting record, concern about immediate issues, and the image of the party leader. Nonetheless, in 2000 the Liberal Party could not have won without the strong support outside Quebec of Catholics (54 per cent) and Canadians of non-European ethnicity (70 per cent; Gidengil et al., 2001: 28). Region was more critical than it had been in earlier elections, with the Alliance powerful west of Ontario (where Liberals were much weaker) but unable to break through in eastern Canada, where Conservatives and especially Liberals were stronger. Women supported the NDP much more than did men, whereas men were more drawn to the Alliance. Age and language were critical to voting in Quebec, where those under 55 and francophones were more likely to support the Bloc Québécois.

Class is not a defining force in contemporary Canadian politics, but economic issues and beliefs do influence the choices of many voters. Thus, outside Quebec, those who believed in giving increased priority to market forces were more attracted to the Alliance and Conservative parties in 2000, while those with the opposite view favoured Liberals and the NDP; social conservatives preferred the Alliance to the Progressive Conservative Party (Gidengil et al., 2001). In the election of 2004, those doubtful of the fairness of the free market were much more likely to be NDP voters, as were those with certain characteristics of lower social status—minimal education and, especially, those who rented (Gidengil et al., 2006: 9–11).

A crude theory in which voting behaviour inevitably follows from social experience is obviously untenable. A more useful sociological account, influenced by **symbolic interactionist** theory, starts from the assumption that voting is an interpretive action to which people carry assumptions from their prior experience, filtered through their social positions and possibly their previous commitments to a party. Usually they have incomplete information and incomplete understanding of how the political system operates. Typically, the strongest parties play down social issues and try to emphasize the quality of their leaders (or record in office) to cope with whatever problems exist. To achieve overall victory, care will be taken not to appear too closely linked to the interests of any particular group. In the end, voters make choices that respond only partially to social and cultural factors. Of course, for decades in Quebec, the priority of cultural concerns and the issue of independence have made political life more ideological and socially influenced. Nonetheless, voting does not really determine state policy—it provides legitimization for those who control it.

Neo-Conservatism and Privatization

After decades of expansion of the welfare state and of standards of living, many countries faced problems of inflation, lower economic growth, and budget deficits in the 1970s and 1980s. Continued demands for better public education and health care were incompatible with pressure to reduce taxes. Many states seemed to be suffering from or on the brink of what some called a 'crisis of legitimation' (Habermas, 1975; Offe, 1984). With welfare state programs under severe stress, political space opened up for more conservative policies. These policies stressed eliminating public deficits by reducing expenditure, stimulating the economy by cutting taxes, and withdrawing the state from the economy by privatizing existing public enterprises and contracting to the private sector for services previously provided by public employees. Sometimes **privatization** sales have been legitimized as contributions to debt reduction. The promotion of 'free' market forces and a smaller state is at the core of this new conservatism, which has found favour with many voters, especially those who would benefit from tax reductions and who have the capacity to purchase services for themselves.

In Canada, this trend has been evident not only in the rise of the Canadian Alliance and now the Conservative Party, but also in practices of various provincial governments, especially Conservatives in Ontario (under Mike Harris) and Alberta (Ralph Klein) and Liberals in British Campbell (Gordon Campbell). However, all levels of government have participated to some degree. For example, the federal government sold Air Canada to the private sector, and Petro-Canada, the highly successful national oil company, can now be purchased on the stock market. Airport security was subcontracted prior to the terrorist attacks of 11 September 2001. The privatization of basic public goods, such as power and water supply, is proving to be controversial: many people are concerned that prices will rise in the long term once supply is in corporate hands. Thus, the decision to sell Ontario Hydro in a mammoth public share offering proved difficult to implement in 2002 as citizen groups mobilized in opposition.

Certainly among the most critical issues is the reform and increased privatization of health care, which was on the political agenda for some years and subject of several investigations, most recently the Romanow Commission on the Future of Health Care in Canada, which reported in 2002. As of 2003, the federal government insisted that it would use its power to maintain standards across Canada, including universal access. Nevertheless, there have been signs of creeping privatization, especially in Alberta, and considerable dispute between the federal government and the more conservative provincial administrations. Canadians worry about what is happening to

Time to Reflect

Have you ever run for public office, or would you ever consider running as a candidate in a local, provincial, or federal election? Explain the reasons for your answer.

OPEN FOR DISCUSSION

Controversy over Health Care Reform

According to various polls, Canadians consider protection of the health-care system to be a priority for public action. Nevertheless, a national poll in 2001 reported that 56.6 per cent were generally satisfied with the existing system and 81.7 per cent were content with services they had received in the previous five years. The main problems that respondents perceived were poor management, inadequate financing, and staff shortages. A majority believed the Canadian system to be superior to that of the United States and were against privatization of hospitals (Leger Marketing, 2001: 2–6).

Although problems are often recognized, many Canadians resist major changes that might affect universal access, especially a reduction in the services that are currently paid from state treasuries. Canadian health care is not, for the most part, socialized because most health-care professionals work in private practice or for independent hospital boards. About 30 per cent of services are not covered by public medicare. Access to health services could be privatized by eliminating state payments so that patients would have to rely on their own resources or a private insurance plan.

The key issue here is whether or not social inequality would affect availability of health care if public services were reduced and access determined by capacity to pay the market rate for the service. Opponents clearly believe this to be the case and prefer other solutions to existing problems. In 2002, the Romanow Commission investigated alternatives prior to the federal government's announcing its plan of action. Preliminary evidence of public opinion on these options indicates that most prefer system reform with a focus on preventative medicine, but nearly half would be willing to accept more private-sector participation (Decima Research, 2002). By 2002, the most radical plan to date to alter the existing system was put forward by Ralph Klein's government in Alberta, which planned to contract out certain services from public hospitals to private clinics. By 1994–5, Alberta had already moved to allow physicians to bill the state for certain core services and to privately sell additional services to their patients. These plans have been bitterly attacked by those concerned about inequities in the emerging health-care system.

their health-care system when they see so many publicized delays in accessing specialist services and when hospital emergency rooms are frequently overflowing. The 2003 SARS outbreak in Toronto again brought such concerns to the forefront as the hospital system appeared close to collapse. Several hospitals had to be diverted from their normal activities, and medical staff were required to function under dangerous and stressful conditions. Some are convinced that privatization or a two-tier system is necessary, while others prefer a reform of the existing system and the injection of the necessary funds to make it work properly. In 2006, the outcome remains unclear but two senior editors of the *Canadian Medical Association Journal* were fired in February 2006, possibly for their pro-medicare opinions, and the Association elected the operator of a private clinic as its head some months later. The federal Minister of Health, Tony Clement, is also on record as favouring private medicine (Canada Health Coalition, 2006; CBC News, 2006b).

Challenging Issues and Political Movements

Political movements are social movements that challenge established state policies and practices in order to bring about social and political changes. Their objectives can vary from moderate reform to radical overhaul of **social institutions**. Similarly, the means vary widely from conventional interest group or party activities to protests outside the existing political norms, including campaigns of violence. **Terrorism** occurs when physical violence is directed against civilians, without regard for who will suffer, in order to promote political objectives. This section reviews a critically important political movement in Canada: Quebec separatism, which has a complex history that includes both peaceful opposition and terrorism.

The Quebec Question: Maîtres chez nous?

It is difficult to create a cohesive nation-state in which a large minority speaks a different language and remains committed to continuing its different culture. To some extent, Canada's federal structure allows for these differences, but the movement for an independent Quebec has threatened for 40 years to split Canada apart.

In the 1950s, a new Quebec started to emerge from a society that had been church-dominated, elitist, and uncomfortable with urban industrial development. Quebec's Quiet Revolution accelerated in the 1960s as the francophone majority became better educated and determined to push ahead with a modern society that would be French-speaking (McRoberts, 1999). Hence the famous provincial Liberal campaign slogan of 1962: *maîtres chez nous*—masters in our own house. Quebec became much more secular and urbanized, but many Québécois felt that more radical changes were necessary to ensure their survival as a distinct, francophone society surrounded by anglophones.

The moderate, federalist segment was led by Liberals, and it brought Pierre Trudeau into the political limelight in 1968 as the champion of an officially bilingual Canada, shortly after the government released the report of the Royal Commission on Bilingualism and Biculturalism (Canada, 1967). The key legislation was the Official Languages Act (1969), which was designed to ensure that public services would be available all over Canada in both languages. One by-product was that bilingualism became critical for higher-level positions in the civil service, which made it easier for Québécois to rise in the bureaucracy.

Although opposed by many anglophones, this accommodation to Quebec's cultural interests did not satisfy a growing force of nationalists who believed that the only solution was for Quebec to become sovereign, that is, to be politically independent and thus in charge of all its own institutions. The most extreme position was taken by a small group known as the FLQ (Front de Libération du Québec), which adopted terrorist means from 1963 to 1970 with a campaign of bombings and culminating in the kidnapping of British diplomat James Cross and the murder of Pierre Laporte, Quebec's Minister of Labour.

Although the FLQ was crushed when Trudeau implemented the War Measures Act in 1970, the idea that Quebec required greater independence than was possible within Canada gained ground. Thus, the Parti Québécois (PQ), dedicated to separatism and generally sympathetic to aspirations of the newly politicized working class, swelled from a minor movement in the late 1960s until it achieved power in 1976 under its charismatic leader, René Lévesque. The PQ moved quickly to introduce legislation that made French the only official language in Quebec and required the children of immigrants and of Canadians moving from other provinces to be educated in French. Anglophones and English business flowed out of the province, but 60 per cent of voters rejected sovereignty-association in the divisive referendum of 1980.

Once more in office, Trudeau's response was to repatriate the Constitution complete with a new Charter of Rights and Freedoms that failed to win support in Quebec. Later, having promised to introduce changes satisfactory to Quebec, the Progressive Conservative government under Brian Mulroney promoted an agreement that increased Quebec's powers (including the right to opt out of federal legislation) and recognized that it was a distinct society. This agreement, the Meech Lake Accord (1987), was almost ratified by the legislatures of the country but collapsed in Manitoba when Elijah Harper, an Oji-Cree chief and the only Aboriginal member of the provincial legislature, on principle over the failure of Aboriginal peoples to achieve their similar objectives, withheld his decisive vote on procedural grounds. This delaying tactic meant that ratification could not be achieved before the three-year deadline.

Clearly, at least to the Mulroney Tories and to the provincial premiers, further action was required, and the process of constitutional reform continued, with many public meetings culminating in the Charlottetown Accord, which included greater rights for both Quebec and Aboriginal peoples. However, a disenchanted public defeated the subsequent referendum in 1992. The rejection of the Charlottetown Accord prompted a strong showing by the separatist movement in the 1993 federal election.

The PQ returned to office in Quebec, and in 1995 held a second referendum in which its proposal for negotiated independence was defeated by the narrowest of margins—50.58 per cent to 49.42 per cent (Pinard, 2002). At this time, some form of separation appeared almost inevitable, but for the government subsequent years were bedevilled with economic and social problems. Both the PQ and separatism in general lost their attraction as opponents made ground with claims that Quebec would suffer excessive economic damage as a separate state. Also, Premier Jacques Parizeau blamed the 'ethnic' vote for the referendum defeat and amid tremendous furor quickly resigned. Lucien Bouchard, the popular leader of the federal Bloc Québécois, became the new PQ leader but resisted any attempt to call another referendum until winning conditions were present—not when the government was engaged in struggles with labour to reduce public spending and services. Discouraged by internal party conflict and especially with signs of anti-Semitic views within the party, Bouchard resigned from the premiership. His more radical successor, Bernard Landry, failed to hold the movement's support. Indeed, in 2003, the Liberals, under the leadership of Jean Charest, won a clear majority of seats based on 44.9 per cent of the popular vote. However, the underlying problems have not been resolved. Indeed, by 2006, the Liberal government had become unpopular and a new poll showed 52 per cent in favour of the same question that failed narrowly in 1995 (Environics, 2006: 5). Quebec independence may still be possible unless Canadians can find a way to accommodate the interests of Quebec inside Canada, but separatists suffered a severe setback when the PQ fell to third place in the provincial election of 2007.

Loss of Legitimacy and Terrorist Opposition

When people believe that their opinions are unwanted and that they can never achieve their objectives by working through the political institutions of their society, established political life has no legitimacy for them. If their commitment is high, they may feel that they have no option but to try any means possible and that the means are justified by the failure of existing authorities. Indiscriminate violence directed against civilians is intended to pressure power-holders to meet the objectives of terrorists and so avoid chaos for and harm to citizens. Perhaps most common are movements to promote independence of ethnic or nationalist groups. Well-known examples are the Irish Republican Army, Basque nationalists in Spain, Kashmiri independence groups, and the Tamils of Sri Lanka. Many parts of the world are unsafe, and many thousands die each year in violent conflicts, usually but not exclusively in less developed countries (see Figure 13.4). Canada has not been free of this problem, as we have seen in the previous section.

Colombia provides an example of this kind of national or internal terrorism, which has changed its focus and lost popular support there after four decades of conflict and over 100,000 deaths. Perhaps because these deaths have occurred over a long time in small numbers per incident, Colombian violence has attracted less attention than its importance warrants, given the threat it poses to South America's oldest democracy.

The roots of crisis include a political system that had to cope with long-standing regional political struggles, from which emerged an elite compromise between liberals and conservatives that effectively eliminated the masses from political life. In a country that was difficult to unite physically and where local power-holders could raise private armies, violence became a normal way of settling disputes. Leftist radicals, both socialist and populist, felt that there was no option in the 1960s but to start a guerrilla campaign against the state. However, in later years, some were reabsorbed into institutional politics, while others turned to the drug trade to finance ongoing struggle against paramilitary forces as well as the army. These paramilitaries sometimes allied with the state against the left, sometimes with drug barons against the state. By the 1990s, the former populist guerrillas had become indistinguishable from drug criminals, and their political objectives seemed simply to achieve a resolution that would solidify their power and acquisition of wealth. Kidnappings, murders, bombings, and brutal attacks on state personnel continued even as peace negotiations were taking place spasmodically from 1999 to 2002. The guerrillas lost almost all their public sympathy, and President Andrés Pastrana was compelled to end negotiations in February 2002. Since then, the Colombian government has tried to combine a tough military campaign with generous reception for those willing to disarm. Although the conflict is far from over, kidnappings, bombings, and killings were much reduced by 2005–6 compared with earlier years, and the paramilitary force has mostly disarmed.

International terrorism differs only in its focus and visibility through the mass media. In the early twenty-first century, the most evident examples are Palestinian attempts to counter the superior military power of Israel and the radical Islamic militants who were behind the events of 11 September 2001 and later attacks in Bali (2002, 2005), Madrid (2004), and London (2005). Most people find it difficult to understand the psychology of those who carry out suicide bombings and hijacking of airliners, and, therefore, the seeming irrationality of such acts makes them extremely hard to prevent. Real danger exists that in response to the desire to avoid terrorist attacks the level of control and surveillance of the affairs

Figure 13.4 Armed Conflicts in 2002

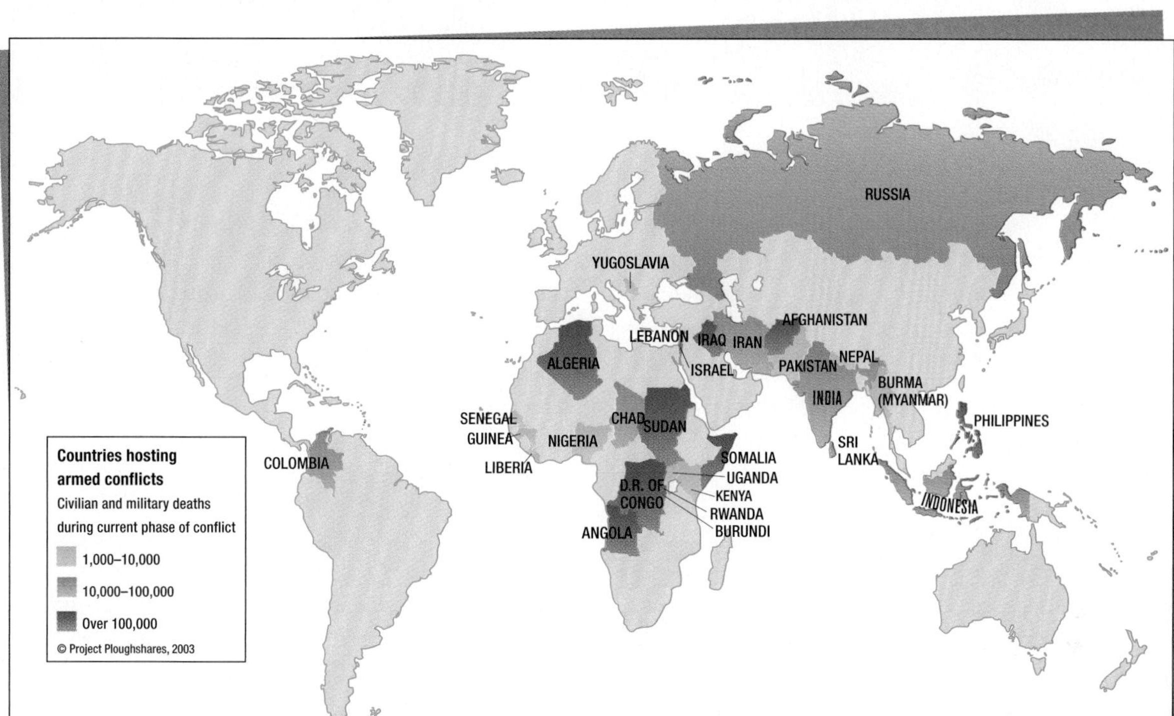

Source: 'Armed Conflicts in 2002', Project Ploughshares, 2003. Reprinted by permission.

and movements of ordinary people will endanger personal freedoms and change the nature of society for the worse.

Environmental Degradation: Coping with Climate Change

Since the 1960s, scientists have been reporting alarming information about the way economic activity has changed and degraded the environment. Non-renewable resources, such as fossil fuels and minerals, have been extracted at an increasing rate to power industrial economies. The pursuit of raw materials and the sprawl of asphalt have destroyed natural habitats. Renewable resources have been taken without, in many cases, the necessary management action to replenish them. Industrial production and consumption pollute the air, soil, and water. Among the most serious problems that have come to the fore is a gradual warming of the earth's atmosphere, which most knowledgeable scientists trace to the greenhouse gas effect—carbon dioxide, methane, and nitrous oxide produced by industrialization. At the same time, forests, which absorb carbon dioxide from the atmosphere, have been seriously depleted.

The solution to the greenhouse gas problem requires international co-ordination to reduce emissions. Everyone will benefit, but costs will vary. This is a major problem that illustrates the continued power of the nation-state: compliance with any international agreement must be voluntary in the absence of any means of enforcement. By 1992, scientific concern about climate change had become so widespread that a Framework Convention on Climate Change was established in which the key strategy was to stabilize greenhouse gases at 1990 levels by the year 2000. The 1997 Kyoto Protocol provides more advanced objectives—specifically, that the developed societies would reduce their emissions to 5.2 per cent less than those prevailing in 1990. Canada was slated for a 6 per cent reduction (Bernstein and Gore, 2001). Although 166 states, including Canada, had signed the agreement by February 2003, and another 22 had indicated their acceptance, most failed to come close to its objectives.

Citing his refusal to endanger the profits of US corporations, President George W. Bush stated, prior to the Bonn meeting on climate change in 2001, that the United States would not ratify the Kyoto Protocol: 'The

GLOBAL ISSUES

Colombia: 'Everybody Is Full of Terror'

Choco is Colombia's poorest province and a battleground for terrorist actions. In May 2002, 119 civilians, including many children, were killed in the little jungle town of Bellavista when a crude mortar exploded in the church where they were hiding to avoid conflict between paramilitary forces and the guerrilla group FARC (the Revolutionary Armed Forces of Colombia). FARC claimed that the civilian deaths were accidental, but this attack appears to have shaken any external political support that FARC had managed to retain up to that time. A few days later, President Pastrana and top officials visited the remote scene, which government troops failed to reach in time to intervene: 'Awed by the evidence of the savage attack—empty storefronts, abandoned homes, war-battered buildings—nobody said a word as they walked down the rubble-filled streets in gloomy silence. "Everybody is full of terror", Emiliano Perera, mayor of nearby Vigía del Fuerte, said afterward' (*Miami Herald*, 19 May 2002).

Two main guerrilla groups, FARC and ELN (the National Liberation Army), as well as paramilitary forces that have operated in Colombia for decades, use terror and intimidation in order to establish their economic and political power. By 2002, their combined forces were estimated at 32,000, up from about 12,000 in 1990. Civil war has been no stranger in the history of this geographically splintered country, but the failure to peacefully resolve political disputes gradually turned into a struggle for power in which ideals of social justice played no role. The conflict claimed an estimated 3,500 lives in 2001 and at least 200,000 over its full history.

More than 30 years ago, groups of left-wing activists became so frustrated with what they considered as elite domination of politics to the exclusion, in practice, of the interests of ordinary people that they began guerrilla actions to bring about change. The inability of the army to suppress them led to the formation of equally violent private armies or paramilitaries, later joined into the United Self-Defence Force. By the 1980s, the main guerrilla groups had become involved in the drug trade in order to finance their activities in what had become a political stalemate with no negotiated end in sight. Colombia's other internal war was being waged against the drug cartels, whose leaders also used terrorism to try to influence state action. Whatever idealistic values promoted initial guerrilla tactics and brought some measure of support inside and outside Colombia evaporated as the revolutionary forces turned into opportunistic seekers of power and wealth (Wagner, 2002).

Kyoto treaty would severely damage the United States' economy, and I don't accept that. I accept the alternative we put out, that we can grow our economy and, at the same time, through technologies, improve our environment' (United States, White House, 2002). The President's statement was a reaction to a report prepared by the Environmental Protection Agency (EPA), which acknowledged that human action was responsible for global warming. A year later, the US government was still resisting the scientific evidence by pressuring the EPA to change statements on climate change in its most recent report.

In December 2002, Canada finally agreed to support the Kyoto agreement despite the resistance of several provinces, spearheaded by Alberta, which feared the effect on oil and gas revenues and, more generally, that Canadian companies will be at a disadvantage until and unless the United States ratifies the treaty—all for a control program that will have little impact. Thus, 'Alberta has warned that Canadian ratification of the Kyoto Accord could cost the economy up to $40 billion, drastically higher than estimates by the federal government' (CBC News, 2002). Since fossil fuels burned in the **developed countries** account for most greenhouse gases, it is no surprise that resistance should come from those who might experience economic contraction if severe measures are taken. Moreover, compliance has become more difficult because high oil prices and concern about future supplies have led to large-scale investment in extracting heavy oil from Alberta's tar sands, a process that is itself a major contributor to greenhouse gases.

Who will pay the costs of coping with climate change is a tricky political issue. In this regard, Kyoto places a greater burden on the developed countries, which were most responsible for creating the problem. To maintain the present industrialized state, new energy sources that do not depend on fossil fuels will need to be introduced on a massive scale. Voluntary measures have little chance of working, and the challenge is becoming ever greater: Canada's actual emissions are expected, on the present course, to exceed its Kyoto commitment by 27 per cent in 2010 (Bernstein and Gore, 2001: 30).

Despite the opposition of some governments and of industry, the environmental movement has been growing in Canada; citizens are concerned about global warming and doing their part to protect the atmosphere. Thus, by 2000, 72 per cent of Canadians were willing to assume a worst-case scenario and take action without waiting for further evidence. This was an increase from 61 per cent in 1997. Residents of Quebec were the most supportive (81 per cent) while residents of Alberta and Saskatchewan, Canada's main oil provinces, were least supportive (57 and 59 per cent, respectively; Environics International, 2000). By 2006, Canadians felt that environmental issues were among the most important facing the country, and 71 per cent felt that the Conservative government was doing too little to deal with air pollution (CBC News, 2006c).

This parody of Michelangelo's painting on the Sistine Chapel ceiling in the Vatican, of God animating Adam, shows Prime Minister Harper being brought to life by the all-powerful American deity, Uncle Sam. (Monaerik/www.lecornichon.qc.ca)

Conclusion: Future Developments

Politics in Canada and around the globe are changing quickly as the people of various societies grapple with major technological, environmental, and social forces that are impinging on their lives. Consider, for example, the capacity to manipulate, even to create, living forms that is based on scientists' discovery of DNA structures and how they may be changed. Already various genetically engineered food products have entered the marketplace, although public resistance has been mobilized, especially in Europe. Proponents point to security of food supply and improved product characteristics. Insofar as they are successful, ownership of this knowledge will generate more centralized control. The landscape and wildlife are also likely to change; the possibility of manufacturing a forest without natural reproduction and without natural undergrowth may have profound effects on the environment as well as on people (Bailey et al., 2004). The same cloning technologies make it possible to create animal life and raise the possibility of radical intervention in human reproduction and health care. While long-term effects are debated, the critical political questions are: Who is in control and what will be permitted?

In the early twenty-first century, there are forces that imply decentralization and fragmentation as cultural groups struggle for political autonomy (like Quebec) and as others advocate a smaller role for the state in many ways, from privatization to more partnerships with non-state actors. Probably these forces are weaker

Time to Reflect

What does the environmental mantra 'think globally, act locally' mean in political terms? Does it apply to you?

than the integrating, regionalizing, and even globalizing tendencies associated with high-speed communication, cultural diffusion of tastes and values, an international division of labour, corporate concentration, world-level environmental problems, North–South inequality, and new or more powerful transnational organizations.

Does this globalization mean the eclipse of the state (Strange, 1996)? Most likely not within the next 20 years. So far, despite the tendencies mentioned, there is little sign that any global decisions, whether taken in political centres such as the United Nations or by other assemblies such as inclusive meetings on AIDS or climate change, can be effective if the most powerful states are unwilling to support them. International organizations such as the World Bank have been able to exert tremendous pressure on debtor countries to mould their domestic policies in return for continued support. The World Trade Organization (WTO) is a key centre of international policy formation that is binding on its members and its free-market orientation is consistent with the policy of the United States. In contrast, the Kyoto Protocol is drastically weakened without US participation.

Regional concentration appears a more powerful force than globalization as such. Regional economic integration through organizations such as the European Union and agreements such as the North American Free Trade Agreement (NAFTA) is certainly a challenge to the capacity of smaller states to influence investment decisions and the functioning of their more local labour markets. The largest transnational corporations operate in any part of the globe where profit is likely and they can put great pressure on smaller states to provide conditions attractive to their business. But there is nothing fundamentally new in this. Moreover, as Grace Skogstad (2000) points out, the changing context need not leave states, even smaller ones, helpless; rather, they may expand policy development into new areas such as information technology.

We live in difficult and dangerous times in which no country is truly isolated from external economic, cultural, and political forces. To that extent, life is internationalized, if not fully globalized. Violent conflicts spill over national borders. Even the powerhouse of world affairs, the United States, is not immune to the most determined assaults of radicals willing to resort to any means. This has placed great pressure on states to control cross-border movement and harmonize policy, including between the United States and Canada (Cilluffo, 2001). In such a situation, Canada, as the weaker state, is put under great pressure to compromise and adjust to the wishes of the United States. Maintaining the civil rights of all people is one of the greatest political challenges that societies face in the early twenty-first century.

Questions for Critical Thought

1. Discuss the ways in which authority can be exercised, providing examples. What sources of bias, if any, can be observed in the organization of the Canadian state?
2 Electoral institutions ensure that political leaders are responsive to the interests of the population as a whole. Do you agree or disagree with this statement?
3. What changes have occurred since 1980 in women's participation in the legislatures and cabinets of liberal democracies? Discuss some of the differences you observe. How would you explain these findings?
4. Assume that a new Royal Commission into the current status of women has been established (a Royal Commission on the Status of Women did report in 1970). Write a brief in which you argue for or against changes in the political process with regard to promoting women's involvement in politics. Compare the current circumstances with what the previous study indicated.
5. Select an issue that has been important during the last year in the province or municipality where you live. Using media sources try to determine who was able to exercise power. What theory of the state best explains what you observed?
6. Collect information on the size of public-sector employment relative to private-sector employment in Canada's provinces. Try to explain any variations among the provinces.
7. Select any five Western democracies. Find out the percentage of electors who voted in at least three general elections since 1970. Try to account for any differences you observe.

Recommended Readings

Michael M. Atkinson and William D. Coleman, *The State, Business, and Industrial Change in Canada* (Toronto: University of Toronto Press, 1989).

Atkinson and Coleman present an excellent case study of Canadian policy and interest groups.

Douglas E. Baer, ed., *Political Sociology: Canadian Perspectives* (Toronto: Oxford University Press, 2002).

Baer has compiled a valuable collection on topics of both Canadian and international interest.

Louise Chappell and Lisa Hill, eds, *The Politics of Women's Interests: New Comparative Perspectives* (London and New York: Routledge, 2006).

This book provides feminist interpretations of key political issues by drawing on experiences in many societies.

Bent Flyvbjerg, *Rationality and Power: Democracy in Practice*, trans. Steven Sampson (Chicago: University of Chicago Press, 1998).

This is an outstanding case study of power in action as a Danish city attempted to grapple with competing demands of business, citizen mobility, and protection of the environment.

Murray Knuttila and Wendee Kubik, *State Theories: Classical, Global and Feminist Perspectives*, 3rd edn (Halifax: Fernwood, 2000).

State Theories is a thorough review of theorizing about the state.

Jacques Lévesque, *The Enigma of 1989: The USSR and the Liberation of Eastern Europe*, trans. Keith Martin (Berkeley: University of California Press, 1997).

Lévesque provides a valuable account of the collapse of state socialism in the Soviet Union and Soviet-influenced areas.

Kenneth McRoberts, *Quebec: Social Change and Political Crisis*, 3rd edn (Toronto: Oxford University Press, 1999).

Grounded in the history of Quebec, this is a sympathetic and insightful account of Quebec politics.

Theda Skocpol, *States and Social Revolutions: A Comparative Analysis of France, Russia, and China* (Cambridge: Cambridge University Press, 1979).

Skocpol's is an outstanding theoretical and empirical contribution to theories of the state and revolution.

Grace Skogstad, 'Globalization and Public Policy', *Canadian Journal of Political Science*, 33 (2000): 805–28.

This article provides insightful commentary on the complex issues around globalization and its implications for state policy, with special attention to Canada.

Recommended Websites

Canada's Parliament
www.parl.gc.ca
This government website provides information on the conduct of parliamentary life and on members of the two houses of Parliament.

Canadian Election Study (CES)
www.ces-eec.umontreal.ca/surveys.html
The results of investigations into federal elections from 1997 to 2006 may be obtained at this site, from which various academic presentations may be downloaded.

Comparative Study of Electoral Systems
www.umich.edu/~cses/
This University of Michigan site maintains an extensive database of US and international election studies.

Electionworld.org
www.electionworld.org
Here you can find results of national elections around the world and links to the websites of political parties, including all parties represented in Canada's House of Commons. The site is updated monthly.

Google News Canada
news.google.ca
This website allows access to a vast database of newspaper articles and news agency reports on any subject.

Peace Pledge Union
www.ppu.org.uk/war/
Here you can click sections of a world map and receive summary information on wars and violent conflict since 1945.

United Nations
www.un.org
The United Nations provides a vast range of information about its activities, as well as databases and bibliographies.

Women in National Parliaments
www.ipu.org/wmn-e/world.htm
The Inter-parliamentary Union's website contains extensive, regularly updated information on women's political participation.

14

Chapter

Social Movements

John Veugelers and Randle Hart

Learning Objectives

In this chapter, you will:

- See how social movements are studied sociologically.
- Review the theoretical approaches to the study of social movements.
- Read about key debates within the study of social movements.
- See how empirical research is used to test and criticize social movement theories.
- Learn how social movements are embedded in national and international (global) politics.
- Understand why social movements have historical importance in the process of social change.

Photo: CP/Fredericton Daily Gleaner/Stephen MacGillivray

LIFE
WARNING
ABORTION
PHOTOS
AHEAD

Introduction

Late one night during the summer of 2006, a rural road in southern Ontario was the scene of a clash between dozens of protestors. Separated by police officers who stood their ground, two groups of Natives and non-Natives hurled taunts and then rocks and golf balls at each other. For the non-Natives, frustration in the face of a standoff between the Native protestors and a local real estate developer was high. That February, members of the Six Nations had occupied land slated for a new housing development. Soon they had expanded their protest by mounting a roadblock near the town of Caledonia. Residents and businesses now faced long and inconvenient detours if they wanted to drive into or out of the area. For the protestors, however, creating trouble for commuters and businesses was meant to right a historical injustice: the loss of land along the Grand River despite an agreement with the British Crown in 1784. By mobilizing not only the members of their community, but also supporters and Native peoples in other parts of Canada, the Six Nations protestors at Caledonia were resorting to politics by other means (CBC News, 2006e).

Writing in the nineteenth century about political associations, Alexis de Tocqueville noted that 'citizens who are individually powerless do not very clearly anticipate the strength that they may acquire by uniting together' (1945 [1835], vol. 2: 124). Tocqueville had identified a curious feature of society: when powerless people lend time, energy, and material resources to an ideological cause, their combined efforts create a new reality with a life and force of its own. This reality becomes a **social movement**. Examples of present-day social movements include Native, women's, peace, gay and lesbian, anti-nuclear, labour, environmental, ethnic, and regionalist movements.

A social movement is a group. Thus, it is more than the sum of the individuals forming it. As a consequence, social movements may take a direction contrary to their members' wishes. Surprisingly, some social movements even betray their supporters by adapting to a social system once seen as corrupt or unresponsive. Others disappear as a result of internal bickering or government repression even though their members' grievances persist.

Since social movements are groups, what they say and do may not reflect their members' attitudes. Furthermore, a psychological analysis of a social movement's members will reveal little about the movement's origins and development, its effect on the social order, or the causes of its successes and failures. A social movement is a distinctive social reality for which sociology offers appropriate tools of analysis.

This chapter opens by looking at the characteristics of social movements. It next considers theoretical approaches to social movements; then examines four social movements of the nineteenth and twentieth centuries. The chapter ends with a discussion about social movements in today's global context.

What Is a Social Movement?

Typically, a social movement depends on the actions of non-elite members of society, those people who have relatively little or no control over major economic, symbolic, political, or military resources—in short, over anything scarce that, if controlled, gives one power over others.

People form a social movement when they voluntarily work together to influence the distribution of social goods. A social good is anything that a particular society values. Familiar examples include money, honour, peace, security, citizenship, leisure time, political power, and divine grace. There are probably no universal social goods, because no two societies have exactly the same set of values. Furthermore, social goods vary historically. They emerge and disappear as values change or traditions lose relevance (Walzer, 1983).

Social goods are scarce—that, in part, is why they are valuable—and some individuals or groups get more of them than others do. How people make sense of such inequalities depends on **ideologies**, sets of ideas that justify how social goods are distributed. *Dominant ideologies* defend existing inequalities by making them seem right. *Counter-ideologies* challenge the justice of the existing social system, promote alternative values and goals, and present a plan for change. Promoting counter-ideologies is a goal of social movements.

Social movements try to achieve change through the voluntary co-operation of the relatively powerless. These people may contribute financial or other material resources, recruit new members, or spread a counter-ideology. They may also participate in strikes, sit-ins, boycotts, demonstrations, protest marches, violent action, or civil disobedience. The efforts of social movements can be focused on changing attitudes, everyday practices, public opinion, or the policies and procedures of business and government.

Environmental movements, for example, have the basic impacts set forth in Figure 14.1. Social change through collective action involves dynamic and complex processes: social movements affect individuals and political policies, but they are influenced also by them. As Figure 14.1 shows, environmental problems are identified usually by natural scientists. Once a problem of this kind is identified, the environmental movement may choose to address the issue. It may lobby the government or appeal to individuals' sense of moral indignation. In some instances, an environmental organization may choose to run in democratic elections, thus forming a political party with ecological issues as its main concern.

Social movements are easier to understand when compared and contrasted with other phenomena studied by sociologists (Diani, 1992). A *social trend*, for example, is simply a changing pattern of social behaviour, whereas a social movement is a co-operative effort to achieve social change from below. The rising labour market participation of women is a social trend; a group of volunteers who fight for gender equality is a social movement. Certainly, social movements influence some social trends. For instance, feminist movements may encourage the trend for women to enter the paid workforce. However, many social trends—such as changing fashions or unemployment patterns—may be scarcely affected by social movements.

A *pressure group* is an organization that aims to influence large institutions, particularly **the state**. A social movement is one kind of pressure group. However, other pressure groups—known as *interest groups*—represent the concerns of specific sets of people. Prominent interest groups include the Canadian Labour Congress, the Canadian Medical Association, Canadian Manufacturers and Exporters (formerly the Canadian Manufacturers Association), and the Consumers' Association of Canada. Interest groups restrict their membership and rely heavily on a professional staff rather than volunteers. Moreover, lobbying politicians and receiving recognition from government can give them semi-official or even official status. Like social movements, interest groups may use public opinion to put pressure on political or economic elites. But membership in social movements is more open, and their ideologies typically appeal to people from different walks of life.

Since social movements depend on voluntary participation, they are voluntary associations. However, not all *voluntary associations* seek deeper changes in the distribution of social goods. Some provide social or health services; others organize leisure activities or unite the followers of a spiritual doctrine. Examples of voluntary associations are groups that help the homeless; run food banks; offer classes in ESL (English as a Second Language) for immigrants; or mobilize residents for annual cleanups of garbage in the public areas of their neighbourhood. Voluntary associations that only help people to accept or enjoy the existing social system are not social movements.

Figure 14.1 The Impact of Environmental Movements

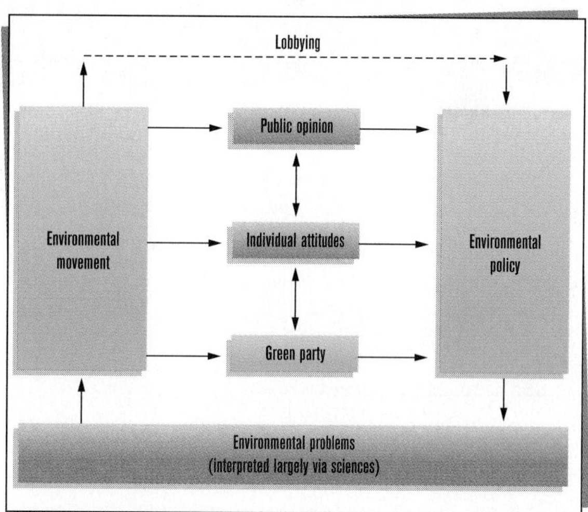

Source: Dieter Rucht, 'The Impact of Environmental Movements in Western Societies', in Marco Giugni et al., eds, *How Social Movements Matter* (Minneapolis: University of Minnesota Press, 1999), 214.

While social movements try to change the distribution of social goods, political parties try to win and keep political power. In principle, a social movement becomes a political party when it fields candidates in elections. The Green parties in Germany, France, and Italy, for example, have grown from environmental movements in these countries. In practice, the difference between social movements and political parties is sometimes hazy. Parties that have grown out of social movements often retain features from their past. They may be more sectarian or rely heavily on grassroots supporters. These features foster a strong party identity, but they may also discourage outsiders from joining.

Finally, not all groups with non-elite, voluntary members who aim to reallocate social goods are necessarily social movements. A counter-movement may have all of the characteristics of a social movement, but with one important difference: a counter-movement arises in response to a social movement. Three conditions must be met for counter-movements to appear:

1. A social movement must be seen as successful (or as gaining success).
2. A social movement's goals must be seen as a threat to another group.
3. Allies must be available to support mobilization of the counter-movement.

SOCIOLOGY IN ACTION

Craig Kielburger and Free The Children

The child shall be protected against all forms of neglect, cruelty and exploitation. He shall not be the subject of traffic, in any form. The child shall not be admitted to employment before an appropriate minimum age; he shall in no case be caused or permitted to engage in any occupation or employment which would prejudice his health or education, or interfere with his physical, mental or moral development.

—From the UN Declaration on the Rights of the Child

One morning when he was searching for the comics section in his local newspaper, 12-year-old Craig Kielburger of Thornhill, Ontario, came across a photo that stopped him short. Beside it was a headline that read 'Battled child labour, boy, 12, murdered' and an article about Iqbal Masik, a Pakistani boy sold to a carpet factory by his parents at the age of four. Unable to attend school, for many years he had been forced to work as many as 14 hours a day, six days a week. After the Pakistani police finally freed Iqbal, the boy wanted to fight the enslavement of child workers. He joined in demonstrations and spoke with journalists so the public would become aware of the plight of child workers. Then, when Iqbal was 12, he paid the price of speaking out: he was murdered.

This news shocked Kielburger. Even though he had never heard about child labour and did not even know where Pakistan was exactly, he decided to act. With friends and classmates in Thornhill, he formed Free The Children. Their goal was to end the abuse and exploitation of children around the world. The young members of this new group faxed world leaders and organized petitions to end child exploitation. To raise funds for their efforts, they also ran car washes, bake sales, and garage sales. In alerting the world to injustice towards children, they learned more about the conditions under which children who are often abused work long hours without having the chance to play or attend school. They also learned about and decided to fight a related injustice: child prostitution.

At the age of 14, Kielburger made a much-publicized visit to South Asia in search of sweatshops. He joined the police during a raid to free children working in a factory. Free The Children wanted Canada to start putting special labels on imported rugs not made by children. The group also wanted a new law that would make it possible for police in Canada to charge a person who had sex with a child prostitute in another country. Two years after it was founded, Free The Children used funds it had raised to set up a centre for children in Pakistan who had escaped from slavery.

Not everybody was pleased. Kielburger was criticized as too young to tell adults in positions of authority what they should be doing. And a social worker in Brazil asked: 'Why is it that North Americans always think they can save the world?' But Kielburger and Free The Children went on. The organization he started has created more than 100 centres and schools worldwide for freed children who are trying to recover after years of physical and psychological abuse.

Today, Free The Children, headed by Craig and his older brother Marc, is involved in the construction of another 420 schools that will provide education for 40,000 children in poor regions of the world. While Kielburger—who is now 24 years old—has received many awards for leadership, good citizenship, and humanitarian service, on three occasions (in 2002, 2003, and 2004) Free The Children itself has been nominated for the Nobel Peace Prize.

Sources: <peaceheroes.com>; <www.freethechildren.com>.

Time to Reflect

Do you consider yourself to be an active participant of any social movement? If not, do you wish you were? What social movement would you become involved in, and what part do you think you could play?

While some counter-movements (such as the National Rifle Association) wish to defend the status quo against a perceived threat by social movements, others (such as the anti-abortion movement) emerge when a state or government agency has ambiguous policies or is internally divided on a particular social issue (Meyer and Staggenborg, 1996).

To sum up: a social movement is an organization that co-ordinates the voluntary actions of non-elite members of society and that offers a program for changing the way society distributes social goods. Though social movements are pressure groups, they differ from interest groups because they have open recruitment, rely on volunteers, and are based outside of elite circles. Social movements are also voluntary associations, but their commitment to social change sets them apart from groups whose main goal is to organize and provide charity, leisure activities, spiritual guidance, and so forth. Unlike political parties, moreover, social movements do not strive for political office. Social movements direct their grievances against the existing distribution of social goods. Counter-movements, by contrast, direct their grievances against the potential success of social movements. Finally, social movements are groups. Hence, knowing the beliefs and behaviours of individual members gives only partial insight into the nature of a social movement.

Theoretical Approaches

Different beliefs about society separate the four main approaches to social movements. The **breakdown approach** assumes that consensus is the basis of social order and that **culture** is the major determinant of action. The **resource mobilization approach** assumes that social order is based on competition and conflict and that interests are the fundamental cause of action. The **identity-based approach** and the **political process approach** draw selectively from the other two. Both assume that social order rests on an unsteady resolution of conflict and that culture is the major determinant of action. Table 14.1 summarizes the assumptions that underlie these four perspectives.

The Breakdown Approach

The breakdown approach builds on a view of society developed by the French sociologist Émile Durkheim (1858–1917) and later by the American founder of **structural functionalism**, Talcott Parsons (1902–79). Both thought that shared **norms** and **values** hold society together. The breakdown approach holds that rapid, thorough, or uneven change in society weakens the

Table 14.1 Approaches to the Study of Social Movements

		Primary Cause of Social Action	
		Culture	Interests
Underlying Societal Dynamic	Consensus	• breakdown approach	• undeveloped approach
	Conflict	• identity-based approach • political process approach	• resource mobilization approach

social bonds that promote social order. Social disintegration, in turn, encourages the formation of groups advocating radical change.

Relative Deprivation Theory

The assumptions of the breakdown approach underlie **relative deprivation theory**, which claims that radical social movements result from feelings of fear and frustration. According to James C. Davies (1962), revolutions and rebellions are preceded by two phases. The first phase is characterized by economic and social progress. More and more social goods become available—food becomes more plentiful, for example, or the rights of citizens expand—and expectations rise. But if a sharp reversal follows—if food suddenly becomes scarce and costly, or if authorities ban opposition parties and the free press after a period of liberalization—rising expectations are no longer met. In the second phase, the gap between what people expect and what they actually get grows ever wider. Rebellion results when anxiety and frustration become widespread and intense.

Critics of relative deprivation theory point out that the most frustrated members of society are not the only people who fight for radical change. Revolutions, especially successful ones, are often led and supported by people from the middle and upper classes. Moreover, relative deprivation theory does not provide a convincing link between people's feelings and revolution. Surely the people of Haiti, for instance, have endured many decades of anxiety and frustration under brutal dictatorships. Yet their dissatisfaction has not led to revolution. A great deal must happen before individual grievances will translate into major changes such as the toppling of a political regime.

The iconic image of the Argentine-born Marxist revolutionary Ernesto 'Che' Guevara has been a symbol of struggle for revolutionary movements around the globe, as in this International Labour Day rally, 1 May 2007, in Karachi, Pakistan. (CP/AP Photo/Shakil Adil)

Systemic Theory

Like relative deprivation theory, Neil Smelser's **systemic theory** highlights the role of social breakdown in the growth of social movements. But instead of focusing on individuals, as relative deprivation theory does, Smelser looks at society as a whole. He sees society as a set of linked elements that work to maintain stability. Social movements reflect the breakdown of stability, but they do not form unless six conditions are met (Smelser, 1963):

1. *Structural conduciveness.* Social conditions must give people a chance to unite for change. If people remain isolated, they cannot pool their efforts.
2. *Structural strain.* The dominant ideology must be viewed with dissatisfaction or uncertainty.
3. *Growth and spread of a generalized belief.* Potential participants in social movements must share a counter-ideology that binds them together.
4. *A precipitating factor.* This is the straw that breaks the camel's back—some event so serious that people finally decide to fight for change.
5. *Mobilization.* People's readiness for action must have an outlet; they must be able to join a social movement.
6. *The response of authorities.* Because the state is so powerful, its response affects a social movement's chances of survival and success.

Smelser's systemic theory improves on relative deprivation theory. It corrects the overemphasis on individuals by specifying group and societal factors involved in the rise of social movements. Moreover, systemic theory recognizes that shared grievances alone will not bind protestors together. For a movement to last, protestors must share a counter-ideology, a set of ideas that gives them guidelines to work together for change. Finally, the theory brings mobilization into the picture. Personal dissatisfaction alone will not form a social movement, no matter how widespread the grievance.

Unfortunately, Smelser's theory does not establish causes and effects, but rests partly on circular reasoning. An example of circular reasoning would be as follows: Suppose you ask someone to explain what caused hail, and the person replies, 'It's frozen rain.' Because hail and frozen rain are the same thing, your respondent's reply is not an explanation, but merely a restatement using different words. Hence, your question has been left unanswered.

Smelser does something similar, though less obviously. On the one hand, he defines social mobilization for action as a response to strain on generalized belief. But he also lists mobilization for action, strain, and generalized belief among the six factors that explain social movements. In this respect, his theory is a restatement of what needs to be explained, not an explanation (Aya, 1990).

Criticisms of the Breakdown Approach

The breakdown approach also has been criticized for forgetting that value consensus and social stability result partly from relations of domination. As Barrington Moore Jr observes, 'To maintain and transmit a value system, human beings are punched, bullied, sent to jail, thrown into concentration camps, cajoled, bribed, made into heroes, encouraged to read newspapers, stood up against the wall and shot, and sometimes even taught sociology' (1966: 486). Contrary to the assumptions of the breakdown approach, social conflict may be a normal feature of social life. If this is so, then the breakdown of value consensus and stability may not explain the formation of social movements.

Breakdown theory has also been accused of treating social movements as ailments. This charge arose during the 1960s, a time when social movements supported by mainstream members of society were flourishing in Western democracies. Many sociologists welcomed the new movements against war, racism, sexism, pollution, bureaucracy, and the educational system as positive signs of healthy protest against injustice and alienation.

Finally, critics have argued it is misleading to treat social movements as outbursts of uncontainable emotion. Experience suggests that participation in social movements may involve the same kind of calm and rational decision-making found in other areas of life. This interpretation underlies the resource mobilization approach.

The Resource Mobilization Approach

The resource mobilization approach challenges the image of social movements as unusual, impermanent, or disorderly. Instead, it assumes that social movements are quite similar to other organizations. They are managed by leaders whose decisions are no less calculating than anyone else's. Some sociologists go so far as to treat social movement organizers as entrepreneurs who have a "product" to sell.

Unlike business entrepreneurs, however, social movement entrepreneurs must deal with free-riding—non-co-operation in the attainment of a good that will be available to all members of the community. For movement leaders, the solution is to make their 'product' appealing in the competitive market for potential members' time, energy, and resources. From this perspective, social movement propaganda is a form of marketing that advertises the benefits of joining (Jenkins, 1983).

IN THE FIRST PERSON

I was first introduced to the study of social movements by William K. Carroll, a sociology professor at the University of Victoria, and I was lucky enough to be admitted into his senior-level sociology seminar, though I had been studying Canadian literature and had very little experience in sociology. With work, I became acclimatized to the sociological imagination and learned how to analyze the social world with a critical eye. I was hooked: I practically ran to the Registrar's office to declare a major in sociology. I remained at the University of Victoria to study for my master's degree in sociology and participated in an interdisciplinary program in cultural, social, and political thought. I continue to be inspired by the possibilities of the sociological study of social movements at the University of Toronto.—Randle Hart

Proponents of the resource mobilization approach argue that the breakdown approach is wrong in assuming that satisfaction with the social order is the normal state of affairs. Instead, dissatisfaction is built into society. There will always be people with grievances because social goods are unequally distributed. But grievances alone do not make a social movement. What social movements do is lift grievances out of the shadows, giving them ideological form and propelling them into public life.

The resource mobilization approach puts **power** at the centre of analysis. Power is not something one has: one can only be in a position that confers power, for power means having the ability to carry out one's wishes. As the German sociologist Max Weber (1864–1920) put it, power refers to a person's or group's chance of fulfilling their goals even when others would have it otherwise (1978 [1908]: 926).

The source of power is control over resources. Control creates leverage, the ability to get others to do what one wants. What represents a resource in any given situation varies, but three kinds of power stand out. One is *economic power*, which is based on control over the means of material production: land, energy, capital, technology, labour, factories, raw materials, and so forth. Another is *political power*, based on control over the legitimate means of violence: the police and the armed forces. A third is *ideological power*, which is based on control over the means of producing and disseminating **symbols**: schools, churches, newspapers, publishing houses, television and radio, film and advertising companies, and the like. The resource base for each of the three kinds of power differs. Nonetheless, control over any resource allows elites to shape the lives of the powerless.

Social movements must compete against other **social institutions** for the scarce resources necessary to start and operate an organization. The resource mobilization approach therefore searches for the social conditions that affect social movements' control over resources, and focuses on the strategies that translate power into success.

There are two perspectives on resource mobilization: the utilitarian and political conflict perspectives (Ramirez, 1981). While both assume that actors (whether individuals or groups) are rational and seek to maximize self-interest, each addresses somewhat different problems.

The Utilitarian Perspective

The **utilitarian perspective** focuses on how individuals promote their own interests. The free-rider problem is a central concern, in particular the question of how and why selective incentives attract volunteers and cut down

Social movements often mobilize against the state. Here, activists protest the threatened closure of a safe injection site for drug addicts.

OPEN FOR DISCUSSION

The Free-Rider Problem

The Fresh Air Coalition is fighting for a reduction in the toxic emissions of Steel City. If the group meets its goal, all of Steel City's citizens will breathe cleaner air: it would be impossible to give the cleaner air only to people who had joined the Fresh Air Coalition, while everyone else—the people who didn't attend the protest rallies, write letters to newspapers and politicians, or contribute to the Fresh Air Coalition's fundraising plant sale—got the same dirty air as before.

Assuming the citizens of Steel City are self-interested, it doesn't make sense for them to join the Fresh Air Coalition. They are free riders: they will benefit even if they don't help, because collective goods such as clean air cannot be divided.

What can the Fresh Air Coalition do? According to free-rider theory, groups can foster co-operation through selective incentives. The Fresh Air Coalition can make co-operation worthwhile by providing rewards. So, in addition to fighting for clean air, the leaders of the Fresh Air Coalition will be sure to organize social events—picnics, parties, camping weekends—that attract and keep members by satisfying their immediate self-interest.

on free-riding. Utilitarians study the relationships between social movements and how rewards motivate social movement entrepreneurs.

Critics of the utilitarian perspective have stressed the limited applicability of the free-rider problem. The assumption that social movements attract support only by providing selective incentives may misconstrue people's reasons for joining. Instead, people may join a movement simply because it seems headed for success. Or, they may join because they identify with other members of the social movement and believe the group will benefit if its members work together (Barry, 1978 [1970]). Finally, norms of fairness may override concerns about efficiency. Pressures to conform may lead people to join social movements, irrespective of selective incentives (Elster, 1989). Such considerations are ruled out by an exclusive focus on the free-rider problem. The utilitarian perspective forgets that people are ruled by more than self-interest. Further, it forgets that social movements are groups, so they cannot be explained by individualistic decisions alone.

The Political Conflict Perspective

The **political conflict perspective** focuses on how parts of society (typically, **classes**) promote collective interests. Although not a Marxist approach, it tends to stress issues central to the Marxist tradition: working-class mobilization, class conflict, and revolution. Hence, analysis from this perspective usually tries to explain the origins of class **solidarity**. Studies in the political conflict tradition also search for factors that determine the success and failure of class-based movements, including class alliances, pre-existing social ties that foster communication and group action, and ties with other groups and political authorities.

In recent decades, sociologists who work from the political conflict perspective have reduced an earlier emphasis on class strength and class alliances. Simultaneously, they have lent more attention to the state. Because it is so powerful, the state can tip the balance in favour of one class over another. Thus, domestic and international events that affect the state may decide the fate of a revolution.

By *the state*, sociologists mean what we commonly call 'the government'—the set of institutions responsible for defending the polity, making and carrying out its laws and public programs, and promoting its interests in foreign affairs. The sociological relevance of the state stems from its domination and influence over social relations. This power is rooted in the state's monopoly over the legitimate use of violence and is expressed in the ability to extract taxes, print money, make and enforce laws, conduct foreign policy, and distribute political office and public funds. Such a high degree of power crucially shapes the milieu in which social movements emerge, mature, and meet with success or failure.

To be sure, the state's power over society differs greatly according to the type of regime, whether monarchy, dictatorship, or democracy. Its power also varies between regimes of the same type. The welfare state is stronger in Sweden than in the United States, for instance, even though both are democracies. History matters as well. Between the 1940s and the 1970s, democratic states increasingly intervened in the economy and provided an ever greater range of welfare services. Finally, the strength of the state varies across different areas of society. For example, the state may control the educational system but leave religious institutions alone.

What do these observations imply? A thorough analysis of social movements will pay attention to the state's power, and a subtle analysis of social movements will respect the complexity of state–society relations.

Criticisms of the Resource Mobilization Approach

The resource mobilization approach represents a clear advance over the breakdown approach. It underscores the normality of social movements by drawing attention to their similarities with other organizations. Nevertheless, this approach has some shortcomings, too.

First, it runs the danger of missing some important differences between social movements and other organizations. Few sociologists still believe that social movements are irrational, exotic, or unusual. However, many are beginning to realize that social movements differ from other types of organizations. They have different resources, career cycles, and relationships with government authorities as well as with other social movements. They also exhibit distinctive modes of acting, organizing, and communicating (Tarrow, 1988).

The image of human action conveyed by the resource mobilization approach has also been criticized as too voluntaristic. It exaggerates the extent to which social movements reflect careful planning and successful strategy. People often behave with vague or conflicting goals in mind. Like any other social group, a successful social movement probably does things the participants never intended in the first place. Further, the goals of social movements often emerge and change as situations evolve.

The voluntarism of the resource mobilization approach contains another drawback: this approach neglects political and international contexts. These matter, for they shape a social movement's chances for success. Devoting greater attention to warfare and the role of the state is one remedy for this oversight (Skocpol, 1979). Critics also point to a more fundamental weakness of the resource mobilization approach: it neglects the manner in which culture shapes—and is shaped by—participation in social movements.

Culture in Social Movements

The analysis of culture in social movement scholarship came about with the so-called 'cultural turn' in the social sciences in the 1980s. Though social movement scholars did not eschew culture before this, it was often left implicit in their analysis. As we discussed above, resource mobilization theory focuses almost entirely on rational action, and largely ignores culture. Cultural approaches to the study of social movements criticize this view for forgetting that neither the goals of social movements nor the ways they calculate the best means of achieving them is self-evident. Since norms and values are created in and by social movements, proponents of the cultural approach believe that the formation of goals needs to be explained (Nedelmann, 1991). The resource mobilization approach also takes for granted the sense of community that creates collective identity and a willingness to work together. How people define themselves depends very much on whom they identify with—on what community, with its unique norms, values, and ways of feeling. Effective social movements redefine identities by changing or reinforcing people's sense of community, and by providing them with opportunities to work together with a shared sense of purpose.

The New Social Movements

European *new social movement* (NSM) theorists (e.g., Melucci, 1989; Touraine, 1981) propose that structural changes in Western societies have fundamentally altered people's identities and cultures. This gives rise, they argue, to social movements that are distinct from older class-based movements. Where resource mobilization theory explains *how* social movements operate, NSM theories explain *why* social movements occur, *why* they are organized differently from the past, and *why* their grievances appear different from movements earlier in the century. Instead of concerning themselves with the politics of redistribution, NSMs are interested in the politics of cultural recognition; they are concerned less with the redistribution of wealth and status than with securing rights to expressive freedoms, symbolic practices, and/or styles of life. In this sense, the appearance of NSMS may be explained by a value shift (Inglehart, 1990b).

The NSM perspective focuses largely on the relationship between culture and collective identity. It proposes that social movements are cultural laboratories where people try out new forms of **social interaction** (Melucci, 1989). The breakdown and resource mobilization approaches define the success of social movements in terms of change in economic or political institutions.

The NSM approach defines success differently. To be sure, it does not deny the desirability of change in dominant institutions. However, for NSM activists more important struggles take place in civil society, those areas of social interaction that stand largely outside of the state and the market. In fact, theorists claim that NSMs have come about since the 1960s because state and economic practices have increasingly encroached on people's everyday lives. Slogans such as 'the personal is political' are meant to express how everyday life is pervaded by government and corporate activities, as well as by dominant cultural ideas that create inequality.

According to this approach, civil society offers greater chances for freedom, equality, and *participatory democracy*, a system of decision-making in which all members of a group exercise control over group decisions. Indeed, NSMs are, in part, characterized by institutional arrangements wherein their members try to organize according to the ideals of equal participation. This is what social movements are good at, and striving for other kinds of success risks perverting these ideals (Cohen, 1985).

Framing Theory

At the same time European NSM scholars were critizing resource mobilization theory, so were some North American researchers, albeit in a different way. Rather than assume that collective action was entirely rational, these scholars were interested in how collective understandings were created, communicated, and used to further a movement's goals. Because they sought to understand the role of cultural meaning in collective action, they looked to the symbolic interactionist tradition for inspiration. The result was **framing theory**, a cultural approach that explains the ways movements create and proselytize their understandings of the world, and how these meanings help form a sense of collective identity and common purpose.

Drawing on Erving Goffman's ideas, these social movement theorists define collective action frames as 'action-oriented sets of beliefs and meanings that inspire and legitimate the activities and campaigns of a social movement organization' (Benford and Snow, 2000: 614). Collective action frames are the communal understandings of a social movement, and these understandings are used to identify and promote grievances.

The process whereby individuals come to adopt the ideology and methods of a particular movement organization is called *frame alignment* (Snow et al., 1986). The alignment of interpretations is a necessary condition for maintaining participation. This is because members can identify with an organization once their cultural understandings are the same as everyone else's in the movement. In other words, collective identity is a product of frame alignment. And, as Gamson suggests, 'any movement that seeks to sustain commitment over a period of time must make the construction of collective identity one of its most central tasks' (Gamson, 1991: 27).

According to framing theory, a social movement must succeed at three core framing tasks in order to mobilize support. First, an organization must articulate *diagnostic* frames that define social problems (or injustices) and their culpable agents. Second, *prognostic* frames must propose solutions to these social problems. Prognostic frames give meaning to specific strategies and are used to persuade potential recruits and members that these actions are the best way to solve or address particular social problems. Third, since agreement with diagnostic and prognostic frames does not necessarily translate into participation, a social movement organization must provide compelling *motivational* frames that convince people to join.

Frame theorists recognize that collective action frames are not simply imposed on members by leaders, but are often changed and agreed on through social interaction and discussion. Though disputes over how to frame something inevitably arises, a minimum level of agreement must be maintained in order for a movement to be viable. There would be little reason to participate in a social movement that could not agree on how to collectively define a social problem or issue.

Criticisms of the Cultural Approach

Like resource mobilization theory, the cultural approach tends to be voluntaristic in its emphasis on people's potential for actively challenging and changing society. It focuses on altering the shared understandings that maintain patterns of domination. Consequently, it too ignores the structures of economic and political opportunity that shape the destinies of social movements.

New social movement theory may explain movement emergence, but it tells us very little about how movements themselves operate, the 'how' of social movement theory. It would seem that in trying to address the deficiencies of resource mobilization theory, NSM theory has created its own blind spot.

Finally, framing theory is quite narrow in its focus, and does not adequately explain how cultural processes external to a movement may influence internal cultural understandings. Framing theory tends to assume that a social movement's framing activities are fully bounded within the movement. A better starting point is to recognize that cultural framings flow easily into (and out of) a movement. Cultural interpretations abound, and analysts must examine all sources of meaning to fully understand the relationships between culture and collective action.

The Political Process Approach

While the breakdown, resource mobilization, and cultural approaches have been very useful for understanding social movements, scholars have attempted to create a synthesis. The political process approach is generally attributed to Peter Eisinger's study of movements during the 1960s. Eisinger (1973) argued that collective action depends on the structure of local political opportunities at the institutional and governmental levels. Charles Tilly (1978), an early proponent of this approach, built on this idea by showing how nation-states can manipulate the political terrain to stymie the activities of social movements. Tilly argues that the rise of nation-states gave rise to the national social movements of the early modern era in Europe. New political ideas that helped to create nation-states also generated grievances that led people to act collectively. These national social movements had characteristics that set them apart from previous forms of collective action (see also Tarrow, 1998).

The political process approach assumes that the polity can be characterized by its opportunities and constraints. Opportunities involve almost anything that provides reasons and resources for people to mobilize—so long as the political climate is not so oppressive that people cannot mobilize without fear or great difficulty. Political opportunities may include economic crises, laws ensuring the right to assemble, a history of previous collective action, even accidents that show the need for social change. Constraints include anything within the polity that may act as a barrier to the mobilization and survival of a social movement. Political constraints include a repressive police state, inexperience with collective action, even a lack of communication among social movement participants. Opportunities and constraints go hand in hand: no polity is completely open or completely closed.

The breakdown approach assumes that some form of social or political crisis is needed for people to act collectively. By contrast, the political process approach proposes that collective action is an ongoing social phenomenon. Where the breakdown approach assumes that social movements arise from outside the polity but enter the political terrain when there are reasons to do so, the political process approach believes that social movements have a historical position within the polity and that the frequency of social movement activity changes according to opportunities and constraints (ibid.).

Fluctuations in the opportunities and constraints that influence the incidence of collective action creates a cycle of contention (ibid.). A rise in the cycle means that social movements have created or met new opportunities and have made room for the rise of other movements. For instance, the rise and decline of collective action by Canadian Aboriginal bands from 1981 to 2000 can be seen in Figure 14.2 (Wilkes, 2001). Protest events among Native groups in Canada rose dramatically between 1989 and 1991, peaking in the 'Indian summer' of 1990. This increase can be attributed to the 78-day armed uprising at Kanesatake (Oka, Quebec) over municipal plans to convert a Mohawk burial ground into a golf course. In support of the Kahnawake, Akwesasne, and Kanesatake, bands across Canada increased their protest activities.

Like the resource mobilization approach, the political process model focuses on institutions. Specifically, this approach looks at mobilizing structures, which include levels of informal and formal organization (McCarthy, 1996). An example of informal organization is a friendship network. When the cycle of contention is at its lowest point—when there are relatively few (or no) active social movement organizations—the network of friendships among demobilized movement participants keeps the spirit of collective action alive. These latent networks explain why social movements arise when political opportunities appear and when constraints are eased (Melucci, 1989). Although informal communica-

Figure 14.2 Number of Protests by First Nations, 1981–2000, Canada

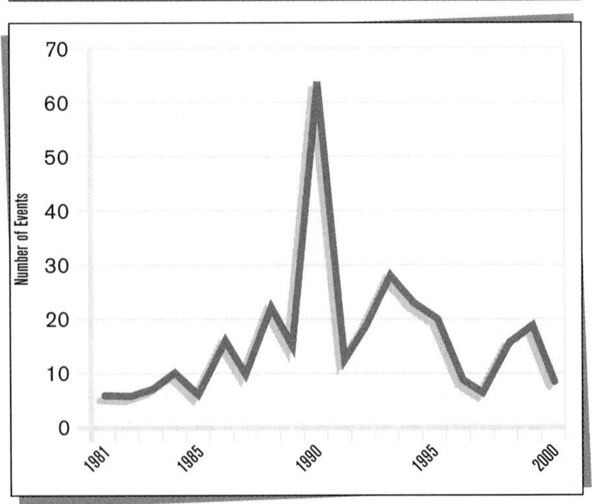

Source: Rima Wilkes, 'Competition or Colonialism? An Analysis of Two Theories of Ethnic Collective Action', Ph.D. thesis (University of Toronto, 2001). Reprinted by permission of the author.

tion alone cannot give rise to a social movement, it can become an important resource for mobilization.

The analysis of formal organization looks at the inner dynamics of social movements. These generally include leadership structures, flows of communication, the entry and exit of members, and the means of identifying, obtaining, and utilizing resources. By studying mobilizing structures, sociologists can understand the institutional processes whereby movements rise, persist, and decline.

The study of social movement organizations also includes inter-organization dynamics, such as movement coalitions. A coalition results when two or more social movement organizations share resources, such as information, in the course of pursuing a common good. Coalitions can be temporary or enduring, and they can bridge different types of movements. Environmental, feminist, gay and lesbian, labour, peace, and anti-poverty organizations in British Columbia, for example, have formed coalitions based on shared understandings of social injustice (Carroll and Ratner, 1996).

Incorporating the insights of framing theory, the political process approach assumes that social movements develop their own cultural understandings of the world. These understandings form the basis for identifying and acting on social grievances, and provide movement participants with the resources needed to create activist identities. In this view, collective action frames can be used to identify appropriate forms of protest. For example, Table 14.2 shows the frequency of types of protest among Native bands in Canada between 1981 and 2000. Clearly, road blockades were the most common protest strategy during this period. This may be due to framing processes: the popularity of roadblocks as a tactic may arise from the cultural significance of this form of protest. As more Native groups block roadways to express their grievances, this form of protest becomes more strongly associated with their social movement. Other Native bands then become more likely to adopt the same tactic.

Social movements may also use collective action frames as strategic resources. To mobilize general sup-

Table 14.2 Frequency of Types of Protest among Native Bands in Canada, 1981–2000

	Number	Percentage
Road blockade	114	36.08
March/demonstration	86	27.22
Train and boat blockade	19	6.01
Boycott	18	5.70
Occupation of land	17	5.38
Illegal fishing/logging	17	5.38
Occupation of building	11	3.45
Hunger strike	5	1.58
Toll booth	5	1.58
Non-strategic violence	4	1.26
Withdrawal from school	3	0.95
English signs changed	2	0.63
Illegal gambling	2	0.63
Invitation of foreign ambassadors	2	0.63
Eviction of police and non-Natives	2	0.63
Dam diversion	2	0.63
Destruction of property	2	0.63
Other	5	1.58
Total	**316**	**100.00**

Source: Rima Wilkes, 'Competition or Colonialism? An Analysis of Two Theories of Ethnic Collective Action', Ph.D. thesis (University of Toronto, 2001). Reprinted by permission of the author.

port for their cause, movements promote their own ideologies in the wider culture. If a social movement's framing of injustice and its solution are accepted in society, then it has created its own political opportunities. If a movement is unsuccessful, however, it risks adding to its own difficulties.

Criticism of the Political Process Approach

One strength of the political process approach is its simultaneous focus on structural, institutional, and cultural conditions. Ideally, such a perspective should provide a robust account of social movement processes. As William Gamson and David Meyer observe, however, the political process model has been 'used to explain so much, it may ultimately explain nothing at all' (1996: 275). While somewhat overstating their case, these critics are concerned that if variable after variable is included in the model, the explanation is no longer parsimonious. The model loses simplicity and, thus, its explanatory appeal.

Doug McAdam (1996) provides two solutions to this problem. First, he suggests restricting the concepts of opportunity and constaint to include only four variables:

- the openness of the state;
- the stability of alliances among elite members of society;
- support within the elite for a particular movement;
- the level of state repression.

Second, McAdam argues that opportunities and constraints are different for each type of social movement. For example, the elements of the political structure that give rise to revolutionary movements will likely be different from those that give rise to identity-based movements. Revolutionary movements are likely to identify most of their political opportunities within the state system, whereas identity-based movements are likely to find most of their opportunities within the cultural practices of civil society (ibid.).

The Analysis of Social Movements

At one time, sociologists argued that successful movements promote their supporters' interests. Nowadays such explanations are rejected, for they fail to recognize that interests are themselves cultural constructs. Moreover, a movement's supporters often have only a schematic or confused understanding of its ideology. But the compelling question remains: Why do some movements succeed, while others fail? To help find an answer to this question, we will examine four social movements: the Canadian women's movement, agrarian social movements in Canada, Nazism in Germany, and socialism in Western Europe.

Unity and Diversity in the Canadian Women's Movement

Social movements need both diversity and unity. In the history of the Canadian women's movement, diversity of membership and experience has helped the movement adapt to a range of situations. Diversity has also encouraged recognition of the many faces of gender inequality. By maintaining a stock of alternative views and ideas, ideological diversity readies the movement for social change. Unity, in turn, gives the movement strength. A one-woman strike, boycott, or sit-in scarcely represents a threat to dominant institutions. But women who are individually powerless gain leverage by acting together. Unified, they can disrupt patriarchal institutions and pressure authorities into finding new solutions.

Though diversity and unity are both beneficial, they pull social movements in opposite directions. Diversity tends to impede unity and may lead to factionalism. Unity tends to suppress diversity and may stifle flexibility and innovation. As in any complex social arrangement, there can be no either/or choice for social movements: survival and efficacy dictate a balance between diversity and unity. The story of the first and second waves of the Canadian women's movement illustrates this dilemma.

The first wave of **feminism** in Canada began in the late nineteenth century and effectively ended in 1918 when women gained the right to vote in federal elections. During this period, women formed organizations for the protection and education of young single women, such as the Anglican Girls Friendly Society and the Young Women's Christian Association (YMCA). Women's groups also protested against child labour and poor working conditions and pressed for health and welfare reforms.

Feminists of the first wave differed in their religious, class, and ethnic backgrounds. While many were Protestant, others were not. Anglo-Saxon women from the middle and upper classes predominated, especially among the leadership, and language divided anglophone and francophone feminists. Moreover, women's organizations had diverse goals. But the battle for women's voting rights unified the movement. One of the earliest women's groups in Canada, the Toronto Women's Literary Club (soon renamed the Women's Suffrage Association), was founded in 1876. By 1916, women had won the right to vote in provincial elections in Alberta, Saskatchewan, and Manitoba. Other provinces soon followed, and Canadian women finally received the federal franchise in 1918.

HUMAN DIVERSITY

Activism After September 11

This story starts with planes flying into buildings on the other coast, in another country. It was just over a year ago, and in the heady months that followed, our elected representatives in Ottawa rushed to approve anti-terrorism legislation intended to protect Canada's national security. In recent months, two Vancouver Island activists found themselves on the wrong side of the Royal Canadian Mounted Police unit created to enforce that legislation.

Early in the morning on September 21, the RCMP's anti-terrorism force, the Integrated National Security Enforcement Team (INSET), followed an anonymous tip and raided John Rampanen's family's empty home in a Port Alberni suburb. They were looking for unauthorized guns.

The INSET team didn't discover anything at the home, says Rampanen, but later, when they found him and his family at his parents' house, they made 'veiled threats towards the safety of our children'. He plans to lodge a formal complaint about the threats. While Rampanen sees the need for the police to investigate such serious allegations as possession of illegal weapons, he says, 'It baffles me that they would be so aggressive in their approach.'

As a member of the West Coast Warriors, an Aboriginal activist group, Rampanen has figured prominently in high-profile confrontations at Cheam on the Fraser River and at Burnt Church in New Brunswick. He also delivers drug and alcohol education programs to First Nations communities. The warriors don't shy from confrontation, he says, but they aren't terrorists and it doesn't make sense for them to be under the scrutiny of INSET. 'It's been over three weeks now, and I still don't understand.'

David Barbarash, former spokesperson for the Animal Liberation Front [ALF], had two computers, computer disks, videos, photos, files, papers, and other documents seized from his home and office in Courtenay on July 30, by INSET officers. He says he understands only too well why INSET might take an interest in activists. 'It used to be people could take these kinds of actions and they'd be labeled protesters', he says. 'At some point in time there was a move to criminalize dissent. What's happening now, post-September 11, is it's shifted again. Now we're not even criminals, we're terrorists.'

The July raid on Barbarash's property stemmed from an ALF action in Maine three years earlier. A group there broke into hunting clubs, spray-painted messages on walls, broke windows and stole stuffed animal heads which they later 'returned to their natural environment to rest in peace.' Damage was estimated at $8,700.

Barbarash acknowledges that the ALF actions were criminal, but stresses the group doesn't physically harm anyone and that what he calls 'economic sabotage' has a long, dignified history that can be traced back to the Boston Tea Party and further.

As with other animal rights actions, Barbarash received information from sources he says he does not know, and has no way to contact, and communicated their message to the media. 'I'm not committing any crimes, I'm simply voicing my support for these kinds of activities', he says. 'I don't see why our resources should be spent in this way, as if this is some kind of terrorist activity. I think it's outrageous.'

'Lets face it', says Barbarash. 'This is Canada. There isn't a lot of terrorism.' So instead of infiltrating al-Qaeda sleeper cells, he says, INSET officers are being used to investigate more mundane criminal matters.

'When they're going after people like me who just speak to the media, it's pretty pathetic', he says. 'They've got to justify their expense account somehow.'

Source: Abridged from Andrew MacLeod, 'Anti-terrorism Police Harass Island Activists', *Monday Magazine*, 24–30 Oct. 2002, 28, 43.

As with many other social movements, success led to decline. The fight for voting rights had given the women's movement a common goal. When this goal was attained, the movement lost unity and momentum. Certainly, women did not stop pushing for change after winning the right to vote. Some worked within the labour movement; others continued to fight for social reform or female political representation. Yet, after 1918, the Canadian women's movement became fragmented, and four decades would pass before it regained strength (Wilson, 1991).

The second wave of the movement rose out of the peace, student, and civil rights movements of the 1960s. In some cases, organizations advanced the women's cause by branching out. For example, a Toronto organization called the Voice of Women (VOW) was founded in 1960 as a peace group. But the VOW gradually adopted other women's issues, and by 1964 it was promoting the legalization of birth control.

The social movements of the 1960s spurred women in other ways. Women in the student movement came to realize that many male activists were sexist. This drove home the extent of gender inequality and the need to organize apart from men. Through the New Left movement, women discovered that socialism helped make sense of gender inequality. More generally, the cultural upheaval of the 1960s encouraged women to question their position in private and public life.

The women's movement has organized around many different issues, including the objectification of women. These women protested against the Miss America Pageant in Atlantic City, NJ, in 1969. (Photo © Jo Freeman, JoFreeman.com)

As a distinct women's movement emerged in the late 1960s and early 1970s, so did internal diversity. Some members were revolutionary Marxists, while others were socialists, liberals, or radical feminists. At times, those who favoured grassroots activism criticized those who worked through high-profile official committees such as the Canadian Advisory Council on the Status of Women. The specific concerns of lesbian, non-white, immigrant, or Native women often were ignored or marginalized by mainstream women's groups. Finally, issues of language and separatism split women's organizations in Quebec from those in the rest of Canada.

Still, the movement found bases for unity. In 1970, a cross-Canada caravan for the repeal of the abortion law attracted much publicity. The caravan collected thousands of petition signatures, showing women what could be achieved through collective action. Other coalitions formed around the issues of daycare, violence against women, labour, and poverty. Women's groups also worked together on International Women's Day celebrations.

To better represent their interests, in 1972 Canadian women formed the National Action Committee on the Status of Women (NAC). The NAC grew and by the late 1980s had become an umbrella organization for over 575 women's groups. At the same time, however, debate over the use of assisted reproductive technologies was growing, too. These technologies include cloning, surrogacy, assisted insemination, *in vitro* fertilization, embryo research, and prenatal diagnosis techniques. During a first round of consultations about these technologies with the federal government (1989–1993), the NAC adopted a position that dissatisfied many of its members. Leaders of the women's organization argued that reproductive technologies were being developed not to meet the needs of ordinary women, but to further the interests of the scientific community and the biotechnology industry. These technologies, claimed the NAC, 'represent the values and priorities of an economically stratified, male-dominated, technocratic science' (NAC, 1990, quoted in Montpetit et al., 2004: 145). Many within the NAC disagreed with this position, which was seen as too simple and out of touch with concerns at the grassroots. Those offended included lesbians and infertile women who wished to bear children.

Between 1993 and 1997, therefore, the NAC adopted a more open approach in reviewing the question. Discussions within the women's organization allowed ample room for the expresssion of diverse views. Rejecting its earlier stance against science, as a result of this more open process the NAC now argued that assisted reproductive technologies are acceptable when they reduce inequalities between women. This stance resulted from a compromise between different perspectives within the NAC. But policy-makers in Ottawa were puzzled because the translation of this stance into actual public policy was not obvious. Losing influence as a result, thereafter the NAC was pushed to the margins relative to other pressure groups involved in making Canadian policy on assisted reproductive technologies (such as the Canadian Bar Association and the Canadian Medical Association; see Montpetit et al., 2004; Scala et al., 2005).

During both its first and second waves, then, the Canadian women's movement has organized around many issues. The diversity of its concerns and perspectives not only reflects the many faces of gender inequality, but also promotes a diffusion of the movement's ideas and its survival in the face of changing social conditions. However, serious internal arguments may exhaust activists. Although factions permit the coexistence of different constituencies, they draw attention and energy away from common interests that unite diverse organizations. When the time for action comes, a movement may lose effectiveness if its factions do not set aside their differences. As with all social movements, the success of the women's movement depends on balancing the trade-offs between diversity and unity (Briskin, 1992).

The Roots of Agrarian Protest in Canada

A study by Canadian sociologist Robert J. Brym (1980) shows why regional differences between farming economies have affected agrarian social movements in Canada. The ideology and popularity of these movements and their links with other social groups all depend on the type of farming found in each region. Brym's study examines regional differences in agrarian protest by comparing farming economies in Alberta, Saskatchewan, and New Brunswick during the Depression years.

During the 1930s, agrarian protest grew rapidly in the Prairie provinces, but not in New Brunswick. Much of this difference can be explained by the degree to which farmers' livelihoods were affected by the market. In the West, farmers concentrated on producing beef or wheat, both for the rest of Canada and for export. Hence, western ranchers and wheat farmers faced similar economic pressures. Eastern Canada set the tariffs on manufactured goods, the rates for railroad freight and bank credit, even the prices of beef and wheat. United by common economic interests, western farmers responded by creating marketing, consumer, and other voluntary associations that stressed co-operation.

In New Brunswick, by contrast, farmers practised mixed agriculture. Their primary productive goal was meeting their economic needs without selling what they produced or buying what they needed—strictly speaking, they were peasants rather than farmers. Since changes in market prices hardly affected them, they had little reason to defend themselves by forming co-operatives. Historical and geographical factors also mattered. While the dominance of shipping and timber interests had hampered the commercialization of agriculture in New Brunswick, the province's poor soil and rugged terrain confined farming to river valleys and the coastline. Finally, New Brunswick farmers not only were more isolated than those in the West, they also had much smaller debts. Farmers in New Brunswick, therefore, were much less likely to form associations. In 1939, for instance, membership in farmers' co-operatives per 1,000 rural residents over 14 years of age was 32 in New Brunswick, compared with 326 in Alberta and 789 in Saskatchewan (Brym, 1980: 346).

Thus, the greater radicalism of western farmers stemmed from high solidarity and a loss of control over their means of production. But the two western provinces diverged in their approach to agrarian protest. Alberta's Social Credit Party was right-wing, while Saskatchewan's CCF (Co-operative Commonwealth Federation, the predecessor of today's New Democratic Party) was left-wing. What accounts for this divergence?

In Alberta, a leftist agrarian party known as the United Farmers of Alberta excluded small-town merchants and others seen as exploiters of farmers. During the

Time to Reflect

In what ways, if any, do you believe the women's movement has altered your life and your attitudes about gender? Has the environmental movement had a greater or lesser effect on you than the women's movement?

difficult Depression years of the 1930s, however, co-operation between farmers and merchants increased when they saw that their economic fortunes were connected—if farmers did badly, so would local businesses, and vice versa. With the support of right-wing merchants, teachers, professionals, and preachers, the new Social Credit Party spread from Calgary to the small towns of southwestern Alberta. Eventually, Social Credit reached farmers and won their support, too, but the party never lost the right-wing ideology of its urban roots.

In Saskatchewan, on the other hand, the CCF maintained strong ties between farmers and the left-wing urban working class. Of the CCF leadership, 53 per cent were farmers and 17 per cent workers, while of the Social Credit Party 24 per cent were farmers and none were workers (ibid., 350). Thus, the differing class backgrounds of the farmers' allies helps to explain differences in the ideologies of agrarian movements in Saskatchewan and Alberta.

Brym's study suggests that economic factors affect the formation of social movements, as well as affecting which ideological direction they take. Agricultural producers such as prairie farmers are more likely to protest if there is a downturn in the capitalist economy because their livelihood, unlike that of producers in New Brunswick, depends on the market. Furthermore, the organization of a protest movement is hampered when potential supporters lack pre-existing social ties or work in isolation from other potential supporters. Finally, the alliances of a social movement affect both its ideology and its chances of success.

The history of agrarian protest in Alberta is linked to a more recent development in Canadian politics, the rise of the Canadian Alliance. This party began as the Reform Party in 1987, and won a staggering 52 seats in the 1993 national election. In many ways, the Reform Party was a protest party. It provided critical opposition to the Progressive Conservatives while appealing to western Canadians' sense of regional pride. Although there are many variables that determined the rise and success of the Canadian Alliance, the early organizers of the Reform Party were able to draw on a right-wing, populist ideology that had already been created and maintained by Alberta's Social Credit Party. In other words, the ideological conditions that made it possible for the rise of a new national conservative party were set many years earlier. Indeed, the Reform Party and the Social Credit Party shared similar bases of support: just prior to the 1993 election, surveys indicated that Alberta's farmers were much more likely than any other group in that province to vote for the Reform Party (Harrison and Krahn, 1995).

The Spread of Nazism

How did so many ordinary Germans come to support the Nazis in the early 1930s? A once-popular explanation, known as **mass-society theory**, holds that the strong social bonds inherent in rural family and village life create psychological security. Modern cities, by contrast, are said to contain masses of individuals uprooted from community and tradition. Feeling lonely and desperate, these isolated individuals readily succumb to extremist movements. Nazism relieved the psychological anxieties of such people with its easy solutions, utopian promises, scapegoating of Jews, and emotion-charged mass gatherings. Mass-society theory also emphasizes the strong manipulative potential of the modern mass media and claims that intolerant ideologies such as Nazism attract marginalized members of the working class (Kornhauser, 1959).

Mass-society theory exhibits the chief deficiency of the breakdown approach: a failure to show a plausible connection between subjective feelings and the spread of a political movement. Surely the Nazis' rise to power required more than supporters who felt isolated and disoriented. Moreover, if mass-society theory is true, why did Nazi-style movements not emerge in other modern societies experiencing social strains similar to Germany's?

These issues have been addressed by a number of studies that conclude that Nazism could not have developed among a mass of isolated individuals (Birnbaum, 1988; Hamilton, 1982; Koshar, 1986). Indeed, these studies show that mass-society theory is wrong in assuming that the solidarity of rural communities raised a barrier to Nazism. In the important German election of 31 July 1932, the proportion of voters supporting the Nazis (the National Socialist Party) was lowest in cities and highest in small communities. In fact, in some villages, all the votes went to the Nazi party. Further, there is no evidence that marginalized working-class people were especially likely to support the Nazis, as mass-society theory claims. To be sure, this question remains unresolved, for the class background of individuals who voted for the Nazis is poorly understood. Nevertheless, electoral support for the Nazis was lower in predominantly working-class districts. This does not prove conclusively that working-class people were less likely to support the Nazis—people from more than one social class may inhabit a district. However, the class pattern of regional voting certainly casts doubt on the mass-society thesis. One other finding has also contributed to the search for an alternative explanation: the fact that the Nazis received far fewer votes in Catholic areas but far more where Protestants predominated.

The spread of Nazism is better explained by first looking at economic conditions in the early 1930s. Like many other countries, Germany was experiencing an economic depression so severe that citizens were eager for new options. In the United States, Depression-era voters turned to the Democratic Party. In the Scandinavian countries, support for socialist parties rose sharply, while in Canada and Britain, voters elected the Conservative parties. Since people exposed to the difficult conditions of the Great Depression wanted substantial change, anti-democratic ideologies also gained strength, especially where liberalism was weak. However, the direction of change was not predetermined. Some countries turned sharply to the left, and even in Germany the left (the Communists and the Social Democrats) presented a radical alternative that attracted many.

But Germany finally turned to the far right, above all because of the effectiveness of Nazi activists. Many were veterans of World War I who had retained military values of comradeship, discipline, obedience, and honour. Rapidly demobilized by the thousands after the Versailles Treaty, they were never reintegrated into German society. These men harboured a wide-ranging resentment against Jews, materialism, democracy, Communism, and capitalism. Through persuasion, intimidation, and thuggery, and by adjusting their propaganda to different audiences, they worked to win support for the Nazis. Elements of the German press also helped by presenting the Nazi cause in a favourable light.

Contrary to the claims of mass-society theory, social ties actually helped the Nazis. It was through their social ties that activists spread the Nazi message and recruited supporters. Nazi activists targeted local leaders and organizations such as clubs, associations, and farmers' and religious groups. These targets were of pivotal importance because of their ties with potential Nazi supporters. If Nazi activists could convert an influential local dignitary or organization leader, then ordinary citizens or organization members were likely to follow. The preponderance of the Protestant vote for the Nazis, especially in the countryside, therefore reflects the activists' success in winning over Protestant religious organizations.

Interestingly, the strength of social ties also explains some of the Nazis' difficulties during the early 1930s. The Catholic Church and strong working-class organizations in the cities resisted Nazi activism. They limited the spread of Nazi support and even organized anti-Nazi resistance. The Nazis were aware of this, and after taking power in 1933 they replaced independent organizations such as unions and youth groups with ones they controlled. The Nazis recognized that the control of social ties amounted to the domination of German society.

Selection for Socialism

The preceding explanations have focused on the roles played by activists, social ties, class alliances, and economic interests. As a comparative study of socialism by Robert Wuthnow (1989) demonstrates, political alliances and the nature of the regime also influence the nature and fortune of ideological movements.

The hope that **capitalism** will one day give way to collective ownership of the means of economic production lies at the heart of socialist doctrines. To this, **Marxism** added two further tenets: first, the belief that class conflict drives history and, second, faith in the industrial working class—the **proletariat**—as the agent of historical progress. While the names of Karl Marx and Friedrich Engels are closely associated with socialism, socialism and Marxism are not synonymous. Various currents of socialist thought had already appeared in Europe by the 1830s and 1840s, and many variants continued to flourish outside of Marxism. Moreover, the ideas of Marx and Engels themselves continued to develop long after they wrote the *Communist Manifesto* in 1848.

European intellectuals were not the only advocates of socialist ideas. Indeed, in some ways they were less influential than the many newspapers and associations affiliated with the movement. Eventually, political parties became the principal promoters of socialism in nineteenth-century Europe. The puzzling question is why some socialist parties in Western Europe were much more successful than others.

Consider the vote for socialist parties prior to World War I. Western European countries fell into three categories on the basis of the level of electoral support for the socialists: *low*, where the socialists got under 15 per cent of the popular vote; *medium*, where they got 15 to 25 per cent; and *high*, where they got over 25 per cent (see Table 14.3). The socialists' electoral performance was a good indicator of their strength in other key areas as well, including party membership, newspaper and book publishing, and the sponsorship of clubs, educational programs, and benevolent societies.

If economic conditions alone affected the success of socialist movements, pre-1914 voting for socialist parties ought to have been stronger in industrialized countries with large working classes. However, voting for the socialists was very low in Great Britain and moderate in France, even though both societies were highly industrialized relative to the rest of Europe. Clearly, industrial-

Table 14.3 Support for Socialist Parties in Western Europe Prior to 1914

Low Support	Medium Support	High Support
Great Britain	France	Germany
Italy	The Netherlands	Sweden
Spain	Norway	Belgium
		Denmark

Source: Based on Robert Wuthnow, *Communities of Discourse: Ideology and Social Structure in the Reformation, the Enlightenment, and European Socialism* (Cambridge, Mass.: Harvard University Press, 1989).

ization and the presence of a large working class do not adequately explain variations in socialist success.

Wuthnow argues for 'the importance of state structures in addition to economic conditions in accounting for the success of the socialist movement' (1989: 446). The main factors he cites are the nature of the regime and the balance of political forces. In a conservative aristocratic regime such as Germany's, the mainly middle-class liberal political parties were weak, unable to forge strong alliances with the industrial working class. Socialist organizers in Germany thus faced less competition in recruiting and organizing the working class. The situation in Belgium paralleled that in Germany. Rule was in the hands of an alliance between industrialists and a monarchic oligarchy. Belgian socialists were helped also by anti-union laws that stifled other working-class organizations. In France, Great Britain, and the Netherlands, by contrast, liberal institutions and forces were well-established by the late nineteenth century. Liberalism and healthy trade unions undercut the socialists' attempt to capture the working-class vote in these nations.

In the Scandinavian countries, the conservative aristocracy was relatively weak by the end of the nineteenth century, but it retained some influence in the towns and cities. In the countryside, the farmers supported liberal parties, especially in Denmark and Norway. Because the conservatives were on the wane and the liberal parties were young and more strongly rooted in the countryside, socialists in Scandinavia had a good chance of organizing the new, urban working class.

Economic factors carried more weight in Italy and Spain, where late industrialization delayed the formation of a working class. To be sure, Italy's socialists made rapid gains after 1898, especially in the industrialized northern regions. Still, they faced strong competition from the church, the liberal parties, and the unions. In Spain, the liberal parties were disorganized, but the socialists had to compete against the anarcho-syndicalists. They also faced a movement for regional autonomy in Catalonia, one of Spain's chief industrial areas. The Catalan movement blocked the socialists by uniting workers with other classes in the region.

European socialism was thus stronger where liberals were weak and industrialists and conservatives were united (Germany and Belgium) or where conservatives and liberals kept each other in check (Scandinavia). Socialism was weaker where conservatives were weak and liberal forces won significant working-class support (France and Britain). In Italy and Spain, socialism remained weak because of late industrialization. More generally, Wuthnow's study shows that the nature of the regime and the type of alliances struck by different political forces crucially affected the socialist movement's chances for success before World War I.

Is the Future of Social Movements Global?

The world is going through an accelerated bout of **globalization**. While this is hardly new, some sociologists claim the level of global interdependence and the scale of global interaction are becoming more complex too. Capital and commodities, information and ideas, people and their cultures are criss-crossing the globe, and these interactions are changing the world's societies.

Many social movements recognize that globalization is changing the political terrain. New opportunities and constraints are appearing that force social movements to adapt their strategies, resources, and ideologies. Recall Charles Tilly's research (1978) on the development of the nation-state in Europe: the rise of new forms of social protest was a product of the rise of nations. Will globalization also give rise to new, global forms of protest?

Some environmental organizations, such as Greenpeace International, Amnesty International, and the Sea Shepherd Society, as well as a variety of anti-globalization movements, claim to operate in a global polity. These organizations take the globe as their site of struggle while simultaneously operating in specific locations. In other words, organizations such as these claim to 'think globally but act locally'. Their strategy is clear: concerted efforts in locations throughout the world will alter the negative social and environmental effects of globalization.

The link between globalization and social movements has not gone unnoticed by sociologists. German sociologist Ulrich Beck (1996) claims that globalization creates opportunities for new forms of collective action

GLOBAL ISSUES
The Clayoquot Standoff

The tourist board markets British Columbia as 'Super, Natural', a Pacific Eden full of lush rainforests and forgotten inlets harbouring killer whales and inexhaustible salmon runs. That wild, virginal image began fading in Clayoquot Sound, on the west coast of Vancouver Island, as loggers and environmentalists battled over the giant cedars and Sitka spruce that have stood on the West Coast since before the time of Columbus.

In the summer of 1993, more than 800 protesters were charged by police after trying to block loggers' attempts to start felling the old-growth stands of Clayoquot Sound. The loggers had the legal right to do so, since the provincial government has decided that 62 per cent of the 270,000 hectare area should be opened up for a timber harvest by forestry giant MacMillan Bloedel Ltd. The rest was to be preserved. The protesters, ranging from teenagers with nose-rings to pensioners in cable-knit sweaters, were carted off in one of the biggest mass arrests in Canadian history. In the courts, some received unexpectedly harsh sentences: up to 60 days in jail and fines as high as $3,000.

But the battle was far from over. Though the environmentalists found themselves on the wrong side of the law, they testified in court that they had the moral high ground. Some used a character in one of Dr Seuss's children's books to illustrate what they viewed as a spiritual quest to save the forests from greedy timber conglomerates: 'I am the Lorax, I speak for the trees.' They settled in outside the Vancouver headquarters of MacMillan Bloedel, where they were to be found most lunch hours, toting billboards in a legal picket. One group planned to take a stump from Clayoquot Sound on a European protest tour in the spring of 1994.

The message of the environmental groups was simple: Forestry companies have been criminally negligent in their stewardship of British Columbia's forestry resource, turning the province into the 'Brazil of the North'. As a result, they do not deserve to be trusted with the logging of Clayoquot Sound, the largest coastal temperate lowland rainforest left in the world. Those in Ireland and Scotland were cut down long ago.

MacMillan Bloedel's response was that the environmentalists simply want to stop logging. Period. Dennis Fitzgerald, a company spokesman, commented, 'I've yet to see them approve of a logging plan anywhere.' To fight back, the forestry industry began doing its own politicking and myth-building. To prove that MacMillan Bloedel is sensitive to the environment, Fitzgerald pointed out that clearcuts no longer stretch over 80 to 100 hectares of forest land, creating eyesores that leave tourists gasping. In the previous five years, the forestry industry reduced clearcuts to between 30 and 40 hectares. MacMillan Bloedel has also stated that it can log in Clayoquot Sound forever, since it will cut at a rate that will give seedlings 80 to 100 years to grow before the chainsaws return.

Ironically, both sides said they want the same thing: sustainable development, the buzzword of the decade. That is easy to overlook, however, given the din of loggers' chainsaws and the TV-savvy theatrics of the environmentalists blocking logging roads.

Source: Adapted from Miro Cernetig, 'The Clayoquot Standoff', *Report on Business* (Jan. 1994), 31–2. Reprinted with permission from The Globe and Mail.

Many environmental groups believe that concerted efforts in locations throughout the world will alter the negative social and environmental effects of globalization. Increasingly, ordinary people are becoming involved in the environmental movement and its many issues. (Photo courtesy of Western Wilderness Committee/Jeremy Williams)

that operate outside the politics of the nation-state, in the politics of what Beck calls a 'world risk society'. Beck suggests that ordinary people in all societies have been socialized to understand that the modern world is full of human-created hazards. Widely publicized dangers, such as the radioactive cloud that drifted from a nuclear reactor in Chernobyl (in Ukraine, at that time part of the Soviet Union) to the rest of Europe in 1986, have forced people to acknowledge that many political issues transcend borders. For Beck, the emerging recognition of global risks marks a new reality for social movements.

Greenpeace International is a good example of a global, or *transnational*, social movement that appears to have adapted to this world risk society. Greenpeace originated in the late 1960s, and its earliest members were environmental activists from Canada and the United States. From the start, this environmental movement was concerned with global issues and it organized protests throughout the world.

Greenpeace has developed its own political opportunities by creating unique forms of global diplomacy (Beck, 1996). It often operates outside the boundaries of the nation-state, such as on the high seas, where individual nations have no legal jurisdiction (Magnusson, 1990). Conscious of the influence of the international media, Greenpeace rallies support by organizing global boycotts that challenge governments and corporations to change their environmental policies and practices. Through these media events, Greenpeace attempts to stir up moral indignation while recognizing that different cultures have various understandings and experiences of global environmental dangers (Eyerman and Jamison, 1989).

Not all sociologists agree that globalization has created a fundamentally new political reality. Leslie Sklair (1994) argues that global politics are very much like national politics, simply on a larger scale. For Sklair, organizations such as Greenpeace International mirror the organizational structures of trans-national corporations. He suggests that the global environmental movement consists of transnational environmental organizations whose professional members make up a global environmental elite. This elite plays an ideological game with the transnational corporate and governmental elite: each side attempts to have its version of the environmental reality accepted as the truth. For Sklair, this is politics as usual.

Sociologists also question whether the rise of supranational organizations, such as the European Union (EU), will bring about new forms of collective action that link activists across national boundaries. Although the EU does constitute a new political terrain, Doug Imig and Sidney Tarrow (2001) have found that collective action in Europe remains strongly rooted within the nation-state. While Europeans have many grievances against the EU, most protest against it is domestic rather than transnational. This may simply indicate that activists have yet to develop new transnational strategies and linkages. Nevertheless, domestic politics remain a viable political arena for voicing concerns about the EU (Imig and Tarrow, 2001).

Today the world is more intricately connected than in the past. A variety of new social issues have arisen as a result, and there are now social movements that attack globalization. Each has to identify guilty institutions and actors, however, and states and corporations remain the best choice because they are largely responsible for the policies and practices that promote globalization.

Generally, two characteristics are needed for a social movement to be truly global. First, a social movement must frame its grievances as global grievances. Many environmental organizations do this. By framing environmental risks as global risks, the environmental movement hopes to demonstrate that environmental degradation affects everyone. Second, to be global a social movement needs to have a worldwide membership and organizational structure. On a global scale, membership and frame alignment probably are supported by communication technologies such as e-mail and the Internet. Alternatively, a global movement can arise through a long-term coalition or network of movement organizations. For example, indigenous peoples across North and South America, Australia, and New Zealand have united against the ongoing effects of colonialism and to ensure that the rights of indigenous populations are recognized.

Conclusion

Sociologists seek to explain how and why social movements form, continue, and dissolve. Comparative studies of movements can help to determine whether or not any common features point to a general explanation or whether existing explanations hold for different situations. And historical studies reveal how social movements change over time.

Figure 14.3 depicts the changes in protest repertoires in Western Europe and North America. Early forms of collective action were poorly organized and relatively sporadic. Often their grievances were tied to local affairs, and usually their targets were local elites. With the rise of nation-states, however, new kinds of social movements appeared. These movements were highly organized and often identified social issues that stemmed from structural conditions such as economic inequality and narrow political representation. They also routinized protest activities: different social movements learned to

Figure 14.3 'Old' and 'New' Repertoires in Western Europe and North America

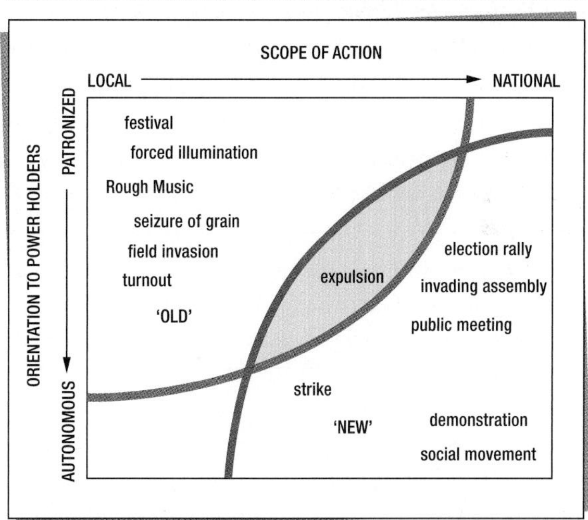

Source: Charles Tilly, 'Speaking Your Mind without Elections, Surveys, or Social Movements', *Public Opinion Quarterly* 47, 4 (1983): 461–78. Reprinted by permission of Oxford University Press.

Time to Reflect

If you lived in Burma (Myanmar), do you think you would have joined in the September 2007 protests for greater freedom and democracy? Why or why not? Can you think of any causes that you would be prepared to go to jail or die for?

apply similar methods of protest, such as the mass demonstration. The rise of NSMs in the second half of the twentieth century marks another change. These movements are more concerned with gaining cultural recognition than with the redistribution of social goods. So, even though NSMs tend to use traditional forms of protest, they are more concerned with the politics of everyday life than with the traditional politics of governance.

While issues and methods of protest have changed over time, the success of collective action always is linked to the social and political climate. In other words, social and political changes can create opportunities for social movements, or they can create constraints. According to a theory developed by Herbert Kitschelt (1993), present conditions in Canada have created opportunities that may lead to an increase in social movement activity. To understand why, short- and long-term social movement dynamics must be distinguished. Support for social movements usually rises when political parties and interest groups fail to channel citizens' demands. Social movements can then mobilize support, attract resources, and forge alliances among protest groups. However, according to Kitschelt, this surge in social movement activity peaks as resources dwindle, as political parties begin to take up citizens' concerns, and as people's interest in collective mobilization wanes. Social movement activity then falls, only to rise again the next time organizers capitalize on frustration with parties and interest groups. In other words, the short-term pattern of movement activity is cyclical.

The long-term trend, by contrast, is towards an increase in the number of social movements. In the wealthy capitalist democracies, social movement activity has grown steadily since the 1960s. Established parties and politicians have proven increasingly incapable of providing satisfactory solutions to such issues as nuclear power, toxic waste disposal, resource management, abortion, pornography, and equal rights. Today, many Canadians share a distrust of established politicians, political parties, and interest groups. The heavy 'No' vote in the constitutional referendum of 1992, the Progressive Conservative Party's brutal fall from power in 1993, and the rise of protest parties in Quebec (the Bloc Québécois) and western Canada (the Reform Party and its successor, the Canadian Alliance) all signal citizens' disenchantment with the political establishment. The extent of citizen discontent should not be exaggerated: recent federal elections have shown that established parties still attract much support. Nevertheless, many burning public questions—around gender, citizen participation, and environmental, ethnic, and Native rights issues—often elude both parties and interest groups. The current climate in Canada, therefore, favours an expansion of social movement activity. Of course, whether organizers actually will exploit this situation remains to be seen. The outcome will depend on social movement leaders and on the political establishment's ability to co-opt them.

Questions for Critical Thought

1. Does economic prosperity encourage or hinder the formation of protest movements? Consider the experience of Canada in the 1930s and the 1960s, or compare capitalist countries in Latin America today.
2. Many people today believe that social movements offer better prospects for democratic participation than political parties or interest groups. However, Roberto Michels's 'iron law of oligarchy' says that organization discourages democratic participation because resources, expertise, and status tend to flow to leaders. Have new social movements (NSMs) successfully broken the iron law of oligarchy? If you were organizing a social movement, what kind of safeguards would you put in place to prevent an oligarchy from forming?
3. Find an ideological statement from a social movement, such as a flyer or leaflet, a brochure or members' newsletter, a website, or an interview with a movement representative. What are the movement's ideals, goals, and plan of action? What social goods does the statement value, disparage, or neglect? How does the statement use emotional appeals to make its message more persuasive? Is the movement offering selective incentives to attract new members? What kinds of people are most and least likely to be persuaded by this statement?
4. Select a chapter of *Political Man* (1981) by Seymour Martin Lipset and write a critique of it based on your sociological understanding of social movements.
5. The political process approach attempts to determine how political opportunities and constraints influence social movement activities. Do you think that McAdam's proposal to restrict the definition of these concepts is useful, or is it too narrow? As an aid, look over the case studies in this chapter and try to identify the most important political opportunities and constraints.
6. All sociological theories make **ontological** assumptions. In other words, theorizing about the social world requires particular assumptions about how it operates (for example, social conflict versus social consensus). How can empirical research on social movements be used to refute or confirm the ontological assumptions of social movement theories?
7. A counter-movement is generally understood to be a response to a social movement. Find an example of a counter-movement and compare it with its associated social movement. What do you think are the main differences? Are there similarities that you think are of sociological importance? What social movement theory do you think is the most appropriate for understanding the relationship between these two forms of collective action?
8. Social movements disseminate ideas and hope to influence the general public. What is the role of the media in this process? How might new media technologies change social movement strategies, processes, and internal organization?

Recommended Readings

William K. Carroll, ed., *Organizing Dissent: Contemporary Social Movements in Theory and Practice*, 2nd edn (Toronto: Garamond, 1997).

The ideological stance, choice of subject matter, analytical styles, and emphasis on identity-based approaches found in this edited volume exemplify the dominant trends in studies of Canadian social movements.

Donatella della Porta, Massimiliano Andretta, Lorenzo Mosca, and Herbert Reiter, *Globalization from Below: Transnational Activists and Protest Networks* (Minneapolis: University of Minnesota Press, 2006).

Challenging the idea that global social movements are merely coalitions of local movements, the authors argue that the global movement against neo-liberalism is a form of collective action that represents important changes in tactics, collective identities, and patterns of organization.

Mario Diani and Jon Eyerman, eds, *Studying Collective Action* (London: Sage, 1992).

This collection of articles by prominent social movement researchers provides detailed discussion of methodological problems in the study of social movements.

Todd Gitlin, *The Whole World Is Watching: Mass Media in the Making and Unmaking of the New Left* (Berkeley: University of California Press, 1980).

Gitlin's vivid account shows why the modern mass media are a mixed blessing for social movements.

Barrington Moore, Jr, *Social Origins of Dictatorship and Democracy: Lord and Peasant in the Making of the Modern World* (Boston: Beacon, 1966).

A classic of historical-comparative sociology, this ambitious, closely argued work connects class alliances and regime outcomes in England, France, the United States, China, Japan, and India.

Theda Skocpol, *States and Social Revolutions: A Comparative Analysis of France, Russia, and China* (Cambridge: Cambridge University Press, 1979).

Skocpol's influential study, which was written partly in rebuttal to Barrington Moore's *Social Origins of Dictatorship and Democracy*, helped to renew interest in the sociological role of the state and the ideas of Max Weber.

Sidney Tarrow, *Power in Movements: Social Movements and Contentious Politics*, 2nd edn (New York: Cambridge University Press, 1998).

An up-to-date survey of social movement studies, written by a scholar versed in theory and empirical work on both sides of the Atlantic.

Eric R. Wolf, *Peasant Wars of the Twentieth Century* (New York: Harper & Row, 1969).

Peasant rebellion and revolt in Mexico, Russia, China, Vietnam, Algeria, and Cuba are explained in terms of the penetration of capitalism.

Recommended Websites

American Sociological Association, Section on Collective Behavior and Social Movements
www.asanet.org/sectioncbsm

This a good starting place for more information on the sociological study of social movements. Read *Critical Mass*, the section's newsletter, to be informed of new publications, conferences, and the latest research.

Assembly of First Nations
www.afn.ca

This very comprehensive site contains detailed information about social issues pertaining to Canada's First Nations.

Canadian Lesbian & Gay Archives (CLGA)
www.clga.ca/archives/

This site provides information that relates to lesbian, gay, bisexual, and transgender movements. Its focus is mostly Canadian, but the archive also provides plenty of information from around the world.

Canadian Race Relations Foundation
www.crr.ca

The Canadian Race Relations Foundation's primary goal is to end race- and ethnic-based discrimination in Canada. This website provides information about current issues and research.

Centre for Social Justice
www.socialjustice.org

This organization was established in 1997 and is based in Toronto. Its goals are to foster national and international social change through research and advocacy.

Global Solidarity Dialogue
www.antenna.nl/~waterman/dialogue.html

This is a good starting place for information on global social movements. The site provides research, news, and discussion on social movements throughout the world, as well as information on globalization.

Greenpeace Canada
www.greenpeace.ca

This site provides information about Greenpeace's past and current campaigns. Peruse the site and try to establish how this organization frames environmental issues.

National Action Committee on the Status of Women
www.nac-cca.ca

NAC is the largest women's movement organization in Canada. This site provides the history of the organization, and it presents current issues and discussion about equity issues in Canada.

Part IV

Social Inequality

ELECTRIC
BLUES

Chapter 15

Class and Status Inequality

Julie Ann McMullin

Learning Objectives

In this chapter, you will:

- Seek to understand Marxist conceptualizations of social class.
- Examine Weberian conceptualizations of social class.
- Differentiate between Marxist and Weberian conceptualizations of social class.
- Learn about the feminist critique of traditional approaches to the study of social class.
- Explore the relationship between social class and inequality in paid work, education, and health.
- Come to understand why 'class matters'.

Photo: Sam Javanrough

Introduction

Kimberly Rogers was born into a working-class family in Sudbury, Ontario, on 20 July 1961. She was raised by her mother and her stepfather; third in a line of four sisters. At the age of 18, Kimberly left Sudbury for Toronto, where she worked as a waitress, bartender, and receptionist. While working in Toronto, she also went to school and completed her high school diploma.

In 1996, she left Toronto and an abusive relationship, and returned to Sudbury. Upon returning to Sudbury, Kimberly could not find work and applied for social assistance. In the fall of 1996, Kimberly registered in the correctional services workers program at Cambrian College. She later changed programs and continued her studies in the social services program, from which she graduated near the top of her class, in the spring of 2000. By all accounts, she was a model student. As one of her teachers remarked, 'She was such an ambitious student . . . very thorough in her work and very supportive of others, which made her extremely popular with her classmates' (MacKinnon and Lacey, 2001: F1).

In order to pay for her education, Kimberly received student loans while receiving benefits under the general welfare program. This violated Ontario provincial law because the general welfare program does not permit recipients to receive student loans, nor does the Ontario Student Assistance Program (OSAP) permit its recipients to receive welfare.

In November 1999, OSAP uncovered the fact that Kimberly had been receiving both OSAP loans and general welfare, and suspended her loan for the remainder of the academic year. Kimberly had to rely on two small grants obtained through the college to pay her tuition and books, and on charity for food. Because of her actions, Kimberly was also unable to benefit from the OSAP loan forgiveness program, and would have to repay the loan in its entirety (approximately $30,000) upon graduation. Ontario Works also began an investigation into Kimberly's actions and, in September 2000, she was charged with welfare fraud.

In April 2001, Kimberly pled guilty to the fraud charge. The judge sentenced her to six months house arrest and required her to pay restitution to welfare for the amount of benefits she received while she was in college, approximately $13,000. Because of her conviction for welfare fraud, Kimberly Rogers was automatically suspended from receiving social assistance for a period of three months. A new regulation, which came into force on 1 April 2000, required that persons convicted of welfare fraud committed prior to 1 April 2000 be suspended for a three- or six-month period, and that persons convicted of welfare fraud committed after 1 April 2000 be subject to a lifetime ban.

As a result of her conviction, Kimberly Rogers was required to stay in her apartment at all times, except for attending medical and religious appointments, and a three-hour period on Wednesday mornings, during which time she could run errands and buy groceries. But Kimberly Rogers had no money to buy the necessities of life. Even after her lawyers succeeded in having the court lift the ban on her benefits, her monthly benefits were reduced to collect a portion of the amount owing under the restitution order. After rent was taken into account, Kimberly Rogers was left with about $18 per month to buy food.

On 9 August 2001, while under house arrest, Kimberly Rogers died. She was eight months pregnant. Sudbury was suffering through a second week of temperatures over 30 degrees Celsius and Kimberly's apartment, which lacked air conditioning, was on the top floor of an old house. Responding to her death, Kimberly's lawyer stated that 'she would have been better off if she had committed a violent crime and been sent to prison. . . . If sentenced to jail, she would have had the necessities of life, she would have had access to medications. If something had happened to her, it wouldn't have been two days before her body was found' (ibid.).

On 20 December 2002, after a three-month coroner's inquest into her death, a coroner's jury determined that Kimberly Rogers had committed suicide. The jury heard testimony from an expert witness in suicidology, who explained that the suspension from benefits, the house arrest, the effects of a criminal conviction—which would effectively act as a bar from employment in the social work field—had acted as a crushing weight on Kimberly Rogers's spirit and played a decisive role in the decision to take her own life. At the conclusion of the inquest, the jury issued 14 recommendations, which they felt would prevent future deaths in similar circumstances. The recommendations included: that the government remove the 3-month, 6-month, and lifetime bans for conviction of welfare fraud from the legislation, and that it increase welfare rates to reflect the actual costs of shelter and basic needs. Although the government initially refused to make these changes, in 2004 the Ontario government removed the lifetime and temporary bans for fraud; three- and six-month suspensions are still in place for failure to comply with other rules.

Activist groups use Kimberly's death as political leverage in their fight against poverty and inequality.

I would like to acknowledge and thank Emily Jovic for her excellent research assistance and critical eye in assisting me with the revisions to this chapter.

IN THE FIRST PERSON

I went to university wanting to become a social worker and save the world. In my first year of undergraduate studies at the University of Western Ontario, I took both introductory social work and sociology. My social work class put me to sleep, but my sociology class was exciting, thanks largely to the excellent teaching skills of Professor Lesley Harman. The lectures in this class set off bells in my mind as I learned that inequality had more to do with the structure of opportunities than with intelligence or ambition. A lot of things happened after Sociology 020 that influenced my decision to become a sociologist. But the thing that inspired me most was my strong belief that, compared to other disciplines, graduate training in sociology would give me a superior set of skills with which to understand social worlds.—Julie McMullin

These groups blame the policies of an ultraconservative Ontario government for Kimberly's death. Indeed, the election of Mike Harris and his neo-conservative government in 1995 led to a 21.6 per cent cut to welfare benefits, a radical dismantling of welfare services, the institution of the Ontario Works Act and workfare program, massive cuts to social spending, and the deregulation of labour and other markets (Walkom, 1997). These social policy changes triggered massive protest movements. For instance, the Ontario Federation of Labour (OFL) sponsored Days of Action in most of Ontario's major cities, with participants from women's groups, unions, anti-poverty groups, and others (Munro, 1997). These were political strikes in which workers stayed 'away from their jobs not to make a point during negotiations in their own work-places or for their own contracts, but for the express purpose of making a point with an elected government' (Munro, 1997: 129). Clearly, this was not a government for the working-class people or those who were otherwise disadvantaged. As Kimberly Rogers's experiences demonstrate, this was a government whose policies helped make the rich get richer and the poor get poorer.

Social class, a structural pillar of inequality in Canadian society, influenced Kimberly Rogers's opportunities and experiences from the moment of her birth. It is not unusual, for instance, for people from working-class backgrounds to finish their education at the end of high school and to work at jobs such as bartending; their opportunities for anything else are often severely restricted. That Kimberly needed to rely on social assistance in the first place is also linked to her social class background.

This chapter considers the relationship between social class and inequality. From its inception, social class has been an important concept in sociology. Much has been written on the relationship between social class and politics and **social movements** (Curtis et al., 2004), voting behaviour (Andersen and Heath, 2002), educational attainment (Ali and Grabb, 1998), family (Bradbury, 1990; Fox, 2001; Luxton, 1980), the nature of paid work (Rinehart, 2006), the process of professionalization (Adams, 2000), health (Davies and McAlpine, 1998; Turner and Avison, 2003), income (Allahar and Côté, 1998), **race** (Allahar, 1995), **gender** (Adams, 1998), and retirement (Myles, 1989; Street and Connidis, 2001). Yet, within this body of work, there is considerable debate about what **class** is and how best to conceptualize it. Hence, the first part of this chapter deals with various conceptualizations of social class. Then we consider the ways in which social class has been measured in the sociological literature and get to a working definition of *social class*. Next we examine the relationship between social class and social inequality. Although many of the topics just listed touch on issues of inequality, it is well beyond the scope of this chapter to discuss all of them. Instead, the focus will be on paid work, education, and health. Finally, I will conclude this chapter by briefly considering an ongoing debate in sociology: Does class matter?

What Is Social Class?

Many first-year sociology students are perplexed when they discover that they are not members of the middle class, as they had been led to believe, even though their family income was sufficient to provide them with the necessities of life and a university education. Unlike lay conceptions of social class that focus on income,

OPEN FOR DISCUSSION

The Lessons of Kimberly Rogers's Death

It was sweltering hot this time last year when Kimberly Rogers, 40 years old and eight months pregnant, died in her Sudbury apartment. She was serving a six-month sentence of house arrest after pleading guilty to defrauding the Ontario Works program (she'd collected welfare while receiving student loans to cover her studies in the social services program at Cambrian College). . . .

What has society learned?

Ontario's welfare rates remain as low as they have been since they were cut by 21.6 per cent in 1995 (there hasn't even been a cost of living adjustment). A single person still receives a maximum of $520 per month.

Just months before Kimberly's death, Ontario introduced further amendments to its social assistance laws. Now, for anyone convicted of welfare fraud committed after April, 2000, there is a lifetime ban. Those convicted can never receive welfare again. Ever. Not even if they need it to survive. The fiscal savings that result from clamping down on welfare remain a greater political priority to government than the lives of citizens who are left without shelter and food.

And the Ontario government is still crowing about the success of 'workfare' in helping welfare recipients return to work. But the reality is different: Instead of integrating people into the new, knowledge-based economy, workfare is geared toward pushing people into low-paying, insecure jobs.

Still, some things have changed.

Opposition to the province's treatment of welfare recipients is growing. To date, 10 Ontario municipalities have passed resolutions to oppose the lifetime ban. Recently, the Court of Appeal determined that the province can't discriminate against welfare recipients simply because they are welfare recipients and dependent on government programs for support—in other words, a government does not have carte blanche to impose stricter conditions on welfare recipients than any other citizen. And later this year the Ontario Superior Court will consider the cases of three people who are appealing their lifetime welfare-benefit bans.

What the government did to Kimberly Rogers, it did in the name of Ontario's citizens. So her case forces all citizens to think about what kind of society we want. One that truly gives us all opportunities to participate in all aspects of society? Or one that condemns the most vulnerable to die alone? We cannot ignore these questions even if we wish to: An inquest into Kimberly Rogers's death is set to begin Oct. 7.

Source: Excerpted from JoAnne Frenschkowski, 'We've Learned Little from Kimberly Rogers's Death', *The Globe and Mail*, 9 Aug. 2002. Reprinted by permission of JoAnne Frenschkowski, staff lawyer, Income Advocacy Centre.

sociologists define *social class* in relation to the paid work that people do. The general idea that people can be members of the working class without being aware that they are is sometimes referred to as **false consciousness**. Members of the working class who are living in a state of false consciousness have not developed a revolutionary, collective sense of their plight in a capitalist world (Hunter, 1981: 47–8).

As students try to make sense of their 'new' social class, a second thing they learn about is **social structure**. In learning about social structures, students begin to understand that individuals are not poor because they are lazy or stupid but because they are not afforded the same opportunities as others. Social life does not provide a level playing field for its players. Tommy Douglas (then Premier of Saskatchewan) nicely made this point at the beginning of one of his political speeches when he said, '"Everyone for himself", yelled the elephant, as he danced among the chickens' (cited in Hunter, 1981: 211). Kimberly Rogers was a chicken. She was a straight-A student who was an ambitious and hard worker. She died, in part, because she was poor.

Time to Reflect

Should Canadians blame individuals for their poverty or should society take some responsibility for ensuring a reasonable standard of living for all?

Sociologists talk a lot about *social structures* in their work, but there is no single definition of them. Some argue that **social institutions**, such as the family and the educational system, are social structures. Others use the term *social structure* to refer to relatively long-lasting patterns that emerge among elements of society that may or may not be directly observable (Abercrombie et al., 2006). It is in the latter sense that the term **structure** is used in this chapter. Hence, *social structures* refer to how society is organized according to patterns of deeply held **beliefs**, of various **roles** and responsibilities of its members, and of sets of social behaviours. Social class may then be considered a social structure because our positioning within the social class system organizes and influences everything that we do. This idea will be developed throughout this chapter, but for now it is important to understand that the terms *social class* and *social structure* are highly interrelated.

Debates about how best to conceptualize social class stem from the sociological traditions of Karl Marx and Max Weber, both of whom arguably might be considered **conflict theorists**. The next sections consider these debates and outline the key themes that emerge from conflict and feminist accounts of social class.

Themes from Conflict Approaches to Social Class

Many of the debates about how to conceptualize social class stem from the work of Karl Marx and the subsequent critiques and elaborations of his views. Interestingly, although Marx discussed social class at length in his work,

Much inequality theory, from Marx to Weber, discusses the proletariat, or working class, but few people realize the devastating and long-lasting effects of such labour ghettoization. This working-class residence, close to Nova Scotia's defunct Sydney steel mill, captures the devastation. (CP/Andrew Vaughan)

nowhere in his writings did he provide us with a succinct definition of what he meant by *social class*. Instead, scholars have had to piece together what they think he meant by the term from the various contexts in which Marx uses the concept. A now-famous quotation from the *Communist Manifesto* is often used in such assessments. Marx and Friedrich Engels (1983 [1848]: 203–4) wrote:

> The history of all hitherto existing society is the history of class struggles. Freeman and slave, patrician and plebeian, lord and serf, guild-master and journeyman, in a word, oppressor and oppressed. . . . Our epoch, the epoch of the bourgeoisie, possesses, however, this distinctive feature: It has simplified class antagonisms. Society as a whole is more and more splitting up into two great hostile camps, into two great classes directly facing each other—bourgeoisie and proletariat.

In these few lines, Marx emphasizes two issues that are central to his work on social class: first, he argues that society is characterized more by conflict than by harmony; second, he suggests that a distinctive feature of **capitalism** is the segregation of society into two central classes.

Few conflict theorists would disagree with Marx's view that society is characterized more by conflict than by harmony. Since the onset of industrial capitalism, workers and owners have fought over working conditions, pay, benefits, required hours of work, and so on (MacDowell and Radforth, 1992; Morton, 1998). Today, struggles continue over job security within the context of globalized economies and the rights of workers in **developing countries**.

The point on which scholars disagree is whether Marx's dichotomous conception of class is—or ever was—accurate. Some argue that these two basic class divisions still exist (Braverman, 1974), while others suggest that Marx's two-class conceptualization needs elaboration (Wright, 1997). Still others argue that Marx's two-category system was simply a theoretical abstraction and that he was well aware of the presence of middling classes and of the historical complexities of class formation (Giddens, 1971). Although such debates are interesting, they are complex and, as yet, unresolved. Hence, rather than delving into debates about how many classes there currently are in Canada, it is more fruitful to discuss the themes that are central to Marxist conceptualizations of social class.

First, Marx and Marxists argue that class is a social relation. Marx believed that society is divided into social classes that are defined by their relationship to the principal **means of production** in society (Giddens, 1971; Zeitlin, 1990). *Relations of production* refers to the idea that individuals who engage in production processes have various rights and powers over the resources that are used in production processes (see Wright, 1999). Under capitalism, those who own the means of the production (the **bourgeoisie**) exploit labourers (the **proletariat**), who have little choice but to sell their **labour power** to the bourgeoisie in order to survive. For Marx, class is not an economic relation but a social one. Hence, unequal access to the rights and powers associated with productive resources are class relations (ibid.).

A second feature of Marxist accounts of class relations concerns who controls production processes (Poulantzas, 1975; Wright, 1997). *Control* refers to a specific form of authority. **Authority**, in turn, is connected to issues of **power**. More will be said on power as we move into a discussion of Weberian accounts of social class. For now, it is important to note that class relations reflect the amount of control that people have, over themselves and others, in doing the work that they do to achieve their means of subsistence. In other words, class relations reflect the relative amount of control that a person has over production processes.

Third, Marxists generally agree that **exploitation** is a central component of social class relations. According to Eric Olin Wright (Wright, 1997: 10), class-based exploitation occurs if the following criteria are met:

1. *The inverse interdependence principle.* The material welfare of one group of people causally depends upon the material deprivations of another.
2. *The exclusion principle.* The inverse interdependence in (1) depends upon the exclusion of the exploited from access to certain productive resources, usually backed by property rights.
3. *The appropriation principle.* Exclusion generates material advantage to exploiters because it enables them to appropriate the labor effort of the exploited.

If the first of these two conditions are met, 'non-exploitative economic oppression' (Wright, 1999: 11) occurs, but it is not technically a situation of class exploitation as such. Exploitation exists only when all three principles are operating simultaneously.

Note the relational component in each of these exploitation principles. Explicit in these statements is the idea that class exploitation involves **social interaction**. This interaction is structured by sets of productive social relations that serve to bind exploiters to the exploited (Wright, 1997). Class exploitation also highlights the presence of inherent conflict in class relations. Put simply, in a profit-driven capitalist system, owners want their workers to work longer and harder than the workers would freely choose to do. Hence, class conflict results, not simply over wage levels, but also over how much 'work effort' is expected (ibid., 18).

In summary, Marxist accounts of social class focus on the relationships between those who appropriate the labour of others to make a profit and those who need to sell their labour power. Furthermore, class relations may be assessed through the concepts of exploitation and control. As we have noted, control is related to power. Hence, one similarity between Marxist and Weberian scholarship, as we shall see, is that both schools agree that power is a central dimension of class relations. Weberians, however, have a somewhat different understanding of power than do Marxists, and Weberians focus more on distribution than on exploitation in their assessment of social class.

For Weber, classes are groups of people who share a common class situation. In *Economy and Society*, Weber (1978 [1908]: 57) defines *class situation* as:

> . . . [the] typical chances of material provision, external position, and personal destiny in life which depend on the degree and nature of the power, or lack of power, to dispose of goods or qualifications for employment and the ways in which, within a given economic order, such goods or qualifications for employment can be utilised as a source of income or revenue.

For Weber, class situations are market situations, and 'a class is simply an aggregate of people sharing common "situations" in the market' (Grabb, 2007: 48).

Weber further argues that there are three types of classes: property classes, income classes, and social classes. A *property class* is one in which differences in property ownership determine class situations. An *income class* is one in which 'the chances of utilising goods or services on the market determines the class situation' (Weber, 1978 [1908]: 57). A *social class* is a combination of the class situations created by property and income, whereby mobility between the social classes is a typical occurrence within either an individual lifetime or over successive generations.

Weber identified four main social classes: (1) the working class as a whole; (2) the petite bourgeoisie; (3) propertyless intellectuals, technicians, commercial workers, and officials who may be socially different from one another depending on the cost of their training; and (4) classes privileged because of property or education. Although these social class distinctions are similar to those put forth by Marx (except with regard to the emphasis on education and the cost of training), Weber employs a different method in assigning groups of individuals to each class. For Weber, the emphasis is on the distribution of resources, whereas Marx is mainly concerned with the social relations of production.

Parties and **status groups** are other pillars of social power according to Weber. By *parties*, Weber means voluntary associations that organize for the collective pursuit of interests, such as political parties or lobbying groups. **Status** reflects an individual's position in society according to the relative prestige, esteem, or honour they are afforded (Clark, 1995; Turner, 1988). Samuel Clark argues that status varies along four dimensions: differentiation, criteria, ascription, and institutionalization. The meanings of these variables are summarized in Table 15.1.

Notably, Clark argues that status is a form of power—the 'power to elicit respect' (Clark, 1995: 15). A *status group* comprises a number of individuals who share a common status situation. Status groups 'are organized to maintain or expand their social privileges by a mechanism of social closure to protect existing monopolies of the privilege against outsiders, and by usurpation to expand the benefits by reference to proximate or superior status groups' (Turner, 1988: 8). Thus, aristocrats and the Hells Angels both are examples of status groups. Although members of a particular class may not be aware of their common situation, members of a status group usually are (Giddens, 1971; Grabb, 2007). And although classes, status groups, and parties sometimes overlap, this is not always the case. In Weberian scholarship, each is analytically distinct and central to class analysis (Weber, 1978 [1908]; see also Giddens, 1971; Grabb, 2007).

Weber's assessment of status groups and parties and the analytical importance that he attaches to these multiple bases of **power** point to the fundamental difference between his analysis of class and that of Marx. According to Weber, although status groups and parties are analytically distinct from classes, they are central to class analysis (Giddens, 1971; Grabb, 2007). For Weber, *status situations* are distinct but related to class situations; this term refers to the social status, prestige, and esteem

Time to Reflect

To which social class do you belong?

Table 15.1 Samuel Clark's Status Variables

Differentiation	The extent to which status is differentiated from other kinds of power, especially economic, cultural, political, and military power.
Criteria	What characteristics or possessions are accorded status (for example, wealth, erudition, military valour, athletic ability).
Ascription	Whether status is ascribed hereditarily.
Institutionalization	The extent to which stable norms and values regulate the distribution of status and the rights and duties associated with it.

Source: Samuel Clark, *State and Status: The Rise of the State and Aristocratic Power in Western Europe* (Montreal and Kingston: McGill-Queen's University Press, 1995), 17. Reprinted by permission.

that are associated with a social position. Unlike Marx, who believed that power is held by those who own the means of production, Weber felt that certain people in high-status groups derive power by virtue of their social position rather than through economic control.

The analytical importance that Weber attaches to the concept of power is evident in the preceding discussion. Unlike Marx, who believed that power relations are structural and cannot be separated from class relations, Weber defines *power* as 'every possibility within a social relationship of imposing one's own will, even against opposition, without regard to the basis of this possibility' (1978 [1908]: 38).

He goes on to clarify this broad definition of *power* by introducing the concept of *domination*. Domination exists in **social relationships** in which one actor (or group of actors) comes to expect that his or her orders will be followed by others or a group of others. *Domination* is a specific power relation in which 'regular patterns of inequality are established whereby the subordinate group (or individual) accepts that position in a sustained arrangement, obeying the commands of the dominant group (or individual)' (Grabb, 2007: 56). Weber states that although relations of domination are usually at work within associations or in cases in which an individual has an executive staff, other non-economic situations are also characteristic of relations of domination. One of the examples Weber mentions in this regard is that the head of the household exercises domination over the members of the household 'even though he does not have an executive staff' (1978 [1908]: 39).

Three themes emerge from Weber's conceptualization of class that separate his work from that of Marx. The first is Weber's insistence that classes, class situations, parties, and status groups must all be considered if we are to understand the class structures of societies and in this he differs significantly from Marx's view. The second is Weber's emphasis on and view of power. Marx felt that power was derived from an economic base and was largely structural. Weber, on the other hand, saw power as a multi-faceted concept that could be derived from many sources and has both structural and individual dimensions. Finally, unlike the social-relational approach to class in Marxist sociology, Weber focuses far more on distributional issues. For Weber, the ability of people to gain access to scarce resources such as income and education is central to class analysis.

Drawing on Weberian scholarship, Canadian sociologist Edward Grabb's work on social inequality and social class is worth considering. According to Grabb power is the 'differential capacity to command resources, which gives rise to structured asymmetric relations of domination and subordination among social actors' (2007: 211). In an elaborate scheme of power, domination, and social inequality, Grabb suggests that there are three means of power—control of material resources, control of people, and control of ideas—which correspond primarily with economic structures, political structures, and ideological structures respectively (see Figure 15.1). These structures of power are intersected by class and non-class bases of inequality that represent the 'human content' of power relations.

Grabb defines *class* on the basis of ownership, education, and occupation. For Grabb, these factors represent a synthesis of the key concepts in class analysis. *Ownership* includes ownership of property but also material possessions and income. *Education* comprises credentials and knowledge. *Occupation* includes distinctions such as manual versus non-manual labour, but also includes issues of skill. Grabb further suggests that, although classes should not be considered in static terms because they vary over time and space (that is, historically and in different regions and countries), there tend to be three main class categories in modern capitalist systems: an upper class, a heterogeneous central category, and a working class. Grabb defines the *working class* as those who do not own capital, who have no special skills or credentials, and who sell their labour to make a living. The *upper class* is made up mostly of capital owners, although individuals with significant political or ideological power fall into this category as well. The *middle class* is a diverse group that may or may not have limited ownership but that is mostly distinguishable from the working class on the basis of credentials.

According to Grabb, the means of power (economic, political, and ideological) are differentially distributed along class lines. Of course, people in the upper classes control the means of material production or the economic structure by virtue of their ownership of the means of production. Middle classes may have some economic power depending on whether their incomes are sufficient to purchase desirable consumer goods and to the extent that their occupation confers upon them a certain amount of authority or autonomy. And working classes tend not to have economic power at all. In Grabb's scheme, class also crosses political and ideological structures of power. Hence, those in the upper class, by virtue of their capital, high levels of education, and good occupations, tend to control political and ideological institutions such as the judiciary and educational systems. Those in the working class tend not to have ideological or political power, and those in the middle vary in the extent to which they hold such power, again on the basis of class-related factors.

Grabb's work holds a great deal of appeal to those who assume that Marxist conceptions of social class do not go far enough in explaining social inequality and that social inequality is, instead, a multi-faceted phenomenon. Why? Because the central focus in his framework is on power, not class. The inherent problem with theories of inequality that begin with issues of class is that other bases of inequality, such as gender, race, **ethnicity**, and age, carry less theoretical significance. Indeed, **feminist** scholarship has been critical of the literature on social class for this reason.

Feminist Approaches to Social Class

Many theorists have worked to perfect the concept of social class. Researchers strive for a specific delineation of social class that corrects what they see as limitations in the classical work. But except among feminist sociologists and

Figure 15.1 Edward Grabb's Theoretical Framework on Social Inequality

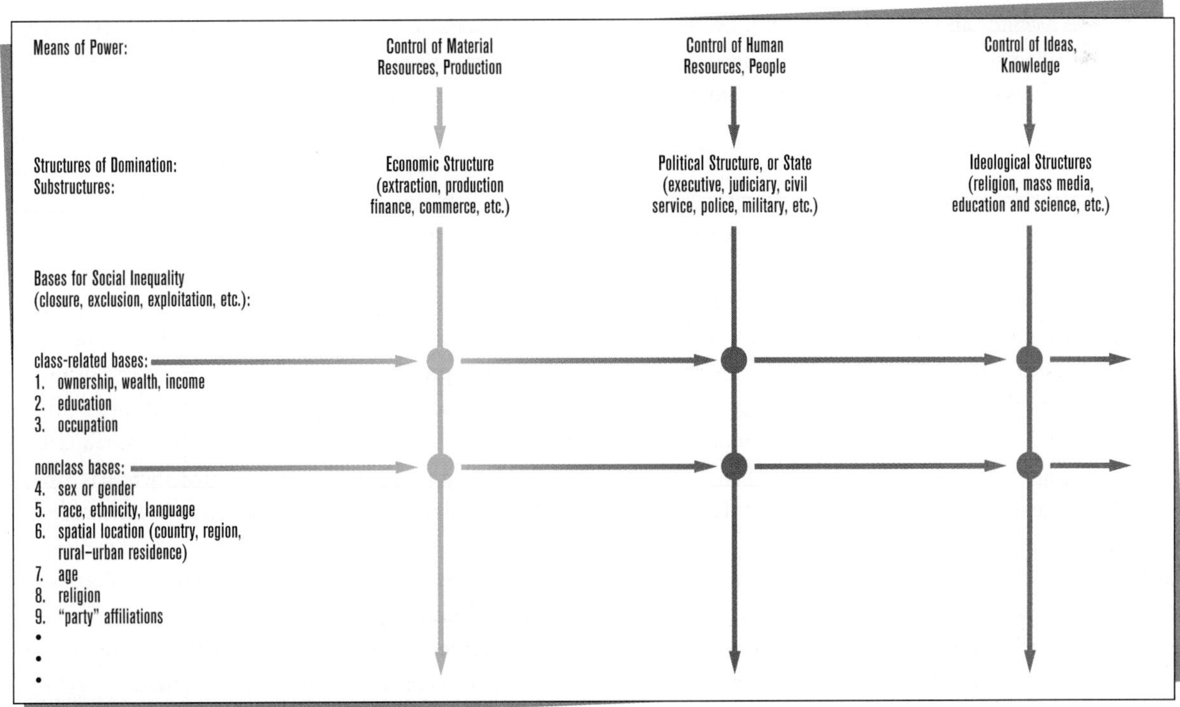

Source: 'The Major Means of Power, Structures of Domination, and Bases for Social Inequality' from *Theories of Social Inequality*, Fourth Edition, by Edward Grabb. © 2002. Reprinted with permission of Nelson, a division of Thomson Learning: www.thomsonrights.com. Fax 800-730-2215.

a few others (for example, Carroll, 1987; Cuneo, 1985), the exclusion of women and gender from class analysis has not traditionally been considered a theoretical limitation. Rather, if the social class of women is mentioned at all, it has been assessed using categories of analysis that were established to study men (Fox, 1989). Unwaged wives are assumed to take on their husband's social class, whereas women involved in the paid labour force are classed like men in what is assumed to be a gender-neutral class system (Acker, 1980, 1988, 1990; Fox, 1989).

Indeed, gender relations are intertwined with class relations in modern industrial capitalism. Particularly telling are the following research findings: (1) Housework and child care, which women are primarily responsible for, are productive activities that are important for capitalist production (Fox, ed., 1980). Hence, 'ignoring gender relations in general, and household labour in particular, produces distorted analyses of "the economy"' (Fox, 1989: 123). (2) Women are segregated into low-paying jobs both across and within broad occupational classifications (Bielby and Baron, 1984; Fox and Fox, 1986, 1987). (3) This segregation cannot be explained by status-attainment variables (England, 1982; England et al., 1988). (4) Often, the relations between men and women at work are antagonistic (Cockburn, 1983; Milkman, 1987). And (5) the responsibilities that women have to their families are inextricably bound to their work lives: wives are more likely than husbands to work at home or to take time off from work to care for a sick child (Hochschild and Machung, 1989; Michelson, 1983), and their wages are influenced by the amount of time they spend engaged in household labour (Coverman, 1983; Shelton and Firestone, 1989).

Although this research demonstrates the prevalence of gender inequality within capitalism, feminists disagree over how these findings should be interpreted. Specifically, there is a theoretical debate among feminists over whether **patriarchy** (male dominance) and capitalism are two systems of oppression that serve to subordinate women (this is called *dual-systems theory*) or whether women's oppression can be best understood by theorizing about a single system of inequality that simultaneously considers gender and social class relations. Patriarchy, an essential concept in dual-systems theories (see Hartmann, 1981), is at the heart of the feminist debates over the appropriateness of single and dual-systems approaches.

Patriarchy refers to 'the system of practices, arrangements and social relations that ensure biological reproduction, child rearing, and the reproduction of gendered subjectivity' (Fox, 1988: 175). The term *patriarchy* and the study of it has served a useful purpose in feminist theory because it gave women (although arguably only white, middle-class women) a political voice and also because it corrected some of the flaws of omission that were prevalent in social theory before the 1970s (that is, women were generally invisible; Acker, 1989). However, the concept of patriarchy is limiting in several respects.

Radical feminists conceptualize patriarchy as a 'universal, trans-historical and trans-cultural phenomenon; women were everywhere oppressed by men in more or less the same ways' (ibid., 235). The tendency in this view is to reduce male oppression of women to biological essentialism, and it is limiting because it does not consider historical or contemporary variations in women's situations (ibid.). In light of these problems, dual-systems theorists attempted to conceptualize a system of patriarchy that was linked to household production. The tendency in this approach was to view patriarchy as a system of domination that operates alongside and interacts with the political-economic system. The roots of patriarchy are thought to be located within the reproductive sphere of the family, whereas the roots of the political-economic system are located in the **mode of production** (ibid.; Fox, 1989). Thus, although surprising given its Marxist roots, this perspective considers gender in a more Weberian manner, as one of several sources of inequality.

Recognizing these problems, some feminists have argued against using the concept of patriarchy (Acker, 1989; Fox, 1988). These researchers argue for a single-system approach whereby the oppression of women cannot be separated from issues of social class. This requires a reconceptualization of social class that adequately considers gendered processes as they structure the class system (Acker, 1988, 1990; Fox, 1989).

Taking issue with dual-systems theory, Joan Acker, for instance, sets out to develop a single-system theory of social relations that places equal emphasis on gender and social class. According to Acker, this requires a reformulation of Marx's conception of class that is best done by taking the social relations of distribution as well as the social relations of production into account. Relations of distribution 'are sequences of linked actions through which people share the necessities of survival' (Acker, 1988: 478). According to Acker, the fact that there has always been a sexual division of labour suggests that in all known societies, the relations of distribution are influenced by gender and take on a gendered meaning. Gendered relations of distribution in capitalist society are historically rooted and they are transformed (like the relations of production) as the means of production change.

Acker suggests that the wage, which is rooted in the relations of production, is the essential component of distribution in capitalist society. The wage has developed historically as a gendered phenomenon because women have always been paid less than men and because gendered job segregation is typical. Thus, 'the wage and the work contexts within which it is earned are gendered in ways that re-create women's relative disadvantage' (ibid., 483).

Personal relations, marital relations, and state relations are the gendered processes through which distribution occurs. According to Acker, *personal relations of distribution* are held together by emotional bonds, usually between blood relatives, and are dependent on the wage. As a result of both the gender-based division of labour and the **ideology** of the family wage, gender serves to organize the personal relations of distribution. In its simplest form, this system requires that at least part of the male wage is distributed to women, who then redistribute it to the dependents in their families. The personal relations of distribution also often extend beyond the household. In instances where economic hardships are typical, women often maintain extensive kinship networks by means of which survival is ensured through the allocation of resources across households. Among the economically advantaged, gender-based personal relations of distribution also occur, helping to ensure the stability and reproduction of class.

Marital relations are the central component of distribution for married women who do not work for pay and are thus dependent on their husbands for their wage. According to Acker, unwaged housewives are connected to the production process through their husbands' wages. Although they share common standards of living with their husbands, they do not assume the same class because their situations, experiences, and activities are different. Unwaged wives have little control over their economic situation, although Acker suggests that this control likely varies by the men's and women's class.

State relations of distribution are the final type of distribution arrangement that Acker considers. The state relations of distribution are based in laws and governmental policies that have historically been developed in gendered ways. Policies and laws, established to alleviate the financial burden of the working class when the market fails, are based on gendered ideologies supporting the 'male breadwinner/dependent housewife' ideal. This renders some groups of women—those who remain unmarried, single mothers, poor working women—particularly disadvantaged. Women are further disadvantaged by the gendered nature of entitlement regulations because many social security programs are based on the labour force experiences of men.

For Acker, the culmination of these gendered relations structures social class. Conceptualizing class in this way allows unwaged persons to be included in the class structure. According to Acker, the aim of class analysis should not be to classify people into different categories; rather, class should be considered as 'processes that produce contradiction, conflict, and different life experiences' (ibid., 496). Thus, to fully understand the 'links between gender and class, divisions must be changed. One way to do this is to see class as rooted in relations of distribution (as well as in relations of production) that necessarily embed gender, both as ideology and material inequality' (ibid.).

Acker (2000) expands her analysis to include race and ethnic relations. Acker argues that to fully understand how class is gendered and racialized, a rethinking of class is necessary. This rethinking, according to Acker, should be informed first by a concept of class anchored within a larger notion of the economic than is now used' (2000: 54). This idea corresponds with Acker's promotion of a conceptualization of class whereby class relations encompass relations of distribution and production. Second, class, gender, race, and ethnicity must be understood from the standpoints of many different people within these categories (see Smith, 1987). In other words, the experiences of men and women of different classes and of different racial and ethnic groups need to inform class analysis. Third, class is not simply an abstraction into which people can be placed. Rather, it is an 'active accomplishment' (Acker, 2000: 53). Everything that people do and say is influenced by their class relations. Class is accomplished by people in interaction with one another. And fourth, class, race and ethnicity, and gender mutually constitute one another. That is, through structural processes and through processes of cultural representation and social interaction, race and ethnicity, class, and gender shape one another; they cannot be considered separately. **Identity** and meaning are not shaped simply by whether one is not a man or black or middle class, but by the interacting influence of all three of these things (see also Glenn, 2000).

To summarize, a central problem in much of the traditional class analysis and the key point of the feminist critique of social class is that the study of class has focused far too much on the relations of production (Acker, 1988, 2000). Feminist scholars argue that class relations are social relations that extend beyond the arena of production and that Marxist approaches that conceptualize social class simply as a relation of production are too restrictive. This is true, in part, because traditional class analysis excludes far too many people who are not directly linked to production processes, such as homemakers and retired individuals. Notably, scholars have tried to reconcile this problem by attributing the social class of homemakers to husbands and by assigning a class to retired persons based on their pre-retirement status. However, these approaches are unsatisfactory because they do not capture important distributive and status differences between a housewife and her husband or between a retired autoworker and her employed counterpart (see Acker, 1988; Estes, 1999).

With these caveats in mind, the remainder of this chapter will nonetheless focus on social class as it has been traditionally defined and conceptualized. The difficulties associated with rethinking social class in light of gender, race, ethnic, and age relations are far too complex for an introductory chapter on social class and inequality. Readers should refer to the chapters on gender, ethnicity, and race for more detail about how these factors structure social inequality.

Defining and Measuring Social Class

Researchers study social class using both quantitative and qualitative methods. Qualitative approaches to social class often draw on the insights of **symbolic interactionism** and place emphasis on issues of meaning, experience, and identity. Such assessments do not attempt to succinctly categorize people into various classes but instead are concerned with the meaning, identity, and experiences of one class in relation to another. Qualitative historical work, for instance, has examined processes of class formation (Comninel, 1987) and how class relations structure professionalization projects (Adams, 1998, 2000). Using observation or in-depth interviewing techniques, other studies have explored the meaning and experiences of class relations in workplaces (Gannagé, 1986; Reiter, 1996; Rinehart et al., 1994) and in schools (Willis, 1977).

Quantitative work on social class tends to focus either on how class affects various outcomes of social inequality or on how the class structure has changed over time. Social class is defined differently depending on which of these particular focuses is at the heart of the research. In work on social inequality, for instance, proxies of social class (that is, such factors as income, education, and occupation that indirectly measure social class) derived from **structural functionalist** approaches to stratification, tend to be used.

Social stratification approaches to social class have been very influential, particularly in American sociology. Stratification approaches conceptualize inequality as a hierarchical order (Davis and Moore, 1945) in which individuals are grouped into strata on the basis of their socio-economic status (SES) as measured through indicators such as income, education, or occupation. As a result, inequality tends to be conceptualized at the level of individual difference rather than in relational terms or on the basis of class structures (Grabb, 2007; Tilly, 1998).

Traditionally, stratification approaches have assumed that the rank ordering of people into socially defined strata is a universal and functionally necessary dimension of society (Davis and Moore, 1945). In other words, an ordering of people according to their worth, variously defined, is required for the smooth functioning of society. Certain positions in society are more valued than others because of the high level of skill that is attached to them. Only a few people can attain the skills required to fulfill these positions, and such attainment requires significant time commitment for the appropriate training. People who choose to invest the time in such training deserve higher-status positions in society and the resultant rewards attached to these positions. Furthermore, there is general agreement or consensus among the members of society that such stratification systems are acceptable (ibid.).

There are two underlying assumptions in stratification research that set it apart from the Marxist or Weberian approaches to inequality. First, is the tendency in stratification research to overemphasize the extent to which society operates on the basis of consensus rather than conflict. Second, and related to the first, is the under-emphasis in stratification research on issues of power and exploitation (see Grabb, 2007, for an extensive discussion of these issues).

The identification of problematic assumptions in stratification research has not, however, led to its demise.

Time to Reflect

Which do you believe contributed more to Kimberly Rogers's disadvantaged situation, gender or social class? Explain.

Instead, it remains influential in studies of inequality and informs much empirical research on the subject. Michael Grimes (1991) argues that many researchers apply stratification measures to the study of class inequality either because they remain committed to certain aspects of functionalist thought or because stratification measures are often used in large surveys. It is important to clarify that stratification researchers do not suggest that they are studying class; class researchers, although they sometimes do stratification research, make the distinction between the two (Grabb, 2007). The point that Grimes makes is nonetheless an important one and stems, perhaps, from a more general observation that researchers whose primary interest lies outside of class and stratification analysis tend to convolute the two approaches. This propensity is most likely a result of the significant overlap between the various social factors that are examined in these approaches. For instance, occupation, defined in various ways, tends to be at the core of research on social class regardless of theoretical perspective. Further, there is a general concern in all conceptual frameworks about the distribution of scarce resources such as income, education, and skill. Hence, the tendency to use stratification measures as indicators of social class likely stems from the continued use of traditional measurements in survey research and also from the fact that the indicators of social class are quite similar, regardless of theoretical perspective.

There is little doubt that stratification measures tell us something about class-based inequality. However, these indicators cannot fully capture the extent to which social class matters in contemporary Canadian society. Instead, a relational understanding of social class is necessary. Such an understanding of social class follows a long tradition in Marxist sociology that suggests that class is not merely an economic relation. Rather, social class manifests itself as people from various classes interact with one another in productive relations. Researchers who are concerned with the macro implications of the organization of the social relations of production **operationalize** social class using concepts such as power, exploitation, oppression, property ownership, and so on that are central in Marxist and Weberian scholarship.

Wright's work is an example of how social class can be assessed quantitatively in this way. For the past 20 years, Wright and his colleagues have been developing a typology of social class that relies on measures of occupation, authority, skill, and the number of employees who work at a particular locale (see Figure 15.2). This latter classification category reflects the number of people who are under the authority of each particular class location. For example, managers tend to have many employees over which they have authority and dominance, while non-managers have authority over no one. Owners are separated from employees in this scheme and are differentiated from one another only on the basis of how many employees they have. Hence, owners who have only a few employees are thought to be different from those who have many and from those who have none. Employees, on the other hand, are differentiated on the basis of number of other employees, skills, and authority. Expert managers have high levels of authority and of skill and tend to supervise many employees. They stand in most stark contrast to non-skilled workers, who have no authority or skill and who supervise no employees.

In this typology, the cells do not represent classes as such, but rather refer to class locations within the capitalist class structure. The distinction here is a subtle but important one that allows Wright to cover all of his bases. Unlike an earlier version of this framework, in which he refers to the various groupings in this model as classes (Wright, 1985), in his more recent work (Wright, 1997, 1999) he makes it clear that these cells represent class locations within an overriding framework of class relations. By doing this, Wright can stay true to a Marxist version of class relations in which exploitation is at the core, and at the same time identify contradictory places within class relations that individuals occupy.

Class has thus been used in many ways in sociological thought. For the purpose of this chapter, stratification measures will be used to assess the relationship between social class and each of income, education, and health. To assess class structure, a modified, more parsimonious version of Wright's conceptualization, as it is put forth by Wallace Clement and John Myles (1994) will be used. Clement and Myles develop a four-class model in which the *capitalist-executive class* controls both the labour power of others and the means of production (see Table 15.2). The *old middle class*—the 'petite bourgeoisie' in Marxist terminology—commands the means of production but not the labour power of others. The *new middle class* controls the labour power of others but not the means of production. And, finally, the *working class* commands neither the labour power of others nor the means of production. The advantage of this approach to social class lies in its simplicity; it accurately reflects the 'relations of ruling' in Canada while at the same time eliminating the unnecessary and often tedious class location distinctions that are contained within Wright's approach.

Figure 15.2 Eric Olin Wright's Class Divisions

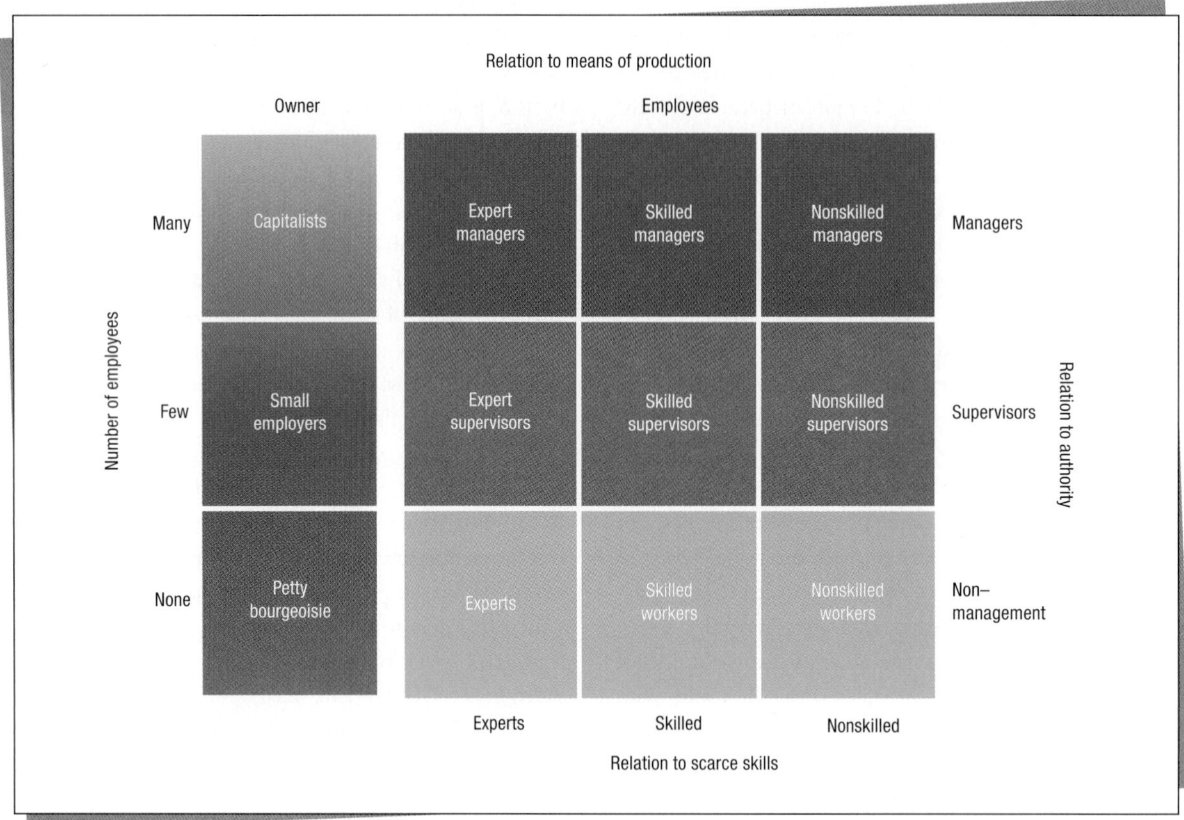

Source: 'Relation to means of production' from *Class Counts: Comparative Studies in Class Analysis* by Erik Olin Wright (Cambridge: Cambridge University Press, 1997). Copyright © Maison des Sciences de l'Homme and Cambridge University Press. Reprinted with the permission of Cambridge University Press.

Social Class and Inequality

Social inequality reflects relatively long-lasting differences between individuals or groups of people that have substantial implications for individual lives, especially 'for the rights or opportunities they exercise and the rewards or privileges they enjoy' (Grabb, 2007: 1; see also Pampel, 1998). So, for example, people who are a part of the working class earn less money, have less fulfilling jobs, do not have the same educational opportunities available to them, and have worse health than do people from the middle and upper classes. The next sec-

Table 15.2 Clement and Myles's Conceptualization of Social Class

	Command Labour Power of Others	
Command Means of Production	Yes	No
Yes	Capitalist-executive	Old middle class
No	New middle class	Working class

Source: Wallace Clement and John Myles, *Relations of Ruling: Class and Gender in Postindustrial Societies* (Montreal: McGill-Queen's University Press, 1994), 16.

tions consider the relationship between social class and each of paid work, education, and health.

Paid Work, Income, and Poverty

Marx argued that as capitalism evolved, there would be an increasing polarization of workers into two central classes, the proletariat and the bourgeoisie. This polarization would involve at least three things: (1) a reduction in the proportion of small business owners and hence a shrinking of the old middle class; (2) increasing proportions of income going to the owners of large businesses and a reduction in the earnings of middle-class workers; and (3) continued deskilling of work and corresponding increases in the **alienation** of workers (Conley, 2004). We will consider each of these issues.

Class Structure in Canada

According to Clement and Myles's definition of social class, a slight majority of employed Canadians in the early 1980s formed the working class (57.6 per cent); almost 25 per cent formed the new middle class, 11.3 per cent the old middle class, and 6.2 per cent the capitalist-executive class (1994: 19).

Since the early twentieth century, the proportion of Canada's class structure comprising small business owners has declined considerably (Clement and Myles, 1994). Between the 1930s and the early 1970s, for instance, the proportion of the workforce comprising small business owners declined from approximately 25 per cent to between 10 and 12 per cent (Conley, 2004). Much of this decline occurred in the agricultural sector, where advances in farm technology made small-farm business unprofitable (Clement and Myles, 1994; Conley, 2004). Nonetheless, for much of the twentieth century it appeared that Marx's prediction regarding the shrinking middle class was right.

Since the mid-1970s, however, this trend has reversed. Indeed, the most significant change in the class structure over the past 20 years in particular has been the

Graffiti protesting health-care cuts is painted on a fence outside the demolition of Wellesley Hospital in Toronto. Many Canadians fear the dismantling of medicare and growth of private medicine. Yet, even with medicare, income, status, and class advantages lead to better health outcomes. (CP/Kevin Frayer)

increase in the proportion of the class structure held by the old middle class. Clement and Myles report that the level of non-agricultural self-employment increased from 5.8 per cent in 1975 to 7.4 per cent in 1990 (1994: 42). When self-employed owners of incorporated businesses are included in this measure, the old middle class made up about 14 per cent of the total labour force in the early 1980s (Lin et al., 1999: 15). By 1997, 17.8 per cent of the total labour force was self-employed in both incorporated and unincorporated businesses (ibid.). The majority of those who are self-employed either work on their own or hire fewer than three employees (Clement and Myles, 1994: 49; Hughes, 1999).

Reactions to recent increases in the proportion of employed Canadians who primarily constitute the old middle class have been mixed. On the one hand, some hail these changes as positive. According to this school of thought, small business owners are free of the control of large capitalist enterprises and as a result have more autonomy in their work. Their conditions of work are less alienating, and this is a positive development of post-industrial capitalism. Others have argued that, far from being a positive occurrence, the rise of small business owners is the result of workplace restructuring whereby workers lose their jobs and are forced to earn a living without some of the rewards (such as pensions and benefits) that are associated with employment in large companies (see Clement and Myles, 1994, for an overview of these opinions). This suggests that the conditions under which one becomes a small business owner are important considerations when discussing the social implications associated with higher proportions of workers in the 'old' middle class.

Notably, the old middle class still includes a relatively small proportion of employed workers. Workers in the new middle class and the working class encompass the overwhelming majority in the Canadian class structure—82.5 per cent, according to Clement and Myles (ibid., 19). The next two sections consider the income, skill, and alienation that are associated with these classes.

Income and Poverty

There is a strong correlation between social class and income. Working-class jobs pay less than middle-class jobs, and owners of capital tend to have higher incomes than others (Krahn et al., 2007). For instance, in 2000, average annual earnings in Canada for dentists ($108,034), lawyers ($94,731), and managers ($61,412 in 2004) were much higher than were the average annual earnings for cashiers ($10,051), hotel clerks ($15,937), and hairstylists ($17,390) (ibid., 109). These earnings stand in stark contrast to the incomes of the chief executive officers (CEOs) of large companies. In 2004, the average compensation package for the CEOs of 160 Canadian companies listed on the Toronto Stock Exchange was $5.5 million (ibid., 111). Notably, a strong correlation between social class and income does not mean that it is a perfect correlation. There are certain jobs that, based on the definitions of social class defined above, would be considered working-class jobs even though they command a relatively high wage. For example, assembly-line workers in any of the 'Big Three' auto manufacturing plants are part of the working class, but because they are members of a relatively strong union they are paid a good wage and have good benefits.

Owners and executives of capital clearly have much higher incomes than do workers. The question that remains unanswered is whether there has been an increasing polarization of income over time. One way to address this issue is to divide Canadians into equal groups (typically either deciles or quintiles) on the basis of their income, calculate the proportion of the total income in Canada that each group accounts for, and then examine whether that proportion changed over time. In 1999, 45.3 per cent of all before-tax income was concentrated in the top quintile of the Canadian population, 24.3 per cent in the fourth quintile, 16.1 per cent in the third (middle) quintile, 10 per cent in the second quintile, and only 4.4 per cent in the lowest quintile. Between 1951 and 1999, there was a 3.0 per cent shift from the second and third quintiles to the two highest quintiles, while the proportion of income concentrated in the lowest quintile remained relatively stable. Moreover, between 1981 and 1999, the second, third, and fourth quintiles lost 3.6 per cent of their before-tax income, a total of $15 billion, to the upper quintile (Urmetzer and Guppy, 2004: 78). These figures support the idea that there is increasing polarization of income in Canada.

The proportion of total before-tax income that is concentrated in the lowest quintile has remained relatively stable since 1951. What these figures do not tell us is that this stability has been maintained largely through government transfers such as tax credits, social assistance, and unemployment insurance. Indeed, for low-income families, the proportion of their total income from labour market earnings has declined since the 1970s (Picot and Myles, 1995). Hence, income polarization is not as serious as it could be because government policies are in place to ensure more equitable income distributions in Canada (Ross et al., 2000). But how equitable is a system in which the lowest quintile receives only 4.4 per cent of all before-tax income? And how equitable is a system in which the $15 billion gain made in the upper quintile during the 1980s and 1990s is equivalent to the amount of money it would take to eliminate poverty in Canada (Osberg, 1992)?

Poverty is a serious social problem in Canada. The National Council of Welfare reports that since a peak at 20.6 per cent in 1996, there were five consecutive years of declines in the poverty rate for all persons; a 12-year low of 15.5 per cent was set in 2001. In 2003, 15.9 per cent of Canadians lived in poverty; poverty rates for families are 12 per cent, and for unattached individuals they are 38 per cent (National Council of Welfare, 2006: 7).

HUMAN DIVERSITY

Images of Child Poverty in Canada

Dirty, bare feet dangle over a licence plate in Prince Albert, Sask. A child plays with a lone tricycle on a cracked driveway in Winnipeg.

Those are images of some of the 1.3 million children in Canada who live in poverty, whose existence a group called PhotoSensitive is documenting in a cross-Canada exhibit.

The show was launched yesterday, in conjunction with a report on child poverty, released by Campaign 2000, that says nearly one in five children [was] living in poverty in 1999, compared with one in seven in 1989.

Campaign 2000 is a coalition of organizations formed to ensure that a 1989 House of Commons resolution to end child poverty by 2000 was implemented, a result still far from being realized, co-ordinator Laurel Rothman said.

'We are no closer [to ending child poverty]', she said. 'In 1989, we were at one in seven children living in poverty. Now we're at almost one in five.'

Ms Rothman said what is disturbing is that child poverty was prevalent even during the economic prosperity of the late 1990s.

'Governments have the option in the boom years of investing in children. Instead they took the strategy of cutting taxes, and in many cases, social services.'

The report says that despite a strong economy between 1998 and 1999, the child-poverty rate dropped only slightly to 18.5 per cent from 19 per cent. And with the latest economic downturn, 'those numbers are going to rocket up again', Ms Rothman said.

One positive number in the bulletin is the decrease in the depth of poverty, said Andrew Jackson, research director for the Canadian Council on Social Development, which compiled the data from several Statistics Canada studies.

Samantha naps in the attic apartment she shares with her mother and three brothers in Edmonton.They will be moving soon. (Chris Schwarz)

In 1999, poor families saw an improvement of more than $500 in their depth of poverty over the previous year (to $9,073 below the poverty line in 1999 from $9,597 in 1998), but the gap between the rich and the poor in Canada is still far too wide, Ms Rothman said.

The report makes several recommendations to government, including the development of a national housing strategy.

And the photographs by the 24 members of PhotoSensitive remind people of the 'faces behind the numbers', Andrew Stawicki, photographer and founder of PhotoSensitive, said.

Source: Allison Dunfield, 'In 1989 We Were at One in Seven Children Living in Poverty. Now We're at Almost One in Five', *Globe and Mail*, 27 Nov. 2001, A11. Reprinted with permission from *The Globe and Mail*.

Poverty rates vary on the basis of gender, family status, age, immigrant and minority status, health, education, and labour-force attachment. For instance, in 2003, the poverty rate for single-parent mothers was 48.9 per cent—more than four times the poverty rate for all families (ibid., 12). Unattached women under the age of 65 are more likely to live in poverty than are their male counterparts (42.8 per cent versus 34.4 per cent), as are unattached women who are aged 65 and over (40.9 per cent versus 31.6 per cent) (ibid., 13). Children (17.6 per cent) and the elderly (15.1 per cent) are somewhat more likely to be poor than are all Canadians (15.9 per cent) (ibid., 8-10).

Gainful employment significantly reduces poverty rates among both unattached individuals and families. Yet more than 30 per cent of families who were living in poverty in 2003 were headed by people who were employed (ibid., 5). The poverty rate for single-parent mothers who worked was 43.1 per cent (ibid., 97). According to the 1996 census, some of the highest rates of poverty are found among Aboriginal peoples (43.4 per cent), members of visible minority groups (35.9 per cent) and persons with disabilities (30.8 per cent) (Ross et al., 2000).

Poverty rates also vary from province to province. In 2003, British Columbia had the highest poverty rate (20.1 per cent), followed by Newfoundland and Labrador (17.3 per cent) and Manitoba and Quebec (both 16.9 per cent). Prince Edward Island had the lowest poverty rate (11.8 per cent), followed by Ontario (14.3 per cent) and Alberta (14.6 per cent). (National Council of Welfare, 2006: 24). Provincial variations in poverty rates are a result of regional differences in economic structures, provincial inconsistencies in government policies regarding social welfare transfers, and access to other social and economic resources (ibid.).

Good Jobs/Bad Jobs

You will recall that Marx's third prediction with respect to the polarization of classes was that as capitalism developed, jobs would become increasingly deskilled and alienated. Indeed, skill and alienation are two characteristics of paid work that vary depending on social class. Generally, working-class jobs are characterized by low levels of skill required to do the job and by often corresponding high levels of alienation, whereas jobs held by those in the 'new middle class' and the 'old middle class' tend to require more skill and to be more intrinsically rewarding. That said, for Marx's prediction to be supported, we must see evidence that middle-class jobs have become increasingly deskilled.

In 1974, Harry Braverman published his classic book *Labor and Monopoly Capitalism*. Taking issue with those who argued that rising white-collar employment was a positive effect of post-industrialism that resulted in an increasingly large middle class, Braverman convincingly argued that most white-collar jobs (such as clerical and retail jobs) should be considered working-class, not middle-class. White-collar jobs, Braverman argued, were increasingly being deskilled and organized according to **scientific management** techniques, thereby eliminating most of the control and autonomy that workers may have had over their work. Advances in new technologies contributed to this process by giving managers sophisticated tools through which they can monitor their employees' work. For example, before the advent of computerized cash registers, cashiers needed to know how to make change. Now cash registers inform cashiers how much change they need to give a customer. Further, cash registers can now monitor the speed of keystrokes and the number of customers that a cashier serves per hour. Managers, in turn, use this information in employee job-performance evaluations. Hence, new technology has been used to both deskill the work process and to monitor and control it.

One year before Braverman published his book, Daniel Bell published what was to become an influential text on post-industrial society. Unlike Braverman, who argued that occupations were becoming increasingly deskilled, Bell (1973) looked to the future and argued that knowledge, and hence skill, would become a highly valued commodity in post-industrial society. According to Bell, knowledge would be a basis of power much as the ownership of property had traditionally been, and knowledge workers would form a significant class (both in number and in power) in their own right. Bell argued that as the proportion of knowledge workers grew, the historical trend towards the polarization of society into

Time to Reflect

Do you think that your university education will protect you from poverty?

two central classes, the bourgeoisie and the proletariat, would lose speed.

In the more than 30 years since Bell and Braverman published their books, debates have ensued over which thesis better explains the relationship between skill and class structure in post-industrial society. Although such debates are far from being resolved, Clement and Myles (1994: 72) note that the debate has unfolded as follows:

> We face either a postindustrial Nirvana of knowledge where everyone will be a brain surgeon, artist, or philosopher (Bell) or, alternatively, a post-industrial Hades where we shall be doomed to labour mindlessly in the service of capital (Braverman). When drawn in these terms, the historical debate is now no debate at all. Bell is the clear winner. Although much less than a knowledge revolution, the net result of the shift to services has been to increase the requirements for people to think on the job.

In Canada, 42 per cent of jobs in the post-industrial service sector are skilled compared to only 26 per cent of those in the goods and distribution sector. And 55 per cent of 'new middle class' jobs are skilled, compared to only 23 per cent of working-class jobs (ibid., 76). Clement and Myles point out that the growth in the service sector has brought both skilled and unskilled jobs, but they underscore the fact that in Canada and the United States, often unskilled service jobs are entry jobs for new workers rather than serving as a basis for working-class formation. This—combined with the fact that these service jobs are now often exit jobs for older workers who have been displaced, discouraged, restructured, or retired early—suggests that age may play a more significant role in labour market inequality in the years to come. Nonetheless, the point is that although the conditions of work in contemporary Canadian capitalism are far from ideal, the proletarianization of the labour force as predicted by Braverman has not occurred even though skilled jobs are concentrated in the new middle and executive classes (ibid.).

In summary, considering debates about the deskilling of work in post-industrial capitalism, about whether the middle class is shrinking, and about the distribution of income and poverty, there is no consensus among sociologists about whether the class structure of Canadian society has become increasingly polarized. On the one hand, overall increases in the skill levels associated with many jobs and recent increases in self-employed small business owners suggests that the polarization thesis is incorrect. On the other hand, huge inequities in the distribution of income in Canada cannot be ignored. Furthermore, regardless of where one comes down on the debate about overall class polarization, the fact is that compared to 'middle-class' jobs, working-class jobs are characterized by low levels of income and other benefits, low levels of autonomy and control in the work process, poor working conditions, low levels of skill, and high levels of alienation. The combination of these things creates social disadvantage for members of the working class relative to members of the middle classes, which carries over to other social domains. Education and health are two areas of sociological study that stand out as sites of class-based inequality.

Education

Many Canadians believe that education is a vehicle through which occupational and income advantages may be attained (Wotherspoon, 2004). Over the last 30 years, more education has come to be required to perform jobs that were done well without as much education in years past (for example, needing a high school degree to work at an auto manufacturing plant). But regardless of this 'credential inflation' (Baer, 2004), there remain strong correlations between education, occupation, and income in Canada (Hunter and Leiper, 1993).

Typically, highly educated people are employed in well-paid jobs (Little, 1995) that have relatively high degrees of autonomy and authority associated with them (Butlin and Oderkirk, 1996). Of course, we have all either heard about or met a taxi driver who holds a Ph.D. or a high school dropout who is the well-paid owner of a successful business. These examples illustrate that, just as with grammar, there are exceptions to the rules. Often, other extraneous factors account for these exceptions. For instance, in the case of the well-educated taxi driver, recent immigration status may affect his or

Time to Reflect

What kind of job do you want after you graduate? Is it a good job or a bad job?

her job prospects because of discriminatory hiring criteria (for example, a hiring requirement of Canadian education or work experience).

In light of the relationship between educational attainment and economic advantage, sociologists have long been concerned with the social determinants of educational attainment. Social class background, usually measured using SES indicators, is one such determinant. Two key measures of educational attainment are often considered in this regard: (1) whether young people complete high school and (2) whether young people continue with post-secondary education.

On average, Canadians are among the most educated people in the world (Looker and Lowe, 2001). High school completion rates continued to increase throughout the 1990s such that only 12 per cent of 20-year-olds did not complete high school in 1999, as compared to 18 per cent in 1991 (Bowlby and McMullen, 2002). The more educated parents are, the more likely their children are to complete high school (ibid.). Figure 15.3 shows data for 18- to 20-year-olds from the Canadian 2000 Youth in Transition Survey. Here we see that the highest proportion of both high school graduates (34.7 per cent) and high school dropouts (45.2 per cent) have at least one parent who graduated from high school. However, among those who have at least one parent who has completed either a college or a university program, the proportion of graduates is twice the proportion of dropouts (56.6 per cent versus 27.9 per cent). Among youth whose parents had not graduated from high school, the proportion of dropouts is three times the proportion of graduates (26.9 per cent versus 8.7 per cent). Furthermore, approximately 7 out of every 10 dropouts, compared to 4 out of 10 graduates, had parents who did not complete high school (ibid., 31).

As tuition freezes expire, students such as Alan Clark at Trent University have taken to the streets in protest, and working-class youth increasingly are barred from higher education. (CP/*Peterborough Examiner*/Clifford Skarstedt)

Similarly, mothers' and fathers' occupations are correlated with whether youth graduate from or drop out of high school. Mothers of high school dropouts were more likely to be working in sales and service jobs or in primary, processing, manufacturing, and utilities jobs. Mothers of graduates were more likely to be working in social science, government, art, culture, health, and applied science jobs. Fathers of dropouts were more likely to be working in trades, transport, and equipment-operating jobs, whereas fathers of graduates were more likely to be working in management jobs (ibid.).

Approximately 65 per cent of high school graduates enter post-secondary educational institutions in Canada (Looker and Lowe, 2001: 4). Among youth, the higher parents' measures of SES, the higher their children's expectations regarding post-secondary educational attainment (ibid.). Plans to attend college or university are correlated with whether youth actually attend such institutions. Hence, educational attainment, including participation in college and university programs after high school completion, is also influenced by class background, regardless of how it is measured (Ali and Grabb, 1998; Wotherspoon, 2004). Several studies have shown that financial situation is listed by youth as a key barrier to pursuing post-secondary studies (Bowlby and McMullen, 2002; see Looker and Lowe, 2001, for an overview). Furthermore, youth who are from families in the highest SES quartile are much more likely to attend university than are those in the lowest SES quartile (Chippendale, 2002; Statistics Canada and CMEC, 2000).

The preceding findings demonstrate that there is a clear relationship between parents' SES and children's educational attainment. A combination of economic, social, and cultural factors helps to explain the relationship between SES and educational attainment (Davies, 2004). In the first place, if parents are poorly educated and have

Figure 15.3 Highest Education Attainment of Parents or Guardians of Dropouts and Graduates

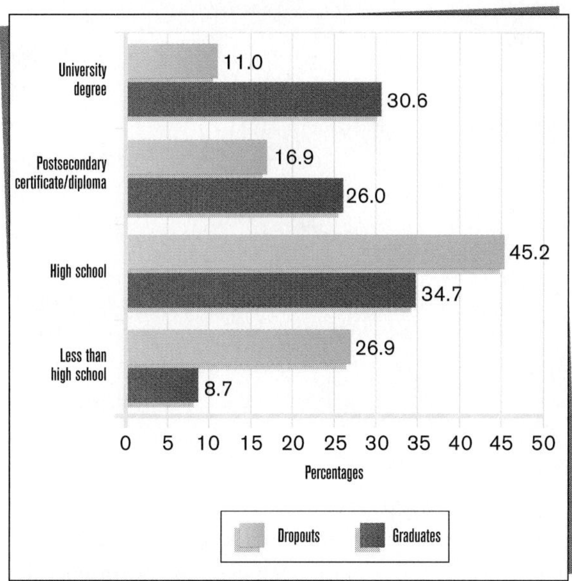

Source: Adapted from Jeffrey Bowlby and Kathryn McMullen, *At a Crossroads: First Results for the 18–20-Year-Old Cohort of the Youth in Transition Survey 2002* (Ottawa: Statistics Canada, 2002), 21.

low-paying jobs, families may not be able to afford to keep children in school. Poor families may need their children to drop out of high school and work to help with the family economy. In other situations, parents may not be able to help with the costs of post-secondary education, and the thought of excessive debt upon school completion may dissuade youth from continuing their studies. Notably, neither of these situations is likely to improve in the short term as rates of child poverty and the costs of post-secondary education continue to rise.

Besides economic factors, other social factors intersect with SES and social class to play a role in the educational attainment. To the extent that children and youth of similar SES and social class backgrounds are segregated into schools based on community residence, they will develop social ties with other children and youth of similar backgrounds. Lack of exposure to middle- and upper-class children and their parents limits access to **social capital**, the resources that are available through our connections to others. In other words, working-class children and youth may not have access to the information gained through social capital that is required for them to succeed in their educational careers. For instance, whereas middle-class children can turn to their parents and friends to learn about the intricacies of the educational system, working-class children do not have those social resources available to them and may not know how to find answers to questions that would help them succeed within school environments.

Finally, **cultural capital** also plays a role in educational attainment. Cultural capital is derived mostly from education and reflects middle- and upper-class **values**, attitudes, and beliefs regarding various aspects of social life. If education and related activities such as reading, discussing politics, and learning about the world and music are valued within a family and by the individuals within it, high levels of educational attainment are more likely. Working-class families tend not to expose their children to these activities to the extent that middle- and upper-class families do. Hence, the value of education is often not as strongly held in working-class families as it is in middle-class families, and working-class children may not be as inclined to continue with their education as a result.

Health

According to the World Health Organization, *health* is broadly defined as 'a state of complete physical, mental, and social well-being and not merely the absence of disease or infirmity' (2003), which suggests that multiple measures of health need to be examined in order to fully understand health and inequality. Income, status, and class advantages lead to better health outcomes within and across countries. Recent media and policy attention regarding the HIV/AIDS epidemics in developing countries suggests that **developed countries** need to pay more attention to the 'have-nots' who live beyond our national borders. Indeed, mortality and **morbidity rates** tend to be higher in developing than in developed countries, and biotechnology researchers are in search of methods to reduce the health gap between rich and poor countries.

Among the many indicators of health, mortality is one of the most studied. There is a well-known and consistent relationship between SES and mortality. Individuals who have lower incomes and less education tend to have lower life expectancies than individuals who have higher incomes and who are better educated (Mustard et al., 1997; Williams and Collins, 1995). Recent evidence suggests that the mortality gap between the rich and the poor is widening; this has been attributed to the more rapid gains for those with high SES relative to those with lower SES (Williams and Collins, 1995).

Erika Klein, with her daughter Morgan, 7, is one of thousands of people in the Ontario Disability Support Program, designed to meet the needs of people with disabilities who are in financial need. (Vince Talotta/Torstar Syndication Services)

Recently, researchers have argued that beyond the simple relationship between SES and mortality, a socio-economic 'gradient' also influences mortality. This *gradient effect* reflects the research finding that regions characterized by high levels of income inequality have higher death rates than do regions in which the income distribution is more equal. This suggests that the experience of disadvantage relative to others in a particular locale has an effect on mortality rates that cannot be explained by SES alone (Kawachi et al., 1999).

Morbidity generally refers to the presence of illness or disease, chronic symptoms, and general malaise. Regardless of how it is measured, there is also a strong and consistent relationship between SES and morbidity such that those who are more disadvantaged experience higher levels of morbidity (Cairney, 1999; Humphries and van Doorslaer, 2000; Jette et al., 1996; MacMillan et al., 1996; Mao et al., 2000; Williams and Collins, 1995). Regional disparities regarding income and poverty have also been found to influence the experience of morbidity (Guernsey et al., 2000). Besides these differences in mortality and morbidity, individuals in lower-SES groups suffer poorer mental health (measured either as the presence of mental illness or as more generalized distress) than do those in higher-SES groups (Turner and Avison, 2003). Although there are debates about whether low SES causes poor mental health or whether poor mental health causes low SES, the correlation is strong.

What explains the strong and consistent relationship between SES and these various measures of health? People with lower levels of income and education and those employed in working-class occupations are more likely to experience malnutrition, disproportionately lack knowledge of health care practices, and are more often exposed to dangerous working and living environments. All of these things negatively affect health status. As well, research has shown that SES is associated with access to health care services even in countries such as Canada that have 'universal' health-care systems (Newbold, 1998).

Conclusion: Does Class Matter?

For decades, sociologists have quibbled over the relevance of social class as a marker of inequality (Clark and Lipset, 1991; Nisbet, 1959; Pakulski and Waters, 1996). Some argue that because false consciousness is so widespread within contemporary capitalism, political distinctions between the middle class and the working class have become negligible. Others suggest that because some working-class jobs are well-paid, distributive distinctions between the classes are becoming less significant. Still others purport that because most people report that they are members of the middle class, not the working class, and because working conditions are better now than they were a century ago, class is losing its significance as a basis of inequality in Canada and other Western industrialized nations (Pakulski and Waters, 1996). Indeed, Jan Pakulski and Malcolm Waters (1996) have gone as far as to proclaim the 'death' of class.

The claims in support of the 'death of class' are true to a certain extent. Indeed, the fact that many students first discover their working-class backgrounds in their first year of university may add some support to the argument that class does not matter. As well, the conditions of, and rewards for, work have mostly improved over the last century. Social security systems are better now than they were during the rise of industrial capitalism in Canada, which has reduced the risk associated with working-class membership.

That said, it is also true that after students are given social class as an explanatory tool, they better understand the circumstances of their lives. Furthermore, if given a choice, most employees would choose to work in non-working-class occupations that are better paid, more autonomous, and less alienating; working-class parents are not able to provide their children with the same educational opportunities that are afforded to middle-class children; and there are unique health risks associated with being a member of the working class. The culmination of this information suggests that although the nature of class-based inequality has changed over time, class remains alive and well.

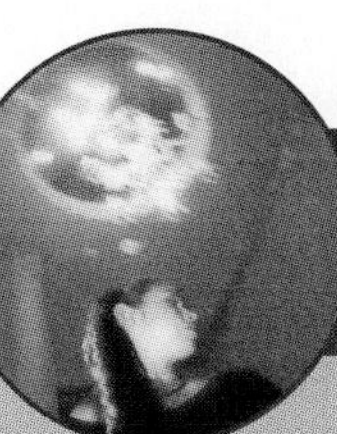

GLOBAL ISSUES

UN Finds Global Inequality Rising

By Susannah Price
(BBC correspondent at the United Nations)

A UN report has found that the world is more unequal today than it was 10 years ago, despite considerable economic growth in many regions.

This year's report on the world's social situation argues that although living standards have improved in some places, poverty remains entrenched.

The authors warned that focusing only on economic growth is an ineffective way of achieving development.

They said wealthy nations are the main beneficiaries of economic development.

The UN report—drawn up by the UN's Economic and Social Affairs Department—found that the gap between rich and poor is now wider than it was a decade ago, and called for immediate action.

The report focuses on worldwide inequality in income and wealth, along with other areas such as health and education.

Redistribution

The report said that although China and India had seen considerable income growth, there was a wide income gap.

It said it would be impossible for the 2.8 billion people living on less than $2 a day to ever match the consumption levels of the rich.

The UN secretary general said the report showed the development agenda could not be advanced without addressing inequality, such as the gap between skilled and unskilled workers and between the formal and informal sectors.

The report recommends expanding opportunities for productive employment, bringing marginalized groups into society and working to distribute the benefits of what it called the increasingly open world economy.

Source: BBC NEWS, 25 Aug. 2005, at: <news.bbc.co.uk/go/pr/fr//2/hi/americas/4185458.stm>.© BBC 2007.

Questions for Critical Thought

1. Some may argue that no one but Kimberly Rogers was to blame for her death. Others would argue that structural circumstances and social policy at least contributed to her death. Compare and contrast these views. Which better explains Rogers's death?
2. Based on what you have learned in this and the preceding chapters, how many social classes are there in contemporary Canadian society? Which makes more sense today, a Weberian or a Marxist view of social class?
3. Discuss the feminist critique of social class. How can social class be reconceptualized so that the experiences of women are fully integrated into a theoretical framework of social class?
4. Why are sociologists concerned about the polarization of social classes? In other words, what are the social implications of a shrinking middle class and a swelling working class?
5. Under the conditions of contemporary capitalism, does small business ownership hold the same appeal as it did for Marx? In other words, assuming that alienation is reduced substantially or even eliminated for small business owners, are there other things that may matter more to one's overall well-being in contemporary capitalism? If so, why do so many Canadians dream of being self-employed?
6. Are there policies that could be put in place that could eliminate poverty? What might some of these policies be? Is the elimination of poverty a desirable social outcome?
7. Are there policies that could be put in place that could eliminate the relationship between social class and education? What might some of these policies be? Is educational equality a desirable social outcome?
8. Are there policies that could be put in place that could eliminate the relationship between social class and health? What might some of these policies be? Is health equality a desirable social outcome?

Recommended Readings

Joan Acker, 'Class, Gender, and the Relations of Distribution', *Signs* 13 (1988): 473–97.

This seminal article tackles the complexities of integrating gender, class, patriarchy, and capitalism into a single system of inequality.

Wallace Clement and John Myles, *Relations of Ruling: Class and Gender in Postindustrial Societies* (Montreal and Kingston: McGill-Queen's University Press, 1994).

This book applies Wright's conceptualization of social class in an analysis of class and gender inequality. Although it focuses primarily on Canada, there are also cross-national comparisons with the United States, Norway, Sweden, and Finland.

James E. Curtis, Edward G. Grabb, and Neil L. Guppy, eds, *Social Inequality in Canada: Patterns, Problems, and Policies* (Toronto: Pearson Prentice-Hall, 2004).

This is an excellent source of information on various aspects of social inequality in Canada.

Bonnie Fox, 'The Feminist Challenge: A Reconsideration of Social Inequality and Economic Development', in Robert J. Brym with Bonnie Fox, *From Culture to Power: The Sociology of English Canada* (Toronto: Oxford University Press, 1989), 120–67.

This chapter provides an excellent overview and analysis of how feminist scholarship provides a more complete understanding of social inequality and development than do 'male-stream' approaches.

Edward G. Grabb, *Theories of Social Inequality*, 5th edn (Toronto: Harcourt, 2007).

Grabb provides an excellent overview and analysis of classical and contemporary theories of social inequality.

Heidi Hartmann, 'The Unhappy Marriage of Marxism and Feminism: Towards a More Progressive Union', in Lydia Sargent, ed., *The Unhappy Marriage of Marxism and Feminism: A Debate on Class and Patriarchy* (London: Pluto, 1981), 2–41.

This classic socialist feminist article brings together, in a dual-systems theory, issues of patriarchy and capitalism.

Desmond Morton, *Working People: An Illustrated History of the Canadian Labour Movement*, 4th edn (Montreal and Kingston: McGill-Queen's University Press, 1998).

This is a great resource book that explores the evolution of the labour movement in Canada from the late nineteenth century until the 1990s.

Erik Olin Wright, *Class Counts: Comparative Studies in Class Analysis*, student edn (Cambridge: Cambridge University Press, 1997).

This comprehensive book outlines Wright's ideas on social class.

Recommended Websites

Canadian Labour Congress (CLC)
www.clc-ctc.ca

Labour-related publications, media releases, and the history of the CLC are among the many resources available on this site.

Canadian Policy Research Networks
www.cprn.ca

This is an excellent source of information regarding the relationship between social policy and social inequality.

Eric Olin Wright
www.ssc.wisc.edu/~wright/

Wright's home page includes an up-to-date listing of his publications, many of which can be downloaded.

Human Resources and Social Development Canada, National Homelessness Initiative
www. homelessness.gc.ca

Information is available on this site on the problem of homelessness among Canadians.

Make Poverty History
www.makepovertyhistory.ca

This site includes information about poverty both in Canada and beyond, as well as ongoing campaigns and resources for anti-poverty activism.

2005 Report Card on Child Poverty
www.campaign2000.ca/rc/rc05/05NationalReportCard.pdf

This site provides interesting data on child poverty in Canada.

National Council on Welfare
www.ncwcnbes.net

This site includes facts and reports on poverty in Canada and information about poverty myths.

Statistics Canada
www.statcan.ca

A wealth of statistical information about income and employment status in Canada is available here.

World Health Organization (WHO)
www.who.int

The WHO website provides definitions of health and world reports about various health topics.

Chapter 16

Gender Relations

Pat Armstrong

Learning Objectives

In this chapter, you will:

- Learn that biology alone does not account for differences between males and females.
- See how ideologies, child-rearing practices, the division of labour by sex, the education system, and the media all influence the physiology, behaviour, and perceptions of both sexes.
- Examine the segregation of the labour force, the political arena, and medical services by sex.
- Consider why the life experiences of women are different from and more limited than those of men.
- Study the issues of housework and caregiving.
- Consider the changing personal relationships between men and women.
- Take into account the effect of changing gender relations on men.

Introduction

'Is it a boy or a girl?' This is the first question asked of new parents. The answer is critical because it has profound implications for an individual's choices and possibilities throughout life.

All known cultures have distinguished between male and female. Furthermore, in all cultures the distinctions have provided the basis for divisions of not only labour, but also most other activities. The distinctions made between **genders** and the divisions of labour have varied enormously through time and across cultures, however, because such distinctions exist within a **social environment**. They result more from social relations and social structures than from biologically determined differences.

This chapter examines gender distinctions and the relations between males and females in Canadian society. We open with a discussion of what is known about biological differences and their implications for behaviour and relationships. Next, we turn to the evidence on sex-specific patterns in behaviour, education, and occupations, evaluating alternative explanations for the established patterns. Finally, we outline some strategies for altering these patterns and reshaping the relations between the sexes in Canada.

Pink or blue? North American birth announcements typically leave no doubt as to the sex of the newborn, despite the obvious difficulty in distinguishing a diapered newborn girl from a boy. (iStockphoto)

Theories of the Sexes

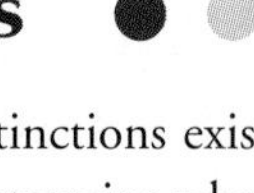

From one perspective, clear biological distinctions exist between the sexes and these distinctions determine what people can be when they grow up. Many sociologists, however, see clear lines to be drawn between distinctions that are biologically determined and those that are socially learned—in short, between nature and nurture. More than 20 years ago, Marlene Mackie explained that 'sex is the biological dichotomy between females and males. It is determined at conception and is, for the most part, unalterable. Gender, on the other hand, is what is socially recognized as femininity and masculinity' (1983: 1). By differentiating between **sex** and **gender**, sociologists sought to stress the **social construction** of distinctions between the sexes. But these terms raised their own problems. First, they implied that biological factors can be separated from social factors and that biological differences are firmly established. Second, they also implied that biology is unchanging, outside history and influence. Third, the distinction suggested that biology is irrelevant to an understanding of social distinctions between males and females.

In an effort to overcome these problems, *gender* has, in the intervening years, increasingly become the only term used. However, the growing popularity of the new genetics and biotechnology has once again encouraged an emphasis on biological differences between the sexes (Grant, 1998). The rest of this section will examine each of the problems in determining biological differences, explaining why it is not always easy to differentiate between sex and gender, biology and learning.

Separating the Boys from the Girls

People throughout the ages have debated the biological differences between the sexes, and they continue to do so today despite extensive research. A 1993 CBC series based on the book *Brain Sex* (Moir and Jessel, 1989) stressed the **biological determinist** side. A more recent article in *Maclean's* magazine begins, 'If there is a gene for murder, it is a safe bet it will be found first in someone who carries XY chromosomes. That is, a man. There may be no such gene. Many experts insist violence is learned, not

Time to Reflect

What does it mean on surveys, questionnaires, and application forms when you are asked to put a check mark in a box indicating gender?

inherited' (Wood and Kar, 2000: 5). Clearly the issue is far from settled (Blustain, 2000; Rhoads, 2004).

Most people would agree that hair length and high heels are socially created distinctions. Fewer would reach a consensus about which aspects of motherhood have biological links. Moreover, some would argue that women are 'naturally' homemakers, men 'naturally' breadwinners. Finally, while most would agree that women and men have different genitals, this difference alone cannot be used to divide all people into two categories. Indeed, the Olympic Committee considers visible genitals so unreliable in establishing sex that it rejects the distinction as a basis for determining who may compete in the women's games. And some known cultures do not understand humans as divided into two categories of male and female or homosexual and heterosexual (Wood, 1997).

Science provides few definitive answers to many points in the debate over biological differences. There is little consensus in the vast research and literature on the topic. The lack of agreement reflects both the problems encountered in conducting the research and the more fundamental problem inherent in the assumption that nature and nurture can be isolated from one another.

Research into human biological differences linked to behaviour is difficult for several reasons. First, children begin learning at birth, if not before, so we cannot be entirely certain that the behaviour even of newborns is innate. Second, while infants have a very limited repertoire for study, as they expand their activities they also increase their opportunities to learn. Moreover, the older the subjects, the more likely they are to respond in terms of their own **values** and expectations. In any event, there are severe restrictions on the kind and amount of experimentation permitted on humans, whatever their age. Third, even when genes or hormones or other biological factors are determined to be different in males and females, there is little basis for assuming that these differences translate into particular behaviours. Perhaps most important, researchers themselves cannot escape their own learning, which helps structure how they do research and interpret results as well as what they accept as evidence (Fausto-Sterling, 2000; Lips, 2004; Messing, 1998).

Research on other species encounters similar problems, even though there are fewer restrictions placed on it. Other animals, such as rodents and birds, learn just as humans do, and there is enormous variety in their behaviour. Males are not universal breadwinners or heroes, and in some species, mothers eat their young. Moreover, researchers' values come into play here, too, often guiding them to select the evidence that best supports their own **hypotheses** (Blustain, 2000). While there are many things to be learned from studying other animals, we cannot be confident that anything we might argue as being innate in another species will be so in humans, for the simple reason that humans are qualitatively different from other species.

Such difficulties have led many observers to contend that an answer to 'Nature or nurture?' can never be found, because the wrong question is being asked. Anne Fausto-Sterling has argued that it is impossible to determine which aspects of our behaviour are biologically determined, because 'an individual's capacities emerge from a web of interactions between the biological being and the social environment. . . . Biology may in some manner condition behaviour, but behaviour in turn can alter one's physiology. Furthermore, any particular behaviour may have many different causes' (1985: 8). This is why, as she has said more recently (Fausto-Sterling, 2000), even with the latest techniques, scientists still disagree about differences and their impact. These debates are not surprising because people do not exist outside their social environment, and what are often called 'biological processes' are influenced by that environment. Jogging or stress may delay a menstrual cycle; tight jeans or a radio carried too often below the waist may reduce sperm counts. The more often women run in marathons, the closer they come to matching the men; the more often men spend their days sitting in office chairs, the less muscle-bound they become.

To argue that nature cannot easily be separated from nurture is not to argue that there are no biological components to people's behaviour or that there are no gender differences that can be related to biological factors. Rather, it is to assert that biological components have no predetermined meaning or value and that they are not unalterable.

The Sexes: What's the Difference?

Researchers do agree on some sex differences. While both sexes have 23 pairs of chromosomes, in most females one pair is made up of two X chromosomes; in most males one pair consists of an X and a Y chromosome. The Y chromosome must be present for the embryonic sex glands to develop in a male direction. Variations can, and do, occur (WHO, 2006). Furthermore, hormones must be present in both sexes for either males or females to reach sexual maturity. Although estrogens are often called 'female' hormones and androgens 'male' hormones, both sexes secrete both types of hormones—'what differs is the ratio of estrogen to androgen in the two sexes' (Rose et al., 151). Hormones, too, come in different degrees within each sex. Between them, the XX and XY chromosomes and the hormones are responsible for the different reproductive capacities of women (menstruation, gestation, and lactation) and men (semen production and impregnation).

It is at this point that agreement ends. Debates rage over the implications of the differences in chromosomes, hormonal ratios, physiology, and reproductive capacities for male and female behaviour and possibilities (see, for example, Bancroft, 2002).

The Genetic Perspective

Sociobiologists and others who are convinced that biology determines a wide range of behaviour attribute a powerful effect to the lone Y chromosome. Some involved in behavioural genetics research have argued that the genetic makeup of men makes them more intelligent than women, superior in visual-spatial abilities and mathematical skills, or more aggressive and dominant. It has also been suggested that women's double X chromosome creates a maternal instinct and makes females more intuitive, nurturant, and moral than men. For supporters of the genetic perspective, then, the hierarchical structure of society and the sexual division of labour are the natural and inevitable result of biological differences (Geary, 1998; Geary and Flinn, 2000, Rhoads, 2004).

So is what is often called the **double standard** in sexual practices. That is, men have a natural sexuality that results, in the words of David Barash, from the 'biologically based need to inject their sperm into as many women as possible' (cited in Messing, 1987: 112). Some have concluded, on the basis of this viewpoint, that rape and violence against women have biological roots: the men cannot help themselves any more than women can stop being nurturant and deceitful. In the eyes of these theorists, women are destined to be mommies and men bosses. Moreover, women should expect to be dominated and sexually harassed.

Study after study has challenged these notions (Fausto-Sterling, 2000; Lips, 2004; Rose et al., 1984). Research in countries other than Canada, for example, reveals an astonishing variety in gender relations that seems to deny biological determinism. Margaret Lock (1998) found that the physical manifestations of menopause vary across cultures, R.A. Anderson and colleagues (1999) that testosterone replacement had a different impact on male sexuality in Hong Kong than it did in North America. And claims that an extra Y chromosome leads to criminal behaviour has been rejected in US courts because the argument lacks scientific support (WHO, 2006).

Within Canadian society, too, considerable differences are evident in gender behaviour over the course of history. Elizabeth Mitchell, for instance, examined Prairie households at the turn of the century and concluded that 'there is no question at all of inequality; the partners have several departments, equally important, and the husband is the first to admit how much he owes his wife, and to own that the burden falls on her heaviest' ([1915] 1981: 48). Mitchell also maintains that city life served to create inequalities and make women subordinate in ways we see today. In addition, **First Nations** families have a long tradition of female independence and of community participation in child-rearing, in contrast to what is assumed as natural for many Caucasian women (Cassidy et al., 2001).

To sum up, research has not revealed any simple dichotomy between the sexes or any direct link between genetics or hormones and the behaviour patterns attributed to each sex. Sociobiology has not succeeded in demonstrating 'that a genetically based human nature or genetically based sex differences exist' (Lowe, 1983: 13). The variability across cultures, the minor differences

Time to Reflect

Given the variation across cultures in regard to sex and gender, does it still make sense to talk about biological determinism?

GLOBAL ISSUES

Changing Views of Men

While most of the research and writing on changing relations between the sexes has focused on women, in the last two decades there has been a flurry of publications that look at emerging patterns for men. Analysis of advertising offers just one example of this trend.

In her examination of the representation of males in advertising, Judith Posner (1987) found that the new male is smaller, has a less pronounced jaw, and is more likely to smile. He is also more likely to be found undressing or partially dressed, and he appears more vulnerable. Yet Posner concludes that this does not reflect a move toward equality, but rather demonstrates 'the increasing commercialization of sexuality' for both men and women (1987: 188).

In another analysis of advertising, Andrew Wernick argues that as women have moved into the labour force, men have become more involved in private consumption; this change has been reflected in 'a steady drive to incorporate male clothing into fashion, and mounting efforts to sell men all manner of personal-care products, from toothpaste and bath oil to hair dye and make-up' (1987: 279). Wernick suggests that men are being subjected to the same kind of 'intense consumerization as women and are no longer defined as breadwinners' (ibid.). More recently, however, Varda Burstyn (1999) has argued that both advertising in sports and the practice of sport promotes what she calls 'hypermasculinity.'

between the sexes in any particular culture, and the variations in patterns within the sexes all challenge notions of simple genetic determinism.

The Hormonal Perspective

Instead of attributing predetermined sex differences to genes, others have looked to hormones as causal agents (Moir and Jessel, 1992). Supporters of this perspective argue that different levels of hormones affect the brain, resulting for males in higher intelligence, more ambition and drive, and more aggressive behaviour. The effect on women is seen as far more negative, inasmuch as menstruation and menopause are viewed as incapacitating them, making them unsuitable for many kinds of work.

Again, research has provided very limited support for this viewpoint. Although the injection of hormones might influence a rodent brain in ways that encourage mating behaviour, in non-human primates it does not create the same results (Lowe, 1983). In the words of Fausto-Sterling, 'the evidence that male hormones control aggression in humans and other primates ranges from weak to non-existent' (1985: 45). A survey of research has concluded that 'there is no known causal relationship between sex hormone levels and other traits, such as intelligence, intuition, and creativity' (Richardson, 1988: 149). Indeed, Lynda Birke (1999) cites evidence that hormone production itself is influenced by the social environment.

Reproductive Capacity

Some feminist theorists have looked to reproductive capacities, rather than to genes or hormones, to explain differences between the sexes. Mary O'Brien, for example, has argued that the very different parts women and men play in reproduction lead to different forms of consciousness and to men's efforts to control women: 'Women's reproductive consciousness is a consciousness that the child is hers, but also a consciousness that she herself was born of a woman's labour, that labour confirms genetic coherence and species continuity. Male reproductive consciousness is splintered and discontinuous, and cannot be mediated within reproductive process' (1981: 59). In O'Brien's view, men experience reproduction mainly as alienation of their male seed, which in turn motivates them to seek control over both mother and child.

This kind of theoretical argument is much more difficult to examine through scientific research than those that attribute sex differences to genes or hormones. What is clear is that the effects of reproductive capacities, like those of genes or hormones, cannot be understood outside the context of time and place. How women experience childbirth, for instance, is related to the available technology and medical care, nutrition, and social support. These factors can transform not only how women feel about giving birth, but also the very biology of the birth process. Women's reproductive capacity makes the consequences of sexual intercourse different for women and men, especially in the absence of safe, effective birth control (Armstrong and Armstrong, 1983a; Hamilton, 1978) and different for women from different racial and cultural groups (Cassidy et al., 2001). Moreover, the consequences are different today than in our grandmothers' time, not only because contemporary women have a better chance of avoiding childbirth, but also because they have a better chance of surviving it. The development of relatively effective birth control has made the implications of sexual intercourse more similar for both sexes and has thereby contributed to changes in sexual practices and in the double standard. In turn, these social changes have affected the workings of our bodies and the meaning of what are often called 'biological processes'.

The recent spread of HIV/AIDS provides another example of the complex relationship between biology and social environment. In making men more vulnerable to the long-term consequences of their sexual activities, HIV/AIDS has altered the sexual practices of at least some men. Furthermore, AIDS can be controlled today primarily by changes in **social relationships** and social practices, not through biological means.

In the end, we are left to conclude that biology cannot be separated from the social environment that influences both its meaning and its structure. Biology is not an independent variable. Moreover, 'female' and 'male' do not constitute opposite sexes. Women and men share both genes and hormones. They differ mainly in reproductive capacities, and the significance of these differences is primarily socially, rather than biologically, structured. Furthermore, 'human biology and behaviour are anything but immutable. Stimulate the brain, and neurons branch out to form new connections. Arouse the senses, and hormonal levels change. Exercise the muscles, and the body becomes stronger and sleeker' (Hales, 2000: 9). As Judith Lorber and Susan Farrell point out, 'it makes more sense to talk of genders, not simply gender, because being a woman and being a man change from one generation to the next and are different for different racial, ethnic, and religious groups, as well as for the members of different social classes' (1991: 1). This does not mean that biology is irrelevant. What it does mean is that sex differences cannot be attributed to biology alone.

Growing Up Feminine or Masculine

When parents answer the question about the sex of their new child, they trigger a range of social responses that have very little to do with genes, hormones, or reproductive capacities. Sex distinctions are a central part of the content and structure of child-rearing practices in the home, and they are just as integral to the content and structure of **social institutions**, such as the formal education system and the **mass media**. The distinctions are reinforced by the dominant **ideology** manifested in all these social contexts. This is not to suggest that children and adults are mere passive recipients or transmitters of ideas and practices. Through interaction with their social and physical worlds, people alter them as well as their ideas about them. Nevertheless, child-rearing practices, educational systems, and dominant ideologies have a powerful influence on the pace and nature of social change, as well as on the distinctions made between males and females.

The Influence of the Home

Once we know the sex identification of a child, we know what toys to bring, what clothes to buy, what colour to paint the baby's room, what stories to read, what games to play, how rough we can be, how much we should talk to the newborn, and what kind of name the child will have, although what is considered appropriate varies with culture (Mackie, 1993). In recent years, unisex clothes, toys, and hairstyles have become popular, and many parents are attempting to raise their children in what is termed a 'non-sexist' manner. Despite some important changes, however, many differences based on sex still persist.

Parents tend to spend more time interacting with little girls, while they not only tend to leave boys alone more often, but also punish them more often. Boys are more likely to have computers and to be shown how to operate them so they can play their adventure games. Girls tend to be more closely supervised, especially when they reach adolescence. Boys are seldom allowed to wear dresses and are taught rough, physical games such as football. Girls are seldom given footballs or guns to play with, but are taught how to play house and dress Barbie in ball gowns. Toughness, aggression, and emotional control are rewarded in boys and sanctioned in girls (Kilmarten, 1994). When tasks are assigned in the house, boys are told to take out the garbage and shovel the walk, girls to clean the toilet and wash the floor—

though more boys are helping with the dishes and operating the microwave. As Jane Gaskell's research on Canadian adolescents shows, the division of household labour contributes to the shared view among young men and women that 'young women will add work outside the home to their domestic work' (2001: 229).

These child-rearing practices help shape the physiology, behaviour, and perceptions of both sexes. Girls and boys learn different skills and develop in different ways. Playing with computers and construction equipment encourages males to develop visual-spatial and mathematical skills. Playing hockey encourages them to be aggressive and dominant. Shovelling snow and lugging garbage develop strength and foster muscle growth. At the same time, playing with dolls encourages girls to develop verbal and relational skills. The wearing of 4-inch heels and tight, low-cut jeans discourages a range of physical activities, while cleaning toilets contributes little to muscle growth. Close supervision limits adventurousness and encourages passivity or trickery.

These differences in experience also lead females and males to view themselves and the other sex in particular ways. Research undertaken for the Royal Commission on the Status of Women found that children 'were more certain about the meaning of masculinity and femininity when they thought in terms of potential jobs or relations than when they thought in terms of personality dispositions' (Lambert, 1971: 69). There is little reason to doubt that this still holds today. What children experience in the area of jobs is a division by sex in which the tasks assigned to females have less value, are less interesting, and have less potential than those done by men. What they experience in the area of relations is greater freedom, more choices, and more **power** for males than for females.

It is in the context of child care that such division along gender lines is most evident. Even though a majority of women now work in the labour force and men help more than they used to with the children, women still bear the primary responsibility for child care (Frederick, 1995; Ghalam, 2000; Sinclair and Felt, 1992). Some theorists (Chodorow, 1978; Pollack, 1998) have argued that this aspect of the division of labour has profound implications for the psyches of females and males. Given that women are child-rearers, females can continue to identify with their mothers and can feel comfortable with intimate or nurturant relations. Men, on the other hand, can find **identity** only by separating themselves from the caregiver. This painful separation helps create the urge to dominate women and to repress intimate or nurturant behaviour.

Mothers around the world typically assume the key caregiving roles in family life, especially when infants are present in the household. This often results in women having to juggle child care with domestic chores and paid work. (Left: Guenter Fischer/World of Stock; Right: Bilodeau/Preston/Masterfile)

Although this explanation simplifies the complex and often contradictory process of gender development (Connell, 1995, 2001), it nevertheless draws our attention to the importance of the division of labour in forming gender distinctions in children. It also suggests the implications of these differences for the perceptions of males and females throughout life.

The Influence of the Educational System

Even if parents try to raise their children in a social environment patterned on equal relations between the sexes, once children enter the educational system they are exposed to sex distinctions and relations in which women are subordinate. Schools often structure classes in ways that encourage girls to focus on courses leading to clerical jobs or other similar work associated with women (Gaskell, 1992; Gaskell and Willinsky, 1995). At the same time, they frequently structure sports in ways that help boys move in other directions and encourage them to be dominant. As former Olympic runner Bruce Kidd (1987: 255) makes clear:

> by giving males exciting opportunities, preaching that the qualities they learn from them are 'masculine,' and preventing girls and women from learning in the same situations, sports confirm the prejudice that males are a breed apart. By encouraging us to spend our most creative and engrossing moments as children and our favorite forms of recreation as adults in the company of other males, they condition us to trust each other more than women.

The very place of women in the educational system is also instructive for the young. Most principals are men. While most elementary school teachers are women, the higher the level, the greater the number of male teachers. Although university programs have long abandoned a quota on the number of women admitted, many less visible barriers remain in place. Women in post-secondary education are still concentrated in health, education, and the social sciences, while the number of women in science and technology remains low relative to their enrolment in other fields (Statistics Canada, 2000).

Various women's groups—some of them made up of teachers—have exposed and successfully attacked such practices. More women are now principals and greater numbers of men teach in elementary schools, though the latter trend may well be more a reflection of higher wages and scarce employment than of feminist action. When quotas on female enrolments were removed, women rushed to take places in faculties of law, medicine, and dentistry. Indeed, in some institutions women now constitute the majority of those enrolled in such traditionally male-dominated programs. Career counsellors discuss non-traditional job possibilities with students, and new courses introduce counsellors to more alternatives for women.

Research revealing the way girls were encouraged to see paid work as secondary to the 'real' work as mothers has been used to bring about some changes within the classroom. Indeed, concerns now are being raised that girls are doing much better in traditional male subjects, leaving the boys behind. However, there is evidence that there is still a hidden curriculum that silently encourages girls and boys in different directions (Bourne et al., 1997; Connell, 2001).

The Influence of the Media

Gender divisions are reflected in and reinforced by the majority of books, magazines, videos games, music, television programs—in short, all the media. Research nearly two decades ago showed that in television and film there were only half as many parts for women as there were for men (Armstrong, 1991). Women were much less likely than men to be portrayed as the initiators of adventures or as the rescuers in the action. They were more often evaluated primarily in terms of their youth, beauty, and ability to attract a man, while men were more often evaluated in terms of their skills, courage, and ability to capture women (Robinson and Salamon, 1987). While some efforts have been made by media regulators and creators to change this imbalance, the major preoccupation of women of every age in many programs and in much music remains being attractive to a man.

The content of some textbooks and some television programs and films has changed. Now women are far more likely to be portrayed as employed outside the home in such fields as medicine or law and as taking the initiative in sexual relationships (changes that reflect a new reality). Nevertheless, in books, as in other media, men still are more powerful and more plentiful, and they are in the society as well (Dines and Humez, 2003; Gauntlett, 2002). Pictures of gatherings of world leaders make this very clear.

The Influence of Ideologies

The practices in the home, the educational system, and the media cannot be separated from the dominant ideologies in a society. Indeed, in many ways they constitute those ideologies. But ideologies are not static—they are constantly being transformed as experiences and interests change. Ideas that do not coincide with people's life experiences or that make little sense of people's lives are difficult to maintain.

Feminist sociologist Dorothy Smith makes it clear that women 'have historically and in the present been excluded from the production of forms of thought, images, and symbols in which their experience and social relations are expressed and ordered' (1975: 353). She goes on to argue that women 'have never controlled the material or social means to the making of a tradition among themselves or to acting as equals in the ongoing discourse of intellectuals' (ibid.).

While many would argue that women have developed some specifically female ideologies, few would challenge the notion that men have been in a far better position than women to have their views of the world and its workings prevail. This has been the case even in the home, traditionally the woman's sphere, because it is men who have most often provided the primary monetary support. Moreover, the male view of the place of both men and women is likely to reaffirm the dominance of men, given their continuing superior place in the home, the educational system, and the media.

Although women do not control what Smith calls 'the means of mental production' (1975: 355), they have nonetheless developed their own perspectives from their own life experiences. For instance, the traditional notion of women focusing exclusively on the home no longer makes sense in light of women's actual experiences. As women gain power in every social institution, their views are likely to become more visible and shared by men. Nevertheless, survey data from 1995 indicated that only one-third of men, as opposed to 41 per cent of women, disagreed with the notion that what most women want is home and family (Ghalam, 2000: 72).

Ideologies, child-rearing practices, the division of labour by sex, the education system, and the media all work together to shape infants into feminine and masculine adults. At the same time, children and adults of both sexes are shaping the practices and ideas of society in response to changes in their daily experiences and the structure of their lives.

The Division of Labour by Sex

Gender divisions still are most obvious in the context of work. Men and women tend to do different work, in different places, for different wages. These differences in work not only create both limits and possibilities, but also help shape the ideas of members of each sex about themselves. In turn, work itself is shaped by the ideas people bring with them to the job, by employers' demands, and by people's responsibilities outside their paid labour.

Paid Work

Like clothing and hairstyles, women's and men's paid work has become increasingly similar in recent years. Women have been moving into the labour force in greater numbers, so the gap between male and female participation rates has been narrowing. In 1976, 42 per cent of women and 73 per cent of men were counted as employed; women constituted just over one-third of the labour market. By 2005, the official employment rates were 62 per cent for women and 73 per cent for men, with women forming 47 per cent of the labour market (Statistics Canada, 2006h). These figures actually underestimate the number of women employed at some point during the year and hide significant variations by marital status, citizenship status, race, culture, and location (Roy, 2006; Statistics Canada, 2004b). And as Figure 16.1 illustrates, participation varies by age, with women's patterns matching those of men when they are young, but diverging in their mid-twenties.

Much of the increase in female labour force participation is accounted for by the movement of married women into the labour market, largely in response to family economic need. Even married women with young children are keeping their paid jobs. In 2005, 72 per cent of women with preschool-aged children were in the labour force (Roy, 2006: Table 1). Edward Pryor points out that between 1971 and 1981 the income of wives 'was the significant factor in preventing family income from declining in real dollars,' although 'by 1979–81, increases in wives' income were no longer able to offset the decline in husbands' average income' (1984: 102). By the end of the 1990s, wives' income accounted for nearly one-third of household income in dual-earner families (Statistics Canada, 2000: 140). Without wives' income, the number of families living in poverty would increase by three-quarters of a million and many more would suffer significant setbacks in lifestyle (Chung, 2004; Statistics Canada, 2000: 146).

Women's increasing participation in post-secondary education and the women's movement have also been factors in rising participation. As Table 16.1 indicates, the higher their level of education, the more likely women are to follow the male labour force participation

Figure 16.1 Rates of Labour Force Participation by Sex and Five-year Age Categories, 2005

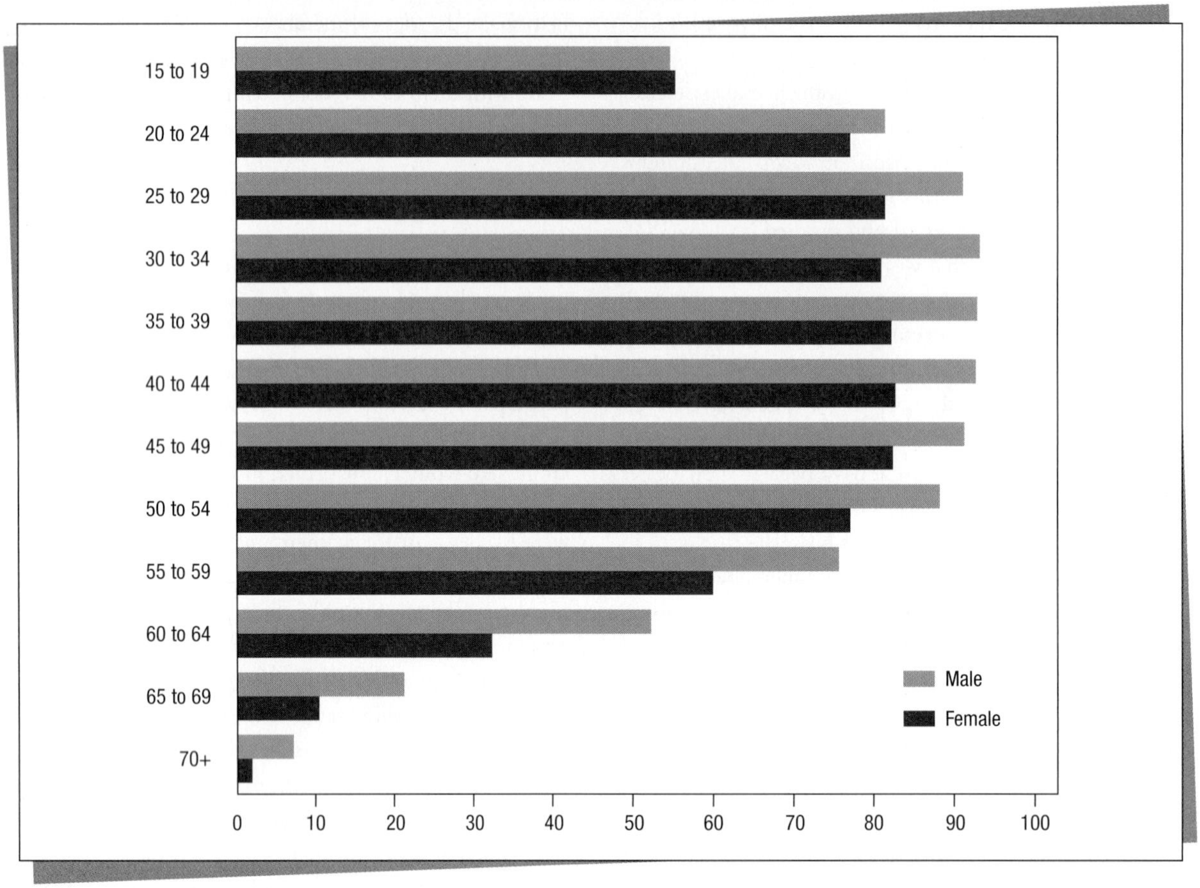

Source: Statistics Canada, *Labour Force Survey*, custom tabulation from public use microdata. Figure prepared by Krista Scott-Dixon.

pattern. More women have taken jobs traditionally done by men. According to Katherine Marshall, 'during the 1971–1981 period, the proportional representation of women increased in all but 1 of the 34 professions identified as male-dominated' (1987: 8). The largest percentage increases were in management, law, veterinary work, and engineering, while the largest numerical increases were in management, pharmacy, law, post-secondary teaching, and medicine (ibid.). This invasion into male-dominated domains was not limited to the professions, but extended to construction, agriculture, mining, and forestry. A few women even acquired licences to operate their own fishing boats. The pace of the movement of women into these occupations has slowed since then, but women do still move into male-dominated fields.

As more women have entered the labour force and followed patterns similar to men's, more of them have joined unions. Indeed, women's unionization rate grew throughout the 1970s and 1980s, while that of men declined. However, the number of employees grew in the 1990s faster than the rate of unionization. By 2001, only 30 per cent of men and women belonged to unions (Statistics Canada, 2002c: 1).

Despite these widely publicized gains, most women have remained doing women's work at women's wages; few have had a choice about taking on paid employment. And many face additional barriers linked to their race, age, or geographical location (Das Gupta, 1996; Statistics Canada, 2000). 'In 2003, 70 per cent of all employed women were working in one of teaching, nursing, and related health occupations, clerical or other administrative or sales and service occupations. This compared with just 31 per cent of employed men' (Statistics Canada, 2004b: 8). In that year, only a quarter of the managers were women but they were three-quarters of those in clerical and administrative work. While women account for nearly nine out of 10 nurses, therapists, and other health workers, they constitute less than a quarter of those in natural and applied sciences (ibid., Table 11). In other words, the labour force remains highly segregated in spite of the gains women have made over the last 40 years. According to the 1996 census, nearly two-thirds of employed women worked in the 40 jobs in which women accounted for 70 per cent or more of the workers. Men were significantly more dispersed and dominated more job categories—67 of them (Armstrong, 2000: 41, 43).

Not only do women and men do different jobs, they often do them in different places. It was still the case in 2003 that three-quarters of those employed in the goods-producing industries were male, while more than half of those working in community, business, and personal services were female (Statistics Canada, 2006h). Women are also more likely than men to do paid work in their homes. If men do work out of their homes, they are far more likely than women to be their own bosses.

Women also have a greater tendency to work part-time or part of the year. In 2003, they account for nearly 70 per cent of those employed part-time, a pattern that has changed little over the last 30 years (Statistics Canada, 2004b: Table 7). Although the proportion of women employed full-time in the labour force has increased over this perod, still, over one-quarter have only part-time paid work. The proportion of men employed part-time has also increased, but only 11 per cent of men work part-time and most of them are young (ibid.).

Shorter work weeks and fewer years of paid employment help account for women's lower wages. But this is only part of the story. In 2004, women's average wages were 63.5 per cent of men's—virtually the same as in 1995 (Statistics Canada, 2006h). These figures include all jobs and thus overstate the wage gap given that so many women have part-time paid work. However, even full-time wages for women averaged only 72 per cent of full-time wages for men (Akyeampong, 2001: 53).

Although large numbers of women have moved into what is classified as managerial and professional work, they earn significantly less than the men in the same occupational categories. The largest wage gaps are in the male-dominated groups. Although unions have helped close the wage gap in some occupational groups, this is not the case for the primarily non-unionized occupations. Table 16.2 shows both the significant difference a union makes to the wage gap and the continuing gap in male/female wages that vary by industry. In health care, women do better than men in part because most of the women are in professional jobs and in part because this female-dominated sector is highly unionized. In the male-dominated construction industry, women do not fare as well even when they are union members. Meanwhile, there are very large gaps both in the finance industry and in professional, scientific, and technical services, especially for the majority without union coverage. And these are the sectors where women's labour force participation is increasing significantly. It is important to note, however, that some women have moved into senior managerial positions and some occupational groups have made significant gains. The result, however, is increasing inequality among women more than growing equity among women and men.

Table 16.1 Rates of Labour Force Participation by Educational Attainment and Sex, 2005

	% in Labour Force	
Highest Level of Educational Attainment	**Male**	**Female**
0–8 years	70.1	50.0
Some secondary	86.2	66.5
High school graduate	92.1	78.9
Some post-secondary	89.1	79.1
Post-secondary certificate or diploma	94.5	86.2
University: bachelor's degree	93.6	86.0
University: graduate degree	93.8	86.9

Source: Statistics Canada, *Labour Force Survey*, custom tabulation from public use microdata prepared by Krista Scott-Dixon.

Table 16.2 Average and Median Hourly Wages by Union Coverage*, Industry, and Sex, 2005

		Mean	Median	Mean	Median
		Agriculture		**Finance, insurance, real estate and leasing**	
Union member	Male	$16.46	$16.00	$20.52	$19.71
	Female	$14.65	$15.61	$18.20	$17.00
Not member or covered	Male	$11.88	$10.00	$23.39	$20.51
	Female	$10.76	$9.75	$17.86	$16.00
		Forestry, fisheries, mining, oil and gas		**Professional, scientific, and technical services**	
Union member	Male	$23.02	$23.92	$28.37	$26.95
	Female	$18.59	$19.67	$21.61	$20.33
Not member or covered	Male	$23.52	$21.35	$26.21	$24.04
	Female	$19.55	$17.31	$19.23	$17.31
		Utilities		**Management, administration, and other support services**	
Union member	Male	$27.31	$26.67	$15.25	$14.05
	Female	$22.45	$21.98	$12.92	$12.00
Not member or covered	Male	$30.17	$28.85	$14.00	$12.00
	Female	$24.32	$22.00	$12.89	$11.00
		Construction		**Educational services**	
Union member	Male	$23.50	$24.00	$26.62	$25.27
	Female	$18.41	$19.00	$23.46	$21.98
Not member or covered	Male	$17.74	$16.00	$21.52	$18.75
	Female	$15.15	$14.00	$18.68	$15.85
		Manufacturing: durables		**Health care and social assistance**	
Union member	Male	$21.11	$20.70	$20.11	$18.50
	Female	$17.31	$16.40	$20.60	$19.00
Not member or covered	Male	$20.52	$18.00	$20.85	$17.55
	Female	$16.75	$15.00	$16.74	$15.00
		Manufacturing: non-durables		**Information, culture, and recreation**	
Union member	Male	$19.86	$19.40	$22.14	$21.44
	Female	$13.78	$13.00	$18.89	$19.00
Not member or covered	Male	$20.36	$17.50	$18.68	$15.23
	Female	$14.86	$12.84	$15.26	$12.98

		Mean	Median	Mean	Median
		Wholesale trade		Accommodation and food services	
Union member	Male Female	$19.23 $15.48	$18.35 $14.87	$12.85 $12.06	$12.00 $11.19
Not member or covered	Male Female	$19.84 $15.98	$17.31 $14.42	$10.94 $9.60	$9.00 $8.17
		Retail trade		Other services	
Union member	Male Female	$14.18 $11.71	$12.50 $10.00	$21.75 $19.20	$20.00 $17.00
Not member or covered	Male Female	$14.23 $10.81	$11.54 $9.00	$16.16 $13.00	$15.00 $10.50
		Transport/warehousing		Public administration	
Union member	Male Female	$21.43 $18.28	$20.00 $19.00	$25.43 $22.08	$24.73 $21.00
Not member or covered	Male Female	$17.89 $15.19	$15.87 $13.57	$27.17 $21.23	$25.75 $18.50

*Statistics Canada uses a three-category breakdown for this variable: union member; not a union member but covered by a collective agreement; and not a union member and not covered by a collective agreement. The second category is not included in this table because only about 2 per cent of workers fall into this category

Source: Statistics Canada, *Labour Force Survey*, custom tabulation from public use microdata prepared by Krista Scott-Dixon

One result of women's lower wages is less power, both within and outside the household. Another is their far greater economic dependence on marriage, to the extent that many women are only a man away from poverty. According to the National Council of Welfare (2006: 4), women 'have consistently higher poverty rates than men mainly due to the high poverty rates of unattached women and single-parent mothers'. While almost half of the single-parent mothers live in poverty, this is the case for one-in-five single-parent fathers. Among seniors, women are twice as likely as men to be poor both because they are less likely to have work-related pensions and more likely to live alone. On the other hand, there are now more women who can leave an unhappy marriage because they have a job that pays them enough to survive on their own.

The fact that men and women do different jobs for different wages means that they often have different life experiences and possibilities. Women are more likely than men to work in jobs that are dull, repetitious, and boring, with little opportunity for training or advancement (Armstrong and Armstrong, 1983b, 1993). Women are more likely to be in employment that includes part-time work (less than 30 hours per week), second jobs, and self-employment (Vosko, 2006). This reflects an ongoing need for wives to supplement family income and, at the same time, fulfill all their family and household responsibilities.

Men and women also tend to face different health hazards in their paid work. Men are more likely to suffer visible physical injury, women to be exposed to cumulative, invisible hazards that are difficult to trace directly to employment. These tend to create effects such as nervousness, headache, and irritability that are often blamed on female physiology rather than on working conditions (Messing, 1998; Messing and Östlin, 2006). Another hazard of the workplace that women are far more likely than men to face is **sexual harassment** (Duffy and Cohen, 2001). To quote Marlene Kadar, 'sexual harassment is almost expected in job ghetto areas where women represent the service and clerical occupations. Here women are most vulnerable to a supervisor's or a co-worker's explicit

Time to Reflect

What kind of research is required to not only expose the links among gender, racialization, culture, and class but also to develop strategies for change?

or implicit demands' (1988: 337). Violence, too, is a common aspect of women's work, especially from patients and customers in traditonal women's work (Armstrong and Daly, 2004). In one important aspect, however, women's and men's jobs are very similar. While both girls and boys are likely to have female caregivers, both men and women are likely to have male bosses.

Research in both the United States (Hochschild, 1989) and Canada has shown that the structure of men's jobs can have a significant effect on family life and gender relations. For example, Meg Luxton's interviews in Flin Flon, Manitoba (1983), show how shift work disrupts social life, making it very difficult for couples to participate together in regularly organized community activities. The frustrations the men interviewed felt over their mining jobs were often brought home and 'taken out' on their wives; they were also reflected in disrupted sleep patterns. Luxton's more recent study of families in Hamilton, Ontario, shows such patterns continue (Luxton and Corman, 2001).

The structure of women's paid work likewise affects gender relations in the home. A study conducted in Toronto suggests that the entry of women into full-time work has profound consequences for relationships. One woman explained, 'My husband works evenings, from 5 p.m. until 1:30 or 2 a.m. My work hours are from 7 a.m. until 4 p.m. We avoid child care expenses and it gives the kids enough time to spend with both parents' (Johnson, 1986: 18). Such arrangements may allow children to spend more time with their parents, but they don't leave the parents much time to spend with each other. In their study of Toronto women, Ann Duffy, Nancy Mandell, and Norene Pupo found that many women who had paid work 'describe such burn-out symptoms as chronic fatigue, depression, apathy, irritability and anxiety' (1989: 37). These symptoms are bound to affect the relationships of couples. A decade later, Bonnie Fox still found that 'parenthood has meant increased differences between the lives of women and men with respect to responsibility, work and time', regardless of whether both had paid employment (2001c: 296). In interviews conducted with workers in long-term care, the women said that the stress of work meant 'no sex' at home (Armstrong et al., 2003).

On the positive side, as employment patterns grow more similar for both sexes, women and men can share their work experiences, which may serve to bring a couple closer together. Parenthood is also more shared. More research is necessary before we have a clear idea about how the conditions of women's and men's work are reflected in their relationships. More research is also necessary on how the work of women and men in different classes, racial and cultural groups, age groups, and locations affects gender relations.

Unpaid Work

Unpaid work, like paid work, is segregated. Women not only do different work from men, they also do more work. As Figure 16.2 shows, regardless of the employment arrangement between the spouses, women do more housework than their husbands.

Figure 16.2 Percentage of Spouses, with Children, Who Do 30 or More Hours of Unpaid Housework per Week, by Labour Force Status, 1996

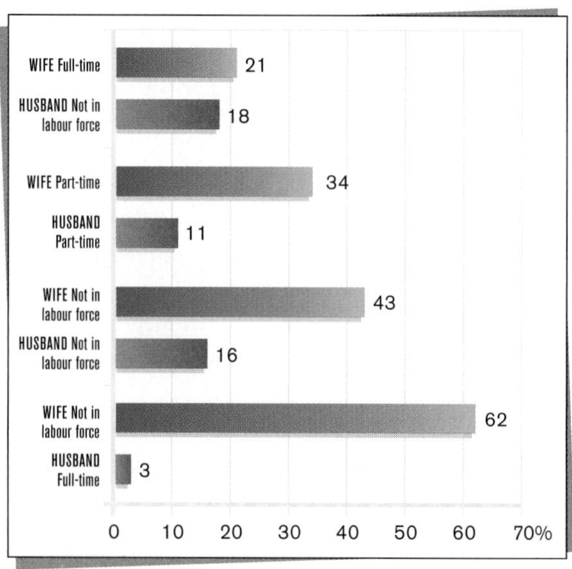

Source: Roger Sauve, 'Tracking the Links between Jobs and Family Job, Family and Stress among Husbands, Wives and Lone Parents 15–64 from 1990–2000', *Connections* (2002). Reprinted by permission of the publisher.

Study after study has shown that women and men do different kinds and amounts of labour in the home. Research conducted in the 1970s in Vancouver concluded that 'most married women do the regular, necessary, and time-consuming tasks in the household every day' (Meissner et al., 1975: 431) and that 'when men's workload and regular housework are plotted against their own job hours . . . and compared with the data for women, men always work less than women' (ibid., 429). On the basis of their Newfoundland research, Peter Sinclair and Lawrence Felt report that women's 'routine housework declines somewhat as hours of employment increase. . . . It is hardly possible for men to reduce their participation' because they are already doing so little (1992: 67).

Luxton's research in Flin Flon, Manitoba (1983), indicates that when husbands do take over work in the home, they tend to do tasks with clearly defined boundaries or those that are the least boring or monotonous. On the basis of a study in Halifax, Nova Scotia, Susan Shaw (1988) suggests that this is why men tend to define cooking and home chores as leisure. Moreover, men's contribution does not seem to significantly reduce women's domestic workload. For example, men are helping more with the children, but the father frequently 'plays with them and tells them stories and other nice things' while the mother performs most of the personal services and other tasks associated with child-rearing (Luxton, 1983: 37).

Even when women have paid jobs outside the home, they still do most of the domestic work. In his Toronto study, William Michelson found that wives do three times as much household work as their husbands: 'In families where the wife has a part-time job, this ratio is approximately 5 to 1, and it increases to 6.7 to 1 when the wife is employed' (1985: 65). In other words, when wives take on paid work, they take on an additional job and get very little help from their husbands. Susan Clark and Andrew Harvey's Halifax research indicates that 'at the present time it appears that the wife does most of the adapting; she reduces her household work and leisure hours quite significantly and is more likely than her husband to hold a part-time job' (1976: 64). Studies among unemployed men in northern Ontario (Wilkinson, 1992) and among immigrant men in Toronto (Haddad and Lam, 1988) do indicate that some men increase their workload when they are unemployed or when their spouses take on paid work, but a clear division of both amounts and types of labour remains. There is little indication that things have changed significantly since this research was done. In 1996, two-thirds of those doing less than five hours a week of unpaid housework were men while over 80 per cent of those doing 60 or more hours were women (Statistics Canada, 2003b). And 'women's share of unpaid work hours has remained quite stable since the early 1960s', in spite of their growing labour force participation (Statistics Canada, 2000: 97). Data from 2005 (Statistics Canada, 2006i: Table 1.1) indicate that women do more of the housekeeping, cooking,

SOCIOLOGY IN ACTION

More Work for Mother

More and more women are taking on paid work in addition to their domestic work. The most recent data indicate that the overwhelming majority of married women had paid work at some time during the year. This second job has important consequences for women and for their relations with men. Research conducted by Graham Lowe for the Canadian Advisory Council on the Status of Women (1989) concluded that 80 per cent of women's illness can be attributed to the stress caused by their double day of paid and unpaid work. This stress may have an impact on relationships with men. When asked if her husband helped at home, one secretary replied:

Are you kidding? That's why I had a big fight with my husband last week because I was fed up. He was complaining about this and that and I turned around and gave it to him. I said, 'I work seven hours a day. I come home, I make supper, I clean up.' I said, 'I do work before I leave in the morning. All weekend I'm working like crazy to get the house clean.' I said, 'You've got the nerve to tell me not to use the bathroom because you want to use it in the morning.'

Source: Pat Armstrong and Hugh Armstrong, *The Double Ghetto: Canadian Women and Their Segregated Work* (Toronto: Oxford University Press, 2001), 207.

Increasingly in industrialized societies, fathers are taking on more parental responsibility—especially when caregiving calls for fun activities with children. (Photo © Sophia Fortier)

washing up, and child care than men and only slightly less maintenance and repair work.

Although women with relatively high-paying careers can afford to hire other women to do much of the domestic work, any remaining tasks are still divided by sex and done disproportionately by women. In her study of career women, Isabella Bassett reports that 'close to half the career women polled say cleaning the house, grocery shopping, and doing the laundry are their responsibility, and over half say the same about cooking. This traditional division of labour applies also to the so-called "male" jobs: two-thirds of career women say household repairs and maintenance are their husband's duties in their households' (1985: 144).

Women take primary responsibility for the sick, disabled, and elderly as well (Grant et al., 2004). As daughters, mothers, partners, friends, or volunteers, women are the overwhelming majority of unpaid primary caregivers and spend more time than men providing care. Women are expected to take time off from work to take care of sick children or other child-related problems and the intensity of the care they provide often makes it difficult to take full-time employment (Pyper, 2006). This in turn greatly hinders women's ability to advance or be promoted in the workplace.

Women are also much more likely than men to do personal tasks such as bathing and toileting, while men are more likely to do household maintenance tasks (Frederick and Fast, 1999; Morris et al., 1999). Moreover, women's caregiving workloads are increasing as governments across Canada reduce hospital and other institutional care (Armstrong et al., 2001). In situations in which women and men provide support to people outside the home, the former tend to do the regular and time-consuming chores such as housework and babysitting, while the latter help with yardwork and transportation. Similar divisions appear in volunteer work. Women work longer hours than men at volunteer jobs, and they are more likely than men to provide personal care. Men who do volunteer work are most likely to coach male teams or to raise and handle funds.

Like paid work, women's and men's unpaid work is often done in different places and under different conditions, resulting in different experiences. Again, women's domestic work tends to be boring and repetitious, as well as fraught with hidden health hazards and the real possibility of sexual harassment. Thus, 'while differences in degree exist among social classes and ethnic groups, women and men in heterosexual partnerships continue to encounter essentially unequal experiences of married life' (Mandell, 2001: 204). We know less about equality in other kinds of partnerships, however.

In unpaid work, like paid work, we see continuity and differences. More men are doing unpaid work, and they are doing more of it. However, women still retain primary responsibility for houses, children, and the sick and the frail and do so in ways that undermine their labour force work and often their health.

Community and Social Life

Relationships between men and women can be said to be characterized by both change and the persistence of traditional patterns of behaviour—in brief, by ambiguity. The 'dating game', politics, and medical services all provide examples of both emerging and lingering patterns in relations between the sexes.

Dating and Sexual Relations

Women are now more likely to pay their own way and open their own doors, and they are even more likely to take the initiative in sexual activity (Wilson, 2001). Women, also, as far as we can tell from the research, are more likely today to engage in premarital or extramarital sex than they were in the past. However, young women still are more likely to justify having sexual relationships on the basis of love, while young men are far more likely to refer to physical grounds for sex.

While women are more likely today than in the past to ask men out and pay their own way, we continue to see some lingering traditional patterns in heterosexual dating and relationships. (iStockphoto)

The old double standard for female and male sexual behaviour has weakened significantly but not disappeared entirely with the advent of better contraceptives and new ideas about women's place. According to a 1992 Gallup Poll, while 74 per cent of men did not think premarital sex was wrong, this was the case for only 65 per cent of the women. More recent US research also suggests differences remain (Greene and Faulkner, 2005).The persistence of the double standard may be related to the failure to develop completely effective and safe birth control techniques and to educate young people about their proper use. The spread of HIV/AIDS may serve to destroy the double standard, however. Both men and women are being educated about and encouraged to use condoms. Moreover, as pointed out earlier, AIDS has given men in particular cause for concern about the consequences of casual sex and may therefore make their sexual practices more similar to those of women, who have had to worry throughout history about the results of sexual contact. AIDS has also contributed to more public discussion of homosexual relationships.

Both the availability of contraception and women's participation in the labour force have given women greater choice about whether, when, and whom to marry. They also have more choice to enter lesbian relationships, although severe pressure against such relationships remains. Men now have greater choice as well because they do not have to assume the main financial burden of maintaining a household when they marry or have children. These changes may help to explain why more and more couples are living in conjugal relationships outside of marriage. Couples may live together without marriage because they want to see whether they are compatible, because they cannot marry for a variety of reasons, to save money, or because they reject the notion of marriage. Living together does not necessarily mean a rejection of marriage, however—many of these couples do marry eventually.

Politics

Women have gained many legal and political rights over the past 100 years, including the right to vote and to be elected or appointed to political office. These rights have, in turn, helped to change laws related to equal opportunity for paid employment, to equal pay, and to property rights, to name but a few (Boyd, 1997; Brodie, 1996).

Women not only vote, they also run for office. The number of women who hold political office has grown enormously in recent decades. Canada's first female Prime Minister, Kim Campbell, was selected by her party in 1993 but she lost a few months later in a devastating federal election that effectively ended the viability of the federal Progressive Conservative Party (though much of the fault for this loss lay with her predecessor, Brian Mulroney), and two women (one elected in a general election) have served as provincial premiers. The active participation of women in politics has significantly altered relations within legislatures, regulatory bodies, and the courts, as well as altering legislation itself. Women's concerns and perspectives are more often taken into account.

But in the political arena, too, the sexes frequently remain segregated. Although women have participated at all levels of government, the largest proportion of women is found in municipal politics, the lowest level of decision-making. Her study of municipal politics led Kathryn Kopinak to conclude that 'women candidates and elected officials occupy positions of greater strength than men on several political dimensions', but also to suggest that this may be related to their smaller numbers at the higher levels (1988: 385). Little has changed in the intervening years. Furthermore, within municipal politics, women are segregated into traditional areas such as school boards, where they can oversee what is happening to the children. The balance of power is shifting, but the seats at the top are still reserved mainly for the men (Bashevkin, 2006).

Medical Services

Attitudes towards the sexes in the area of medical services also are changing, albeit very slowly. Significant differences persist in the treatment of women and men, reflecting old ideas about the relations between the sexes and about women's proper place. Most research is done on male subjects and then generalized to women, and even less research is done on differences among women

Time to Reflect

How can we create egalitarian relationships within households if there are inequalities outside them, in society as a whole?

(Manzer, 2001). Men are less likely than women to use health-care services (*Health Reports*, 2001); when they do, they are more likely to be treated as if they have a 'real', biologically based medical problem. Ruth Cooperstock and Henry Lennard found that 'women consistently receive twice the proportion of prescriptions for tranquilizers as do men' (1987: 314). Such prescriptions have been justified as a way of supporting social relationships, especially those based on sex. The prescription of tranquilizers to women is also 'consistent with the culturally accepted view that it is the role of the wife to control the tensions created by a difficult marriage': Valium is used 'as an aid in the maintenance of the nurturing, caring role' (ibid., 318).

Women's greater use of health services, which is related largely to their reproductive capacity, serves to reinforce the notion of dependency and the need for medical management (DesMeules et al., 2003). But as women move into the labour force or/and attain higher levels of education, traditional medical approaches are coming under attack—from men as well as women. Men now tend to be present not only at the births of their children, but also at prenatal classes. Such developments also influence relations between the sexes, often serving to bring women and men closer together as they share aspects of child-bearing and other life experiences.

Explanations for Inequality: Making Connections

There is at least one woman and one man in every occupational category. Some women are bosses; others are sexual harassers. Some men stay at home and take responsibility for household chores and child care, while most never harass women or batter their wives. These facts reinforce the view that biology is not a major factor determining the division of labour by sex.

Nonetheless, biology is far from irrelevant. The fact that women, not men, have babies does make a difference in society. Childbirth and child-rearing are separate from paid work. Because women bear children and because people have created a distinction between different kinds of work, women are to some extent limited from participating in the labour force as compared to men.

The differences are exaggerated by women's low wages, lack of maternity-leave benefits, and the scarcity and high cost of child care. An examination of paid benefits during and immediately after childbirth shows that few of those with part-time work, self-employment, or part-time jobs are eligible for such benefits (Pulkingham and Van Der Gaag, 2004: 120). Young mothers, recent immigrants, and racialized women are most likely to be without them. In addition, 'licensed or regulated family daycare is still a rarity in Canada' (Baker, 2001: 110). Good child care is not only difficult to find, it is expensive. Daycare fees average almost half the average female wage. Consequently, the families most likely to enjoy access to such care still have 'either an income high enough to pay for the service or an income low enough to qualify for subsidy' (Status of Women Canada, 1986: 72). For the many families who cannot afford or find daycare, it often makes economic sense for the woman to stay at home because she earns the lower wages. The young working-class Vancouver women interviewed by Gaskell (1992: 80) often said they would prefer working for pay to staying home with the children but saw little hope of having their male partners stay at home instead, given women's wages. Fewer women are dropping out of the labour force when they have children and more men provide care, but if anyone leaves the workforce to provide child care, it is almost always the female partner. Indeed, Francine Roy (2006) suggests that the much lower rates of female labour force participation in Alberta compared to Quebec can be understood in terms of the much lower costs and greater availability of day care in Quebec. As pointed out earlier, the same is true when elderly parents and disabled adult children require care. This type of work interruption can serve to boost men's earning potential and to reduce that of women—or at least be used as an excuse to do so.

Women's reproductive capacity and the social arrangements that turn this resource into a liability are not the only factors in the continuing division of labour by sex. The dominant ideology also plays a role. And this ideology is changing, especially for the younger generations. By 1995, the vast majority of women and men under the age of 24 thought paid work was important to personal happiness; however, over half of the men and women surveyed also thought growing children would suffer if both parents were employed (Ghalam, 2000: 70–1). Furthermore, many employers remain convinced that women are physically and mentally suited to some jobs and not others. Career women surveyed by Bassett (1985) cited sex **discrimination** as the most important factor contributing to their failure to win top jobs. A more recent *Psychology Today* article (2000: 18) reports that 'women in male-dominated fields are so intimidated by their work environment that they tend to play down certain typically female traits.' This fits with a Canadian study of women in the legal profession (Brockman, 2001), which found that women faced sexual harassment and discrimination, and were less likely than men to become partners and more likely than men to reduce their hours of paid work when they had children. The very structure of law work, with the relentless demand for billable hours and entertaining, limits the capacity to parent for both women and men. For their part, many women have learned by example and experience that men and women do different work, and this notion has become part of their world view (Gaskell, 1992).

But economic need and the need of employers for employees can overturn ideology. Many married women move into the labour market because their families need the money, but during most of the past century, single women have relied on paid work for personal economic survival. Women who are single parents depend either on wages or on welfare, given that the majority of women do not get support payments after separation but they do get the children (Galarneau and Sturrock, 1997). In addition, employers' need for people with the skills women have traditionally learned, as well as for cheap, often part-time, labour, has increased. Thus, women have provided what Patricia Connelly (1978) described as a 'reserve army'—a large number of workers who are available and who compete with others in their group for the jobs they can get.

Women's subordinate position in the labour market has reinforced their responsibility for domestic work. At the same time, women's domestic responsibilities have reinforced their subordinate position in the market. As women have gained both experience and income—at the same time suffering from the competing demands of paid and unpaid work—their ideas have changed. The resulting protests against male-dominated society and its ideology have changed both society and some of its dominant ideas.

Although large divergences remain, male and female life experiences have become more similar in recent years. Shared experiences open up new possibilities for more egalitarian relationships—though they may also create new areas of tension.

Strategies for Change 

Many women (and some men) have developed a variety of strategies for change. Individual women have pushed men to do more domestic labour. They have entered the labour market, striven for interesting and well-paid jobs, and fought to end discrimination in the workplace. They have had the courage to publicize such previously hidden crimes as sexual harassment, wife abuse, and sexual assault, and to charge men—even their own husbands—with them.

OPEN FOR DISCUSSION

The High Cost of an Interrupted Career

Statistics Canada data reveal that women who interrupt their careers in order to fulfill family responsibilities suffer in terms of pay and promotion. Meanwhile, being married can raise a man's income by 30 per cent. In 1997, married women earned only 68 per cent of married men's wages (Statistics Canada, 2000: 157). When this research was made public, it was suggested that it should be used to convince judges to award higher settlements to women when marriages end in divorce.

Yet career interruptions explain only part of the gap in pay and promotion. A Statistics Canada study concludes,

> Despite the addition of a rich variety of workplace variables, a substantial portion of the gender wage gap remains baffling. After accounting for differences in worker characteristics, women's hourly wage rate is 83.9 per cent of the men's average. . . . Once differences in the characteristics of the workplace to which men and women belong are controlled for, women's average hourly wage rate is 86.9 per cent of men's average. . . . The inclusion of industry and occupation yield considerably larger adjusted gender pay differentials: women earn roughly 91.6 per cent of comparable men. (Drolet, 2001: 42)

In other words, various forms of discrimination combine to create these inequalities.

Collectively, many women have worked—sometimes together with men—to create the conditions in which such individual efforts are possible and effective and to alter the structures that keep women subordinate. Women have succeeded in pressuring governments to pass laws recognizing women's equal contribution to marriage, mandating equal pay for work of equal value, providing maternity leave for employed women, and making job discrimination, sexual harassment, and the sexual assault of wives by their own husbands offences. Women have often succeeded in encouraging schools to develop new materials for classroom use that represent women doing more than domestic and secretarial work. Largely as a result of women's efforts, many of the practices (such as quotas) that prevented many women from entering such programs as law, medicine, and engineering have been ended. Women have also developed education programs to expand female skills and to provide information on birth control and self-protection. They have opened homes for battered women, rape crisis centres, and daycare centres. They have fought for affirmative action programs and for women's right to be heard in union affairs . . . and much more.

At the same time, men have started men's support groups and developed organizations intended to reduce violence against women. Increasing numbers of men are also seeking custody of their children and advocating equal rights for same-sex couples. They have actively worked to include the issues raised by the women's movement in classroom discussions and media presentations. More males in school are taking courses that teach them domestic skills, and some have enrolled in traditionally female university programs such as nursing and domestic science. Some men have taken on their share of domestic work or opted to stay at home to care for the children. More men are caregivers of elderly parents and spouses as well (Kramer and Thompson, 2005). Some attention is being paid to the specifically male aspects of men's health and to differences among men in relation to health.

Certain of these strategies have been successful in altering patterns and relations; many have not. Both men and women have resisted changes in gender relations (Cockburn, 1991; Faludi, 1991, 1999). Many men and many employers in particular have too much at stake to willingly alter the status quo. It cannot be denied, however, that relations between women and men have been fundamentally altered over the past few decades. Some men have learned the joys of child care, the skills involved in domestic work, the strengths of female managers, the value of egalitarian relationships, the relief of not being the sole breadwinner, the negative consequences of sexual harassment and of unprotected sex. It can no longer be assumed that a girl will be a mother and homemaker, or a boy a breadwinner and hero. Nor can it be assumed that all families will consist of partners of different sexes living with their own biological children.

Looking Ahead

Canadian society has been undergoing a fundamental economic restructuring that is bound to have a profound effect on gender relations. Some jobs in resource-based industries, manufacturing, construction, and wholesale trade have disappeared in the face of free trade, new technologies, and new managerial strategies, especially in central Canada. Most of these jobs were held by men, and many were highly paid, unionized, full-time, and relatively permanent. Moreover, their existence was critical in making possible what is called the 'traditional' family, with mother at home and father in the workforce. Recently, however, new jobs in these sectors have emerged in BC, Alberta, and some parts of Altantic Canada, sometimes splitting up households as men seek jobs elsewhere.

While jobs have become more precarious in some male-dominated areas, job growth has been in the service sector, where women dominate and where much of the work is part-time or short-term, insecure, and without union protection. Many service-sector jobs were created by the state, especially in health, social services, and education, where women dominate. But governments are now being restructured, and many of these jobs have disappeared or become precarious (Silver et al., 2004).

These developments have important consequences for both sexes. First of all, women and men are increasingly finding themselves in direct competition for work in all fields. Second, men's employment patterns are becoming more like women's as more men take part-time

Time to Reflect

What other strategies are needed to create more egalitarian relationships, and who should be implementing them?

and short-term jobs in the sectors in which women have traditionally worked and in which more women have full-time employment. A third result is that, with men less able to be breadwinners except perhaps in Alberta, where an economy fuelled by the petroleum industry continues to outstrip those of other provinces, there is even greater pressure on women to take paid work.

These changes in the labour market could lead to greater equality. Men's taking on of women's traditional paid work may develop more of the skills and personality traits relevant to family care; part-time workers may have more time to spend at home. As a result, domestic labour may become more equally shared as many women and men have more time to devote to household work. At the same time, women who become the family breadwinner may better understand the pressures men face; they may also acquire more power and more of the characteristics men develop as a consequence of their paid work.

On the other hand, the same changes could aggravate tensions between the sexes. Competition for scarce wage labour could lead to bitter confrontations between men and women. Indeed, there has already been some backlash against employment and pay equity programs, as well as against public-sector jobs. Women's lower wages mean that families dependent on a female breadwinner sink into poverty. Women are taking on more child care, elder care, and domestic work as a result of cutbacks in government services. Government restructuring of social programs is creating an equality deficit in many areas because many more women than men were dependent on such programs (Day and Brodsky, 1998). The decision of most provinces to close some institutions for those with disabilities means that more women provide home care for those previously institutionalized. At the same time, men who can no longer make a significant contribution to family economic support may leave because they are unable to face what many regard as their failure to act like men. Both tendencies—greater equality and greater tension—are evident today. Which one will prevail depends largely on the responses of men and women themselves.

Conclusion

Relations between women and men have been characterized by both change and lack of change in recent years. Although women have gained certain important rights, greater access to traditionally male-dominated institutions and jobs, and some protection from abuse, they still bear the primary load in domestic work, have lower wages than men, and face a double standard in many relationships. Put another way, although more men are helping with the housework and child care, learning to express their emotions, and treating women as equals, men still dominate the most prestigious jobs in the labour force and seldom take on an equal share of caring work.

Biologically predetermined characteristics provide little explanation for these patterns, both because there are few clearly established biological distinctions between the sexes and because biological factors are influenced by the social and physical environments. Social structures and work relations provide much more useful explanations for both change and lack of change in gender relations. These institutions and interactions are now undergoing significant changes themselves, changes that will have profound consequences for how men and women view one another. But these consequences are not predetermined. They will depend greatly on decisions and actions taken by women and men, individually and collectively, to shape their own lives.

Time to Reflect

In which direction, and in what ways, do you believe the family division of labour—both paid and unpaid—will change in the future, or will it remain essentially the same? Why?

Questions for Critical Thought

1. Why is it disturbing when we cannot readily determine a person's sex? Do you feel this should be disturbing?
2. Do you think it is possible to separate nature from nurture, biology from culture? Explain your reasoning.
3. Do similar clothes and hairstyles for males and females mean similar behaviour?
4. Do we expect the same behaviour from a black man and a white man, a rich woman and a poor woman? Why or why not?
5. Discuss the effect of HIV/AIDS on the double standard in sexual behaviour.
6. How can women's continuing responsibility for domestic work when they take on full-time employment be explained?
7. Select an article from a magazine directed at a female audience, and one from a magazine intended for a male audience. Compare the magazines with respect to the portrayal of women and men themselves and the portrayal of the relations between the sexes.

Recommended Readings

Pat Armstrong and Hugh Armstrong, *The Double Ghetto: Canadian Women and Their Segregated Work* (Toronto: McClelland & Stewart, 1994).

Linking women's paid and unpaid work, this book examines different explanations for patterns in women's jobs.

Martha Bailey, ed., 'Domestic Partnerships', *Canadian Journal of Family Law* 17, 1 (2000).

This special issue explores various aspects of same-sex partnerships.

Tania Das Gupta, *Racism and Paid Work* (Toronto: Garamond, 1996).

This book sets out a theoretical framework for understanding class, racism, and gender at work. It uses nursing and the garment industry to illustrate this framework.

Meg Luxton and June Corman, *Getting By in Hard Times: Gendered Labour at Home and on the Job* (Toronto: University of Toronto Press, 2001).

Based on interviews with household members in Hamilton, Ontario, this book connects class and gender relations, family forms, labour markets, and the process of capital accumulation.

Karen Messing, *One-Eyed Science: Occupational Health and Women Workers* (Philadelphia: Temple University Press, 1998).

This book reveals how different work leads to different health hazards and how these differences are perceived and treated.

Statistics Canada, *Women in Canada: A Gender-Based Statistical Report* (Ottawa: Statistics Canada, 2006).

This compilation of data on the status, health, education, income, and family status of women is accompanied by useful, descriptive text. There are also important chapters on Aboriginal and immigrant women, visible minority women, and senior women.

Leah Vosko, *Precarious Employment: Understanding Labour Market Insecurity in Canada* (Montreal and Kingston: McGill-Queen's University Press, 2006).

This anthology brings together a range of research on new developments in the Canadian labour force, with a particular emphasis on the gendered nature and consequences of these developments.

Stephen M. Whitehead and Frank J. Barrett, eds, *The Masculinities Reader* (Oxford: Blackwell, 2000).

The articles brought together in this text provide an overview of issues linked to being male in North American society.

Recommended Websites

Canadian Centre for Policy Research
http://policyalternatives.ca

The Canadian Centre for Policy Research published policy papers and research on Canadian issues. Much of the material on this website takes gender into account.

Canadian Policy Research Networks
www.cprn.ca

The Canadian Policy Research Networks regularly produce research reports on families, on health, and on work. Their research includes a gender-based analysis of the data.

Canadian Social Research Links
www.canadiansocialresearch.net

This website provides information on social programs in Canada, usually offering links to other sites and sources that provide details. Many of these links are to gender-specific programs.

Centres of Excellence for Women's Health
www.cewh-cesf.ca

This website offers access to a wide range of materials on women's health issues. Women's health is broadly defined to include factors that influence health as well as male/female differences in health.

Gender and Work database
wds.genderwork.ca

This database brings together a range of Statistics Canada data to integrate them in a manner not available elsewhere. The data are grouped in subject area modules and linked to an annotated bibliography. It is possible to use the data to fit your own needs.

Statistics Canada
www.statcan.ca

Statistics Canada provides reliable data on the Canadian population. Almost all of its data are reported by sex, and various research studies on gender are available.

Status of Women Canada (SWC)
www.swc-cfc.gc.ca

SWC is the federal government department that promotes gender equality and the full participation of women in the economic, social, cultural, and political life of the country. SWC focuses its work in three areas: improving women's economic autonomy and well-being, eliminating systemic violence against women and children, and advancing women's human rights.

Women Watch
www.un.org/womenwatch/

The United Nations Convention on the Elimination of Discrimination Against Women can be found on this site, along with routes to a variety of documents the United Nations produces on the current situation of women in the world.

World Health Organization (WHO)
www.who.int

The World Health Organization monitors patterns in population and health around the world. Much of its material reports on issues by gender, and some of its research is gender-specific.

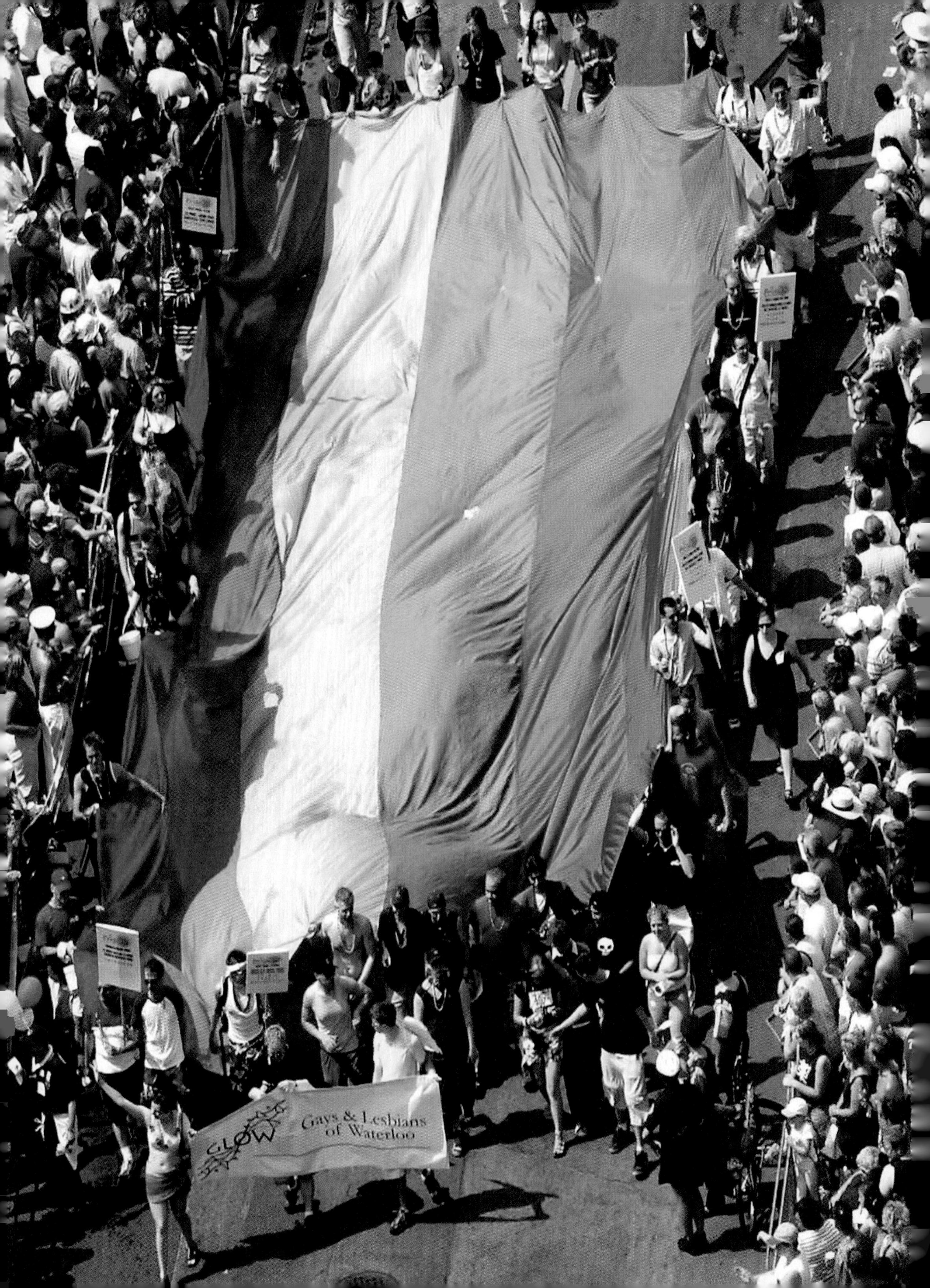
GLOW
Gays & Lesbians of Waterloo

Chapter 17

Sexuality

Patrizia Albanese

Learning Objectives

In this chapter, you will:

- Learn what is meant by sexuality and the diversity it encompasses.
- Appreciate some of the cross-cultural and historical diversity in attitudes and practices surrounding sexuality, particularly as it intersects with spirituality.
- Read about various ways in which sex and sexuality have been studied in the past and across disciplines.
- Compare various theoretical approaches to understanding sexuality.
- See what contributions sociology has made to the study of sexuality.
- Read about recent changes to our (legal) understanding of Canadians as sexual citizens.
- Identify some contemporary issues and trends in sexual attitudes and practices.

CP/Saul Porto

Introduction

Canadians, like many others, spend a considerable amount of time thinking about sex. A key-word Internet search of 'Sex—Canada' resulted in over 50.4 million 'hits'. This included material ranging from Health Canada and CBC reports on changes to same-sex marriage legislation to 'Looking for sex?' at HornyMatches.com. In line with this, in January 2006, the domain name 'sex.com', a valuable piece of Internet real estate, was sold for a reported $12 million US (Van Praet, 2006). Almost in sharp contrast to this, sociology as a discipline has done considerably less thinking about sex—until relatively recently.

As a matter of fact, the *Oxford Dictionary of Sociology* (2005), under the heading 'sociology of sex', explains that the study of sexuality 'was not a major concern in sociology until late in the twentieth century' (Scott and Marshall, 2005: 595). There is some general agreement that only in the 1960s did sociology begin to develop a stance of its own in regard to studying sex and sexuality. On the other hand, important sociological theorizing some decades earlier built the foundations for this development.

Typically, when we talk about sex, sociologists and other social scientists are referring to biological facts associated with being born male or female (including anatomical facts, hormonal facts, etc.). According to the World Health Organization (WHO) 'sex' refers to the biological characteristics that define humans as female or male, but WHO notes that while these are not mutually exclusive categories, as there are individuals who possess elements of both, we nonetheless continue to differentiate humans as either male or female (www.who.int/topics/sexual_health/en/). In other words, considerable evidence indicates that despite the fact that we often think of male/female as a dichotomy, meaning that only two categories exist and that someone is born *either* male *or* female, some infants are born with 'ambiguous' genitalia—or genitalia that are variant or 'difficult to understand' (Morland, 2005: 335). Iain Morland, writing on the **intersexed** body, explains that intersexed infants (previously labelled **hermaphrodites**) are not born ill but instead arrive, as medical historian Alice Domurat Dreger noted, 'with genitals that are pretty confusing to all adults in the room' (ibid.). In other words, intersexed bodies have hormonal, anatomical, and genetic configurations that do not fit our traditional discourses of sexual difference. While these are seemingly biological exceptions, they nonetheless exist universally. What differs, however, is how societies choose to address or treat these 'exceptions', making sex and sexuality political and social issues, rather than mere biological facts or exceptions.

Despite scientific evidence of the existence of diversity, we continue to dichotomize sex into male and female as measured by visible genital facts—the presence of a vagina or penis. And because in our society people often have little tolerance for ambiguity, we typically reconstruct the genitalia, appearance, and personalities of these infants to fit into one of the two boxes. One estimate has it that genital surgery to 'fix' intersexed

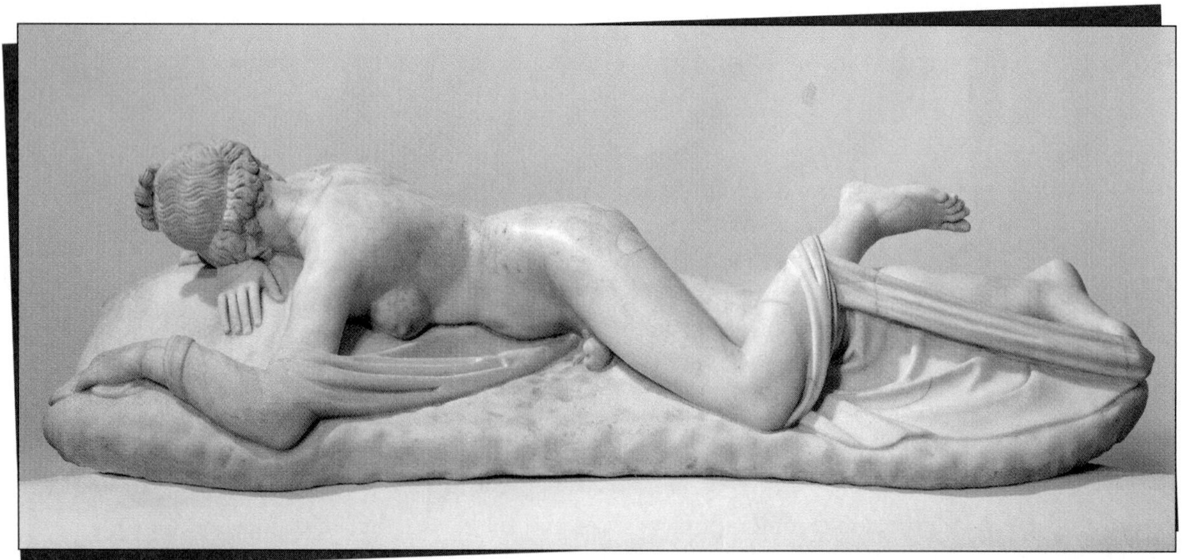

Hermaphroditos, son of the Greek gods Hermes and Aphrodite. When he met the nymph Salmacis, she was so smitten by his appearance that when he started to leave she grabbed him and begged the gods that they might never be parted. The gods assented, merging the two into a single person, both male and female. (Réunion des Musées Nationaux/Art Resource, NY)

Time to Reflect

Why do we as a society react the way we do to intersexed babies and bodies?

OPEN FOR DISCUSSION

Heteronormativity in Nursing

In 2004, a qualitative interview study of gay and lesbian hospital patients and their families was carried out in Sweden (Rondahl et al., 2006). Researchers wanted to know how gay and lesbian patients and their partners experienced nursing in hospital care. Overall they found that heteronormativity was communicated in waiting rooms, in patient documents, and when registering for admission. Nursing staff often showed perplexity when a patient or family member deviated from their heteronormative assumptions. Patients also met nursing staff who showed fear of behaving incorrectly, often impeding communication altogether. Because of heteronormative assumptions, partners of gay patients felt excluded, neglected, and not accepted as 'true' relatives. For example, the researchers found that when informants stated that they were cohabiting, nurses would ask for *his* name (for women's partners) or *her* name (for men's partners), and when they actually heard the names, exhibited reactions of surprise or perplexity.

Study participants candidly shared stories of the heteronormative treatment they received. One study participant, a 60-year-old man, said: 'Since I've been living with a man for 24 years, it was his name I gave and said that he was the partner I lived with. Then the nurse said, "Okay—but you don't have a relative or someone?"'

Lesbian patients in their reproductive years shared personal examples of heteronormative treatment. For example, a 29-year-old woman said:

> They asked if I was on the pill, and I said that 'No, I'm not on the pill'—then they asked, 'No, why not?' and I tell them why, and then it gets weird because they say, 'Well, we always do a pregnancy test'—even though they know—that is extremely insulting—they deny me and how I live—I did the pregnancy test too—I had no choice because it was part of their routine—it seemed like they were thinking, 'Everyone is really heterosexual, so just run along and pee in the bottle now please.'

The narratives of patients' partners were equally filled with examples of heteronormativity. One 30-year-old woman explained:

> In my experience as both patient and close relative, it's been worse to be a relative—as a patient, they pretty much have to take care of me, but as a relative they can ignore me—like my being there makes the patient homosexual—if I weren't there, she would just be another patient in the lot. But since she had me with her—she suddenly became something else—and it's probably easier to just close your eyes and pretend I'm not there—but I can really only interpret it as if they didn't accept that we had a homosexual relationship—they would much rather talk to our parents, even though we are adults.

Rondahl and colleagues note that 'nursing staff may feel torn between an underlying desire to be tolerant towards gay people and a visceral discomfort with gay culture.' These ambivalent attitudes lead to emotional and communicative insecurity and a lack of appropriate behaviour among nursing staff, which in turn may lead to misconceptions for all involved. They recommend more education and opportunities for communication, so that nursing staff might learn to interact in more open and natural ways.

babies happened five times per day to infants in American hospitals in the 1990s (Kessler, 1998).

Once we think of individuals as fitting into one of the two dichotomous sex categories, we also come to see men and women as naturally polar opposites of one another—note the term 'opposite sex'—who are inevitably assumed to be sexually 'drawn' to one another like magnets. As a result, in dichotomizing sex this way, we have also tended to dichotomize sexuality, sexual identity, and sexual orientation into heterosexual ('normal' sexual attraction to the 'opposite' sex) or **homosexual** (less 'normal' attraction to someone of the same sex), when in fact sexuality is considerably more complex than this. Furthermore, in doing this, almost all aspects of social life are constructed on the assumption that all ('normal') people are heterosexual. This has come to be called **heteronormativity**.

Sexuality has been defined by the World Health Organization as being a central aspect of being human, and encompasses sex, gender identities and roles, **sexual orientation**, eroticism, pleasure, intimacy, and reproduction. WHO explains that sexuality is experienced in thoughts, fantasies, desires, beliefs, attitudes, values, behaviours, roles, and relationships. It also adds that sexuality is influenced by the interaction of biological, psychological, social, economic, political, cultural, ethical, legal, historical, religious, and spiritual factors.

Jeffrey Weeks (1993: 16) notes that the meanings we give to sexuality are 'socially organized, sustained by a variety of languages, which seek to tell us what sex is, what it ought to be—and what it could be'. He adds that these languages of sex 'embedded in moral treatises, laws, educational practices, psychological theories, medical definitions, social rituals, pornographic or romantic fictions, popular music and common sense assumptions (most of which disagree) set the horizon of the possible.' Sexuality therefore has to do with who we are and what place we (are allowed to) take within society.

Once people are snuggly packaged into boxes—male or female, masculine or feminine, heterosexual or homosexual—things like **sexism** (the subordination of one sex, usually female, and the perceived superiority of the other) and **homophobia** (an irrational fear and/or hatred of homosexuals and homosexuality) help reinforce rigid boundaries and keep people in their place. For example, a young person who challenges traditional gender ideology or practices is likely to be teased and taunted ('you fag'). In our society, boys, perhaps more than girls, who cross the gender divide are often harassed back into stereotypically masculine behaviour. Children and youth learn quickly to avoid ridicule by conforming to prescribed gender and sexual norms. As a result, we come to see certain types of behaviour as normal, natural, and inevitable—the core or **essence** of femininity or masculinity, heterosexuality or homosexuality—when, in fact, we may have been encouraged or forced to suppress parts of our identities that cross the gender and

IN THE FIRST PERSON

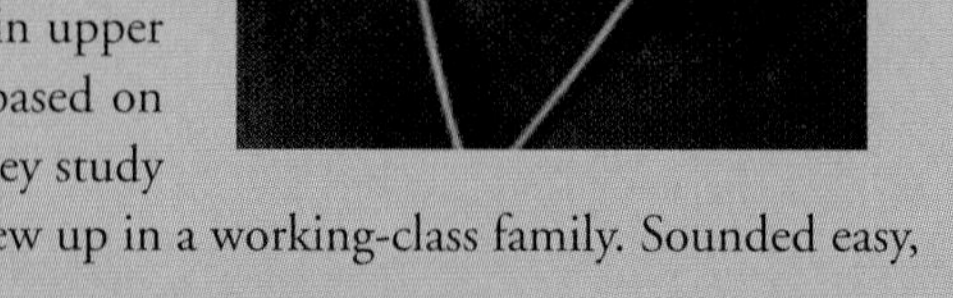

If you asked me in my first year in university what I wanted to do in life, I would probably have said 'teach elementary school or high school history . . . perhaps.' If you pressed me, you'd find that I had no idea what I wanted to do in life. I loved history but what could I do with a history degree? I could do a double major, history and . . . something else.

In my first year I took history, sociology, English, classical studies, and psychology. My English mark was my lowest of the five, so that was out as a second major. Psychology required methods and stats in upper years, so that was out. Sociology seemed straightforward and based on common sense. They study families . . . I'm part of a family. They study ethnicity . . . I'm an immigrant. They study social class . . . I grew up in a working-class family. Sounded easy, and no stats. So history and sociology it was.

Did I say no stats? That was my first mistake. My second was the idea that sociology was based on common sense. It took me awhile (okay, 15 years of university) to figure out that sociology challenges commonsense assumptions about how the world works. I guess that's what I love most about it. Despite my misinformed and rocky beginning, I find myself teaching sociology at Ryerson (and social research methods, to boot!).—Patrizia Albanese sexual divide (see DeLamater and Hyde, 1998). We have learned to treat as natural, inevitable, or **essential** things that are cultural, learned, and open to change.

Sexuality over the Centuries

Sex and Spirituality: Examples of Cross-cultural Diversity and Social Change

Sex and religion/spirituality have been closely linked among some cultures, groups, and belief systems, and certainly all religions have had something to say about our sexual, procreative nature. Theosophy, for example, is a philosophical system professing to achieve knowledge of the divine through spiritual ecstasy. Dozens of cultures throughout history, including ancient Sumerians, Egyptians, and Greeks, and over the past few centuries, some groups in Borneo, the Ibo of Nigeria, the Ewe-speaking peoples of southeast Ghana, Benin, and Togo, and some groups in pre-conquest South and Meso-America, have had sacred male and/or female prostitutes (Bishop, 1996). Many North American Aboriginal societies had transgendered or two-spirited shamans or healers fulfilling religious duties because they were believed to possess spiritual qualities (Baird, 2001).

In ancient China, sex was seen as a form of worship that led to immortality. In other words, sexuality and spirituality were very closely linked. For example, using some of the basic principles of Taoism, the *Su-nu Ching* (an ancient text), believed to have been written around the second or third century AD, noted that 'those who know the Tao of loving and harmonize the yin and yang are able to blend the five joys into a heavenly pleasure' (cited in Bishop, 1996: 140). The Taoist sex guide advised a man to prolong intercourse as long as possible, to arouse a woman to a state of orgasm, allowing him to absorb more of her *yin* (her natural feminine essence) in order to enhance his masculine *yang* (ibid.).

In India, some time between the third and fifth centuries AD, the *Kama Sutra* was written by a lifelong celibate and sage named Vatsyayana. The *Kama Sutra* has been identified as especially significant as a text because it gave as much importance to a woman's active sexual involvement and pleasure as it did to a man's. Women were to be seen and treated as sexual equals to men. As well, the author was obsessed with classifications and the presentation of a huge variety of sexual actions and positions, each with special names and multiple variants (Morris, 1997). Vatsyayana's classifications and instructive illustrations demonstrated the ritualistic and sacred nature of sexual acts. The *Kama Sutra* also equated spirituality with spontaneity in sex (Bishop, 1996).

Tantra, a Sanskrit word meaning web or weaving, is said to have both a Hindu and Buddhist variant, and involves a process of psychosomatic training where the Tantrika tries to attune his/her body and mind to increasingly higher levels of cosmic energy. The process involves activating the energy of the opposite sex in one's own body through ritualized intercourse. *Tantra*, while largely targeting men, is credited for preserving ancient forms of goddess worship and acknowledging, unlike orthodox thinking at the time, that women could attain transcendental bliss. Most of its early followers were also said to have come from the lower castes, and many of its practices were specifically designed to break caste barriers and taboos (ibid.).

Judaism, Christianity, and Islam, while seemingly not as open to the exploration of sexuality, have encouraged followers to use sexual acts to enrich their spiritual lives. Indeed, 'The Song of Solomon' in the Old Testament, dating as far back as the tenth century BC, is one of the earliest writings describing the joy and significance of physical sexuality. The religions that developed in the Middle East particularly extolled the value of the sexual act if linked to procreation in marriage. For example, the Talmud notes that sex in marriage and for the purpose of procreation should be enjoyed, and in some branches of Judaism, sex is considered a blessed duty to be carried out the evening before the Sabbath (ibid.). In Islam, in the Qur'an, sex is encouraged, provided that it is preceded by an act of piety, and parts of the Qur'an describe the 'delights' of men who will be waited on in Paradise by *houris*—bright-eyed maidens with swelling breasts (ibid.). In Christianity, Jesus is presented in the New Testament as being forgiving in regard to sexual sinners so long as they sin no more. Yet the apostle Paul showed a certain personal distaste for sex—if people must marry, have sex, and procreate that was fine, but it was better to remain apart from any physical relationship because such involvement could get in the way of the Christian's total commitment to God. This stance, because of Paul's extensive and influential writings (the epistles of Paul comprise a sizable portion of the New Testament), shaped the sexual moderation embraced by the early Christian church. For the most part, however, Judeo-Christian ideas have done much to forge a sexual morality based on self-denial and on what writer Clifford Bishop (ibid., 78) claims is an 'exaggerated or

Erotic reliefs cover the entire Kandariya Mahadeva Temple in India. The temple was created during the Chandella dynasty, between the years 1025 and 1150. (Borromeo/Art Resource, NY)

unhealthy contempt for the flesh'. Others would suggest, rather, that this religious tradition has sought to teach an awareness of the weaknesses of the flesh.

Many of the examples presented above focused on heterosexuality as a path to heightened spirituality. Over the millennia, religious attitudes towards homosexuality have been quite mixed. Early Buddhist traditions appeared to celebrate Buddha's intimate and loving relationship with his disciple Ananda as depicted in the *Jataka* tales. Some early Chinese and Japanese Buddhists showed considerable tolerance towards homosexuality among their monks and nuns (Baird, 2001). On the other hand, some later variants of Indian Buddhism condemned and expelled homosexual monks and were especially intolerant of transgendered homosexual males, called *pandakas* (ibid.). More modern variants of Hinduism also appear quite hostile to homosexuality, as are some variants of Islam (Sufis were an exception), Judaism, and Christianity. For example, the prophet Muhammad is believed to have said 'no man should look at the private parts of another man and no woman should look at the private parts of another woman.' Similarly, the Old Testament states that 'You shall not lie with a male as with a woman; it is an abomination' (Leviticus 18:22). Christian theologian St Thomas Aquinas identified four categories of vice against nature under the rubric of lust: 'masturbation, bestiality, coitus in unnatural positions and copulation with an undue sex, male with male and female with female' (Baird, 2001: 89–96).

Sex and Knowledge

Homosexuality was not always condemned. When sex and sexuality were used as part of, or in connection to, the acquisition of knowledge we have many cases of homoerotic exchanges and practices. Throughout human history the acquisition and exchange of knowledge also included the exchange of sex and passion (unlike in the typical academy today). The Greek philosopher Plato, for example, has been identified as the first 'Western' thinker to describe the acquisition of knowledge in erotic terms. According to Plato, homosexual love was the fuel that drove the soul towards knowledge. He explained that the mind frees itself from the distractions of the body using the power of Eros. Throughout Plato's *Republic* there are references to the love between a man/teacher and his younger male lover/pupil (Plato, 1980). Similarly, the Greek poet Sappho ran an academy for girls on the island of Lesbos (hence the term 'lesbian') in the seventh century BC, and her sensual poems, it is believed, were written about and for some of her female students. The artists Donatello, Giantantonio Bazzi, Michelangelo, and Leonardo Da Vinci were also believed to either have had sex or felt strong passion for some of their male disciples/students.

Many of Europe's most renowned and powerful men often turned to women other than their wives for sexual and intellectual exchanges. Courtesans, for example, who were often 'respectable' and/or educated prostitutes, were chosen as mistresses by some of the most wealthy and powerful men in Europe, for their skills as lovers but also for their intellectual abilities as well (Richardson, 2000).

Sexual Restraint versus Sexual Freedom

Political economist Thomas Malthus (1766–1834), in *An Essay on the Principles of Population Growth*, first published in 1798, warned that unchecked population growth would outstrip growth of the means of subsistence (food production). In an 1803 edition of the essay, Malthus stressed the importance of 'moral restraint' in keeping population growth in check. He suggested that individuals delay the 'gratification of passion' through sexual abstinence and the postponement of marriage. In contrast to this, one of Malthus's contemporaries, the French aristocrat, Marquis de Sade (1740–1814), famous for his at times violent pornographic texts (the term 'sadism' is derived from his name/work), argued for extreme sexual freedom. Malthus, stressing sexual restraint, and de Sade, the sexual libertine, exemplify extremes that are not uncommon in the history of the scientific study of sex and sexuality. The repression or unleashing of (biologically based or socially constructed) sexual urges or desires has been an underlying theme in a considerable amount of theorizing on sexuality.

The Scientific Study of Sex

Biomedical/Reproductive Approach

For most of human history, the scientific processes connected to procreation have remained a mystery. It was only in the late seventeenth century and early eighteenth

Many artists, like Hieronymous Bosch (*c.* 1450–1516), have been inspired by sex and sexuality. *The Garden of Earthy Delights* is the centre panel of this triptych, on display in the Museo el Prado in Madrid, Spain. (Scala/Art Resource, NY)

century that the Dutch scientist Anton van Leeuwenhoek observed that sperm 'swam' in human semen. And it was not until 1875 that Oscar Hertwig became the first scientist to observe the fertilization of an egg by sperm—in sea urchins. Much of the early scientific research on sex focused on the biomedical aspects of sex and procreation. From there, some scientific work shifted focus towards 'sexual deviance', which included any and all acts that did not have reproduction as a possibility and goal. In other words, the development of sexology involved a shift in focus from reproductive processes to the study of sexual practices. For some time this branch of the field remained medical rather than social in orientation. Beginning in the latter half of the nineteenth century, as physicians sought to strengthen their hold on the medical profession and to extend their professional control over the human body and mind, 'sexual deviance' was seen as a mental illness, to be treated by medical interventions. Indeed, the American Psychological Association only removed homosexuality from its list of psychiatric disorders—found in the *Diagnostic and Statistical Manual of Mental Disorders*—in 1973.

This type of scientific approach to studying sex, which focused on sex for procreation in marriage as normal and all other sexual activity as deviant, was deeply ingrained in the social thinking until fairly recently. A 1967 academic textbook entitled *Human Sexuality: A Contemporary Marriage Manual* (McCary, 1967) included chapters on such topics as 'The Female Reproductive System', 'Fertilization, Prenatal Development and Parturition', 'Techniques in Sexual Arousal', and 'Positions in Sexual Intercourse', and the last chapter, 'Sexual Aberrations', dealt with what was deemed to be deviant: sexual oralism, sexual analism (among a list of abnormal methods), homosexuality, zoophilia, necrophilia, masturbation (among a list of abnormal choices of sexual partners), and frigidity, promiscuity, and seduction (among a list of abnormal degrees of desire). The message of this scholarly text was clear, and not very different from the very earliest studies of sex: not only is human sexuality something that takes place between heterosexuals, but only within marriage, for procreation, and using prescribed and approved methods and positions.

Throughout the 1800s and into the 1900s, a number of prominent thinkers contributed to a growing body of sex research. Sigmund Freud (1856–1939), for example, the founder of psychoanalysis, produced a comprehensive theory of human development with sex at the centre. According to Freud, the development of a healthy adult personality depended on the successful navigation through various stages of psychosocial and psychosexual development, each involving the careful management of various aspects of the sexual instinct. In fact, many of the early theories of sexuality used the metaphor of repression, which comes from hydraulics, and includes the idea or image of a gushing energy that must be held back and controlled. Sexuality, historically, has been perceived as an innate 'force' that needs to be regulated and successfully manipulated or (re)directed towards acceptable channels.

Both scientific and popular examples of this way of thinking about sex and sexuality continue to this day. For example, Jim Popp, head coach and general manager of the Montreal Alouettes of the Canadian Football League, asked his players to refrain from sex during the week leading up to the 2006 Grey Cup championship game (Canadian Press, 2006b). Presumably, he wanted their energy and stamina channelled into hard-hitting play that would lead to a Grey Cup victory (they lost the game, by the way!).

On the scientific side, while not specifically psychoanalytic in focus, Edward Shorter shares with his Freudian predecessors the idea that sexual behaviour is rooted in innate biological drives. Shorter argues in *Written in the Flesh: A History of Desire* that 'sexual behaviour and sensual pleasure are products of biologically driven desire rather than of fashion or social conditioning' (Shorter, 2005: 3–4). He explains that just as our bodies tell us what we might like to eat, they also have brain-driven impulses that direct our sexual desires. According to Shorter, sexual gratification 'springs from unleashed human biology' (ibid., 240).

Another pioneer in the scientific study of sexuality was Henry Havelock Ellis (1859–1939). His is also considered a biological approach to the study of sex; however, unlike most others at the time, he tried to demystify sex and challenge many of the accepted sexual norms of Victorian England, famous for its sexually repressive norms and abundance of clandestine erotic literature (see Kearney, 1982). For example, he assured his readers that masturbation did not lead to illness and homosexuality was not a disease. He argued that homosexuality was simply an innate variation from the norm, not a vice or an amoral choice.

Social Survey Approach

Like Ellis, the American biologist Alfred Kinsey (1894–1956) broke new ground in the scientific study of sex by challenging some of the accepted norms of his time. For example, he argued that 'biologists and psychologists who have accepted the doctrine that the only natural function of sex is reproduction have simply ignored the existence of sexual activity which is not reproductive' (Kinsey et al., 1953: 448). He was critical of biologists and psychologists who assumed that heterosexual responses are part of an animal's innate or instinctive equipment, and was especially critical of their treatment of non-reproductive sexual activity as perversions of normal instincts (ibid.).

In 1947, Kinsey founded the Institute for Research in Sex, Gender and Reproduction at Indiana University, now called the Kinsey Institute. Kinsey is famous for surveying approximately 18,000 Americans in the 1940s on their sexual practices. Through the survey he found, among other things, that there were significantly different class patterns among men in the incidence of masturbation, homosexuality, oral sex, sex with prostitutes, and premarital and extramarital sex. For women, their age and gender ideologies were significantly more important than social class in explaining variations in sexual preferences and practices. He was also famous for his 'Heterosexual–Homosexual Rating Scale', a seven-point continuum representing a considerably more complex approach to understanding sexuality and sexual orientation than was typical at the time.

He proposed that males do not represent two discrete populations—heterosexual and homosexual—and that the living world is a continuum in all its aspects (Kinsey et al., 1948). As such, he emphasized a continuity of the gradations (a scale) between exclusively heterosexual and exclusively homosexual life histories. Note that he did not say 'exclusively heterosexual individuals' but rather 'histories'. This was intentional because Kinsey argued that an individual may be assigned a different position on the scale for different periods in his life. On the scale, zero refers to exclusively heterosexual with no homosexual experiences; 1 is predominantly heterosexual, and only incidentally homosexual; 2 is predominantly heterosexual but more than incidentally homosexual; 3 is equally heterosexual and homosexual; 4 is predominantly homosexual but more than incidentally heterosexual; 5 is predominantly homosexual and only incidentally heterosexual; and 6 is exclusively homosexual (ibid., 638).

Laboratory Approach

Other noted sex researchers include William Masters (1915–2001) and Virginia Johnson (1925–). In 1957, William Masters hired Virginia Johnson as his research assistant in studies of human sexuality. After years of

Figure 17.1 Kinsey's Heterosexual–Homosexual Rating Scale . . . Applied

Heterosexual–Homosexual Rating Scale

One theoretical construct designed by Alfred Kinsey is the 'Heterosexual–Homosexual Rating Scale', a seven-point continuum originally published in Kinsey's *Sexual Behavior in the Human Male* (1948).

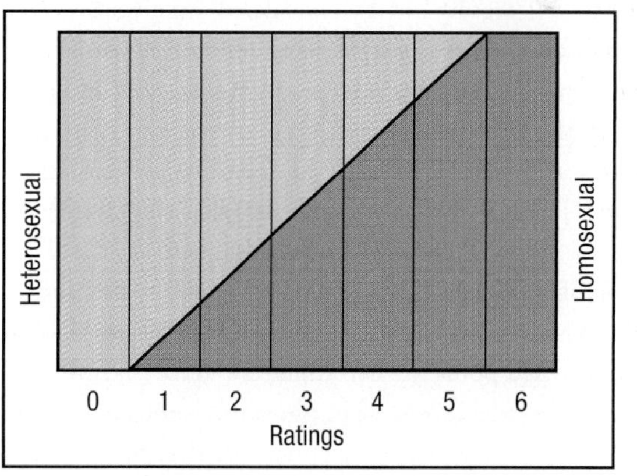

Fernando Luiz Cardoso (2002) applied this scale to his six-month field study of 41 men living in a remote fishing village in southern Brazil. Cardoso found that in this society many 'straight' men customarily had sex with local 'gay' men, called '*paneleiros*'. He found at least three different categories of male sexuality: men who have sex only with men, men who have sex only with women, and men who have sex with men and women. Cardoso noted that 'they believe, a "real" man is somebody "who has never been @#$%&* but can @#!* whoever is available"' (ibid., 57). For them, masculinity is determined by sexual function and position, and not by the sex of the partner. The same was true in ancient Greece, where social class and authority determined who would penetrate and who would be penetrated.

Source: Diagram from <www.kinseyinstitute.org/about/photo-tour.html>. Reprinted by permission of the Kinsey Institute for Research in Sex, Gender, and Reproduction, Inc.

working together, Masters divorced his wife and married Johnson (Masters and Johnson divorced in 1993). Together, they founded the Reproductive Biology Research Foundation in St Louis, Missouri, later renamed the Masters and Johnson Institute. In their early laboratory research they recorded data, based on direct observation, on the anatomy and physiology of human sexual response (including the nature of female arousal and orgasm). They began by observing and documenting the stages of sexual arousal and orgasmic responses of 382 women and 312 men. Among other things, they observed and reported on the sexual responsiveness of older men and women, including elderly individuals—noting that many older men and women are perfectly capable of excitement and orgasm (typically following more direct genital stimulation) well into their seventies. They observed and measured masturbation and sexual intercourse in laboratory settings. In doing this, they treated and wrote about sex as a healthy and natural activity, enjoyed for pleasure and intimacy. They also developed a clinical approach (sex therapy) to the treatment of 'sexual dysfunction' or 'sexual problems', including premature ejaculation, impotence, and female frigidity. Given the voyeuristic nature of this research, it is not surprising that their work was more trendy and 'popular' than of long-lasting importance.

Ethnographic/Anthropological Approach

Although anthropologists such as Margaret Mead (1901–78) would not be considered 'sexologists', they have, nonetheless, done extensive research documenting the sexual lives of people across diverse cultures. In doing so, they have contributed a body of research that challenges the view that sex and sexuality are biological (fixed, innate) facts. Mead, for example, wrote hundreds of articles and dozens of books documenting the lives, including the sexual lives and practice, of diverse cultures of the South Pacific. In *Coming of Age in Samoa* (1928), she shocked some of her American readers (from the 1930s into the 1950s) when she wrote about her observations of young Samoan women who deferred marriage while enjoying casual premarital sex before eventually marrying. She documented the impact of variations in culture (rather than biology) in the construction of sex roles, including sexuality, in *Sex and Temperament in Three Primitive Societies* (1935). Similarly, Clellan Ford and Frank Beach (1951), in an extensive survey of over 200 societies, produced anthropological evidence of striking diversity and variation in sexual practices and norms. The amount of variation across and within cultures is one way in which we know that sexual responses are learned and not innate.

Sociology of Sex: Theoretical and Methodological Approaches

Like Mead, most sociologists today would argue that sexuality involves much more than an understanding of biological aspects of physical attraction. Sociologists, like anthropologists, frequently stress the social and cultural relativity of norms surrounding sexual behaviour and the socio-historical construction of sexual identities and roles. Within sociology, sexuality is typically studied and understood as being intricately connected to cultural, economic, political, legal, moral, and ethical phenomena. Janice Irvine (2003: 431), for example, notes that from a sociological perspective, 'sexuality is a broad social domain involving multiple fields of power, diverse systems of knowledge, and sets of institutional and political discourses.' While sociology may have been comparatively slow to enter this field of study, it has gone a long way to address, explain, and understand some of these diverse issues and dimensions. But it does so from a number of different theoretical and methodological perspectives.

In tracing the history of sociological theorizing and research on sexuality, Irvine identified five broad themes in the sociological literature: (1) the denaturalization of sexuality (a shift away from biological explanations); (2) the historicization of sexuality; (3) the analytic shift from the study of 'sexual deviants' (the individuals) to the study of 'sexual deviance' (the rule-making strategies or social systems that define people as deviant or stigmatize them), thus challenging the pathologizing categories of sexuality and blurring the status of insider/outsider; (4) the destabilization of sexual categories and identities, with new emphasis on the fluid and diverse meanings of sex and sexuality; and (5) the theorizing of sexuality (and gender) as performance.

Denaturalization

Structural Functionalist

Early sociologists, especially some structural functionalists, made liberal use of biological models and metaphors but did not wholeheartedly embrace simple biological explanations of social reality. When the American structural functionalist Kingsley Davis wrote about human sexuality, he looked at sexual intercourse as more

HUMAN DIVERSITY

Incest and Taboo

In the following excerpt, Clifford Bishop (1996: 120–1) describes the variation in the practices and beliefs of different peoples surrounding the issue of incest.

Some form of prohibition against incest is the nearest thing to a universal human taboo. People such as the !Kung of Southern Africa think of incest as 'dangerous, like going up to a lion,' and the Comanche of North America used to consider it neither a crime nor a sin, but simply impossible. However, there are numerous examples of incest being allowed, or even encouraged, in a culture. The most famous instances are the incestuous marriages of the royal houses of ancient Egypt and Inca Peru, in which brother and sister were required to continue the dynastic line. Half-sibling marriages were quite common in the ancient Near East and Europe, among the Persians, Greeks and Hebrews. In Bali, although half- and full-sibling marriages are forbidden, it is assumed that opposite sex twins have already been intimate in the womb, so they are allowed to marry as adults; by contrast, the Marshallese of the Pacific believe that such *in-utero* incest is cause to kill the male twin. Other peoples, such as the Lamet of Asia, define kinship socially rather than by blood, and allow sibling marriage if the boy and girl have been raised in different households.

Sex between a father and his daughter is more rarely sanctioned in any society, but is, in practice, the most frequent form of incest. A survey in the United States in the mid-1980s concluded that 10 to 14 per cent of under-18-year-olds had experienced some form of incestuous attention, and that most were girls and young women abused by their fathers and stepfathers.

The rarest matings of all are between mother and son. Travelers' tales relate examples of this union worldwide, but there are probably only two plausible institutionalized examples. The Kubeo of South America require a boy to sleep with his mother to mark the beginning of his official sex life (although marriage between them is forbidden), and an east African Tutsi cure for impotence on the marriage night involves the man sleeping with his mother.

But even those societies that selectively sanction breaches of the incest taboo enforce it in all other cases . . . .

Source: Clifford Bishop, *Sex and Spirit* (Alexandria, Va: Time-Life Books, 1996), 120–1.

than a biological exchange or a simple response to natural urges. He instead saw it as a social exchange, often involving 'the employment of sex for non-sexual ends within a competitive-authoritarian system' (Davis, 1937: 746). In his classic article, 'The Sociology of Prostitution', Davis asked the question: why is it that a practice so thoroughly disapproved, so widely outlawed in Western civilization, can yet flourish so universally?

Davis noted that where the family is strong, there tends to be a well-defined system of prostitution. He explained that the family is an institution of status that limits the variety, amount, and nature of a person's satisfaction. Through prostitution, a man is paying for the privilege to demand what he wants. Davis suggested that 'the sole limitation on [a man's] satisfaction is not morality or convention, but his ability to pay the price' (ibid., 753). To a certain extent, then, prostitution served to keep nuclear families together and 'strong'. When men could not have their sexual needs met within marriage, prostitution functioned to fill that role. He also added that prostitution served a number of other functions in economical ways: 'enabling a small number of women to take care of the needs of a large number of men, it is the most convenient sexual outlet for an army, and for the legions of strangers, perverts and physically repulsive in our midst. It performs a function apparently, which no other institution fully performs' (ibid., 755). He warned, however, that a decline of the family and a decline of prostitution are both associated with a rise of sexual freedom, and explained that 'unrestricted indulgence in sex for the fun of it by both sexes is the greatest enemy, not only of the family, but also of prostitution' (ibid.).

Time to Reflect

What do you think of Davis's argument? Do you have any sense from his work of how a woman's/wife's sexual and marital satisfaction might be constructed? Is he warning against sexual freedom of *both* sexes? Why do you think this?

More recently, using a structural-functionalist perspective, Davidson and Hoffman (1986) conducted a survey of 212 married female graduate and undergraduate students at a Midwestern commuter university in the United States to see what meaning and function sexual fantasies played in marital satisfaction. They found that, contrary to popular belief and some previous studies, engaging in sexual fantasies did not negatively affect married women's mental health, including level of guilt, sexual adjustment, and overall satisfaction with their current sex life. They found no significant differences between frequency of sexual fantasizing and marital satisfaction. Respondents who reported being satisfied with their current sex life fantasized about their current sex partner, and those who were dissatisfied were much more likely to fantasize about a more affectionate partner. Davidson and Hoffman concluded that their data strongly suggest that sexual fantasies function to help achieve sexual arousal irrespective of satisfaction or dissatisfaction with married women's current sex lives.

Conflict Approaches

We often think of Friedrich Engels in relation to his work with Karl Marx, writing about social class inequality. However, his famous work, *The Origin of Family, Private Property and the State* (1990 [1884]), has a great deal to say about sexuality, private property, power, and subordination. Engels notes that in tribal societies with no concept of private property, promiscuous intercourse prevailed so that 'every woman belonged equally to every man and every man to every woman' (Engels, 1990 [1884]: 142). He adds that among the Iroquois, for example, a man considered his own and his brother's children his children, and they would all call him father. Paternity was no mere honorary title linked to procreation, but rather carried serious mutual obligations, essential for the social constitution of these people (ibid., 141). Engels explains that with the advent of private property, this changed. As the desire for the accumulation of wealth increased, men gained greater status in the family than women. This also created a stimulus for men to overthrow traditional communal forms of inheritance in favour of their children. To do this, men would have to ensure paternity as a biological rather than social category, and did so through the introduction of monogamy, the repression of women's sexual freedom, and the rise of the patriarchal family as a dominant family form (ibid., 164–5).

Engels states that the final outcome of 3,000 years of monogamy is the bourgeois family, where men have exclusive domination over women, including over women's sexual autonomy. He predicted that monogamy and women's sexual oppression would disappear when the economic cause—private property ownership—disappears. The revolutionary overthrow of capitalism and the abolition of private property would mean that the individual family would cease to be the economic unit of society. Engels explains that then 'society takes care of all children equally' and 'the anxiety about the "consequences," which is today the most important social factor—both moral and economic—that hinders a girl from giving herself freely to the man she loves, disappears.' He then proclaims: 'Will this not be cause enough for a gradual rise of more unrestrained sexual intercourse, and along with it, a laxer public opinion regarding virginal honour and female shame?' (ibid., 183). Engels's views on 'individual love sex' or free love were adopted by a number of others, including left-wing feminists Alexandra Kollontai and Emma Goldman.

More recent conflict theorists have focused less on sexual freedom and more on understanding the link between sexuality and social class differences. For example, Gordon, Schroeder, and Abrams (1990) assessed the sexual knowledge of 130 American children, ages two to seven, and found significant differences in knowledge across the social classes. They found that children from lower-class families (with family incomes below $10,000) had less knowledge of sexual body parts, pregnancy, and sexual abuse prevention than children from 'Class 2' (family income $15,000–$25,000) and 'Class 3' (family $30,000 to $40,000) families. As well, children in Class 2 had less sexual knowledge than those in Class 3. Mothers in Class 1 (the lowest class) reported having taught less sex education to their children and reported (correctly or incorrectly) that their children had less sexual experience (for example, sex play with other children and exposure to sexually explicit material) than mothers in Classes 2 and 3.

Similarly, an American study of sexual behaviour and attitudes found that people from higher social classes and white men had greater access to sexual capital than black men and black women, white women, and men and women in lower classes (Gonzales and Rolison, 2005). Gonzales and Rolison found, among other things, that study respondents with higher socio-economic status (SES) reported thinking about sex more frequently than other respondents. They also found that the higher a respondent's SES, the more frequently he or she reported masturbating and the more likely the individual was to report finding a significantly greater variety of sexual acts more appealing than others. Gonzales and Rolison concluded that sexual behaviour and attitudes in the US reflect patterns of dominance and inequality, and these 'structures of sexual inequality are enshrined in taken-for-granted American moral dispositions' (ibid., 716). In other words, these differences reflect their position in a stratified society, and 'private' choice is conditioned by race, class, and gender dominance.

The Chicago School

In the first four decades of the twentieth century the Chicago School was famous for its sociological studies of the city. Sociologists such as Robert Park did extensive ethnographic research on urban life. When using the city as a natural laboratory, Park examined, among other things, vice districts, urban environments, and other social structures that produced unique sexual worlds. While Park, like many of his time, believed that sexuality and sex drives were biologically based, he nonetheless noted that they were shaped and constrained by social forces.

Interactionist Sociology and Sexual Scripts

John Gagnon and William Simon, both of whom trained at the University of Chicago and later worked at the Kinsey Institute (1965–8), have been identified as 'fathers' of the sociological study of sex in North America. Going much further than Park, they openly challenge the biological determinism of most sexologists, arguing that if sex does play an important part in shaping human affairs it is because societies have created its importance, not because of rigid biological grounding (Simon and Gagnon, 2003). For them, sex is neither a dangerous instinct that needs curbing nor a passionate impulse that needs liberating. They further argue that neither sexual activities nor body parts are inherently sexual; rather they become sexual when social meanings are attributed to them. While sexual activity most often takes place in private settings, they argue that 'the sexual encounter remains a profoundly social act in its enactment and even more so in its antecedents and consequences' (ibid., 492). In other words, the language and actions that make up sexual encounters, and their rules, restrictions, and **taboos**, are socially constructed and part of socially defined **sexual scripts** or road maps for sexual activity (Gagnon and Simon, 1986). The script concept implies a complex construction of culturally defined socio-sexual roles. For example, while this may be changing (also evidence of the fact that these are constructed roles), men are/have been expected to conduct themselves assertively and to make the first move, and women are/have been expected to be passive, compliant, and more responsive as the interaction progresses. Scripts also include internal dialogues about desire and resistance (Weis, 1998).

Historical Sociology and Sex

A number of sociologists have sought to understand sex and love in historical perspective, and, in doing so, have argued that sexual desire and intimate relations have not always been understood in the same way (Brickell, 2006). Researchers like Jeffrey Weeks (1993) have mapped the historical origins of sexual categories, subcultures, belief systems, and language to understand how we have arrived at social arrangements that prevail today. Particular emphasis has been placed on how sexual meanings have been negotiated within specific historical moments.

One historical moment of significance, and focus of study in the West, is the sexual revolution of the 1960s. Leisa Meyer (2006) notes that the history of sexuality was a subfield of the new social history that emerged in the 1960s. This period was characterized by a cultural shift in attitudes, an increased ability to control reproduction (legal changes and the introduction of the birth control pill), challenges to conventional definitions of masculinity and femininity, and the investigation of groups that had been little studied. This took place in a climate of change, marked by a new emphasis on questions of power raised through the civil rights, anti-war, feminist, and other movements for social justice. Both Canada and the United States were seemingly becoming more sexually liberal, and the courts reflected some of this through more progressive rulings, for example, in

SOCIOLOGY IN ACTION

Sexual Scripts and Sexual Double Standards in Popular Magazines

A number of content analyses of women's and men's magazines have found that stories, advice columns, and advertising reinforce dominant gender and sexual norms (Carpenter, 1998; Reichert and Lambiase, 2003; Jackson, 2005; McCleneghan, 2003). For example, Jackson (2005), analyzing young women's letters to the advice pages of a magazine (and the published responses from 'agony aunts'), found that while young women's letters suggest attempts to 'do' (and understand their) sexual desire, agony aunts often contributed to an 'undoing' of desire. Discourses of romance, sexual safety, and adolescence functioned to undermine the young women's expressions of desire. For example, compulsory heterosexuality was reinforced when one young woman asked about her attraction to girls over boys. Similarly, masturbation was endorsed, particularly as a substitute for sexual contact with others, and expressions of sexual desire were sidestepped, often by advocating the need for a loving relationship (Jackson, 2005).

In contrast to this, the relatively new and rapidly growing popular genre of men's magazines (often referred to as lad magazines, which include *Maxim*, *Stuff*, and *FHM*), while seeming to focus on what women want sexually, actually often privilege a fairly narrow male heterosexuality, oriented towards sexual variety (Taylor, 2005), and reinforce the objectification of women (Krassas et al., 2003). In brief, while the magazines targeting young women promoted heterosexual exclusivity and traditional sexual scripts, the men's magazines promoted more permissive (hetero)sexual attitudes and the desire to seek sexual sensation more frequently and with a greater number of sexual partners.

cases overturning laws against interracial marriages in some American states and those making contraception legal (ibid.). Sexual freedom became symbolic of other types of freedom, and sexuality became central to many westerners' understanding of themselves (ibid.). This was especially true among the youth. More on Canadian legal changes that took place during this period are outlined below.

From Sexual Deviants to Deviance to Margins to Mainstream

Sociology is noted for its theoretical explanations of deviance. From its theorizing and research on deviance, sociology has exposed diverse sexual cultures, producing a number of significant insights about sexuality (Irvine, 2003). From the Chicago School onward, researchers studying sexual minorities argued for the necessity to concurrently study dominant sexual institutions and definitions. After all, sexuality is governed and regulated by social norms, or shared expectations about what is considered to be culturally desirable and appropriate, and, at the same time, by what is considered to be culturally deviant. But cultural norms change. Sharon Marcus, for example, notes that library shelves tell interesting stories. Thirty years ago it took no time to get from feminism to homosexuality in the stacks in libraries, and homosexuality was 'sandwiched between bestiality and incest, on one side, and prostitution, sadism, fetishism, masturbation and emasculation, on the other' (Marcus, 2005: 192).

Time to Reflect

Do you agree with Simon and Gagnon's idea of sexual scripts? Can you think of any examples where the society in which you live, or the cultures and subcultures that touch your life, also affect your sexual behaviour? Choice of partner? How you approach or don't approach others sexually? What you say/don't say? What you do/don't do?

Time to Reflect

What role do you think pornography plays in our understanding of men's and women's sexuality?

However, the work of deviance theorists, some of whom, like Michel Foucault, have been themselves outspoken members of sexual minorities, challenged assumptions about 'deviant' sexual categories and the individuals who inhabited them. Consequently, a large and growing body of literature on sexuality also challenges various systems of oppression. Some writers, for example, examined the role of stigma in the social control of sexuality (Plummer, 1975). One of the most (in)famous sociological studies of sexual stigma, Laud Humphreys's *Tearoom Trade* (1970), controversially examined the dehumanizing role of stigma on the lives of men who sought sexual pleasure in public washrooms (see Chapter 7). While some continue to study sexual stigma and our understanding of sexual deviance, many have since come to problematize the very notion of sexual deviance. Plummer (2003), for example, critiques and contests the language of perversion.

Destabilizing Sexual Categories: Feminists, Queer Theory, and Beyond

Many feminists have questioned and challenged, among other things, the social construction of sex and sexuality, the control of women's bodies and reproduction, the objectification of women, sexual double standards, the link between sex and power, and sexual abuse and oppression (Millett, 1969; Greer, 1984; Weitz, 2002). Holly Benkert notes that 'the basis for oppression of women is deeply rooted to our sexuality, the very source of our primary "difference"' (Benkert, 2002: 1197). Some, however, have pointed out that, since the 1960s, feminists in North America have understood sexuality as both 'an arena for women's liberation' and 'a crucial vector of women's oppression' (Marcus, 2005: 193). Some feminists have attempted to deconstruct and then reclaim women's rights to sexual pleasure, autonomy, and knowledge (Bell, 1994; Eaves, 2002), while others have challenged the forces that stood against women's autonomy, including pornography, rape, and sexual harassment (Brownmiller, 1975; Dworkin, 1981; MacKinnon, 1989).

The debates around pornography have been especially divisive. Some, like Dworkin and MacKinnon, consider pornography to be demeaning and degrading to women and representative of male power over women. For others, the freedom to explore diverse representations of sexuality, including pornography or erotica, is seen as liberating to women, and challenges restrictions placed on women's sexuality (Bell, 1994; Sprinkle, 1991). The African-American social theorist and feminist critic bell hooks explains that many feminists, in fact, stopped talking about sex publicly because it exposed 'our differences' (hooks, 1994: 79); however, challenging patriarchal definitions and restrictions on women's sexual autonomy has been a unifying theme within feminism.

Writers such as Judith Butler (1990) have argued that categories like 'heterosexual' and 'homosexual' are used to control and constrain individuals and therefore should be challenged on a number of fronts. Some, like Carr, promote the notion of a 'fluid conception of sexual identification' that is subject to 'the flux and flow of life' (Carr, 1999: 17), allowing for the possibility of individuals to change from one identification to another. Queer theory calls for this type of challenge and change.

The use of the term 'queer' within the gay community began as a ploy to reclaim a slur and highlight the multiple ways that sexual practices, sexual fantasy, and sexual identity 'fail to line up consistently' and 'expresses an important insight about the complexity of sexuality' (Marcus, 2005: 196). Queer theory derives part of its philosophy from the ideas of Michel Foucault (1990), who saw homosexuality as a strategically situated marginal

Time to Reflect

Why do you think the word 'queer' was adopted in the gay community and among homosexual writers? Does this help us to rethink sexuality? How? Why?

position from where it may be possible to see new and diverse ways of relating to oneself and others. Queer politics rejects forms of gender and sexual oppression, but it intentionally does so from the margins in order to maintain a critical outsider perspective (Baird, 2001).

Sexuality and Ethno-racial Diversity

Another critique from the margins comes from those who study the racialization of sexuality and the sexualization of minorities. Benkert (2002: 1205) notes that 'comprehensive conversations about race and sexuality together and separately have been taboo topics universally.' Writers such as bell hooks (1992) and Kamela Kempadoo (1998), for example, have explained that sexuality has been experienced and treated differently when it intersects with race. From this perspective, images of 'the exotic' are critically assessed, and the experiences of gays and lesbians of colour who experience racism within white-dominated gay organizations are also a focus of discussion (Baird, 2001). These authors challenge false universalisms that do not reflect the complex reality and lived experiences of minorities. Some have also been critical of the cultural imperialism of American media and the Westernization of sexuality (Nelson and Paek, 2005; Hesse-Biber, 2007). Still others have studied the explicit and implicit sexual dimensions of race, ethnicity, and nationality, arguing that the borderlands at the edges of racial, ethnic, and national boundaries are *ethnosexual frontiers* patrolled, policed, protected, and at times penetrated by invaders (Nagel, 2006; also see Yuval-Davis and Anthias, 1989; Yuval-Davis, 1997; Gamson and Moon, 2004). Emerging from this, a number of feminists and queer theorists have raised radical challenges to mainstream approaches to citizenship (Langdridge, 2006).

Sexual Trafficking: An Intersection of Inequalities

> 'Lena' was 26 when she was brought from Thailand to Japan with the promise of a job as an 'entertainer.' But when she arrived her passport was confiscated; her job, she quickly learned, was to have sex with men in seedy hotel rooms. Her good looks made her a popular choice among clients; she earned 1 million yen (US $9,100) in the first month alone. She needed money. She owed 6 million yen ($55,000) to her traffickers and minders in Japan—a debt she was expected to pay back in full under the constant threat of violence. She was allowed to keep just 10,000 yen ($90) a month pocket money and was confined to a cramped one-room flat. (McCurry, 2004: 1393)

Lena's story is by no means unique. In 2003, *The Lancet*, a UK-based medical journal that features stories on global medical issues, reported that an estimated 800,000 to 900,000 men, women, and children are illegally transported across international borders and forced to work as virtual slaves in the sex trade or in low-paying, dangerous jobs each year (*Lancet*, 2003). Another source estimated that 1.2 million women and girls enter the global commercial sex market (within and across borders) every year (Roby, 2005). Clearly, the trade of women and children has become a booming industry. For example, estimates reveal that about 15,000 women from the former Eastern bloc states alone worked in Germany's red-light districts at the end of the 1990s (Alalehto, 2002).

Women are often abducted, sold (the same is true for children, see Davidson, 2005), or lured through what appear to be legitimate business and employment opportunities as au pairs and as restaurant and child-care workers (ibid.). Some pay thousands of dollars to recruiters who help them obtain travel documents, arrange transport, and get contacts abroad. Women and children are often trafficked from Central and South America, West and Central Africa, South Asia, the Middle East, Eastern Europe, China, and parts of Southeast Asia. Trafficked workers seem to have a few things in common—they are often fleeing poverty, joblessness, and/or the social dislocation characteristic of transitional economies, as seen after the collapse of the Soviet Union (Orlova, 2004; Alalehto, 2002; Kempadoo and Doezema, 1998).

Roby (2005) notes that the factors contributing to the global sex trade include international, national, and local demographic, social, economic, ethnic, and cultural environments, with economic injustice and poverty among the major factors. Similarly, Bertone (2000) suggests that the global sex trade and the trafficking of women are but another manifestation of the international inequality found in the North/South, East/West political-economic divide. She explains that the international subculture of docile and/or exotic women from underdeveloped nations is sustained by the international, patriarchal capitalist market system. While efforts to combat this type of exploitation have been made by supranational bodies like the United Nations (see Roby, 2005) and some states (often in the name of national security, Alalehto, 2002), on a smaller scale some trafficked workers and sex workers are organizing to fight forms of exploitation and oppression, both within and outside the sex trade (see Gayen, 2006; Petzer and Issacs, 1998).

The sex trade and poverty are worldwide phenomena that seem to go hand in hand. Here, sex workers buy fresh goat milk while waiting for clients outside their rented rooms on '*La Linea*' ('The Strip') in Guatemala City. (CP/AP Photo/Alexandre Meneghini)

Sexual Citizenship and Sexuality in Canada

Former Prime Minister Pierre Trudeau, when he was Justice Minister in 1967, played a key role in helping to legally redefine sexuality for Canadians. For the first 100 years after Confederation, homosexuality was illegal in Canada and considered to be a mental illness. In December of 1967, Trudeau introduced a controversial new omnibus bill in the House of Commons (Bill C-150) that challenged this and some other restrictions placed on sexuality. Trudeau's legislation brought issues like abortion, homosexuality, and the divorce law to the forefront, changing the sexual landscape of Canada. At the time, Trudeau famously stated that 'there's no place for the state in the bedrooms of the nation.' Despite considerable opposition, by 1969 homosexual acts had been decriminalized and women had more control over sexual reproduction and their bodies. It was not until the year 2000, however, with the passing of Bill C-23, that same-sex couples were granted the same rights and obligations as common-law couples, and 2005, when the Liberal government passed 'equal marriage' legislation. On 20 July 2005, Bill C-315, The Civil Marriage Act, recognized the right of same-sex couples to have access to civil marriage, without discrimination.

Over the past 40 years there have also been changes to the laws governing the legal age of consent to have sex in Canada, with major changes in 1988. That year, the introduction of Bill C-15 created the offence of 'sexual interference' and prohibited adults from engaging in virtually any kind of sexual contact with either boys or girls under the age of 14, regardless of consent. The notion of

Time to Reflect

Despite legal changes, in the spring of 2002 the Durham Catholic School Board unanimously voted to deny a gay Oshawa high school student, Marc Hall, the right to attend his high school prom with his same-sex partner. In light of the legal changes, do you support the school board decision? Why? Why not?

Groups like the Coalition for the Rights of Sex Workers—shown here—have been organizing to fight forms of exploitation and oppression. (CP/Paul Chiasson)

'sexual exploitation' was also included, making it an offence for an adult to have any sexual contact with boys or girls ages 14 to 18, where a relationship of trust or authority exists (teachers, coaches, etc.). The law added that consensual sex with those 12 to 14 'may not be an offence' if the accused is under 16 and less than two years older than the complainant. This clearly attempted to reflect some of the trends in early sexual engagement among teenagers today.

Sexual Activity among Youth

Findings from the National Longitudinal Survey of Children and Youth in Canada revealed that an estimated 12 per cent of boys and 13 per cent of girls have had sexual intercourse by the age of 15 (Garriguet, 2005; Statistics Canada, 2005c). The study also found that characteristics associated with early sexual activity differed for boys and girls. That is, the odds of early intercourse among girls were high for those who at 12 or 13 had reached puberty, or were not overweight, but also for girls whose self-esteem was weak at ages 12 and 13. In regards to self-esteem, the opposite was true for boys. The association between smoking and early intercourse was also strong. Furthermore, for girls, having tried drinking alcohol by the age of 12 or 13 was also associated with having intercourse by age 15, while drinking alcohol was not associated with boys' sexual activity (Statistics Canada, 2005c). Girls in the eastern provinces and Quebec were more likely to report being sexually active than those in Ontario and the western provinces (Garriguet, 2005). Boys with poor relationships with their parents were more likely to report early sexual activity.

A study of teenagers' perception of parental disapproval of their initiation of sexual intercourse found that well over half of the 2,353 Grade 10 and 12 students interviewed anticipated parental disapproval of their behaviour, but about 44 per cent of the total had had sexual intercourse nonetheless (Hampton et al., 2005). Coincidentally, a report by the Vanier Institute of the Family found that Canadian adults under the age of 35 were considerably less likely than older Canadians to express disapproval and non-acceptance of their children having premarital sex at any age, engaging in homosexual acts, learning that their children are gay or lesbian, the arrival of grandchildren when their sons and daughters are not married, and having their children live together (Bibby, 2004; see Table 17.1). In fact, it has been found that attitudes towards sexuality have shifted considerably when we look across various generations of Canadians (see Tables 17.2 and 17.3). Some historical examples demonstrate that the shift or change has more to do with perceiving rather than with 'doing' sex differently. Let us look at a specific case of the rescue of prostitutes in Toronto in the late Victorian period.

English Canada, in the late 1800s, embraced many of Victorian England's repressive and contradictory views in regard to sexuality. When William Lyon Mackenzie King, later Prime Minister of Canada, was an undergraduate student at the University of Toronto in the 1890s he embarked on a quest, as a prostitute rescuer, to rehabilitate women who lived 'wicked lives' (Graham, 1999). He was not alone. A number of organizations sprang up in the economically bustling city of Toronto to save women from prostitution. Many were headed by members of Canada's Protestant business, social, and political elite (ibid.). In the fall of 1893, a number of King's diary entries reported that he and his fellow undergraduate friends visited 'jolies femmes' on King Street as customers/clients. But by the spring of 1894, King undertook his first attempt at rehabilitating a local prostitute through intensive visits, praying with her, having long talks, and ministering to the girl's family (ibid.). He convinced her to become a 'missionary of God', but the young woman returned to the streets and then to a reformatory months later. King's career as prostitute rescuer did not end with her, but it gradually dissipated. He was first elected Prime Minister in 1921, and at his retirement in 1948 had been the longest-serving head of government in the Commonwealth. The key point here is not that King, like some men today, used the services of prostitutes, but rather that he did so in a climate of profound hypocrisy, where heightened morality intersected with sexual impropriety and where attitudes about sex and sexuality conflicted with actual practice.

Table 17.1 Disapproval and Non-Acceptance of Children's Sexual Behaviour by Age, Gender, and Religious Service Attendance

	Total	18–34	35–54	55+	18–34			
					Female	Male	Weekly+	<Weekly
Engaging in premarital sex proir to age 18	29%	19	28	40	18	20	57	11
Engaging in premarital sex when 18 or older	11	9	9	18	8	10	37	3
Engaging in homosexual acts	45	27	45	63	24	31	71	18
Informing you that they are gay or lesbian	22	12	23	32	12	13	29	9
Having children without being married	17	8	16	30	8	7	28	3
Living with partner without being married	12	9	10	17	8	10	37	3
Having sexual relations other than with spouse	74	69	74	79	74	63	90	65

Notes: Percentages are for those who disapprove and do not accept. Gender breakdown and religious service attendance shown only for 18–34 age group.

Source: Bibby (2004), at: <www.vifamily.ca/library/future/section_2.pdf>. Reprinted by permission of the Vanier Institute of the Family.

Table 17.2 Discussing Sexuality by Age and Region

'Do you—or did you, or do you plan to—talk about sexuality with your children?'

	A Fair Amount	A Bit	Little/None	Totals
Nationally	**54%**	**34**	**12**	**100**
18–34	66	31	3	100
35–54	35	39	26	100
55+	35	39	26	100
Atlantic	60	28	12	100
BC	57	32	11	100
Prairies	57	32	11	100
Ontario	54	33	13	100
Quebec	47	41	12	100
18–34	*62*	*34*	*4*	*100*
35–54	*47*	*42*	*11*	*100*
55+	*33*	*48*	*19*	*100*

Source: Bibby (2004), at: <www.vifamily.ca/library/future/section_2.pdf>. Reprinted by permission of the Vanier Institute of the Family.

While attitudes seem to have liberalized, are young people today actually more sexually active than those in the recent past? Contrary to popular belief, the Sex Information and Education Council of Canada reports that for Grade 9 males, the percentage who reported sexual intercourse actually declined from 31 per cent in 1988 to 23 per cent in 2002 (McKay, 2004). Figure 17.2 similarly shows that the numbers have declined for Grade 9 girls as well. The trend of declining rates of early intercourse is mirrored in US data as well (ibid.). There are also decreases in the percentage of Grade 11 male and female students with multiple sexual partners (see Figure 17.3). Teenagers may well be more cautious, knowing that HIV/AIDS (and other sexually transmitted diseases) disproportionately affect young people (ibid.). A 20-year study of sexual behaviour among students at Okanagan University College in British Columbia certainly supports this, reporting a steady increase in safer sexual practices among students (Netting and Burnett, 2004).

Statistics Canada notes that 28 per cent of 15–17-year-olds reported having had sexual intercourse at least once, and by the ages of 20–4, 80 per cent had had sexual intercourse. One-third of 15–24-year-olds reported having had more than one sexual partner in the previous year, and 30 per cent of those who had sex with multiple partners in the past year had not used a condom the last time they had intercourse (Statistics Canada, 2005c). Having sex without a condom was more common among older youth: 44 per cent of sexually active 20–4-year-olds reported having sex without a condom compared to 33 per cent of those aged 18 and 19, and 22 per cent of those 15 to 17 (ibid.). Researchers speculate that those in older age groups are more likely to be in longer-term relationships and so perceive condom use as less necessary. Indeed, Netting and Burnett (2004) found that condom use tended to be low among monogamous sexually active students.

Studies of youth attitudes and practices in regard to sex in a world with HIV/AIDS tell interesting stories about how we think about and 'do' sex differently. For example, a study of young people's sexuality and risk-taking behaviours in Thailand reveals that neither young men nor

Time to Reflect

Do you believe that young people in the past were much less likely to engage in sexual activity before marriage? Why? Why not?

Table 17.3 Acceptance of Sexual Relations and Approval of Legal Abortion by Age Cohorts, 1975 and 2000*

	1975	2000
PREMARITAL RELATIONS		
Nationally	**68%**	**84**
18–34	90	93
35–54	65	89
55+	42	74
HOMOSEXUAL RELATIONS		
Nationally	**28**	**73**
18–34	42	75
35–54	25	64
55+	12	42
LEGAL ABORTION A POSSIBILITY . . .		
"If her own health is seriously endangered"		
Nationally	**94**	**94**
18–34	97	98
35–54	92	95
55+	93	90
"If she is married and doesn't want more children"		
Nationally	**45**	**52**
18–34	47	51
35–54	43	44
55+	45	48

*Sexual relations: % indicating '*not wrong at all*' or '*sometimes wrong*' versus 'always wrong' or 'almost always wrong'; legal abortion: % indicating '*yes*', it should be possible.

Source: Bibby (2004), at: <www.vifamily.ca/library/future/section_2.pdf>. Reprinted by permission of the Vanier Institute of the Family.

young women, from across different social classes, view themselves as being in an at-risk group, nor do they consider their sexual behaviours to be at-risk behaviours (Thianthai, 2004). Young people admitted screening potential sexual partners as being HIV/AIDS-free using images of 'good girls/boys'. Those labelled 'good girls' and 'good boys' were believed to be HIV/AIDS-free. Interestingly, the ideal image of a 'good girl' involved being loyal and obedient, being a virgin before marriage, and avoiding allowing more than one man to 'have access to their body' (ibid., 191). Being a 'bad girl' implies being promiscuous and sexually skilled at luring men. 'Good boys', as defined by both male and female respondents, are self-confident gentlemen. One respondent explained: 'good boys can visit prostitutes. Good boys can have as many sexual partners as they want. What is important is that they are good at heart' (ibid., 193). Indeed, 'good boys' were actually encouraged to go out and 'enjoy expe-

Time to Reflect

Does our society continue to have sexual double standards, that is, do we think differently about sexually active young women compared to sexually active young men? Is virginity still an 'asset' for young women but a liability for young men? Would you react differently to a young woman who bragged about having multiple sexual partners compared to a young man?

Figure 17.2 Percentage of Canadian Grade 9 and 11 Students Who Have Had Intercourse, 1988, 2002

60
50
40
30
20
10
0
1988
2002
Grade 9 Male
Grade 9 Female
Grade 1 Female
Grade 11 Female

Source: Boyce et al. (cited in McKay, 2004: 74, at: <www.sieccan.org/pdf/mckay.pdf>).

riencing the real world' (including visiting prostitutes) in order to become leaders. These and related views made some considerably more vulnerable than others to contracting and spreading HIV.

While there are clearly shifts in attitudes and practices when it comes to sex and sexuality, do these amount to another sexual revolution? Connell and Hunt (2006) note the sexual revolution of the 1960s weakened the link between sex and marriage. In their analysis of sex advice literature, they identify a clear shift from 'marriage manuals' to 'sex manuals', with the new sex manuals investing heavily in the ideology of interpersonal responsibility and mutuality, and often emphasizing the giving or sharing of pleasure. Connell and Hunt suggest that these new manuals consciously refused to confine sexual pleasure to marriage, yet the traditional script persisted of the male as initiator and the female as responding to his initiative. They explain that the idea that men need to court women with romantic tactics continued to 'pervade the discursive construction of heterosexuality', and this dominant paradigm was only occasionally challenged (ibid., 37). Despite the fact that newer and even recent manuals more openly discuss the female orgasm and women's sexual desires, the dominant

Figure 17.3 Number of Sexual Partners among Grade 11 Students Who Have Had Intercourse, 1988, 2002

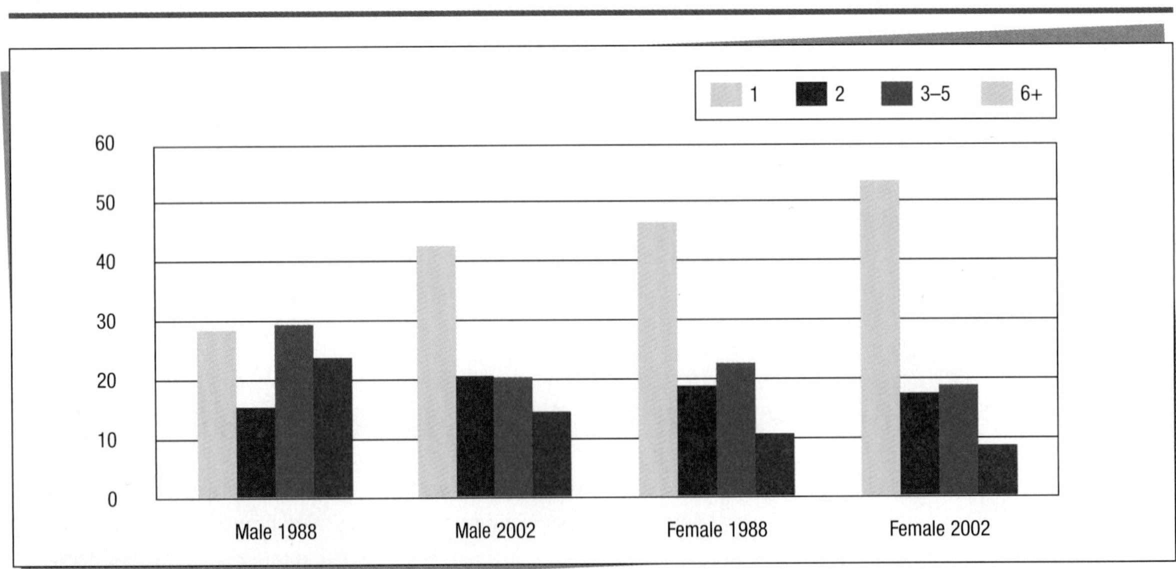

Source: McKay (2004: 74), at: <www.sieccan.org/pdf/mckay.pdf>.

gendered paradigm of the heterosexual encounter has shown remarkable persistence. Connell and Hunt conclude their analysis of sex advice literature by stating that 'the cult of sexual pleasure retained much of its gendered configuration and thus undermined the apparent commitment to sexual egalitarianism' (ibid., 41).

Sex and the Workplace

A number of scholars of sex and gender have argued that many different workplace and organizational cultures play key roles in creating, maintaining, and undermining sexual identity and inequality at work (Hearn and

GLOBAL ISSUES

HIV/AIDS: A Global Crisis

In 2001 there were approximately 5 million people newly infected with HIV, according to UNAIDS and the World Health Organization. Since the beginning of the AIDS epidemic it is estimated that 21.8 million people have died in the pandemic, including about 4.3 million children (UNAIDS/WHO, 2000). Approximately half of the people who become infected do so before they turn 25. Globally, this means that more than one out of 100 adults aged 15–49 is HIV-positive. At least 80 per cent of these infections result from heterosexual transmission (Health Canada, 2000, in Bulman et al., 2004: 142). In fact, according to the Canadian International Development Agency, 3,000 women a day contract HIV, and in Africa there are six HIV-positive women for every five HIV-positive men (CIDA, 2000, in Bulman et al., 2004: 141).

On the twentieth anniversary of the release of the first published reports of what later came to be called AIDS, Eleanor Maticka-Tyndale (2001) published a paper highlighting the importance of sociological research to the understanding of AIDS as a global phenomenon. Maticka-Tyndale notes that, for sociologists, it is not so much the number of people infected, but the distribution of infection that sets the sociological imagination in motion. 'HIV is not an equal-opportunity virus when it comes to gender and age. Nearly 90 percent of new infections are in those in their most productive stage in life, between 15 and 49 years of age' (Maticka-Tyndale, 2001: 17).

She explains that 'psychological perspectives on how attitudes influence behaviours and models of individual learning and behaviour change are the foundations of prevention programming' (ibid., 19), yet, despite the success of these programs, they fall short when addressing factors that affect large numbers (communities and nations), the relationship between communities, relationships between communities and other organizations, such as corporations, and relationships between nations. That's where sociology comes in. Sociology can help in the understanding 'of vulnerabilities, community systems and structures, social systems, power differentials, cultural contexts, social change, social movements, mobilization'.

Maticka-Tyndale states that 'as an academic sociologist, what I have witnessed in all of this is an arena that needs both sociological analysis and input and one that provides a rich environment for application and testing of a wide array of sociological theories' (ibid., 18). She suggests that sociologists from various theoretical backgrounds could contribute to understanding AIDS by drawing on theories of 'collective behaviour and social movements; of social capital's impact on community responses to crisis; of health and well-being in the face of disease and of meaning-making in the face of apparent disaster; of stigma and responses to stigmatization; of power differentials and inequality, their consequences and reversals; of globalization and its impacts; of alternative forms of development; of community and social change' (ibid., 19).

Bulman, Coben, and Van Anh (2004), who focused their research on Canada, the UK, and Vietnam, have taken a sociological approach by looking at the issues and strategies involved in educating women about HIV/AIDS. They noted that, internationally, HIV/AIDS prevention education for women has been influenced by a variety of different approaches to health care as well as widely divergent educational, political, economic, moral, and legal systems that often have different implications for men and women.

Parkin, 1987; Woods and Lucas, 1993; Welsh, 1999; Dellinger, 2002). Dellinger suggests that instead of simply looking at sexuality as something individuals bring to work, we can, and some have, examine how customs and practices in a workplace constitute a type of **organizational sexuality** or social practice that determines explicit and culturally elaborated rules of behaviour to regulate sexual identities and personal relationships. In other words, different occupational cultures hold different and specific social rules about what constitutes 'appropriate' or acceptable sexuality. Workplace norms about sexuality regulate who we say we are, who we 'date', how we dress, and how we understand and experience sexual harassment in the workplace.

Woods and Lucas (1993) write about the 'corporate closet', which strongly encourages gay men in some professions to keep their sexual identities and relationships hidden. In such work contexts, gays and lesbians intentionally pass as heterosexuals because of the pervasiveness of heteronormative discourses and **heterosexism** in the workplace (Johnson, 2002).

Ironically, heterosexist norms in the workplace, which assume that everyone is heterosexual, may at times make sexual interaction between co-workers of the same sexual orientation somewhat less problematic than sexual interaction between heterosexual co-workers. Some workplaces actively discourage the sexual involvement of heterosexual colleagues even when there is sexual consent between the individuals involved. The issue is, of course, very complex. Some 'pro-sex' feminists argue that women should be free to express their sexuality, and that women are oppressed by restrictions on sexual expression, including in the workplace, since such restrictions often are supported by social and political conservatives seeking to promote the image of women as pure and virtuous (Williams et al., 1999). In contrast, Catherine MacKinnon and Andrea Dworkin, among others, argue that heterosexuality is oppressive to women and that sexual consent is only possible between equals and, therefore, impossible in workplaces dominated and controlled by men. Williams and colleagues (1999: 76) explain that 'workers themselves often conceive of sexual behaviors at work along a continuum, ranging from pleasurable, to tolerable, to harassing.'

Sandy Welsh (1999), writing on sexual harassment, explains that some organizations actually mandate the sexualization of their workers, and as a result, in some sexually charged work cultures, degrading and/or sexual behaviours become an institutionalized component of work. Thus, for example, a waitress at Hooters is required to wear short shorts and a top that shows cleavage, but this is not considered sexual harassment. Of course, for some women who work at Hooters bar-restaurants such a requirement may be demeaning and objectifying; for others, however, this might not be the case. Researchers such as Dellinger (2002) have noted that most workplaces, either formally or informally, convey rules of dress, and that dress is a well-recognized site of gender construction and sexual identity. Dellinger finds that dress norms and local workplace norms 'influence people's definition of pleasurable, acceptable, and unacceptable sexuality at work' (ibid., 23). As a result, workplace norms and organizational culture affect how sexuality is negotiated at work and, in part, determine what counts as sexual harassment.

Welsh (1999) reminds us that heterosexual norms in the workplace often exclude or sexualize women, silence or closet gay man and lesbians, and work to constrain the behaviour of heterosexual men who are at times labelled 'unmasculine' when they choose not to participate in 'hypermasculine' stereotypical behaviour.

Cybersex, Pornography, and the Internet

With the spectacular growth in the availability of sexually explicit material on the Internet (Barak and Fisher, 2001), some have claimed that it has revolutionized sex yet again. No doubt, people today have easy (free and for-fee) access to many diverse sites and formats, with varying levels of 'interactivity', featuring very different, and at times unusual, types of sexual acts and preferences (some legal, others not). Cybersex and Internet porn can be had without leaving the safety and privacy

Time to Reflect

If an employer required you to dress in a sexually provocative manner, would you consider this a form of sexual harassment? Why? Why not?

of our homes or offices, all under a perceived cloak of anonymity. Knowing this, some researchers have written about compulsive viewing (Cooper et al., 2000). Others argue that this anonymity expands most people's expression of their sexuality (Barak and Fisher, 2001; Fisher and Barak, 2001). The question remains, does our access to technology change the nature and our understanding of sexuality?

Sociologists Lisa Byers, Ken Menzies, and William O'Grady (2004) surveyed approximately 500 students at a Canadian university and found, among other things, that male students engaged in significantly more viewing of sexually explicit material on the Internet than female students. They also found that people who viewed more non-Internet pornographic material also viewed substantially more on the Internet, suggesting that our society's existing patterns of sexuality, and not Internet technology, will be the dominant determinant of future sexual patterns. Clearly, gendered patterns persist. Morrison and colleagues note that much of the research on sex on the Internet has taken a harm-based approach, focusing on how it negatively affects male viewers' attitudes towards women. Their study, in contrast, shifts the focus away from the impact of Internet porn on male attitudes towards women to its impact on male attitudes towards themselves. They surveyed close to 200 men enrolled at a Canadian college and found significant negative correlations between exposure to pornographic imagery on-line and their levels of genital and sexual self-esteem (Morrison et al., 2006). Those who reported greater exposure to Internet porn were more likely to have lower levels of self-esteem.

Terrie Schauer did a comparative textual analysis of nine pornographic Internet sites, three of which labelled themselves 'for straight women'. She finds that the nude solo male in 'soft-core' porn directed towards women generally conforms to the erotic conventions used in gay male porn, which in turn mirrors conventions used to sexualize and objectify women in heterosexual soft-core porn directed towards men. The male models in porn for women also co-opt symbols from traditionally 'manly' or masculine trades—firemen, cowboys, and police (Schauer, 2005). With the more 'hard-core' couples photos in porn sites aimed at women, Schauer surmises that many images and scenes were taken directly from heterosexual male sites. In other words, if the Internet is indeed revolutionary, it has not yet been so for heterosexual women, where the visual coding of women's pornography has not yet broken away from traditional forms and developed a unique set of representations or conventions.

Sexual Offences

For some radical feminists, such as Andrea Dworkin and Catherine MacKinnon, pornography on- or off-line 'reveals that male pleasure is inextricably tied to victimization, hurting, exploiting' (Dworkin, 1981: 69). Others have not gone so far, but have pointed out that pornography often contains sexual violence (Barron and Kimmel, 2000; Palys, 1986) and that this may have a negative effect on men's attitudes towards women (Allen et al., 1995). But whether pornography actually causes its consumers to engage in sexual violence is still debated. Having said this, sexual assault and abuse continue to be a problem in Canada, especially for younger victims.

In 1983, Bill C-127 introduced a three-tiered structure of sexual assault offences designed to improve legal processing of rape cases (see DuMont, 2003). Today, under Canadian criminal law, a broad array of activities qualify as sexual assault, ranging from unwanted touching to sexual violence resulting in serious injury, with penetration not being an essential component (Johnson, 2005). A Statistics Canada report pointed out that the rate of sexual offences, including sexual assaults, reported to police declined by 36 per cent between 1993 and 2002 (Kong et al., 2003). In contrast, sexual offences against children and youth were alarmingly high. Police reports and victimization surveys reveal that young women and girls are at the highest risk of sexual assault victimization, and rates of sexual offending were highest among male teenagers (ibid.). As a result, a majority of sexual assaults today are committed against children and youth (AuCoin, 2005). In Canada, six of every 10 victims of sexual offences reported to police in 2002 were children and youth under 18 (Statistics Canada, 2005d). Girls made up the majority of victims (85 per cent), with the highest rates among those aged 11–19 (with the peak at 13 years of age). For male victims, rates were highest for boys aged 3–14 (Kong et al., 2003). Boys aged 13–14 were at highest risk of committing level 1 sexual offences (level 1: minor or no physical injuries to victim; level 2: sexual assault with weapon; level 3: wounding or endangering the life of victim).

Younger victims were more likely to be sexually assaulted by a family member. In fact, only 4 per cent of female victims under the age of six and about 10 per cent of victims 6–13 years old were sexually assaulted by a stranger (Statistics Canada, 2005d). Those of ages 12–17 were most often sexually victimized by peers and acquaintances (Kong et al., 2003). In sum, 86 per cent of cases of sexual assaults were perpetrated by an individual known to the victim (AuCoin, 2005). At the same time, it should be noted that increased attention is being placed on the sexual victimization of children and youth by strangers via the Internet. Future research is likely to focus on this relatively new and growing form of sexual exploitation.

Conclusion    

This chapter began by noting that sociology has been a relative latecomer to the study of sex and sexuality, but over the course of the chapter we have seen that the discipline has come a long way in (re)defining, theorizing, and researching sex and sexuality.

Most sociologists today, unlike many early sexologists, would argue that sexuality involves much more than an understanding of biological aspects of (heterosexual) physical attraction (in marriage and for procreation), and would, like many anthropologists, stress the social and cultural relativity of norms surrounding sexual behaviour, identities, and roles. As a result, many sociologists would accept the World Health Organization's broad definition of sexuality, which stresses the importance of understanding sexuality as intricately linked to and influenced by the interaction of biological, psychological, social, economic, political, cultural, ethical, legal, historical, religious, and spiritual factors. Sexuality is therefore understood and studied as a 'broad social domain involving multiple fields of power, diverse systems of knowledge, and sets of institutional and political discourses' (Irvine, 2003: 431). Sociological theorizing and research on sexuality have taken a multiplicity of forms, including the study of sexual scripts, sexual stigma, sexual oppression, and the critical destabilization of sexual categories by feminists and queer theorists.

Furthermore, the amount of historical and cross-cultural diversity and change found in sexual attitudes and practices, both within Canada and around the world, should be further evidence of sexuality's socio-cultural dimensions. In other words, nature, to be sure, has a significant role in people's experience of sexuality, but nurture or social conditioning is of greater importance than earlier theorists and sexologists suggested. Your own experiences are also evidence of this. For example, if you found yourself reading this chapter and saying 'it's not like that any more', you, too, have provided evidence in support of socio-cultural explanations over fixed, biological ones.

Finally, the issues of sex and the media, especially the Internet, and of sexual violence and sexual offences are likely to be areas of debate and research in years to come.

Questions for Critical Thought

1. How has the common, binary (dichotomized) definition of 'sex' affected our understanding of sexuality?
2. The World Health Organization and many sociologists have noted that sexuality is influenced by the interaction of biological, psychological, social, economic, political, cultural, ethical, legal, historical, religious, and spiritual factors. What does all of this mean? Give an example of the influence on sexuality for each of these definitional terms.
3. There is considerable historical and cross-cultural diversity in regard to sexuality and spirituality. Identify some of the variations. Why do you think sex and sexuality have been linked to spirituality? Why do you think some groups try to keep the two far apart?
4. There are clearly very different scientific approaches to the study of sex and sexuality. How do biological and psychoanalytic explanations compare to social survey and ethnographic approaches? What are the key factors that set them apart? Do you see any similarities? Which approach do you think best explains sexuality?
5. Select two different sociological approaches to understanding sexuality. How are they similar? How do they differ? Which do you think provides a better explanation? Why?
6. Identify some of the trends in youth sexual behaviour. What do you think accounts for them? Is there cause for alarm?
7. Welsh (1999) noted that heterosexual norms in the workplace often exclude or sexualize women, silence or closet gay man and lesbians, and work to constrain the behaviour of heterosexual men. What does she mean by this? How are these norms manifested? What should be done, if anything, to address these issues?
8. Has the Internet 'revolutionized' sex? What evidence do we have that it has? What evidence is there that it has not?

Recommended Readings

Mary Louise Adams, *The Trouble with Normal: Post-War Youth and the Making of Heterosexuality* (Toronto: University of Toronto Press, 1999).
Adams writes about the social construction of heterosexuality and the discourse surrounding the notions of 'normal' and 'heterosexuality' as they were imposed on youth in post-war Canada.

Vanessa Baird, *The No-Nonsense Guide to Sexual Diversity* (Toronto: Between the Lines, 2001).
This book, one in a series of 'No-Nonsense Guides', provides a history of sexuality, with international examples of the 'war' against sexual non-conformity.

Donna Bulman, Diana Coben, and Nguyen Van Anh, 'Educating Women about HIV/AIDS: Some International Comparisons', *Compare* 34, 2 (2004): 141–59.
The authors note that the determinants of HIV infection include gender and status, poverty and inequity, education, access to health care, including reproductive care, human rights, and social disruption. They compare strategies in Canada, the UK, and Vietnam, arguing that the creation and implementation of gender-specific and gender-sensitive strategies are essential in preventing the spread of HIV.

Judith Butler, *Gender Troubles: Feminism and the Subversion of Identity* (New York: Routledge Classics, 2006 [1990]).
Butler's groundbreaking work challenges some traditional feminists' assumptions about the 'naturalness' and essentialism of sex and gender. She argues that the masculine and feminine are not biologically fixed categories, but rather are culturally determined.

Michel Foucault, *The History of Sexuality: An Introduction* (New York: Vintage Books, 1990).
This is the first volume of Foucault's three-volume study of sexual history, presenting a detailed, critical, and provocative account of the changing attitudes and discourses surrounding sexuality and sexual repression. His purpose is 'to show how deployments of power are directly connected to the body' (p. 151).

Sharlene Nagy Hesse-Biber, *The Cult of Thinness* (New York: Oxford University Press, 2007).

This book goes beyond psychological explanations of eating disorders. It looks at social, political, and economic pressures on women, and increasingly on men as well, that contribute to the cult of thinness. Hesse-Biber also discusses what is happening to preteens, masculine, and gay and lesbian body images.

Marilyn Myerson, Sara Crawley, Erica Hesch Anstey, Justine Kessler, and Cara Okopny, 'Who's Zoomin' Who? A Feminist, Queer Content Analysis of "Interdisciplinary" Human Sexuality Textbooks', *Hypatia* 22, 1 (2007): 92–113.

This article presents findings from a content analysis of textbooks used in post-secondary introductory human sexuality courses. The authors found that most texts present a covert ideology reinforcing dominant heteronormative narratives of sexual dimorphism, male hegemony, and heteronormativity.

Edward Shorter, *Written in the Flesh: A History of Desire* (Toronto: University of Toronto Press, 2005).

In contrast to other books listed here, *Written in the Flesh*, a finalist for a Governor General's literary award in non-fiction, argues that sexual behaviour is a product of biologically driven desire rather than of fashion or social conditioning. In other words, Shorter supports the nature side of the nature–nurture debate, underscoring that desire is a brain-driven longing for sensuality.

Jeffrey Weeks, *Against Nature: Essays on History, Sexuality and Identity* (London: Rivers Oram Press, 1991).

Weeks presents a historical overview of the study and regulation of sexuality in general and homosexuality in particular. He also explores the personal and cultural impact of the AIDS crisis and the politics and values of the postmodern Western world.

Shannon Winnubst, *Queering Freedom* (Bloomington: Indiana University Press, 2006).

Winnubst looks at contemporary categories of difference such as sexuality, race, gender, class, and nationality and how they operate within the politics of domination.

Recommended Websites

Egale Canada
www.egale.ca

Egale Canada is a national organization that advances equality and justice for lesbian, gay, bisexual, and trans-identified people and their families across Canada. The site includes summaries of key court cases, press releases, and information on local, national, and international campaigns and events.

Joint United Nations Program on HIV/AIDS (UNAIDS)
www.unaids.org/en/

UNAIDS brings together the efforts and resources of 10 UN organizations to the global AIDS response. The website includes international data on HIV and an extensive range of publications/materials (research reports, best practices, etc.) on a variety of topics related to HIV/AIDS.

Kinsey Institute for Research in Sex, Gender and Reproduction
www.indiana.edu/~kinsey/

The Kinsey Institute at Indiana University promotes interdisciplinary research and scholarship in the fields of human sexuality, gender, and reproduction. The website includes an abundance of resources and information on research and publication, interdisciplinary conferences and seminars, opportunities for graduate students, etc.

Pivot Legal Society
www.pivotlegal.org/Issues/sextrade.htm

Pivot Legal Society, a non-profit legal advocacy organization located in Vancouver's Downtown Eastside, takes a strategic approach to social change, using the law to address the root causes that undermine the quality of life of those most on the margins. Pivot's main campaigns are directed towards addiction, housing, policing, and sex work, and the group helped to co-ordinate sex workers' participation in the parliamentary review of prostitution laws in 2005.

Public Health Agency of Canada: 'Talk to Me—Sexuality Education for Parents'
www.phac-aspc.gc.ca/publicat/ttm-pm/index.html

'Talk to Me' is an on-line sexuality education program designed to help parents talk to their children about sexuality. The site contains information for parents on five themes: Attitudes Toward Sexuality; Puberty and 'the Changing Adolescent'; Sexually Transmitted Infections and HIV/AIDS; Contraception; and Communication.

Sex Information and Education Council of Canada (SIECCAN)
www.sieccan.org

SIECCAN is dedicated to informing the public and professionals about diverse aspects of human sexuality. It also publishes the *Canadian Journal of Human Sexuality*.

Sex Workers Education and Advocacy Task Force (SWEAT)
www.sweat.org.za

SWEAT, a not-for-profit organization based in Cape Town, South Africa, works with sex workers around health and human rights. The organization provides safer-sex educational outreach as well as legal advice and skills training, and its site contains fact sheets, resources for sex workers, and recent research and publications related to sex work.

Society for the Scientific Study of Sexuality (SSSS)
www.sexscience.org

This international organization dedicated to the advancement of knowledge about sexuality consists of an interdisciplinary group of professionals who believe in the importance of both the production of quality research and the clinical, educational, and social applications of research related to all aspects of sexuality.

World Health Organization (WHO)—Sexual Health
www.who.int/topics/sexual_health/en/

The World Health Organization, a UN agency, provides information on a wide range of health topics, including sexual health and sexual violence. Included here are fact sheets, reports, and publications on a wide range of topics such as adolescent sexual and reproductive health, sexually transmitted diseases, female genital mutilation, etc.

Chapter 18

Ethnic and Race Relations

Nikolaos I. Liodakis

Learning Objectives

In this chapter, you will:

- Learn that the meaning of the terms 'ethnicity' and 'race' are historically specific, and are important bases for the formation of social groups.
- Discover that ethnic and racial hierarchies exist in society.
- Understand how Canada has been shaped by the colonization of Aboriginal peoples, the requirements of 'nation-building', capitalist economic development, and discriminatory immigration policies.
- Find out that multiculturalism and interculturalism are ideological frameworks within which government policies and programs attempt to manage ethnic and race relations and provide social cohesion.
- Come to appreciate how, despite improvements in immigration policy and government integration efforts, discrimination and racism continue to permeate many aspects of Canadian social, political, and economic life.
- Learn about different theoretical approaches that attempt to explain the economic inequalities among and within ethnic and racial groups.

Photo: World of Stock

Introduction

Canada is, demographically, one of the most multicultural countries in the world. Our population is now approximately 32 million people. Today, almost one in four people in Canada has been born outside the country. Over the past 100 years, more than 13 million immigrants have arrived here from all corners of the earth to start a new and hopefully better life for themselves and their children (Statistics Canada, 2007b). With the exception of Aboriginal peoples, everyone else is either an immigrant to this country or the descendant of one. Recent data show there are over 200 different ethnic groups in Canada, speaking more than 100 languages (Statistics Canada, 2007c). Since Confederation, the majority of immigrants have come mainly from Europe, especially during the first half of the twentieth century. More recently, non-Europeans have been accepted in larger numbers either as skilled workers, business immigrants, refugees, or family members of previous immigrants (Statistics Canada, 2007b).

The examination of ethnic and race relations is crucial in our understanding of Canadian society. As sociologists, we are interested in analyzing social relations, that is, relations of power (domination and subordination) among individuals and social groups. We cannot understand current economic, political, and social relations or conflicts in Canada without a comprehensive understanding of ethnic and race relations. For example, we cannot understand the current struggles of Aboriginal peoples with various levels of Canadian government over their land and self-determination without examining the legacy of colonization and the long-lasting effects it has had on their cultural, economic, and social lives. We cannot begin to talk about the formation of the Canadian state without reference to historical British–French conflicts. Modern Canada is constituted as a political entity, in large part, as a result of the struggles and the uneasy union between the charter groups—the French and English—at the expense of Aboriginal peoples. Moreover, our existing demographic makeup is a product of our history; it is a reflection of Canada's immigration policies and practices even before Confederation, many of which have been outright discriminatory and racist, at least until the mid-1960s.

Similarly, current problems in the economic, social, and political integration of visible minority groups may be attributed in part to racism. The economic and social

Children play street hockey in Inuvik, Northwest Territories, Canada. (Lowell Georgia/Corbis)

hardships facing migrant agricultural labourers in Canada today may be the result—to a great extent—of current neo-racist immigration policies of the federal government (Simmons, 1998). It is not surprising, then, that the field of ethnic and race relations has been central and continues to enjoy growth and importance within Canadian sociology. Let us begin by briefly examining how sociologists define the concepts of ethnicity and race, and how we can approach the study of ethnic and race relations theoretically.

A Brief History of Ethnicity and Race

Sociologists argue that the terms 'ethnicity' and 'race' have historically specific significations, i.e., their meanings differ in time and space. They mean different things to different people at different times and in different places. Ethnicity and race are not constant or monolithic concepts, but represent dynamic social relations in flux. Thus, as people's understandings of these two terms vary considerably, they are not readily or succinctly defined. Popular uses of the terms tend to differ from social scientific definitions (Miles and Torres, 1996). **Ethnicity** refers to social distinctions and relations among individuals and groups based on their cultural characteristics (language, religion, customs, history, etc.), whereas **race** refers to people's assumed but socially significant physical or genetic characteristics (Satzewich and Liodakis, 2007: 10). The term 'ethnicity' comes from the Greek word *ethnos* and means a large group of people. The ancient Greek historian Herodotus, in the fifth century BC, was the first to study **ethnic groups**. In his *Histories*, we find many passages where several ethnic groups are mentioned, some of which reside in the large urban Canadian centres today (e.g., Greeks, Persians, Arabs, Egyptians, Chaldeans, Assyrians, Indians, Ethiopians, Libyans, etc.). He described their languages, gods, some of their customs, their 'idiosyncrasies', their geography and contacts with other groups, their history, politics, other social arrangements, and economies (Herodotus, 1996: Books 1–9). He also provided an explanation of what comprises an ethnic group. For example, recognizing that ancient Greeks were geographically and politically fragmented, still, he argued, they constituted an ethnic group because they were of common biological descent, had a common language, common gods, sacred places, and sacrificial festivals, and customs or ways of life and 'the common character they bear'—their sameness (ibid., Book 8). In short, they shared a sense of 'belonging together'.

Émile Durkheim, one of the founders of sociology, used the concept of collective consciousness as a primary source of identity formation. In his famous *The Division of Labour in Society* (1964 [1893]), he tried to explain what made pre-modern societies so cohesive and emphasized the importance of community or group sentiments over individual ones. Social solidarity is based on sameness and the conformity of individual consciousness to the collective. Furthermore, similarities among members or sameness within the social group lead members to differentiate between themselves and others (non-members) and to prefer their 'own kind' over others. Durkheim believed that the collective consciousness of people leads them to 'love their country . . . to like one another, seeking one another out in preference of foreigners' (ibid., 60). This is an 'us' versus 'them' feeling, important in social group formation, reproduction, and maintenance.

Max Weber, another famous sociologist, argued that social group formation is associated with social practices of inclusion/exclusion, important in turn for the production and distribution of scarce valuable resources (goods, services, wages, social status and status symbols, economic and political power, equality, voting rights and citizenship, access to social programs, human rights, self-determination, autonomy, etc.). This practice of inclusion/exclusion constitutes the basis upon which decisions about rewards and sanctions are made. According to Weber (1978 [1908]), common descent, tribe, culture (which includes language and other symbolic codes), religion, and nationality are important *ethnic markers* and determinants of ethnicity. He wrote:

> We shall call 'ethnic groups' those human groups that entertain *a subjective belief in their common descent* because of similarities of physical type or of customs or both, or because of memories of colonization and migration; this belief must be important for the propagation of group formation; conversely, *it does not matter whether or not an objective blood relationship exists.* Ethnic membership differs from the kinship group precisely by being a *presumed identity.* (Ibid., 389; emphasis added)

Ethnicity should be seen as a subjective and presumed identity based on what Weber called a 'folk-feeling', not (necessarily) on any blood ties. Ethnic identity is often linked to people's 'primordial attachment'. Whereas *hard primordialism* holds that people are attached to one another and their communities of origin because of their blood ties, *soft primordialism*, as Weber

IN THE FIRST PERSON

I am an immigrant to this country. I have always been interested in the study of power relations. After graduating from high school in Greece, I decided to study politics at York University. Canada's international reputation as an ethnically diverse and tolerant society influenced my decision to choose Canada. The large presence of Greek Canadians and their legendary role in the resistance against the dictatorship of 1967–73 made Toronto a logical choice. The first social democrat Prime Minister of my home country, Andreas Papandreou, had been the worldwide leader of that resistance, and he had been a professor at York University. Thus, it made sense to attend York. Fascinated by Canadian society, I decided not to return but to stay and pursue graduate work at McMaster University, where I soon developed an interest in the social and economic aspects of inequality, and consequently switched to sociology. My research today examines the class and gender dimensions of economic inequalities among and within ethnic groups.—Nik Liodakis

argues, proposes that people's feelings of affinity, attachment, acceptance, trust, and intimacy towards their 'own kind' are not mediated by blood ties (Allahar 1994). Here is a historical example of presumed identity: in early Christian times, like today, people's religion was important in designating social groups, social positions, and hierarchies. Those who were not Christians were called *ethnics* (a stigmatizing, derogatory term at that time), although, of course, none of these large groups shared common, identifiable blood ties.

Weber used the term 'race' to denote common identity of groups based on biological heredity and endogamous conjugal groups. Not only customs but also visible similarities and differences, however minor, serve as potential sources of affection and appreciation or repulsion and contempt (Driedger, 1996: 5). Weber wrote: 'Almost any kind of *similarity or contrast of physical type* and of habits can induce the belief that affinity or disaffinity exists between groups that attract or repel each other' (Weber, 1978 [1908]: 386; emphasis added). Cultural and physical differences, produced and reproduced over time, constitute the foundations upon which a 'consciousness of kind' can be built. Such traits, in turn, 'can serve as a starting point for the familiar tendency to monopolistic closure' (ibid.). Monopolistic closure refers to economic, political, and social processes and practices, often institutionalized, whereby members of the in-group ('we'/'Self') have access to the scarce valuable resources mentioned above, while members of the out-group ('they'/'the Other') are excluded. The former monopolize, the latter are left out. Social boundaries, then, have been set and reproduced over time.

Today, sociologists use the term **racialization** to refer to sets of social processes and practices through which social relations among people are structured 'by the signification of human biological characteristics in such a way as to define and construct differentiated social collectivities' (Miles and Brown, 2003: 99). Invariably, these 'collectivities' are the majority, who are advantaged by racialization of others, and visible minorities, who are disadvantaged by their observable difference from the majority. We can also speak of ethnic or minority labelling in general, since cultural and other social characteristics also are used to identify social collectivities. An important part in long, historical processes of this labelling of social groups is the creation of hierarchical social dichotomies by the attribution of negative intellectual, moral, and behavioural characteristics to subordinate populations and the attribution of positive or not-negative characteristics to the dominant group(s) (those who label or stereotype). Social *positions* of superiority and inferiority are thus created; a social order is built (Li, 1999).

Ethnicity and race, therefore, are central factors in relations of power; they are socially constructed categories used to classify human populations and create social hierarchies. Like most social relations of power, they are not only setting boundaries, but they are also designating hierarchical positions of superiority and inferiority among and within social collectivities. As such, the meanings of the categories and the populations they describe or 'contain' are not fixed in time and space. In ancient Greece and Rome, unlike today, physical characteristics such as skin colour did not appear to be socially important in setting group boundaries or in creating social positions of superiority and inferiority (Snowdon, 1983). Herodotus, for example, differentiated between Greeks and 'barbarians', but his was not a racial hierarchy but one based one the notion of freedom (Goldberg, 1993). The Greeks were free; the barbarians were not. The former had desired characteristics, often deemed superior (a better language, cleverness, bravery, adventurousness, piety, cleanliness, the favour of [their] gods, etc.) to those of the barbarians (lacking in intellectual capacity, dressing strangely, dirtiness, cowardice, trickiness, irreverence, bloodthirstiness, raw-meat eaters, etc.).

When I ask my students how many races there are, they usually answer only one: the human race. But when we begin to discuss the legacy of colonialism, or issues of inequality among social groups, terms such as 'white', 'black', 'visible minorities', 'Asians', and 'Aboriginals' cannot be avoided. These terms connote race as real. The physical characteristics of humans that have been used to classify social groups have included skin colour, eye colour, hair type, nose shape, lip shape, body hair, and cheekbone structure (Driedger, 1996: 234–5). Using the term 'race' as a means of categorizing human populations is definitely linked to the European 'voyages of discovery' or, to be historically accurate, to the colonization, exploitation, domination, and often the extermination of indigenous peoples by the colonizers.

The meanings of the term 'race' have been and are shifting even today. Here are a few historical examples. For a long time, race simply meant descent or lineage and was attributed to groups with a common history. It was not seen as a real, objective biological category (Banton, 1987). But by the end of eighteenth century in Europe, there was an obvious shift in the meaning of 'race'. European pseudo-science was preoccupied with the explanation and classification of the physical and cultural diversity of the newly 'discovered' peoples, just as researchers in the natural sciences, led by Linnaeus, sought to classify and give Latin names to the flora and fauna of the natural world. Categorizing and naming the previously unknown and exotic helped to make it known and understandable—and within the namer's control. The concept of race was increasingly used to explain human physical, social, moral, and intellectual variation among peoples. Under conditions of colonialism, the 'racialization of the world', a scientific error according to Banton (1977), took place. In pre-revolutionary France, race denoted common lineage but was also used in a legal sense to protect aristocratic privileges. Guillaumin (1995) has shown that the aristocracy used the term 'race' to differentiate themselves, their offspring, and their ancestors from those who did not share their (presumably glorious) lineage. Aristocratic families were seen as different races by virtue of their common blood and descent. Later, in post-revolutionary France, the term 'race' was used to separate social classes. The *sans-culottes* (lower classes) were considered to belong to inferior races, the aristocracy to a superior one. Changes in the class structure of post-revolutionary France gave rise to changes in the meaning of 'race'. The social *content* of the term (the people and the social relations to which it referred) was altered. The French bourgeoisie, lacking the pedigree, privilege, divine right, or royal connections of the aristocracy, and without access to an ideology of superiority, slowly began to characterize *others* (social groups without the economic and political power that the bourgeoisie was now enjoying) as races (ibid.). Race, then, had a *class* content also. Not only did it apply to non-French 'others', but also to the manual working class and the peasantry (Satzewich, 1998: 28–9).

After the era of colonization and during the advent of capitalism as a new mode of production, a new social dichotomy slowly emerged, one based on definitions of 'Self' and 'Other'. The 'Self' referred to dominant European populations and cultures and was considered superior; the 'Other' referred to non-Europeans, who were seen as inferior and subordinate. Prior to the emergence of capitalism, race was used in a legal sense to describe people with common lineage and as a self-identification label for the aristocracy (a category that defined the Self), but with the emergence of the bourgeoisie in France the term was used to define 'Others', 'others' being 'Negroes', 'Jews', 'Arabs', 'Asiatics', etc. It became an externally imposed label. The classification of certain groups as races was coupled with negative evaluations of their members' biological and social characteristics, just as Herodotus had characterized the barbarians more than 2,000 years earlier.

Time to Reflect

Do you believe that races exist? If so, how many races are there? Could all human populations be categorized in terms of inherited physical characteristics? Should they be?

If we look closely into Canadian history, we find that notions of ethnicity and race have also changed over time. For example, in the aftermath of the Upper and Lower Canada rebellions of 1837, Lord Durham attempted to explain the British–French conflict in terms of racial, not ethnic, differences. It was believed, then, that despite their physical similarities, the British and the French constituted different races, not different ethnic groups, as we call them today (Satzewich and Liodakis, 2007: 28, 32–3). In the first half of the twentieth century in Quebec, this notion of the British and French as different and *unequal* races (i.e., the inferiorizing of the latter) found social expression in the reality of 'capital speaking English' and 'workers speaking French' (Whitaker, 1993: 22).

In Canada, social class position, coupled with prevailing notions of femininity and masculinity, has also been used to 'describe' and define races as social groups. In British Columbia, at the beginning of the twentieth century, the Chinese immigrants were labelled a 'feminine' race by European-origin Canadians because of the large numbers of Chinese males found in occupations traditionally associated with 'female labour': doing laundry, cooking, cleaning, or waiting tables in restaurants (Vorst et al., 1991). Canadian immigration policies—for a very long period of time—were saturated with notions of race as a real biological category, with the idea that certain ethnic and racial groups are superior to others, and with practices of inclusion/exclusion. As a consequence, until policy changes in 1967, members of 'preferred' groups were allowed to immigrate to Canada freely; 'non-preferred' groups could not make Canada their home so easily, as we will see below.

Building One Nation or Two: Canada's Development through Immigration

Canada is not, of course, the only country in the world that has admitted in the past and continues to admit large numbers of immigrants, but we are a major immigrant-receiving country, and for good reason. Why do we admit immigrants in the first place? Today's reasons are not that much different from those of the nation-building era. State formation requires more than a stable political territory, an army, political institutions, and government buildings. It also needs people. It needs the creation and management of human populations, national identities, and citizens. In the late nineteenth and early twentieth centuries the federal government endeavoured to increase its population base, build the country's infrastructure, and develop the economy by promoting capitalist development, domestic and international trade, manufacturing, commercial farming, mining and other resource extraction industries, and generally, to engage in the activities that build nations. Today, in the context of global economic competition, Canada still needs a growing population to keep labour costs down, increase the tax base, finance social programs, increase international competitiveness, and maintain its comparative advantage in the oil and gas industries and in other resource extraction. In short, it needs immigrants. But what explains the present demographic constitution of Canada? In other words, what could account for the cultural, ethnic, and racial makeup of the country today? Why are certain groups in Canada more populous than others? Why have there been dramatic changes in the patterns of immigration to Canada? Some answers to these questions are provided below, where we examine briefly the particular role that immigration policies have played in Canadian nation-building.

Until the 1960s, the image of Canada as a nation was based on the idea that the British and French peoples founded this country. These two **charter groups**, by this thinking, built the country; everyone else 'joined in' later. The 'two founding nations' thesis endures even today, but, in part, it is historically inaccurate. To be sure, the French and the British colonized Canada and sent settlers to this land. But this was done at the expense of the Native peoples who were already here. Not only did they lose their lands through colonization, warfare, and deceitful treaties, but 'efforts to assimilate *them*' into the dominant aspects of the British and French cultures (Christianity, private property, competitive individualism, etc.) left Aboriginals with long-lasting cultural trauma and without the communal economies that had sustained them for centuries. In addition, immigration from other countries began in earnest around the time of Confederation. Nation-building required the creation of a national transportation infrastructure (roads, railways, canals), the development of commercial agriculture in western Canada, and capitalist industry in major urban centres. In the minds of government policy-makers, these requirements, in turn, necessitated the large influx of mostly Northern and Central European and American immigrants (except blacks), since, what was left of the once-thriving Aboriginal population, it was believed, either did not have the necessary skills or could not adapt to the British/French 'ways of doing things'. More often than not, Canada's first peoples were seen and treated as 'uncivilized savages'—very much 'others'. Cultural compatibility was a requirement for immigration to Canada. The offer of free land to European and American settlers (land that was taken away from Aboriginals) resulted in the first wave of immigration to Canada, from 1896 to the beginning of World War I. The federal government passed Immigration Acts (1906, 1910) that set the terms under which immigrants other than the charter groups, called *entrance groups*, were accepted in Canada. In 1913, 400,000 immigrants arrived in Canada. During the years of World War I, the Great Depression, and World War II, immigration almost ceased (see Figure 18.1).

Immigration picked up again in the 1950s, when Canada admitted almost half a million immigrants from Europe. As mentioned earlier, however, not everyone has always been welcomed in Canada. The Immigration Act of 1910 prohibited the immigration of people who were considered 'mentally defective', 'idiots, imbeciles, feeble-minded, epileptics, insane, diseased, the physically defective, the dumb, blind, or otherwise handicapped' (McLaren, 1990: 56). A 1919 amendment to the Immigration Act decreed that people with 'dubious' political loyalties were also excluded outright, or, if already in Canada, were subject to deportation. Individuals who sought to overthrow by force or violence Her Majesty's governments or possessions, or who promoted the destruction of private property, by words or acts, or attempted to create riots or public disorder, were 'deemed to belong to the prohibited or undesired classes' (Roberts, 1988: 19). Early immigration policies, therefore, created categories of desired and undesired immigrants. Race and ethnicity were also critical in determining who was allowed into Canada and who was not. Until the liberalization of immigration in the 1960s, successive Canadian governments, Liberal or Conservative, exercised exclusionary policies. At the end of the nineteenth century and the beginning of the twentieth century, the admission of immigrants was based on a social hierarchy of ethnic and racial groups. Some groups were preferred (mostly Northern and Central Europeans, as well as Americans). Others were labelled as 'non-preferred' and were thus systematically excluded (the Chinese, black Americans, Eastern and Southern Europeans, people from India, etc.). Members of the former groups were seen as good workers, law-abiding people, and desirable future citizens, whereas the latter were regarded as culturally, ethnically, or racially 'unsuitable' and only would be admitted to Canada as a last resort.

Immigrants from China and India were of particular 'concern' to xenophobic immigration authorities since the former were seen as unassimilable and thus unsuitable for permanent residence. In the 1880s, Chinese immigrants were allowed into the country because of the growing demand for cheap and disposable labour in the

Figure 18.1 Immigration in Historical Perspective, 1860–2004

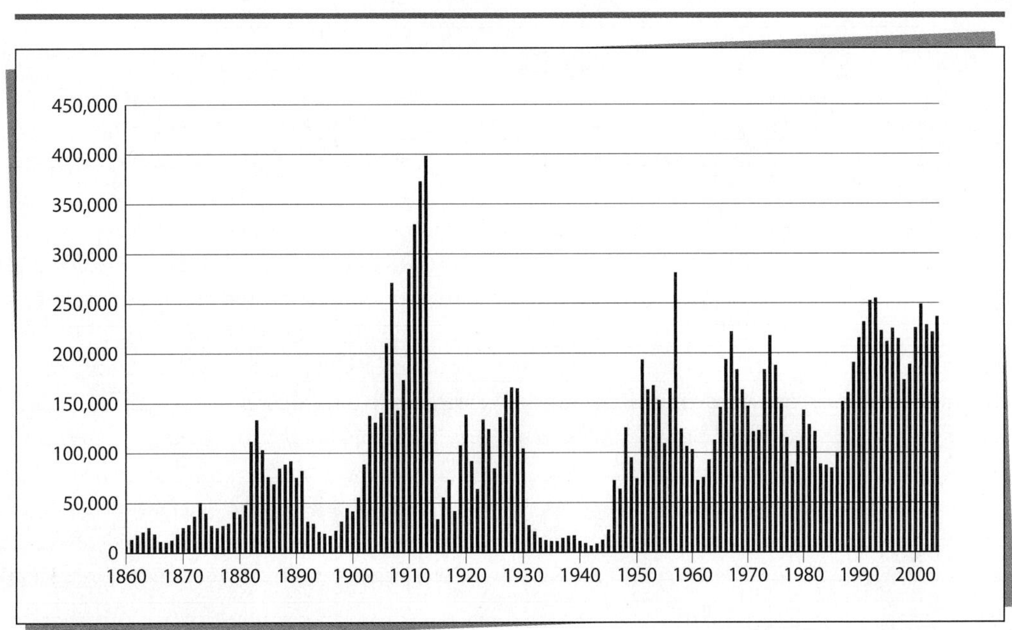

Source: Citizenship and Immigration Canada, *Immigration Overview, 2004*, at: <www.cic.gc.ca/english/pdf/pub/facts2004.pdf>. Reproduced with permission of the Minister of Public Works and Government Services Canada, 2007.

building of the transcontinental railway. From 1880 to 1884, approximately 16,000 Chinese immigrants arrived in Canada, mainly in British Columbia, to work in railroad construction. Employers and railroad contractors saw an opportunity to exploit Chinese labourers and called for increases in Chinese immigration; labour unions, on the other hand, opposed the influx of Chinese workers since increases in the supply of immigrant labour led to stiffer labour market competition and kept wages low. The government, exploiting xenophobia, popular anti-Chinese sentiments, and unfounded fears ('worries' about the 'dilution of our British character', the presumed cultural, ethnic, and racial homogeneity of Canada), restricted immigration from China by imposing the now-infamous Chinese head tax. Introduced first in 1885 at $50, it increased to $100 in 1890 and to $500 per person in 1903. By 1923, Chinese immigration was prohibited until after World War II. In other words, only the Chinese who could afford the head tax could immigrate to Canada. Their social class background and gender were especially important since Chinese businessmen who either invested or established businesses in Canada were exempt from the head tax and were allowed to immigrate to Canada even after 1923. The immigration of Chinese women was also restricted since—it was feared—they would reproduce the 'yellow peril' and lead to the propagation of 'alien' cultures and races, thus undermining the image of Canada as a 'white' settler society. It is believed that the federal government collected a total of $23 million for the period the head tax was in effect (Satzewich and Liodakis, 2007). In today's dollars, this would amount to approximately $1.2 billion.

The case of immigrants from India also demonstrates the **racism** prevalent in immigration policies. By the 1910s, around 5,000 immigrants from India had arrived in British Columbia to work in the lumber and mining industries. The government could not introduce outright anti-Indian immigration legislation since India was part of the British Empire, so, for the sake of appearances, it opted for the covertly discriminatory policy of the so-called 'continuous journey stipulation'. An Order-in-Council passed on 9 May 1910 stipulated that only people who had made a non-stop journey from their country of origin to Canada would be allowed in as immigrants (Basran and Bolaria, 2003: 99). Not sur-

Sikh passengers aboard the *Komagata Maru*. (Vancouver Public Library, Special Collections, VPL6231)

prisingly, there were no direct sailings between India and Canada. Canadian steamship companies were 'persuaded' by the government to end all direct travel from India. Indians who wanted to come to Canada as immigrants had to travel via Hong Kong or Hawaii, but that did not constitute a continuous journey. Immigrants from India, thus, were not admitted. Indeed, when this policy was tested by an enterprising Sikh, Gurdit Singh, who organized the immigration to Canada of 340 fellow Sikhs, the Japanese-registered freighter, the *Komagata Maru*, which sailed from Hong Kong in April 1914, with stops in Shanghai and Japan, was refused landing at the Port of Vancouver. After a tense standoff lasting two months, extensive world press coverage, and rapidly deteriorating conditions aboard the vessel anchored in Vancouver harbour, the *Komagata Maru* returned to Asia with its passengers (Buchignani et al., 1985: 54–61).

The end of World War II saw some minor improvements in Canadian immigration policy. It did not end **discrimination**—that started slowly in the 1960s—but Canada began by repealing the Chinese Immigration Act (1947) and the continuous journey stipulation. A quota of 150 Indian immigrants per annum was set in 1952, which was later raised to 300 (Basran and Bolaria, 2003: 104). Gradually, some non-whites were allowed to immigrate. Small numbers of black women were admitted as domestic workers, typists, and nurses. But even as late as 1952, the government could still (and did) prohibit immigration based on people's nationality, citizenship, ethnic group, occupation, class, geographical area of origin, 'peculiar' customs, habits, modes of life and methods of holding property, low probability of becoming readily assimilated or to assume the duties of citizenship, and unsuitability to the climatic, economic, social, industrial, health, and educational conditions prevailing in Canada (Satzewich, 1991: 124–5). In short, the government could choose from a large pool of legally sanctioned 'reasons' to reject certain 'types' of (undesired) immigrants. It was not until 1962 that the government initiated the elimination of racist criteria in the immigrant selection process, and not until 1967 that the familiar points systems was introduced, which relied on more objective criteria and assigned more weight to the applicant's age, educational credentials, job skills, work experience, and English- and/or French-language abilities, not to a person's country of origin. These changes eventually led to a large increase in the numbers of Southern Europeans (Italians, Greeks, Portuguese, and, to a smaller extent, Spanish) in the late 1960s and early 1970s, and the moderate rise of non-white immigration to Canada.

The New Mosaic: Recent Canadian Immigration Trends

The 'colour' of Canadian immigration has changed since the 1980s. Immigration from the traditional European (white) source countries has diminished substantially, since their standard of living has improved markedly, even in Southern Europe and especially after the emergence of the European Union. As shown in Table 18.1, there has been a remarkable shift in the geographical regions from which Canada admits immigrants. During the 1950–5 period, for example, the United Kingdom and the rest of Europe accounted for 88 per cent of all immigration to Canada, but for the 2000–4 period the percentage of European immigration had dropped to 19.7 per cent. US immigration has dropped from 6.3 per cent to 2.6 per cent. Similarly, when comparing these two periods, we find that immigrants from Africa and the Middle East accounted for only 0.4 per cent of all immigration in the first period, but 50 years later these source regions accounted for 19.1 per cent of all immigration. Most remarkable is the change for Asia

Table 18.1 Percentages of Immigrants to Canada by Major Source Area, 1950–5 and 2000–4

Area	1950–5 (%)	2000–4 (%)
Africa and the Middle East	0.4	19.1
Asia and the Pacific	3.6	50.3
South and Central America	1.5	8.3
United States	6.3	2.6
Europe and the United Kingdom	88.0	19.7
Other/not stated	0.2	0.0

Sources: Figures for 1950–5 compiled from Canada, Department of Manpower and Immigration, *Immigration Statistics*; figures for 2000–4 compiled from Citizenship and Immigration Canada, *Facts and Figures 2004: Immigration Overview*, at: <www.cic.gc.ca/english/pub/facts2004/permanent/12.html>.

and the Pacific. The percentage of all immigration for the aforementioned periods has increased from 3.6 to 50.3 per cent. For South and Central America the percentages are 1.5 and 8.3, respectively.

Canada today admits approximately 260,000 immigrants per year. Table 18.2 lists the top 10 source countries of immigrants to Canada for 2005. Together, these 10 countries accounted for more than 55 per cent of all immigrants. The top source country is China (16.1 per cent of all admitted immigrants that year), and the second highest percentage belongs to India (12.6 per cent). We have certainly come a long way since the era of the Chinese head tax and the continuous journey policy. The UK, France, and the US are still found in the top 10 source countries, but their percentage contributions are small (2.2, 2.1, and 3.5 per cent, respectively).

Table 18.2 Top 10 Source Countries Immigrants to Canada, 2005

Source Countries	Number	% of Total Immigrants
China, People's Republic of	42,291	16.1
India	33,146	12.6
Philippines	17,525	6.7
Pakistan	13,576	5.2
United States	9,262	3.5
Colombia	6,031	2.3
United Kingdom	5,865	2.2
Korea, Republic of	5,819	2.2
Iran	5,502	2.1
France	5,430	2.1
Top 10 source countries	144,447	55.1
Other countries	117,789	44.9
Total	262,236	100

Source: Citizenship and Immigration Canada, *Facts and Figures, 2005: Immigration Overview*, at: <www.cic.gc.ca/english/pub/facts2005/permanent/12.html>. Reproduced with permission of the Minister of Public Works and Government Services Canada, 2007.

Immigrants are divided into four major categories (often called immigration classes): skilled workers, business immigrants, the family class, and refugees. Figure 18.2 shows the numbers and percentages for each category of immigrants admitted to Canada in 2005. Contrary to public misconceptions about the people admitted, the largest immigration class is that of skilled workers (142,842 people), who constituted 54.5 per cent of total immigration in 2005. Skilled workers are independent applicants who are admitted by the use of the points system (based on the criteria mentioned above; see 'Global Issues' box).

The family class in 2005 (63,352 people) was second, with 14.2 per cent of total immigration to Canada. These immigrants are admitted if they have close relatives (spouses or parents) in Canada who are willing to sponsor them to come and to support them financially for a period of 3–10 years after they arrive. Refugees (35,768 people) follow, representing 13.6 per cent. Canada is a signatory to international treaties and is obliged by international law to provide asylum to those who have demonstrably genuine refugee claims. Usually, these are people who come from countries with known records of human rights violations. They are called convention refugees since they fall under the provisions of the 1951 United Nations Convention relating to the Status of Refugees and the 1967 Protocol to the Convention that extended its scope and time frame beyond refugees in Europe following World War II. Finally, business immigrants (13,469 people), comprising 5.1 per cent of the total 2005 immigrants to Canada, are divided into three subcategories: investors who have business experience, are worth at least $800,000, and must invest at least half of that in the country; entrepreneurs who are worth at least $300,000 and must create and manage a company that will create at least one full-time job in the country (other than their own); and the self-employed category, who must demonstrate to immigration officials that they have the skills and experience to start up a business that will create employment for themselves.

Once in Canada, most immigrants in 2006—nearly 85 per cent—settled in Ontario, British Columbia, and Quebec (Table 18.3). The distribution of immigrants across Canada, therefore, is decidedly uneven. From Ontario's high of 50 per cent of all immigrants, after Quebec (17.8 per cent) and BC (16.7 per cent), only Alberta (8.2 per cent) and Manitoba (4 per cent) attracted more than 1 per cent of the total immigration. This uneven distribution, of course, influences variably the ethnic and racial makeup of certain parts of Canada. There is also a clear urban/rural divide. Immigrants are attracted more to major urban centres

GLOBAL ISSUES

The Points System for Skilled Workers: Would You Make It?

Do you think you would qualify as an immigrant to your own country? Test yourself to find out if you would qualify as a skilled worker for admission to Canada. The table below outlines the various categories of qualification for which points are rewarded. For example, if at present your education consists of a secondary school diploma, but no further diplomas, certificates, or degrees, you will get 5 points in this category; under language, if you can read, write, speak, and understand English with complete proficiency, you will get 16 points, and total proficiency in French will give you an additional 8 points. You will need at least 67 points (out of a possible 100) to be admitted to Canada as a skilled worker. For a complete breakdown of the points system, go to the following website: <www.canada-immigration.biz/permanent_skilled.asp>.

Selection Criteria	Points Awarded
Education	up to 25
Knowledge of official language(s)	up to 24
Work experience	up to 21
Age (applicants 21–49 years of age receive maximum points; 2 points are deducted for each year under 21 or over 49, so that someone 16 or younger or 54 or older will receive no points)	up to 10
Arranged employment in Canada	up to 10
Adaptability	up to 10
Spouse's or common-law partner's education	3 to 5
Minimum one-year full-time authorized work in Canada	5
Minimum two years post-secondary study in Canada	5
Maximum points awarded	100
Minimum required to pass for skilled worker immigrants	67

because there they usually find more economic opportunities and other immigrants from their own part of the world. Today, for example, the majority of Torontonians have been born outside Canada, whereas almost all of the residents of Hérouxville, a small farming community in Quebec, are Canadian-born (see 'Open for Discussion' box).

Time to Reflect

Why does Canada admit immigrants? If you were to (re)design Canada's immigration policy, what criteria would you use for admitting immigrants? Why are these criteria of most importance?

Figure 18.2 Categories of Immigrants Admitted to Canada, 2005

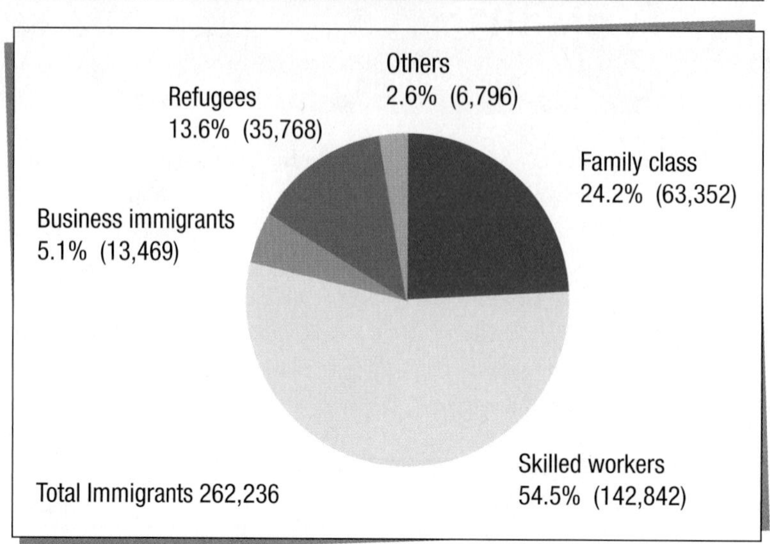

Source: Citizenship and Immigration Canada, *Facts and Figures 2005: Immigration Overview*, at: <www.cic.gc.ca/english/pub/facts2005/overview/1.html>.

Multiculturalism and Its Discontents

As discussed above, part of the problems facing prospective immigrants in the past had to do with their so-called 'unsuitability', namely, that there existed in Canada strong anti-immigrant sentiments and fears, as well as outright racist policies aimed at curbing the influx of 'undesirable foreigners'. But even those who are readily admitted as immigrants today continue to face problems. Some members of ethnic and racial minorities, usually their most vulnerable segments, have problems of limited access to language programs, training and educational opportunities, social and health services, and employment, and frequently, once in the workforce, they encounter poor working conditions and inadequate compensation. Canada may not be as racist as it used to be in the past (Levitt, 1994) but it is still racist, capitalist, and patriarchal (Liodakis, 2002). For example, evidence suggests that recent immigrants, mostly visible minority working-class women, continue to face discrimination and unequal treatment in the labour market (Galabuzi, 2006; Hum and Simpson, 2007; Krahn et al., 2007). But what makes an individual a visible minority? Who is a 'true' Canadian? Why are Aboriginals not considered visible minorities? Are they simply just another ethnic group? Are the Québécois an ethnic group like all others? What defines your identity? What are you? In the 2001 census almost one in three respondents identified their ancestry as Canadian. Are Canadians an ethnic group? More importantly, who decides, who makes the definitional rules, who sets the criteria? These are tough questions, and simplistic approaches usually do not provide satisfactory social scientific answers. Let us examine a few important aspects of the formation and meanings of ethnic and racial identities in the Canadian context of multiculturalism.

As noted earlier, the meanings and social content of ethnicity and race are not monolithic or static but dynamic and fluid. There is no simple, one-to-one correspondence between individual people, their culture and ethnicity, and the 'nation' to which they belong. Culture is not static, uniform, or homogeneous. Rather, it is a set of dynamic social processes and practices; it is a collective response of socially constituted individuals to their ever-changing external conditions, largely determined by pre-existing social structures. Cultural values in Canada have changed over time. Prior to the advent of official **multiculturalism** in 1971, to which we are so used today, there had been the long, hard years of Anglo- and/or Franco-cultural conformity. It is historically inaccurate to believe that the values and attendant practices of ethnic pluralism, tolerance for others, and multiculturalism have been always present or dominant in Canada. Canadian society has been characterized by ethnocentrism from the era of colonization to the early 1970s. An individual is ethnocentric when he

Table 18.3 Immigration to Canada by Province or Territory of Permanent Settlement, 2006

Province/Territory	% of Total Immigration
Alberta	8.2
British Columbia	16.7
Manitoba	4.0
New Brunswick	0.7
Newfoundland and Labrador	0.2
Northwest Territories	0.0
Nova Scotia	1.0
Nunavut	0.0
Ontario	50.0
Prince Edward Island	0.2
Quebec	17.8
Saskatchewan	1.1
Yukon	0.0

Source: Citizenship and Immigration Canada, *Facts and Figures, 2006*, at: <www.cic.gc.ca/english/resources/statistics/facts2006/permanent/17.asp>. Reproduced with permission of the Minister of Public Works and Government Services Canada, 2007.

or she evaluates (usually negatively) the culture of others based on criteria derived from his/her own. The charter groups have set the terms for the entrance of all others into the country. There has always been sustained pressure on Aboriginals and minority group newcomers to adopt the dominant British and French cultural values, customs, and symbols. In short, 'others' had to conform; they had to assimilate to the norms of the 'Self'.

'Assimilation', a term always encountered in race and ethnic relations discourses, is usually defined as the processes and social practices by which members of minority groups are incorporated into the dominant culture of a society (Isajiw, 1999: 170). Sociologists distinguish between behavioural assimilation ('acquiring' the values of dominant groups) and structural assimilation (the integration of 'others' into the economic, social, and political life of a country).

But assimilation has not always been a simple matter of choice for minorities; often it was forceful and violent, as was the case with Aboriginals, for example, through the residential schools and the banning of Native customs and ceremonies such as the thirst dance and the potlatch. Early Canadian government efforts to assimilate Aboriginals and other immigrants somewhat resemble American **melting-pot policies**. Robert Park, the noted Chicago School sociologist, argued that when members of different ethnic groups come into contact (because of colonization or migration), competition and conflict usually occurs among their members. Writing in the US of the early twentieth century, and having worked with blacks in the South and Polish immigrants in Chicago, Park (1914) represented the interaction of whites and blacks in terms of a race relations cycle. The same cycle has also been applied to ethnic relations. It included several stages, two different routes, but one outcome: that of fusion or assimilation, where the subordinate minority groups assimilate to the dominant majority group. Initially, contact between the two groups creates competition for access to and acquisition of scarce valuable resources. This competition can lead either to accommodation and eventually fusion/assimilation, or to conflicts over the social and material resources (remember Weber's monopolistic closure) that in turn lead to accommodation and then fusion/assimilation. Underlying this cycle is the position that the 'new' culture that emerges from their fusion is good for both and certainly good for the 'nation'. Fusion also implies social harmony, even equality. This is the melting-pot metaphor of American society. The present generation in Canada has been brought up within the multicultural framework and even the idea of a melting pot is alien. But multiculturalism is a fairly recent policy development.

'Multiculturalism' is one of those elusive terms that we use everyday, but it means different things to different people. In sociology, we understand the term as having four interrelated meanings:

> It is a demographic reality.
> It is part of pluralist ideology.
> It is a form of struggle among minority groups for access to economic and political resources.
> It is a set of government policies and accompanying programs (Fleras and Elliott, 1996: 325).

It can be defined as an ideology, based on Canadian social reality, that gives rise to sets of economic, political, and social practices, which in turn define boundaries and set limits to ethnic and racial group relations in order to either maintain social order or manage social change (Liodakis and Satzewich, 2003: 147).

First, when we say that multiculturalism is a fact of Canadian society, we mean that the Canadian population comprises people who come from over 200 ethnic groups. Canadian society has never been ethnically homogeneous, as some would like to believe. Demographically, Canada was a multicultural country long before the implementation of multiculturalism as policy. Second, as an ideology, multiculturalism includes normative descriptions about how Canadian society *ought to be*. The basis of multiculturalist ideology is cultural pluralism, which advocates tolerance of cultural diversity and, most importantly, promotes the idea that such diversity is compatible with national goals, especially those of national unity and socio-economic progress (Fleras and Elliot, 1996). The basic principles of multiculturalism rest on the notion of cultural relativism, as opposed to ethnocentrism. Cultural relativism promotes tolerance and diversity in order to achieve the peaceful coexistence of groups in ethnically and racially heterogeneous societies. As opposed to ethnocentrism, cultural relativism argues that we should not judge other cultures by our own norms and criteria. If we recognize the right of all people to self-identify and promote their own culture, then, it is hoped, the same courtesy would be extended to individuals who share different cultural norms and values. Third, multiculturalism is also a process and a terrain of competition among and between minority groups for valuable economic and political resources. As such, it is used by governments as a mechanism for conflict management and resolution. Multiculturalism was not exactly given as a gift to minority groups; historically, it emerged for several reasons:

> During the 1960s, immense political pressure was exerted on the federal government by the 'other' ethnic groups (e.g., the Ukrainians and Germans in the West, who were dissatisfied with the Royal Commission on Bilingualism and Biculturalism of 1963–9) for the recognition of their contributions to Canadian society.
>
> It became a political necessity to counterbalance western alienation and Quebec nationalism, and multiculturalism appeared to be a logical avenue for this counterbalancing.
>
> The Liberal Party of Canada sought to acquire greater electoral support from immigrants in urban centres, and this was a logical step in that direction. (Ibid., 335)

Finally, multiculturalism refers to all government initiatives and programs that seek to realize multiculturalism as ideology and to transform it into a concrete form of social intervention.

As policy, it is a relatively recent aspect of Canadian state activity. It was introduced in 1971 by a very charismatic Canadian Prime Minister, Pierre Elliott Trudeau. Ironically, and contrary to what we may think today, it was not the historical legacy of racism, discrimination, and **prejudice** in Canada that multicultural policy initially aimed to redress. In fact, these issues did not figure at all into the framework for the initial development of multicultural policy. Three stages of multicultural policy development have been identified by Fleras and Elliott. From 1971 to 1980, policy was essentially folkloric (ethnic food, costume, and dance) and focused on 'celebrating our differences'. At this time, cultural diversity was seen as the core of 'Canadian identity', of being Canadian. The years of Anglo- and Franco-conformity had passed. We no longer had an official culture. All cultures were seen as equal. Four basic principles guided federal multiculturalism at this time:

> The federal government would support all of Canada's cultures and seek to assist the development of those cultural groups that had demonstrated a desire and effort to continue to develop a capacity to grow and contribute to Canada as well as a clear need for assistance.
>
> The government would assist all cultural groups to overcome the cultural barriers to full participation in Canadian society.
>
> The government would promote creative encounters and interchange among all Canadian cultural groups in the interest of national unity.
>
> The government would continue to assist immigrants to acquire at least one of Canada's two official languages in order to become full participants in Canadian society. (Hawkins, 1989: 220)

Culture had become an issue of personal choice, and there was no shortage in the Canadian ethnic supermarket. In this light, individuals were protected against any discrimination stemming from their cultural choices, and they were strongly encouraged to cultivate and promote their cultures, and to participate fully in all aspects of Canadian life.

In the 1980s, the second phase of multicultural policy—the process of institutionalization—was developed. This phase entailed a number of new developments. First, there emerged an explicit concern over race relations. Second, in 1988 the Progressive Conservative government passed the Multiculturalism Act, which essentially turned a de facto policy into a de jure legal framework, thus elevating multiculturalism to equality with the principle of bilingualism. Third, renewed calls of Quebec nationalism were countered by the repatriation of the Constitution (1982) and the inclusion of the Charter of Rights and Freedoms in the Constitution Act, 1982. Section 27 of the Charter stated that its interpretation, i.e., in Canadian courts and legislatures, 'shall be . . . in a manner consistent with the preservation and enhancement of the multicultural heritage of Canadians.' In other words, multiculturalism had become a fundamental and legally contestable characteristic of Canadian society.

Finally, multiculturalism was increasingly cast in economic terms. Consistent with neo-conservative economic doctrines was the attempt to justify the 1988 Multiculturalism Act not only in terms of pluralist ideology, but also in terms of potential economic benefits to the country. This involved a shift in emphasis away from a 'culture for culture's sake' perspective towards a more instrumentalist view of the benefits of multicultural policy. Canada is full of people who speak innumerable languages and keep in touch with their homelands. Simply put, the Mulroney government of the day strongly believed that multiculturalism could and did mean business—increased business, more economic opportunities, and greater prosperity for all. Cultural pluralism and the image of Canada as an equal, tolerant, and fair society were defined by the government as a unique Canadian asset within the emerging global economy (Moodley, 1983). What the Conservatives failed to recognize was that most of Canada's global competitors are now multicultural in fact, if not in official policy terms, and so this might not have been as much of an advantage as initially thought.

Since the 1990s, a third stage of multiculturalism has developed. This 'civic multiculturalism' can be defined as a stage during which folkloric and institutional multiculturalism are coupled with notions of social equality and citizenship. The focus of civic multiculturalism is society-building; today, fostering a common sense of identity and belonging is considered essential for the participation and inclusion of all Canadians in national institutions (Fleras and Elliott, 1996: 334–5). During this stage, governments have moved away from the initial folkloric focus, which has meant a withdrawal from all programs associated with it (e.g., funding for cultural festivals).

The policy of multiculturalism has been critiqued since its introduction. There has never been agreement about the effectiveness, desirability, or necessity of the policy and its accompanying programs. Simply put, some argue that multiculturalism makes Canada a unique and great country, while others say that multiculturalism is useless, unnecessary, and ineffective. In the post-9/11 context, debates about multiculturalism have acquired renewed political importance.

Criticisms of Multiculturalism

Early criticisms of multiculturalism focused on the policy's inherent inability to deliver the goods and to solve the problems it set out to address. Some critics argued that too great an emphasis was placed on depoliticized 'song and dance' activities that were non-threatening to British and/or French economic, political, and cultural hegemony, and that the policy mystified social reality by creating the appearance of change without actually changing the fundamental bases of ethnic and racial inequality within Canada (Bolaria and Li, 1988; Moodley, 1983). Furthermore, the identification of only 'cultural barriers' to the full participation of immigrants in Canadian society precluded the examination of racism and discrimination as barriers (Bolaria and Li, 1988). Economic barriers were not recognized, nor were they examined (Stasiulis, 1980: 34). The exclusive focus on cultural and linguistic barriers to equality conceals other, perhaps more fundamental, social inequalities based on people's property rights, position in the labour market, education, gender, age, and so on. In fact, Canadian society is characterized by clear ethnic- and gender-based class hierarchies and socio-political struggles, which of course are not addressed by multiculturalism, because such struggles challenge, if not threaten, such hierarchies. Multiculturalism obfuscates these antagonisms and shifts the struggle to the cultural realm. In addition, in practical terms, many sociologists argue that the programs associated with the policy are mismanaged and are rightfully skeptical of how an average of $60 million per annum allotted to multicultural programs could possibly address the range of problems and issues such funding seeks to address, especially when it appears to cost the government almost as much to administer the programs (Li, 2003).

In the 1990s, critics claimed that the policy of multiculturalism helps to reproduce stereotypes of ethnic groups, undermines Canadian unity, ghettoizes minority issues, and takes away from the special claims that francophones and Aboriginal peoples have within Canadian society. A policy that had as one of its underlying intentions the improvement of inter-group relations was seen by many as a policy leading to deteriorating inter-group relations and as a threat to the coherence and stability of Canada. 'Caravans', 'folk fests', and other multicultural festivals do not promote serious cultural exchanges;

instead, they are superficial and have the effect of commodifying cultures and reproducing cultural, ethnic, and racial stereotypes (Bissoondath, 1994: 83). By placing individuals in preconceived stereotypes, multiculturalism diminishes the autonomy and role of the individual. According to Neil Bissoondath (1994: 224), we have become a nation of cultural hybrids. He argues that '[w]e are . . . of so many colours, that we are essentially colourless' (ibid., 73). Indeed, in this view, no evidence indicates that intercultural exchanges take place or have assisted in the 'harmonization' of racial and ethnic relations in Canada. Not only have the 'problems' of minority relations not been defined, but the little intercultural exchanges that do take place are superficial and, at best, celebrate quaint ethnocultural differences (Fleras and Elliott, 1996: 330–1). In fact, multiculturalism appears to focus on 'saris, samosas and steel-bands' in order to defuse 'resistance, rebellion and rejection' (Li, 1999: 98).

Another criticism has been that multiculturalism promotes cultural relativism and hence undermines Canadian values and social cohesion. This criticism has been developed by sociologist Reginald Bibby. Canadian society has changed as a result of multiculturalism, but not in entirely positive ways. Until the 1950s Canadians—in policy and practice—had emphasized community and the collectivity, but since then, according to Bibby, the focus has been on the individual. Pluralism, although imperative for coexistence, does not offer a subsequent vision of the country, does not set national goals, and does not have a cause. He has argued that one of the main social trends of our postmodern era is that we value collective and individual freedom a lot. While freedom is good in and of itself, the consequence of this increased emphasis is the promotion of individualism, pluralism, and relativism. Cultural relativism undermines social cohesion. We have enshrined into law our 'good intentions' of bilingualism, multiculturalism, and anti-racism by institutionalizing appropriate policies. But in consequence, we have become a fractious nation that lacks a sense of community (Bibby, 1990: 15). Canada, in attempting to promote peaceful coexistence, effectively promotes the breakdown of group life. As both Bibby and Bissoondath have viewed it, we have ended up with a value system that contains nothing exclusively Canadian. Although Bissoondath does not advocate a return to the years of Anglo-conformity, he argues that multiculturalism does not offer a vision of unity and it encourages division by ghettoizing people into ethnic groups. It imposes social controls and employs divide-and-conquer strategy and tactics (ibid., 44).

Criticizing the Critics: Multicultural Policy as a Reflection of Reality

These criticisms share an appeal to the 'national' character of Canada, which is never defined. The implication is that the current system is somehow biased in favour of 'non-whites' and 'non-Europeans' and that it should not be. In addition, the critics seem silent or purposefully vague in describing what constitutes Canadian culture, the definition of what and who is or should be Canadian, or what are Canadian values, and there is no definition of what constitutes 'the Canadian nation, culture, or character', who defines it, or whose interests it serves.

Rhoda Howard-Hassmann has pointed to a basic fault in the critiques of Bibby and Bissoondath: they both assume that Canadian multiculturalism calls for individuals to retain their ancestral identities. But the Canadian policy is 'liberal', not 'illiberal', that is, it does not impose the idea of maintaining ethnic differences, nor does it force individuals to identify with ancestral cultural groups. In her view:

> Multiculturalism 'normalizes' a wide range of customs and makes the enjoyment of such customs part of what it means to be a Canadian. . . . Liberal multiculturalism acknowledges the social need for difference, for smaller, more close-knit communities separated from the Canadian mainstream. But it does not mandate such difference. (Howard-Hassmann, 1999: 533)

She also argues that, far from promoting disloyalty to Canada and things Canadian, multicultural policy has the seemingly ironic consequences of integrating immigrants to the dominant society, promoting national unity, and encouraging 'a sense of connection with other Canadians' (ibid., 534). The rising numbers of people who identify themselves as Canadians in recent censuses tend to support her argument.

Pluralism does not inevitably lead to relativism. Multiculturalism, as we experience in our daily lives, does not encourage an 'everything goes' mentality or attitude. It may help create some ambiguity about what is acceptable and what is not, but these issues are usually contested and resolved in the courts and other domains of political struggle. According to Fleras and Elliot (1996: 354), multiculturalism operates within limits; 'it rejects any customs that violate Canadian laws, interfere with the rights of others, offend the moral sensibilities of most Canadians, or disturb central institutions or core values.' For example, female circumcision is a cultural practice in parts of Africa and Asia and, presumably, part of the cultural heritage of some Canadians. In May

1997, an amendment to the Criminal Code of Canada outlawed female genital mutilation precisely because that practice violates the human rights of young women and offends notions of equality, human integrity, and other core values prevalent in Canada and internationally. The Canadian legislation links this practice to criminal harassment and regards it as a threat to the life, liberty, and security of Canadian women.

Aboriginal Peoples, Québécois, and Multiculturalism

Another criticism is that multiculturalism detracts from the special claims that francophones and Aboriginal peoples have in Canadian society. In Quebec, multiculturalism was seen as an attempt by the federal government to undermine the legitimate Quebec aspirations for 'nationhood'. Indeed, its direct growth out of the fourth volume of the Bilingualism and Biculturalism Commission report, on the 'other' ethnic groups, which seemed to be an extension beyond the mandate the Commission name implied, made this a reasonable charge. By severing culture from language, multiculturalism rejected the 'two founding nations' metaphor of Canada's historical development and reduced the status of French Canadians from that of 'founding people' to just another ethnic group (Abu-Laban and Stasiulis, 1992: 367). Multiculturalism also became a mechanism to buy allophone votes. Multiculturalism, it is claimed, has had an adverse effect on the Quebec collectivity by reducing the Québécois to one of many minorities within Canada. Assimilationist Quebec language policies directed towards allophones can be understood in this context.

Successive Quebec governments have pursued a policy of *interculturalism* (prominent in Europe), instead of multiculturalism. According to Kymlicka (1998), interculturalism operates within three important principles: (1) it recognizes French as the language of public life; (2) it respects the liberal-democratic values of political rights and equality of opportunity for all; and (3) it respects pluralism, openness to, and tolerance of the differences of others. These principles constitute a 'moral contract' between the province of Quebec and immigrant groups. Interculturalism may sound a lot like the federal policy of multiculturalism, but there are some nuanced differences. For example, it promotes *linguistic assimilation.* The 'centre of convergence' for different cultural groups in Quebec is the 'collective good' of the French language, which is seen as an indispensable condition for the creation of the *culture publique commune* (common public culture) and the cohesion of Quebec society. The French language needs to be protected and promoted. It constitutes the basis for the self-definition of Quebec as a political community and as a nation. Particular emphasis is placed on the educational system. As Stéphane Lévesque (1999: 4) has argued, 'common blood or ethnicity hardly creates social cohesion or nationhood, but an education system with a common language does make a "homeland". . . . It is language, more than land and history, that provides the essential form of belonging.' Federal multiculturalism promotes individualist approaches to culture, whereas interculturalism focuses on the collectivity.

Interculturalism does not reduce calls for Quebec separation or more political autonomy to an ethnic phenomenon; it discourages ethnic enclaves (Abu-Laban and Stasiulis, 1992: 368). Like multiculturalism, it promotes cultural exchanges in the hope that, as people of different cultures are exposed to various elements of other cultures, the ensuing dialogue may lead to an understanding and acceptance of the 'Other', not merely to tolerance. The result should lead to a fusion of all commonalities of cultures (in a francophone framework). As a policy, interculturalism also aims to overcome prejudices and fight racism.

Finally, some researchers have argued that interculturalism is the most advanced form of pluralism today (Karmis, 2004: 79). It is claimed that it combines multiculturalism and multinationalism and is more inclusive than either. It does not apply only to ethnic groups or nations but also to 'lifestyle' cultures and world views associated with new social movements, including cultural gay, punk, environmental, feminist, and other non-ethnic-based identities. In principle, no cultural community is excluded from Québécois identity. Whereas multiculturalism is believed to undermine the national claims of peoples within Canada by juxtaposing communities composing the Canadian mosaic, interculturalism seeks to intertwine them, recognizing that most individuals have multiple identities and that no one identity is so dominant as to subordinate others (ibid., 79–80).

Canadian Aboriginal peoples and their organizations are similarly critical and have similar reservations about multiculturalism. Aboriginal leaders argue that multiculturalism reduces them to 'just another minority group' and undermines their aspirations for self-government (Abu-Laban and Stasiulis, 1992: 376). They claim that they possess a distinct and unique set of rights—now enshrined in the Constitution—that stem from their being the first occupants of Canada. Since Aboriginal peoples do not consider themselves to be part of the so-called mainstream Canadian pluralist society, but as

Time to Reflect

Are Aboriginal Canadians and the Québécois just ethnic groups? If not, why not?

being distinct peoples, multiculturalism is seen as an actual threat to their survival. They prefer to negotiate their futures in a binational framework with federal (and provincial) governments that recognizes their collective rights to special status and distinctiveness (Fleras and Elliott, 1996: 343).

Multiculturalism in a Changing World

Many countries now officially celebrate their multicultural makeup, and some have policies designed to promote the peaceful coexistence of diverse groups. However, a number of events over the past few years have provided a context for renewed questions about, and attacks on, policies of multiculturalism both in Canada and abroad. Certainly, the attacks on the World Trade Center in New York and the Pentagon on 11 September 2001 put many Western governments on alert about the threats that cultural and religious 'Others' may pose to the 'peace and security' of their countries. In the post-9/11 era of Islamophobia and 'big brother' surveillance, two criticisms of multiculturalism are also prevalent: (1) that multiculturalism encourages and tolerates the promotion of cultures and religions that are decidedly intolerant; and (2) that multiculturalism is a recipe for homegrown terrorism. Such critiques are often concealed forms of racism. No country has arrived at an ideal management of ethnic and racial diversity. Canada's multicultural approach to diversity issues may not be perfect, indeed, it is rather limited, but many other far more problematic approaches to diversity exist (the US and France spring readily to mind) that we can take pride in having avoided so far. Let us now turn, then, to the unresolved issues of racism.

Prejudice and Racism

Racism is based on 'othering' (Simmons, 1998). According to Stuart Hall, it is 'not a set of false pleas which swim around in the head . . . not a set of mistaken perceptions . . . . [Racist ideas] have their basis in real material conditions of existence. They arise because of the concrete problems of different classes and groups in society. Racism represents the attempt ideologically to construct those conditions, contradictions, and problems in such a way that they can be dealt with and deflected at the same moment' (in Li, 1999: 325). Many sociologists have suggested (e.g., Bolaria and Li, 1988; Li, 1999) that race problems often begin as labour problems. Competition for employment among workers from different ethnic/racialized (and gender) groups keeps wages low and profits for employers high. Workers usually participate in a *split labour market*, in which more members of the dominant groups may have more secure, full-time, and high-paying jobs, whereas minorities are found in largely part-time, low-paying, insecure, and menial occupations. Expressions of working-class racism may be attributable to labour market conditions of inequality (see Dunk in Satzewich, 1998).

This labour market split develops over long periods of time and is reproduced by prejudice and discrimination. Processes of racialization are coupled with preconceived notions of what people are, not who they are, and are associated with everyday racist social practices. Often, we have preconceived notions about ethnic/racialized groups. Members of some groups are seen through the prism of stereotypes (Driedger, 1996). Some are deemed as hard-working, law-abiding, smart, moral, etc. Others are seen as 'lazy', 'smelly', 'dirty', 'stingy', 'criminals', 'promiscuous', 'uncivilized', and the like. Ethnic jokes, which might amuse us uncritically, are based on these stereotypes. Negative stereotypes are often reserved, by the majority group, for minority groups; positive stereotypes are related to dominant groups, although minority groups use positive self-stereotypes to resist racism. Discrimination refers to behaviours and policies that reproduce ethnic and racial social stereotypes as well as economic and political inequalities. We also use the term 'prejudice' to refer to the negative views of and attitudes about members of various minority groups. 'Prejudice' comes from the Latin word for 'prejudgement'. Also associated with this term is the *ecological fallacy*, i.e., the assumption that an individual member of a social group (in our case, an ethnic/racialized group) has the social characteristics associated with that group. As such, stereotypes, discrimination, and prejudice maintain and reproduce racism.

We can speak of two types of discrimination against minorities: de jure (i.e., by law) and de facto (in fact). Historically, in Canada and elsewhere, government policies have explicitly discriminated against specific groups, as against blacks during the apartheid era in South Africa, in Nazi Germany, where the Nuremberg Laws of 1935 restricted the movement, occupations, education opportunities, and other rights and freedoms of Jewish people, and in the US, where in the South, especially, until the 1960s blacks were segregated from other Americans and often were denied the right to vote. In Canada, many Aboriginals experience varying degrees of racism in their daily lives, but as a group, First Nations people have been singled out for unequal treatment by Canadian governments. Their lands have been taken away (presumably legally, through 'treaties'), they have been forcefully segregated in reserves, and, for many, their children were sent to residential schools for most of a century, depriving generations of their own cultural heritage. During the two world wars of the twentieth century, members of other ethnic groups (Germans, Italians, and Japanese) were singled out for internment by Canadian authorities, and members of other ethnic groups (e.g., Russians, Ukrainians, Jews) were seen as harbouring Communist political beliefs and often were not allowed to immigrate to Canada, or, when they were involved in labour strife, they were quickly deported. Canada would accept only a relative handful of European Jewish refugees in the 1930s, and, as we saw earlier, government policy in the first half of twentieth century excluded Chinese and South Asians.

Today, a more subtle type of discrimination permeates Canadian life. De facto discrimination is more difficult to resist and fight against, since it is covert. Canadian law prohibits overt discriminatory acts in employment, social services, and education, but the reality is that some members of minority groups face issues of *systemic discrimination*—impersonal, covert practices that penalize members of certain groups. Also called *institutional racism*, this is the outcome of the inner workings of institutions (the economy, education systems, the government) that disadvantages particular individuals and groups. For example, in the labour market, a minimum educational requirement of a high school diploma may exclude from unskilled jobs some members of minority groups with low educational attainment (e.g., Aboriginals and blacks). Recent immigrants may be excluded from getting good jobs when government and employers require long years of 'Canadian experience'. Members of some minority groups may be excluded from Canadian police or firefighting forces on the basis of a minimum height requirement (similar regulations have kept large numbers of women out of these forces for a long time). Not recognizing the educational credentials of immigrants attained abroad (especially from developing countries) keeps large segments of visible minority immigrants from secure, well-paying jobs. In aggregate terms, we can often detect systemic discrimination in the under-representation of minorities in some better-paid, more prestigious segments of the workforce.

A lot of people believe that, since the term 'race' has been discredited today, and its analytical utility is limited, modern Canadian society is not as racist as it used to be (Levitt, 1994) and that racism may be a thing of the past. This view is wrong. Many modern versions of individual and institutional racism exist. For example, in terms of immigration policy, despite changes to immigration regulations that were considered anti-racist, Simmons (1998) has noted that the Canadian government still is not granting migrant agricultural workers from the Caribbean landed immigrant status. This is a neo-racist policy. In addition, although we do not have lists of preferred and non-preferred countries from

Racism has always been a part of Canadian society. In this historical photograph, dated 1942, Vancouver police harass a Japanese man and confiscate his vehicle. After Pearl Harbor, Canada expelled or interned 22,000 Japanese immigrants and Japanese Canadians. (Vancouver Public Library, Special Collection, vpl 1362)

which we choose immigrants today, Canadian governments do not invest in adequate personnel and the required resources for immigration offices in developing nations, thereby setting systemic limits to the numbers of (racialized) immigrants we accept into the country.

In addition, as Henry and Tator (2005) argue, there is a peculiar form of racism in Canada today: *democratic racism*. Democratic racism is not necessarily based on old racist notions of the biological and social superiority of whites over racialized minorities, but, rather, on contradictions about and conflicts over social values. For example, Canada supposedly is committed to justice, equality, and fairness, but these values coexist with differential treatment and discrimination against minorities. Democratic racism is an ideology and a mechanism for reducing the conflict inherent in maintaining a commitment to both liberal and non-egalitarian values. As an ideology, it permits and sustains the rationalization, justification, and maintenance of two apparently conflicting sets of values (liberal-democratic versus negative judgements about people of colour).

Attitudes, values, and assumptions about minorities may lead to their differential treatment and discrimination. Racism is reflected in the systems of cultural production and representation and in the codes of behaviour of the dominant culture. Henry and Tator argue that they are 'embedded in the values and meanings, policies and practices of powerful institutions' (ibid., 90). Racialized discourse and racist practices in Canada are marked by the history of oppression, domination, and resistance. Society gives voice to racism through words, images, stories, explanations (or silences), categorizations, justifications, and rationalizations, which in turn produce a shared understanding of the world and of the (inferior) status of people of colour in that world (ibid., 91). This discourse is used to extend or defend the traditional interests of the dominant culture.

Some examples of democratic racism include the following. (1) Many people, usually members of dominant groups, claim that they do not 'see' colour. This claim of colour-blindness may be true, but it obfuscates the reality of the pervasiveness of the historical 'baggage' of colour in our everyday lives—the policies, programs, and practices that continue to be racist. (2) The discourse of equal opportunity expresses a value dear to Canadians, but it is often assumed that we do not have to dismantle dominant (white) institutions of power in order to achieve it. Egalitarianism somehow will manifest itself without any social or political struggle. (3) Just because we exalt tolerance of others through the language and policy of multiculturalism, this does not mean that multiculturalism necessarily leads to social harmony. The new buzzword—'reasonable accommodation'—is a hoax (see 'Open for Discussion' box). We continue to use the dominant values, beliefs, and ideas as measuring sticks for evaluating others. In addition, multiculturalism conceals the structural, economic, and political inequalities in Canada. Multiculturalism does not combat racism. (4) The discourse of national identity tends to be racist since it erases or silences the contributions to the Canadian national identity of ethnic/racialized minorities. When we continue to reproduce the two founding nations concept of Canada, this myth ignores the 'First Nations'—Aboriginal groups (Satzewich and Liodakis, 2007: 155–6).

OPEN FOR DISCUSSION

Reasonable Accommodation, Xenophobia, and Islamophobia

'Reasonable accommodation' is the new mantra used by proponents of Quebec interculturalism. The term implies that government policies and programs will endeavour not just to tolerate, but also to accommodate the cultural differences, the 'otherness', of new immigrants, in the spirit of pluralism. The debate on the usefulness of this policy is ongoing. The Quebec government has actually institutionalized this debate by holding public hearings. Not all Quebecers agree with reasonable accommodation. In fact, a clear urban/rural cultural split reflects current socio-demographic realities: urban centres, like Montreal, have sizable immigrant populations and are more accepting of difference; rural areas are largely homogeneous and culturally conservative, and they would like to keep it that way. For example, in January 2007, Hérouxville, a small (population 1,338) Quebec farming community of almost exclusively white, francophone, nominally Catholic residents located 180 kilometres north of Montreal, gained notoriety when its town council passed a resolution prescribing a code of conduct for potential immigrants. It set conditions under which new immigrants could admitted to their town. Specifically, the resolution stated that immigrants who 'cover their face', 'carry weapons to school', 'stone or burn alive women', or 'perform female genital mutilation' were not welcome in their community. As André Drouin, a town councillor, put it, reasonable accommodation had reached a state of emergency in Quebec. The implication was clear: apparently, interculturalism and reasonable accommodation have gone too far, since, it is presumed, they 'allow everything'. Quebec Premier Jean Charest suggested that Hérouxville's 'measures' may be drastic and exaggerated, and not representative of Quebec society.

The reaction of minority communities was swift. A delegation of women from the Canadian Islamic Congress visited Hérouxville and met with the town council and some local residents to discuss the issue, in the spirit of cultural understanding. The resolution was clearly directed against Muslims and other peoples from Northern Africa, the Middle East, and Asia. Its intentions were discriminatory. It was a concrete example of xenophobia and Islamophobia. After the exchange of niceties and gifts, the town resolution was watered down, but the controversy remained and sparked debates in other parts of the country among politicians, the media, students, professors, and many others.

The Hérouxville incident is not the only example of attempts to discriminate against Muslims. In the post 9/11 world, xenophobia and Islamophobia are on the rise worldwide. In particular, the 'veil' issue has sparked debates in the UK and France. Politicians such as former UK Prime Minister Tony Blair and his ex-Minister of Foreign Affairs, Jack Straw, have asked Muslim women to remove their veils in their presence 'in order to improve communication'. A Muslim teacher in the UK was required by law to remove her veil in the classroom, since, it was argued, 'it hindered student learning.' In France, Nicolas Sarkozi, the new President, has made similar calls and is now considering proposals for DNA tests to 'scientifically ascertain the blood relationship of parents and kids' from Muslim North Africa (ex-French colonies with mostly Muslim populations) before they are admitted to France as family members of legal immigrants.

In Canada, no one has called for such DNA testing (yet). But the veil issue attracted media attention recently. In September 2007, three federal by-elections took place in Quebec. Marc Mayrand, Canada's Chief Electoral Officer, was under pressure from politicians, the media, and 'concerned citizens' to take a stance against allowing veiled Muslim women to vote unless they first showed their faces. Should women with their faces covered be allowed to vote? How could their identity be verified? He decided, in the spirit of being reasonable, that veiled Muslim women have the same rights as everyone else. After this decision, Mayrand held a press conference in Ottawa to address some of the criticisms he had received. Allegedly, the Chief Electoral Officer had 'flouted the will of Parliament' by his loose interpretation of the Elections Act (*National Post*, 10 Sept. 2007). According to Mayrand, there is nothing in the current electoral law to prevent veiled people from voting. Moreover, the law allows citizens—for religious reasons—to vote with their face covered provided they show two pieces of valid ID and swear an oath. After all, said Mayrand, in the previous federal election, 80,000 people cast votes by mail (*Toronto Star*, 10 Sept. 2007). Prime Minister Stephen Harper and Official Opposition leader Stéphane Dion disagreed with this interpretation of the law, and argued that people must show their faces when voting to maintain integrity in the election process. Mayrand countered that if parliamentarians did not like his interpretation, they should have changed the law when they had the chance. On the other hand, John Ivison, a writer for the *National Post*, pointed out that neither has Parliament ruled 'on voting by comic book characters but if Batman and Robin turned up in the polling booth, one hopes that Elections Canada staff would force them to reveal their secret identities' (*National Post*, 10 Sept. 2007).

Do you think that veiled women want to hide their identities? Or is veiling based on religious beliefs and/or cultural traditions? Canada is considered a tolerant society, has an official policy of multiculturalism, and freedom of religion is protected by the Charter of Rights and Freedoms. So, should we allow veiled citizens to cast ballots? Before you grapple with this last question, you should know that both the Canadian Islamic Congress and the Canadian Council of Muslim Women agreed that veiled women should show their faces before voting. What do you think are the implications of this issue for the study of race and ethnicity in Canada? Who decides what is 'reasonable' in reasonable accommodation? What are the criteria? What should they be?

Finally, it should be kept in mind that racism is not found exclusively among members of dominant groups. There also exist intra- and inter-group racisms. For example, some members of the same group may exhibit racism towards other members because of regional, linguistic, religious, or political differences. We often encounter inter-minority group racism. Members of groups who had been marginalized in the past (Irish, Greeks, Italians, etc.) identify today more with their skin colour than with their ethnic background and thus reproduce the racial dichotomy of 'us' versus 'them'. They have changed from being 'micks' and 'wops' and 'macaronis' to being racists. There is a broader theoretical issue here: the tendency to view racism as a binary opposition between racists and those who are racialized.

This is a false dichotomy, since it confounds the paradox of minority group racism. 'White European ethnics' ('Euro-ethnics') attributed their inferior social and ethnocultural status to their immigrant status. They usually fragment the categories of immigrant and ethnic into 'benign' and 'malign'. There is a development of a 'reverence' for their 'whiteness' (we are different, and better than those who came recently and happen to be 'darker', i.e., 'Othered'). Their skin colour appears to bring them closer to the dominant groups and creates a social distance from the subordinate ones, supposedly excluding themselves from the latter. They use their common colour (with the British and the French) to reinforce social and political identities and alliances with the dominant groups. Noivo, studying members of the Italian and Greek communities in Montreal, argues (in Satzewich, 1998) that for a long time they had been relegated to entrance status (low pay, manual and menial jobs, without much education, doing 'black labour' for long periods). In the 1960s and 1970s, typical racist attitudes towards them included characterizations of being 'stocky and dark-skinned', 'too emotional', 'wops', and *voleurs de job* (job thieves). They were given minority status within the dominant culture. But today, since some of their members appear to do better than the recently arrived and racialized minorities, they exhibit ethnocentrism and ethnic racism (e.g., will not rent to people of colour, hold racist views, etc.) by uninformed comparisons of their presumed ethnocultural 'traits' and their early experiences in Canada, with those who have arrived recently, the racialized new immigrants. The lines go as follows: 'We' have built this country; 'they' haven't. 'We' feed it; 'they' live on social assistance. When 'we' arrived, 'we' worked hard; 'they' are lazy. 'We' learned the language; 'they' have not.

Culturalism and Political Economy: Explanations of Socio-economic Inequalities

Broadly speaking, two major theoretical frameworks attempt to explain ethnicity and race as social phenomena. One emphasizes the role of culture; the other that of social structures, which is often linked with a political economy perspective. Culturalism has been an important discourse in the social sciences. It attempts to explain the behavioural, moral, intellectual, and socio-economic characteristics of ethnic and racial group members in terms of their culture. Its central argument can be summarized as follows: ethnic and racial groups share common values, religion, beliefs, sentiments, ideas, languages, historical memories and symbols, leaderships, a common past, and often the same geographical territory. They have specific and distinct ways of responding to their external conditions that vary and are shaped by their own environment. In short, they have a common culture. If we want to explain their differential socio-economic achievements, we must look into their culture, the key to understanding their differences. Culture is considered the *explanans* (that which explains), not the *explanandum* (that which must be explained). Cultural values (often linked to biological traits) affect the psychological composition of their members and produce, it is claimed, 'differences in cognitive perception, mental aptitude, and logical reasoning' (Li, 1999: 10). In turn, such differences are thought to affect subsequent educational and economic achievements. Thus, some groups, on average, are doing better than others in school and the labour market. Some cultures foster values conducive to economic achievement (in capitalist conditions); others do not.

Two examples from the 1950s are instructive in this regard. Rosen (1956, 1959) studied the relative upward social mobility of six groups—Greeks, Jews, white Protestants, French Canadians, Italians, and blacks—and found that the former three groups had higher mobility rates than the latter three because of what he asserted were differences in achievement motivation, achievement values, and educational aspirations. He did not examine or show differentials *within* these groups. Presumably, then, if all members of an ethnic group share the same culture and have the same achievement motivation, values, and educational aspirations, there should not have been any differences *within* these groups. Did all Greeks score high on his scales? Did all French Canadians score low? Weren't there any highly motivated Italians in the sample? How could we explain, based on culture alone, those French Canadians with high educational credentials? How could we explain, based on culture alone, variations in the educational and economic achievement within the same ethnic or racial group?

Wagley and Harris (1959) used the term 'adaptive capacity' as an explanatory device. Some groups, according to this line of thinking, are able to adapt to their new external conditions better and more readily, and perform better in education and the labour market than others, because their own cultural values prepare them to do so. They argued, for example, that the French-Canadian and Jewish cultures had higher adaptive capacity than those of Aboriginals and blacks. Hence, the former groups enjoyed higher socio-economic status than the latter. Again, however, there seem to be important differences *within* these groups that cannot be accounted for by culture alone. Not all Jewish Canadians or French Canadians are well-educated and/or have high incomes. Some Aboriginal and black people in Canada are well-educated and/or earn high incomes. By itself, culture cannot account for the internal socio-economic differences of ethnic/racial groups. It has been argued that the links between culture and ethnicity are tenuous at best (Li, 1988). Moreover, culture is not static, monolithic, uniform, or homogeneous. It is a set of ever-changing social processes and practices; it is a dynamic response of socially constituted individuals to their ever-changing external conditions, largely determined by social structures.

Political economy approaches, on the other hand, tend to focus more on the historical development of the terms 'ethnicity' and 'race', as well as on the social inequalities among and within such social groups. The political economy perspective encompasses a wide and varied corpus of literature with the following characteristics: (1) it tends to be rooted in the conflict theories of Marx and Weber and their contemporary variations and proponents; (2) as such, it focuses on the study of differential allocation of economic, political, and ideological power among individuals and groups in society; (3) in turn, social relations based on the ownership and control of private property, their historical development, and their manifold ideological and social manifestations and/or embodiments are examined. The political economy perspective begins with the tenet that socially constituted individuals belong to inherited social structures that enable but also constrain their social actions. Examples of these structures include those built on social relations of class, gender, race/ethnicity, age, sexual preference, physical ability, mental health/illness, etc. Societies are characterized by the unequal distribution of property, power, and other resources (both natural and socio-political). Who owns and controls what, when, why, and how are central concerns of political economy (Satzewich, 1999: 314). The analysis of intergenerational endowments of these resources is also imperative in understanding relations of social inequality. To paraphrase Marx, individuals are born into a web of unequal social relations, inherited from the past, and beyond their immediate control, at least until they understand them and try to change them. Although these social relations are malleable, it takes concerted social action—it takes social *praxis*—to bring about social change.

With regard to ethnic and race relations, then, we must begin by trying to understand historically what processes have brought about the differentiation and classification of human populations, their social impact, and their conditions. Hence, political economy approaches the subject by asking, for example: Who has historically defined certain human populations as superior? Which ones have been defined as inferior, and on what basis? Peter Li has argued that skin colour, for instance, becomes a physical characteristic of classifying human populations only if it is deemed *socially important* (1988). What makes it socially important? Why isn't people's shoe size a socially or culturally 'necessary' criterion? That would definitely signify a discernibly *different* classification of human populations. We must look into the legacy of colonialism and slavery to understand the historical roots of the social construction of the term 'race', as well as the racialization/ethnicization or the reduction to minority status of social groups by dominant groups and their hegemonic ideologies. Historically, under capitalism in the West, the white (see how we cannot escape racist language?), male, capitalist class has been in control of the means of production and reproduction, as well as the political and ideological tools of domination. This domination, by and large, has been a catalyst in creating and sustaining the coupling of people's cultural and physical characteristics with presumed behavioural, moral, and intellectual traits, justified by racism. As Brown (1995) has argued, the assignment of significance to biological or physical attributes (and arguably cultural ones) is itself a cultural, ethnocentric choice.

The political economy approach perceives race and ethnicity as *relational* concepts. Goldberg has argued that race (and ethnicity also) can be seen as social status in the

Weberian sense and as class in the Marxist sense. Goldberg writes that social status, race, and ethnicity can be seen as an 'index of social standing or rank reflected in terms of criteria like wealth, education, style of life, linguistic capacity, residential location, consumptive capacity, or having or lacking respect. Status has to do with one's ranking in a social system *relative to the position of others*, where the ranking involves . . . [positive] self-conception and (de)valuations of others' (Goldberg, 1993: 69; emphasis added). Most immigrant groups have been primarily associated with the lower classes because of the menial (yet highly important) jobs they have done upon arrival in the host country—the Irish 'navvies' laboured in the building of canals in central Canada in the first half of the nineteenth century; Chinese workmen were instrumental in the completion of Canada's first transcontinental rail line; Ukrainians and other Central and Eastern Europeans settled and farmed the prairies; Italians were among the principal labourers when the Toronto subway system was first constructed in the 1950s.

In contrast, members of the charter groups have been associated with the upper classes and with less labour-intensive and more prestigious occupations. There appeared to be an overlap between lower-class membership and membership in a minority ethnic/racial group. John Porter, in *The Vertical Mosaic* (1965), although he emphasized structural conditions in explaining income inequalities (e.g., patterns of immigration, labour market participation, occupational attainment, monopolistic closure), could not resist the temptation of relying—to some extent—on cultural explanations as well. He argued that people's ethnic affiliation was a determinant of their social class membership and prevented the upward mobility of certain groups, partly because they had not *assimilated culturally* to the new conditions of capitalist development in Canada. This is the 'blocked mobility thesis'. We shall examine the economic dimensions of ethnic/racial inequalities below.

The Vertical Mosaic Then and the Colour-coded Mosaic Today

Over the years, most research on social inequality in Canada has focused on the economic performance of ethnic groups to determine whether Canadian society is hierarchically structured (Agocs and Boyd, 1993: 337). Prior to Porter's famous work, *The Vertical Mosaic*, the attention of most politicians and researchers focused on the role of ethnicity in Canadian society, underestimating the importance of social class in determining the location of ethnic group members in the social hierarchy. Porter argued that immigration and ethnic affiliation were important factors in the process of social class formation in Canada, especially at the bottom and elite layers of the stratification system (Porter, 1965: 73). His argument was based on an analysis of census data from 1931, 1951, and 1961. As the title suggests, Porter argued that Canadian society, understood as an ethnic mosaic, is hierarchically structured in terms of the differential distributions of wealth and power among its constituent ethnic groups. Examining the Canadian labour market from a Weberian perspective, Porter found that ethnic groups were unequally represented in the occupational structure.

Four of his findings are noteworthy. First, the charter groups (British and French) had appropriated positions of power and advantage in the social, economic, and political realms and had designated the 'entrance status' groups to lower, less preferred positions. Over time, reinforced by stereotypes and social images, these divisions in status were hardened and perpetuated. Second, 'less preferred' groups that arrived in Canada later than the charter groups were relegated to a lower, 'entrance status'. That is, they were employed in lower-status occupations and were subject to the assimilation processes laid down by the charter groups (ibid., 63–4). Third, ethnic affiliation implied blocked social mobility. Upward mobility of ethnic groups depended on the culture of the ethnic group in question and the degree to which it conformed to the rules of assimilation set by the charter groups. The improvement in the position of entrance status groups over time could be determined by their 'assimilability' or their behavioural and structural assimilation (ibid., 67–73). In terms of the relative hierarchical position of ethnic groups in the occupational structure, which he regarded as a crude substitute for class, Porter found a persistent pattern of ethnic inequality. Canadians of Jewish and British origin were at the top. They were persistently over-represented in the professional and financial occupations (higher status and income) and under-represented in agricultural and unskilled jobs (lower status and income). The Germans, Scandinavians, and Dutch were closest to the British. Italians, Polish, and Ukrainians were next, with other Southern Europeans (Greeks and Portuguese) near the lower end of the spectrum (ibid., 90). The French, somewhere between the Northern and Southern Europeans, were under-represented in professional and financial occupations and over-represented in agricultural and unskilled jobs, a result of historical and socio-political factors. Aboriginal people were at the bottom of the hierarchy. Fourth, in regard to the charter groups, the British were more powerful than the French (ibid., 73–103). In fact, despite the considerable influence exerted on the political system by French Canadians, not only in Quebec but also at the federal level (ibid., 417–56), and their access to high-status political positions and the media, the British dominated Canada's economic life and were over-represented in elite positions (ibid., 201–308, 337–416, 520–59).

Since Porter's influential publication, sociologists have paid attention to the relationship between ethnic origin and class in Canadian society, and a number of significant questions have been raised regarding his findings and treatment of the data. Subsequent analyses have shown that his claims might have been exaggerated (Brym and Fox, 1989: 93–9, 103–19). A detailed account of criticisms of Porter is not our aim here (see, e.g., Ogmundson 1991, 1993; Ogmundson and McLaughlin, 1992). Some researchers have suggested that, since the 1960s, an equalization of earnings has occurred among ethnic groups. Others argue that ethnic earnings inequalities persist. Ornstein (1981) has shown that ethnicity alone does not explain much of the variation in earnings. He argues that much of what appear to be ethnic differences in earnings may be attributed to place of birth, place of education, and language. Subsequent research (Ornstein, 1983) has demonstrated that class and gender, along with labour market variables, are more important determinants of earnings than ethnicity.

Weinfeld (1988), examining 1971 and 1981 census data, has argued that in that 10-year period income inequalities among ethnic groups diminished. When sex, nativity, occupation, age, education, and number of weeks worked are statistically controlled, ethnic groups not considered visible minorities had almost the same income, whereas the earnings gap experienced by visible minorities had narrowed. What mattered, according to Weinfeld, was the percentage of the foreign-born within visible minorities and their amount and type of educational attainment (ibid., 603–5).

Even though questions have been raised about the persistence of the **vertical mosaic** for European-origin ethnic groups, some suggest that the vertical mosaic persists in a racialized form and that Canada is characterized today by a *colour-coded vertical mosaic* (Galabuzi, 2006: 7). In 1984, the Royal Commission on Equality in Employment, using 1981 census data, found that among men, visible minorities such as the Indo-Chinese, Central and South Americans, and blacks had incomes below the national average and were at the bottom of the income hierarchy. Among women, Aboriginal people, Central and South Americans, the Indo-Chinese, and Koreans had the lowest incomes (Royal Commission on Equality in Employment, 1984: 84–5). These income disparities were attributed to **systemic discrimination** in the workplace. Visible minorities were sometimes denied access to employment because of unfair recruitment procedures and were more likely to be unemployed. Often, education credentials acquired outside Canada were not recognized in the labour market or by governments. Sometimes, Canadian experience was required unnecessarily (ibid., 46–51). For Aboriginal peoples, the situation was even worse. Aboriginal men earned 60 per cent of the earnings of non-Aboriginal men; Aboriginal women made 72 per cent of what non-Aboriginal women earned (ibid., 33), and this spoke only of those who had jobs—a high percentage of Aboriginal people then and now, isolated in peripheral locations far from job markets, are unemployed and not seeking employment, and therefore are not counted in unemployment statistics. Educational opportunities and training for Aboriginals were seen as inadequate responses to the problem of inequality (ibid., 34–5). Aboriginal people were more likely to be found in part-time or seasonal employment and less likely to move up the promotional ladder (ibid., 37).

Lian and Matthews (1998) examined 1991 census data and analyzed ethnic inequalities in earnings, studying the relationship between ethnicity and education and between education and income. They argue that race is now *the* fundamental basis of income inequality in Canada. The French now earn more than the British, and there is a general trend of convergence of earnings among the European groups. Visible minorities, however, in all educational levels receive lower rewards, substantially below the national average (Lian and Matthews, 1998: 471, 475). Controlling for a number of variables, such as gender, age, marital status, province and place of residence, and year of immigration, Lian and Matthews suggest that in most of the 10 categories of educational level they examined, visible minorities make less than non-visible minorities (ibid., 473, Table 5). These findings led them to conclude that the old ethnic vertical mosaic may be disappearing, but it is being replaced by a strong 'coloured mosaic' (ibid., 476).

Li (2003) has shown that in 1996 immigrant men and women in medium-sized and large metropolitan areas earned less than their Canadian-born counterparts. Also, the earnings of Canadian-born and immigrant men exceed the earnings of comparable groups of Canadian-born and immigrant women. In addition, Li found that white

Canadian-born men tend to do better than white immigrant men, and that visible minority Canadian-born men do better than visible minority immigrant men. On the other hand, although white Canadian-born men do better than visible minority Canadian-born men, visible minority Canadian-born women tend to do better than white Canadian-born women. This is an interesting finding that tends to undermine the colour-coded vertical mosaic thesis. Finally, Li showed that white and visible minority immigrant women have roughly the lowest levels of earnings of all groups. These patterns are complex, but one of the things that Li has demonstrated is that when other individual and job market variables are taken into account, immigrants do less well in every Canadian CMA than the Canadian-born. Yet, if Canadian society rewarded everyone equally on the basis of the training and skills that they bring to the labour market, the net differences between groups should be minimal.

More recently, Galabuzi (2006) has found substantial evidence to support the colour-coded vertical mosaic claim. Comparing after-tax income of racialized and non-racialized persons in Canada in 2000, he demonstrated that the average after-tax income for racialized persons was $20,627, 12.3 per cent less than the average after-tax income of $23,522 for non-racialized persons. Differences in after-tax income can even be found when higher education is taken into account. Among university degree-holders in 2000, racialized individuals had an after-tax income of $35,617, while non-racialized individuals had an after-tax income of $38,919, an 8.5 per cent difference.

Earnings Differentials within Ethnic Groups: The Role of Class and Gender

Apart from a few notable exceptions (Li, 1988, 1992; Nakhaie, 1999, 2000), the class dimension of ethnic earnings inequality in Canada has not been adequately examined. Porter (1965: 73) argued that ethnic groups have internal hierarchies and are themselves stratified. They are not homogeneous. Among other characteristics, they are differentiated by religion, dialects, regions of origin, whether they are recent or earlier arrivals to Canada (ibid., 72), by social class (Li, 1988, 1992), gender (Boyd, 1992), age, and place of birth (Liodakis, 1998, 2002). Even if we accept that there was a period in the history of Canada when ethnic group membership overlapped with class position, there was never a one-to-one correspondence of the concepts and their social content. In other words, despite the fact that there was never empirical evidence to support the notion that one ethnic group was associated with one class only, ethnicity became a proxy of class. Ethnic groups became 'statistical classes' that exhibited differential socio-economic performance and held differential amounts of political and economic power.

The vertical mosaic thesis should be questioned, not because we now have more ethnic equality but arguably because inequality in Canada is still very much based on social class and gender, and ethnicity and race serve as sources of division within the broader class structure (Li, 1992). Ethnic inequality cannot be analyzed outside the class context (Li, 1988: 141). For example, Nakhaie (1999, 2000) has adopted a Marxian model of class to examine the composition of ethnic groups. Using data from the 1973 Canadian Mobility Survey and the 1989 General Social Survey, he has demonstrated significant changes to the class compositions of ethnic groups between 1973 and 1989 for both men and women. During this period, the English were not over-represented in the ownership class categories (bourgeoisie, petite bourgeoisie, self-employed) compared to other ethnic groups. Ethnic differences in the managerial classes declined, especially for the French. The British, however, still dominated the business elite and were over-represented in the managerial classes. The French and Italians were persistently over-represented in the working class (Nakhaie, 2000: 168, 170). Nakhaie concluded that the effect of ethnicity in determining class position has declined (ibid., 174). The relationship between ethnicity and class is in flux, and no ethnic group dominates the top of the Canadian class structure. But his analysis also shows that ethnic groups are not homogeneous. They are internally stratified in terms of class, and they are also stratified in terms of gender and place of birth.

Another problematic issue in the analysis of social inequality in Canada is that there is sometimes a lack of definitional parsimony in relation to the colour-coded mosaic thesis. Although many researchers argue that there is a clear-cut division in Canadian society along racial lines, more often than not, the groups under examination, ethnic or racial, are defined in terms of Statistics Canada census categories. Categories such as visible minorities, racialized groups, non-racialized groups, or even whites and blacks do not always have a clear social referent. This may be explained in part by two factors. First, over time, increased rates of exogamy among groups who immigrated to Canada before the 1980s have led to a decrease in the number of census

Increasing numbers of immigrants to Canada have impressive credentials and work experience, yet they often are underemployed because their schooling and experience were gained abroad. These posters were part of a public awareness campaign for hireimmigrants.ca, the Toronto Region Immigrant Employment Council (TRIEC). (Photo courtesy of TRIEC)

respondents who report single ethnic origins. In addition, since the 1980s, the number of visible minority immigrants has increased. These two trends make it increasingly difficult to compare single-origin, multiple-origin, and visible minority respondents when analyzing census data. Second, the classifications used by Statistics Canada in the census tend to lump together groups from different ethnic backgrounds, often based on racial markers like skin colour. This makes it easier (both theoretically and statistically) to construct a dichotomy between visible and non-visible groups by adding their 'constituent' parts together, irrespective of their internal ethnic or cultural differences. For example, the category 'Caribbean' includes people from various parts of that geographical area, from countries such as Cuba, Jamaica, Trinidad and Tobago, the Dominican Republic, and Haiti. The category 'Latin American' includes people from Brazil, Argentina, Uruguay, Colombia, Venezuela, and so on. 'Arabs' could come from numerous countries across North Africa, the Middle East, the Pacific, or the Balkans. In 1996, Statistics Canada (1996c) defined the following groups as part of the 'collectivity' of visible minorities: black, South Asian, Chinese, Korean, Japanese, Southeast Asian, Filipino, Arab/West Asian, Latin American, visible minority not included elsewhere, and multiple visible minority.

For the 2006 census, the variable visible minority contained the categories Chinese, South Asian, black, and other visible minority. This taxonomy creates categories so broadly defined that the considerable internal socio-economic heterogeneity within groups is concealed (Boyd, 1992: 281; Liodakis, 2002). The term 'visible minority' emerged in the 1970s in response to the use of pejorative terms such as 'coloured' or non-white and was used by activists and scholars who were fighting racism and other forms of social inequality. The term is now embedded not only in census questions but also in state policies of employment equity and multiculturalism (Synnott and Howes, 1996: 137), and, by extension, in the language of social scientists and non-academics. A person is officially a member of a 'visible minority' group if s/he is 'non-white' in 'colour' or 'non-Caucasian' in 'race', other than Aboriginal.

The problem with this social construction of the concept of 'visible minority', according to Synnott and Howes, is that when attempts are made to refer the concept of 'visible minority' back to the social reality it is supposed to describe, 'it falls apart' (ibid., 138). It does not have a social referent. It tends to homogenize and racialize diverse groups of people. Census-taking is not an innocent exercise of simply counting people. As Melissa Nobles (2000) has argued, censuses help to shape and reproduce a racial discourse that in turn affects public policies that either restrict or protect the rights, privileges, and experiences we commonly associate with citizenship. Statistics Canada is not necessarily a politically neutral institution that simply 'counts' Canadians in an objective sort of way. It creates the conditions under which people will identify themselves so that Statistics Canada can count them afterwards. The terms 'ethnicity', 'visible minority', 'whites', and 'non-whites' are, irreducibly, political categories that construct racial and ethnic groups, often with government approval (Nobles, 2000). In general, the term 'visible minorities' also homogenizes the 'non-visible' category. Synnott and Howes argue that visible minority groups are diverse in terms of their place of birth and place of residence as well as their length of residence in Canada, not to mention their age, class, and gender composition. This is also true, of course, of non-visible groups. Such divisions, however, have important implications for their employment and level and type of education, as well as earnings. For example, there are different unemployment rates within the category of visible minority. In 1991, the unemployment rate of people who reported Japanese ancestry was only 6 per cent, below the national average, whereas that of Latin Americans was 20 per cent, almost double the national average (Synnott and Howes, 1996: 139, Table I).

The colour-coded vertical mosaic thesis does not fully explain the patterns of earnings inequality in Canada. In fact, the racialized vertical mosaic thesis seems to overlook anomalies that undermine the thesis. In much of the literature on social inequality, Southern European groups—the Greeks, Portuguese, and to a lesser extent the Italians—are not as well educated as the rest of the European groups and do not earn as much; many studies have shown that they are not as well educated and are earning less than some visible minority groups (Li, 1988: 76, 78, 82, 84, 88, Tables 5.1–5.5). In Boyd's (1992) research, non-visible minority women of Greek, Italian, Portuguese, other European, and Dutch origin made less than the average earnings of all women. Finally, as noted above, Li's data from the 1996 census show that visible minority native-born women make more than their non-visible counterparts.

Central to the analysis of social inequality is the understanding that the production and reproduction of the conditions of people's existence is social. Individuals are interacting social subjects, situated in class, gender, and ethnic social locations (Satzewich and Wotherspoon, 1993: 13). Social inequality is a social reality. In most advanced, liberal-democratic societies like ours, all social relations have class, gender, and race/ethnic elements. It is not claimed that class is the only, or the most important, dimension of social inequality. We do claim, however, that, along with gender, it accounts more for the earnings differentials among and within ethnic and racial groups than do any of the other dimensions. Ethnicity or visibility alone is not a good 'predictor' of earnings inequality in Canada (Li, 1988, 1992).

In actual societies, class locations (bourgeoisie, petite bourgeoisie, proletariat) contain sets of real people: men and women who come from different ethnic backgrounds and whose actual lives do not fit neatly into one exclusive category. Whereas earlier traditions have tended to emphasize the 'mosaic' dimension of inequality and to examine the earnings inequalities *among* ethnic groups, the 'vertical' dimension also is worthy of examination to discover the earnings inequalities both among and *within* ethnic groups. These ethnic inequalities do not occur in a social vacuum but take place within a class society. The approach proposed here suggests that within each structural locational basis of inequality (ethnicity, gender, or class), the other two coexist. All classes have gender and ethnic segments. Gender groups have class and ethnic segments. All ethnic groups are permeated by class and gender differences.

To simplify our argument, we do not examine the class structure of every ethnic group in Canada. Instead, we selectively examine the social class composition of the following groups: Aboriginal (not considered a 'visible minority' by Statistics Canada), British, Caribbean, Chinese, Filipino, French, Greek, Italian, Jewish, Portuguese, and South Asian. These choices are based on the fact that the British and the French are the so-called charter groups, were part of the original vertical mosaic thesis, and feature prominently in all subsequent analyses of ethnicity. They have conventionally constituted the frame of reference for all comparisons. Jews, on the other hand, albeit accorded an 'entrance status', have tended to outperform both charter and all other groups in terms of educational attainment and earnings. They represent an 'anomalous' case for proponents of the vertical mosaic thesis and/or its assimilationist versions. The three Southern European groups—Greek, Italian, and Portuguese—are undoubtedly the least studied European groups. Some evidence indicates that Greeks may represent an anomalous case as well, which poses problems for the proponents of the racialized vertical mosaic argument (Liodakis, 2002). Often, because of their poor socio-economic performance, they do not

Table 18.4 The Class Composition of Ethnic Groups, 2001 (%)

Ethnic Group (n)	Workers	Professionals	Managers, Supervisors	Petite Bourgeoisie	Small Employers
Aboriginal (3,856)	68.2	17.0	8.8	4.0	2.0
British (32,895)	51.3	21.2	14.5	7.8	5.3
Caribbean (2,348)	63.4	21.0	9.5	4.6	1.5
Chinese (10,740)	47.8	28.2	10.0	6.9	7.1
Filipino (2,811)	68.8	19.6	7.3	2.5	1.8
French (13,750)	51.7	24.4	12.1	7.2	4.5
Greek (1,801)	48.8	19.2	13.4	7.2	11.4
Italian (9,179)	51.7	20.0	15.2	6.2	6.8
Jewish (1,958)	27.2	32.5	15.6	11.5	13.2
Portuguese (3,241)	67.4	11.5	11.8	4.7	4.6
South Asian (2,106)	64.2	18.7	8.5	3.8	4.8
Canada (347,020)	52.9	22.0	12.5	7.5	5.1

Note: The number of people, in this table and for Tables 18.5 and 18.6, is a 1 per cent sample of those 25–60 years old who worked at least one week in the previous year in Canada, excluding the territories and Atlantic Canada.
Source: Adapted from Public Use Microdata File on Individuals, 2001 Census.

very well fit the visible/non-visible dichotomy used by some researchers (Li, 1988; Hou and Balakrishnan, 1999; Lian and Matthews, 1998). The four visible minority groups—Caribbean, Chinese, South Asian, and Filipino—represent the most populous of all other single-origin 'visible' groups in Canada.

Table 18.4 provides contemporary confirmation that ethnic groups are not homogeneous in regard to class composition. If we look at social inequality from the perspective of class composition, it appears that in the case of the proletariat there is no clear-cut visible–non-visible distinction. The Chinese, for example, are less proletarianized than the Portuguese, the Italians, the Greeks, the British, and the French. The Portuguese are more proletarianized than the Chinese, the Caribbeans, and the South Asians. Aboriginal Canadians are more likely to be found in the working class and less likely to be found in the other classes. Aboriginal, British, Caribbean, Filipino, French, and Portuguese individuals are under-represented in the ranks of employers, while Chinese, Greeks, and Jews are variously over-represented among the ranks of the petite bourgeoisie. In the professional category, the Chinese are well above the national average, second only to Jews. In the small employer category, the Chinese are over-represented, but all other visible groups are under-represented, along with the Portuguese, the French, and Aboriginals.

Despite these patterns of over- and under-representation, two important points stand out. First, as one should expect, members of each of the 11 ethnic groups are distributed across the range of class sites. No single group is *exclusively* one class or another. Second, the dividing line is muddied between groups traditionally conceived as visible minorities and those traditionally conceived as non-visible minorities. In short, there is great diversity within ethnic groups in terms of their class composition. There is no consistent pattern of distribution across class locations; at the same time, considerable class heterogeneity exists both among and within these ethnic groups. If analytical primacy is given to only one of the three dimensions we have examined, the important internal, within-group class divisions that affect their earnings are obfuscated. In addition, ethnic groups have different gender and nativity compositions. For example, in terms of gender, the Caribbean and Filipino categories have more women than men in the labour market. In all visible groups, the percentage of foreign-born exceeds 90 per cent, whereas in the non-visible category, the percentages are much lower (less than 50 per cent). These differences affect their earnings but are concealed if we only look at them as homogeneous entities.

If, as Table 18.4 shows, ethnic groups differ in their class composition, do they also differ in the rewards they receive from participating in the economy? In other words, is there variation in their earnings? And if so, are the differences among them greater than the differences within them? In fact, there are considerable differences in the earnings of classes. The petite bourgeoisie and the proletarians have mean earnings below the sample mean, while small employers, semi-autonomous workers, and managers and supervisors have earnings considerably above the mean. These results are consistent with the findings of similar research using 1986, 1991, and 1996 Canadian census data (Li, 1988, 1992; Liodakis, 2002). In percentage terms, those of the petite bourgeoisie make 29.3 per cent less and workers make 18.6 per cent less than the sample mean. On the other hand, small employers make 24.8 per cent more than the mean, professionals 22.1 per cent more, and managers and supervisors 47.9 per cent more. The latter group represents the highest-paid class. Gender differences were also greater: women made $14,895 less than men, more than double the visibility difference. Foreign-born respondents made $2,110 less than the native-born. In all ethnic groups, the class, gender, and nativity patterns of earnings inequalities hold. Tables 18.5 and 18.6, using 2001 census data, reveal various earnings differentials among and within the ethnic groups. As becomes apparent, substantial internal variations of earnings *within* ethnic/racialized groups are greater than the earnings differentials among them.

Conclusion: The Future of Race and Ethnicity

In this chapter we have argued that ethnicity and race are social relations. As such, they are about power among individuals and social groups. Notions of ethnicity and race are about domination and subordination; they are rooted in the history of colonialism and associated with the development of capitalism. Historical processes that have made some people 'minorities' have

Table 18.5 Earnings Differentials among Ethnic Groups, 2001

Ethnic Group	Number	Average Earnings ($)	Median Earnings ($)	SD* ($)	±% of National Average
Jewish	1,958	52,953	40,182	44,898	+48.50
Italian	9,179	39,375	35,000	29,235	+10.50
British	32,895	39,006	33,882	31,363	+09.44
French	13,750	36,033	31,039	27,870	+01.10
Portuguese	3,241	33,466	30,000	21,904	–07.00
Greek	1,801	32,438	28,000	27,632	–09.00
Chinese	10,740	31,379	25,121	27,616	–19.20
Caribbean	2,348	28,789	25,943	21,759	–24.17
Filipino	3,723	27,024	25,000	18,342	–24.90
South Asian	2,106	26,215	21,784	23,073	–26.44
Aboriginals	3,856	21,986	18,000	19,469	–38.30
Canada	**347,020**	**35,639**	**30,000**	**28,781**	

*SD = standard deviation above or below the mean (average) of earnings.
Source: Adapted from Public Use Microdata File on Individuals, 2001 Census.

Table 18.6 Earnings Differentials within Ethnic Groups, 2001

Ethnic Group	Mean Earnings and Differences within Group
Jewish	
Canadian-born, small employers, males	105,539
Foreign-born, working-class, females	27,315
Difference	78,224
British	
Foreign-born, managers and supervisors, males	71,714
Canadian-born, petit bourgeois, females	18,294
Difference	53,420
Italian	
Foreign-born, managers and supervisors, males	63,531
Foreign-born, petit bourgeois, females	21,648
Difference	41,883
French	
Canadian-born, managers and supervisors, males	61,106
Canadian-born, petit bourgeois, females	18,856
Difference	42,250
Portuguese	
Foreign-born, managers and supervisors, males	52,445
Foreign-born, petit bourgeois, females	15,579
Difference	36,866
Greek	
Foreign-born, professionals, males	57,064
Foreign-born, petit bourgeois, females	15,695
Difference	41,369
Chinese	
Canadian-born, managers and supervisors, males	62,002
Foreign-born, petit bourgeois, females	17,125
Difference	44,877
Caribbean	
Canadian-born, managers and supervisors, males	52,352
Foreign-born, petit bourgeois, females	19,822
Difference	32,530
Filipino	
Canadian-born, managers and supervisors, males	46,830
Foreign-born, petit bourgeois, females	12,509
Difference	34,321
South Asian	
Canadian-born, managers and supervisors, males	55,500
Foreign-born, petit bourgeois, females	19,220
Difference	36,280
Aboriginals	
Employers, males	35,802
Petit bourgeois, females	14,300
Difference	21,502
Canada	
Canadian-born, managers and supervisors, males	59,810
Canadian-born, petit bourgeois, females	17,834
Difference	41,976

Source: Adapted from Public Use Microdata File on Individuals, 2001 Census.

led to and continue to inform and reproduce the formation of the social, political, and economic dichotomies of the 'Self' and the 'Other'. Canada's current socio-demographic makeup is linked to the historical (and ongoing) 'othering' of Aboriginal peoples, the usurpation of their lands, the destruction of their cultures, and government policies of forced assimilation. It is also intertwined with racist immigration policies that, for a long time, excluded visible minorities and other 'non-preferred' groups from immigrating to Canada.

Race and ethnicity are bases of social inequality. They inform and are part of its class and gender dimensions. In Canada, some groups are doing better than others. If we consider ethnic and racial groups as homogeneous entities, there appears to be a binary social hierarchy based on visibility. When we examine the internal class and gender differences among groups, it is apparent that the Canadian-born, males, managers and supervisors, professionals, and small employers do better than the foreign-born, females, workers, and the petite bourgeoisie. Canada now has an official policy of multiculturalism that attempts to integrate minorities to the social fabric. But the policy does little to address the economic inequalities of Canadian society, and has not been very successful in combatting racism or promoting the institutional integration of minorities.

Recent efforts of 'reasonable accommodation' have sparked more debates. This is by no means an exclusively Canadian phenomenon. The wider global context is interesting: in the postmodern, globalized world, the hegemonic economic, political, and cultural powers (e.g., the US, the European Union, Japan) have increasingly pushed for world economic integration through free trade, the free movement of capital across nation-states, the control and surveillance of international labour migration, the weakening of the role of the nation-state, as well as the rise of supranational organizations like the World Bank, the International Monetary Fund, and the World Trade Organization. A trend towards global cultural homogenization is partly attributable to the export of consumer popular culture to developing nations.

In the past two decades the world has witnessed the destruction of the Soviet Union, the triumph of capitalism, and the dominance of Western culture. And yet, the world does not seem to be any more peaceful or more egalitarian. Nor have ethnic/racial and cultural identities or racism disappeared. On the contrary, in the past two decades we have witnessed the rise of nationalisms; ethnic cleansing; the rise of racism, xenophobia, and Islamophobia (especially after 9/11); the war in Afghanistan; the war in Iraq; and a general thrust against the protection of individual and group rights and freedoms in all Western, liberal-capitalist democracies—all in the name of fighting 'terrorism' and 'exporting' what is claimed to be democracy. At the heart of all these matters are race and ethnicity, a major field of study within the social sciences, especially within sociology.

Questions for Critical Thought

1. What criteria would you use to differentiate human populations and why?
2. What makes you a member (or not) of an ethnic and/or racial group? Should Ontarians be considered an ethnic group? If yes, why? If not, why not? Try to apply the criteria listed in the first part of this chapter to answer these questions.
3. The Canadian policy of multiculturalism is better than the American view of their society as a melting pot. Do you agree or disagree with this statement? Why?
4. With which criticisms of multiculturalism do you agree or disagree, and why?
5. Can the policy of multiculturalism alone provide solutions to the problems of racism and the attendant issues of immigrant and minority group integration into Canadian political, social, and economic institutions? Explain.
6. What else should policy-makers do to address the issues of racism and immigrant integration into Canadian society?
7. What accounts for the earnings differentials among different ethnic/racial groups—cultural or structural differences? Assume, for the sake of argument, that all members of ethnic/racial groups share the same cultural and behavioural characteristics. If culturalist explanations could account for the economic inequalities among ethnic/racial groups, what would explain the marked economic inequalities within ethnic/racial groups?
8. What is the notion of reasonable accommodation? Who decides what is reasonable? With this in mind, try to explain the rise of xenophobia and Islamophobia in the post 9/11 world of control and surveillance in the US, Canada, and other parts of the world. Choose a particular issue (e.g., the veil) and survey the opinions of your friends and family. What do you conclude?

Recommended Readings

Tanya Basok, *Tortillas and Tomatoes: Transmigrant Mexican Harvesters in Canada* (Montreal and Kingston: McGill-Queen's University Press. 2002).

This book examines the role of Mexican seasonal workers in Canadian agriculture and provides a critique of the ways they have been treated by employers and the Canadian government.

Grace-Edward Galabuzi, *Canada's Economic Apartheid: The Social Exclusion of Racialized Groups in the New Century* (Toronto: Canadian Scholars' Press, 2006).

In this controversial argument that supports the view of Canada as characterized by a new colour-coded vertical mosaic, Galabuzi presents evidence of persistent income inequalities between racialized and non-racialized Canadians.

Frances Henry and Carol Tator, *The Colour of Democracy: Racism in Canadian Society*, 3rd edn (Toronto: Thomson Nelson, 2005).

This thorough and caustic critique of racism in Canadian policies and institutions points to the contradictions of multiculturalism and democratic racism in Canadian society.

Peter Li, *Destination Canada: Immigration Debates and Issues* (Toronto: Oxford University Press, 2003).

This is an excellent and up-to-date review of the major debates about the social and economic consequences of immigration to Canada.

Katharyne Mitchell, *Crossing the Neoliberal Line: Pacific Rim Migration and the Metropolis* (Philadephia: Temple University Press, 2004).

This is an excellent account of the debates and controversies surrounding Chinese business immigration to British Columbia in the 1980s and 1990s.

Vic Satzewich and Nikolaos Liodakis, *'Race' and Ethnicity in Canada: A Critical Introduction* (Toronto: Oxford University Press, 2007).

This work summarizes theoretical approaches to the study of race and ethnicity, Canadian immigration policies, Aboriginal/non-Aboriginal relations, economic inequalities among and within ethnic groups, multiculturalism, racism, and transnationalism.

Stephen Steinberg, *The Ethnic Myth: Race, Ethnicity, and Class in America*, 2nd edn (Boston: Beacon Press, 1989).

The author argues that cultural 'traits' often considered 'ethnic' may be more directly related to class, locality, and other social conditions and provides a caustic commentary on the conditions of recent immigrants and a penetrating reappraisal of the black underclass in the United States. You also may want to look at his latest study: *Race Relations: A Critique* (Stanford, Calif.: Stanford University Press, 2007).

Anthony Synnott and David Howes, 'Canada's Visible Minorities: Identity and Representation', in V. Amit-Talai and C. Knowles, eds, *Re-situating Identities: The Politics of Race, Ethnicity and Culture* (Peterborough, Ont.: Broadview Press, 1996).

In this critique of the concept of visible minority, Synnott and Howes question whether it makes sense to lump together so many different groups, with different immigration histories and backgrounds, into a single category of dubious analytical value.

Recommended Websites

Assembly of First Nations
www.afn.ca/

This excellent website of the national organization for status Indians, established in 1982 out of the earlier National Indian Brotherhood, includes press releases, publications, news, policy areas, information on past and future annual assemblies, and links to provincial and territorial organizations. You also might want to check out the fine websites for the other two national Aboriginal organizations in Canada: Inuit Tapiriit Kanatami, at <www.itk.ca>, and Métis National Council, at <www.metisnation.ca/>.

Canadian Heritage: Multiculturalism
www.canadianheritage.gc.ca/progs/multi/index_e.cfm

This federal department site includes information on multicultural programs, definitions of multiculturalism and diversity, news releases, publications, and links to numerous Canadian and international organizations.

Canadian Race Relations Foundation
www.crr.ca/

The CRRF, established by an Act of Parliament in 1991, is the lead government agency that aims to eliminate racism in Canada. Its site outlines programs, includes publications, and has useful links to other sites.

Global Networks
www.globalnetworksjournal.com/

Global Networks journal, founded at Oxford University in 2001, provides links to sites on transnational movements of goods and people and on globalization, as well as journal contents.

Greek Community of Toronto
www.greekcommunity.org

Operated by the largest local Greek organization in Canada, this site is representative of ethnic organization at the metropolitan level, and provides information on employment opportunities, social happenings, political action of interest to the Greek community, and information on the various departments within the organization, such as cultural affairs, women's issues, education, and social services.

International Organization for Migration
www.iom.ch/

This intergovernmental organization, with 120 member countries, provides news of interest and information on policy and research, as well as 'Quick Links' to such topics as international migration law and United Nations resolutions and reports related to migration. The organization is premised on the liberal-capitalist belief that 'humane and orderly migration benefits migrants and society.'

Justicia for Migrant Workers—J4MW
www.justicia4migrantworkers.org/

This non-governmental organization, founded in 2001 and based in Toronto, with an office in Vancouver, seeks to promote the rights of Mexican and Caribbean migrant workers in Canada. The website, which is bilingual English/Spanish, provides notices on upcoming events, press releases, description of ongoing campaigns, and a 'Wall of Shame' of public statements by politicians and other stakeholders showing 'the face of racism in Canada'.

Québec interculturel
www.quebecinterculturel.gouv.qc.ca/fr/index.html

This Quebec government Ministry of Immigration and Cultural Communities site, in French, provides information on associations in Quebec, employment, the province's ethnocultural diversity, and much more.

Ukrainian Canadian Congress
www.ucc.ca

The Ukrainian Canadian Congress is one of the oldest and largest national ethnic organizations, and was among the several older national ethnic groups that profited significantly from the introduction of official multiculturalism policy in 1971. The UCC site includes background and history of Ukrainian immigration, information for prospective immigrants from Ukraine, updates on Canada–Ukraine relations, and news of relevance to the broad Ukrainian-Canadian community.

Part V

Canadian Society and the Global Context

19 Chapter

Global Society

Michael Smith

Learning Objectives

In this chapter, you will:

- Identify the major international organizations that are the focus for much of the debate on globalization.
- Learn the four main forms of globalization: international political agreements, trade and capital flows, the mobility of populations, and cultural diffusion.
- Distinguish between globalization effects in rich and poor countries.
- See how constraint on policy choice is present whether or not countries enter into treaties.
- See that, in appraising the effects of globalization, it is necessary to distinguish between consequences for parts of populations versus consequences for populations as a whole.
- Examine how global cities play a critical role in the globalization process.
- Explore the two main forms of the cultural diffusion argument.
- Set current concerns with globalization within a broader historical context.

Photo: CP/AP/Ng Han Guan

翅(2块) ¥5
¥7
YAO

巨无霸
大有滋味大有趣味
"巨无霸
百分百

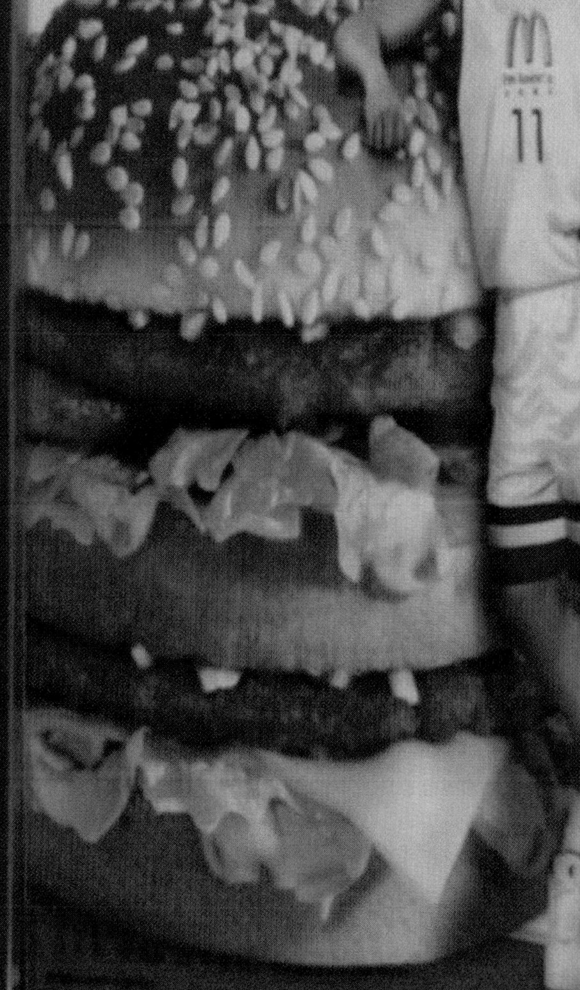

11

Introduction

On 12 August 1999, a group of about 200 people vandalized a McDonald's restaurant under construction in Millau in southern France. They were led by José Bové, a sheep farmer from the region. Bové is a different sort of farmer. He spent most of his childhood in Berkeley, California, while his French parents were teaching at the University of California, before returning to France at the age of 15. Prior to the McDonald's incident, he had led several agriculture-related protests—to recover agricultural land used by the French military, to ban the feeding of growth hormones to calves, to destroy a stock of transgenic (genetically modified) corn. He was in Seattle in 1999 to protest at a World Trade Organization (WTO) meeting, and returned to North America to protest at another one in Quebec City in 2001. In 2002, while awaiting the outcome of his appeal against a prison sentence for the McDonald's incident, he led a group in Brazil that, among other things, pulled up crops of genetically modified corn and soybeans. Bové has become a symbol of anti-globalization protest. His targets reflect a number of the areas of concern about the process.

There is the WTO itself. Created through negotiations between governments, it enforces international trade rules on member countries. Anti-globalization protestors criticize the lack of citizen involvement in such negotiations, claiming that corporations have privileged access to governments so that treaties reflect corporate interests rather than the interests of the broader population.

Countries use tariffs (taxes on imported goods), quotas (restrictions on the quantity of incoming goods), and subsidies (cash transfers or tax relief) to protect domestic producers. The WTO's assumption is that international trade is a good thing and that tariffs, quotas, and subsidies obstruct international trade. The WTO is a forum for negotiating their reduction or elimination.

The WTO also has a quasi-judicial responsibility. Governments that think other countries are protecting their industries in ways incompatible with treaty obligations can appeal to it. The WTO then rules on the matter and may authorize sanctions on the offending country, including the right to impose retaliatory tariffs. Canada's Bombardier and Brazil's Embraer produce competing regional jets. Since 2000 each country has sought and been granted by the WTO the right to impose retaliatory tariffs on the other's goods in response to complaints from each country that the other subsidizes its own company.

Then there is the issue of health and safety. In 2003 it was discovered that a cow raised on an Alberta farm had bovine spongiform encephalitis (BSE, or 'mad cow disease'). BSE can sometimes be transmitted to humans. In the 1990s, significant numbers of cases of the always-fatal human form of the disease were diagnosed in Britain. The US, to which much of Canada's cattle production is exported, responded to the Alberta case by promptly closing its borders to Canadian cattle. This was a catastrophe for Canadian cattle producers but was consistent with WTO rules that allow governments to act to protect the health and safety of their citizens. Other health or safety issues are less clear. In North America, for example, hormones often are added to livestock feed to accelerate the animals' growth. This is less common in Europe. Several European governments claim that hormone-fed beef is a health hazard to those who consume it. North American producers contest that claim, arguing that European cattle producers are asserting this health effect as a pretext, that the real European objective is to protect domestic producers against more efficient North American competition. Bové and others contest the right of the WTO to adjudicate this sort of issue.

Finally, there is a broader resistance to the diffusion of a foreign **culture**, particularly US culture. France uses subsidies to maintain a (relatively) strong national movie industry. Prompted by the Motion Picture Association of America, the industry lobby group, the US has contested the French right to support its domestic industry with subsidies. At a round of trade negotiations in the 1990s France, supported by Canada, secured the right to a 'cultural exception'—a right to exclude cinema and other forms of audiovisual entertainment from any obligation to eliminate protectionist measures. The US continues to push for the narrowing or the abandonment of the 'cultural exception'. José Bové is, in fact, substantially motivated by a concern to protect cultural distinctiveness. He can wax lyrical on the virtues of small-scale local production and high-quality food. On his own farm, he produces one particular culinary gem: Roquefort cheese. The contrast with the industrial agriculture and standardized distribution that underpins the success of McDonald's Corporation is obvious. Bové and his supporters vandalized a McDonald's because they regarded it as a symbol of the intrusion of American culture.

Clearly, Bové is not enthused by globalization, at least in its current form. The same animus with respect to globalization that has expressed itself in his activism stimulates much of the academic, and quasi-academic, debate on the subject. It is an area of diatribes. On one side of the debate, globalization (in its current form) is iniquity incarnate (see, for example, Klein, 1999). On the other side, critics of globalization are treated as fools

Time to Reflect

What have you read about globalization? Did what you read present globalization in a positive or negative light? Identify the positive or negative features of globalization identified in what you read.

or knaves, or both (for example, Wolf, 2004). Let us try to bring some detachment to the issue.

What Is Globalization?

There is debate on what **globalization** means (see Martin et al., 2006), but the underlying idea is fairly clear: international processes intrude on the preferences and behaviour of national and local populations. The word *intrusion* is chosen deliberately: it has a pejorative connotation. In much of the relevant writing, so does *globalization*. That writing often associates globalization with the loss of things that ought to be valued. Beyond this, things get more complicated: globalization takes many forms. We will consider it as political arrangement, economic process, mobility and transnational social networks, and cultural diffusion.

Globalization as Political Arrangement

After World War II, the United States, Britain, and, to a lesser extent, other countries negotiated the framework for subsequent international economic arrangements. They produced the Bretton Woods agreement, named after the resort in New Hampshire where the main negotiations took place. Bretton Woods created the International Monetary Fund and the World Bank. Each has become a *bête noire* to anti-globalization protestors.

The IMF and the World Bank encourage '**sound economic policies**' in the **Third World**, usually including cuts to government expenditures and the reinforcement of the private sector (see 'Open for Discussion'). The WTO (successor to the General Agreement on Tariffs and Trade, GATT) acts to limit the discretion of governments with respect to tariffs, quotas, and subsidies. Critics oppose these organizations because of their definition of 'sound economic policies' and also because of the role of rich, powerful countries in their design. The Bretton Woods agreement was only one of several proposed arrangements for managing post-war international trade, but the relative economic power of the United States after World War II meant that its preferences largely prevailed (Skidelsky, 2000). The IMF, World Bank, and WTO commitments to market solutions reflect the policy preferences of a set of Western nations—in particular, the United States.

Moreover, beyond international organizations, outcomes are also shaped by naked **power**. Take, for example, the softwood lumber dispute between Canada and the United States. For a number of reasons, but particularly because of the depreciation of the Canadian dollar in the 1990s and into the first few years of the twenty-first century, the US lumber industry lost market share to Canadian producers. In response, it pressured US politicians to look hard at Canadian practices, claiming that, in violation of trade rules, Canadian governments had found ways to subsidize the industry. Using threats, the US government forced Canada to adopt policies that raised the price of lumber exports into the United States, including, at various times, both export taxes and quotas (Grafton et al., 1998).

Globalization as Economic Process

Consider, first, rich countries. Trade exposes business owners and employees to competition. Competitors in Third World countries usually pay markedly lower wages, allowing them to price their products lower. They may either drive rich-country producers out of business or force them to cut the wages of their employees in order to compete (Wood, 1994). In the process of doing so employers dealing with unions may seek concessions on both wages and work rules (Munck, 2002: 77–83).

Then, there are **multinational corporations**; Nortel, Bombardier, and Inco are Canadian examples. Other things being equal, managers of these companies are likely to locate factories and offices where costs are lower and the political environment more congenial. Low taxes, less restrictive labour laws and environmental regulations, and government reticence to intervene in the economy are likely to attract them. So, in competition for investment, countries may cut taxes, reduce services, weaken labour laws (health and safety regulations,

OPEN FOR DISCUSSION

The International Monetary Fund and the World Bank

The Bretton Woods negotiations had an ambitious objective: to create an international economic framework that would prevent some of the policy failures of the period before World War II and facilitate post-war economic growth. Two of the major organizations created as a result of these negotiations have become the *bêtes noires* of anti-globalization protestors—the International Monetary Fund (IMF) and the World Bank, which began as the International Bank for Reconstruction and Development (IBRD).

During the Great Depression of the 1930s many people lost their jobs in Europe and North America. Several countries tried to create employment by devaluing their currencies: if the value of the Canadian dollar falls relative to the US dollar, people and businesses in the US can buy more Canadian goods and that, in turn, creates more employment. But any advantage gained by Canada's devaluing its currency is lost if its commercial rivals devalue their currencies. Something like this happened during the 1930s wave of competitive devaluations (Kindleberger, 1986). Export industries were damaged and jobs were lost by competitive devaluations because exporting and importing become much riskier where prices are subject to substantial change through relative currency price changes.

The IMF was set up to help to stabilize currencies. Suppose that an early frost damages the coffee crop in a developing country that is substantially dependent on coffee exports. This will usually lead to a fall in government revenues because there is less income to tax. The IMF was set up to help with this sort of *temporary* problem. It makes loans to countries—at less than commercial rates—to allow the government to cover its temporary revenue shortfall.

The IBRD was set up to assist with the post-war reconstruction of Europe. After World War II the large European countries were in appalling financial shape. Countries such as the United States and Canada were in better economic shape but needed European countries rich enough to absorb their exports. The IBRD was created to provide loans to governments to fund investments in devastated European countries—for example, the reconstruction of a rail network. By the mid-1950s European countries had substantially recovered economically and the IBRD shifted its attention to providing loans to 'credit-worthy poor countries'. It targeted its loans at the Third World.

The IBRD is now part of the World Bank Group. Other elements of the Group were established: the International Financial Corporation (1956), which helps to finance the private sector in the Third World; the International Development Association (1960), which funds programs to alleviate long-term poverty (in recent years it has funded female education and anti-AIDS programs); the International Centre for Settlement of Investment Disputes (1966), which mediates disputes between private investors and countries; and the Multilateral Investment Guarantee Agency (1988), which encourages investments in developing countries by providing insurance against such political risks as civil war.

Described in this way, neither the IMF nor the World Bank seems very controversial. Why, then, the protests against them? Suppose a country like Argentina accumulates a large debt over a substantial period of time. The IMF may make a loan nevertheless, but in such cases it is mandated to encourage governments to adopt 'sound economic policies'. This usually means reductions in government expenditures. It also often means privatization, since loss-making government enterprises may have contributed to government debt. The IBRD also directs its loans to 'credit-worthy countries', which pressures governments to balance budgets. But cutting government expenditures usually means reducing education and welfare spending, and privatization often precipitates layoffs. Measures like these represent suffering for significant parts of the populations of countries receiving financial support from these international organizations. This is one source of hostility towards the IMF and the World Bank. At the same time, both organizations tend to encourage the expansion of the private sector. Those who would prefer a larger role for the public sector in development object to this.

statutory protections against dismissal, trade-union protections), choose not to impose or enforce environmental standards, and refrain from other policies offensive to foreign investors.

Enormous amounts of **finance capital** flow between countries. So-called **hot money** usually accumulates in countries where interest rates are higher and the local currency more stable (Sassen, 2002). This also limits policy options. Government policies designed to stimulate the economy normally involve lower interest rates, but lower interest rates may lead to a flight of 'hot money' out of the country as investors seek the highest rate (for a given level of political and economic stability).

A government confronting a high **unemployment rate** may wish to reduce interest rates, hoping that doing so will create jobs. Lower interest rates imply lower mortgage payments, which stimulate the housing market. Lower rates also reduce entrepreneurs' cost of borrowing, which encourages job-creating investment. But interest-rate reductions may precipitate a decline in the value of a country's currency. For various reasons, a government may be reluctant to see the value of its currency fall. Insofar as this is the case, it may avoid policies that lead to a reduction in interest rates (Andrews, 1994). Thus, although the unemployment rate in Canada in the early 1990s was well over 10 per cent, the government of the time did not substantially stimulate the economy. It chose, instead, policies that had the effect of supporting the value of the Canadian dollar, and the unemployment rate rose fairly dramatically (see Fortin, 1996). The anti-globalization interpretation of this is that Canadian government policy was limited by the development of an international market for capital, with ever-larger flows of 'hot money' between countries.

Parallel damage may be inflicted on Third World countries. Despite lower labour costs, Third World

An anti-globalization protest during the Summit of the Americas in Quebec City, April 2001, showed that—here and elsewhere—many people continue to view globalization as a form of imperialism that works mainly to advance the interests of Western capitalism. (CP/AP Photo/John Moore)

producers are sometimes undercut by exports from rich countries. Here is a particularly pathetic example: rich-country charities receive donations of second-hand clothes, but 'with more donations than they can use, the charities unload their surplus on wholesalers who buy it in the West for a few pennies a pound, then ship it [to Zambia] and sell bales of it to . . . street retailers at a markup of 300 to 400 per cent' (Jeter, 2002: A1). The local population buys the goods for reasons of both price and taste. Items with sports logos are particularly popular in some African markets. There used to be relatively lively textile and apparel industries in Zambia. These have now been seriously damaged by competition from second-hand European and North American goods.

Most damage, however, comes from **capital-intensive** industries. Capital-intensive production in rich countries—particularly agriculture—can often lead to lower sale prices, despite the relatively high cost of labour in the rich countries. The effects are compounded where agriculture is heavily subsidized, as is the case for many US and European agricultural products. Some analysts believe that it is possible for Third World countries to establish their own industries only if those industries are protected or encouraged—with tariffs, quotas, or subsidies. But doing so would go against the policy preferences of the WTO, the World Bank, and the IMF, all of which press for liberalized trade and have sanctions available if a country chooses protectionism.

This brings us to the Third World and capital markets. Lenders often regard Third World countries as too risky for investment, so those countries are compelled to turn to international organizations—the World Bank or, during financial crises, the IMF —as sources of loans or as guarantors of private-sector loans. But these loans come with strings attached, of the sort discussed earlier—requirements that markets be opened and that the country adopt a 'sound economic policy'.

Globalization as Mobility and Transnational Social Networks

Products imported from the Third World might force down rich-country wages, but migration from the Third World to rich countries may have the same effect. In either case, wages of unskilled (usually meaning poorly educated) employees in rich countries are most likely to be affected. There has been a large unskilled migration into the United States, both legal and illegal. One result of this is competition between less educated Latin American migrants and, disproportionately, less educated African Americans. Some think that this competition has forced down wages of unskilled workers in the United States and of African Americans in particular (Stevans, 1998).

The Canadian situation is a little different. A points system determines eligibility for some immigrant classes. Would-be migrants are given points for education and in-demand skills (as well as other things). Those with enough points are admitted. This system for selecting immigrants is thought to have reduced the magnitude of unskilled immigration to Canada (but see Reitz, 1998). Europe has also experienced post-war migrations. The fundamental point, though, is that international migration—mainly from poor to rich countries—is common.

These migrations create transnational social networks. Most migrants settle in cities. The main destinations of migrants to Canada are Toronto, Montreal, and Vancouver, where they create their own communities, sometimes retaining close ties with other members of their family or ethnic group in other cities in the world. The same thing happens on a larger scale in New York, Los Angeles, and London. This creates what Alejandro Portes (1997) calls *transnational communities*, with identities and economic interests shaped by their inter-city relations.

At the other end of the social scale, claims Saskia Sassen (2002), international cities develop a distinctive elite. This elite manages international commercial flows—the movements of goods, services, and capital that have become these cities' main economic vocation—and, to some degree, becomes detached from national loyalties. Bankers in London engaged in the financing of international trade, for example, become less concerned with British domestic policy issues. Rather, their transnational economic and social ties become increasingly important (Sassen, 2002; see also Arthurs, 1999, on Canada).

Globalization as Cultural Diffusion

Hollywood is the most conspicuous worldwide projector of a particular culture, through the process called **cultural diffusion**. The US movie and television industry has aggressively marketed itself throughout the Americas and Europe (Segrave, 1998). It probably shapes the world views of receiving populations. What Hollywood projects is heterogeneous (contrast, for example, *A Prairie Home Companion* with *Rocky Balboa*), but it cannot reflect the range of preferences and opinions in the rest of the world. It must substantially embody cultural judgements, knowledge, or ignorance of those producing movies and television. Hollywood's ignorance extends even to its most immediate northern neighbour;

IN THE FIRST PERSON

I was drawn into sociology because it engaged the sorts of larger issues of inequality, efficiency, and fairness that interested me when I was a student. I've remained a sociologist because the discipline provides a broad enough tent to accommodate the various interests that I've since developed and followed. My approach to sociology has been substantially shaped by my colleagues at McGill, and by others whose work I know and admire. The lesson that I've drawn from those colleagues is that facts matter. It's easy to construct large, general theories of the social and economic world. People do so all the time. Good tests of theories, however, require lots of hard work. So they're less abundant. We need more of them. Using one research method or another, that's what I work on.—Michael Smith

Pierre Berton (1975) describes one film for which the setting was a blizzard in Saskatchewan—in July!

American cultural influence is not confined to Hollywood. US universities train graduate students from the rest of the world and produce a disproportionate share of the world's academic output. US multinational companies transmit employment practices to other countries (Merten, 1997). That is to say, American multinational corporations have similar ways of hiring (recruitment and evaluation methods), of promoting, and of dealing with grievances (among other things). When they set up branches in Belgium, or Brazil, or Barbados, they bring

American cultural influence extends across the globe. This photograph was taken in an open-air market in Kabul, Afghanistan. Even in countries where America is not favoured, an impressive array of US-brand running shoes are ready for sale. (Steve McCurry/Magnum Photos)

Time to Reflect

Are you more or less likely to watch a movie because it is made in Canada? What about your friends? What characteristics (positive or negative) do you associate with Canadian-made movies? Ask yourself the same question with respect to the music you listen to.

those practices with them. They change the culture of employment in those countries. To varying degrees, so do multinationals based in other countries.

The Effect of Globalizing Mechanisms

Two linked themes run through this discussion so far. One is that globalization is a homogenizing process. Political, economic, and cultural pressures create societies that look increasingly similar. Such homogenization may be regarded as undesirable in general—a process through which the diversity and richness of cultures is replaced with the monotone of a standard international practice. A displacement of consumption from, say, Roquefort cheese to Kraft Velveeta or from similarly distinctive local fare to McDonald's might be symbols of this process. The other theme specifies what seem to be identifiably bad outcomes of the globalization process. The destruction of Zambia's indigenous clothing industry might be an example of this. The limits placed on government choices of economic and social policy by international organizations and by international trade and capital flows often are also regarded in this way.

Let us consider the four broad globalizing mechanisms identified above in light of these concerns.

Treaties and International Organizations

Constraint in Principle

International organizations and common markets are created through treaties. Treaties are international contracts, so, like the contracts associated with a mortgage, a marriage, or a mutual fund purchase, they impose constraints on signatories. Further, sovereign nations can sign or not sign such agreements. Several European countries, for example, chose not to become members of the European Economic Community (now the European Union, EU) when it was first created. Some (in 2007, Norway, Switzerland, and Iceland) still remain outside it. Had the 1988 federal election in Canada gone differently—and it could easily have done so—the Canada–US Free Trade Agreement (FTA) would not have been signed. The initiative to create the North American Free Trade Agreement (NAFTA) came from the United States and Mexico. The Canadian government inserted itself into the process when it seemed it would be left out (Robert, 2000)—it was concerned that a NAFTA without Canada might mean that Mexico would replace Canada as the principal trading partner of the United States.

Of course, a picture of sovereign governments free to choose between courses of action would be a gross misrepresentation. Self-defence motivated the Canadian government to negotiate the FTA. Rising protectionist sentiment in the United States in the 1980s led to threats of unilateral imposition of tariffs and quotas. The FTA was conceived to shelter Canadian exporters from this protectionist wave. The threat of protectionism, then, constrained the Canadian government to pursue a trade agreement.

Similarly, Third World countries that borrow from the World Bank, or rich or poor countries that borrow from the IMF, do so because other options seem less appealing. There is no such thing as unconstrained choice. Still, there is some choice. The core of the debate on globalization is about whether or not the constraint has increased.

Constraint in Practice

Do the sorts of treaties associated with globalization imply increased levels of constraint? To answer this question we need first to determine *when* constraint might or might not have increased.

Consider these two examples. From 1876 to 1884, King Leopold of Belgium created his own personal second kingdom in what became the Congo, ushering in a period of spectacular brutality (Anstey, 1966; Hochschild, 1998). Indigenous males were conscripted into the production of rubber, or their lives were disrupted as they fled the Belgian troops sent to conscript them. Among other atrocious acts, mutilation was used as a form of labour discipline. In areas of British conquest in southern Africa, European farmers displaced the indigenous population.

Time to Reflect

Are you for or against the provision of Canadian government subsidies to Canadian firms? Or are you for them under some circumstances and against them under others? If so, when are you for them and when are you against them?

That population was then subjected to taxes. The idea was that the need to pay taxes in cash would force the native population to seek employment on settler farms (Crush, 1987). Coercive activities of various sorts were common across the various European empires in Africa and elsewhere. *These* were constraints.

Treaties and international organizations often are intended as methods for escaping or limiting other sorts of constraint. For example, part of the Bretton Woods agreement of 1944 committed its signatories to maintain approximately fixed rates of exchange between their currencies. This ruled out (or made more difficult) one particular policy choice: competitive devaluation. Bretton Woods was a means of escaping the macroeconomic policy constraints imposed by competitive devaluations, with which governments had to deal during the inter-war period.

Treaties, then, embody chosen constraints. How binding are those constraints? Post-war trade agreements were supposed to create a level playing field across countries, so that only the most efficient producers would thrive, irrespective of country of location. However, democratic governments have to worry about getting re-elected. The livelihoods of parts of their electorates may be put at risk by exposure to foreign competition. Consequently, the governments are under pressure to find ways to offset the effects of the successive tariff reductions negotiated through the GATT and the WTO. They have done so by using the non-tariff barriers discussed earlier. Across democracies, as tariffs have fallen the use of non-tariff barriers has risen (Kono, 2006). Governments have harassed foreign competitors by accusing them of 'dumping' (selling below the cost of production) or of subsidizing (as the US government has done in the softwood lumber dispute) and then imposing retaliatory tariffs. They have developed quality standards like labelling, packaging, inspection, testing, and quarantine often more to make life difficult for would-be importers than to protect domestic consumers. They grant subsidies to domestic producers.

No rich country is innocent of these sorts of activities. In 1999 the Quebec government attempted to lure a Taiwanese computer chip company to Montreal with a generous array of subsidies (Smith, 2001b). The United States aggressively subsidizes its agriculture and in March 2002 imposed a 30 per cent tariff on steel imports that was ruled illegal by the WTO a year later. The European Union is no better. Treaties do constrain signatories, but it is important to understand that the degree of compliance is highly variable. Further evidence of this is the substantial body of legal writings dealing precisely with the problem of increasing the likelihood of treaty compliance. We live in a world where treaty violation is frequent (Chayes and Chayes, 1995).

Governments regularly confront choices. On the one hand, there is the possibility of inconsistent mutual regulation through a treaty. On the other hand, there is the possibility of inconsistent mutual regulation in the absence of a treaty. The latter, no-treaty, situation will often involve a tit-for-tat approach to disputes—one country limits trade to protect its vulnerable industries, another country punishes the first country by closing off its domestic market to the first country's major export industries, and so on. Or countries might consecutively devalue their currencies, as during the inter-war period. Or they might do both.

Constraint is present in both situations. What matter are the relative benefits of different kinds of constraints. Since treaties spell out rules for international relations, they may be preferable—unless the treaties are grossly one-sided. Joseph Stiglitz (2002, 2006) has argued, powerfully, that one-sidedness has been the case for Third World countries. The outcomes at the consecutive rounds of the GATT and the WTO depend on the relative resources that participating countries bring to the bargaining. Richer countries bring more financial muscle and technical expertise than their poorer counterparts. Consequently, the bargains substantially reflect their interests. *With a level playing field*, poor countries could produce and export a range of agricultural products. But rich countries have preferred to reduce tariffs on industrial goods, preserve them on many agricultural products, and further reinforce their domestic agricultural producers with subsidies. According to Stiglitz these treaties, then, have favoured rich countries and disadvantaged poor ones (see 'Global Issues' box).

GLOBAL ISSUES

Stiglitz on Globalization and the Third World

Joseph Stiglitz writes with considerable authority. He is a Nobel prize-winning economist who served as President of the Council of Economic Advisors during the administration of US President Bill Clinton and he was Chief Economist at the World Bank. He has become, arguably, the most important contemporary critic of globalization. Here are some of his criticisms.

First, there is the *selectiveness* of the issues and industries dealt with in trade negotiations. Cotton is produced in Burkina Faso at a very low cost: the income of the farmers is less than $300 per year and they cannot afford to invest in irrigation, fertilizer, tractors, or high-quality seeds. They ought to be able to out-compete US producers in world markets and within the US itself. They cannot. This is because US cotton farmers receive subsidies in two forms. Governments have incurred the costs of providing irrigation and they transfer cash directly. The dollar value of these subsidies is very large indeed—more than $3 billion per year in cash transfers alone. Stiglitz's point is that trade has been liberalized for the industrial goods in the production of which rich countries specialize. Agriculture—in which the developing countries could compete—remains protected.

Second, international trade agreements assume that what works for rich countries works in the same way for poor ones. This is well illustrated with policies on intellectual property. In general, it is widely accepted that in North America, Europe, and Japan the right to patent—that is, grant exclusive rights to an innovation for a period of time—encourages innovation. Patents make it possible for the company or person incurring the costs of innovating to get a return on that investment. (Copyright provides related protections for the ideas embedded in artistic production and software, among other things.) Patent rights have been built into GATT and WTO agreements. These rights limit the capacity of developing countries to produce or use generic equivalents of brand-name drugs—for example, drugs to treat AIDS—that the populations desperately need. Stiglitz concedes that there are costs involved in the development of drugs but argues that incomes in developing countries are sufficiently low that the companies that developed them have no chance of recouping any significant part of their investment in those countries. So, he says, the enforcement of drug patents in the Third World does nothing to assure the stream of pharmaceutical company revenues that can be used to finance research and development for new treatments *and* leads to the withholding of life-saving drugs from most of the world.

Finally, the possibilities for rapid growth in income in Third World countries are often related to the availability of mineral resources—for example, oil in Nigeria, gold in Papua New Guinea, and diamonds in Sierra Leone. Despite this considerable mineral wealth, living standards for most of the population in these countries remain abysmal, even before the appalling effects of civil war in countries like Sierra Leone. The fact that resource richness does not lead to broadly spread rising living standards has something to do with political deficiencies within the resource-rich countries themselves. But the extraction and marketing of these resources often require the technical expertise of companies based in rich countries. Securing a licence to extract and sell resources has often entailed bribes and rich-country companies have been entirely willing to provide bribes, often through 'facilitators' who are nationals of the resource-rich country. Stiglitz comments: 'bribes were not only legal but tax-deductible in a large number of countries (France, Switzerland, Luxembourg, Austria, Belgium, Japan, and the Netherlands); in effect, the government was paying a substantial part of the bribe . . . . There is now an OECD convention on bribery, but enforcement is difficult and incomplete. As of December 2005, there had yet to be a single prosecution outside the United States under national legislation enacted to implement the convention' (Stiglitz, 2006: 139). Rich countries, in other words, play a major role in subverting the political and commercial morality of poor countries.

Trade and Investment: Rich Countries

Critics of globalization, when they consider the impacts on wealthy countries, tend to focus on two sources of negative consequences: increased trade and more mobile investment. One suggests that increased trade—particularly with developing countries—worsens the pay and employment situation of the less skilled and of workers in general. Another argues that, to create an investment-friendly environment and attract increasingly footloose capital, rich countries adopt less generous social policies. This is the **race to the bottom** argument.

Employment and Wages

In assessing the effects of trade and investment on rich countries it needs to be borne in mind that most trade is between rich countries. Roughly speaking, the world's rich countries are members of the Organization for Economic Co-operation and Development (OECD). Figure 19.1 shows that from 1970 to 1998, over two-thirds of imports into OECD countries originated in other OECD countries. There was no downward trend in the share of OECD-originating imports. Finally, imports from members of the Organization of Petroleum Exporting Countries (OPEC) account for a significant share of total non-OECD imports. But the bulk of imports from these countries is petroleum. Few OECD countries compete in the oil market. All of this is to say that, to a very substantial degree, rich countries are competing among themselves.

However, within the pool of rich countries there are variations in living standards. For example, the gap between wages in Canada and the US, on the one hand, and Greece and Portugal, on the other, is fairly wide. Yet, is it possible that the variation in wage levels between rich countries is sufficient to have undermined Canadian and US wages? Do we have evidence of a deteriorating labour market situation of employees in the richer OECD countries of the sort that might be produced by competition with either Third World or lower-income OECD countries?

In most rich countries the proportion of employees who are members of unions (union density) has tended to fall (Visser, 2006). It is likely that some of this decline was caused by a loss of jobs in unionized sectors caused by trade competition. Other things being equal, belonging to a union tends to increase pay. So the decline in union membership may itself be evidence of a negative effect of globalization on employment and wages. Interestingly, in Canada the fall in union density has been rather small. Nonetheless, as in many other countries, Canadian union membership has been increasingly concentrated in the public sector, which is, of course, substantially sheltered from the global marketplace. Even in Canada, then, the evidence on trends in union membership is consistent with a negative effect of globalization on employees.

Closer analysis reveals a more complicated picture. Price competition is supposed to put pressure on wages in richer countries. Low-wage countries should be able to sell into high-wage countries at a lower price. If this process were underway, one might expect those industries in rich countries exposed to more trade to be less able to raise their prices than industries exposed to less trade or altogether sheltered from trade. They might even be forced to lower them. Research on the US and Europe, however, suggests that there is no link between the amount of trade in the goods of a particular industry and price trends in that industry (Slaughter and Swagel, 1997). In fact, rich-country prices have proven to be robust in the face of international competition, a situation that suggests trade exerts little pressure on rich-country wages.

What is the effect of trade on unemployment? For Canada we can consider two tests of this. World trade and investment flows have grown. Canadian manufacturers compete against other firms within the same industry in other countries, most of which have lower wages than ours. So, as a first test, should this not have led to a growth in unemployment in Canada that matches the rise in trade and investment flows? In fact, trends in unemployment over the post-war period have been complex. They were low until the mid-1970s, rose from then until the mid-1990s, and have since fallen

Figure 19.1 OECD Imports

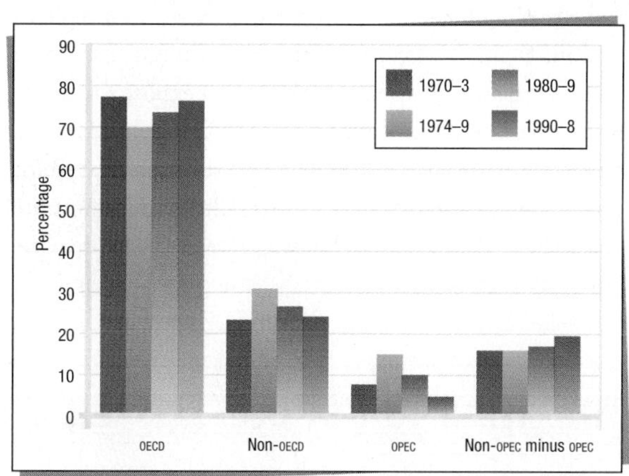

Source: Based on OECD total*: 'Imports by partner country group', from *OECD Historical Statistics: 1970/2000* (2001), © OECD 2001. *OECD total includes Mexico from 1990, Hungary and Poland from 1992, Czech Republic from 1993, Korea from 1994, Slovak Republic from 1997.

abruptly. Note that this pattern is approximately matched by a number of other countries—for example, the US, Australia, and the United Kingdom, all of which have economies that are substantially exposed to trade. There is little evidence of a negative effect of globalization there. A second test is provided by events following the FTA and NAFTA (Smith, 2001b), which came into force on 1 January 1989 and 1 January 1994, respectively. Each agreement reduced barriers to competition with the United States. The second also reduced barriers with Mexico, a low-income country. Unemployment in Canada did rise after the FTA, but the FTA's implementation coincided with a recession—unemployment rose elsewhere at the same time. NAFTA, in contrast, was implemented in the early part of an upswing in the economy. Unemployment was falling before it was signed and continued to fall after it was signed. There is evidence, however, that the largest post-FTA declines in employment were concentrated in industries that had been subject to the largest tariff cuts. These agreements' *aggregate* net effect on unemployment was negligible, though some workers certainly lost their jobs because of them. The complexity of the effects of trade liberalization on employment is illustrated by the case of the Canadian clothing industry (see 'Human Diversity' box).

But if particular workers were damaged by these agreements, perhaps this is evidence of trade's generally harmful effect on unskilled employees in particular? Rising earnings inequality within a country is usually cited in support of this interpretation (e.g., Bernard and Jensen, 2000). It is sometimes thought to reflect the downward pressure on the earnings of the unskilled (the uneducated) exerted by Third World competition. It *is* true that earnings inequality in rich countries in the last two decades of the twentieth century more often trended upward than downward (Atkinson, 2000; OECD, 2004: 141). However, in some rich countries exposed to trade and capital flows, earnings inequality seems to have fallen (Finland, France, Japan) or remained constant (Germany, Denmark). In countries like Canada and the US, where the broad trend was upward, the increase either slowed or stopped in the last part of those two decades (Wolfson and Murphy, 1998; Baker and Solon, 2003; Autor et al., 2005). So, despite rising trade and capital flows, earnings inequality has not risen in all countries and the rise has tailed off in other countries. This is not overwhelming evidence for a perverse effect of globalization.

The Race to the Bottom

Social programs rest on tax collections. But corporations are lured by cuts in corporate taxes and in the income taxes to which high-earning managers are liable. So, it is argued, competitive tax cuts cause cuts to social programs.

This argument is plausible, but the available evidence tends not to support it. On the revenue side, Nancy Olewiler (1999) has found that there were large differences between OECD countries in the tax rates imposed on corporations and individuals, that there were large differences between tax rates in Canada and the United States, that there was no evidence of a convergence in tax rates over time across OECD countries, and that taxes had tended to rise rather than fall in the periods studied.

On the expenditure side, notwithstanding claims to the contrary, '[s]ince 1980, out of the twenty-one leading OECD countries, only three have cut the share of GDP spent on public health care, only two have cut the share spent on public pensions, only four have cut the share spent on welfare, and only three have cut the share spent on unemployment. Overall, only two of the twenty-one countries (Spain and Portugal) have cut the shares spent on social transfers' (Lindert, 2004: 307). Note that between 1960 and 1998 social expenditures as a percentage of GDP in Canada rose by 4.8 per cent, an above-average increase among OECD countries, despite the fact its main commercial competitor is the US (Castles, 2004: 25). Within this context of relative stability in expenditures, huge social policy divergences persist. The income protection provided to those who lose their jobs, get sick, or incur hard-to-manage family obligations (for example, those of single mothers) remain much more generous in Sweden and Germany than in the United States. A substantial literature documents the persistence of social policy variation despite globaliza-

Time to Reflect

What has been happening to the earnings of the people in your family? Have they risen by more than the cost of living or by less than the increase in cost of living? What has been the employment experience of people in your family? Have they moved into better or worse jobs? Have they experienced episodes of unemployment? If they moved into worse jobs or experienced unemployment, do you know what caused this to happen?

tion (see, e.g., Kitschelt, 1999). Figure 19.2 shows just how wide the variation in social spending remains, with social spending as a percentage of GDP (gross domestic product) in Sweden about twice that of Japan. Note, furthermore, the variation in methods of social spending: all of Norway's involves direct spending by the government, whereas about one-quarter of spending in the United States involves private social benefits, either legally stipulated (such as occupational health and safety premiums) or voluntarily provided (such as employer-funded pensions).

What Prevents Convergence?

There are three main reasons why a race to the bottom seems not to be taking place despite increasing trade and investment flows.

First, within capitalist economies many jobs are both destroyed and created (Davis et al., 1996). Changing technology and tastes, as well as globalization, lead to declines in employment in some firms and industries. These declines in employment sometimes involve layoffs, but they are also often managed through attrition. The same changes in technology, taste, and opportunities on

HUMAN DIVERSITY

Foreign Competition: The Case of the Canadian Clothing Industry

As compared to other industries (say, steel or automobiles) the manufacture of clothing is labour-intensive—it requires relatively more labour and less capital equipment. This is the sort of industry that ought to be most vulnerable to competition from low-wage regions—from the Third World or from employees in the southern US working in states with no or weak unions and without or with negligible minimum wages. Trade liberalization might be expected to have devastated the industry. In fact, it has. But the pattern of effects of trade liberalization on the industry indicates some of the complexities of the process (Wyman, 2006).

From about the 1960s Canadian clothing producers were increasingly subject to competition from Hong Kong, South Korea, and Taiwan. In response, along with the United States and the European Union, beginning in 1974 Canada negotiated *quotas* with these countries. This import-limiting agreement was the Multi-Fibre Arrangement (MFA), which was made more stringent during the 1970s and 1980s.

The next change in the situation of the industry came with the Canada–US FTA, implemented in 1989. It eliminated trade restrictions between the two countries. *Both* countries' clothing industries flourished in response to this agreement. The growth in exports from Canada to the US was particularly strong and from the beginning of the 1990s to 2001 employment in the Canadian industry grew by about 20,000, an increase of more than 25 per cent. Note that this increase occurred under both the FTA, which was confined to Canada and the US, and NAFTA (1994), which included low-wage Mexico within the tariff-free trading zone.

In the mid-1990s both Canada and the US were parties to WTO negotiations that, after a delay, provided for the phasing out of the MFA quotas as well as reductions in tariffs. The results of this are interesting. First, Third World countries have occupied a larger and larger share of the market in both countries. Second, the sources of clothing imports have changed. Hong Kong, South Korea, and Taiwan have been displaced by Bangladesh, India, and mainland China. Third, Mexico, a relatively high-income developing country, has also increased its clothing exports to Canada. Fourth, with market share occupied by very low-wage countries the shares in each other's markets of Canada and the US have fallen.

These outcomes are interesting for several reasons. On the one hand, the Canadian industry has been substantially damaged by low-wage competition. Employment has collapsed to about two-thirds of its previous level. On the other hand, the international treaties relevant to this industry have served the interests of some Third World countries. Bangladesh is a desperately poor country—but a little less so because it can sell clothing into the North American market. The fact that Mexico has increased its share of the Canadian market demonstrates that in clothing production, at least, NAFTA served Mexico's interests.

Figure 19.2 Net Public and Private Social Expenditures as a Percentage of GDP

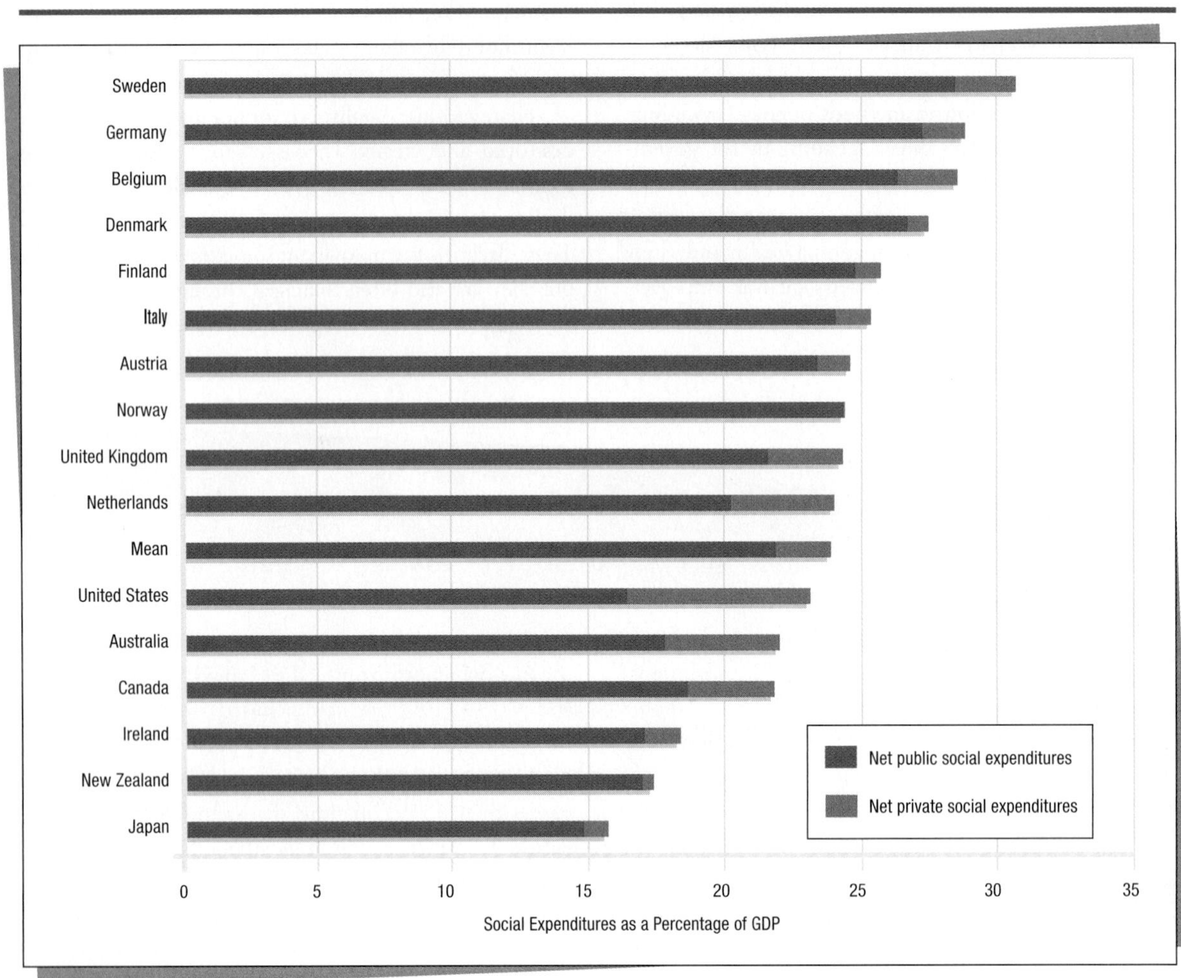

Note: Social benefits include old-age cash benefits, disability cash benefits, occupational injury and disease benefits, sickness benefits, services for the elderly and the disabled, survivors' benefits, family cash benefits, family services, active labour market policies, unemployment compensation, housing benefits, public health expenditures, and other contingencies, such as cash benefits to those on low incomes.
Source: Based on Table 7, 'Net social expenditure indicators, 1997' (p. 27–8), from Willem Adema, *Net Social Expenditure*, 2nd edn, *Labour Market and Social Policy—Occasional Papers* 52, © OECD 2001.

the international market, however, lead to expansions in employment in other sectors. As a result, while particular groups of employees may be harmed by globalization (as has been the case for the Canadian clothing industry), the aggregate effect may be modest.

Second, many governments of countries with greater exposure to the international market have chosen to invest more heavily in social programs than have those with less exposure. Other things being equal, trade as a percentage of GDP is higher in countries with smaller GDP, such as the Netherlands, Belgium, Sweden, and Canada, than it is in economically larger countries such as Germany, the United Kingdom, or, in particular, the United States (perhaps because of economies of scale). At the same time, social programs are, on average, more generous in the first set of countries than in the second (though Germany diverges from the second group pattern). Dani Rodrik (1997) explains this association as follows: countries with a large share of their economy engaged in trade are likely to be particularly hard hit during downturns in the economic activity of their principal trading partners; to compensate for this vulnerability governments of small countries like the Netherlands have developed generous welfare states. In their case, globalization has led to more generous social policy rather than to a race to the bottom.

Third, social expenditures may be efficient. In terms of investment decisions, the 'bottom' may not be the outcome preferred by managers of multinational corporations. Suppose that you are a manager of a multinational company. What factors might affect your decision with respect to where to locate your head office? You would certainly prefer a reasonably safe city—it is harder to recruit and keep high-quality employees who confront a significant likelihood of being mugged, assaulted, or burgled. So investments in a police force are required, as well, probably, as investments in social programs that provide a living standard adequate to reduce the likelihood that the poor will feel inclined to mug, assault, or burgle. Since few people enjoy being solicited by beggars or passing people sleeping in doorways, you may want to see some programs established to help the homeless.

In addition, you almost certainly do not want to be exposed to infectious diseases. Investments in public health reduce the likelihood of contracting, say, tuberculosis. You would want traffic jams kept under control. In a large **metropolitan area**, that would require (very costly) investments in mass transit. You might also like to see a rich cultural life in your city. Universities tend to elevate the cultural lives of their host cities. Even in the United States, universities are substantially funded through taxes. If you want an opera, ballet, symphony orchestra, a set of museums, and a theatre district, you would also have to expect to be taxed to make possible subsidies to these cultural institutions. Along these lines, there are more high-paid head office jobs in New York City than in, say, Birmingham, Alabama. Taxes are markedly lower in Birmingham than in New York, but so are public services. Many would think that the quality of life is also inferior in Birmingham. The preservation of better jobs certainly requires some public spending, possibly a lot of it.

Trade and Investment: Poor Countries

What about the Third World? Is the case of the Zambian apparel industry exemplary? The answer to this question is yes—and no.

The Indian textile industry in the early nineteenth century provides a classic example of destructive trade. It was destroyed by competition from Britain, causing considerable suffering among local weavers (Rothermund, 1993). Contemporary writers within the 'fair trade' tradition are convinced that there are many more such examples (e.g., Suranovic, 1997). It is clear that the export from the United States and Europe of (often subsidized) agricultural products makes more difficult the development of a viable commercial agriculture in several Third World countries. Stiglitz makes a powerful case to the effect that the Third World does not reap anything like the benefits from globalization that it ought to (see 'Global Issues' box). That is the 'yes' part of the answer.

But the issue is complicated. In an exhaustive review of evidence, Peter Lindert and Jeffrey Williamson (2001) show that, over two centuries, between-country inequality has risen. By the mid-1990s, the gap between rich and poor countries was greater than it had been at the beginning of the nineteenth century. Clearly, this rise coincides with a huge increase in economic integration at the international level. Is this evidence of the harmful effects on poor countries of globalization?

Not really. The long-term rise in inequality between countries originates in the improvement in average incomes in those countries that integrated into the world economy. Inequality rose as the European countries that created the modern world economy became rich after 1600. It increased further as countries like Japan, Taiwan, Singapore, Korea, Mexico, and Brazil opened up to the world economy and competed successfully. Japan's success in the 1980s in the export of automobiles and consumer electronics would be a good example of this. Japan, Taiwan, and countries like them became richer than did the Third World countries that, for whatever reasons, failed to become integrated into the global economy. The populations of countries that maintained closed economies failed to get richer. This pattern is reflected in Figure 19.3.

Stiglitz argues powerfully that inequality *within* Third World countries has tended to increase because of corruption, the source of which is rich-country companies that offer bribes to secure and manage the extraction of resources. Still, part of this rise of inequality within Third World countries is consistent with relatively

Time to Reflect

Suppose you were a senior executive in a large Canadian firm and you had been charged with the responsibility for choosing where to relocate your firm's head office. Would you recommend it be located in your home town? In the town in which you are currently studying (if you are studying outside your home town)? What factors would you take into account in your decision?

Figure 19.3 Trade Policy and the Third World

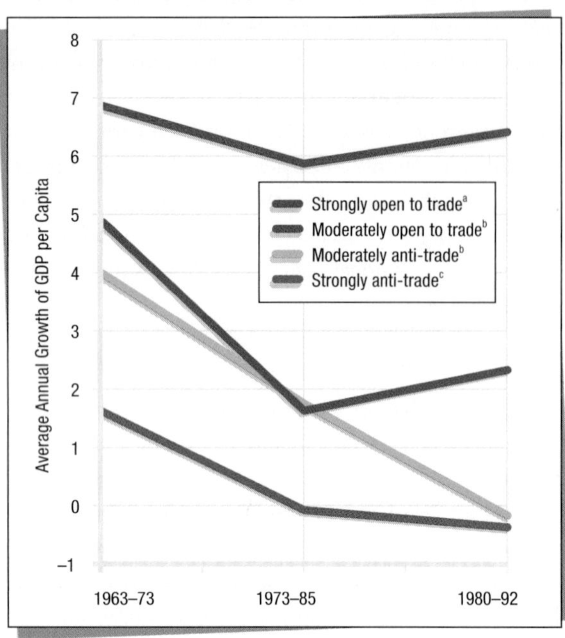

[a][Strongly open] Hong Kong, South Korea, and Singapore.
[b]The composition of the intermediate groups can be found in the original World Bank source used by Lindert and Williamson.
[c][Strongly anti-trade] 1963–73: Argentina, Bangladesh, Burundi, Chile, Dominican Republic, Ethiopia, Ghana, India, Pakistan, Peru, Sri Lanka, Sudan, Tanzania, Turkey, Uruguay, and Zambia. In the two later periods, Chile, Pakistan, Sri Lanka, and Turkey became more open, while Bolivia, Madagascar, and Nigeria joined the strongly anti-trade group.
Source: Peter H. Lindert and Jeffrey G. Williamson, 'Does Globalization Make the World More Unequal?', in M. Bordo, A.M. Taylor, and J.G. Williamson, eds, Globalization in Historical Perspective (Chicago: University of Chicago Press, 2003). Reprinted by permission of the authors.

benign effects of globalization. Inequality has risen within the so-called East Asian tigers as well as in China, Mexico, and Brazil. This is, in part, because regions that are more integrated into the world economy have become richer while the regions that have not been integrated remain as poor as they ever were. For example, it is in the southern coastal part of China, where export industries are located, that incomes are rising. In the interior and the north, which remain largely unintegrated into the world economy, incomes have failed to rise. The Chiapas region in Mexico provides another interesting case. There is significant political unrest there—and it is also a region where persistent poverty coincides with relative exclusion from the international economy, as compared to other parts of the country (Lynn, 2002).

For both the Third World and for rich countries, then, *in aggregate* the character of the economic effects of globalization seems broadly similar. Some workers (and their families) have been harmed by processes associated with globalization—for example, weavers in the nineteenth-century Indian textile industry, agricultural producers in Third World countries excluded from commercial markets by cheap food imports from rich countries, and many employees in the clothing industries of rich countries since World War II.

But within a larger historical perspective it is difficult to discern harmful net and aggregate economic effects of globalization. On the contrary, international trade has been the main route to the relative prosperity of the currently richer countries in the world economy, which includes a set of countries (in particular in East Asia) that, as recently as 60 years ago, were desperately poor. Nor does the evidence yet suggest that trade and investment flows lead to a race to the bottom in social policy, in part because relatively generous social programs and other forms of government spending may often be a requisite for trade and investment, at least where higher-paid jobs are involved.

Social Networks and the Movement of Populations

'Global Cities' and Global Networks

Globalization creates economic opportunities that have been successfully exploited within some—most notably Asian—Third World countries. It is often also a disruptive force (Sassen, 2000). When agricultural producers in rich countries export into the Third World they sometimes displace the small holders who produced for local markets—displacing them from agriculture and obliging them to work for wages. Something like this seems to have happened in both the Caribbean and Mexico. When multinational corporations create manufacturing jobs in developing countries the recruitment of a local labour force disrupts established social relationships, perhaps especially because the plants have often disproportionately recruited women. Global economic and political interests induce rich countries to intervene militarily in developing countries. This is a second form of disruption. Such interventions may create large flows of refugees—something that is currently happening in Iraq. When governments get into economic trouble and the IMF provides loans to them contingent on economic austerity measures, the outcome is usually a wave of employment reductions that lead those displaced to consider their options. In response to each of these forms of disruption some of those displaced will seek to migrate to richer countries

At the same time, the dispersal of economic activities creates a problem of co-ordination (Sassen, 1991, 1998,

2002). The international flow of goods and contracts and the financing of that flow require 'a system for the provision of such inputs as planning, top-level management, and specialized business services' (Sassen, 1991: 29). These inputs are most efficiently co-ordinated within a small number of very large cities. New York, London, and Tokyo are at the top of the global hierarchy of cities providing this co-ordination. Toronto falls in the upper part of the hierarchy, with Montreal some way behind.

The development of global cities has, then, created two sorts of network, each globally oriented. One is made up of the economic decision-makers in global cities—bankers, specialists in commercial insurance, international lawyers, brokers of various kinds, and so on. Because in their day-to-day work they deal with issues that are international, and because this implies that they are part of international social networks, their political orientations also tend to be international. Their loyalties shift towards their international network and away from the nation-state in which they are located.

At the other end of the social hierarchy are the migrants displaced by investment, trade, international organization policies, and military action. They are attracted to the global cities that co-ordinate the international network. In those cities there is a demand for the sorts of labour they can provide. Those who co-ordinate global economic flows have high incomes. They consume lots of personal services; 'the increase in the numbers of expensive restaurants, luxury housing, luxury hotels, gourmet shops, boutiques, French hand laundries, and specialty cleaners that ornament the urban landscape illustrates this trend' (ibid., 9). Many of these activities are both labour-intensive and poorly paid. They provide jobs that immigrants are willing, and that native labour is often unwilling, to fill. The arrival of immigrants willing to work for low wages puts pressure on the wages of similarly unskilled native-born employees and contributes to an increase in overall inequality.

The immigrants filling these low-paid service-sector jobs are usually distinguished by skin colour, language, or both. They tend to be the objects of discrimination. Imperfectly integrated into the host society because of discrimination, immigrants retain their loyalties to family and former neighbours in their countries of origin. They, too, are part of larger transnational networks. Once immigrant communities become established in a global city, they facilitate the migration of others by providing information, cash, sponsorship (for example, through the family reunification component of Canadian immigration policy), contacts, or employment. The result of all this is immigrant communities that are substantially estranged from their host society but that remain part of, and contribute to, the nurturing of a dense pattern of social relations with their countries of origin.

In Sassen's account, these ties with the country of origin often provide economic opportunity to migrants. They can use them to develop more or less lucrative business relationships. They can involve themselves in the import and export of goods from their home countries. Relatives brought in to work in family businesses provide both cheap and reliable labour. Like the elites, the immigrants in global cities develop an extra-national orientation, but, obviously, for different reasons.

Global Cities and Global Networks: Hypotheses and Evidence

Sassen suggests a number of globalization-related hypotheses: that the importance of cities is increasingly related to their role in co-ordinating international exchanges; that migration to rich countries is substantially a consequence of rich-country disruption of ways of life in the Third World; that the effect of the migrant flows is to create profound inequality within global cities both because migrants accept low wages and because their arrival puts pressure on the wages of the native-born with similarly low levels of education; and that residents of these cities are increasingly detached from the politics of the nations within which they live. This sort of argument can be extended (e.g., Rumford, 2006) to suggest that important social and economic borders coincide less with those of the nation-state than was previously the case—for example, that those living in New York and Toronto have more in common than either has with those living in their respective national hinterlands. There is clearly something to all of these arguments. Still, some qualification is necessary.

Jeffrey Reitz (1998) has compared the effects of immigration on inequality within cities in three countries—the United States, Canada, and Australia. He shows that outcomes depend heavily on the particular institutional environment within which immigration takes place. Immigrants, in fact, have done relatively (but not absolutely) worse in the United States. That is, over the period he studied their income difference with the native population was larger in the United States than it was in Canada or Australia. This is because stronger unions and higher minimum wages prop up immigrant earnings in these latter two countries. Sassen may have overgeneralized the particular case of the United States.

The US has received a very large flow of *unskilled* immigrants. The evidence tends to suggest that the *aggregate* effect of this on the earnings of unskilled native-born

Tokyo is at the top of a global hierarchy of cities, along with London and New York, providing co-ordination of international economic activities and networks. (Courtesy http://philip.greenspun.com)

employees has been negative but of modest size (e.g., Borjas et al., 1997) but that the effects on earnings within the global cities that are the principal destination of migrants has been quite large (Enchautegui, 1997).

How is it that such a large flow of mainly unskilled immigrants can have such a small *aggregate* effect on the wages and employment probabilities of native unskilled workers? Gregory DeFreitas (1998) proposes the following explanations. The arrival of immigrants increases not only the supply of labour, but also the demand for all sorts of goods being produced by non-immigrants. The proportion of the self-employed among immigrants is high. Many create their own jobs. In addition, and related to the sort of argument made by Sassen, immigrants often occupy jobs that native labour avoids. Many of these jobs would remain unfilled for longer, or not be created at all, were immigrants unavailable to occupy them. Overall, the evidence tends to suggest smaller employment and wage effects of immigration than some of the writing inspired by Sassen would suggest.

As for the question of the location of loyalty within global cities, the political orientations of powerful city elites may shift from the national to the global. They may, for example, become preoccupied with the elimination of obstacles to international trade and investment flows. The sequence of liberalizing policies associated with the GATT and its successor, the WTO, as well as the creation of regional trade associations and agreements such as the EU and NAFTA, would be broadly consistent with this. But protectionist forces remain strong in all countries, including the United States. Because the small size of their domestic markets requires that they engage heavily in trade, much of the pressure to restrict discretionary protectionism originates in countries such as Canada and Australia, where the leading global cities are not located.

With respect to the political orientation of immigrants at the lower end of the income distribution, Portes (Portes, 1999; Portes et al., 1999) has made the following observations. First, immigrant groups vary in the extent to which their members remain oriented to their country of origin. Second, they are more likely to do so where the group was formed by a political convulsion, leading to the simultaneous migration of large numbers of people (for example, Cubans in the United

States); where the group arrives with a culture that provides it with the skills and motivations to develop businesses with contacts to the homeland; where the group confronts fairly clear discrimination in the destination country; and where the government of the country of origin expends funds and effort to develop and maintain ties with expatriate communities.

Third, concerns with the 'cultural integrity and solidarity of the receiving society' are probably exaggerated (Portes, 1999: 469). Foreign-born people make up 17 per cent of the population in Canada, and less than 10 per cent in the United States. Even if their relationship to the host society is problematic, as an aggregate, immigrants are fragmented into their different ethnicities so that it is hard for them to avoid converging with the majority (host) culture to some degree. Finally, where the cultivation of transnational commercial activities enriches members of a particular immigrant group, it decreases the likelihood of the development of a hostile, adversarial culture within subsequent generations.

Cultural Homogenization

Causes of Cultural Convergence

In response to the collapse of the Soviet Union and its empire at the end of the 1980s and the beginning of the 1990s Francis Fukuyama produced his *End of History* (1992). In it he argued that in the competition between institutions liberal democracy had demonstrated its superiority. Communism was discredited and so, more generally, was dictatorship. He did not mean that dictatorships had disappeared, but that the idea of dictatorship was intellectually discredited—something that had certainly *not* been the case during the 1930s when significant numbers of intellectuals were enamoured of either Benito Mussolini or Joseph Stalin. *Here* is a hypothesis of cultural convergence at the grandest scale!

The hypothesis has been subject to vigorous attack. Fukuyama has to some degree retreated from it. Perhaps the most influential alternative originates with Samuel Huntington's *Clash of Civilizations* (1996), which derives much of its influence from the events of 11 September 2001 and their aftermath. Huntington argued that the world is divided into eight major civilizations distinguished by some combination of culture in general, and religion in some cases. The Muslim world is one alternative civilization that is particularly important because of rapid population growth. That growth increases the global weight of Islam. And since, other than those producing oil, Islamic countries are characterized by generally slow economic growth, the population growth creates an increasingly discontented population—a source of political disorder both nationally and internationally. Huntington also identified a 'Sinic' civilization that includes China, other parts of East Asia, and the Chinese diaspora. Here is a thesis of global fragmentation—since in Huntington's view much of what animates political leaders in the Islamic and Sinic civilizations is a resentment of the wealth and hegemony of the West.

Fukuyama and Huntington propose very general and contradictory visions of convergence or divergence. We can perhaps more usefully approach the issue by considering sources of convergence and divergence in more detail and will start with sources of *convergence*.

First, **capitalism** itself has standardizing effects. It implies common economic and social structures: property ownership, a labour force with varying skills, banks and stockbrokers that mobilize and transfer capital, and so on (Holton, 1998; see also Bromley, 1999).

Second, countries have used force to impose cultural practices on other countries. When they decolonized, France and Britain bequeathed boundaries, education systems, civil services, and government institutions to a range of countries in Africa and the Middle East. Modern Japanese institutions bear the heavy stamp of practices imposed by the United States after World War II.

Third, a large volume of more specialized communication between nations—publications, conferences, diplomatic transactions—is concerned with a range of broader political issues. Since there is no single power centre, no world government, controlling those communications, multiple models are introduced into political debate. For John Meyer (2000), this has allowed many non-governmental organizations (NGOs) to insert themselves into political debate and develop alternative policy models that sometimes change government policy. Examples of this are the emergence to policy salience at the international level of issues concerning human rights and the environment, producing more or less binding international agreements (the Kyoto Accord, the Convention on International Trade in Endangered Species, the Ottawa Convention on the Prohibition of Anti-Personnel Mines), coercive political measures (NATO's bombing of the former Yugoslavia), and shared policy priorities (a commitment to create the education system required by a 'knowledge society'). These are a source of social, economic, and political convergence.

Fourth, the policies of many governments in the 1980s shifted to the right, Patricia Marchak (1991) argues, in response to the concerted urging of a set of conservative think-tanks located in several countries, but with links among them. The Cato Institute in the United

States, the Kiel Institute in West Germany, the Mont Pélérin Society in Switzerland, the Institute for Economic Affairs in Britain, and the Fraser Institute in Canada celebrated and advocated free-market solutions to problems, or what they saw as problems. They continue to do so. This common, well-financed network, Marchak claims, generated policy convergence across countries. There was **privatization** (in Canada, for example, the CN railroad network was privatized). There was deregulation, in particular of financial markets. And by the 1990s, some countries had scaled down the magnitude of government expenditures, and more were trying to.

Alternatively, increasing similarities across countries may reflect US hegemony. There is a rising volume of communication between countries using the Internet (Holton, 1998). A disproportionate share of it is in English. This increases the value of the language and the exposure to ideas and preferences originating in English-language media. But while the English language is the primary medium of communication in several societies (including Canada), the sheer volume of communication originating in the United States arguably swamps all other sources. Moreover, businesses and consecutive US administrations have deliberately attempted to break down regulatory obstacles to US cultural products. Jack Valenti, who served for 38 years, until 2004, as the president of the Motion Picture Association of America, a US lobby group, was an indefatigable crusader for the removal of barriers to the entry of US-produced films (McCarthy, 2002). From Henry Ford to McDonald's, the success of the mass marketing of US companies has transformed the tastes and behaviour of consumers and the menu of business models from which investors can draw (Fantasia, 1995; Ritzer, 2000). Some part of whatever cultural convergence may be taking place is likely to reflect the sheer pervasiveness of the United States and its institutions. Table 19.1, which summarizes shares of cultural imports into Canada by country or region of origin, documents the relative dominance of the United States.

These are all real sources of cultural convergence. However, there are reasons to think their effect may be overstated.

Table 19.1 Shares of Cultural Imports[a] into Canada, 1996–2000

	Share (%)[b]					% Change 1996 to 2000
	1996	1997	1998	1999	2000	
North America						
United States	85.5	85.5	84.2	83.4	82.2	–3.9
Other	0.2	0.3	0.4	0.4	0.6	200.0
Total North America	85.7	85.8	84.6	83.8	82.8	–3.4
Western Europe						
United Kingdom	3.0	3.3	3.5	3.3	3.6	20.0
France	3.3	3.3	3.6	3.6	3.6	9.1
Germany	0.8	0.6	0.8	0.8	0.8	0.0
Other	2.5	1.9	2.0	2.2	1.9	–24.0
Total Western Europe	9.6	9.1	9.9	9.9	9.9	3.0
Asia	4.1	4.5	4.8	5.5	6.4	56.1
Other Regions[c]	0.6	0.7	0.7	0.8	0.9	50.0
Total	**100.0**	**100.0**	**100.0**	**100.0**	**100.0**	

[a]'Cultural industries' are defined as books and printing services, newspapers and periodicals, other written materials, music and other recordings, printed music, visual arts, architectural plans, other pictorial material, advertising material, and exposed film.

[b]Columns may not add up to 100 because of rounding.

[c]'Other regions' include European countries not listed above, Middle East, Africa, Central and South America, and the Antilles.

Source: Statistics Canada, 'Market opportunities: International trade of culture goods and services Focus on Culture', Cat. 87-004, Winter 2000, vol. 12 no. 04, at <http://www.statcan.ca/english/freepub/87-004-XIE/0040087-004-XIE.pdf>.

First, while capitalism does imply some common practices, significant differences between capitalist countries persist (Hall and Soskice, 2001). The German and Japanese banking systems tend to provide longer-term credit to their industrial clients than their North American counterparts. Labour law provides greater protections to unions in most of continental Europe and in parts of Canada (particularly Quebec) than in the United States. The size of the public sector in economies varies hugely. The emergence of China as a major economic force further complicates things. There are different views on the character of institutional change in China (cf. Angresano, 2005; Angresano and Fogel, 2006). What is clear is that while, on the one hand, China has substantially become a market economy with private property, a large part of its output continues to originate in state-owned enterprises and the government attempts to control flows of capital (both within the country and from China to other countries) in a way that is much less present in North America or Europe (*The Economist*, 2006). Furthermore, the Chinese government appears interested in extending its influence, including through the endorsement of economic and political models that diverge from those of the West. The US, in other words, is not the only model available to the Third World.

Second, the legacies of colonial powers—both institutional and territorial—have been very much less than immutable. The influence of China described above is one of the mechanisms producing changes. For decades before the 1990s the Soviet Union was a source of pressure for change in the West's former colonies. Internal political processes within former colonies have no doubt been as important in securing changes as have the external influence of the West's political rivals. Many of those in political office in Africa seem willing consumers of illiberal political messages.

Third, since the 1960s nationalist sentiments have grown in a number of countries and regions—in Quebec, in the Basque region in Spain, in Scotland within the United Kingdom, and in a tragically virulent form in the Balkans. Nationalism can be viewed as a forcible assertion of distinctness (Anderson, 1983) and suggests exactly the opposite of cultural convergence. So, for that matter, does the flow of migrants into global cities, where those migrants retain strong connections not only within their migrant communities but also with their countries of origin. Moreover, since many of those migrants are flowing into the United States and shaping US culture, it seems implausible to argue that cultural diffusion is a one-way street.

Fourth, the existence of right-wing think-tanks has certainly not ensured right-wing policies in either rich countries or in the Third World. As we saw above, in rich countries spending on the welfare state has remained generally robust. In recent years left-leaning politicians in South America have won office in Venezuela, Brazil, Bolivia, Chile, and Ecuador.

Fifth, notwithstanding sterling work by a range of well-meaning non-governmental organizations, the track records on human rights of a number of countries in the world suggest that whatever agreement exists at the level of rhetoric, *in practice* there has been no convergence towards a humane rule of law.

The case for cultural convergence or for US cultural hegemony is not overwhelming. Yet, in a thoughtful article, Christoph Brumann says that it strikes him 'how much the general debate relies on *ad hoc* impressions instead of more systematic empirical observation' (1998: 498), but that 'pending further empirical support, I still think that a slow decrease in the total number of distinct cultural elements or traits . . . paralleling a rampant increase of the possible as well as the actual combinations of these elements is the best working hypothesis about current world cultural developments' (ibid., 499).

What Brumann means by this is that modern communications diffuse cultural traits (a process called cultural diffusion) between countries (hence the 'combinations') but that the number of traits tends to decline as the diffused traits replace or modify others in the recipient countries. Popular music in many countries, for example, absorbs musical characteristics from other countries, creating new combinations that appear across those countries. But some of the original national musical forms disappear as these combinations replace them. This process is well illustrated by the conservation work of several late nineteenth- and early twentieth-century European composers: Leoš Janáček and Zoltán Kodály in Czechoslovakia, Béla Bartók in Hungary, and Gustav Holst and Ralph Vaughan Williams in England, all of whom travelled to the countryside of their respective nations to discover and record examples of folk musical forms. They feared the loss of their national musical traditions because of the cultural dominance of Germany, Italy, and France (Schonberg, 1997). Even in France, which has resisted US cultural influences with some vigour, American cinema, cuisine, language, and management practices now exist alongside what might be regarded as 'authentic' French forms (Gordon and Meunier, 2001). And some have noted that many of the policies adopted by ostensibly left-wing governments in Latin America are not very distinct from those that would be adopted by a right-wing government. Thus: 'What's . . . particularly interesting about the recent cycle of elections is how much the economic options of the "leftist" winners, such as Brazil's Luiz Inacio Lula da Silva and Chile's Michelle Bachelet, may resemble those of newly installed "rightist" Mexican President Felipe Calderon' (Frankel, 2006).

At the global level, processes of convergence and divergence seem underway at the same time, depending on the institution (say, mass media versus political structures) and the country (say, Taiwan versus Pakistan). Overgeneralization is, as always, to be avoided!

Conclusion

Different groups of humans have been bumping into each other throughout human history. Thirty thousand years ago, Neanderthals were driven to extinction, probably through contact and competition with the earliest form of modern humans, the Cro-Magnons (Balter, 2001). Two thousand years ago, the Roman Empire was influencing lives from Western Europe to the Middle East (Gibbon, 1994 [1776–88]). Five hundred years ago, a set of European explorers (Magellan, Columbus, Champlain, and others) pushed further the limits of Western influence (Fernández Armesto, 1995) and the settlements that followed brought diseases that devastated the indigenous populations of the New World (Diamond, 1997). One hundred years ago, the European empires were attempting to regulate and were disrupting lives in areas of conquest spanning the globe (Samson, 2001). The time between those events was filled with contact and disruption, often involving amounts of taken-for-granted brutality that challenge modern sensibilities. All this is to say that the facts of contact, constraint, and disruption do not in themselves make distinct what we call contemporary globalization.

What is clearly distinctive about modern relations between individuals and organizations in different countries is the speed and capacity of communication. 'Hot money' flows are usually seen as the clearest expression of this (but see Smith, 2001a). More important, though, is the fact that modern communications have enhanced the degree to which control can be effectively exercised over large distances and have made it possible to run a multinational corporation; a single organization can coordinate production and marketing in different countries. This seems not to imply homogeneity of social and economic policies across countries, but there are strong reasons to believe that the multinational corporation is an effective vehicle for diffusing both business practices and tastes. One need not endorse Bové's actions to recognize that the McDonald's Corporation has had an impact on consumer preferences in many countries and that in doing so it is forcing indigenous competitors in those countries to change their way of doing business.

Still, the idea of a global society is a chimera, an illusion. It certainly does not yet exist, and there is no prospect of its happening in the medium term. The range of social and economic forms remains huge—the WTO and the IMF notwithstanding. What we do confront, as in the past, is a set of international influences and options that constitute both constraints and possibilities. An intelligent reaction to the processes associated with globalization involves discussion of which responses to those constraints are most sensible and which options should be embraced.

Questions for Critical Thought

1. Four components of globalization have been identified: political arrangements, economic processes, the mobility of populations, and cultural diffusion. Do they all have to move in the same direction? For example, is it possible to have common practices created by treaties and liberalized trade while populations are prevented from moving and cultures are protected against processes of diffusion from elsewhere?
2. Would Third World countries be better off without the IMF and the World Bank?
3. Is it sensible to expect investors to always prefer lower taxes? If not, for what purposes are they likely to favour taxes, and for what purposes are they likely to oppose them?
4. Sassen argues that the development of global cities changes the political context in the countries in which the cities are located. Suppose her analysis is correct. Do you judge the implications of her analysis to be good, bad, or neutral? For whom?
5. Over the post-war period, treaties and the international organizations those treaties have created (such as the WTO) have been designed to limit the capacity of governments to use law (through tariffs and quotas) and taxpayers' money (through subsidies) to protect their domestic industries from international competition. Suppose those treaties and international organizations did not exist. Who would gain and who would lose?
6. The Third World is filled with desperately poor people who work at very low wages. In a context of free trade, how is it possible for rich-country employees to keep their jobs?
7. How do the processes associated with globalization affect labour markets and social policy in rich countries?
8. Does Hollywood matter? If so, how?

Recommended Readings

Gary Burtless, *Globophobia: Confronting Fears About Open Trade* (Washington, DC: Brookings Institution, 1998).

Most economists hold favourable views of globalization. This book is one example, providing a generally non-technical and empirical examination of the subject.

Thomas J. Courchene, ed., *Room to Manoeuvre? Globalization and Policy Convergence* (Montreal: McGill-Queen's University Press, 1999).

This is an excellent collection of essays dealing with the implications for Canada of trade agreements and technology, including suggestions by William Watson that the claims about globalization are overstated.

Mauro Guillén, 'Is Globalization Civilizing, Destructive or Feeble? A Critique of Five Key Debates in the Social Science Literature', *Annual Review of Sociology* 27 (2001): 235–60.

This is a quite even-handed treatment of the issue by a sociologist who allows that the process may be thought of as going back 'to the dawn of history'.

Robert J. Holton, *Globalization and the Nation-State* (New York: St Martin's, 1998).

This excellent, balanced treatment of globalization contains a very useful analysis of the process of cultural diffusion.

Naomi Klein, *No Logo: Taking Aim at the Brand Bullies* (New York: Picador, 1999).

This book made Naomi Klein famous. It opposes a number of features of 'corporate rule', including the effects of marketing by multinationals of culture, of globalization on the characteristics of jobs, and of commerce on cities.

John W. Meyer, John Boli, George M. Thomas, and Francisco Ramirez, 'World Society and the Nation-State', *American Journal of Sociology* 103 (1997): 144–81.

Many sociologists are convinced that there is a world culture developing that includes a concern with human rights, democratic forms, and various sorts of entitlements. This article provides a reasonably clear exposition of this position.

Saskia Sassen, *The Global City* (Princeton, NJ: Princeton University Press, 1991).

Sassen is the main source on the social and political consequences of international migration. She attributes large political and economic effects to it.

Adrian Wood, *North–South Trade, Employment and Inequality* (Oxford, UK: Clarendon, 1994).

This is the classic statement on the effects of trade liberalization and competition from the Third World on unskilled wages in rich countries.

Recommended Websites

Canadian Heritage
www.pch.gc.ca

The mandate of the government department Canadian Heritage is to promote Canadian culture, which in practice often means finding ways of resisting US culture. For example, the site lists ways that the department subsidizes the Canadian film, magazine, and book publishing industries.

Council of Canadians
www.canadians.org

This nationalist organization has been uniformly hostile to the two North American trade agreements. Its website provides a good guide to the range of preoccupations of skeptics of the benefits of a more integrated world economy. See, in particular, the discussion of water as a tradable commodity.

Culture et Communications Québec
www.mcc.gouv.qc.ca

This is the website of the Ministry of Culture of the government of Quebec. While the federal government is promoting Canadian culture in general, the Quebec government is, for the most part, promoting French-language culture in particular.

Fair Trade Watch
www.fairtradewatch.org

This website maintained by the United Steel Workers of America provides useful, though unsympathetic, information on the WTO and other international organizations and agreements. It can also be used as a glossary for trade jargon.

International Monetary Fund (IMF)
www.imf.org

This site provides a summary description of the organization, as well as reports on its recent loans to countries and on the conditions imposed on the countries in exchange for the loans.

Motion Picture Association of America (MPAA)
www.mpaa.org

The Motion Picture Association of America is a tireless advocate of the removal of obstacles to the diffusion of that quintessential vehicle of American culture, the cinema. It is also concerned with the protection of copyright.

World Bank
www.worldbank.org

The World Bank is as unpopular with anti-globalization protestors as the IMF, and its website provides some evidence of its concern with its image.

World Trade Organization (WTO)
www.wto.org

The WTO provides both a forum for the negotiation of liberalized trade and investment and a quasi-judicial apparatus issuing judgements on complaints about infractions of trade laws. This website is an extremely useful source on what the WTO actually does.

Chapter 20

Population and Society

Frank Trovato

Learning Objectives

In this chapter, you will:

- Learn the definition of demography and the balancing equation for population change.
- Explore various demographic phenomena, the aggregate expressions of individual behaviour, conditioned by culture and social structure.
- See how the 'population explosion' is a relatively recent phenomenon.
- Study the demographic transition theory, which summarizes the long-term historical trends in birth and death rates and population growth in three stages.
- Compare the demographic transition histories of industrialized and developing countries.
- Explore the implications of Malthusian theory of population growth and available resources.
- Consider the Marxist perspective on population.
- Examine the growth of Canada's population and changing life expectancies over the last century and into the future.

Photo: Reuters/China Daily Information Corp, CDIC

Introduction

At just over 6.5 billion, the population of the world in 2006 is growing at a rate of 1.2 per cent per annum. At this rate of growth, the population increases by about 79 million persons annually. Some scholars view figures such as these with alarm because of the potentially devastating impact continued growth might have on the long-term sustainability of the planet's environment and resources (Meadows et al., 2005). More optimistic pronouncements in the literature suggest that population growth may actually serve as a stimulus to economic growth and, indirectly, to human well-being (Lomborg, 2001; Simon, 1995). As we shall see, a number of competing perspectives exist on the question of population and its relationship to resources and human welfare.

To demographers—scientists who study the census and vital statistics of societies—the term *population* encompasses a number of interrelated dimensions. Samuel Preston, Patrick Heuveline, and Michel Guillot (2001) define *population* as a collection of persons, alive at a specified point in time, that meets certain criteria, of which national and geographic boundaries are two of the most obvious. As a collectivity, a population persists through time even though its members are continuously changing as a result of *attrition* (losses through out-migration and death) and *accession* (gains through births and immigration). A population also entails the aggregate of persons who have ever been alive in a designated national or geographic area, and possibly those yet to be born there. Populations can be projected into the future by using mathematical procedures guided by sound assumptions concerning anticipated changes in fertility, mortality, and migration.

Demographers study the growth, distribution, and development of populations with respect to their geographic concentration and compositional characteristics, of which age, sex, and marital status are especially relevant (though other characteristics such as language, religion, and ethnicity also are important). The natural processes of fertility and mortality, plus *net migration* (the net exchange between numbers of incoming and outgoing migrants), determine change in population size for a specified area or territory over some defined time interval. This is illustrated with the **demographic components equation**:

$$P_{t2} - P_{t1} = (B_{t1,t2} - D_{t1,t2}) + (IN_{t1,t2} - OUT_{t1,t2})$$

Letting P_{t1} and P_{t2} represent the population at the beginning and the end of some specified time interval, the change over this period ($P_{t2} - P_{t1}$) is a function of the difference between births and deaths ($B_{t1,t2} - D_{t1,t2}$) plus the net exchange between the numbers of immigrants ($IN_{t1,t2}$) and emigrants ($OUT_{t1,t2}$) during the interval. The component ($B_{t1,t2} - D_{t1,t2}$) represents natural increase because it measures the difference between the two natural processes of births and deaths; net migration is measured by the term ($IN_{t1,t2} - OUT_{t1,t2}$).

Populations also change as a result of the reclassification of people across distinct statuses. Examples of reclassification include a change in marital status from single to married or from married to divorced. The distribution of the population in accordance with characteristics such as age and sex is also subject to change as a function of changes in fertility, mortality, and migration.

Demographic Change and Social Change

Aggregate demographic phenomena are the collective expression of individual behaviour conditioned by cultural **norms** and **social structure** (Davis and van den Oever, 1982). Often, novel behaviours develop into widespread demographic phenomena. One such behaviour concerns the growing preference among recent generations of youth to form cohabiting unions rather than marriages. In Canada during the early part of the 1970s, only about 17 per cent of couples entering their first union were common-law relationships. By the early

Time to Reflect

The common experience over most of the twentieth century has been for populations to experience growth. However, in recent decades some populations have been experiencing negative natural increase. Can you think of some actual examples of this? Why do you think such populations have negative rates of natural increase? What are the societal factors behind this pattern of population change, and what are the long-term societal consequences of continued negative natural growth?

1980s, the corresponding figure had risen to 40.5 per cent. During the latter part of the 1980s, over half of all first-union couples were common-law (Wu, 2000: 51). Coinciding with the generalized acceptance of cohabitation, there has been a precipitous decline in the total marriage rate of single persons, and the median age at marriage has been going up.

Other examples may be used to illustrate the interconnectedness of demographic factors with societal change. One could, for instance, discuss the evolution of Canadian society into a multicultural and multi-racial nation as a function of shifts in the regional origins of immigrants, from the once-dominant European sending areas to the current predominance of Asia, Africa, and South America as sending regions.

We could also examine how the majority of today's population is alive because of the mortality improvements that took place at the turn of the twentieth century in the industrialized world. As a result of many developments in public health, medicine, and standards of living in the early twentieth century, newborns at that time enjoyed unprecedented gains in survival probabilities over earlier generations in history. Under preceding historical conditions, large proportions of infants and children succumbed to the ravages of infectious and parasitic diseases. Improved socio-economic conditions and public health programs helped babies and young children overcome the dangerous stages of infancy and early childhood. More infants and children would live to adulthood to eventually have their own children, who would later bear progeny of their own under even more favourable health conditions. Kevin White and Samuel Preston (1996) show that approximately half of the population alive today in the United States owe their existence to twentieth-century mortality improvements. In other words, half of the current population would never have been born had it not been for the significant progress in health and disease prevention that took place around the turn of the twentieth century.

David Herlihy (1997) gives another interesting account of how demography and social-structural change are related. He describes how mortality conditions in European history helped provoke lasting social-structural and cultural transformations in Western society. Among other things, he attributes indirect responsibility for the development of the national university system in Europe and for the rise of nationalism to the Black Death (bubonic plague) that struck Europe in 1348 and several times into the fifteenth century. The population of Europe may have been reduced by two-thirds between 1320 and 1420 as a result of this highly infectious disease. Under the spectre of early death, many wealthy people bequeathed their fortunes to institutions such as the church and the educational system. This helped the creation of new national universities throughout Europe. As many of the teachers in the newly created universities were at first unfamiliar with Latin (the language of higher learning at that time), they used the local languages in their teaching. This, according to Herlihy, stimulated the development of strong nationalistic sentiments in the population and the eventual rise of nationalism in Europe.

World Population

The current population of the world and its projected future must be understood in the broader context of human history. Ansley Coale (1974) divides population history into two broad segments of time: the first, from

IN THE FIRST PERSON

When I first entered university, my intention was to eventually study architecture. However, during my first year, I became interested in population studies, a subfield of sociology. I went on to do graduate work in this field and obtained the Ph.D. in 1983. This area of sociology has held my interest for two important reasons: first, it is highly applied and therefore of practical use in a vast array of areas, from urban planning to forecasting future markets, public policy analysis, and health-care planning for governments. Second, demography is immensely interesting because of its interdisciplinary nature and the intellectual challenges it offers.— Frank Trovato

the beginning of humanity to around 1750 CE, was a very long era of slow population growth; the second, relatively brief in broad historical terms, is one of explosive gains in human numbers. According to Coale (1974: 17), the estimated average annual growth rate between 8000 BCE and 1 CE was only 0.036 per year. Between 1 CE and 1750, the average rate of growth rose to 0.056 per cent, and from 1750 to 1800 it went up to 0.44 per cent. In modern times, the trajectory of population growth has followed an exponential pattern (1, 2, 4, 8, 16, . . .): since the early nineteenth century, each successive billion of world population has arrived in considerably less time than the previous one. It took humanity until about 1750 CE to reach a population size of approximately 800 million. The first billion of population occurred in 1804, the second 123 years later in 1927. Thirty-four years beyond that point, the world witnessed its third billion. The 4 billion mark was reached in 1974, only 14 years later, and 13 years passed before the earth welcomed its five-billionth person in 1987 (Birg, 1995: 85; UN Population Division, 1999: 8). In 1999, the globe's population turned 6 billion (see Figure 20.1).

World population growth rates peaked at just over 2.0 per cent during the 1960s and early 1970s. In recent decades the growth rate has been declining to its present level of 1.2 per cent (Population Reference Bureau, 2006). This trend is expected to proceed into the foreseeable future, such that by the year 2050, the growth rate of the world might be as low as 0.5 per cent per year—a rate of growth not seen since the 1920s (Bongaarts and Bulatao, 2000: 20; Eberstad, 1997; Lutz, 1994). This remarkable reduction will come about as a result of anticipated declines in fertility and mortality over the next half-century. The latest medium variant projection of the United Nations (a projection that assumes change in fertility and mortality thought to be most likely, given past trends) assumes that the total fertility rate at the world level will decline from 2.65 children per woman in 2000–5 to about 2.05 children per woman in 2045–50. The change in **life expectancy at**

Most industrialized nations have been experiencing a baby dearth in recent years. In Italy, the pope has urged the population to have more children in order to solve the 'birth rate problem'. In Spain, women are being asked to reproduce for the sake of the nation. (Vince Streano/Corbis/Magmaphoto.com)

Figure 20.1 The World Population Explosion

Most of the world's population increase has taken place in the past two centuries. It took hundreds of thousands of years for the human race to reach its 1960 total of about 3 billion people. But in the 40 years that followed, it grew by another 3 billion people, to its present total of over 6 billion.

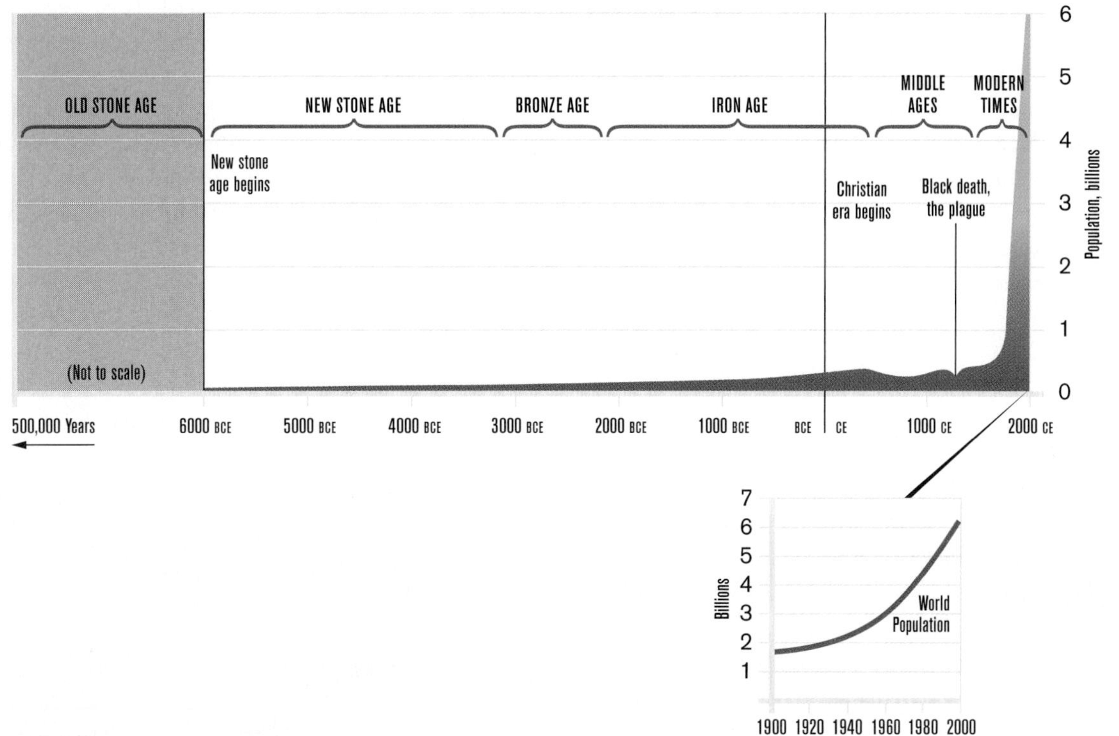

Source: Adapted from Glenn Trewartha, *A Geography of Population: World Patterns* (New York: Wiley, 1969), 29.

World Population Growth through Broad Historical Periods and Projections

Period	Estimated population	Estimated average annual growth rate (%)	Years to add 1 billion
1 million BC–8000 BC	8 million	0.010[1]	
8000 BC–AD 1	300 million	0.036[1]	
AD 1–AD 1750	800 million	0.056[1]	
1804	1 billion	0.400[1]	all of humanity
1927	2 billion	0.540[1]	123
1950	2.5 billion	0.800[1]	—
1960	3 billion	1.7–2.0[2]	33
1974	4 billion	2.0–1.8[2]	14
1987	5 billion	1.8–1.6[2]	13
1999	6 billion	1.6–1.4[2]	12
2013 (projected)	7 billion	1.04[3]	14
2028 (projected)	8 billion	0.90[3]	15
2050 (projected)	9 billion	0.57[3]	22

Note: For the years 2013, 2028, and 2054, the projected populations are based on the UN 2004 revision of World Population Prospects, medium variant (UN, 2006a).

[1] Estimated average population or average rate of growth at the end of the period.

[2] Range of growth rates between specified periods.

[3] Estimated.

Sources: Adapted from Coale (1974); Trewartha (1969); Bongaarts and Bulatao (2000); Population Reference Bureau World Population Data Sheets (various years).

birth during this same period is expected to be from 64.5 years in 2000–5 to 75.1 years in 2045–50 (UN, 2006). This 'central' scenario projection suggests a population in 2050 of just over 9 billion (see Table 20.1).

During this century, population growth will occur unevenly across the major regions of the world. Most of the projected growth will take place in the **developing countries**, especially in the poorest nations, where rates of natural increase remain high. Though fertility has been declining in many developing countries, natural increase is high because of the faster pace of the mortality declines. Although some of the African countries have been hit hard by the HIV/AIDS epidemic and are consequently experiencing either low or negative rates of natural increase (e.g., Botswana, Zimbabwe, Lesotho, South Africa, Swaziland), Africa's share of the world's population will increase rapidly regardless, and is projected to account for 21 per cent of the world's population in 2050 (UN, 2006). The growth rate for the **developed** countries is only 0.1 per cent per year; in nations such as Germany, Italy, and Japan, for example, annual rates of natural increase have been close to zero or slightly negative (Population Reference Bureau, 2006).

Some of the anticipated population growth for the world over the next 50 years is unavoidable. Even if current fertility rates worldwide were to decline suddenly to the replacement level of 2.1 children per woman, substantial population growth would occur. This unavoidable growth is due to the powerful effects of **population momentum** (Bongaarts and Bulatao, 2000; Lutz, 1994). That is, because of past high fertility and mortality declines, the proportion of the world's population in the reproductive ages (roughly ages 15–49) has been growing and is expected to continue to grow over the next several decades. Even with their much reduced fertility rates, large parental cohorts will be bringing more babies into the world than ever before. Even the 'low variant' projection by the United Nations (2006), which assumes substantial declines in fertility, shows a population of about 7.7 billion in 2050. But under this low variant, the population of the world would peak around 2040, then start a course of decline. The projected 7.7 billion number in 2050 under the 'low variant' scenario would be part of a downward trend in world population. Of course, we must recognize that predicting population growth over the long term is an inexact science; the projections depend largely on changes in fertility, which can be a rather unpredictable **variable**. Even small changes in fertility can have dramatic effects on the projected population numbers.

Over the course of this century, all populations in the world will become older as a result of decades of fertility declines worldwide. Countries with more rapid and sustained fertility reductions will experience greater degrees of demographic aging. For example, in 2005, Japan and Italy had the oldest median ages in the world (42.9 and 42.3, respectively). In 2050, the median variant projections for these two countries show their median ages increase to 52.5 and 52.3, respectively (UN, 2006: 31). Italy will see its potential support ratio—the number of persons of working age (15–64) per older person—drop by the year 2050 to less than 2, from its current ratio of about 4. For the Republic of Korea—a society that has also been experiencing rapid fertility declines—the fall in the magnitude of its potential support ratio will be even more dramatic. The United Nations has estimated that Korea's potential support ratio of 12.62 in 1995 will likely reduce to between 2 and 3 by 2050 (UN, 2000a: 7). In 2050, it is anticipated that the world will see 16 per cent of its population being over the age of 65. (In 2005, the percentage was just over 7.) Seniors will account for

Most of the population growth in the coming years will occur in the poorest countries, where rates of natural increase remain high. (Reuters)

Table 20.1 Estimated and Projected Population of the World, Major Development Groups and Major Areas, 1950, 2000, and 2050 According to Different Projection Variants

Major area	Estimated population (millions)		Population in 2050 (millions) by Type of Variant			
	1950	2005	Low	Medium	High	Constant
World	**2,519 (100)**	**6,465 (100)**	**7,680 (100)**	**9,076 (100)**	**10,646 (100)**	**11,658 (100.0)**
More developed regions	813 (32.2%)	1,211 (18.7%)	1,057 (13.8%)	1,236 (13.8%)	1,440 (13.6%)	1,195 (10.3%)
Less developed regions	1,707 (67.6%)	5,253 (81.3%)	6,622 (86.2%)	7,840 (86.2%)	9,206 (19.1%)	10,463 (89.7%)
Least developed countries	201	759	1,497	1,735	1,994	2,744
Other less developed countries	1,506	4,4949	5,126	6,104	7,213	7,719
Africa	224 (8.9%)	906 (14.0%)	1,666 (21.7%)	1,937 (21.7%)	2,228 (21.3%)	3,100 (26.6%)
Asia	1,396 (55.4%)	3,905 (60.4%)	4,388 (57.1%)	5,217 (57.1%)	6,161 (57.5%)	6,487 (55.6%)
Europe	547 (21.7%)	728 (11.3%)	557 (7.2%)	653 (7.2%)	764 (7.2%)	606 (5.2%)
Latin America/Caribbean	167 (6.6%)	561 (8.7%)	653 (8.5%)	783 (8.5%)	930 (8.6%)	957 (8.2%)
Northern America	172 (6.8%)	331 (5.1%)	375 (4.9%)	438 (5.6%)	509 (4.8%)	454 (3.9%)
Oceania	13 (0.5%)	33 (0.5%)	41 (0.5%)	48 (0.5%)	55 (0.5%)	55 (0.5%)

Note: The sum of least developed and other less developed countries adds up to the total population for the less developed countries. The sum of the six regions adds up to the overall world total population. The United Nations (2003: xiv) considers as 'less developed regions' the regions of Africa, Asia (excluding Japan), Latin America and the Caribbean, as well as Melanesia, Micronesia, and Polynesia. The 'more developed' regions comprise Australia/New Zealand, Europe, Northern America, and Japan. The 'least developed' countries consist of 49 nations: Afghanistan, Angola, Bangladesh, Benin, Bhutan, Burkina Faso, Burundi, Cambodia, Cape Verde, Central African Republic, Chad, Comoros, Democratic Republic of the Congo, Djibouti, Equatorial Guinea, Eritrea, Ethiopia, Gambia, Guinea, Guinea-Bissau, Haiti, Kiribati, Lao People's Democratic Republic, Lesotho, Liberia, Madagascar, Malawi, Maldives, Mali, Mauritania, Mozambique, Myanmar, Nepal, Niger, Rwanda, Samoa, Sao Tome and Principe, Senegal, Sierra Leone, Solomon Islands, Somalia, Sudan, Togo, Tuvalu, Uganda, United Republic of Tanzania, Vanuatu, Yemen, and Zambia.

Source: UN (2006a: xviii).

Time to Reflect

What does it mean to say that some of the projected population growth of the world into the next half-century or so is 'unavoidable'?

almost 26 per cent of the population in the developed countries, while in the developing regions as a whole, this proportion will rise to almost 15 per cent (Bongaarts and Bulatao, 2000: 23; UN, 2006: 24).

Age Compositions of Developed and Developing Countries

The different demographic experiences of the developed and developing countries are reflected in their respective **age compositions**. Fertility plays a greater role than mortality in determining the age composition of a population (Coale, 1964; Coale and Hoover, 1958; Frejka, 1973; Keyfitz, 1968). The higher a population's fertility, the larger the percentage of the population in the younger ages. Low-fertility populations have proportionately fewer people in the younger ages and relatively more in the older ages (see Figure 20.2).

The age distribution of the developed countries manifests a slow-growing population, with relatively few people below age 15. Sustained low fertility rates in these countries are responsible for this. On the other hand, the age distribution of the least developed countries characterizes a rapidly growing population, approximating the shape of a pyramid: a wide base and a narrow top. For the other developing countries there is evidence of recent fertility declines, as the bottom of the pyramid has narrowed. However, in comparison to the developed countries, both categories of developing countries show a larger proportion of their population as being under the age of 15.

Owing to decades of high fertility and rapid population growth, the societies of the developing world must cope with huge waves of young people seeking productive work (Cleland, 1996). Assuming that sufficient work is made available, a youthful labour force would actually help boost productivity, economic growth, and prosperity. The key is for governments to provide economic growth and jobs for their burgeoning youthful labour force. Failure to do so may provoke extreme social unrest and political instability. Widening regional inequalities in wealth and resources would help promote illegal and clandestine migrations, possibly exacerbating existing political tensions between nations (Clarke, 1996; Cleland, 1996; Homer-Dixon et al., 1993; McCarthy, 2001; Meadows et al., 1992, 2005; Peterson, 1999; Pimentel and Pimentel, 1999).

Theories of Population Change

Two influential themes can be identified in the literature regarding the interrelationship of population and resources. The first proposes that curbing population growth is essential for maintaining a healthy balance between human numbers, resources, and the sustainability of the environment; the second characterizes population as a minor or inconsequential factor in such matters. Thomas Malthus and Karl Marx (with Friedrich Engels) are the principal thinkers representing these opposing views. Before examining their ideas, let us review another influential theory of population dynamics: the demographic transition theory.

Demographic Transition Theory

The **demographic transition** theory was first developed on the basis of the experience of Western European countries with respect to their historical pattern of change in birth and death rates in the context of socioeconomic modernization. In general terms, the theory can also describe the situation of the developing countries, though the structural conditions underlying changes in vital rates are recognized as being substantially different from the European case (Kirk, 1996; Teitelbaum, 1975). The demographic transition of Western societies entailed three successive stages: (1) a pre-transitional period of high birth and death rates with very low population growth; (2) a transitional phase of high fertility, declining death rates, and explosive growth; (3) a final stage of low mortality and fertility and low natural increase. (The second stage may be divided into early and late Stage 2.) By the early 1940s, most European

Figure 20.2 Comparison of Age Structures: Population by Age, Sex, and Development

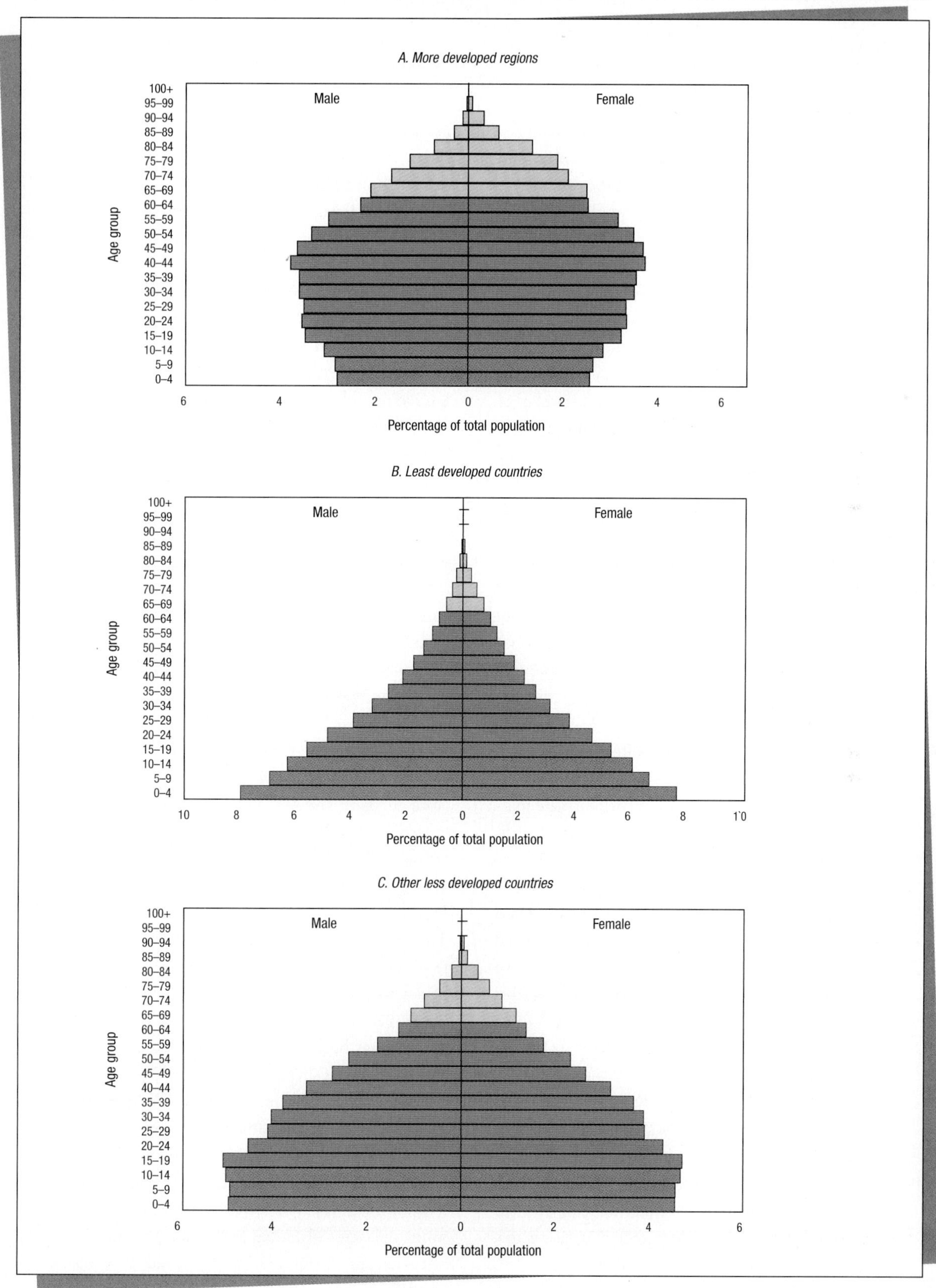

Source: UN (2006a: 27).

OPEN FOR DISCUSSION

Sex Ratio Imbalances and the Marriage Market

A population's age distribution mirrors its experience with respect to fertility, mortality, and migration. The **sex ratio** measures the balance of males and females in a population (males/females = 100). A sex ratio of 100 indicates an equal number of males and females, whereas a ratio below 100 denotes that the number of women exceeds the number of men. Values in excess of 100 mean there are more men than there are women.

In most populations, the overall sex ratio is usually just below 100. This is due to the interplay of three demographic factors: (1) the sex ratio at birth favours males, as for every 100 baby girls, there are usually 105 baby boys; (2) in most populations, the death rates for males are greater than the death rates for females; (3) in some populations, males have greater rates of emigration than do females. Distortions in the overall sex ratio can occur from any or all of these conditions. Severe distortions in these factors can cause the sex ratio to be substantially above or below 100. For instance, in a balanced population, a sudden influx of male workers might raise the sex ratio. On the other hand, a large-scale emigration of males could have the opposite effect.

Sex ratio imbalances can also occur in specific age categories. In some situations, the marriage market (that is, the balance of eligible young men to eligible young women) is affected as a result of either a shortage or a surplus of males or females in the prime marriageable ages. This type of phenomenon is not uncommon. For example, it has been reported recently that in China there is a serious deficit of young women for the number of eligible young men to marry—the number of young men is much greater than that of potential brides (Tuljapurkar, Li, and Feldman, 1995).

According to demographers, this problem stems from the Chinese government's implementation of the one-child policy, initiated in the late 1970s. The Chinese have a traditional preference for sons. Given the government's one-child directive, over the past several decades many couples, it is suspected, have been resorting to sex-selective abortion to ensure having a sole male child (Tuljapurkar, Li, and Feldman, 1995). As explained in the following article, over the course of two or more decades, this situation has helped produce in China a highly distorted marriage market: too few young women for marriage to eligible young men.

With Women So Scarce, What Can Men Do?

Years of female infanticide help shatter the taboo on incestuous marriages

Liu Dehai and Hai Hongmei's matrimonial bed is laid with a thick quilt embroidered with the characters for 'double happiness', words meant to augur good fortune for just-married Chinese couples. This should be a room of joy and hope, but Liu's mother doesn't want anyone investigating too closely. 'Please,' she says, 'do not speak of this room.' The marriage of Liu and Hai is a subject of shame, for they are not just husband and wife; they are also first cousins.

Their marriage, and others of cousins and even siblings, is the latest consequence of China's profound shortage of females. For two decades, the government has tried to control population by limiting most rural families to one child, two if the first is a girl. Because boys are prized in rural areas—they can work the land and give more support to their families—this has led many couples to abort female fetuses, kill newborn daughters, or neglect them to death. The result: China, according to the World Health Organization, is short 50 million females. The first wave of children born under the policy is reaching marriageable age, and there are far too few brides to go around. The most desperate bachelors have taken to marrying relatives. In a few places, the practice has become so common, the communities are referred to as 'incest villages'.

Liu Dehai never imagined he would marry his shy first cousin Hai. Though intramarriage was common in imperial days, it is taboo in modern China. But at age 20, with his friends already paired off, Liu found himself the odd man out. His parents, farmers in the village of Nanliang in Shaanxi province, could not raise the $2,000 required to attract a woman to Nanliang to marry their son. With so many men to choose from, women are loath to settle in hardscrabble villages like Nanliang. Desperate, Liu's mother contacted her sister and requested a favour: Could she ask Hai to be Liu's bride? Young women like Hai are not apt to defy their parents. And so Liu and Hai were wed. While a recent US study concluded that the odds of first cousins producing children with birth defects may have been overstated, the risk is still almost double that for unrelated couples. Denizens of the incest villages see ample evidence of this. Near the city of Yan'an, a brother and sister squat in the mud-brick slums, signing a secret language to each other: both Cao Shuai and Cao Jing were born deaf, to parents who are first cousins. Early this year in Yan'an county, a severely retarded newborn girl was found abandoned beside a road. Her parents, it turned out, were brother and sister.

The female shortage in China is only worsening. In 2000, 900,000 fewer female births were recorded than should have been, based on male births. In 1990 the shortfall was 500,000. Some of that owes to parents giving up daughters for adoption without registering their birth. But population experts at the Chinese Academy of Social Sciences in Beijing estimate that up to one-third of the girls are missing because of gender-based abortions. Rural Chinese women also tend to breast-feed girls for shorter periods, providing less hope for survival. Chinese demographers estimate that in some rural areas, 80 per cent of children ages 5 to 10 are boys.

In Shaanxi's Qiaogou village, children play under a dusty apple tree. The noise is the raucous glee of boys being boys. There is only one girl among them. Asked what he thinks his future will hold, Xiaochun, 7, replies, 'I'll get married and be a good farmer, of course.' Where will he get a wife? 'I think in other villages far away, there are many more girls', Xiaochun says. 'I will get my wife from there.' Across China, millions of boys are hoping the same thing, but only a few will ever meet the woman of their dreams.

Source: Hannah Beech/Nanliang, 'With Women So Scarce, What Can Men Do?', *Time*, 1 July 2002, 8. ©TIME Inc. Reprinted by permission.

societies had completed their demographic transitions (see Figure 20.3).

Crude birth and death rates in the ancient world probably fluctuated between 35 and 45 per 1,000 population (Coale, 1974: 18). With gradual improvements in agriculture and better standards of living, the death rate declined, though fertility remained high. During the second stage, the excess of births over deaths was responsible for the modern rise of population—the so-called population explosion (McKeown, 1976). With gradual modernization and socio-economic development, during the middle and later years of the nineteenth century, birth rates in Europe began to fall, first in France and then in other countries. In the early 1930s, Western nations had attained their lowest birth rates up to that point in their histories; the death rate was also quite low by historical standards, and a new demographic equilibrium had been reached. In pre-transition times, the low growth rates were the result of humans' lack of control over nature; the end of the demographic transition came from incremental controls over nature—agricultural development, industrialization, **urbanization**, economic growth, and modern science and medicine.

Modifications to Demographic Transition Theory

Coale (1969, 1973) undertook an extensive investigation to re-examine the causes of the European fertility transition. Theorists had proposed that in pre-transitional societies, conscious use of family limitation was absent, that economic development and urbanization preceded the onset of fertility declines, and that a drop in mortality always occurred prior to any long-term drop in the birth rate (Davis, 1945; Notestein, 1945; Thompson, 1929, 1944). But some of the empirical evidence uncovered by Coale failed to support some of these propositions. For instance, one important discovery was that economic development is not always a precondition for a society to experience the onset of sustained declines in fertility (though economic development would help speed up the transition). Coale concluded that sustained fertility declines in a society would take place when three preconditions were met: (1) fertility decisions by couples must be within the calculus of conscious choice; that is, cultural and religious norms do not forbid couples to practise family planning, nor do they promote large families; (2) reduced fertility must be viewed by couples as economically advantageous; and (3) effective methods of fertility control must be known and available to couples (Coale, 1969, 1973; Coale and Watkins, 1986).

Having long completed their mortality and fertility transitions, the industrialized countries have gained widespread economic success; their populations enjoy a

HUMAN DIVERSITY

Youth in the International Labour Market

As the world's population surges past the six-billion mark . . . 700 million young people will enter the labour force in developing countries—more than the entire workforce of the developed world in 1990—the United Nations says.

And as the largest-ever group of young people enters its child-bearing and working years, the number of people over the age of 65 continues to swell as health and longevity improve, according to the UN's annual State of the World Population report. . . .

If jobs can be found or created for the global bulge of one billion people between the ages of 15 and 24—the result of past high fertility—there is a chance to increase human capital so that the dependent young and elderly age groups can be better cared for, the report said.

But without investment in jobs for the young, better education for children, especially girls, and better health care for both young and old, social unrest and instability are inevitable.

'The rapid growth of young and old "new generations" is challenging societies' ability to provide education and health care for the young, and social, medical and financial support for the elderly', the report says. . . .

Some developing nations, particularly in Southern Asia and Northern Africa, could reap an economic windfall in the next couple of decades as the bulge in 15- to 24-year-olds swells the workforce in comparison to dependent age groups, the report says.

To avoid squandering this one-time 'demographic bonus', these countries will have to ensure their young people can find jobs and don't start families too soon.

Stan Bernstein, chief author of the UN report and a research adviser at the UN Population Fund, said developing countries need both private and public, domestic and international investment in their basic social services to ensure they don't miss this 'window of opportunity'.

Global Population Growth by Age Group

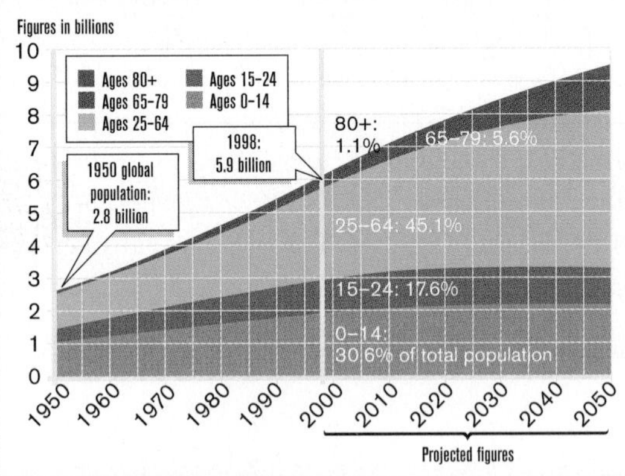

Source: : United Nations, *State of the World Population Report.*

It is in the interest of wealthier nations and private companies to make this investment, Mr Bernstein said in a phone interview from New York yesterday.

'These countries, if given the opportunity to accelerate their development now, are going to be significant economic, trade and social partners in the future. It's a win-win situation.'

However, with most developed nations steadily reducing the amount of foreign aid they provide, and cutting their own social-service budgets, other sources of investment are needed. . . .

At the other end of the age spectrum, a rapidly growing population over the age of 60—578 million this year—is seeing more years of healthy life, is able to work longer and is moving toward greater independence from grown children. . . .

Source: From Jane Gadd, 'Record Numbers of Youth Will Seek Work: UN', *Globe and Mail,* 2 Sept. 1998. Reprinted with permission from The Globe and Mail.

Figure 20.3 The Classical Demographic Transition Model and Corresponding Conceptual Types of Society

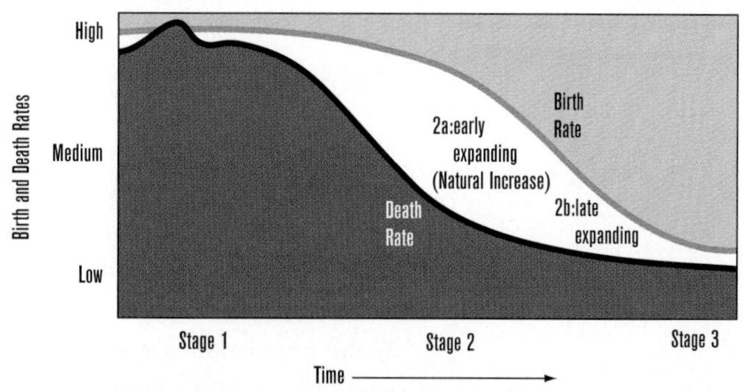

Stage	Fertility	Mortality	Population Growth	Economy
1. Pre-industrial	High, fluctuating	High, fluctuating (low life expectancy)	Static to very low	Primitive or agrarian
2. Early industrial	High	Falling	High, explosive	Mixed
3. Modern urban industrial	Controlled: low to moderate to sub-replacement levels	Low (high life expectancy)	Low to moderate to negative	Urban industrial to post-industrial

Source: Adapted from Glenn Trewartha, *A Geography of Population: World Patterns* (New York: Wiley, 1969), 45, 47.

great deal of social and economic security and well-being. Couples in these societies see little need to have large families. In many developing countries, however, entrenched cultural norms and traditions favour high fertility; parents tend to view children as a source of security in an insecure environment (Cain, 1983; Caldwell, 1976). Nevertheless, over recent decades much progress has been made in raising the prevalence levels of contraceptive practices. Organized family planning programs have played a major role in this trend (Caldwell et al., 2002). New evidence suggests a growing number of developing nations are now approaching the end of their demographic transitions, and others in the poorer regions of the world (for example, sub-Saharan Africa) have recently begun their fertility transitions (Bulatao, 1998; Bulatao and Casterline, 2001).

Demographic Transitions of Industrialized and Developing Countries

Figure 20.4 displays in schematic form the demographic transitions of the West and of the contemporary developing countries, the latter subdivided into 'transitional' and 'delayed transition' societies. Examples of transitional populations are India, Turkey, China, Indonesia, Taiwan, Thailand, Mexico, and countries in Latin America and the Caribbean. Delayed transition societies are found in sub-Saharan Africa, southern Africa, and southwest Asia (for example, Afghanistan, Pakistan, and Bangladesh). In both these cases, mortality reductions have been fairly rapid. In the European historical context, health improvements occurred more gradually in response to incremental socio-economic advancements and economic modernization. In the developing countries, declining

Time to Reflect

Do you think it is possible for a country to experience significant economic growth in the absence of having completed the demographic transition? Is the completion of demographic transition a prerequisite for economic and social development in a country?

Figure 20.4 Schematic Representation of Demographic Transition: Western, Delayed, and Transitional Models

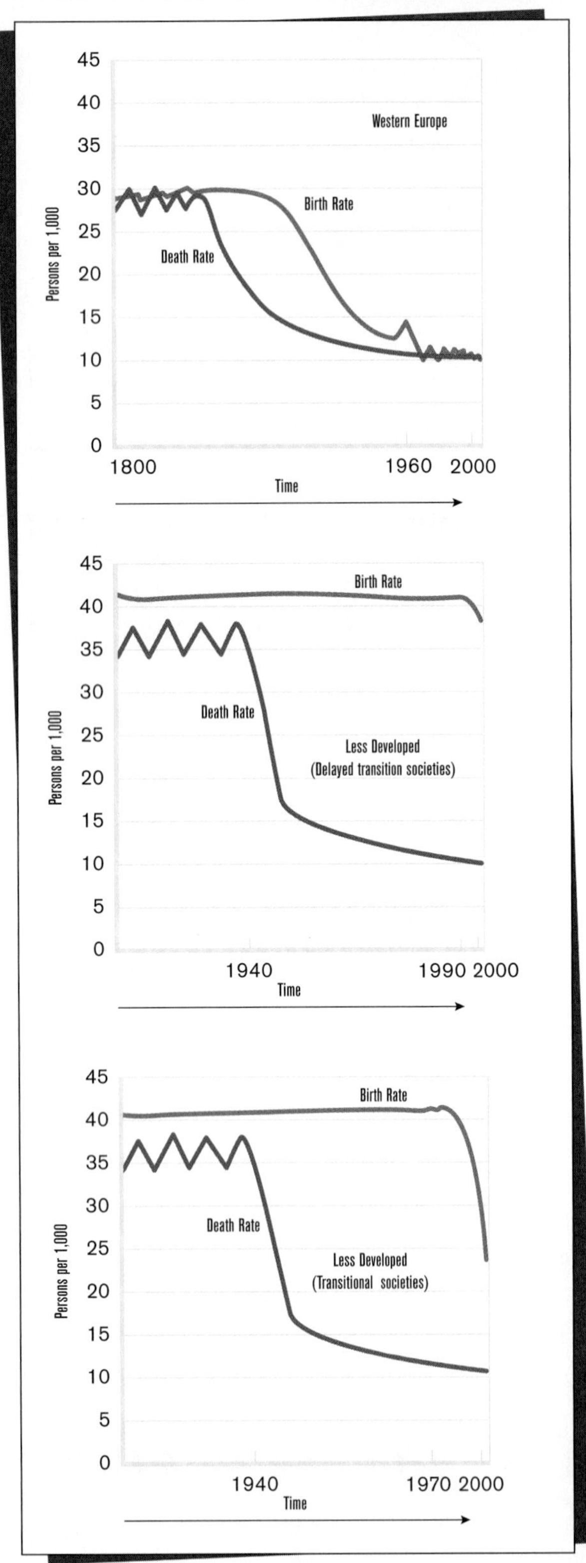

Source: Adapted from Glenn Trewartha, *A Geography of Population: World Patterns* (New York: Wiley, 1969), 45, 46.

death rates have been achieved through family planning, public health programs, and other medical interventions offered by the industrialized countries (Preston, 1986b).

Malthusian Theory

Thomas Malthus (1766–1834) was an ordained Anglican minister and professor of political economy in England. His most famous work, *An Essay on the Principle of Population,* was published in 1798. This important treatise has had a lasting influence on subsequent theorizing about population matters. At the time that Malthus wrote his *Essay,* a number of scholars had already contributed serious thoughts on the question of population and resources. For instance, the Enlightenment theorists Jean-Jacques Rousseau, Marie-Jean-Antoine-Nicolas de Caritat Marquis de Condorcet, and William Godwin viewed population growth as a positive development (Overbeek, 1974). A growing population would help stimulate economic growth, and with further advances in civilization, there would be a natural tendency for subsistence to increase faster than population. Malthus reacted strongly to such optimistic views; he was less optimistic about humanity's capacity to maintain a sustainable balance between available resources and population growth. He set out to warn humanity about the dangers of unchecked population growth.

Citing directly from the work of Malthus, Alan Macfarlane identifies three fundamental themes in the *Essay.*

> The first is that human beings are very strongly motivated by a desire for sexual intercourse:
>
>> 'The passion between the sexes has appeared in every age to be so nearly the same, that it may always be considered, in algebraic language, as a given quantity.
>>
>> 'All else being equal, men and women will mate as soon as possible after puberty. If such mating is only permitted within marriage,
>>
>> 'Such is the disposition to marry, particularly in very young people, that, if the difficulties of providing for a family were entirely removed, very few would remain single at twenty-two . . . .'
>
> The second fact is the high fertility of humans. If this high fertility is combined with a reasonable rate of mortality, such early and frequent mating will lead to rapid population growth. . . . The third fact is that economic resources, and in particular food production, cannot

> keep pace with this population growth within a basically agrarian economy largely dependent on human labour. This is due to the law of diminishing marginal returns. While there may be periods when rates of growth in agriculture rise to three or four per cent per annum, which is equivalent to a doubling of food in a generation, such periods cannot be sustained for more than a few decades. (Macfarlane, 1997: 12–13)

Malthus assumed an inherent tendency in humans to increase in numbers beyond the means of subsistence available to them. Mankind, he argued, lives at the brink of subsistence. Population, left unchecked, tends to double once every generation; it thus follows a geometric, or exponential, progression (1, 2, 4, 8, 16, 32, . . .). The food supply, on the other hand, tends to grow arithmetically (1, 2, 4, 6, 8, 10, . . .). Under this scenario, in the long term, population would eventually outstrip food and other essential resources.

As a solution to this problem, Malthus proposed that population could be kept in equilibrium through the activation of two different mechanisms. The first is what he called positive checks (also referred to as vice and misery). These are conditions that raise the death rate and thus serve to reduce population—famine, pestilence, war, and disease. The second, and more desirable alternative, would be widespread exercise of preventive checks (also referred to as moral restraint) to curb population growth—the imposition of the human will to deliberately curtail reproduction through celibacy, postponed marriage, and sexual abstinence. By postponing marriage until people were in an adequate position to maintain a family, individuals and society would gain economically: by working longer before marriage, people would save more of their incomes, thus helping to reduce poverty and raise the overall level of well-being. Malthus considered abortion and contraception to be immoral.

Criticism of Malthusian Theory

Malthusian theory has provoked strong reactions. One criticism is that Malthus failed to fully appreciate the resilience of humanity when faced with difficult problems. Throughout history, humanity has shown a remarkable ability to solve many of its predicaments. Writers point out that progress in science, technology, and socio-economic well-being has evolved in tandem with explosive population growth and that the agricultural and industrial revolutions arose in response to problems and demands arising from a rapidly growing population (Boserup, 1965, 1981; Fogel and Costa, 1997; Simon, 1995, 1996).

Malthus suggested that population and food supply must be in balance. But exactly what constitutes an 'optimum' population size is difficult, if not impossible, to specify. Perceptions of the 'optimal', in this sense, are highly dependent on available resources to a society, as well as on consumption patterns and the degree of economic activity and production. Consumption and production are closely tied to a society's cultural standards for material comfort and demand for consumer products. As described by Paul Ehrlich and J.P. Holdren (1971), the potential impact of population on the environment is multiplicative. That is, the effect of the population depends partly on its size and growth, but also on a society's level of affluence and technological complexity. In a slow-growing population with strong material expectations, the potential for environmental and resource depletion may be greater than in a fast-growing population with lower levels of material aspirations and technological sophistication. The more developed the society, the higher the expected standard for 'basic' necessities. As material aspirations rise, so do levels of consumption and expenditures by the public. Increased consumer demand for material goods spurs economic activity; greater levels of economic activity heighten the risk of environmental damage because of increased pollution and resource depletion (Ehrlich and Ehrlich, 1970, 1990).

It has been proposed that industrial societies may be facing an inversion of the Malthusian scenario (Woolmington, 1985). In these societies, overpopulation is no longer the threat Malthus advocated. Rather, the seeds of systemic instability in these societies may lie more in their reliance on endless economic growth and consumption. Rather than population pressing on resources, as was proposed by Malthus, the economy now presses the population to consume—economic growth and stability depend on this. However, in the long term, the spiral of consumption and production may not be sustainable in slow-growing or declining populations (ibid.).

Finally, Malthus's insistence on the unacceptability of birth control is inconsistent with his advocacy of curbing rapid population growth. The reality is that people throughout the centuries have always resorted to some means of birth control at one time or another. As stated by Eric Ross (1998: 3):

> Malthus recognized that a desire for children could be moderated by human reason and ingenuity, but failed to advocate any particular method, including non-coital sex, coitus interruptus, abortion and contraception, and actually branded them as 'vice' or 'improper acts'. Nev-

> ertheless, one of these so-called vices—coitus interruptus, or 'withdrawal' . . . continued to be one of the most popular and effective forms of contraception well into the second half of the twentieth century . . . largely because it was safe, free, and remarkably effective.

The Marxist Perspective on Population

Marxist scholars have refuted the Malthusian principles. They contend that population is a secondary issue to the pernicious problems of widespread economic inequality and poverty. Large families arise from poverty. With Friedrich Engels, Marx advocated the elimination of hunger, poverty, and human suffering through the radical restructuring of society to ensure the equitable distribution of wealth and resources (Marx and Engels, 1970 [1845–6]). As for poor developing nations, their population predicament can be traced to their relative economic deprivation. In response to Malthus's principle that population grows geometrically, it also is the case that scientific and technological solutions tend to progress geometrically. Scientific and technological progress could be used to relieve human suffering.

The Marxist perspective is grounded in the idea that socio-economic inequality is a root cause of human problems and suffering. However, in matters of population control, Marxist skepticism towards the role of population in human problems is now largely ignored (Petersen, 1989). China—a Communist state—has outwardly rejected the Marxist doctrine of population. Chinese officials have recognized that slowing population growth through concerted family planning policies is, in the long term, essential to societal well-being (Bulatao, 1998; Caldwell et al., 2002; Haberland and Measham, 2002). With few exceptions, developing countries now embrace population policies that are consistent with neo-Malthusian principles. Family planning and reproductive health programs are recognized by governments as critical means in their quest to curb population growth.

Contemporary Perspectives on Population

Neo-Malthusian scholars—the contemporary followers of Malthus—believe that the world's population has been growing too fast and that the planet is already close to reaching critical ecological limits. Unlike Malthus, however, neo-Malthusians view contraception and family planning as a key element in population control (Ehrlich and Ehrlich, 1990). The neo-Malthusian perspective inherently implies that the world would be a better and safer place if it contained fewer people. An expanding population in conjunction with excessive consumerism and economic production will, in the long term, lead to the depletion of essential resources and to ecological breakdown.

Neo-Marxist scholars place less emphasis on the centrality of population as a source of human predicaments. Focusing on population as the root cause of human suffering obscures the reality that the world is divided into wealthy and relatively poor regions and that this divide is widening rather than narrowing. Neo-Marxists alert us to the extreme consumerism of wealthy regions and their overwhelming economic and political influence over less advantaged nations. It is also argued that the **globalization** of capital—seen by many other observers as the key to emulating the 'success story' of the West—often exacerbates, rather than diminishes, socio-economic disparities within and across societies. Investigations by neo-Marxist scholars tend to focus their analyses on regional inequalities in resources and wealth and on the political and economic dependence of developing countries on the developed nations. Some nations enjoy inordinate power and influence over others (Gregory and Piché, 1983; Wimberley, 1990). In this connection, Andre Gunder Frank (1991) has coined the phrase 'the underdevelopment of development' to refer to the overwhelming influence and control the world's major economic powers hold over the developing countries. Development, it is argued, serves mostly the interests of the most powerful nations. Aid received by the poor nations comes at the cost of being in a persistent state of dependence on the providers.

Other writers concerned with the complex interactions of population, environment, and resources take a revisionist stance on such questions. Revisionists are neither neo-Marxists nor neo-Malthusians (Ahlburg, 1998; Cincotta and Engelman, 1997; Clarke, 1996; Evans, 1998; Furedi, 1997; National Research Council, 1986). Julian Simon (1995, 1996), for instance, has written that population growth historically has been, on balance, beneficial to humankind—people are the 'ultimate resource', Simon contends.

The US National Research Council's report on population, environment, and resources (1986) exemplifies a revisionist perspective. This committee has proclaimed that, in some cases, population may have no discernable relationship to some of the problems often attributed to it. The report also concludes that population's relationship to depletion of exhaustible resources is statistically

Is the poverty shown in this photograph a result of overpopulation or of unequal access to resources and opportunities? This is a shantytown just outside of the commercial district in Buenos Aires, Argentina. (Mariana Bazo/Reuters)

weak and often exaggerated. Indeed, income growth and excessive consumption are more important factors in this sense: a world with rapid population growth but slow increases in income might experience slower resource depletion than one with a stationary population but rapid increase in income. It was found, also, that reduced rates of population growth would increase the rate of return to labour and help bring down income inequality in a country.

The National Research Council committee also suggested that while rapid population growth is directly related to the growth of large cities in the **Third World**, its role in urban problems is most likely secondary. Ineffective or misguided government policies may play a more important role in the development of urban problems. Moreover, the committee has noted that although it is often assumed in the literature that reducing population growth leads to a reduction in poverty and income inequality, in fact this relationship holds to a certain point only. For instance, if the population of Bangladesh were halved, its status as a poor nation would not change appreciably; it would move from being the second poorest nation in the world to thirteenth poorest (National Research Council, 1986). Many factors beyond rapid population growth are responsible for poverty (Keyfitz, 1993).

Canada's Population: An Overview

Components of Growth

Canada is the second largest territory in the world (only Russia is larger). It is a sparsely populated country. Its population density in 2001 was 3.3 inhabitants per

Time to Reflect

Reflect on your own views regarding the relationship of population to environment and resources. Is your view more consistent with Malthus or Marx? Or is your view perhaps different from that of either of these two thinkers?

square kilometre, one of the lowest in the world. According to the 2001 census, Canada's population was just over 30 million (Statistics Canada, 2003d). In July of 2006, the population stood at 32.6 million (Statistics Canada, 2006j). At the time of its first national census, in 1851, the country had only 2.4 million residents. In the 1931 census, Canada recorded its first 10 million inhabitants. By 1967, the year of its first centennial as a country, the population had grown to over 20 million (Statistics Canada, 2003d).

What is the role of the demographic components of fertility, mortality, and migration in this development? Table 20.2 looks at the components of population growth from 1851–61 to 1996–2001. Historically, natural increase has been the principal driving force behind population growth (see the second-last column in the table). However, since the middle of the 1980s, the contribution of net migration has been rising in prominence, such that in the interval between 1986–91 and 1996–2001, net migration accounted for 56 per cent of the growth in Canada's population during this interval, and natural increase contributed 44 per cent. Declining birth rates coupled with rising levels of international migration account for this fact. This situation highlights the importance of immigration for the long-term maintenance of Canada's population in a context of sub-replacement fertility.

Mortality

Changes in mortality can be monitored by examining measures such as the crude death rate, life expectancy, and infant mortality. The crude death rate is the number of deaths in a given year divided by the mid-year population, usually expressed per 1,000 population. Canada's crude death rate in 2001 was 7 per 1,000 population. Since the early 1920s, Canada has witnessed a steady decline in its crude death rate, from 11.6 per 1,000 population in 1921 to 10.1 in 1941 and 7.7 in 1961, the latter being very close to the 2002 rate.

Unfortunately, the crude death rate is not the best indicator of mortality as it fails to take into account the confounding effects of age composition. In some cases, reliance on this measure can seriously distort comparative analyses of mortality. Measures such as life expectancy at birth and the infant mortality rate provide more accurate accounts of mortality conditions as they mirror a society's overall level of socio-economic development and standard of living. Life expectancy at birth represents the average number of years of life remaining for a newborn baby under prevailing mortality conditions in society. Infant mortality is defined as the number of deaths of infants in a given year divided by the number of live births in that year. These two measures are inversely related: when infant mortality is high, life expectancy at age zero will be relatively low, and vice versa. In 2006, Canadians (men and women combined) enjoyed a life expectancy at birth of 80 years. By comparison, the corresponding life expectancy for Mexicans was 75 years. Closely tied to this survival gap is the wide discrepancy in the infant mortality rates of these two societies—5.3 infant deaths per 1,000 live births in Canada versus 21.0 in Mexico (Population Reference Bureau, 2006).

In general, women live longer than men (El-Badry, 1969; Vallin, 1983). The literature emphasizes the interaction of biology and environment as the underlying basis of this differential (Gove, 1973; Nathanson, 1984; Perls and Frets, 1998). The Population Reference Bureau (2006) reports that life expectancies for men and women in the more developed regions of the world are 73 and 80, respectively. For the less developed countries (excluding China), the corresponding life expectancies are much lower—65 and 69 years, respectively. Since the 1990s there have been setbacks in life expectancy gains in sub-Saharan Africa (comprising countries in eastern, central, western, and southern Africa but not North Africa) because of the HIV/AIDS epidemic, as well as periodic famines and social unrest (Lamptey et al., 2002; UN, 2006).

Epidemiological Transition

In Canada and in other advanced societies, the majority of deaths on an annual basis are accounted for by a few leading 'killers'—cardiovascular disease, cancer, acci-

Table 20.2 Canada's Population and Growth Components, 1851–2001[1]

Period	Census Population at End of Period (000s)	Total Population Growth (000s)[1]	Average Annual Growth Rate (%)	Births (000s)	Deaths (000s)	Immi-gration (000s)	Emigration (000s)	Natural Increase (NI) (000s)	Net Migration (NM)(000s)	Ratio: NI/Total Growth x 100	Ratio: NM/Total Growth x 100
1851–61	3,230	793	2.5	1,281	670	352	170	611	182	77.0	23.0
1861–71	3,689	459	1.2	1,370	760	260	410	610	–150	132.6	–32.6
1871–81	4,325	636	1.5	1,480	790	350	404	690	–54	108.5	–8.5
1881–91	4,833	508	1.1	1,524	870	680	826	654	–146	128.7	–28.7
1891–1901	5,371	538	1.0	1,548	880	250	380	668	–130	124.2	–24.2
1901–11	7,207	1,836	2.5	1,925	900	1,550	740	1,025	810	55.9	44.1
1911–21	8,788	1,581	1.8	2,340	1,070	1,400	1,089	1,270	311	80.3	19.7
1921–31	10,377	1,589	1.5	2,415	1,055	1,200	970	1,360	230	85.5	14.5
1931–41	11,507	1,130	1.0	2,294	1,072	149	241	1,222	–92	108.1	–8.1
1941–51[2]	13,648	2,141	1.6	3,186	1,214	548	379	1,972	169	92.1	7.9
1951–6	16,081	2,433	3.0	2,106	633	783	185	1,473	598	71.1	28.9
1956–61	18,238	2,157	2.4	2,362	687	760	278	1,675	482	77.7	22.3
1961–6	20,015	1,777	1.8	2,249	731	539	280	1,518	259	85.4	14.6
1966–71[3]	21,568	1,553	1.4	1,856	766	890	427	1,090	463	70.2	29.8
1971–6	23,450	1,882	1.6	1,755	824	1,053	358	931	695	57.3	42.7
1976–81	24,820	1,371	1.1	1,820	843	771	278	977	493	66.5	33.5
1981–6	26,101	1,280	1.0	1,872	885	678	278	987	399	71.2	28.8
1986–91	28,031	1,930	1.4	1,933	946	1,164	213	987	986	50.0	50.0
1991–6	29,611	1,580	1.1	1,936	1,024	1,118	338	912	908	50.1	49.9
1996–2001	31,021	1,410	0.9	1,705	1,089	1,217	376	609	781	43.8	56.2

[1]Total population growth is the difference in census population counts at the end and beginning of each period.

[2]Beginning in 1951, Newfoundland is included.

[3]Beginning in 1971, the population estimates are based on census counts adjusted for net census undercount and the reference date is 1 July instead of census day. The 1 July 1971 population adjusted for net census undercount is 21,962,000. Immigration figures include immigrants, returning emigrants, and net non-permanent residents. Population growth calculated using the components will produce a different figure from that reported in the table. Prior to 1971, the emigration figures are 'residual' estimates and include the errors in the other three components of growth—births, deaths, and immigration—as well as errors in the census counts. Beginning in 1971, an independent estimate of emigration is produced. From 1991 on, emigration includes emigrants and net temporary emigrants.

Source: Statistics Canada, at: <http://www.statcan.ca/l01/cst01/demo03.htm>. Average annual growth rate and last four columns calculated by author. The ratios in the last two columns are based on the sum of natural increase plus net migration for a given period as denominators.

dents, and violence. Infectious and parasitic diseases such as typhus, cholera, smallpox, and tuberculosis are rare causes of premature mortality. In the past, these ailments predominated as leading killers, over the chronic, degenerative, and 'man-made' causes of death (Omran, 1971). In 1921, out of 67,722 deaths in Canada, malignant neoplasms and diseases of the circulatory system accounted for 20.9 per cent of all deaths. Of the 210,733 deaths recorded in 1991, these same diseases represented 66.5 per cent of this total (McVey and Kalbach, 1995: 206).

The historical shift in Canada's cause-of-death distribution is part of a general phenomenon that all societies typically undergo in the context of their demographic and socio-economic transformations. Abdel Omran's epidemiological transition theory (1971) states that industrialized societies have gone through three epidemiological stages: (1) During stage one, in prehistoric times, life was ruled by Malthusian *positive checks*—famine, misery, pestilence. Life was brutish and short; infectious and parasitic diseases were the leading killers, along with violence and accidents. (2) With the advent of the modern era, the development of agriculture, better systems of food production, and general improvements in the standard of living, humanity developed the ability to resist many infectious diseases, and people lived on average longer than in the preceding stage. This period of epidemiological history in the Western world, 'the stage of receding pandemics', began around 1750 CE and ended around the turn of the twentieth century. (3) The third stage, that of 'man-made and degenerative diseases', began in the 1930s; its main feature was a rising dominance of the chronic and degenerative ailments, such as cancer and heart disease, as the leading killers. Infectious and parasitic diseases receded in relative importance in claiming lives on an annual basis. During this stage, accidents, violence, and suicide also took a prominent position as causes of premature mortality, though overall life expectancy reached unprecedented levels, in the vicinity of 70 years.

At present, the industrialized societies of Western Europe, North America, Japan, Australia, and New Zealand are situated in the fourth stage of epidemiological transition (Olshansky and Ault, 1986). Essential features of this stage include (1) life expectancy at birth in excess of 70 years, (2) continuation of cancer and heart disease as the leading causes of death, (3) increased survival by people with these conditions as a result of effective medical therapies and interventions, (4) unprecedented survival improvements among the old, and (5) the compression (postponement) of the majority of deaths on an annual basis to the advanced ages, as relatively few deaths take place in infancy, early childhood, and young adulthood; over two-thirds of all deaths occur at the ages beyond 65 (Kannisto et al., 1994). Some analysts believe that these societies are now close to attaining the maximum attainable average lifespan for humans (Fries, 1980; Olshansky et al., 1990).

Fertility

The most basic measure of fertility is the crude birth rate (CBR), the number of births in a given year divided by the mid-year population times 1,000. Currently, the Canadian crude birth rate is 11 per 1,000 population—the lowest in the history of the country (Bélanger, 2006). Between the early years of the 1920s and the present, some of the highest crude birth rates were recorded during the peak years of the **baby boom**, the period between the end of World War II and 1966. Between 1947 and 1966, a total of 8,571,376 babies were born, constituting the largest generation in the history of this country (Foot and Stoffman, 1998: 24–5; Romaniuc, 1984: 121–2). From 1966 onward, Canada experienced a **baby bust** followed by a more recent period of sub-replacement fertility levels (Bélanger, 2006; Grindstaff, 1975, 1994; Romaniuc, 1984, 1994).

There have been other low-fertility periods in Canadian history. In 1933, births in Canada had fallen to a low point, with only 229,791 registered that year. One year after the cessation of the war (that is, in 1947), the number of newborns rose to 372,589, a 62 per cent jump from 1933. A steady increase in births occurred during the 1950s, peaking at 479,275 in 1959, at the height of the baby boom. As the 1960s unfolded, Canadians embarked on a long-term trend towards having smaller families. By

Time to Reflect

The Western world has passed through four stages of epidemiological transition. Do you think there will be a fifth stage? If so, what would be the key features of this fifth stage?

GLOBAL ISSUES

The HIV/AIDS Epidemic: A Snapshot

According to the United Nations (2006a), AIDS has become the leading cause of death for adults aged 15 to 59 worldwide. At the end of 2005, 40.3 million people worldwide were living with human immunodeficiency virus (HIV). The top 15 countries with the largest number of HIV cases are: South Africa (5,100,000), India (5,000,000), Nigeria (3,300,000), Zimbabwe (1,600,000), Tanzania (1,500,000), Ethiopia (1,400,000), Mozambique (1,2000,000), Kenya (1,100,000), Democratic Republic of Congo (1,000,000), United States (940,000), Russia (860,000), Zambia (830,000), Malawi (810,000), Cote d'Ivoire (530,000), and Cameroon (520,000).

In its 2004 revision of *World Population Prospects*, the United Nations (2006a) took explicit account of the impact of HIV/AIDS for 60 countries, which in total account for 33.7 million of the 35.7 million HIV-infected adults aged 15–49 in the world at the end of 2003 (i.e., 90 per cent of the total HIV cases). In 56 of these countries, HIV prevalence in the population in this age range was estimated at 1 per cent or higher. The remaining four countries—Brazil, China, India, and United States—had prevalence rates below 1 per cent but had large numbers of infected people because of their large populations. Of the countries considered in the 2004 *Revision*, 40 are in Africa, 5 in Asia, 12 in Latin America and the Caribbean, 2 in Europe, and 1 in North America.

Across the world's regions, sub-Saharan Africa, with 25.8 million HIV-infected people of all ages, remains the worst affected (ibid., 65). Sixty-six per cent of HIV-infected persons (adults and children combined) worldwide at the end of 2003 were in sub-Saharan Africa. Within this region, a small group of countries share a disproportionate burden of the HIV epidemic. These are countries with a prevalence rate of between 10 and 20 per cent or more of the adult population aged 15 and older. Among these are the countries of Swaziland, Botswana, Lesotho, Zimbabwe, and South Africa, where prevalence rates are the highest in the world.

The UN estimated the effect on life expectancy at birth of AIDS across the four countries with the highest per capita HIV prevalence in the world (i.e., Swaziland, Botswana, Lesotho, Zimbabwe) by comparing the resultant life expectancy if AIDS were non-existent as opposed to life expectancy in the presence of AIDS. The computations were made for the periods of 1990–5 and 2000–5, and also were projected to 2045–50 by introducing assumptions about change in the incidence of HIV in these countries, given past and current prevalence trends. The United Nations computations are displayed in the table below.

The differences in life expectancy between the medium variant and the 'no-AIDS' scenario are striking. Life expectancy at birth in 2000–5 was 27.2 years lower in the medium variant than in the 'no-AIDS' scenario. The projections indicate that the worst is likely to come in the period 2010–15, when the impact of AIDS will bring life expectancy down by almost 29 years. Although the effect of AIDS is

Life Expectancy at Birth, Worst-Affected Countries, Estimates and Medium Variant ('with AIDS') and No-AIDS Scenario ('without AIDS'), 1990–2050

Countries with adult HIV prevalence above 20 per cent (Swaziland, Botswana, Lesotho, Zimbabwe)	Life expectancy at birth				
	1991–5	2000–5	2010–15	2020–5	2045–50
With AIDS	57.2	36.8	38.1	43.4	54.4
Without AIDS	64.6	64.0	66.5	69.3	74.1
Absolute difference	–7.4	–27.2	–28.5	–25.9	–19.6
Percentage difference	–11.5	–42.5	–42.8	–37.4	–26.5

Source: Adapted from UN (2006a: 74).

projected to reduce somewhat in the following periods, by 2045–50, life expectancy in these countries will be nearly 20 years below what it could be if AIDS were eliminated.

Among the demographic consequences of the devastating impact of the HIV/AIDS epidemic in these countries (and other affected countries) is the large percentage of children dying under the age of five, as well as a projected deficit in population growth as a function of increased mortality. The four worst-affected populations are projected to decline by 344 million by 2050 (ibid., 79).

It should be mentioned that besides the HIV/AIDS epidemic, countries in sub-Saharan Africa also experience recurrent epidemics of other infectious diseases, including influenza, tuberculosis, whooping cough, measles, chicken pox, typhoid fever, intestinal diseases, cholera, malaria, yellow fever, and other sexually transmitted diseases. Malnutrition remains a major problem, especially among young children. And although not nearly as prevalent as in the industrialized countries, cancer and heart disease have been rising steadily (Kibirige, 1997; Olshansky et al., 1997).

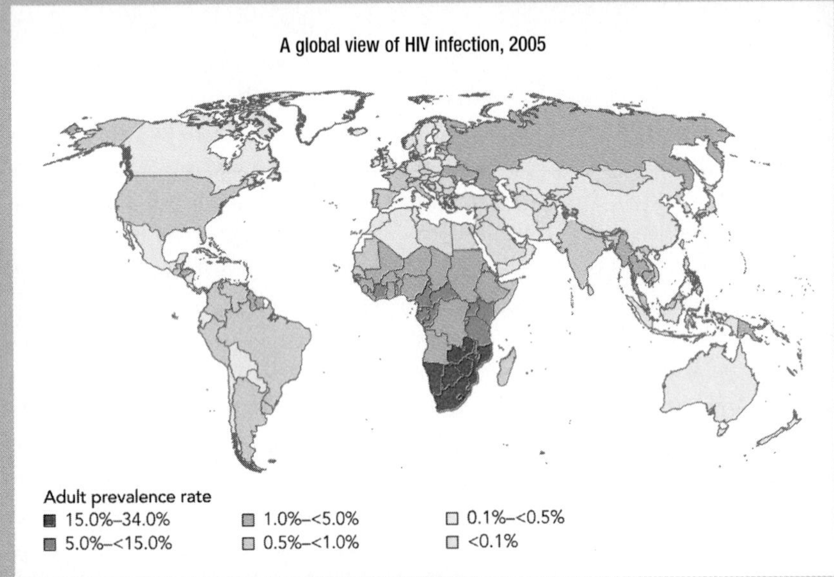

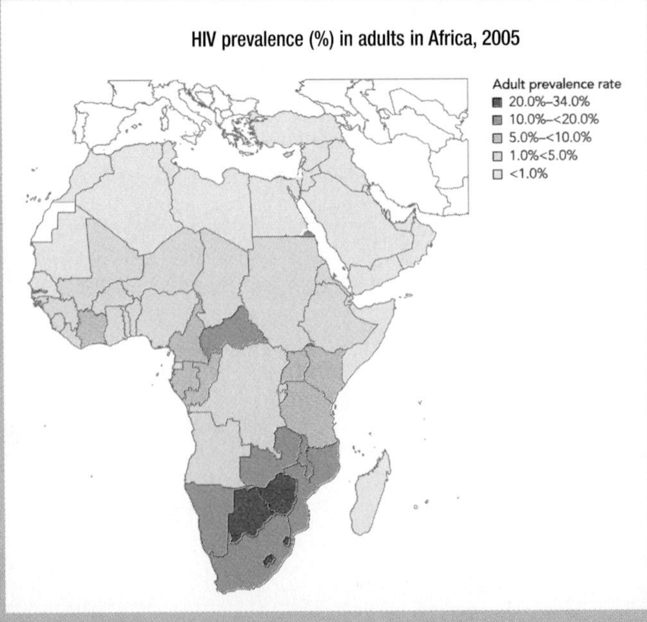

Source: UNAIDS (2006: 14).

1966, the eve of Canada's centennial, the decline was underway; 387,710 babies were born that year, a 19 per cent decline from 1959. The annual numbers of births kept dropping until 1990, when for the first time since 1966, more than 400,000 babies were born. But this was a temporary surge; 1993 saw a return to fewer babies being born (388,394), and the number dropped even further in 2000, to 327,882, the lowest since 1946. In 2003, there were 335,200 births registered in Canada (Bélanger, 2006: 25; Statistics Canada, 2002a: 2).

The total fertility rate (TFR) measures the number of children a woman would bear throughout her reproductive lifetime if she experienced the prevailing age-specific birth rates in a given period. In 1959, at the peak of the baby-boom period, the TFR had climbed to 3.94. But by 1966, it had reduced to 2.81 children per woman. The year 1972 marks an important turning point in Canadian fertility: the TFR fell for the first time to below 2.1, the number of children needed to ensure long-term replacement of the generations. Canada's *total fertility rate* in 2000 was 1.49, the lowest in the country's history. In 2003, it rose slightly to 1.53 (Bélanger, 2006: 31; Statistics Canada, 2002a: 2). If this trend persists, the future of the Canadian population is a precarious one. Other industrialized nations share this prospect as a result of their common pattern of sub-replacement fertility (UN, 2000a, 2006).

Explanations of Fertility Change

The baby-boom and baby-bust phenomena were precipitated by changes in the intermediate variables—a set of variables through which social, cultural, and biological factors operate to determine a society's overall fertility rate (Davis and Blake, 1956). John Bongaarts (1978) has shown that four of these intermediate variables (also known as *proximate determinants*) account for most of the fertility variation across societies: the extent of non-marriage (the higher the number of people who remain unmarried, the lower the overall fertility), the level of contraceptive use (the greater the use of contraception, the lower the fertility), the degree to which abortion is practised (high rates of abortion translate into reduced overall fertility), and the level of postpartum amenorrhea (the longer women breast-feed their babies, the later the return of ovulation, and hence the lower the societal fertility rate). Changes in the extent of marriage and contraceptive use have played leading roles in the historical rise and fall of the Canadian birth rate (Grindstaff, 1975, 1994, 1995; Romaniuc, 1984). Sociological, cultural, and economic factors have also played an important role in the observed changes in Canadian fertility, though indirectly, through the proximate determinants.

The Baby Boom

Following the marriage downturn of the early 1930s associated with the economic depression, the number of Canadians marrying rose substantially during the 1940s. Although the Canadian marriage rate has followed an uneven historical trend, between 1940 and the late 1950s it was well above the rates recorded for the 1920s and the early 1930s.

According to Richard Easterlin (1969, 1980), the economic recovery and prosperity of the post-war period was a major factor explaining the rise of marriage and early procreation among young couples during the baby-boom period. Young men could find abundant work, and their prospects in the labour market looked exceptionally promising. As well, the major institutions—the church, the economy, and the state—provided the individual with a strong sense of security and stability, as governments were in the midst of creating safety-net systems to enhance the welfare of their populations (universal health care, education, employment insurance, and so on). As well, the church exerted a strong moral influence on the people, reinforcing pro-natalist values. These conditions promoted early marriage and childbearing (Ariès, 1980; Lesthaeghe and Surkyn, 1988; Simon, 1980). As described by Easterlin (1969, 1980), demographic conditions in the post-war period were also favourable. The relatively small cohorts of young male workers, born during the low-fertility period of the 1930s, would enter the labour market in the late 1940s and 1950s, a period of increased demand for workers in a rapidly expanding economy.

Changes in **gender roles** also contributed to the baby-boom phenomenon. In her study of the 'feminine mystique', Betty Friedan (1963) outlined the tendency of women in the 1950s to be preoccupied with marriage to a successful husband, motherhood, and a new home in the suburbs. Their self-concept was tied to this 'mystique', presented and reinforced by the society. Early marriage and early parenthood were common, therefore. The male role was predominantly that of the breadwinner. This traditional system of gender roles began to collapse in the 1960s and was eventually supplanted by a more egalitarian system.

At the outset of the 1960s, women began their 'flight' from domesticity, seeking to redefine themselves as full participants in the economic and educational spheres of society. In 1951, only slightly more than

The period between the end of World War II and 1966 was one of high birth rates and came to be known as the baby boom. Since then, like many other industrialized countries, Canada has experienced a baby bust. (David Tanaka)

20 per cent of Canadian women of working age held paid jobs. By 1960, the proportion of women in the paid labour force rose to almost 29 per cent, and it increased over 38 per cent in the following decade. With the advent of the 1980s and the 1990s, the proportion of women working was fast approaching 60 per cent (Mills and Trovato, 2001: 108; Romaniuc, 1994: 221). The rise of female employment has been most pronounced among those in the prime child-bearing ages of 20–34 (Beaujot et al., 1995). Improvements in birth-control methods helped women gain greater control of their reproductive and productive lives (Davis, 1984; Davis and van den Oever, 1982; Murphy, 1993).

Women have been pursuing higher levels of education, careers, and jobs. In the new sex-role system, men are no longer the sole economic providers. In a growing number of Canadian families, the earnings of wives now equal or exceed those of their husbands. During the early 1970s, wives' earnings exceeding or equalling those of their husbands characterized only about 6 per cent of working couples in Canada. By 1997, this proportion had changed to 25 per cent (Grindstaff and Trovato, 1990: 236; Little, 2000: A2).

The Baby Bust

Economists have enunciated theories to help explain the current low-fertility environment of post-industrial societies. A central postulate of economic theories of the family concerns the rising material and non-material costs of parenting (Becker, 1960; Willis, 1987). Easterlin's cyclical theory (1969, 1980) also suggests that there is an interaction of economic factors with demographic and sociological variables in the explanation of family change. As described by Easterlin, the baby boom and the baby bust represent a natural sequence in a self-regulatory process, whereby periods of low fertility give rise to periods of high fertility, and vice versa. The driving forces for this cyclical pattern include economic and sociological forces—how well the economy performs in meeting the material aspirations of young adults, the size of one's birth cohort, and the strength of material preferences among young people of parental age.

The baby bust resulted from the growing gap between high material aspirations among the baby-boom cohorts and declining socio-economic opportunities for these cohorts as compared to their parental generation. As well, the large size of the baby-boom cohorts would represent a further source of insecurity among this generation. In an uncertain economic environment, large cohorts do not fare as well as small cohorts in finding permanent work and in gaining job promotions. The labour pool is large, as is the number of persons seeking advancement in the workplace. These conditions have instilled in young people a reluctance to enter matrimony, and among the married a tendency to postpone having children. One common strategy adopted by couples is to delay child-bearing and to have a completed family size of one or two children on the average. This allows couples to maximize their socio-economic opportunities while fulfilling their parental obligations (Ram and Rahim, 1993).

Following theoretical premises developed by Gary Becker (1960), William Butz and Michael Ward (1979) have suggested that low fertility rates in advanced societies in recent decades are linked to the rising value of time for women. Unlike in the past, most women are now gainfully employed in the labour market. This means that the economic value of their time is now greater. Having children therefore means having to forgo not only potential income, but also career opportunities. Looking at the United States as a case study, Butz and Ward determined that a rise in the average incomes of males induces couples to have more children, presumably because of greater affordability. The same trend for women was found to be inversely associated with fertility, overriding the positive income effect of men. This finding is explained in terms of women's rising opportunity costs, such as lost career opportunities, associated with having children. Besides material considerations, there are also psychic costs—the perceived complications and stresses associated with having to care for children, often while maintaining a job or career, and the restricted freedom that goes along with being a parent.

Sociologically based explanations of fertility decline are grounded on the assumption that social change is largely a function of diffusion processes, whereby new ideas and values gradually spread throughout the society and supplant old ones. Such theories recognize the important interactions of structural and economic forces with ideational factors. The traditional sources of authority in matters of family and procreation—religion, community, extended family—have weakened considerably in recent decades. Individualism is now the dominant ethos guiding personal actions (Ariès, 1980; Keyfitz, 1986; Lesthaeghe and Surkyn, 1988; Preston, 1986a; Simons, 1980; Trovato, 1988b; van de Kaa, 1987). Contemporary values, attitudes, and lifestyles seem incompatible with early marriage and raising large families, as the pro-natalist forces of the past have given way to the small family ideal of the present. According to Ron Lesthaeghe and Johan Surkyn (1988), during the baby-boom period, people generally felt optimistic about their economic future. However, there now exists among the young a generalized skepticism of social institutions, including traditional marriage. Cohabitation, for instance, is seen by many of the young of today as a less restrictive form of sexual union than traditional marriage. In the postmodern society, diverse family forms are increasingly tolerated and accepted. It is no longer unusual for young couples to consciously avoid having children or for individuals to forgo matrimony altogether.

To summarize, social forces of germane importance in explaining the persisting pattern of sub-replacement fertility in industrialized societies are (1) the rise of individualism as a dominant aspect of our culture, which emphasizes detachment of the individual from traditional sources of regulation such as religion; (2) the rise of a consumerist ideology emphasizing strong material preferences and aspirations over early marriage and family building; (3) increasing levels of divorce and the growing preference of the young to enter alternative living arrangements rather than legal marriage; and (4) the sex-role revolution and the increasing levels of emancipation of women and men from traditional roles, allowing young adults a wider range of alternatives to traditional roles as sources of self-fulfillment.

Demographic and Societal Implications of Sub-replacement Fertility

For a society, one of the most profound long-term outcomes of continued low fertility is demographic aging. The 2001 Canadian census confirms that the median age of the population—the point where exactly one-half of the population is older and the other half is younger—is 37.6. The 1996 census showed a median age of 35.3. In 1901 it was only 22.7 years (*National Post*, 2002: A9). The Canadian situation is not unique, as other industrialized nations are experiencing the same trend. For the world, the median age in 2001 was 26.5 (ibid.; UN, 2006).

Figure 20.5 shows a typology of age pyramids, juxtaposed with Canada's actual and projected population age structure to 2036. This typology outlines in schematic form the long-term progression of expected change in the age pyramids of societies as they pass through their demographic transitions. The true pyramid has a wide base and a narrow top, typical of rapidly growing populations with characteristically high reproductive rates and a high percentage of the population below age 15. Some developing nations exemplify this structure, particularly those in sub-Saharan Africa and parts of Asia (for example, Kenya and Afghanistan). The constrictive pyramid is indicative of populations experiencing continued declines in fertility. A number of developing nations have recently begun sustained fertility declines; for this reason, their population pyramids will eventually take on the look of something intermediate to the true and constrictive types. With continued fertility declines, the transitional societies will in time enter a stage at which the shape of their population structures will approximate those of the industrialized nations, whose age pyramids are gradually approaching the stationary form. The Canadian population has gone through this evolution and is projected to attain the stationary form in 2036.

On a practical level, a youthful population means that governments have to plan and devote considerable resources to the needs of children and youth. In an aging society, the dependency burden shifts gradually from the youth to the elderly. Central in such a context are issues related to retirement planning, pension security and management, and adequate provision of geriatric health care and services. The greying of the population is bound to play a critical role in shaping the long-term collective futures of Canada and other demographically mature societies. An article in one of Canada's major newspapers on the 2001 census figures begins by saying that as a consequence of the aging trend, 'Canadians could face delayed retirement, even higher health-care costs, more school closings and a shortage of skilled workers' (Lewington, 2002). According to Peterson (1999), in some societies, demographic aging will induce growing pres-

Figure 20.5 Typological Age-Sex Pyramids and Actual and Projected Age-Sex Pyramids of Canada, 1881, 1921, 1951, 1991, 2011, and 2036

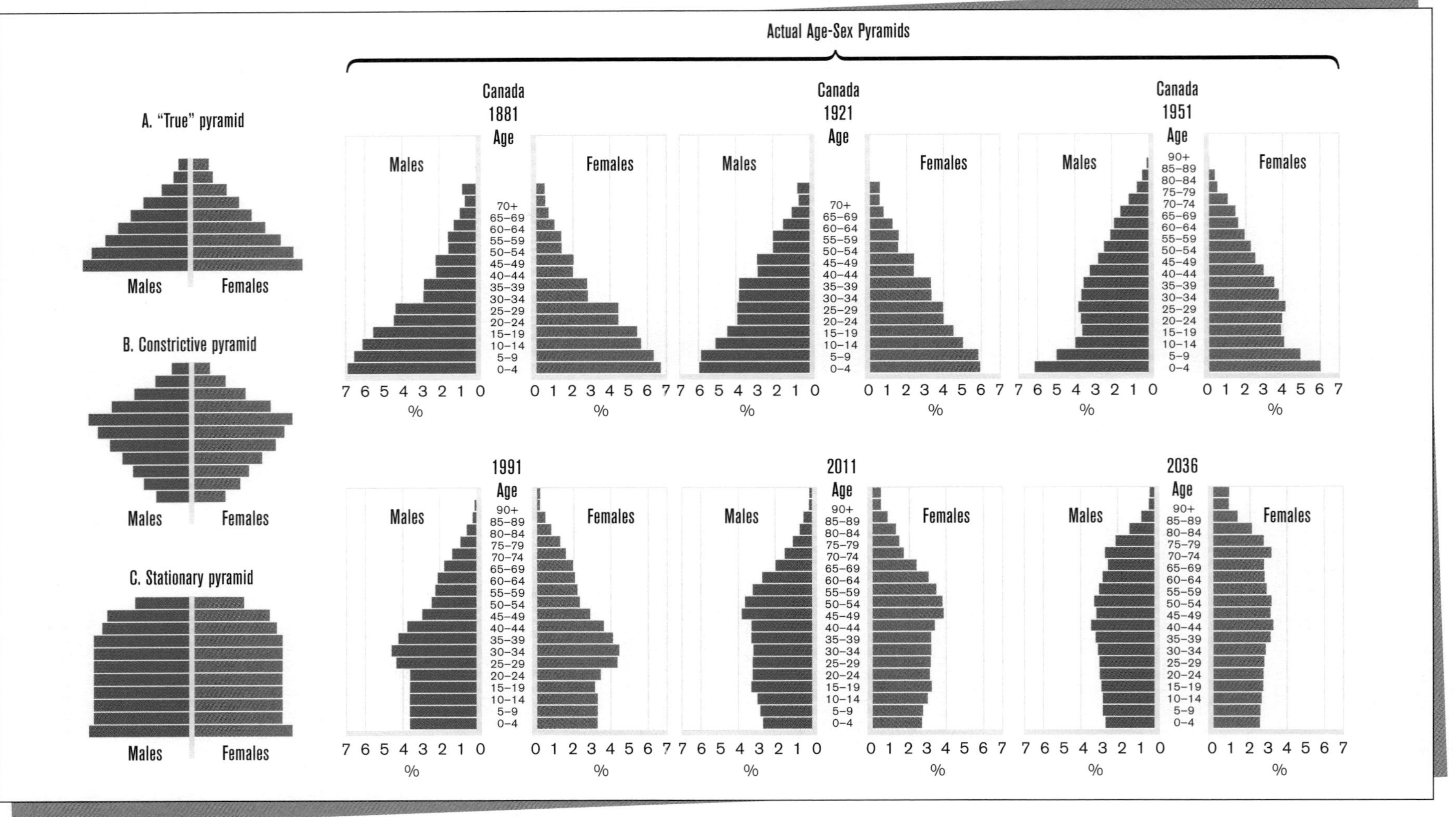

Source: Adapted from Bertrand Desjardins, *Population Aging and the Elderly: Demographic Analysis* (Ottawa: Statistics Canada, 1993), 18; C.W. Kammayer and Helen L. Ginn, *An Introduction to Population*, 2nd edn (Chicago: Dorsey, 1986), 89.

sures on the old age retirement benefit system as the costs of maintaining it will escalate to unprecedented levels. Widening public pension deficits could consume the economic savings of the developed world. As well, reforms of health-care systems will be needed to take into account the growing health needs of an aging population. The growth of the 'old-old' component (the population 85 and older) will be much faster than that of the 'young old' (65–84). In the long term, these societies will be facing an unprecedented economic burden on their working-age populations as the proportion in the working ages shrinks while that of old-age dependants keeps growing. Demographically mature societies will require large numbers of immigrants to supplement their diminishing labour-force populations (Denton et al., 2002; Kennedy, 1993; UN, 2000b; UN Economic Commission for Europe, 1992).

Migration

Canada is a country made up almost exclusively of immigrants and their descendants. The history of the nation is closely tied to immigration (C. Brown, 2002). Currently, about 19 per cent of our population is first-generation immigrants.

Immigration to Canada has fluctuated significantly over the years. In 1852, this country welcomed 29,307 people; in 1913, there were 400,000 newcomers—an annual figure not yet surpassed. Since the early 1970s, immigration levels have been in the range of 80,000 to 250,000 per year. Fluctuations in the annual immigration levels are set by government, usually in response to economic conditions and other policy considerations. From the time of Confederation to 1967, more than 8 million people were admitted to Canada (McVey and Kalbach, 1995: 83). Until recently, most immigrants were from Britain, other northwestern European areas, and the United States. After World War II, immigration started to diversify, and Canada welcomed many people from all regions of Europe, including Italians, Germans, Hungarians, Dutch, and Portuguese. Since the early part of the 1970s, the major source areas have been Asia, South America, the Caribbean, Central America, and Eastern Europe (ibid.; Samuel, 1990).

Immigration has been a significant factor in the growth of Canadian cities (Stone, 1967). The majority of immigrants settle in the largest metropolitan areas of Ontario (about 50 per cent), British Columbia (15 per cent), and Quebec (15 per cent). This rank order of preference has remained fairly stable over time (Bélanger, 2006; Dumas, 1990); it reflects variations in economic and social pulls across Canada's regions. The more economically advantaged locations receive the majority of immigrants. According to Statistics Canada (2003c), one-third of the Canadian population in 2001 was concentrated in the **census metropolitan areas** (CMAs) of Toronto (4.7 million), Montreal (3.4 million), and Vancouver (2 million). Thus, over 60 per cent of new Canadians make their homes in these three areas of the country.

Studies on immigrants' internal migration patterns indicate little movement out of the large urban areas of the country (Trovato, 1988a). The general reluctance of immigrants to relocate to smaller centres in Canada is largely due to the combined effects of economic and social advantages large cities afford and to the strong attraction represented by immigrant ethnic communities in large urban locations. The presence of like ethnic members provides material and psychological comfort and support to immigrants (Breton, 1964; McDonald and McDonald, 1964; Trovato, 1988a).

Although the volume of interprovincial migration has been declining over time (possibly due to aging of the population), the number of people in Canada that change province annually remains substantial. In 2004, 271,037 persons moved across the provinces (Bélanger, 2006: 55). Between 1951 and 2000, almost 20 million people moved interprovincially (see Table 20.3). Internal migration is predominantly from the economically disadvantaged to the economically prosperous regions. The literature describes this as a core/periphery phenomenon: underdeveloped regions (the periphery) export people, and economically developed areas (the core) import labour (Massey et al., 1993). Core/periphery migratory systems arise from unequal regional development. In the Canadian case, the Atlantic region has been a net loser in terms of migration; Ontario, British Columbia, and Alberta have been net gainers. However, as economic conditions across these regions fluctuate periodically, boom periods translate into large net migration gains while declining economic conditions usually provoke high rates of out-migration. Currently, owing to its booming economy, Alberta is the province attracting the majority of internal migrants. According to Statistics Canada (2006j), during the period from July 2005 to July 2006, the population of Alberta increased at the rate of 29.5 per 1,000, the fastest in the country and almost three times the national average. Most of this increase was due to the net internal migration of 57,000 persons, which was 22,700 more than in the previous year. This record migratory gain accounted for 58 per cent of Alberta's population growth during this interval.

Factors of Migration

People are more prone to changing residence during certain stages of the life cycle. The intensity of life-cycle events is greatest in the young adult years, particularly between the ages of 20 and 34. Indeed, besides sex and marital status, one of the most predictive variables for migration is age—a variable that is strongly correlated with life-cycle stage (Lee, 1966; Rogers and Willekens, 1981).

During childhood, the predominant basis of relocation is tied to family migration decisions. In the late teens up to the early thirties, this stage of the life cycle involves a number of important life events for most people, such as graduating from high school, attending university or college, post-secondary graduation, entering the labour force, and marriage. These types of events often dictate having to relocate (for example, for a job in another city). The likelihood of migration diminishes considerably after the late thirties and early forties as during this part of life, persons are established with work and family.

Conclusion

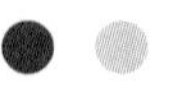   

Population is the foundation of society and its subsystems. The social world cannot be understood in isolation from demography, nor can demography be properly understood devoid of a proper understanding of society. Given the centrality of population to the study of society, sociologists pay particular attention to the dynamics of population change. Fertility, mortality, and migration are the basic demographic variables. In combination, they determine whether a population experiences growth, stability, or decline. Aggregate change in fertil-

Table 20.3 Interprovincial Migratory Balance in Canada over Five Decades, 1950 to 2000

	1951–60	1961–70	1971–80	1981–90	1991–5	1996–2000	1991–2000
Newfoundland	–9,816	–34,557	–20,840	–30,626	–19,814	–32,590	–52,404
Prince Edward Island	–7,938	–5,732	2,927	378	1,414	194	1,608
Nova Scotia	–28,851	–43,521	4,165	3,331	–4,415	–4,412	–8,827
New Brunswick	–25,360	–45,277	6,441	–5,915	–3,094	–7,269	–10,363
Quebec	–72,877	–142,594	–234,163	–122,143	–50,758	–71,509	–122,267
Ontario	148,036	236,081	–96,391	184,649	–42,570	57,698	15,128
Manitoba	–40,587	–64,161	–68,977	–37,968	–26,558	–19,563	–46,121
Saskatchewan	–87,938	–123,492	–50,603	–67,475	–28,917	–22,631	–51,548
Alberta	32,858	30,022	244,991	–61,203	5,753	134,470	140,223
British Columbia	93,075	192,713	216,486	144,345	169,608	–27,452	142,156
Yukon and Northwest Territories[a]	–600	519	–4,036	–7,373	–649	–6,936	–7,585
Total movements	**2,962,004**	**3,660,061**	**3,849,741**	**3,168,426**	**1,482,443**	**1,471,878**	**2,954,321**

[a]Includes data for Nunavut beginning in 1992.

Source: Alain Bélanger, *Report on the Demographic Situation in Canada 2001: Current Demographic Analysis* (Ottawa: Statistics Canada 2002), 58; Jean Dumas, *Report on the Demographic Situation in Canada 1990* (Ottawa: Statistics Canada, Demography Division, 1990), 106.

Time to Reflect

Should the government of Canada increase its immigration targets from their current levels? Can you think of reasons why immigration targets should not be increased?

ity, mortality, and migration results from change in individual behaviour in accordance with conditions in the social structure.

The history of the human population can be subdivided into two broad stages: a very long period of very slow growth, from the beginning of humankind to about 1750 CE, followed by a relatively recent phase of explosive growth. As a legacy of the population explosion that took place in the modern era and currently is ongoing in many developing countries, the world faces challenges heretofore unforeseen in the history of humanity. The earth's population (just over 6.5 billion in 2006) is expected to reach 9 billion by the year 2050. Most of the projected growth will be in the developing countries, particularly in Africa and also in Asia and Latin America. Some of the developing countries are close to completing their demographic transitions; others are just beginning to experience sustained fertility declines after decades of mortality reductions.

Three demographic trends seem inevitable over the course of this new century: the population of the world will become older; the developing countries will grow much more than the developed countries; and there will be intense pressure on highly industrialized countries to accommodate an even larger share of immigrants from developing countries than they do currently. The implications of this eventuality will be far-reaching: with increased immigration, the highly industrialized receiving nations will become even more racially and ethnically heterogeneous. Given its relatively long history of immigration and its multicultural orientation, Canada seems well-positioned to deal with this reality. For the countries that are relatively new immigrant-receiving societies in Western Europe (many of which until recently were sending nations), the adjustment process to this emerging reality poses difficult challenges. Their conceptions of nationhood may need to be modified in view of the changing racial and ethnic composition of their societies.

Questions for Critical Thought

1. Describe how populations change. What are the demographic components of change?
2. What is atypical about the current stage of the demographic history of the world? Describe the relationship of demographic transition to the history and projected future of the human population. Are there any certainties about the future population of the world?
3. Assess the theories of Malthus and Marx on the matter of population and its relationship to contemporary issues concerning resources and the environment. Discuss how contemporary perspectives on population matters relate to the classical Malthusian and Marxist theories of population.
4. What are some sociological determinants of fertility change over the last half-century in Canada?
5. What is the relative importance of fertility and mortality in determining the age distribution of a population?
6. Explain how the epidemiological profile of Canadian society differs today from that of the early part of the century.
7. Why do immigrants to Canada prefer to settle in the largest metropolitan areas of the country?
8. Regional inequalities in socio-economic development explain differential migratory flows within Canada. Explain.
9. What are some of the social and economic implications of increased immigration for the future of Canadian society and other receiving countries in the Western world?

Recommended Readings

Roderic Beaujot and Don Kerr, *Population Change in Canada*, 2nd edn (Toronto: Oxford University Press, 2004).

This book is an important introduction to Canada's population and its demographic trends.

John I. Clarke, *The Future of Population* (London: Phoenix, 1997).

This is an excellent introduction to some of the most critical issues concerning the population of the world.

David K. Foot with Daniel Stoffman, *Boom, Bust and Echo 2000: Profiting from the Demographic Shift in the New Millennium* (Toronto: Macfarlane Walter & Ross, 1998).

The revised edition of this best-selling book examines many potential practical applications of demography to business. It gives a wide range of insights on how demographic shifts affect key sectors of the economy, from the state of the housing market to consumer demand for sports, travel, leisure, and financial investing.

Bjorn Lomborg, *The Skeptical Environmentalist* (Cambridge, Mass.: Harvard University Press 2001).

An anti-Malthusian perspective on the state of world.

Wayne McVey Jr and Warren E. Kalbach, *Canadian Population* (Toronto: Nelson, 1995).

This is an updated version of a classic Canadian text on population first published in the early 1970s. It gives technical and substantive explanation of demographic concepts, with specific reference to Canada.

Anatole Romaniuc, *Fertility in Canada: From Baby-Boom to Baby-Bust* (Ottawa: Statistics Canada, 1984).

Although this study's primary focus is Canadian fertility, the theories and explanations reviewed by the author have broader application to the other industrialized countries.

W.W. Rostow, *The Great Population Spike and After: Reflections on the 21st Century* (New York: Oxford University Press, 1998).

The author takes a careful look at the populations of the industrial and developing countries, how they have been changing, and how they will change over the course of the new millennium. Rostow examines key challenges the industrialized societies are likely to face in the near future as the populations of emerging economies will assert a greater influence on the global economy while the industrial societies face the prospect of depopulation.

Frank Trovato, ed., *Population and Society: Selected Readings* (Toronto: Oxford University Press, 2002).
Twenty-five readings are presented, covering a broad range of topics central to the field of population studies. These selected works emphasize the interrelation between population, culture, and social structure.

———, *Canada's Population in a Global Context: An Introduction to Social Demography* (Toronto: Oxford University Press, 2008).
This textbook introduces the field of social demography—its concepts, measures, and theories—with a focus on both Canada and the international demographic scene.

Recommended Websites

Health Canada: Population Health
www.hc-sc.gc.ca/hppb/phdd/docs/social/
Mortality and other population health information on Canadians can be found at the Health Canada website.

POPLINE Digital Services
www.jhuccp.org/popline
POPLINE is an important on-line bibliographic database on population research and related topics, based at Johns Hopkins University.

Population Index
http://popindex.princeton.edu
This very useful and comprehensive bibliographic source for population research and related disciplines is no longer published in print form.

Population Reference Bureau
www.prb.org
The Population Reference Bureau issues a series of excellent publications on a regular basis, including *Population Bulletin* and the annual *World Population Data Sheet.*

Statistics Canada
www.statcan.ca
Statistics Canada is the authoritative source for Canadian census and other population data.

United Nations Population Division
www.unpopulation.org
The annual *United Nations Demographic Yearbook* contains a wealth of demographic information by country. Another important product from the United Nations is the *Human Development Report.*

United States Bureau of the Census
www.census.gov
This is one of the best sources of demographic information for the United States and other countries. Check out their population clock, which gives continuous updates on the population of the world.

World Health Organization
www.who.int/en/index.html
Another important source of mortality data is the *World Health Organization Statistics Annual.* This publication contains deaths by cause, age, and sex for a large number of countries.

Chapter 21

Cities and Urbanization

William Michelson

Learning Objectives

In this chapter, you will:

- See how the existence and prevalence of cities reflects societal and world conditions.
- Examine the extent and ways that cities and urbanization impact people's characteristic behaviours.
- Begin to understand how built environments facilitate and constrain everyday life.
- Examine characteristic parts of cities and their potential patterns.
- Learn what cities are intended to do as social organizations.
- Study the basis for conflict and change within cities.
- Consider the known implications of different forms of municipal structure—and their restructuring.
- Gain an appreciation of Canadian cities in historical and comparative perspective.

Photo: Courtesy of the West Edmonton Mall

Introduction

Remember: for every urban problem, there is a solution that is clear, simple, and wrong.

—Terry Nichols Clark (2002)

The 80 per cent of Canadians living in urban areas are bombarded with glib remedies for the difficulties cities and city dwellers regularly undergo. Everyone has an opinion. Some of these opinions are informed. Sociologists have assembled considerable knowledge gained from their long-standing application of sociological perspectives and research tools to cities. Moreover, sociological insights on cities are highly diverse and complementary.

Sociologists' fields of interest in cities run the gamut from the place of cities in society to the interiors of dwelling units. The effects of industrialization and deindustrialization, why women feel safe in some places and unsafe in others, the allure of shopping centres for youth, the rationales for regional government—all are valid matters for study within urban sociology. But an understanding of one phenomenon does not automatically explain others. No single theory is sufficient to describe, explain, or solve all problems. A mixture of sociological perspectives is needed to help us understand and deal with the many unique, challenging situations in urban life.

Cities and urbanization will therefore be viewed in this chapter according to four perspectives. The first of these is **urbanization**, the nature, extent, and distribution of cities in the larger society or nation. The second perspective is **urbanism**, behaviour patterns associated with cities. The third is **ecology**, the internal makeup and patterning of cities. Our final perspective is **structural analysis**, which focuses on the functions cities perform, as well as on who has what effect on the decisions and outcomes involving cities.

Individually and together, these perspectives help us to understand cities and to deal more adequately with their woes. Canadians may also understand their urban conditions in the context of historical and international perspectives.

Urbanization

We are familiar with cities from current observations and personal experiences. The concept of urbanization, however, focuses our attention on the place of cities in the greater society, from nation to nation, and over time.

The First Cities

The emergence of cities in about 3500 BC truly represented something new under the sun. Perhaps the most elementary conception of a city is that it must contain at least some non-agricultural workers. The effect of cities on the rest of the society was therefore immediate and direct: the rural sector had to grow a surplus of food to feed the urbanites. Creating stable and predictable agricultural surpluses required simultaneous developments throughout the whole of society in technology and social structure in such geographic areas as Mesopotamia and the Indus Valley that could support intensive agriculture (Adams, 1966).

Technological innovations of importance for urbanization included irrigation; bronze metallurgy for plowing and cutting instruments; animal husbandry for use in agriculture; stone mortars; the selective cultivation of rich, non-perishable foods such as grains and dates; wheeled carts and sailing vessels for transport; and building bricks for permanent settlements.

Alongside of technology, social organization evolved, and the division of labour beyond age and sex became a legacy to later cities and societies. One aspect of the enhanced division of labour was *vertical stratification*, differentiation in the degrees of responsibility and power. For instance, it became the responsibility of some individuals to see to it, by providing technological support and controlling delivery, that the farmers produced surpluses for the non-agricultural workers. Another aspect of the division of labour was *horizontal stratification*, different job specializations even at the same level of power and prestige. Full-time soldiers, artists, and producers of consumer goods appeared in the urban settlements, while farmers became ever-more specialized. From the beginning, then, cities had heterogeneous populations with complex, usually coercive relationships with the rest of society. Although the farmers did obtain products and the often dubious benefits of laws and protection, they relinquished some of their food under terms beyond their control.

This relationship between urban and rural people may appear like what we experience currently. However, there have been enormous changes over time in the balance between the two groups, reflecting developments in the central elements of technology and social organization. At first, technology was barely adequate for producing the necessary food surplus; 50 to 90 farmers were needed to produce enough surplus food for one urbanite. Today, a single farmer in a technologically developed country produces food for about nine urbanites.

In the first few thousand years after the appearance of cities, even the largest urban settlements were very small. Archaeological evidence suggests the largest were between 5,000 and 30,000 in population. Their size was limited by the distance over which a labour-intensive transportation technology could bring food from outlying areas, by how far coercion could be extended, and by the state of sanitation and public health. With refinements in technology and social structure, some ancient cities grew much larger. Athens had about 150,000 residents in 500 BC. At its height, Rome grew to between 250,000 and a million inhabitants.

City-states often dominated vast tributary areas. The size and prosperity of these cities depended on the extent to which people could travel safely to and from these hinterlands. Such dependence on peaceful connections to the outside world has been reflected in the rise and fall of cities throughout history—a relationship reconfirmed by the impacts of violence and epidemics on cities during the current decade. Fostering a climate of violence in the 'outside' world is no recipe for security and prosperity at home!

Although many aspects of urbanization appear to be timeless, the kind of urbanization we know today did not develop until after the Middle Ages.

Paths to Urban Development

The development of industry, based on non-living energy sources such as coal and steam, is commonly given credit for a substantial shift in the population balance from rural to urban. Powered industry reflected societal developments in technology and accentuated the division of labour. The same advances in science and engineering that made possible large-scale factories with machinery also led to innovations in agricultural technology that enabled fewer farm workers to grow food more intensively and on larger holdings.

In technologically advanced societies, therefore, a surplus of agricultural labour became available for newly emerging, specialized city jobs. These workers were *pushed* from the countryside and *pulled* to cities. They became specialists—in housing, food, transportation, financial services, and warehousing distribution, for example—and several specialists were needed to provide services and supplies for every factory worker. This led to a growth in urban population by what is called the *multiplier effect*: population growth several times the number accounted for by factory workers alone.

Technically, observers think of urbanization as the percentage of a nation's population living in settlements of a certain minimum size, usually defined as 5,000 and over. Just two centuries ago, only about 3 per cent of the world's population lived in settlements of 500 or more inhabitants. A city about the size of the current Vancouver metropolitan area would have been the largest in the world. Today's technologically advanced nations have urbanization levels exceeding 75 per cent.

If you look at the development of urbanization in historical perspective, as in the timeline in Figure 21.1, you see that it took many thousands of years of human life for the prerequisites for cities to occur and to lead to the establishment of urban settlements in various parts of the world. The ingredients of modern cities have become known only in 'the last few minutes in the day' of the human timeline. Indeed, the predominantly urban society is largely a phenomenon only of the past 60 years of the 50,000 or so years of recorded human history. During this recent time, however, the tempo of technological innovation and societal adaptation has grown phenomenally. Considering that powered industry

IN THE FIRST PERSON

I have always been interested in patterns: in music, in sports, and in sociology. But it was only through the study of sociology that I discovered that our everyday lives could be better understood as part of social and contextual patterns. Cities are a major example of this. They consist of many kinds of social and physical patterns, and these patterns vary greatly according to time and place. I have long been fascinated by the extent to which understanding cities and urbanization can help unlock the doors of understanding to people's lives. By so doing, we can make cities more humane places.—William Michelson

Figure 21.1 Timeline of Significant Events in the Development of Urbanization[a]

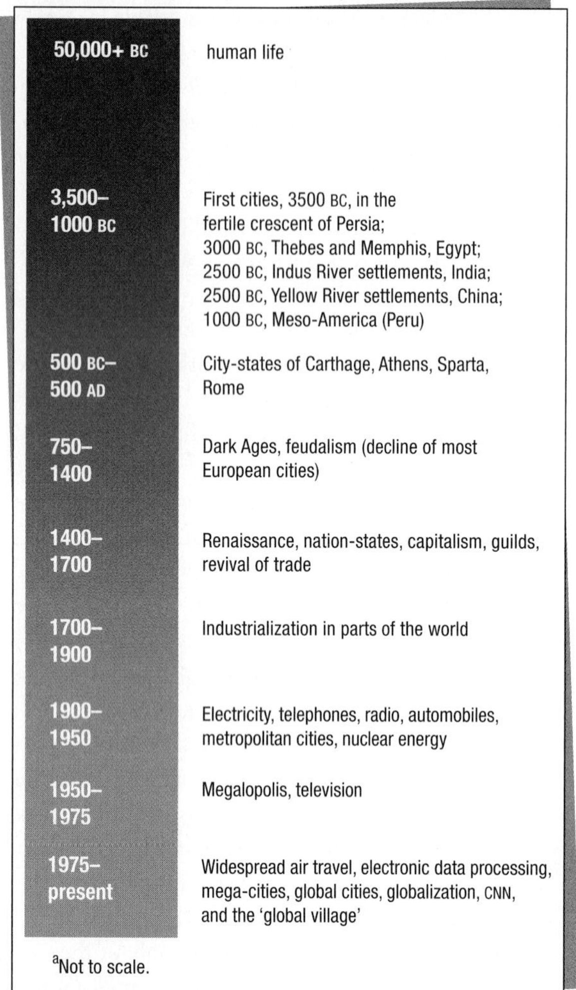

[a]Not to scale.

came about in the eighteenth century, electricity in the nineteenth, and the automobile, telephone, radio, television, airplane, computer, and nuclear power in the twentieth century, it is difficult to predict or imagine what cities and society will be like even in the next decade.

Urbanization in Modern Industrial Nations

Canada and the United States belong to a club of industrial nations with reasonably similar, high rates of urbanization. According to the United Nations Population Division (2005), the more developed nations of the world had a mean urbanization percentage of 74.1 in the year 2005, compared to 42.9 for less developed regions. Canada is slightly above this level, with 80.1 per cent urbanization, as is the US with 80.8 per cent as of 2005.

Table 21.1 shows that the highly industrialized continents of the Americas, Europe, and Oceania all have mean urbanization levels of over 70 per cent, compared to much lower levels (under 40 percent) for Africa and Asia.

Figure 21.2 shows that urbanization levels in the more and less developed nations have risen in parallel patterns from 1950 to 2005. However, this means that the less developed areas, starting at a very low level of urbanization, have encountered a greater *degree* of change in existing levels of urbanization over these years.

Nonetheless, a concentration on such large land masses obscures differences in levels of industrialization within them. Hence, a focus on national urbanization levels shows that Western Europe has some of the highest levels in the world (for example, Belgium, 98 per cent in 2005; United Kingdom, 90 per cent), while some nations in Eastern Europe have less urbanization (for example, Romania, 56 per cent; Croatia, 59 per cent). Australia and New Zealand are at the 92 and 86 per cent levels, respectively, while the smaller islands in Oceania bring down the regional mean level. Japan has a markedly higher urbanization rate, at 79 per cent, than many other Asian nations that have not as yet achieved the same level of industrialization (World Bank, 2005: Table 3.10).

Nations with low urbanization rates may nonetheless have very large cities. Indeed, as Table 21.2 indicates, many of the largest cities in the world are found in less developed nations. Knowing the economic and technological contexts in which cities become established is important to understanding their size and distribution within the nation.

Table 21.1 Urbanization by Continents, 2005

North America	80.7%
Latin America & Caribbean	77.4%
Europe	72.2%
Oceania	70.8%
Asia	39.8%
Africa	38.3%

Source: Population Division of the Department of Economic and Social Affairs of the United Nations Secretariat, *World Population Prospects: The 2004 Revision and World Urbanization Prospects: The 2005 Revision*, at: <wsa.un.org/unup>.

Figure 21.2 Urbanization by Development Level, in Five-Year Intervals

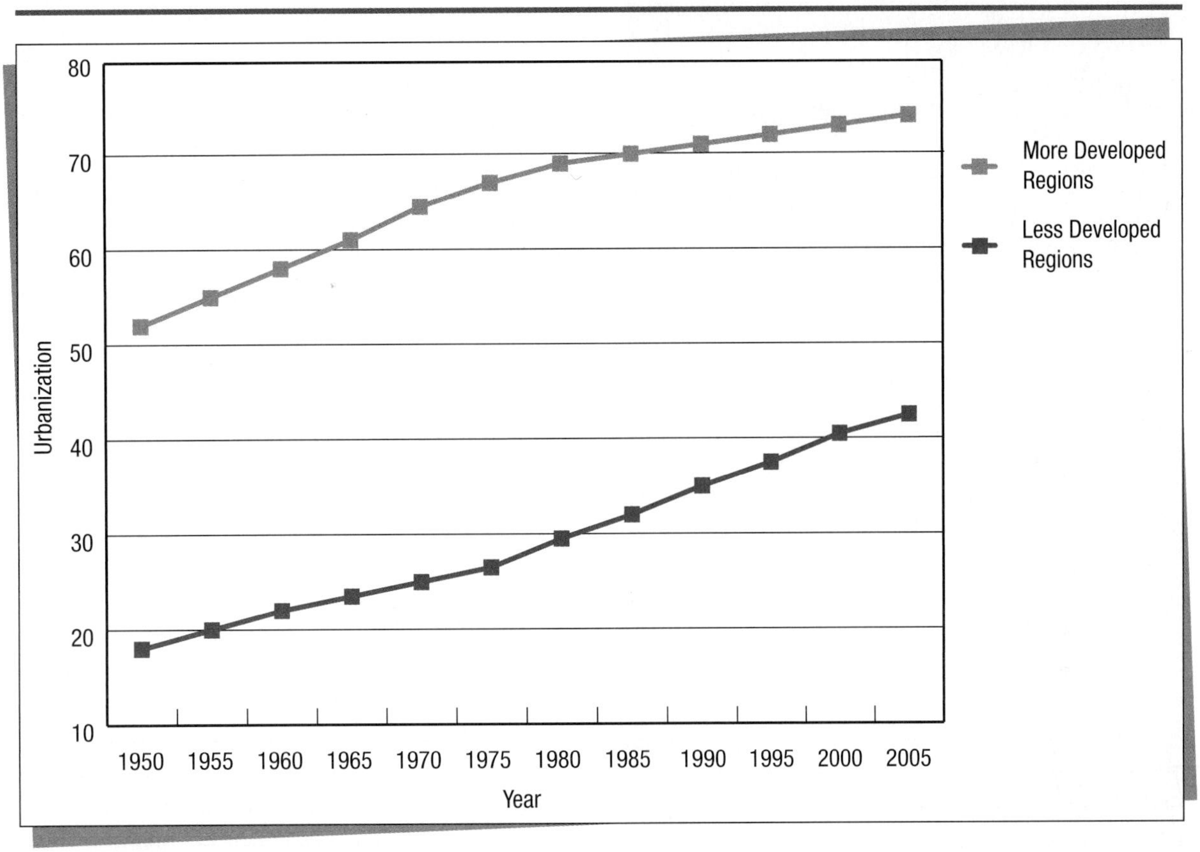

Source: UN (2006c).

The urban population in Western industrial societies is distributed quite evenly among a number of reasonably sized settlements, as capital and technology are diffused. In less developed nations, it is concentrated in the single very large metropolis in the country or in a region. Most of the extremely large cities in the developing world, such as Bombay, Calcutta, and Shanghai, were centres from which foreign imperial powers exported the nation's or region's raw materials for industrial production in the home countries. This system is called *imperialism.* Dogon and Kasarda (1988) suggest that these urban settlements grew to such size as they became obvious destinations for the rural poor, despite the virtual absence of an industrial economic base either in the cities or in the countries at large. Urban populations in such situations typically are underemployed, poor, and predominantly male. When more people reside in a city than would be expected from its economic base, *overurbanization* is said to occur.

When the technology and infrastructure catch up to overurbanized cities that are already large, as a second stage of growth, they become huge. Cities of 10 million or more persons are called **mega-cities**, and the majority of them are in less developed nations. Often their expansion is accompanied by environmental degradations of air, water, hazardous wastes, road accidents, noise, and various social problems such as substandard housing and poor health (Hardoy et al., 2001).

Globalization and Global Cities

Although industrialization is largely held responsible for high rates of urbanization, the recent trend of **globalization**—of corporations expanding their production and sales to many nations of the world, exporting investment capital to take advantage of lower-paid employees in other nations, and exploiting non-traditional markets for the resultant products—has led to added growth and wealth in a few cities. Such cities have witnessed extensive development of corporate organization, finance, telecommunications, and air transportation. These favoured cities, known as **global cities**, manifest high levels of technology. As David Thorns puts it, 'Global cities are now the key sites for the control, coordination,

Table 21.2 The 20 Largest Cities in the World in 2005

	Population (in millions)
1. Tokyo	35.2
2. Mexico City	19.4
3. New York City	18.7
4. São Paulo	18.3
5. Mumbai (Bombay)	18.2
6. Delhi	15
7. Shanghai	14.5
8. Kolkata (Calcutta)	14.3
9. Jakarta	13.2
10. Buenos Aires	12.6
12. Dhaka	12.4
13. Karachi	11.6
14. Rio de Janeiro	11.5
15. Osaka/Kobe	11.3
16. Al-Qahirah (Cairo)	11.1
17. Lagos	10.9
18. Beijing	10.7
19. Manila	10.7
20. Moskva (Moscow)	10.7
47. Toronto	5.3
75. Montreal	3.6
167. Vancouver	2.2

Source: Compiled from UN (2006b).

processing and distribution of knowledge that makes them the engines of growth within the present stage of capitalist development' (2002: 54). They are vital centres for the flow of information, direction, and money, and do not have to be on the doorstep of the heavy industries that they indirectly control and co-ordinate. Global cities reflect the presence of interacting financial enterprises through highly concentrated and prominent office buildings (Castells, 1989; Sassen, 1991).

Saskia Sassen (1991) argues that such cities as New York, London, and Tokyo have achieved more prominence than might be projected from their manufacturing base, while large cities based more fully on manufacturing, such as Detroit in the United States and Manchester in England, do not gain global status because they do not need the same degree of white-collar employment right at hand. Toronto is considered a minor global city, and Vancouver is similarly active on the Pacific Rim.

Can globalization be viewed as a modern form of imperialism, in which profits and consumer products flow from around the world to the home country, rather than the traditional imperialism where raw materials were imported for home-country industries and their wage workers? Globalization provides return on capital to corporate investors in the economically advantaged countries, while exporting productive jobs to the developing nations. The process puts large numbers of people in the latter nations into a growing international economic market that increasingly supersedes the social and political policies and actions of sovereign nations. One impact of this free-wheeling commerce is increasing polarization between rich and poor on a global scale.

In Canada, as in the United States, economic factors pull people to cities rather than push them away from rural areas. Figure 21.3 shows that, as of 2006, the majority of people in every Canadian province and territory except Prince Edward Island and Nunavut were city dwellers. Thus, high levels of urbanization are not confined to Ontario and Quebec, with Canada's two largest cities. There is a predominant urban presence in British Columbia, the Prairie provinces, and in most of the Atlantic provinces, too. The relatively large recent growth of Toronto and Vancouver is related to major global factors, while cities such as Winnipeg, Montreal, and Hamilton, though major centres within the Canadian context, lack comparable levels of international roles with which to boost their employment and population. For more detail on Canadian urbanization, see Hiller (2005).

Time to Reflect

To what extent do you think you can predict future developments in urbanization from an understanding of past trends? Why or why not?

GLOBAL ISSUES

The Gap between the Real World and Statistical Measures

The documenting of various aspects of urbanization demonstrates many of the measurement challenges facing sociologists more generally. For example, the basic measure of urbanization—percentage of persons in a nation living in urban areas—depends on a standard definition of what constitutes an urban area. In some nations, it means residing in a municipality of 5,000 persons. In others, the threshold is only 1,000 persons, while in some others it is as high as 10,000 persons. Beijing, for example, is known to have at least 3 million undocumented residents in addition to the nearly 11 million officially reported as legal residents.

The degree to which census organizations are able to accurately count urban and rural populations is variable. The size of large cities also reflects how wide an area of settlement is considered to be part of a given city. Urban regions, larger than a named municipality, are often considered a logical unit for which to present demographic statistics. But how such regions are defined and then measured varies greatly from place to place and from time to time. For example, Tokyo could lose nine million people while New York would gain three million by virtue of a different set of definitions (see *Statistics Norway*, 2005: Table 53). Despite such revision Tokyo would still be largest and New York just slightly less. Therefore, descriptive and analytic numbers should be understood in terms of the best efforts of researchers and knowledge of the criteria they employ, rather than as absolutely objective and fully comparable facts.

Urbanism

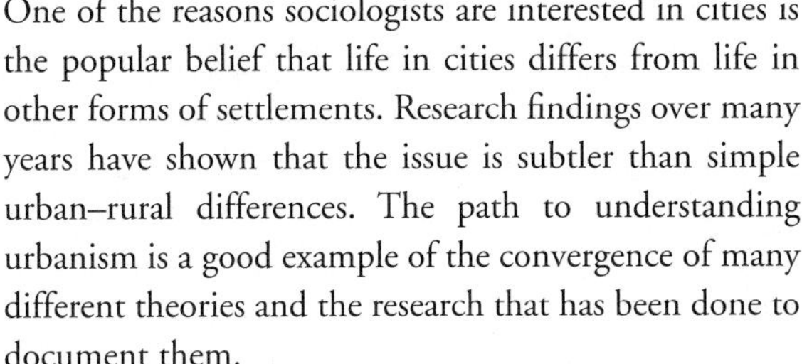

One of the reasons sociologists are interested in cities is the popular belief that life in cities differs from life in other forms of settlements. Research findings over many years have shown that the issue is subtler than simple urban–rural differences. The path to understanding urbanism is a good example of the convergence of many different theories and the research that has been done to document them.

Classical Approaches

Early approaches to urbanism seemed to make the assumption that urban contexts cause certain forms of behaviour in a very direct way. This viewpoint is known as *determinism*, since it supposes that a given set of conditions determines behavioural outcomes. Does life in an urban context differ systematically from that in a rural context? Sjoberg (1960) found that job specialization and the complexity of production and marketing that accompanied industrialization required standardization in weights, measures, currencies, pricing, and financial interaction. For the system to work, rational, exact actions became necessary. Classical theorists such as Max Weber, Sir Henry Maine, Ferdinand Tönnies, and Émile Durkheim used different words, but made similar observations that urban life is more likely to involve rational, universalistic, impersonal, and logistically oriented behaviours than had been the case in earlier rural settings. Noting that German urbanites had to pay constant attention to contextual signals—lights, signs, footsteps, whistles, and the like—Georg Simmel (1950) summarized these observations by saying that the head, rather than the heart, dictates most urban behaviours.

The best-known ideas on urbanism may be attributed to Louis Wirth's 1938 article 'Urbanism as a Way of Life'. Wirth believed that cities have three defining characteristics—large numbers of inhabitants, high densities, and heterogeneous populations—each accounting for important aspects of an urban way of life. Large numbers lead to the impossibility of knowing all persons, and hence to the relative absence of intimacy in most interpersonal relationships. Human relations become segmented into many largely anonymous, superficial, transitory contacts. At the same time, high density fosters human diversification and specialization. Social distance is established to maintain personal space

Figure 21.3 Urbanization of Canada, by Province and Territory, 2001

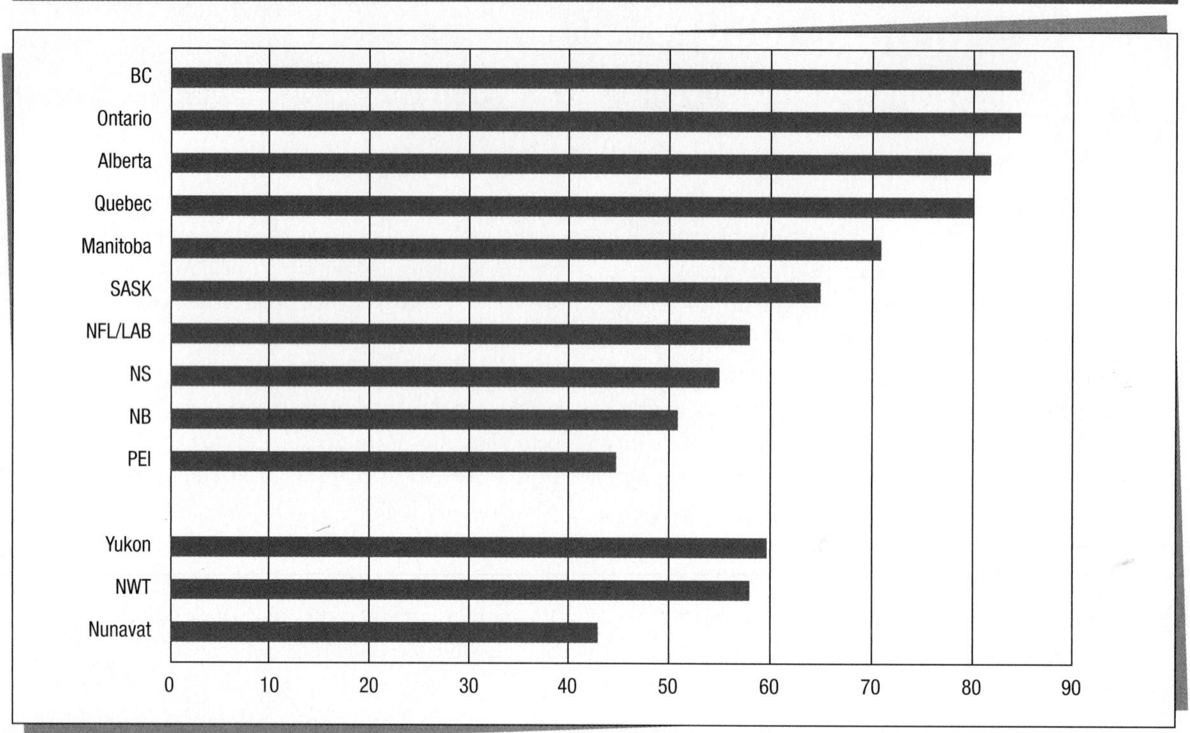

Source: Adapted from data in Statistics Canada (2007a).

in response to the inescapable presence of close physical contact with diverse persons. Nonetheless, accentuated friction inevitably arises, and formal means of social control, notably uniformed police, assume prominence in cities. Despite, or perhaps because of, such close proximity, complex patterns of segregation take shape. Finally, heterogeneity makes it difficult for individuals to be constricted by rigid social structures, as in rural areas. Urban individuals more often find themselves in varied social settings and groups. Both upward and downward mobility, with the resultant greater feelings of instability and insecurity, are more likely in cities.

Although classical approaches to urbanism never achieved total consensus among sociologists, the classical legacy was sobering. Any societal gains derived from greater division of labour, rationality, and personal freedom seemed counterbalanced by unending suspicion, distrust, and isolation.

Modern Social-Psychological Approaches

Modern social psychologists have been particularly taken by the earlier theoretical themes dealing with urban life as situated in the impersonal presence of great numbers of strangers, some of whom represent annoyance at the least and, more seriously, risk. Lyn Lofland wrote a valuable analysis of how people relate to each other in cities, with the germane title, *A World of Strangers* (1985). In it, she stressed that people minimize interpersonal interaction as a way to maximize public order (that is, safety). In more recent work (Lofland, 1998), she delves into how urbanites have a love–hate relationship with public spaces. She suggests that even though people potentially access unparalleled experiences in the congregating spaces of large cities, the public realm has been largely neglected as a result of the ambivalence urbanites have about contact with strangers.

Stanley Milgram (1970: 1462) made a noteworthy contribution to Simmel's notion of impersonal signals bombarding urbanites. Using modern systems analysis, Milgram characterized it as sensory overload: 'City life, as we experience it, constitutes a continuous set of encounters with overload, and of resultant adaptations.' He went on to describe a variety of ways in which urbanites cope with overload. All of them are literally textbook examples of the *Gesellschaft* side of Tönnies's classical theoretical dichotomy between *Gemeinschaft* and *Gesellschaft*—figuratively, 'heart' *versus* 'head' as describing social interaction in societies.

Urban life in a world of strangers: a subway station. (William Michelson)

One common strategy for coping with overload is to tune out what is found to be overburdening: anything from drunks, through poverty, to negative consequences of public- or private-sector policies or practices that benefit only some. Increasing numbers of persons literally live on the streets of Canada. Many citizens have taken active ameliorative roles in food drives, food banks, and night patrols for the homeless, but the context of everyday life for most people involves passively working around difficult situations.

In another coping strategy, urbanites are said to avoid aiding strangers who need help in order to avoid trouble themselves. Much research followed the public shock that resulted when Kitty Genovese was murdered after appealing for help outside the windows of at least 38 onlooking neighbours in a New York City apartment house. The research suggested that the more people there are, the less likely any individual will intervene. People are more likely to intervene if they feel that they are needed in the absence of others.

Urbanites also minimize involvement by taking action to remove themselves from easy contact with strangers. They buy telephone-answering devices or subscribe to voice-mail services, institute scripted menus to provide information, fail to list their telephone numbers (this is certainly the case for ubiquitous cellphones), preview incoming calls, filter visitors through secretaries and assistants, travel by private automobile, and live in segregated (increasingly, guarded) buildings and **neighbourhoods**. Ironically, the same people are in greater contact than ever with those they know, through the medium of electronic mail.

People use a range of coping procedures in public places. They pretend not to see each other (for example, on beaches), and tolerate other lifestyles except where these represent clear and present dangers. They follow unspoken but definite rules about how much distance to keep from others for particular purposes, where they sit (for example, on buses or in libraries), and the way they walk (Hall, 1966; Sommer, 1969).

Urbanites, however, are not totally isolated beings. There are public settings where people come to expect to interact with other persons in ways that they don't during most public encounters. Churches, bars, and sporting events, for example, all provide the opportunity for positive interactions among persons with similar interests and objectives. When people want to communicate to others their personal identity, they once relied on clothing in general and uniforms in particular to provide a basis for secure interaction without previous personal acquaintance. In smaller settings, the family name was noteworthy, and it still is in some circles. However, in urban circles in which consumer goods like clothing are rampant and family connections may be obscure, personal credentials (transcripts, credit cards, etc.) and home addresses help complete the introduction, for good and for ill. According to Abu-Lughod (1991: 338), 'the larger neighborhood or even the city can take on an important symbolic and social meaning, serving as a source of identity ("I come from Grosse Pointe").' However, government-issued photo identification has become *de rigueur*. Even people without cars have driver's licences for personal identification. And, increasingly, this is not sufficient.

The Subcultural Theory of Urban Life

Is it really some aspect of the city that calls for coping behaviours such as those described by Milgram? Albert J. Reiss Jr (1959) found that the anonymous, segmented, and impersonal relations noted by Wirth reflected occupation more than residence. For instance, men living in rural areas with non-farm jobs had daily contact patterns resembling those of their urban counterparts.

In contrast to the deterministic approach of the classical thinkers, other sociologists adopt a *compositional* perspective, according to which behaviour reflects the composition of the population. Herbert Gans (1967), for example, explained suburban behaviour not in terms of the physical nature of the area, but in terms of the social class background and life-cycle characteristics of the population in the suburb he studied. The nature and extent of their contact with neighbours, their participation in organizations, and their interest in schools all reflected middle-class background and the presence of families with young children, according to Gans. In short, exponents of the compositional approach believe that urban life reflects the most salient features (for example, class, ethnic background or race, religion, age, and sex) of the particular population groups living in particular cities and/or their constituent parts.

In *The Urban Experience* (1976), Claude Fischer attempted to reconcile deterministic and compositional theories and to go beyond them. Fischer argues that Wirth was right in stressing the significance of large numbers of persons in cities. But Fischer does not see the numbers as providing various direct effects; rather, he considers their primary importance as providing the nucleus for various specialized *subcultures* within cities. It is the particular compositions of the various subcultures that influence so-called urban lifestyles.

Fischer calls his approach the *subcultural theory* of urban life. Which subcultures become significant in a given city depends on many macroscopic characteristics of cities: their economic base, sources of migration, climate, and more. Within highly urbanized societies, cities of different sizes and in different locations may be functionally specialized. This does not mean that they are monolithic in terms of their activities or resident populations; but there are distinct tendencies regarding who chooses to live and work there and, hence, which subcultures take root. It is unusual even for a city spe-

OPEN FOR DISCUSSION

Individual Identity in a World of Strangers

In response to the unprecedented taking of American civilian lives on 11 September 2001, the issue of individual identity has arisen not only in the United States but in Canada and other nations as well. The fear of strangers has been made a public issue by some political leaders. The public sector has stepped into the void of personal acquaintance to screen persons more thoroughly at fixed locations such as airline check-in counters and border crossings, though photo ID scrutiny has increased in countless other situations. Personal searches of those entering clubs and sporting events have increased.

Do you think that the circumstances of 9/11 and subsequent developments justify proactive public intervention into the largely impersonal world of urban residents? Compare political reactions to the tragic loss of life on 9/11 to the considerably greater morbidity each year in cities from firearm violations and automobile accidents (not least from drunk drivers). How does the fear of strangers alter public reaction to these different situations?

Time to Reflect

Which theory of urbanism do you find most compelling? What does it explain?

cializing in industry to have more than 25 per cent of its jobs in manufacturing because of the need for complementary and supportive activities; yet the difference between 25 per cent in manufacturing and 10 per cent spells a big difference in the *critical mass* of a blue-collar subculture. Hamilton, with its huge steel mills, differs substantially in its ways of life from nearby London, an insurance and financial centre and both differ from Victoria, with its combination of government jobs, retirees, mild weather, and afternoon tea! However, the largest national cities tend to be diverse economically, with their population size supporting varied subcultures and lifestyles. It takes a Toronto, not a Truro, to supply the critical masses for creating the world's most ethnically diverse city, where the varied ethnic communities enjoy rich, visible cultural lives—some manifestations of which are shared with the city population at large—and where these cultural groups exist side-by-side with youth, yuppie, gay, sports, criminal, and endless other subcultures.

Does Fischer's subcultural theory invalidate the generalizations made by urban social psychologists about such problems as overload, anonymity, and coping adaptations? In subsequent work, Fischer (1982) shows that the personal contact patterns of urbanites are more firmly concentrated in specialized groupings (which in cities means subcultures) than those of people living in smaller communities and rural areas. Similarly, big-city dwellers are likely to trust their closest neighbours, but not urbanites in general.

Visible signs of an Asian ethnic community in Toronto. (William Michelson)

Ecology

You have already seen much evidence that urban behaviour patterns reflect subcultural cleavages. You might expect, therefore, that the physical structure of cities will reflect and reinforce these patterns. Examining the city in ecological terms strongly supports such an expectation. We know that most cities comprise distinct parts.

HUMAN DIVERSITY

Gender and the Everyday Use of Urban Contexts

Regularities in the way people manage their interactions with others in public areas become most evident in times of social change. It is then that unstated assumptions are challenged, and the implications of emerging behaviours are felt most strongly. It is perhaps noteworthy in this connection that some of the most dramatic episodes in the long-term trend towards greater racial integration have focused on the shared use of public facilities: buses, beaches, and bathrooms. While such facilities are a tangential part of everyday life, they strongly symbolize differential assumptions about who mingles with whom, where, and for what purpose.

One of the major social changes of the past 20 years is the increase in the percentage of women with young children who undertake paid employment. Their numbers have risen from a minority (clearly thought of as an exception to the norm of women staying home to care for children) to a majority approaching 70 per cent, even among mothers of preschool children. Among the many explanations for the change are greater support for gender equality, higher education among women, increases in the cost of living (particularly housing), a rising divorce rate, and a growing incidence of childbirth among single women. Much attention is given to how women balance traditional household responsibilities and the demands of the paid employment sector, as well as to the availability of child care and other relevant support facilities.

A relatively neglected aspect of the growing employment of mothers is the revolution in women's use of non-traditional urban spaces and their interaction with other persons there. When women were more likely to 'stay home', far more emphasis was placed on the nature of their neighbourhoods. The local area was a cocoon, containing (to the extent that could be arranged) the 'right' kind of neighbours and stores, in a setting conducive to safety. Errands away from home occurred during the day, unless a woman was accompanied by her husband. Women therefore spent much time alone, with their children, or with immediate neighbours, when not with their husbands. For employed women, the pattern of daily life is very different. Relatively little time is spent with neighbours (less than was previously spent with relatives), but much more is spent with other types of people on the job. Most women now spend a significant part of the day in non-domestic settings, usually outside their own neighbourhoods, and they travel at non-traditional times on non-traditional routes, usually without spousal accompaniment.

Past understandings about whom people meet, how they differentiate themselves, and who might be expected to be found in what location (and for what purpose) are in a state of flux. The results are ambiguity, concern, and, unfortunately, danger. Adaptation to social change lags behind the overt change itself. How long will it take for women to be able to travel safely home from work, through areas where women aren't expected to be out after dark?

A major national study in 1993 by Statistics Canada found that more than 80 per cent of women fear entering parking garages; 76 per cent worry about using public transportation after dark; and 60 per cent are afraid to walk in their neighbourhoods after dark. In her report on the Statistics Canada data, Rosemary Speirs notes, '42 per cent said they have no choice in walking alone on dark streets at least weekly. Young women living in large cities are most fearful of situations in which they are alone after dark' (1993: A29).

Perhaps it is not surprising that sociologists and geographers have discovered this neglected aspect of the interaction between social change and urban space (Hanson, 1992; Michelson, 2005; Wekerle, 2005).

The ecological perspective addresses the nature of these parts and what kinds of patterns they form.

Cities, Suburbs, and Metropolitan Areas

While urbanization levels in Canada show that Canadians live predominantly in cities, they do not reveal in what types of settlements or where within them we live. Do most Canadians live in large or small cities, in central cities or suburbs?

A common pattern in technologically advanced societies has been the build-up of population beyond the borders of older cities and into newer municipalities immediately adjacent. These are commonly called *suburbs*, although the word is often applied to areas that simply look newer and less crowded than the centres of the traditional cities. Montreal and Vancouver, for example, have many suburbs, while much of Calgary and Edmonton appear suburban.

Large cities and their suburbs may represent different municipalities, but, in terms of everyday behaviour and economic activity, they form an entity known as a **metropolitan area**. Many people live in one part of a metropolitan area and work in another; there is, for instance, an active interchange between Vancouver and New Westminster.

Statistics Canada defines a *census metropolitan area* (CMA) as an area comprised of one or more large cities (totalling at least 100,000 inhabitants at the previous census) in the centre (the urban core) together with surrounding areas that are economically and socially integrated on a day-to-day basis with the urban core (1992: 29). On the basis of these criteria, some CMAs include a central city with many municipalities extending a considerable distance from the urban core, while others consist of a single municipality. The makeup of a CMA reflects the size of the urban area, its history, and the amount of land suitable for expansion under the control of the central city. Toronto extends as a functional entity almost as far as Hamilton (that is, through Oakville), while the formal city of Saskatoon not only includes nearly all the residents in its vicinity but also controls undeveloped land for future development. There are 33 CMAs in Canada. Although these metropolitan areas take up only a tiny fraction of the land in Canada, in 2006 they were home to approximately 21.5 million of Canada's population of 31.6 million—more than two-thirds of the national population (Statistics Canada, 2007a). Canada's urban population is not characterized by dispersal into many small cities and towns across the landscape; it is highly concentrated within metropolitan areas. This is especially true when we realize that nearly 11 million people live in Canada's three largest cities—Toronto, Montreal, and Vancouver.

Many people have an image of the city as an older municipality with a high density and buildings that are large and striking or old and grey. The suburbs are, somehow, something else. This view needs revision. Table 21.3 presents Canadian CMAs with about 300,000 residents or more in order of size in 2006, indicating in the final column the percentage of inhabitants living outside what is currently designated as the central city; this varies from 0 to 76 per cent of CMA population. Within all of these 16 cities, 44.2 per cent of residents are suburbanites by this measure. However, this considerably underestimates the extent of suburban presence in CMAs, as the current central-city boundaries of Toronto, Montreal, Ottawa, Quebec City, Hamilton, and Halifax have recently been expanded to include substantial numbers of suburban municipalities that had grown outside original central-city boundaries; thus, until now, these amalgamated municipalities were considered as suburban. It is not an exaggeration to confirm the conclusion drawn from previous analyses that most residents of Canadian (and American) metropolitan areas are suburbanites.

This distribution is essential to an understanding of the pattern of local areas and lifestyles in metropolitan areas. Whereas previously people focused on the central city and spoke in stereotypical terms about the suburbs and suburbanites, now it is essential to recognize that the majority of the urban population live outside of traditional central cities.

Metropolitan Population and Land-Use Patterns

How are people and their subcultures patterned within metropolitan areas? Several theories have been proposed to answer this question.

From studies of Chicago, Ernest Burgess (1925) identified the *concentric ring* land-use and stratification pattern of cities. At the heart of this pattern is the *central business district* (CBD), consisting of the principal private- and public-sector offices, department stores, and hotels. The CBD is serviced by public transit to make it the most accessible place in the city. Burgess assumed that the CBD would be the only major centre in the city, and that it would continue to grow indefinitely.

Because of this growth, the land around the CBD would be held speculatively for future profit. Before upgrading, the *zone in transition* would be used, with-

Table 21.3 The Size and Suburban Proportion of Canada's Largest Census Metropolitan Areas, 2006

Census Metropolitan Area	Total Population in 2006	Per cent of Population Outside Central City
1. Toronto	5,113,149	51
2. Montreal	3,635,571	55
3. Vancouver	2,116,581	73
4. Ottawa–Gatineau	1,130,761	28
5. Calgary	1,079,310	8
6. Edmonton	1,034,945	29
7. Quebec City	715,515	31
8. Winnipeg	694,668	9
9. Hamilton	692,911	27
10. London	457,720	23
11. Kitchener	451,235	33
12. St Catharines–Niagara	390,317	45
13. Halifax	372,858	0
14. Victoria	330,088	76
15. Oshawa	330,594	57
16. Windsor	323,342	33

Source: Calculated from Statistics Canada, Population and dwelling counts, for Canada, census metropolitan areas, census agglomerations and census subdivisions (municipality), 2006 and 2001 censuses – 100% data, at: <www12.statcan.ca/english/census06/data/popdwell>.

out maintenance or improvement, for rooming houses, transient hotels, and other impermanent uses. This zone would contain the poorest, newest migrants, the criminal element, and prostitutes—all subcultures requiring short-term affordable housing and, in many cases, anonymity. The more regularized sectors of the population would be distributed in rings around both the CBD and the zone in transition, in proportion to their ability to pay for greater amounts of land increasingly far from these two areas, as well as for the cost and time involved in longer commutes. Thus, working-class communities would be surrounded by the middle class, which in turn would be surrounded by the upper class.

In short, according to Burgess, major land uses would claim the city centre through market-mechanism competition, while residential areas would be distributed at varying distances from the CBD according to income.

Another member of the Chicago School of urban sociology, Robert E. Park (1925), labelled as **community** the forms of behaviour thought to arise because 'birds of a feather flock together.' Within a given ring, local communities that were homogeneous by ethnic or religious background would form within boundaries formed by major streets, railways, parks, and the like. Park called these communities *natural areas* because no one rationally planned their location—they were simply a function of land value (thought to lie beyond the control of individuals) and incidental boundaries. According to this view, by the physical proximity of people to one another in the natural area the critical mass of people in subcultures could exercise a strong influence on individual behaviour.

Unfortunately for theorists, the concentric ring pattern is far from universal; it has been demonstrated to exist in few places outside Chicago. Indeed, in many settings outside the United States, the rich occupy the city centres, while the poor are left outside of the benefits of urban infrastructure.

Ironically, it was right in Chicago that another researcher, Homer Hoyt (1939), discovered a rather different pattern. Hoyt's *sectors* resemble pieces of a pie, extending from the centre outward without interruption. Hoyt noted that certain amenities, such as waterfront parks, and eyesores, such as freight railways, extended outward. People of means would try to live within view of the amenities; those of few means would follow the tracks; still others would locate themselves in-between. One side of town would become better than another, if only because it was upwind from centrally located industries.

A third approach is Harris and Ullman's *multiple nuclei theory* (1945), which states that each land use or subculture is located according to unique criteria having to do with the proximity of other land uses. Heavy industry, for example, wants to be near railroads and highways, but doesn't need to be as accessible to consumers as do retailing land uses. Head offices draw fine restaurants, banks, and law offices to their vicinity, while universities attract fast-food and coffee chains, copy shops, computer outlets, and bookstores. The result is a city with many diverse centres whose locations are not in a fixed geometric pattern.

A statistical process called *factorial ecology* lets sociologists analyze census statistics for local areas of a given city to determine the patterns shown by such dimen-

Central business districts are common in cities throughout the world. Pictured is the CBD in contemporary Singapore in Southeast Asia. (William Michelson)

sions. Robert Murdie (1969) drew a number of conclusions in his pioneering analysis of Metro Toronto: that family size increased with distance from the centre; that social class segregation was in sectors from the centre outward; and that ethnic groups lived in unique clusters of multiple nuclei. He demonstrated that a single city could show several different patterns, depending on the criterion. No one pattern of land use characterizes all cities.

Neighbourhood and Community

The various approaches discussed above might lead you to conclude that every city dweller lives in a tightly knit neighbourhood made up of people similar in social class, family size, and ethnicity. While this is not the case, it is true that the concepts of neighbourhood and community help to clarify urban settlement patterns. A **neighbourhood** is a specific physical area within a city that may or may not have formal boundaries, though people may have an image of it even without any consensus on its exact territory. *Community* refers to tangible interpersonal contact patterns; the term has primarily social connotations.

Traditionally, neighbourhood and community were synonymous. In the old days, or in small communities, people centred their interpersonal relationships within the physical areas where they lived. According to the deterministic view of urbanism, this kind of community was lost in the city. However, later researchers, such as Gans (1962), found extremely strong ethnic subcultures in cities that appeared to re-establish the identity between community and neighbourhood. Barry Wellman and Barry Leighton (1979) declared community regained. More penetrating analyses of interpersonal networks went on to show that many people in cities have specific types of contact patterns that often reflect subcultures but have no reference to the boundaries of neighbourhoods (Hampton, 2005). Close associates may be all over the map, yet may easily be reached by telephone or computer, or met at work, bars, parties, or conventions. Webber (1963) called this phenomenon *community without propinquity*; Wellman and Leighton (1979) termed it *community liberated* or *unbound*.

Urban neighbourhoods take various forms, starting with the *ideal type*, where everybody interacts with everyone else (Hallman, 1984; Wireman, 1984). A *conscious neighbourhood* is something that developers and designers work to achieve in newly built areas by trying to construct unifying symbols, so that residents will treat the area well and interact with each other. Clarence Perry (1966) created the *neighbourhood unit plan* in 1927. It was an area of about 400 homes surrounded by traffic arteries but with only local roads inside, focusing on an elementary school and communal facilities. Although Perry's plan has been shown ineffective in its most grandiose social engineering objectives, for the reason that people often have greater interpersonal loyalties elsewhere, it has been highly influential in suburban development. The most common urban neighbourhoods represent what Janowitz (1952) called the *community of limited liability*. People recognize that they live in a specific area that has identifiable institutions, yet is the limit neither to their contact patterns nor to their everyday activities.

A Closer Look at Selected Urban Neighbourhoods

Within the inner areas of cities, planners have noted the crucial differences between slums and low-income ethnic subcultural neighbourhoods. The former, typified by the skid row (or *skid road*), is what Burgess meant by his zones in transition. People go to such areas to avoid contact, usually for short periods. Intense personal networks are uncommon, and there is little or no proprietary interest in buildings or neighbourhood areas apart from their pragmatic, short-term function. Skid rows contrast greatly in their interpersonal communities with other areas that may also have older buildings, poor maintenance, and people of modest means, but where well-established kinship and neighbourhood relationships exist. Gans (1962) and Whyte (1943) have written extremely detailed accounts of the high degree of organization in two Italian-American communities in central Boston. Gans called such neighbourhoods *urban villages*, a term fitting many neighbourhoods with ethnic communities in Canadian cities, including the Italian (Sidlofsky, 1969), Jewish (Shaffir, 1974), and Portuguese (Anderson, 1974).

Gentrification, studied in Canada by David Ley (1991), is a different phenomenon. To take Rosenthal's (1980) description, upper-middle-class professionals move into and transform formerly working-class areas of the central city. Gentrification is well developed in Canada, the United States, Britain, and other nations. The trend shows certain characteristics: it occurs less frequently in new cities; its extent is highly variable; it normally occurs in cities with centralized white-collar and professional jobs, where the suburbs are extending farther and farther, and where the housing stock in one or more relatively central areas is fundamentally sound and has aesthetic potential and historic interest.

The gentrification process begins when wealthier individuals purchase, restore, and modernize the older buildings in a given neighbourhood for personal use or for sale at enormous markups. As more members of the upper middle class move in, the neighbourhood changes. Local businesses shift towards the tastes of well-heeled adults: trendy restaurants, health food stores, art galleries, computer boutiques, and similar concerns appear. In Toronto, a rundown area known for decades as Cabbagetown has, with gentrification, assumed the more upscale name of Don Vale.

While some Canadian cities have witnessed the slow but mellow transformation of existing neighbourhoods through gentrification, the subsequent condominium boom is more obvious. This currently ongoing boom in the larger cities involves a radical intensification of building, both in the central cities and in suburbs, whereby land that is underutilized is covered by (usually) high-rise buildings in which apartments are created for purchase. In some instances, ground-level space is rented to commercial enterprises such as grocers, coffee shops, and home furnishing stores. Many purchasers of condo units are doing so for speculative purposes, with the result that these units become an informal part of the rental market—but expanding only the more expensive part of the market, not adding generally affordable rental housing to scarce supply. Although the condo boom is upgrading the urban streetscape and expanding the tax base for cities, neither this nor the gentrification trend offers any hope to the less affluent segment of the population. Vacated housing does not work its way down to use by the destitute in Canada's growing cities.

The suburbs also provide a diversity of urban neighbourhoods. The old suburban stereotypes came from studies of middle- and upper-middle-class areas. But other segments of the population seek suburban residence as well; many blue-collar families have sought affordable housing away from what some regard as disreputable elements in the central city. Clark (1966) has pointed out that suburban lifestyles end up reflecting diversity in the composition of their residential populations.

Three new trends have appeared in the past decade. The first is the transformation of centrally located former industrial and warehousing sites and railway yards, the original uses for which have become outdated by changes in production and transportation technologies and the relocation of manufacturing to other parts of the world as part of globalization. These areas are called

Toronto: (left) Condominium apartments and sports facilities on former brownfields (right). Current construction is ongoing on adjacent brownfields, with an earlier generation of such redeveloped brownfields behind (and bordering Lake Ontario). (William Michelson)

brownfields. Brownfields are increasingly replaced by condominium buildings, sports and convention facilities, and shopping centres, and the momentum for these changes is being felt in many cities on both sides of the border, as well as in European cities. The Canada Mortgage and Housing Corporation (2006) details contemporary brownfield conversion into housing in such diverse cities as Richmond and Kelowna, British Columbia; Edmonton, Alberta; Cambridge, Dundas, and Hamilton, Ontario; Montreal, Quebec; and Charlottetown, Prince Edward Island.

A second trend is the **edge city**. This is the creation of highly concentrated business, commercial, and high-technology centres on lower-cost land on the fringes of urban areas, which suburbanites find easier to access than the traditional central business district. The edge city becomes a competitor to the original central city, with comparative economic advantages and an absence

Left: Brownfield redevelopment in port area of Montreal in foreground. Old Montreal is in background. (William Michelson) Right: The Yaletown Urban Renewal Project in Vancouver, on the north shore of False Creek brownfield. (© Steve Allen/BrandX/MAGMA)

of central-city costs and difficulties. Joel Garreau (1992) describes edge cities in such differing places as Boston, the state of New Jersey, Washington, DC, and Atlanta. Edge cities are evident north and west of Toronto and south of Vancouver.

Another trend emerging primarily in the United States is the development of occasional planned towns under the guiding theories of the *new urbanism* (Duany et al., 2000). These are towns or settlements on the outer fringes or entirely away from existing cities, built with a unifying design reflecting a period of historical gentility and emphasizing public spaces to be shared by wealthy owners of the private homes built according to the plan. They have become refuges for affluent people seeking alternatives to contemporary cities, on the premise that the solution to urban problems is to ignore them in congenial company elsewhere. In the southern United States, Georgian architecture is popular. The city of Seaside, Florida, is an early icon of the new urbanism (and the location of the popular 1998 film *The Truman Show*). The Disney Corporation has created a rendition of this kind of development in a new town called Celebration, which has been criticized for over-regimentation and control by the developer and a lack of diversity due to the deliberate unavailability of affordable housing (Gold, 2002). A subdivision called Cornell built according to new urbanism principles has been built in the suburban belt north of Toronto; after much discussion, Victorian architecture was chosen, as found historically in Cabbagetown/Don Vale.

Less developed nations, whose large cities typically receive immigrants fleeing rural poverty, add another suburban variation, the *shantytown* (also known as the *favela* or *bidonville*). A shantytown is built in extremely short order with a miscellany of salvaged materials on found land in poorly accessible areas outside the actual cities. It has little or no infrastructure and is an illegal first foothold giving residents some access to the city without the requirements of money, jobs, or legitimacy. Planners and other observers despair of these communities, but development agencies have learned that the most responsible reaction is to try to help the residents by installing such basic aspects of infrastructure as sewage, water, and electricity. As the economic situation of the shantytown dwellers starts to improve, so too does their quality of life, and mobility to better housing and/or location becomes a possibility (Van Vliet et al., 1985)—as is the gradual normalization of housing quality in the peripheral areas.

Shantytown in far suburban hill township outside Durban, South Africa. (William Michelson)

These glimpses of selected urban neighbourhoods have been extremely brief. Still, they serve to prove that a huge variety of factors—far more than just the growth of the central business district—accounts for differentiation among metropolitan areas. Many kinds of rational human intervention establish and change local areas, beyond the invisible reach of land economics. Developers cultivate new neighbourhood images; real estate agents help reinforce or change the composition of older ones. Banks and insurance companies can influence who enters, leaves, and stays in neighbourhoods through their lending and insuring policies. Planning and zoning activities affect stability and change, while ratepayers' associations, tenant groups, and trade organizations influence planning and zoning bodies.

The variation in neighbourhood mix is accentuated by a non-random distribution of population in residential space. Affordability is linked to socio-economic status. Different types of housing and location come with different household structure; families with children often have different criteria in choosing housing than do elderly persons and couples. People with the same backgrounds are more likely than not to live together, and this is clearly exemplified in regard to ethnicity, whether by choice or by compulsion.

Paul Jargowsky's work in the United States (1997) suggests the presence of economic and racial segregation working together. Many areas in American central cities and inner suburbs are designated as high-poverty areas (when 40 per cent or more of residents live in poverty) but distinguished as being black ghettos, Hispanic barrios, or white slums—different names according to the nature of the occupants. Recent research suggests the emergence during the past several decades of such high-poverty areas in Toronto, reflecting an increase in the polarization of local areas between high and low economic groups (United Way of Greater Toronto and the Canadian Council on Social Development, 2004).

Critical masses of persons having diverse ethnicities are common to Canadian cities (Fong, 2005; Reitz and Lum, 2006). But their locations and characteristics within cities are not as constant as in American cities (Fong, 2006; Michelson, 2006). A tradition is evident in Halifax of black versus white residential clustering. Montreal is residentially divided between French, English, and allophone. Toronto finds distinct, but certainly not total, ethnic clustering of Portuguese, Jews, Italians, Chinese, East Indians, Maltese, Ukrainians, Greeks, Russians, and many other groups. In Vancouver, the Chinese ethnic population has traditionally been residentially segregated, though now the Chinese in Vancouver are becoming a significant proportion of the population. Native Canadians are significantly segregated throughout many cities (see Ponting, 2005).

Although there is much clustering in Canadian cities by ethnicity, this does not mean that a great percentage of single groups are necessarily in a single place or in the central city. Different age and economic levels of groups like Chinese, Jews, and Italians may be found in different types of housing, locations, and levels of prosperity throughout the Toronto area, for example.

Some grouping comes about as a voluntary expression of education and lifestyle. Caulfield (1994), for example, shows how clustering in Canada can occur as a result of willed human action, or human agency, over time by like-minded people, rather than as a function of determination by either economics or external parties.

Built Environments and Behaviour

The components of the urban pattern are many and complex, as are the forces influencing them. Nevertheless, the social composition of sub-areas of cities is not the only influence on human behaviour within urban settlements. The built environment and the organization of its infrastructure also have important effects. In many instances, both the design and the planning of buildings, neighbourhoods, and cities can facilitate or constrain behaviours.

The Design of Housing and Other Institutions

Families differing in age, composition, size, and ethnic background choose or are forced to live in homes varying by size, density, layout, and amenities. Apart from connotations of status and identity, does it matter who lives where?

Numerous studies have confirmed that housing design does have an effect on people's lives (Arias, 1993; Marcus and Sarkissian, 1986). Research on middle-class married couples living in high-rise apartments and single-family homes in both downtown and suburban areas of Metro Toronto (Michelson, 1977) concluded that behaviours among those living in combinations of housing type and location differed because of the respective opportunities in housing, such as space for entertainment or hobbies within the home, and differing access by location to urban amenities and services.

Research by C. Ray Jeffery (1971) and Oscar Newman (1972) empirically confirmed prior observations by Jane Jacobs (1961) and suggested that enlightened designs for residential buildings and grounds can help prevent such crimes as vandalism and muggings, which occur where perpetrators believe they can get away with them. For example, apartment houses with stairways out of the public view provide opportunities for muggings; glass-walled stairways take away an intruder's protection. Long, anonymous hallways make it possible for strangers to lurk unchallenged, unlike small apartment groupings, where residents are more likely to know each other and their respective guests. Well-lit, open lobbies situated in view of many apartments are less a target than those that are out of sight. By extension, Robert Gifford (1987) has commented that it takes no stretch of the imagination to consider what difference the amount and design of space in schools, hospitals, offices, and factories can make to the people there.

Neighbourhood Design

Neighbourhoods have been shown to be of considerable salience to housewives, children, and others whose daily routines or resources restrict them to the areas where they live. Consider the scope of the child's world. It starts with a crib in a room and expands slowly; typically, only with adolescence does it expand beyond the neighbourhood for independent activities, and even then only by the grace of adults in the absence of good public transportation (Michelson and Roberts, 1979).

From the time they can walk until they are considered capable of negotiating the greater urban context, children are expected to conduct the sum of their daily non-school or non-daycare play and social interaction within their own neighbourhoods. How safe are these areas from grown-ups and from other children, from automobiles, from pollutants? What is there for the children to interact with? If play areas are provided, under what weather conditions can they be used? Are the play areas physically safe; interesting; available to all relevant age groups? To what extent can parents observe and control their child's situation from their dwelling unit? Is the child's play restricted by parental availability for supervision? Numerous guidelines have been set out suggesting how local neighbourhood designs can fruitfully accommodate the needs of families with children (Marcus and Sarkissian, 1986).

Comparative international research has confirmed the importance of local area characteristics in the daily lives of children, even as the particular characteristics of such neighbourhoods vary greatly from country to country, as do the cultures in which the children grow up (Chawla, 2002).

A resurgence of research attention to the characteristics of local areas within cities has been seen in recent years. Some of this emerged with respect to the risks encountered by relatively fragile sectors of the population, such as children and the elderly, to environmental perils. Air pollution, heavy traffic, vermin, and hazardous waste are distributed no more randomly than are the population groups most exposed to them. As a result, disease and accidents impact more greatly the sectors of the population with fewer economic means to have choices in where to live (Fitzgerald and LaGory, 2000).

Furthermore, research has shown that some decision-makers in both the private and public sectors consciously decide to locate noxious land uses (euphemistically known as locally unwanted land uses, or LULUs) proximate to those population groups least able to defend themselves politically against them (Bryant and Mohai, 1992). In the United States, such discrimination has been largely directed against African

SOCIOLOGY IN ACTION

Improving Women's Safety

It is becoming more common to conduct a *safety audit* in and around multiple-family dwelling areas, office buildings, universities, and transit systems. The intention is to learn from those who use these facilities the circumstances in which they feel afraid of being victimized, so that appropriate environmental changes might be made. Women's safety has become a particular concern. Toronto's subway system, for example, has responded by creating designated waiting areas on the platforms. They are monitored by television cameras, and are positioned to be adjacent to the cars of incoming trains where the conductors are stationed. City buses will halt after dark between designated bus stops so that female passengers can alight closer to home.

Americans. In Canada, powerless groups have been less specifically targeted (but see Michelson, 1997a). Native Canadians have observed more than their share of this decision-making. Attention to such practices goes under the academic heading of *environmental justice.*

Considerable attention also is being given to the aggregate social characteristics of local areas within cities, just as was the case 80 years ago in Chicago with the work of Robert Park and his colleagues at the University of Chicago. The concentration of people, problems, and varying availability and quality of support facilities is being explored, as, for example, by Peter Dreier, John Mollenkopf, and Todd Swanstrom, in *Place Matters* (2001: 1):

> Where we live makes a big difference in the quality of our lives, and how the places in which we live function has a big impact on the quality of our society. The evidence shows that places are becoming more unequal. Economic classes are becoming more spatially separate from each other, with the rich increasingly living with other rich people and the poor with other poor. The latter are concentrated in central cities and distressed inner suburbs, and the former are in exclusive central-city neighborhoods and more distant suburbs.

A new generation of researchers at the University of Chicago developed modern methods to assess the aggregate social characteristics of local areas (Raudenbush and Sampson, 1999; Sampson and Raudenbush, 1999). They examined what is popularly known as the *broken glass theory.* Espoused by a former mayor of New York City, Rudolph Giuliani, it suggests that minor physical manifestations of disorder in city neighbourhoods such as broken glass and graffiti should be responded to immediately after occurring, lest they reinforce and accentuate trends towards a greater scale of social and urban disorder, including crime. These researchers, however, suggest that this theory is a reversal of reality. City leaders should instead concentrate on improving their citizens' economic and social situations—and then less glass will be broken. Mark Hutter (2007: ch. 10) presents a valuable integration of insights into this type of issue, considering such factors as the types of property and social groups involved.

Macro Urban Design and Organization

It is somewhat difficult to grasp how urban design on a scale greater than the neighbourhood affects individual behaviour. The late Swedish geographer Torsten Hägerstrand (1970) provided some insight into this matter, as has Tommy Carlstein (1978). The spatial dimensions of the greater urban area—that is, the degree of mixture or separation of its land uses, its densities, and the layout and operation of private and public transportation—are *capability constraints* that serve to make combining different daily activities such as work, shopping, and entertainment either easier or harder to manage. The time dimensions of community—working hours, school and daycare hours, medical and dental office and bank hours, the opening and closing times of stores, services, and bureaucracies, and so forth—are *authority constraints* that likewise impinge on what people can do on a given day. These two types of constraints combine with others to limit daily activity and to serve as the basis for habit formation (Cullen, 1978; van Paasen, 1981).

Structural Analysis

Cities do not consist 'merely' of people and their behaviour occurring in and between land uses. The land uses have to be determined, transportation and infrastructure have to be built, and decisions have to be made and funds provided so that the whole complex can be provided and maintained. For this reason, a *socio-spatial* approach to cities has been advocated in recent years (Gottdiener and Hutchison, 2000). Cities do not appear and run without social organization and process.

Cities must take collective action with respect to both social and physical policies. They must make decisions about which political jurisdictions are relevant; which actions to take; whose interests are to be served; and who will take initiatives. Cities are formed and are granted their powers and responsibilities according to the laws and decisions of the provincial and federal governments in Canada, and of the state and federal governments in the United States. In short, what cities do and how they do it are functions of the attitudes and actions of higher levels of government.

Time to Reflect

What single aspect of urban ecology do you find most salient for people's everyday lives? Why?

Schools have traditionally been organized at the municipal level and have always accounted for the greatest portion of municipal spending. Among other longstanding municipal responsibilities are police and fire protection; public works such as roads, parks, water, and sewage; and public health, including the prevention of epidemics, the maintenance of sanitary standards, and, more recently, pollution control. Planning, transportation, recreation, child care, and welfare have become increasingly important municipal responsibilities. Performing these varied functions are government bureaucracies that oversee the writing, processing, and maintenance of by-laws, records, permits, licences, and so on, as well as the collection of taxes and the payment of bills.

Figure 21.4 shows the allocation of the average Toronto residential property tax payment for various long-standing and recent types of municipal responsibilities. There are many, diverse categories of function. Even though education financing has been assumed by the provincial government in Ontario in exchange for a downloading of other functions to the municipality, the half of the provincial education budget still collected as part of municipal property taxes is still almost twice the amount of the second largest expenditure, for police services, and many more times the amount of all the lesser municipal budget items. An innovation accompanying the transfer of the education component of the property tax to provincial auspices is that the funds collected in

Figure 21.4 Payment by Average Residential Property Owner in Toronto (2006) for Types of Service (in dollars)

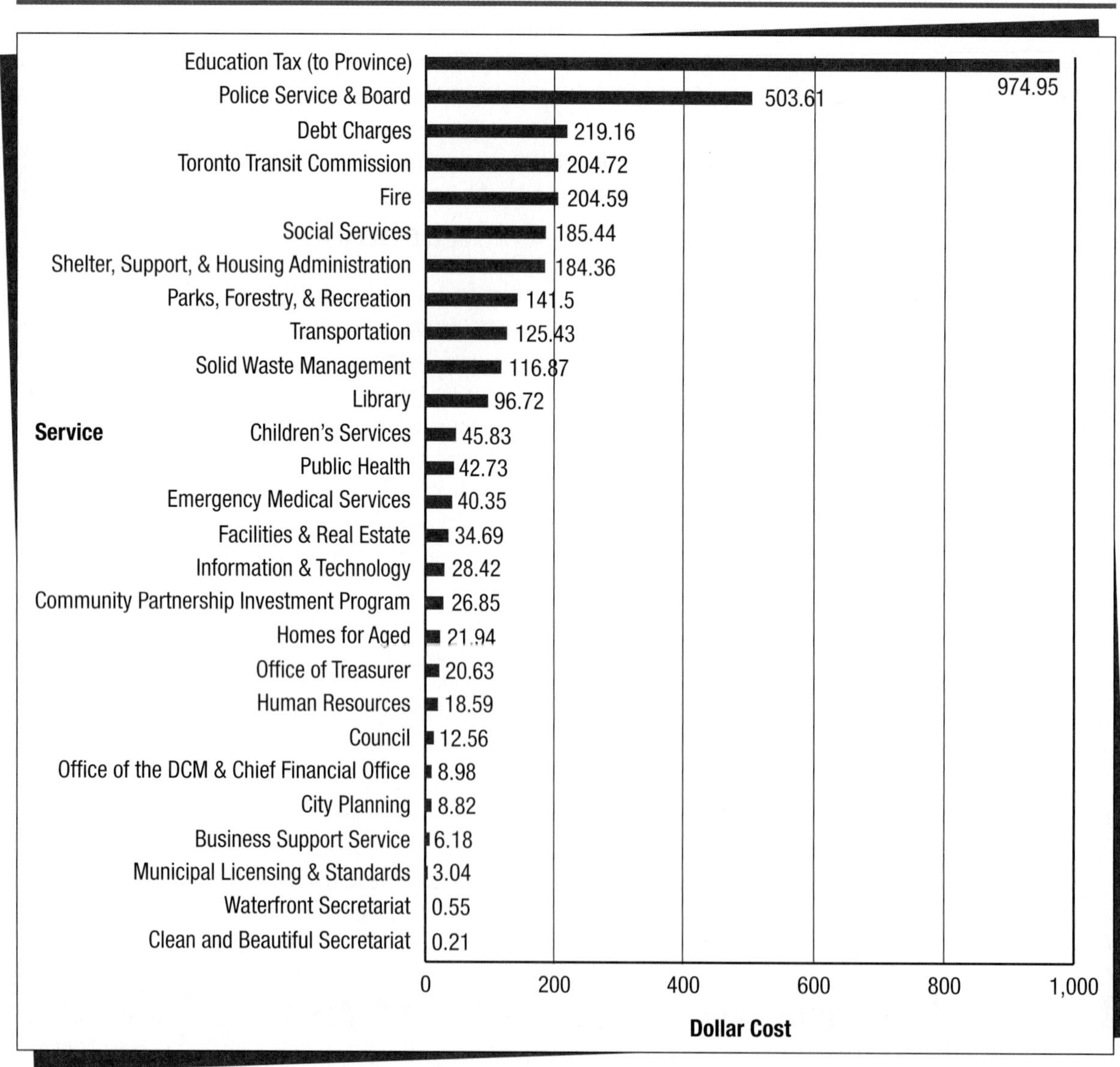

Source: Derived from City of Toronto, *Fact Sheet: How Your Tax Dollar Will Work for You in 2006*, 30 Mar. 2006.

any given municipality need not be—and are not—targeted for the direct benefit of the schoolchildren there.

Conflicts within the System

It is possible to view the functioning of municipal government as a harmonious application of rational laws—but only by doing no more than reading descriptions of how the system is formally structured and by never attending a meeting of city council! There are several reasons why urban structure should be viewed through a conflict perspective, in which disagreements emerge naturally within the system.

The primary source of conflict is that the money required for what cities do is always limited, so different functions have to compete for funds. For instance, in a given year, a new daycare centre may have to compete with a new stadium, or with the basic maintenance of existing facilities and services. Or, perhaps, none of these can be done if a higher level of government changes the rules of the game.

Second, municipalities have a mandate to preserve and enhance health, welfare, and safety, providing the greatest good for the greatest number. However, specific issues typically carry costs and benefits that affect different sectors of the population differentially. Employed mothers (not to speak of their children and spouses) are most affected by decisions related to child care, while the construction of a stadium affects the development and hospitality industries more directly. When any decision is made, one part of town may receive the benefits and another the costs. For example, building a superhighway from a suburb to the city centre provides greater access for the suburbanites but gives the highway itself and more cars and pollution to the central area.

Our final point brings us back to the matter of funds, specifically, to their transfer. In response to difficulties and inequities in financing many municipal programs, governmental structures in Canada and the United States have adapted to raising money at higher, more broadly based levels and transferring it downward to guarantee that essential programs are provided, regardless of varying local resources. But when ideologies and budgets are less generous, transfers decline or disappear altogether. Declining transfers leave lower levels of government with decisions as to how to manage responsibilities on which people have come to depend, without the financial support that stimulated their creation and growth. The level and perhaps the very continuation of local services are at stake. In such a situation, conflict arises between levels of government and among program sectors.

This conflict is exacerbated even more when the higher level of government constrains its grants as a result of lowering income taxes. In this situation, relatively affluent people gain economically while those most dependent on municipal programs have no way to replace those programs.

Such a situation is more than theoretical. Within Canada over the past decade, federal grants to provinces have declined at the same time that some provinces restructured their support to municipalities because of ideological priorities. Municipalities have recently responded by banding together and collectively demanding a regularized share of federal and provincial levies, such as the gasoline tax for local transportation needs. However, the success of such municipal initiatives is subject to the interests of the upper-level governments *du jour*. Promises made during political heat have fleeting lifespans.

Power

Into this diversity of interests enters the exercise of **power**—the ability of individuals or groups to get others to do what they want them to do. The formal structure of government grants power to elected representatives and to those who implement policies and laws. However, sociological studies by Willis Hawley and Frederick Wirt (1968) and by William G. Domhoff (1980), among others, have documented a host of ways in which this formal system is swayed by informal power structures. Power has been found centralized in the hands of a few in some cities and dispersed among different interest groups in others. Obviously, no two cities are the same in this regard, given the range of conditions in each. Norton Long (1958) has argued persuasively that the city is an 'ecology of games'—meaning that the outcome of any policy issue is never totally predictable. Each issue will draw a unique combination of protagonists whose influence and power are cast in different combinations on the formal decision-makers. According to this view, urban politics is kaleidoscopic, forming a different pattern with various combinations of elements each time.

Roger Friedland and Donald Palmer (1984) and William Tabb and Larry Sawers (1984) have suggested that, in this context, one should focus primarily on major actors in the economic system and on associated motives for profit and control. A convincing case has been made that there is a coalition of persons believing in and usually benefiting personally from continuous urban growth, which they unflaggingly foster. John Logan and Harvey Molotch (1987) have called this neo-Marxist view the *urban growth machine.* Analyses of Toronto by Lorimer (1978) and many others have placed the interests of large property owners at the centre. Recent transaction patterns in Vancouver indicate that the urban growth machine there is increasingly fuelled from outside of Canada.

It is ironic that the production of numerous costly new buildings by the urban growth machine, creating upward pricing pressures throughout the urban real estate market, has been accompanied by an unprecedented increase in the number of homeless persons. Homelessness is the more serious because most people in North America assume that it can't happen here (Bingham et al., 1987). David Hulchanski (1991) reminds us of the important point that what's good for the functioning of the economic market is not necessarily positive for the objectives of social welfare in cities. Homelessness has spread from older men to women, children, and whole families, in part related to economically rational policies in both the private and public sectors that undermine job security and rates of pay. The tragedy of Hurricane Katrina in New Orleans has left in its wake a rebuilding program in housing that gives every evidence of purposefully avoiding the provision of housing for the poverty-stricken minorities that became homeless, so that they will not remain a part of the future population mix in that city (Ouroussoff, 2006). Gerda Wekerle (2005) examines the even larger question as to the ways in which neo-liberal urban restructuring contributes to social exclusion, bringing gender also into this picture. Economic rationality can be socially inhumane when its manifestations are wielded only by self-selected sectors of the population.

There is no questioning the presence and impact of economic forces and factors. Nonetheless, economics does not always win. In recent decades in Montreal, Vancouver, Toronto, and other cities, many decisions have gone in the opposite direction from what an ideologically pure economic determinist perspective would have predicted.

The Scope of Urban Functions and Organization

Many municipalities exist side by side in metropolitan areas. Should decisions and operations be kept close to home in each municipality, where the local population can exercise the greatest degree of control for its particular interests? Or should they be the responsibility of the higher level of the metropolitan area?

Many functions and responsibilities of municipal government transcend boundaries. Polluted water or toxic emissions in one municipality have tangible effects in other jurisdictions; pollution is seldom a local concern. Roads, policing, and licensing would be chaotic without clear organization and co-ordination at higher levels.

While the different parts of a metropolitan area may share responsibility for many activities, their historical boundaries can divide efforts to solve problems facing the area as a whole. For instance, the tax money that can be gathered by an individual municipality has traditionally reflected its wealth and the intensity of activity within its borders. Research has shown that many people differentiate clearly between adjacent municipalities (Michelson, 1997) and that they choose where to live in view of the long-standing images of different municipalities (Weiher, 1991). But the needs of a given municipality for funds for such operations as education, welfare, and police and fire protection are not always in line with its tax base. Indeed, the relationship is often inverse; municipalities with poor and aging populations may need greater levels of service yet have less of a basis for raising money.

The purely fiscal solution to the inequitable availability of funds is to let higher levels of government (federal or provincial) collect taxes and provide grants to municipalities with special needs. But even when the funding tap is flowing, objectives can be distorted in actual operation. School financing, for example, relies more and more on provincial grants in response to local inequities. However, the strings attached often bind the recipients more than they might wish—perhaps by requirements for larger student–teacher ratios or curriculum reforms to reflect the ideology of the provincial government of the day. Even when grants have few strings, benefits do not always go where intended. Federal transfers for higher education can end up in more mundane coffers, for instance.

Metropolitan Government

One structural response to municipal conflicts and inequities is the creation of metropolitan government. A higher level of government is superimposed on existing municipalities, which can remain as they were or be reconfigured. The metropolitan level carries out the functions for which higher-level co-ordination and financing are needed. The functions chosen vary with both place and time.

Examples of metropolitan government abound in Canada. Metropolitan Toronto ('Metro') was formed in 1953 to care for water, sewage, transportation arteries, parks, school financing, welfare, co-ordinated planning, policing, business licensing, and air pollution control. The metropolitan government was run—until it was abolished by the provincial government in 1998—by a council elected from wards in the various municipalities and a chairperson elected by council members. Metro collected tax money from its constituent cities and boroughs and distributed it where needed. Periodic reviews increased the powers of the metropolitan government and decreased those of the lower-level municipalities. The metropolitan government of Winnipeg has even more responsibility, while that of Montreal has less. The power of the Greater Vancouver Regional District has waxed and waned over the decades.

The turn of the millennium has seen considerable restructuring of municipal government in Ontario and Quebec. In Toronto, the recommendations of a Royal Commission to abolish the boundaries of the Metro government and to extend the functions of a metropolitan government to the much larger area now constituting the de facto Toronto area, while maintaining the lower-level municipalities as a form of direct democracy, were countermanded by the government of Ontario, which instead abolished the local municipalities and created a unified City of Toronto with the existing Metro boundaries, in the process all but ignoring the presence of a larger population outside than inside those boundaries. Although many of the functions of the new, larger City of Toronto were already being carried out at the Metro level, the job of governing was made more difficult by a downloading of increasingly costly services from the provincial level, in return only for the province assuming the untraditional role of its paying (what turned out to be only half) the costs of schools while controlling school budgets tightly. Ottawa and Hamilton each were compelled to implement the consolidation of existing municipalities into single, larger ones. The looser federation of the City of Montreal and its surrounding suburbs was changed on 1 January 2002 to a consolidation into a single City of Montreal, though within short order some individual municipalities sought to opt out.

The sociological lessons of informal systems should not be forgotten when formal solutions are evaluated—even such a highly rational structure as metropolitan government is affected by human interests and influences.

Other Structural Solutions

In situations where people fear alterations in municipal jurisdictions but urgently require area-wide services, commonly special authorities, commissions, or districts are set up. These entities are charged with specific responsibilities. Depending on their location and function, they may have taxation rights or public subsidies, as well as the right to charge the public for services. Such bodies usually are shielded from the direct control or scrutiny of city officials. They generally function more efficiently than local municipal services, but are often more remote from constituency demands as well.

Nonetheless, even when a good match is made between types of needs and governmental level and structures, governments may not be adequately responsive, if only due to lack of appropriate information and communication. Klinenberg (2002), for example, documents the disconnect between disadvantaged residents of Chicago and the government when a long, severe heat wave hit the city. The government had difficulty recognizing how poor, old, minority-group residents of the city were hindered in taking adaptive survival steps to protect themselves against the searing heat. As a consequence, many people died in the absence of a prompt public response to the heat wave. Fortunately, the lessons learned through Klinenberg's research were applied with better results in a subsequent heat wave in 2005.

There is no perfect form of government, though some are surely better suited to achieve certain needs than others. Sociological examination of municipal experiences with different structures is a resource that all too often goes untapped by decision-makers with their own agendas. In deciding what is most appropriate, certain factors must always be taken into consideration: what needs to be done; what type of structure is appropriate for achieving each objective; and what interests are mobilized in the de facto operation.

Urban Planning in Structural Perspective

Planning is a profession practised by members of municipal staffs or by private consultants hired to contribute services and reports; planners are not elected officials. In most municipalities, planning is found within a number of city structures. It may be done in a separate city department, parallel to public works or licensing; it may be advisory to the mayor; or it may take place under the supervision of an elected or selected commission that reports to city council. Planning activities usually also take place within other organizations, including transit agencies, school boards, and public housing agencies.

Planners help to create long-range, comprehensive plans, which, if adopted by city governments, should facilitate the orderly growth of cities. They also help in designing transportation networks. In addition, they are highly visible in planning interventions within existing city areas.

Urban renewal occurs when the nature or use of an area changes and improvements are made to buildings and/or land use. City officials disapprove of areas whose property values and, hence, tax base potential are low. When existing buildings or activities are considered outdated or no longer viable and are unlikely to be changed by means of private-sector initiatives, cities often intervene. One form of urban renewal is *redevelopment*. A block or larger area is levelled, and a new land use is arranged in co-operation with public- or private-sector organizations. This is the most frequently practised approach to brownfields. Another is *rehabilitation*, in which existing buildings are modernized and either resold or rented at higher levels. American cities have seen much publicly planned and implemented renewal of residential and commercial areas. By contrast, major Canadian projects have tended to the reuse of former brownfields.

When money is short, support for sports and entertainment arenas, convention centres, or hotels is much greater than support for housing. The urban growth machine is common in cities throughout North America. This approach to planning has been referred to as the creation of a 'Fantasy City' (Hannigan, 1998).

Not all planning activities involve such radical intervention as redevelopment or even rehabilitation; preventive medicine is preferable to surgery. Much planning activity is devoted to liaisons with specific neighbourhoods in hopes that minor site-by-site improvements, such as off-street parking, can maintain or upgrade existing areas.

Yet, whatever they do, planners are caught in a strange structural position. Their recommendations always involve economic benefits to some parties and losses to others. Moreover, they have no political decision-making power. R.E. Pahl (1970) points out that influences on the essentially redistributive processes with which planners deal can enter the decision-making process from above their heads and from outside the formal decision-making structure. Furthermore, while planners may honestly support the point of view of neighbourhood residents and groups, deviation from their employers' positions may be at the risk of their jobs.

Ambiguity about the role of planners and their conflicts with other interest groups concerned with urban developmental decisions during times of municipal austerity have led to actions to cut out planning functions entirely.

Citizen Participation

It is commonly felt that citizens need to express their interests to those in power in an organized and active way, just as large corporate groups do. The best-known approach to citizen participation is that of Saul Alinsky and his many North American followers, documented by Reitzes and Reitzes (1987). Their *conflict approach* recognizes the difficulty of inducing largely apolitical people to unite in a public stand on technical matters. The answer, according to Alinsky, lies in the uniting effect of conflict. People will join together during a crisis. Trained conflict agents are brought in to discover (or invent) problems besetting the local community that could bring them into conflict with others (often the city government). Through such conflict, latent power can be used to pursue planning interests. The problem in this approach lies in the difficulty of keeping organizational momentum after the main conflict is resolved.

An alternative to the conflict approach is the *coalition approach*, in which an effort is made to create a local citizens' group, perhaps a ratepayers' association or tenants' union. Rather than acting independently, such groups join with other interests and organizations for mutual support. It is true that they gain a broader base of support. But it is unclear how broad a coalition can be if interests within it clash over issues.

Many other techniques for citizen participation have developed. Some, using videotaped opinions, were developed in Canada. Given that planners have technical expertise and that elected city officials represent the people, it may seem surprising that so many efforts appear necessary to represent the ordinary Canadian's interests in planning issues. Once again, however, we must keep in mind the diversity of persons and interests in urban areas, and recall that informal processes occur within formal institutional structures. Such a diversity of actors and interests has raised its head in a current planning controversy in Toronto over a very limited proposal to make a dedicated right-of-way for streetcars (trolley cars) in the middle of a busy street through a neighbourhood shopping area, to speed up travel to and through the area. Organizational innovation and animation are often essential, if the legitimate needs and wants of citizens are to be promoted to the same extent as those of strong economic interests, so that decisions can respect them both.

Time to Reflect

If you were elected to be the mayor of a major Canadian city right now, what is the first action you would commit yourself to take on behalf of the city?

Nonetheless, recent research on environmental justice shows that even successful citizen participation in conflictual planning situations may consume huge amounts of time and emotional cost—something that ordinary people are less equipped to endure than are large corporations with professional support (Roberts and Toffolon-Weiss, 2001). A measure of the decision-making apparatus is what it demands of citizens to make their voices and interests heard.

Conclusion

The diversity in nature and scale of urban considerations and problems taxes the scope of the sociological imagination. This chapter is necessarily a summary. No single sociological theory or perspective addresses all urban problems or phenomena. No two matters are likely to draw on the same combination of factors for their solution or understanding. Yet, it is useful to start thinking through questions about cities and urban living in light of the logic of four perspectives: urbanization, urbanism, ecology, and structural analysis.

No matter which of these perspectives is taken, cities are not immutable structures with predictably deterministic effects on human beings. Cities are a part of societies and social changes, reflecting the conscious actions of people like you and me. Cities may be large and complex, but—for good or for ill—they are subject to human agency and organization. In many respects, cities mirror at an impressive scale the interacting agendas of individuals, groups, cultures, and nations. As in other areas of sociological inquiry, analyses and research help to clarify what goes on around us and provide a basis for shaping contexts and structures in useful ways. It remains for more people to benefit from such knowledge by taking conscious steps for the common good.

There is now so much known about cities and how they function that it is unconscionable for informed citizens to allow charismatic advocates to provide solutions that are clear, simple, and wrong.

Questions for Critical Thought

1. Has the coercive relationship of city dwellers over those living in their hinterlands changed materially over the span of history? If so, in what ways? Why?
2. What role does technology play in contemporary urbanization and in the growth or decline of specific Canadian cities?
3. Do you think that everyday interpersonal behaviour varies more in an urban–rural comparison or between critical masses of subcultures within cities?
4. What are the largest subcultures in your area? Do they have different ways of life that make an impact on the city?
5. How would you describe the macro spatial pattern or infrastructure of the city you know best? What differences in everyday life are possible outcomes of the opportunities and constraints presented by this pattern of infrastructure?
6. If you were an architect, to what extent would your residential designs vary according to specific characteristics of the people expected to live there? What differences in characteristics are significant in this regard? How would your designs vary accordingly?
7. If you were a city planner, to what extent would you take gender differences into account in your plans for the city? What aspects of the city do you think are pertinent in this regard?
8. Are there brownfields in a city with which you are familiar? What land uses there have become outmoded? What is happening to these brownfields?
9. Evaluate the governmental structures (and restructuring) of cities you know in terms of how effectively they can carry out what cities are expected to do.

Recommended Readings

Kevin Fitzgerald and Mark LaGory, *Unhealthy Places: The Ecology of Risk in the Urban Landscape* (New York: Routledge, 2000).

This is an unusual and pioneering examination of some sources of physical and social risk in cities. It shows how exposure to risks is greater among otherwise disadvantaged segments of urban populations.

John Hannigan, *Fantasy City: Pleasure and Profit in the Postmodern Metropolis* (New York: Routledge, 1998).

Hannigan gives many examples of how cities are persuaded to solve their fiscal and land-use problems by giving priority to the creation of entertainment districts catering to tourists.

Harry Hiller, ed., *Urban Canada: Sociological Perspectives* (Toronto: Oxford University Press, 2005).

An up-to-date examination of many aspects of Canadian cities by authors with special knowledge of them.

Nancy Kleniewsky, ed., *Cities and Society* (Malden, Mass.: Blackwell, 2005).

A superb collection of readings illuminating many current issues concerning contemporary cities.

Lyn Lofland, *The Public Realm: Exploring the City's Quintessential Social Territory* (New York: Aldine de Gruyter, 1998).

Lyn Lofland is one of the leading students of urbanism. In this recent book, she examines in a thorough and engaging way how people adapt to urban spaces.

John Macionis and Vincent Parrillo, *Cities and Urban Life*, 4th edn (Upper Saddle River, NJ: Pearson/Prentice-Hall, 2007).

A comprehensive and highly readable text, American based but with copious international (including Canadian) examples.

David Thorns, *The Transformation of Cities: Urban Theory and Urban Life* (New York: Palgrave Macmillan, 2002).

This is a sophisticated, well-written book on how cities have changed as a result of recent global trends. It is particularly strong in its international content, perspectives, and documentation.

United Nations Centre for Human Settlements (HABITAT), *Cities in a Globalizing World* (London: Earthscan, 2001).

The United Nations has made available a treasure chest of information on cities throughout the world. It provides detailed documentation for any number of specific interests and inquiries concerning urbanization.

Recommended Websites

Children, Youth, and Environments
www.colorado.edu/journals/cye/index.htm
A high-quality e-journal on children and their urban environments.

Earth from Space
earth.jsc.nasa.gov/sseop/efs/city.htm
This site contains stunning bird's-eye views of a number of North American and international cities. Montreal and Vancouver are included.

Google Earth
earth.google.com
Zoom in on the place of your choice through satellite imagery and maps.

Metropolis
www.metropolis.org
The World Association of the Major Metropolises provides interesting information about large cities and their problems and prospects.

Statistics Canada
www.statcan.ca
Increasing amounts of information and data about Canadian communities, cities, and urbanization are available from Statistics Canada.

The Social Explorer
www.socialexplorer.com
Get vital social and economic data about your choice of urban and suburban sub-areas, at the scale you wish, within the United States, making whatever comparative analyses you find useful.

United Nations Centre for Human Settlements
www.unchs.org
The United Nations Centre for Human Settlements (HABITAT) provides information about housing and infrastructural considerations.

World Urbanization Prospects
esa.un.org/unup
Uniquely up-to-date and complete statistics on urbanization and its manifestations.

Bell
Making it simple.™

Give an mp3 phone.
Bell
Making it simple.™
On your
Cellphone

SEA
Dundas
SEARS

Chapter 22

Mass Media and Communication

David Young

Learning Objectives

In this chapter, you will:

- Learn about different theories sociologists have used to analyze the mass media.
- Identify various forms of media ownership and critically understand concerns about deepening ownership concentration among media companies.
- Study the role of the state in relation to media policy and media organizations.
- Consider how economic and cultural globalization is connected to the mass media.
- Grasp how media content represents relatively powerless groups in society, such as the working class, women, and ethno-racial minorities.
- Discover how media content is interpreted by audience members.
- Become aware of the conflicts that exist over media policy and media content.
- Examine how the Internet reflects long-standing issues in the sociology of mass media.

Photo: Ivy Images

Introduction

The mass media include newspapers, magazines, recorded music, motion pictures, radio, and television. We are exposed to the mass media frequently in contemporary society. In light of this, a number of questions may come to mind when you think about the mass media. What is the role of the mass media in society? Who has power over what we read, see, or hear in the mass media? What kinds of messages exist in media content, and how do people react to them? What are the social implications of the Internet, which is associated with the 'new media'? Sociology provides the tools to grapple with such questions. Throughout this chapter, you will be introduced to answers developed by media sociologists.

Sociological Theories of the Media

The classical theorists who have informed sociological research—Karl Marx, Émile Durkheim, and Max Weber—did not write specifically about the mass media. All three men were aware of newspapers, and Marx even spent some time working as a journalist (Ryan and Wentworth, 1999). However, Marx died in 1883 and did not live to see even the emergence of motion pictures. Motion pictures had been in existence for some time when Durkheim and Weber died, in 1917 and 1920 respectively, but radio was only beginning to emerge as a form of mass communication. Consequently, the three thinkers who offered sociologists so much specific guidance in approaching such issues as class and status inequality or religion were not in a position to provide an analysis of the mass media. Nevertheless, at least some of the classical theorists presented ideas that sociologists have applied to the study of mass communication. Four sociological perspectives on communication and media can be identified: symbolic interactionism, structural functionalism, conflict theory, and feminism.

Symbolic Interactionism

The theoretical perspective known as symbolic interactionism was named by Herbert Blumer, and its key elements were further developed by a number of sociologists. This approach focuses on the microsociological issue of interaction among individuals through the use of symbols. Symbols can be verbal (such as the words used in spoken language) or non-verbal (including forms of body language such as a smile, frown, or gesture). All of these symbols carry meaning, which the members of a society come to understand and share through the process of socialization. Without this shared understanding of symbols, interaction among people would not be possible. An aspect of symbolic interactionism known as *social constructionism* suggests that we construct our own social reality through symbols. Reality consists not of something that objectively exists but rather what we subjectively perceive through our interpretation of symbols, and this interpretation in turn shapes our social behaviour. For example, from your interpretation of verbal and non-verbal cues, you may believe that a friend is angry at you. This may not in fact be the case, but it is the reality you have constructed and it will affect how you respond to your friend.

Especially since the 1970s, symbolic interactionism has been used in research on communication and media. Faules and Alexander (1978) identified how symbolic interactionist theory could be employed to study different forms of communication, including mass communication. They indicated that symbolic interactionism can be applied to *interpersonal communication* (face-to-face interaction between two individuals that involves the reciprocal exchange of verbal and non-verbal symbols); *group communication* (face-to-face interaction among several individuals in a context, such as a seminar discussion, that still permits the mutual exchange of verbal and non-verbal cues); *public communication* (sending messages to large groups in a face-to-face setting, as in a lecture, where the participants have a much more limited opportunity for the exchange of verbal and non-verbal symbols); and *mass communication* (which exists through the use of mass media such as newspapers, motion pictures, radio, or television).

Faules and Alexander (ibid., 11) noted that mass communication is different from the other forms of communication since it does not involve direct, face-to-face interaction and 'there is no opportunity for immediate mutual exchange of verbal and nonverbal cues between the initiator of a message and the recipients of that message.' However, since much of our interpretation of the world is based on our previous experience with direct and indirect forms of communication, they concluded that 'the media are a prime source of indirect experience and for that reason have impact on the construction of social reality' (ibid., 23).

Symbolic interactionism is not one of the principal theories employed by media sociologists. Its microsociological focus is the reason for this. An approach that addresses interaction through symbols can be useful in certain areas of sociology, such as the analysis of socialization, and it can also be useful to scholars who study various forms of face-to-face communication. However, in terms of research on mass communication, symbolic interactionist theory has more limited applicability. It does not allow sociologists to address macrosociological concerns such as the role of media institutions in society.

Structural Functionalism

Structural functionalism is inspired by the ideas of Émile Durkheim, but the theory took shape in the work of later sociologists. As a macrosociological framework, structural functionalism focuses on social order. The order and stability of society is facilitated by consensus (agreement) among its members regarding norms and values. Stability is also facilitated by the interconnected parts of society. According to structural functionalists, the maintenance of society depends on its different parts fulfilling their particular functions. Structural functionalists make this point through an analogy between society and a biological organism. The body of any person or animal is made up of different parts (organs such as the heart or the lungs), and all of these parts must continue to perform their specific functions if the person or animal is to survive. Similarly, social institutions make up the different parts of society, and these institutions must carry out certain functions for the entire society to endure.

Structural functionalism frequently was used in studies of the mass media during the 1950s. Unlike symbolic interactionism, this theoretical approach enabled sociologists to examine the role of media institutions. Building on the work of Lasswell (1948), Wright (1959) argued that media institutions contribute to the maintenance and survival of society by performing four functions: surveillance of the environment; correlation of the parts of society; transmission of the social heritage; and entertainment.

Surveillance of the environment involves the collection and distribution of information about events that occur inside and outside a particular society. This surveillance is provided by news media organizations, and it is functional for society in several ways. The flow of information through the news helps institutions or individuals to organize their activities, and the population can be warned of imminent danger (such as a hurricane or military attack).

Correlation of the parts of society refers to interpretation of information about the environment and prescription for behaviour in response to events. Editorials in the news or commentaries through other media, such as televised speeches by political leaders, are functional for society because they help people to make sense of what is happening. They are also functional because they aim to integrate society by building consensus. A specific example is the patriotic tone of the American media after the terrorist attacks on 11 September 2001.

Transmission of the social heritage involves communicating information, norms, and values from one generation to another or from the members of a group to new members. Various mass media are functional for society since they contribute to the socialization process and help to ensure that the culture of a society or group will continue across time.

Entertainment involves forms of communication that are mainly intended to provide amusement or diversion. Entertainment is functional for society because it provides relaxation and enables the release of emotional tensions that may generate conflict and threaten social order.

IN THE FIRST PERSON

When I started my first year of studies at Queen's University in Kingston, I had already decided to major in psychology. I also took a course in sociology, even though I had far less idea of what this subject was about. To my surprise, while I found that psychology was nowhere near as interesting as I thought it would be, I was fascinated by sociology—particularly by that guy named Marx. By my second year, my major had switched to sociology. I sampled various areas of sociology over the next three years and was intrigued enough to pursue graduate studies at Queen's. It was while working on my master's degree that I finally found what I wanted to make my life's work: the sociology of mass media.—David Young

Although structural functionalism offered some important insights, media sociologists had largely abandoned this theoretical approach by the 1970s. It was seen as having several problems, including a conservative orientation. The conservative nature of structural functionalism is evident in the value it places on the order and stability of society. Structural functionalist theory stresses the role of media institutions (and other social institutions) in maintaining society as it is. The theory makes little attempt to question media institutions and their role.

Conflict Theory

Conflict theory is rooted in the work of Karl Marx. Like structural functionalism, it provides a macrosociological framework. However, conflict theory differs from structural functionalism by emphasizing social change rather than social order. Marx theorized that social change occurs through conflict in society. In capitalist society, the conflict is between the bourgeoisie and the proletariat. Members of the *bourgeoisie* (the capitalist class) own the means of production (such as the factories, technology, and capital needed in the production process). Because members of the *proletariat* (the working class) do not own the means of production, they have to sell their labour to capitalists in exchange for a wage so that they have money to live. Marx also recognized the *petite bourgeoisie*, a middle class of farmers and small business people who own the means of production but hire little or no wage labour. However, the focus of his analysis was on the conflict that stemmed from the exploitation of workers by capitalists. Marx expected that the working class eventually would lead a revolution against the capitalist class and capitalism would be replaced by socialism.

Conflict theory has provided the basis for numerous studies of the mass media since the 1960s. In contrast to structural functionalism, this theoretical approach made it possible for sociologists to question the role of media institutions. For instance, conflict theory enabled sociologists to see how media institutions are tied to power and inequality in capitalist society. Marx's recognition of a middle class also led some sociologists to examine the growth of a new middle class made up of managers (including those in media institutions) and professionals (such as journalists). Members of the new middle class work for an annual salary rather than an hourly wage and some of them, as supervisors of the labour of the working class, may be ideologically aligned with capitalists (Wright, 1985).

The growing popularity of conflict theory during the 1960s had much to do with the inability of structural functionalism—with its focus on social order—to address the social conflict that had taken shape between various social institutions (including media institutions) and social movements. In the 1960s, the labour movement was joined by other movements that had emerged to struggle against social inequality—especially the women's movement and the civil rights movement. These movements were aware of the role the media played in oppressing women or racial minorities, and they were aware also of the potential to use media in ways that might help to generate social change. However, because Marxism focuses on the analysis of class relations, it has had difficulty explaining other aspects of social inequality that are connected to or reinforced by the mass media.

Feminism

By offering analysis of inequality between women and men, feminism has made a valuable contribution to sociology. Feminism can be used to understand microsociological issues associated with the lives of women and their experience with inequality, but it also has a strong focus on addressing macrosociological conditions that account for the oppression of women. Especially with regard to the macro level of analysis, *patriarchy* is a key concept in feminism. Patriarchy refers to a society or form of social organization based on male domination. Due to considerable debate among feminists about patriarchy and the origins or nature of women's oppression, a number of feminist theories have emerged. Some of these theories have informed research on the mass media.

Liberal feminism, which is rooted in liberal philosophy, suggests that the inequality between women and men stems from inappropriate ideas that can be corrected through argument, legislation, and socialization. Many liberal feminists have objected to prevalent ideas about 'masculinity' and 'femininity' that affect young boys and girls. For example, while our culture has traditionally regarded certain behaviours and jobs to be 'masculine' (such as being rational or being a doctor), it has regarded others to be 'feminine' (such as being irrational or being a nurse). Consequently, media research based on liberal feminism has included content analysis of how gendered socializing is evident in television programs that children are exposed to. The research has led to calls for legislation that governs the depiction of gender in television programs aimed at children. Although liberal feminism draws attention to the sexist ideas that circulate in society, it does not challenge the capitalist nature of society (Steeves, 1987).

Marxist feminism (also referred to as *socialist* or *materialist feminism*) has attempted to overcome Marxism's failure to address the inequality experienced by women. Marxist feminists contend that the oppression of women stems from connections between two systems that generate inequality—capitalism and patriarchy—both of which must be overcome through political struggles (ibid.). A great deal of media research based on Marxist feminism has examined media content to show how 'representations reinforce nuclear families and class distinctions that sustain capitalism and women's secondary status' (ibid., 113). Fewer Marxist feminist studies have focused on the role of capitalist patriarchal media institutions and their role in the production of this content or the exploitation of female workers.

Radical feminism is less concerned with explaining the origins of women's oppression. It concentrates on developing radical alternatives. Radical feminists seek separation from men as a solution to the problem of male domination. Little media research has been based on radical feminism, but its proposed political solution implies the need for feminist media with separate processes and audiences (ibid.).

More recently, feminist theories have addressed three themes in relation to the analysis of media and communication. Wackwitz and Rakow (2004) identify these themes as difference, voice, and representation. *Difference* raises several issues, including the notion of differences between women and men. Feminists have shown that patriarchy justifies inequality between women and men by asserting supposedly biological differences—men being 'naturally' more aggressive than women, for example—even though these differences are actually products of culture and socialization. The theme of difference also refers to differences among women with regard to class, race/ethnicity, sexual preference, or other aspects of identity. Feminists have increasingly examined these elements of difference in order to overcome the deficiencies of earlier feminist theories, which minimized or ignored diversity among women. The second theme identified by Wackwitz and Rakow focuses on exclusion. *Voice* concerns the degree to which women are denied an opportunity to speak in various forms of communication (including interpersonal or group communication) or given a voice only to have their ideas ignored. The third theme considers the portrayal of women in the media. *Representation* draws attention to the way women are depicted in media content and the way this negatively affects them. Wackwitz and Rakow (ibid., 9) see these three themes as overlapping because 'systems of difference and exclusion are linked with the process of representation.'

Critical Perspectives on the Media

Conflict theory and feminism have contributed to critical perspectives on the media. Critical perspectives challenge the type of society we have and analyze the media in relation to power, inequality, conflict, and change.

Critical perspectives on the media are often divided into two categories: political economy and cultural studies. Political economy focuses on ownership and control of the media. It examines private corporations and the state in relation to the media as well as the opposition of subordinate groups to the role of powerful media organizations. In contrast, work within cultural studies addresses the ideological aspects of the media. This approach analyzes the ideology embedded in media content, the interpretation of media content by audience members, and efforts to change media representations or disseminate alternative media messages. Adapting the themes that Mosco (1989) associated with political economy and cultural studies, we will now turn to these two critical perspectives.

Political Economy of the Media

While placing a strong emphasis on historical analysis, researchers who specialize in the political economy of media devote particular attention to several issues. The main issues are forms of media ownership; the state and media policy; globalization and the media; and conflict over ownership, policy, and globalization.

Time to Reflect

Compare and contrast symbolic interactionism, structural functionalism, conflict theory, and feminism (especially in relation to analysis of the mass media).

Forms of Media Ownership

There are different forms of media ownership. We can distinguish between public and private ownership as well as various types of ownership that are private.

Public ownership—ownership of media by the government—has a long history in Canada. Examples of public media ownership in this country include the National Film Board of Canada (NFB), the Canadian Broadcasting Corporation/Société Radio-Canada (CBC/SRC), and the educational television broadcasters operated by some provincial governments: TV Ontario, Radio-Québec, and the Knowledge Network (which serves British Columbia). The goal of these organizations is to provide a public service by utilizing the media to satisfy social objectives. Such objectives include providing media that are freely available to citizens, using the media for educational purposes, and ensuring a Canadian voice in the media. Media organizations under public ownership are often supported by government funding, but additional funding may come from advertising or user fees (such as memberships). Public ownership of the media in Canada frequently takes the form of a Crown corporation, a business owned by the federal or provincial government but operating at arm's length (independently) from government (Lorimer and Gasher, 2001).

Critical scholars have often expressed support for public ownership of the media, as when Taras (2001: 26) indicated that the CBC/SRC has played a crucial role as one of the 'public squares' where Canadian citizens can meet. However, these scholars are also aware that public ownership is not without its problems. For instance, Raboy (1990) has argued that public broadcasting must be re-imagined so that it goes beyond the federal or provincial levels of jurisdiction and an emphasis on 'national' or 'Canadian' identity.

Private ownership refers to ownership of the media by commercial firms, and it too has a long tradition in Canada. Most of the mass media in Canada, ranging from newspapers to radio and television stations, are under private ownership. The prevalence of private ownership is illustrated by Table 22.1, which presents a list of the leading media organizations in Canada. Only one of these organizations, the CBC/SRC, is a public corporation. The ownership of a private media company may be held by an individual or a small group (such as a family). Alternatively, the ownership may be held by many shareholders through the stock market. The goal of the private media company is 'survival and growth in a marketplace driven by profit' (Lorimer and Gasher, 2001: 223).

Critical researchers argue that private ownership has significant implications for media content. The interests of private media companies mean that media content 'is regarded by their management not as a public service, but as a business cost to be met as inexpensively as possible' (Hackett et al., 1996: 260). For example, the private television network CTV can purchase the rights to broadcast popular American shows like *Desperate Housewives* or *Law & Order* for approximately one-tenth the cost of producing a Canadian series. As Taras (2001: 189) has indicated, this explains why private television broadcasters in Canada 'put as little as possible into Canadian content and squeeze the most out of imported Hollywood productions.' While noting that private media have done little to reflect Canadian culture in their programming, critical scholars have also been concerned about several specific types of private ownership.

Independent ownership is the most basic and least problematic of these types. It exists when the owners of a media company confine themselves to that one company and are not involved in the ownership of other firms. Their media company usually operates on a small scale. It is often closely associated with a local community and aims to serve that community. This form of ownership means that the newspaper, radio station, or television station in a small town or city might be owned by an entrepreneur who lives in the area. Independent ownership was once quite common in the Canadian media, but it has diminished as large companies have bought small media firms (Lorimer and Gasher, 2001). This can be illustrated through the case of CHCH, which was for many years an independently owned television station in the Ontario city of Hamilton. The station was acquired by Western International Communications (WIC) in 1990 and became one of several television stations owned by this company. WIC was purchased by CanWest Global Communications in 2000, and CH (as the station is now known) is currently among CanWest Global's many holdings in television.

Such developments bring us to **horizontal integration**, a second form of private ownership. Horizontal integration, which is also known as chain ownership, exists when one company owns a number of media organizations in different locations that are doing the same type of business. One company may own several newspapers, for example. Critical scholars contend that this form of ownership has negative implications. For instance, if a company owns a chain of newspapers, it could cut costs by using syndicated news stories across the chain and reducing the number of journalists and local stories at each of the newspapers (Hackett and Gruneau, 2000). Therefore,

Table 22.1 The Leading Media Organizations in Canada, 2005

Organization	Revenues (2005)
BCE	$19,105,000,000
The Thomson Corp.	$10,539,333,000
Quebecor	$10,208,500,000
Rogers Communications	$ 7,482,154,000
CanWest Global Communications	$ 3,072,542,000
Shaw Communications	$ 2,209,810,000
Torstar	$ 1,566,943,000
Lions Gate Entertainment	$ 1,076,824,000
Alliance Atlantis Communications	$ 1,043,400,000
Corus Entertainment	$ 683,069,000
COGECO	$ 675,605,000
CHUM Ltd	$ 628,392,000
Canadian Broadcasting Corp.	$ 546,706,000
Osprey Media	$ 222,525,000
IMAX	$ 175,510,000

Source: Adapted from Financial Post Business, FP500 Online 2006 Database, at: <www.canada.com/nationalpost/npb/500/index.html>.

when an independently owned newspaper becomes part of a chain, a number of jobs disappear along with some of the newspaper's local flavour. We can see this in the case of the *Kingston Whig-Standard*. When this newspaper was under independent ownership, it provided excellent coverage to the local community in Ontario where I grew up. However, in 1990, the *Whig-Standard* became part of a chain when it was purchased by Southam. Southam began cutting the journalistic staff of the newspaper while supplying a number of stories through its syndicated Southam News Service. As Fetherling (1993: xii) has noted in his historical analysis of the *Whig-Standard*, the newspaper was the victim of an 'obsession with profit at any price'.

Vertical integration is a third form of private ownership. It exists when one company owns media firms or divisions that are part of the overall process linking production, distribution, and exhibition. A good example is provided by the structure of the Canadian company Alliance Atlantis Communications before its different holdings were recently sold. Alliance Atlantis was involved with television production, film and television distribution, and television broadcasting. The company co-produced (with CBS Productions) the television series *CSI: Crime Scene Investigation* and its two spin-offs, and one of its divisions distributed the three shows in all territories outside the United States. Repeat episodes of the *CSI* shows were broadcast through Showcase, which was among the many specialty television channels that Alliance Atlantis owned in Canada. Such vertical integration enables a company to have a guaranteed market for its production activities and a guaranteed supply of content for its exhibition outlets. However, critical researchers have been concerned about the implications of vertical integration. They suggest that this form of ownership can result in content from other sources being shut out (Croteau and Hoynes, 2000). For instance, if a record company owned several radio stations, those stations might prominently feature the record company's music and give more limited exposure to music produced by competing record companies.

Cross-ownership exists when one company owns organizations that are associated with different types of media. CTVglobemedia (formerly Bell Globemedia) provides an example. The holdings of this company include the television network CTV; print media (the *Globe and Mail* newspaper and the magazine *Report on Business*); and specialty television channels (such as CTV Newsnet, The Comedy Network, and Report on Business Television). Cross-ownership has certain advantages for a company, including the opportunity to share resources or personnel among its media outlets, but critical researchers argue that it can limit the variety of journalistic opinions or media messages that are presented (Hackett et al., 1996). When one company owns the number of media outlets that CTVglobemedia has, the concern is that the same news stories and television shows will appear across the range of its holdings. These large companies may provide us with lots of media choices but less diversity in media content (Taras, 2001).

Finally, it is necessary to consider **conglomerate ownership**. A conglomerate is a company containing many firms engage in a variety of (usually) unrelated business activities. This form of ownership may combine different linkages (horizontal and vertical integration and even cross-ownership). There are also different types of conglomerates. A media conglomerate does most of its business in the media. A non-media conglomerate has its foundation in other types of business, but it might also own one or more media organizations (Lorimer and Gasher, 2001). Critical researchers have been concerned about the content of the news media held by both types of conglomerates. In this regard, Hackett and Gruneau (2000: 60–1) identify 'two worrying implications'. First, news media owned by a conglomerate may be required to carry promotional material for other parts of the company. Second, and even more significantly, news stories could be suppressed if they contain negative and damaging information about other aspects of the corporate empire.

These points can be illustrated through reference to particular firms. The Walt Disney Company is one of the world's best-known media conglomerates. Disney's holdings include different media (such as the Walt Disney film studio and the ABC television network) and theme parks (like Disney World). The company has promoted its theme parks or upcoming films through programming on ABC and ABC News. In an even more troubling development, ABC News reportedly cancelled a segment of its news magazine series *20/20* that would have addressed lapses in security at Disney World (Wasko, 2001). Similar concerns have been raised about General Electric (GE), a non-media conglomerate that owns the NBC television network while primarily being involved with other enterprises. These include the manufacturing of consumer appliances and military or aviation equipment. Although most of the known or suspected cases of suppressed news involve companies like Disney and GE, such cases raise disturbing questions about the ownership of news media by Canadian conglomerates such as the Irving Group. The Irving family has various business interests, including oil and newspapers (Hackett and Gruneau, 2000).

The suppression or slanting of news stories might occasionally stem from orders at the top of a conglomerate, but it is more likely to emerge from self-censorship by journalists or directions from editors when journalists present their stories. These news workers realize that corporate executives do not want such stories broadcast or published and act in a way that protects their jobs (ibid.; Wasko, 2001).

The State and Media Policy

The concept of **the state** is sometimes confused with that of the government. However, for sociologists, the state is actually a much broader term. Cuneo (1990) defines the state in Canada as encompassing various institutions: the federal, provincial, and local levels of government; the administration (including the civil service and regulatory agencies); parliamentary assemblies; the armed forces and police; intelligence agencies, such as the Canadian Security Intelligence Service (CSIS); the legal, judicial, and court systems; prisons, reform institutions, and asylums; Crown corporations; and the institutions associated with public education, public health care, and public media that are under different levels of government.

While the state includes public media, other parts of the state have implications for both public and private media. As prepared by governments and passed by par-

Time to Reflect

What forms of media ownership exist, and what concerns have researchers raised about them?

liamentary assemblies, various acts associated with the legal system set out certain requirements for media organizations. For example, the Broadcasting Act indicates what is expected of organizations that provide public and private radio or television in Canada. The legislation makes it clear that these organizations must present Canadian programming. The latest version of the legislation, the 1991 Broadcasting Act, sets out a broadcasting policy that includes the following clause: 'each broadcasting undertaking shall make maximum use, and in no case less than predominant use, of Canadian creative and other resources in the creation and presentation of programming' (Canada, 1991: 3.1.f). Regulatory agencies are components of the state that have consequences for the media. For instance, historically Canada has had two independent regulators in relation to broadcasting. The Board of Broadcast Governors (BBG) was established in 1958 and replaced in 1968 by what is now referred to as the Canadian Radio-television and Telecommunications Commission (CRTC).

These regulatory state agencies were created to help ensure that media organizations comply with media legislation by setting specific rules for the organizations to follow. For example, in relation to the Broadcasting Act, the requirement that radio and television undertakings must utilize Canadian resources in programming has been reflected in Canadian content regulations. These regulations were established first by the BBG in 1960, and they initially required that at least 45 per cent of television programming be Canadian. The CRTC maintained the regulations for television and established similar regulations for radio in 1970. At first, a minimum of 30 per cent of the music on popular music stations had to be Canadian. Over the years, the CRTC has set various percentages of required Canadian content for different types of radio and television programming, but Canadian-content regulations remain a key aspect of the agency's policy.

Analysis of media policy is often based on a key point in Marxist theories of the state. As Gold et al. (1975: 31) noted, 'Marxist treatments of the state begin with the fundamental observation that the state in capitalist society broadly serves the interests of the capitalist class.' The state in Canada has served the interests of private media companies in a number of ways. For instance, the federal government responded to the cable industry's desire for vertical integration by placing a clause in the 1991 Broadcasting Act that identified cable companies as distributors and programmers. While cable companies distributed television channels on their systems, the clause paved the way for these companies also to own and program television channels (Raboy, 1995). This is now the case, as is illustrated by the ownership of the OMNI stations and Rogers Sportsnet by Rogers Communications. The CRTC's regulatory process has also done much to assist private media companies. According to Mosco (1989: 57), 'this formal regulatory process generally serves the interests of communications companies and large corporate users of communications systems.' For example, since the CRTC has taken 'a permissive attitude to industry mergers' (ibid., 212), the agency usually has given regulatory approval to the deepening concentration of ownership that worries critical scholars.

Some critical scholars suggest that the role of the state has been decreasing as a result of neo-liberalism. **Neo-liberalism** is an economic doctrine influential since the late 1970s that is favoured by private companies and has been adopted by many governments around the world. The doctrine of neo-liberalism supports free trade between countries, cuts in social spending, and measures such as deregulation and privatization. Deregulation means that regulatory agencies reduce or even eliminate rules they had previously imposed on organizations. For instance, under its 1998 Commercial Radio Policy, the CRTC reduced restrictions on how many radio stations private companies could own in a single market (Canada, 1998). Privatization, which means that organizations under public ownership are transferred to private ownership, has also been apparent in the Canadian media; during the 1990s, the government of Alberta sold the Access Network, its educational television broadcaster, to the CHUM Group (which rebranded the service as Access: The Education Station).

While some argue that such developments reveal the decreasing role of the state, other critical scholars contend that terms such as deregulation and privatization obscure the complexity of changes in the state. They suggest that the state's role has also been increasing in some ways, and this, too, has assisted private capital (Salter and Salter, 1997). For example, I have documented the deepening use of government funding to support the Juno Awards ceremony for the Canadian music industry. While the Junos received some federal funding during the 1980s, provincial and municipal levels of government have also spent a great deal of money on the ceremony since the 1990s to facilitate moving the Junos to cities such as Vancouver and Hamilton. Financial support from provincial and municipal governments deepened further after the Canadian Academy of Recording Arts and Sciences (CARAS), the organization that administers the Juno Awards, began to encourage competitive bidding among Canadian cities for the rights to host the annual ceremony. Cities with the highest bids have won

Time to Reflect

What is the state, and in what ways is the state connected to the mass media?

the opportunity to host the Junos. Increasing government funding for the Juno Awards has benefited the music industry, but it has also benefited host cities and private companies in those cities through economic spin-off effects for hotels and other local businesses as people come to town for the Junos (Young, 2004).

Globalization and the Media

In recent decades, the issue of globalization has been the focus of much analysis by sociologists. **Globalization** involves the flow of goods, services, media, information, and labour between countries around the world. Researchers often examine different but interrelated aspects of globalization. *Economic globalization* concerns worldwide production and financial transactions while *cultural globalization* refers to 'the transmission or diffusion across national borders of various forms of media and the arts' (Crane, 2002: 1).

Several factors are associated with the deepening impact of globalization. Developments in information and communications technologies are certainly among these factors. Computers and telecommunications technologies make possible the instantaneous transfer of data, which has contributed to the formation of a transnational financial system and facilitated the worldwide production undertaken by the multinational corporations that are central to economic globalization. Linkages between satellite and cable technologies have played an important role in cultural globalization by enabling the news media to make us almost immediately aware of important events as they are occurring even half a world away (Nash, 2000).

While technological factors are significant, it is crucial to realize that globalization is also being driven by a complex mixture of economic and political factors. Economic factors include deepening ownership concentration within countries and across national borders as well the international impact of neo-liberalism and free trade between countries. These economic factors are tied to political factors. The latter include the role of the state in assisting private capital, partly through the negotiation of the North American Free Trade Agreement (NAFTA) and similar international treaties. Political factors also include the emergence of the World Trade Organization (WTO), an international institution that enforces trade rules on member countries and has thereby reduced the control of governments over their own economies (Karim, 2002). These various developments have generated a number of issues that concern critical media sociologists.

Cultural Globalization

In relation to cultural globalization, critical researchers are concerned about the historically deepening and worldwide impact of media industries.

We can illustrate this through reference to the American motion picture industry. The dominance of the American film industry was established soon after the earliest Hollywood productions at the beginning of the twentieth century. By 1939, Hollywood was already supplying 65 per cent of the films shown in theatres worldwide. This export flow expanded dramatically after World War II, and the United States was providing over 80 per cent of the world's films in the 1990s (Miller et al., 2001). Major importers of Hollywood films include Canada, Japan, the Netherlands, and the United Kingdom. American films generate at least half of the total box-office receipts in all their major markets and sometimes even more than two-thirds of total receipts (Scott, 2004). In Canada, Hollywood films account for over 95 per cent of Canadian box office and video receipts during an average year (Magder and Burston, 2001).

Several factors help to explain the dominance of the American film industry. To begin with, the ownership structure of the industry has played a crucial role. The vertical integration of production, distribution, and exhibition during the early history of the Hollywood studios ensured that the films these studios made were seen in the United States and in many international markets. In Canada and elsewhere, this made it more difficult for domestic films to secure theatrical exhibition (Miller et al., 2001; Pendakur, 1990). Hollywood production companies usually do not own movie theatres any more, but they still have substantial distribution operations around the world. Furthermore, as the Hollywood studios have increasingly come under conglomerate ownership since the 1980s, massive and often non-American multinational firms such as Sony Corporation (which owns Columbia Pictures) have developed strategies to pursue global audiences (Miller et al., 2001).

It is also important to note that the state in various countries has contributed to the global dominance of Hollywood. The film industry in the United States has prospered internationally in part because it has 'a willing servant in the state' (ibid., 24). Under pressure from the Motion Picture Association of America (MPAA), which represents the major film studios, American federal bureaucracies have pushed governments in other countries to satisfy Hollywood's interests (Scott, 2004). In Canada, this has historically resulted in several successful efforts to discourage the federal government from establishing measures to protect the Canadian film industry, including quotas that would place limits on the importation of American films (Magder, 1993).

Especially given the import quotas in other countries, it must be recognized that pressure for free trade aims to further deepen Hollywood's global influence. Ever since the 1940s, American media companies have tried to justify their access to foreign markets on the grounds that there should be a free flow of information rather than quotas or other restrictions (Smythe, 1981). However, the pressure for free trade in culture has mounted since the 1980s due to the influence of neo-liberalism and the emergence of the WTO (Miller et al., 2001; Scott, 2004).

GLOBAL ISSUES

The Global Music Industry

Worldwide, the music industry is dominated by a handful of large groups. The 'Big Four' record groups are the Universal Music Group, Sony BMG Music Entertainment, the Warner Music Group, and the EMI Group. These groups are made up of record companies, record labels (various brand names on recordings), and music publishers. Music organizations not held by the Big Four are considered to be independent.

Most of the Big Four are part of massive conglomerates. The Universal Music Group is owned by the French conglomerate Vivendi. Since purchasing Universal from the Canadian company Seagram in 2000, Vivendi has sold most of its interests in Universal Entertainment (which became NBC Universal) while retaining the Universal Music Group. The latter has the largest collection of record labels in the world (including such well-known names as A&M Records and Geffen Records). Sony BMG Music Entertainment was created in 2004 through a merger of the music divisions in two companies. Sony Music is part of the Sony Corporation, a Japanese conglomerate, while BMG is a component of the German conglomerate Bertelsmann.

The merger between Sony Music and the Bertelsmann Music Group (BMG) reduced the Big Five to the current Big Four. The Warner Music Group was once part of the conglomerate AOL/Time Warner, but the music division of the company was purchased in 2004 by a number of investors led by Canadian businessman Edgar Bronfman Jr. Like the Warner Music Group, the EMI Group is not held by a conglomerate (Bishop, 2005). In 2006, the two companies entered talks about joining forces through a merger that would reduce the Big Four to the Big Three.

The Big Four music groups control most of the world music market. The Universal Music Group is in the leading position, with 25.5 per cent of the market in 2004. It was followed by Sony BMG Music Entertainment with 21.5 per cent, the EMI Group with 13.4 per cent, and the Warner Music Group with 11.3 per cent. The independent sector held the remaining 28.4 per cent of the global market (International Federation of the Phonographic Industry, 2005).

As they operate globally, the Big Four make use of various marketing strategies. One of these strategies is *glocalization*. Glocalization involves creating and distributing a product for a global market while making modifications to the product so that it reflects local culture (Nash, 2000). For instance, during the 1990s, Sony Music released albums by Céline Dion and other artists in several slightly different editions that were tailored to different countries or regions. A specific case is the Latin American edition of Dion's 1996 album *Falling Into You*, which featured a Spanish-language version of the song 'All By Myself'.

The global domination of the Big Four and the possibility of further ownership concentration raise several issues of concern. To begin with, the concentration of *ownership* in the music industry is also the concentration of *power* (Bishop, 2005). Fewer and fewer companies get to make decisions about the recorded music heard by people around the world. Many of these decisions are based on generating massive sales from a relatively small number of artists who have enough mainstream appeal to become global superstars. Consequently, the power of the Big Four has implications for the degree of diversity and innovation in music.

In various countries, independent record companies are more willing than the Big Four to take risks on less mainstream music and artists (ibid.). However, these small companies face difficulties stemming from the presence of their multinational competitors. The difficulties are familiar to the Independent Music Publishers and Labels Association (IMPALA), which represents the interests of the independent music sector in Europe. Martin Mills, the chair of IMPALA, argued that 'four big companies can impose their will on retail and media in a way that 15 did not. In battling each other for space and attention—and leveraging their strength—they intentionally or unintentionally reduce opportunities for smaller players' (Mills, 2006: 8). As a result, Mills noted that a new artist on a small label can easily get squeezed out. He concluded that 'a concentrated market carries dangers to musical diversity, to smaller companies and to music fans' (ibid.).

As a result of these concerns, domination by the Big Four has generated conflicts that are being addressed by regulatory authorities and the courts. Since IMPALA is opposed to any further ownership concentration in the music industry, it challenged the European Commission's 2004 decision to grant regulatory approval to the Sony BMG merger. In 2006, Europe's Court of First Instance ruled that the merger had been allowed on the basis of inadequate evidence about its impact. This gave Sony BMG three options. It could undo the merger, appeal the court's decision, or reapply to the European Commission for approval of the merger (*The Economist*, 2006b). At the time of writing, it appears that Sony BMG is pursuing the last two options (Ferguson and Cendrowicz, 2006). Meanwhile, given that a merger between EMI and Warner might also be rejected, these two companies have put their merger talks on hold until a final decision is made about Sony BMG (Cardew, 2006).

While such mergers in the global music industry have an impact on companies and even fans (at least in terms of the diversity of music available to listeners), we must not forget the impact they can have on workers. It has been suggested that a merger between EMI and Warner would lead to job cuts (ibid.). Clearly, the global music industry raises a number of issues that are of interest to media sociologists.

Economic Globalization

With regard to economic globalization, critical researchers are concerned about the emergence of an *international division of labour.* Sociologists and other scholars have analyzed how multinational corporations, including those with holdings in the media and information industries, have spread their production operations around the world. The standard view of this process suggests that it involves shifting jobs from developed, rich countries (such as the United States) to developing, poor countries (like India). Although the trend is certainly in the direction of moving jobs to the developing world, Mosco (2005: 52) has pointed to 'an increasingly complex international division of labour involving far more than simply the transfer of service jobs from high- to low-wage nations'.

This is illustrated by the fact that several developed countries, especially Canada and Ireland, have been the recipients of much outsourcing and offshoring of jobs in the media and information industries. *Outsourcing* occurs when a company shifts a portion of its production to another entity, typically independent local companies in a foreign country. *Offshoring* exists when a company has one of its own foreign affiliates handle the production. Although developing countries offer cheaper labour and other advantages, multinational corporations maintain some outsourcing or offshoring in developed countries like Canada because they need certain jobs to be filled by workers with higher levels of skill or education (ibid.). Due to the value of the dollar and wage rates in these other developed countries, multinationals can still enjoy considerable savings on production costs compared to keeping production in the United States. These factors explain the existence of so-called 'runaway' productions. Hollywood studios have moved a number of film and television productions

Time to Reflect

What are economic globalization and cultural globalization? How do these concepts help us to understand issues associated with the mass media?

from Los Angeles to Canadian cities—everything from the *X-Men* movie trilogy to *The X-Files* television series—in order to cut costs while utilizing the expertise of Canadian companies and production crews (Elmer and Gasher, 2005; Magder and Burston, 2001).

We can illustrate some aspects of the international division of labour through the case of Disney. Wasko has shown that Disney arranges to have some of its film, television, and animation production done in countries such as Canada and Australia. However, where manual labour is involved, as in the production of toys or clothing that feature Disney characters, Disney has most of the work done in less developed countries to take advantage of cheap labour. The products are designed by Disney in the United States, but the actual manufacturing is licensed to independent subcontractors in developing countries. Many of the toys and clothing sold in the Disney Store at your local shopping mall are made 'in Third World countries where workers are paid poverty-level wages and often work in inhumane conditions' (Wasko, 2001: 69).

Mickey doesn't have a monopoly yet, but like other media conglomerates the Disney Corporation seeks to gain greater market share for its various enterprises. (Ivy Images)

Conflict Over Ownership, Policy, and Globalization

It is also important to consider the issue of conflict. Capitalist interests in ownership, policy, and globalization have generated conflict between private companies and various subordinate groups. Although the state serves the interests of the capitalist class, Marxist theory suggests that the state makes some concessions to the working class and its allies. Consequently, despite the power of corporate capital and its influence on the state, we must realize that subordinate groups have occasionally won victories through their struggles and resistance.

A Canadian example involves the historical conflict over public and private ownership of broadcasting in Canada. Broadcasting in this country began during the 1920s with private radio stations, but a commission appointed by the federal government (the Royal Commission on Radio Broadcasting) recommended in 1929 that all broadcasting in Canada should be publicly owned and operated by a Crown corporation. Smythe (1981: 165) noted that the period from 1930 to 1936 was marked by 'a struggle between the popular forces in Canada fighting for public service broadcasting and those seeking private profit'.

The 'popular forces' were organized around the Canadian Radio League (CRL), which was headed by two nationalistic young men named Graham Spry and Alan Plaunt. Those who joined with the CRL to call for public broadcasting included trade unions, farm groups, women's organizations, churches, and educational leaders. The advocates of using broadcasting for private profit were led by the Canadian Association of Broadcasters (CAB), a lobbying organization that represented the existing private radio stations in Canada. Supporters of the CAB included the major newspapers (which often owned the stations) and many large corporations or manufacturers that wanted to use private radio for advertising (Raboy, 1990; Smythe, 1981). In the end, the CRL and its allies were successful in their struggle for public broadcasting. The federal government established the Canadian Radio Broadcasting Commission (CRBC) as Canada's first public broadcaster in 1932, and the CRBC paved the way for the emergence of the CBC as a Crown corporation in 1936. However, private broadcasting was allowed to continue and grow in Canada.

The Canadian content regulations for television and radio that were referred to earlier are important aspects of regulatory policy, and they have long provided the basis for conflict. Private broadcasters do not want the regulations; in the pursuit of profit, they are more interested in maximizing audiences and advertising revenues by offering popular American television shows and music. A different position has been taken by Canadian nationalists as well as unions representing actors, musicians, and other workers in Canadian media industries. They contend that Canadian content regulations are necessary to provide jobs for Canadian artists and ensure that Canadian culture is presented over the Canadian airwaves. In the late 1950s, the BBG's proposal for a minimum percentage of Canadian content on television was opposed by the CAB as well as advertisers (Peers, 1979). However, the proposal was supported by the Canadian Broadcasting League (CBL)—an organization that had been inspired by the CRL—and the Canadian Labour Congress, which represented workers (Raboy, 1990). Similarly, while the CAB was against the CRTC's notion of having Canadian content regulations for radio, those in favour of such regulations included labour unions.

The efforts of private broadcasters to get around the regulations or get them reduced have provided the basis for further conflict. Conflict has also taken the form of ongoing debate about whether or not these regulations are needed—a debate that is especially fierce in relation to radio and support for Canadian music (Young, 2008).

In recent years, much conflict associated with the media has been connected to globalization. This is most obvious in the protests against economic and cultural globalization that various social movements have held at WTO meetings and at the meetings of other international bodies that focus on economic growth, but conflict over globalization also takes other forms. For instance, in developed countries like the United States, and even in developing countries such as India, trade unions have resisted outsourcing in the media and information industries. Although workers in the developing world appreciate the jobs that outsourcing provides, they are concerned about the low wages and poor working conditions that often come with these jobs. While trade unions in developed countries have resisted the loss of jobs to the Third World, they have also challenged the shifting of work to other developed countries (Mosco, 2005). For example, there has been considerable opposition from labour in the United States to the movement of film and television production to Canada (Magder and Burston, 2001). These 'runaway' productions, many of which are shot in Vancouver, have generated contradictions and conflicts in the Canadian context. A member of the Union of British Columbian Performers (UBCP) made this quite clear: 'All of us are constantly making an effort to woo Hollywood [production companies], but as unions we also have to fight them because they want to exploit' (cited in Coe, 2000: 91).

Opponents of Canadian content regulations, especially private broadcasters, claim that these CRTC regulations are an attack on the freedom of broadcasters. (Reprinted with permission. Torstar Syndication Services)

Conflict is reflected further in the opposition of many countries—including Canada—to the insistence of the United States on a free flow of information. Along with France, Canada led efforts to establish an international agreement upholding the rights of countries to support and promote the diversity of cultural expression

Time to Reflect

What kinds of conflict have emerged over ownership, policy, and globalization?

OPEN FOR DISCUSSION

Do We Need CanCon Regulations for Radio?

Canadian content regulations for radio stations in Canada were established in 1970. The regulations are administered by the Canadian Radio-television and Telecommunications Commission (CRTC). Currently, CanCon regulations (as they are often known) stipulate that at least 35 per cent of the music on radio stations featuring popular music must be Canadian. The amount of Canadian content required by the CRTC has varied over time and in accordance with the type of music played by a station. To qualify as Canadian, a piece of music must generally meet at least two of the following four criteria: the music is composed entirely by a Canadian; the lyrics are written entirely by a Canadian; the music or lyrics are performed principally by a Canadian; or the musical selection consists of a live performance that is either recorded wholly in Canada or performed wholly in Canada and broadcast live in Canada.

There has been considerable debate about whether or not we need Canadian content regulations. Opponents of CanCon include private radio broadcasters and some Canadian musicians. Supporters of the regulations include other Canadian musicians, labour unions that represent Canadian musicians, Canadian nationalists, and the owners of Canadian independent record companies. The debate between the opponents and supporters of CanCon has focused on several issues, two of which are outlined below.

The first issue concerns whether or not radio stations should be forced to play Canadian music. Opponents of CanCon, especially owners of private radio stations, contend that CanCon regulations are an attack on the freedom of broadcasters. They maintain that radio broadcasters should have the right to play whatever music they want and whatever music their listeners want to hear. Supporters of CanCon argue that the owners of private radio stations are making money off of the Canadian airwaves, which are public property and subject to legal requirements under the Broadcasting Act. In exchange for being given the opportunity to use the public airwaves for profit, they point out that it is reasonable for private radio broadcasters to meet some public service obligations by playing music that is Canadian.

The second issue concerns whether or not Canadian artists need CanCon regulations. Opponents of CanCon argue that, if Canadian artists have talent, they will make it on their own without assistance from the CRTC. In their view, radio stations will be happy to play music by Canadian artists as long as their music is good. Supporters of CanCon maintain that Canadian artists will not get on the radio unless they are already well known or unless they are signed to or distributed by one of the multinational conglomerates that dominate the music industry. They contend that developing artists (those who are unsigned or signed to small, independently owned Canadian record companies) will not receive airplay unless there are regulations to force radio stations to give them a chance to be heard.

Now that you have learned about some of the points made on each side of the debate, which side do you agree with? Do we need CanCon regulations for radio or not?

Source: Adapted from Young (2008).

(Azzi, 2005). The resulting Convention on Cultural Diversity was drafted through the United Nations Educational, Scientific, and Cultural Organization (UNESCO). In a vote held by UNESCO members during October 2005, 148 countries approved the convention while two countries (including the United States) were against it and four countries abstained from voting. It is hoped that this convention will become an effective counterweight against pressure from the United States for free trade in culture (Young, 2008).

Cultural Studies of the Media

As noted earlier, while political economy focuses on ownership and control of the media, cultural studies address the ideological aspects of the media. Three key issues in cultural studies need to be discussed. These are representation in mainstream media; interpreting and resisting mainstream media; and opposition through alternative media.

Representation in Mainstream Media

The mainstream media include the newspapers, magazines, radio stations, or television channels that most people are exposed to every day. These means of communication are owned by private companies or by the government. The mainstream media present *texts* (such as newspaper and magazine articles or television shows) that convey certain messages about society and groups in society. Critical media sociologists and other scholars argue that these messages reflect the **dominant ideology**. In other words, the messages express the viewpoints of the capitalist class and other powerful groups. Capitalist, patriarchal, or racist ideologies are some specific forms of the dominant ideology that have been embedded in media texts.

We can investigate aspects of the dominant ideology by considering the representation of social class, gender, and race/ethnicity in the mainstream media. Less powerful groups in society —the working class, women, and racial or ethnic minorities—receive poor representation in media content. This takes the form of *under-representation* (since members of disadvantaged groups are usually not seen in the media as frequently as they actually exist in society) and *misrepresentation* (because members of these groups often are portrayed in ways that are both stereotypical and negative).

Representation of the Working Class

Critical media sociologists and other researchers have been concerned about the representation of social class in the mainstream media. In particular, they have been concerned about the portrayal of the working class and labour unions. The representation of these groups can be illustrated through reference to some North American studies.

Butsch conducted a series of studies on the representation of social classes in American domestic situation comedies. After researching all of the domestic situation comedies that had appeared on American television between 1946 and 1978, Butsch identified the class position of the family in each show through the occupation of the household head (usually the lead male character). The family was considered to be working class if the lead character was a blue-collar worker, clerical worker, retail sales worker, or service worker. The criteria for indicating that the family was middle class included the existence of a professional or salaried manager as the household head. Some comedies fell outside these categories because they featured a lead character who was self-employed or independently wealthy, and it was not possible to identify the occupation of the household head in a number of shows (Butsch and Glennon, 1983). Once he had categorized the comedies, Butsch examined what they revealed about the representation of social classes.

Butsch demonstrated that there were significant differences in the extent to which social classes were represented in domestic situation comedies. He could not specify the occupation of the household head in 10.1 per cent of the comedies, but he found that 4.8 per cent featured a family that was independently wealthy and 13.2 per cent portrayed a family led by someone who was self-employed. However, his key findings were that 63.5 per cent of domestic situation comedies were about a middle-class family and only 8.4 per cent centred on a working-class family. Butsch noted that these figures were out of line with the existence of both classes in American society; based on census data, 28.7 per cent of actual household heads in the United States were middle class while 65.0 per cent were working class (ibid.). Thus, based on research Butsch conducted in the early 1980s, the middle class was over-represented in domestic situation comedies and the working class was under-represented. Unfortunately, no studies have been done to update these findings.

In his later research, Butsch found sharp differences in the way that social classes were represented in domestic situation comedies. Much of his analysis focused on the portrayal of working-class and middle-class men. Working-class men were generally represented in negative ways; the emphasis was on their 'ineptitude, immaturity, stupidity, lack of good sense, or emotional outburst' (Butsch, 1992: 391). The women in working-class comedies (and sometimes even the children) were portrayed as being much more intelligent and level-headed. In these comedies, the humorous situation typically involved the husband/father. The situation was often one of his own making, and he was usually helped out of it by his wife (Butsch, 1992). As Butsch (1995) pointed out, this scenario describes various working-class domestic situation comedies and their lead male characters in decades from the 1950s through to the 1980s. Consider *The Honeymooners* (Ralph Kramden), *The Flintstones* (Fred Flintstone), *All in the Family* (Archie Bunker), and *The Simpsons* (Homer Simpson).

In contrast, Butsch found that middle-class men were often represented in positive ways. They were portrayed as being 'intelligent, rational, mature, and responsible' (Butsch, 1992: 391). The women in middle-class families were shown as also having these characteristics in their roles as wives and mothers. In middle-class domestic situation comedies, the humorous situation typically involved one of the children. The parents guided the child through the situation, and they often provided a moral lesson in the process. Examples of these comedies from the 1950s to the 1980s include *Father Knows Best*, *My Three Sons*, *The Brady Bunch*, and *The Cosby Show* (Butsch, 1992). Butsch (1995: 404) argued that the stark differences between the representation of working-class and middle-class men ideologically justify inequality in our class-divided society: 'Blue-collar workers are portrayed as requiring supervision, and managers and professionals as intelligent and mature enough to provide it.'

The problematic representation of the working class in the entertainment media is an important issue, but it is even more significant that there is under-representation and negative representation of workers and trade unions in the news media. Inspired by British research conducted by the Glasgow University Media Group (1976), Canadian media scholars have done a number of studies on news coverage of labour issues. They have found that capitalists receive more representation in the news than workers. Indeed, it is telling that most newspapers have a 'Business' section but no 'Labour' section (Hackett et al., 1996). Issues of particular concern to organized labour—such as low wages, unemployment, layoffs, industrial safety, poor working conditions, discrimination in the workforce, and minimum wage laws—are rarely covered in the news. Workers and unions receive significant attention in the news only when they are on strike (Hackett, 1992).

Since much of the negative representation of labour is connected to strike coverage, it is important to consider aspects of this coverage. First, there is a focus on the effects rather than the causes of labour strikes, and the main effect is the inconvenience to the public when particular services are no longer available. Second, to the extent that the causes of strikes are addressed, the emphasis is on organizational or individual causes; unions and workers are usually held responsible for initiating the strike action. Structural causes of strikes, such as the exploitation that exists in capitalist society, are ignored. Third, the focus on blaming labour for strikes is reinforced by the very different words used to describe unions and employers. Unions are said to make 'demands' (implying they are arrogant) while employers make 'offers' (suggesting they are generous). Businesses are described in objective terms (such as their size), but workers are associated with subjective terms that have emotional connotations. Some examples uncovered by researchers include 'angry', 'furious', 'militant', and 'upset' (ibid.; Knight, 1992).

Representation of Women

Critical media sociologists and feminist researchers have been concerned about gender issues in media content, particularly about the representation of women. Many studies have been done in this area, and on a wide variety of specific topics, but we can illustrate the representation of women in the mainstream media through a few studies of American and Canadian media content.

In a study titled 'Woman with a Gun', Dole (2000) examined the representation of women as law enforcers in American motion pictures that were released during the 1980s and 1990s. Dole (2000: 11) argued that the women in these films had 'types of power culturally coded as masculine'. The women had power because they occupied the position of law enforcer and because they carried a gun (two characteristics socially defined as 'masculine' within our culture). Dole saw the genre of women cop films as emerging in two phases. The earlier films (1987–91), such as *Blue Steel* and *Impulse*, often imitated the physicality and violence of male action films by showing the women using their guns. Because many of these films were commercially unsuccessful, the later films (1991–5) took a softer approach. These films, including *The Silence of the Lambs* and *Copycat*, were more inclined 'to privilege intellectual over physical power' (ibid., 12). Rather than using their guns, the female law enforcers in the later films relied on their sleuthing skills.

Several other techniques were employed to play down 'the threatening image of Woman with a Gun' (ibid., 16). These techniques included *domestication* (portraying the female cops as single mothers or at least as women who have 'maternal instincts'), *infantilization* (representing the women as being dependent, vulnerable, helpless, or in need of rescue), and *sexualization* (emphasizing the bodies of the women through the provocative way they are dressed). Finally, those films that focused on intellectual power utilized what Dole called *splitting strategies*. Splitting strategies distributed among multiple characters the power that would otherwise be concentrated in one character. Through the use

FBI agent Clarice Starling, played here by Julianne Moore, wields her firearm in the movie *Hannibal* (2001). Dole, citing films including *Hannibal*'s prequel, *The Silence of the Lambs*, argues that Hollywood has preferred to show women cops using their wits and dependent on males; this scene of a 'woman with a gun' is an exception to the rule. (Reuters/Ho Old)

of splitting strategies, the power of the female law enforcer was reduced. This can be illustrated by *The Silence of the Lambs*. In that film, intellectual power was split between Clarice Starling (Jodie Foster) and Hannibal Lecter (Anthony Hopkins). Although Starling was intelligent, she needed male assistance in the form of Lecter (ibid.). The ideological message was that a woman is incapable of solving the case and catching the killer on her own. Although female cop films gave women more representation than most movies (because they occupied central roles rather than peripheral roles), the stereotypical and patriarchal misrepresentation of women was still quite evident in these films.

Dole's analysis has implications for understanding the representation of female characters in other motion pictures or even television shows. Consider, for example, the character of Dana Scully in the 1990s television series *The X-Files*. Scully (Gillian Anderson) was endowed with even more 'masculine' features than the characters Dole discusses. Apart from being an FBI agent who carried a gun, Scully was also a medical doctor and scientist who placed a strong emphasis on rationality and logic. For all of these reasons, the character of Scully was a particularly threatening image of Woman with a Gun. Because Scully was so heavily endowed with 'masculine' properties, there were efforts to reduce her power and make her less threatening. This happened in a variety of ways throughout the history of the series. From the very beginning, Scully's power was undercut through sexualization. A scene in the first episode had Scully appearing before her new male partner, Fox Mulder (David Duchovny), wearing only a bra and panties. Infantilization was also employed to reduce her power. For example, in the 1998 motion picture based on the series, Mulder spent the last half of the movie trying to rescue Scully. Scully's power was further undercut through domestication. In the final year of the long-running series, Scully was often seen at home taking care of the baby she had just given birth to. The mother role slotted Scully into more traditional representations of women. Finally, throughout the series, Scully's intellectual power was undermined through splitting strategies. In *The X-Files*, intellectual power was split between Scully and Mulder. Each of them had an explanation for the strange goings-on they were investigating, but Mulder's interpretation of events was almost always proven to be correct. Once again, the representation of a female law enforcer is riddled with contradictions; the portrayal of a strong, independent woman is undercut by patriarchal elements that reassert male domination.

It is also important to consider how the news media are connected to the representation of women or issues associated with women, and some Canadian research in this area has focused on news coverage of what is often referred to as the Montreal Massacre. On 6 December 1989, 25-year-old Marc Lépine walked into l'École polytechnique (the School of Engineering) at the University of Montreal with a semi-automatic rifle. He entered a classroom, ordered the men to leave, and accused the women of being 'a bunch of feminists' before shooting six of them to death. Lépine then walked through the hallways of the building, entered other classrooms, and murdered eight more women. He also injured nine women and four men. At the end of his shooting rampage, he killed himself. In a suicide note found on his body, Lépine cited 'political reasons' for the murders: he blamed 'the feminists, who have always ruined my life' (cited in Eglin and Hester, 1999: 256). There was much coverage of the Montreal Massacre in the news media, and some studies have been done of this coverage.

In one study, Hayford compared newspaper coverage of the Montreal Massacre at the time of the murders to coverage of a similar incident in Chicago during 1966 when eight women were killed by a man named Richard Speck. She found that the killings in Chicago were often interpreted by journalists in individualistic terms as the act of a madman. However, by the time the murders in Montreal occurred 23 years later, the women's movement had experienced some success in raising public awareness about the prevalence of wife-beating, rape, and other acts of violence against women in a patriarchal society. Since this had an impact on at least some journalists, there was media debate about individual versus societal explanations for the murders. Hayford (1992: 209) indicated that 'the question of whether Lépine was no more than a demented individual or a reflection of broader social patterns of male violence against women, a question never raised about Speck, became a central issue in coverage of the Montreal killings.'

In another study, Rosenberg examined news coverage of the tenth anniversary of the Montreal Massacre. One aspect of her study addressed the 'emblematic' characteristics that the coverage had taken on by this point. She noted that, in order to contest individualistic and psychological explanations for Lépine's actions, many feminists had encouraged interpretation of the Montreal Massacre as an emblem or symbol of violence against women. However, by this time, some feminists had come to see the 'emblematic' interpretation of the Montreal Massacre as problematic due to the growing emphasis within feminism on the issue of difference. These feminists argued that taking the murders of 14 middle-class, white women as emblematic obscured diversity among women in terms of their experiences with violence through other class positions and racial or ethnic backgrounds. However, Rosenberg (2003: 15) found that the 'critiques of emblemization by feminists' were 'largely absent in tenth anniversary coverage'.

Representation of Racial and Ethnic Minorities

We also need to consider the under-representation and misrepresentation of racial and ethnic minorities in the mainstream media. From its beginnings in the 1960s, research on media–minority relations has largely focused on these issues (Mahtani, 2001).

Many studies have documented the under-representation of racial and ethnic minorities in Canadian mass media. Researchers have found that, although Canadian society features growing cultural diversity, this diversity usually is not reflected in media content (ibid.). For example, my own research shows that ethno-racial minorities have rarely been seen at the annual and nationally televised Juno Awards ceremony for the Canadian music industry. Francophones, blacks, and Aboriginal peoples were almost never among the musical artists who appeared on the ceremony or won Junos during the 1970s and 1980s. There has been some improvement since then, but the Juno Awards ceremony still does not adequately reflect the cultural diversity of artists in Canada's music scene (Young, 2006). Other scholars have arrived at similar findings. The general absence of racial and ethnic minorities (relative to their existence in the actual population) is apparent in advertisements, magazines, news, television series, and other forms of media content (Fleras and Kunz, 2001; Mahtani, 2001). The under-representation of these minorities is significant because it means that their contributions to Canadian society are trivialized and their roles as Canadian citizens are devalued (Mahtani, 2001).

Studies have also shown that racial and ethnic minorities have experienced misrepresentation in Canadian mass media. To the extent that they are seen, ethno-racial minorities are portrayed in stereotypical and negative ways. Especially in the news media, this often takes the form of identifying them as social problems; racial and ethnic minorities are depicted as 'having problems or creating problems in need of political attention or costly solutions' (Fleras and Kunz, 2001: 145).

Members of these minorities, particularly any who are immigrants, are presented as social problems in a variety of ways. They are seen to be participating in illegal activities, clashing with police, cheating on welfare, creating difficulties for immigration authorities, and having other undesirable effects (ibid.). Specific groups—blacks, Asians, and Aboriginal people—are often singled out. For instance, Grenier (1994: 313) noted that Aboriginal people are 'portrayed by mass media as strange, as unpredictable threats to social order, and as heavily engaged in emotive and largely deviant forms of conflict.' However, especially since the 9/11 terrorist attacks, Muslims have become the favourite target in media content. The news and entertainment media have depicted Muslims as religious fanatics who have little regard for human life. In the process, an entire group has been demonized for the actions of a few (Fleras and Kunz, 2001). The various portrayals of ethno-racial minorities described above are all based on positioning 'us' (an assumed mainstream audience) against 'them' (the minorities that are seen as posing threats to the majority). As a result, these negative representations may contribute to deepening divisions in society (Mahtani, 2001).

Explaining the Representation

How can we explain the under-representation or misrepresentation of the working class, women, and racial or ethnic minorities in media content? To begin, we must reject the notion that there is a plot or 'conspiracy' by powerful groups against less powerful groups. The circumstances are far more complex than that, and we must return to the concept of the dominant ideology in order to understand this. According to Hall, the dominant ideology is woven into media texts through **encoding**. Messages are constructed within the economic and technical frameworks of media institutions through a complicated production process that involves (among other things) organizational relations or practices and 'meanings and ideas' drawn from the production structure (the media institutions) and 'the wider socio-cultural and political structure' (Hall, 1980: 129). Therefore, in order to grasp the representation of subordinate groups, we need to consider some of these factors in more depth.

Economic factors associated with media or cultural institutions help to partially account for the representation of subordinate groups in the entertainment media. Butsch (1995) noted that the under-representation of the working class in domestic situation comedies has much to do with the need for producers and broadcasters to develop programs that will attract advertisers by providing a good atmosphere for products. There is a tendency, then, to create shows that feature middle-class characters and occupational groups that can afford to buy the products appearing in the ads. Furthermore, to the limited extent that working-class domestic situation comedies have been made, their persistently negative representation of working-class men exists in part because producers and broadcasters avoid financial risk by relying on formulas that have proven to be successful. Thus, the popularity of *The Honeymooners* in the 1950s spawned *The Flintstones* in the 1960s.

Dole also draws attention to economic factors when addressing the representation of female law enforcers in motion pictures. She explains that 'Hollywood has experimented with various levels of violence, muscularity, and sexualization in women's action films in order to achieve a mix that will produce big profits' (Dole, 2000: 12). Producers have tried to expand the female audience for types of entertainment that more frequently appeal to a male audience without losing that male audience. This helps to account for the contradictions in films and television dramas that feature female law enforcers.

Finally, economic factors clearly affect the representation of racial and ethnic minorities. The quantity and quality of media representation of minorities is affected by the commercial imperatives of institutions, including the need to attract the largest possible audience (Fleras and Kunz, 2001). For example, the Canadian Academy of Recording Arts and Sciences (CARAS) has attempted to generate the largest possible audience for the telecast of the Juno Awards by getting high-profile musical artists to appear on the ceremony, and this has left few spots for lesser-known artists from minority groups (Young, 2006).

Factors associated with production and ideology also help to explain the problematic representation of subordinate groups in the entertainment media. Members of less powerful groups often do not occupy important positions associated with media production. For example, as an American communications scholar has shown, women have little control over production in the film industry; women comprised only 17 per cent of all directors, executive producers, producers, writers, cinematographers, and editors who worked on the top 250 grossing American films in the United States for the year 2005 (Lauzen, 2006). Such exclusion from the process of media production can have a substantial impact on media content. Butsch (1995) makes this clear in his analysis of domestic situation comedies. He notes that the under-representation of the working class in these

Time to Reflect

How are less powerful groups in society represented in the content of the mass media, and why are they represented in these ways?

comedies, along with the negative representation of working-class men, can partially be explained by the middle-class background of most producers and writers. Middle-class people develop shows based on what is familiar to them and, when they occasionally focus on working-class characters, they rely on the negative stereotypes of the working class that circulate in our culture as part of the dominant system of meanings and ideas.

Some of the same factors also help to explain the representation of subordinate groups in the news media. The need to attract advertising revenues by capturing large numbers of readers or viewers has contributed to the under-representation of the working class and ethno-racial minorities in news stories. For instance, since affluent middle-class audiences are desired by advertisers, the content of the news is designed to attract these audiences by reflecting their interests or concerns (Hackett and Uzelman, 2003). The middle-class, male, white backgrounds of many news personnel also have at least some consequences for how less powerful groups are covered (Mahtani, 2001). Like producers and writers in the entertainment media, the work of journalists is partially shaped by their socio-demographic backgrounds and the dominant meanings and ideas they are exposed to. As Mahtani (ibid., 115) has indicated, 'journalists are largely bound by the dominant cultures within which they operate, including embedded societal prejudices, stereotypes, and populist frames of thinking.'

An additional factor unique to the news media is that the routines of gathering news through sources can also affect media representation. When preparing a story, journalists first seek information from *primary sources*. These are the powerful voices of private capital or the state such as corporate representatives, government officials, and the police. Primary sources draw on the dominant ideology to 'define the situation, and establish what the event or issue is essentially about; the terms in which it should be understood' (Knight, 1998: 99). Once the key terms of the story have been established by the primary sources, journalists then get reactions from *secondary sources*. These are less powerful individuals such as trade union leaders, spokespeople for women's groups and minority groups, or representatives of oppositional social movements. Secondary sources provide reactions to the event or issue within the boundaries set by the primary sources. Compared to primary sources, 'they speak less often; and they rarely speak as fully and autonomously' (Knight, 1988: 20). As a result, the routines associated with using sources mean that the news is structured more favourably towards the views of the powerful (Knight, 1982). The less powerful receive less representation and, since they are more likely to be paraphrased than quoted, their views may be misrepresented.

Interpreting and Resisting Mainstream Media

In cultural studies, research has gone beyond studying representation in mainstream media to considering interpretation of this representation and resistance to representation. We have seen that the dominant ideology—the perspective of powerful groups—is embedded in media texts through the process of encoding, but it is also important to consider the **decoding** of media content by audience members. As part of his encoding/decoding model, Hall argued that the dominant ideology is inscribed as the *dominant or preferred meaning* within media content.

Since Hall recognized that audience members may not always adopt this meaning when they interpret media messages, he identified three possible ways of decoding media texts. A *dominant-hegemonic* reading involves taking the preferred meaning while an *oppositional* reading involves resisting a message by interpreting it through an alternative ideological framework. A *negotiated* reading contains a mixture of the dominant-hegemonic and oppositional readings. According to Hall (1980: 137), it reflects 'the dominant definition of events' while refusing to accept every aspect of the definition. Consequently, 'this negotiated version of the dominant ideology is shot through with contradictions' (ibid.). For example, a worker may accept the argument of government officials (as presented by the news media) that the 'national interest' requires citizens to make economic sacrifices while opposing the related argument that such sacrifices must be made through legislation imposing wage freezes (ibid.).

Studies have been done on the decoding of media content by relatively powerless or disadvantaged groups, and some of this research has documented the resistance of groups to their representation in media texts or their resistance to other aspects of media messages. In order to examine the decoding positions that Hall identified, Morley (1980) conducted a now-classic study of how groups interpreted the British current affairs television series *Nationwide*. Morley demonstrated that decoding is affected by one's class position. For instance, in relation to a *Nationwide* program that discussed the effects of budget policy on families of different class backgrounds, Morley found that none of the middle-class groups adopted an oppositional reading while working-class groups produced more oppositional and negotiated readings.

Although the research on *Nationwide* is often remembered for analysis of how class position affects interpretation of media texts, Morley (2006) has stressed that his aim was to examine how decoding is also influenced by other types of social position (such as gender, race/ethnicity, and age). These elements of Morley's study have come through more clearly in a statistical re-analysis of his data conducted by Kim. For example, in relation to age, Kim (2004: 88, 91) found that 'the *younger* working-class viewers are, the more probability they have of producing *dominant* readings . . . . The more youthful viewers' consent to the preferred meanings can be explained by their relatively low-level of political consciousness, which is commonly found among youths in general.'

In another study, Press discovered differences in the way that working-class and middle-class women interpreted television shows. Her findings indicated that middle-class women tended to respond to television in ways that were gender-specific (connected to patriarchy) while working-class women were more inclined to respond in class-specific terms. Paradoxically, middle-class women accepted 'television's portrayals of independent women and television's stereotypically sexy females' (Press, 1991: 138). Press (ibid., 96) concluded that, for these women, 'television is both a source of feminist resistance to the status quo and, at the same time, a source for the reinforcement of many of the status quo's patriarchal values.' Working-class women resisted the representation of working-class life in television shows, seeing it as unrealistic, but Press (ibid., 175) noted that it was 'more surprising and disturbing' that these women thought many shows about middle-class life presented 'accurate pictures of reality'.

Some studies have addressed resistance to representation in a different way by examining the efforts of subor-

SOCIOLOGY IN ACTION

Watching Homeless Men Watch *Die Hard*

Fiske and Dawson (1996: 297) wanted to examine 'audiencing', which they defined as 'the process in which audiences selectively produce meanings and pleasures from texts'. They were especially interested in studying how texts associated with the dominant culture were used, through audiencing, by subordinate groups. Fiske and Dawson decided to focus their analysis on how homeless men watched and interpreted television.

The researchers began by getting access to homeless men. They approached the authorities who ran a homeless shelter in an American city. After the researchers convinced the authorities that their work would be done with sensitivity towards the plight of the homeless, they were given permission to conduct their study. Fiske and Dawson then spent time at the shelter (at least twice a week for three months) until the homeless men felt more comfortable with their presence. Eventually, they started collecting data on how the men made use of a television set and videocassette recorder in a lounge at the shelter.

Fiske and Dawson tried to make their observations unobtrusively. They just watched television with the homeless men and only talked with those who wanted to talk. The researchers carefully observed the reactions of the men to what was being watched and made notes in private as soon as possible afterwards. By choosing these particular observational strategies, Fiske and Dawson hoped that their presence would not significantly affect the behaviour of the men as they watched television.

The homeless men often borrowed violent action films from the local public library, and one of the films they watched during the study was *Die Hard*. Fiske and Dawson analyzed the reactions of the men to this movie. The main character of the movie is John McClane (Bruce Willis), an off-duty detective who happens to be in the office tower of the Nakatomi Corporation at the time a gang of terrorists invades a Christmas party and takes the company's executives hostage. Although they profess to have political motives, these 'terrorists' turn out to be thieves who want the millions of dollars held in the company's vaults. The plot of the film involves McClane's efforts to kill off the terrorists/thieves one by one as the police unsuccessfully try to contend with the situation from outside the building.

Fiske and Dawson made some interesting observations about the reactions of the homeless men to *Die Hard*. They found the men paid the most attention to 'violence that was directed against the social order' (ibid., 301). For instance, the first scene that captured the interest of the homeless men was the one in which the terrorists/thieves invade the party being held by the corporate executives. The homeless men cheered at the climax of the scene, which showed the thieves killing the head of the Nakatomi Corporation after he refuses to give them a computer code to access the company's vaults.

The men had a similar reaction to another scene. In one part of the movie, the police attempt to retake the building with an armoured vehicle. While hidden and in radio communication with the terrorists, McClane could see the terrorists preparing to fire a rocket that would destroy the vehicle and kill the men in it. McClane begs them not to fire their weapon, but they do it anyway. The homeless men cheered in response. Fiske and Dawson (ibid., 306) note that 'the hero's plea works to position the viewer inside the norms of the dominant social order against the excessive violence of terrorists, but the homeless refused this positioning.' In contrast to the way people are intended to interpret the film, the homeless men were enthusiastic about the attacks on corporate capital and the police.

What explains the reactions of homeless men to *Die Hard*? Their reactions must be understood in terms of their position in society and the reasons for their position. Although the dominant way of thinking about the homeless assumes that these people are to blame for the situation they are in, Fiske and Dawson stress that homelessness is rooted in structural conditions rather than individual failings or inadequacies. This means that homelessness emerges from the structure and conditions of capitalist society.

As they indicate, 'the contemporary conditions of US capitalism . . . have produced and then exacerbated the gap between the privileged and the deprived' (ibid., 301). In the years prior to their study, policies associated with **neo-liberalism** had 'minimized the role of the state in social life and maximized that of capital and the market' (ibid., 302). Millions of jobs had disappeared, many of them at the lower end of the pay scale, and government assistance to the poor was reduced. As a result, poverty increased. Government tax incentives for investment in low-income housing were reduced, also, which meant that average rents doubled and low-income housing decreased. All of these conditions within capitalist society generated an increase in the number of homeless people.

While capitalism has had a negative impact on the homeless, the police have had a parallel impact as agents of social control. As Fiske and Dawson point out, violence 'may be initiated by the social order to control the homeless' (ibid., 303). They note that riot police have been used to clear the homeless from parks in American cities, and the police have also confronted activist homeless groups that organize illegal squats in empty houses.

The experiences of the homeless with capitalism and the police make it possible to understand their reactions to some of the violence in *Die Hard*. Fiske and Dawson conclude that 'certain representations of violence enable subordinated people to articulate symbolically their sense of opposition and hostility to the particular forms of domination that oppress them' (ibid., 304).

dinate groups to change their representation through conflicts with cultural organizations. Tator et al. (1998) examined several cases of conflict over racism in the arts. These cases included the opposition of blacks to negative stereotypes in *Show Boat* and the resistance of Asians to the way they were portrayed in *Miss Saigon*. Both musicals were performed on stage in Toronto during the early 1990s, and Tator et al. found a consistent pattern among the events associated with these two cases and most of the others they examined. They identified a five-stage process that is more fully outlined in Table 22.2. After a white-dominated cultural institution stages an event that misrepresents minorities, such as *Show Boat* or *Miss Saigon*, there is resistance from ethno-racial minorities. Once the positions have hardened into two opposing factions, the cultural institution engages in counter-resistance. This is effective, and one of the immediate outcomes is that the resistance of minorities soon disappears (ibid.).

In my work on the Juno Awards, I found that the resistance of ethno-racial minorities is not crushed so easily. Ethno-racial minorities have struggled for years to overcome their under-representation at the Juno Awards ceremony. They have used various forms of opposition, such as staging protests at the ceremony and lobbying the Canadian Academy of Recording Arts and Sciences (CARAS) for awards that reflect their music. The struggles of ethno-racial minorities have resulted in some successes, including the creation of awards for black music and Aboriginal music, but conditions have necessitated ongoing resistance. For example, CARAS has repeatedly responded to pressure from blacks for more opportunities to perform on the Junos only to withdraw these opportunities in subsequent years, and this has forced black artists to engage in continuing struggles with the organization (Young, 2006).

Opposition through Alternative Media

While relatively powerless or disadvantaged groups have engaged in resistance to problematic representation and messages in mainstream media, some of these groups have turned to opposition through alternative media. **Alternative media** are forms of communication used by subordinate groups and social movements to present their own messages, which often involve challenging existing conditions in society.

Many types of alternative media have been employed by groups and movements committed to social change, but community broadcasting has historically played a particularly important role in Canada. Beginning in the late 1960s, the terms *alternative* or *community* broadcasting were used to describe a new approach to radio and

Table 22.2 Stages in Conflict between Cultural Institutions and Ethno-racial Minorities over Representation in the Arts

Stage	Key Characteristics
Stage 1: Selection and staging of the event	• A cultural institution decides to produce an event that is problematic because of the way it depicts ethno-racial minorities. • Members of the institution are typically from the white majority, so they often do not see the problematic aspects of the event. • The institution plans, organizes, produces, and markets the event.
Stage 2: Resistance mounted by ethno-racial minorities	• The resistance effort begins as minorities express concerns about how they are portrayed in the cultural event. • Minorities try to generate support for their resistance through pamphlets, the ethnic media, demonstrations, etc.
Stage 3: Development of two distinct factions	• The institution defends its cultural event, deflects criticisms, and rejects alternatives. • The two sides clash over the correctness of their different positions. • The positions become more polarized, and resentment or anger grows.
Stage 4: Counter-resistance by the majority	• The institution fights back with the aim of maintaining the cultural event. • Alliances with other power elites and access to the mainstream media are used to suppress the resistance of minorities.
Stage 5: Immediate outcomes	• The resistance effort led by minorities is crushed and disappears. • The resistance results in little or no change, and the institution is victorious.

Source: Adapted from Tator et al. (1998).

Norman Otis Richmond of the Black Music Association protests the lack of separate music categories for reggae and calypso at the 1989 Juno Awards in Toronto. (John Mahler/Torstar Syndication Services)

television that differed from *public* broadcasting—a phrase that had come to be associated with the centralized, hierarchical, and government-owned approach exemplified by the CBC (Raboy, 1990). During the early 1970s, community broadcasting started operating through small radio stations or 'public access' television channels on privately owned cable systems. These new forms of communication strongly emphasized democratic principles. For instance, the community television channels on many cable systems were run by an advisory board of community members (especially in Quebec), and any groups or individuals from the local community could prepare their own programs.

Operated in this fashion, community television enabled social activists and members of marginalized groups to express themselves. However, as Goldberg (1990: 38) noted, community television was 'a collectivist, pluralist, egalitarian concept embedded in a hierarchical, privately controlled, corporate structure'. As private cable companies started to assert their ultimate control over community channels in the late 1970s, the community advisory boards virtually disappeared (at least in English Canada) and groups committed to social change largely gave up using community television to achieve their goals (ibid.). Although community television lost its focus on the disadvantaged and social change, community radio still plays an important role in these respects. For instance, Vancouver Co-operative Radio is a non-commercial station that is owned and run jointly by its members. According to its website (www.coopradio.org), the station is 'a voice for the voiceless that strives to provide a space for under-represented and marginalized communities'.

Other types of alternative media have also been used by oppositional movements in Canada. Carroll and Ratner (1999) investigated the political strategies of three social movement organizations, including their use of alternative media. One of the organizations they studied was Greenpeace. Even though Greenpeace usually created spectacles that received widespread coverage in the mainstream media, this environmental group had been involved in the production of magazines and video footage that permitted more control over the presentation of its messages. Carroll and Ratner noted that The Centre, an organization for gay men and lesbians in Vancouver, was even more involved with alternative media. It had established the monthly newspaper *Angles* and the *Coming Out Show* on Vancouver Co-operative Radio. The final organization that Carroll and Ratner examined was End Legislated Poverty (ELP). Committed to mobilizing the poor and fighting various state policies that perpetuate poverty, ELP had engaged in popular education through alternative media directed at the poor and the general public. ELP's alternative media included 'Fighting Poverty Kits' and a newspaper, *The Long Haul.*

Documentaries provide an effective way for progressive social movements to present their messages. For instance, during the summer of 1993, environmental activists filmed their protests against the clear-cutting of trees at Clayoquot Sound in British Columbia by the logging company MacMillan Bloedel. This enabled the activists to document their actions and express their con-

Time to Reflect

How is the content of the mass media interpreted and sometimes resisted?

Time to Reflect

What are alternative media, and how are they different from mainstream media?

cerns without potentially being misrepresented in the mainstream news media, where they would be limited to the role of secondary sources. Filming a documentary also gave the activists, many of whom were women, an opportunity to record how the state dealt with their opposition. The activists underwent mass arrests by the police as well as mass trials. Some of them even served prison terms. The resulting documentary film, *Fury for the Sound: The Women at Clayoquot*, is often shown on Canadian university campuses. There is a continuing need for such alternative media. As Hackett et al. (1996: 271) have indicated, 'establishment of alternative media is essential to building popular democratic movements, without which the hope of progressive social transformation is in vain.'

The Internet: Extending Political Economy and Cultural Studies

The critical perspectives of political economy and cultural studies have long been utilized by sociologists and other researchers to study so-called 'old media' like newspapers, motion pictures, and television. It is sometimes argued that new approaches are needed to examine the 'new media' of digital communications such as the Internet (an interconnected computer network) and the World Wide Web (interconnected documents accessible through the Internet).

However, it is quite clear that the old theoretical tools can still be very useful for understanding the 'new media'. For instance, despite the futuristic discussion of these media through technological rather than sociological theories, the emphasis that political economy places on historical analysis reminds us that industrial capitalist society has generated similar waves of technological and media change before. Furthermore, since much theoretical discussion of the Internet and other 'new media' returns us to the notion of *technological determinism*—the view that technologies themselves transform the world—it is worth keeping in mind that cultural studies have long challenged this asocial notion and the way its ideology conceals the role of private companies and the state in generating and using these media or technologies (Morley, 2006).

While the Internet has opened up fresh areas of research into media and communications, we must consider what the old perspectives can teach us about the 'new media'. Research on the Internet provides opportunities to extend work in political economy and cultural studies.

The Internet and Political Economy

Through research on the Internet, media sociologists and other scholars have given renewed emphasis to an issue in political economy that was not addressed in our earlier discussion—namely, social inequalities in access to information and communications technologies (ICTs). This issue had been important in political economy up to the late 1980s. Critical scholars investigated how private ownership and control of ICTs helped to 'deepen social class divisions nationally and internationally, as people now divide into those who can afford the technology, services and content—the *information rich*—and those who cannot—the *information poor*' (Mosco, 1989: 80). The research encompassed social class differences in access to such technologies as cable, video-cassette recorders, direct-to-home satellite receivers, and the initial personal computers.

With the further development of personal computers and the explosive growth of the Internet that began in the mid-1990s, scholars in political economy have revived the issue of inequalities in access through research on the **digital divide**. However, there has been much debate among researchers about the meaning of this concept. It is often seen as referring to inequalities in access to computers and/or the Internet, but some academics extend the concept to inequalities in the skills needed to use computers or to assimilate information transmitted through the Internet. Scholars also disagree about the types of inequalities that are the basis for the digital divide. Most sociologists view the digital divide in terms of divisions in access by socio-economic status and social class. Feminists prefer to focus on gender, arguing that the digital divide represents another way in which women have experienced exclusion from equal opportunities with men (Cuneo, 2002). With these different types of inequalities in mind, let us consider some recent data.

The data presented in Figure 22.1 support the view of sociologists that there is an economic and class

Figure 22.1 Home Computer Access, Ages 16–65, by Household Income Quartiles, 2003

Per cent
100
80
60
40
20
0

Highest quartile
Second quartile
Third quartile
Lowest quartile

Bermuda Norway Canada Switzerland United States Italy

Countries are ranked by the rate of access among those in highest income quartile.
Source: Statistics Canada, 'Learning a Living: First Results of the Adult Literacy and Life Skills Survey', Cat. 89-603, released 11 May 2005, available at <http://www.statcan.ca/english/freepub/89-603-XIE/2005001/pdf/89-603-XWE-part1.pdf>, p. 186.

dimension to the digital divide. The figure shows home computer access by household income quartiles in different countries for the year 2003. In all countries, the highest quartile (the top 25 per cent of households in terms of income) had considerably more access to home computers than the lowest quartile. In Canada, while 91.8 per cent of the highest income group had access, only 54.6 per cent of the lowest group did (Canada, 2005a). Clearly, as a recent study concluded from this data, 'income is a key factor shaping the digital divide. It determines whether households can afford to purchase computers and access to the Internet as well as other ICTs' (ibid., 183).

In relation to gender, the data provided in Figure 22.2 offer some support for the argument of feminists that a digital divide exists between women and men. The figure shows male and female use of computers in 2003 for task-oriented purposes (such as writing or editing text and preparing spreadsheets or statistical analyses). Clear differences by gender were evident in Switzerland, Norway, and Italy. However, the differences were much smaller in Canada as well as in the United States and in Bermuda. Men also had higher rates of computer and Internet access than women in the three European nations while differences in these rates were

School pupils in Alexandra Township, Johannesburg, South Africa, learn computer skills. Poverty and lack of resources often hamper the development of technicalskills in the developing world. (Reuters/Corbis/Mike Hutchings)

Figure 22.2 Use of Computers for Task-Oriented Purposes, by Gender, Ages 16–65, 2003

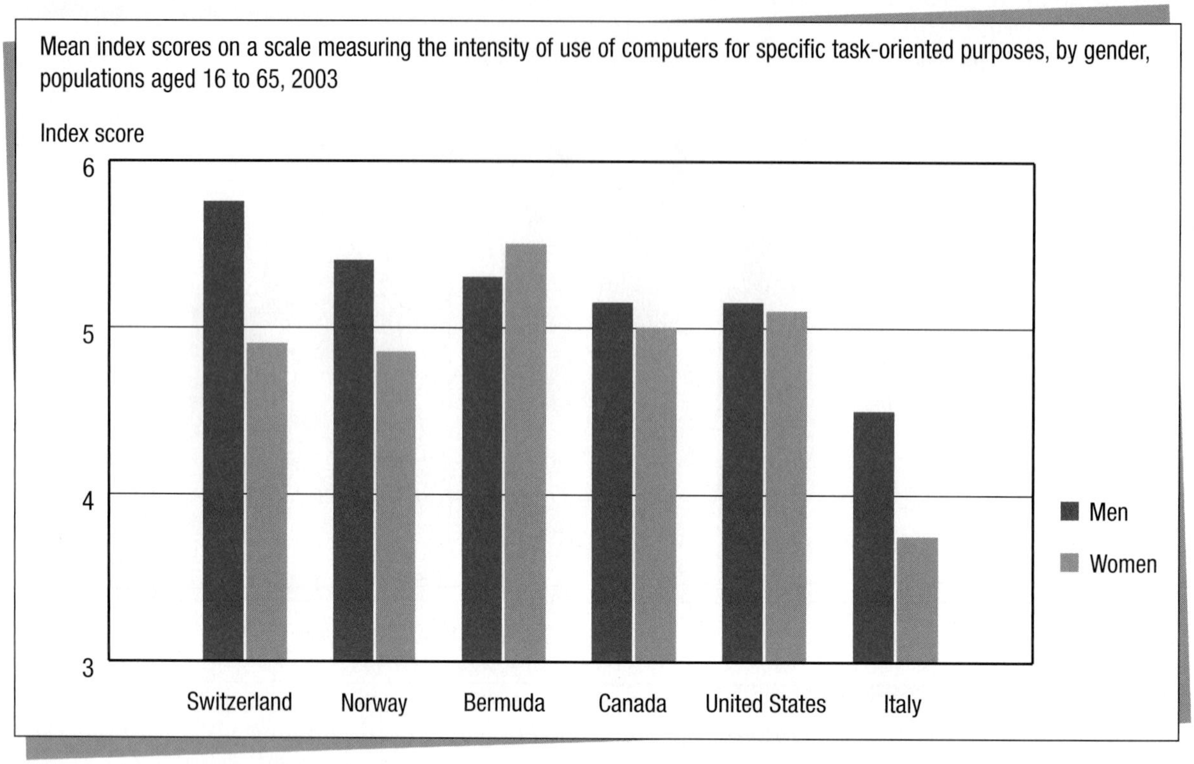

Countries are ranked by mean index scores for men.
Source: Statistics Canada, 'Learning a Living: First Results of the Adult Literacy and Life Skills Survey', Cat. 89-603, released 11 May 2005, available at <http://www.statcan.ca/english/freepub/89-603-XIE/2005001/pdf/89-603-XWE-part1.pdf>, p. 186.

almost non-existent in the North American countries. Therefore, although some evidence suggests the existence of a digital divide by gender, the evidence is only apparent in certain national contexts (Canada, 2005b).

The Internet can also be understood through other long-standing issues in political economy. Analysis of the Internet must consider the state as well as globalization and private ownership. The state was crucial to the origins of the Internet. The Internet had its beginnings in the late 1950s when the US Department of Defence established the Advanced Research Projects Agency (ARPA) to ensure that the Soviet Union would not develop military superiority over the United States, especially in relation to computers and communications technologies. ARPA developed a means to interconnect computers in such a way that an attack on one server and one part of the network would not knock out other servers or the rest of the network. That aspect of the Internet is one reason why national governments have found it difficult to regulate or censor information flowing through the network of computers (Cuneo, 2002). Indeed, in 1999, the CRTC announced that it would not attempt to regulate the Internet (Canada, 1999). Therefore, while the Internet began with the state, it has also had implications for regulatory control through the state.

As the Internet has grown, it has joined satellite communications systems and other technologies in contributing to cultural globalization. However, rather than simply being the product of a technological process, the global impact of the Internet is closely tied to private ownership. Like the 'old media', the 'new media' have become associated with deepening ownership concentration. For instance, in 2000, America Online (AOL) took over the global media conglomerate Time Warner to form AOL/Time Warner. This allowed AOL to combine its role in Internet services with Time Warner's involvement in film, television, music, and magazine and book publishing. AOL's objective was to attract advertisers with multimedia deals and promote its own services across a range of media (Taras, 2001).

The Internet and Cultural Studies

Key issues associated with cultural studies also provide a basis for thinking about the Internet and its implications. These issues highlight how the content of the

Time to Reflect

How does analysis of the Internet extend key issues in political economy and cultural studies?

Internet is linked in contradictory ways to mainstream media and alternative media.

Mainstream Media

On the one hand, the Internet represents an extension of mainstream media and the content provided by powerful groups. Mainstream media content and the dominant ideology within this content have spread onto the Internet. Recorded music, motion pictures, and television shows are available for download. The advertising that is crucial for supporting many of the mainstream media is appearing with increasing frequency on websites. Newspapers and television news channels have websites where they can reproduce news stories. While offering stories that reflect the dominant ideology, the websites maintained by news organizations also have a promotional role; they are a form of advertising that encourages people to view upcoming specials on a news channel or to examine the greater variety of stories offered in the hard-copy edition of a newspaper. Similarly, radio stations, television networks (such as CTV), and specialty channels on cable (including Much Music and Space: The Imagination Station) have established websites where they can promote their programming.

Various companies have set up websites for promoting themselves, their products or services, and their activities. The use of the Internet for such promotion is strikingly evident in the case of Nike, a corporation that has its shoes and other products manufactured in Third World sweatshops—factories employing people to work for long hours and little pay under poor conditions. Nike has received more negative attention than other companies for exploiting workers in developing countries, and it has attempted to contend with this criticism through its website. The corporation has used its website to provide a 'Frequently Asked Questions' page on wages and labour rights issues and to offer a virtual video tour of Nike factories in Asia (Knight and Greenberg, 2002).

Alternative Media

On the other hand, the Internet can also be seen as a new form of alternative media that subordinate groups use to present their own content and messages. The anti-sweatshop movement consists of various groups, and they have drawn on different tactics—including public protests and use of the Internet—to raise awareness about Nike's labour practices. For instance, in their efforts to counter Nike's promotionalisms, these groups have used the Internet to distribute accounts of abuse told by Nike factory workers (ibid.).

Another example is provided by the global justice movement—the various social movements that are opposed to neo-liberalism and other aspects of the agenda that multinational corporations have adopted in relation to globalization. Sometimes referred to as the anti-globalization movement, particularly in the mainstream media, these activists have made considerable use of the Internet. For instance, the Independent Media Centre established a website just before the Ministerial Conference of the World Trade Organization in Seattle during 1999. The aim was to provide coverage and analysis that would counter news of the conference offered by the corporate-dominated mainstream media (Downey and Fenton, 2003). Through the website, which was known as Indymedia, journalists broke stories about the brutality of the police in relation to the demonstrators. The website had received over one million hits from individual users by the end of the conference. The success of the website spawned other Indymedia websites around the world. Within a year, there were 24 new Indymedia sites. As of 2005, Indymedia was a network of over 150 websites in 50 countries across six continents (Pickard, 2006).

Although the focus here has been on 'left-wing' social movements, the Internet has also been used by extreme 'right-wing' movements. These include neo-Nazis and other racist groups. The Internet is useful to movements on the political left and right in a number of ways. For instance, through e-mail and websites, members of these groups can communicate with each other and organize protests or other off-line political activities. The Internet may even enhance solidarity among the group members (Downey and Fenton, 2003).

Conclusion

Several questions were posed at the beginning of this chapter. We are now in a position to review these questions and provide sociological answers to each of them.

In the process, we will be reminded of some of the issues that have been addressed.

What is the role of the mass media in society? Sociologists provide different answers to this question. Inspired by Durkheim's ideas, structural functionalists suggest that the mass media perform key functions for society by contributing to its order and stability. In contrast, drawing on Marx's work, conflict theorists indicate that the mass media help to sustain the power and inequality that characterize capitalist society. Media institutions and media content, therefore, are a basis for conflict between unequal groups. Feminists also focus on power and inequality by indicating that the mass media are an aspect of patriarchal society. They contend that media institutions and media content contribute to the oppression of women.

Who has power over what we read, see, or hear in the mass media? The critical perspective of political economy holds that much of this power is held by private companies through their ownership and control of media organizations. Ownership by private companies is becoming concentrated—falling into fewer and fewer hands—through horizontal or vertical integration, cross-ownership, and conglomerate ownership. These interrelations raise concerns about the diversity and suppression of media content and its use for promoting specific agendas. Private ownership also raises concerns about the amount of American media content in Canada and other countries, especially in view of globalization. The state in Canada has countered some of these tendencies through public ownership of the media and media regulations. However, since the state generally serves the interests of the capitalist class, these types of measures were implemented only because groups with little power pushed for them or supported them.

What kinds of messages exist in media content, and how do people react to them? According to the critical perspective of cultural studies, media content reflects the dominant ideology in society. Media texts are encoded with capitalist, patriarchal, and racist ideology through a complex mixture of economic and production factors. However, these texts are decoded by audience members in a variety of ways. Dominant, negotiated, and oppositional readings are possible. Oppositional readings point to the issue of resistance to media content. It is clear that some members of subordinate groups object to certain messages or representations in media texts, but they also struggle against their misrepresentation (and even their under-representation) by directly challenging dominant cultural and media institutions. Subordinate groups have gone beyond resisting mainstream media to express their own messages through alternative media.

What are the social implications of the Internet, which is associated with the 'new media'? Inequalities in access to media technologies have long existed in society, and the digital divide indicates that these inequalities are continuing through the Internet. Furthermore, as Taras (2001: 113) has noted, 'the Internet seems more and more to be an instrument that reflects and reinforces the power of the powerful.' This is evident, for instance, in the way it has become tied to deepening ownership concentration as well as to the distribution of mainstream media content and the dominant ideology embedded in this content. However, the Internet clearly presents new opportunities for movements on the left to challenge social inequality and generate social change.

Questions for Critical Thought

1. Consider how symbolic interactionism, structural functionalism, conflict theory, and feminism might be used to study a particular media institution (like a private broadcasting company) or a television program (such as a children's show). Would some of these sociological theories be more useful than others? What might they suggest about the institution or the program?
2. Research the background and current status of a media organization identified in Table 22.1 (by visiting its website or using your university library's resources). What types of media have been associated with the organization? Can you connect the organization to one or more forms of ownership and the concerns raised about these ownership forms?
3. Compare the evening television schedules of the CBC, CTV, and Global by looking at their websites or your local television listings. How much Canadian and American content do you see being scheduled? What differences exist when you compare the CBC's schedule to that of the two private broadcasters? Is there too much American content on Canadian television? Do we need more Canadian content? Why or why not?
4. Find a newspaper article that reports on a regulatory decision the CRTC has made about radio or television. Does the CRTC's decision favour powerful groups or less powerful groups? What do sociological ideas about the state suggest about the reasons for the CRTC's decision? Do you agree with the decision made by the CRTC? Why or why not?
5. Review Butsch's findings on the representation of the working class and the middle class in domestic situation comedies. Do you agree with his analysis? If so, can you apply his analysis to more recent shows?
6. Review Dole's analysis of how female law enforcers are represented in motion pictures as well as the extension of her analysis to *The X-Files*. Do you agree with these points? If so, can you think of more recent movies or television shows where a female character is represented in a similar way?
7. Examine the content in some form of alternative media (such as Vancouver Co-operative Radio or an Indymedia website). Identify specific ways in which the content is different from that of the mainstream media.
8. Examine the content of websites that you often visit. In what ways do they involve an extension of mainstream media and the content provided by powerful groups?

Recommended Readings

Augie Fleras, *Mass Media Communication in Canada* (Scarborough, Ont.: Thomson Nelson, 2003).

Fleras presents sociological perspectives on a variety of media issues. Since the book is intended for use in first- or second-year courses, it provides a good next step for students who would like to learn more about the sociology of mass media.

——— and Jean Lock Kunz, *Media and Minorities: Representing Diversity in a Multicultural Canada* (Toronto: Thompson Educational Publishing, 2001).

Fleras and Kunz offer a sociological approach to the representation of minorities in the Canadian media. Their book is especially appropriate for sociology students who want to learn more about these issues in second- or third-year media or race and ethnicity courses.

Robert A. Hackett and Richard Gruneau, *The Missing News: Filters and Blind Spots in Canada's Press* (Aurora, Ont.: Garamond Press, 2000).

Although this book is outdated in some respects (because it addresses news events and ownership of news organizations during the 1990s), the issues that Hackett and Gruneau raise are still very much relevant. Their book provides undergraduate students with an easy-to-read and thought-provoking analysis of how the content of the news is affected by ownership of the news media, reliance on advertising, the practices of journalists, and other factors.

Naomi Klein, *No Logo: Taking Aim at the Brand Bullies* (New York: Picador, 2000).

In this very readable book, Klein examines several issues associated with brands and logos (such as the Nike Swoosh and the Golden Arches of McDonald's). She discusses the expansion of branding by companies, the role of giant corporations in relation to globalization, and forms of resistance to these developments.

Vincent Mosco, *The Political Economy of Communication: Rethinking and Renewal* (London: Sage, 1996).

Mosco discusses a number of issues connected to political economy. His analysis is advanced, but undergraduate students can benefit from Chapter 2 (which describes political economy), Chapter 3 (which identifies issues and key thinkers in the political economy of communication), and Chapter 7 (which situates political economy in relation to cultural studies and policy analysis).

Bohdan Szuchewycz and Jeannette Sloniowski, eds, *Canadian Communications: Issues in Contemporary Media and Culture*, 2nd edn (Toronto: Prentice-Hall, 2002).

Szuchewycz and Sloniowski present a collection of articles on Canadian media and culture that were previously published in magazines or newspapers. This book provides good background for students who want to explore a variety of contentious issues.

David Taras, *Power and Betrayal in the Canadian Media*, updated edn (Peterborough, Ont.: Broadview Press, 2001).

Taras examines what he sees as a crisis facing the Canadian media system. This interesting, easy-to-read book considers the problems confronting public broadcasting, the detrimental impact of private broadcasting, and the implications of developments such as ownership concentration and audience fragmentation.

Serra Tinic, *On Location: Canada's Television Industry in a Global Market* (Toronto: University of Toronto Press, 2005).

Tinic examines television production in Vancouver, particularly in terms of the tensions that exist between meeting the needs of Hollywood and reflecting culture in Canada. Since her analysis draws on political economy and cultural studies, the book may be of particular interest to students who want to learn more about these two approaches.

Recommended Websites

Adbusters
www.adbusters.org

Adbusters is a group of artists, activists, writers, educators, and others who provide anti-corporate criticism on a range of issues. Its website features parodies of corporate ads or logos as well as information about the group's magazine.

Alliance of Canadian Cinema, Television, and Radio Artists (ACTRA)
www.actra.ca

ACTRA is a labour union that represents more than 21,000 performers working in the English-language media. Among other things, ACTRA's website includes the collective agreements the union has with various media organizations.

Canadian Broadcasting Corporation/Société Radio-Canada (CBC/SRC)
www.cbc.radio-canada.ca

The website for the CBC/SRC will enable you to find out more about Canada's national public broadcaster. The site supplies the broadcaster's annual reports, corporate documents and policies, background on the CBC/SRC, and other information.

Canadian Media Guild (CMG)
www.cmg.ca

The CMG is a labour union that represents nearly 6,000 workers who help to create information and entertainment programming for media organizations such as the CBC/SRC. The website for the CMG features the union's policies and newsletters.

Canadian Radio-television and Telecommunications Commission (CRTC)
www.crtc.gc.ca

The CRTC's site will help you to learn more about this federal regulatory agency and its various policies regarding radio, television, and telecommunications in Canada.

Department of Canadian Heritage
www.pch.gc.ca

The Department of Canadian Heritage is the federal government agency responsible for broadcasting, film, and other aspects of media or culture. Canadian Heritage's website provides access to relevant government policies and legislation as well as studies and reports.

Independent Media Center
www.indymedia.org

You can find out more about Indymedia through this website. It also provides links to Indymedia sites in various areas and cities around the world.

Vancouver Co-operative Radio
www.coopradio.org

The website for Vancouver Co-operative Radio (CFRO 102.7 FM) will enable you to learn more about community radio as a form of alternative media. You can get more information about CFRO and listen to the station through its site.

Chapter 23

The Environment

G. Keith Warriner

Learning Objectives

In this chapter, you will:

- Examine global population growth and its relationship to poverty and development.
- Differentiate theories of environmental sociology and their basic assumptions.
- Critically assess such terms as 'sustainable development', 'scarcity', and 'carrying capacity'.
- Understand the theory of 'risk society'.
- Learn about the social constructionist perspective as it is applied in environmental sociology.
- Appreciate the distribution of environmental benefits and impacts.
- Differentiate the various sides of the environmental movement.

Photo: CP/Adrian Wyld

Introduction

Saving the environment is often in the forefront of public concern, but few people associate sociology with the study of environmental problems. Typically, people assume that overcoming these problems requires an understanding of the natural world and knowledge of biology, chemistry, physics, bioengineering, and geography, areas in which sociologists tend to have little expertise. In fact, students may be surprised to learn that a field of sociology associated with the study of environmental issues even exists.

No one denies that science and technology play vital roles in the fight to protect the environment. However, it takes only a little thought to appreciate the very significant connection between social conditions and environmental quality. Consider the ongoing debate over the Kyoto Protocol. This international agreement was negotiated between more than 160 countries in 1997, establishing targets for the reduction of gases believed to be contributing to global climate change. Global warming may have very significant social implications for the future, eradicating some low-lying Pacific island nations, altering agriculture and food consumption patterns in the world, and triggering catastrophic regional weather disturbances with resulting economic disaster and destruction of human life. The natural sciences of physics, chemistry, biology, and geography are all closely associated with attempts to understand global warming, but almost all agree that human society is among the root causes of global climate change, as well as being significantly affected by it. Industrialization, population growth, and even the eating habits of much of the world all are to a degree responsible for the production of greenhouse gases that lead to global warming. Greenhouse gases, therefore, exist as one of the largely human-induced environmental problems that threaten the **carrying capacity** of the Earth—its ability to provide the resources to sustain all of humankind.

That human beings contribute to environmental problems through our social systems comes as no surprise. But the issue of global warming is sociologically far more profound than simply that humans contribute to it. The debate on the nature and extent of climate change, and its solution, has emerged as among the most significant social controversies during the first decade of this century, with scientists, business leaders, policymakers, environmentalists, the media, and members of the public at large all vying to have their version of the evidence accepted, thus providing an example of how even so-called objectively determined environmental problems are social constructions.

In addition, how societies define global warming affects responses. In Canada, some groups argue that achieving Kyoto's emissions reduction targets will be prohibitively expensive and harmful to Canadian economic competitiveness. Finally, the Kyoto Protocol is responsible, to a degree, for rekindling long-standing regional tensions in Canada, reflected largely by Alberta's strong opposition to the federal government's ratification of the convention. Hence, sociological implications surround every point in the global climate change question, from debates over whether global warming even exists to who is responsible, what can be done, and how the costs of solutions will be shared. The sociological complexity of the climate change issue means that science and technology alone are not likely to solve the environmental problem of global warming.

The example of climate change is typical of the societal debate around most environmental problems, and over the last several decades the field of environmental science has become interdisciplinary, spanning the natural and social sciences. Researchers, policymakers, and environmentalists all have come to accept that the complexity of the environment defies the ability of any single field of science to solve environmental problems. Environmental sociology makes its contribution by seeking to understand those aspects of societies, organizations, and people that contribute to environmental degradation, as well as by assessing the prospects for social change necessary for improving environmental quality.

Environmental sociologists have tended to draw on the traditional theories and approaches of sociology and at the same time to challenge and suggest alternatives to certain of sociology's basic assumptions. Thus, not only the subject matter of environmental sociology but also its approaches are somewhat unorthodox within the broader field of sociology.

This chapter opens with a look at the basic assumptions of environmental sociology and at its origins, then examines the theory and practice of environmental sociology. Various topics of current relevance to research in the discipline are described in the following section, with an emphasis on sustainable development. Next, we look at the environmental movement, its history and contemporary forms. The chapter closes with a discussion of the future of the environment and the global changes affecting it.

The Basics of Environmental Sociology

Environmental sociology as a distinct subfield of the larger discipline is generally acknowledged as having originated in the mid-1960s in connection with the rise of the environmental movement. Sociologists of the day were fascinated by this rich, new social movement that emerged in the United States during the late 1960s and rapidly spread worldwide.

Environmentalism among US college students of the 1960s was as much a result of the social climate of American society as of any startling understanding of or revelation about environmental concerns (Hays, 1987). The long wave of economic prosperity following World War II helped to deflect the attention of youth from material concerns to social conditions, particularly to the uneven distribution of political and economic power. This new awareness, together with obvious environmental problems such as smog and the influence of Rachel Carson's *Silent Spring* (1962), which detailed the effects of pesticides on the environment and human health, made environmental protection a cause. Two earlier causes, the civil rights and anti-war movements, provided background, helping the environmental movement's leadership to gain experience in activism and providing the organizational framework needed to launch a successful new movement. According to Craig Humphrey and Frederick Buttel (1982: 7–8):

> Students who participated in [these] causes registered limited successes, but they were reaching political impasses with respect to ending racism and the Vietnam War. As successes became more elusive, the movements became more radical in their ideologies and tactics. Universities were polarized. Pivotal events such as the Santa Barbara oil spill then directed the anti-corporate predilections of the civil rights and anti-war activists to another area of importance for human survival, the problems of pollution, resource depletion and eventually energy.

As the environmental movement escalated, leading to such events as the first Earth Day in 1970, many sociologists became interested in studying it. The field of social movements has long been important in sociology, and the environmental movement allowed sociologists to bring established theories and approaches to an exciting new social phenomenon. Some researchers investigated the composition of the movement and the ideologies and tactics of its participants (Dunlap and Gale, 1972). Others questioned how the environmental movement had so successfully supplanted the civil rights and anti-war movements (Gale, 1972; Morrison et al., 1972). Still others applied theories of social problems to environmental concerns (Albrecht and Mauss, 1975).

Along with the environmental movement, the development of environmental sociology was aided by the theoretical tradition of **human ecology**. Developed by Robert Park and Ernest Burgess of the Chicago School of sociology of the 1920s and 1930s, human ecology was the prevailing sociological tradition prior to being supplanted by the structural functionalism of Talcott Parsons and Robert Merton in the 1940s (Michelson, 1976). For environmental sociology, the legacy of human ecology provided a theoretical perspective capable of being reactivated at the moment when the environmental movement crystallized a broadly based sociological interest in the environment. The approach allowed an optimistic vision of applied problem-solving based on functional adaptation to dominate the field of environmental sociology at its inception.

A third formative influence for environmental sociology was rural sociology (Humphrey and Buttel, 1982). Rural sociologists tend to be involved with applied, quantitative research aimed at problem-solving in rural settings; they frequently work with interdisciplinary teams of planners, geographers, economists, wildlife managers, and agronomists. Their interest in such matters as rural communities, agriculture, urban–rural migration, and underdevelopment in the Third World creates inevitable contact with resource development and its consequences, including the pollution caused by new human settlement, modern agricultural practices, and economic growth. When the environment came to the forefront of public concern in the mid-1970s, an experienced body of professional researchers in rural sociology already were in a position to deal with environmental problems.

As is usually the case for sociologists in other subfields of the discipline, environmental sociologists tend to be diverse with respect to their research interests, theoretical approaches, and methodological practices. Considering the very wide range of possible issues, a broad distinction is made between those who primarily study the 'built' environment versus those whose main interests are with the natural environment (Dunlap et al., 2002). By **built environment** we mean that which largely has been created by humans, including buildings, factories, neightbourhoods, roads, and other infrastructure and the modified landscapes that surround them. There is a decided tendency for research on the built environment to focus on urban settings, particularly with respect to how urban forms affect people's activities, values, and relationships, along with questions of design and scale as, for example, with neighbourhood planning. Environmental sociology, therefore, contributes to the fields of urban and regional planning. Natural environments, on the other hand, include ecosystems and largely unmodified settings, possibly impacted by human intrusion. Among the topics investigated here are environmental values and behaviours, environmentalism and environmental activism, environmental policy and change, pollution and health, conservation, environmental hazards and natural disasters, energy, resouces, and population. Obviously, the two branches of environmental sociology often overlap—for example, environmental protest may as often occur in connection with a built feature (e.g., a proposed subdivision) as with a natural one (e.g., protecting an endangered species). Nevertheless, the built versus natural bifurcation still distingishes different groups of environmental sociologists with respect to research settings, the types of problems addressed, professional allegiances, and membership in professional bodies.

Despite the broad distinction between built and natural environments, environmental sociologists share a number of assumptions. Environmental sociology studies the interrelationships between society and the environment. The focus is on the relationship between human social organization and the physical environment. This focus effectively amounts to an important distinction between environmental sociology and other sociological fields having to do with some defined aspect of environment. Within sociology, the term 'environment' generally refers to a socio-cultural or symbolic system—a particular social context, its organizational framework, and the relationships among and meanings shared by the individuals involved. Sociologists have been reluctant to extend the term to include the physical environment, preferring to leave this usage to natural scientists. Environmental sociology, however, seeks to consider 'environment' as *both* a physical entity and a socio-cultural (symbolic) phenomenon. This does not mean that environmental sociologists are scientific experts; indeed, their work has sometimes been challenged on the grounds of their naïveté in the natural sciences. What it does mean is that environmental sociology typically acknowledges physical environmental factors along with socio-cultural factors as vital for understanding the (physical) environmental consequences of social organization, as well as for predicting such organization. This position is not without controversy, resulting in sociology's 'essential dualism', according to Alan Irwin (2001: 3), meaning that environmental sociologists are critical of their colleagues from other sociological fields for treating the physical environment as little more than backdrop to social activity or a context in which it occurs, while in turn they are themselves criticized for advocating a scientific approach that seems impossible because it is too encompassing.

Environmental sociologists agree that environmental issues are by and large social problems, even though these problems often affect the biophysical world of animals, plants, landforms, and water, while other social problems affect humans almost exclusively. This may seem obvious, but requires further consideration. Environmental problems, like other social problems, such as war, crime, and inequality, exist and persist largely because of the way societies and the global social order are organized. Consider, for instance, the fact that modern industrial and post-industrial societies contain within their central logic the enhancement of such values as individualism, universalism, and achievement. These values are part of the socialization of citizens, and have resulted in social differentiation and material abundance. At the same time, the positive values attached to economic growth and structural differentiation fuel an expansionist society. The expansionist tendency, in turn, causes myriad environmental problems. This does not have to be —the environmental problems associated with the 'treadmill of production', as it has been labelled by sociologist Allan Schnaiberg (1980: 227), could be avoided, but to do so would involve a fundamental change in ideology.

Too often there has been a tendency to see environmental problems as inevitable consequences of the process of modernization. People have tended to consider social processes and structures as being beyond their ability to change. From this perspective, many are satisfied with attempting to keep environmental problems in check, without believing that they can be eliminated altogether. Moreover, societies tend to adapt to scarcities imposed by environmental destruction rather than to seek fundamental social change. Environmental sociologists want to challenge these attitudes. They argue that the environment has fallen victim to a process of collective social definition that has accepted the inevitability of environmental damage and that simultaneously fails to question the social system that allows it—a system that in itself is neither right, best, nor inevitable. Society can choose to deal with environmental problems, as with other social problems, through deliberate social change.

Time to Reflect

Does economic prosperity create environmental problems or solve them? Think of an environmental problem that has largely occurred as a result of economic growth, as well as one that has been mitigated or solved by it. What conditions should apply to sustainable development in order for this to serve as an approach for alleviating environmental degradation?

Achieving environmental integrity may mean sacrifices, but it is a choice people can make.

A complication arises in that environmental issues are likely to be the focus of conflict between competing social groups. Resources such as air and water tend to be considered common property, freely available to everyone and having economic, recreational, and aesthetic uses. But competition for such resources arises with increasing frequency. The net result is to make solutions to environmental problems all the more difficult, since the usual response of the authorities has been to compromise environmental integrity in order to satisfy competing social demands.

Chief among the social processes and structures questioned by environmental sociology are the benefits of economic growth. In the past, sociologists, together with other scientists, tended to be enamoured of social progress, which was regarded as the means for achieving uniform prosperity and thereby eliminating class differences. Today's environmental sociologists are of two minds. On the one hand, economic expansion has adverse consequences for the environment: pollution, waste, and the destruction of non-renewable resources. On the other hand, the expansion of economic markets, besides helping to provide economic and social well-being, also provides the prosperity societies need to deal with environmental problems. The conundrum of economic growth versus environmental protection has been recognized by Schnaiberg (1975) as the 'socio-environmental dialectic'. Schnaiberg points out that economic policies that are 'regressive' in their effects—that is, that lead to reductions in economic benefits because of stagnant or negative growth—are more likely to result in environmental policies that are less sensitive to the environment. When times are hard, politicians, encouraged by corporations, see stimulating the economy as the first priority, with environmental protection being put on hold. Hence, there are grounds for believing that a healthy, growing economy is needed for environmental preservation.

Support for this viewpoint was offered by the report of the 1987 World Commission on the Environment and Development, *Our Common Future*, which strongly supported the principle of **sustainable development**. According to this principle, only through significant improvements in the economic conditions of developing nations can global ecological disaster be averted. Sustainable development approaches have emerged as indispensable to economic planning at many levels, but at the cost of falling short of providing a set of agreed-on 'best practices', operating principles, and goals. Professing support for the environment while doing little about it is one way many projects gain political and public approval. On these grounds, while still acknowledging the importance of a healthy economy for environmental matters, most environmental sociologists remain skeptical about the wisdom of constant economic expansion, especially in the guise of sustainable development, and advocate both redirection and some curtailment in growth.

The Environment and Ecological Scarcity

Issues of ecological scarcity have been of considerable interest to environmental sociologists. Scarcity has to do with problems associated with the overuse of natural resources, leading to their exhaustion, or with their waste or destruction by contamination or misuse. The immense reliance of societies on natural resources and the extent to which this reliance influences social arrangements as well as prospects for social change often go unrecognized. Sociological interest in resource scarcity therefore addresses questions of world population growth, the limits of global carrying capacity, and the relationship between development and scarcity.

Population Growth

There are presently more people living on the Earth than throughout all of human history. It took over 1 million years for the population to reach 1 billion, around the mid-nineteenth century. In the century and a half since then, the figure has grown to approximately

6.6 billion (in 2006). Some 77 million people are added each year, at a rate of around 3 people per second. Although the rate of world population increase is slowing, the absolute amount of growth continues to be substantial. By 2050, the world's population will have increased by more than half its size today, to 9.4 billion people (US Bureau of the Census, 2006). These startling statistics explain why world population has been likened to a time bomb threatening to destroy the planet. Population pressure is regarded as one of the most serious environmental threats, contributing to resource exhaustion, destroying species and habitat, causing pollution, and taxing the capacity of agricultural systems. It is a major factor in such diverse ecological disasters as famines in Africa, global warming, acid rain, the garbage crisis, and the spread of disease. While we have not yet arrived at the theoretical limits for food production on the planet, they will be reached by the year 2100, with a projected population of 11.2 billion (World Commission on Environment and Development, 1987: 98–9).

The most serious environmental problems affect mainly the more than 5 billion people in the developing countries of Africa, Asia, Latin America, and the Caribbean—more than 80 per cent of the global population (see Table 23.1). The 172 countries classified by the United Nations as the 'less developed regions' (LDRs) account for 99 per cent of global population natural increase—the difference between numbers of births and numbers of deaths. By the end of the first quarter of the twenty-second century, the world's more developed countries (MDCs) will be experiencing negative natural increase, and all of the global population increase will come from the less developed world (UN Department of Economic and Social Affairs, 2006: 5). It is not surprising, then, that environmental scientists and population experts generally agree that the way to avoid reaching

Located close to the wealthy suburb of Sandton, Alexandra Township, on the outskirts of Johannesburg, is one of the poorest urban areas in South Africa and suffers from numerous environmental shortcomings and health problems, resulting from a lack of basic infrastructure—clean water, sewerage, garbage disposal. (Hervé Collart/Sygma/Corbis)

the limits of the global carrying capacity is to reduce the birth rates of developing nations.

How can the differences in birth rates between developed and developing nations be accounted for? The **demographic transition** theory is widely used to explain the dynamic relationship between fertility and mortality, which is based on economic and social progress in societies (Notestein, 1967). During the first stage, pre-transition, a society experiences high rates of both fertility and mortality. Medicine, science, and agriculture are not sufficiently developed to keep deaths from disease, injury, starvation, or childbirth in check, while lack of contraception means fertility remains high. Births are offset by deaths, so natural increase is slow and the population remains stable or grows slowly. At the second stage, transition, mortality rates decline due to scientific and technological advances, while fertility rates remain high. Births outstrip deaths, so the population grows rapidly. In the final stage of the demographic transition, post-transition, the death rate remains low, but the birth rate also decreases because of contraception and societal changes. Births are again offset by deaths, so natural increase is low, and the population remains stable or grows slowly.

After the post-war baby boom (1947 to 1966), industrialized nations moved rapidly into the third stage of the demographic transition and remain there today. The social bases for this transition are quite clear. The modernization process in these countries was accompanied by improvements in sanitation, nutrition, water, medicine, housing, and social programs, all of which help to increase life expectancy substantially. The reasons for the corresponding decline in fertility are more difficult to pin down. They probably centre on changes in institutional structures and cultural and personal values. Examples of the former are the entry of women into the workforce, which tends to be associated with later marriage and child-bearing, and the rise of the nuclear family, which made the services of extended family members for child care less available. Examples of changes in values include the preference of many couples for emphasizing the quality of their children's upbringing instead of having large families and the tendency for children to remain dependent on their parents into early adulthood.

Developing countries have benefited to some extent from the same technological and social improvements. However, mortality rates remain high in comparison with the developed world. Moreover, these societies are largely agrarian and based on the extended family. Large numbers of children are needed to guarantee the

Table 23.1 Population by Level of Development and World Regions, 1950, 2005, and 2050

Level of Development	Population (millions)			Percentage Distribution		
	1950	2005	2050	1950	2005	2050
World	2,519	6,465	9,076	100.0	100.0	100.0
More developed regions	813	1,211	1,236	32.3	18.7	13.6
Less developed regions	1,707	5,253	7,840	67.7	81.3	86.4
Least developed countries	201	759	1,735	8.0	11.7	19.1
Other less developed countries	1,506	4,494	6,104	59.8	69.5	67.3
World Regions						
Africa	224	906	1,937	8.9	14.0	21.3
Asia	1,396	3,905	5,217	55.4	60.4	57.5
Europe	547	728	653	21.7	11.3	7.2
Latin America & the Caribbean	167	561	783	6.6	8.7	6.6
North America	172	331	438	6.8	5.1	4.8
Oceania	13	33	48	0.5	0.5	0.5

Source: UN (2006a: Table I.1, 5).

economic survival of the family by working and performing household tasks, as well as to support the parents in old age. In some cases, an entire family may be carried by an exceptional child, who is given access to higher education and a secure, well-paying job. Although birth control is widely available and, in many cases, strongly encouraged by the state, a variety of compelling cultural, religious, and lifestyle reasons militate against contraception. As a result of all these factors, fertility levels have remained relatively high, and most developing nations remain at the second stage of the demographic transition, with fertility outpacing mortality.

At present, only some 20 to 30 per cent of the world population has attained the stable third stage. A significant question for social scientists concerns the prospects for the remainder of the world reaching post-transition. It is generally felt that for this change to occur, the requisite social and cultural conditions of industrialization must first appear, including a complex division of labour, more labour specialization and increased employment opportunity, and a more efficient system of agricultural production capable of freeing families from the necessity of providing just their own basic needs. But long-standing relations of inequality between developed and developing countries, stemming from colonialism and from political and economic imperialism, have distorted and weakened the ability of poorer nations to move towards full-fledged industrialization. Without the accompanying fundamental improvements, the chance of reducing birth rates is small.

Some gains have been made through programs of public education about birth control, the dispensing of free contraceptives, and coercion by the state through laws enforcing birth control policies, most notably in China. However, as noted, contraception has had limited success. Sociologists such as Karen Michaelson (1981) have suggested that the main reason these countries remain in the transitional stage is poverty. Bearing many children to support the family is seen as the only option for escape. Thus, the most direct means of solving the world population problem is to eradicate poverty, as difficult as this may be. Environmental planners have increasingly come to accept this argument. Both the 1987 report of the World Commission on Environment and Development, chaired by Norwegian Prime Minister Gro Harlem Brundtland, and the 1992 and 2002 United Nations conferences on environment and development (the 'Earth Summits') have based their recommendations on the same proposition.

Only improvements to the economies of developing nations that help them move to the final stage of the demographic transition will end the poverty underlying high birth rates. It is clear that programs for economic improvement will require co-operation between developed and developing nations. But many factors stand in the way. Industrialized nations have traditionally benefited from access to cheap resources and labour in Third World countries, and so have contributed greatly to their economic problems. Furthermore, wealthier nations laud their overseas investments in developing countries as helpful, but studies show that there is no guarantee that the benefits will be shared equally in the face of historically rigid class divisions and traditional concentrations of wealth among a tiny elite. Industrialized nations may also view economic improvements in less developed countries as a potential threat. For all these reasons, the task of altering socio-economic arrangements in these countries—giving families a greater measure of financial security and more control over their lives—is daunting. But without a more equitable distribution of economic, social, and technological benefits, people in developing nations will have little incentive for having fewer children, and the world will have little hope of achieving environmental integrity by defusing the population bomb.

The Limits to Growth

The concept of limits to growth—the extent of the planet's ability to sustain its population—is an important basis for much environmentalism and for the scientific arguments underlying conservationism. The metaphor of 'Spaceship Earth' readily evokes the image of a shimmering orb floating in the vast void of space, reminding us of the fragility of the planet and of our dependence upon it.

That the Earth's natural resources are finite is accepted by almost everyone. Nonetheless, debate has raged for decades about how to ascertain the ecological limits of the planet and pinpoint their implications for economic growth. The controversy is highly significant, since it influences much of present-day resource use and planning, including population planning. Some observers, including ecologist Paul Ehrlich (1981) and sociologist William Catton (1980), believe that the Earth's capacity to sustain itself in the face of population expansion and resource exploitation is rapidly nearing the limit and that ecological collapse is a possibility unless growth is curbed very soon. Others, such as economist Julian Simon (1981), regard this perspective as needlessly alarmist, arguing against any immediate, or even long-term, crisis and claiming that resources are abundant and people have the inventiveness to adapt to shortages. The continuum of environmental concern defined by these two poles is the basis of calls for either continued economic expansion or economic restriction.

The controversy over the issue of limits to growth was initiated by the publication in 1972 of a study entitled *The Limits to Growth* (Meadows et al., 1972). The research team attempted to model the interplay among five factors affected by economic growth on the planet: population, agricultural production, natural resources, industrial production, and pollution. One assumption of the model was that the components of the system grow geometrically (2, 4, 8, 16, 32, . . .). Another was that the five variables affect one another reciprocally through feedback loops of cause and effect. As you can see in Figure 23.1, the model is highly complex.

The model was used to generate the baseline projection of outcomes on the five variables until the year 2100, given the assumption that no significant changes in human values or in global population and economic functioning would occur over the next 50 years. The results were startling. According to the model, sometime before 2100, 'overshoot'—the team's term for ecological disaster—was imminent. By the middle of the twenty-first century, the world's population would overtake food production and resources. The resultant predicted collapse of the industrial system would, in all likelihood, be followed by famine, poverty, war, and significant population loss.

When assumptions about values, population, and the economy were changed, more optimistic models resulted. Still, even when the team assumed inexhaustible natural resources, a 75 per cent reduction in pollution, perfect birth control, and more output from food production, global ecological collapse was still predicted, although it would be delayed until after the twenty-second century. The most optimistic (and preferred) model was premised on significant changes in population and industrial growth occurring before the end of the twentieth century. In this model, equilibrium or sustainability was achieved and ecological disaster was avoided.

The release of the study unleashed intense debate between its supporters and critics. The latter pointed to the naïveté of certain of the model's assumptions and the inadequacies of many of its measures. Nevertheless, *The Limits to Growth* generated an international furor over environmental issues. In so doing, it had a notable impact as a warning against unchecked growth and was responsible for creating much of today's widespread opposition to economic expansion.

The growth-versus-no-growth debate remains central to discussion on the environment. But the debate has become anything but clear-cut. Some scientists who favour continued expansion have close ties to the environmental movement. Their argument is that growth is essential for ameliorating the conditions of the poor in the Third World, that it will lead to reduced population growth and ultimately to the preservation of soil, water, and other resources. An extension of this argument is that, even in industrialized nations, limits on growth will have the most adverse effects on the working class and the poor. Yet another view is that economic growth is necessary to provide the profits to invest in technologies for reducing waste and controlling pollution. Thus, where economic growth and environmental quality were once considered irreconcilable, this is no longer the case. Nor can the proponents of growth or no growth be easily located along the continuum of environmental concern.

Sustainable Development

The concept of sustainable development grew out of the perspective that economic development and environmental conservation are compatible goals. First appearing during the 1972 United Nations Conference on the Human Environment in Stockholm, the principle gained widespread support over the three decades that followed while being the focus of various international conferences and reviews, including the 1987 Brundtland Commission and the 1992 and 2002 Earth Summits. Sustainable development calls for the conciliation of several apparently competing ends: environmental integrity; the protection of ecosystems and biodiversity, and the meeting of human needs; and positive economic growth and equitable distribution of the benefits of the environment and resources among social classes and across nations. While the idea of the existence of ecological limits is clearly ingrained in sustainable development, and while there is an insistence on strict resource husbandry, the principle is unabashedly pro-development. In the words of the World Commission on Environment and Development (1987: 45):

> Growth has not set limits in terms of population or resource use beyond which lies ecological disaster. Different limits hold for the use of energy, materials, water and land. Many of these will manifest themselves in the form of rising costs and diminishing returns, rather than in the form of any sudden loss of a resource base. The accumulation of knowledge and development of technology can enhance the carrying capacity of the resource base. But ultimate limits there are, and sustainability must ensure equitable access to the constrained resource and reorient technological efforts to relieve pressure.

Figure 23.1 The World Model from The Limits to Growth

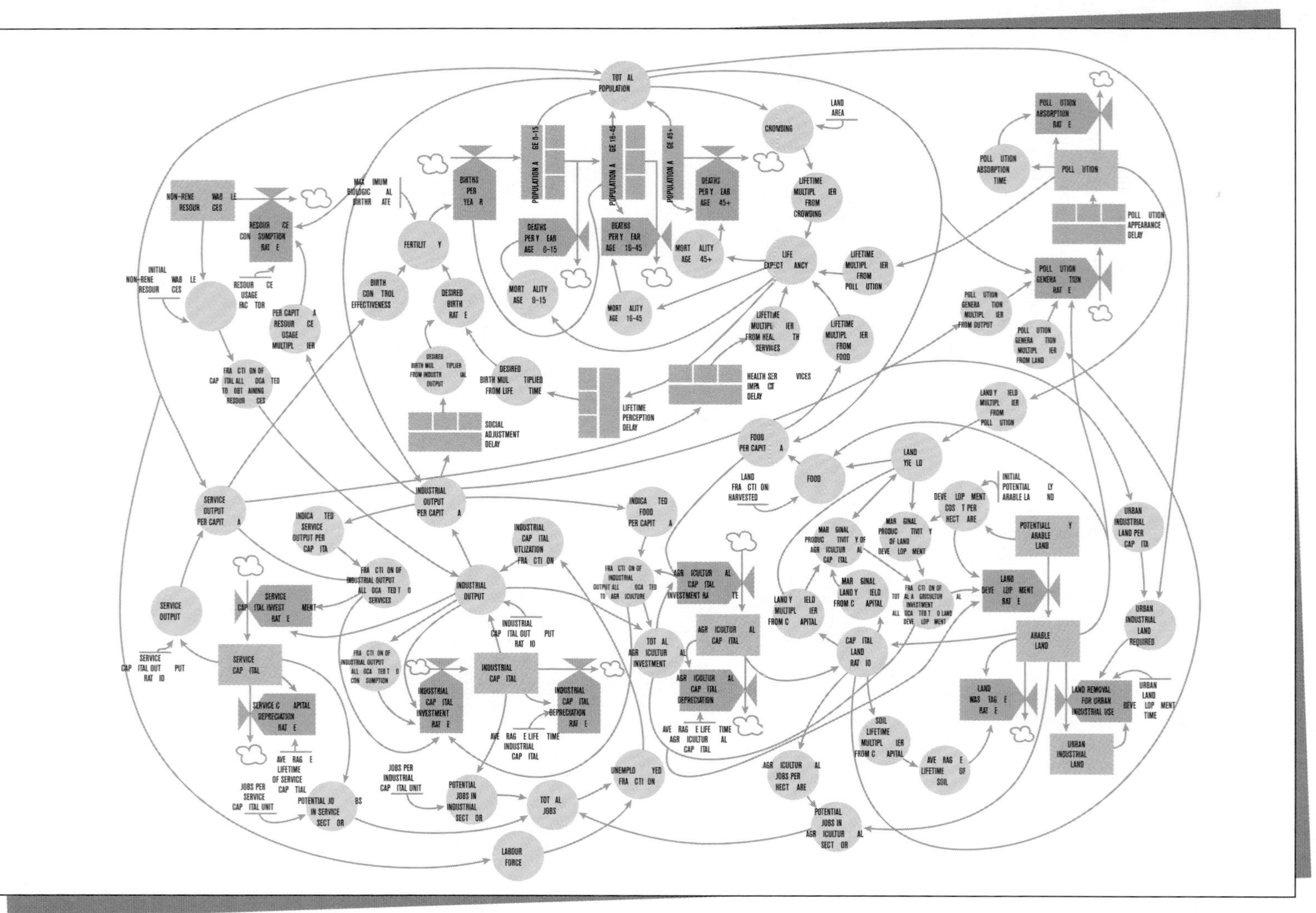

Source: Donella Meadows, Dennis L. Meadows, Jorgen Randers, and William Behrens III, *The Limits to Growth* (New York: Universe, 1972), 101–3. By permission of Donella Meadows.

After initial enthusiasm, certain environmentalists have come to regard sustainable development with skepticism. Some see it as no more than a legitimization of development under the guise of enviromental stewardship. An extension of this view is that sustainable development is an excuse for further incursions by Western nations into the Third World for the sole purpose of profit. In the words of Wolfgang Sachs, 'Capital, bureaucracy and science . . . the venerable trinity of Western Modernization declare themselves indispensable to the new crisis and promise to prevent the worst through better engineering, integrated planning and sophisticated models' (1991: 257). Others claim that the principles of ecology, together with the scientific community, are being co-opted to support the further destruction of nature on the grounds of scientific rationality. While such criticisms are undoubtedly sometimes valid, it is nevertheless the case that the concept of sustainable development has become so widely adopted as a planning goal that it should be considered a new benchmark to thinking on human–environment interactions.

The Environment and Social Theory

Environmental sociology has its theoretical bases in several sociological traditions. Among these is the field of human ecology, a sociological perspective with important ties to the work of Émile Durkheim. More recently, human ecology has been revised for the insights it provides for environmental sociology. Another theoretical topic debated by environmental sociologists concerns whether their field should be seen as constituting a paradigm shift for sociology in general. The division between the order and conflict schools so prevalent elsewhere in sociology is also a characteristic feature of environmental sociology. More generally, there has been broad debate over the relevance of sociology's classical theoretical traditions to the study of environmental issues. Contemporary theoretical approaches include the concept of the risk society, developed by Ulrich Beck. Finally, social constructionism, a perspective found elsewhere in sociology, has developed to become a prominent approach within environmental sociology. In this section, we review these theoretical positions.

Human Ecology

The science of ecology is central to the study of environmental issues; human ecology is the application of the same approach to sociological analyses. Human ecology emerged under the direction of Robert Park and Ernest Burgess at the University of Chicago during the 1920s (Park and Burgess, 1921; Park and McKenzie, 1925; Theodorson, 1961, 1982). Much as the science of ecology studies plant and animal communities, human ecology sought to explain human spatial and temporal organization by concentrating on the dynamic processes of competition and succession that influence human social organization. Park and Burgess and their students concentrated on studying how Chicago's rapidly changing society physically accommodated increases in population and changes in the industrial and cultural organization of the city. Their approach, and that of their successors, was to focus on symbiosis, the dynamic interdependencies that bind people together in communities and lead to particular living arrangements.

In developing the concept of human ecology, Park was greatly influenced by Durkheim's *The Division of Labor in Society* (1964 [1893]). Durkheim addressed the development of social complexity from human population growth and density. As populations grow, the threat to available resources is crucial from a sociological viewpoint because it leads to competition and conflict. Problems of resource scarcity can therefore affect societal organization.

Durkheim's work was appealing to early human ecologists because of their interest in sustenance activities—the routine functions necessary to ensure the survival of a population from generation to generation (Hawley, 1950). Humans have a greater capacity for adapting to resource scarcity than any other organism, an ability labelled competitive co-operation. Adaptive responses include reductions in per capita consumption,

Time to Reflect

What is your position on the future of the planet in terms of its likelihood of reaching its ecological limits? Can current patterns of population growth and development be sustained or will these lead eventually to ecological collapse? If collapse is to be avoided what steps by societies are required?

GLOBAL ISSUES

Energetics

Energetics is the study of the flow of solar energy through the biosphere, and especially of the various processes by which it is transformed into other forms of energy capable of performing work for humans. As early as 1955, sociologist Fred Cottrell noted that modern societies have developed without a full appreciation of their dependence on the energy resources of the physical environment. Cottrell recognized that the forms of energy used by a given society influence its organization and ideological characteristics. Each transformation from lower to higher energy forms throughout history (for example, wood to coal to hydroelectricity) has been accompanied by fundamental changes in the social, economic, political, and psychological makeup of the society.

In short, most people fail to realize that the survival of any society depends on its characteristic energy flows. Disruptions in these flows foreshadow social dislocation and change. 'Energy crises' are no new phenomenon. In the eighteenth century, for instance, the depletion of wood in England provided the stimulus for the development of coal and steam as energy resources, which in turn led to the Industrial Revolution with its massive social disruptions.

The 1973 oil embargo of the Organization of the Petroleum Exporting Countries (OPEC) was responsible for rekindling sociological interest in energetics. The resulting body of microsociological research focused on energy consumption and programs as sociologists responded to the energy crisis by attempting to demonstrate the relevance of their work in solving or helping to avoid future energy shortages. Other studies examined such matters as the beliefs and attitudes of energy consumers about conservation and pricing programs, the effectiveness of information campaigns on changing attitudes, the social-demographic correlates of reduced energy use, and the relationship between attitudes and conservation behaviours. Still other researchers focused on general issues of energy policy for society, particularly on alternative forms of energy.

In this connection, a distinction is often made between 'hard' and 'soft' energy paths. *Hard energy paths* involve the generation and distribution of energy through large-scale, centralized production systems relying mainly on non-renewable energy forms such as oil, gas, coal, and nuclear energy. Such systems prevail in the industrialized world today. *Soft energy paths* comprise systems relying mainly on renewable energy sources: solar power, wind, tidal power, hydroelectricity, and energy from biomass; these systems also involve conservation and recycling. Because of the nature of these fuels, these systems are more likely to be small and decentralized; examples include solar panels on a building, a community hydroelectric dam, and windmills. The essence of a soft energy path is to use the resources available locally to produce energy to be consumed locally.

(One Word Photography)

increases in production through technology or more intensive resource exploitation, changes to distribution networks, and decreases in competition because of emigration from the community or an increased division of labour (Micklin, 1973; Schnore, 1958). Through such adaptive mechanisms, involving reciprocal cause-and-effect processes between the population and its vital resources, a state of equilibrium is reached. Park and Burgess (1921) postulated that competition and co-operation are the key forms of human exchange by which organized populations seek to maintain equilibrium within a dynamic environment.

Park and Burgess's theory underwent significant revision beginning in the mid-1950s to correct what are commonly regarded as major shortcomings: an overemphasis on the spatial arrangements of populations at the expense of understanding societal–environmental relations, and the neglect of culture and values (Dunlap and Catton, 1979a, 1979b; Hawley, 1981). Moreover, while highly influenced by the conceptual approaches and terminology of ecology, early human ecologists concentrated on human social organization and patterns and did not include other species or aspects of the natural world in their analyses. They veered away, therefore, from a concern about environmental issues. During the 1950s, the ecological complex (Duncan and Schnore, 1959; Hawley, 1950), which viewed societies as being constituted of four interrelated dimensions—population, organization, environment, and technology (POET)—substantially revised the conceptual basis of human ecology. But even after this reformulation, human ecologists continued to use the concept of environment in socio-cultural, symbolic terms (Dunlap and Catton, 1983; Michelson, 1976).

Human Exemptionalism and the New Environmental Paradigm

Paradigms are metatheoretical (that is, broad and comprehensive) frameworks of understanding based on a set of shared assumptions by practitioners in a given field. Because paradigmatic assumptions are widely shared, they tend not to be questioned. At the same time, they influence the direction and scope of the field by defining the nature both of the questions asked and of those that are resisted (Kuhn, 1970).

Sociology has long been characterized by paradigmatic divisions that have led to hot debates. Environmental sociology was at the centre of one such paradigmatic clash in the early 1980s that has never been fully resolved. In several influential articles, William Catton and Riley Dunlap (Catton and Dunlap, 1978, 1980; Dunlap and Catton, 1979a, 1983) forcefully advanced the thesis that 'the numerous competing theoretical perspectives in contemporary sociology—e.g., functionalism, symbolic interactionism, ethnomethodology, conflict theory, Marxism, and so forth—are prone to exaggerate their differences from each other' (1978: 42). That is, Catton and Dunlap argued that, while purporting to be paradigms in their own right, all these approaches really were variants of a larger paradigm. The basis of their similarity was their 'shared anthropocentrism'. The authors argued that this assumption—that humans are separate from and superior to other things in nature—is the product of 500 years of Western culture in which societies have behaved as though nature existed primarily for human use (Dunlap and Catton, 1983; White, 1967). Catton and Dunlap referred to this world view as the **human exemptionalism paradigm (HEP)**, arguing that it comprises several assumptions that sociologists, regardless of their orientation, implicitly accept (see Table 23.2). This failure, even in the face of the contradictions suggested by contemporary environmental events, suggested that sociologists were unequipped to deal meaningfully with ecological problems.

For Catton and Dunlap, the assumptions and approaches of the newly emerging environmental sociology constituted a paradigm shift, or a challenge to orthodox sociology. A paradigm shift occurs in science when a previously unrecognized framework of understanding replaces the dominant world view and redirects the given field on a qualitatively new course involving different research propositions and methods. Catton and Dunlap referred to the new approach as the **new environmental paradigm (NEP)**. Its assumptions are compared to those of the human exemptionalism paradigm in Table 23.2. The essential difference between them can be summed up as anthropocentrism (HEP) versus ecocentrism (NEP).

According to the NEP's supporters, sociologists and others who adopt the NEP world view must limit their faith in the ability of social progress and culture to overcome contemporary social problems, including environmental problems, while striving to appreciate the realities of humans within nature. Moreover, environmental problems cannot just be expected to go away; rather, societies must learn to minimize the environmental harm they inflict and be willing to rely less on nature to increase material comforts and prosperity. Since human society and nature can never really be separated, the implication for sociology in general is that the NEP

Table 23.2 A Comparison of the Human Exemptionalism Paradigm and the New Ecological Paradigm

Assumptions	Human Exemptionalism Paradigm (HEP)	New Ecological Paradigm (NEP)
About the nature of human beings	Humans have cultural heritage in addition to (and distinct from) their generic inheritance, and so are quite unlike all other animal species.	While humans have exceptional characteristics (culture, technology, etc.), they remain one among many species that are interdependently involved in the global ecosystem.
About social causation	Social and cultural factors (including technology) are the major determinants of human affairs.	Human affairs are influenced not by social and cultural factors, but also by intricate linkages of cause, effect, and feedback in the web of nature; purposive human actions therefore have many unintended consequences.
About the context of human society	Social and cultural environments are the crucial context for human affairs, and the biophysical environment is largely irrelevant.	Humans live in and are dependent upon a finite biophysical environment which imposes potent physical and biological restraints on human affairs.
About constraints on human society	Culture is cumulative; therefore, technological and social progress can continue indefinitely, making all social problems ultimately solvable.	Although human inventiveness and the powers derived from it may seem for a while to extend carrying capacity limits, ecological laws cannot be repealed.

Source: William Catton Jr and Riley Dunlap, 'A New Ecological Paradigm for Post-exuberant Society', *American Behavioral Scientist* 24 (1980): 34. Copyright 1980 SAGE Publications. Reprinted by permission of Sage Publications Inc.

should be accepted as the only framework within which sociologists can understand the laws that shape the development of modern societies. Therefore, according to Catton and Dunlap, the HEP/NEP distinction should be recognized as the principal paradigmatic cleavage in sociology; moreover, the HEP should be considered obsolete.

NEP vs Classical Sociological Theory

The debate over HEP and NEP and whether environmental sociology constitutes a paradigm shift for sociology as a whole has raised further questions over the relevance of classical sociological theory for understanding environmental problems. One concern is whether the HEP/NEP distinction should be regarded as anything but a further manifestation of the long-running theoretical debate in sociology over order versus conflict. Many environmental sociologists, including Frederick Buttel (1976) and Craig Humphrey (Humphrey and Buttel, 1982), disagreed with Catton and Dunlap's belief that environmental sociology represented a paradigm shift. Instead, they argued that environmental sociology is still characterized by paradigmatic cleavages, primarily between structural functionalism (order) and Marxism and neo-Marxism (conflict). The two approaches offer competing views on both the social origins of environmental problems and their solutions.

The structural functionalist school of sociology, stressing the rational functioning of society, has been summarized by Buttel (1976). The image of society is that of a social system with needs. Individual actors and institutions within the system have competing needs, and the state acts as an impartial arbitrator to smooth out differences and relieve stress and misalignment. From this perspective, environmental problems are associated with the process of modernization or progress. The positive functions associated with the needs of economic growth, abundance, and social stratification sometimes get out of hand, leading to environmental harm. Social reform or adjustment is then called for. The public's values must be modified, usually through public education, so that society may remain within its survival base and adapt to environmental exigencies. Protective environmental legislation is also enacted. The goal is to create an environmental ethos based on rights and the rational use of resources. Appropriate environmental use is maintained through state laws, social norms, and collective action. Possible adverse distributional effects on certain social groups as a result of environmental laws are regarded as the unfortunate, but necessary, trade-off for protection of the resource base, and they are not seriously questioned.

By contrast, the conflict approach takes the view that environmental problems are irrationalities within the capitalist system leading to societal contradictions (Schnaiberg, 1980). The key proposition here is that economic growth under capitalism has been a historical necessity in order to allow the corporate class to maintain its dominant position and its control of private property. Class struggle is the permanent condition of society, because the state has favoured and promoted the interests of the upper classes. Everyone works so that capitalists may receive profits. Growth is mandatory, and the environment is the victim. Arrangements for maintaining growth and profits—including planned obsolescence, disposable products, private transportation, and the military—promote waste and excessive resource exploitation and lead to environmental destruction. In short, Marxists and neo-Marxists see environmental destruction as inherent in capitalism. The working class cannot help because of its powerlessness, the control of the state, and the co-optation of workers through high wages earned at the expense of the environment. Orthodox approaches to solving environmental problems do not help because the necessary social reorganization will be resisted. Conflict theorists tend to be hostile to reform solutions, arguing that they do not treat the root causes of environmental destruction and mislead the public into believing something is being done. Environmental laws and regulations passed by elites call only for 'reasonable' conservation, the conditions of which are most easily met by large corporations, so that wealth and power are further concentrated. Finally, the costs of such reforms are carried mainly by the poor and the working class through losses of resource jobs and through higher prices and taxes for environmental protection.

After reading these summaries of the order and conflict approaches, you may agree with Buttel and Humphrey that the HEP and the NEP are nothing other than a new expression of these classical approaches. Such a conclusion would refute Catton and Dunlap's view that environmental sociology represents a paradigm shift in sociology. Moreover, the order/conflict controversy raises questions about the evidence for environmental damage by various political-economic systems. Following the collapse of the Soviet bloc in 1989, it became abundantly clear, if it was not already known, that neither Communist (conflict perspective) nor capitalist (order perspective) societies are manifestly superior in regard to environmental sensitivity—all industrialized nations have created the environmental problems associated with industrial technologies.

Finally, the debate over HEP/NEP versus order/conflict provokes further questions concerning the benefits of classical theoretical approaches in sociology for understanding and addressing environmental problems. It has already been noted that the Durkheimian tradition was important to the formulation of early human ecology, which helped to guide the new field of environmental sociology at its beginnings. But human ecology is not without its critics, and today, despite recent reformulation, it is largely seen as relevant only in certain areas of study of the built (that is, urban) environment. By and large, the classical theorists, Marx, Weber, and Durkheim—so important for their contributions to the conceptual foundations of much of sociology—do not appear nearly so relevant to the field of environmental sociology (Goldblatt, 1996; Redclift and Benton, 1994).

Weber, for example, is known to have vigorously opposed the inclusion of 'naturalistic or biologistic concepts' within the conceptual framework of sociology, partly in order to enhance the status of sociology as a new and separate discipline, as well as to avoid any descent into biological determinism (Stehr and Grundmann, 1996). Durkheim's dictum that all human circumstances could be explained eventually through knowledge of 'social facts' is further evidence of the tendency for the classical theorists to see a clear separation between the social and the natural worlds (Redclift and Woodgate, 1994).

The Marxist approach of dialectical materialism, which includes among its arguments the logic that new ideas can be achieved only through knowledge of the real or material world, has been quite relevant to the developments of a critical new branch of environmental philosophy known as 'green' political thought (for example, Dickens, 1992, 1996; Eckersley, 1992), which is of interest to many environmental sociologists. As well, Marx did argue that natural conditions, such as climate and region, contribute to the division of labour, while both he and Friedrich Engels were forceful in their condemnation of capitalism for its appalling effects on the health and living conditions of workers.

Nevertheless, the tendencies of the founders of sociology were, for the most part, to focus on distinguishing between social and natural conditions while emphasizing the social and ignoring the dynamic interplay between the two. For this reason, environmental sociology has not benefited from the classical writings to the degree found elsewhere in sociology, and there is ongoing and pressing need for new theories for understanding this relationship. The risk society as outlined by Ulrich Beck and social constructionist applications for the analysis of environmental problems are two areas of significant new theoretical development within environmental sociology.

The Risk Society

Ulrich Beck's conception of the **risk society** was initially outlined in *Risk Society: Towards a New Modernity* (1992). Originally published in German in 1986, this text has had considerable impact in sociology as well as in the social sciences and philosophy in general, while also drawing wide public debate and media attention.

The central thesis of the risk society concerns the evolution towards a new modernity, referred to by Beck as 'late modernity' (1992: 10), reflecting social change on a global scale. The impetus for this transformation is risk, hence the term 'risk society'. According to this theory, the world has evolved beyond the industrial state, with its successor, late modernity or postmodernity, being essentially the outcome of the success of the period preceding it. For affluent Western societies, the success of industrialization has meant, in practical terms, the end of scarcity. Wealth, science, and technology combine to provide for the needs of those in prosperous countries. At the same time, however, a multitude of problems, or risks, face individuals on a daily basis, which can be traced directly to industrialization. These involve all sorts of uncertainties—to do with changing workplace and gender roles, the nature of the family, social class relations, crime, environmental dangers, and more—all confronting the individual and for which there are no obvious solutions. This creates uncertainty, doubt, and confusion.

How should people respond? In industrial society, the primary concern involved the distribution of 'goods', with class action as the resulting collective response to inequities. Within late modernity, however, the concern is with the distribution of the 'bads'—the risks and dangers confronting individuals, which are the by-products of the success of industrialization. Social class and class relations are no longer relevant to the extent they once were. Rather, the defining perception is with respect to one's risk position. In a class-based society, one's material position determines consciousness, making one aware of one's access, along with that of others, to scarce resources and being prepared to act collectively to secure a greater share. In a risk-based society, consciousness around issues of risk defines individual well-being and the struggle to exist. With this comes a decline in importance of structures like social class that previously served to support a direction to be taken on the person's behalf, while at the same time there is increased emphasis on the individualization of the actor, who now is forced to choose from a range of ambiguous options.

'Reflexive modernity' is the term used to describe the response to this new reality. Problems faced by individuals are no longer clearly externally imposed (for example, resource scarcities), nor are solutions founded on some kind of 'natural' order (for example, gender roles). Instead, we must reflect on our options, while struggling to make the best choice. Uncertainty, alienation, and loneliness may result. Where alliances exist, they are less likely to be defined on socio-economic grounds, and they are more likely to be ideologically determined and 'strategic', as in the example of the European Green Party, in which the anti-establishment forces of the environmental, feminist, and anti-nuclear movements combine to form a pragmatic alliance in opposition to the traditional parties. Thus, while modernity has freed Western society from material want, we are confronted with new challenges and fewer guideposts to understanding.

Reflexive modernity must also be considered in light of the new and ambiguous role of science. Science and technology are irrevocably tied to the success of industrialization. Hence, science is in part responsible for the growth of hazards and risks, while at the same time it is the body called on to provide knowledge claims needed to overcome or avoid risk (Dietz et al., 2002). However, in the period of late modernity, the notion of the existence of simple truth and certainty seems naive. One only has to reflect briefly on the scientific debates and controversies that have raged over such issues as global warming, genetically modified foods, ozone depletion, hazardous waste, acid rain, and the risks of nuclear energy to realize that there is no single scientific position on these issues, or even an agreed-to set of facts. Rather, scientific knowledge is often revealed to be a body of contested claims, with the supremacy of any position largely linked to the skills of its advocates and their resources for advancing it, more so than to evidence of any overt truth. This absence of a clear and unequivocal knowledge system means that science, rather than solving the problems of the risk society, only adds to them by increasing uncertainty.

The premise of the risk society advanced by Beck has important implications with respect to the study of environmental problems by environmental sociologists. On the one hand, the theory represents a serious challenge to what has emerged as the most widely supported position on how to deal with the environmental crisis, that of sustainable development. The logic of sustainable development sees the need for fine-tuning of the existing system. Industrialization and development are not in themselves considered inimical to environmental preservation. Indeed, the position typically is that economic development needs to be expanded, especially in the case of the developing world, while still adhering to sustainability principles. Notwithstanding the lack of any widely agreed-on model of sustainability, even 30 years after the publication of *Our Common Future* (World Commission on Environment and Development, 1987), the sustainable development thesis is in stark contradiction to the risk society. The underlying assumption on which sustainable development is based is that the existing system can cope. The risk society represents an entirely different perspective, that of a society imbued with uncertainty and self-doubt. On what grounds, Beck asks, is society likely to right itself and overcome environmental risks? The continued expansion of industry and development in the name of prosperity only increases environmental risk rather than solving it, and science, the henchman of this advancement, increases the odds of risk further while proving incapable of providing solutions or reducing uncertainty.

The risk society thesis has numerous other implications for society and the environment. It strongly emphasizes the interconnections between society and nature, rejecting any anthropocentric tendency to see humans as distinct from and superior to nature while requiring us to question conventional assumptions about both society and nature. The theory is one of epochal-level change, and preparation for this new age requires challenging social traditions and taken-for-granted conventional ways of life. This invites uncertainty, but living with risk and ambiguity is something that each one of us must learn to accept (Beck, 1992).

In addition, there are profound implications for existing social institutions and social actions in connection with the risk society. Beck is generally hostile to any notion of existing institutions—government, corporations—responding effectively to the environmental crisis. Rooted to an earlier age, they are insensitive and ill-suited for dealing with contemporary problems of such complexity. Generally, political systems create more problems than they solve. Where progress has occurred, it has been in the guise of environmental movements, coalitions, and local networks. This, therefore, calls for new forms of political action that rely on grassroots protest and for strategic alliances demanding more openness and access to the decision-making process while bypassing existing political systems, parties, and the civil service.

Social Constructionism and Environmental Sociology

Social constructionism is a perspective often applied in other areas of sociology, one that has recently become established within environmental sociology as well. This establishment has stirred new debates. Social constructionism argues that social reality is more a matter of perception than of objective determination (Best, 1989, 1993; Blumer, 1971; Spector and Kitsuse, 1977). In other words, reality is what we think it is rather than what it is. While most people assume social problems are recognized and dealt with because their existence is obvious, social constructionists argue that such recognition only occurs following a process of negotiation by which the 'reality' of the problem becomes recognized. What is real is contested among parties with competing claims struggling to frame their version of the situation in order that the broader public will come to accept it. In these negotiations, the media play an important role, allowing the means for claims to be reported and providing important interpretation and emphasis, which may assist one or another of the competing parties to be successful in defining the problem and the approaches for dealing with it.

Time to Reflect

To what extent do you feel Beck's description of the 'risk society' accurately reflects reality? Do you think it represents your own life experience? What are the implications for environmental solutions? Does the idea of the 'new environmental paradigm' contradict the risk society or complement it?

Social constructionism has been widely applied in sociology in areas such as crime and deviance, homelessness, gender inequality, sexual orientation, illness and health care, and race and ethnicity. The perspective is appealing to some environmental sociologists, as well. John Hannigan (1995: 55), for example, argues that the 'successful construction' of environmental problems requires that six conditions be met:

1. scientific 'authority for and validation of claim' by parties;
2. the existence of 'popularizers' who can bridge environmentalism and science;
3. media attention in which the problem is framed as novel and important;
4. the dramatization of the problem 'in symbolic and visual terms';
5. economic 'incentives for taking positive action';
6. the emergence of an 'institutional sponsor who can ensure both legitimacy and continuity'.

In other words, an environmental problem is only the result of the success of the claims-making of those who advocate its existence. The implication here concerns the sociological process that underlies the 'discovery' of the environmental problem. Social dynamics replace objective existence of scientific risk as the object of scholarly interest since the social process is the basis for what we believe the problem to be.

Does this make sense when environmental problems are associated with such catastrophic threats that the very life of the planet is considered at risk? The social constructionist approach has provided abundant insight with respect to a variety of environmental debates, including global warming, acid rain, ozone depletion, environmental racism, globalization in general, and a host of local and regional industrial contamination and development debates. Examine any recent environmental controversy in your community and you likely will be able to apply a social constructionist perspective. Issues such as new industrial development, chemical contamination, or the siting of a landfill invariably pit against one another residents, politicians, factory managers, government officials, and scientific experts in a struggle to get their version of 'the truth' accepted. The media provide the means for broadcasting the competing views, while arbitrating what will be presented. Science has an authoritative voice in these debates, but all sides struggle to mount compelling scientific and/or moral/emotional arguments, and it is unlikely that science alone will determine the outcome. The result may be perceived by many as objective truth, but it is clear that such so-called reality is largely a social product.

Concerns over social constructionist analyses as applied to environmental problems have been expressed by a number of environmental sociologists, including Ted Benton (1994), Riley Dunlap and W. Richard Catton (1994), Raymond Murphy (1994), and Peter Dickens (1996). These authors argue that there are objective, independent, and physical qualities to environmental problems that cannot be accounted for simply on the grounds of being 'social constructions'. For example, chemical contamination of groundwater from industry and radiation from nuclear energy constitute absolute and deadly threats to individuals and should not be treated simply as perceived concerns. Murphy accuses social constructionists within environmental sociology of having lost touch with nature and 'gone overboard' (1994: 970), and Benton laments the 'over-socialized' view of environmental risks by social constructionists (1994: 44). Further, these 'realist' critics consider environmental sociology to be positioned to assist in overcoming environmental problems, and express alarm over whether the constructionist perspective is deflecting scholarly interest away from such work by focusing only on the moral and political issues surrounding the way a problem becomes defined.

Environmental social constructionists respond by noting that their position is not strict constructionism, as sometimes found in other areas of sociology (Burningham and Cooper, 1999). Such extreme relativism sees all reality in terms of linguistic and social constructs and is of interest mainly to such areas of theoretical reasoning as postmodernism, areas that have little following within environmental sociology. Rather, for environmental sociology, the constructionist approach has been a more mild relativism, or contextual constructionism,

Time to Reflect

What are the implications of the social constructionist approach to defining environmental problems for the identification of legitimate problems? Is society attempting to 'solve' problems that objectively do not exist, while failing to recognize other valid problems? Can you think of examples in each case?

which attempts to draw attention to the social processes involved in the development of societal recognition and response to environmental problems but does not claim that environmental problems do not objectively exist. For example, numerous sociological studies have reviewed the political discourse around the acid rain debate, along with the process by which scientists came to accept its existence and impacts (Zehr, 1994), and while there was strong interest in studying how the denials around acid rain were overcome, there was always recognition of the existence of dying lakes and forests and a desire to help end this.

The Environment and Social Movements

Fascinated by the environmental movement from its inception, environmental sociologists continue to be deeply interested in it. It has proven to be among the most successful and enduring social movements of all time. Few other recent movements can match it in terms of sustained activity, size of following, and ability to affect the lives of so many people. It has even changed our language, with such terms as NIMBY ('not in my back yard') and 'environmentally friendly product' entering the vernacular. The first Earth Day, staged 22 April 1970, was impressive, drawing some 20 million people (Dunlap and Gale, 1972), and Earth Day has since grown to become an international annual event—Earth Week, celebrated in 180 countries. Today few people admit to not supporting environmentalism; in fact, most people claim to be environmentalists (Dunlap, 1992). The environmental lobby, institutionalized as a significant player in government decision-making, is further evidence of the movement's impressive success.

The environmental movement has changed significantly over the years, often appearing to share little with its student-activist beginnings. The movement seems less angry today, but at the same time far more meticulous and deliberate in its approaches, often more at home in the corridors of power than on the protest line. The discussion that follows offers a look at the several strands of the contemporary environmental movement.

Progressive Conservation

Contemporary environmentalism traces its roots to the **progressive conservation** movement of the late-nineteenth-century United States (Fox, 1985; O'Riordan, 1971). Led by such reformers as Gifford Pinchot and John Muir, the founder of the Sierra Club, progressive conservation was a reaction against the unchecked destruction of nature during this period of freewheeling capitalism. The wanton environmental damage caused by private ownership of resources led to widespread public support for placing limits on the private use of land. Progressive conservation was instrumental in the creation of the national parks system in the United States, the increase of government control over public lands, and the founding of such conservation groups as the Sierra Club and the Audubon Society.

Reflecting a period in which science and technology were revered, progressive conservation sought to formulate and implement 'scientific management' of the environment. Two alternative science-based approaches to environmental management emerged. The preservationists, led by John Muir, advocated setting aside and protecting wilderness so that its natural, aesthetic, recreational, and scientific values could remain undisturbed for the benefit of future generations. Consumptive wildlife users, on the other hand, promoted conservation for utilitarian ends. Led by Pinchot and supported by President Theodore Roosevelt, this group wanted lands to be set aside mainly for recreational needs, but also for logging, mining, and grazing. American conservation policies in the early twentieth century tried to accommodate both sides of the debate through the creation of a liberal policy of greater government control over both private enterprise and public lands.

Mainstream Environmentalism

One legacy of the progressive conservation movement was the legitimation of government involvement in the economy and the environment. The responsibility for maintaining some balance between environmental preservation and economic growth is mainly the province of government planners and politicians. Hence, progressive conservation set the scene for the current relationship between business and government. The main beneficiaries of this policy are the large corporations, which, while gaining controlled access to resources, have paid little in resource rents. Some observers regard the sustainable development movement as a new expression of the principle of consumptive wildlife use. Meanwhile, the voices of the early preservationists, calling for environmental protection on moral, scientific, and aesthetic grounds, have largely gone unheard.

According to Robert Cameron Mitchell, Angela Mertig, and Riley Dunlap (1992), the other legacy of

A grove of cedars in Hesquiat Lake Creek, Clayoquot Sound, on Vancouver Island. Although Clayoquot Sound's rainforest is a UNESCO Biosphere Reserve, commercial activities such as logging continue. (Torfino Photography—W.C. Barnes)

progressive conservation can be seen in the relationship between contemporary mainstream environmentalists and the government. Early preservationists quickly learned that they had to co-operate with the consumptive wildlife users and the Roosevelt administration or they would have little hope of making progress towards environmental protection. By now, environmentalists have become highly skilled at working as partners with government and developers in reaching compromise on environmental decisions. The inevitable result is trade-offs on preferred environmental solutions. Rik Scarce (1990: 15) reports that most environmental organizations admit to having no specific approach or plan for the environment other than saving what they can. Such 'muddling through' has resulted in some checks on development, but also in serious environmental losses. Rarely have the mainstream environmental groups been in a position to claim complete victory in their efforts to stop a development or save an ecosystem.

Contemporary mainstream environmentalism is increasingly in the form of inside lobbying, politicking, and consultation, and relies mainly on its well-organized bureaucracies for success (Mertig et al., 2002). The leaders tend to be highly educated environmental professionals, often having backgrounds in public administration or environmental law and holding permanent, salaried positions. Fundraising and research are essential to successful competition with large corporations over the fate of resources. The individual member is far more likely to write a cheque or the occasional letter to an elected representative than to take part in a sit-in or blockade.

Many mainstream environmentalists argue that it has only been through these increasingly well-organized, well-funded, professional organizations that environmental review and assessment have become a permanent part of economic planning. Critics such as William Devall (1992) have suggested, however, that these same organizations are too accommodating to development interests, their leaders too close to their opposite numbers in business and government and too secure in their professional status. Still others are critical of mainstream environmentalism in general, arguing that it has long suffered from elitism. Various writers have pointed out the middle- or upper-class origins and high educational levels of environmental leaders and members of mainstream environmental organizations (Humphrey and Buttel, 1982; Morrison and Dunlap, 1986). However, supporters of the environmental movement—if not those actually involved in it—tend to be drawn widely from across the social class spectrum (Mertig and Dunlap, 2001). A related criticism levelled at mainstream environmentalism is that the programs or policies advocated may lead to reductions in resource-based jobs or even in wholesale plant closures because of the high costs of environmental regulation or the protection of a given wilderness area (Schnaiberg, 1975). Such economic events are likely to have the most adverse effects on the working class and the poor.

The New Ecologies

Mainstream environmentalism is one wing of the larger environmental movement, which includes various alternatives. The new ecologies are a range of approaches within environmentalism with a number of common features. First, they are critical of mainstream environmentalism for its failure to address ecological problems by taking into account the systems of dominance in social relations that help to create those problems. Inequality among nations and regions serves to enhance competition for scarce resources and thereby increases environmental harm. The new ecologies argue that central to solving environmental problems is the promotion of social equity and self-determination, which will allow peoples and nations to meet their human needs while maintaining ecological integrity (Gardner and Roseland, 1989).

Another distinguishing feature of the new ecologies, according to Nicholas Freudenberg and Carol Steinsapir (1992), is their devolved character. Hierarchical relations of authority between the membership and leaders or between the branches of each organization are rejected as being inconsistent with the prevailing thesis of human equality with nature rather than domination over it. This essentially ecocentric (and preservationist) stance is yet another characteristic of these groups, which tend to be sharply critical of any anthropocentric tendency to 'manage' the environment—an approach mainstream environmentalists seem all too willing to accept.

Finally, the new ecologies tend to outline specific principles for environmental reform consistent with their broad vision of the human–nature relationship, rather than simply muddling through. They are also far less willing than the mainstream to accommodate solutions in the interest of political and economic expediencies. Indeed, some radical arms of the new ecologies movement advocate the use of illegal, even violent, actions in order to win environmental disputes. While these radicals are in the minority, mainstream environmentalists admit to having been helped by them in reaching compromises more favourable to the environment—they appear reasonable in comparison to the unbending demands and extremism of the radicals (Scarce, 1990).

Thus far, we have enumerated the similarities among the new ecologies. Now we look at three of these movements in order to highlight their differences.

Eco-feminism

Eco-feminism represents the partnership of ecology and feminism. It is founded mainly on mutual opposition to hierarchy and domination. Feminists argue that the subordination of women by men has been achieved through the ability of men to employ conceptual frameworks that place women at a disadvantage. According to Val Plumwood (1992), these include hierarchical frameworks that justify inequality; dualism, which justifies exclusion and separation; and rationality, which justifies logic and control. By advancing these three conceptual preferences, men have succeeded in legitimizing their domination over both women and nature.

The logic of domination holds that by virtue of the distinctiveness of men from nature and of men from women, together with the supposed greater rationality of men, the domination of men over both women and nature is 'reasonable'. In other words, eco-feminists argue that exactly the same male-controlled value system is used to justify both patriarchal human relations and the exploitation of nature.

Feminism and environmentalism connect, then, at the point of recognizing the similarities in the ways men treat women and nature. If one form of domination—of men over women—is wrong, then all forms of domination are wrong, including that of humans over nature. To be a feminist, therefore, compels one to be an environmentalist. Moreover, eco-feminists argue, inasmuch as environmentalists recognize and reject the domination of men over nature, they must also reject the domination of men over women. Therefore, all environmentalists must be feminists (Warren, 1990).

Social Ecology

Social ecology is a body of philosophical thought appealing to many in the contemporary environmental movement who are seeking to understand the interplay between humans and nature. Founder Murray Bookchin

The forests, lakes, and rivers north of Kenora, Ontario, have sustained the people of Grassy Narrows First Nation for thousands of years. Clear-cut logging threatens their traditional way of life, as did mercury pollution from a paper mill 40–50 years ago. In 2007, Amnesty International (Canada) called for the provincial government to respect a moratorium on logging declared by the people of Grassy Narrows.

articulated this philosophy during nearly five decades until his death in 2006. Social ecology advances a holistic world view of the human–nature partnership, one based on community. Bookchin identifies the dualism and domination informing current human–nature relations as products of human ideology and culture through which society has come to be defined as distinct from and superior to nature. While he acknowledges that culture and technology do distinguish society from nature, Bookchin rejects the idea that they are separate. Rather, society springs from nature, reworking it into the human experience. Society always has a naturalistic dimension, and social ecology is largely involved with attempting to describe how both the connectedness and the divergences between society and nature occur. Appropriate technology, reconstruction of damaged ecosystems, and human creativity will combine with equity and social justice to produce an ecological society in which human culture and nature are mutually supportive and evolve together. Social ecology envisions a society in harmony with nature, combining human-scale sustainable settlement, ecological balance, community self-reliance, and participatory democracy. Social ecology is not the sole advocate of many of these objectives by any means, which are shared by various environmental schools of thought, including the writings of David Suzuki, Eurpoean Greens, and several branches of green political thought. What social ecology, along with these other schools, shows is how deeply philosophical various segments of the environmental movement are while seeking to establish an intellectual foundation for social change and environmental improvement.

Deep Ecology

Deep ecology is among the more intriguing of the new ecologies, as well as the most controversial. The name was coined in 1973 by Norwegian philosopher Arne Naess. Defining contemporary environmentalism as 'shallow' ecology, Naess (1973) argued that its advocacy of social reforms to curb problems of pollution and resource depletion identifies it as concerned mainly with protecting the health and affluence of the developed countries. By contrast, deep ecology is concerned with the root causes of environmental crisis and inspired by the understanding derived through personal experiences as humans in nature. The most distinctive aspect of deep ecology is its biocentric emphasis. Deep ecologists claim to hold all forms of life equally valuable, but at the same time raise non-human life forms beyond the human. Therefore, while deep ecology shares with the other new ecologies the rejection of anthropocentrism, it goes beyond the humanistic, ecocentric ecology of human–nature coexistence. Deep ecologists desire humans to have the least possible effect on the planet and respect ecological integrity above all else (Tokar, 1988).

Deep ecology also places heavy emphasis on self-realization, the extension of the environmentally conscious individual's self beyond his or her personal needs to include the environment as a whole. The idea that human insight and experience are enhanced by contact with nature follows logically from biocentrism.

Deep ecologists believe that an important practical consequence of self-realization is the obligation to strive actively to prevent environmental destruction. The emphasis on direct action has particularly inspired the best-known of the deep ecology groups, Earth First!, which advocates the use of whatever means are necessary to save wilderness areas. Earth First! has garnered much attention—and criticism—for the use of ecological sabotage ('ecotage'), that is, illegal force intended to block actions perceived as harming the environment (Taylor, 1991). 'Monkey wrenching'—disruption by such covert and unlawful means as removing survey stakes, destroying machinery, or spiking trees—is controversial even within Earth First! These tactics stand in sharp contrast with the more widely accepted civil disobedience strategies of other radical environmentalists. Civil disobedience involves public protest for a cause, and while the marches or blockades may result in the protestors' being charged with civil crimes, there is a strong commitment to non-violence.

Grassroots Environmentalism

While the roots of environmentalism date back to the preservationist movement of the nineteenth century, it was the publication of Rachel Carson's *Silent Spring* in 1962 that led to human health risks assuming significance along with conservation and preservation as environmental goals. The current era of environmentalism has increasingly focused on the dangers associated with industrial pollution and the occurrence of pollution

The University of Waterloo's Midnight Sun Solar Car Team unveils their entry at the 2007 World Solar Challenge in Australia.

sources in residential communities. Recent years have seen the emergence of new grassroots forms of environmentalism with this focus as their mandate.

The Toxic Waste Movement

The toxic waste movement is a branch of environmentalism unlike either the mainstream environmental movement or the new ecologies. On the one hand, the well-funded and organized mainstream environmental organizations, such as the Sierra Club, rely on professional leadership and a skilled staff, along with well-placed connections within the power structure, savvy insight into the political process, and a large public base of followers willing to provide financial support or to lend their voices to back a cause. On the other hand, the new ecologies are far less resourced but are inspired and maintained by the ideology and shared values of the members.

The toxic waste movement reflects few of the tendencies of either of these more general arms of the environmental movement. The movement is, in a sense, all the disputes and protests by myriad groups opposed to perceived environmental threats present in their own communities and neighbourhoods. Diffuse in its focus, the toxic waste movement is associated with all manner of protest against everything from proposed developments, such as a new landfill, factory, or highway, to those affected by pollution caused by an existing industry. What unites the toxic waste movement is a common focus on perceived health threats to the community. The movement is intrinsically grassroots in its composition and approach, constituted typically of groups of formerly uninvolved citizens now struggling in their cause to stop a development or clean up pollution while facing the efficient and well-funded opposition of industry and/or government.

The toxic waste movement may be the fastest-growing branch of environmentalism (Szasz, 1994). It is also in many ways far less distinguishable than the other types of environmentalism. For one thing, there is little in the way of national organizing bodies or even communication among the various local groups. This extreme decentralization means that local protestors have very few resources, outside of their own means, on which to draw in developing their plans of opposition. Mainstream environmental organizations typically employ professional social movement organizers in order to guide their agendas, but local toxic waste protestors rarely have the backgrounds or resources required to mount a well-managed and effective campaign. Valuable skills may be learned as the protest develops, but as these campaigns are often short-lived, such knowledge may not be passed on.

SOCIOLOGY IN ACTION

Cancer City

The only thing missing from disaster is the bodies on the streets of Whitney Pier.

On a drive through the neighborhood, the quiet homes reveal no clues about the hundreds who have died prematurely over the years.

But those who live here can tell you how cancer and heart disease have stalked this area for decades.

'Heart attack and cancer in these houses here,' says Eric Brophy, 65, pointing to a group of homes along Lingan Road.

'My wife, who died 2-1/2 years ago, this was her grandfather's home. Her aunt who lived in this house died of cancer. Her dad died of a heart attack. He was 58.'

Pointing a stubby finger down the road, Mr Brophy indicates yet another home.

'The Hotter girl that I mentioned, she lived in this house. That was cancer.'

He continues to drive, hooded eyes focused on memories.

'Cancer through there. I know there was cancer here, I don't know the years. This is where my wife grew up. My wife was 56 when she died. She died of cancer.'

House after house. Street after street. Block after block.

Why?

Finding the answer is what drives the health studies working group of the Joint Action Group, a community-driven effort to clean up the largest toxic waste site in North America.

For almost 90 years, smoke stacks at Sydney Steel belched carcinogens daily over Sydney, blanketing Whitney Pier and adjoining neighborhoods.

The mill's coke ovens were torn down a decade ago, but the pollution stayed.

Leachate from a hilltop municipal dump still flows into the 50-hectare coke ovens site, mixing with the heavily contaminated soil and bedrock.

The resulting chemical cocktail—a witch's brew of heavy metals, poisonous hydrocarbons and other toxins—creeps steadily downhill, finally draining into the infamous tar ponds, two pools holding 700,000 tonnes of hazardous goo, including 50,000 tonnes of PCBs.

Since the tar ponds are actually a tidal estuary, every day the ocean flushes more contaminants out to sea.

'Last week I buried a second family member in a year from cancer,' says Michelle Gardiner, a young, expectant mother and interim chair of the health studies group'. 'I live with the same things that people in this community do, but I want the truth.'

Ms Gardiner, who lives in Ashby, bordering Whitney Pier, leans forward, her voice weary yet earnest.

'What a legacy to pass on to this baby I'm carrying right now. "You were born in the cancer capital." I'm sorry, there's so much else at risk here. There's a future.'

Despite dozens of studies done through the years, scientists and JAG officials agree there's not enough evidence to conclusively identify what's causing the health problems.

Only one report has ever been published in the scientific literature, a 1985 study by Health Canada scientist Yang Mao on mortality in Cape Breton County.

Using death certificate data from 1971 to 1983, Mr Mao's team found rates of cancer and circulatory disease higher than the provincial average among both men and women, particularly in Sydney.

While the link between environmental factors and health remains largely unstudied, a 1987 provincial study of lifestyle factors associated with cancer and heart disease found many Cape Breton County residents smoked too much, had poor diets, were overweight and did not exercise enough.

That report is derisively known in Sydney as the Broccoli Study because of a perception the study concluded local residents needed to eat more broccoli.

Meanwhile, studies in other parts of the world—Pennsylvania, the United Kingdom and Ontario—have established a link between coke oven emissions and cancer, especially of the lungs.

But, explains Don Ferguson, Health Canada's director general for the Atlantic region, more studies are needed to determine the precise role that pollution played in the Sydney area.

'Exposed to what? Through what conditions? For what period of time?' Mr Ferguson said. 'In order to get to "what happened", you need to know these three things.'

Even when all the studies are complete, he said, the best you'll be able to say is that there's a high probability that exposure to hazardous waste contributed to the high rates of cancer and other diseases.

'The reality is you will probably never find the smoking gun because health is impacted by genetics, it's impacted by lifestyle and, clearly, environmental and occupational exposures.'

JAG members acknowledge that scientifically proving a connection between pollution and disease might be extremely difficult.

Still, they're determined to try.

At JAG's request, two Health Canada scientists launched a multiyear study in May, reviewing cancer mortality and incidence rates over a 30-year period, as well as reproductive health outcomes, including birth defects.

The first results, to be released in late September, will show some diseases are definitely more common in Sydney than the rest of the province, says team co-leader Pierre Band.

Other disease rates are higher in Cape Breton County than Nova Scotia, and higher still in Sydney, he said.

'At the end, we'll have a reasonably complete picture of what stands out,' Mr Band said. 'And based on that, one would then need to develop other studies to try and answer why.'

Finding answers will likely take three to five years, he said.

'I have no problem with three to five years, if it's done right,' Ms Gardiner said. 'We deserve to know what the hell is going on.'

The coke ovens site, bordering Whitney Pier, is largely barren today.

Two towering smokestacks still rise from the ground like bleached ribs. A rusting warehouse stands in the distance.

On the northwest corner of the site, a large steel tank similar to those used at refineries sits beside a gravel ramp once used by dump trucks.

Inside are some 4,000 tonnes of toxic liquid and sludge, including lead, mercury, various hydrocarbons and PCBs.

When the coke ovens were demolished in 1988, 16 other tanks belonging to the coal tar company Domtar were torn down and their contents transferred to the largest remaining tank.

'It's full, right to the top,' said Mike Britten, JAG's overall program coordinator. 'Every time it rains and the wind blows, the material blows over the side.

'You can see the black staining down along the side of the tank from the hydrocarbons.'

The tank's structural integrity is unknown, he said. Removing the tank's top in 1988 to simplify dumping weakened the structure. And the tank was not designed for its current contents.

Discussions on removing the tank and its contents are under way, he said. 'I'd say this fall that tank would be gone.'

But what if the tank ruptured?

There would be a public outcry and an emergency cleanup, say both Mr Britten and Germaine LeMoine, public information officer for JAG.

But it's Mr Britten's frank assessment of the relative impact of the contamination that speaks volumes about the size of the overall problem.

You'd be adding 4,000 tonnes to literally millions of tonnes of contamination already in the ground, he said.

'In the big picture, given a couple of days, you probably wouldn't even see it.'

Conveying the immensity of the problem to the public is a challenge, say JAG members.

'The tar ponds are barely one-fifteenth of the problem,' said Francois Sirois, a member of JAG's environmental data gathering and remedial options working group.

Including the heavily contaminated soil at the coke ovens site and surrounding areas, 'you're looking at up to 10 million tonnes of potentially contaminated sediment.'

The tar ponds have been extensively tested, but officials say they know little about the rest of the site.

That problem is compounded by the roughly 13 kilometers of steel pipe, used to carry byproducts like benzene, still buried underground.

'If you were operating a high hoe [used for excavating], would you want to start digging in the coke ovens [site] not knowing what's down there?' asks John Steele, a member of JAG's environmental group.

'And [if] you run into a benzene line or possibly a pocket of coke ovens gas that might be in there—Boom!'

JAG must also evaluate various methods for cleaning up the mess, Mr Sirois said.

People are already sending in ideas for disposal, including firing the mess into space aboard a rocket, Ms LeMoine said. 'For every idea, there are 10 behind it.'

The cleanup will take decades, Mr Sirois said, and afterwards the area will only be suitable for industrial use, not housing.

'You can't, with the fact the bedrock is contaminated.

'You can't dig into that bedrock forever. It would be prohibitive. You'd have to be blasting in the middle of Sydney to break up the rock.

'Not possible.'

Source: Paul Schneidereit, *Halifax Herald*, 26 July 1998. Republished with permission from The Halifax Herald Limited.

What is characteristic of the toxic waste movement is the high proportion of its members who are women and homemakers, minorities, and those from lower socio-economic backgrounds (Brown and Masterson-Allen, 1994). Toxic waste activists also tend to be older, politically conservative, and trusting of existing institutions, laws, and regulations. The movement's high composition of women and homemakers is in keeping with its principal focus on preserving human health, especially that of children, in the face of an immediate threat from a nearby development or pollution source. These groups' membership is on average less educated than that found within mainstream environmentalism and the new ecologies, and their protests are more emotional than those of these other groups, which prefer to emphasize rational opposition based on scientific and legal evidence.

Unlike the new ecologies, ideology is not a prominent factor relating either to the formation or to the reasoning of toxic waste groups. Toxic waste activists are motivated by the presence of a nearby environmental threat and are conditioned by their experiences in responding to it. Initially apolitical and inexperienced in the art of protest, these activists have learned lessons at the hands of the authorities and corporations that compel a loss of innocence leading to personal transformations (Aronson, 1993). Along with bringing lifestyle and value changes, such personal reconsideration may also prompt new skepticism about the political process, along with mistrust of the authorities, business, and scientific experts.

Grassroots toxic waste protest is often dismissed as NIMBYism by those who disagree with its ends, and it is true that it often does appear that self-interest is an underlying motivation on which such protests are based. Nevertheless, if the threat is real, why should self-interest depreciate the legitimacy of the group's goal? It is also the case that a general increase within society in concerns over health risk from pollution and development is helping to move the toxic waste movement towards a more formally defined foundation of support and new allegiances. This is seen, for example, in connection with the general movement to supplant NIMBY with NIABY—'not in anyone's back yard'—indicative of the reduced emphasis on self-interest, as well as with LULU ('locally unwanted land uses'), reflective of the greater sensitivity to the broader public interest currently sought in the development of many municipal land-use plans (Freudenburg and Pastor, 1992).

Environmental Justice

Recently, another new grassroots movement, known as the **environmental justice** (EJ) movement, has emerged, with an agenda going beyond the traditional concerns of conservation and preservation common to most environmentalism. The EJ movement has ties to the toxic waste movement, but is also altering the focus of environmentalism generally to include broader concerns with regard to the societal inequities that result from industrial facility-siting and industrial development. Lois Gibbs, a leader in the fight over the chemical contamination of the Love Canal neighbourhood in Niagara Falls, New York, and founder of the Citizens' Clearing House for Hazardous Waste (1993: ix–x), has written:

> This movement, in hundreds of local and regional organizations, is typically led by women, working-class people, and people of color. Many, particularly the women, have never been involved in any political issue before and have been galvanized primarily by their concern for their children's safety. . . . Although these leaders became involved because of a single issue or problem, they quickly recognized the interconnections with other injustices they face daily. They realize that the root of their problem is the lack of organized political power, deteriorating neighborhood conditions, poverty and race. . . . As a result, these leaders now build bridges with civil-rights and labor organizations, housing groups, and those fighting for adequate health care for all. . . . As they battle with various bureaucracies to resolve the crisis that brought them together, they begin to identify links among issues and build an even broader coalition for change. . . . These new alliances and cooperative work can achieve real democracy.

While the environmental movement has long been concerned with the risks to human health from industrial pollution, only recently has that awareness developed over the distributional risks associated with these effects. Various US studies have documented the inequitable distribution of environmental hazard (Bryant and Mohai, 1992; Bullard, 1990; Hofrichter, 1993), showing that, for the most part, people of low income and racial minorities are disproportionately being affected by poor environmental quality resulting from exposure to industrial pollution, workplace pollution, and contaminated water and lands. A similar finding for low-income people and the likelihood of exposure to contamination risk was found in a comparison of pollution sites across Toronto, Hamilton, and Niagara Falls, Ontario (Nabalamba, 2001), and lower socio-economic status has often been found to be a prevalent condition within Canada's worst-polluted neighbourhoods.

Various explanations revolve around the processes that result in the inequitable distribution of environmental burdens. One position reflects economic or market dynamics, suggesting that 'sound' business decisions and the need to reduce costs may be grounds for locating potentially polluting industrial facilities (Kriesel et

HUMAN DIVERSITY
Environmental Justice

Much of the environmental justice literature is based on US findings. In a Canadian study, Alice Nabalamba (2001) focuses on southern Ontario, in particular, Toronto, Hamilton, and the Niagara region. Using 1996 data from the Canadian census and municipal records, Nabalamba investigates the link between visible minority status, socio-economic status, and the location of pollution sources. Five types of polluted sites were included: contaminated sites, industrial discharges, hazardous waste treatment and storage facilities, polychlorinated biphenyl (PCB) storage and treatment facilities, and other waste treatment, disposal, and storage facilities.

Nabalamba found that 'people of lower socio-economic means were more likely than the general population to live near a pollution source and industrial land use' (2001: 141). Visible minority status was also related to increased exposure to certain types of pollution sources, but the relationship is clouded by the lower socio-economic status of many visible minority groups. The location of pollution sources was related to decreased real estate values, decreased home ownership (versus renting), and the age of housing. The relationship between pollution siting and older, poorer neighbourhoods reflects a lack of political and organizational clout to defend against these types of uses. Therefore, Nabalamba predicts, future siting of these kinds of facilities will continue to effect these types of neighbourhoods more so than wealthier, newer, and 'whiter' areas.

al., 1996; Oakes, 1996). It points to economic efficiency within the marketplace as the central criterion that guides what results as the unfair distribution of environmental risks to the poor. Industry's desire to minimize costs specifically associated with land or property values is seen as a major contributing factor to the disproportionate exposure to environmental pollutants. The suggestion is that this unequal risk occurs because cost-efficient industrial areas with low property values also are likely to be near areas with low residential property values or affordable housing and, therefore, a concentration of low-income populations.

Another rationale given for why the poor face greater pollution risk is the 'path of least resistance' argument (Higgins, 1994; Hofrichter, 1993). This suggests that low-income and minority communities end up with a disproportionate share of disposal and polluting industrial facilities and poor environmental quality in general because they have less political clout than the more affluent communities.

Finally, a more contentious explanation cites 'environmental racism' among private industry and government decision-makers as being behind the disparities found in the uneven distribution of polluting industrial facilities (Bryant and Mohai, 1992; Bullard, 1994). This position draws largely on interpretations of evidence from the United States that show race to be a major factor in who is likely to be exposed to pollution risk. Hence, it is concluded that when race stands out as being significantly associated with the location of new disposal and polluting industrial facilities, it is racism that is influencing the decision-making process.

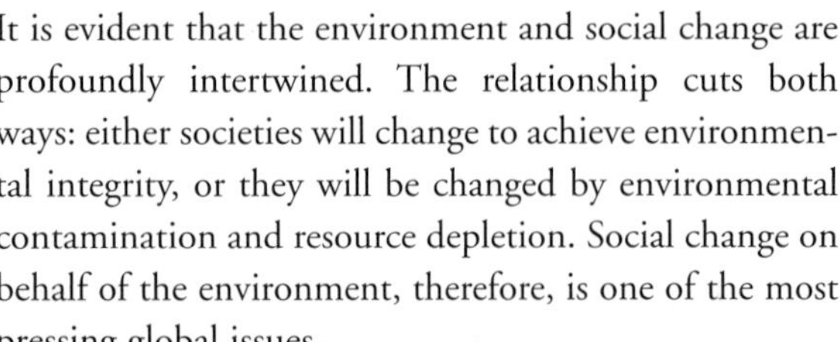

Conclusion

It is evident that the environment and social change are profoundly intertwined. The relationship cuts both ways: either societies will change to achieve environmental integrity, or they will be changed by environmental contamination and resource depletion. Social change on behalf of the environment, therefore, is one of the most pressing global issues.

If sociology can make one substantial contribution to the understanding of ecological crisis, it is the recognition that environmental problems are social products. This understanding goes beyond descriptions of how individuals or firms contribute to environmental degra-

Time to Reflect

According to many public opinion surveys, most people claim to be environmentalists. What kind of environmentalist are you? In the context of the broad umbrella of the environmental movement encompassing everything from national environmental lobbying groups to local neighbourhood associations, what is your place? Do you see this changing? How?

dation, and the solutions suggested involve more than promoting more environmentally responsible behaviours or technologies. While such approaches may help deal with an immediate situation, they ultimately do more harm than good by deflecting attention from the real roots of environmental problems and the discovery of long-term solutions.

In short, social systems must change so that global disaster may be averted. Frederick Buttel and Peter Taylor (1992) have pointed out that one promising development in this direction has been the globalization of environmental discourse. The 1972 UN conference on the environment held in Stockholm initiated the process, helping to shift the attention of governments to the global nature of environmental problems, boosting public concern for the environment, and spawning a number of treaties and other institutional innovations to reduce marine pollution, control acid rain, protect the atmosphere, and preserve wetlands.

Almost as important as the actual steps taken to check environmental damage has been the extension of such talks to include global social relations and their connection to environmental threats. The 1972 conference dealt mainly with industrial pollution in the developed world, but at the Earth Summits held two and three decades later, Third World development, sovereignty, foreign aid, poverty, debt, and social justice were central to the negotiations. Indeed, these issues had become so dominant by the time of the 2002 Earth Summit, held in South Africa, that the United States refused even to attend, arguing that the process had been 'hijacked' by anti-globalization interests.

It is now widely accepted that the eradication of poverty in the less developed world is among the keys to solving environmental problems. Yet this realization has served to kindle both old and new tensions between industrialized and developing nations. The former continue to promote such traditional mechanisms for economic improvement as foreign investment, new trading relations, and foreign aid. In some cases, it has been suggested that foreign assistance be tied to population control or environmental improvements. Third World countries tend to be deeply suspicious of such tactics, referring to them as environmental colonialism and arguing they are little more than a new version of the historical patterns of domination that have been responsible for most underdevelopment. The refusal also by the United States to sign the biodiversity convention at the 1992 Earth Summit in Rio de Janeiro, on the grounds that it could restrict US international commercial interests, was widely interpreted as demonstrating a willingness to abandon the environment if its protection involved any threat to the existing global distribution of power.

Developing countries are also sensitive to any threats to their sovereignty perceived to result from intrusive foreign aid or investment, and are distrustful of the World Bank, the International Monetary Fund, the Food and Agriculture Organization, and other global bodies traditionally involved with Third World programs. Finally, many developing countries have crushing foreign debts and are compelled to earn hard currency through the export of raw resources or agricultural products in demand in industrialized nations. The harvesting of the resources and the farming practices used to grow the crops often cause considerable environmental damage while doing little to improve the long-term economic prospects of poorer countries.

Another source of tension is the fact that the industrialized nations have failed to demonstrate sufficient financial commitment to solving global environmental problems. It has been estimated that a total of $600 billion (US) annually would be needed to make progress towards the environmental improvements outlined in the work plan, Agenda 21, agreed to by the 150 nations attending the 1992 Earth Summit. Of this total, $125 billion was expected to come through development assistance or loan relief from the industrialized world. These amounts have never been pledged, and foreign aid still remains a controversial, and largely low-priority, item for countries such as Canada and the United States.

On a smaller scale, the principle of sustainable development is becoming ingrained in the policy and planning frameworks of developed and less developed countries. Many herald this tendency as a breakthrough in attitudes towards the environment. Others are more skeptical, suggesting that the concept of sustainable development may be hijacked by development interests and used to legitimize unnecessary economic expansion. These critics cite the Business Council for Sustainable Development, created at the 1992 Rio Summit and comprising 48 CEOs from the world's corporations. The Council was intended to represent business interests in global sustainable development negotiations and to sensitize world business leaders to issues of development and the environment. However, its many detractors regard the Council as demonstrating all too clearly the real interests the sustainable development movement will serve.

The potential for deflecting such a hijacking, if one is planned, could rest with the success of the new ecologies and grassroots environmentalism. The intensely participatory focus of these organizations, together with their high levels of commitment to local control of ecosystems, could go far towards curtailing economically driven environmental exploitation. As noted earlier, the influence of such movements in environmental planning is increasing, and if Ulrich Beck's risk society thesis is correct, then such involvement is destined to grow. The less conventional approaches of the new ecologies to environmental planning are also considered to represent the new forms of thinking necessary for achieving true sustainable development (Gardner and Roseland, 1989). By reflecting alternatives to current forms of social organization and changing environmental values and aspirations, contemporary environmentalism may be in the vanguard of social change on behalf of the environment and of social improvement generally.

Questions for Critical Thought

1. Despite the recognition that significant environmental problems persist, there still exists a spirit of optimism in many quarters, a feeling that humankind is making progress towards environmental quality. Should we be optimistic or pessimistic about the view that societies are succeeding in overcoming environmental problems?
2. Some individuals argue that environmental problems are inherent in the process of modernization, which involves urbanization, economic progress, and population growth. Do you feel that the inevitability of environmental damage is a valid assumption?
3. The concept of sustainable development is key to much economic planning, but its critics often argue that it is being used mainly as a rationale for allowing more economic growth at the expense of the environment. Can economic growth and environmental quality coexist, in your opinion?
4. When, if ever, is illegal protest, such as the ecotage practised by Earth First!, justifiable for protecting the environment?
5. Eco-feminists see similarities between environmentalists' fight to preserve the environment and women's struggle to achieve equality. Do you agree that there is a connection between these two social movements? Should all feminists be environmentalists, and vice versa?
6. Population growth is frequently likened to an ecological time bomb and one of the most virulent threats to the future of the planet. Are such claims valid? What are the various sides to this controversy? Discuss ways in which the global population problem could be solved.
7. Social constructionists see environmental problems as something formed by perception—basing their view on the extent to which these problems are recognized and validated by the greater part of society, measured in terms of the responses provided by such groups. How helpful is this perspective in alleviating environmental problems? Consider environmental controversies both at the local and international levels. How does the constructionist viewpoint contribute to their understanding?
8. How valid is the claim that being poor or a member of an ethnic minority increases one's degree of environmental threat in Canada? Aside from these populations, who else might face environmental risk? Are these risks reasonable or should steps be taken to ensure that when dangers to health exist from the environment these should be shared equally across the population? Is inequitable distribution of environmental hazard inevitable?
9. Ulrich Beck's theory of the risk society is a challenge to conventional thinking with regard both to the organization of society in the twenty-first century and to how environmental problems are viewed. How could Beck's theory alter the course of environmentalism and the manner by which environmental problems are addressed?

Recommended Readings

Ronald Bailey, *Eco-scam: The False Prophets of Ecological Apocalypse* (New York: St Martin's Press, 1993).

Not everyone agrees with environmentalism, and some are adamantly critical of its claims, particularly with respect to carrying capacity, or the Earth's ability to sustain its resource base. This book is a response to environmentalism's assumptions, claiming environmental alarmism and extremism are actually serving to undermine the future of the planet.

Robert D. Bullard, *Dumping in Dixie: Race, Class and Environmental Quality* (Boulder, Colo.: Westview Press, 1990).

This series of case studies of five black, southern communities chronicles the increased environmental risks associated with being poor, black, and female in the United States, and is one of the principal works leading to the development of the field of environmental social justice.

Jared Diamond, *Collapse: How Societies Choose to Fail or Succeed* (New York: Viking, 2005).
Diamond's writing is thoughtful, comprehensive, and scientific and he draws on history, natural science, paleontology, and archaeology to address the issue of why societies fail due to the collapse of the ecological system on which they depend. Diamond introduces the idea of 'progress traps'—innovations that give societies a competitive advantage, but ultimately undermine their existence and result in their demise. The volume contains a number of excellent, detailed reviews of societal collapses due to ecocide, with examples of some amazingly enduring civilizations.

Paul R. Ehrlich, *The Population Bomb* (New York: Ballantine, 1968).
Ehrlich's book was among the first analyses of the global ecological consequences of overpopulation. It received widespread attention for its prediction of imminent ecological collapse, leading to the founding of the zero population growth (ZPG) movement.

Lois Gibbs, *Love Canal: My Story* (Albany: State University of New York Press, 1982).
Love Canal is the most famous incident of chemical hazardous waste contamination in the United States and the struggle of neighbourhood residents to have it recognized. For years Love Canal, an abandoned hydroelectric canal built in Niagara Falls, New York, in 1890, was used first as a municipal landfill by the City of Niagara Falls, and later as a chemical dump by the Hooker Chemical Company. Houses and a school were built on the site after it was closed. In the mid-1970s contamination and health problems began plaguing the neighbourhood. Lois Gibbs emerged as the leader of the struggle to have the contamination recognized and compensation provided to its victims.

Robert Hunter, *The Greenpeace to Amchitka: An Environmental Odyssey* (Vancouver: Arsenal Press, 2004).
This is the story of the 1971 trip by 12 environmental protestors sailing from Vancouver aboard the vessel *Greenpeace* in an attempt to stop US nuclear weapons testing on the island of Amchitka in Alaska. The protest failed when their ship could not reach the site prior to the time the test took place, but the legacy of that trip was the founding of the international environmental group Greenpeace by Hunter and others taking part in the protest. This highly personalized account was published shortly before Hunter's death in 2005. Hunter also wrote an earlier history of Greenpeace, *Warriors of the Rainbow: A Chronicle of the Greenpeace Movement* (New York: Holt, Rinehart and Winston, 1979).

Rik Scarce, *Eco-Warriors: Understanding the Radical Environmental Movement* (Chicago: Noble Press, 1990).
A review of the histories, actions, and philosophies of the various groups constituting the radical arm of contemporary environmentalism, including Greenpeace, Earth First!, the Sea Shepherds, and Animal Liberation. Comparisons are made with non-radical, grassroots environmentalism and the mainstream environmental lobby.

Allan Schnaiberg and Kenneth Alan Gould, *Environment and Society: The Enduring Conflict* (New York: St Martin's Press, 1994).
Schnaiberg is the foremost conflict-oriented environmental sociologist, whose earlier book *The Environment: From Surplus to Scarcity* (1980) largely defined the critical approach in environmental sociology. This more recent book contains many of the essential ideas of the earlier work, while updating them in the context of sustainable development.

Mathis Wackernagel, and William Rees, *Our Ecological Footprint: Reducing Human Impact on the Earth* (Gabriola Island, BC: The New Catalyst, 1996).
This book introduces the metaphor of the *ecological footprint*, a term used to refer to the productive land needed in order to sustain different lifestyles. If everyone in the world lived like the average Canadian in terms of their consumption patterns, housing, and transportation, we would need two additional planets to provide for all our needs. This book provides an accounting measure by which each individual can measure his or her own ecological footprint.

Recommended Websites

Center for Health, Environment and Justice
www.chej.org/

The Center for Health, Environment and Justice website is an on-line extension of the public campaign to promote environmental justice through community actions and public awareness of toxins. The site provides information and practical advice on community mobilization against toxic products, processes, and wastes.

David Suzuki Foundation
www.davidsuzuki.org/

Canada's most famous environmentalist, David Suzuki, began a foundation in 1990, which focuses on climate change, biodiversity, and forest and fishery issues. The website offers information on public action and advocacy, a regular column by Dr Suzuki, and media releases and community events information.

Earth Day
www.Earthday.net/footprint/index.asp

A number of websites allow on-line calculation of one's ecological footprint—the amount of productive land needed to sustain each individual's own lifestyle. This one from the Earth Day organization calculates your ecological footprint based on information you provide on your consumption, housing, and travel patterns.

Environmental Defence Canada
www.environmentaldefence.ca/

Environmental Defence Canada is a charitable organization with broad-based membership of university, private, and corporate sponsorship. The organization advocates community and individual actions on environmental problems, and the website contains links to their newsletter, action alerts, and media releases.

Foundation for Deep Ecology
www.deepecology.org/

The Foundation for Deep Ecology supports 'education, advocacy, and legal action on behalf of wild Nature and in opposition to the technologies and developments . . . destroying the natural world'. The website describes news, publications, programs, and grants in connection with the deep ecology movement.

Greenpeace
www.greenpeace.ca/

Greenpeace's website provides information on the group's various campaigns as well as public information guides and press releases on environmental problems.

100 Mile Diet
www.100milediet.org

The food eaten daily by typical North Americans travels an average of 2,400 kilometres from the farm to the place it is consumed. In 2005 two Vancouver residents, Alisa Smith and James MacKinnon, attempted to see if they could eat and drink for a year on products only from within a radius of 100 miles of their home. The result has been a minor social movement comprising '100 milers', all attempting to replicate this feat in connection to products found in proximity to their own communities. This website recounts their stories while also providing advice and information for those wishing to accept the challenge.

Pembina Institute
www.pembina.org/

The Pembina Institute is an independent, not-for-profit environmental policy research and education organization located in Alberta. The website states: 'the Institute's major policy research and education programs are in the areas of sustainable energy, climate change, environmental governance, ecological fiscal reform, sustainability indicators, and the environmental impacts of the energy industry.'

United Nations Environmental Program
www.unep.org/

The UNEP website offers students and other researchers access to maps, UN publications, and many databases from various sources including the World Bank, UNICEF, UNESCO, and UNPOP. Databases can be downloaded in many different formats for student use and investigation.

Glossary

Accountability The expectation that public education, like other state-provided services, has clearly defined objectives that members of the public can identify and assess how well and how cost effectively they are being met.

Aesthetics A system of rules for the appreciation of the beautiful.

Age composition The distribution of the population with respect to age (and usually also sex); typically displayed graphically as a population pyramid.

Agents of socialization Those groups in a child's environment that have the greatest effect on his or her socialization.

Alienation A concept derived from Marx's analysis of the position of workers under capitalism, referring to the separation of workers from the products of their labour, from the control of the work process, from owners, managers, and other workers, and even from themselves.

Allopathic medicine Conventional medicine that treats by opposing something, whether germs, bacteria, cells, organs, or other pathology.

Altercasting The counterpart of impression management. In impression management actors self-cast, whereas in altercasting actors force on others identities that are in the altercaster's interests.

Alternative media Types of communication that have been used by subordinate groups and social movements to present their own messages, which often involve challenging existing conditions in society. Examples include community radio, documentary films, and the Internet.

Anticipatory socialization Explicit or implicit learning, in preparation for a future role; in Merton's definition, the acquisition of values and orientations found in statuses and groups in which one is not yet engaged but that one is likely to enter.

Authority Power considered legitimate by those subject to it.

Baby boom The dramatic rise in the birth rate in Canada following World War II and lasting until well into the 1960s.

Baby bust The continuing decline in fertility following the end of the baby boom in the industrialized world.

Behavioural school An approach within organizational theory that developed out of human relations theory and a psychological conception of human needs.

Beliefs Any statement or part of a statement that describes an aspect of collective reality. Beliefs are ideas and explanations of what is commonly accepted as the truth. Beliefs may also be normative, saying what ought—or ought not—to be done.

Bilateral descent pattern A system under which a married couple is considered part of both the female's and the male's kin groups.

Biological determinism The view that nature dominates nurture.

Bourgeoisie Owners of the means of production; the merchant (economically dominant) or ruling class.

Breakdown approach An approach to social movements that assumes rapid, thorough, or uneven change in social institutions weakens social bonds and encourages the formation of groups advocating radical change.

Bride price Money, property, or labour provided by the groom or his family to a bride's family for permission to marry the bride.

Brownfields Large tracts of urban land, usually central, whose original uses have become outdated by changes in production and/or transportation technology.

Built environment Tangible settings, such as buildings, streets, and other, often urban, settings constructed by humans for their repeated use.

Bureaucracy A type of formal organization, found in government and private industry and in capitalist and socialist societies alike, that has the following six characteristics: a division of labour; a hierarchy of positions; a formal system of rules; a separation of the person from the office; hiring and promotion based on technical merit; and the protection of careers. Administrative efficiency is achieved by depersonalized treatment and mass processing of cases, as dictated by regulations and filed information.

Capital-intensive production All production involves both labour and capital, but the proportions of the two used can vary considerably across different goods and services. In dollar terms, the inputs of capital into the production of aluminum are enormous (plant, equipment, electricity, bauxite) but the labour inputs are modest—a capital-intensive industry. In contrast, hairdressers use negligible amounts of capital equipment (a chair, sink and water, scissors, a mirror, some chemicals). The bulk of the cost of that activity is labour—a labour-intensive industry.

Capitalism An economic system characterized by a relationship of unequal economic exchange between capitalists (employers) and workers. Because they do not own the means of production, workers must sell their labour to employers in exchange for a wage or salary. Capitalism is a market-based system driven by the pursuit of profit for personal gain.

Carrying capacity The ability of the earth to provide the resources to sustain all of humankind.

Census A complete count of the population at one point in time, usually taken by a country every 5 or 10 years. The census is distinguished from the vital statistics system, a continuous registration system of births, deaths, marriages, and divorces.

Census family The Statistics Canada definition of the family used in the census, which usually includes married or long-term cohabiting couples, with or without never-married children, as well as single parents living with never-married children.

Census metropolitan areas (CMAs) Statistics Canada term for large urban agglomerations of 100,000 or more people, sometimes consisting of more than one political jurisdiction or municipality, interconnected in relatively close proximity by systems of roadways. Today in Canada there are 33 CMAs.

Ceremonial theories Building on the later work of Durkheim, a series of theories that stress the unifying function of rituals, holidays, and sporting events in society for the maintenance of social cohesion and community.

Charismatic authority Power considered legitimate because those subject to it believe in the exceptional qualities of an individual person, who appears exemplary or heroic and able to solve what others cannot.

Charter groups Canadians of British and French origin are known as charter groups because they have a special status entrenched in the Canadian constitution and have effectively determined the dominant cultural characteristics of Canada. Each of these groups has special rights and privileges, especially in terms of the language of the legislature, of the courts, and of education.

Claims-making The social constructionist process by which groups assert grievances about the troublesome character of people or their behaviour.

Class Inequality among groups of people based on the distribution of material resources and social capital.

Coherence Interrelationships that link parts to make a whole.

Collective conscience; collective consciousness Durkheim's term for the collective intellectual property of a culture; something that we can all share in and contribute to but that no one person can know or possess. The cognitive-moral system of shared symbols, beliefs, and sentiments of a social group. Individuals think and feel what they learn and internalize as members of a collective. The content of the conscience collective is determined by the structural organization of the society in question.

Collective effervescence The experience of psychological excitement and empowerment that often happens to individuals caught up in large crowd activities such as political rallies, sporting events, or rock concerts.

Common-sense knowledge Facts of life accepted without being fully researched and understood.

Community Tangible interpersonal contact patterns.

Compensators Things that are provided in place of some real but unattainable goal or object, for example, the religious promise of life after death in lieu of actual immortality in one's present existence.

Concept An abstract idea that cannot be tested directly. Concepts can refer to anything, but in social research they usually refer to characteristics of individuals, groups, or artifacts, or to social processes. Some common sociological concepts include religiosity (strength of religious conviction), social class, and alienation.

Conflict theory A theoretical paradigm linked to the work of Marx and Weber that emphasizes conflict and change as the regular and permanent features of society, because society is made up of various groups that wield varying amounts of power. Conflict theorists often stress the importance of status, economic inequality, and political power.

Conglomerate ownership A form of ownership in which one company has many firms that engage in a variety of often unrelated business activities. It may combine *horizontal integration, vertical integration,* and even *cross-ownership.*

Control theory A category of explanation that maintains that people engage in deviant behaviour when the various controls that might be expected to prohibit them from doing so are weak or absent.

Cross-ownership A form of ownership in which one company owns organizations associated with different types of media. For instance, a company might own a newspaper and a television network.

CRTC The Canadian Radio-television and Telecommunications Commission, which governs the broadcasting as well as the telecommunications business in Canada, setting the rules for operation based on principles of scarcity, public resource, and national importance.

Cults Religious groups, usually very small, that have either been newly created or imported into a society from a quite different culture.

Cultural capital A term coined by Pierre Bourdieu for the cultural and linguistic competence, such as prestigious knowledge, tastes, preferences, and educational expertise and credentials, that individuals possess and that influence the likelihood of their educational and occupational success.

Cultural diffusion The process whereby the beliefs and customary behaviours of one society spread to, and are adopted within, another society.

Cultural support theory A category of explanation that argues people become and remain deviant because the cultural environments in which they find themselves teach deviance and define such behaviour as appropriate.

Culture At its broadest, the sum total of the human-produced environment (the objects, artifacts, ideas, beliefs, and values that make up the symbolic and learned aspects of human society) as separate from the natural environment; more often refers to norms, values, beliefs, ideas, and meanings; an assumption that different societies are distinguished by their shared beliefs and customary behaviours; the products and services delivered by a number of industries—theatre, music, film, publishing, and so on.

Decoding The process of interpreting or 'reading' media content. It may involve a dominant-hegemonic reading, an oppositional reading, or a negotiated reading. See *Encoding*; *Encoding and decoding.*

Deep ecology Term coined by Norwegian philosopher Arne Naess referring to a philosophical approach to environmentalism calling for fundamental social change in contrast to the more reformist orientation of mainstream environmentalism, referred to by Naess as 'shallow ecology'. Deep ecology has been criticized for its biocentric emphasis claiming nature to be separate from and superior to human society, and used by some environmental organizations to justify any means, even illegal, for addressing environmental problems.

Demographic components equation A method of estimating population size by adding births, subtracting deaths, and adding net migration occurring in an interval of time, then adding the result to the population at the beginning of the interval; also knows as a balancing equation.

Demographic transition The process by which a country moves from high birth and death rates to low birth and death rates. The shift in fertility rates is often referred to as the fertility transition, while the complementary change in death rates is referred to as the mortality transition. The epidemiological transition theory is a complementary theory to demographic transition theory.

Developed countries The most industrialized countries of the world. According to the United Nations, these are the countries in Europe and in North America, as well as Australia, New Zealand, and Japan.

Developing countries All the countries not in the developed world. A subdivision of developing countries is the least developed countries, defined by the United Nations as countries with average annual incomes of less than $9,000 (US). See also *Third World.*

Deviance People, behaviours, and conditions subject to social control.

Digital divide Inequalities in access to computers and/or the Internet; also used to describe inequalities in the skills needed to use computers or information transmitted through the Internet. Inequalities associated with social class, gender, national origin, and other characteristics are seen as the basis for the digital divide.

Discourse A way of talking about and conceptualizing an issue, presented through ideas, concepts, and vocabulary that recur in texts.

Discrimination An action whereby a person is treated differently (usually, unfairly) because of his or her membership in a particular group or category.

Disease, illness, and sickness Distinguished from one another in the sociology of health, illness, and medicine. Disease is the disorder that is diagnosed by the physician. Illness is the personal experience of the person who acknowledges that he or she does not feel well. Sickness is the social action taken by a person as a result of illness or disease.

Doctrine of emergence A key ontological principle in the social realist perspective: new properties or realities are created by the combination of elements.

Dominant ideology The ideas and viewpoints held by the capitalist class or other powerful groups in society. Specific forms of the dominant ideology include capitalist, patriarchal, and racist ideology.

Double standard Expecting or requiring different behaviour from women than men, and from boys than girls.

Dowry Money or property provided by a bride's family upon her marriage, to help obtain a suitable husband and to be used by her new household (or sometimes to support her in case of divorce or widowhood).

Ecology In the context of urban studies, the internal makeup, patterning, and dynamics of cities. See also *Human ecology.*

Edge city Highly concentrated business, commercial, and high-technology centre on lower-cost land on the fringe of an urban area.

Education The process by which human beings learn and develop capacities through understanding of their social and natural environments, which takes place in both formal and informal settings.

Encoding The process of embedding ideology in media content. Encoding emerges through the complex interplay of economic and technical conditions associated with a media institution, the organizational relations and practices of the institution, and the ideology existing within the institution and the wider society. See also *Decoding*; *Encoding and decoding.*

Encoding and decoding The embedding and subsequent interpretation of cues, meanings, and codes in cultural productions.

Environmental justice The branch of environmentalism that focuses on the inequitable distribution of environmental risks affecting the poor and racial minorities.

Epistemology A branch of philosophy concerned with the nature of knowledge, how it is obtained, and the means for establishing its validity.

Essence; essentialism; essential nature The idea that a 'true' or core reality lies behind appearances, which makes something what it is and which, once identified, can establish its 'truth'. In the study of sexual and gender identities, for example, many challenge the idea that there is an essence of 'femaleness' (something all women share/are) or 'maleness' that sets females and males apart from each other.

Ethnic group People sharing a common ethnic identity who are potentially capable of organizing and acting on their ethnic interests.

Ethnicity Sets of social distinctions by which groups differentiate themselves from one another on the basis of presumed biological ties. Members of such groups have a sense of themselves as a common 'people' separate and distinct from others.

Ethnocentric bias The tendency to think that the beliefs, values, and customs of one's own culture are universal (that is, that they can be applied to others).

Ethnomethodology A type of qualitative research founded by Harold Garfinkel that analyzes the methods people use in relation to one another to make sense of social life and conceptual order at the everyday level.

Exploitation At the heart of Marxist sociology, the situation under capitalism in which the bourgeoisie takes advantage of the proletariat. Class-based exploitation occurs when the bourgeoisie appropriates the labour effort of the proletariat to create its own material advantage.

Extended family Several generations and/or married siblings and their children sharing a residence and co-operating economically.

Face The positive presentation of self projected by an individual.

False consciousness Condition in which the working class does not recognize its exploitation and oppression under capitalism.

Feminism A theoretical paradigm, as well as a social movement, that focuses on causes and consequences of inequality between men and women, especially patriarchy and sexism.

Finance capital In contrast to physical capital, instruments that can be used to purchase physical capital—bank loans, equity (voting shares in a company), fixed interest bonds, and so on; the monetary expression of physical capital.

First Nations 'Indians' in Canadian law; together with Métis and Inuit, they constitute Canada's Aboriginal peoples.

Flexible specialization Another component of the new flexible approach to management; involves multi-skilling, job rotation, the organization of workers into teams, and concentrated yet decentralized decision-making power within work organizations.

Formal organization A deliberately formed social group in which people, resources, and technologies are consciously co-ordinated through formalized roles, statuses, and relationships to achieve a division of labour intended to attain a specific set of objectives.

Forms of association An approach to sociology founded by German scholar Georg Simmel that focuses on identifiable generic patterns to discover how people interact with each other in groups; distinct from the content of associations, which vary much more widely.

Functionalism A theoretical approach stressing order, consensus, social stability, and the positive functions of certain levels of inequality in social life, with a major emphasis on shared values and norms and on the importance of community.

Gender Socially recognized distinctions of masculinity and femininity.

Gender stereotyping Beliefs about differences in the natural capabilities and attributes of women and men.

Generalized other In Mead's theory, the 'internalized audience' with which we, as 'minded selves', dialogue or converse during the reflective prelude to action. It represents the acquired collective attitudes and sentiments of our society or group.

Global cities Cities favoured under globalization that are at high levels of technology, finance, and international transportation, serving as the focal points for multinational corporations but not for local manufacturing.

Globalization The flow of goods, services, media, information, and labour between countries around the world; different but interrelated aspects include economic globalization and cultural globalization. Worldwide control and co-ordination by large private-sector interests not constrained by local or national boundaries.

Globalization of work The relocation of production and consumption beyond national borders to various parts of the globe done in the interest of increasing profits by decreasing labour costs and maximizing employer control of the overall work process.

Hawthorne effect The finding that when people know they are subjects of an important experiment and receive a large amount of special attention, they tend to behave the way they think the researchers expect them to.

Health Defined by the World Health Organization (WHO, 2003) as a 'state of complete physical, mental, and social well-being'.

Hermaphroditism A term no longer used in the social sciences (but still used in the natural sciences in sexual differentiation) to refer to individuals born with 'ambiguous' genitalia.

Heteronormativity The assumption that heterosexuality is a universal norm, therefore making homosexuality invisible or 'abnormal'.

Heterosexism A set of overt and covert social practices in both the public and private spheres that privileges heterosexuality over other sexual orientations.

Hidden curriculum The understandings that students develop as a result of the institutional requirements and day-to-day realities they encounter in their schooling; typically refers to norms, such as competition, individualism, and obedience, as well as to a sense of one's place in school and social hierarchies.

Historical-comparative theory An approach that stresses how societies evolve, temporally and over large areas of geography, in particular ways based on the specific history of the unit (city, region, or nation) under consideration.

Homophobia A term coined by George Weinberg, in 1972, to refer to the psychological fear of homosexuality; tends to neglect the wider structural sources of the homosexual taboo.

Homosexual Someone who has sex with or is attracted to a person of the same sex.

Horizontal integration A form of ownership in which one company owns a number of media organizations in different locations that are doing the same type of business; also known as 'chain ownership'; e.g., a company might own several radio stations across Canada.

Hot money Liquid assets that can be turned into cash quickly and with negligible cost. They can, consequently, be moved between investment locations—including countries—rapidly and easily.

Household People who share a dwelling, whether or not they are related by blood, adoption, or marriage.

Human capital The notion that education, skills development, and other learning processes are investments that enhance our capacities. Human capital theory builds on this notion.

Human ecology The science of ecology, as applied to sociological analyses. See also *Ecology*.

Human exemptionalism paradigm (HEP) The term used by Catton and Dunlap in arguing that the competing theoretical perspectives in sociology, including functionalism, conflict theory, and symbolic interactionism, all share a world view based on anthropocentrism.

Human relations school An approach within organizational theory that focuses on relationships within informal groups and assumes that happy group relationships produce job satisfaction, which, in turn, produces high productivity.

Hypermasculinities An excessive emphasis on practices associated with being male in any culture.

Hypotheses Testable statements composed of at least two variables and how they are related.

Identity How we see ourselves and how others see us. How we view ourselves is a product of our history and of our interpretation of others' reactions to us. How others view us is termed 'placement' and is other people's reactions to our projections of ourselves, which is termed 'announcement'.

Identity-based approach An approach to social movements that assumes dominant interpretations of reality preserve class, gender, racial, and other inequalities. The central task of social movements is to challenge and reformulate the dominant culture by reshaping identities.

Ideology A system of beliefs, ideas, and norms, reflecting the interests and experiences of a group, class, or subculture, that legitimizes or justifies the existing unequal distribution of power and privilege; ways of seeing and of understanding the world and its actors. Ideologies function by making the social appear natural or functional rather than constructed for partisan interests and advantage.

Illness See *Disease, illness, and sickness.*

Impression management Goffman's term for the 'dramatic moves' individuals make in trying to advance 'definitions of the situation' favourable to their interests and self-image. It is achieved by carefully manipulating the elements of appearance, manner, and setting.

Informal economy A wide range of legal and illegal economic activities that are not officially reported to the government.

Informal organization Complex personal and informal networks that develop among people within a bureaucracy who interact on the job.

Institutional completeness A measure of the degree to which a community offers a range of services to its members.

Institutional discrimination Discrimination built into how an institution is structured or how it operates.

Interpretive theory An approach that pays close attention to the cultural meanings held by actors, derived from socialization in the group, which is seen as the key to understanding human behaviour and patterns of action.

Intersexed (bodies) Infants born with genetic, hormonal, and anatomical configurations that do not coincide with normative anatomical sexual difference (male/female).

Labour power Marx argued that labour is work and labour power is the capacity to work. The only real power that the proletariat has under capitalism is the power to choose whether to work.

Labour process theory A neo-Marxist approach to organizations and the conduct of work that focuses on the alienation of the worker and on power relationships between capitalists and workers.

Level of analysis Refers to the scale and size of population being looked at in a work of empirical research. Large-scale historical trends and data about large populations of people (macro), organizational processes (meso), or small groups (micro) are the most common levels of analysis, though any one study may bridge or move between these three levels as necessary.

Life expectancy at birth The average number of years left to live for a newborn in a given period. Life expectancy is distinct from life span, which is the oldest age humans can attain.

Lifelong learning The ongoing expectations for people to acquire new knowledge and capacities through learning that occurs in various levels and kinds of formal education as well as in other learning contexts; associated with increasing emphasis on the new economy and the continuing transitions that individuals undergo throughout their lives.

Lifeworld A concept in phenomenology referring to the lived, intersubjective experiences of people sharing a way of life. It is characterized by taken-for-granted assumptions about their constructed social reality.

Looking-glass self In Cooley's symbolic interactionist approach, the idea that self-concept is based on a person's perceptions of the opinions that others hold about him or her.

Macro See *Micro; macro.*

Macrosociology The study of social institutions and large social groups; the study of the processes that depict societies as a whole and of the social structural aspects of a given society.

Marxism Based on the work of Karl Marx, the historical materialist school of thought that posits a structural explanation for historical change, namely, that the economic base of society determines change in all other realms.

Mass-society theory An argument that holds that modern life creates isolated, disoriented individuals who are easily manipulated by the media and extremist politicians.

Master status A status characteristic that overrides other status characteristics. When a person is assigned a label of 'deviant' (for example, 'murderer', 'drug addict', 'cheater'), that label is usually read by others as signifying the most essential aspects of the individual's character.

Matrifocal A family life system focused around the women, who earn most of the money and hold the family together (often in the absence of a male breadwinner).

Matrilineal descent The tracing of relationships and inheritance through the female line.

Means of production Wealth-generating property such as land, factories, and machinery.

Medicalization The tendency for more and more of life to be defined as relevant to medical diagnosis and treatment.

Mega-cities Cities of 10 million or more residents.

Melting-pot policies Policies that are most notable for their failure to recognize difference among communities and ethnic/racial groups, derived from American liberal individualistic ideology that assumes that immigrants should discard all of the traditions and distinctions they brought to the United States with them, such as their ethnic language or national identity, and become nothing but 'Americans'.

Metropolitan area With respect to everyday behaviour and economic activity, the unified entity formed on a de facto basis by a large city and its suburbs. See also *Census metropolitan areas.*

Micro; macro Used analytically to distinguish small-scale, face-to-face interaction settings (micro) from institutional arrangements such as the economy or state and from large-scale collective processes like revolutions and religious movements (macro).

Microsociology The analysis of small groups and of the face-to-face interactions that occur within these groups in the everyday.

Middle-range theory Developed by American sociologist Robert Merton, theories of the middle range consider levels of analysis above the micro and somewhat below the whole society in order to develop manageable theories that can be tested. Theories of suicide, theories regarding the relationship between Protestantism and capitalism, and theories of revolutions are examples of such middle-range theories.

Mind In Mead's theory, a 'social emergent' created through symbolic interaction, consisting of the ability to think, to carry on an internal conversation. Mind is made possible through the internalization of language.

Mode of production Marx's concept referring to the economic structure of society, consisting of the forces and relations of production; the 'base' that conditions the 'superstructure' of politics, law, religion, art, and so on.

Modified extended family Several generations who live near each other and maintain close social and economic contact.

Monarchy Rule by a single individual who claims legitimacy based on royal lineage.

Morbidity rate The sickness rate per a specified number of people over a specified period of time.

Mortality rate The death rate per a specified number of people over a specified period of time.

Multiculturalism In Canada, a government policy to promote tolerance among cultural groups and to assist ethnic groups in preserving the values and traditions that are important to them; multiculturalism became official policy in 1971, following the report of the Royal Commission on Bilingualism and Biculturalism.

Multinational corporations Companies that have significant production facilities in more than one national jurisdiction; those detached from any particular country, with loyalty to no country, are sometimes labelled 'transnational corporations'.

Multivariate theory A theoretical approach that stresses how society can be understood as being made up of certain 'variables' that interact with each other, producing results that can be measured in order to develop a theory of society. Durkheim's analysis of the various 'variables' of religion and marital status that help predict suicide rates is probably the most influential early version of multivariate theory.

Naturalistic attitude Schütz's term for the common-sense mindset of people inhabiting a lifeworld. It is grounded in an intersubjective agreement that their world is as it appears to the members of a group or community—that is, a collective suspension of doubt that permits a taken-for-granted practicality.

Negotiation A discussion intended to produce an agreement.

Neighbourhood A recognizable physical area within a city, with or without formal boundaries.

Neo-liberalism An economic doctrine that supports free trade between countries, cuts in social spending, and measures such as deregulation or privatization.

New economy A term used to highlight the shift in emphasis from industrial production within specific industries, firms, and nations to economic activities driven by information and high-level technologies, global competition, and international networks, and knowledge-based advancement.

New environmental paradigm (NEP) The term used by Catton and Dunlap in arguing that environmental sociology constitutes a paradigm shift within general sociology based on the understanding that human societies cannot be separate and distinct from nature.

Nominalism An ontological position that insists that only flesh-and-blood individuals are real and have the capacity to act; collective terms like 'the state' or 'economy' are mere verbal expressions and consist only of aggregated individual actions.

Non-standard work Jobs that are characterized by an increasingly tenuous or precarious relationship between employer and employee, including part-time employment, temporary employment, contract work, multiple job-holding, and self-employment; also termed 'contingent work' and 'casual work'.

Norms The rules and expectations of appropriate behaviour under various social circumstances. Norms create social consequences that have the effect of regulating appearance and behaviour.

Nuclear family A husband, wife, and their children, sharing a common residence and co-operating economically.

Numerical flexibility Part of a new general managerial approach that rests on flexibility in employment; involves shrinking or eliminating the core workforce (in continuous, full-time positions) and replacing them with workers in non-standard employment.

Objective Something completely unaffected by the characteristics of the person or instrument observing it. 'Objective' observations were used in the past to establish the truth of scientific theories until it became clear that completely objective observations are impossible.

Ontology Inquiry that deals with the fundamental nature of things—of reality or existence—and that specifies the essential properties or characteristics of phenomena.

Operationalization The translation of abstract theories and concepts into observable hypotheses and variables. Once abstract ideas are operationalized, we can test them in a study.

Organization A group of people participating in a division of labour that is co-ordinated by communication and leadership to achieve a common goal or goals; includes both spontaneous and formal organizations.

Paradigm A set of assumptions used to view society and people's behaviour. A paradigm serves as a model for which questions sociologists should ask and how they should interpret the answers.

Parties Voluntary associations that organize for the collective pursuit of interests such as political parties or lobbying groups; common in Weberian scholarship.

Patriarchy A society or family system in which men have more authority than women.

Patrilineal descent The tracing of relationships and inheritance through the male line.

Pedagogy Processes associated with the organization and practice of teaching; more generally, various kinds of interactions (and how these are understood and organized) in teaching/learning situations.

Political conflict perspective A resource mobilization approach that focuses on how groups (typically classes) promote collective interests.

Political institutions Established rules and procedures for the conduct of political affairs.

Political movements Social movements that challenge established state policies and practices in order to bring about social and political changes.

Political party An organization dedicated to winning political power by controlling government.

Political process approach An approach that assumes that political constraints and opportunities influence the rise and fall of social movements, as well as their institutional organization.

Politics The process in which individuals and groups act to promote their interests, often in conflict with others.

Polyandry The practice of being legally married to more than one husband at a time.

Polygamy The practice of being legally married to more than one spouse at a time.

Polygyny The practice of being legally married to more than one wife at a time.

Population momentum The tendency for population to keep growing even when the fertility rate drops to just the replacement level of 2.1 children per woman, as a consequence of a high proportion of persons in the child-bearing ages.

Power In Marxist sociology, a social relationship that has a material base. Those who own the means of production have the power to exploit workers through the appropriation of their labour efforts. In Weberian sociology, power is more broadly defined and can reflect an individual's or group's capacity to exert their will over others.

Prejudice An attitude by which individuals are prejudged on the basis of stereotyped characteristics assumed to be common to all members of the individual's group.

Primary socialization The most intense socialization, which occurs from birth to adolescence and which takes place in or is strongly influenced by the family.

Privatization The movement away from a completely universally available and state-funded medical system to one that includes profit-making components.

Progressive conservation The movement originating in the nineteenth century that sought to check environmental destruction caused by unbridled economic growth and that resulted in the founding of such modern environmental organizations as the Audubon Society and the Sierra Club.

Proletariat People who sell their labour power to capitalists in return for a wage; the working class.

Protestant ethic thesis Weber's argument that aspects of the Protestant religion originally imbued people with a sense of dedication to their work that helped to lay the foundations for capitalism.

PYLL 'Potential years of life lost'; refers to premature mortality and taking into account the average age of death from a particular cause.

Queer A once derogatory term reclaimed by the LGBT (lesbian, gay, bisexual, transgendered) community to galvanize and help forge a public collective identity and to take apart and blur sexual boundaries. The term is used to stress the inessential, fluid, and multiple-sited forms of sexual identity.

Race A group that is defined on the basis of perceived physical differences, such as skin colour.

Race to the bottom The outcome produced by competitive tax-cutting motivated by the desire to attract (and keep) investors.

Racialization Sets of social processes and practices whereby social relations among people are structured according to visible physical difference among peoples, to the advantage of those in the visible majority and the disadvantage of those who are visible minorities.

Racism A belief that groups that differ in physical appearance also differ in personality characteristics, intelligence, honesty, reliability, law abidingness, and so on. Racism also implies a belief that these differences make one group superior to another.

Rationalization In Weber's view, the movement away from mystical and religious interpretations of the world to the development of human thought and belief based on the systematic accumulation of evidence; associated with the emergence of impersonal authority.

Rational-legal authority Power considered legitimate because those subject to it believe commands are based on formally established rules, procedures, and certified expertise.

Reductionism An analytical strategy that explains wholes or totalities by reducing them to the aggregated properties of their constituent parts; for example, attempts to explain social facts in strict psychological terms (behaviourism) or as the consequence of underlying biological factors (sociobiology).

Relative deprivation theory A breakdown approach that claims radical social movements result from people's subjective feelings of fear and frustration.

Relativism The idea that there is no single, unchangeable truth about anything; all things are either true or false only relative to particular standards. Many sociologists who do not view sociology as a science take their stance persuaded by relativism.

Reliability The consistency of a measure, indicator, or study. Note that reliability is different from validity and does not refer to the accuracy of a measure or study.

Resocialization The process of learning new roles in response to changes in life circumstances.

Resource mobilization approach An approach that assumes social movements are quite similar to other organizations.

Risk society A theory of the new modernity that argues that perception of risk is modernity's defining feature, creating uncertainty and compelling individuals to seek new strategic allegiances.

Rites of passage Rituals performed by all cultures to mark major transitions in life; these rites usually display a three-part structure: a symbolically marked departure from an old identity or phase of life, a symbolically marked period of innocent non-involvement, and a symbolic incorporation into the rights and responsibilities of a new identity or phase of life.

Role expectations The expected characteristics and social behaviours of an individual in a particular position in society.

Role-making The continual improvising and revising of our actions as others' reactions to them change and are imputed.

Roles The specific duties and obligations expected of one who occupies a specific status.

Role-taking The construction in our mind of what others mean by their actions.

Sample The group of people or objects drawn from the whole population that will be studied. In quantitative research, a great deal of time and effort is devoted to the selection of truly random samples, while in qualitative research, samples are often selected based on the theoretical importance of the people or objects.

Schooling Processes that take place within formal educational institutions.

Scientific management A managerial method developed in the early twentieth century by F.W. Taylor that rests on breaking up work processes into their smallest constituent parts in an effort to maximize efficiency in productivity, resulting in the separation of mental from manual labour and in the deskilling of workers; assumes that workers are motivated by economic rewards alone and that specialists know more than workers about how a task can most effectively be performed; also known as Taylorism.

Secondary socialization The ongoing lifelong process of socialization, based on the accumulated learning of childhood and adolescence.

Sects Religious groups, still usually relatively small, that come into being as a result of a disagreement between the members of an established church.

Secularization The social process resulting in the declining presence and influence of religious beliefs, practices, symbols, and institutions.

Self In Mead's theory, an emergent entity with a capacity to be both a subject and an object, as reflected upon in one's own mind. In Goffman's dramaturgical theory, the self is a more shifting 'dramatic effect', a staged product of the scenes one performs in.

Serial monogamy A pattern of marriage, divorce, and remarriage, resulting in having more than one spouse over a lifetime, but only one at a time.

Service economy The economic sector in which most Canadians currently are employed. In comparison to primary industry (the extraction of natural resources) and manufacturing (processing raw materials into usable goods and services), the service economy is based on the provision of services rather than a tangible product, ranging widely from advertising and retailing to entertaining to generating and distributing information. Also called the 'tertiary sector'.

Sex The biological differences between females and males, determined at conception.

Sex ratio; primary sex ratio; secondary sex ratio The number of males in relation to the number of females in a population. The primary sex ratio is the sex ratio at birth, typically in the range of about 105 baby boys per 100 baby girls. The secondary sex ratio is the sex ratio beyond infancy.

Sexual harassment Unwanted attention linked to the gender of the person receiving that attention.

Sexuality The ways in which we experience and express ourselves as sexual beings.

Sexual orientation An individual's sexual preference(s), which could include partners of the opposite sex, same sex, both sexes, or neither.

Sexual scripting An approach that argues that socio-cultural processes are fundamental in determining what is perceived as sexual and how individuals should behave sexually.

Sickness See *Disease, illness, and sickness.*

Situated identity According to symbolic interactionist theory, social life is in a constant process of change, imposing changes in, and new forms of, identity announcement and identity placement. A particular announcement–placement identity at any point in time is referred to as a situated identity.

Situated transaction A process of social interaction that lasts as long as the individuals find themselves in each other's company. As applied to the study of deviance, the concept of the situated transaction helps us to understand how deviant acts are social and not just individual products.

Social capital A concept widely thought to have been developed by American sociologist James Coleman in 1988, but discussed by Pierre Bourdieu in a similar way in the early 1980s; reflects the power that is derived from ties to social networks.

Social constructionism The sociological theory that argues that social problems and issues are less objective conditions than they are collective social definitions based on how they are framed and interpreted.

Social control The various and myriad ways in which members of social groups express their disapproval of people and behaviours. These include name-calling, ridicule, ostracism, incarceration, and even killing.

Social environment The people and relationships that surround us.

Social facts Patterns of social life and forces external to the individual that shape behaviour (e.g., religion, age distribution, ethnicity, rates of suicide, crime, or divorce); drawing causal connections between these larger social facts becomes a main sociological tool to explain behaviour, rather than individual or psychological explanations.

Social group A number of individuals, defined by formal or informal criteria of membership, who share a feeling of unity or are bound together in stable patterns of interaction; two or more individuals who have a specific common identity and who interact in a reciprocal social relationship.

Social institution A stable, well-acknowledged pattern of social relationships that endures over time, including the family, the economy, education, politics, religion, the mass media, medicine, and science and technology. Social institutions are the result of an enduring set of ideas about how to accomplish various goals generally recognized as important in a society.

Social interaction The process by which people act and react in relationships with others.

Social movement The co-ordinated, voluntary action of non-elites (those people with no control over major resources) for the manifest purpose of changing the distribution of social goods.

Social networks Based on kinship, friendship, or economic ties, these may include social transactions (shared recreation, communication, gift exchanges, mutual assistance) and shared tastes and values.

Social realism The ontological position that collective terms—such as 'patriarchy', the 'economy', 'the church'—correspond to real emergent entities, to structures that exert causal influence on individual lives.

Social relationships Interactions of people in a society. Because people share culture and a sense of collective existence, these interactions will to some extent be recurrent and predictable.

Social reproduction A range of unpaid activities that help to reproduce workforces daily and over generations; typically, though not exclusively, performed by women in the family household.

Social revolution A rapid, fundamental transformation of a society's state and class structures, often accomplished through violent means.

Social structure Patterns of behaviour or social relationships developed and accepted through time in a given group, organization, or society.

Social support The various ways people support each other through interactions.

Socialization The process by which people learn to become members of society. Scc also primary socialization; secondary socialization.

Society The largest collection of social relationships in which people live their lives; some very encompassing international relationships among nations (such as the European Common Market or the North American Free Trade Agreement), but these cover only a narrow range of types of activities (for example, economic relationships) compared to societies.

Sociological imagination A term coined by American sociologist C Wright Mills that calls on sociologists and on all people to attempt to fit so-called individual circumstances (private troubles) appropriately within their social and historical context, thus moving them to the level of public issues.

Sociology The systematic study of social behaviours in human societies.

Socio-technical systems theory An approach within organizational theory that holds that the social and technological aspects of an organization should be developed simultaneously. It also focuses on semi-autonomous work groups rather than on individual workers.

Solidarity The quality of an integrated and well-functioning society that is brought into harmony through an adaptive cultural foundation.

'Sound economic policies' As understood by a number of international economic organizations, these usually imply assurance that government budgets are not in deficit, a dominant role for the private sector in the provision of most goods and services, and policies of openness to trade. See also *Neo-liberalism.*

Spontaneous organization An organization that arises quickly to meet a single goal then disbands when that goal is achieved or perceived to be beyond reach, or when the organization becomes absorbed by a formal organization.

State Institutions associated with governing over a specific territory as well as establishing and enforcing rules within that territory. The state in a number of countries (including Canada) also is involved with providing various public services. Procedures and organizations concerned with creating, administering, and enforcing rules or decisions for conduct within a given territory.

Status A socially defined position that a person holds in a given social group or organization, to which are attached certain rights, duties, and obligations; a relational term, as each status exists only through its relation to one or more other statuses filled by other people.

Status degradation ceremony The rituals by which formal transition is made from non-deviant to deviant status. Examples include the criminal trial and the psychiatric hearing.

Status groups Organized groups comprising people who have similar social status situations. These groups organize to maintain or expand their social privileges by excluding outsiders from their ranks and by trying to gain status recognition from other groups.

Strain theory A category of explanation that seeks to understand how deviant behaviour results as people attempt to solve problems that the social structure presents to them.

Stratification The hierarchical patterns of inequality found in social life, in terms of gender, economic well-being, status, and political power.

Structural analysis or approach An approach within organizational theory in the Weberian tradition; focuses on the structural characteristics of organizations and their effect on the people within them; in the context of urban studies, the analysis of the functions cities perform, the size and shape of their governments, and who has what bearing on decisions and outcomes involving cities.

Structural discrimination See *Institutional discrimination.*

Structural functionalism A theoretical paradigm that emphasizes the way each part of a society functions to fulfill the needs of society as a whole.

Structure The 'concrete' elements of society that are embodied and enacted by things and people, in opposition to the cultural elements of society.

Subculture A subset of cultural traits of the larger society that also includes distinctive values, beliefs, norms, style of dress, and behaviour.

Supply-side theory The notion that a product available in a society is determined as much by how it is being supplied as by the demand for the product; the state of religion can be viewed through supply-side theory as a product like any other.

Sustainable development The principle that economic growth and environmental conservation are compatible goals.

Symbolic ethnicity Ethnicity that has become purely a matter of personal identification and that has little or no impact upon how people live their lives or relate to one another.

Symbolic interactionism An intellectual tradition in sociology akin to interpretive theory, founded in the early twentieth-century work of Charles Horton Cooley and George Herbert Mead, although the term itself was not coined until years later by Herbert Blumer. Symbolic interactionism emphasizes the importance of understanding the meanings of social action, and uses ethnographic methods to discover these meanings for individuals in an effort to explain human conduct.

Symbols The heart of cultural systems, for with them we construct thought, ideas, and other ways of representing reality to others and to ourselves; gestures, artifacts, or uses of language that represent something else.

Systemic discrimination Discrimination that is built into the fabric of Canadian life, as in the case of institutional self-segregation.

Systemic theory A breakdown approach, advanced by Neil Smelser, that views society as a set of interrelated elements that work together to maintain stability.

Systems theory An approach within organizational theory that sees organizations as open systems and that views organizations and their goals as shaped by the interests of their participants and their environments.

Taboo Behaviour that is prohibited, such as incest and sexual relations with specific categories of kin, from the Tongan word meaning 'sacred' or 'inviolable'.

Technology The practical things we as humans make and use, and the knowledge we require to build, maintain, and enhance them.

Terrorism Physical violence directed against civilians, without regard for who will suffer, in order to promote political objectives.

Theory An integrated set of concepts and statements that specify relations of ordered dependence and causal connection between phenomena. At the most general level, theories are perspectives, or ways of seeing, that conceptualize and highlight certain patterns and relations among complex realities. Theories are not tested directly. They may also be simple or complex: the more complex a theory, the more difficult it is to operationalize and test it.

Third World Poor countries; an element of a classification in which the First World was made up of Western Europe, North America, Australia, and New Zealand, the Second World of the various Communist countries (the Soviet Union, the numerous Soviet satellites, and China), and the Third World of poorer countries in Asia, Africa, and Latin America. See also *Developing countries.*

Totalitarianism Form of the state that involves intervening in and controlling all aspects of life both public and private.

Traditional authority Power considered legitimate because those subject to it believe that is the way things have always been done.

Transitions The pathways that people follow from family life, into and out of education, and into various jobs or other social situations throughout their life course.

Unemployment rate People are considered to be unemployed only if they do not have a job and are actively looking for a job. The unemployment rate is the number of people who meet those two conditions divided by the labour force (which includes both the employed and unemployed) expressed as a percentage. Those who do not have a job and are not looking for one are considered to be not in the labour force.

Urbanism Behaviour patterns associated with cities.

Urbanization The nature, extent, and distribution of cities in the larger society or nation.

Urban renewal A general term for improving buildings and land use; can include redevelopment, rehabilitation, or both.

Utilitarian perspective A resource mobilization approach that focuses on how individuals promote self-interest.

Validity The accuracy of a measure, indicator, or study; many different dimensions to validity can be established through formal tests, logic, or depth of understanding.

Values Shared ideas about how something is ranked in terms of its relative social desirability, worth, or goodness; what a group or society views as right and wrong, good and bad, desirable and undesirable.

Variable The operational or observable equivalent of concepts. Many concepts require more than one variable for proper operationalization. The key characteristic of variables is that there must be a range of different values that can be observed.

Verstehen Popularized by Max Weber, the German word for 'understanding' emphasizes the need to understand the cultural meanings actors carry (in Weber's context, the meanings associated with Calvinist religious values) to develop an adequate explanation of their behaviour.

Vertical integration A form of ownership in which one company owns firms or divisions that are part of the overall process; in media production firms would be integrated by linking production, distribution, and exhibition, e.g., a company that owns a movie studio, a movie distributor, and movie theatres.

Vertical mosaic A view of Canadian society as constituting an ethnically divided stratification system, with the charter groups at the top, Native people at the bottom, and other ethnic immigrant groups fitting in depending on their entrance status; from John Porter's *The Vertical Mosaic* (1965).

References

Abercrombie, Nicholas, Stephen Hill, and Bryan S. Turner. 2006. *The Penguin Dictionary of Sociology*, 5th edn. Toronto: Penguin.

Abrahams, Roger D. 2006 [1964]. *Deep Down in the Jungle: Black American Folklore from the Streets of Philadelphia.* New York: Aldine de Gruyter.

Abu-Laban, Baha, and Daiva Stasiulis. 1992. 'Ethnic Pluralism under Siege: Popular and Partisan Opposition to Multiculturalism', *Canadian Public Policy* 27, 4:365–86.

Abu-Lughod, Janet L. 1991. *Changing Cities: Urban Sociology.* New York: HarperCollins.

Acker, Joan. 1980. 'Women and Stratification: A Review of Recent Literature', *Contemporary Sociology* 9: 25–34.

———. 1988. 'Class, Gender, and the Relations of Distribution', *Signs* 13: 473–97.

———. 1989. 'The Problem with Patriarchy', *Sociology* 23: 235–40.

———. 1990. 'Hierarchies, Jobs, and Bodies: A Theory of Gendered Organizations', *Gender and Society* 4: 139–58.

———. 1991. 'Hierarchy, Jobs, Bodies: A Theory of Gendered Organizations', in Judith Lorber and Susan Farrell, eds, *The Social Construction of Gender.* Newbury Park, Calif.: Sage, 162–79.

———. 2000. 'Rewriting Class, Race, and Gender: Problems in Feminist Rethinking', in Myra Marx Ferree, Judith Lorber, and Beth Hess, eds, *Revisioning Gender.* New York: AltaMira, 44–69.

Acker, Sandra. 1999. *The Realities of Teachers' Work: Never a Dull Moment.* London: Cassell.

Adamic, L., and Eytan Adar. 2005. 'How to Search a Social Network', *Social Networks* 27: 187–203.

Adams, Mary Louise. 1999. *The Trouble with Normal: Post-War Youth and the Making of Heterosexuality.* Toronto: University of Toronto Press.

Adams, Michael. 1997. *Sex in the Snow: Canadian Social Values at the End of the Millennium.* Toronto: Viking.

Adams, Robert M. 1966. *The Evolution of Urban Society.* Chicago: Aldine.

Adams, Tracey L. 1998. 'Combining Gender, Class, and Race: Structuring Relations in the Ontario Dental Profession', *Gender and Society* 12: 578–97.

———. 2000. *A Dentist and a Gentleman: Gender and the Rise of Dentistry in Ontario.* Toronto: University of Toronto Press.

Adelson, N. 2005. 'The Embodiment of Inequity: Health Disparities in Aboriginal Canada', *Canadian Journal of Public Health* 96: S45.

Adler, Patricia A., and Peter Adler. 1995. 'Dynamics of Inclusion and Exclusion in Preadolescent Cliques', *Social Psychology Quarterly* 58, 3: 145–62.

——— and ———. 2006. 'The Deviance Society', *Deviant Behavior* 27: 129–48.

Agnew, Robert. 1985. 'A Revised Strain Theory of Delinquency', *Social Forces* 64, 1: 151–67.

———. 2006. 'General Strain Theory: Current Status and Directions', in F.T. Cullen, J.P. Wright, and K.R. Blevins, eds, *Taking Stock: The Status of Criminological Theory.* New Brunswick, NJ: Transaction.

——— and Lisa Broidy. 1997. 'Gender and Crime: A General Strain Theory Perspective', *Journal of Research in Crime and Delinquency* 34: 275–306.

Agocs, Carol, and Monica Boyd. 1993. 'The Canadian Ethnic Mosaic Recast for the 90s', in James Curtis, Edward Grabb, and Neil Guppy, eds, *Social Inequality in Canada: Patterns, Problems, Policies*, 2nd edn. Scarborough, Ont.: Prentice-Hall Canada, 330–52.

Ahlburg, Dennis A. 1998. 'Julian Simon and the Population Growth Debate', *Population and Development Review* 24: 317–27.

Akyeampong, Ernest B. 2001. 'Fact Sheet on Unionization', *Perspectives on Labour and Income* 13, 3: 46–54.

Alalehto, Tage. 2002. 'Eastern Prostitution from Russia to Sweden and Finland', *Journal of Scandinavian Studies in Criminology and Crime Prevention* 3, 1: 96–111.

Albanese, Patrizia. 2006. 'Small Town, Big Benefits: The Ripple Effect of $7/day Child Care', *Canadian Review of Sociology and Anthropology* 43, 2: 125–40.

Albas, Dan, and Cheryl Albas. 1995. 'Avoiding the Label of Cheater during Exams', in Lorne Tepperman and James Curtis, eds, *Sociology Everyday Life: A Reader*, 2nd edn. Toronto: McGraw-Hill, 217–23.

——— and ———. 2003. 'Aces and Bombers: The Post-exam Impression Management Strategies of Students', in Ramón S. Guerra and Robert Lee Maril, eds, *A Social World: Classic and Contemporary Sociological Readings*, 3rd edn. Boston: Pearson Custom Publishing, 27–36.

——— and ———. 2005. 'Disclaimer Mannerisms of Students: How to Avoid Being Labelled as Cheaters', in Bruce Ravelli, ed., *Exploring Canadian Sociology: A Reader.* Toronto: Pearson/Prentice-Hall, 22–32.

Albrecht, Stan L., and Armand L. Mauss. 1975. 'The Environment as a Social Problem', in Armand L. Mauss, ed., *Social Problems as Social Movements.* Philadelphia: Lippincott, 556–605.

Albury, Rebecca M. 1999. *The Politics of Reproduction.* Sydney, Australia: Allen & Unwin.

Alford, Robert. 1998. *The Craft of Inquiry: Theories, Methods, Evidence.* New York: Oxford University Press.

Ali, Jennifer, and Edward Grabb. 1998. 'Ethnic Origin, Class Origin and Educational Attainment in Canada: Further Evidence on the Mosaic Thesis', *Journal of Canadian Studies* 33: 3–21.

Allahar, Anton. 1994. 'More Than an Oxymoron: The Social Construction of Primordial Attachment', *Canadian Ethnic Studies* 16, 3: 15–63.

———. 1995. *Sociology and the Periphery: Theories and Issues*, 2nd edn. Toronto: Garamond.

——— and James E. Côté. 1998. *Richer and Poorer: The Structure of Inequality in Canada.* Toronto: Lorimer.

Allcorn, Seth. 1997. 'Parallel Virtual Organizations: Managing and Working in the Virtual Workplace', *Administration and Society* 29: 412–39.

Allen, Judith. 1990. 'Do We Need a Theory of the State?', in Sophie Watson, ed., *Playing the State: Australian Feminist Interventions.* London: Verso, 21–37.

Allen, Mary, and Chantal Vaillancourt. 2004. *Class of 2000: Profile of Post-Secondary Graduates and Student Debt.* Ottawa: Statistics Canada.

Altman, Dennis. 1986. *AIDS in the Mind of America.* New York: Doubleday-Anchor.

Alvarez, Rodolfo. 2001. 'The Social Problem as an Enterprise: Values as a Defining Factor', *Social Problems* 48: 3–10.

Alwin, Duane F. 1984. 'Trends in Parental Socialization, Detroit, 1958–1983', *American Journal of Sociology* 90: 359–82.

———. 1990. 'Historical Changes in Parental Orientations to Children', in Patricia Adler and Peter Adler, eds, *Sociological Studies of Child Development*, vol. 3. Greenwich, Conn.: JAI, 65–86.

Amato, Paul. 2004. 'Parenting through Family Transitions', *Social Policy Journal of New Zealand* 23 (Dec.): 31-44.

——— and S.J. Rezac. 1994. 'Contact with Non-resident Parents, Interparental Conflict, and Children's Behavior', *Journal of Family Issues* 15, 2: 191–207.

Andersen, Robert, and Anthony Heath. 2002. 'Class Matters: The Persisting Effects of Contextual Social Class on Individual Voting in Britain, 1964–97', *European Sociological Review* 18: 125–38.

Anderson, Benedict. 1983. *Imagined Communities: Reflections on the Origin and Spread of Nationalism.* London: Verso.

Anderson, Grace. 1974. *Networks of Contact: The Portuguese and Toronto.* Waterloo, Ont.: Wilfrid Laurier University Press.

Anderson, R.A., et al. 1999. '7a-Merhyl-19-Notestosterone (MENT) Maintains Sexual Behavior and More in Hypogonad Men', *Journal of Clinical Endocrinology and Metabolism* 78: 711–16.

Andres Bellamy, Lesley. 1993. 'Life Trajectories, Action, and Negotiating the Transition from High School', in Paul Anisef and Paul Axelrod, eds, *Transitions: Schooling and Employment in Canada.* Toronto: Thompson Educational, 136–57.

Andrews, David M. 1994. 'Capital Mobility and State Autonomy: Toward a Structural Theory of International Monetary Relations', *International Studies Quarterly* 38: 193–218.

Angresano, James. 2005. 'China's Development Strategy: A Game of Chess That Countered Orthodox Development Advice', *Journal of Socio-Economics* 34: 471–98.

Anisef, Paul, Paul Axelrod, Etta Baichman-Anisef, Carl James, and Anton Turritin. 2000. *Opportunity and Uncertainty: Life Course Experiences of the Class of '73.* Toronto: University of Toronto Press.

Anstey, Roger. 1966. *King Leopold's Legacy: The Congo under Belgian Rule, 1908–1960.* London: Oxford University Press.

Antonovsky, Aaron. 1979. *Health, Stress and Coping.* San Francisco: Jossey-Bass.

Apple, Michael W. 1997. 'What Postmodernists Forget: Cultural Capital and Official Knowledge', in A.H. Halsey, Hugh Lauder, Phillip Brown, and Amy Stuart Wells, eds, *Education: Culture, Economy, and Society.* New York: Oxford University Press, 595–604.

Appleton, Lynn M. 1995. 'Rethinking Medicalization: Alcoholism and Anomalies', in Joel Best, ed., *Images of Issues: Typifying Contemporary Social Problems,* 2nd edn. New York: Aldine de Gruyter, 59–80.

Arai, A. Bruce. 2000. 'Changing Motivations for Home-schooling in Canada', *Canadian Journal of Education* 25, 3: 204–17.

Arat-Koc, Sedef. 1990. 'Importing Housewives: Non-citizen Domestic Workers and the Crisis of the Domestic Sphere in Canada', in Meg Luxton, Harriet Rosenberg, and Sedef Arat-Koc, eds, *Through the Kitchen Window: The Politics of Home and Family,* 2nd edn. Toronto: Garamond, 81–103.

———. 1999. 'Gender and Race in "Non-Discriminatory" Immigration Policies in Canada: 1960s to the Present', in Enakshi Dua and Angela Robertson, eds, *Scratching the Surface: Canadian Anti-Racist Feminist Thought.* Toronto: Women's Press.

Archibald, W. Peter. 1976. 'Face-to-Face: The Alienating Effects of Class, Status and Power Divisions', *American Sociological Review* 41: 819–37.

———. 1978. *Social Psychology as Political Economy.* Toronto: McGraw-Hill Ryerson.

Arias, Ernesto, ed. 1993. *The Meaning and Use of Housing.* Aldershot, UK: Avebury.

Ariès, Philippe. 1980. 'Two Successive Motivations for Declining Birth Rates in the West', *Population and Development Review* 6: 645–50.

Armstrong, Pat. 1991. 'Understanding the Numbers: Women in the Film and Television Industry', in Toronto Women in Film and Television, *Changing Focus: The Future for Women in the Canadian Film and Television Industry.* Toronto: Toronto Women in Film and Television, 3–38.

———, Carol Amaratunga, Jocelyne Bernier, Karen Grant, Ann Pederson, and Kay Willson, eds. 2001. *Exposing Privatization: Women and Health Reform in Canada.* Aurora, Ont.: Garamond.

——— and Hugh Armstrong. 1983a. 'Beyond Sexless Class and Classless Sex', *Studies in Political Economy* 10: 7–43.

——— and ———. 1983b. *A Working Majority: What Women Must Do for Pay.* Ottawa: Canadian Advisory Council on the Status of Women.

——— and ———. 1993. *The Double Ghetto: Canadian Women and Their Segregated Work.* Toronto: McClelland & Stewart.

——— and Tamara Daly. 2004. "There are not enough hands': Conditions in Ontario's Long-Term Care Facilities', Report prepared for the Canadian Union of Public Employees (Toronto).

———, Irene Jansen, Erin Connell, and Mavis Jones. 2003. 'Assessing the Impact of Restructuring and Work Reorganization in Long-Term Care', in Penny Van Esterik, ed., *Head, Heart and Hand: Partnerships for Women's Health in Canadian Environments,* volume 1. Toronto: National Network on Environments and Women's Health, 175–217.

Aronson, Hal. 1993. 'Becoming an Environmental Activist: The Process of Transformation from Everyday Life into Making History in the Hazardous Waste Movement', *Journal of Political and Military Sociology* 1: 63–80.

Arthurs, Harry. 1999. 'Constitutionalizing Neo-conservatism and Regional Economic Integration', in Thomas J. Courchene, ed., *Room to Manoeuvre? Globalization and Policy Convergence.* Montreal: McGill-Queen's University Press, 17–74.

Asbridge, M., R.E. Mann, and R. Flam-Zalcman. 2004. 'The Criminalization of Impaired Driving in Canada: Assessing the Deterrent Impact of Canada's First Per Se Law', *Journal of Studies in Alcohol* 65, 4: 450–9.

Assembly of First Nations. 2006. *Royal Commission on Aboriginal People at 10 Years: A Report Card.* Ottawa: Assembly of First Nations.

Atkinson, Anthony B. 2000. *Increased Income Inequality in OECD Countries and the Redistributive Impact of the Government Budget.* Helsinki: World Institute for Development Economics Research, United Nations University.

Atkinson, Michael M., and William D. Coleman. 1989. *The State, Business, and Industrial Change in Canada.* Toronto: University of Toronto Press.

Atwood, Margaret. 1994 [1968]. *The Edible Woman.* Toronto: McClelland & Stewart.

AuCoin, Kathy. 2005. 'Children and Youth as Victims of Violent Crime', *Juristat* 25, 1. Ottawa: Statistics Canada Catalogue no. 85–022–XIE.

Autor, David H., Lawrence F. Katz, and Melissa S. Kearney. 2005. *Trends in US Wage Inequality: Re-assessing the Revisionists.* Cambridge, Mass.: National Bureau of Economic Research, Working Paper 11627.

Axelrod, Paul. 1997. *The Promise of Schooling: Education in Canada, 1800–1914.* Toronto: University of Toronto Press.

Aya, Rod. 1990. *Rethinking Revolutions and Collective Violence: Studies on Concept, Theory, and Method.* Amsterdam: Het Spinhuis.

Azzi, Stephen. 2005. 'Negotiating Cultural Space in the Global Economy: The United States, UNESCO, and the Convention on Cultural Diversity', *International Journal* 60, 3: 765–84.

Babbie, Earl R. 1988. *The Sociological Spirit: Critical Essays in a Critical Science.* Belmont, Calif.: Wadsworth.

Badets, Jane, and Tina W.L. Chui. 1994. *Canada's Changing Immigrant Population.* Ottawa: Statistics Canada.

Baer, Doug. 2004. 'Educational Credentials and the Changing Occupational Structure.' in James Curtis, Edward Grabb, and Neil Guppy, eds, *Social Inequality in Canada: Patterns, Problems, and Policies*, 4th edn. Toronto: Pearson Prentice-Hall, 115–30.

Bafoil, François. 1998. 'Weber critique de Marx: Elements d'une interpretation de la crise des systèmes bureaucratiques communistes', *L'Année sociologique* 48: 385–415.

Bailey, C.B., P.R. Sinclair, and M. Dubois. 2004. 'Future Forests: Forecasting Social and Environmental Consequences of Genetic Engineering in Forestry', *Society and Natural Resources* 17: 641–50.

Baines, Carol T., Patricia M. Evans, and Sheila Neysmith, eds. 1998. *Women's Caring: Feminist Perspectives on Social Welfare*, 2nd edn. Toronto: Oxford University Press.

Baird, P. 1997. 'Individual Interests, Societal Interests, and Reproductive Technologies', *Perspectives in Biology and Medicine* 40, 3: 440–52.

Baird, Vanessa. 2001. *The No-Nonsense Guide to Sexual Diversity.* Toronto: Between the Lines.

Bakan, Abigail, and Daiva K. Stasiulis. 1994. 'Foreign Domestic Worker Policy in Canada and the Social Boundaries of Modern Citizenship', *Science and Society* 58, 1: 7–33.

Baker, Maureen. 1995. *Canadian Family Policies: Cross-national Comparisons.* Toronto: University of Toronto Press.

———. 2001. *Families, Labour and Love: Family Diversity in a Changing World.* Vancouver: University of British Columbia Press.

———. 2005. 'Medically Assisted Conception: Revolutionizing Family or Perpetuating a Nuclear and Gendered Model?', *Journal of Comparative Family Studies* 36, 4: 521–43.

———. 2006. *Restructuring Family Policies: Divergences and Convergences.* Toronto: University of Toronto Press.

———. 2007. *Choices and Constraints in Family Life.* Toronto: Oxford University Press.

——— and David Tippin. 1999. *Poverty, Social Assistance and the Employability of Mothers: Restructuring Welfare States.* Toronto: University of Toronto Press.

Baker, Michael, and Gary Solon. 2003. 'Earning Dynamics and Inequality among Canadian Men, 1976–1992: Evidence from Longitudinal Income Tax Records', *Journal of Labor Economics* 21: 289–321.

Baker, P.M. 1991. 'Socialization after Death: The Might of the Living Dead', in B.B. Hess and E.W. Markson, eds, *Growing Old in America.* New Brunswick, NJ: Transaction, 539–51.

Bales, Robert F. 1950. *Interaction Process Analysis: A Method for the Study of Small Groups.* Chicago: University of Chicago Press.

Balnke, D.D., and V. Silva. 2004. *Tobacco Control Legislation: An Introductory Guide.* Geneva: World Health Organization.

Balter, Michael. 2001. 'What—or Who—Did in the Neanderthals?', *Science* 293: 1980–1.

Bancroft, John. 2002. 'Biological Factors in Human Sexuality', *Journal of Sex Research* 39: 15–21.

Bandura, Albert. 1973. *Aggression: A Social Learning Analysis.* Englewood Cliffs, NJ: Prentice-Hall.

Banton, Michael. 1977. *The Idea of Race.* London: Tavistock.

———. 1987. *Racial Theories.* Cambridge: Cambridge University Press.

Barak, Azy, and William Fisher. 2001. 'Toward an Internet-driven, Theoretically-based, Innovative Approach to Sex Education', *Journal of Sex Research* 38, 4: 324–32.

Barker, John. 2003. 'Dowry', in James J. Ponzetti, ed., *International Encyclopedia of Marriage and Family*, 2nd edn. New York: Thomson Gale, 495–6.

Barnes, Barry. 1988. *The Nature of Power.* Cambridge: Polity.

Barron, Martin, and Michael Kimmel. 2000. 'Sexual Violence in Three Pornographic Media: Towards a Sociological Explanation', *Journal of Sex Research* 37, 2: 161–8.

Barry, Brian. 1978 [1970]. *Sociologists, Economists and Democracy.* Chicago: University of Chicago Press.

Bartsch, Robert, Theresa Burnett, Tommye Diller, and Elizabeth Rankin-Williams. 2000. 'Gender Representation in Television Commercials: Updating an Update', *Sex Roles* 43: 735–43.

Bashevkin, Sylvia. 1985. *Toeing the Lines: Women and Party Politics in English Canada.* Toronto: University of Toronto Press.

———. 2006. *Tales of Two Cities: Women and Municipal Restructuring in London and Toronto.* Vancouver: University of British Columbia Press.

Basran, Gurcharn, and B. Singh Bolaria. 2003. *The Sikhs in Canada: Migration, Race, Class and Gender.* New Delhi: Oxford University Press.

Bassett, Isabella. 1985. *The Bassett Report.* Toronto: Collins.

Baumrind, Diana. 1971. 'Current Patterns of Parental Authority', *Developmental Psychology Monographs* 4: 1–107.

Baxter, Janine. 2000. 'The Joys and Justice of Housework', *Sociology* 34, 4: 609–31.

Beaujot, Roderic. 2000. *Earning and Caring in Canadian Families.* Peterborough, Ont.: Broadview.

———, Ellen M. Gee, R. Fernando, and Z.R. Ravanera. 1995. *Family over the Life Course: Current Demographic Analysis.* Ottawa: Statistics Canada, Demography Division.

——— and Kevin McQuillan. 1982. *Growth and Dualism: The Demographic Development of Canadian Society.* Toronto: Gage.

Beauvoir, Simone de. 1957 [1949]. *The Second Sex,* trans. H.M. Parshley. New York: Vintage.

Beck, Ulrich. 1992. *Risk Society: Towards a New Modernity,* trans. Mark Ritter. London: Sage.

———. 1996. 'World Risk Society as Cosmopolitan Society? Ecological Questions in a Framework of Manufactured Uncertainties', *Theory, Culture, and Society* 13, 4: 1–32.

Becker, Gary. 1960. 'An Economic Analysis of Fertility', in *Demographic and Economic Change in Developed Countries: A Conference of the Universities–National Bureau Committee for Economic Research.* Princeton, NJ: Princeton University Press, 209–40.

Becker, Howard. 1952. 'Social Class Variations in the Teacher–Student Relationship', *Journal of Educational Sociology* 25: 451–65.

———. 1963. *Outsiders: Studies in the Sociology of Deviance.* New York: Free Press.

———. 1982. *Art Worlds.* Berkeley: University of California Press.

Beck-Gernsheim, Elisabeth. 2002. *Reinventing the Family: In Search of New Lifestyles.* Cambridge: Polity.

Beiser, Morton, Feng Hou, Ilian Hyman, and Michel Tousignant. 1999. 'Immigrant Mental Health', Human Resources Development Canada, *Applied Research Bulletin* (Fall): 20–2.

Bélanger, Alain. 2002. *Report on the Demographic Situation in Canada 2001: Current Demographic Analysis.* Ottawa: Statistics Canada.

———. 2006. *Report on the Demographic Situation in Canada 2003 and 2004.* Ottawa: Statistics Canada Catalogue no. 91–209–XIE.

Bell, Daniel. 1973. *The Coming of Post-industrial Society.* New York: Basic Books.

———. 1975. 'Ethnicity and Social Change', in Nathan Glazer and Daniel P. Moynihan with Corinne Saposs Schelling, eds, *Ethnicity: Theory and Experience.* Cambridge, Mass.: Harvard University Press, 141–74.

———. 1979. *The Cultural Contradictions of Capitalism,* 2nd edn. London: Heinemann.

Bell, Edward A. 1993. *Social Classes and Social Credit in Alberta.* Montreal: McGill-Queen's University Press.

Bell, Shannon. 1994. *Reading, Writing and Rewriting the Prostitute Body.* Bloomington: Indiana University Press.

Bellah, Robert. 1996. *Habits of the Heart: Individualism and Commitment in American Life.* Berkeley: University of California Press.

Belsky, Jay. 1985. 'Exploring Individual Differences in Marital Change across the Transition to Parenthood: The Role of Violated Expectations', *Journal of Marriage and the Family* 47: 1037–44.

Bendix, Reinhard. 1956. *Work and Authority in Industry.* New York: Harper and Row.

Benford, Robert D., and David A. Snow. 2000. 'Framing Processes and Social Movements: An Overview and Assessment', *Annual Review of Sociology* 26: 611–39.

Benkert, Holly. 2002. 'Liberating Insights from a Cross-Cultural Sexuality Study about Women', *American Behavioral Scientist* 45, 8: 1197–1207.

Bensman, Joseph. 1987. 'Mediterranean and Total Bureaucracies: Some Additions to the Weberian Theory of Bureaucracy', *International Journal of Politics, Culture and Society* 1, 1: 62–78.

Benton, Ted. 1994. 'Biology and Social Theory in the Environmental Debate', in Michael Redclift and Ted Benton, eds, *Social Theory and the Global Environment.* London: Routledge, 28–50.

Berger, Peter L. 1967. *The Sacred Canopy: Elements of a Sociological Theory of Religion.* Garden City, NY: Doubleday.

———, ed. 1999. *The Desecularization of the World: Resurgent Religion and World Politics.* Grand Rapids, Mich.: Eerdmans.

——— and Brigitte Berger. 1975. *Sociology: A Biographical Approach,* 2nd edn. New York: Basic Books.

——— and Thomas Luckmann. 1966. *The Social Construction of Reality: Treatise in the Sociology of Knowledge.* Garden City, NY: Anchor.

Bernard, Andrew B., and J. Bradford Jensen. 2000. 'Understanding Increasing and Decreasing Wage Inequality', in Robert C. Feenstra, ed., *The Impact of International Trade on Wages.* Chicago: University of Chicago Press, 227–61.

Bernburg, J.G., M.D. Krohn, and C.J. Rivera. 2006. 'Official Labeling, Criminal Embeddedness, and Subsequent Delinquency: A Longitudinal Test of Labeling Theory', *Journal of Research in Crime and Delinquency* 43, 1: 67–88.

Bernstein, Basil. 1977. 'Class and Pedagogies: Visible and Invisible', in Jerome Karabel and A.H. Halsey, eds, *Power and Ideology in Education.* New York: Oxford University Press, 511–34.

Bernstein, Steven, and Christopher Gore. 2001. 'Policy Implications of the Kyoto Protocol for Canada', *ISUMA: Canadian Journal of Policy Research* 2, 4: 26–36.

Berton, Pierre. 1975. *Hollywood's Canada: The Americanization of Our National Image.* Toronto: McClelland & Stewart.

Bertone, Andrea Marie. 2000. 'Sexual Trafficking in Women: International Political Economy and the Politics of Sex', *Gender Issues* 18, 1: 4–22.

Berwick, Donald. 2002. 'We All Have AIDS: Case for Reducing the Cost of HIV Drugs to Zero', *British Medical Journal* 324: 214–18.

Bessel, Richard. 2004. 'The Nazi Capture of Power', *Journal of Contemporary History* 39: 169–88.

Best, Joel. 1989. 'Extending the Constructionist Perspective: A Conclusion—and an Introduction', in Joel Best, ed., *Images of Issues: Typifying Contemporary Social Problems.* New York: Aldine de Gruyter, 243–53.

———. 1993. 'But Seriously Folks: The Limitations of the Strict Constructionist Interpretation of Social Problems', in James A. Holstein and Gale Miller, eds, *Reconsidering*

Social Constructionism: Debates in Social Problems Theory. New York: Aldine de Gruyter, 129–47.

———. 1999. *Random Violence: How We Talk About New Crime and New Victims.* Berkeley: University of California Press.

———. 2001. *Damned Lies and Statistics: Untangling Numbers from Media, Politicians and Activists.* Berkeley: University of California Press.

———, ed. 2001. *How Claims Spread: Cross-National Diffusion of Social Problems.* New York: Aldine de Gruyter.

———. 2004. 'Deviance May Be Alive But Is It Intellectually Lively? A Reaction to Goode', *Deviant Behavior* 25: 483–92.

———. 2008. *Social Problems.* New York: Norton.

Beyer, Peter. 1997. 'Religious Vitality in Canada: The Complementarity of Religious Market and Secularization Perspectives', *Journal for the Scientific Study of Religion* 36: 272–88.

———. 2000. 'Modern Forms of the Religious Life: Denomination, Church and Invisible Religion in Canada, the United States, and Europe', in David Lyon and Marguerite Van Die, eds, *Rethinking Church, State, and Modernity: Canada between Europe and America.* Toronto: University of Toronto Press, 189–210.

Bibby, Reginald. 1987. *Fragmented Gods: The Poverty and Potential of Religion in Canada.* Toronto: Irwin.

———. 1993. *Unknown Gods: The Ongoing Story of Religion in Canada.* Toronto: Stoddart.

———. 2001. *Canada's Teens: Today, Yesterday and Tomorrow.* Toronto: Stoddart.

———. 2002. *Restless Gods: The Renaissance of Religion in Canada.* Toronto: Stoddart.

———. 2004. 'Section 2–Dating, Sexuality and Cohabitation', *The Future of Families Project: A Survey of Canadian Hopes and Dreams.* Ottawa: Vanier Institute of the Family, 11–24.

———. 2006. *The Boomer Factor: What Canada's Most Famous Generation Is Leaving Behind.* Toronto: Bastion Books.

Bielby, William, and James Baron. 1984. 'Men and Women at Work: Sex Segregation and Statistical Discrimination', *American Journal of Sociology* 91: 759–99.

Bies, Robert J., and Thomas M. Tripp. 1996. 'Beyond Distrust: "Getting Even" and the Need for Revenge', in Roderick M. Kramer and Tom R. Tyler, eds, *Trust in Organizations: Frontiers of Theory and Research.* Thousand Oaks, Calif.: Sage, 246–60.

Bingham, Richard D., Roy E. Green, and Sammis B. White, eds. 1987. *The Homeless in Contemporary Society.* Beverly Hills, Calif.: Sage.

Birg, Herwig. 1995. *World Population Projections for the 21st Century: Theoretical Interpretations and Quantitative Simulations.* Frankfurt: Campus Verlag; New York: St Martin's.

Birke, Lynda. 1999. *Biology, Bodies and Feminism.* Edinburgh: Edinburgh University Press.

Birnbaum, Pierre. 1988. *States and Collective Action: The European Experience.* Cambridge: Cambridge University Press.

Bishop, Clifford. 1996. *Sex and Spirit.* Alexandria, Va: Time-Life Books.

Bishop, Jack. 2005. 'Building International Empires of Sound: Concentrations of Power and Property in the "Global" Music Market', *Popular Music and Society* 28, 4: 443–71.

Bissoondath, Neil. 1994. *Selling Illusions: The Cult of Multiculturalism.* Toronto: Penguin.

Bittman, Michael, and Jocelyn Pixley. 1997. *The Double Life of the Family: Myth, Hope and Experience.* Sydney, Australia: Allen & Unwin.

Blackledge, David, and Barry Hunt. 1985. *Sociological Interpretations of Education.* London: Routledge.

Blain, Michael. 1992. 'Fighting Words: What We Can Learn from Hitler's Hyperbole', in Gary Alan Fine, John Johnson, and Harvey A. Farberman, eds, *Sociological Slices: Introductory Readings from the Interactionist Perspective.* Greenwich, Conn.: JAI, 171–92.

Blau, Peter M. 1963. *The Dynamics of Bureaucracy.* Chicago: University of Chicago Press.

Bleecker, E. Timothy, and Sarah K. Murnen. 2005. 'Fraternity Membership, the Display of Degrading Sexual Images of Women, and Rape Myth Acceptance', *Sex Roles: A Journal of Research* 53, 7/8: 487–93.

Bliss, Michael. 1991. *Plague: A Story of Smallpox in Montreal.* Toronto: HarperCollins.

———. 1992. *Banting: A Biography*, 2nd edn. Toronto: University of Toronto Press.

Block, Fred. 1980. 'Beyond Relative Autonomy: State Managers as Historical Subjects', in Ralph Miliband and John Saville, eds, *The Socialist Register, 1980.* London: Merlin, 227–40.

Bloemraad, Irene. 2002. 'The North American Naturalization Gap: An Institutional Approach to Citizenship Acquisition in the United States and Canada', *International Migration Review* 36: 193–228.

Blumer, Herbert. 1937. 'Social Psychology', in E.P. Schmidt, ed., *Man and Society: A Substantive Introduction to the Social Sciences.* New York: Prentice-Hall, 148–98.

———. 1969. *Symbolic Interactionism: Perspective and Method.* Englewood Cliffs, NJ: Prentice-Hall and Berkeley: University of California Press.

———. 1971. 'Social Problems as Collective Behavior', *Social Problems*, 8, 3: 298–396.

Blustain, Sarah. 2000. 'The New Gender Wars', *Psychology Today* (Nov.–Dec.): 43–8.

Bohm, Robert M. 1997. *A Primer on Crime and Delinquency.* Belmont, Calif.: Wadsworth.

Bolaria, B. Singh, and Peter Li. 1988. *Racial Oppression in Canada*, 2nd edn. Toronto: Garamond.

Bongaarts, John. 1978. 'A Framework for Analyzing the Proximate Determinants of Fertility', *Population and Development Review* 4, 1: 105–32.

——— and Rodolfo Bulatao, eds. 2000. *Beyond Six Billion: Forecasting the World's Population.* Washington: National Academy Press.

Bookchin, Murray. 1989. *Remaking Society.* Montreal: Black Rose.

Booth, Alan, and John N. Edwards. 1990. 'Transmission of Marital and Family Quality over the Generations: The Effect of Parental Divorce and Unhappiness', *Journal of Divorce* 13: 41–58.

Boritch, Helen. 1997. *Fallen Women: Women, Crime and Criminal Justice in Canada.* Toronto: Nelson.

Borjas, George J., Richard B. Freeman, and Lawrence F. Katz. 1997. 'How Much Do Immigration and Trade Affect Labor Market Outcomes?', *Brookings Papers on Economic Activity* 1: 1–67.

Boserup, Ester. 1965. *The Conditions of Agricultural Growth: The Economics of Agrarian Change under Population Pressure.* Chicago: Aldine.

———. 1981. *Population and Technological Change: A Study of Long-Term Trends.* Chicago: University of Chicago Press.

Bostock, L. 2002. '"God, She's Gonna Report Me": The Ethics of Child Protection in Poverty Research', *Children and Society* 16, 4: 273–83.

Boston Women's Health Collective. 1971. *Our Bodies, Our Selves.* Toronto: New Hogtown Press.

Bottomore, Tom. 1979. *Political Sociology.* London: Hutchinson University Press.

Bouchard, Brigitte, and John Zhao. 2000. 'University Education: Recent Trends in Participation, Accessibility and Returns', *Education Quarterly Review* 6, 4: 24–32.

Bourdieu, Pierre. 1984 [1979]. *Distinction: A Social Critique of the Judgement of Taste,* trans. Richard Nice. London: Routledge.

———. 1997a. 'The Forms of Capital', trans. Richard Nice, in A.H. Halsey, Hugh Lauder, Phillip Brown, and Amy Stuart Wells, eds, *Education: Culture, Economy, and Society.* Oxford: Oxford University Press, 46–58.

———. 1997b. 'From the Royal House to the State's Logic: A Model of the Genesis of the Bureaucratic Field / De la maison du roi a la raison d'état: un modèle de la genese du champ bureaucratique', *Actes de la recherché en sciences sociales* 118 (June): 55–68.

——— and Jean-Claude Passeron. 1979. *The Inheritors: French Students and Their Relations to Culture,* trans. Richard Nice. Chicago: University of Chicago Press.

Bourne, Paul, Liza McCoy, and Myra Novogrodsky, eds. 1997. 'Gender and Schooling', *Orbit* 28, 1 (special issue).

Bowlby, Jeffrey, and Kathryn McMullen. 2002. *At a Crossroads: First Results for the 18- to 20-Year-Old Cohort of the Youth in Transition Survey.* Ottawa: Human Resources Development Canada.

Bowles, Samuel, and Herbert Gintis. 1976. *Schooling in Capitalist America: Education Reform and the Contradictions of Economic Life.* New York: Basic Books.

Boyd, Monica. 1992. 'Gender, Visible Minority, and Immigrant Earnings Inequality: Reassessing an Employment Equity Premise', in Vic Satzewich, ed., *Deconstructing a Nation: Immigration, Multiculturalism and Racism in '90s Canada.* Halifax: Fernwood, 279–321.

———. 1999. 'Integrating Gender, Language and Visible Minority Groups', in Shiva S. Halli and Leo Driedger, eds, *Immigrant Canada: Demographic, Economic and Social Challenges.* Toronto: University of Toronto Press, 282–306.

Boyd, Susan B., ed. 1997. *Challenging the Public/Private Divide: Feminism, Law and Public Policy.* Toronto: University of Toronto Press.

Bozeman, Barry, and Hal G. Rainey. 1998. 'Organizational Rules and the "Bureaucratic Personality"', *American Journal of Political Science* 42: 163–89.

Bradbury, Bettina. 1982. 'The Fragmented Family: Family Strategies in the Face of Death, Illness, and Poverty, Montreal, 1860–1885', in Joy Parr, ed., *Childhood and Family in Canadian History.* Toronto: McClelland & Stewart, 109–28.

———. 1993. *Working Families: Age, Gender, and Daily Survival in Industrializing Montreal.* Toronto: McClelland & Stewart.

———. 2005. 'Social, Economic, and Cultural Origins of Contemporary Families', in M. Baker, ed., *Families: Changing Trends in Canada,* 5th edn. Toronto: McGraw-Hill Ryerson, 71–98.

Braithewaite, John. 1979. *Inequality, Crime and Public Policy.* London: Routledge & Kegan Paul.

Brannigan, Augustine, and William Zwerman. 2001. 'The Real "Hawthorne Effect"', *Society* 38, 2: 55–60.

Braverman, Harry. 1974. *Labor and Monopoly Capital: The Degradation of Work in the Twentieth Century.* New York: Monthly Review Press.

Brehony, Kevin J. and Rosemary Deem. 2005. 'Challenging the Post-Fordist/Flexible Organization Thesis: The Case of Reformed Educational Organizations', *British Journal of Sociology of Education* 26, 3: 395–414.

Breton, Raymond. 1983. 'West Indian, Chinese and European Ethnic Groups in Toronto: Perceptions of Problems and Resources', in Jean Leonard Elliott, ed., *Two Nations, Many Cultures: Ethnic Groups in Canada.* Scarborough, Ont.: Prentice-Hall, 425–43.

———, Jean Burnet, Norbert Hartmann, Wsevolod Isajiw, and Jos Lennards. 1977. 'The Impact of Ethnic Groups on Canadian Society: Research Issues', in Wsevolod Isajiw, ed., *Identities: The Impact of Ethnicity on Canadian Society.* Toronto: Peter Martin, 191–213.

———, Wsevolod Isajiw, Warren Kalbach, and Jeffrey G. Reitz. 1990. *Ethnic Identity and Equality: Varieties of Experience in a Canadian City.* Toronto: University of Toronto Press.

Brickell, Chris. 2006. 'A Symbolic Interactionist History of Sexuality', *Rethinking History* 10, 3: 415–32.

Briskin, Linda. 1992. 'Socialist Feminism: From the Standpoint of Practice', in M. Patricia Connelly and Pat Armstrong, eds, *Feminism in Action: Studies in Political Economy.* Toronto: Canadian Scholars' Press, 267–93.

Brock, Deborah R. 1998. *Making Work, Making Trouble: Prostitution as a Social Problem.* Toronto: University of Toronto Press.

Brockman, Joan. 2001. *Gender in the Legal Profession: Fitting or Breaking the Mould.* Vancouver: University of British Columbia Press.

Brodie, Janine. 1985. *Women and Politics in Canada.* Toronto: McGraw-Hill Ryerson.

———. 1996. *Women and Canadian Public Policy.* Toronto: Harcourt Brace.

Bromley, David G., and Anson D. Shupe Jr. 1981. *Strange Gods: The Great American Cult Scare.* Boston: Beacon.

Bromley, Simon. 1999. 'Marxism and Globalization', in Andrew Gamble, David Marsh, and Tony Tant, eds, *Marxism and Social Science.* Urbana: University of Illinois Press, 280–301.

Brook, Barbara. 1999. *Feminist Perspectives on the Body.* London: Longman.

Brower, Ralph S., and Mitchel Y. Abolafia. 1997. 'Bureaucratic Politics: The View from Below', *Journal of Public Administration Research and Theory* 7: 305–31.

Brown, Archie. 1996. *The Gorbachev Factor.* Oxford: Oxford University Press.

Brown, Craig, ed. 2002. *The Illustrated History of Canada.* Toronto: Key Porter.

Brown, Louise. 2002. 'Two-Tier Grade Schooling Feared', *Toronto Star*, 31 May, A1, A26.

Brown, Phil, and Susan Masterson-Allen. 1994. 'The Toxic Waste Movement: A New Type of Activism', *Society and Natural Resources* 7, 3: 269–87.

Brown, Rupert. 1995. *Prejudice: Its Social Psychology.* Oxford: Blackwell.

Brownmiller, Susan. 1975. *Against Our Will: Men, Women and Rape.* New York: Simon & Schuster.

Bruce, Steve. 1996. *Religion in the Modern World.* Oxford: Oxford University Press.

———. 2001. 'The Curious Case of the Unnecessary Recantation: Berger and Secularization', in Linda Woodhead, ed., *Peter Berger and the Study of Religion.* London: Routledge, 87–100.

Brumann, Christoph. 1998. 'The Anthropological Study of Globalization: Towards an Agenda for the Second Phase', *Anthropos* 93: 495–506.

Bryant, Bunyon, and Paul Mohai, eds. 1992. *Race and the Incidence of Environmental Hazard: A Time for Discourse.* Boulder, Colo.: Westview.

Bryant, Heather. 1990. *The Infertility Dilemma: Reproductive Technologies and Prevention.* Ottawa: Canadian Advisory Council on the Status of Women, Feb.

Brym, Robert J. 1980. 'Regional Social Structure and Agrarian Radicalism in Canada: Alberta, Saskatchewan and New Brunswick', in Alexander Himelfarb and C. James Richardson, eds, *People, Power and Process: A Reader.* Toronto: McGraw-Hill Ryerson, 344–53.

——— and Bonnie Fox. 1989. *From Culture to Power: The Sociology of English Canada.* Toronto: Oxford University Press.

Brzozowski, J.A., A. Taylor-Butts, and S. Johnson. 2006. 'Victimization and Offending among the Aboriginal Population in Canada', *Juristat* 26, 3.

Bulatao, Rodolfo. 1998. *The Value of Family Planning Programs in Developing Countries.* Santa Monica, Calif.: Rand.

——— and John Casterline, eds. 2001. 'Global Fertility Transition', *Population and Development Review* 27 (suppl.).

Bullard, Robert. 1990. *Dumping in Dixie: Race, Class and Environmental Quality.* Boulder, Colo.: Westview.

Bullock, Cathy Ferrand, and Jason Culbert. 2002. 'Coverage of Domestic Violence Fatalities by Newspapers in Washington State', *Journal of Interpersonal Violence* 17: 475–99.

Bulman, Donna, Diana Coben, and Nguyen Van Anh. 2004. 'Educating Women about HIV/AIDS: Some International Comparisons', *Compare* 34, 2: 141–59.

Bunge, V.P., H. Johnson, and T.A. Baldé. 2005. *Exploring Crime Patterns.* Ottawa: Canadian Centre for Justice Statistics and Time Series Analysis Centre, Statistics Canada.

Burgess, Ernest. 1925. 'The Growth of the City: An Introduction to a Research Project', in Robert E. Park, Ernest Burgess, and R. McKenzie, eds, *The City.* Chicago: University of Chicago Press, 47–62.

Burningham, Kate, and Geoff Cooper. 1999. 'Being Constructive: Social Constructionism and the Environment', *Sociology* 33: 297–316.

Burstyn, Varda. 1983. 'Masculine Domination and the State', in Ralph Miliband and John Saville, eds, *The Socialist Register, 1983.* London: Merlin, 45–89.

———. 1999. *The Rites of Men: Manhood, Politics and the Culture of Sport.* Toronto: University of Toronto Press.

Burt, Ronald S., and Marc Knez. 1996. 'Trust and Third-Party Gossip', in Roderick M. Kramer and Tom R. Tyler, eds, *Trust in Organizations: Frontiers of Theory and Research.* Thousand Oaks, Calif.: Sage, 68–89.

Burtless, Gary. 1998. *Globaphobia: Confronting Fears about Open Trade.* Washington: Brookings Institution.

Bush, Diane Mitsch, and Roberta G. Simmons. 1981. 'Socialization Processes over the Life Course', in Morris Rosenberg and Ralph Turner, eds, *Social Psychology: Sociological Perspectives.* New York: Basic Books, 133–64.

Bussière, Patrick, Fernando Cartwright, Robert Crocker, Xin Ma, Jillian Oderkirk, and Yanhong Zhang. 2001. *Measuring Up: The Performance of Canada's Youth in Reading, Mathematics and Science.* Ottawa: Statistics Canada.

———, ———, and Tamara Knighton. 2004. *Measuring Up: Canadian Results of the OECD PISA Study: The Performance of Canada's Youth in Mathematics, Reading, Science and Problem Solving, 2003. First Findings for Canadians Aged 15.* Ottawa: Minister of Industry.

Butler, Judith. 1992. 'Contingent Foundations: Feminism and the Question of "Postmodernism"', in Judith Butler and Joan W. Scott, eds, *Feminists Theorize the Political.* New York: Routledge, 3–21.

———. 2006 [1990]. *Gender Troubles: Feminism and the Subversion of Identity.* New York: Routledge Classics.

Butlin, George, and Jillian Oderkirk. 1996. *Educational Attainment: A Key to Autonomy and Authority in the Workplace.* Ottawa: Statistics Canada.

Butsch, Richard. 1992. 'Class and Gender in Four Decades of Television Situation Comedy: Plus ça Change . . .', *Critical Studies in Mass Communication* 9: 387–99.

———. 1995. 'Ralph, Fred, Archie and Homer: Why Television Keeps Recreating the White Male Working-Class Buffoon', in Gail Dines and Jean M. Humez, eds, *Gender, Race and Class in Media: A Text-Reader.* Thousand Oaks, Calif.: Sage, 403–12.

——— and Lynda M. Glennon. 1983. 'Social Class: Frequency Trends in Domestic Situation Comedy, 1946-1978', *Journal of Broadcasting* 27, 1: 77–81.

Buttel, Frederick. 1976. 'Social Science and the Environment: Competing Theories', *Social Science Quarterly* 57: 307–23.

———. 1978. 'Environmental Sociology: A New Paradigm?', *American Sociologist* 13: 252–6.

———. 1987. 'New Directions in Environmental Sociology', *Annual Review of Sociology* 13: 465–88.

——— and Peter J. Taylor. 1992. 'Environmental Sociology and Global Environmental Change: A Critical Assessment', *Society and Natural Resources* 5: 211–30.

Butters, Jennifer, and Patricia Erickson. 2002. 'Addictions as Deviant Behaviour: Normalizing the Pleasures of Intoxication', in Lori G. Beaman, ed., *New Perspectives on Deviance: The Construction of Deviance in Everyday Life.* Toronto: Prentice-Hall Allyn and Bacon, 67–84.

Butz, William P., and Michael P. Ward. 1979. 'The Emergence of Countercyclical US Fertility', *American Economic Review* 69: 318–28.

Byers, Lisa, Ken Menzies, and William O'Grady. 2004. 'The Impact of Computer Variables on the Viewing and Sending of Sexually Explicit Material on the Internet: Testing Cooper's "Triple-A Engine"', *Canadian Journal of Human Sexuality* 13, 3/4: 157–69.

Cain, Mead. 1983. 'Fertility as an Adjustment to Risk', *Population and Development Review* 9: 688–702.

Cairney, John. 1999. 'Socio-economic Status and Self-Rated Health among Older Canadians', *Canadian Journal on Aging* 19: 456–77.

Calavita, K., and H.N. Pontell. 1991. '"Other People's Money" Revisited: Collective Embezzlement in the Savings and Loan Insurance Industries', *Social Problems* 38, 1: 94–112.

Caldwell, John C. 1976. 'Toward a Restatement of Demographic Transition Theory', *Population and Development Review* 2: 321–66.

——— and Pat Caldwell. 1996. 'The African AIDS Epidemic', *Scientific American* (Mar.): 62–8.

———, James F. Phillips, and Barkat-e-Khuda, eds. 2002. 'Family Planning Programs in the Twenty-First Century', *Studies in Family Planning* 33, 1 (special issue).

Calliste, Agnes. 1993. 'Sleeping Car Porters in Canada: An Ethnically Submerged Split Labour Market', in Graham S. Lowe and Harvey Krahn, eds, *Work in Canada: Readings in the Sociology of Work and Industry*. Scarborough, Ont.: Nelson, 139–53.

Calvert, Barbara, and Warren R. Stanton. 1992. 'Perceptions of Parenthood: Similarities and Differences between 15-Year-Old Girls and Boys', *Adolescence* 27: 315–28.

Campbell, Donald T., and Julian C. Stanley. 1970. *Experimental and Quasi-experimental Designs for Research*. Chicago: Rand McNally.

Campey, John. 2002. 'Immigrant Children in Our Classrooms: Beyond ESL', *Education Canada* 42, 3: 44–7.

Canada. 1991. Broadcasting Act. *Statutes of Canada* 1991, c. 11.

———. 2006. *Senators and Members—Occupations of Parliamentarians*. Ottawa: Library of Parliament. At: <www.parl.gc.ca/information/about/people/key/occupations/index.asp?lang=E&hea=1&leg=1>.

———, Citizenship and Immigration Canada. 2004. *Immigration Overview, 2004*. At: <www.cic.gc.ca/english/pdf/pub/facts2004.pdf>.

———, Royal Commission on Bilingualism and Biculturalism. 1967. *Report of the Royal Commission on Bilingualism and Biculturalism*. Ottawa: Queen's Printer.

Canada Health Coalition. 2006. 'Health Minister Clement Must Divest or Resign', press release, 20 June. At: <www.healthcoalition.ca/2tierTony.html>.

Canada Mortgage and Housing Corporation. 2006. 'Brownfield Redevelopment for Housing: Case Studies', *CMHC Research Highlight*, Socio-economic series 06–015, Aug.

Canadian Health Services Research Foundation. 2001. *Myth: The Aging Population Will Overwhelm the Healthcare System*. Ottawa: Canadian Health Services Research Foundation.

———. 2002. *Myth: For-Profit Ownership of Facilities Would Lead to Better Health Care*. Ottawa: Canadian Health Services Research Foundation.

Canadian Institute of Child Health. 1994. *The Health of Canada's Children: A CICH Profile*. Ottawa: Canadian Institute on Child Health.

Canadian Press. 2006a. 'Provinces Should Keep Gas Revenues: McGuinty'. At: <www.ctv.ca/ArticleNews/print/CTVNews>.

———. 2006b. 'Alouettes Coach Popp Hoping His Players Refrain from Sex during Grey Cup Week', 15 Nov. At: <www.cbc.ca/cp/football/051115/f111527A.html>.

Canadian Radio-television and Telecommunications Commission. 1998. *Commercial Radio Policy*. Broadcasting Public Notice 1998-41, 30 Apr. Ottawa: CRTC.

———. 1999. *New Media*. Broadcasting Public Notice 1999-84, 17 May 1999. Ottawa: CRTC.

Card, David E., and John DiNardo. 2002. *Skill Biased Technological Change and Rising Wage Inequality: Some Problems and Puzzles*. Cambridge, Mass.: National Bureau of Economic Research.

Cardew, Ben. 2006. 'EMI Puts Merger on Hold', *Music Week*, 5 Aug., 1.

Cardoso, Fernando Luiz. 2002. '"Fishermen": Masculinity and Sexuality in a Brazilian Fishing Community', *Sexuality and Culture* 6, 4: 45–72.

Carley, Kathleen. 1989. 'The Value of Cognitive Foundations for Dynamic Social Theory', *Journal of Mathematical Sociology* 14, 2/3: 171–208.

———. 1991. 'A Theory of Group Stability', *American Sociological Review* 56: 331–54.

Carlstein, Tommy. 1978. 'A Time-Geographic Approach to Time Allocation and Socio-ecological Systems', in William Michelson, ed., *Public Policy in Temporal Perspective*. The Hague: Mouton, 69–82.

Carpenter, Laura. 1998. 'From Girls into Women: Scripts for Sexuality and Romance in *Seventeen* Magazine, 1974–1994', *Journal of Sex Research* 35, 2: 158–68.

Carr, Lynn. 1999. 'Cognitive Scripting and Sexual Identification: Essentialism, Anarchism, and Constructionism', *Symbolic Interactionism* 22, 1: 1–24.

Carre, Dominique, and Sylvie Craipeau. 1996. 'Entre delocalisation et mobilité: analyse des strategies entrepreneuriales de teletravail', *Technologies de l'information et société* 8: 333–54.

Carroll, Michael. 2005. 'Who Owns Democracy? Explaining the Long-Running Debate over Canadian/American Value Differences', *Canadian Review of Sociology and Anthropology* 42, 3: 267–82.

Carroll, William K. 1987. 'Which Women Are More Proletarianized Than Men?', *Canadian Review of Sociology and Anthropology* 24: 465–95.

——— and Robert S. Ratner. 1996. 'Master Framing and Cross-movement Networking in Contemporary Social Movements', *Sociological Quarterly* 37: 601–25.

——— and ———. 1999. 'Media Strategies and Political Projects: A Comparative Study of Social Movements', *Canadian Journal of Sociology* 24, 1: 1–34.

Carson, Rachel. 1962. *Silent Spring*. Boston: Houghton Mifflin.

Cassidy, Barbara, Robina Lord, and Nancy Mandell. 2001. 'Silenced and Forgotten Women: Race, Poverty and Disability', in Nancy Mandell, ed., *Feminist Issues: Race, Class and Sexuality*, 3rd edn. Toronto: Prentice-Hall, 75–107.

Castellano, Marlene Brant, Lynne Davis, and Louise Lahache. 2000. 'Conclusion: Fulfilling the Promise', in Castellano, Davis, and Lahache, eds, *Aboriginal Education: Fulfilling the Promise*. Vancouver: University of British Columbia Press, 251–5.

Castells, Manuel. 1989. *The Informational City: Information Technology, Economic Restructuring, and the Urban-Regional Process*. Cambridge, Mass.: MIT Press.

Castilla, Emilio J. 2005. 'Social Networks and Employee Performance in a Call Center', *American Journal of Sociology* 110, 5: 1243–83.

Castles, Frances G. 2004. *The Future of the Welfare State*. Oxford: Oxford University Press.

Catton, William, Jr. 1980. *Overshoot: The Ecological Basis of Revolutionary Change*. Urbana: University of Illinois Press.

——— and Riley Dunlap. 1978. 'Environmental Sociology: A New Paradigm', *American Sociologist* 13: 41–9.

——— and ———. 1980. 'A New Ecological Paradigm for Post-exuberant Sociology', *American Behavioral Scientist* 24: 15–47.

Caulfield, Jon. 1994. *City Form and Everyday Life: Toronto's Gentrification and Critical Social Practice*. Toronto: University of Toronto Press.

CBC News. 2002. 'Alberta Oil Industry Predicts Losses after Kyoto', 22 Feb. At: <www.cbc.ca/stories/2002/02/22/kyoto_alberta020222>.

———. 2006a. 'Day Care in Canada'. At: <cbc.ca/news/printablestory.jsp>.

———. 2006b. 'Canadian Medical Association Journal Fires 2 Editors'. At: <www.cbc.ca/health/story>.

———. 2006c. 'Environment a Priority for More Canadians, Poll Suggests'. At: <www.cbc.ca/canada/story/2006/11/08/environment-poll.html>.

———. 2006d. 'Include Resource Money in Equalization Program, Experts Say'. At: <www.cbc.ca/story/Canada/national/2006/06/05/equalization-report.html>.

———. 2006e. 'Caledonia Land Claim—Timeline'. At: <www.cbc.ca/news/background/caledonia-landclaim/>.

Chalmers, A.F. 1999. *What Is This Thing Called Science? An Assessment of the Nature and Status of Science and Its Methods*, 3rd edn. Indianapolis: Hackett.

Chappell, Neena L., and Nina L. Colwill. 1981. 'Medical Schools as Agents of Professional Socialization', *Canadian Review of Sociology and Anthropology* 18, 1: 67–79.

Charrad, Mounira. 2001. *States and Women's Rights: The Making of Postcolonial Tunisia, Algeria, and Morocco*. Berkeley: University of California Press.

Chasteen, Amy L. 2001. 'Constructing Rape: Feminism, Change, and Women's Everyday Understandings of Sexual Assault', *Sociological Spectrum* 21: 101–39.

Chawla, Louise. 2002. *Growing Up in an Urbanising World*. London: Earthscan.

Chayes, Abram, and Antonia Chayes. 1995. *The New Sovereignty: Compliance with International Regulatory Agreements*. Cambridge, Mass.: Harvard University Press.

Cheal, David. 1991. *Family and the State of Theory*. Toronto: University of Toronto Press.

Chen, Wenhong, and Barry Wellman. 2004. 'The Global Digital Divide—Within and Between Countries', *IT and Society* 1, 7: 39–45. At: <www.stanford.edu/group/siqss/itandsociety/v01i07/v01i07a03.pdf>.

Childers, Thomas. 1983. *The Nazi Voter: The Social Foundations of Fascism in Germany, 1919–1933*. Chapel Hill: University of North Carolina Press.

Chippendale, Nigel. 2002. *Access to Post-secondary Education in Canada: Facts and Gaps: Conference Report*. Ottawa: Canadian Policy Research Networks for the Canadian Millennium Scholarship Foundation. At: <www.cprn.ca/en/doc.cfm?doc=59>.

Chodorow, Nancy. 1978. *The Reproduction of Mothering*. Berkeley: University of California Press.

———. 1989. *Feminism and Psychoanalytic Theory*. New Haven: Yale University Press.

Christiano, Kevin J., William H. Swatos Jr, and Peter Kivisto. 2002. *Sociology of Religion: Contemporary Developments*. Walnut Creek, Calif.: AltaMira.

Chubb, John E., and Terry M. Moe. 1990. *Politics, Markets, and America's Schools*. Washington: Brookings Institution.

Chung, Lucy. 2004. 'Low-Paid Workers: How Many Live in Low-Income Families?', *Perspectives on Labour and Income* (Oct): 5–14.

Cilluffo, Frank J. 2001. 'Terrorism and the Canada–US Border', *ISUMA: Canadian Journal of Policy Research* 2, 4: 104–10.

Cincotta, Richard P., and Roberta Engelman. 1997. *Economics and Rapid Change: The Influence of Population Growth*. Washington: Population Action International.

Citizenship and Immigration Canada. 2001. *Canada's Recent Immigrants: A Comparative Portrait Based on the 1996 Census*. At: <www.cic.gc.ca/english/srr/research/res3ci.html>.

Clark, S.D. 1966. *The Suburban Society*. Toronto: University of Toronto Press.

———. 1995. *State and Status: The Rise of the State and Aristocratic Power in Western Europe*. Montreal: McGill-Queen's University Press.

Clark, Susan, and Andrew S. Harvey. 1976. 'The Sexual Division of Labour: The Use of Time', *Atlantis* 2, 1: 46–65.

Clark, Terry Nichols. 2002. Contribution to American Sociological Association's Section on Community and Urban Sociology list-server, 26 Nov.

Clark, Terry, and Seymour Martin Lipset. 1991. 'Are Social Classes Dying?', *International Sociology* 6: 397–410.

Clark, Warren. 2000. 'Education', *Canadian Social Trends* (Winter): 3–7.

Clarke, Harold D., Jane Jensen, Lawrence Leduc, and Jon H. Pammett. 1991. *Absent Mandate: The Politics of Discontent in Canada*, 2nd edn. Toronto: Gage.

Clarke, John I. 1996. 'The Impact of Population Change on Environment: An Overview', in Bernardo Colombo, Paul Demeny, and Max F. Perutz, eds, *Resources and Population: Natural, Institutional, and Demographic Dimensions of Development*. Oxford: Clarendon, 244–68.

Clarke, Juanne N. 2000. *Health, Illness, and Medicine in Canada*, 3rd edn. Toronto: Oxford University Press.

——— and P. Fletcher. 2004. 'Parents as Advocates: Stories of Surplus Suffering When a Child Is Diagnosed and Treated for Cancer', *Health and Social Work* 39, 3/4: 107–27.

——— and G. Van Amerom. Forthcoming. 'The Differences between Parents and People with Aspergers', *Social Work in Health Care.*

Cleland, John. 1996. 'Population Growth in the 21st Century: Cause for Crisis or Celebration?', *Tropical Medicine and International Health* 1, 1: 15–26.

Clement, Wallace. 1975. *The Canadian Corporate Elite.* Toronto: McClelland & Stewart.

———. 1988. 'The Labour Process', in James Curtis and Lorne Tepperman, eds, *Understanding Canadian Society.* Toronto: McGraw-Hill Ryerson, 161–84.

——— and John Myles. 1994. *Relations of Ruling: Class and Gender in Postindustrial Societies.* Montreal: McGill-Queen's University Press.

Clevedon, Gordon, and Michael Krashinsky. 2001. *Our Children's Future: Child Care Policy in Canada.* Toronto: University of Toronto Press.

Cloward, Richard A., and Lloyd E. Ohlin. 1960. *Delinquency and Opportunity: A Theory of Delinquent Gangs.* New York: Free Press.

Coale, Ansley J. 1964. 'How a Population Ages or Grows Younger', in Ronald Freedman, ed., *Population: The Vital Revolution.* Chicago: Aldine, 47–58.

———. 1969. 'The Decline of Fertility in Europe from the French Revolution to World War II', in S.J. Berhman, Leslie Corsa, and Ronald Freedman, eds, *Fertility and Family Planning: A World View.* Ann Arbor: University of Michigan Press, 3–24.

———. 1973. 'The Demographic Transition Reconsidered', in International Union for the Study of Population, *Proceedings of the International Population Conference,* vol. 1. Liège, Belgium, 53–72.

———. 1974. 'The History of the Human Population', *Scientific American* (special issue): 15–25.

——— and Edgar M. Hoover. 1958. *Population Growth and Economic Development in Low-Income Countries.* Princeton, NJ: Princeton University Press.

——— and Susan Cotts Watkins, eds. 1986. *The Decline of Fertility in Europe: The Revised Proceedings of a Conference on the Princeton European Fertility Project.* Princeton, NJ: Princeton University Press.

Coats, Patricia B., and Steven Overman. 1992. 'Childhood Play Experiences of Women in Traditional and Nontraditional Professions', *Sex Roles* 26, 7/8: 261–71.

Cockburn, Cynthia. 1983. *Brothers: Male Dominance and Technological Change.* London: Pluto.

———. 1990. 'Men's Power in Organizations', in Jeff Hearn and David Morgan, eds, *Men, Masculinity and Social Theory.* London: Unwin Hyman, 72–89.

———. 1991. *In the Way of Women: Men's Resistances to Sex Equality in Organization.* Ithaca, NY: ILR Press.

Cockett, Monica, and John Tripp. 1994. *The Exeter Family Study: Family Breakdown and Its Impact on Children.* Exeter, UK: University of Exeter Press.

Coe, Neil M. 2000. 'On Location: American Capital and the Local Labour Market in the Vancouver Film Industry', *International Journal of Urban and Regional Research* 24, 1: 79–94.

Cohen, Albert K. 1966. *Deviance and Control.* Englewood Cliffs, NJ: Prentice-Hall.

Cohen, J.L., and J.H. Davis. 1973. 'Effects of Audience Status, Evaluation, and Time of Action on Performance with Hidden-Word Problems', *Journal of Personality and Social Psychology* 27: 74–85.

Cohen, Jean L. 1985. 'Strategy or Identity: New Theoretical Paradigms and Contemporary Social Movements', *Social Research* 53: 663–716.

Coker, Naaz. 2001. *Racism in Medicine.* London: King's Fund.

Collier, Gary, Henry L. Minton, and Graham Reynolds. 1991. *Currents of Thought in American Social Psychology.* New York: Oxford University Press.

Collins, Randall. 1975. *Conflict Sociology: Toward an Explanatory Science.* New York: Academic Press.

———. 1979. *The Credential Society: An Historical Sociology of Education and Stratification.* New York: Academic Press.

———. 2004. *Interaction Ritual Chains.* Princeton, NJ: Princeton University Press.

Comack, E., V. Chopyk, and L. Wood. 2000. *Mean Streets: The Social Location, Gender Dynamic and Patterns of Violent Crime in Winnipeg.* Ottawa: Canadian Centre for Policy Alternatives.

Comninel, George C. 1987. *Rethinking the French Revolution: Marxism and the Revisionist Challenge.* New York: Verso.

Conley, James. 2004. 'Working-Class Formation in Twentieth-Century Canada', in James Curtis, Edward Grabb, and Neil Guppy, eds, *Social Inequality in Canada: Patterns, Problems, and Policies.* Toronto: Pearson Prentice-Hall, 38–54.

Connell, Erin, and Alan Hunt. 2006. 'Sexual Ideology and Sexual Physiology in the Discourses of Sex Advice Literature', *Canadian Journal of Human Sexuality* 15, 1: 23–45.

Connell, R.W. 1995. *Masculinities.* Berkeley: University of California Press.

———. 2001. *Gender.* Cambridge: Polity.

Connelly, Patricia M. 1978. *Last Hired, First Fired.* Toronto: Women's Press.

Connolly, Paul. 2002. *'Race' and Racism in Northern Ireland: A Review of the Research Evidence.* Belfast: Office of the First Minister and Deputy First Minister. At: <www.research.ofmdfmni.gov.uk/raceandracism/index.htm>.

———, Siobhan Fitzpatrick, Tony Gallagher, and Paul Harris, 2006. 'Addressing Diversity and Inclusion in the Early Years in Conflict-affected Societies: A Case Study of the Media Initiative for Children 1—Northern Ireland', *International Journal of Early Years Education* 14, 3: 263–78.

Conrad, Peter, and Joseph Schneider. 1980. *Deviance and Medicalization: From Badness to Sickness.* St Louis: Mosby.

Constant, David, Lee Sproull, and Sara Kiesler. 1996. 'The Kindness of Strangers: The Usefulness of Electronic Weak Ties for Technical Advice', *Organization Science* 7, 2: 119–35.

Cook, J. 2001. 'Practical Guide to Medical Education', *Pharmaceutical Marketing* 6: 14–22.

Cool, Julie. 2006. 'Women in Parliament', Library of Parliament, Government of Canada. At: <www.parl.gc.ca/information/library/PRBpubs/prb0562-e.htm>.

Cooley, Charles Horton. 1902. *Human Nature and Social Order.* New York: Scribner.

———. 1962 [1909]. *Social Organization: A Study of the Larger Mind.* Glencoe, Ill.: Free Press.

Cooperstock, Ruth, and Henry Lennard. 1987. 'Role Strain and Tranquilizer Use', in David Coburn, Carl D'Arcy, George M. Torrance, and Peter New, eds, *Health and Canadian Society: Sociological Perspectives,* 2nd edn. Markham, Ont.: Fitzhenry & Whiteside, 314–32.

Cottrell, Fred. 1955. *Energy and Society.* New York: McGraw-Hill.

Council of Ministers of Education, Canada. 1996. *Enhancing the Role of Teachers in a Changing World.* Report in response to the International Survey in Preparation for the Forty-Fifth Session of the International Conference on Education. Toronto: Council of Ministers of Education, Canada.

———. 2001. *The Development of Education in Canada: Report of Canada.* Toronto: Council of Ministers of Education, Canada.

Coverman, Shelly. 1983. 'Gender, Domestic Labour Time and Wage Inequality', *American Sociological Review* 48: 623–37.

Crane, Diana. 2002. 'Culture and Globalization: Theoretical Models and Emerging Trends', in Diana Crane, Nobuko Kawashima, and Kenichi Kawasaki, eds, *Global Culture: Media, Arts, Policy, and Globalization.* New York: Routledge, 1–25.

Crockett, Lisa, Mike Losoff, and Anne C. Petersen. 1984. 'Perceptions of the Peer Group and Friendship in Early Adolescence', *Journal of Early Adolescence* 4, 2: 155–81.

Crompton, Susan. 2000. 'Health', *Canadian Social Trends* 59: 12–17.

Crossley, Michelle L. 2002. 'The Perils of Health Promotion and the "Barebacking" Backlash', *Health* 6, 1: 47–68.

Croteau, David, and William Hoynes. 2000. *Media/Society: Industries, Images, and Audiences,* 2nd edn. Thousand Oaks, Calif.: Pine Forge.

Crozier, Michel. 1964. *The Bureaucratic Phenomenon.* Chicago: University of Chicago Press.

Crush, Jonathan. 1987. *The Struggle for Swazi Labour, 1890–1920.* Montreal: McGill-Queen's University Press.

Cullen, Ian. 1978. 'The Treatment of Time in the Explanation of Spatial Behavior', in Tommy Carlstein, Don Parkes, and Nigel Thrift, eds, *Human Activity and Time Geography.* New York: Halstead, 27–38.

Cuneo, Carl. 1985. 'Have Women Become More Proletarianized Than Men?', *Canadian Review of Sociology and Anthropology* 22: 465–95.

———. 1990. *Pay Equity: The Labour-Feminist Challenge.* Toronto: Oxford University Press.

———. 2002. 'Globalized and Localized Digital Divides along the Information Highway: A Fragile Synthesis across Bridges, Ramps, Cloverleaves, and Ladders', 33rd Annual Sorokin Lecture, University of Saskatchewan. 31 Jan.

Cunningham, Mick. 2001. 'The Influence of Parental Attitudes and Behaviors on Children's Attitudes toward Gender and Household Labor in Early Adulthood', *Journal of Marriage and the Family* 63, 1: 111–23.

Curra, John. 2000. *The Relativity of Deviance.* Thousand Oaks, Calif.: Sage.

Currie, Dawn. 1988. 'Starvation amidst Abundance: Female Adolescents and Anorexia', in B. Singh Bolaria and Harley D. Dickinson, eds, *Sociology of Health Care in Canada.* Toronto: Harcourt Brace Jovanovich, 198–215.

Curtis, James, Edward Grabb, Thomas Perks, and Tina Chui. 2004. 'Public Involvement, Civic Engagement, and Social Inequality', in James Curtis, Edward Grabb, and Neil Guppy, eds, *Social Inequality in Canada: Patterns, Problems, and Policies,* 4th edn. Toronto: Pearson Prentice-Hall, 431–49.

Daenzer, Patricia, 1993. *Regulating Class Privilege: Immigrant Servants in Canada, 1940s–1990.* Toronto: Canadian Scholars' Press.

Dahl, Robert. 1961. *Who Governs? Democracy and Power in an American City.* New Haven: Yale University Press.

Darder, Antonia, Marta Baltodano, and Rodolfo D. Torres, eds. 2003. *The Critical Pedagogy Reader.* New York: Routledge Falmer.

Das, Mallika. 2000. 'Men and Women in Indian Magazine Advertisements: A Preliminary Report', *Sex Roles* 43: 699–717.

Das Gupta, Tania. 1996. *Racism and Paid Work.* Toronto: Garamond.

Davey, Ian E. 1978. 'The Rhythm of Work and the Rhythm of School', in Neil McDonald and Alf Chaiton, eds, *Egerton Ryerson and His Times.* Toronto: Macmillan, 221–53.

Davidson, James, and Dean Knudsen. 1977. 'A New Approach to Religious Commitment', *Sociological Focus* 10, 2: 151–73.

Davidson, Julia O'Connell. 2005. *Children in the Global Sex Trade.* Malden, Mass.: Polity.

Davidson, Kenneth, and Linda Hoffman. 1986. 'Sexual Fantasies and Sexual Satisfaction: An Empirical Analysis of Erotic Thought', *Journal of Sex Research* 22, 2: 184–205.

Davie, Grace. 1994. *Religion in Britain Since 1945: Believing without Belonging.* Oxford: Blackwell.

———. 2000. *Religion in Modern Europe: A Memory Mutates.* Oxford: Oxford University Press.

Davies, James C. 1962. 'Toward a Theory of Revolution', *American Sociological Review* 27: 5–19.

Davies, Lorraine, and Patricia Jane Carrier. 1999. 'The Importance of Power Relations for the Division of Household Labour', *Canadian Journal of Sociology* 24, 1: 35–51.

Davies, Lorraine, and Donna McAlpine. 1998. 'The Significance of Family, Work, and Power Relations for Mothers' Mental Health', *Canadian Journal of Sociology* 23: 368–88.

Davies, Scott. 2004. 'Stubborn Disparities: Explaining Class Inequalities in Schooling', in James Curtis, Edward Grabb, and Neil Guppy, eds, *Social Inequality in Canada: Patterns, Problems, and Policies,* 4th edn. Toronto: Pearson Prentice-Hall, 173–86.

Davies, Scott, Janice Aurini, and Linda Quirke. 2002. 'New Markets for Private Education in Canada', *Education Canada* 42, 3: 36–8.

Davis, Charles R. 1996. 'The Administrative Rational Model and Public Organization Theory', *Administration and Society* 28: 39–60.

Davis, Kingsley. 1937. 'The Sociology of Prostitution', *American Sociological Review* 2, 5: 744–55.

———. 1945. 'The World Demographic Transition', *Annals of American Academy of Political and Social Sciences* 237: 1–11.

———. 1984. 'Wives and Work: The Sex Role Revolution and Its Consequences', *Population and Development Review* 8: 495–511.

——— and Judith Blake. 1956. 'Social Structure and Fertility: An Analytic Framework', *Economic Development and Cultural Change* 4, 4: 211–35.

——— and Wilbert E. Moore. 1945. 'Some Principles of Stratification', *American Sociological Review* 10: 242–9.

——— and Pietronella van den Oever. 1982. 'Demographic Foundations of New Sex Roles', *Population and Development Review* 8: 495–512.

Davis, Steven J., John C. Haltiwanger, and Scott Schuh. 1996. *Job Creation and Destruction.* Cambridge, Mass: MIT Press.

Dawe, Alan. 1970. 'Two Sociologies', *British Journal of Sociology* 21: 207–18.

Day, Shelagh, and Gwen Brodsky. 1998. *Women and the Equality Deficit: The Impact of Restructuring Canada's Social Programs.* Ottawa: Status of Women Canada.

DeLamater, John, and Janet Shibley Hyde. 1998. 'Essentialism vs. Social Constructionism in the Study of Human Sexuality', *Journal of Sex Research* 35, 1: 10–18.

de la Torre, Isabel. 1997. 'La formacion y las organizaciones. Los acuerdos nacionales de formacion continua', *Revista Espanola de Investigaciones Sociologicas* 77–8 (Jan.–June): 15–33.

Decima Research. 2002. 'Canadians Favour Fundamental Changes to Health Care System over Other Romanow Commission Options', press release, 7 Mar.

DeFreitas, Gregory. 1998. 'Immigration, Inequality, and Policy Alternatives', in Dean Baker, Gerald Epstein, and Robert Pollin, eds, *Globalization and Progressive Economic Policy.* Cambridge: Cambridge University Press, 337–56.

Dei, George J. Sefa. 1996. *Anti-racism Education: Theory and Practice.* Halifax: Fernwood.

———. 2006. 'Black-focused Schools: A Call for Re-visioning', *Education Canada* 46, 3: 27–31.

———, Irma Marcia James, Leeno Luke Karumanchery, Sonia James-Wilson, and Jasmin Zine. 2000. *Removing the Margins: The Challenges and Possibilities of Inclusive Schooling.* Toronto: Canadian Scholars' Press.

DeKeseredy, Walter. 2005. 'Patterns of Family Violence', in M. Baker, ed., *Families: Changing Trends in Canada*, 5th edn. Toronto: McGraw-Hill Ryerson, 229–57.

——— and Linda MacLeod. 1997. *Woman Abuse: A Sociological Story.* Toronto: Harcourt Brace.

Dellinger, Kirsten. 2002. 'Wearing Gender and Sexuality "On Your Sleeve": Dress Norms and the Importance of Occupational and Organizational Culture at Work', *Gender Issues* 20, 1: 3–25.

Dempsey, Ken. 1999. 'Resistance and Change: Trying to Get Husbands to Do More Housework', paper presented at the Australian Sociologists Association annual meetings, Monash University.

———. 2002. 'Who Gets the Best Deal from Marriage: Men or Women?', *Journal of Sociology* 38, 2: 91–110.

DeNora, Tia. 1991. 'Musical Patronage and Social Change in Beethoven's Vienna', *American Journal of Sociology* 97: 310–46.

Denton, Frank T., Christine H. Feaver, and Byron G. Spencer. 2002. 'Alternative Pasts, Possible Futures: A "What If" Study of the Effects of Fertility on the Canadian Population and Labour Force', *Canadian Public Policy* 28, 3: 443–59.

Dery, David. 1998. '"Papereality" and Learning in Bureaucratic Organizations', *Administration and Society* 29: 677–89.

Desjardins, Richard, Scott Murray, Yvan Clermont, and Patrick Werquin. 2005. *Learning a Living: First Results of the Adult Literacy and Life Skills Survey.* Ottawa and Paris: Statistics Canada and OECD.

DesMeules, Marie, et al. 2003. *Women's Health Surveillance Report.* Ottawa: Health Canada and Canadian Institute for Health Information.

Deutschmann, Linda. 2007. *Deviance and Social Control*, 4th edn. Toronto: Thomson Nelson.

Devall, William B. 1992. 'Deep Ecology and Radical Environmentalism', in Riley Dunlap and Angela G. Mertig, eds, *American Environmentalism.* Philadelphia: Taylor and Francis, 51–62.

Devereaux, P.J., et al. 2002. 'A Systematic Review and Meta-analysis of Studies Comparing Mortality Rates of Private For-Profit and Private Not-for-Profit Hospitals', *Canadian Medical Association Journal* 166: 1399–1406.

Dhalla, Irfan A., et al. 2002. 'Characteristics of First-Year Students in Canadian Medical Schools', *Canadian Medical Association Journal* 166: 1029–35.

Diamond, Jared. 1997. *Guns, Germs, and Steel: The Fates of Human Societies.* New York: Norton.

Diani, Mario. 1992. 'The Concept of Social Movement', *Sociological Review* 40: 1–25.

Dias, K. 2003. 'The Ana Sanctuary: Women's Pro-anorexia Narratives in Cyberspace', *Journal of International Women's Studies* 4, 2: 31–45.

Dickens, Peter. 1992. *Society and Nature: Towards a Green Social Theory.* Hemel Hempstead, UK: Harvester Wheatsheaf.

———. 1996. *Reconstructing Nature: Alienation, Emancipation and the Division of Labour.* London: Routledge.

Diekman, Andreas, Monika Jungbauer-Gans, Heinz Krassnig, and Sigrid Lorenz. 1996. 'Social Status and Aggression: A Field Study Analyzed by Survival Analysis', *Journal of Social Psychology* 136: 761–8.

Dietz, Thomas, R. Scott Frey, and Eugene A. Rosa. 2002. 'Risk, Technology and Society', in Riley Dunlap and William Michelson, eds, *Handbook of Environmental Sociology.* Westport, Conn.: Greenwood, 329–69.

Di Martino, Vittorio. 1996. 'Télétravail: à la recherche des règles d'or', *Technologies de l'information et société* 8: 355–71.

Dines, Gail, and Jean M. Humez, eds. 2003. *Race, Gender and Class in the Media.* Thousand Oaks, Calif.: Sage.

Djelic, Marie-Laure. 2004. 'The Banyan Tree of Globalization. McKinsey at the Rise of the Advisory Industry' [L'arbre banian de la mondialisation. McKinsey et l'ascension de l'industrie du conseil], *Actes de la recherche en sciences sociales* 151/152 (Dec.): 107–13.

Dobash, R. Emerson, Russell P. Dobash, Margo Wilson, and Martin Daly. 1992. 'The Myth of Sexual Symmetry in Marital Violence', *Social Problems* 39: 71–91.

Dogon, Mattei, and John Kasarda, eds. 1988. *The Metropolis Era*. Beverly Hills, Calif.: Sage.

Doherty, Gillian, Martha Friendly, and Mab Oloman. 1998. *Women's Support, Women's Work: Child Care in an Era of Deficit Reduction, Devolution, Downsizing and Deregulation*. Ottawa: Status of Women Canada.

Dole, Carol M. 2000. 'Woman with a Gun: Cinematic Law Enforcers on the Gender Frontier', in Murray Pomerance and John Sakeris, eds, *Bang Bang, Shoot Shoot! Essays on Guns and Popular Culture*, 2nd edn. Needham Heights, Mass.: Pearson Education, 11–21.

Domhoff, G. William, ed. 1980. *Power Structure Research*. Beverly Hills, Calif.: Sage.

———. 1990. *The Power Elite and the State: How Policy Is Made in America*. Hawthorne, NY: Aldine de Gruyter.

Doob, Anthony N., and Alan E. Gross. 1968. 'Status of Frustrator as an Inhibitor of Horn-Honking Responses', *Journal of Social Psychology* 76: 213–18.

Dooley, Martin. 1995. 'Lone-Mother Families and Social Assistance Policy in Canada', in Martin Dooley, Ross Finnie, Shelley A. Phipps, and Nancy Naylor, eds, *Family Matters: New Policies for Divorce, Lone Mothers, and Child Poverty*. Toronto: C.D. Howe Institute, 35–104.

Downes, D., and P. Rock. 2003. *Understanding Deviance*, 4th edn. Toronto: Oxford University Press.

Downey, John, and Natalie Fenton. 2003. 'New Media, Counter Publicity and the Public Sphere', *New Media & Society* 5, 2: 185–202.

Doyal, Lesley. 1995. *What Makes Women Sick: Gender and the Political Economy of Health*. New Brunswick, NJ: Rutgers University Press.

Drago, Robert, et al. 2006. 'The Avoidance of Bias against Caregiving: The Case of Academic Faculty', *American Behavioral Scientist* 49, 9: 1222–47.

Dreeben, Robert. 1968. *On What Is Learned in School*. Reading, Mass.: Addison-Wesley.

Dreier, Peter, John Mollenkopf, and Todd Swanstrom. 2001. *Place Matters: Metropolitics for the Twenty-First Century*. Lawrence: University Press of Kansas.

Driedger, Leo. 1996. *Multi-ethnic Canada: Identities and Inequalities*. Toronto: Oxford University Press.

Drolet, Marie. 2001. *The Persistent Gap: New Evidence on the Canadian Gender Wage Gap*. Ottawa: Statistics Canada.

Duany, Andres, Elizabeth Plater-Zyberk, and Jeff Speck. 2000. *Suburban Nation: The Rise of Sprawl and the Decline of the American Dream*. Boston: North Point.

Du Bois, W.E.B. 1899. *The Philadelphia Negro: A Social Study*. New York: Lippincott.

———. 1903. *Souls of Black Folk*. New York: Penguin Books.

———. 1935. *Black Reconstruction in America, 1860–1880*. New York: Atheneum.

Duffy, Ann, and Rina Cohen. 2001. 'Violence against Women: The Struggle Persists', in Nancy Mandell, ed., *Feminist Issues: Race, Class and Sexuality*. Toronto: Prentice-Hall, 134–65.

———, Dan Glenday, and Norene Pupo. 1997. *Good Jobs, Bad Jobs, No Jobs: The Transformation of Work in the 21st Century*. Toronto: Harcourt Brace.

———, Nancy Mandell, and Norene Pupo. 1989. *Few Choices: Women, Work and Family*. Toronto: Garamond.

——— and Norene Pupo. 1992. *Part-Time Paradox: Connecting Gender, Work and Family*. Toronto: McClelland & Stewart.

Dumas, Jean. 1990. *Report on the Demographic Situation in Canada 1990*. Ottawa: Statistics Canada, Demography Division.

DuMont, Janice. 2003. 'Charging and Sentencing in Sexual Assault Cases: An Exploratory Examination', *Canadian Journal of Women and the Law* 15, 2: 305–30.

Duncan, Otis Dudley. 1959. 'Human Ecology and Population Studies', in Philip Hauser and Otis Dudley Duncan, eds, *The Study of Population*. Chicago: University of Chicago Press, 678–716.

———. 1961. 'From Social System to Ecosystem', *Sociological Inquiry* 31: 140–9.

———. 1985. *Notes on Social Measurement: Historical and Critical*. New York: Russell Sage Foundation.

——— and Leo F. Schnore. 1959. 'Cultural, Behavioral and Ecological Perspectives in the Study of Social Organization', *American Journal of Sociology* 65: 132–45.

Dunlap, Riley. 1992. 'Trends in Public Opinion toward Environmental Issues: 1965–1990', in Riley Dunlap and Angela G. Mertig, eds, *American Environmentalism*. Philadelphia: Taylor and Francis, 89–116.

——— and W. Richard Catton. 1994. 'Struggling with Human Exemptionalism: The Rise, Decline and Revitalization of Environmental Sociology', *American Sociologist* 25 (Spring): 5–30.

——— and William Catton Jr. 1979a. 'Environmental Sociology', *Annual Review of Sociology* 5: 243–73.

——— and ———. 1979b. 'Environmental Sociology: A Framework for Analysis', in Timothy O'Riordan and R.C. d'Arge, eds, *Progress in Resource Management and Environmental Planning*, vol. 1. Chichester, UK: Wiley, 57–85.

——— and ———. 1983. 'What Environmental Sociologists Have in Common (Whether Concerned with "Built" or "Natural" Environments)', *Sociological Inquiry* 53, 2/3: 113–15.

——— and Richard P. Gale. 1972. 'Politics and Ecology: A Political Profile of Student Eco-activists', *Youth and Society* 3: 379–97.

———, William Michelson, and Glenn Stalker. 2002. 'Environmental Sociology: An Introduction', in Riley Dunlap and William Michelson, eds, *Handbook of Environmental Sociology*. Westport, Conn.: Greenwood Press, 1–32.

Dunn, Judy. 1986. 'Growing Up in a Family World: Issues in the Study of Social Development in Young Children', in Martin Richards and Paul Light, eds, *Children of Social Worlds: Development in a Social Context*. Cambridge: Polity, 98–115.

Durkheim, Émile. 1964 [1893]. *The Division of Labor in Society*, trans. George Simpson. New York: Free Press.

———. 1958, 1964 [1895]. *The Rules of Sociological Method*, trans. S. Solovay and John Mueller. New York: Free Press.

———. 1951 [1897]. *Suicide: A Study in Sociology*, trans. John A. Spaulding and George Simpson. New York: Free Press.

———. 1965 [1912]. *The Elementary Forms of Religious Life*, trans. Joseph Ward Swain. New York: Free Press.

———. 1995 [1912]. *The Elementary Forms of Religious Life*, trans. Karen E. Fields. New York: Free Press.

———. 1956 [1922]. *Education and Society*, trans. Sherwood W. Fox. Glencoe, Ill.: Free Press.

Dworkin, Andrea. 1981. *Pornography: Men Possessing Women.* New York: Perigee.

Dworkin, Ronald W. 2001. 'The Medicalization of Unhappiness', *The Public Interest* (Summer): 85–99.

Easterlin, Richard A. 1969. 'Towards a Socio-economic Theory of Fertility: A Survey of Recent Research on Economic Factors in American Fertility', in S.J. Berhman, Leslie Corsa, and Ronald Freedman, eds, *Fertility and Family Planning: A World View.* Ann Arbor: University of Michigan Press, 127–56.

———. 1980. *Birth and Fortune: The Impact of Numbers on Personal Welfare.* New York: Basic Books.

Eaves, Elizabeth. 2002. *Bare: On Women, Dancing, Sex and Power.* New York: Knopf.

Ebaugh, Helen. 1988. *Becoming an Ex: The Process of Role Exit.* Chicago: University of Chicago Press.

——— and Janet Saltzman Chafetz, eds. 2000. *Religion and the New Immigrants.* Walnut Creek, Calif.: AltaMira.

Eberstadt, Nicholas. 1997. 'World Population Implosion?', *The Public Interest* 129: 3–20.

Eckersley, Robyn. 1992. *Environmentalism and Political Theory: Toward an Ecocentric Approach.* Albany: State University of New York Press.

Economist, The. 2006. 'Let's Try That Again: Mergers in Europe', 22 July, 68.

——— . 2006. 'Change in Africa: Never Too Late to Scramble', 381, 8501: 53–6.

Edin, Kathryn, and Maria J. Kefalas. 2005. *Promises I Can Keep: Why Poor Women Put Motherhood before Marriage.* Berkeley: University of California Press.

Edwards, Nigel, Mary Jane Kornacki, and Jack Silversin. 2002. 'Unhappy Doctors: What Are the Causes and What Can Be Done?', *British Medical Journal* 324: 835–8.

Edwards, Richard. 1979. *Contested Terrain: The Transformation of the Workplace in the Twentieth Century.* New York: Basic Books.

Eglin, Peter, and Stephen Hester. 1999. '"You're All a Bunch of Feminists": Categorization and the Politics of Terror in the Montreal Massacre', *Human Studies* 22: 253–72.

Ehrenreich, Barbara. 2001. *Nickel and Dimed: On (Not) Getting By in America.* New York: Henry Holt.

Ehrlich, Paul R. 1981. 'Environmental Disruption: Implications for the Social Sciences', *Social Science Quarterly* 62, 1: 7–22.

——— and Anne H. Ehrlich. 1970. *Population, Resources, Environment: Issues in Human Ecology.* San Francisco: Freeman.

——— and ———. 1990. *The Population Explosion.* London: Hutchinson.

——— and J.P. Holdren. 1971. 'The Impact of Population Growth', *Science* 171: 1212–17.

Eichler, Margrit. 1996. 'The Impact of New Reproductive and Genetic Technologies on Families', in Maureen Baker, ed., *Families: Changing Trends in Canada,* 3rd edn. Toronto: McGraw-Hill Ryerson, 104–18.

———. 1997. *Family Shifts: Families, Policies, and Gender Equality.* Toronto: Oxford University Press.

———. 2005. 'Biases in Family Literature', in Maureen Baker, ed., *Families: Changing Trends in Canada,* 5th edn. Toronto: McGraw-Hill Ryerson, 121–42.

Eisenberg, David M., et al. 1998. 'Trends in Alternative Medicine Use in the United States, 1990–1997: Results of a Follow-up National Survey', *Journal of the American Medical Association* 280: 1569–75.

Eisinger, Peter K. 1973. 'The Conditions of Protest Behaviour in American Cities', *American Political Science Review* 67: 11–28.

El-Badry, M.A. 1969. 'Higher Female Than Male Mortality in Some Countries of South Asia: A Digest', *Journal of the American Statistical Association* 64: 1234–44.

Eliade, Mircea. 1969. *The Quest: History and Meaning in Religion.* Chicago: University of Chicago Press.

Elias, Norbert. 1994. *The Civilizing Process,* trans. Edmund Jephcott. Oxford: Blackwell.

Elizabeth, Vivienne. 2000. 'Cohabitation, Marriage, and the Unruly Consequences of '"Difference"', *Gender and Society* 14, 1: 87–100.

Elliot, Faith Robertson. 1996. *Gender, Family, and Society.* London: Macmillan.

Elliott, J., and M. Richards. 1991. 'Parental Divorce and the Life Chances of Children', *Family Law* 481–4.

Elmer, Greg, and Mike Gasher, eds. 2005. *Contracting Out Hollywood: Runaway Productions and Foreign Location Shooting.* Lanham, Md: Rowman and Littlefield.

Elster, Jon. 1989. *The Cement of Society: A Study of Social Order.* Cambridge: Cambridge University Press.

Emerson, Joan. 1970. 'Behavior in Private Places: Sustaining Definitions of Reality in Gynecological Examinations', in Hans P. Dreitzel, ed., *Recent Sociology 2.* London: Macmillan, 73–97.

Emery, Robert. 1994. 'Psychological Research on Children, Parents, and Divorce', in Robert Emery, ed., *Renegotiating Family Relationships: Divorce, Child Custody, and Mediation.* New York: Guildford, 194–217.

Enchautegui, Maria E. 1997. 'Immigration and Wage Changes of High School Dropouts', *Monthly Labor Review* (Oct.): 3–9.

Engels, Friedrich. 1994 [1845]. *The Condition of the Working Class in England,* trans. W.O. Henderson and W.H. Chaloner. Stanford, Calif.: Stanford University Press.

———. 1942 [1884]. *The Origin of the Family, Private Property and the State.* New York: International Publishers.

———. 1990 [1884]. *The Origin of the Family, Private Property and the State,* vol. 26 of *Karl Marx and Frederick Engels Collected Works.* New York: International Publishers.

England, Paula. 1982. 'The Failure of Human Capital Theory to Explain Occupational Sex Segregation', *Journal of Human Resources* 17: 358–70.

———, George Farkas, Barbara Kilbourne, and Thomas Dou. 1988. 'Explaining Occupational Sex Segregation and Wages: Findings from a Model with Fixed Effects', *American Sociological Review* 53: 544–58.

Ennett, Susan T., and Karl E. Bauman. 1996. 'Adolescent Social Networks: School, Demographic, and Longitudinal Considerations', *Journal of Adolescent Research* 11: 194–215.

Entwhistle, N.J., and D. Entwhistle. 1970. 'The Relationship between Personality, Study Methods, and Academic Performance', *British Journal of Educational Psychology* 40: 131–40.

Entwisle, Doris, and Leslie Hayduk. 1988. 'Lasting Effects of Elementary School', *Sociology of Education* 61: 147–59.

Environics. 2000. 'Canadian Opinion on Climate Change Action in Advance of COP-6'. At: <www.rockies.ca/election/Environics_Climate_eFlash.pdf>.

———. 2006. 'Environics Has Conducted a New Poll for the CBC on Issues Important to the Country', press release, 9 Nov. At: <erg.environics.net/media_room/default.asp?aID=615>.

Epstein, Debbie, Jannette Elwood, Valerie Hey, and Janet Maw. 1997. *Failing Boys? Issues in Gender and Achievement.* Buckingham, UK: Open University Press.

Erasmus, Georges. 2002. 'Why Can't We Talk', from the 2002 Lafontaine-Baldwin Lecture, *Globe and Mail*, 9 Mar., F6–7.

Erikson, Erik. 1982. *The Life Cycle Completed: A Review.* New York: Norton.

Erikson, Kai T. 1966. *Wayward Puritans: A Study in the Sociology of Deviance.* New York: Wiley.

Ermann, M. David, and Richard J. Lundman. 1996. 'Corporate and Governmental Deviance: Origins, Patterns, and Reactions', in M. David Ermann and Richard J. Lundman, eds, *Corporate and Governmental Deviance: Problems of Organizational Behavior in Contemporary Society.* New York: Oxford University Press, 3–44.

Estes, Carroll L. 1999. 'The New Political Economy of Aging: Introduction and Critique', in Meredith Minkler and Carroll L. Estes, eds, *Critical Gerontology: Perspectives from Political and Moral Economy.* Amityville, NY: Baywood, 17–35.

Evans, L.T. 1998. *Feeding the Ten Billion: Plants and Population Growth.* Cambridge: Cambridge University Press.

Eyerman, Ron, and Andrew Jamison. 1989. 'Environmental Knowledge as an Organizational Weapon: The Case of Greenpeace', *Social Science Information* 28, 1: 99–119.

Ezzell, Carol. 2002. 'Hope in a Vial: Will There Be an AIDS Vaccine Anytime Soon?', *Scientific American* (June): 38–45.

Falkenberg, Loren. 1988. 'The Perceptions of Women Working in Male-Dominated Professions', *Canadian Journal of Atlantic Studies* (June): 77–83.

Faludi, Susan. 1991. *Backlash: The Undeclared War against American Women.* New York: Doubleday-Anchor.

———. 1999. *Stiffed: The Betrayal of the American Man.* New York: HarperCollins.

Fantasia, Rick. 1995. 'Fast Food in France', *Theory and Society* 24: 201–33.

Faules, Don F., and Dennis C. Alexander. 1978. *Communication and Social Behaviour: A Symbolic Interaction Perspective.* Reading, Mass.: Addison-Wesley.

Fausto-Sterling, Anne. 1985. *Myths of Gender.* New York: Basic Books.

———. 2000. *Sexing the Body: Gender Politics and the Construction of Sexuality.* New York: Basic Books.

Featherstone, Liza. 2004. *Selling Women Short: The Landmark Battle for Workers' Rights at Wal-Mart.* New York: Basic Books.

Feld, Scott L. 1982. 'Social Structural Determinants of Similarity among Associates', *American Sociological Review* 47: 797–801.

Ferguson, Kathy E. 1984. *The Feminist Case against Bureaucracy.* Philadelphia: Temple University Press.

Ferguson, Tom, and Leo Cendrowicz. 2006. 'Indie Ambush: Impala's Challenge of Sony BMG Merger Indicative of Larger Consolidation Battle', *Billboard*, 23 Dec., 38.

Fernández Armesto, Felipe, ed. 1995. *The European Opportunity.* Aldershot, UK: Variorum.

Fetherling, Douglas. 1993. *A Little Bit of Thunder: The Strange Inner Life of the Kingston Whig-Standard.* Toronto: Stoddart.

Filion, Normand.1998. 'The Management of Self-Discipline: Social Norms and Cultural Surveillance', paper presented at the annual meeting of the International Sociological Association.

Fineman, Martha A. 1995. *The Neutered Mother, the Sexual Family, and Other Twentieth Century Tragedies.* New York: Routledge.

Finke, Roger. 1997. 'The Consequences of Religious Competition: Supply-Side Explanations for Religious Change', in Lawrence A. Young, ed., *Rational Choice Theory and Religion: Summary and Assessment.* New York: Routledge, 45–64.

———, A. Guest, and Rodney Stark. 1996. 'Mobilizing Local Religious Markets: Religious Pluralism in the Empire State, 1855 to 1865', *American Sociological Review* 61: 203–18.

——— and Rodney Stark. 1992. *The Churching of America, 1776–1990.* New Brunswick, NJ: Rutgers University Press.

Firey, Walter. 1977. *Man, Mind and Land: A Theory of Resource Use.* Glencoe, Ill.: Free Press.

Fischer, Claude S. 1976. *The Urban Experience.* New York: Harcourt Brace Jovanovich.

———. 1982. *To Dwell Among Friends: Personal Networks in Town and City.* Chicago: University of Chicago Press.

Fisher, William, and Azy Barak. 2001. 'Internet Pornography: A Social Psychological Perspective on Internet Sexuality', *Journal of Sex Research* 38, 4: 312–23.

Fiske, John, and Robert Dawson. 1996. 'Audiencing Violence: Watching Homeless Men Watch *Die Hard*', in James Hay, Lawrence Grossberg, and Ellen Wartella, eds, *The Audience and Its Landscape.* Boulder, Colo.: Westview, 297–316.

Fitzgerald, Kevin, and Mark LaGory. 2000. *Unhealthy Places: The Ecology of Risk in the Urban Landscape.* New York: Routledge.

Fleras, Augie, and Jean Leonard Elliott. 1996. *Unequal Relations: An Introduction to Race, Ethnic and Aboriginal Dynamics in Canada.* Toronto: Prentice-Hall.

——— and Jean Lock Kunz. 2001. *Media and Minorities: Representing Diversity in a Multicultural Canada.* Toronto: Thompson Educational Publishing.

Flood, Gavin. 1999. *Beyond Phenomenology: Rethinking the Study of Religion.* London: Cassell.

Flyvbjerg, Bent. 1998. *Rationality and Power: Democracy in Practice.* Chicago: University of Chicago Press.

———. 2001. *Making Social Science Matter.* Cambridge: Cambridge University Press.

Fogel, Robert W. 2006. *Why China Is Likely to Achieve Its Growth Objectives.* Cambridge, Mass.: National Bureau of Economic Research Working Paper 12122.

——— and Dora L. Costa. 1997. 'A Theory of Technophysio Evolution, with Some Implications for Forecasting Population, Health Care Costs, and Pension Costs', *Demography* 34: 49–66.

Fong, Eric. 2005. 'Immigration and the City', in Hiller (2005: 117–37).

———. 2006. 'Residential Segregation of Visible Minority Groups in Toronto', in Eric Fong, ed., *Inside the Mosaic.* Toronto: University of Toronto Press, 51–75.

Foot, David, with Daniel Stoffman. 1998. *Boom, Bust and Echo 2000: Profiting from the Demographic Shift in the New Millennium.* Toronto: Macfarlane Walter & Ross.

Ford, Clellan, and Frank Beach. 1951. *Patterns of Sexual Behavior.* New York: Harper & Row.

Ford, J., N. Nassar, E. Sullivan, G. Chambers, and P. Lancaster. 2003. *Reproductive Health Indicators, Australia, 2002.* Sydney: Australian Institute of Health and Welfare.

Fortin, Pierre. 1996. 'The Great Canadian Slump', *Canadian Journal of Economics* 29: 761–87.

Foschi, Martha, Larissa Lai, and Kirsten Sigerson. 1994. 'Gender and Double Standards in the Assessment of Job Applicants', *Social Psychology Quarterly* 57: 326–39.

Foucault, Michel. 1990. *The History of Sexuality: An Introduction.* New York: Vintage Books.

Fox, Bonnie, ed. 1980. *Hidden in the Household: Women's Domestic Labour under Capitalism.* Toronto: Women's Press.

———. 1988. 'Conceptualizing "Patriarchy"', *Canadian Review of Sociology and Anthropology* 25: 163–83.

———. 1989. 'The Feminist Challenge: A Reconsideration of Social Inequality and Economic Development', in Robert J. Brym with Bonnie J. Fox, *From Culture to Power: The Sociology of English Canada.* Toronto: Oxford University Press, 120–67.

———, ed. 2001a. *Family Patterns, Gender Relations,* 2nd edn. Toronto: Oxford University Press.

———. 2001b. 'The Formative Years: How Parenthood Creates Gender', *Canadian Review of Sociology and Anthropology* 38: 373–90.

———. 2001c. 'Reproducing Difference: Changes in the Lives of Partners Becoming Parents', in Fox (2001a: 217–302).

——— and John Fox. 1986. 'Women in the Labour Market, 1931–1981: Exclusion and Competition', *Canadian Review of Sociology and Anthropology* 23: 1–21.

——— and ———. 1987. 'Occupational Gender Segregation of the Canadian Labour Force, 1931–1981', *Canadian Review of Sociology and Anthropology* 24: 374–97.

——— and Pamela Sugiman. 1999. 'Flexible Work, Flexible Workers: The Restructuring of Clerical Work in a Large Telecommunications Company', *Studies in Political Economy* 60: 59–84.

Fox, James Alan, and Jack Levin. 2001. *The Will to Kill: Making Sense of Senseless Murder.* Boston: Allyn and Bacon.

Fox, Jo. 2004. 'Resistance and the Third Reich', *Journal of Contemporary History* 39: 271–83.

Fox, John, and Michael Ornstein. 1986. 'The Canadian State and Corporate Elites in the Post-war Period', *Canadian Review of Sociology and Anthropology* 23: 481–506.

Fox, Stephen. 1985. *The American Conservation Movement: John Muir and His Legacy.* Madison: University of Wisconsin Press.

Frank, Andre Gunder. 1991. 'The Underdevelopment of Development', *Scandinavian Journal of Development Alternatives* 10, 3: 5–72.

Frankel, Ken. 2006. 'Forget about Right, Left . . . It's Latin America', *Globe and Mail,* 12 Dec., A23.

Fraser, Nancy. 1997. 'After the Family Wage: A Postindustrial Thought Experiment', in Nancy Fraser, *Justice Interruptus: Critical Reflections on the 'Postsocialist' Condition.* New York: Routledge, 41–66.

——— and Linda Nicholson. 1990. 'Social Criticism without Philosophy: An Encounter between Feminism and Postmodernism', in Linda Nicholson, ed., *Feminism/Postmodernism.* London: Routledge, 19–38.

Frauen Computer Zentrum Berlin (FCZB). 2001. 'European Database: Women in Decision-Making. Fact Sheet: Women in the National Governments of the EU-Member States—2001'. At: <www.db-decision.de/FactSheets/FactSheets_E.htm>.

Frederick, Judith. 1995. *As Time Goes By . . . : Time Use of Canadians.* Ottawa: Statistics Canada.

——— and Janet E. Fast. 1999. 'Eldercare in Canada: Who Does How Much?', *Canadian Social Trends* (Autumn): 27–30.

——— and Jason Hamel. 1998. 'Canadian Attitudes to Divorce', *Canadian Social Trends* 48: 6–11.

Freidson, Eliot. 1970. *The Profession of Medicine: A Study in the Sociology of Applied Knowledge.* New York: Harper & Row.

Freire, Paulo. 1970. *Pedagogy of the Oppressed,* trans. Myra Bergman Ramos. New York: Herder and Herder.

Frejka, Tomas. 1973. *The Future of Population Growth: Alternative Paths to Equilibrium.* New York: Wiley.

Freud, Sigmund. 1974 [1923]. *The Ego and the Id,* trans. James Strachey. London: Hogarth.

———. 1961 [1927]. *The Future of an Illusion,* trans. James Strachey. New York: Norton.

———. 1973 [1938]. *An Outline of Psychoanalysis,* trans. James Strachey. London: Hogarth.

Freudenberg, Nicholas, and Carol Steinsapir. 1992. 'Not in Our Backyards: The Grassroots Environmental Movement', in Riley Dunlap and Angela G. Mertig, eds, *American Environmentalism.* Philadelphia: Taylor and Francis, 27–38.

Freudenburg, William, and Susan Pastor. 1992. 'NIMBYs and LULUs: Stalking the Syndromes', *Journal of Social Issues* 48, 4: 39–61.

Friedan, Betty. 1963. *The Feminine Mystique.* New York: Norton.

Friedland, Roger, and Donald Palmer. 1984. 'Park Place and Main Street: Business and the Urban Power Structure', *Annual Review of Sociology* 10: 394–416.

Friedman, Debra, and Michael Hechter. 1988. 'The Contribution of Rational Choice Theory to Macrosociological Research', *Sociological Theory* 6: 201–18.

Friendly, Martha. 2001. 'Child Care and Canadian Federalism in the 1990's: Canary in a Coal Mine', in Gordon Cleveland and Michael Krashinsky, eds, *Our Children's Future: Child Care Policy in Canada.* Toronto: University of Toronto Press.

Fries, James F. 1980. 'Aging, Natural Death, and the Compression of Morbidity', *New England Journal of Medicine* 303: 130–5.

Friesen, John W., and Virginia Lyons Friesen. 2001. *In Defense of Public Schools in North America*. Calgary: Detselig.

Froese, Paul. 2001. 'Hungary for Religion: A Supply-Side Interpretation of the Hungarian Religious Revival', *Journal for the Scientific Study of Religion* 40: 251–68.

Fukuyama, Francis. 1992. *The End of History and the Last Man*. New York: Free Press.

Fuller, Colleen. 1998. *Caring for Profit: How Corporations Are Taking Over Canada's Health Care System*. Vancouver: New Star.

Funder, Kathleen. 1996. *Remaking Families: Adaptation of Parents and Children to Divorce*. Melbourne: Australian Institute of Family Studies.

Furedi, Frank. 1997. *Population and Development: A Critical Introduction*. New York: St Martin's.

Furstenberg, Frank F., S. Philip Morgan, and Paul D. Allison. 1987. 'Paternal Participation and Children's Well-Being after Marital Dissolution', *American Sociological Review* 52: 695–701.

Gagnon, J., and W. Simon. 1986. 'Sexual Scripts: Performance and Change', *Archives of Sexual Behavior* 15: 98–104.

Gaines, Donna. 1991. *Teenage Wasteland: Suburbia's Dead End Kids*. New York: Pantheon Books.

Galabuzi, Grace-Edward. 2006. *Canada's Economic Apartheid: The Social Exclusion of Racialized Groups in the New Century*. Toronto: Canadian Scholars' Press.

Galarneau, Diane, and Jim Sturrock. 1997. 'Family Income after Separation', *Perspectives on Labour and Income* 9, 2: 19–28.

Gale, Richard P. 1972. 'From Sit-ins to Hike-ins: A Comparison of the Civil Rights and Environmental Movements', in William R. Burch Jr, Neil H. Cheek Jr, and Lee Taylor, eds, *Social Behavior, Natural Resources and the Environment*. New York: Harper, 280–305.

Gallup Organization. 1992. '70% Believe Premarital Sex Not Wrong', *Gallup Report*, 27 Aug.

Gamson, Joshua, and Dawne Moon. 2004. 'The Sociology of Sexualities', *Annual Review of Sociology* 30: 47–64.

Gamson, William. 1991. 'Commitment and Agency in Social Movements', *Sociological Forum* 6: 27–50.

——— and David S. Meyer. 1996. 'Framing Political Opportunity', in Doug McAdam, John McCarthy, and Mayer Zald, eds, *Comparative Perspectives on Social Movements: Political Opportunities, Mobilizing Structures, and Cultural Framing*. New York: Cambridge University Press, 275–90.

Gannagé, Charlene. 1986. *Double Day, Double Bind: Women Garment Workers*. Toronto: Women's Press.

Gannon, M., K. Mihorean, K. Beatie, A. Taylor-Butts, and R. Kong. 2005. *Criminal Justice Indicators, 2005*. Ottawa: Canadian Centre for Justice Statistics, Statistics Canada.

Gans, Herbert J. 1962. *The Urban Villagers: Group and Class in the Life of Italian-Americans*. New York: Free Press.

———. 1967. *The Levittowners: Ways of Life and Politics in a New Suburban Community*. New York: Pantheon.

———. 1979. 'Symbolic Ethnicity: The Future of Ethnic Groups and Culture in America', *Ethnic and Racial Studies* 2: 1–20.

———. 2003. *Democracy and the News*. New York: Oxford University Press.

Gardner, Julia, and Mark Roseland. 1989. 'Thinking Globally: The Role of Social Equity in Sustainable Development', *Alternatives* 16, 3: 26–35.

Garfinkel, Harold. 1956. 'Conditions of Successful Status Degradation Ceremonies', *American Journal of Sociology* 61: 420–4.

———. 1967. *Studies in Ethnomethodology*. Englewood Cliffs, NJ: Prentice-Hall.

———. 1997. 'A Conception of and Experiments with "Trust" as a Condition of Concerted Stable Actions', in J. O'Brien and P. Kollock, eds, *The Production of Social Reality: Essays and Readings in Social Interaction*. Thousand Oaks, Calif.: Pine Forge, 396–407.

Garreau, Joel. 1992. *Edge City: Life on the New Frontier*. New York: Anchor.

Garriguet, Didier. 2005. 'Early Sexual Intercourse', *Health Reports* 16, 3: 9–19. Statistics Canada Catalogue no. 82-003-XPE.

Garson, Barbara. 1972. *All the Livelong Day: The Meaning and Demeaning of Routine Work*. New York: Doubleday.

Garwood, Shae. 2002. 'Working to Death: Gender, Labour, and Violence in Ciudad Juarez, Mexico', *Peace, Conflict and Development* 2 (Dec.): 1–23.

Gaskell, Jane. 1992. *Gender Matters from School to Work*. Milton Keynes, UK: Open University Press.

———. 1993. 'Feminism and Its Impact on Educational Scholarship in Canada', in Leonard L. Stewin and Stewart J.H. McCann, eds, *Contemporary Educational Issues: The Canadian Mosaic*, 2nd edn. Toronto: Copp Clark Pitman, 145–60.

———. 2001. 'The Reproduction of Family Life: Perspectives of Male and Female Adolescents', in Bonnie Fox, ed., *Family Patterns, Gender Relations*, 2nd edn. Toronto: Oxford University Press, 217–32.

——— and John Willinsky, eds. 1995. *Gender In/forms Curriculum: From Enrichment to Transformation*. Toronto: OISE Press.

Gauntlett, David. 2002. *Media, Gender and Identity*. London: Routledge.

Gaventa, John. 1980. *Power and Powerlessness: Quiescence and Rebellion in an Appalachian Valley*. Urbana: University of Illinois Press.

Geary, David. 1998. *Male, Female: The Evolution of Human Sexual Differences*. Washington: American Psychological Association.

——— and Mark V. Flinn. 2001. 'Evolution of Human Parental Behavior and the Human Family', *Parenting, Science and Practice* 1: 5–61.

Geertz, Clifford. 1957. 'Ritual and Social Change: A Javanese Example', *American Anthropologist* 59, 1: 32–54.

Gergen, Kenneth. 2001. 'From Mind to Relationship: The Emerging Challenge', *Education Canada* 41, 1: 8–11.

Ghalam, Nancy. 2000. 'Attitudes toward Women, Work and Family', *Canadian Social Trends* 3.

Ghosh, Sabriti. 2002. 'AIDS in Canada', *Voices* 9, 10: 1–3.

Gibbon, Edward. 1994 [1776–88]. *The History of the Decline and Fall of the Roman Empire*. London: Allen Lane.

Gibbs, Lois. 1993. Foreword to Richard Hofrichter, ed., *Toxic Struggles: The Theory and Practice of Environmental Justice*. Philadelphia: New Society, ix–xi.

Giddens, Anthony. 1971. *Capitalism and Modern Social Theory: An Analysis of the Writings of Marx, Durkheim, and Max Weber*. Cambridge: Cambridge University Press.

———. 1979. *Selected Problems of Social Theory*. London: Macmillan.

———. 2000. *Introduction to Sociology*, 3rd edn. New York: Norton.

Gidengil, Elisabeth, Andre Blais, Joanna Everitt, Patrick Fournier, and Neil Nevitte. 2006. 'Back to the Future? Making Sense of the 2004 Canadian Election Outside Quebec', *Canadian Journal of Political Science* 39: 1–25.

———, ———, Richard Nadeau, and Neil Nevitte. 2001. 'Making Sense of the Vote: The 2000 Canadian Election', paper presented at the annual meeting of the Association for Canadian Studies in the United States.

Gidney, R.D. 1999. *From Hope to Harris: The Reshaping of Ontario's Schools*. Toronto: University of Toronto Press.

Gifford, Robert. 1987. *Environmental Psychology: Principles and Practice*. Toronto: Allyn & Bacon.

Gilbert, Neil. 1997. 'Advocacy Research and Social Policy', *Crime and Justice* 22: 101–48.

Gilligan, Carol. 1982. *In a Different Voice: Psychoanalytic Theory and Women's Development*. Cambridge, Mass.: Harvard University Press.

Giroux, Henri. 1997. *Pedagogy and the Politics of Hope: Theory, Culture, and Schooling: A Critical Reader*. Boulder, Colo.: Westview.

Glasgow University Media Group. 1976. *Bad News*. London: Routledge & Kegan Paul.

Glassner, Barry. 1999. *The Culture of Fear: Why Americans Are Afraid of the Wrong Things*. New York: Basic Books.

Glenmary Research Center. 2002. 'Religious Congregations and Membership: 2000'. At: <www.glenmary.org/grc/RCMS_2000/release.htm>.

Glenn, Evelyn Nakano. 2000. 'The Social Construction and Institutionalization of Gender and Race: An Integrative Framework', in Myra Marx Feree, Judith Lorber, and Beth B. Hess, eds, *Revisioning Gender*. New York: AltaMira, 3–43.

Glock, Charles, and Rodney Stark. 1965. *Religion and Society in Tension*. Chicago: Rand McNally.

Goffman, Erving. 1959. *The Presentation of Self in Everyday Life*. Garden City, NY: Doubleday-Anchor.

———. 1961a. *Asylums: Essays on the Social Situation of Mental Patients and Other Inmates*. New York: Doubleday.

———. 1961b. *Encounters: Two Studies in the Sociology of Interaction*. Indianapolis: Bobbs Merrill.

———. 1963a. *Behavior in Public Places: Notes on the Social Organization of Gatherings*. Glencoe, Ill.: Free Press.

———. 1963b. *Stigma: Notes on the Management of Spoiled Identity*. Englewood Cliffs, NJ: Prentice-Hall.

———. 1967. *Interaction Ritual: Essays on Face to Face Behavior*. Garden City, NY: Anchor.

———. 1971. *Relations in Public: Microstudies of the Public Order*. New York: Basic Books.

———. 1986. *Frame Analysis: An Essay on the Organization of Experience*. Boston: Northeastern University Press.

Gold, David A., Clarence Y.H. Lo, and Erik Olin Wright. 1975. 'Recent Developments in Marxist Theories of the Capitalist State', *Monthly Review* 27: 29–43.

Gold, Harry. 2002. *Urban Life and Society*. Upper Saddle River, NJ: Prentice-Hall.

Goldberg, David Theo. 1993. *Racist Culture: Philosophy and the Politics of Meaning*. Oxford: Blackwell.

Goldberg, Kim. 1990. *The Barefoot Channel: Community Television as a Tool for Social Change*. Vancouver: New Star Books.

Goldblatt, David. 1996. *Social Theory and the Environment*. Cambridge: Polity.

Goldenberg, Sheldon. 1992. *Thinking Methodologically*. New York: HarperCollins.

Goldthorpe, J.E. 1987. *Family Life in Western Societies: A Historical Sociology of Family Relationships in Britain and North America*. Cambridge: Cambridge University Press.

Goldthorpe, J.H., David Lockwood, Frank Bechhofer, and Jennifer Platt. 1969. *The Affluent Worker in the Class Structure*. Cambridge: Cambridge University Press.

Gonzales, Alicia, and Gary Rolison. 2004. 'Social Oppression and Attitudes toward Sexual Practices', *Journal of Black Studies* 35, 6: 715–29.

Goode, E. 2003. 'The MacGuffin That Refuses to Die: An Investigation into the Condition of the Sociology of Deviance', *Deviant Behavior* 24: 507–33.

———. 2004. 'The "Death" MacGuffin Redux: Comments on Best', *Deviant Behavior* 25: 493–509.

Goode, William J. 1960. 'A Theory of Role Strain', *American Sociological Review* 25: 483–96.

Gordon, Betty, Carolyn Schroeder, and Michael Abrams. 1990. 'Age and Social-Class Differences in Children's Knowledge of Sexuality', *Journal of Clinical Child Psychology* 19, 1: 33–43.

Gordon, Philip H., and Sophie Meunier. 2001. 'Globalization and French Cultural Identity', *French Politics, Culture and Society* 19: 22–41.

Gordon, Robert M., and Jacquelyn Nelson. 2000. 'Crime, Ethnicity, and Immigration', in Robert A. Silverman, James J. Teevan, and Vincent F. Sacco, eds, *Crime in Canadian Society*, 6th edn. Toronto: Harcourt Brace.

Gorski, Philip S. 1995. 'The Protestant Ethic and the Spirit of Bureaucracy', *American Sociological Review* 60: 783–6.

Gorz, Andre. 1999. *Reclaiming Work: Beyond the Wage-Based Society*, trans. Chris Turner. Cambridge: Polity.

Gottdiener, Mark, and Ray Hutchison. 2000. *The New Urban Sociology*, 2nd edn. Toronto: McGraw-Hill.

Gottfedson Michael, and Travis Hirschi. 1990. *A General Theory of Crime*. Stanford, Calif.: Stanford University Press.

Gove, Walter. 1973. 'Sex, Marital Status and Mortality', *American Journal of Sociology* 79: 45–67.

GPI Atlantic. n.d. 'The Economic Value of Housework and Child Care'. At: <www.gpiatlantic.org/ab_housework.shtml>.

Grabb, Edward G. 2007. *Theories of Social Inequality*, 5th edn. Toronto: Thomson Nelson.

——— and James Curtis. 2005. *Regions Apart: The Four Societies of Canada and the United States*. New York: Oxford University Press.

Grafton, R. Quentin, Robert W. Lynch, and Harry W. Nelson. 1998. 'British Columbia's Stumpage System: Economic and Trade Policy Implications', *Canadian Public Policy* 24 (suppl.): S41–50.

Graham, Hilary. 1984. *Women, Health and the Family*. Brighton, UK: Wheatsheaf.

Graham, John A. 1999. 'William Lyon Mackenzie King, Elizabeth Harvie and Edna: A Prostitute Rescuing Initiative in Late Victorian Toronto', *Canadian Journal of Human Sexuality* 8, 1: 47–60.

Gramsci, Antonio. 1992. *Prison Notebooks*, vol. 1, trans. Joseph A. Buttigieg and Antonio Callari. New York: Columbia University Press.

Granovetter, Mark S. 1974. *Getting a Job: A Study of Contacts and Careers*. Cambridge, Mass.: Harvard University Press.

———. 1982. 'Alienation Reconsidered: The Strength of Weak Ties', *Connections* 5, 2: 4–16.

Grant, Karen. 1998. 'It's All in Your Genes', in Wayne Antony and Les Samuelson, eds, *Critical Thinking about Canadian Social Issues*. Halifax: Fernwood, 200–17.

———, Carol Amaratunga, Pat Armstrong, Madeline Bosco, Ann Pederson, and Kay Garamond, eds. 2004. *Caring For/Caring About Women: Home Care and Unpaid Caregiving*. Aurora, Ont.: Garamond.

Gray, Gary, and Neil Guppy. 2003. *Successful Surveys: Research Methods and Practice*, 3rd edn. Toronto: Thomson Nelson.

Gray, Herman. 1989. 'Popular Music as a Social Problem: A Social History of Claims against Popular Music', in Joel Best, ed., *Images of Issues: Typifying Contemporary Social Problems*. New York: Aldine de Gruyter, 143–58.

Grbich, Carolyn. 1992. 'Societal Response to Familial Role Change in Australia: Marginalisation or Social Change', *Journal of Comparative Family Studies* 23, 1: 79–94.

Greeley, Andrew. 1989. *Religious Change in America*. Cambridge, Mass.: Harvard University Press.

Greene, Kathryn, and Sandra Faulkner. 2005. 'Gender, Belief in the Sexual Double Standard, and Sexual Talk in Heterosexual Dating Relationships', *Sex Roles. A Journal of Research* 53, 3/4: 239–51.

Greer, Germaine. 1984. *Sex and Destiny: The Politics of Human Fertility*. London: Martin Secker & Warburg.

Gregory, J.W., and V. Piché. 1983. 'Inequality and Mortality: Demographic Hypotheses Regarding Advanced and Peripheral Capitalism', *International Journal of Health Services* 13: 89–106.

Grenier, Marc. 1994. 'Native Indians in the English-Canadian Press: The Case of the "Oka Crisis"', *Media, Culture & Society* 16: 313–36.

Grimes, Michael D. 1991. *Class in Twentieth-Century American Sociology: An Analysis of Theories and Measurement Strategies*. New York: Praeger.

Grindstaff, Carl F. 1975. 'The Baby Bust: Changes in Fertility Patterns in Canada', *Canadian Studies in Population* 2: 15–22.

———. 1994. 'The Baby Bust Revisited: Canada's Continuing Pattern of Low Fertility', in Frank Trovato and Carl F. Grindstaff, eds, *Perspectives on Canada's Population: An Introduction to Concepts and Issues*. Toronto: Oxford University Press, 168–72.

———. 1995. 'Canada's Continued Trend of Low Fertility', *Canadian Social Trends* (Winter): 12–16.

——— and Frank Trovato. 1990. 'Junior Partners: Women's Contribution to Family Income in Canada', *Social Indicators Research* 22: 229–53.

Griswold, Wendy. 1987. 'A Methodological Framework for the Sociology of Culture', *Sociological Methodology* 17: 1–35.

Grosjean, Michele, and Michele Lacoste. 1998. 'L'oral et l'écrit dans les communications de travail ou les illusions du "tout ecrit"', *Sociologie du travail* 40: 439–61.

Gross, Edward, and Gregory P. Stone. 1981. 'Embarrassment and the Analysis of Role Requirements', *American Journal of Sociology* 70: 1–15.

Guernsey, Judith Read, Ron Dewar, Swarna Weerasinghe, Susan Kirkland, and Paul J. Veugelers. 2000. 'Incidence of Cancer in Sydney and Cape Breton County, Nova Scotia 1979–1997', *Canadian Journal of Public Health* 91: 285–92.

Guillaumin, C. 1995. *Racism, Sexism, Power and Ideology*. London: Routledge.

Guillebaud, Jean-Claude. 2002. 'Definition of Man: What Is Left of the Nuremburg Code?', *Diogenes* 195: 7–12.

Guppy, Neil, and Scott Davies. 1998. *Education in Canada: Recent Trends and Future Challenges*. Ottawa: Statistics Canada.

———, Sabrina Freeman, and Shari Buchan. 1987. 'Representing Canadians: Changes in the Economic Backgrounds of Federal Politicians', *Canadian Review of Sociology and Anthropology* 24: 417–30.

Gusfield, Joseph R. 1963. *Symbolic Crusade: Status Politics and the American Temperance Movement*. Urbana: University of Illinois Press.

———. 1981. *The Culture of Public Problems: Drinking-Driving and the Symbolic Order*. Chicago: University of Chicago Press.

———. 1989. 'Constructing the Ownership of Social Problems: Fun and Profit in the Welfare State', *Social Problems* 36: 431–41.

Haas, Jack, and William Shaffir. 1978. 'The Professionalization of Medical Students: Developing Competence and a Cloak of Competence', in Haas and Shaffir, eds, *Shaping Identity in Canadian Society*. Englewood Cliffs, NJ: Prentice-Hall.

Haas, Peter M., Marc A. Levy, and Edward Parson. 1992. 'Appraising the Earth Summit: How Should We Judge UNCED's Success?', *Environment* 34, 8: 7–11, 26–33.

Haberland, Nicole, and Diana Measham, eds. 2002. *Responding to Cairo: Case Studies of Changing Practice in Reproductive Health and Family Planning*. New York: Population Council.

Habermas, Jürgen. 1975. *Legitimation Crisis*, trans. Thomas McCarthy. Boston: Beacon.

———. 1984. *The Theory of Communicative Action*, 2 vols, trans. Thomas McCarthy. Cambridge: Polity.

Hackett, Robert A. 1992. 'The Depiction of Labour and Business on National Television News', in Marc Grenier, ed., *Critical Studies of Canadian Mass Media*. Markham, Ont.: Butterworths, 59–82.

——— and Richard Gruneau. 2000. *The Missing News: Filters and Blind Spots in Canada's Press*. Aurora, Ont.: Garamond.

———, Richard Pinet, and Myles Ruggles. 1996. 'News for Whom: Hegemony and Monopoly versus Democracy in Canadian Media', in Helen Holmes and David Taras, eds, *Seeing Ourselves: Media Power and Policy in Canada*, 2nd edn. Toronto: Harcourt Brace Canada, 257–72.

——— and Scott Uzelman. 2003. 'Tracing Corporate Influences on Press Content: A Summary of Recent NewsWatch Canada Research', *Journalism Studies* 4, 3: 331–46.

Hadaway, C. Kirk, Penny Long Marler, and Mark Chaves. 1993. 'What the Polls Don't Tell Us: A Closer Look at United States Church Attendance', *American Sociological Review* 58: 741–52.

Haddad, Tony, and Lawrence Lam. 1988. 'Canadian Families—Men's Involvement in Family Work: A Case Study of Immigrant Men in Toronto', *International Journal of Comparative Sociology* 29: 269–79.

Hagan, John, and Ruth D. Peterson, eds. 1995. *Crime and Inequality*. Stanford, Calif.: Stanford University Press.

Hägerstrand, Torsten. 1970. 'What about People in Regional Science?', *Papers of the Regional Science Association* 24: 7–21.

Hales, Dianne. 2000. *Just Like a Woman: How Gender Science Is Redefining What Makes Us Female*. New York: Bantam.

Hall, Edward T. 1966. *The Hidden Dimension*. Garden City, NY: Doubleday.

Hall, Emmett. 1964–5. *Report of the Royal Commission on Health Services*. Ottawa: Queen's Printer.

Hall, Peter A., and David Soskice, eds. 2001. *Varieties of Capitalism: The Institutional Foundations of Comparative Advantage*. Oxford: Oxford University Press.

Hall, Stuart. 1980. 'Encoding/Decoding', in Stuart Hall, Dorothy Hobson, Andrew Lowe, and Paul Willis, eds, *Culture, Media, Language: Working Papers in Cultural Studies, 1972–79*. London: Hutchinson, 128–38.

———. 2000. 'Conclusion: The Multi-cultural Questions', in Barnor Hesse, ed., *Un/settled Multiculturalism: Diasporas, Entanglements, 'Transruptions'*. London: Zed Books.

Hallett, Tim, and Marc J. Ventresca. 2006. 'How Institutions Form: Loose Coupling as Mechanism in Gouldner's Patterns of Industrial Bureaucracy', *American Behavioral Scientist* 49, 7: 908.

Hallman, Howard W. 1984. *Neighborhoods: Their Place in Urban Life*. Beverly Hills, Calif.: Sage.

Hamilton, Richard F. 1982. *Who Voted for Hitler?* Princeton, NJ: Princeton University Press.

Hamilton, Roberta. 1978. *The Liberation of Women*. London: Allen and Unwin.

Hampton, Keith. 2005. 'Social Ties and Community in Urban Places', in Hiller (2005: 95–116).

Hampton, Mary, Bonnie Jeffery, Barb McWatters, and Pamela Smith. 2005. 'Influence of Teens' Disapproval and Peer Behaviour on Their Initiation of Sexual Intercourse', *Canadian Journal of Human Sexuality* 14, 3/4: 105–21.

Handel, Gerald, ed. 1988. *Childhood Socialization*. New York: Aldine de Gruyter.

Hannigan, John. 1995. *Environmental Sociology: A Social Constructionist Perspective*. London: Routledge.

———. 1998. *Fantasy City: Pleasure and Profit in the Postmodern Metropolis*. New York: Routledge.

Hanson, Susan. 1992. 'Geography and Feminism: Worlds in Collision?', *Annals of the Association of American Geographers* 82: 569–86.

Hardey, Michael. 2002. 'The Story of My Illness: Personal Accounts of Illness on the Internet', *Health* 6, 1: 31–46.

Hardin, Garret. 1968. 'The Tragedy of the Commons', *Science* 162: 1243–8.

———. 1974. 'Lifeboat Ethics: The Case Against Helping the Poor', *Psychology Today* 8: 33ff.

Harding, Sandra. 1986. *The Science Question in Feminism*. Ithaca, NY: Cornell University Press.

Hardoy, Jorge E., Diana Mitlin, and David Satterthwaite. 2001. *Environmental Problems in an Urbanizing World*. London: Earthscan.

Harris, Chauncy, and Edward L. Ullman. 1945. 'The Nature of Cities', *Annals of the American Academy of Political and Social Science* no. 242: 7–17.

Harris, Judith. 1998. *The Nurture Assumption*. New York: Free Press

Harris, Martin. 2006. 'F.W. Taylor and the Legacies of Systemization, Information', *Communication & Society* 9, 1: 109–20.

Harrison, Trevor, and Harvey Krahn. 1995. 'Populism and the Rise of the Reform Party in Alberta', *Canadian Review of Sociology and Anthropology* 32: 127–50.

Hartmann, Heidi. 1981. 'The Unhappy Marriage of Marxism and Feminism: Towards a More Progressive Union', in Lydia Sargent, ed., *The Unhappy Marriage of Marxism and Feminism: A Debate on Class and Patriarchy*. London: Pluto, 2–41.

Harvey, David. 1989. *The Condition of Postmodernity: An Enquiry into the Origins of Cultural Change*. New York: Routledge.

Hathaway, A.D. 2004. 'Cannabis Users' Informal Rules for Managing Stigma and Risk', *Deviant Behavior* 25, 6: 559–77.

Hawkins, Freda. 1988. *Canada and Immigration: Public Policy and Public Concern*, 2nd edn. Montreal: McGill-Queen's University Press.

Hawley, Amos A. 1950. *Human Ecology: A Theory of Community Structure*. New York: Ronald Press.

———. 1981. *Urban Society*, 2nd edn. New York: Wiley.

Hawley, Willis, and Frederick M. Wirt. 1968. *The Search for Community Power*. Scarborough, Ont.: Prentice-Hall.

Hayford, Alison. 1992. 'From Chicago 1966 to Montreal 1989: Notes on New(s) Paradigms of Women as Victims', in Marc Grenier, ed., *Critical Studies of Canadian Mass Media*. Markham, Ont.: Butterworths, 201–12.

Hays, Samuel. 1987. *Beauty, Health and Permanence: Environmental Politics in the United States, 1955–1985*. New York: Cambridge University Press.

Health Canada. 2002. *A Report on Mental Illness in Canada*. Ottawa: Health Canada.

———. 2003. *HIV/AIDS Epidemiology Update: HIV and AIDS among Women in Canada*. Ottawa: Health Canada.

———. 2004. *Canadian Addiction Survey*. Ottawa: Canadian Centre on Substance Abuse.

———. 2005. *Canadian Addiction Survey*. Ottawa: Canadian Centre on Substance Abuse

Health Reports. 2001. 'Women's Health Needs', *Health Reports* 12, 3: 34.

Hearn, Jeff, and Wendy Parkin. 1987. *'Sex' and 'Work': The Power and Paradox of Organizational Sexuality*. New York: St Martin's.

Heimer, Robert. 2002. *Social Problems: An Introduction to Critical Constructionism*. New York: Oxford University Press.

Held, David. 1980. *Introduction to Critical Theory: Horkheimer to Adorno*. Berkeley: University of California Press.

Helwig, David. 2000. 'NWT Residents Are Accident Prone, Live Shorter Lives', *Canadian Medical Association Journal* 162: 681–2.

Henry, Frances, and Effie Ginzberg. 1985. *Who Gets the Work: A Test of Racial Discrimination in Employment.* Toronto: Urban Alliance on Race Relations and Social Planning Directorate.

——— and Carol Tator. 2005. *The Colour of Democracy: Racism in Canadian Society*, 3rd edn. Toronto: Thomson Nelson.

Herlihy, David. 1997. *The Black Death and the Transformation of the West.* Cambridge, Mass.: Harvard University Press.

Herodotus. 1996. *Histories.* Hertfordshire: Wordsworth.

Hesse-Biber, Sharlene Nagy. 2007. *The Cult of Thinness.* New York: Oxford University Press.

Hewitt, John P. 2000. *Self and Society: A Symbolic Interactionist Social Psychology*, 8th edn. Boston: Allyn and Bacon.

Hickman, B. 1988. 'Men Wise Up to Bald Truth', *Australian*, 21 May, 4.

Hier, Sean P. 2002. 'Raves, Risks and the Ecstasy Panic: A Case Study in the Subversive Nature of Moral Regulation', *Canadian Journal of Sociology* 27: 33–52.

Higgins, Robert R. 1994. 'Race, Pollution and the Mastery of Nature', *Environmental Ethics* 16: 251–64.

Hilberg, Raul. 1996. 'The Nazi Holocaust: Using Bureaucracies, Overcoming Psychological Barriers to Genocide', in M. David Ermann and Richard J. Lundman, eds, *Corporate and Governmental Deviance: Problems of Organizational Behavior in Contemporary Society.* New York: Oxford University Press, 158–79.

Hilgartner, Stephen, and Charles Bosk. 1988. 'The Rise and Fall of Social Problems: A Public Arenas Model', *American Journal of Sociology* 94: 53–78.

Hiller, Harry. 1979. 'The Canadian Sociology Movement: Analysis and Assessment', *Canadian Journal of Sociology* 4: 125–50.

——— ed. 2005. *Urban Canada: Sociological Perspectives.* Toronto: Oxford University Press.

Hirschi, Travis. 1969. *Causes of Delinquency.* Berkeley: University of California Press.

Hobbes, Thomas. 1968 [1651]. *Leviathan.* Baltimore, Md: Penguin.

Hochschild, Adam. 1998. *King Leopold's Ghost: A Story of Greed, Terror, and Heroism in Colonial Africa.* Boston: Houghton Mifflin.

Hochschild, Arlie. 1983. *The Managed Heart: Commercialization of Human Feeling.* Berkeley: University of California Press.

———. 1997. *The Time Bind: When Work Becomes Home and Home Becomes Work.* New York: Metropolitan Books.

———. 2001. 'The Third Shift', in Bonnie J. Fox, ed., *Family Patterns, Gender Relations*, 2nd edn. Toronto: Oxford University Press, 338–51.

——— and Anne Machung. 1989. *The Second Shift: Working Parents and the Revolution at Home.* New York: Viking.

Hodson, Randy. 2001. *Dignity at Work.* Cambridge: Cambridge University Press.

Hofrichter, Richard, ed. 1993. *Toxic Struggles: The Theory and Practice of Environmental Justice.* Philadelphia: New Society.

Holden, Michael. 2006. 'Equalization: Implications of Recent Changes', Library of Parliament, Parliamentary Information and Research Service. At: <www.parl.gc.ca/information/library/PRBpubs/prb0591-e.htm>.

Holmes, Malcolm D., and Judith A. Antell. 2001. 'The Social Construction of American Indian Drinking: Perceptions of American Indian and White Officials', *Sociological Quarterly* 42: 151–73.

Holmes, Mark. 1998. *The Reformation of Canada's Schools: Breaking the Barriers to Parental Choice.* Montreal: McGill-Queen's University Press.

Holton, Robert J. 1998. *Globalization and the Nation-State.* New York: St Martin's.

Homans, George. 1951. 'The Western Electric Researchers', in Schyler Dean Hoslett, ed., *Human Factors in Management.* New York: Harper, 210–41.

———. 1961. *Social Behavior: Its Elementary Forms.* New York: Harcourt, Brace, and World.

Homer-Dixon, Thomas F., Jeffrey H. Boutwell, and George W. Rathjens. 1993. 'Environmental Change and Violent Conflict', *Scientific American* (Feb.): 38–45.

hooks, bell. 1992. *Black Looks: Race and Representation.* Toronto: Between the Lines.

———. 1994. *Outlaw Culture.* New York: Routledge.

Hope, Steven, Chris Power, and Bryan Rodgers. 1998. 'The Relationship between Parental Separation in Childhood and Problem Drinking in Adulthood', *Addiction* 93, 4: 505–14.

Hou, Feng, and T.R. Balakrishnan. 1999. 'The Economic Integration of Visible Minorities in Contemporary Canadian Society', in James Curtis, Edward Grabb, and Neil Guppy, eds, *Social Inequality in Canada: Patterns, Problems, and Policies*, 3rd edn. Scarborough, Ont.: Prentice-Hall Canada, 214–43.

Hout, Michael, and Claude S. Fischer. 2002. 'Why More Americans Have No Religious Preference: Politics and Generations', *American Sociological Review* 67: 165–90.

Howard, Judith. 1995. 'Social Cognition', in Karen S. Cook, Gary Alan Fine, and James S. House, eds, *Sociological Perspectives on Social Psychology.* Boston: Allyn and Bacon, 90–117.

Howard-Hassmann, Rhoda. 1999. '"Canadian" as an Ethnic Category: Implications for Multiculturalism and National Unity', *Canadian Public Policy* 25, 4.

Hoyt, Homer. 1939. *The Structure and Growth of Residential Neighborhoods in American Cities.* Washington: Federal Housing Administration.

Hughes, Diane, and Deborah Johnson. 2001. 'Correlates in Children's Experiences of Parents' Racial Socialization Behaviors', *Journal of Marriage and Family* 63: 981–96.

Hughes, Everett C. 1945. 'Dilemmas and Contradictions of Status', *American Journal of Sociology* 50: 353–9.

Hughes, Karen. 1999. *Gender and Self-Employment in Canada: Assessing Trends and Policy Implications.* Ottawa: Canadian Policy Research Networks.

Hulchanski, David. 1991. 'Social Welfare versus Market Welfare', in Kent Gerecke, ed., *The Canadian City.* Montreal: Black Rose, 207–16.

Hull, Jeremy. 2005. *Post-Secondary Education and Labour Market Outcomes, Canada 2001.* Ottawa: Minister of Indian Affairs and Northern Development.

Hum, Derek, and Wayne Simpson. 2007. 'Revisiting Equity and Labour: Immigration, Gender, Minority Status, and

Income Differentials in Canada', in S. Hier and B. Singh Bolaria, eds, *Race and Racism in 21st Century Canada*. Peterborough, Ont.: Broadview.

Human Fertilisation and Embryology Authority (HFEA). 1997. *Sixth Annual Report*. United Kingdom: HFEA.

Human Resources Development Canada (HRDC). 2002. *Knowledge Matters: Skills and Learning for Canadians*. Hull, Que.: HRDC.

——— and Statistics Canada. 1998. *High School May Not Be Enough: An Analysis of Results from the School Leavers Follow-up Survey 1995*. Ottawa: Minister of Public Works and Government Services Canada.

Humphrey, Craig R., and Frederick R. Buttel. 1982. *Environment, Energy and Society*. Belmont, Calif.: Wadsworth.

Humphreys, Laud. 1970. *Tearoom Trade: Impersonal Sex in Public Places*. Chicago: Aldine.

Humphries, Karin H., and Eddy van Doorslaer. 2000. 'Income-Related Health Inequality in Canada', *Social Science and Medicine* 50: 663–71.

Hunter, Alfred A. 1981. *Class Tells: On Social Inequality in Canada*. Toronto: Butterworths.

——— and Jean McKenzie Leiper. 1993. 'On Formal Education, Skills and Earnings: The Role of Educational Certificates in Earnings Determination', *Canadian Journal of Sociology* 18: 21–42.

Hunter, Floyd. 1953. *Community Power Structure: A Study of Decision Makers*. Chapel Hill: University of North Carolina Press.

Hunter, James Davison. 1991. *Culture Wars: The Struggle to Define America*. New York: Basic Books.

Huntington, Samuel P. 1996. *The Clash of Civilizations and the Remaking of the World Order*. New York: Simon and Schuster.

Hurrelmann, Klaus, ed. 1989. *The Social World of Adolescents*. Berlin: Walter de Gruyter.

Hutter, Mark. 2007. *Experiencing Cities*. New York: Pearson Education.

Idinopulos, Thomas A., and Edward A. Yonan, eds. 1994. *Religion and Reductionism*. Leiden, Netherlands: E.J. Brill.

Ihinger-Tallman, Marilyn, and David Levinson (revised by J.M. White). 2003. 'Definition of Marriage', in J. Ponzetti Jr, ed., *International Encyclopedia of Marriage and Family*, 2nd edn. New York: Macmillan Reference and Thomson Gale.

Illich, Ivan. 1976. *Limits to Medicine*. Toronto: McClelland & Stewart.

Imershein, Allen W., and Carroll L. Estes. 1996. 'From Health Services to Medical Markets: The Commodity Transformation of Medical Production and the Non-profit Sector', *International Journal of Health Services* 26: 221–38.

Imig, Doug, and Sidney Tarrow. 2001. 'Mapping the Europeanization of Contention: Evidence from a Quantitative Data Analysis', in Imig and Tarrow, eds, *Contentious Europeans: Protest and Politics in an Emerging Polity*. New York: Rowman and Littlefield, 27–49.

Income Security Advocacy Centre. 2002. 'The Inquest into the Death of Kimberly Rogers.' At: <www.incomesecurity.org/index_html>.

Inglehart, Ronald. 1977. *The Silent Revolution: Changing Values and Political Styles among Western Publics*. Princeton, NJ: Princeton University Press.

———. 1990a. *Culture Shift in Advanced Industrial Society*. Princeton, NJ: Princeton University Press.

———. 1990b. 'Values, Ideology, and Cognitive Mobilization in New Social Movements', in R.J. Dalton and M. Kuechler, eds, *Challenging the Political Order*. New York: Oxford University Press, 23–42.

International Federation of the Phonographic Industry. 2005. 'IFPI Releases Definitive Statistics on Global Market for Recorded Music'. At: <www.ifpi.org/content/section_news/20050802.html>.

International Labour Organization. n.d. Multinational Corporations. At: <www.itcilo.it/english/actrav/telearn/global/ilo/multinat/multinat.htm>.

Irvine, Janice. 2003. '"The Sociologist as Voyeur": Social Theory and Sexual Research, 1910–1978', *Qualitative Sociology* 26, 4: 429–56.

Irving, John A. 1959. *The Social Credit Movement in Alberta*. Toronto: University of Toronto Press.

Irwin, Alan. 2001. *Sociology and the Environment*. Cambridge: Polity.

Isajiw, Wsevolod. 1999. *Understanding Diversity: Ethnicity and Race in the Canadian Context*. Toronto: Thompson Educational Publishing.

Jablin, Frederic M. 1984. 'Assimilating New Members in Organizations', in R.N. Bostrom, ed., *Communication Yearbook*. Newbury Park, Calif.: Sage, 594–626.

Jackson, Andrew, and David Robinson. 2000. *Falling Behind: The State of Working Canada, 2000*. Ottawa: Canadian Centre for Policy Alternatives.

Jackson, Sue. 2005. '"I'm 15 and Desperate for Sex": "Doing" and "Undoing" Desire in Letters to a Teenage Magazine', *Feminism & Psychology* 15, 3: 295–313.

Jacobs, Jane. 1961. *The Death and Life of Great American Cities*. New York: Random House.

James, Daniel Lee, and Elizabeth A. Craft. 2002. 'Protecting One's Self from a Stigmatized Disease . . . Once One Has It', *Deviant Behavior* 23: 267–99.

Jamieson, Lynn. 1998. *Intimacy: Personal Relationships in Modern Societies*. Cambridge: Polity.

Janis, Irving Lester. 1982. *Groupthink: Psychological Studies of Policy Decisions and Fiascoes*, 2nd edn. Boston: Houghton Mifflin.

Janowitz, Morris. 1952. *The Community Press in an Urban Setting*. Chicago: University of Chicago Press.

Jargowsky, Paul A. 1996. *Poverty and Place: Ghettos, Barrios, and the American City*. New York: Russell Sage Foundation.

Jeffery, C. Ray. 1971. *Crime Prevention through Environmental Design*. Beverly Hills, Calif.: Sage.

Jenkins, J. Craig. 1983. 'Resource Mobilization Theory and the Study of Social Movements', *Annual Review of Sociology* 9: 527–53.

Jenkins, Philip. 1994. *Using Murder: The Social Construction of Serial Homicide*. New York: Aldine de Gruyter.

———. 2002. *The Next Christendom: The Coming of Global Christianity*. New York: Oxford University Press.

Jeter, Jon. 2002. 'Zambia Reduced to a Flea-Market Economy: Cheap Foreign Imports Have Destroyed the Once Thriving Textile Industry', *Washington Post*, 22 Apr., A1.

Jette, Allan M., Sybil L. Crawford, and Sharon L. Tennstedt.

1996. 'Toward Understanding Ethnic Differences in Late-Life Disability', *Research on Aging* 18: 292–309.

Johnson, Carol. 2002. 'Heteronormative Citizenship and the Politics of Passing', *Sexualities* 5, 3: 317–36.

Johnson, Chalmers, Laura D'Andrea Tyson, and John Zysman. 1990. *Politics and Productivity: How Japan's Development Strategy Works.* New York: Harper Business.

Johnson, Holly. 1990. 'Wife Abuse', in Craig McKie and Keith Thompson, eds, *Canadian Social Trends.* Toronto: Thompson Educational, 173–6.

———. 1996. *Dangerous Domains: Violence against Women in Canada.* Toronto: Nelson.

———. 2005. 'Assessing the Prevalence of Violence against Women in Canada', *Statistical Journal of the United Nations ECE* 22: 225–38.

Johnson, Laura. 1986. *Working Families: Workplace Supports for Families.* Toronto: Working Families Project of the Social Planning Council of Metropolitan Toronto.

Johnson, Terence. 1972. *Professions and Power.* London: Macmillan, 1972.

Jones, Jennifer M., Susan Bennett, Marion P. Olmsted, Margaret L. Lawson, and Gary Rodin. 2001. 'Disordered Eating Attitudes and Behaviours in Teenaged Girls: A School-Based Study', *Canadian Medical Association Journal* 165: 547–52.

Jose Castillo, Juan, and Pablo Lopez Calle. 2002–3. 'Women at the End of the Assembly Line: The Labor Process of VW-Navarra' [Mujeres al final de la cadena: El entorno productivo de VW-Navarra], *Sociologia del Trabajo* 47 (Winter): 3–42

Junger, Marianne, Peter van der Heijden, and Carl Keane. 2001. 'Interrelated Harms: Examining the Association between Victimization, Accidents and Criminal Behaviour', *Injury Control and Safety Promotion* 8, 1: 13–28.

Kachur, Jerrold L. 1999. 'Quasi-Marketing Education: The Entrepreneurial State and Charter Schooling in Alberta', in Dave Broad and Wayne Antony, eds, *Citizens or Consumers? Social Policy in a Market Society.* Halifax: Fernwood, 129–50.

Kachur, Jerrold L., and Trevor W. Harrison. 1999. 'Introduction: Public Education, Globalization, and Democracy: Whither Alberta?', in Harrison and Kachur, eds, *Contested Classrooms: Education, Globalization, and Democracy in Alberta.* Edmonton: University of Alberta Press and Parkland Institute, xiii–xxxv.

Kadar, Marlene. 1988. 'Sexual Harassment as a Form of Social Control', in Arlene Tigar McLaren, ed., *Gender and Society.* Toronto: Copp Clark Pitman, 337–46.

Kannisto, Vaino, Jens Lauritsen, A.R. Thatcher, and J.W. Vaupel. 1994. 'Reflections in Mortality at Advanced Ages: Several Decades of Evidence from Advanced Countries', *Population and Development Review* 20: 793–810.

Kanter, Rosabeth Moss. 1977. *Men and Women of the Corporation.* New York: Basic Books.

Kanungo, Shivraj. 1998. 'An Empirical Study of Organizational Culture and Network-Based Computer Use', *Computers in Human Behavior* 14, 1: 79–91.

Karim, Karim H. 2002. 'Globalization, Communication, and Diaspora', in Paul Attallah and Leslie Regan Shade, eds, *Mediascapes: New Patterns in Canadian Communication.* Scarborough, Ont.: Thomson Nelson, 272–94.

Karmis, Demetrios. 2004. 'Pluralism and National Identity(ies) in Contemporary Quebec: Conceptual Clarifications, Typology, and Discourse Analysis', in Alain-G. Gagnon, ed., *Quebec: State and Society.* Peterborough, Ont.: Broadview, 69–96.

Kashefi, Max. 2005. 'The Relationship between Work Values and Job Rewards: Is Satisfaction of Extrinsic Job Rewards a Pre-Condition for the Salience of Intrinsic Rewards?', *International Review of Modern Sociology* 31, 2: 233–50.

Kasper, Anne S., and Susan J. Ferguson, eds. 2000. *Breast Cancer: Society Shapes an Epidemic.* New York: St Martin's.

Kassebaum, Donald G., and Ellen R. Cutler. 1998. 'On the Culture of Student Abuse in Medical School', *Academic Medicine* 73: 1149–58.

Katzmarzyk, Peter T. 2002. 'The Canadian Obesity Epidemic: 1995–1998', *Canadian Medical Association Journal* 166: 1039–40.

Kawachi, Ichiro, Bruce P. Kennedy, Vanita Gupta, and Deborah Prothrow-Stith. 1999. 'Women's Status and the Health of Women and Men: A View from the States', *Social Science and Medicine* 48: 21–32.

Kearney, Patrick. 1982. *A History of Erotic Literature.* Hong Kong: Parragin Books.

Kelley, Maryellen R., and Susan Helper. 1997. 'Interorganizational Learning and the Environment: The Influences of Regional Agglomeration and Local Institutional Linkages on the Adoption of New Technologies', paper presented at the annual meeting of the American Sociological Association.

Kempadoo, Kamala. 1998. 'Introduction: Globalizing Sex Workers' Rights', in Kempadoo and Doezema (1998: 1–28).

——— and Jo Doezema, eds. 1998. *Global Sex Workers: Rights, Resistance, and Redefinition.* New York: Routledge.

Kennedy, Paul. 1993. *Preparing for the Twenty-First Century.* Toronto: HarperCollins.

Kenway, Jane, and Helen Modra. 1992. 'Feminist Pedagogy and Emancipatory Possibilities', in Carmen Luke and Jennifer Gore, eds, *Feminisms and Critical Pedagogy.* London: Routledge, 138–66.

———, Sue Willis, Jack Blackmore, and Leonnie Rennie. 1998. *Answering Back: Girls, Boys, and Feminism in Schools.* New York: Routledge.

Kershaw, Ian. 2004. 'Hitler and the Uniqueness of Nazism', *Journal of Contemporary History* 39: 239–54.

Kessler, S. 1998. *Lessons from the Intersexed.* New Brunswick, NJ: Rutgers University Press.

Keyfitz, Nathan. 1968. *Introduction to the Mathematics of Population.* Reading, Mass.: Addison-Wesley.

———. 1986. 'The Family That Does Not Reproduce Itself', *Population and Development Review* 12 (suppl.): 139–54.

———. 1993. 'Are There Ecological Limits to Population?', *Proceedings of the National Academy of Sciences* 90: 6895–9.

Kibirige, Joachim S. 1997. 'Population Growth, Poverty and Health', *Social Science and Medicine* 45: 247–59.

Kidd, Bruce. 1987. 'Sports and Masculinity', in Michael Kaufman, ed., *Beyond Patriarchy.* Toronto: Oxford University Press, 250–65.

Kiernan, Kathleen. 1997. *The Legacy of Parental Divorce: Social, Economic, and Demographic Experiences in Adulthood.* London: Centre for Analysis of Social Exclusion.

Kilgour, David. 1998. 'From Informal Economy to Microenterprise: The Role of Microcredit', Address to Results/Résultats Canada convention, Ottawa, 24 Oct. At: <www.david-kilgour.com/ssap/informal.htm>.

Killingsworth, B. 2007. '"Drinking Stories" from a Playgroup: Alcohol in the Lives of Middle-Class Mothers in Australia', *Ethnography* 7, 3: 357–84.

Kilmarten, Christopher T. 1994. *The Masculine Self.* Toronto: Maxwell Macmillan.

Kim, Sujeong. 2004. 'Rereading David Morley's *The "Nationwide" Audience*', *Cultural Studies* 18, 1: 84–108.

Kindleberger, Charles P. 1986. *The World in Depression, 1929–1939.* Berkeley: University of California Press.

King, Samantha. 2006. *Pink Ribbons, Inc.* Minneapolis: University of Minnesota Press.

Kinney, David. 1993. 'From Nerds to Normals: The Recovery of Identity among Adolescents from Middle School to High School', *Sociology of Education* 66: 21–40.

Kinsey, Alfred, Wardell Pomeroy, and Clyde Martin. 1948. *Sexual Behavior in the Human Male.* Philadelphia: W.B. Saunders.

———, ———, ———, and Paul Gebhard. 1953. *Sexual Behavior in the Human Female.* Philadelphia: W.B. Saunders.

Kirk, Dudley. 1998. 'Demographic Transition Theory', *Population Studies* 50: 361–87.

Kiser, Edgar, and Joachim Schneider. 1995. 'Rational Choice versus Cultural Explanations of the Efficiency of the Prussian Tax System', *American Sociological Review* 60: 787–91.

Kitschelt, Herbert. 1993. 'Social Movements, Political Parties, and Democratic Theory', *Annals of the American Academy of Political and Social Science* 528 (July): 13–29.

———, ed. 1999. *Continuity and Change in Contemporary Capitalism.* Cambridge: Cambridge University Press.

Kivimaki, M., T. Feldt, J. Vahtera, and J.E. Nurmi. 2000. 'Sense of Coherence: Evidence from 2 Cross-lagged Longitudinal Samples', *Social Science and Medicine* 50, 4: 583–97.

Klandermans, Bert. 1991. 'New Social Movements and Resource Mobilization: The European and the American Approach Revisited', in Dieter Rucht, ed., *Research on Social Movements.* Boulder, Colo.: Westview, 17–46.

Klein, David M., and James M. White. 1996. *Family Theories: An Introduction.* Thousand Oaks, Calif.: Sage.

Klein, Naomi. 1999. *No Logo: Taking Aim at the Brand Bullies.* New York: Picador.

Kleniewski, Nancy, ed. 2005. *Cities and Society.* Malden, Mass.: Blackwell.

Klinenberg, Eric. 2002. *Heat Wave: A Social Autopsy of Disaster in Chicago.* Chicago: University of Chicago Press.

Knight, Graham. 1982. 'News and Ideology', *Canadian Journal of Communication* 8, 4: 15–41.

———. 1988. 'Stratified News: Media, Sources, and the Politics of Representation', in Peter A. Bruck, ed., *A Proxy for Knowledge: The News Media as Agents in Arms Control and Verification.* Ottawa: Carleton International Proceedings, 15–24.

———. 1992. 'Strike Talk: A Case Study of News', in Marc Grenier, ed., *Critical Studies of Canadian Mass Media.* Markham, Ont.: Butterworths, 47–57.

———. 1998. 'Hegemony, the Press and Business Discourse: News Coverage of Strike-Breaker Reform in Quebec and Ontario', *Studies in Political Economy* 55: 93–125.

——— and Josh Greenberg. 2002. 'Promotionalism and Subpolitics: Nike and Its Labor Critics', *Management Communication Quarterly* 15, 4: 541–70.

Knight, Rolf. 1996. *Indians at Work: An Informal History of Native Labour in British Columbia, 1858–1930.* Vancouver: New Star.

Knighton, Tamara, and Sheba Mirza. 2002. 'Postsecondary Participation: The Effects of Parents' Education and Household Income', *Education Quarterly Review* 8, 3: 25–31.

Knobloch, Silvia, Coy Callison, Lei Chen, Annett Fritzsche, and Dolf Zillmann. 2005. 'Children's Sex-Stereotyped Self-Socialization through Selective Exposure to Entertainment: Cross-cultural Experiments in Germany, China, and the United States', *Journal of Communication* 55, 1: 122–38.

Kohn, Melvin L. 1977. *Class and Conformity: A Study of Values, with a Reassessment,* 2nd edn. Chicago: University of Chicago Press.

Kong, Rebecca, Holly Johnson, Sara Beattie, and Andrea Cardillo. 2003. 'Sexual Offences in Canada', *Juristat* 23, 6. Ottawa: Statistics Canada Catalogue no. 85–002–XIE.

Kono, Daniel Y. 2006. 'Optimal Obfuscation: Democracy and Trade Policy Transparency', *American Political Science Review* 100: 369–84.

Kopinak, Kathryn. 1988. 'Women in Canadian Municipal Politics: Two Steps Forward, One Step Back', in Arlene Tigar McLaren, ed., *Gender and Society.* Toronto: Copp Clark Pitman, 372–89.

Kornhauser, William. 1959. *The Politics of Mass Society.* Glencoe, Ill.: Free Press.

Kortenhaus, Carole, and Jack Demarest. 1993. 'Gender Stereotyping in Children's Literature: An Update', *Sex Roles* 28, 3/4: 219–33.

Koshar, Rudy. 1986. 'Political Gangsters and Nazism: Some Comments on Richard Hamilton's Theory of Fascism', *Comparative Studies in Society and History* 28: 785–93.

Krahn, Harvey J., Graham S. Lowe, and Karen D. Hughes. 2007. *Work, Industry, and Canadian Society,* 5th edn. Toronto: Thomson Nelson.

Kramer, Betty J., and Edward H. Thompson Jr. 2005. *Men as Caregivers.* Amherst, NY: Prometheus.

Krane, Julia. 2003. *What's Mother Got to Do With It? Protecting Children from Sexual Abuse.* Toronto: University of Toronto Press.

Krassas, Nicole, Joan Blauwkamp, and Peggy Wesselink. 2003. '"Master Your Johnson": Sexual Rhetoric in *Maxim* and *Stuff* Magazines', *Sexuality and Culture* 7, 3: 98–119.

Kriesel, Warren, Terrence J. Centner, and Andrew Keeler. 1996. 'Neighborhood Exposure to Toxic Releases: Are There Racial Inequities?', *Growth and Change* 27: 479–99.

Kuhn, Thomas S. 1970. *The Structure of Scientific Revolutions,* 2nd edn. Chicago: University of Chicago Press.

Kwong, Jeff C., Irfan A. Dhalla, David L. Streiner, Ralph E. Baddour, Andrea E. Waddell, and Ian L. Johnson. 2002. 'Effects of Rising Tuition Fees on Medical School Class Composition and Financial Outlook', *Canadian Medical Association Journal* 166: 1023–8.

Kymlicka, Will. 1998. 'The Theory and Practice of Canadian Multiculturalism', *Canadian Federation of the Social Sciences and Humanities* 23 (Nov.): 1–10. At: <www.fedcan.ca/english/fromold/breakfast-kymlicka1198.cfm>.

Lambert, Ronald D. 1971. *Sex Role Imagery in Children.* Ottawa: Royal Commission on the Status of Women.

Lambert, Yves. 2004. 'A Turning Point in Religious Evolution in Europe', *Journal of Contemporary Religion* 19, 1: 29–45.

Lamont, Michele. 1992. *Money, Morals, and Manners: The Culture of the French and American Upper-Middle Class.* Chicago: University of Chicago Press.

Lamptey, Peter, Merywen Wigley, D. Carr, and Y. Collymore. 2002. 'Facing the HIV/AIDS Epidemic', *Population Bulletin* 57, 3.

Lancet. 2003. 'Slavery Today', 361: 2093.

Landy, Sarah, and Kwok Kwan Tam. 1996. 'Yes, Parenting Does Make a Difference to the Development of Children in Canada', in Statistics Canada, *Growing Up in Canada.* Ottawa: Human Resources Development Canada and Statistics Canada, 103–11.

Langdridge, Darren. 2006. 'Voices from the Margins: Sadomasochism and Sexual Citizenship', *Citzenship Studies* 10, 4: 373–89.

Langille, David. 1987. 'The Business Council on National Issues and the Canadian State', *Studies in Political Economy* 24: 41–85.

Langlois, S., and P. Morrison. 2002. 'Suicide Deaths and Suicide Attempts', *Health Reports* 13, 2: 9–22.

Larsen, Elena. 2001. *CyberFaith: How Americans Pursue Religion Online.* Washington: Pew Internet & American Life Project. At: <www.pewinternet.org/reports/pdfs/PIP_CyberFaith_Report.pdf>.

Lasswell, Harold D. 1948. 'The Structure and Function of Communication in Society', in Lyman Bryson, ed., *The Communication of Ideas: A Series of Addresses.* New York: Cooper Square, 37–51.

Latour, Bruno, and Steve Woolgar. 1987. *Laboratory Life: The Construction of Scientific Fact,* 2nd edn. Princeton, NJ: Princeton University Press.

Laufer, William S., and Freda Adler. 1994. *The Legacy of Anomie Theory: Advances in Criminological Theory.* New Brunswick, NJ: Transaction.

Lauzen, Martha M. 2006. *The Celluloid Ceiling: Behind-the-Scenes Employment of Women in the Top 250 Films of 2005.* At: <www.moviesbywomen.com/marthalauzenphd/stats2005.html>.

Lawr, Douglas, and Robert Gidney, eds. 1973. *Educating Canadians: A Documentary History of Public Education.* Toronto: Van Nostrand Reinhold.

LeBlanc, J. Clarence. 1994. *Educating Canadians for the New Economy.* Working paper prepared for the Canadian Institute for Research on Regional Development. Moncton, NB.

Lee, Everet. 1966. 'A Theory of Migration', *Demography* 3: 47–57.

Leger Marketing. 2001. 'Canadian Perceptions of Their Health Care System', Canadian Press report, 22 June.

Leitz, Christian, and Harold James. 1999. *The Third Reich: The Essential Readings.* Oxford: Blackwell.

Lemert, Edwin. 1951. *Social Pathology: A Systematic Approach to the Theory of Sociopathic Behavior.* New York: McGraw-Hill.

Lenski, Gerhard E. 1966. *Power and Privilege: A Theory of Social Stratification.* New York: McGraw-Hill.

———, with Patrick Nolan and Jean Lenski. 1995. *Human Societies: An Introduction to Macrosociology,* 7th edn. New York: McGraw-Hill.

Leslie, Gerald, and Sheila K. Korman. 1989. *The Family in Social Context,* 7th edn. New York: Oxford University Press.

Lesthaeghe, Ron, and Johan Surkyn. 1988. 'Cultural Dynamics and Economic Theories of Fertility Change', *Population and Development Review* 14: 1–45.

Lévesque, Stéphane. 1999. 'Rethinking Citizenship and Citizenship Education: A Canadian Perspective for the 21st Century', paper presented at the Citizenship Research Network Symposium, Fourth International Metropolis Conference, Georgetown University, Washington, DC.

Levin, Benjamin, and J. Anthony Riffel. 1997. *Schools and the Changing World: Struggling Toward the Future.* London: Falmer.

Levitt, Cyril. 1994. 'Is Canada a Racist Country?', in Sally F. Zerker, ed., *Change and Impact: Essays in Canadian Social Sciences.* Jerusalem: Magnes Press, Hebrew University, 304–16.

Lewicki, Roy J., and Barbara Benedict Bunker. 1996. 'Developing and Maintaining Trust in Work Relationships', in Roderick M. Kramer and Tom R. Tyler, eds, *Trust in Organizations: Frontiers of Theory and Research.* Thousand Oaks, Calif.: Sage, 114–39.

Lewington, Jennifer. 2002. 'Canada Facing Age Crunch', *Globe and Mail,* 17 July, A1, A8.

Lewis, David L. 1993. 'Canada's Native Peoples and the Churches', in W.E. Hewitt, ed., *The Sociology of Religion: A Canadian Focus.* Toronto: Butterworths, 235–51.

Lewis, Jone Johnson. 2002. 'Women Prime Ministers and Presidents: Twentieth Century', *Women's History Guide.* At: <womenshistory.about.com/library/weekly/aa010128a.htm>.

Ley, David. 1991. 'Gentrification: A Ten Year Overview', in Kent Gerecke, ed., *The Canadian City.* Montreal: Black Rose, 181–96.

Li, Peter. 1988. *Ethnic Inequality in a Class Society.* Toronto: Thompson Educational Publishing.

———, ed. 1999. *Race and Ethnic Relations in Canada,* 2nd edn. Toronto: Oxford University Press.

———. 2003. *Destination Canada: Immigration Debates and Issues.* Toronto: Oxford University Press.

Lian, Jason Z., and Ralph Matthews. 1998. 'Does the Vertical Mosaic Still Exist? Ethnicity and Income in Canada, 1991', *Canadian Review of Sociology and Anthropology* 35, 4: 461–81.

Liazos, A. 1972. 'The Poverty of the Sociology of Deviance: Nuts, Sluts and Preverts', *Social Problems* 20:103-20.

Library of Parliament. 2002. 'Women—Party Standings in the House of Commons: Current List'. At: <www.parl.gc.ca/information/about/people/house/StandingsHofCwm.asp>.

Lieberman, Seymour. 1956. 'The Effects of Changes in Roles on the Attitudes of Role Occupants', *Human Relations* 9: 385–402.

Lieberson, Stanley. 2000. *A Matter of Taste: How Names, Fashions, and Culture Change*. New Haven: Yale University Press.

——— and Freda B. Lynn. 2002. 'Barking up the Wrong Branch: Scientific Alternatives to the Current Model of Sociological Science', *Annual Review of Sociology* 28: 1–19.

Liebow, Elliot. 1993. *Tell Them Who I Am: The Lives of Homeless Women*. New York: Free Press.

Lin, Zhengxi, Janice Yates, and Garnett Picot. 1999. *Rising Self-employment in the Midst of High Unemployment: An Empirical Analysis of Recent Developments in Canada*. Ottawa: Statistics Canada.

Lindert, Peter H. 2004. *Growing Public: Social and Economic Growth since the Eighteenth Century*. Cambridge: Cambridge University Press.

——— and Jeffrey G. Williamson. 2001. *Does Globalization Make the World More Unequal?* Cambridge, Mass.: National Bureau of Economic Research.

Linton, Ralph. 1936. *The Study of Man: An Introduction*. New York: Appleton-Century-Crofts.

Liodakis, Nikolaos. 1998 'The Activities of Hellenic-Canadian Secular Organizations in the Context of Canadian Multiculturalism', *Études Helléniques/Hellenic Studies* 6, 1: 37–58.

———. 2002. 'The Vertical Mosaic Within: Class, Gender and Nativity within Ethnicity', Ph.D. dissertation, McMaster University.

——— and Victor Satzewich. 2003. 'From Solution to Problem: Multiculturalism and "Race Relations" as New Social Problems', in Wayne Antony and Les Samuelson, eds, *Power and Resistance: Critical Thinking about Canadian Social Issues*, 3rd edn. Halifax: Fernwood, 145–68.

Lipman, Ellen L., David R. Offord, and Martin D. Dooley. 1996. 'What Do We Know about Children from Single-Parent Families? Questions and Answers from the National Longitudinal Survey on Children', in *Growing Up in Canada*. Ottawa: Human Resources Development Canada, 83–91.

Lips, Hilary. 2004. *Sex and Gender*. New York: McGraw-Hill.

Lipset, Seymour Martin. 1950. *Agrarian Socialism*. Berkeley: University of California Press.

———. 1981. *Political Man: The Social Bases of Politics*, 2nd edn. Baltimore: Johns Hopkins University Press.

———. 1990. *Continental Divide: The Values and Institutions of the United States and Canada*. New York: Routledge.

Little, Bruce. 2000. 'Female Boomers Led March into the Paid Work Force', *Globe and Mail*, 14 Feb., A2.

Little, Don. 1995. 'Earnings and Labour Force Status of 1990 Graduates', *Education Quarterly Review* 2, 3: 10–20.

Livingston, Jessica. 2004. 'Murder in Juarez: Gender, Sexual Violence, and the Global Assembly Line', *Frontiers* 25, 1: 59–76.

Livingstone, D.W. 2004. *The Education–Jobs Gap: Underemployment or Economic Democracy*. Aurora, Ont.: Garamond.

Lock, Margaret. 1998. 'Menopause: Lessons from Anthropology', *Psychosomatic Medicine* 60: 410–19.

Lofland, Lyn H. 1985. *A World of Strangers: Order and Action in Urban Public Space*. Prospect Heights, Ill.: Waveland.

———. 1998. *The Public Realm: Exploring the City's Quintessential Social Territory*. New York: Aldine de Gruyter.

Logan, John, and Harvey Molotch. 1987. *Urban Fortunes: The Political Economy of Place*. Berkeley: University of California Press.

Long, Norton. 1958. 'The Local Community as an Ecology of Games', *American Journal of Sociology* 64: 251–61.

Looker, E. Dianne, and Graham S. Lowe. 2001. *Post-secondary Access and Student Financial Aid in Canada: Current Knowledge and Research Gaps*. Ottawa: Canadian Policy Research Networks. At: <www.cprn.ca/en/doc.cfm?doc=192>.

——— and Victor Thiessen. 1999. 'Images of Work: Women's Work, Men's Work, Housework', *Canadian Journal of Sociology* 24, 2: 225–54.

Lorber, Judith, and Susan Farrell. 1991. *The Social Construction of Gender*. London: Sage.

Lorimer, James. 1978. *The Developers*. Toronto: Lorimer.

Lorimer, Rowland, and Mike Gasher. 2001. *Mass Communication in Canada*, 4th edn. Toronto: Oxford University Press.

Loseke, Donileen R. 2003. *Thinking about Social Problems: An Introduction to Constructionist Perspectives*. New York: Aldine de Gruyter.

Losh-Hesselbart, Susan. 1987. 'Development of Gender Roles', in Marvin B. Sussman and Suzanne K. Steinmetz, eds, *Handbook of Marriage and the Family*. New York: Plenum, 535–63.

Loughlin, Julia. 1993. 'The Feminist Challenge to Social Studies of Science', in Thomas Brante, Steve Fuller, and William Lynch, eds, *Controversial Science: From Content to Contention*. Albany: State University of New York Press, 3–20.

Lowe, Graham S. 1987. *Women in the Administrative Revolution: The Feminization of Clerical Work*. Toronto: University of Toronto Press.

———. 1989. *Paid/Unpaid Work and Stress: New Directions in Research*. Ottawa: Canadian Advisory Council on the Status of Women.

———. 2000. *The Quality of Work: A People-Centred Agenda*. Toronto: Oxford University Press.

Lowe, Marion. 1983. 'Sex Differences, Science and Society', in Jan Zimmerman, ed., *The Technological Woman*. New York: Praeger, 7–17.

Luckenbill, David F. 1977. 'Criminal Homicide as a Situational Transaction', *Social Problems* 25: 176–86.

Luckmann, Thomas. 1967. *Invisible Religion: The Problem of Religion in Modern Society*. New York: Macmillan.

Lukes, Steven. 1974. *Power: A Radical View*. London: Macmillan.

Lutz, Wolfgang, ed. 1994. *The Future Population of the World: What Can We Assume Today?* London: Earthscan.

Luxton, Meg. 1980. *More Than a Labour of Love*. Toronto: Women's Press.

———. 1983. 'Two Hands for the Clock: Changing Patterns in the Gendered Division of Labour in the Home', *Studies in Political Economy* 12: 27–44.

———. 2001. 'Family Coping Strategies: Balancing Paid Employment and Domestic Labour', in Bonnie Fox, ed., *Family Patterns, Gender Relations*, 2nd edn. Toronto: Oxford University Press, 318–37.

——— and June Corman. 2001. *Getting By in Hard Times: Gendered Labour at Home and on the Job*. Toronto: University of Toronto Press.

Lynch, Kathleen. 1989. *The Hidden Curriculum: Reproduction in Education, A Reappraisal.* London: Falmer.

Lynch, Michael. 1985. 'Discipline and the Material Form of Images: An Analysis of Scientific Visibility', *Social Studies of Science* 15, 1: 37–66.

Lynn, Stephen. 2002. *Zapata Lives! Histories and Cultural Politics in Southern Mexico.* Berkeley: University of California Press.

McAdam, Doug. 1996. 'Conceptual Origins, Current Problems, Future Directions', in McAdam, John McCarthy, and Mayer Zald, eds, *Comparative Perspectives on Social Movements.* New York: Cambridge University Press, 23–40.

McCarthy, John D. 1996. 'Constraints and Opportunities in Adopting, Adapting, and Inventing', in Doug McAdam, John McCarthy, and Mayer Zald, eds, *Comparative Perspectives on Social Movements.* New York: Cambridge University Press, 141–51.

McCarthy, Kevin R. 2001. *World Population Shifts: Boom or Doom?* Santa Monica, Calif.: Rand.

McCarthy, Shawn. 2002. 'Valenti Pitches to Film Makers', *Globe and Mail,* 8 Feb., A1.

McCary, James Leslie. 1967. *Human Sexuality: A Contemporary Marriage Manual.* Toronto: D. Van Nostrand.

McCauley, Martin. 1993. *The Soviet Union: 1917–1991.* London: Longman.

McCleneghan, Sean. 2003. 'Selling Sex to College Females: Their Attitudes about *Cosmopolitan* and *Glamour* Magazines', *Social Science Journal* 40: 317–25.

Maccoby, Eleanor. 1992. 'Trends in the Study of Socialization: Is There a Lewinian Heritage?', *Journal of Social Issues* 48, 2: 171–86.

——— and Carole Jacklin. 1974. *The Psychology of Sex Differences.* Stanford, Calif.: Stanford University Press.

McCurry, Justin. 2004. 'Smuggling for Sex', *Lancet* 364: 1393–4.

McCutcheon, Russell T., ed. 1999. *The Insider/Outsider Problem in the Study of Religion: A Reader.* New York: Cassell.

McDaniel, Susan. 1988. 'Women's Roles, Reproduction and the New Reproductive Technologies: A New Stork Rising', in Nancy Mandell and Ann Duffy, eds, *Reconstructing the Canadian Family.* Toronto: Butterworths, 175–206.

——— and Lorne Tepperman. 2004. *Close Relations: An Introduction to the Sociology of Families,* 2nd edn. Toronto: Pearson/Prentice-Hall.

McDonald, John, and L.D. McDonald. 1964. 'Chain Migration, Ethnic Neighborhood Formation and Social Relationships', *Milbank Memorial Fund Quarterly* 42: 82–7.

MacDowell, Laurel Sefton, and Ian Radforth, eds. 1992. *Canadian Working Class History: Selected Readings.* Toronto: Canadian Scholars' Press.

Macek, S. 2006. *Urban Nightmares.* Minneapolis: University of Minnesota Press.

Macfarlane, Alan. 1997. *The Savage Wars of Peace: England, Japan and the Malthusian Trap.* Oxford: Blackwell.

McFaul, Michael. 2001. *Russia's Unfinished Revolution: Political Change from Gorbachev to Putin.* Ithaca, NY: Cornell University Press.

McGilly, Frank. 1998. *An Introduction to Canada's Public Social Services: Understanding Income and Health Programs,* 2nd edn. Toronto: Oxford University Press..

McGregor, Douglas. 1960. *The Human Side of Enterprise.* New York: McGraw-Hill.

McIntosh, Mary. 1978. 'The State and the Oppression of Women', in Annette Kuhn and Ann Marie Wolpe, eds, *Feminism and Materialism.* London: Routledge & Kegan Paul, 254–89.

Macionis, John J., and Vincent N. Parrillo. 2007. *Cities and Urban Life,* 4th edn. Upper Saddle River, NJ: Prentice-Hall.

McKay, Alexander. 2004. 'Adolescent Sexual and Reproductive Health in Canada: A Report Card in 2004', *Canadian Journal of Human Sexuality* 13, 2: 67–81.

McKeown, Thomas. 1976. *The Modern Rise of Population.* London: Edward Arnold.

Mackie, Marlene. 1983. *Exploring Gender Relations.* Toronto: Butterworths.

———. 1987. *Constructing Women and Men: Gender Socialization.* Toronto: Holt, Rinehart and Winston.

———. 1993. 'Primary Socialization in Socio-cultural Context', in G.N. Ramu, ed., *Marriage and the Family in Canada Today.* Scarborough, Ont.: Prentice-Hall, 96–112.

MacKinnon, Mark, and Keith Lacey. 2001. 'Bleak House', *Globe and Mail,* 18 Aug., F1.

McLaren, Angus. 1990. *Our Own Master Race: Eugenics in Canada, 1885–1945.* Toronto: McClelland & Stewart.

McLaren, Peter. 1998. *Life in Schools: An Introduction to Critical Pedagogy in the Foundations of Education,* 3rd edn. New York: Longman.

McLellan, Janet. 1999. *Many Petals of the Lotus: Five Asian Buddhist Communities in Toronto.* Toronto: University of Toronto Press.

McMahon, Anthony. 1999. *Taking Care of Men: Sexual Politics in the Public Mind.* Cambridge: Cambridge University Press.

MacMillan, Harriet L., Angus B. MacMillan, David R. Offord, and Jennifer L. Dingle. 1996. 'Aboriginal Health', *Canadian Medical Association Journal* 155: 1569–78.

McRoberts, Kenneth. 1988, 1999. *Quebec: Social Change and Political Crisis.* Toronto: McClelland & Stewart/Oxford University Press.

McVey, Wayne, Jr, and Warren E. Kalbach. 1995. *Canadian Population.* Toronto: Nelson.

Magder, Ted. 1993. *Canada's Hollywood: The Canadian State and Feature Films.* Toronto: University of Toronto Press.

——— and Jonathan Burston. 2001. 'Whose Hollywood? Changing Forms and Relations Inside the North American Entertainment Economy', in Vincent Mosco and Dan Schiller, eds, *Continental Order? Integrating North America for Cybercapitalism.* Lanham, Md: Rowman and Littlefield, 207–34.

Magnusson, Warren. 1990. 'Critical Social Movements: Decentring the State', in Alain G. Gagnon and James Bickerton, eds, *Canadian Politics: An Introduction.* Peterborough, Ont.: Broadview, 525–41.

Mahtani, Minelle. 2001. 'Representing Minorities: Canadian Media and Minority Identities', *Canadian Ethnic Studies* 33, 3: 99–133.

Malinowski, Bronislaw. 1922. *Argonauts of the Western Pacific.* New York: Dutton.

Malthus, Thomas R. 1970 [1798]. *An Essay on the Principle of Population.* Harmondsworth, UK: Penguin.

Mandell, Nancy. 2001. 'Women, Families and Intimate Relations', in Mandell, ed., *Feminist Issues: Race, Class and Sexuality,* 3rd edn. Toronto: Prentice-Hall, 193–218.

Mankoff, Milton. 1971. 'Societal Reaction and Career Deviance: A Critical Analysis', *Sociological Quarterly* 12: 204–18.

Manzer, Jenny. 2001. 'Clinical Guidelines Ignore Gender Differences', *Medical Post* 37, 13: 2, 65.

Manzer, Ronald. 1994. *Public Schools and Political Ideas: Canadian Educational Policy in Historical Perspective.* Toronto: University of Toronto Press.

Mao, Y., J. Hu, A.M. Ugnat, and K. White. 2000. 'Non-Hodgkin's Lymphoma and Occupational Exposure to Chemicals in Canada', *Annals of Oncology* 11, suppl. 1: 69–73.

Maquiladora Solidarity Network. 2000. 'Child Labour and the Rights of Youth'. At: <www.maquilasolidarity.org/resources/child/issuesheet.htm>.

March, Karen. 2003. 'Who Do I Look Like? Gaining a Sense of Self-Authenticity through the Physical Reflections of Others', in J. Holstein and J. Gubriam, eds, *Inner Lives and Social Worlds: Readings in Social Psychology.* New York: Oxford University Press, 317–23.

Marchak, Patricia. 1991. *The Integrated Circus: The New Right and the Restructuring of Global Markets.* Montreal: McGill-Queen's University Press.

Marcil-Gratton, Nicole. 1998. *Growing Up with Mom and Dad? The Intricate Family Life Courses of Canadian Children.* Ottawa: Statistics Canada.

Marcus, Clare Cooper, and Wendy Sarkissian. 1986. *Housing as If People Mattered: Site Design Guidelines for Medium-Density Family Housing.* Berkeley: University of California Press.

Marcus, Sheron. 2005. 'Queer Theory for Everyone: A Review Essay', *Signs* 31, 1: 191–218.

Markin, K.M. 2005. 'Still Crazy after All These Years: The Enduring Defamatory Power of Mental Disorder', *Law and Psychology Review* 29: 155–85.

Marmot, Michael G., Geffrey Rose, Martin Shipley, and P.J. Hamilton. 1978. 'Employment Grade and Coronary Heart Disease in British Civil Servants', *Journal of Epidemiological Community Health* 32: 244–9.

———, George Davey Smith, Stephen Stansfeld, Chandra Patel, Fiona North, Jenny Head, Ian White, Eric Brunner, and Amanda Feeney. 1991. 'Health Inequalities among British Civil Servants: The Whitehall II Study', *Lancet* 337: 1387–93.

Marr, William L. 1992. 'Post-war Canadian Immigration Patterns', in Steven Globerman, ed., *The Immigration Dilemma.* Vancouver: Fraser Institute, 17–42.

Marsden, Peter V., Cynthia R. Cook, and Arne L. Kalleberg. 1996. 'Bureaucratic Structures for Coordination and Control', in Arne L. Kalleberg, David Knoke, Peter V. Marsden, and Joe L. Spaeth, eds, *Organizations in America: Analyzing Their Structures and Human Resource Practices.* Thousand Oaks, Calif.: Sage, 69–86.

Marshall, Katherine. 1987. 'Women in Male Dominated Professions', *Social Trends* (Winter): 7–11.

———. 1993. 'Employed Parents and the Division of Labour', *Perspectives on Labour and Income* 5, 3: 23–30.

———. 1994. 'Balancing Work and Family Responsibilities', *Perspectives on Labour and Income* 6, 1: 26–30.

———. 1998. 'Stay-at-Home Dads', *Perspectives on Labour and Income* 10, 1: 9–15.

Marshall, Sheree. 1995. 'Ethnic Socialization of African American Children: Implications for Parenting, Identity Development, and Achievement', *Journal of Youth and Adolescence* 24: 377–96.

Martin, David. 2000. 'Canada in Comparative Perspective', in David Lyon and Marguerite Van Die, eds, *Rethinking Church, State, and Modernity: Canada between Europe and America.* Toronto: University of Toronto Press, 23–33.

Martin, Dominique, Jean-Luc Metzger, and Philippe Pierre. 2006. 'The Sociology of Globalization: Theoretical and Methodological Reflections', *International Sociology* 21: 499–521.

Martínez, Javier, and Alvaro Díaz. 1996. *Chile: The Great Transformation.* Washington and Geneva: Brookings Institution and UN Research Institute for Social Development.

Marx, Karl. 1957 [1844]. 'Contribution to the Critique of Hegel's Philosophy of Right—Introduction', in *On Religion: Karl Marx and Friedrich Engels.* Moscow: Progress.

———. 1967 [1867]. *Capital: A Critique of Political Economy.* New York: International Publishers.

———. 1976 [1867]. *Capital,* vol. 1. Harmondsworth, UK: Penguin.

———. 1887. *Capital: A Critical Analysis of Capitalist Production,* ed. Friedrich Engels. London: Lowry and Company.

———. 1956. *Selected Writings in Sociology and Social Philosophy,* ed. T.B. Bottomore and Maximilien Rubel, trans. T.B. Bottomore. New York: McGraw-Hill.

———. 1964. *The Economic and Philosophical Manuscripts of 1844,* ed. Dirk J. Struik, trans. Martin Milligan. New York: International Publishers.

——— and Friedrich Engels. 1970 [1845–6]. *The German Ideology,* Part I, with Selections from Parts 2 and 3, trans. C.J. Arthur. New York: International Publishers.

——— and ———. 1948 [1848]. *Manifesto of the Communist Party.* New York: International Publishers.

——— and ———. 1983 [1848]. 'Manifesto of the Communist Party', in Eugene Kamenka, ed., *The Portable Karl Marx.* New York: Penguin, 197–324.

Maslovski, Mikhail. 1996. 'Max Weber's Concept of Patrimonialism and the Soviet System', *Sociological Review* 44: 294–308.

Maslow, Abraham. 1954. *Motivation and Personality.* New York: Harper & Row.

Massey, Douglas S., Joaquin Arango, Graeme Hugo, Ali Kouauci, Adela Pellegrino, and J. Edward Taylor. 1993. 'Theories of International Migration: A Review and Appraisal', *Population and Development Review* 19: 431–65.

Maticka-Tyndale, Eleanor. 2001. 'Twenty Years in the AIDS Pandemic: A Place for Sociology', *Current Sociology* 49, 6: 13–21.

Matza, D., and Gresham Sykes. 1957. 'Techniques of Neutralization: A Theory of Delinquency', *American Sociological Review* 5: 1–12.

Maume, David J. 2006. 'Gender Differences in Taking Vacation Time', *Work and Occupations* 33, 2: 161.

Maxim, Paul S., and Paul C. Whitehead. 1998. *Explaining Crime*, 4th edn. Newton, Mass.: Butterworth-Heinemann.

Mead, George Herbert. 1934. *Mind, Self, and Society from the Standpoint of a Social Behaviorist.* Chicago: University of Chicago Press.

Mead, Margaret. 1935. *Sex and Temperament in Three Primitive Societies.* New York: Dell.

Meadows, Donella H., Dennis L. Meadows, and Jorgen Randers. 1992. *Beyond the Limits: Confronting Global Collapse, Envisioning a Sustainable Future.* Post Mills, Vt: Chelsea Green.

———, ———, ———, and William H. Behrens III. 1972. *The Limits to Growth.* New York: Universe.

———, Jorgen Randers, and Dennis Meadows. 2005. *The Limits to Growth—The 30-Year Update.* London: Earthscan.

Meissner, Martin, Elizabeth Humphries, Scott Meis, and William Schell. 1975. 'No Exit for Wives: Sexual Division of Labour and the Culmination of Household Demands', *Canadian Review of Sociology and Anthropology* 12: 424–39.

Meller, Patricio. 2000. *The Unidad Popular and the Pinochet Dictatorship: A Political Economy Analysis.* New York: St Martin's.

Melucci, Alerbero. 1989. *Nomads of the Present: Social Movements and Individual Needs in Contemporary Society.* Philadelphia: Temple University Press.

Ménoret, Pascal. 2005. *The Saudi Enigma: A History*, trans. P. Camiller. London: Zed.

Merten, Hans-Joachim. 1997. 'Lex Mercatoria: A Self-Applying System beyond National Law?', in Gunther Teubner, ed., *Global Law without a State.* Aldershot, UK: Dartmouth, 31–43.

Mertig, Angela, and Riley Dunlap. 2001. 'Environmentalism, New Social Movement and the New Class: A Cross-national Investigation', *Rural Sociology* 66, 1: 113–36.

———, ———, and Denton Morrison. 2002. 'The Environmental Movement in the United States', in Riley Dunlap and William Michelson, eds, *Handbook of Environmental Sociology.* Westport, Conn.: Greenwood, 448–81.

Merton, Robert K. 1938. 'Social Structure and Anomie', *American Sociological Review* 3: 672–82.

———. 1949, 1957. *Social Theory and Social Structure.* Glencoe, Ill./New York: Free Press.

Messing, Karen. 1987. 'The Scientific Mystique: Can a White Lab Coat Guarantee Purity in the Search for Knowledge about the Nature of Women?', in Greta Hofmann Nemiroff, ed., *Women and Men: Interdisciplinary Readings on Gender.* Toronto: Fitzhenry & Whiteside, 103–16.

———. 1998. *One-Eyed Science: Occupational Health and Women Workers.* Philadelphia: Temple University Press.

——— and Piroska Åslin. 2006. *Gender Equality, Work and Health: A Review of the Evidence.* Geneva: WHO.

Meyer, David, and Suzanne Staggenborg. 1996. 'Movements, Countermovements and the Structure of Political Opportunity', *American Journal of Sociology* 101: 1628–60.

Meyer, John W. 2000. 'Globalization: Sources and Effects on National States and Societies', *International Sociology* 15: 233–48.

Meyer, Leisa. 2006. 'Sexual Revolutions', *OAH Magazine of History* 20, 2: 5–6.

Meyerson, Debra, Karl E. Weick, and Roderick M. Kramer. 1996. 'Swift Trust and Temporary Groups', in Roderick M. Kramer and Tom R. Tyler, eds, *Trust in Organizations: Frontiers of Theory and Research.* Thousand Oaks, Calif.: Sage, 166–95.

Michaelson, Karen L., ed. 1981. *And the Poor Get Children: Radical Perspectives on Population Dynamics.* New York: Monthly Review Press.

Michels, Robert. 1962. *Political Parties.* New York: Free Press.

Michelson, William. 1976. *Man and His Urban Environment: A Sociological Approach.* Reading, Mass.: Addison-Wesley.

———. 1977. *Environmental Choice, Human Behavior, and Residential Satisfaction.* New York: Oxford University Press.

———. 1983. *From Sun to Sun: Daily Obligations and Community Structure in the Lives of Employed Women and Their Families.* Totowa, NJ: Rowman and Allanheld.

———. 2005. *Time-Use: Expanding Explanation in the Social Sciences.* Boulder, Colo.: Paradigm.

———. 2006. 'Metropolitan Government and the Social Ecology of Minority Residential Distribution: The Experience of Metropolitan Toronto', in Fong (2006: 76–98).

——— and Ellis Roberts. 1979. 'Children and the Urban Physical Environment', in William Michelson, Saul Levine, and Anna-Rose Spina, eds, *The Child in the City: Changes and Challenges.* Toronto: University of Toronto Press, 410–77.

Micklin, Michael, ed. 1973. *Population, Environment and Social Organization: Current Issues in Human Ecology.* Hinsdale, Ill.: Dryden.

Mihorean, K. 2005. 'Trends in Self-Reported Spousal Violence', in K. AuCoin, ed., *Family Violence in Canada: A Statistical Profile.* Ottawa: Canadian Centre for Justice Statistics, Statistics Canada.

Miles, Robert, and Malcolm Brown. 2003. *Racism*, 2nd edn. London: Routledge.

——— and Rudy Torres. 1996. 'Does "Race" Matter? Transatlantic Perspectives on Racism after "Race Relations"', in V. Amit-Talai and C. Knowles, eds, *Re-situating Identities: The Politics of Race, Ethnicity and Culture.* Peterborough, Ont.: Broadview, 24–46.

Milgram, Stanley. 1970. 'The Experience of Living in Cities', *Science* 167: 1461–8.

———. 1974. *Obedience to Authority.* New York: Harper and Row.

Milkman, Ruth. 1987. *Gender at Work: The Dynamics of Job Segregation by Sex during World War II.* Chicago: University of Illinois Press.

Miller, Gale, and James A. Holstein. 1993. *Constructionist Controversies: Issues in Social Problems Theory.* New York: Aldine de Gruyter.

Miller, John R. 1996. *Singwaulk's Vision: A History of Native Residential Schools in Canada.* Toronto: University of Toronto Press.

Miller, Toby, Nitin Govil, John McMurria, and Richard Maxwell. 2001. *Global Hollywood.* London: British Film Institute.

Millett, Kate. 1969, 1970. *Sexual Politics.* New York: Doubleday; Avon.

Mills, C. Wright. 1956. *The Power Elite.* New York: Oxford University Press.

———. 1959. *The Sociological Imagination.* New York: Oxford University Press.

Mills, Martin. 2006. 'Sony-BMG Annulment Good for Business', *Billboard*, 2 Sept., 8.

Mills, Melinda, and Frank Trovato. 2001. 'The Effect of Pregnancy in Cohabiting Unions on Marriage in Canada, the Netherlands, and Latvia', *Statistical Journal of the United Nations Economic Commission for Europe* 18: 103–18.

Miranda, Dave, and Michael Claes. 2004. 'Rap Music Genres and Deviant Behaviors in French-Canadian Adolescents', *Journal of Youth and Adolescence* 33, 2: 113–22.

Mitchell, Ann. 1985. *Children in the Middle: Living through Divorce*. London: Tavistock.

Mitchell, Elizabeth. 1981 [1915]. *In Western Canada before the War*. Saskatoon: Western Producer Prairie Books.

Mitchell, Robert Cameron, Angela G. Mertig, and Riley E. Dunlap. 1992. 'Twenty Years of Environmental Mobilization: Trends among National Environmental Organizations', in Dunlap and Mertig, eds, *American Environmentalism*. Philadelphia: Taylor and Francis, 11–26.

Moir, Anne, and David Jessel. 1992. *Brain Sex: The Real Difference between Men and Women*. London: Michael Joseph.

Mondschein, E.R., K.E. Adolph, and C.S. Tamis-LeMonda. 2000. 'Gender Bias in Mothers' Expectations about Infant Crawling', *Journal of Experimental Child Psychology* 77: 304–16.

Montpetit, Eric, Francesca Scala, and Isabelle Fortier. 2004. 'The Paradox of Deliberative Democracy: The National Action Committee on the Status of Women and Canada's Policy on Reproductive Technology', *Policy Sciences* 37: 137–57.

Moodie, Susannah. 1995 [1852]. *Roughing It in the Bush*. Toronto: McClelland & Stewart.

Moodley, Kogila. 1983. 'Canadian Multiculturalism as Ideology', *Ethnic and Racial Studies* 6, 3: 320–31.

Moore, Barrington, Jr. 1966. *Social Origins of Dictatorship and Democracy: Lord and Peasant in the Making of the Modern World*. Boston: Beacon.

———. 1969. *Social Origins of Dictatorship and Democracy*. London: Peregrine.

Morell, Carolyn M. 1994. *Unwomanly Conduct: The Challenges of Intentional Childlessness*. New York: Routledge.

Morgan, Laurie A., and Karin A. Martin. 2006. 'Taking Women Professionals Out of the Office: The Case of Women in Sales', *Gender & Society* 20, 1: 108.

Morgan, Stephen, and Aage B. Sorensen. 1999. 'Parental Networks, Social Closure and Mathematics Learning: A Test of Coleman's Social Capital Explanation of School Effects', *American Sociological Review* 64: 661–81.

Morland, Iain. 2005. '"The Glans Opens Like a Book": Writing and Reading the Intersexed Body', *Continuum: Journal of Media and Cultural Studies* 19, 3: 335–48.

Morley, David. 1980. *The 'Nationwide' Audience*. London: British Film Institute.

———. 2006. 'Unanswered Questions in Audience Research', *Communication Review* 9: 101–21.

Morris, Desmond. 1997. *The Human Sexes: A Natural History of Man and Woman*. New York: St Martin's.

Morris, Marika, Jane Robinson, and Janet Simpson with Sherry Galey. 1999. *The Changing Nature of Home Care and Its Impact on Women's Vulnerability to Poverty*. Ottawa: Status of Women Canada.

Morrison, Denton, and Riley E. Dunlap. 1986. 'Environmentalism and Elitism: A Conceptual and Empirical Analysis', *Environmental Management* 10: 581–9.

———, Kenneth E. Hornback, and W. Keith Warner. 1972. 'The Environmental Movement: Some Preliminary Observations and Predictions', in William R. Burch Jr, Neil H. Cheek Jr, and Lee Taylor, eds, *Social Behavior, Natural Resources and the Environment*. New York: Harper, 259–79.

Morrison, Todd, Shannon Ellis, Melanie Morrison, Anomi Bearben, and Rebecca Harriman. 2006. 'Exposure to Sexually Explicit Material and Variations in Body Esteem, Genital Attitudes and Sexual Esteem among a Sample of Canadian Men', *Journal of Men's Studies* 14, 2: 209–22.

Morton, Desmond. 1998. *Working People: An Illustrated History of the Canadian Labour Movement*, 4th edn. Montreal: McGill-Queen's University Press.

Mosco, Vincent. 1989. *The Pay-per Society: Computers and Communication in the Information Age*. Toronto: Garamond.

———. 2005. 'Here Today, Outsourced Tomorrow: Knowledge Workers in the Global Economy', *Javnost—The Public* 12, 2: 39–55.

Moss, Kathleen. 2004. 'Kids Witnessing Violence', *Canadian Social Trends* no. 73 (Summer): 12–16.

Moynihan, Ray, Iona Heath, and David Henry. 2002. 'Selling Sickness: The Pharmaceutical Industry and Disease Mongering', *British Medical Journal* 324: 886–91.

Muncie, John, and Margaret Weatherell. 1995. 'Family Policy and Political Discourse', in John Muncie, Margaret Weatherell, Rudi Dallos, and Allan Cochrane, eds, *Understanding the Family*. London: Sage, 39–80.

Munck, Ronaldo. 2002. *Globalization and Labour: The New 'Great Transformation'*. London: Zed Books.

Munro, Marcella. 1997. 'Ontario's "Days of Action" and Strategic Choices for the Left in Canada', *Studies in Political Economy* 53: 125–40.

Murdie, Robert. 1969. *Factorial Ecology of Metropolitan Toronto*. Department of Geography Research Paper 116. Chicago: University of Chicago.

Murdock, George. 1949. *Social Structure*. New York: Macmillan.

Murphy, Elizabeth. 2000. 'Risk, Responsibility and Rhetoric in Infant Feeding', *Journal of Contemporary Ethnography* 29: 291–325.

———. 2007. *Childhood* 14, 1: 105–27. At: <search1.scholarsportal.info/ids70/view_record.php?id=2&recnum=3&SID=dd5cc57671b4400ab13563fc5427839d>.

Murphy, Michael. 1993. 'The Contraceptive Pill and Women's Employment as Factors in Fertility Change in Britain 1963–1980: A Challenge to the Conventional View', *Population Studies* 7: 221–44.

Murphy, Raymond. 1994. 'The Sociological Construction of Science without Nature', *Sociology* 28: 957–74.

Mustard, Cameron A., Shelley Derkson, Jean-Marie Berthelot, Michael Wolfson, and Leslie L. Roos. 1997. 'Age-Specific Education and Income Gradients in Morbidity and Mortality in a Canadian Province', *Social Science and Medicine* 45: 383–97.

Mustard, Fraser. 1999. 'Health Care and Social Cohesion', in Daniel Drache and Terry Sullivan, eds, *Market Limits in Health Reform: Public Success, Private Failure.* London: Routledge, 329–50.

Myerson, Marilyn, Sara Crawley, Erica Hesch Anstey, Justine Kessler, and Cara Okopny. 2007. 'Who's Zoomin' Who? A Feminist, Queer Content Analysis of "Interdisciplinary" Human Sexuality Textbooks', *Hypatia* 22, 1: 92–113.

Myles, John. 1989. *Old Age in the Welfare State: The Political Economy of Public Pensions*, rev. edn. Lawrence: University Press of Kansas.

Nabalamba, Alice. 2001. 'Locating Risk: A Multivariate Analysis of the Spatial and Socio-demographic Characteristics of Pollution', Ph.D. dissertation, University of Waterloo.

Naess, Arne. 1973. 'The Shallow and the Deep, Long Range Ecology Movement', *Inquiry* 16: 95–100.

Nagel, Joane. 2006. 'Ethnicity, Sexuality and Globalization', *Theory, Culture and Society* 23, 2/3: 545–7.

Nagel, Thomas. 1986. *The View from Nowhere.* New York: Oxford University Press.

Nakhaie, M. Reza, ed. 1999. *Debates on Social Inequality: Class, Gender and Ethnicity in Canada.* Toronto: Harcourt Canada.

———. 2000. 'Ownership and Management Position of Canadian Ethnic Groups in 1973 and 1989', in Madeline A. Kalbach and Warren Kalbach, eds, *Perspectives on Ethnicity in Canada.* Toronto: Harcourt Canada.

———, Robert A. Silverman, and Teresa C. LaGrange. 2000. 'An Examination of Gender, Ethnicity, Class and Delinquency', *Canadian Journal of Sociology* 25: 35–59.

Nanda, Serena. 1991. *Cultural Anthropology.* Belmont, Calif.: Wadsworth.

——— and Richard L. Warms. 2004. *Cultural Anthropology*, 8th edn. Belmont, Calif.: Wadsworth/Thomson Learning.

Nash, Kate. 2000. *Contemporary Political Sociology: Globalization, Politics, and Power.* Oxford: Blackwell.

Nathanson, C.A. 1984. 'Sex Differences in Mortality', *Annual Review of Sociology* 10: 191–213.

Nathe, Patricia. 1978. 'The Flux, Flow, and Effluvia of Bohemia', *Urban Life* 6: 387–416.

National Council of Welfare. 2001–2. *The Cost of Poverty.* Ottawa: National Council of Welfare.

———. 2002. *Poverty Profile 1999.* Ottawa: Minister of Public Works and Government Services.

———. 2006. *Poverty Profile 2002 and 2003.* Ottawa: Minister of Public Works and Government Services.

National Longitudinal Survey of Children and Youth (NLSCY). 1996. *Growing Up in Canada.* Ottawa: Human Resources Development Canada and Statistics Canada.

National Post. 2002. 'Census: How You Fit into the National Picture', 17 July, A9.

National Research Council, Committee on Population and Working Group on Population Growth and Economic Development. 1986. *Population Growth and Economic Development: Policy Questions.* Washington: National Academy Press.

Navarro, Véase Vicente. 1975. 'The Industrialization of Fetishism or the Fetishism of Industrialization: A Critique of Ivan Illich', *Social Science and Medicine* 9: 351–63.

———. 1999. *NWT Health Status Report.* Ottawa: Department of Health and Social Services, Statistics Canada.

Nedelmann, Birgitta. 1991. 'Review of *Ideology and the New Social Movements*, by Alan Scott', *Contemporary Sociology* 20: 374–5.

Nelson, Adie, and Barrie W. Robinson. 2002. *Gender in Canada*, 2nd edn. Toronto: Pearson Educational.

Nelson, Fiona. 1999. 'Maternal Identities, Maternal Practices and the Culture(s) of Motherhood', paper presented at the annual meeting of the Canadian Sociology and Anthropology Association, Lennoxville, Que., 8 June.

Nelson, Michelle, and Hye-Jin Paek. 2005. 'Cross-Cultural Differences in Sexual Advertising Content in a Transnational Women's Magazine', *Sex Roles* 53, 5/6: 371–83.

Nett, Emily. 1981. 'Canadian Families in Social-Historical Perspective', *Canadian Journal of Sociology* 6, 3: 239–60.

Netting, S. Nancy, and Matthew Burnett. 2004. 'Twenty Years of Student Sexual Behaviour: Subcultural Adaptations to a Changing Health Environment', *Adolescence* 39, 153: 19–38.

Newbold, K. Bruce. 1998. 'Problems in Search of Solutions: Health and Canadian Aboriginals', *Journal of Community Health* 23, 1: 59–73.

Newman, Oscar. 1972. *Defensible Space: Crime Prevention through Urban Design.* New York: Macmillan.

Nicholson, Linda, and Steven Seidman, eds. 1995. *Introduction to Social Postmodernism: Beyond Identity Politics.* Cambridge: Cambridge University Press.

Nielsen, Tracy. 2002. 'Streets, Strangers and Solidarity: A Study of Lesbian Interaction in the Public Realm', Ph.D. dissertation, University of Manitoba.

———. 2007. 'Streets, Strangers, and Solidarity', in John J. Macionis, Nijole V. Benokraitis, and Bruce Ravelli, eds, *Seeing Ourselves: Classic, Contemporary, and Cross-Cultural Readings in Sociology*, 2nd Canadian edn. Toronto: Pearson/Prentice-Hall, 173–87.

Nisbet, Robert A. 1959. 'The Decline and Fall of Social Class', *Pacific Sociological Review* 2: 11–17.

Nobles, Melissa. 2000. *Shades of Citizenship: Race and the Census in Modern Politics.* Stanford, Calif.: Stanford University Press.

Notestein, Frank. 1945. 'Population: The Long View', in Theodore W. Schultz, ed., *Food for the World.* Chicago: University of Chicago Press, 36–57.

———. 1967. 'The Population Crisis: Reasons for Hope', *Foreign Affairs* 46, 1: 156–80.

Oakes, J.M. 1996. 'A Longitudinal Analysis of Environmental Equity in Communities with Hazardous Waste Facilities', *Social Science Research* 25: 125–48.

Obesity Canada. 2001. 'What Is Obesity?' At: <www.obesitycanada.com>.

O'Brien, Mary. 1981. *The Politics of Reproduction.* London: Routledge & Kegan Paul.

Occhionero, Marisa Ferrari. 1996. 'Rethinking Public Space and Power', *International Review of Sociology* 6 (n.s.): 453–64.

O'Connor, Dennis R. 2002. *Report of the Walkerton Inquiry: The Events of May 2000 and Related Issues: Part One: A Summary.* Toronto: Ontario Ministry of the Attorney General.

O'Connor, Julia S., Ann Shola Orloff, and Sheila Shaver. 1999. *States, Markets, Families: Gender Liberalism and Social Policy in Australia, Canada, Great Britain and the United States.* Cambridge: Cambridge University Press.

Offe, Claus. 1984. *Contradictions of the Welfare State.* Cambridge, Mass.: MIT Press.

Offer, Daniel, Eric Ostrov, Kenneth Howard, and Robert Atkinson. 1988. *The Teenage World: Adolescents' Self-Image in Ten Countries.* New York: Plenum.

Ogmundson, Richard. 1991. 'Perspective on the Class and Ethnic Origins of Canadian Elites: A Methodological Critique of the Porter/Clement/Olsen Tradition', *Canadian Journal of Sociology* 15, 2: 165–77.

———. 1993. 'At the Top of the Mosaic: Doubts about the Data', *American Review of Canadian Studies* (Autumn): 373–86.

———. 2005. 'Does it Matter If Women, Minorities and Gays Govern? New Data Concerning an Old Question', *Canadian Journal of Sociology* 30: 315–19.

——— and J. McLaughlin. 1992. 'Trends in the Ethnic Origins of Canadian Elites: The Decline of the Brits?', *Canadian Review of Sociology and Anthropology* 29, 2: 227–42.

O'Leary, K. Daniel, J. Barling, Ilena Arias, Alan Rosenbaum, J. Malone, and A. Tyree. 1989. 'Prevalence and Stability of Physical Aggression between Spouses: A Longitudinal Analysis', *Journal of Consulting and Clinical Psychology* 57: 263–8.

Olewiler, Nancy. 1999. 'National Tax Policy for an International Economy: Divergence in a Converging World?', in Thomas J. Courchene, ed., *Room to Manoeuvre? Globalization and Policy Convergence.* Montreal: McGill-Queen's University Press, 345–72.

Olsken, Daniel V.A. 1999. 'Religious Pluralism and US Church Membership: A Reassessment', *Sociology of Religion* 60: 149–73.

Olsen, Denis. 1980. *The State Elite.* Toronto: McClelland & Stewart.

Olshansky, S. Jay, and Brian A. Ault. 1986. 'The Fourth Stage of the Epidemiological Transition: The Age of Delayed Degenerative Diseases', *Milbank Quarterly* 46: 355–91.

———, Bruce A. Carnes, and Christine Cassel. 1990. 'In Search of Methuselah: Estimating the Upper Limits to Human Longevity', *Science* 250: 634–40.

———, ———, Richard G. Rogers, and Len Smith. 1997. 'Infectious Diseases: New and Ancient Threats to World Health', *Population Bulletin* 52, 2.

Olson, Mancur. 1965. *The Logic of Collective Action: Public Goods and the Theory of Groups.* Cambridge, Mass.: Harvard University Press.

Olzak, Susan. 1983. 'Contemporary Ethnic Mobilization', *Annual Review of Sociology* 9: 355–74.

Omran, Abdal R. 1971. 'The Epidemiologic Transition', *Milbank Memorial Quarterly* 49: 509–38.

Organization for Economic Co-operation and Development (OECD). 2001. *OECD Economic Outlook* 70 (Dec.). Paris: OECD.

———. 2004. 'Wage-setting Institutions and Outcomes', *OECD Employment Outlook.* Paris: OECD.

———. 2005. *Society at a Glance: OECD Social Indicators 2005.* Paris: OECD.

———. 2006. *Education at a Glance: OECD Indicators 2006.* Paris: OECD.

O'Riordan, T. 1971. 'The Third American Environmental Conservation Movement: New Implications for Public Policy', *Journal of American Studies* 5: 155–71.

Orlova, Alexandra. 2004. 'Insiders and Outcasts: From Social Dislocation to Human Trafficking—The Russian Case', *Problems of Post-Communism* 51, 6: 14–22.

Ornstein, Michael. 1981. 'The Occupational Mobility of Men in Ontario', *Canadian Review of Sociology and Anthropology* 18, 2: 181–215.

———. 1983. *Accounting for Gender Differentials in Job Income in Canada: Results from a 1981 Survey.* Ottawa: Minister of Supply and Services.

Osberg, Lars. 1992. 'Canada's Economic Performance: Inequality, Poverty, and Growth', in Robert C. Allen and Gideon Rosenbluth, eds, *False Promises: The Failure of Conservative Economics.* Vancouver: New Star, 39–52.

Osborne, Ken. 1999. *Education: A Guide to the Canadian School Debate: Or, Who Wants What and Why?* Toronto: Penguin.

Ottawa Citizen. 2002. 'Aboriginals More Likely to Get AIDS, Study Shows', 8 June: A7.

Otto, Rudolph. 1923. *The Idea of the Holy.* Oxford: Oxford University Press.

Ouroussoff, Nicolai. 2006. 'All Fall Down', *New York Times,* 19 Nov. At: <www.nytimes.com/2006/11/19/weekinreview/19ouroussoff.html?ex=1164776400&en=538ca5fe9d9c64a5&ei=5070&emc=eta1>.

Overbeek, Johannes. 1974. *History of Population Theories.* Rotterdam: Rotterdam University Press.

Page, Randy M., and Michelle O'Hegarty. 2006. 'Type of Student Residence as a Factor in College Students' Alcohol Consumption and Social Normative Perceptions Regarding Alcohol Use', *Journal of Child and Adolescent Substance Abuse* 15, 3: 15–31.

Pahl, R.E. 1970. *Whose City? And Other Essays on Sociology and Planning.* New York: Longman.

Pais, José Machado. 2000. 'Transitions and Youth Cultures: Forms and Performances', *International Social Science Journal* 52: 219–33.

Pakulski, Jan, and Malcolm Walters. 1996. *The Death of Class.* London: Sage.

Paletta, Anna. 1992. 'Today's Extended Families', *Canadian Social Trends* (Winter): 26–8.

Palys, T.S. 1986. 'Testing the Common Wisdom: The Social Content of Video Pornography', *Canadian Psychology* 27: 22–35.

Palys, T., and J. Lowman. 2000. 'Protecting Research Participant Confidentiality: Toward a Research Participant Shield Law', *Canadian Journal of Law and Society* 21, 1: 163–85.

Pampel, Fred C. 1998. *Aging, Social Inequality, and Public Policy.* Thousand Oaks, Calif.: Pine Forge.

Pandey, Sanjay K., and Stuart I. Bretschneider. 1997. 'The Impact of Red Tape's Administrative Delay on Public Organizations' Interest in New Information Technologies', *Journal of Public Administration Research and Theory* 7: 113–30.

Panitch, Leo, ed. 1977. *The Canadian State: Political Economy and Political Power*. Toronto: University of Toronto Press.

Park, Kristin. 2002. 'Stigma Management among the Voluntarily Childless', *Sociological Perspectives* 45, 1: 21–45.

Park, Robert E. 1914. 'Racial Assimilation in Secondary Groups', *American Journal of Sociology*: 607

———. 1925. 'The City: Suggestions for the Investigation of Human Behavior in the Urban Environment', in Park et al. (1925: 1–46).

——— and Ernest Burgess. 1921. *Introduction to the Science of Sociology*. Chicago: University of Chicago Press.

———, ———, and Roderick D. McKenzie, eds. 1925. *The City*. Chicago: University of Chicago Press.

Parsons, Talcott. 1937. *The Structure of Social Action*. New York: McGraw-Hill.

———. 1949. *Essays in Sociological Theory*. New York: Free Press.

———. 1951. *The Social System*. Glencoe, Ill.: Free Press.

———. 1955. *Family, Socialization and Interaction Process*. New York: Free Press.

———. 1959. 'The School Class as a Social System: Some of Its Functions in American Society', *Harvard Educational Review* 29: 297–318.

——— and Robert F. Bales. 1955. *Family Socialization and Interaction Process*. New York: Free Press.

Pearce, Frank, and Laureen Snider, eds. 1995. *Corporate Crime: Contemporary Debates*. Toronto: University of Toronto Press.

Peers, Frank W. 1979. *The Public Eye: Television and the Politics of Canadian Broadcasting, 1952–1968*. Toronto: University of Toronto Press.

Pendakur, Manjunath. 1990. *Canadian Dreams and American Control: The Political Economy of the Canadian Film Industry*. Detroit: Wayne State University Press.

Penha-Lopes, Vania. 2006. '"To Cook, Sew, to Be a Man": The Socialization for Competence and Black Men's Involvement in Housework', *Sex Roles* 54, 3/4: 261–74.

Perls, Thomas T., and Ruth C. Fretts. 1998. 'Why Women Live Longer Than Men', *Scientific American Presents* 9, 2: 100–3.

Perrow, Charles. 1972. *Complex Organizations: A Critical Essay* Glenview, Ill.: Scott, Foresman.

Perry, Clarence. 1966. 'The Neighborhood Unit Formula', in William Wheaton, ed., *Urban Housing*. New York: Free Press, 94–109.

Petersen, William. 1989. 'Marxism and the Population Question: Theory and Practice', *Population and Development Review* 14 (suppl.): 77–101.

Peterson, Peter G. 1999. 'Grey Dawn: The Global Aging Crisis', *Foreign Affairs* 78, 1: 42–55.

Peterson, Richard A. 1994. 'Culture Studies through the Production Perspective: Progress and Prospects', in Diana Crane, ed., *The Sociology of Culture: Emerging Theoretical Perspectives*. Oxford: Blackwell, 163–89.

Petzer, Shane, and Gordon Issacs. 1998. 'SWEAT: The Development and Implementation of a Sex-Worker Advocacy and Intervention Program in Post-Apartheid South Africa', in Kempadoo and Doezema (1998 192–6).

Pfohl, Stephen J. 1977. 'The Discovery of Child Abuse', *Social Problems* 24: 310–23.

Pfuhl, Erdwin H., and Stuart Henry. 1993. *The Deviance Process*, 3rd edn. New York: Aldine de Gruyter.

Phillips, Lynne, and Suzan Ilcan. 2003. '"A World Free from Hunger": Global Imagination and Governance in the Age of Scientific Management', *Sociologia Ruralis* 43, 4: 434–53.

Pickard, Victor W. 2006. 'Assessing the Radical Democracy of Indymedia: Discursive, Technical, and Institutional Constructions', *Critical Studies in Media Communication* 23, 1: 19–38.

Picot, Garnett, and John Myles. 1995. *Social Transfers, Changing Family Structure, and Low Income among Children*. Ottawa: Statistics Canada.

Pierce, Marie. 2003. 'Canada's Crossroads: Radical Change Has Left Canadian School Boards Facing New Challenges', *American School Board Journal* 190, 4: 46–8.

Piliavin, Erving, and S. Briar. 1964. 'Police Encounters with Juveniles', *American Journal of Sociology* 70: 206–14.

Pimentel, David, and Marcia Pimentel. 1999. 'Population Growth, Environmental Resources and the Global Availability of Food', *Social Research* 66: 417–28.

Pinard, Maurice. 2002. 'The Quebec Independence Movement: From Its Emergence to the 1995 Referendum', in D. Baer, ed., *Political Sociology: Canadian Perspectives*. Toronto: Oxford University Press, 238–68.

Plato. 1980. *The Republic*. London: Fitzhenry & Whiteside.

Plummer, Ken. 1975. *Sexual Stigma: An Interactionist Account*. London: Routledge & Kegan Paul.

———. 2003. 'Queers, Bodies and Postmodern Sexualities: A Note on Revisiting the "Sexual" in Symbolic Interactionism', *Qualitative Sociology* 26, 4: 515–30.

Plumwood, Val. 1992. 'Feminism and Ecofeminism: Beyond the Dualistic Assumptions of Women, Men and Nature', *Ecologist* 22, 1: 8–13.

Pollack, William. 1998. *Real Boys: Rescuing Our Sons from the Myths of Boyhood*. New York: Random House.

Pomerleau, Andrée, Daniel Bolduc, Gerard Malcuit, and Louise Cossess. 1990. 'Pink or Blue: Environmental Gender Stereotypes in the First Two Years of Life', *Sex Roles* 22: 359–67.

Ponting, J. Rick. 2005. 'Urban Aboriginal People', in Hiller (2005: 139–67).

Population Reference Bureau (PRB). 1995. *World Population Data Sheet for 1995*. Washington: PRB.

———. 2000. *World Population Data Sheet for 2000*. Washington: PRB.

———. 2001. *World Population Data Sheet for 2001*. Washington: PRB.

———. 2002. *World Population Data Sheet for 2002*. Washington: PRB.

———. 2003. *World Population Data Sheet for 2003*. Washington: PRB.

———. 2006. *World Population Data Sheet for 2006*. Washington: PRB.

Porter, John. 1965. *The Vertical Mosaic: An Analysis of Social Class and Power in Canada*. Toronto: University of Toronto Press.

Portes, Alejandro. 1997. *Globalization from Below: The Rise of Transnational Communities*. Princeton, NJ: Centre for Migration and Development.

———. 1999. 'Conclusion: Towards a New World: The Origins and Effects of Transnational Activities', *Ethnic and Racial Studies* 22: 463–77.

———, Luis E. Guarnizo, and Patricia Landolt. 1999. 'The Study of Transnationalism: Pitfalls and Promise of an Emergent Research Field', *Ethnic and Racial Studies* 22: 217–37.

Posner, Judith. 1987. 'The Objectified Male: The New Male Image in Advertising', in Greta Hofmann Nemiroff, ed., *Women and Men: Interdisciplinary Readings on Gender.* Markham, Ont.: Fitzhenry & Whiteside, 180–8.

Potuchek, Jean L. 1997. *Who Supports the Family: Gender and Breadwinning in Dual-Earner Marriages.* Stanford, Calif.: Stanford University Press.

Poulantzas, Nicos. 1975. *Classes in Contemporary Capitalism,* trans. David Fernbach. London: New Left Books.

———. 1978. *State, Power, Socialism,* trans. Patrick Camiller. London: New Left Books.

Press, Andrea L. 1991. *Women Watching Television: Gender, Class, and Generation in the American Television Experience.* Philadelphia: University of Pennsylvania Press.

Presthus, Robert V. 1973. *Elite Accommodation in Canadian Politics.* Toronto: Macmillan.

Preston, Samuel H. 1986a. 'Changing Values and Falling Birth Rates', *Population and Development Review* 12 (suppl.): 176–200.

———. 1986b. 'Mortality and Development Revisited', *United Nations Population Bulletin* 18: 34–40.

———, Patrick Heuveline, and Michel Guillot. 2001. *Demography.* Malden, Mass.: Blackwell.

Price, Robert. 1975. 'Bureaucrat and Kinsman', in Price, *Society and Bureaucracy in Contemporary Ghana.* Berkeley: University of California Press, 56–82.

Pringle, Rosemary. 1988. *Secretaries Talk: Sexuality, Power and Work.* London: Verso.

Prus, Robert. 1987. 'Generic Social Processes: Maximizing Conceptual Development in Ethnographic Research', *Journal of Contemporary Ethnography* 16: 250–93.

Pryor, Edward. 1984. 'Canadian Husband–Wife Families: Labour Force Participation and Income Trends, 1971–1981', *Labour Force* (May): 93–109.

Pryor, Jan, and Bryan Rodgers. 2001. *Children in Changing Families: Life after Parental Separation.* Oxford: Blackwell.

Psychology Today. 2000. 'Makeup vs. Math' (Nov.–Dec.): 18.

Pulkingham, Jane, and Tanya Van Der Gaag. 2004. 'Maternity/Parental Leave Provisions in Canada', *Canadian Women's Studies* 23, 3/4: 116–26.

Putney, Norella, and Vern Bengtson. 2003. 'Socialization and the Family Revisited', in Richard Settersten, ed., *Invitation to the Life Course.* Amityville, NY: Baywood, 165–94.

Pyper, Wendy. 2006. 'Balancing Career and Care', *Perspectives on Labour and Income* (Nov.): 5–15.

Quadagno, Jill. 1990. 'Race, Class, and Gender in the US Welfare State', *American Sociological Review* 55: 25–7.

Quine, Lyn. 1999. 'Workplace Bullying in NHS Community Trust: Staff Questionnaire Survey', *British Medical Journal* 318: 228–32.

———. 2002. 'Workplace Bullying in Junior Doctors: Questionnaire Survey', *British Medical Journal* 324: 878–9.

Raadschelders, Jos C.N. 1997. 'Size and Organizational Differentiation in Historical Perspective', *Journal of Public Administration Research and Theory* 7: 419–41.

Raboy, Marc. 1990. *Missed Opportunities: The Story of Canada's Broadcasting Policy.* Montreal: McGill-Queen's University Press.

———. 1995. 'The Role of Public Consultation in Shaping the Canadian Broadcasting System', *Canadian Journal of Political Science* 28, 3: 455–77.

Radway, Janice. 1984. *Reading the Romance: Women, Patriarchy and Popular Literature.* Chapel Hill: University of North Carolina Press.

Ram, Bali. 1990. *New Trends in the Family: Demographic Facts and Figures.* Ottawa: Minister of Supply and Services Canada.

——— and Rahim. 1993. 'Enduring Effects of Women's Early Employment Experiences on Child-Spacing: The Canadian Evidence', *Population Studies* 47: 307–18.

Ramirez, Francisco O. 1981. 'Comparative Social Movements', *International Journal of Comparative Sociology* 22: 3–21.

Ramsay, Patricia. 1999. *Making Friends in School: Promoting Peer Relationships in Early Childhood.* New York: Teachers College Press, Columbia University.

Ranson, Gillian. 2005. 'Paid and Unpaid Work: How do Families Divide Their Time?', in Maureen Baker, ed., *Families: Changing Trends in Canada,* 5th edn. Toronto: McGraw-Hill Ryerson, 99–120.

Raphael, Dennis. 2001. 'From Increasing Poverty to Societal Disintegration: The Effects of Economic Inequality on the Health of Individuals and Communities', in Pat Armstrong, Hugh Armstrong, and David Coburn, eds, *Unhealthy Times: The Political Economy of Health Care.* Toronto: Oxford University Press, 223–46.

Raudenbush, Stephen, and Robert J. Sampson. 1999. '"Ecometrics": Toward a Science of Assessing Ecological Settings, with Application to the Systematic Social Observation of Neighborhoods', *Sociological Methodology* 29: 1–41.

Redclift, Michael, and Ted Benton, eds. 1994. *Social Theory and the Global Environment.* London: Routledge.

——— and Graham Woodgate. 1994. 'Sociology and the Environment: Discordant Discourse?', in Redclift and Benton (1994: 51–66).

Reichert, Tom, and Jacqueline Lambiase. 2003. 'How To Get "Kissably Close": Examining How Advertisers Appeal to Consumers' Sexual Needs and Desires', *Sexuality and Culture* 7, 3: 120–36.

Reimer, Samuel H. 1995. 'A Look at Cultural Effects on Religiosity: A Comparison between Canada and the United States', *Journal for the Scientific Study of Religion* 34: 445–57.

Reinarman, Craig. 1996. 'The Social Construction of an Alcohol Problem', in Gary W. Potter and Victor E. Kappeler, eds, *Constructing Crime: Perspectives on Making News and Social Problems.* Prospect Heights, Ill.: Waveland, 193–220.

Reiss, Albert J., Jr. 1959. 'Rural–Urban and Status Differences in Interpersonal Contacts', *American Journal of Sociology* 65: 182–95.

Reiter, Ester. 1991. *Making Fast Food: From the Frying Pan into the Fire.* Montreal: McGill-Queen's University Press.

———. 1996. *Making Fast Food: From the Frying Pan into the Fryer*, 2nd edn. Montreal: McGill-Queen's University Press.

Reitz, Jeffrey G.. 1998. *The Warmth of the Welcome: The Social Causes of Economic Success for Immigrants in Different Nations and Cities*. Boulder, Colo.: Westview.

——— and Janet Lum. 2006. 'Immigration and Diversity in a Changing Canadian City: Social Bases of Intergroup Relations in Toronto', in Fong (2006: 15–50).

Reitzes, Donald, and Dietrich Reitzes. 1987. *The Alinski Legacy: Alive and Kicking*. Greenwich, Conn.: JAI.

Reskin, Barbara. 2003. 'Including Mechanisms in Our Models of Ascriptive Inequality: 2002 Presidential Address', *American Sociological Review* 68, 1: 1–12.

Rhoads, Steven E. 2004. *Taking Sex Differences Seriously*. San Francisco: Encounter Books.

Richardson, Joanna. 2000. *The Courtesans: The Demi-Monde in 19th Century France*. London: Phoenix.

Richardson, Laurel. 1988. *The Dynamics of Sex and Gender*. New York: Harper and Row.

Richardson, R. Jack. 1992. 'Free Trade: Why Did It Happen?', *Canadian Review of Sociology and Anthropology* 29: 307–28.

Rifkin, Jeremy. 1995. *The End of Work: The Decline of the Global Labour Force and the Dawn of the Post-market Era*. New York: Putnam.

Rinehart, James. 2006. *The Tyranny of Work: Alienation and the Labour Process*, 5th edn. Toronto: Thomson Nelson.

———, Christopher Huxley, and David Robertson. 1994. 'Worker Commitment and Labour–Management Relations under Lean Production at CAMI', *Industrial Relations* 49: 750–75.

Ritzer, George. 2000. *The McDonaldization of Society*, 3rd edn. Thousand Oaks, Calif.: Pine Forge.

Robert, Maryse. 2000. *Negotiating NAFTA: Explaining the Outcome in Culture, Textiles, Autos, and Pharmaceuticals*. Toronto: University of Toronto Press.

Roberts, Barbara. 1988. *Whence They Came: Deportation from Canada, 1900–1935*. Ottawa: Ottawa University Press.

Roberts, J. Timmons, and Melissa M. Toffolon-Weiss. 2001. *Chronicles from the Environmental Justice Frontline*. Cambridge: Cambridge University Press.

Roberts, Keith. 1995. *Religion in Sociological Perspective*, 3rd edn. Belmont, Calif.: Wadsworth.

Robertson, Ann. 2001. 'Biotechnology, Political Rationality and Discourses on Health Risk', *Health* 5: 293–310.

Robertson, David, James Rinehart, Chris Huxley, Jeff Wareham, Herman Rosenfeld, A. McGough, and Steven Benedict. 1993. *The CAMI Report: Lean Production in a Unionized Auto Plant*. North York, Ont.: CAW Research, 1993.

Robertson, Heather-Jane. 1998. *No More Teachers, No More Books: The Commercialization of Canada's Schools*. Toronto: McClelland & Stewart.

Robinson, B.W., and E.D. Salamon. 1987. 'Gender Role Socialization: A Review of the Literature', in Salamon and Robinson, eds, *Gender Roles: Doing What Comes Naturally?* Toronto: Methuen, 123–42.

Robinson, Tracy L. 2001. 'White Mothers of Non-White Children', *Journal of Humanistic Counseling, Education and Development* 40, 2: 171–85.

Roby, Jini. 2005. 'Women and Children in the Global Sex Trade: Toward More Effective Policy', *International Journal of Social Work* 48, 2: 136–47.

Rodgers, Bryan, and Jan Pryor. 1998. *Divorce and Separation: The Outcomes for Children*. York, UK: Joseph Rowntree Foundation.

Rodrik, Dani. 1997. *Has Globalization Gone Too Far?* Washington: Institute for International Economics.

Rogan, Mary. 1999. 'Acts of Faith', *Saturday Night* 114, 5: 42–51.

Rogers, Andrei, and Frans J. Willekens, eds. 1981. *Migration and Settlement: A Multiregional Comparative Study*. Dordrecht, Germany: Reidel.

Romaniuc, Anatole. 1984. *Current Demographic Analysis: Fertility in Canada: From Baby-Boom to Baby-Bust*. Ottawa: Statistics Canada.

———. 1994. 'Fertility in Canada: Retrospective and Prospective', in Frank Trovato and Carl F. Grindstaff, eds, *Perspectives on Canada's Population: An Introduction to Concepts and Issues*. Toronto: Oxford University Press, 213–30.

Romanow, Roy J. 2002. *Building on Values: The Future of Health Care in Canada*. Final Report of the Royal Commission on the Future of Health Care in Canada. Ottawa. At: <www.hc-sc.gc.ca/english/care/romanow/hcc0086.html>.

Rondahl, Gerd, Sune Innala, and Marianne Carlson. 2006. 'Heterosexual Assumptions in Verbal and Non-verbal Communication in Nursing', *Journal of Advanced Nursing* 56, 4: 373–81.

Roof, Wade Clark. 1999. *Spiritual Marketplace: Baby Boomers and the Remaking of American Religion*. Princeton, NJ: Princeton University Press.

——— and William McKinney. 1987. *American Mainline Religion*. New Brunswick, NJ: Rutgers University Press.

Rosa, Eugene, Gary Machlis, and Kenneth Keating. 1988. 'Energy and Society', *Annual Review of Sociology* 14: 149–72.

Rose, Steven, Leon J. Kamin, and R.C. Lewontin. 1984. *Not in Our Genes: Biology, Ideology, and Human Nature*. New York: Penguin.

Rosen, Bernard C. 1956. 'The Achievement Syndrome: A Psychocultural Dimension of Social Stratification', *American Sociological Review* 21: 203–11.

———. 1959. 'Race, Ethnicity, and the Achievement Syndrome', *American Sociological Review* 24: 47–60.

Rosenberg, Sharon. 2003. 'Neither Forgotten nor Fully Remembered: Tracing an Ambivalent Public Memory on the 10th Anniversary of the Montreal Massacre', *Feminist Theory* 4, 1: 5–27.

Rosenthal, Carolyn J. 1985. 'Kinkeeping in the Familial Division of Labour', *Journal of Marriage and the Family* 47: 965–74.

Rosenthal, Donald B., ed. 1980. *Urban Revitalization*. Beverly Hills, Calif.: Sage.

Ross, David P., and Paul Roberts. 1999. *Income and Child Well-Being: A New Perspective on the Poverty Debate*. Ottawa: Canadian Council on Social Development.

———, Katherine J. Scott, and Peter J. Smith. 2000. *The Canadian Fact Book on Poverty 2000*. Ottawa: Canadian Council on Social Development.

Ross, Eric B. 1998. *The Malthus Factor: Poverty, Politics and Population in Capitalist Development*. London: Zed Books.

Rossi, Alice. 1984. 'Gender and Parenthood', *American Sociological Review* 49: 1–18.

Rotermann, Michelle. 2001. 'Wired Young Canadians', *Canadian Social Trends* (Winter): 4–8.

Rothermund, Dietmar. 1993. *An Economic History of India: From Pre-colonial Times to 1991*, 2nd edn. London: Routledge.

Roy, Francine. 2006. 'From She to She: Changing Patterns of Women in the Canadian Labour Force', *Canadian Economic Observer* (June): 1–9.

Royal Commission on Aboriginal Peoples. 1996. *Report of the Royal Commission on Aboriginal Peoples*, vol. 3: *Gathering Strength*. Ottawa: RCAP.

Royal Commission on Bilingualism and Biculturalism. 1970. *Report of the Royal Commission on Bilingualism and Biculturalism*, vol. 4: *The Cultural Contribution of the Other Ethnic Groups*. Ottawa: Queen's Printer.

Royal Commission on Equality in Employment. 1984. *Report*. Ottawa: Supply and Services Canada.

Ruble, Diane N., and Carol Lynn Martin. 1998. 'Gender Development', in William Damon, ed., *Handbook of Child Psychology*, 5th edn. New York: Wiley, 933–1016.

Rudner, L.M. 1999. 'Scholasitc Achievement and Demographic Characteristics of Home School Students in 1998', *Education Policy Analysis Archives* 7, 8. At: <http://epaa.asu.edu/epaa/v7n8/>.

Rumford, Chris. 2006. 'Theorizing Borders', *European Journal of Social Theory* 9: 155–69.

Ryan, John, and William M. Wentworth. 1999. *Media and Society: The Production of Culture in the Mass Media*. Needham Heights, Mass.: Allyn and Bacon.

Sabini, John, and Maury Silver. 2005. 'Destroying the Innocent with a Clear Conscience: A Sociopsychology of the Holocaust', in Jason A. Nier, ed., *Taking Sides: Clashing Views on Controversial Issues in Social Psychology*. Dubuque, Iowa: McGraw-Hill/Dushkin, 198–207.

Sacco, Vincent F. 1992. 'An Introduction to the Study of Deviance and Control', in Sacco, ed., *Deviance: Conformity and Control in Canadian Society*. Scarborough, Ont.: Prentice-Hall, 1–48.

———. 2005. *When Crime Waves*. Thousand Oaks, Calif.: Sage.

——— and K. Ismaili. 2001. 'Social Problem Claims and the Undefended Border: The Case of Canada and the United States', in Best (2001).

Sachs, Wolfgang. 1991. 'Environment and Development: The Story of a Dangerous Liaison', *Ecologist* 21: 252–7.

Sadovnick, Alan R., ed. 1995. *Knowledge and Pedagogy: The Sociology of Basil Bernstein*. Norwood, NJ: Ablex.

Said, Edward W. 1978. *Orientalism*. London: Routledge & Kegan Paul.

Salazar, Lilia P., Shirin M. Schuldermann, Eduard H. Schuldermann, and Cam-Loi Huynh. 2001. 'Canadian Filipino Adolescents Report on Parental Socialization for School Involvement', *Canadian Ethnic Studies* 33, 2: 52–76.

Salter, Liora, and Rick Salter. 1997. 'The New Infrastructure', *Studies in Political Economy* 53: 67–102.

Sampson, Robert, and Steve Raudenbush. 1999. 'Systematic Social Observation of Public Spaces: A New Look at Disorder in Urban Neighborhoods', *American Journal of Sociology* 105: 603–51.

Samson, Jane, ed. 2001. *The British Empire*. New York: Oxford University Press.

Samuel, John T. 1990. 'Third World Immigration and Multiculturalism', in Shiva S. Halli, Frank Trovato, and Leo Driedger, eds, *Ethnic Demography: Canadian Immigrant, Racial and Cultural Variations*. Ottawa: Carleton University Press, 383–414.

Sartorius, N. 2001. 'The Economic and Social Burden of Depression', *Journal of Clinical Psychiatry* 62 (suppl. 15): 8–11.

Sassen, Saskia. 1991. *The Global City: New York, London, Tokyo*. Princeton, NJ: Princeton University Press.

———. 1996. *Losing Control? Sovereignty in an Age of Globalization*. New York: Columbia University Press.

———. 2000. 'Regulating Immigration in a Global Age: A New Policy Landscape', *Annals, American Academy of Political and Social Science* 570: 65–77.

———. 2002. 'Introduction: Locating Cities on Global Circuits', in Sassen, ed., *Global Networks: Linked Cities*. New York: Routledge, 1–36.

Sasson, Theodore. 1995. *Crime Talk: How Citizens Construct a Social Problem*. Hawthorne, NY: Aldine de Gruyter.

Satzewich, Vic. 1991. *Racism and the Incorporation of Foreign Labour: Farm Labour Migration to Canada since 1945*. London: Routledge.

———, ed. 1998. *Racism and Social Inequality in Canada*. Toronto: Thompson Educational Publishing.

———. 1999. 'The Political Economy of Race and Ethnicity', in Li (1999: 311–46).

——— and Nikolaos Liodakis. 2007. *'Race' and Ethnicity in Canada: A Critical Introduction*. Toronto: Oxford University Press.

——— and Terry Wotherspoon. 1993. *First Nations: Race, Class and Gender Relations*. Scarborough, Ont.: Nelson.

Scala, Francesca, Eric Montpetit, and Isabelle Fortier. 2005. 'The NAC's Organizational Practices and the Politics of Assisted Reproductive Technologies in Canada', *Canadian Journal of Political Science* 38, 3: 581–604.

Scarce, Rik. 1990. *Eco-warriors: Understanding the Radical Environmental Movement*. Chicago: Noble.

Schauer, Terrie. 2005. 'Women's Porno: The Heterosexual Female Gaze in Porn Sites "For Women"', *Sexuality & Culture* 9, 2: 42–64.

Schecter, Tanya. 1998. *Race, Class, Women and the State: The Case of Domestic Labour*. Montreal: Black Rose.

Scheid, T.L. 2005. 'Stigma as a Barrier to Employment: Mental Disability and the American Disabilities Act', *International Journal of Law and Psychiatry* 28, 6: 670–90.

Schiller, Herbert I. 1984. *Information and the Crisis Economy*. Norwood, NJ: Ablex.

Schissel, Bernard, and Terry Wotherspoon. 2003. *The Legacy of School for Aboriginal People: Education, Oppression, and Emancipation*. Toronto: Oxford University Press.

Schnaiberg, Allan. 1975. 'Social Synthesis of the Societal-Environmental Dialectic: The Role of Distributional Impacts', *Social Science Quarterly* 56: 5–20.

———. 1980. *The Environment: From Surplus to Scarcity*. New York: Oxford University Press.

Schnore, Leo F. 1958. 'Social Morphology and Human Ecology', *American Journal of Sociology* 63: 620–34.

Schonberg, Harold C. 1977. *The Lives of the Great Composers*, 3rd edn. New York: Norton.

Schütz, Alfred. 1967 [1932]. *The Phenomenology of the Social World*, trans. George Walsh and Frederick Lehnert. Evanston, Ill.: Northwestern University Press.

Schweingruber, David. 2006. 'Success through a Positive Mental Attitude? The Role of Positive Thinking in Door-to-Door Sales', *Sociological Quarterly* 47, 1: 41.

Scott, Allen J. 2004. 'Hollywood and the World: The Geography of Motion-Picture Distribution and Marketing', *Review of International Political Economy* 11, 1: 33–61.

Scott, Marvin B., and Stanford M. Lyman. 1968. 'Accounts', *American Sociological Review* 33: 46–64.

Sears, Alan. 2003. *Retooling the Mind Factory: Education in a Lean State.* Aurora, Ont.: Garamond.

Segrave, Kerry. 1998. *American Television Abroad: Hollywood's Attempt to Dominate World Television.* Jefferson, NC: McFarland.

Seiber, Timothy, and Andrew Gordon. 1981. *Children and Their Organizations.* Boston: G.K. Hall.

Seidman, Steven. 1994. 'Introduction', in Seidman, ed., *The Postmodern Turn: New Perspectives on Social Theory.* Cambridge: Cambridge University Press.

Seltzer, Judith, and Debra Kalmuss. 1988. 'Socialization and Stress Explanations for Spouse Abuse', *Social Forces* 67: 473–91.

Selznick, Philip. 1949. *TVA and the Grass Roots.* Berkeley: University of California Press.

Sennett, Richard. 1998. *The Corrosion of Character: The Personal Consequences of Work in the New Capitalism.* New York: Norton.

Settersten, Richard. 2003 'Socialization and the Life Course: New Frontiers in Theory and Research', in Settersten, ed., *Invitation to the Life Course.* Amityville, NY: Baywood, 39–40.

Sev'er, Aysan. 2002. *Fleeing the House of Horrors: Women Who Have Left Abusive Partners.* Toronto: University of Toronto Press.

Shaffir, William. 1974. *Life in a Religious Community: The Lubavitcher Chassidim in Montreal.* Toronto: Holt, Rinehart and Winston.

Shaw, Susan. 1988. 'Gender Difference in the Definition and Perception of Household Labour', *Family Relations* 37: 333–7.

Shelton, Beth Anne, and Juanita Firestone. 1989. 'Household Labor Time and the Gender Gap in Earnings', *Gender and Society* 3, 1: 105–12.

——— and Daphne John. 1996. 'The Division of Household Labor', *Annual Review of Sociology* 22: 299–322.

Shively, JoEllen. 1992. 'Cowboys and Indians: Perceptions of Western Films among American Indians and Anglos', *American Sociological Review* 57: 725–34.

Shorter, Edward. 2005. *Written in the Flesh: A History of Desire.* Toronto: University of Toronto Press.

Sidlofsky, Samuel. 1969. 'Post-war Immigrants in the Changing Metropolis, with Special Reference to Toronto's Italian Population', Ph.D. dissertation, University of Toronto.

Sieber, Sam. 1981. *Fatal Remedies: The Ironies of Social Intervention.* New York: Plenum.

Siegel, Lloyd, and Arthur Zitrin. 1978. 'Transsexuals in the New York City Welfare Population: The Function of Illusion in Transsexuality', *Archives of Sexual Behavior* 7: 285–90.

Siegel, M. 2005. *False Alarm: The Truth about the Epidemic of Fear.* New York: Wiley.

Sills, David L. 1975. 'The Environmental Movement and Its Critics', *Human Ecology* 3: 1–41.

Silva, Elizabeth B., and Carol Smart, eds. 1999. *The New Family?* London: Sage.

Silver, Susan, Sue Wilson, and J.M. Shields. 2004. 'Job Restructuring and Worker Displacement: Does Gender Matter?', *Canadian Women's Studies* 23, 3/4: 7–13.

Simmel, Georg. 1950a. 'The Metropolis and Mental Life', in Simmel (1950b: 400–27).

———. 1950b. *The Sociology of Georg Simmel*, trans. Kurt Wolff. New York: Free Press.

———. 1957. 'Fashion', *American Journal of Sociology* 62: 541–58.

Simmons, Alan. 1998. 'Racism and Immigration Policy', in Satzewich (1998).

Simon, Herbert. 1986. *Decision Making and Problem Solving.* Washington: National Academy Press.

———. 1997. *Administrative Behavior: A Study of Decision-Making Processes in Administrative Organizations*, 4th edn. New York: Free Press.

Simon, Julian. 1981. 'Environmental Disruption or Environmental Improvement?', *Social Science Quarterly* 62: 30–43.

———, ed. 1995. *The State of Humanity.* Cambridge, Mass.: Blackwell.

———. 1996. *The Ultimate Resource 2.* Princeton, NJ: Princeton University Press.

Simon, William, and John Gagnon. 2003. 'Sexual Scripts: Origins, Influences and Changes', *Qualitative Sociology* 26, 4: 491–7.

Simons, John. 1980. 'Reproductive Behavior as Religious Practice', in Charlotte Höhn and Rainer Mackensen, eds, *Determinants of Fertility Trends: Theories Re-examined.* Liège, Belgium: Ordina, 133–45.

Sinclair, Peter R. 1982. 'Towards a Class Analysis of Contemporary Socialist Agriculture', *Sociologia Ruralis* 22: 122–39.

———. 1987. *State Intervention and the Newfoundland Fisheries.* Aldershot, UK: Avebury.

——— and Lawrence Felt. 1992. 'Separate Worlds: Gender and Domestic Labour in an Isolated Fishing Region', *Canadian Review of Sociology and Anthropology* 29: 55–71.

Singer, Dorothy, and Jerome Singer. 2001. *Handbook of Children and the Media.* Thousand Oaks, Calif.: Sage.

Sjoberg, Gideon. 1960. *The Preindustrial City: Past and Present.* New York: Free Press.

Skidelsky, Robert. 2000. *John Maynard Keynes: Fighting for Britain, 1937–1946.* London: Macmillan.

Sklair, Leslie. 1994. 'Global Sociology and Global Environmental Change', in Redclift and Benton (1994: 205–27).

Skocpol, Theda. 1979. *States and Social Revolutions: A Comparative Analysis of France, Russia, and China.* Cambridge: Cambridge University Press.

Skogstad, Grace. 2000. 'Globalization and Public Policy', *Canadian Journal of Political Science* 33: 805–28.

Slaughter, Matthew J., and Phillip Swagel. 1997. *Does Globalization Lower Wages and Export Jobs?* International Monetary Fund Economic Issues 11. Washington: IMF.

Smelser, Neil J. 1963. *Theory of Collective Behavior*. New York: Free Press.

Smith, Adam. 1976 [1776]. *An Inquiry into the Nature and Causes of the Wealth of Nations*, ed. W.B. Todd. Oxford: Oxford University Press.

Smith, Dorothy. 1975. 'Ideological Structures and How Women Are Excluded', *Canadian Review of Sociology and Anthropology* 12: 353–69.

———. 1987. *The Everyday World as Problematic: A Feminist Sociology*. Boston: Northeastern University Press.

———. 1990. *The Conceptual Practices of Power: A Feminist Sociology of Knowledge*. Toronto: University of Toronto Press.

———. 1993. *Earnings of Men and Women*. Ottawa: Statistics Canada.

———. 1999. *Writing the Social: Critique, Theory, and Investigations*. Toronto: University of Toronto Press.

Smith, Michael R. 1999. 'What Is the Effect of Technological Change on Earnings Inequality?', *International Journal of Sociology and Social Policy* 19: 24–59.

———. 2001a. 'La mondialisation à-t-elle un effet important sur les marchés du travail des pays riches?', in Daniel Mercure, ed., *Une société monde? Les dynamiques de la mondialisation*. Quebec City: Presses de l'Université Laval, 201–14.

———. 2001b. 'What Have the FTA and the NAFTA Done to the Canadian Labor Market?', *Forum for Social Economics* 30: 25–50.

Smith, Philip. 2001. *Cultural Theory: An Introduction*. Oxford: Blackwell.

Smith, Raymond T. 1996. *The Matrifocal Family: Power, Pluralism and Politics*. New York: Routledge.

Smith, Tom W. 2002. 'Religious Diversity in America: The Emergence of Muslims, Buddhists, Hindus, and Others', *Journal for the Scientific Study of Religion* 41: 577–85.

Smith, Wilfred Cantwell. 1959. 'Comparative Religion: Wither—and Why?', in Mircea Eliade and Joseph M. Kitagawa, eds, *The History of Religions: Essays in Methodology*. Chicago: University of Chicago Press, 31–58.

Smyth, Bruce, ed. 2004. *Parent–Child Contact and Post-Separation Parenting Arrangements*. Research Report #9. Melbourne: Australian Institute of Family Studies.

Smythe, Dallas. W. 1981. *Dependency Road: Communications, Capitalism, Consciousness, and Canada*. Norwood, NJ: Ablex.

Snow, David A., and Leon Anderson. 1993. *Down on Their Luck: A Study of Homeless Street People*. Berkeley: University of California Press.

———, E. Burke Rochford Jr, Steven K. Worden, and Robert D. Benford. 1986. 'Frame Alignment Processes, Micromobilization, and Movement Participation', *American Sociological Review* 51: 464–81.

Snowdon, Frank. 1983. *Before Color Prejudice: The Ancient View of Blacks*. Cambridge, Mass.: Harvard University Press.

Sommer, Robert. 1969. *Personal Space: The Behavioral Basis of Design*. Toronto: Prentice-Hall.

Sontag, Susan. 1978. *Illness as Metaphor*. New York: Farrar, Straus & Giroux.

Spector, Malcolm, and John I. Kitsuse. 1977. *Constructing Social Problems*. Menlo Park, Calif.: Cummings.

Speirs, Rosemary. 1993. 'Violence Affects Half of Women, Study Says', *Toronto Star*, 19 Nov., A1, A29.

Spittler, Gerd. 1980. 'Abstract Knowledge as a Basis of Power: The History of the Evolution of Bureaucratic Power in the Prussian Peasant State', *Kolner Zeitschrift fur Soziologie und Sozialpsychologie* 32: 574–604.

Spitzer, Steven. 1975. 'Toward a Marxian Theory of Deviance', *Social Problems* 22: 638–51.

Spreitzer, G.M., and S. Sonenshein. 2004. 'Toward the Construct Definition of Positive Deviance', *American Behavioral Scientist* 47, 6: 828–47.

Sprinkle, Annie. 1991. *Post Porn Modernism*. Amsterdam: Torch Books.

Stack, John F., Jr. 1986. 'Ethnic Mobilization in World Politics: The Primordial Perspective', in Stack, ed., *The Primordial Challenge: Ethnicity in the Contemporary World*. New York: Greenwood, 1–11.

Stanton, Elizabeth Cady. 1972 [1895]. *The Woman's Bible*. New York: Arno.

Staples, Clifford L., and William G. Staples. 2000. 'Rereading Harry Braverman's *Labor and Monopoly Capital* after Twenty Years', *Social Thought & Research* 23, 1/2: 227–38.

Stark, Rodney. 1996. *The Rise of Christianity*. Princeton, NJ: Princeton University Press.

——— and William Sims Bainbridge. 1985. *The Future of Religion*. Berkeley: University of California Press.

——— and ———. 1996. *A Theory of Religion*. New Brunswick, NJ: Rutgers University Press.

——— and Roger Finke. 2000. *Acts of Faith: Explaining the Human Side of Religion*. Berkeley: University of California Press.

——— and Laurence Innaccone. 1994. 'A Supply-Side Reinterpretation of the "Secularization" of Europe', *Journal for the Scientific Study of Religion* 33: 230–52.

Stasiulis, Daiva. 1980. 'The Political Structuring of Ethnic Community Action', *Canadian Ethnic Studies* 12, 3: 19–44.

Statistics Canada. 1973. *Education in Canada 1973*. Ottawa: Statistics Canada.

———. 1992. *Census Metropolitan Areas and Census Agglomerations: Population and Dwelling Counts*. Ottawa: Statistics Canada.

———. 1993. *Earnings of Men and Women*. Ottawa: Statistics Canada.

———. 1996a. *Canada Year Book 1997*. Ottawa: Statistics Canada.

———. 1996b. *Growing Up in Canada*. Ottawa: Human Resources Development Canada and Statistics Canada.

———. 1996c. Public Use Microdata File on Individuals User Documentation. Ottawa: Ministry of Supply and Services.

———. 1998a. *Characteristics of Dual-Earner Families 1996*. Ottawa: Statistics Canada.

———. 1998b. '1996 Census: Education, Mobility and Migration', *The Daily*, 14 Apr.

———. 1999a. *Annual Demographic Statistics*. Ottawa: Statistics Canada.

———. 1999b. *Canada Year Book 1999*. Ottawa: Statistics Canada.

———. 2000. *Women in Canada, 2000: A Gender-based Statistical Report*. Ottawa: Minister of Industry.

———. 2001a. *Canada Year Book 2001*. Ottawa: Statistics Canada.

———. 2001b. *The Changing Profile of Canada's Labour Force*. Ottawa: Statistics Canada.

———. 2001c. 'Internet Use on the Cusp of the 21st Century', *Canadian Social Trends* (Winter): 2–3.

———. 2002a. 'Births: 2000', *The Daily*, 26 Sept.

———. 2002b. 'Education at a Glance', *Education Quarterly Review* 8, 4: 46–51.

———. 2002c. 'Fact Sheet on Unionization', *Perspectives on Labour and Income* 13, 3: 1–25.

———. 2002d. *Life Tables: Canada, Provinces and Territories 1995–1997*. Ottawa: Statistics Canada.

———. 2002e. *Perspectives on Labour and Income: Fact-Sheet on Unionization*. Ottawa: Statistics Canada.

———. 2003a. *Canada's Ethnocultural Portrait: The Changing Mosaic*. Ottawa: Statistics Canada.

———. 2003b. 'Population 15 Years and Over by Hours Spent on Unpaid Housework, 1996 Census'. At: <www.statcan.ca.80/english/Pdgb/famil56_96a.htm>.

———. 2003c. 'Population of Census Metropolitan Areas'. At: <www.statcan.ca/english/Pgdb/demo05.htm>.

———. 2003d. *A Profile of the Canadian Population: Where We Live*. At: <geodepot.statcan.ca/Diss/Highlights/>.

———. 2004a. 'Education at a Glance', *Education Quarterly Review* 9, 4: 53–8.

———. 2004b. *Women in Canada: Work Chapter Updates*. Ottawa: Statistics Canada.

———. 2005a. 'Back to School . . . by the Numbers', Statistics Canada Media Advisory, 29 Aug. At: www42.statcan.ca/smr08/smr08_009_e.htm.

———. 2005b. 'University Degrees, Diplomas and Certificates, 2003', *The Daily*, 11 Oct.

———. 2005c. 'Early Sexual Intercourse, Condom Use and Sexually Transmitted Diseases', *The Daily*, 3 May.

———. 2005d. 'Children and Youth as Victims of Violent Crime', *The Daily*, 20 Apr.

———. 2005e. *Literacy and Digital Technologies: Linkages and Outcomes*. Ottawa: Minister of Industry.

———. 2006a. 'Television Viewing', *The Daily*, 31 Mar.

———. 2006b. 'Canadian Internet Use Survey', *The Daily*, 15 Aug.

———. 2006c. 'General Social Survey: Paid and Unpaid Work', *The Daily*, 19 July.

———. 2006d. 'Study: Changing Patterns of Women in the Canadian Labour Force', *The Daily*, 15 June.

———. 2006e. *Education in Canada: School Attendance and Levels of Schooling*. Ottawa: Statistics Canada Catalogue no. 97F0017XCB2001001.

———. 2006f. 'National Longitudinal Survey of Children and Youth: Early Reading Ability and Later Literacy Skills 1994/1995 to 2004/2005', *The Daily*, 5 Dec.

———. 2006g. *Canada Year Book*. Ottawa: Statistics Canada.

———. 2006h. *Labour Force Survey*. At: <www40.statcan.ca/101/cst01/lanor05.html>.

———. 2006i. *Overview of the Time Use of Canadians 2005*. Ottawa: Minister of Industry.

———. 2006j. 'Canada's Population as of July 1, 2006', *The Daily*, 27 Sept.

———. 2007a. *Population and Dwelling Counts, for Canada, Provinces, and Territories by the Statistical Area Classification, 2006 and 2001 Censuses—100% Data*. At: <www12.statcan.ca/english/census06/data/popdwell>.

———. 2007b. Employment and Immigration. At: <www41.statcan.ca/2007/30000/ceb30000_000_e.htm>.

———. 2007c. Employment and Immigration. At: <www41.statcan.ca/2007/50000/ceb50000_000_e.htm>.

——— and Council of Ministers of Education Canada (CMEC). 2000. *Education Indicators in Canada: Report of the Pan-Canadian Education Indicators Program 1999*. At: <www.cmec.ca/stats/pceip/1999/Indicatorsite/index.html>.

——— and Human Resources Development Canada (HRDC). 2001. *A Report on Adult Education and Training in Canada: Learning a Living*. Ottawa: Statistics Canada and HRDC.

——— and Organization for Economic Co-operation and Development. 2005. *Learning a Living: First Results of the Adult Literacy and Life Skills Survey*. Ottawa and Paris: Minister of Industry, Canada and OECD.

Status of Women Canada. 1986. *Report of the Task Force on Child Care*. Ottawa: Status of Women Canada.

Steeves, H. Leslie. 1987. 'Feminist Theories and Media Studies', *Critical Studies in Mass Communication* 4, 2: 95–135.

Steffensmeier, Renee. 1982. 'A Role Model of the Transition to Parenthood', *Journal of Marriage and the Family* 44: 319–34.

Stehr, Nico, and R. Grundmann. 1996. 'Classical Social Science Discourse and the Impact of Climate on Society', unpublished paper, Wall Institute for Advanced Studies, University of British Columbia.

Stein, Janice Gross. 2002. 'Choice and Public Education: A Core Civic Challenge', *Education Canada* 42, 3: 4–7.

Stern, Nicholas. 2002. 'Keynote Address: A Strategy for Development', in Boris Pleskovic and Stern, eds, *Annual World Bank Conference on Development Economics 2001/2002*. Washington and New York: World Bank and Oxford University Press, 11–35.

Stevans, Lonnie K. 1998. 'Assessing the Effect of the Occupational Crowding of Immigrants on the Real Wages of African American Workers', *Review of Black Political Economy* 26: 37–46.

Stevenson, Kathryn. 1999. 'Family Characteristics of Problem Kids', *Canadian Social Trends* 55 (Winter): 2–6.

Stewart, M.W. 2002. *Ordinary Violence: Everyday Assaults against Women*. Westport Conn.: Bergin and Garvey.

Stiglitz, Joseph E. 2002. *Globalization and Its Discontents*. New York: Norton.

———. 2006. *Making Globalization Work*. New York: Norton.

Stoddart, Kenneth. 1986. 'The Presentation of Everyday Life: Some Textual Strategies for "Adequate Ethnography"', *Urban Life* 15, 1: 103–21.

Stokes, Randall, and John P. Hewitt. 1976. 'Aligning Actions', *American Sociological Review* 1: 838–49.

Stone, Gregory P. 1981. 'Appearance and the Self: A Slightly Revised Version', in Stone and Harvey A. Farberman, eds, *Social Psychology through Symbolic Interaction*. New York: Wiley, 187–202.

Stone, Leroy O. 1967. *Urban Development in Canada*. Ottawa: Dominion Bureau of Statistics.

Storey, Robert. 2002. 'From Capitalism to Socialism', unpublished paper, McMaster University, Hamilton, Ont.

Strange, Susan. 1996. *The Retreat of the State*. Cambridge: Cambridge University Press.

Strauss, Murray A., and Richard J. Gelles. 1990. *Physical Violence in American Families: Risk Factors and Adaptations to Violence in 8,145 Families*. New Brunswick, NJ: Transaction.

Street, Debra, and Ingrid Connidis. 2001. 'Creeping Selectivity in Canadian Women's Pensions', in Jay Ginn, Street, and Sara Arber, eds, *Women, Work and Pensions: International Issues and Prospects*. Buckingham, UK: Open University Press, 158–78.

Sugiman, Pamela. 1994. *Labour's Dilemma: The Gender Politics of Auto Workers in Canada, 1937–1979*. Toronto: University of Toronto Press.

———. 2001. 'Privilege and Oppression: The Configuration of Race, Gender, and Class in Southern Ontario Auto Plants, 1939 to 1949', *Labour/Le Travail* 47 (Spring): 83–113.

Sumner, C. 1994. *The Sociology of Deviance: An Obituary*. New York: Continuum.

Suominen, S., H. Helenius, H. Blomberg, A Uutela, and M. Koskenvuo. 2001. 'Sense of Coherence as a Predictor of Subjective State of Health: Results of 4 Years of Follow-up of Adults', *Journal of Psychosomatic Research* 50, 2: 77–86.

Suranovic, Steven M. 1997. 'Why Economists Should Study Fairness', *Challenge* 40: 109–24.

Sutherland, Edwin. 1947. *Principles of Criminology*, 4th edn. Chicago: Lippincott.

Sydie, Rosalind. 1987. 'Sociology and Gender', in M. Michael Rosenberg, William B. Shaffir, Allan Turowetz, and Morton Weinfeld, eds, *An Introduction to Sociology*. Toronto: Methuen.

Synnott, Anthony, and David Howes. 1996. 'Canada's Visible Minorities: Identity and Representation', in V. Amit-Talai and C. Knowles, eds, *Re-situating Identities: The Politics of Race, Ethnicity and Culture*. Peterborough, Ont.: Broadview.

Szasz, Andrew. 1994. *Ecopopulism: Toxic Waste and the Movement for Environmental Justice*. Minneapolis: University of Minneapolis Press.

Tabb, William K., and Larry Sawers. 1984. *Marxism and the Metropolis*, 2nd edn. New York: Oxford University Press.

Tannenbaum, Frank. 1938. *Crime and the Community*. Boston: Ginn.

Tanner, Julian. 2001. *Teenage Troubles: Youth and Deviance in Canada*, 2nd edn. Toronto: Nelson.

Tannock, Stuart. 2001. *Youth at Work: The Unionized Fast-Food and Grocery Workplace*. Philadelphia: Temple University Press.

Tapscott, Don. 1998. *Growing Up Digital: The Rise of the Net Generation*. New York: McGraw-Hill.

Taras, David. 2001. *Power and Betrayal in the Canadian Media*, updated edn. Peterborough, Ont.: Broadview.

Tardy, Rebecca. 2000. 'But I Am a Good Mom: The Social Construction of Motherhood through Health-Care Conversations', *Journal of Contemporary Ethnography* 29: 433–73.

Tarrow, Sidney. 1988. 'National Politics and Collective Action: Recent Theory and Research in Western Europe and the United States', *Annual Review of Sociology* 14: 421–40.

———. 1998. *Power in Movements: Social Movements and Contentious Politics*, 2nd edn. New York: Cambridge University Press.

Tator, Carol, Frances Henry, and Winston Mattis. 1998. *Challenging Racism in the Arts: Case Studies of Controversy and Conflict*. Toronto: University of Toronto Press.

Taylor, Bron. 1991. 'The Religion and Politics of Earth First!', *Ecologist* 21: 258–66.

Taylor, Frederick W. 1911. *Principles of Scientific Management*. New York: Harper.

Taylor, Laramie. 2005. 'All for Him: Articles about Sex in American Lad Magazines', *Sex Roles* 52, 3/4: 153–63.

Teitelbaum, Michael S. 1975. 'Relevance of Demographic Transition Theory for Developing Countries', *Science* 2 (May): 420–5.

Ten Bos, Réné. 1997. 'Essai: Business Ethics and Bauman Ethics', *Organization Studies* 18: 997–1014.

Theodorson, George A. 1961. *Studies in Human Ecology*. New York: Harper and Row.

———. 1982. *Urban Patterns: Studies in Human Ecology*. University Park: University of Pennsylvania Press.

Thianthai, Chulanee. 2004. 'Gender and Class Differences in Young People's Sexuality and HIV/AIDS Risk-Taking Behaviours in Thailand', *Culture, Health & Sexuality* 6, 3: 189–203.

Thiessen, Joel, and Lorne L. Dawson. 2008 (forthcoming). 'Is There a "Renaissance" of Religion in Canada? A Critical Look at Bibby and Beyond', *Studies in Religion/Sciences Religieuses* 37.

Thomas, Derrick. 2001. 'Evolving Family Living Arrangements of Canada's Immigrants', *Canadian Social Trends* (Summer): 16–22.

Thomas, Eleanor. 2006. *Readiness to Learn at School among Five-year-old Children in Canada*. Ottawa: Statistics Canada Catalogue no. 89–599–MIE no. 004.

Thomas, W.I., and D.S. Thomas. 1928. *The Child in America*. New York: Knopf.

Thompson, Kevin, and Leslie Heinberg. 1999. 'The Media's Influence on Body Image Disturbance and Eating Disorders: We've Reviled Them, Now Can We Rehabilitate Them?', *Journal of Social Issues* 55: 339–53.

Thompson, Warren S. 1929. 'Population', *American Journal of Sociology* 34: 959–75.

———. 1944. *Plenty of People*. Lancaster, Penn.: Jacques Cattel.

Thomson, Elizabeth, Sara McLanahan, and Roberta Curtin. 1992. 'Family Structure, Gender and Parental Socialization', *Journal of Marriage and the Family* 54: 368–78.

Thorne, Barry. 1982. 'Feminist Rethinking of the Family: An Overview', in Thorne with Marilyn Yalom, eds, *Rethinking the Family: Some Feminist Questions*. New York: Longman, 1–24.

Thorns, David C. 2002. *The Transformation of Cities: Urban Theory and Urban Life.* New York: Palgrave Macmillan.

Tilleczek, K.C., and D.W. Hine. 2006. 'The Meaning of Smoking as Health and Social Risk and Adolescence', *Journal of Adolescence* 29, 2: 273–87.

Tilly, Charles. 1978. *From Mobilization to Revolution.* Reading, Mass.: Addison-Wesley.

———. 1998. *Durable Inequality.* Berkeley: University of California Press.

Titchkosky, Tanta. 2001. 'Disability: A Rose by Any Other Name? "People-First" Language in Canadian Society', *Canadian Review of Sociology and Anthropology* 38, 2: 125–40.

Tittle, C.R., W.J. Villemez, and D.A. Smith. 1978. 'The Myth of Social Class and Criminality: An Empirical Assessment of the Empirical Evidence', *American Sociological Review* 43: 643–56.

Tocqueville, Alexis de. 1945 [1835, 1840]. *Democracy in America.* New York: Vintage.

Tokar, Brian. 1988. 'Exploring the New Ecologies', *Alternatives* 15, 4: 31–43.

Tönnies, Ferdinand. 1957 [1887]. *Community and Society* (*Gemeinschaft und Gesellschaft*). New York: Harper and Row.

Torres, Carlos Alberto. 1998. *Democracy, Education, and Multiculturalism: Dilemmas of Citizenship in a Global World.* Lanham, Md: Rowman and Littlefield.

Touraine, Alain. 1981. *The Voice and the Eye: An Analysis of Social Movements.* Cambridge: Cambridge University Press.

Traill, Catherine Parr. 1966 [1836]. *The Backwoods of Canada.* Toronto: McClelland & Stewart.

Tremblay, Manon. 1998. 'Do Female MPs Substantively Represent Women? A Study of Legislative Behaviour in Canada's 35th Parliament', *Canadian Journal of Political Science* 31: 435–65.

Tremblay, Mark S., and J. Douglas Willms. 2000. 'Secular Trends in the Body Mass Index of Canadian Children', *Canadian Medical Association Journal* 163: 1429–33.

Tremblay, Richard E., Bernard Boulerice, Philip Harden, Pierre McDuff, Daniel Perusse, Robert Pihl, and Mark Zoccolillo. 1996. 'Do Children in Canada Become More Aggressive as They Approach Adolescence?', in Statistics Canada (1996b: 127–38).

Trovato, Frank. 1988a. 'The Interurban Mobility of the Foreign Born in Canada, 1976–81', *International Migration Review* 22, 3: 59–86.

———. 1988b. 'A Macrosociological Analysis of Change in the Marriage Rate: Canadian Women, 1921–25 to 1980–85', *Journal of Marriage and the Family* 50: 507–21.

———. 1998. 'The Stanley Cup of Hockey and Suicide in Quebec', *Social Forces* 77, 1: 105–26.

Troyer, Ronald, and Gerald Markle. 1983. *Cigarettes: The Battle over Smoking.* New Brunswick, NJ: Rutgers University Press.

Tuggle, Justin L., and Malcolm D. Holmes. 1997. 'Blowing Smoke: Status Politics and the Shasta County Smoking Ban', *Deviant Behavior* 18: 77–93.

Tuljapurkar, Shripad, Nan Li, and Marcus W. Feldman. 1995. 'High Sex Ratios in China's Future', *Science*, 10 Feb., 874–6.

Turk, Austin T. 1976. 'Law as a Weapon in Social Conflict', *Social Problems* 23: 276–92.

Turner, Bryan S. 1988. *Status.* Minneapolis: University of Minnesota Press.

Turner, R. Jay, and William R. Avison. 2003. 'Status Variations in Stress Exposure: Implications for the Interpretation of Research on Race, Socioeconomic Status and Gender', *Journal of Health and Social Behaviour* 44, 4: 488–505.

Turner, Ralph. 1962. 'Role-Taking: Process versus Conformity', in Arnold Rose, ed., *Human Behavior and Social Processes.* Boston: Houghton Mifflin, 20–40.

Tylor, Edward. 1871. *Primitive Culture: Researches into the Development of Mythology, Philosophy, Religion, Language, Art and Custom.* London: John Murray.

———. 1903. *Primitive Culture: Researches into the Development of Mythology, Philosophy, Religion, Language, Art, and Custom*, vol. 1. London: John Murphy.

Tyrell, Hartmann. 1981. 'Is Weber's Type of Bureaucracy an Objective, True Type? Remarks on a Thesis by Renate Mayntz', *Zeitschrift fur Soziologie.*

UNAIDS. 2001a. *Children and Young People in a World of AIDS.* Geneva: Joint United Nations Programme on HIV/AIDS.

———. 2001b. *Gender and HIV Fact Sheet.* Geneva: Joint United Nations Programme on HIV/AIDS.

———. 2002. *Epidemiological Fact Sheets on HIV/AIDS and Sexually Transmitted Infections: Canada.* Geneva: Joint United Nations Programme on HIV/AIDS.

———. 2006. *2006 Report of the Global AIDS Epidemic.* At: <data.unaids.org/pub/GlobalReport/2006/2006_GR_CH02_en.pdf>.

Ungar, S. 1992 [1986]. 'Self Mockery: An Alternative Format Self-Presentation', in Gary Alan Fine, John Johnson, and Harvey A. Farberman, eds, *Sociological Slices: Introductory Readings from the Interactionist Perspective.* Greenwich, Conn.: JAI, 45–58.

United Nations. 1990. *The World's Women: Trends and Statistics.* New York: UN.

———. 1999. *The World at Six Billion.* New York: UN Dept. of Economic and Social Affairs, Population Division.

———. 2000a. *The World's Women. Trends and Statistics.* New York: UN.

———. 2000b. *Replacement Migration.* New York: UN Dept. of Economic and Social Affairs, Population Division.

———. 2001. *World Population Prospects: The 2000 Revision*, 2 vols. New York: UN Dept. of Economic and Social Affairs, Population Division.

———. 2002. *World Population Ageing: 1950–2050.* New York: UN Dept. of Economic and Social Affairs, Population Division.

———. 2003. *World Population Prospects: The 2002 Revision. Highlights.* New York: UN Dept. of Economic and Social Affairs, Population Division.

———. 2006a. *World Population Prospects—The 2004 Revision. Volume III: Analytical Report.* New York: UN Dept. of Economic and Social Affairs, Population Division.

———. 2006b. *Urban Agglomerations 2005.* New York: UN Dept. of Economic and Social Affairs, Population Division. At: <www.un.org/esa/population/WUP2005/2005WUP_agglo.htm>.

———. 2006c. *World Urbanization Prospects: The 2005 Revision.* At: <esa.un.org/unup>.

United Nations Economic Commission for Europe. 1992. *Demographic Causes and Economic Consequences of Population Aging*, ed. George Stolnitz. New York: UN.

United Nations Educational, Scientific and Cultural Organization (UNESCO). 2006. *Strong Foundations: Early Childhood Care and Education. Education for All Global Monitoring Report 2007.* Paris: UNESCO.

United States, Bureau of Census. 1999. *World Population Profile: 1998.* Report WP/98. Washington: US Government Printing Office.

———. 2003. *World POPClock Projection.* At: <www.census.gov/cgi-bin/ipc/popclockw>.

———. 2006. *International Data Base, 2006.* At: <www.census.gov/ipc/www/idbnew.html>.

United States, White House. 2002. 'Remarks by the President to the Travel Pool'. At <www.whitehouse.gov/news/releases/2002/06/20020604-16.html>.

United Way of Greater Toronto and the Canadian Council on Social Development. 2004. *Poverty by Postal Code: The Geography of Neighbourhood Poverty, City of Toronto, 1981–2001.* Toronto: United Way of Greater Toronto.

Urmetzer, Peter, and Neil Guppy. 1999. 'Changing Income Inequality in Canada', in James Curtis, Edward Grabb, and Guppy, eds, *Social Inequality in Canada: Patterns, Problems, and Policies.* Toronto: Pearson Prentice-Hall, 75–84.

Urry, John. 2005. 'The Complexity Turn', *Theory, Culture & Society* 22, 5: 1.

Ursel, Jane. 1992. *Private Lives, Public Policy: 100 Years of State Intervention in the Family.* Toronto: Women's Press.

Vallin, Jacques. 1983. 'Sex Patterns of Mortality: A Comparative Study of Model Life Tables and Actual Situations with Special Reference to the Case of Algeria and France', in Alan D. Lopez and Lado T. Ruzicka, eds, *Sex Differences in Mortality.* Canberra: Australian National University, 443–76.

Van de Kaa, Dirk J. 1987. 'Europe's Second Demographic Transition', *Population Bulletin* 42, 1.

———. 1994. 'The Second Demographic Transition Revisited: Theories and Expectations', in Gijs Beets, Hans van den Brekel, R. Cliquet, G. Dooghe, and J. de Jong Gierveld, eds, *Population and Family in the Low Countries 1993: Late Fertility and Other Current Issues.* Lisse, Netherlands: Swets & Zeitlinger, 81–126.

Van Delinder, Jean. 2005. 'Taylorism, Managerial Control Strategies, and the Ballets of Balanchine and Stravinsky', *American Behavioral Scientist* 48, 11: 1439.

Van Paasen, C. 1981. 'The Philosophy of Geography: From Vidal to Hägerstrand', in Alan Pred, ed., *Space and Time Geography: Essays Dedicated to Torsten Hägerstrand.* Lund, Sweden: Gleerup, 17–29.

Van Praet, Nicolas. 2006. 'Sex.com Fetches $12 Million as a Domain Name', *Montreal Gazette*, 27 Jan.

Van Vliet, Willem, Elizabeth Huttman, and Sylvia Fava, eds. 1985. *Housing Needs and Policy Approaches.* Durham, NC: Duke University Press.

Vanier Institute of the Family. 2000. *Profiling Canada's Families II.* Ottawa.

———. 2004. *Profiling Canadian Families III.* Ottawa.

Vaughan, Dianne. 1986. *Uncoupling: Turning Points in Intimate Relations.* New York: Vintage Books.

Veenstra, Gerry. 2001. 'Social Capital and Health', *Canadian Journal of Policy Research* 2: 1672–81.

Videla, Nancy Plankey. 2006. 'It Cuts Both Ways: Workers, Management and the Construction of a "Community of Fate" on the Shop Floor in a Mexican Garment Factory', *Social Forces* 84, 4: 2099–2120.

Visser, Jelle. 2006. 'Union Membership Statistics in 24 Countries', *Monthly Labor Review* (Jan.): 38–49.

Vold, George B., Thomas J. Bernard, and Jeffrey B. Snipes. 2002. *Theoretical Criminology*, 5th edn. New York: Oxford University Press.

Vorst, Jesse, et al., eds. 1991. *Race, Class, Gender: Bonds and Barriers.* Toronto: Garamond.

Vosko, Leah. 2000. *Temporary Work: The Gendered Rise of a Precarious Employment Relationship.* Toronto: University of Toronto Press.

———. 2003. 'Gender Differentiation and the Standard/Non-Standard Employment Distinction in Canada, 1945 to the Present', in Danielle Juteau, ed., *Patterns and Processes of Social Differentiation: The Construction of Gender, Age, 'Race/Ethnicity' and Locality.* Toronto: University of Toronto Press.

———. 2006. *Precarious Employment: Understanding Labour Market Insecurity in Canada.* Montreal: McGill-Queen's University Press.

Wackwitz, Laura A., and Lana F. Rakow. 2004. 'Feminist Communication Theory: An Introduction', in Rakow and Wackwitz, eds, *Feminist Communication Theory: Selections in Context.* Thousand Oaks, Calif.: Sage, 1–10.

Wagley, Charles, and Marvin Harris. 1959. *Minorities in the New World.* New York: Columbia University Press.

Wagner, David. 1997. *The New Temperance: The American Obsession with Sin and Vice.* Boulder, Colo.: Westview.

Wagner, Nicoletta. 2002. 'Wars Old and New in Colombia', NZZ online (Neue Zürcher Zeitung), 19 May. At: <www.nzz.ch/english/editorials/2002/05/07_colombia.html>.

Waksler, Frances. 1991. *Studying the Social Worlds of Children: Sociological Readings.* London: Falmer.

Walkom, Thomas. 1997. 'The Harris Government: Restoration or Revolution?', in Graham White, ed., *The Government and Politics of Ontario*, 5th edn. Toronto: University of Toronto Press, 402–17.

Waller, Willard. 1965 [1932]. *The Sociology of Teaching.* New York: Wiley.

Walliss, John. 2002. 'Loved the Wedding, Invite Me to the Marriage: The Secularization of Weddings in Contemporary Britain', *Sociological Research Online* 7, 4. At: <www.socresonline.org.uk/7/4/walliss.html>.

Walzer, Michael. 1983. *Spheres of Justice: A Defense of Pluralism and Equality.* New York: Basic Books.

Waring, Marilyn. 1996. *Three Masquerades: Essays on Equality, Work and Human Rights.* Toronto: University of Toronto Press.

Warner, R. Stephen, and J.G. Wittner, eds. 1998. *Gatherings in Diaspora: Religious Communities and the New Immigration.* Philadelphia: Temple University Press.

Warren, Karen. 1990. 'The Power and Promise of Ecological Feminism', *Environmental Ethics* 12, 2: 125–46.

Wasko, Janet. 2001. 'The Magical-Market World of Disney', *Monthly Review* 52, 11: 56–71.

Weatherall, Ann. 2002. *Gender, Language, and Discourse.* New York: Routledge.

Webber, Melvin M. 1963. 'Order in Diversity: Community without Propinquity', in Lowden Wingo, ed., *Cities and Space.* Baltimore: Johns Hopkins University Press, 23–54.

Weber, Max. 1958 [1904]. *The Protestant Ethic and the Spirit of Capitalism*, trans. Talcott Parsons. New York: Scribner.

———. 1978 [1908]. *Economy and Society*, trans. Ephraim Fischoff, eds Guenther Roth and Claus Wittich. Berkeley: University of California Press.

———. 1951 [1916]. *The Religion of China: Confucianism and Taoism*, trans. H.H. Gerth. Glencoe, Ill.: Free Press.

———. 1958 [1916–17]. *The Religion of India: The Sociology of Hinduism and Buddhism*, trans. H.H. Gerth and Don Martindale. Glencoe, Ill.: Free Press.

———. 1952 [1917–19]. *Ancient Judaism*, trans. H.H. Gerth and Don Martindale. Glencoe, Ill.: Free Press.

———. 1963 [1922]. *The Sociology of Religion*, trans. E. Fischoff. Boston: Beacon Press.

———. 1946 [1922]. *From Max Weber: Essays in Sociology*, trans. and ed. H.H. Gerth and C. Wright Mills. New York: Oxford University Press.

———. 1958 [1922]. *Essays in Sociology*, trans. H.H. Gerth and C. Wright Mills. New York: Oxford University Press.

———. 1961 [1923]. *General Economic History*, trans. Frank H. Knight. New York: Collier.

Weeks, Jeffrey. 1991. *Against Nature: Essays on History, Sexuality and Identity.* London: Rivers Oram Press.

———. 1993. *Sexuality.* London: Routledge.

———, Catherine Donovan, and Brian Heaphy. 1998. 'Everyday Experiments: Narratives of Non-heterosexual Relationships', in Elizabeth B. Silva and Carol Smart, eds, *The New Family?* London: Sage, 83–99.

Weiher, Gregory R. 1991. *The Fractured Metropolis.* Albany: State University of New York Press.

Weinberg, E., and P. Deutschberger. 1963. 'Some Dimensions of Altercasting', *Sociometry* 26: 545–66.

Weinberg, Martin S. 1997. 'The Nudist Management of Respectability', in Jodi O'Brien and Peter Kollock, eds, *The Production of Reality: Essays and Readings on Social Interaction*, 2nd edn. Thousand Oaks, Calif.: Pine Forge, 511–19.

Weiner, Gaby. 1994. *Feminisms in Education: An Introduction.* Buckingham, UK: Open University Press.

Weinfeld, Morton. 1988. 'Ethnic and Race Relations', in James Curtis and Lorne Tepperman, eds, *Understanding Canadian Society.* Toronto: McGraw-Hill Ryerson, 587–616.

Weis, David. 1998. 'Conclusion: The State of Sexual Theory', *Journal of Sex Research* 35, 1: 100–14.

Weitz, Rose, ed. 2002. *The Politics of Women's Bodies: Sexuality, Appearance and Behaviour*, 2nd edn. Oxford: Oxford University Press.

Wekerle, Gerda. 2005. 'Gender and the City: Urban Restructuring, Social Exclusion, and Gender Claims', in Hiller (2005: 205–44).

Wellman, Barry, and Barry Leighton. 1979. 'Networks, Neighborhoods, and Communities: Approaches to the Study of the Community Question', *Urban Affairs Quarterly* 14: 363–90.

Welsh, Sandy. 1999. 'Gender and Sexual Harassment', *Annual Review of Sociology* 25, 1: 169–90.

Wepman, Dennis, Ronald B. Newman, and Murray B. Binderman. 1976. *The Life: The Lore and Folk Poetry of the Black Hustler.* Philadelphia: University of Pennsylvania Press.

Werbner, Pnina, and Tariq Modood. 1997. *The Politics of Multiculturalism in the New Europe: Racism, Identity and Community.* London: Zed Books.

Wernick, Andrew. 1987. 'From Voyeur to Narcissist: Imaging Men in Contemporary Advertising', in Michael Kaufman, ed., *Beyond Patriarchy.* Toronto: Oxford University Press, 277–97.

Wertham, Frederic. 1954. *Seduction of the Innocent.* New York: Rinehart.

West, G. Page, III, and G. Dale Meyer. 1997. 'Communicated Knowledge as a Learning Foundation', *International Journal of Organizational Analysis* 5: 25–58.

Westhues, Kenneth. 1982. *First Sociology.* New York: McGraw-Hill.

Whitaker, Reginald. 1993. 'From the Quebec Cauldron to the Canadian Cauldron', in Alain-G. Gagnon, ed., *Quebec: State and Society*, 2nd edn. Toronto: Nelson Canada.

White, David Manning. 1950. 'The "Gatekeeper": A Case Study in the Selection of News', *Journalism Quarterly* 27: 383–90.

White, Kevin M., and Samuel H. Preston. 1996. 'How Many Americans Are Alive Because of Twentieth-Century Improvements in Mortality?', *Population and Development Review* 22: 415–30.

White, Lynn, Jr. 1967. 'The Historical Roots of Our Ecological Crisis', *Science* 155: 1203–7.

Whyte, William Foote. 1943. *Street Corner Society: The Social Structure of an Italian Slum.* Chicago: University of Chicago Press.

———. 1949. 'The Social Structure of the Restaurant', *American Journal of Sociology* 54: 302–8.

Wignall, Robert A. 2004. 'An Investigation of Job Satisfaction of Florida State Prison Industry Workers: An Examination of Herzberg Two-Factor Theory', *Dissertation Abstracts International, A: The Humanities and Social Sciences* 65, 4 (Oct.): 1549A.

Wilkes, Rima. 2001. 'Competition or Colonialism? An Analysis of Two Theories of Ethnic Collective Action', Ph.D. dissertation, University of Toronto.

Wilkins, Russell, Owen Adams, and Anna Brancker. 1989. 'Change in Mortality by Income in Urban Canada from 1971 to 1986', *Health Reports* 1: 137–74.

Wilkinson, Derek. 1992. 'Change in Household Division of Labour Following Unemployment in Elliot Lake', paper presented to Learned Societies, Charlottetown.

Williams, A. Paul. 1989. 'Social Origins and Elite Politics in Canada: The Impact of Background Differences on Attitudes towards the Welfare State', *Canadian Journal of Sociology* 14: 67–87.

Williams, Christine, Patti Giuffre, and Kirsten Dellinger. 1999. 'Sexuality in the Workplace: Organizational Control, Sexual Harassment and the Pursuit of Pleasure', *Annual Review of Sociology* 25, 1: 73–93.

Williams, David R., and Chiquita Collins. 1995. 'U.S. Socioeconomic and Racial Differences in Health: Patterns and Explanations', *Annual Review of Sociology* 21: 349–86.

Willis, J.R. 1987. 'What Have We Learned from the Economics of the Family?', *American Economic Review* 77, 2: 68–81.

Willis, Paul. 1977. *Learning to Labour: How Working Class Kids Get Working Class Jobs.* Farnborough, UK: Saxon House.

Wilson, Bryan. 1966. *Religion in Secular Society.* London: Watts.

———. 1982. *Religion in Sociological Perspective.* Oxford: Oxford University Press.

Wilson, Susannah J. 1991. *Women, Families, and Work,* 3rd edn. Toronto: McGraw-Hill Ryerson.

———. 2001. 'Intimacy and Commitment in Family Formation', in Maureen Baker, ed., *Families: Changing Trends in Canada,* 4th edn. Toronto: McGraw-Hill Ryerson, 93–114.

Wimberley, Dale W. 1990. 'Investment Dependence and Alternative Explanations of Third World Mortality', *American Sociological Review* 55: 75–91.

Winnubst, Shannon. 2006. *Queering Freedom.* Bloomington: Indiana University Press.

Wireman, Peggy. 1984. *Urban Neighborhoods, Networks, and Families.* Toronto: Lexington.

Wirth, Louis. 1938. 'Urbanism as a Way of Life', *American Journal of Sociology* 44: 1–24.

Witz, Anne. 1992. *Professions and Patriarchy.* London: Routledge.

Wolejszo, Stefan. 2002. 'Gender Trouble and the Construction of Gender Identity on Internet Chat Sites', MA thesis, University of Manitoba.

Wolf, Martin. 2004. *Why Globalization Works.* New Haven: Yale University Press.

Wolfe, David A., and Meric S. Gertler. 2001. 'The New Economy: An Overview', discussion paper produced for the Social Sciences and Humanities Research Council of Canada.

Wolfgang, Marvin, and Franco Ferracuti. 1967. *The Subculture of Violence: Towards an Integrated Theory in Criminology.* Beverly Hills, Calif.: Sage.

Wolfson, Michael C., and Brian B. Murphy. 1998. 'New Views on Inequality and Trends in Canada and the United States', *Monthly Labor Review* (Apr.): 3–23.

Wollstonecraft, Mary. 1986 [1792]. *Vindication of the Rights of Women.* Middlesex, UK: Penguin.

Wood, Adrian. 1994. *North–South Trade, Employment and Inequality.* Oxford: Clarendon.

Wood, Chris, with Rima Kar. 2000. 'Why Do Men Do It?', *Maclean's,* 7 Aug., 5–7.

Wood, Julia T. 1997. *Gendered Lives: Communication, Gender and Culture,* 2nd edn. Belmont, Calif.: Wadsworth.

Woodiwiss, M. 2005. *Gangster Capitalism.* New York: Caroll and Graff.

Woods, James, with Jay Lucas. 1993. *The Corporate Closet: The Professional Lives of Gay Men in America.* New York: Free Press.

Woods, Peter. 1979. *The Divided School.* London: Routledge & Kegan Paul.

Woodward, Kath. 2003. *Understanding Identity.* London: Arnold.

Woolmington, Eric. 1985. 'Small May Be Inevitable', *Australian Geographical Studies* 23: 195–207.

World Bank. 2005. *World Development Indicators.* Washington: World Bank.

World Commission on Environment and Development. 1987. *Our Common Future.* New York: Oxford University Press.

World Health Organization (WHO). 1996. *Statistics Annual for 1995.* Geneva: WHO.

———. 2001. 'Obesity Epidemic Puts Millions at Risk from Related Diseases', press release. Geneva: WHO.

———. 2003. 'WHO Definition of Health'. At: <www.who.int/about/definition/en/>.

———. 2006. 'Gender and Genetics'. At: <who.int/genomics/gender/en/printi.html>.

Wortley, Scott. 1999. 'A Northern Taboo: Research on Race, Crime and Criminal Justice in Canada', *Canadian Journal of Criminology* 41: 261–74.

Wotherspoon, Terry. 1995. 'The Incorporation of Public School Teachers into the Industrial Order: British Columbia in the First Half of the Twentieth Century', *Studies in Political Economy* 46: 119–51.

———. 2000. 'Transforming Canada's Education System: The Impact on Educational Inequalities, Opportunities, and Benefits', in B. Singh Bolaria, ed., *Social Issues and Contradictions in Canadian Society.* Toronto: Harcourt Brace, 250–72.

———. 2004. *The Sociology of Education in Canada: Critical Perspectives,* 2nd edn. Toronto: Oxford University Press.

Wright, Charles R. 1959. *Mass Communication: A Sociological Perspective.* New York: Random House.

Wright, Erik Olin. 1983. *Class, Crisis and the State.* London: Verso.

———. 1985. *Classes.* London: Verso.

———. 1997. *Class Counts: Comparative Studies in Class Analysis.* Cambridge: Cambridge University Press.

———. 1999. 'Foundations of Class Analysis: A Marxist Perspective', paper presented at the annual meeting of the American Sociological Association.

Wrong, Dennis. 1961. 'The Oversocialized Concept of Man in Modern Sociology', *American Sociological Review* 26: 183–93.

Wu, Zheng. 2000. *Cohabitation: A New Form of Family Living.* Toronto: Oxford University Press.

Wuthnow, Robert. 1989. *Communities of Discourse: Ideology and Social Structure in the Reformation, the Enlightenment, and European Socialism.* Cambridge, Mass.: Harvard University Press.

Wyman, Diana. 2006. 'Trade Liberalization and the Canadian Clothing Market', *Canadian Economic Observer* (Dec.). (Statistics Canada Catalogue no. 11-010.)

Yalnizyan, Armine. 1998. *The Growing Gap: A Report on the Growing Inequality between Rich and Poor in Canada.* Toronto: Centre for Social Justice.

Yinger, Milton J. 1970. *The Scientific Study of Religion.* New York: Macmillan.

Young, David. 2004. 'The Promotional State and Canada's Juno Awards', *Popular Music* 23, 3: 271–89.

———. 2006. 'Ethno-racial Minorities and the Juno Awards', *Canadian Journal of Sociology* 31, 2: 183–210.

———. 2008 (forthcoming). 'Why Canadian Content Regulations Are Needed to Support Canadian Music', in Charlene Elliott and Joshua Greenberg, eds, *Communications in Question: Canadian Perspectives on Controversial Issues in Communication Studies.* Scarborough, Ont.: Thomson Nelson.

Yuval-Davis, Nira. 1997. *Gender and Nation.* London: Sage.

——— and Floya Anthias, eds. 1989. *Women-Nation-State.* New York: St Martin's.

Zang, Xiaowei. 1998. 'Elite Transformation and Recruitment in Post-Mao China', *Journal of Political and Military Sociology* 26, 1: 39–57.

Zehr, Stephen. 1994. 'The Centrality of Scientists and the Transition of Interests in the U.S. Acid Rain Controversy', *Canadian Review of Sociology and Anthropology* 31, 3: 325–53.

Zeitlin, I.M. 1990. *Ideology and the Development of Sociological Theory,* 4th edn. Englewood Cliffs, NJ: Prentice-Hall.

Zimbardo, Philip G. 1972. 'Pathology of Imprisonment', *Society* 9: 4–8.

Zola, Irving Kenneth. 1972. 'Medicine as an Institution of Social Control', *Sociological Review* 20: 487–504.

Zucker, Lynne G., Michael R. Darby, Marilynn B. Brewer, and Yusheng Peng. 1996. 'Collaboration Structure and Information Dilemmas in Biotechnology', in Roderick M. Kramer and Tom R. Tyler, eds, *Trust in Organizations: Frontiers of Theory and Research.* Thousand Oaks, Calif.: Sage, 90–113.

Zukin, Sharon. 1995. *The Culture of Cities.* Cambridge, Mass.: Blackwell.

Contributors

Patrizia Albanese is associate professor in the Department of Sociology at Ryerson University and is the co-director of the Centre for Children, Youth and Families at Ryerson.

Cheryl Albas teaches in the Department of Sociology at the University of Manitoba.

Daniel Albas is professor of sociology at the University of Manitoba.

Bruce Arai teaches courses in research methods, statistics, and the sociology of work at Wilfred Laurier University.

Pat Armstrong is professor of sociology at York University.

Maureen Baker is professor of sociology at the University of Auckland.

Shyon Baumann is assistant professor of sociology at the University of Toronto.

Juanne Clarke is professor of sociology at Wilfred Laurier University.

Lorne L. Dawson is associate professor of sociology and chair of the Department of Religious Studies at the University of Waterloo.

Randle Hart is assistant professor in the Department of Social Sciences at the University of Toronto.

Nikolaos I. Liodakis is assistant professor of sociology at Wilfrid Laurier University.

Neil McLaughlin is associate professor of sociology at McMaster University.

Julie Ann McMullin is associate professor in the Department of Sociology at the University of Western Ontario.

William Michelson is S.D. Clark Professor of Sociology Emeritus at the University of Toronto.

Antony Puddephatt is a postdoctoral fellow in the Department of Science and Technology Studies at Cornell University.

Vincent F. Sacco is professor of sociology and teaches courses relating to crime, deviance, and social control at Queen's University.

Peter R. Sinclair is professor of sociology at Memorial University of Newfoundland.

Michael R. Smith is James McGill Professor of Sociology at McGill University.

Pamela Sugiman teaches in the Department of Sociology at Ryerson University.

Lorne Tepperman is professor of sociology at the University of Toronto and past president of the Canadian Sociological Association.

Frank Trovato is professor of sociology at the University of Alberta.

John W.P. Veugelers is associate professor in the Department of Sociology at the University of Toronto.

G. Keith Warriner is associate professor of sociology at the University of Waterloo.

Susannah Wilson is professor and associate dean of the Faculty of Community Services at Ryerson University.

Terry Wotherspoon is professor of sociology at the University of Saskatchewan.

David Young is assistant professor of sociology at McMaster University.

Index

Aalborg project, 373–4
Aberhart, William, 375
Aboriginal peoples, 516; assimilation and, 527; colonization and, 520; constitution and, 393; earnings of, 539; education and, 266, 271–2; health of, 323, 326; multiculturalism and, 531–2; protest by, 404, 414–15; racism and, 533; religion and, 355; sex and gender and, 462; work and, 302
abortion, 418
Abrams, Michael, 496–7
Abu-Lughod, Janet L., 620
accidents: 'normal', 175–6, 178; workplace, 291–2
accountability, 708
accounts: identity and, 146–7
acid rain, 693
Acker, Joan, 179, 300, 442–3
Adams, Michael, 29–30
Adler, Patricia and Peter, 196
Adolph, K.E., 117
adoption, 230
Advanced Research Projects Agency (ARPA), 668
advertising: sex and gender and, 463; socialization and, 108
aesthetics: culture and, 85–7, 708
Afghanistan, 372
age: culture and, 71, 72; deviance and, 205; median, 584, 603
age composition, 586, 708
Agenda 21, 703
age pyramid, 603–4
Agnew, Robert, 198–9
AIDS Committee of Toronto (ACT), 72–3
Albas, Daniel and Cheryl, 212
alcohol, 167
Alexander, Dennis C., 642–3
alienation, 290, 351, 450–1, 708; labour process theory and, 176–8; role and, 137–40
Alinsky, Saul, 636
Allen, Judith, 385
Allende, Salvador, 377
Alliance Atlantis Communications, 647
altercasting, 145, 708
Alwin, Duane F., 121–2
American Psychological Association, 492
American War of Independence, 29
America Online (AOL), 668
analysis: content, 56–7; latent content, 57; level of, 712; manifest content, 57; secondary data, 56
Anderson, Hans Christian, 148
Anderson, Leon, 148
Anderson, R.A., 462
anthropocentrism, 687–90
anti-globalization movement, 554, 669
Antonovsky, Aaron, 328
Aquinas, St Thomas, 490
Archibald, W. Peter, 137–40
art: culture and, 85–7
Assembly of First Nations, 271
assimilation, 527; linguistic, 531
association: forms of, 27, 711
Atkinson, Michael, 385
Atwood, Margaret, 320
authority, 131, 150–2, 708; charismatic, 375, 709; class and, 438; family, 224; rational-legal, 375, 714; traditional, 374–5, 717
Axelrod, Paul, 264

Babbie, Earl, 7
baby boom, 598, 601–2, 708; education and, 249
baby boom echo generation, 111
baby bust, 598, 602–3, 708
Bainbridge, William, 359–60
Baker, P.M., 106
Bales, Robert R., 163, 225
Bandura, Albert, 105
banking model: education and, 263
Banton, Michael, 519
Barash, David, 462
Barbarash, David, 417
Barrett, Dave, 145
Bartsch, Robert, 108
Bashevkin, Sylvia, 386
Bassett, Isabella, 474, 477
Baumrind, Diana, 106
Beck, Ulrich, 424, 685, 690–1
Becker, Gary, 602
Becker, Howard, 208, 211, 257
Beech, Hannah, 588–9
behavioural school, 174–5, 708; socialization and, 105
beliefs, 708; culture and, 68; religious, 346, 347–8
Bell, Daniel, 292–3, 450–1
Bell Globemedia, 648
Belsky, Jay, 123
Benkert, Holly, 499, 500
Bennett, W.A.C., 145
Benton, Ted, 692
Berger, Peter L., 100, 358
Bernstein, Basil, 257
Bernstein, Stan, 590
Bertelsmann Music Group (BMG), 651–2
Bertin, Oliver, 306
Berton, Pierre, 559
Bertone, Andrea Marie, 500
Best, Joel, 194
Beyer, Peter, 363
bias: acquiescent, 47; ethnocentric, 710; research and, 46–7; respondent, 47; social desirability, 47; systematic, 47
Bibby, Reginald, 112, 114, 349, 358, 361–5, 363–5, 530
bidonville, 628
bilingualism, 91, 393
bin Laden, Osama, 372
biocentrism, 697
biodiversity convention, 703
biology: sex and gender and, 460–4, 486, 488–9
Birke, Lynda, 463
Birmingham School, 78
birth control, 593–4, 682
birth rate, 586, 589, 680–2; future, 241; *see also* fertility
Bishop, Clifford, 489–90, 495
Bissoondath, Neil, 530
Black, Conrad, 185
Blau, Peter M., 186
Block, Fred, 384
Bloc Québécois, 388, 389, 390
Blumer, Herbert, 19, 20, 22, 143
Board of Broadcast Governors (BBG), 648, 654
Bongaarts, John, 601
Bookchin, Murray, 695–6
Bouchard, Lucien, 394
Bourdieu, Pierre, 261
bourgeoisie, 281, 438, 708
Bové, José, 554
bovine spongiform encephalitis (BSE), 554
Bowles, Samuel, 257–8
Boyd, Monica, 299
Brannigan, Augustine, 173
Braverman, Harry, 176, 258, 450–1
breakdown approach, 407–9, 420, 708
Bretton Woods agreement, 555, 556, 561
bride price, 224, 708
British–French conflict, 520
broadcasting, alternative/community, 664–5
Broadcasting Act, 648, 655
broken glass theory, 631
Brown, Malcolm, 518
Brown, Rupert, 537
brownfields, 626–7, 636, 708
Brumann, Christoph, 573
Brundtland Commission, 679, 682, 683
Brym, Robert J., 419–20
Buchan, Shari, 383
Buddhism, 346, 348
bullying, 166; workplace, 334–5
Bulman, Coben and Van Anh, 507
bureaucracies, 158, 167–73, 708; actual working of, 180–7; authority and, 375–6; flexibility and, 181, 183; rationality and, 183–5
bureaucratic personality, 172, 183
bureaucratization, 178
Burgess, Ernest, 623–4, 677, 685, 687
Burstyn, Varda, 385
Bush, Diane, 102
Bush, George W., 372, 395–6
business: environment and, 693–5, 703–4

Business Council for Sustainable Development, 704
Business Council on National Interests, 384–5
Butler, Judith, 499
Butsch, Richard, 656–7, 660–1
Buttel, Frederick, 677, 688, 689, 703
Butz, William, 602
Byers, Lisa, 509

Calliste, Agnes, 303
Calvert, Barbara, 123
Calvin, John, 19, 354
Campaign 2000, 449
Campbell, Kim, 476
Canada: capitalism and state in, 384–5; class structure in, 447–8; culture in, 28–30, 91–5; equalization payments in, 382; immigration and, 520–5; medical care system in, 331; mortality rates in, 320–2; population of, 516, 595–607; population density in, 595–6; religion in, 361–5, 366; urbanization levels in, 616
Canada Assistance Plan, 233
Canada Child Tax Benefit, 239
Canada Health Act, 331
Canada Pension Plan, 239
Canadian Aboriginal Health Network, 323
Canadian Academy of Recording Arts and Sciences (CARAS), 649–50, 660, 664
Canadian Alliance, 388–9, 390–1, 420
Canadian Association of Broadcasters (CAB), 653–4
Canadian Broadcasting Corporation (CBC), 654
Canadian Broadcasting League, 654
Canadian Council of Muslim Women, 535
Canadian Council on Social Development, 449
Canadian Health Services Research Foundation, 335
Canadian International Development Agency, 507
Canadian Islamic Congress, 535
Canadian Labour Congress, 654
Canadian Medical Association Journal, 392
Canadian Radio League (CRL), 653–4
Canadian Radio-television and Telecommunications Commission (CRTC), 649, 655, 668, 709
Canadian Teachers' Federation, 264
Canadian Urban Victimization Study, 236
cancer: breast, 318–19; Sydney tar ponds and, 698–70
CanCon, 649, 654, 655
CanWest Global Communications, 646
capital: cultural, 86, 453, 709; finance, 557, 710; human, 256, 711; social, 327–8, 453, 715
capital-intensive production, 558, 708
capitalism, 279, 281–3, 438, 708; bureaucracy and, 168–9; corporate, 282; culture and, 76–7; education and, 257–8; environment and, 689; family, 282; health and, 316–17; industrial, 281–2; international, 372; monopoly, 282; religion and, 19–20, 353–4; state and, 384–5; welfare, 282–3; women and, 442
Cardoso, Fernando Luiz, 493
career: bureaucracy and, 171; concept of, 301; deviant, 212–14
caregiving, 465–6, 474; *see also* child care
Carlstein, Tommy, 631
Carr, Lynn, 499
Carrier, Patricia Jane, 229
Carroll, William, 665
carrying capacity, 676, 708
Carson, Rachel, 677
Castellano, Marlene Brant, 271
categories, 158–60; deviant, 206–13
Catholicism, 362–3
Catton, William, 682, 687–8, 689, 692
Caulfield, Jon, 629
census, 708; cities and, 617; definitions used, 541–2
census metropolitan areas (CMAs), 623, 708
ceremonial theories, 26, 708–9
Cernetig, Miro, 423
Chappell, Neena, 124
Charest, Jean, 394, 535
Charlottetown Accord, 393
Charrad, Mounira, 25
Charter of Rights and Freedoms, 393, 529
Chicago School, 497, 623–4, 677
child care, 226, 228–9, 232–3, 465–6, 477
children: aggression and, 113–14; cities and, 630; divorce and, 233–6; gender and, 464–6; immigrant, 115; poverty and, 325–6; sexual assault and, 509–10; socialization and, 100–1, 105–15; special needs, 233; trafficking of, 500; as workers, 284–6, 406
Child Tax Benefit, 239
Chile, 377
China: globalization and, 573; immigrants from, 521–2; Nike in, 285; revolution in, 25; sex ratio in, 588–9; youth culture in, 93–4
Chinese Immigration Act, 523
chiropractic, 315
Chodorow, Nancy, 226
Christianity, 346, 348, 355, 359, 489–90
chromosomes: sex and gender and, 462–3
CHUM Group, 649
cigarette smoking, 208, 315
cities, 611–39; built environments in, 629–31; central business district (CBD) in, 623–4; citizen participation in, 636–7; classical approaches to, 617–18; community and, 161–2, 624, 625–9; compositional perspective on, 620; concentric ring in, 623–4; crime and, 630, 631; edge, 627–8; environment and, 620; first, 612–13; funding of, 633, 634–5; global, 568–71, 615–16, 711; government of, 631–7; land use in, 623–5; macro urban design and, 631; mega-, 615, 712; multiple nuclei theory of, 624; population in, 623–5; poverty in, 629; power and, 633–4; redevelopment of, 636; rehabilitation of, 636; sectors in, 624; social-psychological approaches to, 618–20; socio-spatial approach to, 631; strangers in, 618–20; subcultural theory of, 620–1; zone in transition in, 623–4
Citizens' Clearing House for Hazardous Waste, 701
city-states, 613
Civil Marriage Act, 501
Claes, Michael, 110
claims-making, 208–10, 709
Clark, S.D., 439, 626
Clark, Susan, 473
Clark, Terry Nichols, 612
Clarke, Harold, 390
class, 281, 433–47, 709; capitalist, 383, 384; capitalist-executive, 445, 447; culture and, 71; definition of, 444–5; deviance and, 198, 205–6; ethnic relations and, 537–8, 540–4; income, 439; mass media and, 644, 656–7, 660–1; measurement of, 444–5; middle, 435–6, 455; new middle, 445, 447–8; old middle, 445, 447–8; property, 439; role and, 136–40; sexuality and, 496–7; social, 439; socialization and, 121–2; state and, 383; theories of, 437–44; working, 435–6, 445, 447–8, 455
class locations, 445
Clayoquot Sound, 423
Clement, Tony, 392
Clement, Wallace, 176, 381, 383, 445, 447–8, 451
clientelism, 168, 183, 184
climate change, 395–7, 676
clique, 163, 164–7
clothing industry, 565
Cloward, Richard, 198
Coale, Ansley, 581–2, 589–90
Coats, Patricia, 119
Coburn, David, 327
Cockburn, Cynthia, 179, 300
Cohen, J.L., 138
coherence, 709; 'sense of', 328
Coleman, William, 385
collective agreement, 305
collective conscience, 353, 709

collective consciousness, 86, 709
collective effervescence, 353, 709
collectivism, 29
Collins, Randall, 16, 32–3
Colombia, 394, 396
colonialism: racialization and, 519
'colour line': problem of, 33–5
Colwill, Nina, 124
common sense knowledge, 4, 9, 709
communication: computer-mediated, 181; culture and, 78, 82–3; group, 642; interpersonal, 642; mass, 642; organizations and, 163, 167, 170; public, 642; *see also* mass media
communism, 284
Communist Party, 378–9
community, 160–2, 709; cities and, 161–2, 624, 625–9; religious, 350–1
compensators, 359–60, 709
complementary and alternative medicines (CAMs), 315, 316
computers: access to, 666–7; communication and, 181
computing, distributed or grid, 182
concepts, 43, 709; operational definitions of, 45
condominium boom, 626
Confederation of National Trade Unions, 306
Conference on the Human Environment, 683, 703
conflict theories, 14, 19, 24, 709; class and, 437–41; deviance and, 209–10; education and, 257–8; health issues and, 316–17; mass media and, 644; new environmental paradigm and, 689; role and status and, 136–40; sexuality and, 496–7
conformity, 199
connections, direct/indirect, 159–60
Connell, Erin, 506–7
Connelly, Patricia, 478
Connolly, Paul, et al., 118
consent: age of, 501–2; informed, 60
Conservative Party of Canada, 387, 389, 390–1
constituency system, 389
constitution, Canadian, 393
constraint, 132
consumption: population theory and, 592–5
control: self, 202; technical, 290; workplace, 176–8
control theory, 201–2, 709
Convention on Cultural Diversity, 655
convergence: cultural, 571–4; economic, 565–7
Cooley, Charles H., 104, 141, 158, 162, 226
Co-operative Commonwealth Federation (CCF), 28–9, 387, 419–20
Cooperstock, Ruth, 477
co-optation, 175
copyright, 561
corporations: cities and, 615–16; Crown, 283, 646, 653; definition of, 282; multinational, 284–6, 555, 557, 559–60, 713
Cottrell, Fred, 686
counter-movements, 405, 407
counter-secularization, 359
credentials, educational, 258
crime, 630, 631; corporate, 198, 201; juvenile, 198, 201; theories of, 198, 201–2; *see also* deviance
Crozier, Michel, 180
CTVglobemedia, 648
cults, 360, 709
cultural appropriation, 72–3
'cultural exception', 554
culturalism, 536–7
cultural realms, 82–7
cultural studies, 78, 80; Internet and, 668–9; mass media and, 656–66
cultural support theory, 199–201, 709
culture, 66–96, 180, 709; Canadian, 91–5, 530–2; changes in, 87–91; conflict and, 80; diffusion of, 554, 558–60, 709; economic change and, 88; families and, 221–2; French and English, 91; globalization and, 93–5, 284; high, 86; homogenization of, 571–4; meaning of, 68–76; national, 70; organizational, 181, 183; popular, 84–5, 86, 93–5; as 'reflection', 79, 80; regional, 70–1; as self-expression, 89–90; social movements and, 412–14; sociology of, 75–6; structure and, 74–5; as symbolic, 74–5; technological change and, 88–9; theories of, 76–82; time and, 73–4; urban, 70; youth, 87, 88
culture industry, 77
Cuneo, Carl, 648
currencies: stabilization of, 556, 557, 561
curriculum, hidden, 115, 263, 711
Curtin, Roberta, 106
Curtis, James, 29
cybersex, 508–9

Dahl, Robert, 381
Das, Mallika, 108
data: existing, 56–7; historical-comparative, 16; observational, 16; statistical, 16
dating, 475–6
Davey, Ian, 245
Davidson, Kenneth, 495
Davie, Grace, 358
Davies, James C., 408
Davies, Lorraine, 229
Davies, Scott, 268, 269
Davis, J.H., 138
Davis, Kingsley, 494–5
Davis, Lynne, 271
Dawe, Alan, 103
Dawson, Robert, 663–4
Day, Stockwell, 388
death: causes of, 321, 322, 596, 598, 599–600; crude rate of, 596; rates of, 586, 589, 596; *see also* mortality
De Blij, Harm, 81–2
decoding, 78, 661–2, 709, 710
DeFreitas, Gregory, 570
Dei, George Sefa, 252
DeKeseredy, Walter, 236
Dellinger, Kirsten, 508
Demarest, Jack, 119
democracy, 24–5, 379; bureaucracy and, 186; direct, 379; in Canada, 386–92; participatory, 413; spread of, 379–80
demographic components equation, 580, 709
demographic transition theory, 586, 589–92, 681–2, 709–10
demography, 580–1; *see also* population
Dempsey, Ken, 229
denaturalization: sexuality and, 494–7
descent: bilateral, 224, 708; matrilineal, 712; patrilineal, 223, 224, 713
deskilling, 176
determinism: biological, 117, 460, 708; technological, 666
Devall, William, 694
developed countries, 710; cities in, 614–16; demographic transition in, 591–2; environment and, 703–4; population growth in, 584
developing countries, 710; cities in, 614–17; demographic transition in, 591–2; environment and, 703–4; globalization and, 284–6, 557–8, 561–2, 567–8; population in, 584, 680–2; youth in, 590
deviance, 130–1, 191–216, 710: bureaucracies and, 184–5; causes of, 197–8; as claims-making process, 208–10; diffusion of, 194; as harm, 193; labelling and, 194, 210–12; objective/subjective aspects of, 193–4, 197; ownership of, 209; primary, 212–13; research and, 195–7; secondary, 212–13; sexual, 492, 498–9; as sociological concept, 193–5; statistics and, 192–3; theories of, 197–203
deviancy amplification, 212–13
Dias, K., 318
Dickens, Peter, 692
dictatorship, 24–5, 377
Diekman, Andreas, et al., 139
digital divide, 112, 267, 268, 666–7, 710
Dion, Stéphane, 535
disaster, ecological, 683
disclaimers, 146–7, 212
discourse, 710; culture and, 82–3; individualist/collectivist, 83
discrimination, 710; de facto/de jure, 532–3; institutional, 712; racial, 120–1; sex, 477–8; structural, 716; systemic, 533, 716

disease, 710; infectious, 317, 320, 321; metaphors and, 330; occupational, 291–2
disease mongering, 333–4
divorce, 27–8, 233–41
documentaries, 665–6
documents: field research and, 55; historical, 56–7
Dogon, Mattei, 615
Dole, Carol M., 657–9, 660
domestication, 657, 658
Domhoff, William G., 381, 633
domination: class and, 440; environment and, 695
Doob, Anthony, 139
double standard, 462, 476, 710
Douglas, Tommy, 436
dowry, 224, 710
Drago, Robert, et al., 180
dramaturgical theory, 22–3, 77–8, 141, 144–5
Dreeben, Robert, 255–6
Dreger, Alice Domurat, 486
Dreier, Peter, 631
dual-systems theory, 442
Du Bois, W.E.B., 16, 33–5
Dueck, Tyrell, 333
Duffy, Ann, 472
'dumping', 561
Dunfield, Allison, 449
Dunlap, Riley, 687–8, 689, 692, 693–4
Dunn, Judy, 105
Durkheim, Émile, 15, 17–18, 1312, 407, 517, 642; cities and, 617; education and, 255; environment and, 685, 689; religion and, 85, 343–4, 347, 349, 351, 352–3; suicide and, 30, 201
Dworkin, Andrea, 499, 508, 509

Earth Day, 677, 693
Earth First!, 697
Earth Summits, 682, 683, 703
Easterlin, Richard, 601, 602
eating, disordered, 119, 317–18, 328–9
Ebaugh, Helen, 149
ecocentrism, 687–90, 695, 697
eco-feminism, 695
ecological fallacy, 532
ecology, 710; cities and, 612, 622–31; deep, 696–7, 709; factorial, 624–5; new, 695–7; social, 695–6; *see also* human ecology
economy, 276–311; definition of, 278–9; environment and, 678–9, 682–3, 689; global, 284–6; informal, 289, 712; knowledge-based, 251–5; new, 251–5, 713; sectors of, 286–9; service, 287–8, 715; subsistence, 279–80; types of, 279–84; underground, 289
education, 245–75, 710; adult, 251; alternatives in, 252; amalgamation in, 249; anti-racism, 261; attainment in, 247–8, 452; class and, 440, 451–3; enrolment and, 249–50; formal, 245; funding for, 264–6; global progress in, 254; high-school, 452; inequalities in, 267–72; informal, 245; international comparisons in, 252, 253; 'new sociology of', 257; new technologies and, 266–7; participants in, 262–3; policies on, 263–6; post-secondary, 249–51, 258, 452–3; as 'product', 264, 266; reports on, 253; sex and gender and, 465, 479; theories of, 255–61; work and, 266, 304; *see also* schools
Edwards, Richard, 177, 290
egalitarianism, 534
ego, 105
Ehrlich, Paul, 593, 682
Eichler, Margrit, 230–1
Eisinger, Peter, 414
elections, 379, 390–1; 'veil' issue and, 535
Elections Act, 535
electoral system, Canadian, 389
elites: corporate, 380–1; ruling, 380–3; state, 385
elite competition, 381–3
elite concessions, 382
Elliott, Jean Leonard, 527–8, 530
Ellis, Henry Havelock, 492
ELN (National Liberation Army), 386
embarrassment, 145–6
emergence: doctrine of, 710
emergent behaviour, 182
EMI Group, 651–2
employment: Canadian, 282, 283; economic sectors and, 287–9; ethnicity and, 532–4, 538–40; gender and, 467–75, 477–80; globalization and, 297, 563–4; self-, 294; socialization and, 124; *see also* labour; work
encoding, 78, 660, 710
energetics, 686
Engels, Friedrich, 225, 421, 438; health and, 316–17; population and, 594; sexuality and, 496
Enron, 185
Entwisle, Doris, 115
environment, 675–707; built, 629–31, 677–8, 708; degradation of, 395–7; ecological scarcity and, 679–85; economic growth and, 678–9, 682–3, 689; health and, 324–5, 697–702; natural, 678; 'problem' in, 692; social theory and, 685–93; as term, 678
environmental justice, 631, 637, 701–2, 710
environmental movement, 387, 677; grassroots, 697–702; mainstream, 693–5
Environmental Protection Agency (US), 386
environmental sociology, 676–9, 702–4; assumptions of, 678; theories in, 677, 685–93
epidemiological transition, 596, 598
epistemology, 16, 710
Erikson, Erik, 105
essence: sexuality and, 488–9, 710
essentialism, 710
ethics: deviance research and, 195–7; religion and, 350; research, 60–1
ethnic and race relations, 515–49; multiculturalism and, 526–32; theories of, 536–8; *see also* ethnicity; race
ethnicity, 710; class and, 443; concept of, 517–20; culture and, 71; deviance and, 205–6; education and, 269, 271–2; media representation of, 659–60, 663–4; symbolic, 716; *see also* race
ethnocentrism, 526–7, 528, 710
ethnography, 22–3; feminist, 31–2; institutional, 31
ethnomethodology, 31, 710; education and, 257
Europe: socialism in, 421–2
European Commission, 652
European Union, 425, 560
exchange theory, 359
experiments, 47–8
exploitation, 438–9, 710
exteriority, 131–2

face, 146, 710; -work, 146
fallacy, ecological, 532
false consciousness, 436, 710
families, 218–43; aggression and, 113–14; census, 221, 708; definitions of, 220–2; dual-earner, 228–9, 299; education and, 266; extended, 221–2, 710; future, 239–41; gender and sex and, 464–6; matrifocal, 224; modified extended, 222, 712; nuclear, 221, 496, 713; policies on, 238–9; single-earner, 233; single-parent, 234–5; as social institution, 221; socialization and, 101, 106–7, 124; step-, 235–6; theories of, 224–7; types of, 220–4
Family Allowance, 239
FARC (Revolutionary Armed Forces of Colombia), 386
farmers: protest by, 419–20
Farrell, Susan, 464
fashion: culture and, 72–3, 89–90
Faules, Don F., 642–3
Fausto-Sterling, Anne, 460, 463
favela, 628
Felt, Lawrence, 473
females, 486; biology and, 460–4; deviance and, 204–5; education and, 268–9; *see also* women
feminism, 14, 416–19, 710; class and, 441–4; deviance and, 205; ecology and, 695; education and, 258–62; ethnography and, 31–2; families and, 226–7; health issues and, 317, 318–19; liberal, 644; Marxist, 645;

mass media and, 644–5, 657–9, 667; multivariate theory and, 19; organizations and, 179–80; radical, 645; reproductive technology and, 231; research methods and, 59–60; sexuality and, 499–500; socialist, 645; socialization and, 104; state and, 385–6; work and, 299–301
Ferguson, Kathy, 179
Ferguson, Susan, 318
fertility, 580, 582, 584, 586; Canada's population and, 598, 601–5; low, 229–31; sub-replacement, 603, 605; total rate, 582, 601; *see also* birth rate
Fetherling, Douglas, 647
film industry, 650–1, 652–3, 654, 660
Fineman, Martha, 227
First Nations, 710; *see also* Aboriginal peoples
Fischer, Claude, 620–1
Fiske, John, 663–4
Fitzgerald, Dennis, 423
Fleras, Augie, 527–8, 530
flexibility: functional, 296–7; numerical, 293–6, 713; work and, 293–7, 304
flexible specialization, 296–7, 710
Flyvbjerg, Bent, 373–4
Ford, Henry, 290
Fordism, 174, 178
Foucault, Michel, 499–500
Fox, Bonnie, 286, 472
Fox, John, 383, 384
framing theory, 413
Frank, Andre Gunder, 594
Frankfurt School, 77
Fraser, Nancy, 227
fraternities, 167
Freedom House, 379–80
Freeman, Sabrina, 383
free-rider problem, 410–11
Free The Children, 406
Free Trade Agreement (FTA), 560, 564, 565
French–British conflict, 520
Frenschkowski, JoAnne, 436
Freud, Sigmund, 105, 492
Freudenberg, Nicholas, 695
Friedan, Betty, 601
Friedland, Roger, 633
Friendly, Martha, 233
front, 144
Front de Libération du Québec (FLQ), 393
Fukuyama, Frances, 571
functionalism, 14, 18–19, 711; culture and, 77, 80; deviance and, 198–203; socialization and, 103–4; technical, 256; *see also* structural functionalism
fundamentalism, 358–9
Furneaux, W., 134

Gadd, Jane, 590
Gagnon, John, 497
Gaines, Donna, 23, 30
Galabuzi, Grace-Edward, 540
game stage, 105, 141
Gamson, William, 413, 416
Gans, Herbert, 174, 620, 625, 626
Garfinkel, Harold, 31, 60, 130–1
Garreau, Joel, 628
Gaskell, Jane, 465, 477
Gaventa, John, 373
Geertz, Clifford, 351
Gelles, Richard, 236
Gemeinschaft, 161–2, 618
gender, 19, 71, 459–82, 711; biology and, 460–4; class and, 441–4; definition of, 460; deviance and, 204–5; education and, 258–62, 268–70, 465; families and, 225, 226–7; patriarchy and, 31–2; socialization and, 104, 108, 114–15, 116–17, 119–20, 464–6; *see also* sex; sexuality
General Agreement on Tariffs and Trade (GATT), 555
General Electric, 648
genes: sex and gender and, 462–3
genetic engineering, 387
genitalia, 'ambiguous', 486, 488
Genovese, Kitty, 619
gentrification, 626
Gesellschaft, 161–2, 618
Ghana, 184
Gibbs, Lois, 701
Giddens, Anthony, 284
Gifford, Robert, 620
Gilligan, Carol, 226
Gintis, Herbert, 257–8
Ginzberg, Effie, 303
Giuliani, Rudolph, 631
glasnost, 379
GlaxoSmithKline, 334
globalization, 93–5, 284–6, 398, 552–76, 711; cities and, 615–16; cultural, 558–60, 650–2; economic, 555–8, 650, 652–3; education and, 252–5; effect of, 560–74; environment and, 703–4; mass media and, 650–3, 654–5; as mobility, 558; as political arrangement, 555; population movement and, 568–71; social movements and, 422–5; social networks and, 558, 568–71; social programs and, 564–7
global warming, 676
goals: deviance and, 198
Goffman, Erving, 22–3, 33, 77–8, 137–9, 141, 144–8, 150, 186, 212, 413
Gold, Harry, 649
Goldberg, David Theo, 537–8
Goldenberg, Sheldon, 58
Goldman, Emma, 496
Goldthorpe, J.H., 290
Gonzales, Alicia, 497
Goode, Erich, 196
Goode, William, 133
Gorbachev, Mikhail, 378–9
Gordon, Andrew, 102
Gordon, Betty, 496–7
Gosine, Andil, 73
Gottfredson, Michael, 201–2
Gouldner, Alvin, 178–9
Grabb, Edward, 29, 440–1, 446
gradient effect, 454
Graham, Hilary, 317
Gramsci, Antonio, 76–7
Granovetter, Mark, 159
Great Depression, 421
greenhouse gases, 395, 676
Green Party (European), 690, 696
Greenpeace International, 424
'green' political thought, 689, 696
Grenier, Marc, 660
Grimes, Michael, 445
Griswold, Wendy, 46
Gross, Alan, 139
Gross, Edward, 146
groups, 156–89; charter, 520–1, 527, 538, 709; culture and, 68; entrance status, 538–9; entrance, 521; ethnic, 517–18, 710; informal, 174; interest, 381, 405; lobby, 381, 405; peer, 112–14; pressure, 405, 407; primary, 104, 162–3; secondary, 162–3; social, 68, 715; social movements and, 404, 405; status, 439, 716; 'virtual', 181, 182; work, 163
'groupthink', 165, 186
Gruneau, Richard, 648
Guillaumin, C., 519
Guillot, Michel, 580
Guppy, Neil, 268, 269, 383

Hackett, Robert, 648, 657
Hägerstrand, Torsten, 631
Hales, Dianne, 464
Hall, Stuart, 78, 532, 661
Hallett, Tim, 178–9
Handel, Gerald, 112
Handwerk, Brian, 81–2
Hannigan, John, 692
Harding, Sandra, 40
Harper, Elijah, 393
Harper, Stephen, 535
Harris, Chauncy, 624
Harris, Judith, 114
Harris, Marvin, 537
Harris, Mike, 435
Harvey, Andrew, 473
Hawkins, Freda, 528
Hawley, Willis, 633
Hawthorne effect, 172, 711
Hawthorne studies, 172–3, 174, 178, 292
Hayduck, Leslie, 115
Hayford, Alison, 659
head tax, 522
health, 711; class and, 453–4; environmental issues and, 324–5, 697–702; meanings of, 315; personal expenditures on, 331–2; policy on, 327; public, 317, 320;

sex and gender and, 471, 476–7; *see also* illness; medicine
health and medical issues, 312–39; privatization and, 391–2; theories of, 313–19
Health Canada, 699
Heath, Iona, 333
hegemony: culture and, 78
Heinberg, Leslie, 119
Henry, David, 333
Henry, Frances, 303, 534
Herlihy, David, 581
hermaphrodites, 486, 711
Herodotus, 517, 519
Hérouxville, Que., 535
Hertwig, Oscar, 492
heteronormativity, 487, 488, 711
heterosexism, 711
'Heterosexual–Homosexual Rating Scale', 493
heterosexuality, 488
Heuveline, Patrick, 580
Hewitt, John, 140–1
hierarchy: bureaucracy and, 170; cultural, 86–7; 'of needs', 174–5
Hinduism, 490
Hirschi, Travis, 201–2
historical-comparative theory, 15, 17, 23–5, 28, 30–5, 711
Hitler, Adolf, 377–8
HIV/AIDS, 87, 316, 322–3, 464, 476, 504–6, 507; population and, 599–600
Hochschild, Arlie, 134, 288, 301
Hoffman, Linda, 495
Holdren, J.P., 593
Hollinger International, 185
Homans, George, 172
homelessness, 634, 663–4
home-schooling, 52
homicide, 202–3, 236
homophobia, 488, 711
homosexuality, 488, 499–500, 501, 711; as deviance, 193, 492; knowledge and, 490–1; religion and, 490; workplace and, 508
hooks, bell, 499, 500
hormones: sex and gender and, 463
Hospital Insurance and Diagnostic Services Act, 331
hot money, 557, 711
household, 221, 711
housing, 629–30
Howard, Judith, 141
Howard-Hassmann, Rhoda, 530
Howe, Julia Ward, 344
Howes, David, 541–2
Hoyt, Homer, 624
Hughes, D., 120
Hughes, Everett, 19, 133
Hulchanski, David, 634
human capital theory, 256
human ecology, 677, 685, 687, 689, 711; *see also* ecology
human exemptionalism paradigm (HEP), 687–90, 711
human relations school, 174, 292, 711
Humphrey, Craig, 677, 688, 689
Humphreys, Laud, 195, 499
Hunt, Alan, 506–7
Huntington, Samuel, 571
Hurrelmann, Klaus, 112
Hussein, Saddam, 81–2
Hutter, Mark, 631
hypermasculinities, 711
hypotheses, 43–4, 711

I: Mead's view of, 104, 142
id, 105
identity, 100, 128–54, 711; authority and, 150–2; contemporary views of, 143–5; deviant, 212–13; dominant, 146; ethnic, 517–18; management of, 145–8; relict, 146; reserve, 146; role and, 148–9; situated, 140–1, 715
identity-based approach, 407, 412–14, 711
ideology, 711; dominant, 76, 404, 710; mass media and, 656, 660, 661; religion and, 352; sex and gender and, 465–6
Illich, Ivan, 332
illness, 710; experience of, 329–30
Imig, Doug, 425
immigrants: education and, 266, 269; families and, 222, 223; religion and, 366; work and, 299–303
immigration, 516, 520–5; Canada's population and, 596, 605–6; classes of, 524, 525; 'continuous journey stipulation' and, 522–3; culture and, 92–3; globalization and, 558, 569–71; points system and, 523, 525; policies on, 520, 521–3; source areas of, 523–4
Immigration Acts, 521
imperialism: cities and, 615, 616; US cultural, 93–5; *see also* globalization
impression management, 145, 711–12
incest, 495
income: class and, 442–3, 448–50, 451–3; ethnicity and, 539–44; families and, 234–5; gap in, 299, 302, 303; gender and, 468–71, 477, 478; globalization and, 563–4; health and, 325; meaningless work and, 290, 291; unions and, 307
Independent Music Publishers and Labels Association, 652
India: immigrants from, 522–3
individualism, 29
industrialization, 281–2; bureaucracy and, 169; cities and, 612–13; population and, 682; risk society and, 690–1
Indymedia, 669
inequalities: class and, 433–47; economic, 282; education and, 267–72; environment and, 701–2; global, 455; health and, 325–7; social, 33; work and, 293, 296–304
infantilization, 657, 658
infertility, 230
information and communication technologies (ICTs), 666–7
innovation: deviance and, 199
institutional completeness, 712
institutionalization, 175
institutions: education, 245–75; electoral, 379; family, 218–43; political, 376, 713; social, 715; state 376–80; total, 102, 186
insurance: hospital, 239; unemployment, 239
integration: economic, 398; horizontal, 646–7, 711; vertical, 647, 717
intellectual property, 562
interculturalism, 531
interest rates: globalization and, 55
International Bank for Reconstruction and Development (IBRD), 556
International Centre for Settlement of Investment Disputes, 556
International Development Association, 556
International Financial Corporation, 556
International Labour Organization, 289, 307–8
International Monetary Fund (IMF), 555
Internet, 666–70; bullying and, 166; education and, 267; globalization and, 668; religion and, 356–7; sexuality and, 508–9, 510; social networks and, 160; use of, 111–12; virtual groups and, 182
interpretive theory, 15, 16–17, 19–23, 30–5, 712
intersexed (bodies), 486, 712
interviews, 54–5
in vitro fertilization (IVF), 230, 231
Iran, 377
Iraq, 81–2
Irvine, Janice, 494, 510
Irving Group, 648
Irwin, Alan, 678
Islam, 346, 359, 489–90
Islamophobia, 535
Israel, 394–5
Ivison, John, 535

Jablin, Frederic, 124
Jacklin, Carole, 117
Jackson, Andrew, 296
Jackson, Sue, 498
Jacobs, Jane, 629–30
Janis, Irving, 165
Janowitz, Morris, 626
Jargowsky, Paul, 629
Jeffrey, C. Ray, 629–30
Johnson, D., 120
Johnson, Terence, 305
Johnson, Virginia, 493–4
Judaism, 346, 489–90
Juno Awards, 649–50, 659, 660, 664, 665

Kadar, Marlene, 471–2
Kalmuss, Debra, 122
Kama Sutra, 489
Kanter, Rosabeth Moss, 179
Kasarda, John, 615
Kasper, Anne, 318
Kempadoo, Kamela, 500
Kidd, Bruce, 465
Kielburger, Craig, 406
Kiernan, Kathleen, 234
Killingsworth, B., 53–4
'kin keepers', 228
King, Samantha, 319
King, William Lyon Mackenzie, 503
Kinney, David, 115
Kinsey, Alfred, 492–3
Kitschelt, Herbert, 426
Klinenberg, Eric, 635
Knight, Graham, 661
Knobloch, Silvia, 111
knowledge society, 245, 292–7
Koebel, Stan and Frank, 325
Kollontai, Alexandra, 496
Komagata Maru, 523
Kopas, Matt, 164
Kopinak, Kathryn, 476
Korea, 93–4
Kortenhaus, Carole, 119
Kurds, 81–2
Kymlicka, Will, 531
Kyoto Protocol, 395–7, 398, 676

labelling: deviance and, 194, 210–12; ethnic, 518
labour: child, 284–6, 406; division of, 169–70, 173–4, 612–14; free and unfree, 298; gendered division of, 119–20, 226, 227, 460, 464–6, 467–75; organized, 305–9; *see also* employment; unions; work
labour power, 290, 712
labour process theory, 176–8, 712
Lahache, Louise, 271
Lancet, The, 500
Landry, Bernard, 394
Landy, Sarah, 106
Langille, David, 384–5
language: culture and, 82–3; globalization and, 572; Quebec and, 531; socialization and, 100
law: employment equity, 299; environmental, 689; gender and, 479; health and safety, 291–2; labour, 307, 308–9
Lay, Kenneth, 185
leadership, 166, 175; organizations and, 163, 167, 175; theory of, 43
learning society, 245, 251–5
legitimacy, political, 379, 394–5
Leighton, Barry, 625
Lennard, Henry, 477
'less developed regions' (LDRs), 680
Lesthaeghe, Ron, 603
Lévesque, René, 393
Lévesque, Stéphane, 531
Levin, Benjamin, 263, 267
Ley, David, 626
Li, Peter, 536, 537, 539–40, 542
Lian, Jason Z., 539
Liazos, Alexander, 196
Liberal Party, 387, 389, 390–1
Lieberman, Seymour, 140
Lieberson, Stanley, 41
life expectancy at birth, 582, 584, 596, 599–600, 712; rising, 320–2
lifelong learning, 251, 712
lifestyle behaviours: health and, 328–9
lifeworld, 712
limits to growth, 682–3
Lindert, Peter, 567
Linton, Ralph, 131
Lipset, Seymour Martin, 25, 28–30, 75
locally unwanted land uses (LULUs), 630–1, 701
Lofland, Lyn, 137, 618
Logan, John, 633–4
Long, Norton, 633
'looking-glass self', 104, 141, 712
Lorber, Judith, 464
Lorimer, Rowland, 634
Losh-Hesselbart, Susan, 117, 119
Love Canal, 701
Lowe, Graham, 278, 293
Lucas, Jay, 508
Luckenbill, David, 202–3
Luther, Martin, 354
Luxton, Meg, 301, 472, 473
Lyman, Stanford M., 147

Maccoby, Eleanor, 101, 106, 117
McCurry, Justin, 500
McDonald's, 306
Macfarlane, Alan, 592–3
McGregor, Douglas, 174–5
Machung, Anne, 134, 301
McIntosh, Mary, 385
Mackie, Marlene, 105, 460
McKinney, William, 361
MacKinnon, Catherine, 499, 508, 509
McLanahan, Sara, 106
MacLeod, Andrew, 417
MacMillan Bloedel Ltd, 423
macrosociology, 5–7, 712
mad cow disease, 554
magazines: sexual scripts and, 498
Mahtani, Minelle, 661
Maine, Henry, 617
males, 486; biology and, 460–4; deviance and, 204–5; education and, 268–9; *see also* men
Malthus, Thomas, 491, 586, 592–4
Malthusian theory, 592–4
Mandell, Nancy, 472
mannerisms: disclaimer, 212; motive, 147
Maquiladora Solidarity Network, 284, 286
March, Karen, 142
Marchak, Patricia, 571–2
Marcus, Sharon, 498
market system, 281
marriage, 222–4, 227; arranged, 223–4; common-law, 580–1; culture and, 68; equal, 501; future of, 240–1
Marshall, Gordon, 486
Marshall, Katherine, 467
Martin, David, 362
Martin, Karin A., 180
Marx, Karl, 15, 23, 24, 28, 136, 281, 283–4, 290, 642; class and, 437–8; environment and, 689; population and, 586, 594; religion and, 351–2
Marxism, 31, 33, 712; culture and, 76, 80; new environmental paradigm and, 689; *see also* conflict theories
Maslow, Abraham, 174–5
mass collaborations, 182
mass media, 641–73; Canadian content in, 649, 654, 655; cultural studies of, 656–66, 668–9; culture and, 83–5, 93–5; dominant-hegemonic reading of, 661; environment and, 692; globalization and, 93–5, 284, 650–3, 654–5; Internet and, 669; laboratory studies of, 109–10; mainstream, 669; minorities and, 659–60, 663–4; negotiated reading of, 661; oppositional reading of, 661; ownership of, 646–8, 651–2, 653–4; policy on, 648–50; political economy of, 645–55; representation in, 656–61; sex and gender and, 465; socialization and, 108–12; theories of, 642–5
mass-society theory, 420–1, 712
Masters, William, 493–4
Maticka-Tyndale, Eleanor, 507
matriarchy, 224
matrifocal, 712
Matthews, Ralph, 539
Maume, David J., 179–80
Mayo, Elton, 172–3, 292
Mayrand, Marc, 535
me: Mead's view of, 104, 142
Mead, George Herbert, 19, 20, 104–5, 135–6, 141–2, 226
Mead, Margaret, 47
means of production, 281, 712
media: alternative, 664–6, 669, 708; 'new', 666; *see also* mass media
medical care system, 331; *see also* health; health and medical issues; medicine
medicalization, 330, 332–3, 712; deviance and, 209
medicine: allopathic, 315, 316, 708; alternative, 315, 316; evidence-based, 335–6; homeopathic, 315; naturopathic, 315; sociology of, 330–6
Meech Lake Accord, 393
Mehta, Deepa, 73
melting pot policies, 527, 712
men: changing gender relations and, 479–80; changing views of, 463; children and, 123–4, 230–1, 235; deviance and, 204–5; education

and, 268–9; families and, 225, 228–9; feminist theory and, 227; life expectancy of, 321, 596; media representation of, 656–7; organizations and, 179–80, 180–1; ratio of, 588–9; spousal abuse and, 236–8; stereotypes of, 108; violence against, 236; work and, 281–2, 297, 299–301, 467–75; *see also* males
Menzies, Ken, 509
Merck, 333–4
Mertig, Angela, 693–4
Merton, Robert K., 18–19, 102, 132, 133, 134, 172, 198, 199
metropolitan area, 623, 712
Meyer, David, 416
Meyer, John, 571
Meyer, Leisa, 497–8
Michaelson, Karen, 682
Michels, Robert, 186
micro/macro, 712
microsociology, 5–7, 20, 712; education and, 256–7
middle-range theory, 19, 712
migrant farm workers, 298, 533–4
migration, 580, 605–6
Miles, Robert, 518
Milgram, Stanley, 150–1, 618
Mills, C. Wright, 4, 7, 14, 380–1
Mills, Martin, 652
mind: Mead's view of, 135, 712
Miranda, Dave, 110
misrepresentation, 656, 659–60
Mitchell, Elizabeth, 462
Mitchell, Robert Cameron, 693–4
mode of production, 712
modernity: 'late', 690; 'reflexive', 690; religion and, 344–5, 351, 353–61
Mollenkopt, John, 631
Molotch, Harvey, 633–4
monarchy, 376, 377, 712; constitutional, 379
Mondschein, E.R., 117
monogamy, 222, 496, 715
Montreal Massacre, 659
Moodie, Susannah, 320
Moore, Barrington, 24–5, 409
moral entrepreneurs, 208–9
moral panic, 194
morbidity rate, 453–4, 712
'more developed regions' (MDRs), 680
Morgan, Laurie A., 180
Morland, Iain, 486
mortality, 453–4, 580, 581; Canada's population and, 596–8; infant, 596; rates of, 320–2, 586, 589, 681–2, 713; *see also* death
Mosco, Vincent, 649, 652, 666
Mothers'/Widows' Pensions, 239
Motion Picture Association of America, 554, 572, 650
Moynihan, Ray, 333
Muir, John, 693
multiculturalism, 91–3, 526–32, 713; civic, 529; meanings of, 527–8
Multiculturalism Act, 528–9
Multi-Fibre Arrangement, 565
Multilateral Investment Guarantee Agency, 556
multivariate theory, 15, 16, 17–19, 26, 30–5, 713
municipalities, 631–7; conflict and, 633; functions of, 634–5; *see also* cities
Murdie, Robert, 625
Murphy, Elizabeth, 54–5
Murphy, Raymond, 692
music industry, 651–2, 655
Myles, John, 445, 447–8, 451

Nabalamba, Alice, 702
Naess, Arne, 696–7
Nakhaie, M. Reza, 540
Nathe, Patricia, 165
National Action Committee on the Status of Women (NAC), 418
National Council of Welfare, 449–50, 471
nationalism: globalization and, 573
National Labor Committee, 285
National Longitudinal Survey of Children and Youth, 106–8, 112–14, 234, 502
National Research Council (US), 594–5
National Strategy on Child Care, 233
naturalistic attitude, 713
nature/nurture debate, 117, 460–1
Navarro, Vincente, 332–3
Nazism, 377–8, 420–1; bureaucracy and, 185, 186
needs: hierarchy of, 174–5
negotiation, 713
neighbourhoods, 713; cities and, 625–9; conscious, 625–6; design of, 630–1
neo-conservatism, 391–2
neo-liberalism, 649, 713
neo-Malthusian theory, 594
neo-Marxism: culture and, 76–7, 80; new environmental paradigm and, 689; organizations and, 176–8; population and, 594; state and, 383–5; *see also* conflict theories
Net generation, 111
networks: global, 568–71; social, 159–60, 715
New Christian Right, 359
New Democratic Party (NDP), 383, 387–8, 390–1
new ecologies, 695–7
new environmental paradigm (NEP), 687–90, 713
Newman, Oscar, 629–30
New Managerialism, 178
New Right, 388–9
news: negative representation in, 657; suppression of, 648
new social movement (NSM), 412–13
NIABY (not in anyone's back yard), 701
Nielsen, Tracy, 143–4
Nike, 285, 669
NIMBY (not in my back yard), 701
Nobles, Melissa, 542
nominalism, 713
non-governmental organizations (NGOs), 571
norms, 713; education and, 255–6; gender and sexual, 488–9, 498, 508; socialization and, 100
North American Free Trade Agreement (NAFTA), 560, 564, 565
North Atlantic Treaty Organization (NATO), 372
Northern Ireland, 118
nurses, 303, 487

obesity, 328–9
objectivity, 41–2, 713; feminism and, 59
O'Brien, Mary, 463
occupations, 300; class and, 450–3, 440; members of Parliament and, 383; sex and gender and, 467–8
O'Connor, Dennis R., 325
offices, bureaucratic, 168, 170
Official Languages Act, 393
offshoring, 652
Ogden, Russel, 196–7
O'Grady, William, 509
Ohlin, Lloyd, 198
oil sands, Alberta, 324
Old Age Pension, 239
O'Leary, K., 237
Olewiler, Nancy, 564
oligopoly, 282
Olsen, Denis, 383
Omran, Abdel, 598
Onishi, Norimitsu, 93–4
Ontario Labour Relations Board, 308–9
Ontario Student Assistance Program, 434
Ontario Works, 434–5, 436
ontology, 713
operationalization, 42–4, 713
'opium of the people', 352
organizations, 158, 163–4, 713; formal, 163, 167–8, 711; informal, 163–4, 172–3, 712; international, 556, 560–2; non-governmental, 571; spontaneous, 163, 716; stigma and, 213; theories of, 173–80; voluntary, 164
organization charts, 168, 170, 171
Organization for Economic Co-operation and Development (OECD), 563
Organization of Petroleum Exporting Countries (OPEC), 563, 686
Ornstein, Michael, 383, 384, 539
other, generalized, 105, 136, 141, 711
Our Bodies, Our Selves, 318
outsourcing, 652
overload, sensory, 618–19
Overman, Steven, 119
overtime, unpaid, 295–6
overurbanization, 615

ownership: chain, 646–7; class and, 440; conglomerate, 648, 651–2, 709; cross-, 648, 709; independent, 646; private, 646–8, 653–4; public, 646, 653–4

Pahl, R.E., 636
Pais, José Machado, 122
Palmer, Donald, 633
paradigm, 131, 713; shift, 687–8
parenting: school and, 115; socialization and, 106–7, 123–4
Parizeau, Jacques, 394
Park, Robert, 19, 22, 497, 624, 677, 685, 687
Parliament: members of, 383, 386
Parsons, Talcott, 18, 19, 103–4, 131, 225, 255, 315, 407
participant observation research, 53–4
parties, 713; class and, 439; political, 381, 386–9, 405, 421–2, 713
Parti Québécois, 388, 393–4
Pastrana, Andrés, 394, 396
patents, 561
paternity, 496
patriarchy, 31, 224, 442, 644, 713
pedagogy, 713; critical, 261
Penha-Lopes, Vania, 119–20
pensions, 239
'people of colour', 299–300, 302–3
Perrow, Charles, 173, 175, 178
Perry, Clarence, 626
Peterson, Peter G., 603, 605
Peterson, Richard A., 79
Pew Internet and American Life Project, 356–7
pharmaceutical industry, 333–4
Pinchot, Gifford, 693
Pinochet, Augusto, 377
Plato, 490–1
Plaunt, Alan, 653
play stage, 105, 141
Plumwood, Val, 695
pluralism: cultural, 528–9; elite competition and, 381–3
Pluralism Project, 366
political conflict perspective, 411–12, 713
political economy approaches: ethnic relations and, 537–8; families and, 225; Internet, and, 666–8
political movements, 392–7, 713
political process approach, 407, 414–16, 713
politics, 370–400, 713; in Canada, 386–92; concepts in, 372–7; culture and, 74; gender and, 476; participation in, 390–1; party, 386–9; power and, 372–4; religion and, 367; urban, 633–7
polls, 49
pollution, 697–702, 703
polyandry, 223, 713
polygamy, 223
polygyny, 222–3, 713
Pomerleau, Andrée, 117

Popp, Jim, 492
population, 578–609; aging, 241, 335, 584, 586, 603, 605; Canada's, 595–607; definition of, 580; ecological scarcity and, 679–82; 'explosion', 589; 'momentum', 584; movement, 713–14; growth rate of, 582, 584; theories of change in, 586–95; world, 580, 581–6
pornography, 499, 508–9
Porter, John, 383, 538–9, 540
Portes, Alejandro, 558, 570–1
'positive mental attitude' (PMA), 177–8
post-Fordism, 178
post-industrialism, 450–1
postmodernism, 227, 690
potential years of life lost (PYLL), 321–2, 714
Poulantzas, Nicos, 384
poverty, 234, 302, 303, 629; 'child', 239, 449; class and, 448–50; environment and, 703; health and, 325–6; population and, 682; women and, 471
power, 714; class and, 438, 439–41; definition of, 372–3; economic, 410; ideological, 410; political, 410; role strain and, 134; social movements and, 410
prejudice, 532–6, 714
pre-play stage, 104–5
Presthus, Robert, 385
prestige, 33, 131
Preston, Samuel, 580, 581
Price, Robert, 184
primary resource industry, 286–7
primordialism, hard/soft, 517–18
Pringle, Rosemary, 300
prison experiment, 138
privatization, 283, 714; globalization and, 556, 572; health care and, 331–2, 391–2; mass media and, 649
'production of culture perspective', 78–80
profane: sacred and, 353
professionalization, 305
progressive conservation, 693, 714
Progressive Conservative Party, 389
proletariat, 281, 438, 714
prostitution, 495, 503
protectionism, 560
Protestant ethic thesis, 353–4, 714
Protestantism, 19–20, 359, 361–2
Pryor, Edward, 467
pseudo-surveys, 49–50
psychological theories: socialization and, 105
psychology, social, 7
Pupo, Norene, 472
PWAs (persons with AIDS), 87
PYLL (potential years of life lost), 321–2, 714

al-Qaeda, 372
Quadagno, Jill, 385

Quebec: family in, 224, 232; multiculturalism and, 531; 'reasonable accommodation' in, 534–5; religion in, 362–3; separatism in, 393–4; suicide in, 25–6
queer theory, 499–500, 714
questionnaires, 50
questions: double-barrelled, 51; structured/unstructured, 54–5; survey, 50–1
Quiet Revolution, 363, 393
Quine, Lyn, 334–5
quintiles, 448–9
quotas, 554

Raboy, Marc, 646
race, 33–5, 714; class and, 443; concept of, 517–20; culture and, 71; education and, 269, 271–2; employment and, 299–300, 302–3; media representation of, 659–60, 663–4; as objective category, 519–20; socialization and, 120–1; work and, 299–303; *see also* ethnic and race relations; ethnicity
'race to the bottom', 561–7, 714
racialization, 518, 519, 714
racism, 516–17, 532–6, 714; democratic, 534; 'environmental', 702 ; institutional, 533; intra- and inter-group, 536; portrayal of, 663–4
radio, community, 665
Radler, David, 185
Rakow, Lana F., 645
Rampanen, John, 417
Rand formula, 305
randomization, 51–3
rape, 509
rape supportive attitude scale (RSA), 167
rational choice theory, 359
rationality: bureaucracies and, 183–5
rationalization, 169, 714
Ratner, Robert S., 665
Reams, James P., 81–2
rebellion: deviance and, 199
reductionism, 714
Reform Party, 388, 420
refugees, 524
regulation theory, 178
Reinhart, James, 176
Reiss, Albert J., Jr, 620
Reiter, Esther, 290
Reitzes, Donald and Dietrich, 636
relations of distribution, 442–3
relations of production, 438
relative deprivation theory, 408, 714
relativism, 41, 714; cultural, 528, 530
reliability: research and, 46, 714
religion, 341–69; capitalism and, 19–20; in China, 93–4; church attendance and, 356–8, 362, 363–4; classical theories of, 351–4; conservative, 358–9, 362–3, 356–8; culture and, 72–3, 85; decline of,

361–5; definition of, 345–7; experience of, 349–50; future of, 365–7; as group identity, 359, 361; modernity and, 354–61; new, 356–7; 'no religion' category and, 364–5; privatization of, 358; renewal of, 360, 361; as social solidarity, 352–3; study of, 342–5; suicide and, 18; theories of, 351–61
representation: mass media and, 656–61; political, 386; proportional, 389
repression, sexual, 491, 492
reproduction: assisted, 229–31, 418–19; economy and, 289; sex and gender and, 463–4, 477; social, 288–9, 715
research: context of, 58–61; ethics and, 60–1; ethnographic, 53–4; existing data and, 56–7; explanatory, 58–9; exploratory, 58; field, 53–6; historical, 56–7; methods of, 39–63; participant observation, 53–4; participatory action, 59; purposes of, 58–9; qualitative, 40, 46, 47, 53–6; quantitative, 40, 56; quasi-experimental, 48; theory and, 42–7
Reskin, Barbara, 19
resocialization, 102–3, 714
resource mobilization approach, 407, 409–12, 714
Ressam, Ahmed, 144
retreatism: deviance and, 199
revolutions, 408, 715
rewards: extrinsic/intrinsic, 175; religion and, 359–60
Richardson, Jack, 385
Riffel, J. Anthony, 263, 267
Rifkin, Jeremy, 287–8
ripple effect, 176
risk society, 690–1, 714
rites of passage, 342, 348–9, 364, 714
ritual, religious, 348–9, 353
ritualism: deviance and, 199
Robinson, David, 296
Robinson, Tracy, 120–1
Roby, Jini, 500
Rodrik, Dani, 566
Rogers, Kimberly, 434–5, 436
Rogers Communications, 649
role, 128–54, 714; adult, 122–4; authority and, 150–2; expressive, 225; groups and, 163; identity and, 144, 148–9; instrumental, 225; reproductive technology and, 230–1; sick, 315–16; socialization and, 100; socio-sexual, 497
role competition, 134
role conflict, 134, 179–80
role distance, 148
role embracement, 148
role exit, 148–50
role expectations, 130, 714
role-making, 135–6, 714
role set, 132, 134
role strain, 133–4
role-taking, 135–6, 714
Rolison, Gary, 497
Romanow Commission, 391, 392
Rondahl, Gerd, et al., 487
Roof, Wade Clark, 361
Rosen, Bernard C., 536–7
Rosenberg, Sharon, 659
Ross, Eric, 593–4
Rossi, Alice, 123
Roy, Francine, 477
Royal Canadian Mounted Police (RCMP), 417
Royal Commission on Aboriginal Peoples, 271
Royal Commission on Bilingualism and Biculturalism, 393, 528, 531
Royal Commission on Equality in Employment, 539
Royal Commission on Radio Broadcasting, 653
Rudner, L.M., 52
rules: bureaucracy and, 170, 183–4
'ruling elite approach', 380–3
Ryan, Isobel, 162

Sabini, John, 151
Sachs, Wolfgang, 685
sacred: profane and, 352
Sade, Marquis de, 491
Salazar, L.P., 115
sample, 714; pseudo-surveys and, 49; random, 45, 51–3; representative, 51–3; simple random, 51–2; size of, 51–3; validity and, 45–6
Sappho, 491
Sassen, Saskia, 558, 568–70, 616
Satzewich, Vic, 298
Saudi Arabia, 377
Sawers, Larry, 633
Scarce, Rik, 694
scarcity, ecological, 679–85, 687
Schauer, Terrie, 509
Schnaiberg, Allan, 678, 679
Schneidereit, Paul, 698–700
schooling, 246, 714
schools: black-focused, 252; cliques in, 166–7; socialization and, 114–15; *see also* education
Schroeder, Carolyn, 496–7
Schweingruber, David, 177–8
science: environment and, 690–1, 692; gender and, 460–4, 486, 488–9; feminism and, 59; sexuality and, 491–4; sociology and, 40–2; techniques of, 47–58
scientific management, 290–1, 714
Scott, John, 486
Scott, Marvin B., 147
secondary sector, 287
sects, 360, 715
secularization, 344–5, 351, 715; in Canada, 361–5; as cyclical, 360; theory of, 354–61
segregation, economic and racial, 629
Seiber, Timothy, 102
self, 715; deviance and, 213; looking-glass, 104, 141, 712; role and, 135–6; socialization and, 104
Seltzer, Judith, 122
Selznick, Philip, 175
Sennett, Richard, 296, 297
September 11, 343, 372, 394
service sector, 287–9, 293, 451, 715
Settersten, Richard, 101, 103, 106
sex, 715; definition of, 460, 486; safe, 504–6; sociology of, 486; *see also* gender; sexuality
Sex Information and Education Council of Canada, 503
sexism, 488
sex ratio, 588–9, 715
sexual harassment, 471–2, 478, 715
sexuality, 485–513, 715; biomedical approach to, 491–4; in Canada, 501–7; definition of, 488, 510; ethnographic approach to, 494; historical perspective on, 497–8; laboratory approach to, 493–4; organizational, 508; social survey approach to, 492–3; spirituality and, 489–91; theories of, 494–500; workplace and, 507–8
sexualization, 657, 658
sexual offenses, 509–10
sexual practices, 462, 464, 475–6
sexual revolution, 497–8
sexual scripts, 497, 715
shantytown, 628
Shaw, Susan, 473
Shiite Muslims, 81–2
shocking experiment, 151
Shorter, Edward, 492
sickness, 710
Siegel, Lloyd, 165
Sierra Club, 693
Silva, Elizabeth, 227
Silver, Maury, 151
Simmel, Georg, 15, 19, 20, 21, 27, 90, 617
Simmons, Alan, 533–4
Simmons, Roberta, 102
Simon, Herbert, 178
Simon, Julian, 594, 682
Simon, William, 497
Sinclair, Peter, 473
Singh, Gurdit, 523
Sjoberg, Gideon, 617
skid row/road, 626
skill: employment and, 176, 450–1
Sklair, Leslie, 424–5
Skocpol, Theda, 25, 384
Skogstad, Grace, 398
slavery, 298
Smart, Carol, 227
Smelser, Neil, 408–9
Smith, Adam, 169
Smith, Dorothy, 16, 31–2, 466
Smith, Philip, 74, 78
Smythe, Dallas, 653
Snow, David, 148
social constructionism, 642, 715;

deviance and, 207–13; environment and, 685, 691–3; families and, 226
social control, 715; deviance and, 192, 193, 201–2; organizations and, 158; religion and, 351–2
Social Credit, 375, 419–20
social environment, 69, 715
social facts, 17, 715
social goods, 408; social movements and, 404, 407
social interaction, 100, 715
socialism, 283–4, 421–2
socialization, 69, 99–127, 715; agents of, 101, 105–15, 708; anticipatory, 102, 123, 124, 708; education and, 245; forms of, 101–3; gender, 104, 108, 114–15, 116–17, 119–20, 152; inadequate, 133; primary, 101, 714; racial, 120; reciprocal, 101; secondary, 101–2, 714; theories of, 103–5
social movements, 402–28, 715; environment and, 693–702; mass media and, 644, 669; theories on, 407–16
social realism, 642, 715; *see also* social constructionism
social relationships, 715
social sciences: science and, 40–1
social structure, 436–7, 715
society, 715–16
sociobiology, 462–3
socio-economic status (SES), 444–5, 452–4
'sociological imagination', 4, 7, 14, 716
sociological theory, 16–17, 12–37; levels of, 14
sociology, 4–9, 716; assumptions of, 7–8; definition of, 5–7; other fields and, 7–8; qualitative, 40; quantitative, 40; rural, 677; as science, 40–2; *see also* environmental sociology
socio-technical systems theory, 716
solidarity, 716
Sontag, Susan, 330
Sony BMG Entertainment, 651–2
sororities, 167
'sound economic policies', 555, 556, 558, 716
Southam News Service, 647
Soviet Union, 284, 378–9
Speirs, Rosemary, 622
splitting strategies, 657–8
Spouses Allowance, 239
Spry, Graham, 653
standpoint theory, 31–2, 59–60
Stanton, Warren, 123
Stark, Rodney, 359–60, 362
state, 716; authoritarian, 377; bureaucracy and, 168; capitalism and, 282–3; culture and, 74, 75; definition of, 376; democratic, 380–8; education and, 251–5, 263–6; environment and, 693–5, 703–4; families and, 232–3, 237, 238–9; Internet and, 668; liberal-democratic, 379–80; mass media and, 648–50; partially autonomous, 384; power of, 372; religion and, 356, 362–3; social movements and, 411–12; socialist, 378–9; theories of, 380–6; totalitarian, 186, 377–9, 717; welfare, 385
statistics: analysis of, 56
Statistics Canada, 110–11, 112, 221, 478, 504, 509–10, 541–2, 622
status, 33, 128–54, 716; authority and, 150–2; class and, 439–40; culture change and, 90; divorce and, 234–5; health and, 327–8; identity and, 144; master, 133, 210, 712; rights and duties of, 131
status degradation ceremony, 210–11, 716
status sequence, 132, 133
status set, 134, 132
status situations, 439–40
Steffensmeier, Renee, 123
Steinsapir, Carol, 695
stereotypes: ethnic, 532; gender, 108, 117, 119–20, 711
Stiglitz, Joseph, 561–2, 567
stigma, 209, 210–14; health and, 318; managing, 213; sexual, 499
Stone, Gregory P., 146
Storey, Robert, 284, 291–2
strain theory, 198–9, 716
stratification, 716; vertical/horizontal, 612; theory of, 32–3, 444–5
Strauss, Murray, 236
stress, 133
strikes, 305, 306, 657
structural analysis, 716
structural approach: cities and, 612, 631–7; families and, 226; organizations and, 178–9
structural functionalism, 716; authority and, 150; class and, 444–5; education and, 255–6; families and, 225–6; health issues and, 315–16; mass media and, 643–4; new environmental paradigm and, 688–9; sexuality and, 494–6; status and role and, 131–4
structure, 716
subcultures, 72, 78, 165, 716
subsidies, trade, 554, 561, 562
suburbs, 623, 626
suicide, 17–18, 23, 30, 201, 205, 206; in Quebec, 25–6
Sumner, Colin, 196
Sunni Muslims, 81–2
superego, 105
supernatural, 359–60
superordinate, 168
supply-side theory, 360, 362, 716
Surkyn, Johan, 603
surnames, 224
surveys, 48–53; pseudo-, 49–50; questions for, 50–1
sustainable development, 683–5, 691, 693, 703–4, 716
Sutherland, Edwin, 199–200
Suzuki, David, 696
Swanstrom, Todd, 631
Sydney tar ponds, 325, 698–700
symbolic interactionism, 14, 20–1, 716; authority and, 150; class and, 444; culture and, 77–8, 80; education and, 256–7; families and, 226; health issues and, 317–18; identity and, 143–4; mass media and, 642–3; socialization and, 103, 104–5; status and role and, 134–6
symbols, 642, 716
Synnott, Anthony, 541–2
systemic theory, 408–9, 716
systems theory, 175–6, 226, 716

Tabb, William, 633
taboo, 716
Tam, Kwok Kwan, 106
Tamis-LeMonda, C.S., 117
Tannock, Stuart, 304
Tantra, 489
Taoism, 489
Tapscott, Don, 111
Taras, David, 646, 670
tariffs, trade, 554
tar ponds, 325, 698–700
Tarrow, Sidney, 425
Tator, Carol, 534, 663
tax: child care and, 233, 239; cigarette, 315; property, 632–3, 634
Taylor, Frederick W., 173–4, 290
Taylor, Paul, 703
Taylorism, 173–4, 290
technology, 716; cities and, 612–14; education and, 266–7; information and communication, 666–7; reproductive, 229–31, 418–19; work and, 287–8, 292–3
television: community, 664–5; culture and, 88; gender and, 117, 119; socialization and, 110–12; violence on, 109, 111
teleworking, 296
Tennessee Valley Authority (TVA) study, 175
terrorism, 372, 392–3, 394–5, 417, 716
theodices, 342
theory, 7, 716–17; research and, 42–7; *see also* sociological theory
theosophy, 489
Thianthai, Chulanee, 504–6
Thiessen, Joel, 349
think-tanks, 571–2
Third World, 717; *see also* developing countries
Thompson, Ken, 182
Thompson, Kevin, 119
Thomson, Elizabeth, 106
Thorns, David, 615–16
Tilly, Charles, 414
Tocqueville, Alexis de, 23–4, 164, 404

Tönnies, Ferdinand, 161, 617, 618
totalitarianism, 186, 377–9, 717
toxic waste movement, 698, 700–1
trade, international, 554–76
trafficking, sexual, 500
Traill, Catharine Parr, 314
trait theory, 305
transaction, situated, 202–3, 715
transitions, 717
Tremblay, Manon, 386
Tremblay, Richard, 113
Trovato, Frank, 25–7
Trudeau, Pierre, 393, 501, 528
trust: bureaucracies and, 181; swift, 181
Tunisia, 25
Turner, Ralph, 135–6
Tylor, Edward, 346

Ullman, Edward L., 624
under-representation, 656, 657
unemployment, 302–4; globalization and, 563–4; rate of, 717
Unemployment Insurance, 239
unions, 305–9; 'advantage', 307–8; globalization and, 563; mass media and, 654, 656–7; membership in, 307
United Farmers of Alberta, 419–20
United Nations, 455, 507
United Nations Declaration on the Rights of the Child, 406
United Nations Education, Science and Cultural Organization (UNESCO), 254
United States: African Americans in, 33–5; Chile and, 377; cultural hegemony of, 93–4, 554, 558–60, 572–3, 650–2, 654–5; culture of, 28–30, 93–5; democracy in, 24; environment and, 395–6, 703; immigration and, 569–70; religion in, 343, 345, 356–9, 361–4, 366; terrorist attack on, 372
Universal Music Group, 651–2
urban growth machine, 634
urbanism, 70, 612, 617–21, 717; new, 628
urbanization, 612–17, 717; levels of, 614–15; measure of, 617
urban planning, 635–6
urban renewal, 636, 717
urban-rural differences, 612
urban villages, 626
Urry, John, 176
utilitarian perspective, 410–11, 717

Valenti, Jack, 572
validity, 44–6, 717; construct, 45; content, 45; external, 45–6, 48; face, 45; internal, 46
values, 717; deviance and, 199–201
Vanier Institute of the Family, 502–3
van Leeuwenhoek, Anton, 492
variables, 717; dependent/independent, 43–4; experiments and, 48
Vaughan, Diane, 25, 27–8, 30
'veil issue', 535
Ventresca, Marc J., 178–9
verstehen, 19, 47, 717
vertical mosaic, 538–9, 717; colour-coded, 539–40
Videla, Nancy Plankey, 176–7
violence: children and, 107, 122–3; 'courtship', 237; domestic, 236–8; 'family', 236; homeless men's view of, 663–4; mass media and, 85, 108–9, 111; sexual, 509–10; 'spousal', 236–8; against women, 472, 479, 659; youth, 112–13
'visible minority': as term, 541–2
voluntary associations, 405, 407

Wackwitz, Laura A., 646
wages: *see* income
Wagley, Charles, 537
Waksler, Frances, 102
Walkerton water crisis, 324–5
Waller, Willard, 256–7
Walliss, John, 349
Walt Disney Company, 648, 653
war: culture and, 68; health and, 319
War Measures Act, 393
'War on Terror', 372
Ward, Michael, 602
Waring, Marilyn, 289
Warner Music Group, 651–2
water, contaminated, 324–5
Webber, Melvin M., 625
Weber, Max, 15, 19–20, 47, 642; authority and, 374–6; bureaucracy and, 168–9, 186; cities and, 617; class and, 439–41; environment and, 689; ethnicity and, 517–18; power and, 372–3; religion and, 85, 342, 351, 353
Weeks, Jeffrey, 488, 497
Weinfeld, Morton, 539
Wellman, Barry, 625
Welsh, Sandy, 508
Wertham, Frederic, 109
Westhues, Kenneth, 7
White, Kevin, 581
Whyte, William, 53, 173, 139, 626
Williams, A. Paul, 382
Williams, Christine, et al., 508
Williamson, Jeffrey, 567
Wirt, Frederick, 633
Wirth, Louis, 617
Wittgenstein, Ludwig, 347
Wollstonecraft, May, 259
women, 180–1; Aboriginal, 299; cities and, 622, 630; class and, 441–4; 'of colour', 299–300; deviance and, 204–5; education and, 258–62, 268–9; environmental movement and, 700–1; families and, 225, 227, 228–9, 234–5; film industry and, 660; globalization and, 284–6; health and, 318–19, 330; immigrant, 299–300; life expectancy of, 321, 596; media representation of, 656–9; organizations and, 179–80; politics and, 386, 387; ratio of, 588–9; rights of, 25, 385–6, 416–19; state and, 385–6, 443; stereotypes of, 108; as teachers, 260–1; trafficking of, 500; unions and, 307, 467; violence against, 236–8, 472, 479, 659; work and, 282, 288–9, 294, 297, 299–301, 467–75
Woods, James, 508
Woods, Peter, 257
work, 276–311; class and, 447–51; contingent, 293; domestic, 227, 228–9, 288–9, 303, 442–3, 472–5; 'double day of', 301; emotional, 288; flexible, 293–7; gendered, 297, 299–301; 'hidden', 289, 300; management of, 290–7; meaning in, 278, 290, 291, 304–5; non-standard, 293–7, 713; overtime, 295–6; paid, 301, 467–72; part-time, 294, 299, 468; polarization of, 296–7; racialized, 299–303; religion and, 354; satisfaction and, 304; sociology of, 278; teams and, 296; unpaid, 288–9, 301, 443–4, 472–5; *see also* employment; labour
workers' compensation boards, 291–2
workfare, 435
Workplace 2000, 278
World Bank, 555
World Commission on the Environment and Development (Brundtland), 679, 682, 683
World Health Organization (WHO), 486, 488, 507, 510, 453
World Trade Organization (WTO), 398, 554, 650, 651
World Wide Web, 666; *see also* Internet
Wright, Charles R., 643
Wright, Eric Olin, 438–9, 445
Wrong, Dennis, 104
Wuthnow, Robert, 421–2

Yelaja, Prithi, 73
Yeltsin, Boris, 379
Yinger, Milton, 346–7
youth: labour market and, 590; sexual assault and, 509–10; sexuality and, 502–7; work and, 294, 299, 303–4
Youth in Transition Survey, 452

Zimbardo, Philip, 138
Zitrin, Arthur, 165
Zola, Irving, 332
Zwerman, William, 173

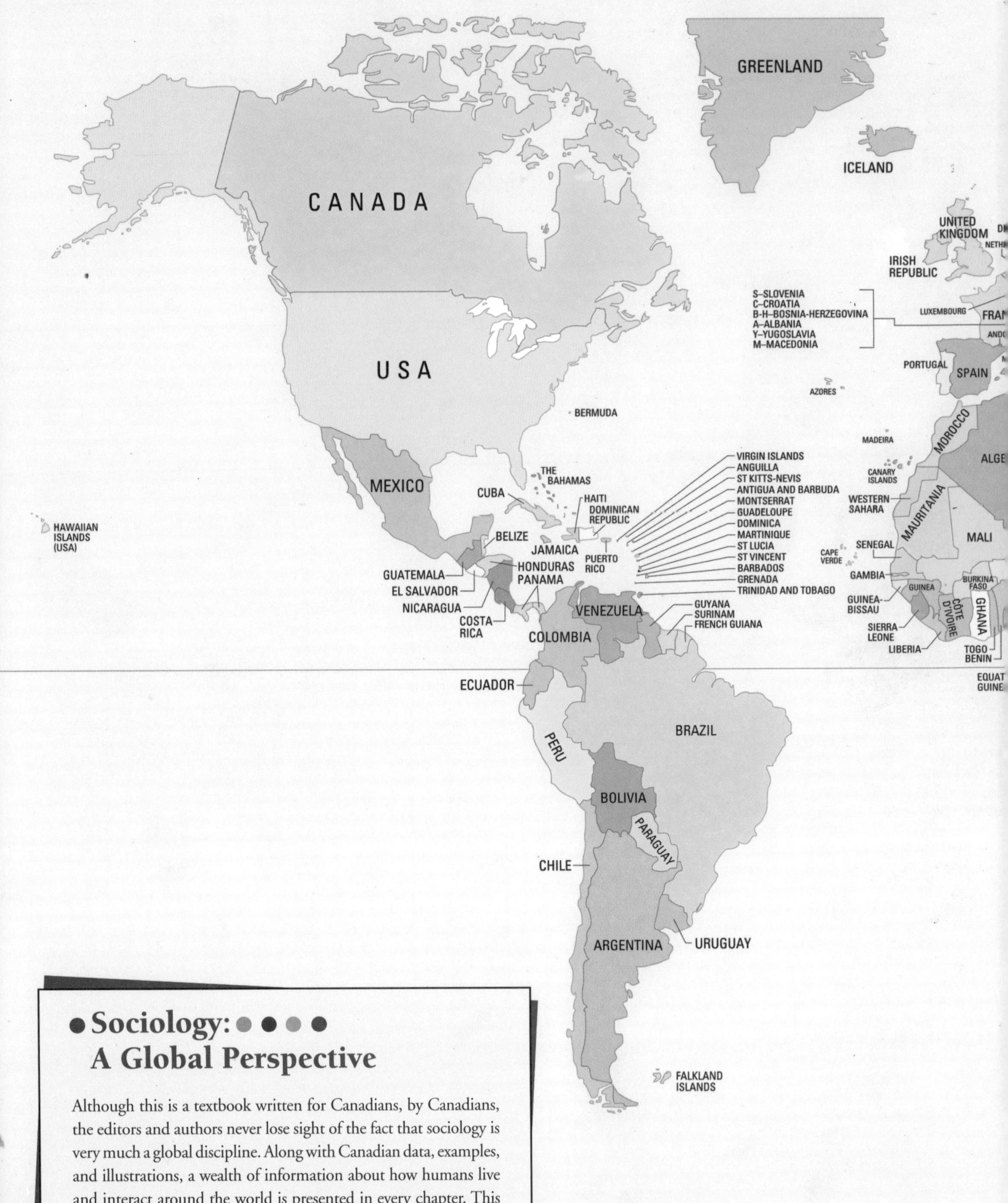

Sociology: A Global Perspective

Although this is a textbook written for Canadians, by Canadians, the editors and authors never lose sight of the fact that sociology is very much a global discipline. Along with Canadian data, examples, and illustrations, a wealth of information about how humans live and interact around the world is presented in every chapter. This map will help you situate those references in their global context.